White Supremacy Confronted

White Supremacy Confronted:

U.S. Imperialism and Anti-Communism vs. the Liberation of Southern Africa, From Rhodes to Mandela

Gerald Horne

INTERNATIONAL PUBLISHERS
New York

Library of Congress Cataloging-in-Publication Data

Names: Horne, Gerald, author.
Title: White supremacy confronted : U.S. imperialism and anti-communism vs. the liberation of southern Africa, from Rhodes to Mandela / Gerald Horne.
Description: New York : International Publishers, 2019.
Identifiers: LCCN 2019008352 | ISBN 9780717807635 (pbk.) | ISBN 0717807630 (pbk.)
Subjects: LCSH: Civil rights movements—Africa, Southern. | Civil rights movements—United States. | African Americans—Relations with Africans—History—20th century. | Anti-communist movements—United States. | Anti-communist movements—Africa, Southern. | Decolonization—Africa, Southern. | Africa, Southern—Foreign relations—United States. | United States—Foreign relations—Africa, Southern.
Classification: LCC DT1105.U6 H66 2019 | DDC 327.680730904—dc23
LC record available at https://lccn.loc.gov/2019008352

ISBN 10: 0-7178-0763-0 ISBN-13 978-07178-0763-5
Typeset by Amnet Systems, Chennai, India

Table of Contents

Abbreviations

AAI	African American Institute
AALC	African American Labor Center
ACOA	American Committee on Africa
ADL	Anti-Defamation League of B'Nai B'Rith
AFL-CIO	American Federation of Labor-Congress of Industrial Organizations
AFSC	American Friends Services Committee
AIPAC	American Israel Public Affairs Committee
ANC	African National Congress
AME	African Methodist Episcopalian
ALSC	African Liberation Support Committee
AZAPO	Azanian Peoples Organization
BCM	Black Consciousness Movement
CAA	Council on African Affairs
CCNY	Carnegie Corporation of New York
CFR	Council on Foreign Relations
CIA	Central Intelligence Agency
COREMO	Revolutionary Committee of Mozambique
COSATU	Congress of South African Trade Unions
CPSA	Communist Party of South Africa
CPUSA	Communist Party of United States of America
FDR	President Franklin D. Roosevelt
FNLA	Front for the National Liberation of Angola
FRELIMO	Front for the Liberation of Mozambique
FRG	Federal Republic of Germany
FROLIZI	Front for the Liberation of Zimbabwe
GDR	German Democratic Republic
GOP	Grand Old Party {Republican Party of U.S.)
GRAE	Revolutionary Government of Angola in Exile
ICJ	International Court of Justice
JFK	President John F. Kennedy
KGB	Committee for State Security—Soviet Intelligence Agency
LBJ	President Lyndon B. Johnson
MIT	Massachusetts Institute of Technology
MK	Umkhonto We Sizwe (Armed Wing of the ANC)
MNR/ RENAMO	Mozambique National Resistance

MPLA	Popular Movement for the Liberation of Angola
NAACP	National Association for the Advancement of Colored People
NAIMSAL	National Anti-Imperialist Movement in Solidarity with African Liberation
NATO	North Atlantic Treaty Organization
NCBL	National Conference of Black Lawyers
NCC	National Council of Churches
OAU	Organization of African Unity
PAC	Pan Africanist Congress of Azania
PAIGC	African Party for the Independence of Guinea and Cape Verde
SABC	South African Broadcasting Corporation
SACP	South African Communist Party
SCLC	Southern Christian Leadership Conference
SNCC	Student Non-Violent Coordinating Committee
SWAPO	SouthWest Africa Peoples Organization
UDI	Unilateral Declaration of Independence
U.K.	United Kingdom
UN	United Nations
UNITA	Union for the Total Independence of Angola
U.S.	United States of America
U.S.S.R.	Union of Soviet Socialist Republics
WACL	World Anticommunist League
WCC	World Council of Churches
ZANU	Zimbabwe African National Union
ZAPU	Zimbabwe African Peoples Union

White Supremacy Confronted

Introduction

THIS is a book about peoples of African descent separated by thousands of miles, who forged common bonds based in no small measure on bruising encounters with white supremacy and imperialism. It is also a book about the role of U.S. imperialism—and its handmaiden, anticommunism—in the epochal process that led to the liberation of Southern Africa,[1] culminating with the first democratic elections in South Africa in 1994. Its thesis is that it is difficult to understand the decolonization of Southern Africa if one ignores contemporaneous events in North America and, indeed, the global correlation of forces more generally.

South Africa is not the book's sole topic. That country, however, stands like a sun around which revolve other bodies—including Namibia, Zimbabwe, Angola, Mozambique, Tanzania, Zambia, Botswana, Lesotho and Swaziland. Like Eduardo Mondlane, the Founding Father of modern Mozambique, I agree that the subregion of Southern Africa is best contemplated as a whole (though one should not lose sight of individual peculiarities).[2] Like Baleka Mbete, one of the highest-ranking women politicians in today's South Africa, I agree that "South African history is [more than] what happened within the borders of South Africa."[3] Thus, the 1974 overthrow of the dictatorship in Portugal led inevitably, like falling dominoes, to the decolonization of Mozambique and Angola, then the fall of Rhodesia (Zimbabwe), followed by South Africa, the major

---

1. See e.g. Saul Dubow, *Apartheid, 1948-1994,* New York: Oxford University Press, 2014.

2. Harry Ododa and Jerome Stewart Legge, Jr., "The Political Thought of Eduardo Mondlane," *Black Scholar,* April 1974, Box 4, Subgroup II, *Herbert Shore Collection, Oberlin College, Oberlin, Ohio.* Given its proximity to both Rhodesia and South Africa, Mondlane's homeland was noticeably vulnerable to pressure and destabilization.

3. Oral History, Baleka Mbete, 9 May 2001, *University of Connecticut-Storrs.*

prize. Of course, the preceding decolonization of the other nations in the region impelled this entire process.

* * *

"I thank Prof. Gerald Horne who started interviewing me in the early 1990s," said Andimba Toivo ya Toivo, a Founding Father of modern Namibia, in regard to his recently published autobiography, "although due to his many commitments he could not proceed."[4] These words indicate that the pages that follow not only adhere to the norms of contemporary historiography but also draw upon the author's lengthy experience, stretching over at least a half-century.[5]

---

4. Andimba Toivo ya Toivo, *On Trial for My Country*, as told to Ellen Namhila, et.al., Windhoek: University of Namibia Press, 2016, 4. See also the Transcript of Interview of Toivo ya Toivo conducted by the author, March 1997, Box 169, *Gerald Horne Papers, Schomburg Center, New York Public Library*: "I was delighted," says this African leader, "when in 1985 NCBL under the leadership of Mr. Gerald Horne, organized a trip for me [to the United States] to .....publicize [then illegally occupied Namibia]...." It was then that he met the woman, who was to become his spouse, my colleague and fellow lawyer, Vicki Erenstein. As shall be seen, their marriage was one of many trans-Atlantic bonds that linked Southern Africa and North America. See e.g. Report by Bill Sutherland, 7 January 1976, IAD 1976, ADMINISTRATION AFRICA PROGRAMS ADMINISTRATION ......*American Friends Services Committee-Philadelphia*: At this conference on Namibia in Dakar, Senegal, he noticed that "more [Namibian liberation] fighters seem to have married Afro-Americans than have other African freedom fighters." At the same site see David Sogge to File, 14 June 1976, ID 1977 ADMINISTRATION AFRICA PROGRAMS ADMINISTRATION SOUTHERN MOZAMBIQUE.....*AFSC*: José Carlos Lobo, then serving as Mozambique's chief envoy at the United Nations, was a graduate of California State University-Long Beach: "His American 'family' lives in Akron, Pennsylvania and is Mennonite....." See also *Cape Times*, 15 August 1981: Eunice Bradley of U.S. marries Dr. Mandla Amos Tshabalala of South Africa in Florida. Of course, influential Euro-Americans at times married those of the European minority in Southern Africa. See Kenneth Towsey to S.D. O'Connell, 17 December 1971, Box 2, *Kenneth Towsey Papers, University of Mississippi-Oxford*: Chester Crocker, the leading U.S. diplomat in the region during the presidency of Ronald Reagan, was—said Towsey, Rhodesia's key operative in Washington—"married to Ben Baron's daughter" (speaking of a prominent member of the colonial elite there) and "therefore takes a close interest in Rhodesian affairs."

5. In 1968 as a student at Princeton, I was involved in a building takeover driven by the university's holdings in corporations invested in apartheid South Africa. See e.g. William Bowen to Robert Goheen, 22 November 1968,

Readers should note that this book makes use of the author's personal memories, which may—or may not—be footnoted (though a close reading of my personal papers at the New York Public Library, will substantiate my remembrances).

* * *

We do not need to go as far back as the 17th century, when the process that led to European settlement in North America was linked to a similar process at the southern tip of Africa, to identify connections between these regions.[6] In 1953 Hayden Raynor of the U.S. State Department, was instructed that the "surplus population of Europe" should now be settled in Africa, not the U.S., since the ruling class centered in Pretoria was seen to need bolstering. "The early American settlers were able to suppress the Indians," Raynor was told, so "why cannot the British [with] the assistance of the other Europeans do likewise" in Africa? One useful tactic would be to string "electric wire…fences between the settlers and [Africans]," an update from

---

Box 278, *Records of the Office of the President, Robert F. Goheen, Princeton University, Princeton, New Jersey*: "John Schrecker just came in to report on last evening's meeting of the ABC," the Association of Black Collegians, of which I was a leading member: "he had never before felt so much hostility when speaking to a group….some of the black freshmen, in particular, are very unhappy here and are really alienated from the University…..they do not fear expulsion…..angry militant students…..more moderate black students feel unable to take any position counter to the position of the militants……a real crisis in the making." See also Gerald Horne and Melba Smith to "Dear Friends," 26 January 1980, Box 6, *George Houser Papers, Michigan State University, East Lansing, Michigan:* On the eve of the first democratic elections in Zimbabwe, the Committee to Support the Patriotic Front of Zimbabwe—sited in New York City—which I chaired, turned over tens of thousands of dollars split evenly between the two major African majority parties—the Zimbabwe African Peoples Union [ZAPU] and the Zimbabwe African National Union [ZANU], which prevailed then and continues to rule. As noted in the letter I drafted, "the outcome [of this election] will affect the whole of Africa and possibly the course of world events." The concert we organized that led to this donation featured a stellar array of musicians including Hugh Masekela, Abdullah Ibrahim, Jimmy Owen, Beaver Harris, Machito and the choreographer, Rod Rodgers. The event was endorsed by e.g. Harry Belafonte; Tanzanian diplomat Salim Salim and pugilist, Muhammad Ali: in this collection, see the Press Release, 25 January 1980.

6. See e.g. Gerald Horne, *The Apocalypse of Settler Colonialism: The Roots of Slavery, White Supremacy and Capitalism in Seventeenth Century North America and the Caribbean*, New York: Monthly Review Press, 2018.

the 17th century. "If they"—the Africans— "tried to get into the white territory, they would be electrocuted," the memo noted with cool dispassion.[7] [emphasis-original]

This callous thinking was not unusual during the high tide of colonialism, which—after all—was premised on the now discredited notion that there were those (principally Europeans) who were destined to rule, not least over Africans and others not ushered into the hallowed halls of "whiteness." Testifying before a congressional panel in 1966, the eminent U.S. military man S.L.A. Marshall dismissed airily the idea that the very concept of apartheid was ready for the dung heap of history: "As to [the] white autocracy bit," he sniffed, "many of us have forgotten that in the period following the Revolutionary War [in North America] only 6 percent of the white people of the United States had the vote;" thus, "we [sic] were a white autocracy" and, as such, could hardly object to unsightly events in Southern Africa.[8] Yes, asserted General Marshall, the Unilateral Declaration of Independence in November 1965 by the European minority in Rhodesia, was wholly comparable to 1776—one sought to evade African majority rule, the other abolition of slavery. "The Declaration of Independence did not free one Negro slave or save the life ...of one local Indian;" again, he stressed "the United States began as a white autocracy." So why object to apartheid?[9] The comparison of UDI to 1776 was a frequent rhetorical device of certain U.S. patriots.[10] Still, General Marshall's harsh words should remind us that it was not easy to compel Washington to retreat from its untenable support for minority rule in Southern Africa.

From the opposite shore, there were Africans like me—and some non-Africans too—in the racist wilds of North America who were

---

7. R. Youngblood to Hayden Raynor, Director, Bureau of European Affairs, Office of the British Commonwealth and European [Affairs], 4 May 1953, Box 3571, Record Group 59, Africa 1950-1954, 645A. 00/3-951, Decimal File, *National Archives and Records Administration, College Park, Maryland*. [Hereinafter denoted as NARA-CP]

8. "Hearings Before the Subcommittee on Africa of the Committee on Foreign Affairs of the House of Representatives....[89th] Congress, Second Session," 23-24, 30 March 1966, Part II, Washington, D.C.: Government Printing Office, 1966, Box 77, Folder 1352, *S.L.A. Marshall Papers, University of Texas-El Paso.*

9. Report, 1965, Box 57, Folder 480, *S.L.A. Marshall Papers.*

10. See Cartoon, in *Dan Smoot Report,* 13(Number 9, 27 February 1967), Box 86, *William Jennings Bryan Dorn Papers, University of South Carolina-Columbia*: Here in a cartoon a bewigged advocate denoted as "England" before a bewigged judge points to "13 American colonies" demanding "sanctions against this rebel who has set up an all-white rule in a nation of Redskins."

magnetically drawn to likeminded movements in Africa. Toivo ya Toivo was not the only liberation leader who found love in North America. Janet Johnson, a Euro-American from the Midwest, was only 17 when she met Eduardo Mondlane, then 31, of Mozambique; they married in 1956 while he was a student in the U.S. Her goal then was to be a missionary doctor in Africa.[11] Mondlane was present, according to the memory of David Finke, at a "quadrennial gathering of the Student Volunteer Movement and the National Student Christian Federation in Athens, Ohio. It was a memorable meeting for me in many ways," he recalled, "in that the speakers' list included [Dr. Martin Luther King, Jr.] ...James Lawson," and other luminaries "who laid a groundwork of preparation for the northern student response to the sit-ins which occurred just one year later" in Greensboro, North Carolina in February 1960.[12]

In short, Mondlane and other Africans were present and instrumental as Jim Crow began to crumble, unavoidably drawing lessons and aspirations for the ongoing battle against colonialism. But even before this fateful confluence, the then leader of the African National Congress of South Africa [ANC], A.B. Xuma, found love and inspiration in the person of North Carolinian Madie Hall Xuma while studying in the U.S. She arrived in South Africa in the early 1940s and quickly became a leader of the Women's League of the ANC.[13]

Then there were families with branches in both the U.S. and South Africa. Amy Schecter, who happened to be Jewish, graduated from Barnard College in Manhattan, became a Communist, then became involved in the trailblazing 1929 cotton mill strike in Gastonia, North Carolina (her sister, Ruth, spent much of her adult life in South Africa and also was a Communist: ironically, their brother Frank, a prominent New York attorney, represented mill interests in Dixie.).[14]

Naturally, Washington was aware of these intimacies and sought to take advantage of them. In a "confidential" 1956 missive from Pretoria, the State Department was informed about Dr. Willem Christiaan Naudé, South Africa's emissary in Switzerland (who had served in Washington at the time of the all-important Bretton Woods

---

11. *New York Post*, 17 November 1967, Box 1, Subgroup II, *Herbert Shore Collection*.

12. David Finke to George Houser, 7 August 1970, Box 1, Subgroup II, *Herbert Shore Collection*.

13. Emily Herring Wilson, *Hope and Dignity: Older Black Women of the South*, Philadelphia: Temple University Press, 1983, 147.

14. John A. Salmond, *Gastonia 1929: The Story of the Loray Mill Strike*, Chapel Hill: University of North Carolina Press, 1995.

accord and was tied to the Broederbond, the fraternity of powerful Afrikaners in his homeland); he was "influenced by life abroad and by his wife," it was announced. She was a "British born naturalized American" who was "well disposed toward the U.S. and U.K. and deeply mistrustful of the Russians," it was added brightly. She was "friendly and impetuous," a tendency facilitated by the fact that she "occasionally over indulges in alcohol," a potential point of leverage that could possibly be enhanced by her U.S. nationality.[15]

The brother-in-law of Helen Suzman, a leader of the so-called "liberal" opposition during the apartheid era, studied at Harvard in the early 1930s, where his son later matriculated. Her nephew, Magnus, was an alumnus of MIT. Their father had a sizeable number of U.S. firms among his clients.[16]

Some of these trans-oceanic ties were more attenuated. For example, like many who joined the South African Communist Party, the father of the leading U.S. novelist Norman Mailer was of Lithuanian Jewish descent; he decamped to South Africa, then served in the British army but after leaving the military, migrated to the U.S. where he had relatives—and where his renowned son was born in New Jersey.[17] A key shaper of U.S. policy toward apartheid, Edwin S. Munger, lived for several years in South Africa and had a wife who was born there.[18]

Mailer was no promoter of Southern African literary creativity. On the other hand, Langston Hughes—the Harlem Bard—was in touch with Richard Rive of South Africa in the 1950s. Lewis Nkosi and Bessie Head were influenced by James Baldwin (Head has also been profitably compared to both Toni Morrison and Alice Walker). Richard Wright was influential in South Africa. Musician and poet Gil Scott Heron, like others, indicted apartheid in his artistic work. Keorapetse Kgositsile was among those who saw the similarities between his homeland, South Africa, and his chosen site of exile, the U.S.; a comparison not unique to his oeuvre.[19] Gwendolyn Brooks, the celebrated African American writer, considered the exiled Kgositsile to

15. "Confidential" Report from "Dulles," 1 November 1956, Record Group 59, Box 3233, Central Decimal Files, 745A.5, *NARA-CP*.

16. Memorandum of Conversation, 24 June 1964, Central Foreign Policy Files, Record Group 59, Box 2628, *NARA-CP*.

17. Carl Rollyson, *The Lives of Norman Mailer: A Biography*, New York: Paragon House, 1991.

18. *Cape Argus*, 14 January 1970.

19. Stephane Pierre Raymond Robolin, *Grounds of Engagement: Apartheid-era African American and South African Writing*, Urbana: University of Illinois Press, 2015, 1, 24-25, 91, 37, 91, 94, 117, 126.

be a founder of the formidable Black Arts Movement in the U.S., while she—in turn—wrote poems about Soweto (which she compared to the Chicago "township" that was Harvey) and Steve Biko, the South African hero.[20]

Then there was Danny Rochman, who was born in Johannesburg in 1960 but wound up residing in Chicago. Of Latvian and Lithuanian Jewish descent, he recalled in 2009 how Nelson Mandela hid in his parents' home when he was on the lam from the authorities in the early 1960s.[21] A fellow Chicagoan, Lisa Brock, moved to Maputo, Mozambique in 1983: "it was rough," she recalled later, "very rough for me personally....I was scared...." The family that she lived with was part of the military wing of the ANC and top leaders like Joe Slovo and Chris Hani were frequently on the scene.[22]

Predating her on the battlefield was Mary Louise Hooper of the U.S. Her family had missionary ties to South Africa and she moved to Durban in 1955 and worked closely with Chief Albert Luthuli of the ANC—before being arrested, jailed, and deported in 1957. This Phi Beta Kappa graduate of Stanford University was, it was said, "elected the first Caucasian member" of the ANC and represented the group at important gatherings in Accra in 1958 and Tunis in 1960 and Cairo in 1961.[23]

Hooper and Madie Hall Xuma were unusual as U.S. nationals arriving in South Africa to partake in the often woeful condition of Africans. More typical were those who arrived to take advantage of this condition through the grossest form of labor exploitation. By 1963, as Jim Crow was in a defensive crouch and apartheid was headed in that direction, the White House contemplated a "confidential" report that detailed that "direct U.S. investment in South Africa at the end of 1962 was $353,000,000," while "if private bank deposit portfolio investments, etc., are added, total U.S. private investment is currently on the order of $600,000,000." Returns were described as "high"— "about 16% per year in the mining industry and from 12 to 20% in the manufacturing and commercial fields. More than 150 U.S. firms have holdings in South Africa," it was said. "Twelve are in the automotive field, 12 in drugs and cosmetics, 12 in the

---

20. Angela Jackson, *A Surprised Queenhood in the New Black Sun: The Life & Legacy of Gwendolyn Brooks*, Boston: Beacon Press, 2017, 131, 167, 170.

21. Oral History, Danny Rochman, 1 December 2009, *Columbia College Chicago*.

22. Oral History, Lisa Brock, 8 December 2009, *Columbia College Chicago*.

23. Information Sheet, 1961, Box 5, *Mary Louise Hooper Papers, Michigan State University-East Lansing*.

electrical equipment and appliance trade and 10 in food processing." The giants there included General Motors, Ford, Studebaker, Chrysler, Firestone, Goodyear, General Electric, Westinghouse, Cal-Tex, (known elsewhere as Esso), International Harvester, American Cyanamide, Kellogg, and Procter and Gamble. These companies were "under some pressure" by Pretoria, which demanded they conform to apartheid priorities, e.g. "bulletproof tires in the case of Firestone...."[24] This massive investment along with the calcified attitudes thereby engendered also made it difficult for U.S. imperialism to bid farewell to apartheid.

Lubricating the path for the deep penetration of U.S. capital into the region was the mass ignorance of North Americans when it came to Southern Africa. In late 1970 U.S. Communists dejectedly told their South African peers that the "struggles of the Portuguese colonies are all but unknown in the United States, even among anti-imperialists. Even the fact there is an African National Congress or a PAIGC [African Party for the Independence of Guinea-Bissau and Cape Verde Islands, then Portuguese colony], is not well known in the U.S." "Most U.S. anti-imperialists including Communists," it was said wondrously, "do not recognize the names of most African countries let alone the movements operating in those countries," while "efforts of white Americans in solidarity with Africa have been sporadic...."[25]

* * *

At the same time U.S. ruling circles were preoccupied with the growing relationship between African Americans and their "kith and kin" in Southern Africa. In 1970 a report from the Ford Foundation concluded with little hint of satisfaction that "there is a growing interest of Americans, particularly Black Americans, in Africa and the potential of the black-white issue in Southern Africa as a source of tension both in Africa and the United States." In this context, wrote Wayne Fredericks, "the withdrawal or substantial reduction of Foundation

24. "Confidential" Report, 30 June 1963, Box 99, *Harlan Cleveland Papers, John F. Kennedy Presidential Library-Boston, Massachusetts.*

25. Charlene Mitchell and Michael Myerson, "Africa's Impact on Black America," *African Communist*, (Number 43, Fourth Quarter 1970): 100-111, 198. See also Kenneth Towsey to N.R. Heathcote, 12 May 1966, Box 1, *Kenneth Towsey Papers*: "Before November last," speaking of the ill-fated secession in Salisbury, "95% of Americans would not have known the difference between Rhodesia and Indonesia.....a school teacher once referred to my mother-in-law as the lady from Rhodonesia [sic]...."

activity in sub-Sahara Africa would entail adverse repercussions in Africa but would also be viewed by groups in the U.S. in which the Foundation has a strong interest as a decision based on race or color," to the detriment of the U.S. ruling elite.[26]

In other words, as the U.S. was compelled to make an agonized retreat from the more egregious aspects of Jim Crow, it continued to support apartheid, placing enormous strain on this system of iniquity, which finally was forced to yield in 1994, as its chief protector was forced to accede to pressure from its own newly energized population. Moreover, the U.S. elite found it hard to reduce spending in Africa because of apprehension of how such a move would be viewed on these shores.

These links between the two citadels of white supremacy had been detected in Washington and there was angst about the prospect that the internationalization of South African racism would contribute to a similar trend within the U.S. In 1963, Dr. King appeared at the U.N. and Secretary of State Dean Rusk was worried. Rusk lobbied to ensure that the cleric would "confine his public testimony entirely to South Africa" and not "veer…into criticism of the domestic United States racial situation." Rusk was blunt: "I have serious reservations about the desirability of Dr. King's appearing before the U.N…in view of the danger that our domestic racial policies will be made the focus…." In a message to President Kennedy, he fretted that this popular leader would be "in some sense [be] appealing to the United Nations" for external "assistance." He recommended that the president "take this up with Dr. King," given the "serious implications of his appearance."[27]

By late 1964, hands were once again wringing in the White House, as Dr. King headed to Europe to receive the Nobel Peace Prize. Presidential aide Lee White worried that he might make "statements …abroad about an economic blockade of the Union [sic] of South Africa and [make] a perhaps unfortunate linkage of Mississippi and South Africa,"[28] since the former bastion of racism

---

26. Report, December 1970, 3255-6161 (fa 739b), Box 267, 005996, *Ford Foundation Records, Rockefeller Archive Center, Sleepy Hollow, New York.*

27. Secretary of State Dean Rusk to President Kennedy, 21 June 1963, Box 159, *Papers of President Kennedy, National Security Files, John F. Kennedy Presidential Library-Boston*. Tellingly, James Earl Ray, the man believed to be Dr. King's assassin, sought to flee to Rhodesia after this cleric's murder: **Washington Post**, 2 May 1997; **London Times**, 8 July 2008.

28. Lee White to President Lyndon B. Johnson, 18 December 1964, WHCF, Subject Files, Gen Co 296, Box 71, *Papers of Lyndon B. Johnson, Lyndon B. Johnson Presidential Library-Austin, Texas.*

was likewise highly vulnerable to a sweeping embargo. As protests heated up in Dixie, yet another presidential advisor—Ulric Haynes, an African American—saw a looming conflict between the White House's "progressive position on domestic race relations" and its failure to confront apartheid boldly. "In order to prevent the Communists from seizing the initiative in Southern Africa," he warned, the U.S. "has no choice but to stand on principle." He chose to "strongly recommend that the President call in Charlie Engelhard [the largest single investor in South Africa and an active Democrat] to express his concern"[29]—and to move a satellite tracking station to colonial Mozambique from apartheid South Africa, an indicator of the limited options the Cold War provided. Yet the fact that they considered confronting a major donor also indicated the heavy pressure delivered by trans-Atlantic racism.

It was in 1967 that U.S. ultra-rightist Dan Smoot cited with alarm, in a widely circulated radio broadcast, a "Carnegie study" which observed that "'if American Negroes increasingly identify the struggle against apartheid with their domestic civil rights struggle, they could bring interest in the South African policy of the United Nations to a level seldom achieved by any foreign policy issue"[30]—which is precisely what occurred.

That same year, U.S. Ambassador to the United Nations Arthur Goldberg conceded mournfully that "the Rhodesian problem causes us difficulties with domestic public opinion" since "there is in the U.S. a very active Rhodesian lobby." Apologetically, he sought to explain a perceived anti-Rhodesian vote that he was "obliged" to cast "as we did because to do otherwise would have caused us domestic racial difficulties and hurt our business interests in every African country…." Translation: increasingly militant U.S. Negroes combined with newly independent African nations to compel Washington to defy the "very active Rhodesian lobby;" a situation which could only cause grief for the ruling Democratic Party for years to come.[31]

By 1969 Kissinger's National Security Council was sounding the alarm. "Because of the multi-racial character of our society and our

---

29. Memorandum from Ulric Haynes, 28 June 1965, Box 3, *Files of Edward K. Hamilton, Lyndon B. Johnson Presidential Library-Austin, Texas.*

30. *Dan Smoot Report*, 13(Number 9, 27 February 1967), Box 86, *William Jennings Bryan Dorn Papers, University of South Carolina-Columbia.*

31. Summary Notes of 567th Meeting of National Security Council, 25 January 1967, 12:10 to 12:45, Box 36, *Dean Rusk Research Collection, University of Georgia-Athens.*

own racial problems," it was noted tremulously, "other countries tend to see our relationship with Southern Africa as reflections of domestic attitudes on race. This situation," said the NSC memorandum, is exacerbated by the "extension of South African racial discrimination to black Americans who may be refused visas or who are subjected to segregated facilities in South Africa...." At stake was U.S. direct investment in the region, which had reached the billion-dollar plateau and "yields a highly profitable return..."[32]

By 1970 U.S. Communists were informing their South African comrades that it was "hardly coincidental that the new character of the Black liberation movement in the U.S. developed simultaneously with the political dependence of most of Africa," providing a basis for pro-Jim Crow and pro-apartheid formations to join hands.[33]

Naturally, Washington sought to take advantage of this easy familiarity between and among anti-apartheid advocates on both sides of the Atlantic. Leo Milas claimed to have been born in Mozambique and was said to have been taken to the U.S. at an early age. In fact, says the progressive, Maputo-based writer Iain Christie, he was Leo Clinton Aldridge of Texas; his parents were U.S.-born and resided in California. Yet somehow he rose to the highest level of the military struggle in southeast Africa where, it was said, he was perpetually "wreaking havoc."[34] He was to become a founding member of the terrorist group known colloquially as the "Mozambique Resistance," RENAMO or MNR, which with the assistance of the U.S. ultra-right was able to attain a degree of respectability as an interlocutor of the ruling FRELIMO, the Front for the Liberation Movement of Mozambique. He was present at the creation of the MNR in 1977, though he was dubbed by one analyst as "African American," a "mysterious figure who had infiltrated FRELIMO in the early 1960s pretending to be a Mozambican".[35]

---

32. National Security Council Memorandum #39, 10 April 1969 in Kenneth Mokoena, ed., *South Africa and the United States: The Declassified History*, New York: New Press, 1993, 201-204, 201.

33. Charlene Mitchell and Michael Myerson, "Africa's Impact on Black America," *African Communist*, (Number 3, Fourth Quarter 1970): 100-111, 100.

34. Iain Christie, *Samora Machel: A Biography*, London: Zed, 1989, 35.

35. William Minter, *Apartheid's Contras: An Inquiry into the Roots of War in Angola and Mozambique*, Johannesburg: Witwatersrand University Press, 1994, 156: The daughter of Ray Cline, a former deputy director of the U.S. Central Intelligence Agency, was also tied to MNR and was married to Robert MacKenzie, who had similar connections. See also Report, 10 August 1973, Box 1, *George Houser Papers, Michigan State University-East Lansing*:

Aldridge—or "Milas"—is but an extreme example of how Washington sought to influence the region using foul means. A more typical relationship was that enjoyed by Joseph Gaboakwe "Joe" Matthews, a son of ANC leader Z.K. Matthews-the latter had spent time in Manhattan in the early 1950s. The younger Matthews had close ties to both the ANC and its partner, the South African Communist Party. Yet, in 1957 Washington was told that this slippery figure was "probably since in his offer to provide Native mailing-lists for [the U.S. Information Service]" to help "combat Communism and promote goodwill towards the United States."[36]

Such ties of singular intimacy between the U.S. and Southern Africa aided the anti-apartheid cause in that so many in North America had unique knowledge of issues there that enhanced their lobbying in Washington. But this cut the other way too in that those sympathetic to Pretoria were also aided by their peculiar knowledge in resisting the winds of change.

* * *

These connections between North America and Southern Africa extended to the earliest days of colonial settlement, when the Cape of Good Hope and the region surrounding Manhattan were both claimed by the Netherlands, easing travel between the two sprawling regions, not to mention the trade in Africans.[37] Travel between the two may have been smoothed further when London claimed control of the southern tip of Africa at the beginning of the 19th century.[38] When London abolished slavery in the 1830s, it drove the slaveholding republic and their comrades in the Cape closer together, not least in enslaving Mozambicans.[39] In fact, the "Great Trek," a phrase describing the strenuous effort by Afrikaners—or Boers,

---

Houser, a leader of the American Committee on Africa, recalled after the death of FRELIMO founder Eduardo Mondlane that the latter met Milas in the U.S. and found that the turncoat "spoke Spanish and not Portuguese." Mondlane supported Milas before ascertaining that he was "a fake."

36. Edward Holmes, U.S. Embassy Pretoria to Secretary of State, 18 March 1957, Record Group 59, Box 3230, Central Decimal File, *NARA-CP*.

37. Gerald Horne, *The Apocalypse of Settler Colonialism*, passim.

38. C.I. Latrobe, *Journal of a Visit to South Africa in 1815 and 1816 with Some Account of the Missionary Settlements of the United Brethren Near the Cape of Good Hope*, New York: Eastburn, 1818.

39. Gerald Horne, *Negro Comrades of the Crown: African Americans and the British Empire Fight the U.S. Before Emancipation*, New York: New York University Press, 2012, passim.

i.e. the descendants of the original Dutch settlers, replenished by the arrival of French Protestants in the late 17th century—to escape London's jurisdiction by heading north, could just as well describe the journey taken by British settlers who fled to the mainland of North America in the 18th century from the Caribbean to escape the fury of revolt by enslaved Africans.[40]

Unsurprisingly, as shall be seen, the so-called Confederate States of America found succor in Cape Town when this outlaw regime sought to secede from the U.S. in order to perpetuate the enslavement of Africans forevermore. The favor was returned during the war between London and the settlers in South Africa at the end of the 19th century. On the day of his arrival in Mozambique, said Richard Harding Davis, speaking of the city that became Maputo, "the town was invaded by the Irish-American ambulance corps from Chicago," eager to wage war against London. Paul Kruger, settler leader, not unlike his counterparts in North America in 1776, claimed that London "turned the black men on the border against us." These Irish-American combatants, said Davis, "traveled many thousand miles to risk their lives for people fighting for their independence", referring to the settlers.[41]

Still, sympathy for the underdog Boers was widespread among Euro-Americans. In 1902 the 8-year-old Allen Dulles, future leader of U.S. intelligence, lavishly praised the Afrikaners in writing that attracted the rapt attention of his uncle, future Secretary of State Robert Lansing, and President Theodore Roosevelt. "I hope that the Boers will win," said the budding conservative, "for the Boers are in the wright [sic] and the British are wrong...."[42]

Rhetoric notwithstanding, the so-called "Anglo-Boer War" by its nature exposed what was evident: the idea of a united "white" South Africa—even surrounded by a sullen African majority—was merely notional. This was the dilemma of the dominant Afrikaners: they were not as successful as their counterparts in North America in constructing a synthetic "whiteness" that could have had a better chance of extending white supremacy than the existent Afrikaner nationalism. F.W. de Klerk, the final apartheid president, recalled in

40. Gerald Horne, *The Counter-Revolution of 1776: Slave Resistance and the Origins of the United States of America*, New York: New York University Press, 2014.

41. Richard Harding Davis, *With Both Armies in South Africa*, New York: Scribner's, 1900, 91, 145.

42. Edwin S. Munger, *Afrikaner and African Nationalism: South African Parallels and Parameters*, London: Oxford University Press, 1967, 6.

1999 that the "Anglo-Boer War burnt itself into the collective consciousness of my people, the Afrikaners, like no other event in our history." He compared the setbacks suffered to what befell Dixie by 1865. He was "strongly anti-British" in his youth[43]—and he was not unique.

Unlike their counterparts, however, the Afrikaners did not have a majority. Still, their stiff-necked Christianity did not allow for overtures to the Jewish population that began to flow southward in the wake of Czarist repression. There was already a steady stream of Jewish migrants, from the Baltic region of Europe most notably. By 1940 the U.S. legation noticed the "swastikas in Pretoria," conspicuously placed on posters seeking to recruit for the British military. "Reports of sabotage, treachery and even threatened uprisings," lamented Washington's man, "are confirmed on a…widening scale." "New internment camps" were being "rapidly established" for these residents, which did not seem to deter new arrivals.[44]

One reason for this was bruited in early 1943 when it was reported that there was in Cape Town growing "bitterness over the Jewish influence in this country." The allegation was that Jan Smuts, the nation's leading figure, was "directly under the control of the Jews," a charge that was also affixed to Washington too, leading to "anxiety regarding our possible intervention in the Native Question after the war." "Nazi anti-Roosevelt propaganda "was overflowing. Reuters and BBC were indirectly responsible as both tended to downplay the U.S. role in fighting in North Africa—excepting setbacks of course—while success was ascribed to the "Allies."[45]

The U.S. envoy in Pretoria chose Christmas Day 1942 to inform the president he addressed as "Dear Franklin" that "there is a Jewish problem here," manifested in "resentment of Jewish intrusion into every line of business particularly real estate." Diplomat Lincoln MacVeagh seemed to sense how this bias was organically connected to the racism designed to exploit Africans, who were "permitted to become fully qualified doctors of medicine and to practice surgery but are debarred from becoming most classes of carpenters and joiners." "This sounds fantastic," he conceded "but it is true," a result of intense lobbying by the "organized European Labour Party," the

---

43. F.W. de Klerk, *The Last Trek—a New Beginning: The Autobiography*, New York: St. Martin's, 1999, 6, 20.

44. L.G. Keena to Secretary of State, 10 June 1940, Record Group 59, Decimal Files, 848A.221/4. Box 5123, *NARA-CP*.

45. Report from Cape Town, 17 March 1943, Record Group 59, Box 5128, Decimal Files, 848A.221/4, *NARA-CP*.

"chief obstacle to reform." There was a "natural gravitation" of Afrikaner republicans "to the side of Nazi Germany" and the perception that there was an ongoing "raising [of] the consuming power of the Native for the benefit of the English trade"— "is still certainly one of the cruder British objectives here…." Like U.S. commentators and leaders during the high tide of anti-apartheid activism decades later, he knew even then that "however distant the affairs of the whites and blacks in South Africa may appear we shall surely have to take account of them on the other side of the Atlantic someday…."[46] South African bigotry could not be quarantined, and barring Africans from being carpenters but allowing them to become surgeons reflected this bigotry's working class base—a reality that had a counterpart in the U.S. too.

At the same time there was the growth of the pro-fascist Ossewa-Brandwag Broederbond, symbolized by Oswald Pirow. "German is spoken exclusively in his home," it was said forebodingly of this man who attained postwar notoriety by persecuting the ANC and their Communist allies. He was "very intimate with [Antonio] Salazar," the Portuguese ultra-rightist, and Hermann Goering of Nazi infamy. Becoming "Dictator of South Africa" was his goal, it was said in 1942 when this ambition did not seem unrealistic. Pirow collaborated with "German agents" with "sinister designs," some of which were formulated in "Von Ribbentrop's office in Berlin during 1935," a reference to one of Adolf Hitler's top lieutenants. The OBB had "dynamite" and "made attempts" to "blow up bridges and plants" and "beat up soldiers on the streets," and conducted "espionage at the ports". South African Broadcasting had been "controlled by them up to about a year ago," which was quite helpful to their dastardly plans. Such "gangsterism" meant that a "real armed rebellion" was not out of the question. "Political murders" were proliferating. By 1939 OBB membership was said to be an astounding 200,000.[47] In the 1950s the influential Communist Rusty Bernstein continued to affirm that Pirow had "always been an admirer of Hitler and still sponsors an influential pro-Nazi periodical called 'The New Order.'"[48]

46. Lincoln MacVeagh to "Dear Franklin," 25 December 1942, Box 51, *PSF Diplomatic, Franklin D. Roosevelt Presidential Library,*Hyde Park, New York.

47. Lincoln MacVeagh Pretoria to Secretary of State, 11 December 1942, Record Group 59, Box 5121, Decimal File, *NARA-CP*.

48. Rusty Bernstein, *Memory Against Forgetting: Memoirs from a Life in South African Politics*, London: Penguin, 1999, 183.

Clearly, the fact that certain pro-fascist leaders were interned during the war had not discredited their ideology. Shortly after the war ended, a U.S diplomat met with one of these men and his spouse for three hours, "speaking quite freely of the sabotage and violence committed by his followers during the war years." The "Stormjaers or Storm Troopers had been formed within the Ossewa Brandwag," holding a firm commitment to the "National Socialist philosophy." This leader, Hans van Rensburg, had visited Germany in the 1930s and met the top leadership, including Joseph Goebbels— "whom he admired very much," said his interlocutor. He planned to "bring five to ten thousand homeless German children to South Africa," which would have the bonus of bolstering the constituency in neighboring Namibia, initially colonized by Berlin.[49]

In 1959, the liberal leader Helen Suzman objected to what Washington's delegate termed "brutality and mistreatment" of Africans—which "provoked a Nationalist anti-Semitic outburst more violent than any seen in the House [of Assembly] since World War II...."[50] By 1968 Washington's man in Johannesburg had exposed why his nation was so reluctant to distance itself from apartheid, despite official revulsion: there were an "inordinately high number of Jews among listed Communists,"[51] it was reported.

The obvious sympathy in Pretoria for the Nazis complicated Washington's attempt to ally with apartheid. As the U.S. moved awkwardly away from fascism's close relative—Jim Crow—overt embrace of Nazis became only more difficult.

In addition, there was fervent sympathy for the odious likes of Pirow. In 1976, when Secretary of State Henry Kissinger was frantically seeking to hold back the surging tide of anti-colonialism, a South Carolina Congressman was instructed bluntly by a constituent, "please remember that a man acts according to his own background. Kissinger is a Jew and this race has survived for the last 2000 years by compromising, giving up their property and moving on rather than stand and fight," the preferred option of Attorney Hugh Beasley of Greenwood. "He is doing the same thing with our

49. "Confidential" Report, 17 June 1946, Record Group 59, Box 6190, Decimal Files, *NARA-CP*.

50. Report from Cape Town, 24 June 1959, Reel 6, *Confidential U.S. State Department Files, South Africa, 1955-1959, Internal Affairs, Decimal Numbers 745A, 745A and 945 A and Foreign Affairs, Decimal Numbers 645 A and 611.45 A, NARA-CP.*

51. Consul Geneal-Johannesburg to Secretary of State, 29 August 1968, Record Group 59, *Central Foreign Policy Files, Political and Defense*, Box 2467, *NARA-CP*.

country," Beasley insisted; "South Africa will be next and that is when the 'dung' is going to hit the fan" since the "Negroid race of Africa is the only race on the face of the earth that has never developed an independent civilization...."[52]

In some ways, obdurately incoherent apartheid was its own gravedigger. Afrikaner nationalism made it difficult to absorb those fleeing Europe; indeed, apartheid was, among other things, an attempt to elevate poorer Afrikaners and wall them off from competition. But with growing international investment and increasing ties to the U.S., which was being compelled to retreat from its own form of apartheid, Pretoria came into conflict with the anticommunist superpower that was keen to back South Africa against the perceived threat represented by the growth of the African majority—which was influenced by Communists and backed in turn by Moscow. Moreover, growing U.S. investment meant a more developed economy in South Africa and a real need for more skilled laborers, making it difficult to avoid recruiting among skilled Africans. Chafing under apartheid restrictions, Africans became more susceptible to the blandishments of Communists—all of which was creating a virtuous circle, insofar as the strangulation of apartheid was concerned.

The U.S. elite was aware of the strategic importance of South Africa and the perceived danger presented by the ouster from

52. Hugh Beasley to Butler Derricks, 29 September 1976, Box 2, *Butler Derricks Papers, University of South Carolina-Columbia.* Of course, the threshold question is why anticommunism—peppered with racism—was so appealing to the U.S. ruling elite. Though often forgotten it was the U.S. elite that endured one of the largest expropriations of private property without compensation in world history in 1865 when investment in enslaved Africans was nullified. The socialism which Communists promised was thought to mean more expropriation. When Paul Robeson, who also happened to be a fluent speaker of Russian and is a major character in this book, zoomed to the forefront of the struggle for socialism, this fear of what socialism was thought to portend, metastasized. And this was occurring in the context of a nation where the fiercest class struggle historically had been that between the enslaved and the slaveholders, culminating in a debacle for the latter, with the struggle now featuring Robeson leading to a result exceeding 1865 exponentially—or so it was thought. To that extent, anticommunism was a logical response by Washington and Wall Street to the "threat" they perceived they were facing. When Robeson became the most visible champion of an anti-apartheid struggle in which Communists played a leading role, this enhanced the ineffable tie between white supremacy and anticommunism. Unfortunately, the understandable focus on "race" in discussing the torturous relation that was enslavement, has obscured too frequently the similarly explosive "class" aspects.

power of the European minority regime and its replacement by a Communist-influenced African majority. U.S. General S.L.A. Marshall was petrified in 1967 by the prospect of what he termed the "Congolization of Africa from the Cape upward," and how the latter region was linked with Suez as a grand chokepoint of the planet. "Seeing the globe as a whole," he asserted, "the Cape is an anchor position." The recently concluded war prosecuted by Israel, he said, "heightened [the] importance of [the] Cape."[53]

* * *

Yet another factor complicating the regional hegemony of Pretoria was the staunch opposition of Communists at home and abroad. At the same time in the U.S., there was a small but influential cadre of Communists that included within its orbit a host of prominent personalities, including Paul Robeson,[54] W.E.B. Du Bois,[55] Shirley Graham Du Bois,[56] William Patterson,[57] Ben Davis,[58] and a host of others. The granting of anti-Jim Crow concessions to the constituency they represented undermined their base of support, but also made it more problematic for U.S. imperialism to align with its appointed guardian of the Cape.

African Communists on both sides of the Atlantic were in turn sympathetic to Moscow, a tendency that inflamed passions in Washington and Pretoria alike. As the Cold War unfolded, this made it more difficult for the superpower to forge an entente with the African National Congress [ANC], which harbored Communist leadership. It also made it more difficult for African American groupings to endorse the ANC too for fear of absorbing the presumed Red taint.

---

53. "A Special Study of South Africa: The Strategic View," for the American Affairs Association, November 1967, Box 41, Folder 430, *S.L.A. Marshall Papers*.

54. Gerald Horne, *Paul Robeson: The Artist as Revolutionary*, London: Pluto, 2016.

55. Gerald Horne, *W.E.B. Du Bois: A Biography*, Santa Barbara: ABC-CLIO, 2010.

56. Gerald Horne, *Race Woman: The Lives of Shirley Graham Du Bois*, New York: New York University Press, 2001.

57. Gerald Horne, *Black Revolutionary: William Patterson and the Globalization of the African American Freedom Struggle*, Urbana: University of Illinois Press, 2013.

58. Gerald Horne, *Black Liberation/Red Scare: Ben Davis and the Communist Party*, Newark: University of Delaware Press, 1994.

Hysteria about Moscow in North America stretched back to the founding of the republic, where as early as 1775 there was a regnant fear of an anti-Yankee coalition of "Indians, Negroes, Russians" designed to "humble America," an apprehension shaped by fears of London's European allies, notably the Hessians.[59] The Bolshevik Revolution of 1917 caused this fright to metastasize, as Moscow moved aggressively to influence those pummeled by imperialism, Africans most notably. Even the heralded leader of the ANC—and global symbol of resistance and integrity—Nelson Mandela was said to be part of the CP.[60] This was confirmed by leading ANC member, Bawo Andrew Mlangeni, who joined the Young Communist League himself in 1945 where—he recalled later—he was "in the same cell with Ruth First," a leading radical intellectual. He only joined the ANC in 1949. Yes, he conceded in 2003, "Madiba [Mandela] was part of this," meaning the CP leadership. Since, he said, "Madiba's [prison] cell was Number 7" and "mine was Number 5," he was in a position to know.[61] While in Budapest in the early 1950s, Ahmed Kathrada, one of Mandela's closest Communist comrades, recalled, "I sent a great deal of Communist literature" to "Madiba" who "was a voracious reader."[62] (Kathrada may have known that Mandela had pored over Marxist classics, e.g. *Das Kapital* and *The Communist Manifesto*).[63] About a decade later, Communist Party member Rusty Bernstein "lent" Mandela "a Chinese booklet called 'How to be a Good Communist'" written by "Liu Shao Chia" and a book by Communist intellectual William Pomeroy on the Huk Rebellion in the Philippines; the former became a major issue in the trial that led to the ANC leader's lengthy incarceration.[64]

---

59. Robert G. Parkinson, *The Common Cause: Creating Race and Nation in the American Revolution*, Chapel Hill: University of North Carolina Press, 2016, 55.

60. Stephen Ellis and Tsepo Sechaba, *Comrades Against Apartheid: The ANC & the South African Communist Party in Exile*, Bloomington: Indiana University Press, 1992. Paul S. Landau, "Controlled by Communists? (Re) Assessing the ANC in its Exile Decades," *South African Historical Journal*, 67(Number 2, June 2015): 222-241, 223: The author agrees with the thesis that Mandela was part of the CP leadership. See also Tom Lodge, "Secret Party: South African Communists Between 1950 and 1960," *South African Historical Journal*, 67(Number 4, December 22015): 433-464.

61. Oral History, Bawo Andrew Mlagenia, 5 November 2003, *University of Connecticut-Storrs*.

62. Ahmed Kathrada, *Memoirs*, Cape Town: New Holland, 2004, 92.

63. David James Smith, *Young Mandela: The Revolutionary Years*, New York: Little Brown, 2010, 94.

64. Rusty Bernstein, *Memory Against Forgetting*, 229.

When the visiting Frank Loescher of the Philadelphia-based American Friends Service Committee spoke with Mandela in 1953 for an hour, he was struck by the fact that he "followed the straight Marxist interpretation of the causes of change."[65] Unsurprisingly, about a quarter of a century later Vice President Walter Mondale was told that Mandela became a part of the "underground [Communist Party] in the mid-1950s" and "has since adhered to Marxist philosophy. He was strongly influenced by the Castro rebellion in Cuba" and, filling out this combative image, it was added that he "enjoys boxing."[66] Official Washington had reason to know what Mandela's sympathetic biographer revealed: i.e. not only was the derided Paul Robeson "much loved by Mandela and his colleagues" but moreover "anyone who didn't recognize the baritone Paul Robeson was unworthy of their attention." (In addition on the wall of his 1950s home were pictures of not just Franklin Roosevelt and M.K. Gandhi but Josef Stalin.)[67] It was during the darkest days of apartheid in 1954 that Robeson told an ANC gathering that "there should be and must be much closer and stronger bonds between us because of the very nature of our common struggle"[68]—a sentiment that was bountifully reciprocated, not least by Mandela.

"Madiba" was hardly alone. His Communist comrade Mac Maharaj traveled to the then socialist German Democratic Republic [GDR] as early as 1961 for military training and, he recalled, received training for six months in "all aspects of printing and five months in sabotage—how to use dynamite, blow up pylons, cut railway lines and manufacture homemade explosives." He was also involved in smuggling cadre from the "German Communist Party" and "Canadian Communist Party" into South Africa to conduct operations.[69] Eventually the conflict between Moscow and Beijing would tremendously complicate the struggle in Southern Africa, but as Maharaj was headed to Berlin, his Communist comrade Raymond Mhlaba was on his way to China where, he said, "Mao Tse-Tung met and welcomed us," and he "received specialized training in guerilla warfare" and instruction in "how to manufacture and use indigenous

65. Frank Loescher to "Dear Ed," 5 May 1953, Box Foreign Service 1953, *American Friends Service Committee-Philadelphia.*

66. Jay Katzen to Vice President Mondale, 28 April 1977, NLC 133 107 2 50 8, *RAC Project, Jimmy Carter Presidential Library-Atlanta, Georgia.*

67. David James Smith, *Young Mandela: The Revolutionary Years,* New York: Little Brown, 2010, 99, 210.

68. *New Age* [South Africa], 23 December 1954.

69. Padraig O'Malley, *Shades of Difference: Mac Maharaj and the Struggle for South Africa,* New York: Viking, 2007, 35, 88, 90, 255.

weapons," not to mention "hit-and-run techniques" and "how to make and use light weapons for these techniques."[70]

By 1958 the preeminent U.S. academic Edwin S. Munger had detected "Russian submarines surfacing off the isolated Pondoland coast to take aboard Africans and to land secret agents." Until shuttered, the Soviet consulates in South Africa were the "scene of fairly frequent...parties attended by South Africans of all races;" these sites "also served as the focal point for clandestine meetings." He spotted Africans boarding a Soviet "tanker" or "whaler" in South Africa. And Zulus were then "being taught at the University of Leningrad."[71]

Twenty years later, Joe Nhlanhla of the ANC made an urgent request, asking the GDR for aid in "installing at our New Headquarters in Lusaka [Zambia] an internal inter-communication telephone system." He asked that Kurt Kruger in East Berlin "check the whole place against any gadgets and some such electronic devices that might have been planted even before we started using the place..."[72]

Ten years after that, ANC leader Alfred Nzo told a Moscow official that "for a number of years" his group "has had the valuable services of Soviet military experts in the development of our People's Army" and, naturally, "we are very grateful." He was referring to Soviet advisors training ANC cadre in Angola, including both military and intelligence operatives, along with "specialists in organization of transport" and "artillery." There was the provision of "82 mm mortar" and "fire arms specialists" and "radio communication specialists," "specialist physicians," "hand-to-hand fighting specialists," "survival specialists," and a "senior interpreter of the English & Portuguese languages".[73] By one estimate, Moscow provided 90% of the ANC's weapons, amounting to about $80 million annually

70. Thembeka Mufamadi, compiler, *Raymond Mhlaba's Personal Memoirs*, Pretoria: Human Sciences Research Council, 2001, 115.

71. "A Letter from Edwin S. Munger" on "Communist Activity in South Africa," 8 June 1958, Reel 16, #416, *American Committee on Africa Papers, Library of Congress-Washington, D.C.* See also Andimba Toivo ya Toivo, *On Trial for My Country*, 124: "Ben Amathila was "instructed to go and look around the Kunene River, where a Soviet boat could land and offload arms. This was top secret...."

72. Joe Nhlanhla to Kurt Kruger, Solidarity Committee-GDR, 23 June 1978, Part 2, Box 6, *African National Congress Archives, Fort Hare University-South Africa.*

73. Alfred Nzo to "Cde. V. Shubin," 5 March 1988, Part 2, Box 6, *African National Congress Archives, Fort Hare University-South Africa.*

(which does not account for the sums devoted to arming Cuba and Angola and other regional allies).[74]

Even after the fall of apartheid, ANC leader Phyllis Naidoo confessed candidly that "of course, the Soviet Union was our anchor, Cuba was our anchor."[75] Havana notoriously intervened in the region, inflicting hammer blows on white supremacy to the point that by 1976, Washington was soberly contemplating the prospect of what Assistant Secretary of State William Schaufele described to his supervisor, Henry Kissinger, as "the Cuban Spectre," i.e. "direct Cuban involvement in Rhodesia" and, perhaps "intervention" in South Africa itself.[76] This advantage for the anti-apartheid efforts had a downside: what would happen when the ANC came to power in straitened conditions without the fearsome specter of a militant Cuba backed by a Soviet Union to convince the racists of the value of negotiating reasonably?

By the same token, anticommunists in Eastern Europe leaned toward apartheid in response. As the revolt in Hungary was unwinding in 1956, Pretoria dispatched funding to the anti-Soviet forces. "Extensive student protests against events in Hungary," said the U.S. legation in Pretoria, "were confined almost exclusively to the Afrikaans universities."[77] Weeks later, said the legation, "Hungarian refugees" began "arriving in South Africa," and found that "response from employers had been 'terrific'" and the ordinarily xenophobic regime, which looked askance at even non-Boers defined as "white," seemed enthusiastic about their coming.[78]

A quarter of a century later, Pretoria's mouthpiece crowed that "Poles prefer South Africa." By 1981 the South African Broadcasting Corporation was elated to find that in Vienna "the longest of the queues are at the South African Embassy." Unlike the disfavored

74. Masqud Ulhasan Nuri, "Cuban Policy in Africa: The Limits of the Proxy Model," Ph.d. dissertation, University of South Carolina, 1990, 392.

75. Oral History, Phyllis Naidoo, 23 November 2000, *University of Connecticut-Storrs*. See also Christine Hatzky, *Cubans in Angola: South-South Cooperation and Transfer of Knowledge, 1976-1991*, Madison: University of Wisconsin Press, 2014.

76. William Schaufele to Henry Kissinger, 1 April 1976, in Kenneth Mokoena, ed., *South Africa and the United States: The Declassified History*, New York: New Press, 1993, 229-235, 232.

77. Report from U.S. Embassy-Pretoria, 21 November 1956, Reel 1, *Confidential U.S. State Department Files. Internal Afffairs Decimal Numbers 745A and 945A and Foreign Affairs, Decimal Numbers 645A, 1955-1959, NARA-CP.*

78. Report from U.S. Embassy, 3 January 1957, in Ibid., Reel 1, *Confidential U.S. State Department Files, Inernal Affairs.*

Africans in the land of apartheid, "Poles hate communism and they know from their own state-controlled media that South Africa of all countries is anti-communist;" happily, it was reported, "South Africa, as it was 300 years ago," remained "the land of good hope for the victims of oppression in Europe."[79] There was an added bonus for Pretoria, as the *Wall Street Journal* soon reported that an "influx of Polish refugees in South Africa sparks hostility from black community...."[80] By 1990, as apartheid was crumbling, it was reported that "East Europeans" continued to "seek a promised land in South Africa," as in the first quarter of that fateful year, "30,000" from this wracked region nested at the southern tip of the beleaguered continent, thereby fortifying the minority regime and complicating an already beset future for the Africans.[81]

It was precisely at this fraught moment that apartheid rulers made the fateful decision to retreat from the most egregious aspects of white supremacy. President F.W. de Klerk made this clear at the opening of the Second Session of the 9th parliament of the Republic of South Africa on Friday, 2 February 1990. "For South Africa," he asserted, "indeed of the whole world, the past year has been one of change and major upheaval. In Eastern Europe and even the Soviet Union itself, political and economic upheaval surged forward in an unstoppable tide...the year of 1989 will go down in history," he insisted, "as the year in which Stalinist Communism expired" and, he emphasized, this "will also be of decisive importance to Africa...." Tossing down the gauntlet before the ANC leaders and their Communist allies, he declared that this European tumult "serves as a warning to those who insist on [socialism]...." This was a "changed dispensation," he cried, discrediting—he thought—those "who seek to force this failure of a system on South Africa...."[82]

When the socialist camp began to erode in 1989, apartheid rulers chose this moment—adroitly—to negotiate with an ANC that had been weakened globally precisely because of these developments; a decision which in turn set the stage for compromise accords that to this day have hindered the ability of the post-apartheid regime to deliver radical transformation. The collapse of the Soviet Union,

79. SABC Report, 23 December 1981, Box 113, *Leroy Walker Africa News Service Archive, Duke University-Durham, North Carolina.*

80. *Wall Street Journal*, 15 January 1982.

81. *The Independent* [London], 18 January 1990.

82. Address by F.W. de Klerk, 2 February 1990, Box 'Atlanta Regional Office Southern Africa Peace Education Program, 1982-1995', *American Friends Service Committee-Philadelphia.*

which had buttressed the ANC and other liberation movements, was of monumental import. Unfortunately, African Americans, who were forced to turn away from their most globally minded leaders as part of a Cold War bargain—Robeson in the first instance—hardly recognized the importance of these Copernican changes on their own plight.[83] Most of all, they seemed unaware of the import of the events in Eastern Europe for their own flagging destinies.

In brief, the support of the socialist camp was essential to the eventual liberation of Southern Africa. This support was accelerating as the U.S. itself was in the process of retreating from the more egregious aspects of its own apartheid, Jim Crow. This facilitated the rise of a potent anti-apartheid movement on these shores; however, often neglected is the fact that the earlier solidarity represented by early 20th century South Africans studying at Tuskegee, was augmented—if not supplanted—by later 20th century South Africans seeking succor in Moscow, Havana, and East Berlin. This made it more difficult for African-Americans to ally with ANC leaders now demonized as Communists and hampered the ability of certain U.S. activists to lend full-throated support to the ANC. It also meant, in the words of one analyst, that an earlier "transnational black identity that promised modernity linked to racial pride," which yoked Africans across the oceans,[84] was increasingly bolstered—if not replaced—by a kind of socialist solidarity that transcended racial frontiers.

The future ANC leader Albert Xuma was a member of the NAACP by the early 1930s. Decades later such a joint membership would have been unusual at best, since the Cold War ideological barrier effectively separated the U.S. grouping from its South African counterpart.[85]

Thus, by 1954 Walter White of the NAACP leadership was querying Nobel Laureate Ralph Bunche in a "personal and confidential" missive about the political credentials of Mandela's closest comrade,

---

83. Cf. Joaquin M. Chavez, "How did the Civil War in El Salvador End?" *American Historical Review*, 120(Number 5, December 2015): 1784-1797, 1791: "The Soviet-U.S. rapprochement regarding the Central American conflicts, the eventual collapse of the Soviet Union, and the defeat of the Sandinistas in the elections of February 1990 had both direct and indirect impacts on the Salvadoran peace negotiations. Soviet support for the FMLN [liberation force] apparently dwindles in 1989…."

84. Iris Berger, "An African American 'Mother of the Nation': Madie Hall Xuma in South Africa, 1940-1963," *Journal of Southern African Studies*, 27(Number 3, September 2001): 547-566, 555.

85. Roy Wilkins to "Dear Xuma," 11 January 1932, Reel 1, *Albert Xuma Papers, Witwatersrand University-South Africa.*

Walter Sisulu. "As far as we can learn," White stated incorrectly, "the African National Congress...is completely free of any Communist infiltration...." Yes, he knew of the "stories" about the South African Indian Congress and their radical ties and the "Congress of Democrats", also within the ambit of the Communists. On United Nations stationery, Bunche replied that Sisulu, "along with 20 other persons, has been cited as a Communist within the meaning of the Communist Suppression Act of the Union of South Africa"[86]—presumably enough evidence to bar a relationship between him and the ideologically skittish NAACP.

Thus, trans-Atlantic "racial solidarity" was not as sturdy as it appeared, particularly after 1989. But even before then, the Marxist-oriented liberation forces in Southern Africa had reason to be suspicious of their erstwhile "supporters" in Black America. Maida Springer, for example, regarded as a Negro and union stalwart in the U.S., was considered suspect by ANC leaders, as she was accused of working with the Central Intelligence Agency [CIA] in East Africa and Rhodesia [Zimbabwe]. Springer was close to Irving Brown, a U.S. labor leader with ties to intelligence agencies, who despite his ties to Springer counseled U.S. labor organizations to "not assign American blacks to live" in Southern Africa, presumably out of fear that they could be more easily seduced politically.[87] Brown was also close to the ANC's chief ideological competitor, the Pan Africanist Congress[88] and was in contact with George Houser of the American

---

86. Walter White to Ralph Bunche, 9 September 1954, Box HA7, *NAACP Papers* and Ralph Bunche to Walter White, 14 September 1954, Box HA7, *NAACP Papers. Library of Congress, Washington, D.C.*

87. Yvette Richards, *Maida Springer: Pan Africanist and International Labor Leader*, Pittsburgh: University of Pittsburgh Press, 2000, 280, 216; See also Yvette Richards, *Conversations with Maida Springer: A Personal History of Labor, Race and International Relations*, Pittsburgh: University of Pittsburgh Press, 2004. See also R.S. Nyameko, "U.S. Subversion of South African Labor Movement," *African Communist*, (Number 73, Second Quarter 1978): 74-88.

88. Peter Raboroko to "Dear Irving," 28 September 1966, Box 2, *Records of AALC AFL-CIO Offices, Staff Department Division A, Correspondence, 1965-1975, University of Maryland-College Park*: "On behalf of the Pan Africanist Congress and the African people whom I represent I wish to thank you very much for the assistance you have given me....I had understood the position to be that the ICFTU [International Confederation of Free Trade Unions] were responsible for much more than my bare lodgings while I was here [Manhattan] as a guest;" thus, he expected "remuneration" for an article he wrote: "above all I look forward to the strengthening of fraternal ties between the PAC and the African people and the ICFTU....until we meet

Committee on Africa, the liberal grouping that arose as Robeson's more left-wing Council on African Affairs was being driven into liquidation.[89]

Consequently, the premier U.S. Negro leader, Roy Wilkins of the National Association for the Advancement of Colored People [NAACP], won few friends within the ANC when in 1972 he argued that the plight of Africans would worsen if U.S. corporations were forced to depart South Africa. Even his liberal U.S. ally, the American Committee on Africa [ACOA], was "appalled" by this advice.[90] One Atlantan said he was "extremely disappointed and disturbed" by Wilkins' demarche, which he said "defended" U.S. corporate involvement in South Africa.[91] Protestations to the contrary notwithstanding, the scholar Zoe Hyman is no doubt accurate in asserting

---

again..." See also Ben Rathbun, *The Point Man: Irving Brown and the Deadly Post-1945 Struggle for Europe and Africa*, Washington: Minerva Press, 1996.

89. George Houser toi A.B. Ngcobo, PAC, 11 May 1965, Series III, Box 142, *American Committee on Africa Papers, Tulane University-New Orleans*: "Will try to mention to Irving Brown that I heard from you.....we do talk on the telephone...." In the same collection and site, see Box 79: Houser's chief contact in the Congo, Ian Gilchrist to Houser, 19 February 1963, "Irving Brown brought the five hundred dollars from you yesterday...." Houser tended to take an ecumenical approach to liberation movements, which left him vulnerable to charges that he was subject to manipulation by U.S. imperialism: in the same collection and site, see George Houser to Jonas Savimbi of UNITA in Lusaka, 5 May 1967, Box 150: "quite some time since we have been in touch...good to see you and have a chance to talk....messages can be left for me c/o American Embassy in Lusaka...." UNITA quickly became a darling of the U.S. ultra-right-wing forces. I became involved in this controversy when in 1976 I wrote a review of a book by a Soviet author who made similarly explosive charges about Houser, who retained my review of the book with the charges of CIA ties underlined. See Oleg Ignatyev to George Houser, 17 December 1978, Box 7, *George Houser Papers, Michigan State University-East Lansing*: At issue were Houser's connections to Holden Roberto of Angola, who was known to be a U.S. asset. Ignatyev claimed that this evasive African was recruited to the CIA on 25 October 1959 at the Hotel Tudor in Manhattan: "your grievance against me," said the Muscovite, "is therefore groundless and unlawful." See also George Houser to Ian Gilchrist, 19 November 1964, Box 6, *George Houser Papers*: Houser saw no "alternative" to Roberto: "I cannot forget the fact that I have been associated with him in one way or another for about ten years...." In the same box, see also the 15 March 1961 letter by Roberto on ACOA letterhead.

90. *New York Times*, 30 March 1972.

91. Letter from D. Wilkins in *African Agenda*, 1(Number 2, April 1972): 4, *Chicago History Museum*.

that "tangible and working links between the NAACP and black liberation groups in South Africa did not materialize to any significant extent" and the perception of many of the latter as being on the "wrong" side of the Cold War divide was a major reason.[92]

In fact, Hyman's analysis understates the matter, for she may not have noticed the extraordinary occurrence five years prior to Wilkins' arrival in South Africa. Back in Washington, the NAACP chief lobbyist, Clarence Mitchell, Jr., was enmeshed in sensitive negotiations about a "nuclear energy agreement" with Pretoria. He was "originally negative" on the proposal but, according to Herman Pollack of the State Department, "Mr. Mitchell was led by the argumentation to agree that the NAACP would not take the initiative in opposition to the renewal....When asked for advice as to whether the leaders of other organizations should be consulted, his considered response was in the negative." "We intend to follow his advice," the memo continued, "and do not plan any further consultations",[93] effectively stymying the crusade to keep nuclear energy out of the hands of the racist regime. In other words, the NAACP's historic compromise with the U.S. ruling class that led to the organization's effective purge of the left in 1948, including but not limited to Communists,[94] had global implications when a compromise was reached by the group not to raise objection to Pretoria's vast nuclear ambitions.

Thus, though Washington thought it had been quite sagacious in appointing the African American leader Andrew Young U.S. Ambassador to the United Nations in 1977, assuming that the "trans-racial identity" would reap dividends, by this point Southern Africans tied to the socialist bloc were not so moved. When Ambassador Young appeared at the 1977 Maputo conference on Zimbabwe and Namibia, Peter Molotsi of South Africa was among those unimpressed, noting that Young "really tried to sell himself as a sort of comrade in the struggle, failing to recognize that in the eyes of the liberation people and the progressive Africans he is simply a representative of the greatest imperialist country." Young's remarks, it was added

---

92. Zoe L. Hyman, "American Segregationist Ideology and White Southern Africa, 1948-1975," Ph.d. dissertation, University of Sussex, 2011, 28.

93. Herman Pollack to Clifford Alexander, 19 July 1967, Record Group 59, *Central Foreign Policy Files: Social, 1967-1969,* Box 3092, *NARA-CP*. Less than a decade later—if not sooner—the apartheid regime had developed an atomic weapon with the purported provision of U.S. uranium: *Washington Post*, 14 April 1975.

94. Gerald Horne, *Black and Red: W.E.B. Du Bois and the Afro-American Response to the Cold War, 1944-1963*, Albany: State University of New York Press, 1986.

contemptuously, were "both naïve—lacking an historical understanding of the Southern Africa struggle—and racialist—claiming expertise because he is black." Such blather particularly "upset [Samora] Machel," Mozambique's astute leader, especially when the U.S. envoy counseled both non-violence and boycotts as the region's choice tools, simplistically transposing what "worked" in his homeland and rather ignorantly "comparing police clubs, tear gas and vigilante squads...with the full-scale military operations resulting in scores of deaths monthly...." Leslie Harriman of increasingly important Nigeria was "very disappointed" with the emissary's performance and, it was reported, this "view appeared to be shared by most of the delegates from 93 countries" present, as Young's remarks were "met with only polite applause...."[95]

Ambassador Young and a good deal of the African American leadership then did not realize what acolytes of President Ronald Reagan would later acknowledge. A June 1988 position paper submitted to Reagan pointed out with anxiety that "of the 47 independent nations of Africa, 18 are Marxist-Leninist controlled," while "most [African nations] have pro-Soviet leanings...." In Washington there was an utter lack of sympathy with this radical turn of events, but plenty of patience for Pretoria since "it took the United States nearly 100 years to free the slave and nearly 200 years before the blacks were to achieve a true opportunity at equality," The paper's ominous implication being: ease up on apartheid, since "the loss of South Africa to the Communist orbit poses a serious threat to the security of the United States...."[96]

Predictably, despite the apparent closeness between the ANC and its African American backers, ties between the two deteriorated after the presidential election of Nelson Mandela. Randall Robinson, a leader of the U.S. anti-apartheid movement, was bitterly disappointed by this turn of events—though he should have seen it coming. He cited the words of Moeletsi Mbeki, a member of a premier family of South Africa, who observed tartly that "since coming to power, ANC leaders have virtually cut off all contact"

95. Report from Peter Molotsi and David Sogge, 10 June 1977, Box: *ID 1977 Administration, Africa Programs, ...Mozambique...Sou Afr Repress Prog, American Friends Service Committee-Philadelphia*. Hereafter AFSC.

96. "Position Paper....The Military Order of the World Wars....United States Policy Toward South Africa," Alexandria, Virginia," June 1988, WHORM, CO 141, South Africa 59200 and CO 143 Namibia, Box 175, *Ronald Reagan Presidential Library-Simi Valley, California*.

with Robinson's organization and those it represented.[97] By 2016, the self-described "scholar, activist and analyst" Liepollo Lebohango Pheko lamented the "usurpation and distraction of a colonial liberation struggle," meaning South Africa's, "into a black/white issue," presumably by the U.S., "remains one of the greatest fissures in the South African liberation narrative." "It is this," she mourned, "that removed African liberation, decolonization and land restitution from the centre of the debate. It translated the complexity of land occupation into race relations," the latter being a North American specialty, "with the anti-apartheid movement more in keeping with the United States civil rights movement"[98]—a profound setback.

That Robinson and the Trans-Africa group he headed were ultimately shunned by the ANC was more the reflection of a general suspicion of the U.S. itself and its citizenry than of the towering lawyer and activist himself or his cohorts. For during a time when the ANC was in strict solidarity with the ruling Popular Movement for the Liberation of Angola (MPLA) in Luanda, prominent African Americans—e.g. Charles Evers (brother of the martyred Medgar); Ralph Abernathy (Martin Luther King's closest colleague); Dick Gregory, performer and activist; and Hosea Williams (yet another King colleague)—were listed as supporters of the MPLA's fiercest opponents, UNITA (National Union for the Total Independence of Angola), which in turn was backed by the U.S. ultra-right.[99] It was in 1987 that Reagan aide Herman Cohen sought to mobilize African American leaders on UNITA's behalf. The group's leader, Jonas Savimbi, was "highly thought of by centrist Black Political Personalities like Bayard Rustin," a former aide to Dr. King and prominent anti-communist. Yet Cohen knew that despite the apparent popularity of those like Rustin, "his viewpoint" was "definitely a minority one within the Black Community where mainstream opinion considers Savimbi a puppet of the South Africans…."[100]

Over the years, UNITA had styled itself as a "Black Nationalist" formation, an ideological tendency more widely accepted in the U.S.,

97. Randall Robinson, *Defending the Spirit: A Black Life in America*, New York: Dutton, 1998, 187, 190.

98. *Mail and Guardian* [South Africa], 9-14 December 2016.

99. Prexy Nesbitt, "Terminators, Crusaders and Gladiators: [Private and Public] Western Support for RENAMO and UNITA," Paper for Bonn Conference, December 1988. Box 1, Subgroup II, Series 4,*Herbert Shore Collection, Oberlin College—Ohio.*

100. Report by Herman Cohen, 16 April 1987, WHORM, Subject File, CO COUNTRIES CO006 Angola, Box 38, *Ronald Reagan Presidential Library-Simi Valley, California.*

not least as it filled the vacuum created when Robeson and his comrades were sidelined.[101] Meanwhile, the ANC was in an ideological standoff with such forces regionally, not just UNITA but South Africa's own Pan Africanist Congress [PAC]. Suspicion of these groups, as far as Mandela was concerned, was also extended to the Black Consciousness Movement of South Africa. Mandela was among the critics who were "suspicious of the support the movement enjoys from the imperialist countries, particularly the USA, as well as the movement's alleged hostility to Marxism." "Some of the critics", including Mandela presumably, "dismiss the movement as the brainchild of the American Central Intelligence Agency...." Mandela and these unnamed "critics" were skeptical of this "movement's hostility to the Soviet Union." "In this regard," he said in what was deemed to be the ultimate reproach, "the new movement is again in a position like that of the PAC..." After all, these forces, especially the PAC, "joined Western spokesmen and conservatives in accusing us of being a Communist front and the tools of the Soviet Union...." All this was "imported lock, stock and barrel from the USA." Their "dogmatism," said the ANC leader with a scoff, "flows from the fact that the concept of Black Consciousness" itself was "imported from America and swallowed in a lump without regard to our concrete situation" in which "progressive whites, including Marxists" tended to "form part of the liberation movement...." Unimpressed with a founding document of "Black Power"—the text of the same name penned by activist Stokely Carmichael and academic Charles Hamilton—Mandela argued instead, "the history of our country bears out Marxist theory;"[102] a proposition only acceptable in the U.S. to the dwindling number who continued to swear unswerving allegiance to Robeson and those like him.

Yet when Mandela finally arrived in the U.S., this polemic was largely unrecalled in the interests of the final push against apartheid. Hence the famed filmmaker Spike Lee and his associates could importune the ANC leader to appear in his film on Malcolm X, a symbol of "Black Power." Though the underlying misunderstanding doubtlessly led the filmmaker to tell the man he called "Dear

---

101. Gerald Horne, *Fire this Time: The Watts Uprising and the 1960s*, Charlottesville: University of Virginia Press, 1995.

102. Nelson Mandela, "Whither the Black Consciousness Movement," in Mac Maharaj, ed., *Reflections in Prison: Voices from the South African Liberation Struggle*, Amherst: University of Massachusetts Press, 2001, 21-64, 21, 39, 40, 43, 44, 45, 47 [originally written circa 1976].

Nelson" that he was in "shock" about the "misinformation about the film. We do not want you to play Malcolm X," he insisted.[103]

But, once more, Mandela was not alone in his skepticism of the beneficence of U.S. imperialism and its denizens. In 1974, recounts historian Seth Markle, "600 black expatriates, which constituted 75% of African American population in [Tanzania]" were rounded up and arrested on charges of "espionage." This may have been all a misunderstanding as Markle claims,[104] but the veteran activist Prexy Nesbitt of Chicago, who was quite close to the regional leadership, argued that this Pan-African fiasco was driven by a wider plot by certain African-Americans to smuggle arms to UNITA in Angola, a grouping already viewed widely as a Trojan Horse of imperialism.[105] The era's conflict between Africans and African Americans reached a zenith that same year, when the Sixth Pan African Congress met in Tanzania over 12 days, involving 400 delegates and guests from about 30 independent states and 7 liberation movements—and a goodly number from the U.S. The headline was a raging dispute between states and liberation movements then allied tightly with the socialist bloc of Europe and Social Democrats in Scandinavia—and African Americans who believed they were seeking to steer the Africans away from European snares based on "race" but who were seen as confused stalking horses for U.S. imperialism.[106]

This debacle was symptomatic of a wider international trend, rarely interrogated, As Robeson and his comrades were marginalized in the U.S., his ideological soulmates across the ocean remained in the vanguard, a situation bound to cause severe ructions.

It also contributed to a growingly skeptical view of African Americans by Southern African leaders. There was the mainstream NAACP outlook, which steered clear of Communism because of Cold War sensibilities. Then there was its "Black Power" counterpart, many of whose proponents took positions in the developing bitter conflict between the Soviet Union—which was quite close to the ANC and MPLA and whose relations with others in the region varied—and China, which was close to the Tanzanian leaders, ZANU, and, to a

---

103. Spike Lee to "Dear Nelson," circa late 1991, Box 17, *ANC Washington Mission, ANC Archives, Fort Hare University-South Africa.*

104. Seth Markle, "'We Are not Tourists': The Black Power Movement and the Making of Socialist Tanzania, 1960-1974," Ph.d. dissertation, New York University, 2010, 233.

105. Interview with Prexy Nesbitt, 29 February 2016 [in possession of author].

106. Ibid., Seth Markle, 266.

degree, FRELIMO of Mozambique. That is, "Black Power" advocates leaned toward China in its ongoing dispute with Moscow and its allies. President Julius Nyerere in Dar es Salaam may have had second thoughts about allowing in so many representatives of Black Power after the 1974 mass arrests. He also chose to provide exile to Robert F. Williams, the North Carolinian who fled to Cuba then China before arriving in Dar. Williams had departed Cuba in a huff, dispatching a 16-page critique to Fidel Castro, then denouncing what he termed "Moscow Communists" as "revisionists," China's preferred epithet for its former patron. The "Great Proletarian Cultural Revolution," he proclaimed boldly, was "the greatest event in the history of mankind," a view later repudiated by the Chinese Communist Party. That his words were reported by Richard Gibson,[107] yet another African American hostile to Communists—from the apparent "left"—only further twisted the ties between "Black Power" and one of its chief targets: Mandela's ANC. Revealingly, it was observed subsequently that Gibson had close ties to U.S. intelligence agencies at the highest level.[108]

As Williams' complicated itinerary suggests, the developments flowing from what was called the "Sino-Soviet" rupture, also split the Black Liberation Movement—on both sides of the Atlantic. U.S. "Black Power" advocates, as we shall see, downplayed—if not supported—China finding itself in bed with apartheid and U.S. imperialism during the Angola crisis of the 1970s: this occurred despite "Black Power" chest-beating (alleged) hostility to white supremacy.

At an exceedingly important global meeting of Communists that took place in Moscow in mid-1969, J.B. Marks of the South African Communist Party excoriated the "sidetracking and disruption of various international solidarity organizations by Chinese delegations who persisted in dragging into gatherings of non-Communists their

---

107. "Richard Gibson Reports: International News and Features," March 1967, Series II, Box 55, *American Committee on Africa Papers, Tulane University-New Orleans*. Gibson was quite close to the U.S. writer and activist Amiri Baraka [Le Roi Jones], serving as his literary agent in Europe: Contract, 22 March 1976, Box 12, *Richard Gibson Papers, George Washington University, Washington, D.C.* Gibson was also close to Robert F. Williams. See Richard Gibson to Tim Tyson, 20 March 2002. Box 18, *Richard Gibson Papers*. In the same collection, see also Richard Gibson to Tim Tyson, 21 March 2002, Box 18: This shady figure was "pleased" with Tyson's "account of Rob's contribution to the opening of U.S. diplomatic relations with China, which for many Muscovite Leftists in the U.S. and the old nostalgics of Cuba seemed to amount to treason…."

108. **Newsweek**, 15 November 2018.

alleged 'ideological' campaigns" against Moscow "and the world Communist movement…." Thus, "for several years and without reason or explanation, this aid has been withdrawn, instead we find the Maoists subsidizing and actually preserving from complete collapse a group of right-wing renegades from our struggle whose documentary evidence now proves to have been started at the instance and with the support of the CIA."[109]

If the CIA made such a bargain, they may now rue the day since it has eventuated with China in the passing lane in the 21st century. The strength of this Asian juggernaut has yet to fill the vacuum created by the disappearance of the Soviet Union; a vacancy which sheds light on current disgruntlement in a South Africa now ruled by the ANC and their Communist allies. As for African-Americans, sadly enough, there remains to this day little understanding of the impact this global bargain made on their now dismaying destiny.

* * *

Despite the ideological cleavage that often split Africans from African Americans, the movement in solidarity with the liberation of the sub-continent was a mighty force. I have explored this division not only because it sheds light on ongoing problems in both South Africa and Black America but also because scholarship—at least in the U.S.—tends to glide past such ideological disputes. Many scholars on this side of the Atlantic are either influenced by the liberal NAACP tradition or the "Black Power" critique thereof and, for whatever reason, tend particularly to endorse Mandela's global popularity today (or criticize same in a one-sided fashion), as they gloss over a more tortuous history.

The exploration of these divisions should not, however, detract from the mighty force of solidarity revealed when Mandela arrived in the U.S. in 1990, nor that which preceded this epochal event. Given apartheid's powerful constituency in the U.S., changing Washington's policy was neither easy nor simple. It required force and ingenuity and supple organizing. In early 1966 the White House was astir when a report detailed a raucous protest at South Africa's U.N. Mission in Manhattan. Protesters from the Student Non-Violent Coordinating Committee [SNCC] invaded the Mission's sanctum on the 17th floor of a skyscraper at 300 East 42nd Street and "shouted

109. J.B. Marks, "South Africa and the World Communist Movement," 16 June 1969, in A. Lerumo, ed., *Fifty Fighting Years: The Communist Party of South Africa, 1921-1971*, London: Inkululeko, 1987, 156-163, 162.

loudly, declaimed and banged on the doors of the offices," as "policemen made ineffectual attempts to contain the demonstrators." The militants barged into the office, slamming the head of an official against the wall. When police regained control, there were 5 men and 4 women who refused to budge and "had to be carried out."[110] Before being removed the "pickets shouted epithets at members of [the] Mission" as they were "rattling doors to create disturbance...." The demonstration's leader, James Forman, warned sternly that these protests would not cease until apartheid South Africa was forced to "leave" the U.S.[111] Such stormy protests became the norm in the U.S: on campuses, where students interrupted meetings of high-level administrators; at corporate board meetings, which were challenged about their investment decisions; and at sports events, as tennis matches and track meets were interrupted by protestors.

Elizabeth Benson of the staunch solidarity movement in Chicago was among the masses involved in picketing First National Bank because of its sale of the Kruggerrand. "Picketing" took place "for several years, once a week," she recalled later, targeting this illicit gold coin and related matters — "whatever the weather was," no mean feat in a city known for its bone chilling frigidity and gusty winds. What buoyed her? "When I'm with somebody" and "with other people [who] have the same views, they want justice where there is injustice"—"that's a wonderful experience," she enthused, identifying the feeling of collectivity that propelled her.[112] Magnify her example by millions and you may understand how and why solidarity was a corrosive that impelled U.S. imperialism to make an agonized retreat by 1986—during the height of Ronald Reagan's conservatism—and impose biting sanctions on apartheid.

U.S. activists, whose ranks increased over the years thanks to their cascading energy, were quite creative in confronting apartheid. It was in 1967 when a delegation from the liberal American Committee on Africa that was barred from entering illegally occupied Namibia sought to get into the country by air without visas from Pretoria or Windhoek. This, said the ACOA, was "nonviolent direct action" on a global scale, as the delegation chartered two small planes and took

---

110. Stephen Schwebel to Ulric Haynes, 25 March 1966, Box 3, *Files of Edward K. Hamilton, Lyndon B. Johnson Presidential Library.*

111. U.S. Mission to the United Nations to State Department, 24 March 1966, Box 3, *Files of Edward K. Hamilton.*

112. Oral History, Elizabeth Benson, 11 April 2010, *Columbia College Chicago.*

off from Botswana, then almost ran out of fuel near Windhoek and nearly crashed.[113]

Pretoria, facing what it deemed to be a total onslaught, responded in kind, making anti-apartheid activism perilous. In 1981 scores of files were stolen from the Brooklyn office of a grouping of anti-apartheid exiles; that same day, their erstwhile comrade Clifton Westraad vanished and was then accused of turning over these records to Pretoria.[114] In 1984 the Reagan White House was informed that a "terrorist group…the 'Wat Committee' has issued a warning that it will kill Senator [Edward] Kennedy," younger brother of the slain president, and "Jesse Jackson," yet another former aide to the slain Dr. King, if they travelled to South Africa. The National Security Council was "taking this thing seriously, as the Wat Committee is genuine and secretive and has committed terrorist acts before"—though it was "conceivable that this is a ploy by the South Africans to justify close monitoring/surveillance" of the two leaders.[115]

Maybe. But those opposed to apartheid could not be too sure. The 1988 assault by 4 men described as "white…right wing vandals" on the headquarters of the Washington Office on Africa, a stern opponent of apartheid, was not a unique event.[116] At any rate, prominent U.S. press organs often danced to the tune of Pretoria, which meant downplaying or ignoring such outrages. By 1986 it was estimated that the *Washington Times* was subsidized by Pretoria at a rate of $900,000 annually.[117]

* * *

In October 1925, J.L. Pinkerton, U.S. Vice Consul in Port Elizabeth, South Africa provided what was deemed to be sage advice to Pretoria: "exterminate, assimilate or go." That is, liquidate the indigenes—as occurred in North America—merge with the Africans, or depart the country. Espying the rise of a "mulatto race," i.e. "Coloureds," he

113. Memorandum, no date, circa 1967, Series III, Box 94, *American Committee on Africa Papers, Tulane University*.

114. Statement by SAMRAF [South African Military Refugee Aid Fund], 7 October 1981, Box 4, *George Houser Papers*.

115. Report by Phillip Ringdahl, National Security Council, 21 December 1984, Executive Secretariat, NSC, Country File, Africa, S. Africa, Box 4, *Ronald Reagan Presidential Library*.

116. *Guardian* [U.S.], 8 June 1988.

117. Scott and Jon Lee Anderson, *Inside the League: The Shocking Expose of How Terrorists, Nazis and Latin American Death Squads Have Infiltrated the World Anti-Communist League*, New York: Dodd Mead, 1986, 107.

thought the regime was stumbling toward option 2. The "poor white" population was growing, which would probably augment the trend toward assimilation. "What South Africa needs," he advised, "is a flood of immigration to submerge the Bantu as the Negroes have been outnumbered in the United States."[118] As we shall see, Pretoria sought to pursue his advice with mixed results. Yet, this counsel was just another example of how Washington sought to bail out white supremacy in the face of its retreat, particularly with the tool that was anticommunism.

---

118. J. L. Pinkerton, Vice Consul-Port Elizabeth to Secretary of State, 4 October 1925, Reel 4, M583, *Records of the Department of State Relating to Internal Affairs of British Africa, NARA-CP.*

Chapter 1

The U.S. and Southern Africa During the 19th and Early Twentieth Centuries

TIES between Southern Africa and North America stretch back to the acceleration of the African Slave Trade in the 17th century and the snatching of Angolans particularly. As early as 1645 enslaved Africans were being shipped to North America from southeast Africa.[1] There were Zulus enslaved in Virginia by 1719.[2] Many Angolans played an essential role in the bloodiest revolt of the enslaved in the colonial era: Stono's Revolt in South Carolina in 1739.[3] Though Brazilian slave markets were closed—officially—in the 1850s, Cuba and the United States continued to dragoon Angolans and Mozambicans thereafter.[4]

Eschel Rhoodie, an authoritative apartheid spokesman, noted in 1967 that while "to most Americans 'Southern Africa' is like the dark side of the moon," unknown and unknowable, it was actually "in South Africa" that "the historic parallel with the United States of Africa is most fascinating and striking…." He observed that the 1776 war "was a cause of jubilation on the part of the opposition Patriot Party in Holland," which was allied tightly with its compatriots at the Cape; thus, there was an implied recognition of the nascent U.S.A. as early as 1784.[5]

After London's defeat in the 1776 war in North America consideration was given to dumping Africans who sided with the redcoats in

1. Poultney Bigelow, *White Man's Africa*, New York: Harper and Bros., 1900, 70.

2. Adam Hochschild, *The Mirror at Midnight: A South African Journey*, New York: Viking, 1990, 8.

3. Gerald Horne, *The Counter-Revolution of 1776*.

4. Malyn Newitt, *A History of Mozambique*, London: Hurst, 1995, 248, 270; Gerald Horne, *The Deepest South: The U.S., Brazil and the African Slave Trade*, New York: New York University Press, 2008.

5. Eschel Rhoodie, *The Third Africa*, New York: Twin Circle, 1967, 92, 95, 96.

what is now Namibia's Walvis Bay.[6] Religious denominations from the newly born U.S. were to play a major role in the sub-region. The Quakers, prominent in founding Pennsylvania, started a so-called "Meeting Room" in Cape Town in this era, propelled by whalers from Nantucket.[7]

U.S. slave traders continued to be found in the waters of the sub-region in the 19th century, enchaining Africans and dragging them to Cuba, Brazil, and North America too.[8] They were followed—if not preceded—by missionaries who (whatever their ostensibly benign intentions) tended to soften up the indigenes for their eventual crass exploitation.[9]

Beginning in the 1820s at the latest, U.S. vessels, some of which were ravenously eyeing neighboring Mozambique as a source for the enslaved, were bartering with the Zulus due south. Fretting about the growing abolitionist sentiment in London the European minority in South Africa was already suggesting that the U.S. declare the area a sphere of influence for the slaveholding republic. By 1835 some Cape settlers became alarmed at the intensity of U.S. activity in Natal.[10] After all, Washington was the expanding slaveholding power, while London—which had ousted the Netherlands from rule at the Cape earlier in the century—had moved toward abolition of slavery by 1833, compromising the model of development in South Africa and—à la 1776—motivated a wild scramble, a "Great Trek," to seize more indigenous land.[11] Into this distasteful journey for "liberty" came Daniel Lindley, U.S. missionary from Ohio who arrived in Southern Africa in 1835, aided in the trek, and then went on to found the Dutch Reformed Church—a pillar of apartheid—and for his labors had a South African town named after him.[12]

---

6. Cassandra Pybus, *Black Founders: The Unknown Story of Australia's First Black Settlers*, Sydney: University of New South Wales Press, 2006, 66.

7. Memorandum, 1 May 1978, PED PROGRAM RESOURCES SOUTHERN AFRICA 1978, *AFSC*.

8. Gerald Horne, *Race to Revolution: The U.S. and Cuba During Slavery and Jim Crow*, New York: Monthly Review Press, 2014.

9. Captain W.C. Harris, *Narrative of an Expedition into Southern Africa During the Years 1836 and 1837 from the Cape of Good Hope Through the Territories of the Chief Moselekatse to the Tropic of Capricorn*, Bombay American Mission Press, 1836, *Kansas University-Lawrence*.

10. Ibid., Eschel Rhoodie, 96.

11. See e.g. Gerald Horne, *The Counter-Revolution of 1776* and *Negro Comrades of the Crown*.

12. Adam Hochschild, *The Mirror at Midnight*, 80.

As was to be increasingly the case in coming decades, other arriving North Americans were not as lucky as Lindley. There was Jane Wilson, 22, of Richmond, Virginia, a missionary slain in the Transvaal.[13] She may have fallen victim to a growing concern among Africans that these latest arrivals from across the Atlantic were not there to curtail white supremacy. One scholar has detected "American racism" at the Cape as early as the 1830s buoyed precisely by missionaries. They were accused of introducing the odious epithet "Nigger," as a complement to the more frequently used "Kaffir."[14]

U.S. missionaries were flocking to the southern tip of Africa at the same time as the colonial power, London, was imposing anti-slavery measures, compelling Afrikaners—or descendants of the merger between the Dutch and Huguenot settlers—to embark upon the "Great Trek" northward. As that process was unfolding, some of these visitors were contemplating the impact of the fiery revolt of the enslaved led by Nat Turner in Virginia and the onrushing trend of the import of Islam for Africa, notably in the U.S. neo-colony that was Liberia. Monrovia represented a desire to deport en masse "Free Negroes" and these other concerns—Islam, slave revolts, etc.—influenced the appeal of deportation. In a trend that was to last for decades, U.S. nationals were viewing their own nation through the lens of South Africa. Thus, in 1837 U.S. missionaries in Grahamstown argued forcefully that "we may expect that the natives in that region will be compelled to give way to the wishes and interests of the white men. We cannot think of the American Indians and of the natives of this country" without noticing parallels between the dire plight facing both.[15]

Paul Kruger, a chief leader of the anti-London Boers at century's end, said that he was confirmed in his religiosity at the hands of a U.S. missionary—presumably Lindley, whose son Bryant was a successful entrepreneur in Cape Town, founding the American Life Insurance Society by 1900. The elder Lindley was revered by the Afrikaners.[16] As late as 1972, in an attempt to rally Washington to

---

13. Edyth Kaigh-Eustace, *The Tragedy of Mosega: An Account of America's Girl Martyr, Mrs. Jane Wilson, Aged 22, of Richmond, Virginia. The First White Woman to Lay Down her Life in the Transvaal, South Africa for the Cause and Love of Christ*, Richmond: Shepperson, 1930.

14. William Manning Marable, "African Nationalist: The Life of John Langalibalele Dube," Ph.d. dissertation, University of Maryland, 1976, 16.

15. Joint Letter, 2 May 1837 in Ibid., D.J. Kotze, 173.

16. Poultney Bigelow, *White Man's Africa*, New York: Harper and Bros., 1900, 39.

Pretoria's banner, an apartheid official recalled that it was in 1899 that Kruger of "the old Transvaal Republic" declared that it was his "wish ....that the great Republic of America may become the greatest nation on earth...."[17] It is unclear if Piet Uys, one of the prominent Voortrekkers, was en route to Natal when he announced portentously that he and his comrades planned to establish "our settlement on the same principles of liberty as those adopted" in the U.S.[18]

The American Bible Society translated their sacred document into Zulu just as missionaries of the Church of Latter-Day Saints—then fighting a battle for survival in North America—arrived at the Cape by the middle of the 19th century. They created converts and fielded nearly a hundred men, women, and children to sail from Table Bay in 1852 to join Brigham Young's settlement in Utah in 1852.[19]

Near the same time, a mutual congeniality between the two settlements was suggested by the first Transvaal constitution, which, anticipating the notorious Dred Scott decision in the U.S.,[20] promulgated the fundamental inequality of Europeans and Africans—to the dismaying detriment of the latter—was an import from the southern U.S. Afrikaners in the Transvaal established a powerful pro-U.S. tradition: Pretoria, capital of the Transvaal in 1860, originally bore the name Pretoria Philadelphia. The secessionist—and fiercely pro-slavery--Confederate States of America found one of their major global bases of support at the Cape. When a Confederate vessel arrived in Cape Town, a reporter found the "enthusiasm displayed by the inhabitants" created a "frenzy," as the dock was "all day crowded with visitors...."[21] Cape Town was astir, "full of

17. L.E.S. de Villiers, Director of Information, Information Service of South Africa to William Rusher, 16 October 1972, Box 84, *William Rusher Papers, Library of Congress-Washington, D.C.*

18. Adam Hochschild, *The Mirror at Midnight*, 237.

19. Jeffrey G. Cannon, "A Faithful Band: Moses Mahlangu and the First Soweto Saints," *BYU Studies Quarterly*, 55(Number 1, 2016): 31-36; *Washington Post*, 5 October 2011; Farrell Ray Monson, "History of the South African Mission of the Church of Jesus Christ of Latter Day Saints, 1853-1970," M.A. Thesis, Brigham Young University, 1971.

20. Kelly M. Kennington, *In the Shadow of Dred Scott: St Louis Freedom Suits and the Legal Culture of Slavery in Antebellum America*, Athens: University of Georgia Press, 2017.

21. *Our Cruise in the Confederate States' War Steamer Alabama, the Private Journal of an Officer*, Cape Town: South African Advertiser and Mail, 19 September 1863, *University of Georgia-Athens*. In January 1863 this vessel was off the coast of Galveston, Texas and "in anticipation of news being received of Lincoln's [abolition] Proclamation, a tombstone, consisting of a board,

life and motion" as a result of the arrival of these visitors. "Nearly all the city was upon the bay,"[22] though doubtlessly the throng did not include many Africans. The presence of these U.S. rebels was still being felt in 1957 when a grave and tombstone for CSA engineer Simeon W. Cummings of the steamer "Alabama" was uncovered in Saldanha in the Cape Province.[23]

John McIntosh Kell, who was present at the Cape near that time, remained ecstatic years later in recollections penned from Washington. "The reception and welcome we met with there from our 'English cousins' was warm and refreshing." Assembled there, Kell wrote, was a "large number of English people, the soldiers of whose families were engaged in the Kaffir War...." He was overwhelmed by the reality that "we were thronged with visitors" and "all seemed anxious to welcome the sea-rover to their shores...." Such "enthusiasm was beyond description," he gushed and "their hearty welcome and sympathy for our cause truly gratifying..." The crowd amassed could "only be enumerated by thousands!" he exulted. Tellingly, when the ship departed, "some dozen or more" of his comrades chose to remain in Cape Town.[24]

The U.S. Consul, Walter Graham, then in a death match with these traitors, was furious but, said one observer, "all of Cape Town was suffering from 'Alabama Fever'..."[25] John Lowe, a Confederate sailor who arrived in Cape Town, noticed that the deck of his vessel was crowded from the moment anchor was dropped. His companion,

---

about four feet in length and two in breadth, was sent on shore and placed in the most prominent position the largest island afforded. In black letters of a white ground was the following: 'in memory of Abraham Lincoln, President of the late United States, who died of nigger on the brain, 1st January 1863...." At the same site, see also H.W.R. Jackson, *The Southern Women of the Second American Revolution. Our Naval Victories and Exploits of Confederate War Steamers*, Atlanta: Intelligencer Steam Power Press, 1863.

22. Commander R. Semmes, *The Cruise of the Alabama and the Sumter, Volume II*, London: Saunders, Ottley, 1864, Appendix, 347-361, 347, 351.

23. S.D. Boykin to Secretary of State, 30 October 1957, RG 59, Decimal File, Box 4504, *NARA-CP*.

24. John McIntosh Kell, *Recollections of a Naval Life, Including The Cruises of the Confederate Steamers 'Sumter' and 'Alabama'*, Washington: Neale, 1900, 50, 228, 231. Throughout I will quote sources that use the contemptuous epithet, "Kaffir," which—I believe—further exposes the rank racism that drove colonialism and apartheid.

25. William Stanley Hoole, *Four Years in the Confederate Navy: The Career of Captain John Low on the 'CSS Fingal, Florida, Alabama, Tuscaloosa and Ajaz*, Athens: University of Georgia Press, 1964, 85, 86, 87.

Arthur Sinclair, was taken by the "fair lassies of the South African Colony." "Buxom they are" with a "delightful womanly grace," he rejoiced. Yet all was not sweetness and light, as the angry "Hottentots" refused to aid their landing: "all assistance on their part was emphatically refused" he recalled grumpily. Still, the visitors were "constantly entertained at dinner.... quite royally" at that.[26]

The discovery of diamonds in Kimberley in the 1860s precipitated a flood of fortune seekers in South Africa, among them not only disgruntled, hard-bitten pro-slavery rebels, who found crusted bigotry at the Cape to be agreeable, but also some newly freed slaves who had been under the rebels' jurisdiction until quite recently.[27]

Traveling in the opposite direction was John Dube, who arrived in the U.S. as early as 1887 and continued to visit in coming years, before becoming a persistent critic of settler colonialism—though he styled himself without irony as the "Booker Washington of South Africa." The school he established in his homeland was termed the "African Tuskegee."[28] An equivalent to the Jubilee Singers of Fisk University was founded at South Africa's Wilberforce Institute, just as Washington's famed autobiography, *Up from Slavery*, appeared in Zulu translation.[29] The likeminded Virginia Jubilee Singers toured South Africa three times between 1890 and 1899 and were greeted rapturously.[30]

Oberlin College in Ohio, renowned for educating U.S. Negroes, also claimed Dube as an alumnus. His brother was a graduate of Ohio's Wilberforce University, alumni of which founded the similarly named South African school.[31] Also emerging from the Wilberforce campus in Ohio was Charlotte Manye. W.E.B. Du Bois, the premier Negro leader, met her in 1894, later recalling that she was

26. Arthur Sinclair, *Two Years on the Alabama*, Annapolis: Naval Institute Press, 1989, 128, 130, 135, [originally published 1895].

27. Eric Rosenthal, *Stars and Stripes in Africa: Being a History of American Achievements in Africa by Explorers, Missionaries, Pirates, Adventurers, Hunters, Miners, Merchants, Scientists, Soldiers, Showmen, Engineers and Others with Some Account of Africans who Have Played a Role in American Affairs*, Cape Town: Nasionale Boekhandel Beperk, 1968, 129, 130, 122.

28. Ibid., William Manning Marable, 120.

29. Ira Dworkin, *Congo Love Song: African American Culture and the Crisis of the Colonial State*, Chapel Hill: University of North Carolina Press, 2017, 93, 94.

30. Adam Ewing, *The Age of Garvey: How a Jamaican Activist Created a Mass Movement and Changed Global Politics*, Princeton: Princeton University Press, 2014, 168.

31. Charlotte Crogman Wright, *Beneath the Southern Cross: The Story of an American Bishop's Wife in South Africa*, New York: Exposition, 1955, 26.

one of three or four students from South Africa and the only woman. A Basuto born among the Xhosas, Du Bois praised her as the rarity who was a champion of both her "race" and "sex." Her father, said A.B. Xuma, a future leader of the African National Congress, traveled from the Transvaal to the Cape "for the sole purpose of buying guns with which to fight the Boers." By 1901 she returned home to join the struggle, along with her spouse Marshall Macdonald Maxeke. There they worked to build the A.M.E. church—and she established the Women's Christian Temperance Union.[32]

As Dube was arriving in the U.S., John Lewis Waller of the U.S was voyaging within striking distance of Dube's homeland. Reflecting the waning Negro influence on the Republican Party, this African American was sent to Madagascar as a diplomat in 1891, where he served for three years. His travails indicated why European powers were so hostile to visiting Negroes. He obtained a huge land grant—150,000 acres for the purpose of forming a settlement for his fellow U.S. Negroes, which the island's rulers' thought would serve as a firewall of U.S. protection against growing French imperialism—agents of which proceeded to thwart this ambitious plan.[33]

Arriving directly in Dube's homeland was Bishop Henry McNeal Turner of Georgia. He travelled to South Africa for six weeks in 1898 and preached sermons from the Cape to the Transvaal.[34] Unlike those who carped about how U.S. Negroes were treated in South Africa, the bishop found that a "Negro from a civilized country and having the bearing of a gentleman and of a scholar, coming among the English of the Cape Colony or the Boers of the Transvaal, is received with all honor, and his color is no barrier to the proffer of courtesies and hospitalities…." The starry-eyed cleric found not only that the "blight of slavery has never made [the African] cringing, nor has it had the opportunity to make the Africander [sic] unwilling to recognize merit in the non-resident…." He was impressed to find that "many of the natives are engaged in business and some are men of means. I found the President of the Orange Free State," said the bedazzled preacher, "a perfect gentleman in every respect…."

32. A.B. Xuma, "Charlotte Manye: What an Educated African Girl Can Do," Foreword by W.E.B. Du Bois, 1930, *A.B. Xuma Papers, University of Witwatersrand-South Africa.*

33. Randall Bennett Woods, *A Black Odyssey: John Lewis Waller and the Promise of American Life, 1878-1900*, Lawrence: University Press of Kansas, 1981, xvii.

34. Adam Ewing, *The Age of Garvey: How a Jamaican Activist Created a Mass Movement and Changed Global Politics*, Princeton: Princeton University Press, 2014, 168.

He was even impressed by the stiff-necked ideologue, "Oom Paul," his intimate reference to "President Kruger," as he was "fondly called by the Boers...." Like others, Kruger apparently found it opportune to distinguish this visitor from other Africans as he was "treated throughout the Republic with marked consideration and respect...." Kruger "received our church with great cordiality," Turner said; an attitude that would soon no longer be extended to other churches as a matter of policy. This policy, Turner opined, "was not so much from love" as "from distrust of white missionaries whom he greatly dislikes." "Regarding the future of the African Methodist Episcopal Church in South Africa," he concluded optimistically, "I believe it to be assured...." As early as 1895, he recalled, the "Ethiopian Church" there wanted to "unite with us..." As of 1899, the AME had "nearly 100 ministers and a lay membership of 10, 800"—soon to be "12,000 where three years ago we had none." Turner arrived in South Africa just before the war, which doubtlessly shaped his overly sunny views.[35]

Turner may have been unduly optimistic. The U.S. Negro influence in Africa steadily grew,[36] especially in the southern cone of the continent, via missionaries; a development seen by many Africans as something to resist, not encourage. Euro-American missionaries: were jealous of these African-Americans too, sensing that they had an advantage in saving souls because of common experiences with racism.[37] It may not have been just a matter of semantics when Europeans in South Africa balked at using the term "Negro." It was only deployed as a "term of opprobrium" said one close observer, perhaps an indication of disaffection toward those from North America to whom it was traditionally applied. Both "Afrikander" and "Englishmen" had "stopped" this New Yorker abruptly when he used this word.[38]

Ironically—and insultingly—Turner was given the status of "honorary white" upon arrival, a decision driven by an incident in 1893 when John Ross, a U.S. Negro, was mistaken for a "native Kaffir" and given a severe whipping at the hands of a policeman. Shortly

35. Henry McNeal Turner, "My Trip to South Africa," in Edwin Redkey, ed., *Respect Black: The Writing and Speeches of Henry McNeal Turner*, New York: Arno, 1991, 178-181, 179.

36. Ibid., Eric Rosenthal, 202.

37. Catherine Higgs, *The Ghost of Equality: The Public Lives of D.D.T. Jabavu of South Africa, 1885-1959*, Athens: Ohio University Press, 1997, 213.

38. Poultney Bigelow, *White Man's Africa*, New York: Harper and Bros., 1900, 107.

thereafter a Negro barber from Boston was forced by Europeans to step off the sidewalk as he approached them in Johannesburg, leading to a fracas: he resisted and, apparently, got the better of his attackers. His resistance and arrest led local Africans to identify him as a kind of "Moses"—and South African authorities to compel him to return to Boston. In August 1899, Thomas Turnbull, yet another visiting U.S. Negro, was beaten after being mistaken for a local.

Certainly, the Negroes tended to back London during the war with the Afrikaners. A leader of Negroes thought that "one hundred thousand Colored Americans could be raised inside of a hundred days" to fight alongside the redcoats. Some Negroes did join British forces, including H.A. Smith and Howard Scott; the latter becoming a Negro hero for his aggressiveness in confronting the Afrikaners. This support only intensified and polarized domestic politics in the U.S., as the Democratic Party backed the rebels avidly while the Negro Republicans compared them to their ultimate antagonist: Dixie denizens. T. Thomas Fortune, the prominent Negro journalist, claimed that Dixie had "too many Boers". The segregationist Alfred Holt of Mississippi seemed to agree with him when he espied similarities between his state and the Transvaal.[39]

At the turn of the century, American J. Frank Lanning arrived in the Transvaal. He spoke to the U.S. Consul there, who was moonlighting as "Assistant General Manager of the De Beers mine." In the diamond mine he peered "nearly three thousand feet below the surface" and saw "over seven hundred naked savages at work"—"black imps" in his pinched estimation. He was "impressed however by the silence of these people as compared with our Southern Negro—the latter makes a noise of some kind whenever he is doing anything..." But then he was stunned when he was "awakened" one "morning hearing a regular old plantation Negro's crowning song. I looked out the window and there sure enough was a genuine old Virginia Negro sweeping out the porch yard, keeping time with broom and feet with the song," an unusual appearance the origins of which he did not describe.

What really struck Lanning, however, were the indigenous Africans. "I have never looked upon such magnificent types of physical beauty," he exulted, "as are presented by the Zulu race, both men

---

39. Willard Gatewood, "Black Americans and the Boer War," *South Atlantic Quarterly*, 75(1996): 229-244, 229, 230, 235, 236, 239, 244.

and women....as for the legs, arms and bust, especially [of] the latter," he clarified, "well—they don't grow anywhere else...."[40]

There was bilateral fascination: the Afrikaner elite drew upon the U.S. Constitution when erecting their own political structure, intriguingly paying particularly close attention to the veto.[41]

There were clear parallels between reactions to abolitionism on both sides of the Atlantic. "With the Boers as with the American slave-owners," said one Manhattan based writer in 1900, "it was not the emancipation alone which produced the mischief, but the fact that the liberation Negro was at once elevated to a position equal, if not superior to that of the former master."[42]

By 1886 there were, perhaps, 1800 U.S. nationals in the Johannesburg area and little more than a decade later, there were 2500, mostly in that same boomtown, borne on a sea of gold. The opening of U.S. consulates then was a signal of a growing relationship with the settler colony. Local Africans in mining districts were expected to carry a pass and wear an identification badge but U.S. Negroes—physically indistinguishable from those designated locals—were not expected to comply with these regulations, which suggested that the oppressors were as concerned with persecuting those who controlled the land as with their ostensible racist creed. Still, U.S. Negroes—whose polecat status within the republic was seemingly unshakeable—often lacked documentary proof of their citizenship and, consequently, were swept within the racist ambit nonetheless.

These decades of interaction were a prelude to events at century's end: the conflict that is known widely as the "Anglo-Boer War"—however, as in the 1776 revolt against British rule to which it has been compared, the "Boers" who sought to secede from the British Empire were widely opposed by Africans. Still, there were hundreds of sizeable public gatherings throughout the U.S. for the South African rebels.[43] Thanks to lobbying efforts, most notably Irish and German-American groups, most of the U.S. Senate backed the rebels. The Democratic Party—supposed tool of the working man (at least those who were defined as "white")—could claim credit when

---

40. J. Frank Lanning, *My Trip to South Africa*, Richmond: Williams, 1905, 14, 15, 26, 37.

41. Poultney Bigelow, *White Man's Africa*, 100.

42. E. De Waal, "American Black Residents in Visitors in [South Africa] Before 1899," *South African Historical Journal*, 6(1974): 52-55, 52.

43. Ibid., Eric Rosenthal, 149.

by 1900 public opinion in the U.S. was overwhelmingly pro-rebel.[44] The Mississippian Hodding Carter, who termed his 1950s trip to the land of apartheid the "turning point" in his life, was also among those who later on saw "the Boers of 1900" as equivalent to the "outnumbered Confederates of the 1860s." (Lavishing praise upon these embattled settlers, he compared them favorably to the "settlers of Israel.")[45]

In contrast, U.S. Negro editors saw the struggle as a pitiless contest between good and evil, with the rebels cast in the latter role. Tellingly, of all regions on the besieged African continent it was the southern tip that received disproportionate attention from U.S. Negroes, in part because of the common experience of European settlement and white racism. Zulus and their "warrior tradition" were widely admired, and already students from Southern Africa had begun enrolling in all-Negro schools, e.g. Lincoln [Pennsylvania], Hampton Institute, and Tuskegee.[46]

One exception was Frederick Russell Burnham, a Euro-American freebooter who fought on the side of the British during this accursed war. Burnham, who had roots in Southern California, compared the Afrikaners to the Mormons who also had roots in that vicinity of the Golden State, not intending this as a compliment.[47] Burnham's views were typical of the ambition of imperialists of that era, once stating baldly, "I am convinced that the whole of East Africa"—he became involved in the subjugation of the colony of Kenya after fighting the Afrikaners—"from the Cape to Eritrea can be a white man's country and within 50 years support a European population of 10 millions."[48] With no less ambition, during the same era Jan Smuts and his party were advocating "amalgamation" of British colonies in Africa under Pretoria's administration.[49]

By 1900 Burnham was enthused by the possibility of fighting alongside London's forces in South Africa. Accurately, he thought

---

44. John H. Ferguson, *American Diplomacy and the Boer Warm*, Philadelphia: University of Pennsylvania Press, 1939, 177, 189, 192.

45. Ann Waldron, *Hodding Carter: the Reconstruction of a Racist*, Chapel Hill: Algonquin, 1993, 280-281.

46. Charles Alvis Bodie, "The Images of Africa in the Black American Press, 1890=1930," Ph.d. dissertation, Indiana University, 1975, 26, 47.

47. Steve Kemper, *A Splendid Savage: The Restless Life of Frederick Russell Burnham*, New York: Norton, 2016, 243, 248, 275.

48. Major Frederick Burnham to "Uncle Fred" no date, circa 1940s, Box 4, *Frederick R. Burnham Papers, Stanford University-Palo Alto, California.*

49. T. Holcomb, Consul-General, Pretoria to Secretary of State, 9 December 1944, Record Group 59, Decimal File, Box 5121, *NARA-CP*.

that "I might be of use…." Thus, he found "excitement is as high in Canada" duty bound to back London. Elliptically, he thought "mistakes of twenty years will be made right before this [war] is all over…." During this tempestuous time, he became friendly with Winston Churchill, who was also serving in this zone of conflict, finding celebrity in London because of his heroism on the battlefield.[50]

Mustachioed and barely over five feet tall, Burnham was comparable to John Fillmore Blake, born in 1856 in Missouri. The latter grew to adolescence in Texas and by 1871 was studying in Arkansas before decamping to West Point. Along the way, he fought Apaches, which prepared him well to fight Africans, as he joined the Boers in their war with London. He was indignant about the pro-London allegiance of presidents McKinley and Roosevelt "who were acting toward the republics of South Africa as our forefathers had acted toward the republic of Texas," yet another secessionist entity hell-bent on the exploitation of Africans, the slave trade in this instance. He also castigated Burnham, indicative of a strategic rift within the ranks of settler colonialists. He was no fan of Cecil Rhodes either: he found it curious that "in order to amuse his fellow British subjects," Rhodes hung a picture in his office of Africans hung in Bulawayo in 1896. Like many who joined the Boers, Blake was contemptuous of their opponents: "it is just as much of a latter-day Englishman's nature to be treacherous as it is for an American Indian to be suspicious," while adding for emphasis: "I had seen much of the blood work of the Apache Indians far away in Arizona but I had never seen anything that could possibly compare in downright cruelty to this piece of savagery on the part of the English soldiers." He knew the great indigenous American warrior Geronimo and opined that "this old savage chief showed far more humility in his way of waging war than was shown by the two civilized lords," meaning Lord Roberts and Lord Kitchener.

Blake commanded about 300 Irish and Irish American adventurers who had come to fight the redcoats in Africa. He could not understand why London was allowed to recruit soldiers in the U.S.[51] The pro-rebel U.S. national Blake was bitter about this turn of events. He was in South Africa from 1894-1902 and in combat for a good deal of this time. "The Boers lost," he concluded as early as 1903, because the U.S. "allied itself with the English government in London,

---

50. Frederick R. Burnham to H. Rider Haggard, 25 January 1900, Box 2, *H. Rider Haggard Papers, Huntington Library-San Marino, California.*

51. John Y. Fillmore Blake, *West Pointer with the Boers*, Boston: Angel Guardian Press, 1903, vii, 20-21, 26, 50, 126, 216, 266, 359.

England allowed British officers to establish a military camp at Chalmette, New Orleans for recruiting horses, mules and men for the British army in South Africa;" his assessment was that "more than 200,000 horses and mules were sent" southward—"and I don't know how many thousand[s] [of] men"—to the point that a "deficiency" of mules and horses emerged "in our own cavalry regiments...." Though the Afrikaners were notorious for their sulfurous attitudes toward Africans, he accused Queen Victoria of slaying "185,000 of her black subjects" during her reign and, consequently, he backed the fight of the so-called "Mad Mullah" in Somalia.[52] Naturally, this pro-London trend was displeasing to rebel supporters in the U.S. By 1902 they had taken their complaint to Washington, leading to a detailed report about London's emissaries purchasing vast materiel in New Orleans—horses and mules not alone--and shipping same to the Cape. The charges were made by what was described as a "Boer legislative committee" in Philadelphia.[53]

The skills of such Euro-Americans in fighting Apaches, then Matebeles were essential in combating Britons. He was a proud Irishman, commanding others from this group who saw confronting London as akin to a holy crusade. For his troubles he was wounded in the left hand, paralyzing his fingers. His heroism meant that he was part of the highest war councils among the Boers. He was reinforced by the arrival of many more men from North America (Chicago and Massachusetts, particularly) landing at Mozambique, then heading for the Transvaal.[54]

Like moths to a flame, soldiers of fortune began to flock to the sounds of the guns roaring in South Africa. By 1902, one of them, a Euro-American from Norfolk, Virginia, was described as "stranded" by one of his nation's diplomats. He was "ragged and dirty and without funds and," it was added tellingly, "all the rough labor is done by Kaffirs": thus, "a white man has no chance to earn a living unless he is a skilled mechanic...."[55] Thus, by 1903 there was an effort to induce Britain to "allow a free passage home to those Americans now in South Africa, who have served in the British forces in the

52. John Y. Fillmore Blake, *West Pointer with the Boers*, Boston: Angel Guardian, 1903, 369, 393, 395, 401.

53. U.S. Congress, House of Representatives, 57th Congress, 1st Session, Document No. 649, "Alleged Supply Camp in the State of Louisiana," 5 June 1902, *Williams Research Center-New Orleans.*

54. Gustav S. Preller, "Some Notes on Americans in South African Wars," 14 September 1932, Record Group 59, Decimal File, Box 6282, *NARA-CP.*

55. Consul General-Cape Town to State Department, 25 August 1902, Reel 21, *Despatches from U.S. Consuls in Cape Town, NARA-CP.*

war...." There were "many Americans now in Cape Colony," said the U.S. Consul, "who enlisted in the British army as volunteers...."[56]

These guns for hire were essential to the ability of the Afrikaner rebels to survive. A visiting U.S. scribe heard rebel leader Paul Kruger for "the first time.... when he received the Irish-Americans who came from Chicago to join the Transvaal Army...." It was then that Kruger signaled his forces' ultimate defeat: "They are two hundred thousand," he lamented of the redcoats, "we are thirty thousand," with even hired hands from Chicago unable to make up the shortfall. Thus, Kruger urged U.S. "intervention," a proposal doubtlessly buoyed by the fact that the writer, Richard Harding Davis, told him there was "much sympathy in America, that there were many people anxious to help the Transvaal." Kruger was satisfied with the "great deal of money" sent from the U.S. (not to mention the "message of sympathy signed by twenty-nine hundred Philadelphia schoolboys") while the equally pleased Davis thought this leader "reminded me greatly of one of our own presidents, Mr. [Grover] Cleveland." Davis also pointed to non-military aid to the rebels; the manager of the hotel in which he resided was from Ohio, aided by a "lady from Brooklyn"— "her husband, another American, was a prisoner" seized by the redcoats.[57]

Later Deneys Reitz, whose uncle fought in the war, recalled that Blake was a man of "roystering habits and devil-may-care methods," traits useful in the face of the overwhelming strength exhibited by the redcoats and their "many thousands" of Canadians and Australians and others from the far-flung empire. Aid from the likes of Blake, combined with the multi-faceted aid supplied by Russia and Germany to the Boers, seemed to be just enough to make the latter a nuisance, little more. Jan Smuts, perhaps the preeminent Afrikaner of the 20th century, hailed his peers' "genius" in guerilla warfare and, like his fellow Confederates, was not above constructing postbellum mythology, as he spoke of George Washington and Valley Forge and of "other seemingly lost causes that had triumphed in the end."[58]

As a number of U.S. nationals streamed into South Africa, attracted by the immense mineral wealth there, a "Martha Washington Club" was founded by U.S.-born women residing in Johannesburg, then a small mining camp festooned with a large number of Americans.

---

56. Consul General to State Department, 9 April 1903, Reel 21.

57. Richard Harding Davis, *With Both Armies in South Africa*, New York: Scribner's, 1900, 145, 147, 181.

58. Deneys Reitz, *Commando: A Boer Journal of the Boer War*, New York: Praeger, 1970, 11, 93, 100, 112.

"Largely through these Americans," said a U.S. official speaking decades later, "gold mining on the Rand was established in such an efficient manner."[59]

It was as if an umbilical cord tied together the U.S. and Southern Africa. One New York writer compared "the American cowboy of New Mexico or Wyoming" to the "Boer Vortrekker...." Natal, he thought, was a miniature U.S.: "in wooden ware of all kinds," said Poultney Bigelow, "such as houses and frames and oars," the U.S. was the clear leader. "We lead in manufactured tobacco," he boasted and "are the chief shippers of turpentine, petroleum, lard, oil, salt beef and pork." Officially, Britain was the leader in providing clocks and watches to South Africa "but I suspect" he asserted triumphantly, "that a large amount of those imported as from England are really manufactured in America...." Traipsing around the southern protuberance of Africa he felt right at home since "whenever I went in any part of South Africa," he said with wonder, "I found American handicraft represented in ploughs, carriages, mining industry, labor saving implements for domestic purposes, furniture," seemingly everything, making this feisty colony a de facto outpost of U.S. imperialism.

As for many visitors from the U.S., the profusion of U.S. products made Bigelow see South Africa as an extension of the U.S., the putative big brother of settler colonialism. But also, like others he saw Afrikaner nationalism as a stumbling block to the forging of "white" unity, the key to the success of the colonial project. "In my country," he said reveling in post-civil war reconciliation, "the citizens of Virginia and New York call themselves Americans," and, thus, "the Transvaal Dutchmen and the Cape Englishman must in future think less of what each is giving up and more of what all are gaining in common by a United Fatherland...." The "United States of South Africa" was his goal. If that hurdle could be leapt, the future would be bright indeed, since "as compared to the whole continent," South Africa in 1900 "reminds one of the thirteen united colonies of America in 1776," making the Cape Colony the "New England of Africa...." Not for the last time, he saw settler colonialism spreading northward at a rapid clip, in emulation of the U.S. decades earlier. The equivalence was uncanny: "the white man argued in South Africa as much as he did in New England when he landed on Plymouth Rock and cheerfully expelled the heathen...." The perceived success of settler colonialism made Bigelow lament all the more the inflamed

---

59. Report by M.K. Moorhead, U.S. Consul General-Johannesburg, 14 September 1932, Record Group 59, Decimal File, Box 6282, *NARA-CP*.

conflict between Afrikaner and Briton: "that the Boer should today hate the Englishman," he moaned, "is as absurd as if Dutch and England should quarrel on the banks of the Hudson or Delaware…." But they did quarrel—and fight—in the 17th century until the Dutch were ousted, which was precisely the fate their descendants at the Cape were seeking strenuously to avoid.[60]

What Bigelow did not notice was that there were forces driving the respective regional hegemons—the U.S. and South Africa—closer together. It was not just the impending weakening of the British Empire that would see Washington filling the breach. Rubber was in the process of replacing ivory as the chief export from the Congo, climbing from 100 metric tons in 1890 to 1300 by 1896 and 6000 by 1901. The concomitant development of the automobile, and then the airplane, opened the interior of the continent for further exploitation, often of a brutal nature. Perhaps not coincidentally, the African American intellectual George Washington Williams arrived in Luanda, Angola in October 1890, taking a course reverse to that of the unlamented African Slave Trade which had dumped so many of his compatriots in North America. To a degree he was countering those like Henry Stanley, who collaborated with Brussels in concocting what became a postbellum "white national identity" that augured a renewed 20th century thrust into the already bleeding continent. Williams' journey was in this sense unique: during this conflicted era, civil and human rights were being suffocated for those like himself in his homeland, a suffocation which assuredly included curtailment of the right to travel abroad, particularly to Africa.[61]

His arrival was a counterpoint to the activism of the Euro-American Henry Sanford, who had been encouraging U.S. Negroes to migrate to the Congo—and for reasons not benign. Still, Williams—like subsequent generations of African Americans—sought to aid African development by dispatching there Negro clerks, carpenters, blacksmiths, and engineers. He probably knew that Washington, reigniting an interest in Africa that stretched back to the republic's founding and the ignominious African Slave Trade, had sent warships to intimidate the Congo in 1879.[62]

At this time, Williams was outnumbered. Emblematic of what could well be considered a "White Atlantic" brotherhood was the

---

60. Ibid., Poutney Bigelow, iii, v, 106.

61. Ira Dworkin, *Congo Love Song: African American Culture and the Crisis of the Colonial State*, Chapel Hill: University of North Carolina Press, 2017, 32.

62. John Hope Franklin, *George Washington Williams: A Biography*, Chicago: University of Chicago Press, 1985, 182, 191.

man known as Colonel Wemyss Feilden, a friend of Rudyard Kipling who had served at the highest levels of the Confederate military.[63] Born in 1838, he began his martial life with the ill-famed "Black Watch" (42nd Highlanders) during the heroic Mutiny that rocked India; perhaps sensing the incipient unraveling of colonialism, he departed speedily for Natal but somehow—perhaps motivated by the pro-slavery cause—wound up in North America, where he ran blockades expertly and wedded his southern wife at Richmond with a ring hammered out of an English Sovereign coin. His skill in fighting for colonialism swiftly elevated him to top aide to General Robert E. Lee. Later he became friendly with the pro-colonial writer Rider Haggard, who he connected with almost immediately, with—as one writer put it— "South Africa in the early days being their bond."[64]

Bestriding multiple continents, the diehard Feilden fought the war in the southern states to its end, serving with a remnant of the army of Tennessee under General J.E. Johnston until it surrendered to General William T. Sherman. Returning to Britain, he wound up as a naturalist on the British Polar Expedition in 1875. He made it back to South Africa, where he won three medals for valor, before returning to his native Sussex, where he was still to be found in 1919.[65] In between, he found the time to serve in China in 1860 (where he also garnered medals) during a time of great turmoil, and then milk the original cash cow of the British Empire, which stationed him in the Caribbean by 1888.[66]

Feilden was present in South Africa when the Afrikaners and the British clashed violently in 1881, a setback for the latter that emboldened the former. Two decades later he embarked on his final military campaign, serving as Chief Paymaster to the Imperial Yeomanry in South Africa, before retiring to Sussex, where Kipling was one of his neighbors.[67] Despite his travels—and travails—his ultimate allegiance may be gleaned from his marriage to the daughter of the late David McCord of Charleston, South Carolina, a bastion of the slaveholding aristocracy.[68]

As U.S. imperialism began to bloom after the seizures of the Philippines, Hawaii, Cuba, and Puerto Rico, the republic's elite naturally

---

63. State Librarian to Mary Mullins, 13 February 1940, *Henry Wemyss Feilden Collection, University of Georgia-Athens.*

64. Report by Winifred Feilden, no date, *Henry Wemyss Feilden Collection.*

65. Biographical data on H.W. Feilden, no date, *Feilden Collection.*

66. "Who's Who 1919", *Feilden Collection.*

67. Notes on the Career of H.W. Feilden, circa 1919, *Feilden Collection.*

68. "Confederate Veterans", November-December 1921, *Feilden Collection.*

became more globally minded. It was such an outlook that brought future U.S. president Herbert Hoover to South Africa in 1904.[69]

Yet in a presentiment of competing developments, as Feilden was fading into the sunset, U.S. Negroes began flocking to the southern tip of Africa in ever greater numbers. Many were religious, as the Ethiopian Church, which had ties to Detroit and the Wesleyan Church, had established a foundation in South Africa. After Georgia's Henry McNeal Turner came to the region, Reverend James Mata Dwane came to the U.S. and helped to merge the Ethiopian Church with the African Methodist Episcopal Church. One observer asserted that there were "enough Negroes with masters and doctors['] degrees, who are unemployed in this country to aid substantially in giving direction to the training of our brothers in Africa and in thus contributing to their salvation we shall be doing much toward the realization of our own"; echoing a point that was to become increasingly familiar, it was added portentously, "for blackmen in America will never be fully and completely free until they do what they can to bring a larger measure of freedom to their kin of the 'dark' continent."[70]

The increasing influx of U.S. Negroes was disconcerting to some. Edward Blyden, the "Pan-Negro" activist, with roots in the Caribbean, North America, then Liberia,[71] was perceived as emblematic of a deepening problem, insofar as he preached uplift while the model in South Africa was based on the exact opposite. The Ethiopian church movement was seen in similar terms. "Ethiopianism" led in 1896 to the African Christian Union, which advocated emigration of U.S. Negroes to South Africa.[72] This movement was reviled by Afrikaners and their allies, with at least one among them perceiving Basutos as potentially vulnerable to their appeal. This church, said Ambrose Pratt, was "really a secret society having for its object the driving of the white race into the sea" and, shockingly enough, "is meeting with success in all directions"; it "makes scores of converts every day" as "they watch and work and wait…"[73]

69. Eschel Roodie, *The Third Africa*, New York: Twin Circle, 1967, 97.

70. Amos Jerome White and Luella Graham White, *Dawn in Basutoland: An African Experiment or an Account of Missionary Experiences and Observations in South Africa*, Boston: Christopher, 1953, 242, 283.

71. Hollis Lynch, *Edward Wilmot Blyden, Pan-Negro Patriot, 1832-1912*, New York: Oxford University Press, 1970.

72. Amanda Denise Kemp, "'Up from Slavery' and Other Narratives: Black South African Performances of the American Negro (1920-1943)," Ph.d. dissertation, Northwestern University, 1997, 8, 38.

73. Ambrose Pratt, *The Real South Africa*, Indianapolis: Bobbs-Merrill, 1913, 34.

Then there was the Salvation Army, which had arrived in South Africa as early as 1888, principally toiling in Natal—the British bastion—and "Kaffraria," similarly oriented. By 1891 they had invaded Zululand on the premise, sure to bring negative attention in Pretoria, that "The Army knows no colour or creed."[74]

Such sentiments propelled the self-described "Negro sea-captain" Harry Dean to Cape Town at the time of the war with London. This growing city became "my headquarters," he recalled, since it was "the most strategic point in that part of the world and was bound to become as important as the Golden Horn in ancient times." It was also critical, he thought, to "locate in the very midst of the imperialists and learn their game at first hand," to combat them more effectively. There he encountered other U.S. Negroes, including Kid Gardener, a "two fisted buck from Texas with a six shooter and a long knife," recently arrived on a ship from New Orleans. Despite that town's Jim Crow pedigree, the Texan took umbrage to being subjected to the same in Africa and roughed up those who sought to impose this precursor to apartheid. He was jailed as a result, but since he was a major diamond smuggler, in league with the trade's prominent Somali Haji Hassan, his confinement would not be lengthy. Dean also met another "colored man," this one from Georgia, who was also residing at the Cape.

As the Afrikaner–British conflict unfolded, Dean headed to "Pondo land to aid the indigenes," for he had noticed that "for every chivalrous Boer," there were two others "hating the natives like the Devil hates holy water and killing them like flies." This he could not abide. He was in town for the funeral of the "pompous" Cecil Rhodes, an "imperialist to the last," he added contemptuously. The Pondos were "anxious to begin building schools," and he was more than willing to contribute since he knew better than most that "the world in general" was "unaware of the manner in which the natives in South Africa are treated," which shocked the conscience. "At Blomfontein and elsewhere they are segregated from the European element by confinement in compounds where they are forced to wear collars and tags as if they were dogs." He described the Afrikaners as "Dutch mixed with Hottentot with just enough American pirates, slaves and highjackers [sic] added to imbue them with sin and love of the devil...." In fact, these Afrikaners "outdid [the English] in all

74. Brochure on Salvation Army, circa 1891, Reel 1, *A.B. Xuma Papers, University of Witwatersrand.*

forms of iniquity," quite a feat.[75] Dean was not singular in his distaste for Rhodes. This attitude was a staple of the U.S. Negro press.[76]

Dean may have had in mind when denouncing retrograde attitudes, the writer Edward Strathmeyer, then publishing from Boston, who in 1900 announced, "by natives I mean the Boers, for the Kaffirs and Hottentots"—i.e. Africans—"don't count...." He saw this war between London and its foes as akin to the U.S. Civil War, a common assumption of the era[77] shared by the influential Charles Francis Adams.[78]

Unfortunately for U.S. Negroes visiting southern Africa, the distaste was reciprocated. By 1903 a U.S. official had detected "ill treatment of certain colored Americans in Johannesburg." A "Mr. Dean"—presumably Harry Dean—was told that "his passport was not proof sufficient to prove his citizenship" and that he and others of his kind were "heathens." "Under the Boer regime," it was reported "colored people were not permitted to walk on the sidewalks," not unlike Dixie. "Many of these regulations have become relaxed since

75. Harry Dean, *The Pedro Gorino: The Adventures of a Negro Sea-Captain in Africa on the Seven Seas in His Attempts to Found an Ethiopian Empire*, Boston: Houghton Mifflin, 1929, 78, 79, 80, 84, 87, 145, 154, 166, 201, 202, 212, 213, 218, 227. Dean apparently shared the dyspeptic view of Rhodes held by today's South African comedian, Trevor Noah: "if black South Africans," he said in 2016, "could go back in time and kill one person, Cecil Rhodes would come up before Hitler." See Trevor Noah, *Born a Crime: Stories from a South African Childhood*, New York: Spiegel and Grau, 2016, 195.

76. See e.g. Willard Gatewood, "Black Americans and the Boer War," *South Atlantic Quarterly*, 75(1996): 229-244; *Indianapolis Freeman*, 20 February 1897.

77. Edward Stratemyer, *Between Boer and Briton or Two Boys' Adventures in South Africa*, Boston: Less and Shepard, 1900, 25.

78. Charles Francis Adams, *The Confederacy and the Transvaal: A People's Obligation to Robert E. Lee*, Boston: Houghton Mifflin, 1901. Charles Francis Adams, "Before and After the Treaty of Washington: The American Civil War and the War in the Transvaal, An Address Delivered Before the New York Historical Society," New York, 1902, *University of Virginia-Charlottesville*. See also A.T. Mahan, *The War in South Africa: A Narrative of the Anglo-Boer War from the Beginning of Hostilities to the Fall of Pretoria*, New York: Fenelon House, 1900. Arguably, the imminent decline of enslavement of Africans as the basis for society signaled by 1865 led directly to a renewed scramble for Africa as what then ensued was exploiting Africans shamelessly on their home turf; this was indicated by the Belgian monarch then plunging into Congo, a former happy hunting ground for slave traders, followed by the Congress of Berlin in 1884 when the continent was carved up like a turkey by European powers: this was then punctuated by a steady streaming into Southern Africa by Euro-Americans.

the British occupation," further confirmation of the correctness of opposing the rebels during the war. Nonetheless, there were "physical conflicts engendered by this old prejudice" of the rebels as they sought to impose their racist diktat forcibly.[79]

At this juncture, the U.S. legation counted "some 3300 Americans" living in the Orange Free State and Transvaal, with no estimate of the number of "colored."[80] Yet the number was probably growing, if the proliferating number of complaints from U.S. Negroes in the region is any indicator. One notable petition was signed by a dozen U.S. Negroes "and others," writing from Johannesburg.[81] Washington was told that ousting the Negroes from the sidewalks was a product of "custom" not "law," thereby—supposedly—restricting the ability for official protest. "Such prohibition was abrogated with the accession of this colony to the British Crown"; however, "the sentiment which exists in the breast of the average white man in South Africa against the use of sidewalks by people of color is perhaps a greater deterrent than any law could possibly be." But how could the U.S. credibly complain when the "average white man" in Africa was simply emulating his peer in Dixie? It was acknowledged that "the prevailing law relative to railway transportation does not differ in any essential respects from the laws obtaining in many of our Southern States," insofar as Jim Crow was concerned. Afrikaners were simply arguing that U.S. Negroes "must expect the same treatment as is accorded to the African"—so there was no discrimination. African-Americans did not buy this casuistry and "complaints" from them were becoming ever more "frequent," though Joseph Proffit, the consul, had "tried to make the colored men contented with his lot in South Africa...."[82]

Arguably, being forced off the sidewalks was minor compared to other travails endured by touring U.S. Negroes. By 1905 there was a report of the "torturing of an alleged American colored citizen" and other "atrocities" too.[83] In an expression of an ongoing trend that only worsened as time passed, the visiting U.S. Negro Fanny Jackson

79. Report from Consul General, 28 December 1903, Reel 2, Microfilm T660, *NARA-CP*.

80. Consul General to State Department, 17 February 1904, Reel 2, Microfilm T660.

81. Petition, 8 August 1904, Reel 2, T660.

82. Joseph Proffit, U.S. Consul General to State Department, 8 August 1904, Reel 2, T660.

83. Consul General-Pretoria to State Department, 9 January 1905, Reel, T660.

Coppin found herself under surveillance upon arrival in Cape Town in late 1902, a situation that did not cease as she headed northward to Bulawayo in the British colony of Southern Rhodesia. She noticed "spies," and "suspicion was everywhere prevalent"[84]—a lubricant for inchoate violence. A persistent issue for colonizers in Pretoria, London, Brussels, Lisbon, and elsewhere was the presence in their contested realm of U.S. Negroes.[85]

John Blick, a brother-in-law of Burnham, summarized the thoughts of other European interlopers in Africa when he declared that "these swine here"—referring to indigenes in Southern Africa— "are spoiled by missionaries..."[86]—particularly those who were Negroes.

On the other hand, most Afrikaners had a further excuse for seeking to bar U.S. Negroes, since in the postwar environment even the U.S. authorities noticed "depressed business conditions" in Cape Town. "During the war everything here was boomed up to an extravagant imaginary value; money was plenty and business of all kinds was good," which tended to attract migrants of various sorts, including U.S. Negroes. Even the "Kaffirs," it was said, were having trouble finding work. "There are thousands of Americans in this country," the State Department was told, "who are getting into a very bad fix...."[87]

Though understandably the Negroes stood with London during the war, afterward the complaint arose that the British authorities "would not permit colored ministers to baptize by immersion their converts among the Kaffirs...."[88] Still, the U.S. Consul in Cape Town suspected strongly that London was simply capitulating to the staunch sentiment of the Boers. "I know that the government here is not in sympathy with any colored organization that is teaching the Kaffirs," it was announced by Washington's man in early 1904, since "they have the old idea that existed in the Southern States that the colored man should be kept in ignorance...."[89]

84. Fanny Jackson Coppin, *Reminiscences of School Life and Hints on Teaching*, New York: G.K. Hall, 1995 [originally published 1913], 123, 126, 127.

85. Elizabeth I. Normandy, "Black Americans and U.S. Foreign Policy Toward Africa: Two Case Studies from the Pre-World War II Period," Ph.d. dissertation, University of South Carolina, 1987.

86. Entry, circa 1900, Diary of John Blick, Box 6, *Frederick R. Burnham Papers.*

87. Report, 16 February 1904, Reel 21, T191, *Despatches from U.S. Consuls in Cape Town, NARA-CP.*

88. Report, 7 March 1904, Reel 21, T191: Reverend Henry Tate, a "colored preacher from Cleveland.... working under instructions from the Missionary Board of America" denied this claim.

89. Report, 7 March 1904, Reel 21, T191.

As the example of Feilden suggests, settler colonialism in Southern Africa was a joint enterprise, backed not least by the nation that was to contain a plurality of those defined as "white"—the U.S. Sensing a downturn in the U.S. economy in the last decade of the 19th century, John Hammond left his homeland in search of enrichment at the Cape. He partnered with Cecil Rhodes, whose star was then ascending, in mining on the Rand. "I had the good fortune to be intimately associated with Rhodes for seven years," he later acknowledged proudly. "He was my close friend" and "most important of all we were conspirators in a political revolution," a veiled reference to undermining Africans and Afrikaners alike. He "claim[ed] a special knowledge" of this man who named entire nations—including Zambia and Zimbabwe—after himself. Unlike those Irish-Americans who aligned with the Afrikaners, Hammond backed Rhodes' "plan… to form a secret society whose aim would be to extend British rule throughout the world," including the "whole of Africa, Palestine…. all of South America," the "Chinese and Japanese seaboard," all "by perfecting a system of emigration from the British Isles…." Rhodes continued to berate "[King] George III for the loss of America and stated that but for the King's stupidity there … would now be one great country with two great capitals—one in London, the other at Washington…." Finally, the "recovery of the United States as an integral part of the British Empire" was a central goal, not least since considering these capacious plans, there were simply not enough British nationals to settle and administer such vast territories. This would not be easy since the "consensus of opinion in the United States was undoubtedly anti-British," and the former colony had plans of world conquest all its own. Then there were the Germans in what became Namibia, who also had designs on global domination.

More settlers were needed to overawe Africans increasingly disgusted with the maltreatment visited upon them. Hammond confessed openly that it was "frequently necessary to resort to flogging to maintain order among the boys in the compounds," i.e. the brutalizing "mines."[90] Hammond could qualify as an expert witness on the horrors of mining that delivered high mortality rates to Africans. By 1896 half of South Africa's gold mines were run by U.S. engineers,

90. John Hays Hammond, *The Autobiography, Volume I*, New York: Farrar, Straus & Rinehart, 1935, 199, 214, 218, 221, 225, 237, 305, 315: Rhodes' voice "like that of [Theodore Roosevelt] broke into a falsetto whenever he became excited". *Volume II*, 398, 427,

accompanied by hundreds of pimps and prostitutes from North America.[91]

It was Hammond who joined Rhodes in the ill-fated "Jameson Raid" against the Afrikaner republicans led by Paul Kruger,[92] and wound up in prison, where a visiting Mark Twain paid his respects to the man who—according to one analyst— "might have been the highest paid salaried employee in the world." Hammond had toiled on behalf of the Hearst publishing fortune before arriving in Africa and was well versed in the machinations of empire building.[93]

Hammond denied the idea that he was preeminent among his compatriots in rallying to London's cause in South Africa, pointing to Frederick Russell Burnham as a better candidate for that lofty role. This U.S. national left San Francisco for Africa on 1 January 1893 and wound up fighting King Lobengula of the Ndebele, helping to create what became Southern Rhodesia. He was angry that he was not present for Jameson's Raid, feeling that "I might have found some weak point in the line of the Boers…."[94] By 1896 Burnham was capturing headlines as the "slayer of M'Limo, High Priest of the warlike Matbeles…. [sic]"[95] The consensus among U.S. freebooters then was that Burnham's battles with the Ndebele were—as Richard Harding Davis put it—"not unlike the Indian fighting of the early days" in which the rowdy Burnham was also involved.[96]

Writing in 1896 the colonial hero Frederick Courtney Selous hailed Burnham the "American Scout" who displayed heroism in the face of danger, especially when "the Kaffirs nearly surrounded [him] in a very rocky bit of ground…"[97]

---

91. Adam Hochschild, *The Mirror at Midnight*, 122.

92. Charles Van Onselen, *The Cowboy Capitalist: John Hays Hammond, the American West and the James Raid*, Johannesburg: Jonathan Ball, 2017.

93. Richard Sacks, *Chasing the Last Laugh: Mark Twain's Raucous and Redemptive Round the World Comedy Tour*, New York: Doubleday, 2016, 291. Hammond may have been the "mining engineer" deemed by a visiting U.S. journalist to have "received a salary four times as great as that of the President of the United States…." See Richard Harding Davis, *With Both Armies in South Africa*, New York: Scribner's, 1900, 108.

94. Frederick Russell Burnham, *Scouting on Two Continents*, London: Heinemann, 1926, xi, 86, 221.

95. *San Francisco Sunday Examiner*, 27 September 1896, Box 6, *Frederick R. Burnham Papers, Stanford University-Palo Alto, California*.

96. Richard Harding Davis, *Real Soldiers of Fortune*, New York: Scribner's, 1907, 204.

97. Frederick Courtney Selous, *Sunshine and Storm in Rhodesia, Being a Narrative of Events in Matabeleland Both Before and During the Recent Native*

Burnham saw the Ndebele as one of the more formidable foes he had confronted in his warfighting career. The "constant ulcer of rebellion in Matebeland" was bound, he said in 1897, to "stir up these natives again" since "they do not consider that the white man beat them...." Assuredly, he did not "want the Kaffirs to rise again," which meant a concerted campaign to "dispel the idea which they now have that the white man cannot concentrate quickly or catch a Kaffir...."[98]

Like others, Burnham compared how he had "roamed.... far and wide" in Rhodesia with his perambulations on the "western American plains," where he had viciously fought Native Americans. He was elated to be in the future Zimbabwe, especially since the "Matebele had risen, their black soldiers had turned on the whites and were murdering men, women and children," events to which he responded with alacrity, leading to accusations of war crimes. Then it was on to the Klondike of Alaska, where Burnham again searched for wealth and undermined indigenes, before returning in time for the war against the Afrikaners. There he bonded with Winston Churchill before arriving in London at the "invitation" of Queen Victoria. Upon arrival King Edward VII granted him "rank as a Major in the British Army," which he accepted "without renouncing his American citizenship," a sign of concord between the declining and ascending powers. Then it was off to the Gold Coast (today's Ghana) and on to East Africa for the purpose of "quieting the natives" during the formation of Kenya Colony. Afterwards it was on to Mexico, as revolutionary sentiments rose.[99]

Fortunately, he confessed, "my heart was never in the work of extermination...."[100] Burnham was an exemplar of the freelance imperialist, a type honed in the U.S., where subduing indigenes and Africans was valuable training for similar efforts elsewhere. He was also an example of the borderless imperialists, who were willing to make the ultimate sacrifice on behalf of another nation, out of commitment to the larger goal of spreading the ravages of imperialism, to Africa most notably.

Insurrection up to the Date of the Disbandment of the Bulawayo Field Force, London: Rowland Ward, 1896, 201.

98. Frederick R. Burnham to Lord Gifford, 7 June 1907, Box 6, *Frederick R. Burnham Papers, Stanford University-Palo Alto, Claifornia.*

99. H.T. Goodland, "Hail and Farewell", no date, Box 1, *Frederick R. Burnham Papers, Stanford University-reaPalo Alto, California.*

100. Frederick R. Burnham to Baden Powell, 18 September 1909, Box 2, *Frederick R. Burnham Papers.*

Burnham was devoted to the Anglo-American project for surprising reasons. He served on the staff of Lord Roberts in South Africa and, he thought, the only U.S. nationals who might disagree with his stance were the "noisy" Irish. "'Monarchy stands for freedom,'" he claimed, and "Republic for despotism." Besides, he said, the "Boer cause has been closely followed and thoroughly thrashed out in the States."[101]

It was in 1897 that he advised the dispatching of a "large expedition" to "check the encroachment of the Portuguese," then ensconced in Angola and Mozambique "and the Belgians from the north" then feasting in the Congo.[102] Then there were the "Germans pushing in from the west," today's Namibia, who were then "urging the Portuguese to claim…the Zambesi River from the west via Mossamedes…." He sensed that "as soon as the Belgians have quieted their own native row they will again be entering the northern mineral fields…." He was bent on moving northward to what is now Zambia but knew that the "settlers" needed for "occupation" were in short supply, already attracted to North America and Australia. At that point—Spring 1897—the "natives" were "not entirely quiet" but this state of affairs was not eternal, he well knew. Even more, he knew that "these expeditions are expensive for prospecting and not large enough to really take over a country."[103] Yet the vast untapped wealth of the continent made it "worth conquering"; by 1897 he had "fought two wars" there and "endured … pestilence, drought and locust" but was "still…strong" and, importantly, had "no further fear of the Matebele." "They have had quite enough fighting" he concluded prematurely, making the invidious comparison with their neighbors, the "Mashonas," then "living like baboons"[104]—a simian reference quite commonly invoked by Europeans then.

Burnham ignored advice not to throw in his lot with London in the war with the Afrikaners. He was informed in 1900 that Britain was willing to "spend her last shilling" since the "end must be equal rights for English & the world in the Transvaal…." Burnham was told that "no good could ever come from English defeat," a conclusion he evidently shared. During the U.S. Civil War, Washington employed a "loyal element ready to act as scouts who knew the country. But

101. Undated Clipping, *London Telegraph*, Box 6, *Frederick R. Burnham Papers*.

102. Frederick R. Burnham to "Dear Lord" Gifford, 7 May 1897, Box 6, *Frederick R. Burnham Papers*.

103. Frederick R. Burnham to Weston Jervis, 27 May 1897, Box 6.

104. Frederick R. Burnham to R. Haggard, 22 May 1897, Box 6.

there seems to be no Boers loyal to the Queen and scouting will be hard on you in a land unknown…."[105]

Joining the pro-London phalanx was Richard Harding Davis. He knew there was "sympathy" for the "underdog" Afrikaners and "in spite of the wishes of the editors for whom I was acting as a correspondent," forthrightly, he "elected to join the British. I did this," he confessed openly, "because I had never seen so large a body of troops in the field as there were British troops in South Africa…." Still, when he ascertained that this underdog had been "misrepresented and misunderstood," he "sympathized with them entirely."[106]

As Hammond was headed to the Cape, others in that vicinity were considering a move in the opposite direction. By 1901 the U.S. Consul in Johannesburg was mulling over a proposal by "certain [Afrikaners]….to migrate to the United States…as an alternative to their being compelled to take the Oath of Allegiance to the British Crown…." Investigated was "whether land suitable for agriculture or stock raising can be obtained on reasonable terms and if so in what States." The U.S. official David Draper was gung-ho about this prospect, inquiring if "as a first installment about fifty families consisting of about 250 souls would be prepared to leave here…."[107] Several states, it was said, offered "free land" to these would-be migrants, seized from indigenes in a manner not unlike what had befallen South Africans.[108]

At that point it was estimated that "about 95% of the Americans in the country" were sited in the commercial capital of Johannesburg.[109] At that point also there were U.S. officials in London recruiting soldiers returning from the Cape for the purpose of sending them onwards to the still percolating conflict in the Philippines. There were applications from "hundreds of men," it was reported happily, ready to enlist.[110] This may have been an underestimate, since months later the State Department was told that "five thousand trained soldiers," could have been recruited for this dangerous Pacific mission, "all of whom have seen active service" in South Africa.[111] This may not have

105. Letter to "Dear Fred", 21 February 1900, Box 6.

106. Ibid., Richard Harding Davis, 108.

107. David Draper to U.S. Consul, Pretoria, 4 September 1901, Reel 2, *Microfilm 1660: Despatches from U.S. Consul in Pretoria, 1898-1906, NARA-CP.*

108. Ibid., Steve Kemper, 248.

109. Report, 28 January 1902, Reel 2, *Pretoria Despatches.*

110. Report from U.S. Consul-Pretoria to State Department, 22 June 1902, Reel 2.

111. William Gordon to State Department, 22 June 1902, Reel 2.

been an exaggeration. The pro-London fighter Frederick Burnham retained a clipping that argued that "the number of Americans serving in the British ranks must be very considerable…."[112]

Often missed is the fact that beyond racial solidarity or Anglophilia or imperialist bloodlust, there were other reasons for U.S. nationals to become involved in the internal affairs of South Africa. As the war was being initiated between Briton and Boer in 1898, U.S. nationals with roots in Montana, Nevada, Virginia, California, Michigan, Maryland, Georgia, Massachusetts, Illinois, and Maryland were concerned that what they termed their "controlling interest" in the "Electric Tramway" in Johannesburg was being threatened.[113] Other U.S. nationals residing in what was becoming a combat zone were increasingly concerned that "alien residents" could be "required to perform service in a local force raised for the maintenance of the internal order or the defense of the territory from an invasion by savages," meaning Africans eager to take advantage of an intra-European conflict. "They cannot be forcibly enrolled in the regular army of the country," the U.S. consulate advised, "or in any force organized to defend it against a civilized power,"[114] meaning London.

This distinction between the "savage" and the "civilized" became harder to maintain as hostilities flared. For by late 1899 the rebels were irate about "the English arming and drafting Natives…." There was a fight near Mafeking, said H.C. ten Haaf, Under Secretary of State for Foreign Affairs, between his "burgher commandos" and the redcoats who were "strengthened by 100 natives…." In words he suspected would resonate with a Washington deeply influenced by Dixie, he termed this African brigade as "a totally unjustifiable act against all the white races of South Africa"—and he could have added superfluously, the world. This was "an outrage," he thundered, "as all white races will suffer by it and it trusts," he told the U.S. consul, "you will inform your Government of these facts…."[115]

This stinging critique was repeated throughout the conflict. There was an "outbreak of natives in the northern part of the country," said the U.S. consul, in "which natives are said to have been led and officered by British army officers and to have used a Maxim gun…."

112. Undated Clipping, Box 6, *Frederick Russell Burnham Papers.*

113. Petition to Consulate, 17 October 1898, Reel 1, T660, *Despatches from U.S. Consuls in Pretoria, NARA-CP.*

114. Letter to "Mr. Cridler," 6 April 1899, Reel 1, T660.

115. "Translation of Letter forwarded by Charles Macrum, U.S. Consul, to Secretary of State, 7 December 1899, Reel 2, T660.

Sounding sympathetic to the Boers' claim, the consul added that this stunning event "will possibly prove a great menace not only to the property but to the lives of the non-combatants residing in this State...." He implored the State Department to "take steps to show to Great Britain the danger in which we will all be placed" as a result. Pointedly, he attached a missive from the rebels' State Secretary, F.W. Reitz, who observed that "again English officers have incited and lead on Kaffirs to fight our burghers." "Kaffirs," he warned caustically, "once incited to murdering whites, do not make any distinction in nationality...."[116] Apparently, London suspected that such charges were tilting opinion in Washington toward the rebels, which led the consul in Pretoria to object to "systematic efforts of the English press to embitter these people against the Americans"—though as of January 1900, he contended "our people are well liked here...."[117]

This ebullience came no thanks to the British press, thought the U.S. consul. "Ever since this war began," it was charged in early 1900, "Reuter's cable service for this country has been full of false and misleading statements regarding the attitude of the United States in this unhappy war...." Reuters judged that the U.S. was "not neutral" but was "practically at the back of and was encouraging Great Britain in this war against the Boers and that the sentiment of the United States was overwhelmingly against" the rebels. This was not true: Euro-American opinion was split (though it was true that U.S. Negroes were hostile to the rebels). But London's domination of press coverage meant that "the world at large has been made to believe that Kruger and his supporters were little better than a band of pirates" and "that the average Boer was worse than a Kaffir"—the ultimate putdown.

For his part the consul, W. Stanley Hollis, praised the rebels: "these people," he said admiringly, "have always respected and looked up to the American people." Anyway, "logically the war was bound to come," in the way that 1776 and 1861 had also been inevitable. Thus, he had "met hundreds of good honest Americans" who "all praised this country as the ideal country for the working man and for the mining man...." Telling, he thought, was "the bare fact that hundreds of non-British Uitlanders are today fighting in the Republican ranks and that many more are remaining here at work in the mines and elsewhere...." His judgment, which was to be ratified in Washington repeatedly in coming decades, was that the "Africander, Dutch-Huguenot race is to be the ruling race of South Africa and

116. U.S. Consul to State Department, 30 November 1899, Reel 1, T660.
117. Consul General to State Department, 4 January 1900, Reel 1, T660.

that it will absorb the other races possessing less individuality, as the United States has already done....." This conclusion was reached "after more than ten years of careful study" and it was driven by the perception that "there is going to be a big market in this country for goods our American people can supply," particularly since "Boers still have a warm regard for us...."[118]

Hollis could have added that a blooming U.S. imperialism, still in the process of masticating and digesting Hawaii, Cuba, Puerto Rico, and the Philippines, saw a better chance of absorbing the region's untold riches—including diamonds and gold—if allied with Afrikaners and opposing Londoners.[119]

Also tipping opinion in the U.S. toward their fellow republicans across the ocean were the nagging and persistent reports about redcoats arming Africans to attack Afrikaners. "Murdered persons are American citizens" was Hollis' claim in February 1900, speaking of the latest victims of this alliance. "The child Annie Pieters was born in New York," he lamented, while "natives had crossed the border, killed all white people and burned their houses...."[120]

Still, that the socialist Charles Edward Russell, a founder of the National Association for the Advancement of Colored People, also backed the Boers suggests either the blinkered views of certain Euro-Americans, the complicated choice between Boer and Briton, or the similarities between this war and that which republicans revered:1776.[121]

By May 1899 a fervent petition was forwarded by "all 'Uitlanders'—British, Americans, German, French, Dutch and subjects of other nationalities," signed—it seemed—by 21,000 and sent to London. The rebel force, it was claimed by detractors, "gives no protection to life or property" and thus petitioners' "life and property" were "in jeopardy...." They blamed this on unnamed "Capitalists" and argued further that if this amorphous group gained "their object," it would be "detrimental to the whole public including the "'Uitlanders,'" Thus,

118. W. Stanley Hollis, U.S. Consul to State Department, 5 January 1900, Reel 1, T660.

119. Gardner F. Williams, *The Diamond Mines of South Africa*, New York: Buck, 1905. See also Report, circa 1899, DO119/367, *National Archives of the United Kingdom-London:* The U.S. takes charge of British interests in rebel territory.

120. W. Stanley Hollis to State Department, 1 February 1900, Reel 1, T660.

121. Steve Kemper, *A Splendid Savage*, 248.

they were "perfectly satisfied with the Government" and sought "no other Government…."[122]

By this point, David Hill, Assistant Secretary of State, was informed that there were—minimally— "hundreds of Americans …in Johannesburg" alone.[123] Yet in the Transvaal and Mozambique, the State Department was told there were "nearly a thousand American citizens" thereabouts and mail tampering by "Cape Colony authorities" was creating more work for the U.S. legation.[124]

One result of the war in South Africa was that this nation became better known in the U.S. Thus, as early as 1903 there was a growing exodus of Africans to the U.S. with the purpose of enrolling in the significant number of Negro colleges and universities. This in turn fed Pretoria's anxieties about the presumed seditious ideas these students would be subjected to, leading to the formation of Fort Hare University which became a beacon for African students regionally.[125]

* * *

Ultimately, the sad similarity between white U.S. Southerners and Afrikaners also informed attitudes toward the results of the U.S. Civil War and the so-called Anglo-Boer war. In both instances, the force that was defeated militarily actually triumphed politically in that their extremely horrific varieties of racism prevailed.[126] Nonetheless, even then there were signs that the Afrikaners and their fellow republicans had developed fissures that would be difficult to bridge. Whereas the Euro-Americans were moving toward incorporating the Jewish community into a broader category of "whiteness," the Boers were hardly sincere in their purported movements in a similar direction, a failing that was to lead to their ultimate undoing. When a man in Dixie charged in the 1970s that "it was the Jews who fomented the unrest in the Boer Republics," specifically naming Sir Moses Montefiore, who was also blamed for the U.S. Civil War, it was more likely that this inflammatory charge would arouse

122. Petition, 5 May 1899, Reel 1, T660.

123. Consul General to David Hill, 7 July 1899, Reel 1, T660.

124. U.S. Consul, Pretoria, to State Department, 20 November 1899, Reel 1, T660.

125. Daniel Massey, *Under Protest: The Rise of Student Resistance at the University of Fort Hare*, Pretoria: UNISA Press, 2010, 11.

126. Marvin L. Faison, "Pixley ka Isaka Seme, President General of the African National Congress, 1930-1939: A Study of the Impact of His Leadership and Ideology on the Congress," M.A. Thesis, Columbia University, 1983.

Pretoria than Washington. Still the author, John Coleman of the ultra-right redoubt that was Metairie, Louisiana, correctly ascertained the "very definite link between American history and that of South Africa," which would be demonstrated repeatedly throughout the 20th century.[127]

Repeatedly over the years, Euro-Americans sought to build unity between Boer and Briton.[128] According to the Mayor of Cape Town in 1905, "many citizens of the United States served during the late war,"[129] and their influence tended toward binding Boer and Briton but, ultimately, this influence did not prevail altogether. For even after relinquishing power, the final apartheid leader, F.W. de Klerk, conceded that the war with London was still achingly shaping his overall ideological posture, hampering his ability to maneuver diplomatically.[130] Though London sought to bend to the will of the defeated socially and politically, just as Washington did post-1865, reconciliation between these combatants in Africa was not as successful.

Still, by 1910 Boer and Briton had reconciled in the Union of South Africa, to the detriment of Africans. U.S. Negroes too were a loser in this reconciliation. If U.S. Negroes were deprived of the right to vote by fraud and violence, London and its Afrikaner peers argued, then why couldn't Pretoria do the same?[131]

---

127. John Coleman, *The Boer War: How the Jew Seized South Africa*, Metairie, Louisiana: Sons of Liberty, 1970s, *Michigan State University-East Lansing*.

128. Poultney Bigelow, *White Man's Africa*, 259.

129. Report from Consul General-Cape Town, 24 January 1905, Reel 21, *NARA-CP*.

130. F.W. de Klerk, *The Last Trek-A New Beginning: The Autobiography*, New York: St. Martin's, 1999, 6.

131. Bernard Magubane, *The Making of a Racist State: British Imperialism and the Union of South Africa, 1875-1910*, Trenton: Africa World Press, 367.

Chapter 2

The U.S. Lays the Foundation for Apartheid, 1906-1930

LIKE Washington after the U.S. Civil War, in the aftermath of the so-called "Anglo-Boer War," London sought to conciliate the defeated party and to accommodate particularly their bitter maltreatment of Africans. The African uprising of 1906 helped to drive this result, convincing the two major combatants that they should hang together—or hang separately. In what was to become Namibia, Germany was rising, which in the minds of some among the defeated provided a source of leverage against Britain, providing this power more incentive to engage in conciliation. Weeks after the outbreak of world war in 1914, a leading South African general resigned out of unwillingness to back London in its confrontation with Berlin. Another South African general was accused of treason when he joined the Germans in Windhoek, bringing along a large portion of the troops entrusted to his command. Martial law was proclaimed, with the U.S. Consul in Cape Town warning bluntly of the "danger of Civil War."[1] By late October 1914, Washington had detected "organized and armed resistance to government authority" from a "combined force approximating 1500 to 2000 burghers."[2] Within months there was pushback, as reports emerged of "riotous anti-German demonstrations," accompanied by "wholesale burning and destruction of property" and "mob violence."[3] In Cape Town there was evidently an unsuccessful attempt to sell South African gold to a U.S. firm for the benefit of Germany.[4]

---

1. G.H. Murphy, Consul General to Secretary of State, 17 October 1914, Reel 2, M583, *Internal Affairs of British Africa, NARA-CP.*

2. Consul General to Secretary of State, 28 October 1914, Reel 2, M583.

3. Consul General to Secretary of State, 20 May 1915, Reel 2, M583.

4. George Murphy, Consul General-Cape Town to Secretary of State, 12 November 1915, Reel 7, M583.

* * *

At this juncture, three nations—the U.S., Germany, and Britain—were jousting for influence in South Africa. By early 1917 Washington was objecting furiously to a harsh critique of President Woodrow Wilson and complaining of what the U.S. Consul in Cape Town characterized as the "growth of anti-American feeling in this country."[5] In response, Theodore Roosevelt was said to be "preparing to form a division for foreign service" and, said Frederick Burnham, was "flooded with offers of service." Such an outfit being sent to the border between South Africa and the German colony to the north could not be ruled out.[6] But, as so often happened, the various wings of the elite over-reached and by May 1917 Washington was told of an "attempted Socialist anti-war demonstration,"[7] reflecting a growing force that was to share power by 1994.

By April 1918, the U.S. Secretary of State was told of the "Nationalist Party's republican propaganda and its pro-German or at least anti-British attitude," meaning it was "neutral in the present war…."[8] By July Washington was told of the "openly pro-German attitude of 'Die Burger', the Cape Town organ of the Nationalist Party," which rested uneasily with the "recent restlessness among native miners of the Rand…."[9] As so often happened, the Africans had seized upon the turmoil of war in order to stir the pot of impatience. There was a "reported danger of a native rising in the Transvaal," according to a U.S. diplomat.[10] Washington was in a bind since while it was not opposed to undermining London's influence, propelling Berlin was another matter altogether, particularly in a scheme engineered by the ascendant Nationalists, who were to assume a commanding role in the Afrikaner firmament for decades to come.

The wider point was that pro-Berlin sentiment was to grip Pretoria, a factor bolstered by the nearby presence of the Germany colony. It was evident, said one observer during the First World War, that

5. George Murphy, Consul General-Cape Town to Secretary of State, 2 February 1917, Reel 22, M583.

6. Frederick Burnham to Patrick Longan, 20 February 1917, Box 3, *Frederick Burnham Papers*.

7. Consul General to Secretary of State, 4 May 1917, Reel 2, M583.

8. Consul General, Cape Town to Secretary of State, 19 April 1918, Reel 3, M583.

9. Consul General, Cape Town to Secretary of State, 6 July 1918, Reel 3, M583.

10. Consul General, Cape Town to Secretary of State, 2 July 1918, Reel 3, M583.

the "possession of the African continent was the greatest desire of the Teutons," which drove their interest in fomenting "rebellion in South Africa," with many of its denizens all too willing to participate.[11] Days after the armistice in November 1918, the U.S. consul was assailing the dominant Afrikaner elite, which "during the past four years [has] done its utmost to obstruct the successful prosecution of this war" because of "pro-German ...sympathies"—and now expected U.S. assistance "in its efforts to secede from the British Empire."[12] Days later a document in German from residents in what became Namibia demanded that their "Fatherland" remain in Berlin's jurisdiction. They claimed that the "natives" agreed—except for the "Reheboth Bastards who, through English influence, allowed themselves during the war to be seduced into attacking us in the rear...."[13]

Washington thought it had reason to believe that a British subject, R.H. Swale, had been sent by London in 1903 to stir up discord among the Africans of Germany's colony and told to pose as a U.S. agent on the premise that he would be caught, thereby disrupting Berlin-Washington relations. The U.S. Consul in Cape Town doubted this elaborate ruse, however.[14]

Berlin's defeat did push Pretoria closer to Washington, and the latter came to see an advantage in twisting the British lion's tail from time to time in a way that many Afrikaners found pleasing.

Meanwhile, U.S. visitors of various sorts continued arriving in the area, providing yet another source of leverage. By 1905 John Snodgrass, the U.S. diplomat, told his superiors in Washington that Johannesburg was "of more value, many times over, to the American manufacturer and exporter than all the other cities of the continent combined." "It is there," he insisted, that "the American Mining Engineers have taught the representatives of other countries how to work the reefs successfully thousands of feet beneath the surface and it is there that American Mining Machinery has the preference today." This economic foothold could flummox the most rigid

11. J.K. O'Connor, "The Hun in our Hinterland or the Menace of German SouthWestAfrica," Cape Town: Maskew Miller, circa 1915, Box 25, *Western European Theater Pamphlet Collection, Princeton University-Princeton, New Jersey.*

12. Consul General-Cape Town to Secretary of State, 18 November 1918, Reel 22, M583.

13. Translation of document from Keetmanshoop, SouthWest Africa, dated both 28 November 1918 and 6 January 1919, Reel 3, M583.

14. George Murphy, Consul General-Cape Town to Secretary of State, 1 April 1920, Reel 3, M583.

"imperial preference" seeking to lock what was to soon become the Union of South Africa into a market straitjacket fastened tightly by London.[15] Just after this missive, Snodgrass sent a proposal from "an American bank" back to Washington, seeking assistance in establishing a branch in South Africa.[16] Then two U.S. war vessels steamed into Cape Town.[17] This encroachment was sensed further when in 1905 U.S. officialdom in Pretoria was grousing about the "public criticisms heaped upon" H.J. Meyer, a U.S. national and past Vice Consul in Pretoria, "through the agency of the British and Colonial press" and even "members the House of Commons...."[18]

Nevertheless, opportunities were perceived as sufficiently lush that U.S. nationals were inquiring—as they would throughout coming decades—about migrating to South Africa. By 1910, U.S. dentists were looking into migrating to South Africa,[19] followed by medics.[20] Later it was acknowledged by the U.S. consul in Durban that "Natal has long been the place of practice of quite a few American dentists and of many others educated in American dental schools...."[21] Shortly after the founding of the African National Congress of South Africa in 1912, an attorney, D.A. Tomkins of Charlotte, North Carolina, wanted to know if Africans could vote and own land in the Transvaal—and of the ability of Africans to perambulate on the sidewalks (apparently gauging if that region would be as uncomfortable for Africans as his own Dixie, thereby hastening his migration).[22] By

15. John Snodgrass, Consul General-Pretoria to State Department, 1 September 1905, Reel 2, T660.

16. John Snodgrass, Consul General-Pretoria to State Department, 15 September 1905, Reel 2, T660.

17. Horace Washington, Consul General-Cape Town to State Department, 8 January 1906, Reel 21, T191, *Despatches from U.S. Consuls in Cape Town.*

18. John Snodgrass, Consul General-Pretoria to State Department, 25 June 1905, Reel 2, T660, *Despatches from U.S. Consul in Pretoria.*

19. Consul General-Cape Town to Secretary of State, 30 December 1910, Reel 8, M583.

20. Consul General-Johannesburg to Secretary of State, 10 January 1911, Reel 8, M583. The attempt by dentists and nurses too to migrate to South Africa continued in succeeding decades: On the former, see Report, 15 August 1932, Record Group 59, Decimal File, Box 6282, *NARA-CP*. On the latter, see Report from Ralph Totten, 13 January 1930, Record Group 59, Decimal File, Box 6282.

21. Henry Lakin, Consul General-Durban to Secretary of State, 23 April 1925, Reel 23, M583.

22. Consul General-Johannesburg to D.A. Tomkins, 9 April 1912, Reel 6, M583.

that year, there were 30 U.S. nationals residing in Natal, who took time to mark the July 4th holiday.[23]

If these plans of migration were to be executed, arriving U.S. nationals may not have been greeted with open arms by the colonizing power. After the eruption of the World War, U.S. investors were considering pouring capital into yet another gold mine in South Africa. The Secretary of State was informed that although Pretoria and, indeed, "the people are favorably inclined" toward this proposal, "British financiers are opposed," not just to this idea but, more broadly, they were hostile to "the extensive introduction of American capital" generally.[24]

But Britain had certain disadvantages in this latest scramble for Africa. "For the first time in African mining history," chortled the U.S. Consul in Johannesburg in 1927, "airplanes are to be used in making preliminary surveys…on the Congo border of Northern Rhodesia."[25] Washington's growing primacy in technological development was asserting itself in a way that was to leave London sprawling in the dust.[26] Well aware of this advantage, the U.S. monitored carefully Pretoria's regulations concerning airplane flights by their nationals and their airplanes, seeking to avoid being blocked on either score.[27] By the same token, in 1924, Ford—the future auto giant—was slated to open a plant in Port Elizabeth.[28] By then South Africa was well on its way to its present role as the industrial powerhouse of the continent; as early as 1926, a U.S. official was remarking that a "number of Natal's industries manufacture products which compete with American products and eventually will probably force the American goods out of the market."[29]

London faced another, less noticed problem in the form of racial overstretch. In its African colonies particularly, London demanded administrators and officials of European descent. There were only so

23. *Natal Mercury*, 5 July 1912.

24. Consul General, Cape Town to Secretary of State, 10 June 1916, Reel 18, M583.

25. G.K. Donald, Consul General to Secretary of State, 1 March 1927, Reel 19, M583.

26. See also Gerald Horne, *Storming the Heavens: African Americans and the Early Fight for the Right to Fly*, Baltimore: Black Classics Press, 2017.

27. M.K. Moorhead, U.S. Consul General-Johannesburg to Secretary of State, 13 May 1926, Reel 21, M583.

28. Consul General-Port Elizabeth to Secretary of State, 24 January 1924, Reel 21, M583.

29. Henry Lakin, Consul General-Durban to Secretary of State, 22 March 1926, Reel 23, M583.

many of these and more in the U.S. than Britain. Thus, in drawing up regulations concerning U.S. nationals entering "British East Africa and the Southwest Protectorate" recently taken from Germany, no objection was raised to the entrance of Euro-Americans.[30] Increasingly, as London continued to lick the wounds inflicted by the Afrikaners, the empire was turning toward the colony in Kenya[31] but had to rely upon Euro-Americans to supply a growing number of colonizers. In regard to Frederick R. Burnham, the colonial writer Rider Haggard thought that "of the many Americans who have contributed service to the winning of South Africa from barbarism no one is held in higher esteem" than this diminutive U.S. fighter.[32] But he spent time subduing East Africa too—though he confessed that "the real work of my life was not in East Africa, it was with Rhodes" due south.[33] Burnham, who was not above using ugly racial epithets to describe U.S. Negroes, was quite suited for the vicious business of subjugating Africans, South and East.[34]

Burnham was presumably willing to integrate into the British Empire, his U.S. passport notwithstanding. But William Rose of Fort Dodge, Kansas was symbolic of other U.S. nationals who found it more difficult to embrace London so willingly. He had a claim for land in South Africa based on a grant to his father in about 1850. Discharged from the 91st Regiment infantry, he started a village in South Africa and lived there until the dreaded "Kaffirs.... massacred the settlement on Christmas Day. Only two men [and] a few boys escaped," and a "Kaffir war followed this massacre." Rose was born in the neighborhood and now that matters had calmed, wanted to reclaim "his" land but inevitably would face resistance from London, Afrikaners, and Africans alike.[35]

30. John Bray, Consul General-Johannesburg to Secretary of State, 5 January 1917, Reel 8, M583.

31. Gerald Horne, *Mau Mau in Harlem? The U.S. and the Liberation of Kenya*, New York: Palgrave, 2009.

32. Undated comment by Rider Haggard on F.R. Burnham, Box 2, *Frederick R. Burnham Papers*.

33. F.R. Burnham to "My Dear Professor," 24 November 1913, Box 2, *Frederick R. Burnham Papers*: "it was under his [Rhodes'] stimulus that a new object in my life, far greater than even finding of mines, the defeating of savages, or personal success" was found.

34. Frederick Burnham to W. Mackie, 20 September 1916, Box 1, *Frederick R. Burnham Papers*.

35. William Rose to Honorable George Neeley, 7 April 1913, Reel 14, M583.

As Rose's difficult experience exemplified, as matters evolved the squabbling parties—Afrikaners, Germans, Britons and Euro-Americans—had to contend with the rising might of the ultimate victor: Africans. By 1906 there was martial law in Natal— "by reason of the opposition of the natives," meaning an "uprising." The U.S. official making this pronouncement declared that a "careful.... watch" must be "kept upon the native South Africa," an early indication of a sense of where the true power would come to rest.[36] The revolt led by the man known as "Chief Bambata" was thought by the State Department to represent a "more serious condition of unrest.... in Natal than was given publicly...." What was termed "Zululand" was "disaffected" and of that "there can be no doubt" and "the situation may prove to be a very serious one for the native is as good a fighter, presumably as he was" and, importantly, "possesses firearms...."[37] A few years later there was a strike on sugar estates in Natal, deemed "serious" by a U.S. observer, notably when M.K. Gandhi, recently "released from prison," arrived on the scene.[38]

The simmering unrest had been noticed by Burnham, who in 1906 proclaimed that "we in America are greatly stirred up over the Negro problem and some of our 'yellow journals' are howling about Congo atrocities and other excitable subjects," possibly referring to Natal. "The problem of dark races," he warned, "loom[s] larger and larger on our political horizon," a situation which "makes a knotty problem, almost as difficult to solve as you have in South Africa,"[39] the veritable gold standard of race problems.

* * *

By 1910, a kind of reconciliation between the warring parties in South Africa was affected through the formation of the union,[40]

---

36. Report, 6 February 1906, Reel 21, T191. *Despatches from U.S. Consuls in Cape Town-NARA-CP.*

37. Report by Horace Washington, U.S. Consul, 18 April 1906, Reel 21, T191.

38. Consul General-Durban to Secretary of State, 22 December 1913, Reel 23, M583.

39. Frederick R. Burnham to Sir George Farrar, 10 December 1906, Box 4, *Frederick R. Burnham Papers.*

40. Paul Knapland, "The Unification of South Africa: A Study in British Colonial Policy" in *Transactions of the Wisconsin Academy of Sciences, Arts and Letters*, 21(July 1934): 1-21, Box 2, *E. Merlon Coulter Papers, University of Georgia-Athens.*

which—since it had displayed its martial ability and had European leadership—was more likely to be treated by London like Canada or Australia than Gambia. The previous year, the National Association for the Advancement of Colored People was formed in the U.S., with the astute guidance of the man later to be known as the "Father of Pan-Africanism"—W.E.B. Du Bois—playing a leading role. This formation was to signal a more concerted focus of U.S. Negroes on African matters and the new "U.S.A." more particularly. As a direct result, more Africans began crossing the Atlantic to study, inducing Pretoria's establishment of Fort Hare University. As early as 1901, the Ohlange school—known as the South African Tuskegee—opened, creating an additional point of contact for these two oppressed groups of Africans. With the rise of the Universal Negro Improvement Association [UNIA], a Black Nationalist formation initiated by the Jamaican activist Marcus Garvey, ties were strengthened further through the firm links between the New York City headquarters and the growing branch in the Western Cape.[41]

Even in the 1930s, the visiting Ralph Bunche continued to find Africans "all excited about Garveyism and the slogan was 'The American Negroes are coming to save us'"—an earnest expression of the desperate plight faced by Africans and a precursor to the astringent disappointment that Africans would face as African Americans demonstrated that they could hardly save themselves, driving the African National Congress toward the socialist camp and a decolonized Africa.[42]

There was a symbiosis linking the rise of the NAACP, the founding of the African National Congress of South Africa in 1912, and the establishment of the UNIA a few years after that. The revolt in Natal and the spurt in lynchings in the U.S. helped to give rise to these organizational expressions.

Some of the African leaders in the first few decades of the twentieth century had Garveyite sympathies. This included a number who were pioneer members of the Communist Party, including James La Guma, who soared to prominence in Cape Town.[43] Beyond the Americas, the UNIA had its greatest organizational success in South Africa and the closely linked economies of Basutoland and German-occupied South West Africa. This trend was often borne by

41. Alan G. Cobley, *Class and Consciousness: The Black Petty Bourgeoisie in South Africa*, Westport: Greenwood, 1990.

42. Note in Robert R. Edgar, ed., *The Travel Notes of Ralph J. Bunche, 28 September 1937-January 1938*, Athens: Ohio University Press, 1992, 134.

43. Ibid., Alan G. Cobley, 187.

a steady stream of Caribbean and U.S. Negro sailors, migrant workers, and missionaries. Like La Guma, Josiah Gumede, born in 1912, was a Communist who played a leading role in the African National Congress and was also influenced by Garvey, these ostensibly disparate movements being intertwined.[44] Clements Kadalie, a leader of workers in South Africa, may represent the clearest example of Garveyite influence in that the Jamaican referred to Kadalie's publication as "The 'Negro World'" of South Africa, a reference to his own widely circulated periodical.[45] Kadalie, influenced by Booker T. Washington, also served as a correspondent for the socialist oriented journal, *The Messenger*, tied to then militant Negro labor leader A. Philip Randolph.[46]

Garveyites also included Sol Plaatje, another founder of the ANC, whose lectures in South Africa were covered assiduously in UNIA journals. He too crossed the Atlantic and addressed overflowing audiences in Brooklyn, with aisles and seats packed by a spellbound audience. He shared platforms with Garvey himself. Like the Jamaican, he also was taken by Tuskegee, bringing home a portrait of Booker T. Washington's successor Robert Moton to hang on his living room wall in Kimberley. As is evident, Plaatje found it necessary to publicize the plight of his people among the U.S. Negro population.[47]

Plaatje sought to participate in the Pan African Congress organized by the NAACP, indicating the growing ties between U.S. Negroes and Africans. Writing from Detroit in 1921, he asked the NAACP to "render a great service" to his people. He was unable to make it to Paris for the upcoming PAC but wanted an Association official to read his remarks there. Solidarity was his watchword, as he acknowledged that "Tulsa"—site of a recent bloody pogrom in Oklahoma—and "all American race riots are receiving all the publicity they deserve...." The glaring exception was his own homeland, whose own uprisings provided a basis for U.S. Negroes to continue pressing Pretoria, particularly since racist authorities in both countries were acting similarly: "indiscriminate shooting of innocent natives by individual whites or the mowing down of scores of unarmed mothers by a cavalcade of police;" the growing list of victims included "workers

---

44. Adam Ewing, *The Age of Garvey*, 92, 168.
45. Adam Ewing, *The Age of Garvey*, 93.
46. James T. Campbell, *Songs of Zion: The African Methodist Episcopal Church in the United States and South Africa*, 1995, 303.
47. Brian Willan, *Sol Plaatje: South African Nationalist, 1876-1932*, Berkeley: University of California Press, 1984, 266, 267, 279, 281, 292.

whose only crime is passing a resolution to ask their employers for an adequate subsistence allowance in return for their unrequited service...." Please, he implored, "take my speech with you and read it in my absence...."[48]

Plaatje was not the only prominent South Africa who bonded with U.S. Negroes. While visiting South Africa in the 1930s, the scholar Ralph Bunche encountered Pixley ka Seme in Bloemfontein, who recounted how in 1907 he had attended a meeting of Booker T. Washington's Negro Business League and his matriculation at Oxford University alongside Alain Locke, then of Howard University.[49] His early education in the place of his birth came via the American Board Mission Station and with its sponsorship he received higher education in the U.S., including attending the Mount Hermon School and Columbia University. Like many of the pre-Cold War ANC leaders, he was deeply influenced by U.S. Negroes, even visiting Booker T. Washington in Tuskegee. He seemed to harbor an almost romantic view of Black Americans as a role model—though he also anticipated the ANC's subsequent evolution: By 1927 he was attending an anti-imperialist congress in Brussels, then it was on to the Soviet Union, the latter journey portending the post Cold War shift in Southern Africa.[50]

Plaatje, who spent considerable time in the U.S., was aware of the NAACP's global ventures. Their chief operative, Du Bois, had mobilized these Pan African Congresses, goals of which included seeking to shape the postwar settlement at Versailles. The Association then claimed 46,000 members and 173 branches.[51] The closely affiliated "National Association of Loyal Negroes," based in the U.S. colony that was the Panama Canal Zone, argued passionately that the German colonies in Africa be internationalized, especially since "it was Negroes who stopped the Germans at Verdun; it was Negroes who

48. Letter from Sol Plaatje, 11 July 1921, Box C158, *NAACP Papers, Library of Congress-Washington, D.C.*

49. Note in Robert R. Edgar, ed., *The Travel Notes of Ralph J. Bunche, 28 September 1937-1 January 1938*, Athens: Ohio University Press, 1992, 277.

50. Marvin Faison, "Pixley ka Isaka Seme, President-General of the Afri-[...]ational Congress, 1930-1939: A Study of the Impact of His Leadership [...]ogy on the Congress," M.A., Columbia University, 1983, 7, 9, 43. [...]gani Ngqulunga, *The Man Who Founded the ANC: A Biography of [...]eme*, Cape Town: Penguin, 2017.

[...]cretary to John Mitchell, 24 February 1919, Box C158,

helped to stem the tide at Piave" and "it was Negroes who drove Germany out of Africa."[52]

So moved, the Secretary of State was told nervously that a delegation from what came to be called the African National Congress based in the Orange Free State, were headed to Versailles. South African periodicals publicized contrasting views of the expedition, with *Die Burger* charging that this journey was "engineered by anti-republican whites," while the *Cape Argus* editorialized that the "five million" oppressed of the nation were justified in making their views known.[53] In a seeming counterpoint, a sizeable Afrikaner delegation led by "Reverend Dr. Malan," a surname of some heft among Afrikaners, was headed to Europe—and Manhattan.[54]

These naïve Negroes may have thought that their blood sacrifice was enough to induce the imperialist powers to push for anti-colonial freedom, but this was not to be the case—at least any time soon. Instead, writing from Boston, Frank Weston—though blistering in his assessment of German colonialism—was concerned that Berliners "however cruel in punishment" tended to "have an affable way with Africans" and were "not showing the same colour prejudice that so many Britons unfortunately possess." "Germans," he continued, "divide the world into Germans and non-Germans" and not necessarily in the racial manner then underpinning colonialism in Africa. There was even a "proposal to legalize marriage between Germans and Africans," an unthinkable idea, he believed, and potentially disastrous for Zanzibar.[55]

Thus, South West Africa became a de facto colony of South Africa, which may have had the incidental effect of opening the door to further U.S. influence, for if London had difficulty standing up to U.S. imperialism, South Africa certainly faced a similar problem. Indeed, Pretoria had to toggle between London and Washington for its own benefit, which was partially a function of the aftermath of the bitter "Anglo-Boer" War and the anti-British sentiment it generated. By 1924, the U.S. was demanding "equal treatment" for its nationals in

52. Petition, no date, from National Association of Loyal Negroes, Box C158.

53. George Murphy, Consul General-Cape Town to Secretary of State, 22 February 1919, Reel 3, M583.

54. George Murphy, Consul General to Cape Town to Secretary of State, 19 March 1919, Reel 3, M583.

55. Frank Weston, *The Black Slaves of Prussia: An Open Letter Addressed to General Smuts*, Boston: Houghton Mifflin, 1918, *University of Virginia-Charlottesville.*

this huge colony north of South Africa, especially in relation to livestock export—a move toward granting Washington a kind of colonial status there too.[56]

* * *

There were other problems for white supremacy arriving from the east. War brings new weapons, and some had not eluded the grasp of Africans. There was a "gun running trade in Zululand," said the U.S. consul worriedly, stemming "from across the Mozambique border," leading understandably to "much local discussion." The "desire of the Zulu to possess modern firearms is without doubt general and he will resort to any means to obtain them"— "the Zulu is a born hunter and fighter," it was asserted with concern.[57]

These sobering words almost overshadowed a spate of labor unrest. It was in 1922 that the future U.S. president Herbert Hoover was told that a workers' upsurge "culminated in open rebellion" and "had a paralyzing effect on industry and business." It had "effected every section of the South African community—the farmer, wholesale and retail merchant, industrialist, forwarding and shipping agent[s]" and workers most directly. "Business has been badly shaken" and to that point "the air has not been cleared of the 'miasma of industrial unrest.'"[58] The U.S. Negro press, keen to publicize unrest in South Africa, played up these events.[59]

Frederick Burnham histrionically described men "armed and equipped and struggling to bring within their grasp the greatest gold camp on earth," while "inoculated with the idea of Sovietism" and "striving to make another Russia...." In the recent decade alone, he said, "4000 tons" of gold had been extracted from this bonanza, with much more to come, all for the benefit of the self-proclaimed "Ruling Race." Seeking to curry favor with his former antagonist, he saluted the "Boers" since they were "fighting for the British Empire" while "destroying the armies of the Reds and Radicals who would have turned South Africa into another Russia...." He was still ecstatic that

56. D.C. Poole, Consul General, Cape Town to Secretary of State, 12 March 1924, Reel 20, M583.

57. Consul General Durban to Secretary of State, 26 February 1925, Reel 23, M583.

58. Trade Commissioner, Johannesburg to Herbert Hoover, 28 April 1922, Box 560, Secretary of Commerce Files, *Herbert Hoover Papers, Herbert Hoover Presidential Library-West Branch, Iowa.*

59. Ibid., Charles Alvis Bodie, "The Images of Africa in the Black American Press, 1890-1930," 118.

he had fallen "under the spell of Cecil Rhodes" and continued to fret about the demographic challenge of South Africa, which could only fuel radicalism, i.e. the "ever present danger of the teeming black races that outnumbered the whites twenty to one...." Imagine by comparison his own California "with a population of sixty million blacks living with us and on the soil and these blacks were trained to savage warfare"—and backed by Moscow too.[60]

* * *

Given the racial disparity, Washington thought that Pretoria would have an interest in opening the door to an influx of more Hollywood fare, though —as of 1925 —Secretary of State Frank Kellogg was told that "the British have a monopoly in this field...."[61] The fact that within its borders, the U.S. contained an often unruly African population—a domestic pressure largely absent in the U.K.—was an advantage for London. Though Hollywood's depiction of Negroes was often demeaning, U.S. Consul General in Johannesburg, G.K. Donald, thought that "propaganda against American films in the British Empire will bear [unintended] fruit....on the basis of its demoralizing effect on uncivilized races, such as ...the Africans...."[62] He may have had in mind the spiraling unrest among Africans, buoyed by the Russian Revolution and Garveyism alike.

For there was the man known as Wellington Buthelezi, a onetime AME preacher and licensed herbalist, who modeled himself after Garvey and claimed to be a Chicago-born U.S. Negro. His followers called themselves "Americans" and like related millennialists paraded with U.S. flags. Yet another ANC leader who had Garveyite sympathies was James Thaele.[63] He was mirrored by a Garveyite born in Barbados, Dr. John Albert Thorne, who resided periodically in the U.S. and tried to create a colony for fellow Caribbean and U.S. nationals in what is now Malawi.[64]

---

60. Address by Frederick Burnham, 10 April 1922, Box 4, *Frederick R. Burnham Papers*.

61. Jack S. Connolly, Motion Picture Production & Distribution of America to Secretary of State, 14 December 1925, Reel 10, M583.

62. G.K. Donald to Secretary of State, 23 May 1927. Reel 10, M583.

63. Amanda Denise Kemp, "'Up from Slavery' and other Narratives: Black South African Performances of the American Negro (1920-1943), 45, 215, 269.

64. Robert A. Hill, ed., *The Marcus Garvey and Universal Negro Improvement Association Papers; the Caribbean Diaspora, 1921-1922, Volume XIII*, Durham: Duke University Press, 2016, 386-387.

Symbolically, however, Buthelezi tended to overshadow others in obeisance to U.S. Negroes. He helped propagate the popular belief that Africans would be rescued from their misery by African Americans in airplanes. Though he was Zulu, he played up his mythical U.S. Negro origin; when around 1926 the government sent a squadron of planes to impress upon the African masses the strength of its mailed fist, some among the target audience mistakenly saw these planes as precisely the deliverance they had been hoping for.[65]

"'I am an American Negro male adult'," he claimed, a fiction boosted by the existence of about 4 UNIA branches in the Western Cape by 1921 and the presence in the region of the U.S. educated Thaele. (Note however, that there were South Africans who scrutinized the U.S. Negroes who founded Liberia and concluded that the mistreatment of the indigenes there by this ruling elite did not bode well for their treatment of indigenous South Africans.)[66]

Nonetheless, Tomo Nyirenda, a figure comparable to Buthelezi, attained notoriety in what is now the Zambia-Congo border region. In the 1920s he declared that he had been sent from across the ocean to cleanse the nation and that when the North Americans arrived the colonizers and settlers would be driven away or enslaved, leaving vast sums of wealth. During that time certain Christian preachers forecast that Africans would be emancipated by an invading army of U.S. Negroes.[67]

A harbinger of both Buthelezi and Nyirenda was John Chilembwe, who led a fabled anti-colonial uprising in what is now Malawi in 1915. This cleric received financial support from the U.S.— "Coloured people" there, as it was put at the time. His preaching was in the "Ethiopian" tradition, a throwback to the churches inspired by African Americans that had arisen at the turn of the century. He studied in the U.S., where he was exposed not only to Booker T. Washington but the often-contrasting ideas of John Brown and Frederick Douglass. It is a fair to infer that despite the rank oppression of U.S. Negroes, being amongst them made it more difficult for Africans to accept blithely the colonial oppression in their homeland. The authorities firmly held this opinion, blaming the uprising he spearheaded on "a class of American Negro publications imported by Chilembwe the tendency of which was to inflame racial feeling and also religious

---

65. Note in Robert R. Edgar, ed., *The Travel Notes of Ralph J. Bunche, 28 September 1937-January 1938*, Athens: Ohio University Press, 1992, 344.

66. Robert Edgar, "Garveyism in Africa: Dr. Wellington Buthelezi and the Americans' Movemen in the Transkei" **Ufahamu**, 6(1976): 31-57, 33, 34.

67. Adam Ewing, *The Age of Garvey*, 177.

literature of which the 'Watchtower' publication may be taken as an example."[68]

Perhaps seeking to steady his frazzled nervousness, an investigator for the Carnegie Corporation of New York, Bernard Huss, made light of the growth of movements influenced by U.S. Negroes. He began his 1931 report by lamenting that U.S. "white work for the most part…raise no objection to being supervised" by Negroes: "the latter fact is of particular interest to a visitor from South Africa where a European would [not] consent to worker under a Native." This roseate view of the U.S. was a tipoff that his opinions may have been skewed. But while overly generous to the U.S., the comparison reflected the reality that racism in South Africa may have been harsher. "Our Natives can get a great deal of inspiration from the Negroes and imitate or emulate them in several things," he added, a belief already imbibed by Africans. Huss, the principal CCNY investigator, "repeatedly"—he said— "made definite attempts during my tour" of the U.S. "to find out how far Negroes were interested in South Africa and I seldom found any interest at all or only very little, just as our Bantu may [not] be interested in the Maoris or Papuans."

> I was several times told that the Negroes do not like to hear of Africa, that they even hate the word 'Africa' because they do not want to be reminded of their African origin. These facts must be mentioned because I know only too well from personal experience how much some of our Natives expected and still expect, hoping against all hope, assistance from the American Negroes and deliverance from the yoke of the white man. This belief of our Natives in the intervention of the American Negroes on their behalf is not only pathetic but even ridiculous in the eyes of the Negroes. It is known in South Africa as the 'Wellington' movement and I know from the natives themselves how its apostles fleeced their black brothers and reaped golden harvests…

Nonetheless, despite clearing the path for the emergence of apartheid, Carnegie persisted in seeking to draw lessons from the U.S. Negro experience. As the South Africa study was in motion, another

68. Report by Witness, H.R. Cruise, 29 July 1915; Report by Witness, Reverend R.H. Napier, 9 July 1915; Report, 1915, all in John McCracken, ed., *Voices from the Chilembwe Uprising: Witness Testimonies Made to the Nyasaland Rising Commission of Inquiry, 1915*, London: British Academy, 2015, 38-54, 408-426; 586-596.

study funded by CCNY hailed the Negro congressman Oscar de Priest and the scientist George Washington Carver.

This otherwise negative assessment of U.S. Negroes' view of Africa was premature considering the anti-apartheid movement this group would go on to lead in the 1980s, compelling a conservative U.S. regime to impose debilitating sanctions on Pretoria. Huss also neglected to consider how white supremacy's modus operandi was a disparagement of Africa designed to break the bonds between U.S. Negroes and their fellow exploited across the ocean, to the detriment of both. Still, he did say that Africans should import the "idea of self-reliance and of emulating the Negroes in courageously facing and braving their own difficulties and of using all their time, thought and money"—in the manner of Booker T. Washington.[69]

As things evolved, Huss' view illustrated how and why the socialist camp and decolonization became so important to the fortunes of Africans—on both sides of the Atlantic. For U.S. Negroes, despite their valiant struggles, were hardly able to liberate Africans; here Huss had a point—but he did not have enough foresight to envision what would be needed to overthrow what may have been the highest stage of white supremacy.

Pretoria did not embrace this trans-oceanic amity warmly, in any case. Instead, when the U.S. Negro missionary Reverend H.A. Payne arrived at the Cape with his spouse, they were detained as "undesirable immigrants." They had been dispatched by the National Baptist Convention in the U.S. and told at a stopover in London that he would encounter little difficulty in gaining entrance to Cape Town. But such was not the case. Payne told U.S. Consul George Murphy that "the cause of detention was the fact of their being Negroes," for this official well knew, as he stressed, that "*all colored people*, including British East Indians, are excluded" from the union.[70]

Why such rigidity? "The natives of the Union so far exceed in number the white population," said Murphy, "that the question of permitting the admission of other Negroes is considered a serious one," thus despite the tax-paying status of the complainants, he advised solemnly, "I do not feel justified in taking any further

69. Bernard Huss, *Agricultural Economics among American Negroes: Report of a Visit to the United States of America under the Auspices of the Visitors' Grants Committee of the Carnegie Corporation of New York*, Pretoria: CCNY, 1931, *University of Virginia-Charlottesville*.

70. Consul General George Murphy to Secretary of State, 2 March 1917, Reel 14, M5583.

steps in behalf of Mr. and Mrs. Payne..."[71] Pressure on Washington in response by clerics had an impact months later, though barriers remained: Murphy informed Herbert Case of the American Board of Commissioners for Foreign Missions in Boston that "relative to colored missionaries whom your Board desires to send in transit through this country to Angola," he had ascertained that both Pretoria and Luanda would make no objections.[72]

Washington reciprocated by blocking the arrival of U.S. Negroes in the sub-region and there was likewise stern objection to a visit to their shores by South Africa's Clements Kadalie, a labor leader; "his presence," said Ralph Totten, the U.S. man in Cape Town, "could not serve any good purpose and might easily do much harm."[73]

This was an indicator of a growing trend: Africans in South Africa identified closely with African-Americans but contact between the two was blocked systematically and surveilled intently.[74] Africans attended Negro colleges and addressed local audiences. The rise, however, of Communist parties in both lands after the Bolshevik Revolution of 1917 meant the two paths began to diverge, as the ANC was more amenable to Marxism than the NAACP. This trend proceeded fitfully until the start of the Cold War and the proclamation of apartheid in 1948, when these organizations and the constituencies they represented diverged much further, as the NAACP endorsed anticommunism and the ANC opened its doors wider to CP influence. At that point South African Communists, not yet purged from the ANC, began to orient the anti-apartheid movement toward the socialist camp—a prevailing trend in the anti-colonial world generally. By 1989, the association was so firm that when the Berlin Wall crumbled, it gave a signal to Pretoria, which seized the moment to negotiate when the ANC was in a weakened global position. African Americans led by the NAACP, however, did not necessarily benefit from this turn of events either, as the existence of the socialist camp had forced Washington into difficult anti-Jim Crow compromises. It is ironic that although the ANC and NAACP had

71. Consul General George Murphy to Secretary of State, 7 July 1917, Reel 14, M583.

72. Consul General George Murphy to Herbert Case, 15 February 1919, Reel 14, M583.

73. Ralph Totten, Consul General Cape Town to Secretary of State, 3 September 1927, Reel 4, M583.

74. Maurice S. Evans, *Black and White in the Southern States: A Study of the Race Problem in the United States from a South African Point of View*, London: Longmans, Green, 1915; John Walter Gregory, *The Menace of Colour*, London: Seeley, 1925.

embarked on wildly diverging paths after 1948, neither benefited from the collapse of existing socialism—though at least the ANC was left holding the reins of state power, while African Americans found themselves in a familiar position: trapped and surrounded by unfriendly forces.

The pivotal year 1917, in short, marked the onset of a new era for both South Africa and the U.S., as the upset of war led to a reassertion of the question of "class," per the Russian Revolution and the rise of Communist parties, and the renewed attack against racial regimes on both sides of the Atlantic. Looking more broadly, 1917 marked the rise of "class" as the axis of society, just as 1688 had marked the onset of the demise of religion as the axis of society[75] and 1776 marked the rise of "race" as its complement and, at times, in its stead[76], while the triumph of the Haitian Revolution created a general crisis for this latest axis,[77] creating in its wake a precondition for 1917. These developments were not anticipated by Washington's man in Cape Town, who in November 1917 rhapsodized that "more and more capital from the United States is likely to enter South Africa," particularly since "for investment in the mining industry...American ingenuity and management has obtained a strong foothold" and because "this market has long been one of importance to the American manufacturer...."[78] As of 1913, an official report detailed that there were a "large number of Americans engaged in mining and other occupations on the Rand, aggregating at least 500;" this preponderance did not eliminate the danger posed by strikes; in fact, it enhanced the "fears" of "relatives in the United States as to their safety and welfare."[79] Just as the Bolshevik's were seizing power in Russia, the Secretary of State was told that U.S. oil giants, including the firm to be known as Texaco, were supplying South Africa with the lifeblood that was oil but consumers were demanding more since the military was soaking up a disproportionate percentage of the supply.[80]

Thus, on 30 July 1921 the Communist Party of South Africa was formed, a true turning point in the history of this troubled land. As

---

75. See Gerald Horne, *The Apocalypse of Settler Colonialism.*

76. Gerald Horne, *The Counter-Revolution of 1776.*

77. Gerald Horne, *Confronting Black Jacobins.*

78. Vice Consul General-Cape Town to Secretary of State, 21 November 1917, Reel 12, M583.

79. Consul General-Johannesburg to Secretary of State, 11 July 1913, Reel 12, M583.

80. Vice Consul General, Cape Town to Secretary of State, 30 October 1917, Reel 12, M583.

argued by leader W.H. Andrews, in a message to the Communist International in Moscow, the founding represented—revealingly—an "amalgamation" of, e.g. the Jewish Socialist Society of Cape Town and its counterpart in Cape Town.[81] This birth also served to drive Pretoria and Washington closer together as both settler states, inherently insecure given the tawdry circumstances of their births, rather quickly became hysterically anticommunist.

By 4 August 1921 the Secretary of State had access to a report detailing a "large gathering of the discontented" and the "lively meeting" held "at which some Bolshevik utterances were made" by those with "red favors on their coats." Naturally, "150 additional mounted police" were "sent into the city from the northern provinces" for backup.[82]

Edwin Thabo Mofutsanyana, an African, joined the CP in 1928, five years after joining the ANC. "In the early [days]," he recalled, "most of the members of the Party were Jews. There is no getting away from that;" stunningly, "we used to say we belonged to the Jewish organization because of the composition of the Party...." Eventually, he made his pilgrimage to the Soviet Union to study Marxism-Leninism, along with several other future leaders, including Moses Kotane and J.B. Marks. There he met other Africans, notably from Liberia and Ghana but also Jomo Kenyatta of Kenya and George Padmore of Trinidad. During his 18-month stay, Mofutsanyana and the Caribbean leader spoke "daily." His accession to the CP was suggestive of the party's growth and popularity, still in evidence late in the century, he said in a 1983 interview, evidenced by the fact that gangs in Johannesburg continued to refer to themselves as "The Russians...because they thought the Russians were a brave people...."

Unresolved grievances drove him into the ranks of the radicals. "I used to walk on the sidewalks," before being compelled not to, he lamented years later, reviving the charge often made by U.S. Negro visitors who thought they had left this indignity behind in Dixie. He too recalled that the Africans he knew tended to be "pro-English and against the Dutch," as in the turn-of-the-century war. Garvey was "very popular" then too, which seemed to be an adjunct of his association with Harlem: "you see," Mofutsanyana observed, "the American Negroes have always been popular in South Africa;" thus the

81. W.H. Andrews to Secretary of Communist International, 10 August 1921, in *South African Communists Speak: Documents from the History of the South African Communist Party, 1915-1980*, London: Inkululeko, 1981, 65.

82. Alfred A. Winslow, Consul General-Cape Town to Secretary of State, 4 August 1921, Reel 3, M583.

Jamaican "became the hope of the black man." He became intrigued by "Marxism" and, confessed, "I lost interest" in the UNIA. There were "a hell of a lot" of women in the CP, he said, perhaps attracted by the "party library" with "all sorts of books about Marx, Engels, Lenin and so forth...." Like others he backed the controversial idea of a "Native Republic," an analogue to the "Black Belt" thesis in the U.S., both demanding self-determination for oppressed Africans to the consternation of many.[83]

James La Guma, born of French-Malagasy origin in 1894 in Bloemfontein, went on to lead a diamond workers' strike in what became Namibia in 1918 and worked with militant labor in Luderitz there before joining the Communist Party in 1924. He was in the Soviet Union by 1927, one of a steady stream of Communists who made this pilgrimage,[84] a growing list that was to lead many Africans to the Lenin School.[85]

Not least because of prodding by Moscow, within a decade the heavily Jewish and European domination of the CP had been leavened by entry into the ranks by Africans. By 1925 a militant "seamen's strike" in South Africa would be characterized by the U.S. as a "Communist enterprise."[86] By 1926 Ralph Totten of the U.S. legation in South Africa was experiencing a "great deal of anxiety ... because of the activities of Bolshevist agents among the Zulu and other natives in Natal...." He had just visited Addis Ababa where he was told that a "representative of Soviet Russia was soon to arrive" and, obviously, this was a "good base from which to send unofficial agents to the Negroes and natives of Central and South Central Africa."[87] By then, of about 1750 reported Reds in South Africa 1600 were African or Coloured.[88] By 1927, even the U.S. official Totten had noticed that "there is no doubt but that Red agents are quite

83. Interview with Edwin Mofutsanyana by Robert Edgar, 18 February 1983, Reel 6, *Oliver Tambo Papers, University of Witwatersrand-Johannesburg.*

84. Biography of James La Guma, no date, M2.1, *Jack Simons and Ray Alexander Simons Collection, University of Cape Town.*

85. Biography of Edwin Thabo Mofutsanyana, no date, O2, *Jack Simons and Ray Alexander Simons Collection, University of Cape Town.* At the same site, see the Biography of Moses Kotane, born in 1905.

86. D.C. Poole, Consul General, Cape Town to Secretary of State, 12 October 1925, Reel 4, M583.

87. Ralph Totten, Consul General, Cape Town to Secretary of State, 14 December 1936, Reel 4, M583.

88. Resolution on South African Question, Adopted by Executive Committee of Communist International following Sixth Communist International Congress, 1928-1929, in Ibid., *South African Communists Speak*, 93.

active among the black and colored people of Africa," not least in the southern cone of the continent.[89] It was also in that year—1927—that the case of the Italian anarchists in Massachusetts, Sacco and Vanzetti, was creating a stir in South Africa. "Mass meetings of protest against the execution" were held there, said Totten, sponsored by "Labor, Socialist and Communist elements in Cape Town, Johannesburg, Durban," and elsewhere.[90]

Agitation generated by the Sacco-Vanzetti case continued to grip South Africa, leading to ever fiercer attacks on U.S. interests there. This was "arousing the socialistic and communistic elements," said Totten, and even the "capitalistic press" was seeking to "publish their propaganda for the sake of hurting the prestige of the United States," as pro-London attitudes merged with anti-imperialist sentiment. By 1929 the CP claimed with some justification that it contained "already the largest Negro membership of any Communist Party in the world."[91] If Totten had investigated further, he may have discovered that the South African Ruth Schecter—whose sister, Amy, was arrested for murder in Gastonia, North Carolina during the ongoing labor unrest—had written about the Italian activists slated for execution for the press in Cape Town. (Amy had joined the Communist Party of Great Britain in 1920 and the party in the U.S. in 1921).[92]

These stirring events contextualize the words delivered by SACP leader Joe Slovo in Maputo on the 60th anniversary of the founding of his party. FRELIMO, he said prematurely, was the "Communist vanguard" of the nation's working class. He dismissed those South African "white worker[s]" then "well organized and making up the bulk of the 'industrial masses'" who "had not yet won [a] seat at the ruler's table and still expressed a degree of class hostility towards capitalism." The ANC, he asserted, was then marked by "cap-in-hand nationalism" imbued with a "spirit of loyalty to the British Crown." Amazingly, "some of its leaders went as far as to acknowledge 'the superiority of the white race.'" Thus in 1928 its "House of Chiefs" resolved "against cooperation with the Communist Party" arguing that "'the Tsar was a great man in his country, of royal blood like

89. Ralph Totten, Consul General, Cape Town to Secretary of State, 6 January 1927, Reel 4, M583.

90. Ralph Totten, Consul General, Cape Town to Secretary of State, 12 August 1927, Reel 4, M583.

91. "Programme of the [CP] Adopted at the Seventh Annual Congress of the Party on January 1, 1929," in Ibid., *South African Communists Speak*, 97-100, 97.

92. Baruch Hirson, *The Cape Town Intellectuals: Ruth Schecter and Her Circle, 1907-1954*, Johannesburg: Witwatersrand University Press, 2001, 174.

us chiefs....'" But by 1928, he said proudly, the CP was "no longer an all-white affair and its African membership made up 90% of the total."[93]

This radical ascendancy was seemingly inducing as much agita in Washington, as in Pretoria. By early 1919, the U.S. official in Johannesburg had spotted "two Russian Bolshevists," one claiming to be a "'barrister of law of the University of Petrograd and ex-Secretary to the Ministry of Labor and Attorney General in the Ukraine" and the latter representing himself to be "a member of the Peoples Tribunal of Justice." The official, George Murphy, was told that "these Russians were opponents of the Bolshevist Movement" but he was not so sure.[94]

Soon the South African authorities were importuning Murphy for "information concerning existing laws in the United States against Bolshevism," a request with which he complied readily.[95] The Cape Town press reported that the newly installed Soviet regime had set aside large sums of money for the purpose of spreading "Bolshevist propaganda among the American Negroes and African natives," providing yet another rationale for cooperation between Pretoria and Washington. Supposedly, the two oppressed groups were receiving training on Soviet soil.[96] Washington took the claim seriously when a report was filed concerning support by South African Communists of struggles in the Rhodesias and the Congo.[97]

The global reach of the Communist movement compelled Pretoria to broaden its own reach in response, but this effort made it more dependent upon Washington, particularly since lingering anti-London passions yet to be squelched after the war, made it difficult to rely wholly upon the actual colonizing power. Thus, it was from Latvia that Washington transmitted the intelligence about an intense discussion of the "Negro Problem in South Africa," featuring Communists. "A day or two previous," it was added anxiously "a speaker from Indonesia spoke of the possibility of 'bestial' revenge

93. Remarks by Joe Slovo, 30 July 1981, Reel 19, *Oliver Tambo Papers, University of Witwatersrand*

94. George Murphy, Consul General-Cape Town to Secretary of State, 31 March 1919, Reel 12, M583. See also *Cape Times*, 31 March 1919.

95. Consul General George Murphy tio Secretary of State, 19 March 1920, Reel 5, M583.

96. Charles Pisar, Consul General to Secretary of State, 13 December 1922, Reel 5, M583. See also *Cape Times*, 11 December 1922 and *Cape Times*, 18 February 1924.

97. Report by Ralph Totten, U.S. Consul General, Cape Town, 36 January 1929, Reel 5, M583.

being taken by the natives on the whole white population...."[98] Correspondingly, the growing reliance on Washington contributed to a backlash. By 1929 even South African Communists had noticed that "the U.S.A. having become Britain's great capitalist rival, Americans are now called 'too foreign blooded' as the Germans were called 'Huns' by the British press."[99] But it would take more than mere slurs to derail the deepening relationship between Pretoria and a republican rival that ravenously sought to replace London as the leading capitalist power and was encouraged in this task by resentful Afrikaners, still licking their wounds from the beating that had been inflicted upon them decades earlier.

There was also fear that what U.S. official Charles Pisar termed the "so-called Asiatic menace in South Africa"[100] had to be scrutinized considering similar hysterical cries in California. It was recalled that Pretoria had arranged for the "importation of some sixty thousand Chinese coolies to work in the Transvaal," but after the proclamation of the Union—and indicative of the regression it entailed—this policy was "immediately reversed" and "all contract Chinese were repatriated, now... any more Asiatics or Japanese of any description [were not] allowed...."[101]

As with Bolshevism and Chinese migrants, the two racist regimes also compared notes on the project that J.R. McCulloch of the Southern Cooperative League in Washington had requested: the "segregation of Negroes in South Africa, especially as regards the ownership of land."[102]

Pretoria had not blocked all migratory streams from the U.S. I.W. Schlesinger arrived from there in South Africa in 1903 and rather quickly became one of the major businessmen there.[103] Horatio Alger-style, this man of unusually small stature landed in South Africa penniless but after World War I he owned every theatre in South Africa but two and more than sixty cinemas.[104] The State Department found that he had "extensive and varied interests in South Africa,

98. Report on "Negro Problem", 19 October 1928, Reel 10, M583.

99. *The South African Worker*, 31 January 1929 in Ibid., *South African Communists Speak*, 97-100.

100. Charles Pisar, Consul General-Cape Town to Secretary of State, 17 March 1921, Reel 10, M583.

101. Consul General-Lisbon to Secretary of State, 5 August 1921, Reel 10, M583.

102. Alvey A. Adams, Second Assistant Secretary to J.R. McCulloch, 9 January 1922, Reel 10, M583.

103. *New York Times*, 20 January 1964.

104. *Daily Express* [London], 27 July 1921.

including a banking institution of some importance...." Washington thought that since he was "an American," his stature would facilitate the "promotion of commercial relations between South Africa and this country which...will be very helpful in the extension of American interests in that country...."[105] He was tied to the Colonial Bank and Trust Company, which was sited in Johannesburg but was owned and controlled by U.S. nationals.[106] U.S. official Arthur Cawston referred to Schlesinger as "the American capitalist of Johannesburg" after he "just completed the purchase of...one of the largest land deals in the history of South Africa...."[107]

Born in New York, by 1927 Schlesinger's varied interest included theaters, manufacturing, importation and exhibition of motion pictures, banking, insurance, agriculture, canning, and restaurants. He was on good terms with Pretoria, "notably with Mr. Tielman Roos, one of the most influential members of the Nationalist Party and Minister of Justice," according to U.S. Consul G.K. Donald. Despite his U.S. roots, Donald fretted that Schlesinger could back legislation "that would make prohibitive the importation of American films."[108] For despite his national origin, Schlesinger's allegiance to Pretoria, where his fortune was made after all, was not questioned—at least by Roos and those around him. As early as 1921 the wily Schlesinger was deputed "authority to negotiate on behalf" of Pretoria in sensitive talks with leading powers.[109]

As Schlesinger was ascending to the pinnacle of business success, Professor R. W. Kemmerer of Princeton University was arriving in South Africa for a "confidential talk" on "monetary matters."[110] Though London was the ostensible power in Pretoria, with every passing day, it was being supplemented by—if not supplanted by—U.S. imperialism. London's problem was that South Africa resembled the U.S. more than it did the U.K., a fact which tended to undergird republican influence. Thus in 1922 the ravages of the boll weevil in the U.S. led to interest in growing cotton in Natal, a

---

105. Report by Foreign Trade Adviser of the U.S. State Department, 18 April 1921, Reel 13, M583.

106. Report by Foreign Trade Adviser, 12 April 1921, Reel 13, M583.

107. Arthur Cawston, Consul General-Port Elizabeth to Secretary of State, 17 January 1924, M583.

108. G.K. Donald, U.S. Consul General-Johannesburg, 23 May 1927, Reel 10, M583.

109. F.M. Dearing, Assistant Secretary of State to Jerome Greene, 22 April 1921, Reel 13, M583.

110. Report by D.C. Poole, Consul General-Cape Town, 20 January 1925, Reel 13, M583.

project which perforce would necessitate influence from across the Atlantic.[111]

The embrace of the likes of Schlesinger and Kemmerer co-existed oddly with a growing provincialism among the Afrikaner elite, which often frowned upon acceptance of European immigrants, even as Pretoria was desperate to increase the percentage of the population considered "white" to blunt population growth among Africans. Yet by 1928 Washington was receiving well-founded complaints that hundreds were migrating to neighboring Southern Rhodesia in revulsion at the reality of Afrikaner nationalism. The problem was that this nationalism could threaten the "whiteness" project generally.[112]

Months earlier Baden Powell, a noteworthy British colonialist, informed Frederick Burnham, the Yankee who fought the Boers decades earlier, that a "good many settlers are going to take up land" in the Rhodesias, meaning "civilization and industry" would advance "on the foundations which you and others laid there."[113] Unremarked was the underlying tension between Boer and Briton that would complicate the advance of white supremacy for years to come. At times it seemed that figures like Burnham thought they could assume that white supremacy would assert itself even in the face of Boer objection. Still, in praising the celebrated racial theorists Madison Grant and Lothrop Stoddard, Burnham observed offhandedly that "the racial tides are as full of whirlpools and sunken rocks as all the unchartered seven seas"—though this vague reference could just as well be directed toward African rebelliousness, then on the rise.[114]

Washington had its own problem with anti-Jewish fervor and found it difficult to restrain a similar trend in South Africa, which could also weaken the overriding goal of white supremacy. By 1929, the U.S. Consul in Port Elizabeth was noticing an "increasing Jewish immigration into the Union from Southeastern Europe" but, it was said skeptically, this was "not benefiting the interior farmer particularly. In business deals the back-veld Boer is no match for the

111. Memorandum, 6 December 1922, Reel 15, M583,

112. Report from Ralph Totten, U.S. Consul General, Cape Town, 8 March 1928, Reel 5, M583.

113. Baden Powell to Frederick Burnham, 11 May 1927, Box 2, *Frederick Burnham Papers.*

114. Comment by Burnham, no date, Box 2, *Frederick Burnham Papers.*

Hebrew general trader," and therefore, "the poorer farmers are getting enmeshed in a sort of economic slavery."[115]

Writing earlier from Cape Town, U.S.-born Ralph Totten declared without critique that "General Mannie Martiz, a Nationalist member of Parliament" proclaimed that "the Jews because of their monopoly of business and finance were the greatest menace to general progress in South Africa. He said that before many years there would be no longer Nationalists and South Africans but Jew against Gentile" and, indeed, the "future of South Africa lays in the cooperation of Dutch and English against Jewish commercial and financial supremacy…."[116]

Pretoria's racist policies cut in unanticipated directions. Paramount British leader Jan Smuts admitted in 1923 that South Africa had such an "enormous" African population to supply "all the heavy and unskilled labor requirements" that, unlike Canada and Australia for example, there was less of a perceived need for massive numbers of incoming Europeans.[117] However, in the long run this dependence would backfire, since Pretoria was unable to "exterminate" the indigenous population and was incapable of trying to "assimilate" within it, leaving the last remaining option: to "go," i.e. depart or relinquish power.

Then there was the influx from British India; what was referred to as "the Indian Problem in South Africa." These Asians, the Secretary of State was told, were "penetrating into areas occupied for residential or trading purposes by Europeans," exacerbating "racial incompatibility." The counsel noted sympathetically that "the laws of the country had to take account of the feeling of the people," meaning those defined as "white." Recall, it was reported, that in the republic "the Negro had been given certain rights but what the law allowed custom by violence denied," so how could there be meaningful objection to a similar pattern in South Africa?[118]

But the U.S. Consul in Calcutta had found this racist pattern was instigating "resentment" there, not to mention "Tanganyika and Kenya" where sizeable Indian populations resided. This was

---

115. C.E. Macy, Consul General-Port Elizabeth to Secretary of State, 8 April 1929, Reel 5, M583.

116. Ralph Totten, Consul General, Cape Town to Secretary of State, 14 December 1926, Reel 4, M583.

117. Consul General-Cape Town to Secretary of State, 27 June 1923, Reel 11, M583. See also *Cape Times*, 25 June 1923.

118. Consul General-Cape Town to Secretary of State, 15 April 1924, Reel 10, M583.

creating a "most formidable" issue for London, but it may have been a boon for Washington, which because of the festering problem of "the Negro" was bound to be sympathetic to Pretoria at this time of need.[119]

Fortunately for Pretoria, the Union was being bolstered by a steady arrival of Euro-Americans. By 1922 there was a club of 30 women from this group enrolled in the "Martha Washington Club," bent on "promoting," said the U.S. official involved, "the conviviality of the American community and for eleemosynary work;"[120] a few years later there were—at least—400 U.S. nationals in and about Johannesburg alone.[121]

The population defined as "white" had its influence further bolstered in the 1920s with the arrival of a delegation from the Carnegie Corporation of New York to study "the poor white problem." Three decades later, the visiting Philadelphian Frank S. Loescher was told of "job discrimination in the '20s by British business against Afrikaners who were better qualified than British applicants;" the wounded Afrikaners could hardly contain their ire at the idea that the British were "dominant in business and industry" and, worse, "would use cheaper labor rather than white Afrikaners...." So the government in 1924, he said, began to reserve jobs for those defined as "white," many of whom were Afrikaners.[122]

Ultimately, apartheid—which Carnegie helped to implant—sought to improve the status of Afrikaners, at the expense of Africans. Though one scholar argues that the extensive Carnegie study did not provide a "blueprint for apartheid," the weight of the evidence points in the opposite direction. It was a watershed event in South Africa's social and political history when this munificent firm arrived in Cape Town. Pointing South Africa in the same direction as the United States, it sought to unite the destinies of privileged and downtrodden Europeans in a trajectory that led inexorably to apartheid. The study aided the Afrikaner nationalist cause, as well as white supremacy in general, even as the former often undercut the latter. For while Afrikaner nationalism often restricted the European

---

119. Julius Lay, Consul General-Calcutta to Secretary of State, 20 January 1926, Reel 10, M583.

120. Consul General-Johannesburg to Secretary of State, 19 May 1922, Reel 10, M583.

121. M.K. Moorhead, Consul General-Johannesburg to Secretary of State, 21 October 1929, M583.

122. Report by Frank S. Loescher, 21 June 1953, South Africa File, *Records of American Friends Service Committee-Philadelphia.*

immigration that would have augmented white supremacy, Carnegie and its paymasters were not sufficiently alert to this fundamental contradiction.[123]

Again, the U.S. was better positioned than the U.K. to address this matter in an interracial context. "Do the experiences of other countries," it was asked in a 1929 Carnegie meeting, "especially Germany and the United States throw light" on South Africa? "Or are there additional factors present in South Africa, different in kind or degree, that make the problem at least in part specific and unique... do racial heritage, racial competition, racial fears; climate in its influence on the persons; conditions—historical or intrinsic......international economic competition and so on play a major or a minor part in the problem..."?[124]

Carnegie admitted that the word "'poor white' had already come into use in the Southern States in the slavery days and there is little doubt that we received the term from them...." Also uniting the two lands of racism was that in South Africa, Carnegie found that "the influence of the Jews engaged in commerce was often pernicious...."[125]

Carnegie had considered "the native" as a subject of inquiry and presumed amelioration, but as Dr. C.T. Loram of Stellenbosch University was told, the corporation then decided that "in order to play fair with our own trustees," it would feel compelled to "concentrate...attention in South Africa to the Poor White Research."[126] Yet the funds for this massive project might have been better spent if CCNY had taken into account what Sir Frederic de Waal of Cape Town noticed: in his "household," he told a U.S. official, "where both white and colored labor is employed, the whites do nothing but make the colored people perform all the work."[127]

Unleashing researchers on South Africa led to some unusual analyses. Thus, Frederick Keppel of CCNY was told that "South African people" tend to "read far too little." Why? The "climate" was singled

123. Patricia Rosenfeld, *A World of Giving: Carnegie Corporation of New York: A Century of International Philanthropy*, New York: Public Affairs, 2014, 111, 112.

124. Minutes of Meeting, 13 April 1929, Box 295, *Carnegie Corporation of New York Records-Columbia University, New York City*. [hereinafter CCNY Papers]

125. J.W. Grosskopf, *The Poor White Problem in South Africa: Report of the Carnegie Commission, Volume I*, Stellenbosch: Pro Ecclesia-Drukkery, 1932, 17, 115.

126. Frederick Keppel to Dr. C.T. Loram, 2 April 1929, Box 295, *CCNY Papers*.

127. Memorandum from U.S. Vice Consul, 22 February 1923, Reel 3, M583.

out since the "days practically unbroken of sunshine call the youth of our country out of doors practically the whole year round. We lack the cold winter nights," said this Durban correspondent, "which confined one to the easy chair with a book;" this "respect," it was reported, was "where the Northern countries score over us."[128]

Climatology aside, when researchers met in Cape Town in mid-June 1928 at 75 Parliament Street, they mulled over the notion that "nine tenths of the Poor Whites"—the capitalization seemingly signifying the weightiness of the issue— "belong to the Dutch Reformed Church, which had thrown its whole weight into the matter." More than weather, the point stressed was that "prejudice against manual labour which had arisen in the early slave days" was problematic and enhanced "the fact that the natives are supposed to do all the rough work."[129]

The subject to be scrutinized was defined as an "untrained European unemployed or unemployable and so degraded economically that he cannot live like a white man without charitable aid." This "problem" could be addressed by the left and interracial struggle too, both of which would undermine white supremacy ultimately. They were not proud symbols of the racialist doctrine either. Climate did play a role in that "each bad drought [was] increasing their numbers by some thousands." Moreover, "syphilitic children with inefficient parents constitute a grave problem," meaning that "the only effective solution is sterilization, infusion of new blood from Europe by immigration of peasant classes who would intermarry with our own races could be very beneficial...." The problem with the latter solution, which unlike the former was not addition by subtraction, was that it collided with Afrikaner nationalism which often frowned on the arrival of "peasant classes" who happened to be Jewish.

Dr. W.A. Murray of the Union Health Department in Pretoria told the investigators that the "most important root cause" of the problem was "the presence of natives who have provided cheap and abundant labour resulting in cheap and easy food supply for the whites." That is, a main byproduct of white supremacy—paltry wages for Africans—was constructed as problematic. "A fictitious feeling of supremacy amongst" the poorer Europeans led to their "disinclination and even contempt for manual work." This was

128. E. Malherbe to Frederick Keppel, 14 July 1928, Box 295, *CCNY Papers*.

129. Minutes of Meeting of the Board of Research on the Poor White Question, 14 June 1928. Box 295, *CCNY Papers*.

leading to "improvidence and lack of foresight and ambition," worsened by "considerable inbreeding."[130]

CCNY was arriving at the conclusion that "poor whites" were becoming superfluous not least because of the overwhelming presence of "poor Africans." The remedy was not seen in uplifting the latter; instead, the idea was a kind of affirmative action to uplift the targeted group, which paved the way for the proclamation of apartheid in 1948, which was little more than a massive program of "positive discrimination" to propel upward poorer Europeans and rescue them from their seeming destiny of joining class struggle alongside Africans. Poverty among this "white" group was seen to contradict "white" superiority, undermining the dominant societal ideology.

Tellingly, driving CCNY and their comrades was the lurking idea that those defined as "white" were not actually superior—but rather than adjust ideologically to this obvious reality they decided to engage in social engineering. One problem, it was determined, was the "inability of the Poor White of a low standard of intelligence to compete in the unskilled labour market with the intelligent coloured or native worker."[131] Still, it did not take long for the "research" to fit the ideology, as Hugh A. Rayburn of the Department of Psychology argued that "many observers, including magistrates, teachers and psychiatrists have come to the conclusion that the mental growth of the native ceases earlier than that of the European."[132]

The CCNY report was publicized in a major initiative that would be deployed to pave the road to apartheid. Professor H.F. Verwoerd, soon to be the 1950s Prime Minister most identified with apartheid, chaired the body that promulgated this program.[133] Inevitably these troubling events in South Africa influenced similar trends in the south of the U.S. There were explicit reports concerning "rural poverty among whites" in both regions.[134]Dr. W.N.J. Hollander's book on this issue in Dixie was consulted in South Africa.

Given the toxicity of the topic at hand, the researchers waded into murky waters. One of the investigators expressed "surprise that his

---

130. "Poor White Problem: Proposed Investigation", 3 May 1928, Box 295, *CCNY Papers*.

131. Minutes of Meeting, 14 April 1928, 10 A.M., University Buildings, Queen Victoria Street, Cape Town, Box 295, *CCNY Records*.

132. Hugh A. Rayburn to C.T. Loram, 30 April 1928, Box 295, *CCNY Records*.

133. "National Conference on the Poor White Question, 1934. First Annual Report of the Activities of the Continuations Committee (October 1934-December 1935), Box 295, *CCNY Records*.

134. James Sertan to Frederick Keppel, 31 May 1933, Box 295, *CCNY Records*.

remarks on the harmful influence of some Jews"—also accused of undermining "poor whites"—"should be construed as a deliberate libel on Jews in general."[135] J.F.W. Grosskopf admitted to having "quite a number of Jewish friends" yet somehow "an evidently hyper-sensitive Jewish reader had taken offense where none was intended" when all that he did was to refer to the "frequently harmful effect of the business methods of Jewish traders" which were leading directly to the "impoverishment of many old Free State farmers' families." In short, "the type of Jew from Eastern Europe who has become prevalent during the last two or three decades" was far from a "blessing to our pioneer families." To be fair, Grosskopf spoke glowingly of Jewish bosses who favored Afrikaner workers in the name of white supremacy.[136]

Carnegie thought it had a basis for this salty opinion since their investigators had secured Ford vehicles to drive the length and breadth of the nation, hailing the hospitality they enjoyed, which E.G. Malherbe of Carnegie contrasted favorably with the "general absence of this trait of natural hospitality" in Dixie. But on both sides of the Atlantic, he found what was referred to in South Africa as an aversion to "'Kaffir work.'" The presence of Africans in both places was repetitively invoked as the root of the problem in that "poverty in a white man causes more concern than poverty in a black man. That is why the term 'Poor White' is found only in a country like South Africa and in the Southern States of America where there is a preponderance of black people…." This was not just a conceptual matter for this "concern is tinged with fear that in open competition the lower 10% of whites will become subordinate to say, the upper 10% of blacks. This is still a phobia in South Africa."

But poverty among Europeans was not just a function of being surrounded by cheap "native labour." The war decades earlier was thought to have decimated the Afrikaners—meaning "die Englese" and, of course, "the Jews" were culpable. Thus by 1921, Malherbe, who had attended Columbia University in Manhattan, found "over 100,000 so-called poor whites living in our very midst and a menace to the self-preservation and prestige of our white people." Himself a member of the Dutch Reformed Church, he was gravely concerned

135. R.W. Wilcocks to Frederick Keppel, 11 May 1933, Box 295, *CCNY Records*. (The reference to the Hollander book is in this correspondence.) See also R.W. Wilcocks, *Psychological Report, Volume II*, Stellenbosch: Pro Ecclesia-Drukkery, 1932.

136. J.F.W. Grosskopf to R.W. Wilcocks, 2 May 1933, Box 295, *CCNY Records*.

about their presence in this holy temple. He was proud to have been "reared in the bosom" of the DRC and prouder still that his "father" was a minister, along with his grandfather and all his uncles from his father's and mother's sides. Along with Verwoerd, a member of another founding family of apartheid was collaborating with Carnegie: F.S. Malan.[137]

Though Carnegie paved the way for apartheid, as early as 1928 C.T. Loram of Stellenbosch, who was also tied to a study being conducted by the U.S. based Phelps-Stokes Fund—which had multiple interests in Africa—penned a "confidential" missive in which he charged the "whole Stellenbosch group" with harboring an "anti-British attitude": the "Dutch section is opposed to any person from Britain taking part in the study," encouraging a "South Africa only"—meaning Boer only—approach, which could even mean excluding U.S. nationals.[138]

Remarking years later on this five-volume study in which he played a role, Francis Wilson of Cape Town did not shrink from noting that Carnegie laid the foundation for apartheid, as it recommended stiffened segregation and the expropriation of African land to be disbursed to poorer Europeans, the latter mirroring what befell Native Americans. Brusquely, he pointed out in 1999 that "one way of looking apartheid is that it was an anti-poverty program for whites" in which the Manhattan foundation proved to be "important in the Afrikaner drive against poverty…."[139] Another way of looking at apartheid is to view it as a way to heighten race contradictions in order to evade class contradictions.[140] In other words, it was a fevered reaction to 1917 and the rise of class solidarity and a throwback to the late 18th century.

This raw chauvinism, which was birthed in part as a sword and shield to combat Africans and then Britons, was to ultimately prove the undoing of apartheid's ruling clique. Thus, in 1922 Washington was briefed on a proposal for the "admission" of Southern Rhodesia

137. E.G. Malherbe, "The Carnegie Poor White Investigation: Its Origins and Sequels", no date, Box 295, *CCNY Records*. See also E.G. Malherbe, *Education and the Poor White*, Stellenbosch: Pro Ecclesia-Drukkery, 1932.

138. C.T. Loram to Frederick Keppel, 15 April 1928, Box 295, *CCNY Records*.

139. Oral History, Francis Wilson, 3 August 1999, *Columbia University-New York City*.

140. See also Tiffany Willoughby-Heard, *Waste of a White Skin: The Carnegie Corporation and the Racial Logic of White Vulnerability*, Berkeley: University of California Press, 2015.

"into the Union of South Africa."[141] But how could such a proposal ever gain traction if rancor among Boer and Briton continued to inflame?

Moreover, it was unclear if Washington would back this premature Anschluss. In the decades after the turn of the century war, the U.S. was beginning to view the southern cone of the continent as a unit, allowing the republic to galvanize its diplomatic and economic force to particular ends without diffusing it. But even here South Africa was the sun, other colonies were surrounding planets: though Washington's goal was to block London's hegemony, it was not easy given the centuries long tie between Lisbon (dominant in Angola and Mozambique alike) and London. Certainly, an integrated railway network that crossed borders effortlessly was in Washington's interest. By 1922 Sinclair Oil of the U.S. was already invested heavily in Angola, soon to become one of the world's major producers of this precious fluid. South Africa, said the U.S. man in Lisbon with oversight of Angola, "is a long distance from Washington but events are now taking place there which will eventually have a strong repercussion upon London, Lisbon, and Brussels"[142]—not to mention Washington. With oil came cars. Months after this statement was made, a U.S. official was conferring with Sir Frederic de Waal of Cape Town and "one of the first subjects he mentioned was American automobiles. He stated that he had just purchased his second American car," that he exhibited with "much pride" while noting that he "now used American cars almost exclusively," bringing a reprimand from his superiors. Yes, it was reported, that "undoubtedly" an "undercurrent of anti-American feeling" persisted but the rise of U.S. imperialism and the impending decline of the British version would lead to an adjustment.[143]

Across the border in what was to become Namibia, the vaunted firm of J.P. Morgan already had expressed passionate interest in what was to prove one of the motherlodes of diamonds globally.[144] Grabbing this wealth would not be easy if London dominated in Pretoria.

After Sir Frederic's remarks, the paramount leader of South Africa, Jan Smuts, spoke on U.S.-S.A. ties; the relationship was a "subject of

---

141. Report by Charles Pisar, Vice Consul General, Cape Town, 12 April 1922, Reel 24, M583.

142. U.S. Consul General-Lisbon to Secretary of State, 31 August 1922, Reel 21, M583.

143. Report by U.S. Vice Consul, 22 February 1923, Reel 3, M583.

144. Vice Consul, Cape Town to Secretary of State, 4 March 1920, Reel 3, M583.

much discussion during the last two days in Natal," said Lewis Cole of the U.S. in September 1923. A local newspaper was unimpressed, however, with the perceived "acerbity"[145] expressed toward Washington by a man who had experienced the turn of the century war and saw concord between Boer and Briton as essential to the overriding goal of keeping Africans in line.

Hence, Washington felt compelled to stake out political territory to the right of London, backing the rising Nationalists who were to enact apartheid in 1948. "If the Nationalists come into power," said a U.S. official in Port Elizabeth in 1924, this "will be to the interest of the United States [,] because of the anti-British attitude of the Nationalists," still smarting from the whipping administered by London decades earlier. Their victory would mean the dislodging of Sir Edgar Walton, Pretoria's top leader in London and his being "replaced" by a Nationalist. Sir Edgar was "extremely anti-American" and makes sure that "no South African government orders"—from paper clips to cars—were placed in the U.S.[146]

London, however, was severely disadvantaged, not least in provisioning higher education for ambitious young people. Yes, there were Oxford and Cambridge—but across the water was Harvard, Yale, Princeton, Columbia, Stanford, and other rising giants. "A good deal" was being said "privately, especially in British circles," noted D.C. Poole of the U.S., "about the preference which has been shown by the present South African government when filling important technical positions for men educated in the United States;" to that end, Yale was about to start an astronomical observatory in Johannesburg.[147]

By 1925 yet another U.S. official was boasting that the trend in Pretoria was "to move in channels already followed" by Washington, understandable given the parallels in their histories of settler colonialism, slavery, white supremacy, and capitalism. "Consciously or unconsciously," a U.S. official bragged, Pretoria was tending to "accept the [U.S.] as a friend and guide;" this "growing bond" and "growing intimacy" were "more and more evident," since "trade" was "on the increase." In fact, said this Cape Town-based diplomat, "American automobiles fill the South African roads consuming to a

145. Lewis Cole, Consul General, Cape Town to Secretary of State, 7 September 1923, Reel 4, M583. See also *Natal Mercury*, 5 September 1923.

146. Arthur Cawston, Vice Consul, Port Elizabeth to Secretary of State, 15 April 1924, Reel 4, M583.

147. D.C. Poole, Consul General, Cape Town to Secretary of State, 4 March 1925, Reel 4, M583.

great extent American gasoline, while American agricultural implements are regarded as standard" by "South African farmers." Events even thousands of miles away were benefiting Washington in that the "friendly reception given the American fleet in Australia has not gone unnoticed in South Africa." Once Germany had competed for the "more rabidly anti-British" constituency but nowadays Uncle Sam had it all to himself.[148]

As this rainbow of optimism was rising, simultaneously clouds were forming. For by 1927 Totten had found "Germanization" of the region with "100 new settlers per month" arriving in Walvis Bay. With the 1930s and the rise of fascism, Pretoria would discover that it had more in common with Berlin—perhaps—than Washington.[149]

148. Consul General, Cape Town to Secretary of State, 5 August 1925. Reel 4, M583.

149. Ralph Totten, Consul General, Cape Town to Secretary of State, 6 February 1927, Reel 4, M583.

Chapter 3

Pretoria Seeks Alliance with Nazi Germany to Complement Ties with the U.S., 1930-1939

THE rise of fascism in Europe presented a peculiar challenge for Southern Africa. Pretoria had yet to forget the defeat that had been inflicted by London decades earlier and, in any case, Berlin—not least due to anti-London and ideological bias—was sympathetic to the dominant Afrikaners. The fact that Africans traditionally had appealed to London for intervention against Pretoria was serving to corrode the latter's ties to the British Empire.[1] That the U.S. housed a substantial population of African descent hampered the ability of Pretoria to place an unvarnished faith in Washington in the long run—a wager that proved to be farsighted. This left Berlin as the ally most likely to be resolute. In a "strictly confidential" 1932 message, the U.S. legation in South Africa warned that "now being discussed" between Pretoria and Berlin was a "scheme providing for the immigration into the Union of thirty thousand Germans," with Pretoria bearing the expense. Oswald Pirow, a major player in Pretoria, had German parentage, was educated in that European nation and was thought by the U.S. to be "pronouncedly pro-German in his sympathies."[2] The execution of this plan would have not only harmed the interests of London and Washington but would have erected a formidable barrier for Africans too. Thus, the anti-London and anti-African biases so redolent among Afrikaners, said one left wing analyst, made this community uniquely susceptible to influence from Berlin.[3]

1. Amanda Denise Kemp, "'Up from Slavery' and other Narratives," 122.

2. Report by Ernest Ives, 9 September 1932, Record Group 50, Decimal File, Box 6284, *NARA-CP*.

3. *Guardian* [Cape Town], 3 June 1938. Cf. *Guardian*, 14 October 1938: "Nazis boycott Afrikaners" in what is to become Namibia.

Those influenced by the Communist Party charged that there was an ongoing "Nazification" of the Nationalist Party and that its leaders were "prepared to exchange British imperialism for another and worse imperialism, that of Nazi Germany."[4] Indeed, many Africans and Coloureds found it difficult to distinguish between fascism and what they endured daily in South Africa.[5] "Probably nowhere in the world outside the Fascist States," alleged one left-wing writer in 1939, "is there a country so ripe for the abolition of democracy and introduction of a complete Fascist system as the Union of South Africa...."[6] The U.S. Negro missionary couple Amos and Luella White, writing in the mid-20th century, found the Boers to be "very much like the Southern whites of this country of about fifty years earlier"; "their every act of oppression is justified by some passage from the Bible—in just the same way as the Southerners used to justify slavery."[7] This comparison to U.S. slavery was not misleading in that the logic of 1930s South Africa seemed to be heading in this onerous direction. When the right to vote was restricted in the Cape to Europeans only, a result of growing Nazi influence and a counter-reaction to the growth of the left, the comparison to U.S. slavery gained further traction.[8]

Washington, mired in Jim Crow, was hardly disposed to challenge the racism that inhered in colonialism but at the same time, it had an interest in undercutting both London and Berlin. Thus, in 1930, the invitation of Jan Smuts to Washington was hoped to "reduce" the apparent "anti-American feeling of the British South Africans" or, at least, "reduce the number of anti-American articles in the English language newspapers."[9] Apparently, this visit did little good since by 1933 the Secretary of State was told that the "Natal papers have as usual been most outspoken in their criticism of the United States"—Natal being a fountainhead of British influence. "In the main," it was concluded morosely, "the press has been rather more critical of

4. *Guardian*, 27 January 1939.

5. *Guardian*, 4 November 1938.

6. *Guardian*, 1 June 1939.

7. Amos Jerome White and Luella Graham White, *Dawn in Basutoland: An African Experiment or an Account of Missionary Experiences and Observations in South Africa*, Boston: Christopher, 1953, 234.

8. Anthony Sampson, *Drum: An African Adventure and Aftermath*, London: Hodder and Stoughton, 1983, 103.

9. Report by Ralph Totten, 11 January 1930, Record Group 59, Decimal File, Box 6279. *NARA-CP*

American policies than during any period of the last few months."[10] The "monopoly" of Reuters, the British news service, was blamed since its predominance meant that the "American [news] published in the Union is not always entirely unbiased."[11]

Washington was torn. It saw South Africa as a mirrored image of the republic but knew that Pretoria was being courted avidly by Berlin while still ensconced in a legal relationship with London. This contradictory position led to hemming and hawing in the U.S. The fact that U.S. influence was not as strong in the 1930s as it had been decades earlier also weighed heavily on Washington. In the prelude to the 1890s war, there were an estimated 5000 U.S. nationals residing in or near Johannesburg alone; by 1932 there were about 500. Yes, they were able to convert cricket fields to baseball diamonds—yet another indication of one empire declining as another rose and, yes, just before the U.S. national holiday in July 1932, an estimated 4000 fans attended a game where the Yanks defeated the competition, 13-7, but the cheers of the assembled could not drown out the reality that Washington's leverage in South Africa was weaker than it once was.[12]

Then there was the question of how U.S. nationals of Jewish descent would be treated in South Africa. Preeminent among them by 1935 was I.W. Schlesinger, who had arrived in Cape Town earlier in the century and became a major economic force in South Africa. He nevertheless continued to maintain his U.S. citizenship, as if he were hedging against the rise of untoward problems. In some ways his interests included some of the most important in the land, especially in connection with theaters, motion pictures, broadcasting, and amusements. There was also Colonial Banking and Trust Ltd; the African Amalgamated Advertising Contractors, Ltd; African Consolidated Theaters, Ltd; the African Consolidated Films, Ltd; African Consolidated Investments Corporation, which included the African Broadcasting Company—and other businesses, more than 50 altogether. He was, a U.S. envoy said, "naturally disposed to

10. Report by Ralph Totten, 12 July 1933, Record Group 59, Decimal File, Box 6279.

11. Report by Ralph Totten, 8 January 1934, Record Group 59, Decimal File, Box 6279.

12. Report by M.K. Moorhead, 6 July 1932, Record Group 59, Decimal File, Box 6282.

drive a sharp bargain," which given his Jewishness and the regime's ties to Berlin spelled a potential disaster.[13]

Smoothing the way for a closer relationship between Pretoria and the republic was the development of radio. A station operating from San Francisco was receiving, said the operator, "quite a few letters from South Africa commenting very favorably on both the reception and the programs received."[14] Westinghouse Broadcasting in Boston boasted that their transmitter was "doing a remarkable job penetrating to South Africa....our signals rival, if not exceed, those of the much stronger transmitters of Germany, England, Japan and Portuguese East Africa;" moreover, said J.B. Rock of WB, "our programs are well liked by the South African listeners."[15]

Nevertheless, by early 1931, a U.S. official was castigating Pretoria for taking a "short-sighted view of the problem" of survival while reclining on a "great, closed boiling caldron which sooner or later must blow off those of us who are riding the crest so fiercely or must shatter itself into a million pieces by bloody internal strife;" this official was not "secure in the feeling of permanence of ...white supremacy in South Africa"—and he was correct, particularly since often the Afrikaner elite allowed their own ethnic ascendancy to interfere with the racial project.[16]

Consequently, Washington sought to cater to anti-London groups in the guise of a "Republican movement."[17] The problem was that this effort was adding to the intensity of Afrikaner nationalism, which in a few decades jettisoned London and declared the Republic of South Africa, a new stage in the evolution of apartheid. However, once global forces compelled Washington to erode Jim Crow, the Afrikaner nationalism that had been generated created severe problems for the Pretoria-Washington tie.

In short, the Afrikaner elite seemed to be unerring in creating problems for themselves, e.g. when in 1932 there was a move to make many universities exclusively administered in their language, which was designed to boomerang against the Smuts vision of a federation

---

13. Ralph Totten to Secretary of State, 27 March 1935, Record Group 59, Decimal File, Box 6285.

14. B.M. Bullock to G.S. Messersmith, Assistant Secretary State, 6 July 1939, Record Group 59, Decimal Files, Box 6285, *NARA-CP*.

15. J.B. Rock to G.S. Messersmith, 21 December 1939, Record Group 59, Decimal Files, Box 6285.

16. Report, 13 January 1931, Record Group 59, Decimal File, Box 6282.

17. Report by Ralph Totten, 11 December 1931, Record Group 59, Decimal File, Box 6278.

of colonies, which would include the English-speaking Rhodesias, to be dominated by Pretoria.[18]

To push his agenda, Smuts was sufficiently bold to visit Howard University in Washington, D.C., a bulwark of anti-racist sentiment.[19] But he was insufficiently courageous to debate Negro leader W.E.B. Du Bois, while the latter's fellow leader, William Pickens was displeased when this visitor welcomed tourism but evaded the unavoidable question of how "Colored Visitors" would be greeted. "The South African government," Pickens charged, "refuses to visa the entrance of Negroes from anywhere." Worse, he said, European colonizers in Africa generally acted similarly; and when an African made it to the U.S. for education, "he finds it next to impossible to get admitted back into his own native land...." Smuts, said Pickens dismissively, "was about as logical and as impressive as the average politician from Mississippi would be...." He posed as "a man of the world, while on the question of the Negro, he is a man of South Africa," which neatly summed up the contradictions of the figure often praised in London and Washington.[20] This shot across the bow aimed at Smuts apparently affected his compatriot Malan, who spoke haltingly about "compromise" when he addressed an audience at Tuskegee Institute.[21] Negro press baron Claude Barnett piled on, suggesting that his Washington correspondent badger visitors like Smuts, in light of the horrors visited routinely upon Africans.[22]

The U.S. legation was sufficiently forthcoming to acknowledge that the boorishness of U.S. tourists—an analogue to the controversial visits by Smuts and Malan—likewise complicated bilateral relations. Ironically, the repeal of Prohibition "tended to create a better feeling" in South Africa for the U.S., said the republic's representative, in that it allowed the export of wine from the Cape, but alcohol may not have been the ideal tonic for concord.[23] This conciliation of Cape oenophiles was apparently insufficient since these wineries and fruit farmers sought a boycott of U.S. merchandise by 1936;

18. Report by Ralph Totten, 19 October 1932, Record Group 59, Decimal File, Box 6278.

19. Press Release, January 1930, Reel 2, #313, Part I, Press Releases, *Claude Barnett/Associated Negro Press Papers, Chicago History Museum.*

20. Press Release, January 1930, Reel 2, #365, Part I, Press Releases.

21. Press Release, November 1933, Reel 8, #74, Part I, Press Releases.

22. Gerald Horne, *The Rise and Fall of the Associated Negro Press: Claude Barnett's Pan African News and the Jim Crow Paradox*, Urbana: University of Illinois Press, 10, 158.

23. Report by Ralph Totten, 5 December 1934, Record Group 59, Decimal File, Box 6279.

a visit by Thomas Lamont of J.P. Morgan, the fabulously endowed investment firm, did little to curb their rancor.[24] Nicolaas Havenga, Minister of Finance, upbraided the boycotters since it would compromise the sale of increasingly popular U.S. cars and gasoline, not to mention the U.S. purchase of South African diamonds, gold, and the like.[25] He could have added that the boycott could also have hindered Pretoria's ability to gain access to weapons from Remington and Winchester, which would be quite useful in suppressing mass protests by Africans.[26]

Another problematic export matter was cotton. That was the focus of a deputation under the aegis of the U.S. Quakers, who arrived in 1938. "Many similarities exist between economic conditions in South Africa and America," was the headline: "in cotton production, land tenure, urbanization and labor problems, analogies [too] may be found," since "the loss of cotton exports by America as shown in a [sharp] reduction ....during the past sixty years and the rapid rise of cotton culture in Uganda and Kenya colonies and South Central Africa." This had the potential effect of orienting textile production—the initial rung of industrialization—in South Africa toward its neighbors. "America may be moving away from a one-crop plantation system, Africa may be moving into it"[27]—fueling a field-to-factory movement in both the Union and the republic, which was sending Negroes northward where they could enjoy voting rights and influence U.S. policy toward the Union.

The question of wine also broaches the most nettlesome problem in bilateral ties: there were sharp objections to U.S. attempts to gut "imperial preference," the heart of empire and colonialism alike, which gave London advantage over other trading partners. The U.S. was instructed that it comprised 48 states and trades within itself preferentially—and so should the British Empire.[28] By 1938 the U.S. emissary in Cape Town was elated to find that there was "much closer interest in the Union" in the state of the U.S. economy "since the realization was brought home last year of the important influence

---

24. Report by Ralph Totten, 10 August 1936, Record Group 59, Decimal File, Box 6280.

25. Report by Ralph Totten, 9 November 1936, Record Group 59, Decimal File, Box 6280.

26. Report, 2 December 1935, Record Group 59, Decimal File, Box 6281.

27. Report of "The Friends South African Deputation," 1938, General Files 1938, General to Foreign Service, *Records of American Friends Service Committee—Philadelphia.*

28. Report by Ralph Totten, 15 August 1930, Record Group 59, Decimal File, Box 6278.

which conditions in the [U.S.] exert upon South Africa"[29]—a trend that did bode well for continuing republican influence.

* * *

Washington knew of the intensity of anti-Semitism in South Africa but was tongue-tied in confronting it. The shortsightedness of these powers, which made it difficult for them to envision an alternative to the racist status quo, made it difficult for them to understand that they had handed the African majority to Moscow on a golden platter.

Arguably, as Washington sought to ally with South Africa, it was reinforcing retrograde trends in the U.S. itself. Since it had placed a wager on the Afrikaner elite's continuing influence, the U.S. was hitched to their backwardness. By 1935, the U.S. delegate in Pretoria was mulling the noxious thought that the "the fear of the black races has persuaded South Africans to look favorably upon Germany's possible return to the Dark Continent as a Colonial Power."[30] But how could the U.S. make concessions to its own population of African descent when it was living in sin with Pretoria?

Rebelliousness among Africans in Cape Town was also viewed with anxiety by Washington. There were a "very large number of native and colored inhabitants of the Union," it was reported in March 1930, when about "1500 natives and colored, armed with sticks, knives and razors, tried to force their way [in]to Parliament, " followed by "crowd of 2500 non-whites" who "attempted to march to Parliament to protest against the exclusion of native and colored women" from various provisions that included European women. There were of late an "unusual number of riots and conflicts between the whites and the non-whites."[31] Riotousness among Africans was becoming "more acute," Totten advised in May 1930. Communists were blamed. "At a recent Bantu congress in Bloemfontein, the native Communists were in full charge and by heckling and hooligan tactics prevented any speakers from being heard whose views did not please them;" this was accompanied, he said with disgust, by an "actual battle between the [ANC] and the police" that left three policemen wounded, two of them quite seriously, as the officers'

29. Report by L.J. Keena, 28 March 1938, Record Group 59, Decimal File, Box 6280

30. Report by Ralph Totten, 4 June 1935, Record Group 59, Decimal File, Box 6280.

31. Report by Ralph Totten, 20 March 1930, Record Group 59, Decimal File, Box 6279.

rifles and bayonets did not save them.[32] This decade would see the establishment of an interlocking directorate between the ANC and the CP, as evidenced when Moses Kotane of the latter chaired a rally of the former in Cape Town in 1939.[33]

Totten claimed that a leader of the South African Labour Party—an "avowed Communist"— confronted him, "during the excitement connected with the condemnation and execution of Sacco and Vanzetti," and "did not hesitate to threaten me with measures of retaliation in case the execution was carried out."[34] Washington was reassured however when the Labour Party moved toward a "white labour policy," which flummoxed the attempt by Communists to build a "People's Front."[35]

As early as June 1931 there were demonstrations in Johannesburg protesting the attempted frame-up of the Scottsboro 9 defendants, African Americans in Alabama on the fast track to execution—before the forceful intervention of the Communist Party and their global allies.[36] At the same time in Nairobi, the U.S. was tracking an "increase of Bolshevic [sic] propaganda amongst the Kikuyu tribe," as evidenced in "speeches made by natives who received training in Moscow."[37] By 1932 in the Union the U.S. was examining carefully the fact that the CP had decided to put forward African candidates for elections; this, it was noted with relief, "will have very little effect on the final result."[38] The movement led decades earlier by John Chilembwe was continuing to cause upset in 1935; it was not seen as coincidental that the Watchtower movement, which was blamed, had roots in the U.S.[39] Combined with the supposed seditious activity of Negro colleges and newspapers, this fact called into question Washington's reliability as an ally.

32. Report by Ralph Totten, 21 May 1930, Record Group 59, Decimal File, Box 6279.

33. *Guardian*, 23 June 1939.

34. Report by Ralph Totten, 2 July 1931, Record Group 59, Decimal File, Box 6278.

35. Report by H. Earle Russell, 15 September 1937, Record Group 59, Decimal File, Box 6280.

36. Report, 8 June 1931, Record Group 59, Decimal File, Box 6279. Gerald Horne, *Powell v. Alabama: The Scottsboro Case and American Justice*, New York: Franklin Watts, 1997.

37. Report, 2 April 1931, Record Group 59, Decimal File, Box 6279.

38. Report by Ralph Totten, 7 October 1932, Record Group 59, Decimal File, Box 6278.

39. Report by Irving Linnell, 5 September 1935, Record Group 59, Decimal File, Box 6280.

During the decade of the Great Depression, U.S. Negro heroes like the boxing champions Henry Armstrong and Joe Louis and particularly the progressive artist and activist Paul Robeson were lionized among Africans, and their images contributed to a preexisting combativeness. Reuben Caluza, a Zulu with degrees from the historically Black Hampton Institute and Columbia University conferred with both Robeson and his cultural counterpart, the singer Roland Hayes. ANC leader James Moroka planned to leave South Africa to see Louis box but was blocked by Pretoria. Robeson was singled out for special praise, along with his "message of hope." Negro musicians like Duke Ellington and Louis Armstrong were also popular and whose very image of affluence and sophistication served to undermine the lineaments of white supremacy.[40] It was Robeson, however, who had a built-in lobbying arm in the form of the interracial left wing,[41] and who was often the subject of intense interest in South Africa.[42] He was "one of the world's great singers," according to the left-wing tribune of Cape Town. Peter Abrahams, a South African writer of Ethiopian descent, captured the sentiment of his compatriots when he celebrated Robeson in poetry.[43]

It was in 1935 that the *Bantu World*, which addressed Africans, beamed that "there is perhaps no part of Africa where the American Negroes have a warmer corner in the eyes of Africans than in this country."[44] Protest by a delegate from Haiti at the League of Nations in response to a massacre in what was to become Namibia also fueled Pan-African ferment and outreach in these years.[45]

Pretoria worked overtime to make sure that such alliances did not materialize. It was in 1936 that Eslanda Robeson, better known as the spouse of Paul Robeson, arrived in South Africa with her young son in tow. Typically, obtaining a visa was not easy. "If you are a Negro," she said, "you can't make up your mind to go to Africa and just go. Oh, no," she reminded, "not unless you are a missionary." But through wheedling and pressure, this political "missionary" received documentation and departed on 29 May. There she met with Albert Xuma, soon to become a top ANC leader, who shepherded her about in what she described gushingly as a "gorgeous

40. Amanda Denise Kemp, "'Up from Slavery' and Other Narratives," 49, 95, 100, 104,

41. *Guardian*, 12 November 1937.

42. *Guardian*, 1 July 1938.

43. *Guardian*, 3 April 1941.

44. *Bantu World*, 2 February 1935.

45. Ibid., Amanda Denise Kemp, 220.

new 1935 Buick complete with balloon tires…."[46] A diminutive man, dignified with rapidly graying hair sitting atop a high forehead and quick and piercing eyes, Xuma was notorious for walking solemnly and stiffly, often seen eating sandwiches with quiet dignity. He had the lilting accent of the Xhosas from the Eastern Cape.[47] Ms. Robeson was embraced warmly, a trend surely influenced by her generosity. She "gave me my first bicycle," said future ANC leader Joe Matthews.[48]

Xuma was also friendly with Max Yergan, then quite close with the U.S. radical left, as was his good friend Ms. Robeson. "My dear Xuma," he said in 1936, "after a long absence I have just returned [to] South Africa. I have much to discuss with you,"[49] he added portentously. Similarly, when Ms. Robeson journeyed to nearby Swaziland, it was Xuma who contacted the region's leader, "Chief Sobhuza," requesting a "personal favour" to "act as her guide."[50] Likewise, when Xuma headed to London, he was keen to meet with the Robesons.[51]

When the young scholar Ralph Bunche sought to travel to South Africa in 1937, he was not greeted enthusiastically by Pretoria. He recalled later his "trouble in gaining permission to enter" this iniquitous land.[52] He was equally shunned, he recalled, by "these American consuls and legation secretaries" who also tended to act "pretty lousey [sic] when they are confronted with an American Negro."[53]

The Negro missionaries Amos Jerome White and Luella Graham White agreed, adding that "no American Negro can go to South Africa without being impressed at every turn by the eagerness of the Africans to hear about America and to learn more about the Negro"—though "they know far more about us than we do about them." The couple confessed unashamedly that "while we are

46. Eslanda Goode Robeson, *African Journey*, New York: John Day, 945, 18, 19, 65.

47. Anthony Sampson, *Drum: An African Adventure—and Aftermath*, London: Hodder and Stoughton, 1983,

48. Oral History, Joe Matthews, 2 October 2000, *University of Connecticut-Storrs.*

49. Max Yergan to "My Dear Xuma," 22 April 1936, Reel 1, *A.B. Xuma Papers, Witwatersrand University-Johannesburg.*

50. A.B. Xuma to Chief Sobhuza, 23 June 1936, Reel 1, *A.B. Xuma Papers.*

51. A.B. Xuma to Eslanda and Paul Robeson, 21 May 1937, Reel 1, *A.B. Xuma Papers.*

52. Ralph Bunche, "Race Relations—South African and American," 9 December 1938, Box 340, Folder 10, *Ralph Bunche Papers, UCLA-Los Angeles.*

53. Ibid., *The Travel Notes of Ralph J. Bunche*, 79.

feeling that we [are] in no way connected with Africa and wish nothing of it, the Africans' vision is clearer than ours. They look to the future and hear the tramp of millions of American Negroes marching to join with their African kin in their steady progress toward a brighter future, 'for who knows,' says Bernard Shaw, 'but that the next great civilization may be that of the Negro race.'" They saw the AME church—with branches on both sides of the Atlantic—as peculiarly suited to lead this wave, though they neglected the fact that Africans might be better suited to lead, since they were yearning for sovereignty. Still, they opined that "there are enough Negroes with Masters and Doctors degrees, who are unemployed in this country to aid substantially in giving direction to the training of our brothers in Africa and in thus contributing to their salvation we shall be doing much toward the realization of our own, for black men in America will never be fully and completely free until they do what they can to bring a larger measure of freedom to their kin on the 'dark' continent." Even then the idea of U.S. Negroes leading Africans might have been misplaced, for as they noted, Witwatersrand University had already agreed to "admit four Native Africans every year to the medical college" which was "better than some medical colleges" in the U.S.

With hope, the visitors found that Africans "seemed to know every detail" of the "career" of the Brown Bomber, Joe Louis. Many Africans read Negro newspapers, which provided such knowledge. Likewise, while in Windhoek, they heard a "Hottentot band" and "listening one would have thought that it was Fletcher Henderson, Cab Calloway [or] Duke Ellington." They also heard a quartet singing spiritual hymns that "sounded so much like an American spiritual quartet that we felt for the moment we were right in the USA." Coincidentally, they also met there an "elderly man from Jacksonville" who had been "shipwrecked" earlier in the century.[54] Yet, as time passed, and particularly after too many Negro organizations capitulated to the Red Scare, South African comrades found it difficult to forge an alliance with them and accelerated their ties to decolonizing Africa—and the socialist camp.

Traveling in the other direction was Z.K. Matthews, who was to become a prominent shaper of South African politics. Short and heavy, always impeccably dressed in a dark suit with white collar and tie, he was a man of gravitas, moderate, even conservative,

54. Amos Jerome White and Luella Graham White, *Dawn in Basutoland: An African Experiment or an Account of Missionary Experiences and Observations in South Africa*, Boston: Christopher, 1953, 36, 54, 73, 237, 242, 243, 283.

and trusted across the ANC spectrum from left to right.[55] He visited Negro colleges in the 1930s and was subjected to a withering Jim Crow; he also met Bunche. (He recalled being able to elude Jim Crow when he presented himself as an "Abyssinian prince").[56]

Albert Xuma may have been closer to U.S. Negroes than other ANC leaders. As a student at Booker T. Washington's Tuskegee Institute, he joined the Reserve Officer Training Corps—a step away from the U.S. military—and, as he noted later, "rose to the rank of First Sergeant."[57] He married his first wife, Amanda Priscilla Mason, in 1931: she hailed from Liberia, the U.S. neo-colony, and graduated from what became Wilberforce University in Ohio in the early 1920s. The couple became involved in the AME church, a testament to their close ties to U.S. Negroes. By the mid-1930s he was president of the laymen's association in the Transvaal. She died in 1934, after which Xuma married an African American woman. Madie Hall Xuma spent two years at Shaw University in her native North Carolina before receiving a degree from the college in Winston-Salem, and then taught at Bethune Cookman in Florida before receiving an advanced degree at Columbia University in Manhattan.[58] (Sibusisiwe Makhanya of South Africa was matriculating there at the same time. Like many South Africans, she had European ancestry: her grandfather and great-grandfather were defined as "white.")[59]

55. Rusty Bernstein, *Memory Against Forgetting: Memoirs from a Life in South African Politics*, London: Penguin, 1999, 142.

56. Z.K. Matthews, *Freedom for My People: The Autobiography of Z.K. Matthews: Southern Africa, 1901 to 1968*, Cape Town: David Philip, 1981, 161, 96: He added: the "irony is that in 1977 in South Africa holders of foreign passports who are black may be admitted to restaurants and hotels from which black Africans are excluded;" this was at a time when formal Jim Crow had evaporated in the U.S., leaving a still regnant economic Jim Crow—the destiny to which Matthews' homeland was headed then.

57. Peter Limb, ed., *A.B. Xuma: Autobiography and Selected Works*, Cape Town: Van Riebeeck Society, 2012, 17.

58. Steven D. Gish, *Alfred B. Xuma*, 68. See "A Message from Wilberforce Institute", South Africa, circa 1936, Box 18, Folder 2, *Ralph Bunche Papers, UCLA-Los Angeles*: Teachers there were "well qualified and all members of the African Race, some were trained at Wilbeforce University [Ohio]; Tuskegee....Hartshorn College, Virginia."

59. Iris Berger, "An African American 'Mother of the Nation': Madie Hall Xuma in South Africa, 1940-1963," *Journal of Southern African Studies*, 27(Number 3, September 2001): 547-566, 548, 549, 553.

Xuma was a member of the Negro fraternity Alpha Phi Alpha and was asked to form a branch in South Africa.[60] By late 1931 he actually joined the NAACP, thrilling leader Roy Wilkins, who wrote "I do not know when I have had anything to please me as much as having a word from you did."[61] He was well connected on both sides of the ocean and, thus, when the U.S. Negro leader Dr. George Haynes Holmes headed to Cape Town, Xuma was recruited to assist him.[62] When a relative of former U.S. president Ulysses S. Grant visited South Africa, it was Xuma who was asked to show her around.[63] Claude Barnett, the Chicago based press baron and fellow Tuskegee alumnus, thought Xuma could assist in one of his primary concerns: collecting "African objects," notably sculptures. Such a gift would "arouse intense interest among the students and officials from Dr. Moton on down to know that a former student from so far away remembered him."[64]

By 1937, Xuma was headed to Manhattan and Wilkins of the NAACP made an "offer to assist" him on "problems of mutual interest." Attending the Association's annual confab was one of Xuma's objectives for the trip.[65] Another goal was to secure research material from the preeminent Negro historian Carter G. Woodson.[66] Xuma declared that he was "deeply interested" in the "Study of Negro History" and, he told the illustrious scholar, eagerly "anticipate[d] the pleasure of meeting you."[67] He also reached R.R. Moton of Tuskegee, instructing him that he could be contacted in New York City via Wilkins or Yergan; he was interested in "consulting" the successor to Booker T. Washington on "devising means of carrying out a programme," a hint of his soon to be pivotal role with the ANC.

In some ways, Xuma was a transitional figure, representing the influence of U.S. Negroes on South Africans that was to dissipate as the Cold War began, making it difficult for African Americans to ally with an ANC that was moving ever closer to the CP. As he had

60. Raymond Cannon to Alfred Xuma, 15 September 1927, Reel 1, *A.B. Xuma Papers, University of Witwatersrand-Johannesburg.*

61. Roy Wilkins to "Dear Xuma", 11 January 1932, Reel 1, *A.B. Xuma Papers.*

62. J.D.R. Jones to A.B. Xuma, 22 April 1930, Reel 1, *A.B. Xuma Papers.*

63. Grover Little of YMCA to A.B. Xuma, 13 December 1935, Reel 1, *A.B. Xuma Papers.*

64. Claude Barnett to A.B. Xuma, 25 May 1934, Reel 1, *A.B. Xuma Papers.*

65. A.B. Xuma to "My Dear Roy" Wilkins, 5 May 1937, Reel 1, *A.B. Xuma Papers.*

66. A.B. Xuma to Z.K. Matthews, 4 May 1937, Reel 1, *A.B. Xuma Papers.*

67. A.B. Xuma to Carter G. Woodson, 12 May 1937, Reel 1, *A.B. Xuma Papers.*

told Moton, "I am forever indebted to America and Americans, both Black and White for what they have done for me."[68] He repeated this praise to Emmett Scott, Dr. Washington's former top aide, who by the time of his voyage he had not seen in "over twenty years." "My debt of gratitude to America and her people," he insisted, "can never be repaid. They gave me opportunities that my country did not offer."[69]

Mandela and Tambo and the "liberation generation" in South Africa would be able to say something similar about the socialist camp, the Scandinavian nations, and what was then the Organization of African Unity.

By July 1937 Xuma was residing in Harlem on 135th Street, where Yergan was "exceedingly anxious to get in touch...."[70] It was Yergan, according to Wilkins, who was "causing some excitement by his denunciation of British imperialism in Africa" which had struck a "responsive c[h]ord among American colored people who are slowly becoming internationally minded."[71] The year before, at the 27th annual convention of Wilkins' group in Baltimore, those assembled, in line with his reminder, referred contemptuously to fascism as the "last desperate efforts of capitalism to preserve itself at all costs."[72] But Yergan, soon to be one of the most bitter antagonists of the radicals he once embraced, was by then displaying signs of the pressure to which he would be subjected. "I cannot understand what has happened to our correspondence,"[73] he mused to Xuma a few months later, perhaps suggesting dirty tricks by mutual foes.

Yergan was a key figure then, with a foot in Communist circles on both sides of the Atlantic. Govan Mbeki, who was influenced to join the Communist Party of South Africa through his tie to Yergan, admitted that "I formed an association, a relationship with him...we took to each other," as the African "used to visit his home virtually every evening....I would sit in his study, it was a big library, and he would say to me, 'When I leave Fort Hare [University], I'll leave all my books at the library of Fort Hare"—a gesture that was to supply the school's "learning library." Reflecting later he observed cogently

68. A.B. Xuma to R.R. Moton, 12 May 1937, Reel 1, *A.B. Xuma Papers.*

69. A.B. Xuma to Emmet Scott, 12 May 1937, Reel 1, *A.B. Xuma Papers.*

70. Max Yergan to A.B. Xuma, 10 July 1937, Reel 1, *A.B. Xuma Papers.*

71. "Roy" to "My Dear Friend Xuma", 13 March 1937, Reel 1, *A.B. Xuma Papers.*

72. "Fascism and Minority Groups", 2 July 1936, NAACP Convention, Box 340, Folder 2, *Ralph Bunche Papers.*

73. Max Yergan to A.B. Xuma, 17 June 1938,

that the "influence they had on my thinking was there for life," though there was a concomitant "influence" from Edward Roux and African Communists too.[74]

Beyond conferring on weighty matters in Harlem, Xuma had a more prosaic—though no less crucial—issue to pursue. He was then in hot pursuit of Madie Hall Xuma, yet another sign of his fascination with U.S. Negroes. "I am indeed grateful for all the things you have offered me for a prolonged stay in South Africa," she said after his departure; "but," she cautioned, "I am only interested in a career not marriage" and she was, in any case, "expecting some company from the state of Florida…I haven't seen him in several years"—a comment that could either give the rebuffed Xuma hope that this relationship was unserious or, alternatively, make a strong hint that he should seek "company" elsewhere.[75] Removing any ambiguity, she then informed him that it was merely a "platonic" tie with him that captured her fancy.[76]

But the persistent African won over the hesitant U.S. Negro, as she told "Dear Alfred" that "from now on I shall try to write more often" and asking insistently, "have you started negotiations yet relative to my coming over? I am getting keyed up over the expected trip there…." Reassuring him of her commitment, she informed him with emphasis, "once I make up my mind to do a thing, *I never turn back*…I do promise to write every week and you must do the same…."[77]

She was true to her word: soon she was sailing across the Atlantic to wed him. But in a sense, this marked the end of the era. Xuma, soon to be a top leader of the ANC, was to become an outlier in his devotion to U.S. Negroes and the U.S. alike, with the rising generation of Southern African leaders—and African leaders more generally—winning liberation and solidifying ties with Eastern Europe and Scandinavia and a decolonizing Africa.

* * *

Though Pretoria was clearly open to partnership with Germany, its fascist ally in Rome seemed to be creating intractable difficulties for settler colonialism in Africa. There were many turning points in the

74. Oral History, Govan Mbeki, 5 October 2000, *University of Connecticut-Storrs.*

75. Madie Hall Xuma to A.B. Xuma, 8 August 1938, Reel 1, *A.B. Xuma Papers.*

76. Madie Hall Xuma to A.B. Xuma, 26 August 1938, Reel 1, *A.B. Xuma Papers.*

77. Madie Hall Xuma to "Dear Alfred", 11 June 1939, Reel 1, *A.B. Xuma Papers.*

long road to 1994, but one came in 1935 when Africans thought that one of the few sovereign states on the continent was on the verge of being liquidated, which would effectively handicap the ability of indigenous South Africans to follow in the footsteps of Addis Ababa. The invasion of Ethiopia outraged Africans and African Americans alike and doubtlessly energized protest from Cape Town to Durban. The U.S. envoy in Johannesburg watched anxiously as a "Communist meeting" there on 18 July 1935 concluded with the burning in effigy of Benito Mussolini. This was followed by the refusal of Cape Town stevedores to load beef destined for Italy, a maneuver emulated by their peers in Durban. Though the envoy officially fretted about the impact of such actions on "relations between the white and black races throughout Africa," he would have been more insightful if he had contemplated the impact in his own homeland.[78] The deprivation of the franchise in the Cape dovetailing with Rome's aggression was enough to fuel a great leap forward in activism.[79]

Rome's fellow colonizers, including Pretoria, were wary of another power elbowing into the neighborhood, forcing yet another division of the spoils and, perhaps, a smaller share for all. In 1936 Frederick Burnham, the U.S. national who had fought the Boers decades earlier, said that he had "received many letters from South African and Rhodesian friends," who were "excited"—not positively—about the "new menace of Italy." With moroseness, he seemed to indicate that Rome had beaten his coterie to the punch, affirming "we seem to have lost our colonizing and frontier spirit in the last generation."[80] Burnham, then feeling his advanced age, was becoming more philosophical. When his fellow turn of the century combatant, John Hays Hammond, expired, the latter was compared to Herbert Hoover as an engineer, recalling that his report to Cecil Rhodes on the mines of Africa spurred the conflict with Afrikaners, culminating in the infamous Jameson Raid—and a death sentence from the Boers.[81] Burnham was notably proud of the "part played by Americans," e.g. himself, in building South Africa. "When the two great strains of white blood were contending with each other and both [were] menaced by hordes of savages," he reported happily that "very many strong Americans, mostly from beyond the Rockies, several thousand in all" rode to the

78. Report by Irving Linnell, 5 September 1935, Record Group 59, Decimal File, Box 6280.

79. Ibid., Daniel Massey, *Under Protest*, 34.

80. Frederick Burnham to "My Dear Aylmer," 6 November 1936, Box 3, *Frederick R. Burnham Papers.*

81. *New York Herald Tribune*, 9 June 1936.

rescue; "they played an interesting part and Hammond most important of all."[82] As of his passing in 1936 these intra-European tensions had yet to abate, as the rise of Rome demonstrated.

By 1937, the U.S. representative L.J. Keena was furrowing his brow about "native riots at Vereeniging," which led to the "death of two constables and the serious injury of a third." This "aroused bitter resentments among the white population," he proclaimed—though the demand the latter made was the immediate "deportation of overseas Jews who disseminate Communist propaganda among the natives,"[83] as if Africans would not protest but for the presence of Jewish Communists. Differing was the youthful Negro scholar Ralph Bunche, who was told by the African Communist Edwin Thabo Mafutsanyana that in Johannesburg alone there were 200 CP members, "mostly Bantu," while only recently the CP had attracted 500 African members in the Vereeniging "location."[84]

Still, Pretoria thought it had a basis for positing a connection between Jewishness and Communism. Rusty Bernstein, who was to become a premier South African Communist in the 1950s, was born in London in 1915 and arrived in South Africa in 1932 along with his parents of Eastern European Jewish origin. Later he reflected on the fact that CP meetings during this time in various cities would regularly "finish up in a fight with Nationalists and Fascists...."[85] Sarah Carneson of Cape Town was the daughter of founding members of the Communist Party, both of her parents being of Russian Jewish origin.[86] Sadie Forman, born in 1929, had parents of Lithuanian Jewish origin, who arrived in South Africa in 1913. Her father was a member of what she termed the "Bolshevik Party" who had been exiled to Siberia after 1905 and told her repeatedly during Passover that those who were Jewish used to be slaves but now they lived in a nation—South Africa—"where the majority of the people were slaves and it was our task also to put ourselves on the side of the people struggling...."[87]

---

82. Frederick Burnham to "Mrs. Saunders", no date, Box 2, *Frederick Burnham Papers.*

83. Report by L.J. Keena, 12 November 1937, Record Group 59, Decimal File, Box 6281.

84. Ibid., Robert R. Edgar, ed., *The Travel Notes of Ralph J. Bunche*, 12, 72

85. Oral History, Rusty Bernstein, 28 February 2001, *University of Connecticut-Storrs.*

86. Oral History, Sarah Carneson, 11 October 2000, *University of Connecticut-Storrs.*

87. Oral History, Sadie Forman, 19 December 2001, *University of Connecticut-Storrs.*

A comrade of them all was Ben Turok, born in Latvia in 1927, though his parents came from Ukraine. They were Jewish too and, as he said later, "victims of the White Terror of the Cossacks" who fled their homeland in 1921 for Riga. But in 1929 a surge of fascism there sent them fleeing again. "It was the first country of Eastern Europe [to] go fascist," he recalled. By 1934 they were in Cape Town though "our home language was Yiddish" and remained so, though they also spoke German. His mother became South Africa's "foremost Jewish actress," by his recollection. Because in Latvia "we lived very much like Africans live in townships," he was easily attracted to the CP as a tool to fight oppression.[88]

Ray Alexander, also known as Ray Alexander Simons, spoke Russian and German and could write in Yiddish. She too was of Eastern European Jewish extraction and was also a leader of the CP. "I knew of the oppression that the Jewish people had in the ghetto," she recalled later, i.e. "that they were discriminated against in Tsarist Russia." Hence, "race discrimination and job reservations in South Africa [were] very close to me" and "strongly rooted" in her soul the "desire to do away with race discrimination...." Born in 1914 in Latvia in what she called a "Jewish town," she was close to the "leader of the Bolsheviks" there and read early on the revolutionary work of the heroic Rosa Luxembourg. She had been attracted to Zionism before reading the Balfour Declaration, promising a Zionist homeland, which caused her to ask, "what will happen to the Palestinian people"? By 1929 she had arrived in Cape Town.[89]

In sum, Pretoria thought it had reason to believe it was welcoming "whites" when it opened the doors to those fleeing anti-Semitism in Europe but soon discovered with dismay that they may have been importing people bent on burying racism. This helped to generate further anti-Semitism in South Africa, just as it bolstered the position of Africans.

Washington was happy to learn that South Africa was considering legislation that would allow U.S. nationals to be admitted as immigrants on a par with those of the British Empire and twelve other—mostly Western European—nations. Frank Birmingham of Pittsburgh was one of many looking to take advantage of this bill.[90]

---

88. Oral History, Ben Turok, 5 October 2000, *University of Connecticut-Storrs.*

89. See "Transcripts of Interviews for Ray's Autobiography," 22 November 1997 and 23 May 1992, A28, *Jack Simons and Ray Alexander Collection, University of Cape Town.*

90. Letter from Frank Birmingham, 19 January 1937, Record Group 59, Decimal File, Box 6283.

However, the Jewish community erupted in furor when it was learned that excluded from this bill's remit were those from Russia, Lithuania, Poland, Latvia and Palestine—i.e. those likely to have Jewish roots. Totten claimed this was a "necessity" since "the Jewish immigration boom is becoming so heavy that it has become a problem" since "they are largely non-producing middle-men, traders and dealers" and were "becoming too numerous and too are great a drain on the small white population…."[91] Left unmentioned was the white supremacist concern with how this "small white population" could continue to overawe a massive African population without reinforcements, not to mention the injustice of closing the door to those fleeing persecution.

Taking the cue, Nationalist leader D.F. Malan argued vehemently that his opponents were backed by a "section of the Jews who want revenge on the Nationalist Party," moving to "warn" this persecuted grouping of the danger they knew well: "it is very easy to rouse a feeling of hate towards the Jews" and this capability, he thought, was enhanced by an "influx of immigrants from Eastern Europe."[92] With menace unleashed, he warned the minority that "if they want to hit us, they may be assured that we will hit back."[93] Despite this inflammatory verbiage, Totten was struck in 1932 when the Nationalists chose a Jewish man as their candidate for higher office in a district that contained "many shopkeepers and garment workers" but there was "little hope of this being successful, as the Jewish vote in South Africa is strongly anti-Nationalist…."[94] In any case—as Rusty Bernstein and his comrades could well attest--the early 1930s in South Africa featured anti-Nazi demonstrations ending in fistfights,[95] followed by intensified pro-Nazi activism.[96]

91. Report by Ralph Totten, 18 March 1930, Record Group 59, Decimal File, Box 6284.

92. Report by Ralph Totten, 11 November 1931, Record Group 59, Decimal File, Box 6278.

93. Report by Ralph Totten, 11 November 1931, Record Group 59, Decimal File, Box 6284.

94. Report by Ralph Totten, 7 October 1932, Record Group 59, Decimal File, Box 6278.

95. Report by Ralph Totten, 13 November 1933, Record Group 59, Decimal File, Box 6278.

96. Report by Ralph Totten, 1 February 1934, Record Group 59, Decimal File, Box 6278.

Roiling the waters was a tremendous social and economic transformation that was remaking the nation. As farmers and the Chamber of Mines clamored for African labor, Black workers were entering urban areas in enormous numbers. This migration "might lead to revolutionary social and economic changes," said the leftist *Guardian* of Cape Town in 1937. In the 15 years between the census of 1921 and that of 1936 the African population in urban areas had practically doubled from 587,000 to 1.15 million. With the concentration effected by urbanization arrived more opportunities for organization, previously hindered by the scattering of Africans in rural areas. It also increased the likelihood that Africans would be influenced by the most boisterous among them, leading to charges that the majority population was becoming more "cheeky." Concurrently, the growing shortage of Africans in rural areas led to the complementary charge that their bargaining power was increasing. South Africa had been a slave society up to about 1834, after which Africans became a kind of serf, tied to the land and compelled to work for next to nothing by means of vagrancy laws, pass laws, poll taxes. A kind of feudal economy then emerged, with miners recruited as indentured laborers, then mutating into an industrial proletariat. As with developments preceding the U.S. Civil War, South Africa was facing an imminent confrontation between rural neo-slavery and urban capitalism. "Once the black man has been urbanized, proletarianized, westernized," said the *Guardian* commentator, "he will find his own salvation."[97]

The growing U.S. presence was the other side of the coin to African urbanization. General Motors had set up shop in Port Elizabeth and was accused quickly of employing "boss tactics." That firm, along with Ford and Firestone, became the focus of major organizing drives by Communist-influenced labor organizers, capable of proselytizing in a radical vein. Scandalously skimpy starvation wages facilitated their formidable task. The left found that "in no other sector of industry has there been such resistance from the employers as in the motor industry," a testament to the routinization of U.S. hardball tactics, as all firms sought to "imitate" the notorious Henry Ford. The result was the importation from the U.S. of a hardline approach, said the *Guardian*, that "smacks very much of America and not of our own country where workers are legally entitled to organize themselves into trade unions."[98] In an early example of trans-oceanic labor commonality, the South African union highlighted the reality

97. *Guardian*, 15 October 1937.

98. *Guardian*, 29 October 1937.

that GM had spent 250,000 pounds to spy on workers at home, worrying that such invasive tactics were headed in their direction.[99]

Accompanying the growing U.S. presence was the popularity of U.S. popular culture; this was not just the music of Duke Ellington, the exploits of Joe Louis, and the image of Paul Robeson. The South African press raved about Margaret Mitchell's *Gone with the Wind*, the moonlight and magnolias Civil War epic glorifying the enslavement of Africans. "It is seldom" raved the *Johannesburg Star* "that one reads a novel for which one has nothing but praise...."[100] Validating this praise were the "big sales" reported in Cape Town.[101] Johannesburg, generally to the right of the ocean-bound metropolis, spoke glowingly of a "roaring trade" in the book with "every bookshop in town" witnessing this doorstop of a novel flying out of the doors.[102] The novelist herself helped along the booming sales, giving interviews to the South African press[103] and dismissing charges of plagiarism from Susan Lawrence Davis, who wrote an "authentic history" of the heralded Ku Klux Klan. She was "happy" that "Scarlett and Rhett and my other characters were finding friends in South Africa,"[104] which was all too true.

There was, by way of complementarity, a steady influx of Germans into Southern Africa, drawn not only by the once tightly held colony of South West Africa but also Tanganyika, due east, likewise once held by Berlin. By 1934, Washington was told of "outbursts of Nazi enthusiasm" emerging there, along with demands for "recognition of German as an official language."[105] This may have been motivated by the fact that Oswald Pirow, Minister of Defense—who was to torment Mandela in coming years—gave speeches in German regularly, a bouquet tossed at his comrades in Berlin.[106] Pirow nervily visited Spain during the civil war to salute the fascist forces. He welcomed the idea of Germany heightening its colonial interest in Africa and interviewed Adolf Hitler himself. The "Little Hitler of Africa" was his chilling nickname—when he was not referred to as the "Pocket

---

99. *Guardian*, 4 February 1938.

100. *Johannesburg Star*, 17 November 1936.

101. *Cape Argus*, 28 January 1937.

102. *Johannesburg Daily Express*, 24 February 1937.

103. *Natal Daily News*, 2 February 1938.

104. *Cape Argus*, 11 December 1937.

105. Report by Irving Linnell, 5 December 1934, Record Group 59, Decimal File, Box 6279.

106. Report by Irving Linnell, 30 January 1935, Record Group 59, Decimal File, Box 6281.

Fuhrer"—as he continually threatened to install a unique fascism in Southern Africa.[107]

By 1936 the U.S. emissary was clucking about the "financial supremacy of the Jews," the supposed "cause of considerable unrest;" there were "near riots caused by an anti-Jewish organization called the 'grey shirts'," and "many heads [were] broken by the police" as a result—though it wasn't necessarily the fascists who departed with cracked craniums.[108] By 1939 there were credible reports of a "threatened Nazi uprising" in Windhoek.[109] Fascism was so intense in South Africa that there were two ultra-right groups known for how they were clad: not just the "grey shirts" but the "black shirts" too.[110]

The steady influx of Jewish migrants from Europe into South Africa continued, many of them fleeing incipient fascism. Protest meetings ensued. "The average citizen," sniffed Totten, implicitly limiting his view to Europeans, "feels that this large influx of Jews into the small white population of South Africa is not entirely a good thing."[111]

By 1937 Smuts was sending a message of support to a Zionist conference in Kimberley, while expressing doubt about the prospect of partition of Palestine.[112] Reputedly, the Nationalists were more enthusiastic about a kind of *Aliyah*, promoting a Jewish settlement in neighboring Swaziland. Supporters included one of Malan's lieutenants in the Transvaal.[113] Malan, said the Cape Town left, was "anti-British...anti-Coloured, Anti-Native"—and "anti-Jew,"[114] so this apparent sympathy for Zionism should not be viewed benignly.

Undoubtedly, this was the position of South Africa's Jewish Board of Deputies in 1937, which protested the reality that their constituency was "made the object of a systematic campaign of abuse" and "unfounded accusation," presenting a "serious national danger of racial conflict." The JBD was galled by the allegation that their community was seeking "'political revenge'" against those who had sought to bar their admission from Eastern Europe and were

107. F.S. Crafford, *Jan Smuts: A Biography*, Garden City: Doubleday, 1943, 260.

108. Report by Ralph Totten, 11 April 1936, Record Group 59, Decimal File, Box 6280.

109. *Guardian*, 28 April 1939.

110. *Guardian*, 24 March 1939.

111. Report by Ralph Totten, 9 November 1936, Record Group 59, Decimal File, Box 6280.

112. Report by H. Earle Russell, 15 September 1937, Record Group 59, Decimal File, Box 6280.

113. *Guardian* [Cape Town], 12 March 1937.

114. *Guardian*, 9 April 1937.

outraged by the supposed "intimate association between Jewry and Communism" and the allied charge that the "trade unions are controlled by Jewish officials." (There were 104 registered unions in 1935 and "only nine" were led by those who happened to be Jewish, it was contended.) Then in typical bigoted fashion was the "equally insidious suggestion that all Jews are capitalists." This body was founded in 1903 in the Transvaal as the war wound down and migration from Europe accelerated.[115]

There was a natural tie between the Zionists and Smuts, given the antipathy both shared toward the Afrikaner elite, just as the latter enjoyed mutual warmth with Nazi Berlin. Thus, Washington's representative in South Africa was almost giddy in reporting on the tension between the two allies when the Boers took umbrage at allegations in the German press—not inaccurate—that some amongst this group were involved in "miscegenation." This, it was charged, was leading to the "racial and cultural deterioration" of the Afrikaners, making them an unreliable ally for Germany.[116] Perhaps in response, the Afrikaner elite proposed legislation to bar the employment of women defined as "white" by employers of Asian origin.[117]

Yet like its U.S. peer in racialism, Pretoria had difficulty in grasping the rise of Asia, notably Japan. As early as 1913 Smuts had declared, a U.S. envoy recalled, that "all colored persons including Asiatics" were "prohibited immigrants"—but Tokyo railed at this "stigma." A Pretoria journalist countered by stating that "'there is color prejudice and South Africa is not ashamed to admit it;'" besides, he continued, "'there is a fear that by opening the door to Japanese immigrants we are going to add to our racial complications'"[118]—which was both true and unavoidable. A cartoon from a local newspaper, forwarded to Washington in "strictly confidential" terms, suggesting sensitivity, summed up these concerns. The accompanying description drafted by the U.S. observer, spoke of a "happy, smiling Japanese merchant with doffed hat held high in the air, descending the gangway of a ship to the open arms of the Nationalist Government, which exclaims a hardy 'welcome.'!" The caption read: "down the gangway to a 'white man's country'. Nationalists' new solution

115. *Guardian*, 10 December 1937.

116. Report by H. Earle Russell, 15 September 1937, Record Group 59, Decimal File, Box 6280.

117. Report by L.J. Keena, 12 November 1937, Record Group 59, Decimal File, Box 6280.

118. Report by Garret C. Anderson, 16 March 1931, Record Group 59, Decimal File, Box 6281.

to the Asiatic problem.'" Johannesburg merchants, already steaming from the arrival of more Jewish competitors from Europe, were reportedly irate. A member of the Chamber of Commerce warned of the recrudescence of the daunting "Yellow Peril."[119] What Pretoria did not seem to understand was that Japan had upset the calculus for white supremacy. Rather than adjust, once again the Nationalists were compelled to dig in their heels against reality. Thus, the *Rand Daily Mail*, as so often happened on matters racial, looked to the U.S. for guidance and concluded defiantly "California's fate a warning to Africa,"[120], insisting that those of Asian origin were taking over the Golden State and Pretoria should take heed.

Pirow, a close observer of the ebb and flow of whiteness, found white prestige to be falling, a development that would imperil South Africa—which was accurate insofar as white supremacy was concerned. The chief U.S. diplomat in South Africa spoke to Prime Minister J.B. M. Hertzog—a former Boer general during the war against Britain—who concurred.[121] The local press agreed.[122] Yet, despite this insight, these myrmidons of racism saw no alternative to digging in their heels and refusing concessions to the African majority or their assumed Asian allies.

By 1938, however, Albert Luthuli, the future Nobel Laureate and ANC leader, was in India, conferring with fellow stalwarts from Japan and China, in conversations which left a deep impression upon him.[123] These growing ties of solidarity provided further incentive to curtail the travel of Africans and the arrival in South Africa itself by Negro and Asian visitors with potentially subversive messages.

But Pretoria also had to be concerned with residents of South Asian heritage. In 2000 one member of this important community, Indres Naidoo, told an inquiring interviewer that "for all intent and purposes my grandfather is one of those people that made Mahatma Gandhi. My grandfather himself went to jail 14 times" and "my grandmother was among the very first women to go to jail in South Africa…when Gandhi returns to India in 1914, my grandfather hands over four of his sons to Gandhi and that included my father,

119. Report, 3 March 1931, Record Group 59, Decimal File, Box 6284.

120. *Rand Daily Mail*, 4 March 1931.

121. Report by L.J. Keena, 19 August 1939, Record Group 59, Decimal File, Box 6282.

122. *Cape Times*, 12 August 1939; *Johannesburg Star*, 19 August 1939.

123. Interview with Albert Luthuli, date unclear, Box 1, Folder 3, *Mary Benson Research Materials about the African National Congress of South Africa, UCLA-Los Angeles.*

and go to India, they study under.....[Rabindranath]Tagore [Nobel Laureate].....my father returns to South Africa 14 years later" and "my father was very active in the Communist Party of South Africa," as was his mother. And so was he.[124] He was not unique. Shantie Naidook, born in 1935, had a grandfather who, he said, was the "right hand man" of Gandhi, and like other South Asians in South Africa, he had roots in Mauritius.[125]

U.S. imperialism was quite concerned about these global ties to South Africa. As early as 1938, Washington was monitoring the "activities of Nazi organization in South Africa and South West Africa." The Nationalist Party of South Africa had an "anti-Jewish and anti-communist platform" which made this party of the apartheid to come the "best medium" for installing the "objectives" and "the exercise of German influence; and the Germans are extremely active in South Africa just now."[126]

This complexity was combustible. That same year, 1938, the U.S. Secretary of State was told about rioting in Johannesburg, which followed an alleged anti-Semitic assault amid shouts of "Heil Hitler!" The fascists were bearded and had cloaked themselves in the garb of the "Vootrekkers," hailed by many Afrikaners as the embodiment of their unique nationalism. "Johannesburg has never been famous as a 'law and order' town," said the U.S. observer drily, an allusion to the frequent routing and rousting of Africans. The "strength of the so-called Anti-Fascist group," he added, "is to be found in the Jewish community," which in turn had developed links with the Communist Party. The "fascists have, therefore, developed a strong anti-Semitic trend" and the bloc "is very solidly Dutch-South African." The police were "largely drawn" from the latter group too. Thus, the "Jewish element here is facing a most unpleasant situation" and this included some with roots in the U.S. itself.[127]

According to the U.S. envoy L.J. Keena, the Nationalists were gaining strength by "championing the cause of the Afrikaner 'poor whites' who.... they claim have been forced into that position by the Jews" and an elite that was "allowing natives and Orientals to hold

---

124. Oral History, Indres Naidoo, 3 October 2000, *University of Connecticut-Storrs.*

125. Oral History, Shanti Naidoo, 6 October 2000, *University of Connecticut-Storrs.*

126. L.J. Keena to Secretary of State, 8 April 1938, Record Group 59, Decimal Files, Box 6279..

127. H. Earle Russell to Secretary of State, 28 November 1938, Record Group 59, Decimal File, Box 6279.

positions which should be reserved for the white man." Thus, while Pretoria stipulated that immigrants must know at least one European language, apartheid architect Eric Louw sought to amend this to exclude Yiddish from this category, thereby choking off the flow of migrants fleeing Nazism in Europe.[128] It was Louw who would introduce a bill in 1939 that would result in the expulsion of all Jews who entered the Union during the previous nine years (it would also bar Communists from admission); understatedly, the U.S. delegate opined, that this maneuver "indicates the degree to which anti-Semitism has been incorporated in the creed of the Nationalists."[129]

Washington was told of how Louw—who during the 1950s was in and out of the U.S. on a regular basis, lobbying on behalf of his homeland— "linked the Jews with Communism" and "dealt at some length on the communistic menace if those doctrines were disseminated among the natives". Louw found it worrisome that a "disproportionate number of Jews [are] in the professions" in South Africa, alleging that "48%" of the physicians in Johannesburg were Jewish and 31% in Cape Town. There was an "increasing attractiveness," said Keena, "of the idea put forward by Nationalist speakers of replacing Jews in industry, commerce and the professions by Afrikaners,"[130] and this perniciousness too was a taproot of apartheid. Though the Communists were the sternest critics of anti-Jewish fervor, the U.S. legation did not seem terribly upset when Communists Edward Roux and Joseph Ngedhlane were convicted in Durban for contempt of the Crown, after attempting to circulate their periodical, *Umsebenzi*.[131]

Pretoria may have been aware of the credible rumors that the Communist International in Moscow had dispatched their Trinidadian operative George Padmore to South Africa and the Congo in the early 1930s and that, as a result, scores of potential cadres were smuggled out of the sub-continent for training—educational, political, and otherwise. Padmore was reputedly skilled in deploying decoys, codes, and various security stratagems.[132]

128. Report by L.J. Keena, 2 February 1939, Record Group 59, Decimal File, Box 6279.

129. Report by LJ. Keena, 9 February 1939, Record Group 59, Decimal File, Box 6280.

130. Report by L.J. Keena, 10 March 1939, Record Group 59, Decimal File, Box 6279.

131. Report, 31 July 1935, Record Group 59, Decimal File, Box 6279.

132. Holger Weiss, *Framing a Radical African Atlantic: African American Agency, West African Intellectuals and the International Trade Union Committee for Negro Workers*, Leiden: Brill, 2014.

Inevitably, the U.S. was influenced by the tendency in Pretoria to conflate the growing Jewish presence with the growing Communist presence. U.S. officialdom proved not immune to anti-Jewish fervor. Just before the escalation of anti-Semitism in Germany signaled by Kristallnacht,[133] H. Earle Russell declared that "business in Johannesburg is largely Jewish controlled and Jewish business activity permeates and, in many instances, controls not only ordinary commercial enterprise but the stock exchange, the mining industry and the professions...." This meant a "rapid growth of anti-Semitic feeling in the Transvaal and the Orange Free State." In the former province, he said, "much of the wealth...has undoubtedly been developed following the discovery of the reef gold fields by the Jews who in their turn have become wealthy...." This minority was opposed by the Nationalists and dependent on Smuts' United Party, a frail reed indeed, which was "bound to split when Smuts dies." As a result, many among this group were heading to the U.S. and "accepting heavy losses" in the process. A subtle sign was that they no longer were looking to London for help, as many did previously, with many asserting that the growth of anti-Semitism there was "most alarming." Russell continued, "the number of less wealthy individuals of the Jewish race [sic] desiring to proceed to the United States is constantly growing." With understatement, he concluded, "South Africa is a strange country politically."[134]

Just after Kristallnacht, there was an attempt to blow up a synagogue in Benoni, near Johannesburg. This led to synagogues, the German consulate, and various German clubs being placed under police guard. "The Jew, for years, has been very unpopular in South Africa," said L.J. Keena. Why? There was a "general belief," he said, "that if you examine any dirty business in [South Africa] you will find a Jew at the bottom of it." They were perceived to be perpetually outsmarting Afrikaners, though "about 300,000 white persons" in this benighted land were "living below the bread line"— "roughly one third of white population of the Union." Berlin, he said chillingly, "showed how" this matter could be resolved "by direct and violent action" against this beset community, i.e. though looting and displacement.[135]

---

133. Anthony Read, *Kristallnacht: The Night of Nazi Terror*, New York: Times Books, 1989.

134. Report by H. Earle Russell, 29 October 1938, Record Group 59, Decimal File, Box 6282.

135. Report by L.J. Keena, 1 December 1938, Record Group 59, Decimal File, Box 6282.

Contrastingly, 15,000 in Cape Town were marching against precursors to apartheid: Keena listened to a radio broadcast from Berlin in English that described this procession as a provocation by Africans and their Coloured allies "against the cruelty of the English…."[136]

Oswald Pirow, the German-speaking cabinet minister, denied emphatically that he attempted to effect a transfer of territory on the west coast of Africa to Germany at the expense of Belgium and Portugal—probably the oil rich region known as Cabinda—but Washington was skeptical about his adamant denial.[137] For it was during this time that the number of foreigners in Angola was increasing, including Euro-Americans, British—and Germans too.[138]

As this tumultuous decade unfolded, South Africa was being flooded by anti-Jewish propaganda worded in English and Afrikaans. Simultaneously, Germany was increasing its exports to South Africa at a faster pace than Britain, taking advantage of its pre-existing bases in South West Africa and Tanganyika.[139] By late 1937 the Communist intellectual Jack Simons was predicting the rise of a version of the Ku Klux Klan in South Africa and to validate this prediction he need look no further than what was unfolding in Cape Town, Johannesburg, and Durban.[140]

The popularity of Nazis in South Africa did little to dissuade him. He would not have been surprised by the October 1939 report from a leading U.S. envoy that "all amateur wireless transmitting stations" in South Africa had been shuttered, since too many were "communicating with Germany and German nationals in territories bordering the Union," for the purpose of "spreading Nazi propaganda."[141]

A few weeks earlier, in September 1939, Madie Hall Xuma was moaning to "My Dear Alfred" that she was "at a loss," in that "we had things under control until Britain and France declared war."[142] Now she was stuck in North America unable to cross the submarine infested

---

136. Report by L.J. Keena, 29 March 1939, Record Group 59,Decimal File, Box 6282.

137. Report by Division of European Affairs, State Department, 29 March 1939, Record Group 59, Decimal File, Box 6282.

138. Nicol Stassen, *The Boers in Angola, 1928-1975*, Pretoria: Protea, 2011, 83.

139. *Guardian*, 1 October 1937.

140. Ibid., *The Travel Notes of Ralph J. Bunche*, 344.

141. L.G. Keena to Secretary of State, 31 October 1939, Record Group 59, Decimal Files, Box 6285.

142. Madie Hall Xuma to "My Dear Alfred," 22 September 1939, Reel 1, *A.B. Xuma Papers*.

Atlantic to see her beloved, while the world was about to be riven by war.

Worrisome was the sense that Africans, fed up with colonialism, were in no mood to sympathize with London in this confrontation with Berlin. In 1938 Bunche told Yergan that he left Dar es Salaam "impressed with the extent to which pro-German and pro-Nazi propaganda" was "disseminated among the natives," received favorably because of their alienation from Britain. Thus, he was not optimistic about the idea of settling Jewish exiles from Central Europe in East Africa.[143] If Bunche had poked around further, he would have found a similar sentiment in South Africa. Fatima Seedat, a Communist from South Africa, recalled later that when "Hitler was bombing Britain, oh I'm jumping for joy, I say, 'kill these white.... kill them'. I was so excited and happy that Hitler is bombing...."[144] She was not alone. Andimba Toivo ya Toivo, a founding father of modern Namibia, said of his fellow Africans that "their understanding was that Hitler was going to liberate them."[145]

Nevertheless, after war erupted in Europe in 1939, the CP took the time to denounce the blatant "pro-fascism" then prevalent in the ranks of the Nationalists, including their bonding with the "grey shirts and other Nazi organizations" and swallowing whole their program: "anti-Semitism, attacks on 'international ' capital, race theories and the Communist bogey"—and the bankrupt idea that Berlin would defeat London, leading to a reversal of the so-called "Anglo-Boer war."[146]

143. Ralph Bunche to Max Yergan, 13 December 1938, Box 26, Folder 5, *Brian Urqhart Collection on Ralph Bunche, UCLA-Los Angeles.*

144. Oral History, Fatima Seedat, circa 2000, *University of Connecticut-Storrs.*

145. Andimba Toivo ya Toivo, *On Trial for My Country*, 33.

146. "Extracts from 'The War and South Africa'," by J. Morkel, Report Delivered at a Conference of the Communist Party held on March 23 and 24, 1940 in *South African Communists Speak*, 148.

Chapter 4

Pro-Nazi Sabotage in Pretoria, 1940-1945

ON 27 April 1940 Madie Hall Xuma departed Manhattan for her new home, destined for Cape Town and her spouse-to-be. The vessel that carried her headed on toward Singapore and what is now Indonesia after she exited at Cape Town, indicating the British and Dutch colonial heritage that was soon to be disrupted.[1] She did not arrive empty handed, entering South Africa with over $400, a portion of the estate left by her father, Dr. H.H. Hall of Winston-Salem, North Carolina.[2] Hours after disembarking, she married Xuma. She played the wedding march on the church organ, and then moved in to his comfortable 11-room house in Sophiatown, a suburb of Johannesburg. She quickly became an expert witness in comparing the two forms of rancid racism in Dixie and South Africa. The latter form was "worse" than North Carolina's, she thought. Racism was "more radical" in Johannesburg. "It's the worst country I have ever seen for antagonism and hate just because of the color of the skin...." Once, walking down the street en route to the office of her physician spouse, she spotted some pianos in a window, that she stopped to scrutinize— "and then the next thing I know," she said, still startled, "I was l[a]ying on the ground. Three white boys had hooked their feet in mine and pulled me down to the ground. They were just laughing...." Though she "could pass for Coloured," she found "if [I] was the only one standing waiting at the stop, the tram would leave me there...." Though she "lived better...in many ways" in her homeland— "I had four servants," for example—she was better connected in South Africa, with "more white friends, "including

1. List of Passengers, 27 April 1940, Reel 2, *A.B. Xuma Papers*.
2. Madie Hall Xuma to Secretary for Finance, 2 March 1943, *A.B. Xuma Papers*.

"people at the top,"[3] suggesting that a kind of social discrimination may have been more potent in Dixie.

It is instructive to speculate on the impact of U.S. Negroes encountering a land more racist than their own. Comparative analysis may have allowed them to see their homeland more clearly and ignited more sympathy for Africans too. Hall's view was shared by the writer Horace Cayton, who in 1939 bumped into some from the "white" minority in South Africa after traveling to Europe and adjudged them to be worse than the "rabid Negro baiters" of the U.S. South.[4]

She went on to become in 1943 the first President of the ANC's Women's League, though she was faulted for her aloofness and her failure to learn Xhosa, her spouse's tongue. She was re-elected in 1946, but symbolic of the declining importance of U.S. Negroes in African affairs, she was defeated in 1949—along with her spouse, ousted as leader of the ANC. They were a living symbol of a trans-oceanic and transnational identity that promised modernity[5]—but though U.S. Negroes received certain concessions as the Cold War detonated in the aftermath of World War II, part of the price of the ticket was the excision of those like Robeson, which did not sit well with an ANC and CP leadership that chose not to abjure socialism.

The role played by Madie Hall Xuma was refracted through the lens of a cultural extravaganza she wrote and produced in 1943. The *American Negro Revue—Progress of a Race by African Stars* was produced "in aid" of the ANC and included scenes of slavery—and slave markets—Negro spirituals, and more contemporary vignettes featuring the likes of Robeson and Congressman Arthur Mitchell. But also featured was Hattie McDaniel, the Negro actor, then being lambasted by the left because of her role as an enslaved servant in *Gone With the Wind*.[6] In addition to highlighting the questionable contributions of McDaniel, it was Ms. Xuma who sought—thankfully unsuccessfully—to produce in 1943 the repulsive play by Marc Connelly, *The Green Pastures*, which was replete with anti-Negro stereotypes. Rescuing her, the Department of Interior informed her that they were "unable to agree" to staging such

3. Emily Herring Wilson, *Hope and Dignity: Older Black Women of the South*, Philadelphia: Temple University Press, 1983, 147, 148.

4. Press Release, October 1939, Reel 10, #812, Part I, Press Releases, *Claude Barnett Papers*.

5. Iris Berger, "An African American 'Mother of the Nation'," 553, 555.

6. "American Negro Revue," 11 June 1943, Reel 2, *A.B. Xuma Papers*.

a production.[7] To her credit, Ms. Xuma, coming from a land where there were color differences among those of African descent, sought to bridge the gap between Africans and Coloureds in South Africa, observing that the latter "thought I would work with them but I let them know if they worked with me they would have to work with the African people…."[8]

Her language deficiency contributed to her initial social isolation. "I think I must have cried for three months after I arrived," she recalled—though her subsequent election to an ANC post suggests that she quickly adapted. Though the couple was ousted from ANC leadership by the rising tide of militancy borne by the likes of Nelson Mandela, Oliver R. Tambo, Walter Sisulu and their allies, the Xumas—at least A.B. Xuma—did not reject these new leaders either. It was in 1943 that the "Young Turks" spearheaded by Tambo and Mandela organized the ANC Youth League, targeting the presumed fustiness of the leadership symbolized by Xuma and his orientation toward U.S. Negroes. Their colleague, Joe Matthews, recalled a time when Tambo earned his spurs leading a student strike at Fort Hare, aided by the Communist Party: they were among those who sold the left-leaning periodical the *Guardian* on campus.[9] Initially, part of the critique of the Young Turks rested on anti-CP grounds—not unlike that made by the Pan Africanist Congress, which emerged about two decades later. The Communist Govan Mbeki, who was to become an ideological lodestar in coming years, thought that the extreme nationalism that eventuated in apartheid helped to shape a kind of nationalist counter-reaction that eventuated in the Tambo-Mandela challenge in the 1940s.[10]

Despite the Xumas' orientation toward the NAACP, which infamously steered clear of ties to Communists to their detriment and that of their constituency too, the South African couple did not evade Moses Kotane—a premier Communist—who became a valued advisor. During Xuma's tenure with the ANC, he appointed another Communist, Dan Tloome, to the newly created post of secretary-bookkeeper. J.B. Marks and Edwin Mofutsanyana were among his collaborators who happened to be Communists. Still, as

7. Department of Interior to Madie Hall Xuma, a943, Reel 2, *A.B. Xuma Papers*.

8. Emily Herring Wilson, *Hope and Dignity*, 148.

9. Oral History, Joe Matthews, 2 October 2000, *University of Connecticut-Storrs*.

10. Oral History, Govan Mbeki, 5 October 2000, *University of Connecticut-Storrs*.

early as 1942—driven by the uniqueness of the anti-fascist war—Xuma was pressured from the left and he began to see the CP as rivals for grassroots support.[11] When 7000 gathered at a CP rally in Durban in October 1942,[12] it presented a stunning reality that Xuma or any comparable leader would be hard pressed to ignore.

It was wise for Xuma to adopt this policy since the CP had long been stronger organizationally than the ANC. Thus, as the Communist Wolfie Kodesh observed later, his party's innovative tactics included appointing members to discuss events on trains with passengers—as if they had just met—in order to circumvent the issue of illiteracy. The CP was one of the few multiracial groupings in South Africa, which not only helps to account for why so many joined—not just "the philosophy of Marx and Engels," he said—but provided it with an automatic advantage in terms of recruitment and a vision of the future. Even among the business elite, he said, "you never found Afrikaners and Jews and Englishmen on the same committees in the boardroom…."[13]

Among those surrounding Xuma were not only mainstream ANC figures like Z.K. Matthews but Communists like Govan Mbeki, often coordinating "political" matters, and Mofutsanyana, who handled the "economic" portfolio, along with Kotane.[14] Communist comrades, like J.B. Marks and Mofutsanyana, were often nearby during pivotal moments.[15] "My dear Govan," waxed Xuma in late 1943, "we are all proud of you…."[16]

This friendliness toward Communists was reflected when the Council on African Affairs, founded by Robeson, felt sufficiently comfortable with Xuma's politics to make inquiries about his activities.[17] So motivated CAA greeted warmly the "Colored Peoples Conference" being held in South Africa in the summer of 1942.[18]

Xuma's friendliness toward those to his left was understandable. It was in July 1941 that the *Guardian* of Cape Town announced that "one of the most important events in the history of South African

---

11. Steven D. Gish, *Alfred B. Xuma*, 98, 100, 131, 134. See also *Guardian*, 3 July 1941: Kotane is pictured here.

12. *Guardian*, 1 October 1942.

13. Oral History, Wolfie Kodesh, 4 October 2000, *University of Connecticut-Storrs*.

14. Document, no date, circa 1943, Reel 2, *A.B. Xuma Papers*.

15. Minutes of Meeting, 21 June 1943, Reel 2, *A.B. Xuma Papers*.

16. A.B. Xuma to "My Dear Govan", 22 November 1943, Reel 2, *A.B. Xuma Papers*.

17. Frieda Nougebauer to A.B. Xuma, 1 July 1942, Reel 2, *A.B. Xuma Papers*.

18. CAA Press Release, 1 July 1942, Reel 2, *A.B. Xuma Papers*.

working class organization will take place in Johannesburg....when a great conference is to be held for the purpose of inaugurating a Trade Union for African Mine Workers," with a potential membership of 400,000.[19] Already, the left was speaking in words that would not be pleasing to Pretoria, advising by July 1942 that "gold is a non-essential commodity," advocating for the mines to be shut and the labor shifted elsewhere. "[The] position of gold," it was declared forthrightly, "rests...on the maintenance of the American gold buying policy,"[20] a further strike against this valuable industry. That the U.S. was also apparently considering the feasibility of seeking gold elsewhere hardly allayed Pretoria's concern.[21] The latter possibility may have been exaggerated, unduly influenced by the fact that republican gold prospectors were then sniffing for ore in neighboring Angola,[22] which if successful would have hampered Pretoria's bargaining power. The situation in Angola illustrated the major wartime trend that saw Washington pushing London aside. Lisbon and London had a partnership reaching back centuries; seeing Luanda as a British sphere of influence, the U.S. was determined to upset the status quo.[23]

It was assumed that the CP played a vanguard role in this epochal union organizing drive, implying that the ANC and the CP would share a base in the African working class, particularly the proletariat. Therefore it made sense for Xuma to avoid shunning Communists. The fact that the Labour Party in South Africa supported—in the words of one left-winger— "socialism" for "European workers" alone,[24] gave impetus to the contrasting CP view, which in turn made it difficult for the likes of Xuma to ignore their militant inter-racialism. Communist militant Wolfie Kodesh, born in 1918 to a mother from London and father from Belarus, later castigated Smuts and his United Party for their maltreatment of the working class of all stripes, thereby driving the Labour Party into the arms of Malan and the Nationalist architects of apartheid. This was no small thing, he said in an interview in 2000, since "there are more Afrikaans workers and artisans than there are English speaking artisans...."[25]

19. *Guardian*, 24 July 1941.

20. *Guardian*, 16 July 1942.

21. *Guardian*, 28 January 1943.

22. Nicol Stassen, *The Boers in Angola, 1928-1975*, Pretoria: Protea, 2011, 189.

23. "Weekly Morale Survey," circa 1943, Box 57, Folder 8, *Brian Urquhart Collection on Ralph Bunche, University of California-Los Angeles.*

24. *Guardian*, 23 October 1941.

25. Oral History, Wolfie Kodesh, 4 October 2000, *University of Connecticut-Storrs.*

Another reason for Xuma's flexibility was divulged when a U.S. official told the Secretary of State in 1943 that the Communist-led National Maritime Union of the U.S.—a grouping of seafarers—had opened a lodge for their members in Cape Town, which was deemed to be a "disturbing factor."[26] Many of the union's members, including a top leader—Ferdinand Smith[27]—were Negroes, cosmopolitan with money to spend. By September 1942 a visiting U.S. seaman in Cape Town was complaining publicly about the poverty he had witnessed.[28] But the influence was not unidirectional. When the CP in the U.S.A. moved to downsize and become a political association, a maneuver interpreted widely as liquidation,[29] this was strongly criticized by Reds in Johannesburg,[30] criticisms then echoed in London.[31] Repeatedly, the CP in South Africa denounced their U.S. comrades as a result of this disastrous maneuver.[32]

As noted by Rusty Bernstein, a leading Communist and ANC member, "party membership in Johannesburg had grown to around three hundred, rooted in trade unions and the national liberation movements" by the time of Madie Hall Xuma's arrival in Cape Town, and "fraternal relations had been established with Lekgotla la Bafo, a radical peasant movement in Basutoland," soon to be Lesotho, an independent nation where the liberation forces established a toehold. This movement, he said, was "led by the remarkable brothers Maphutseng and Josiel Lefela," their militancy supplemented by "small Communist parties in Mozambique and in Southern Rhodesia." As the 1940s unwound, entering the liberation movement was Oliver R. Tambo, a complete diplomat: gentle, quiet, and undemonstrative, with impeccable diction and manners.[33] His leadership of

26. James Orr Derby, Consul General Cape Town to Secretary of State, 8 May 1943, RG 59, Decimal File, Box 5122. He was citing the *Guardian*, 15 April 1943. See also Gerald Horne, *Red Seas: Ferdinand Smith and Radical Black Sailors in the U.S. and Jamaica*, New York: New York University Press, 2005.

27. Gerald Horne, *Red Seas: Ferdinand Smith and Radical Black Sailors in the U.S. and Jamaica*, New York: New York University Press, 2005.

28. *Guardian*, 10 September 1942.

29. Gerald Horne, *Black Revolutionary: William Patterson and the Globalization of the African-American Freedom Struggle*, Urbana: University of Illinois Press, 2014.

30. *Guardian*, 20 January 1944.

31. *Guardian*, 27 January 1944.

32. *Guardian*, 1 June 1944. See the letter from an "American merchant seaman" defending this maneuver. *Guardian*, 21 June 1945. This view was contested by Cape Town comrade I.O. Horvitch: *Guardian*, 28 June 1945.

33. Rusty Bernstein, *Memory Against Forgetting*, 61, 142.

struggles at Fort Hare presaged his stalwart leadership of the ANC itself.[34]

Like Xuma, Tambo too did not shrink from working with the CP, a wise move on both their parts since even the U.S. legation in Cape Town noticed the party enjoying an "increase among the so-called 'Native' populations." The U.S. observer, Lincoln MacVeagh, was not necessarily sympathetic to this trend, reproving a writer who expressed empathy for the dilemma faced by Africans forced to die for Pretoria in the war: "here again," he spat out venomously, exhibiting the racism and anticommunism that pockmarked his homeland, "the Communist nigger peers out of the woodpile."[35]

* * *

When Madie Hall Xuma arrived in South Africa, she may have noticed a familiar sight: a Hollywood film based on a popular U.S. novel that was accused of glorifying enslavement of her ancestors, a reprise of the controversy surrounding the book's South African publication. In Bulawayo, across the border in Southern Rhodesia, a journalist found *Gone with the Wind* to be the "talk of the town... we have all been discussing Scarlett [O'Hara, the fictional heroine]" as her expressions have already crept into the conversational repertoire...." With every passing day, this blockbuster was becoming more popular: "bookings got heavier as the week progressed," as "many people planned originally to see it twice."[36]

Critics were either too diplomatic—or too purblind—to see that this movie reinforced the most retrograde tendencies in Southern Africa, particularly with its slimy depictions of Negroes. The *Cape Times* praised the role played by the African American actor Hattie McDaniel, apparently finding her portrayal of a servile domestic slave engrossing. It was a "great film," bellowed their critic, imbued with "magnificence." The mildest descriptor deployed was "superb." Escalating, he claimed it "the greatest film ever made"; "one of the most realistic films to come to the screen," which "really needs to be seen a second time." The captivated reviewer found that "when this long film is ended and you part company with your seat

34. Oral History, Joe Matthews, 2 October 2000, *University of Connecticut-Storrs*.

35. Report by Lincoln MacVeagh, 19 January 1943, RG 59, Decimal File, Box 5121.

36. *Bulawayo Chronicle*, 11 October 1940.

you will want to stand up for a long, long time." Stand up for racism, perhaps.[37]

The *Johannesburg Star* also lauded McDaniel's representation of a "motherly Negro [mammy], loyal in her feudal attachment to the Southern family she is proud to serve," perhaps hoping that it would inspire Africans to act similarly. This paper too found the film "magnificent," reporting enthusiastically that it "scales the rarest heights of inspiration." Openly, it declared the "terrible plight of the Southern States" provided a lesson for Pretoria of the perils of retreating from the heights of white supremacy.[38] *Die Burger* concurred, finding it a "great film," and their analyst lamenting the "decline of the proud South of America during the civil war."[39]

The *Cape Argus* synthesized the consensus among elite European opinion, demanding that this work "should not be allowed to die with 1940," emphasizing that "it should be like a precious book that one keeps on one's shelves to read and read again...." Praising the author of the film's source material, Margaret Mitchell, the paper underlined that "she shows people that might be you or I, people making the same mistakes." In other words, the story was seen as a primer for Europeans to avoid the decline of white supremacy.[40]

From another shore, the left-wing *Guardian* praised *The Grapes of Wrath*, another Hollywood product, which in its illustration of "white" poverty may have underscored the ongoing attempt by the Carnegie Corporation of New York to bridge the class divide among Europeans.[41] Unlike Margaret Mitchell, the author of the novel on which this film was based—John Steinbeck—received high praise (along with fellow social realist Theodore Dreiser) in their pages.[42] In contrast to *Gone with the Wind*, the *Guardian* also lavished praise on the movie *Abe Lincoln in Illinois*, though it was not widely shown in South Africa. Why? "[Lincoln] said that the white man could never be free while the black man was in slavery;" "such ideas," it was said, "are not popular today," certainly "not in this country."[43] Similarly, the paper touted the unusually pro-Soviet movie *Mission to*

37. *Cape Times*, 5 July 1940.

38. *Johannesburg Star*, 13 April 1940.

39. *Die Burger*, 6 July 1940.

40. *Cape Argus*, 13 July 1940. The foregoing news items all be found in Box 135, *Margaret Mitchell Papers, University of Georgia-Athens.*

41. *Guardian*, 1 May 1941.

42. *Guardian* , 29 May 1941.

43. *Guardian*, 10 April 1941.

Moscow.[44] However, like the movie glorifying the gangly rail-splitter, the love letter to Moscow was only screened for a few days: ditto for *Stormy Weather*, the rare film with a U.S. Negro cast.[45]

* * *

After war erupted in Europe, swastikas predictably began popping up in Pretoria, placed provocatively on posters designed to attract recruits for London's military. "Reports of sabotage, treachery and even threatened uprisings are confirmed on a...widening scale," said the worried U.S. envoy. Hundreds of rifles were intentionally disabled by rebels, and in response new internment camps for ultra-rightists were being prepared. In a different vein, the so-called "Lend-Lease" program, designed by the U.S. to aid its British ally militarily, also allowed for a deeper penetration by Washington into South Africa.[46] Yet the most worrisome trend was reflected by December 1941, when a leftist journalist was denouncing the rise of pro-Berlin "saboteurs and dynamiters."[47]

By January when the CP met in Johannesburg, their assemblage was disrupted by throaty cries of "Heil Hitler," punctuated with the distinctive salute. Young men in the audience were shouting and interrupting uncontrollably and expressing a conspicuous anti-Jewish bias, as the meeting spiraled downward.[48] By May there were explosions in post offices, cutting of telephone and telegraph wires, sabotage of the railways, mysterious fires which destroyed valuable raw materials, bombs exploding randomly—all on "orders from Nazi spies," said the *Guardian*, as they raised the cry of "death to saboteurs...."[49] Breaking up CP meetings became habitual in Pretoria.[50]

Providing oxygen for Nazi aggression was the support they received from pro-Berlin elements close by in Mozambique.[51] In a "most secret" 1943 missive, London was told that it was "established

44. *Guardian*, 23 September 1943. Interestingly, while a student at Fort Hare Mandela played the role of the assassin, John Wilkes Booth, in a theatre production: David James Smith, *Young Mandela: The Revolutionary Years*, New York: Little Brown, 2010, 44.

45. *Guardian*, 16 March 1944.

46. 10 June 1940, L.G. Keena to Secretary of State, Record Group 59, Decimal File, Box 5123, *NARA-CP*.

47. *Guardian*, 18 December 1941.

48. *Guardian*, 29 January 1942.

49. *Guardian*, 28 May 1942

50. *Guardian*, 6 May 1943.

51. *Guardian*, 12 February 1942.

beyond reasonable doubt that the German Consul-General Paul Trompke in Lourrenco Marques [Mozambique]...and a band of willing assistants have been conducting espionage on a wide scale during the last year." They had "taken full advantage of dissident elements of the Union of South Africa to set up a network of agents" that was "centered in the Transvaal, notably in Pretoria," the seat of power. They were "closely connected with the Ossewa Brandwag Movement" and on "confidential terms with [J.F.J.] van Rensburg, the prominent South African lawyer and head of the O.B."[52]

Similarly, Madagascar was in the hands of pro-Nazi French colonialists; only 800 miles from Durban, at its nearest point it was only 240 miles from southeast Africa. This island, it was stated accurately, was—and is— "immensely important to the safety of South Africa...."[53] By July 1942 there were predictions that submarine activity in Madagascar served warning that South Africa could expect attack any moment.[54] Dar es Salaam continued to harbor pro-Berlin forces, a legacy of German colonialism. The "sinister hand of Germany," groused Frederick Burnham, the pro-London Yankee, "was always against us in the long struggle in Africa"[55]—true to the extent that Germany had dreams of its own for the beleaguered continent.

The U.S. continued to monitor events within the Jewish community there, especially the activity of the Jewish Board of Deputies[56], while taking note of rightist press reports that South Africa was "constantly receiving German immigrants,"[57] a trend that doubtlessly buoyed Pirow's reported plan to establish a "Nationalist Socialist State" in South Africa.[58] The anti-Jewish miasma had become so thick that even the Communist-influenced *Guardian* felt compelled to announce that "there is not a single Jew at the editorial board, circulation and business department" of the journal and "not one of the regular contributors to the paper is Jewish."[59]

---

52. "Most Secret" Report, 5 April 1943, KV 2/758, *National Archives of United Kingdom-London.*

53. *Guardian*, 19 February 1942.

54. *Guardian*, 2 July 1942.

55. Frederick Burnham to Lady Clave, 9 April 1943, Box 1, *Frederick Burnham Papers.*

56. Press Digest of Jewish Board of Deputies, 4 December 1940, Record Group 59, Decimal File, Box 5123.

57. *Die Burger*, 11 October 1940, RG 59, Decimal File, Box 5123.

58. *Die Vaderland*, 14 October 1940, RG 59, Decimal File, Box 5123.

59. *Guardian*, 16 September 1943.

U.S. nationals continued inquiring about migration there too.[60] It was unclear how Washington interpreted the story it filed concerning a German official's assertion that there was no so-called Native problem, only Asiatic and Jewish problems.[61] The official referred to the South Asian population that was concentrated mostly on the Indian Ocean coast, though there were still reportedly thousands of Chinese—"oppressed and victimized," said the left—who stood as the legacy of a policy formulated decades earlier, and later reversed, to exploit their labor.[62] The category of "Asian" was so expansive, said the left, that according to recently promulgated regulations in Durban, the Soviet leader Josef Stalin, being a "Georgian" and "Asiatic," would not be able to reside in certain sections of the city.[63]

In a sense, the extreme bigotry in South Africa boomeranged, creating numerous gravediggers eager to provide an indecent burial for the regime. Among these were Ebrahim Ibrahim born in 1937 in Durban. His parents were from Gujarat, India and in 2000 he recalled a time when "the lifts were only meant for whites. So, if you went up to the tenth floor you had to walk up, if you didn't use the lift at the back." Subsequently, he became a writer for the CP publication, *New Age*.[64]

The foundation for "National Socialism" in South Africa—which would be formally initiated in 1948 with the rise of apartheid—was laid years earlier by the Carnegie Corporation of New York. D.F. Malan, one of the architects of South Africa's exaggerated version of Jim Crow, toured a Johannesburg slum in 1940 and was stunned to find Europeans and Africans living cheek by jowl. Not only did this experience impel him toward apartheid—or a kind of affirmative action for Europeans of various classes, the poor not least—it also soured him on traditional capitalism, prodding him to support a kind of socialism for Europeans only: in other words, National Socialism.[65] Govan Mbeki is accurate in stating that Malan and his cohort were shaped by Nazism; "almost all the top leadership"

60. Ruth Hooper to Secretary of State, 22 April 1940, RG 59, Decimal File, Box 5123: She was a high school teacher in Franklin, Maine and a graduate of Bates College.

61. *Sunday Times*, 27 October 1940, RG 59, Decimal File, Box 5123: Dr. Manfred Zapp, head of the German Trans-Oceanic News Service, made this controversial assertion.

62. *Guardian*, 2 July 1942.

63. *Guardian*, 26 October 1944.

64. Oral History, Ebrahim Ibrahim, 20 October 2000, *University of Connecticut-Storrs*.

65. *Guardian*, 28 November 1940.

surrounding Malan "at one time or another went to Germany," he said.[66]

In short, Washington had to be concerned that the anti-London elite in Pretoria, still licking their wounds in the aftermath of the war decades earlier, would be predisposed to back Berlin during the titanic conflict that had commenced formally in Europe in 1939. The arriving German migrants augmenting those already influenced by Pretoria, installed as they were in nearby Windhoek and Dar es Salaam, provided multiple opportunities for mischief. The Ossewa Brandwag, or Ox Wagon Sentinels—their name a clear echo of the turn of the century war—provided a local version of European fascism and encompassed a goodly number of Afrikaners, claiming an astonishing 500, 000 members. Sabotaging London's war against Berlin was a primary goal.[67]

This group was not dissimilar to another Afrikaner formation, the Broederbond, which was accused of treason during the war.[68] Whereas Smuts' United Party termed the group threatening, some Communists tended to deride them as ludicrous, even childish and impotent. For all practical purposes, the Broederbond was coterminous with the Nationalist Party elite, and all three groups were like Russian dolls, each one nested within another. The kernel of the Broederbond, however, comprised the rising array of Afrikaner capitalists and professional men, who were then bumping against the growing Jewish population in this stratum, contributing to friction.[69] Like the Leninists they so staunchly opposed, they were divided into cells and acted as links between various groups, including the Nationalists and the Sentinels and their members in the press and industry.[70] Yet the essential glue for the Nationalists may have been the Dutch Reformed Church, which gave their ultra-right ideology an intense religious cast and, as the Rhodesian leader, Roy Welensky pointed out at the time, reached across the border.[71]

These ultra-rightists, charged the *Guardian*, were "Nazis in sympathy, in outlook and in aim." There was "evidence of military

66. Oral History, Govan Mbeki, 5 October 2000, *University of Connecticut-Storrs*.

67. Johann van Rooyen, *Hard Right: The New White Power in South Africa*, London: Tauris, 1994, 14.

68. *Guardian*, 3 August 1944.

69. *Guardian*, 7 September 1944.

70. *Guardian*, 21 September 1944.

71. A.E. Gray, Consul General Salisbury to Secretary of State, 9 October 1940, RG 59, Decimal File, Box 3577, *NARA-CP*.

organization and attempts to store arms by members," indicating that they were "getting ready for an attempt to seize power." The plan in Durban was "to carry out an armed attack, to capture and destroy magazines, stores, wireless stations and other key points and to kill off people whose names had been marked on lists...." They were "smuggling guns from Germans" in Mozambique and a "spy network had been established."[72]

Their view did not differ sharply from that of Lincoln MacVeagh, the U.S. emissary in Pretoria. His analysis, however, targeted Pirow, who he suspected may not have been born in South Africa; revealingly, German was spoken exclusively at his home; he was very friendly with Antonio Salazar, the fascist Prime Minister in Lisbon, not to mention Hitler's closest comrades. The Ox Wagon Sentinels were "cleverly designed," said MacVeagh, by German agents, the Broederbond, and Pirow. Their aims were "sinister," as suggested by their 1935 convening in Berlin at the office of Foreign Minister Joachim von Ribbentrop, with an agenda focused on capturing Pretoria—a meeting Pirow "probably attended," in MacVeagh's estimation. These terrorists had dynamite and made attempts to blow up bridges and manufacturing plants. They beat up soldiers on the streets, conducted espionage at ports, controlled South African Broadcasting—the major electronic press organ—and were thought to be infused with "gangsterism," all toward the earnest aim to "start a real armed rebellion." They also committed political murders. MacVeagh said they had 200,000 members in 1939. The 1937 Union Census revealed that of the 2 million-plus Europeans said to be in South Africa, only 17,810 spoke German but it was evident that this deficiency would not necessarily limit the ambition of the steely Sentinels.[73]

These contrasting trends presented the South African left with a complex challenge. The *Guardian* was skeptical of Washington, viewing suspiciously the early 1940 meeting between Sumner Welles of the State Department and Benito Mussolini. U.S. imperialism, it was said, "will encourage the Allies with supplies" while "in the meantime stealing their markets...."[74] Welles came under repeated fire in their pages. "A very rich gentleman with very rich friends who did his best to put through a Munich when he paid a 'mysterious' visit" to Europe in early 1940; like others of his ilk, he "would like to see

72. *Guardian*, 4 December 1941.

73. Lincoln MacVeagh to Secretary of State, 11 December 1942, RG 59, Decimal File, Box 5121.

74. *Guardian*, 21 March 1940.

the present war dropped and a united front made on the USSR...."[75] At this early stage of the war, their opinion of Welles' supervisor—President Franklin D. Roosevelt—was not exactly complimentary either. Their ultimate insult was to compare him invidiously to his predecessor, Woodrow Wilson— "tweedledum or tweedledee." The incumbent former New York governor was full of elevated verbiage but "in deeds as opposed to words, his record is as disgusting as that of [Neville] Chamberlain," the discredited British Prime Minister. Worse, "he helped to murder the Spanish Republic...."[76]

FDR's party comrade, Joseph Kennedy, father of a future president, fared no better. His face was plastered on page 1 of the leftist journal with the caption that he was leader of the "Appeasement International," willing to cut a deal with Berlin against the interests of Moscow. (Henry Ford was also placed in this cabal).[77] Saluted instead was Wayland Rudd, an "American Negro actor who is a naturalized Soviet citizen," who they pictured casting a vote—an exercise from which Africans were generally excluded on both sides of the Atlantic.[78] Like Ford, General Motors had "Nazi connections" and the same could be said of Du Pont of the U.S.[79]

Their prognostications proved to be canny. In December 1940, the *Guardian* predicted that the U.S. would "help Britain to survive," simply to "ensure that if she does John Bull will be Uncle Sam's junior partner not his rival"[80]—precisely what occurred in coming years.

Interestingly, despite its stern anti-fascism, this left-wing organ protested the overly broad brush applied in the internment of proliferating pro-Nazi elements. They thought that Pretoria—which objected to arming Africans despite the national security danger—was engaged in "indiscriminate internment of Germans" generally, among them "anti-Nazis,"[81] including one of their leaders, Fritz Feliner.[82] Washington, it declared, "intends to become Policeman of the whole world in the final stages of this war," i.e. "Protector and Champion in Chief of the Rights of Capital,"[83] which is precisely what was attempted in coming years.

75. *Guardian*, 25 July 1940.
76. *Guardian*, 17 October 1940.
77. *Guardian*, 29 May 1941.
78. *Guardian*, 3 July 1941.
79. *Guardian*, 4 December 1941.
80. *Guardian*, 27 December 1940.
81. *Guardian*, 25 July 1940
82. *Guardian*, 24 October 1940.
83. *Guardian*, 21 January 1941.

* * *

Despite visa difficulties, Negro missionaries continued to arrive in South Africa, notably those representing the AME denomination. Their self-interested view was that their "mission work" there was the "greatest work done by any Negro organization in Africa. It is perhaps the greatest expression and sympathy and helpfulness between American Negroes and Africans…." Emphatically it was stated that *"there is nothing like it in the world.* We have a payroll of teachers not exceeded by many American Negro institutions…."[84] The boastful church claimed that since 1892 it had grown to number 100,000 parishioners in Africa and 600 churches. It was probably because of their influence that King Sobhuza II of neighboring Swaziland, like so many on the continent, was aware of the plunder of U.S. Negroes, as he too labored under the accurate belief that lynchings were commonplace in the republic. On the other hand, the church's presence may explain the not wholly complimentary opinion that U.S. Negroes were like a "white man with black face."[85]

The puffery of the AME aside,[86] the fact that their presence was not wholly embraced by Pretoria was revealed in 1940 when Bishop R.R. Wright found himself stuck in Cape Town after a vessel refused to transport him because—as a journalist put it—they "did not like Negroes" and, anyway, the ongoing war gave the company inordinate bargaining power in determining which passengers they would or would not accept. Though, as was reported, "white Americans found no trouble booking passage home." It was a troubling sign for Pretoria when the White House took the time to intervene on Wright's behalf, assuring him "first class" passage.[87]

Back at his headquarters in Wilberforce, Ohio in early 1943, the bishop was still reflecting nostalgically while telling Xuma about "our work in South Africa and the fine association we had with you and our other South Africa friends…." Though he found "so

---

84. Press Release, April 1940, Reel 1, #760, Part III, Series I, *Claude Barnett Papers.*

85. *Louisville Courier-Journal,* no date, circa 1941, Reel 8, #176, Part III, Series IJ

86. Press Release, February 1939, Reel 6, #981, Part III, Series J: "Cuba hails AME leaders…..extended a royal welcome…marked the first time so large a number of colored American church leaders had come to Cuba…..met at the pier by the personal adjutant of Colonel Batista…."

87. Press Release, February 1940, Reel 8, #100, Part III, Series J.

much ignorance here about our South African people," he remained undeterred.[88]

This rebuff of Bishop Wright may have caused Bishop Frank Madison Reid, just appointed to preside in South Africa, to caution that "conditions make it unwise for me to give out any statement at this time about our anticipated trip" to the southern cone of the continent.[89] Even after this warning, Bishop John Gregg of the AME Church was still unable to find a single hotel in Durban to provide overnight lodging when he stopped en route to visit Negro troops then deployed on Arab soil.[90]

It was not just the AME winning souls through Xuma's good offices. The AME collaborated with the ANC in recruiting members, notably in the area of Lady Selborne, strategically sited close by Pretoria.[91] It was during this era that the church established a foothold in what became Namibia. Andimba Toivo ya Toivo seemed heartened that it was "established" in "opposition to the colonial attitude of the Rhenish Mission" there; "it stood at the beginning of the modern nationalist movement in Namibia and brought forth anti-colonial leaders such as the Reverends Markus Kooper and Bartholomeus Karuaera and Chief Hendrik Witbooi...."[92]

The AME's interest in the continent may have influenced others; thus it was in 1940 that Reid's interlocutor—Claude Barnett of the Associated Negro Press[93]—became the moving force behind the American Negro Exposition in Chicago, a kind of Pan-African equivalent of the World's Fair, though it was subsidized partially by the state of Illinois to the tune of $75,000, itself a testament to the lobbying muscle of U.S. Negroes. It was then that the Christian Council in Pretoria was asked to forward "two or three copies of editions of every African paper, magazine or publication in your district" that had been "printed by, staffed by Africans and where

---

88. Bishop R.R. Wright to A.B. Xuma, 5 February 1941, Reel 2, *A.B. Xuma Papers*.

89. Bishop Frank Madison Reid to Claude Barnett, 10 April 1941, Reel 8, #602, Part III, Series J.

90. Press Release, July 1944, Reel 29, #316, Part I, Press Releases.

91. Representative of AME to A.B. Xuma, 14 August 1943, Reel 2, *A.B. Xuma Papers*.

92. Andimba Toivo ya Toivo, *On Trial for my Country*, 62.

93. See Gerald Horne, *The Rise and Fall of the Associated Negro Press: Claude Barnett's Pan-African News and the Jim Crow Paradox*, Urbana: University of Illinois Press, 2017.

the ownership is African...."[94] Similar letters were sent to Mozambique, Tanganyika, Angola, Gold Coast, Sierra Leone, Kenya, and the Belgian Congo.[95] A leper mission in Cameroon sent a color film to Barnett for the ANE.[96] There were also negotiations for the delivery of Ethiopian paintings.[97] Photographs arrived from Liberia, Nigeria, and Southern Rhodesia, among other nations.[98]

Though innocent on its face, this outreach to colonized Africa was also a signal to colonizers—in Pretoria not least—that potential antagonists in Black America, who had begun voting in large numbers for FDR, were aware of colonialism's exploitative existence, now under stress because of war. Already in 1937, Robeson and Yergan had formed the Council on African Affairs precisely in the service of decolonization. Barnett's news agency had been receiving bundles of newspapers from Africa for some time and had been digesting their reportage into news accounts consumed hungrily by its readers. This did not bode well for the shelf life of colonialism[99]—of the settler variety or otherwise.

Thus, Barnett's agency was well aware of the pro-Nazi sabotage unfolding in South Africa; Barnett asked pointedly "why won't South Africa arm the natives?"[100] The African politico Henry Nxumalo was among those in South Africa writing for the U.S. Negro press—the *Pittsburgh Courier* in his case[101]—which allowed African Americans to keep a thumb on the pulse of colonialism in Southern Africa. In 1944 Julius Malie of the Progressive African News Agency in Johannesburg informed the ANP that there "always and

---

94. American Negro Exposition to J.M. du Toit, 23 April 1940, Reel 1, #869, Part III, Series J.

95. See e.g. American Negro Exposition to M. le Pasteur Patton, Evangelical Missionary Organization, Mozambique, 23 April 1940 and to Reverend J.J. Kakwell of Consultative Board of Federated Missions of Tanganyika and John Rucker, Allianca Evangelica de Angola and J.G.T. Obaka-Torte, Accra, etc., Reel 1, #871, Part III, Series I.

96. Report by Emory Ross, American Mission in Lepers, 24 June 1940, Reel 2, #830, Part III, Series I.

97. Frederick A. Sweet of Art Institute of Chicago to "Mrs. Solobillings," 26 June 1940, Reel 2, #871, Part III

98. Clara Bentley, Secretary of African Welfare Committee to Claude Barnett, 2 July 1940, Reel 2, #991, Part III, Series I.

99. George Arthur to Claude Barnett, 26 February 1941, Reel 5, #1024, Part III, Series G.

100. Claude Barnett to Alvin White, 18 February 1942, Box 141, Folder 1, *Claude Barnett Papers, Chicago History Museum.*

101. Ahmed Kathrada, *Memoirs*, Cape Town: New Holland, 2004, 46.

still is in South Africa on the part of blacks a burning desire to know more of the American Negro," requesting an ANP correspondent to be posted there. Reciprocally, he wanted to represent the ANP as a "Foreign Correspondent" and to distribute U.S. Negro periodicals in South Africa. Symptomatic of the uphill climb he faced was the fact that the envelope came embossed with the foreboding stamp declaring that it "was open when it reached the censor."[102]

The Smuts regime in Pretoria felt pressed on all sides. Restive Africans and pro-Nazi saboteurs appeared to be the main threats. But when the flinty leader mounted the rostrum to address the Union Parliament in March 1942, he was forthright in proclaiming that Japan constituted a more fundamental menace to the status quo than any European power and the situation was unprecedented. Indicating the depth of the problem, he pledged that if Tokyo's forces attacked his nation, he would not hesitate to deploy any weapons at his disposal—including the training and arming Africans, which could backfire spectacularly once the conflict ceased. The statement was so astonishing that the White House chose to retain a copy of his startling remarks.[103] To this end, Smuts wrote FDR, seeking an invitation to Washington to address Congress, seemingly unaware that the New Yorker's growing reliance on Negro voters was making his presence in the republic untenable.[104]

It was on Thanksgiving Day 1942 that Lincoln MacVeagh wrote the man he called "Dear Franklin," warning him "there are problems here of which America will very likely have to take more account in the future than in the past…."South Africa, he suggested, was a giant with feet of clay, "pitifully weak in the prize requisite of man-power," a direct result of the wasted human capital that racism demanded and which the U.S. too had to confront eventually. "On the basis of its population, the Union should be able to put fifty thousand whites and four hundred thousand natives and coloreds into the field as soldiers" but this was not as simple as it seemed at first glance. It was true that "most" of the Africans "all revere the memory of Queen Victoria and are loyal to the British Crown," but this feeling contrasted

102. Julius Malie to ANP, 22 April 1944, Box 175, Folder 1.

103. Pamphlet, "South Africa at War," Compiled by the South African Public Relations and Information Department, 1942, Official File 861, Box 1, *Franklin D. Roosevelt Presidential Library, Hyde Park, New York*. See also Gerald Horne, *Facing the Rising Sun: African Americans, Japan and the Rise of Afro-Asian Solidarity*, New York: New York University Press, 2018.

104. Jan Smuts to Franklin D. Roosevelt, 15 August 1943, Official File 861, Box 1.

sharply with the "fear of the native…still strong in the Afrikaner nation…." In fact, "distrust and dislike of Britain" was "powerful and widespread even today…." The "overmastering anti-Britishism [sic] of the typical Boer has provided a wonderful breeding ground for foreign propaganda," demonstrated by the "great masses" that "are pro-German today…." Indeed, "German allegations as to our imperialistic designs" were "echoed by Dr. Malan." Thus, "there is a lot of Old Kruger still," a reference to the Boer leader who vigorously fought the redcoats decades earlier.

Their fanaticism also led to the inevitable: "Boer prejudice jealously limits immigration," which was self-defeating for white supremacy—especially when "blacks are out breeding the whites at a great rate" and steadily undermining the bedrock concept of "a white man's country…." There was a certain "fanaticism" imbedded in this "fear": "Dr. Malan…has actually stated publicly that God created the blacks to be subject to the whites…." Thus, when General Smuts announced that he would "enroll the natives in the Army should the Japanese invade the Union, he was met with a storm of opposition even among his own supporters…." Already, some Africans had been "trained" to "shoot," unnerving Smuts' backers, not to mention pro-Nazi saboteurs. Their hysteria was extended to "black servicing crews for the anti-aircraft guns in the ports" in which Africans were "reported to be trained [as] gunners as well…." This measure was deemed necessary since "ports are most feebly guarded," indicative of a "very loose security situation…."[105]

Lurking underneath the security situation, however, was the massive waste of human capital tolerated in South Africa. "Natives are permitted to become fully qualified doctors of medicine," which A.B. Xuma could well attest, "and to practice surgery but are debarred from becoming most classes [sic] of carpenters and joiners. This sound fantastic," he asserted with wonderment, "but it is true…." The "organized European Labour Party" was the "chief obstacle," as he saw it, envisioning how it would pave the path for apartheid after the war. The "maintenance of a class privilege of one section of wage earners against another section of wage earners" was at issue. This "would appear to be in flagrant conflict with the fundamental ethics of socialism," he said in a statement that reflected the progressive winds then blowing gustily, a trend driven in part by something else he witnessed: the "natural gravitation" of many Afrikaners to "the side of Nazi Germany," which was utterly polarizing politically.

105. Lincoln MacVeagh to "Dear Franklin," November 1942, PSF Diplomatic, Box 51, *Franklin D. Roosevelt Presidential Library.*

Just as in the U.S., where the lifting of Jim Crow barriers was seen to boost the economy, in South Africa the idea was taking hold that "raising the consuming power of the native for the benefit of English trade is still certainly one of the cruder British objectives here...." MacVeagh instinctively understood the implication of such trends for his own country, informing the president that "however distant the affairs of the whites and blacks in South Africa may appear, we shall surely have to take account of them on the other side of the Atlantic someday..."[106]

MacVeagh sketched fault lines that would bedevil Pretoria-Washington relations for decades to come. Looming ominously for the Malan voter was the rising importance of the African American vote, already buoyed by the powerful dynamics unleashed by the anti-fascist war.[107] African American influence on the ascendant Democratic Party would make it difficult to ally closely with Pretoria. Washington's global obligations in the ideological conflict with Moscow made it difficult to establish a viable partnership with a nakedly racist South Africa. But that was not all.

Ironically, MacVeagh chose Christmas Day in 1942 to extend his dissection of Pretoria. "There is a Jewish problem here," he told "Dear Franklin" bluntly. "Of course," he amended, that problem existed "elsewhere" too but in Pretoria it was noticeably corrosive. There was "resentment of Jewish intrusion into every line of business, particularly real estate" and rather than diminishing, this bile was "growing" uglier daily.[108]

Washington was more flexible than Pretoria in handling what was called the "Jewish Question." When South Africa proved to be more recalcitrant in eliminating the more egregious forms of anti-Jewish fervor, it made it more difficult for Pretoria to curry favor with what had become one of its chief allies.

Inflexibility proved to be one of the South African state's prime defects. Pretoria, an island of whiteness surrounded by those not so endowed, felt that it had less room for compromise. As things turned out, the government might have been better served by pursuing compromise earlier and more deftly. By 1943 MacVeagh was becoming ever more exasperated with Smuts; his latest gambit was

---

106. Lincoln MacVeagh to "Dear Franklin," 25 December 1942 PSF Diplomatic, Box 51.

107. Gerald Horne, *Black Liberation/Red Scare: Ben Davis and the Communist Party*, Newark: University of Delaware Press, 1994.

108. Lincoln MacVeagh to "Dear Franklin," 25 December 1942, PSF Diplomatic.

"demanding a rupture of consular relations with the USSR on account of alleged machinations of the Soviet[s] tending to stir up the natives against the whites...." This effort was coupled with the "rumor" that "President Roosevelt intends to establish a native state in Africa after the war." Under pressure from raucous Africans, Nazi conspirators, the rising Japanese—and more—Pretoria did not respond coolly and competently but instead potentially jeopardized ties to Washington, which was generally sympathetic to the regime.[109]

Smuts' gambit placed Washington in a tricky position. The U.S. was officially friendly to its Soviet wartime ally but simultaneously nervous about the intentions and capacities of this regime. Neither Washington nor Pretoria could ignore the headline in the *Guardian* of September 1941, chortling over the "greatest pro-Soviet meeting yet" in Johannesburg.[110] "For better or worse," chimed the "Friends of the Soviet Union" in South Africa, "the destiny of our country is bound up with the fate of the USSR...."[111] This came after the catastrophic June 1941 invasion of the Soviet Union by the Nazi hordes. By November, thousands were demonstrating in protest, in an event addressed by CP leaders Kotane and William Andrews.[112] "Up to a year ago, " said a 1943 U.S. report from Cape Town, "there was no Russian consular representative in the Union," but things had changed dramatically.[113] "Communism is becoming increasingly attractive to the vast colored majority in South Africa," said another U.S. emissary near the same time.[114]

Pretoria's rigidity made it more difficult for rulers there to analyze the state's objective dilemma, particularly the necessity of reinforcing its vastly outnumbered "white" population. There was a

109. Lincoln MacVeagh to President Roosevelt, 25 March 1943, PSF Diplomatic, Box 51. Pretoria did not help its tenuous case in Washington due to misdeeds of some its delegates. See "Memorandum of Conversation," 23 December 1940, Box 166, *Sumner Welles Papers, Franklin D. Roosevelt Presidential Library.*: The "Commercial Secretary" of the South African legation "had been sending through the mail obscene literature" and, thus, "his official activities in this country should be terminated and that he should leave" the U.S.

110. *Guardian*, 11 September 1941.

111. Pamphlet, no date, Box 1, *Communist Party of South Africa Collection, Stanford University-Palo Alto, California.*

112. *Guardian*, 13 November 1941.

113. Lincoln MacVeagh to Secretary of State, 7 August 1943, RG 59, Decimal File, Box 5121.

114. Goodhue Livingston to Secretary of State, 13 July 1943, RG 59, Decimal File, Box 5121.

ferocious debate on immigration during the war at the parliament headquartered in Cape Town. At one point, the assertion was made that South Africa could "support a population of 10,000,000 Europeans" but Afrikaners fearful about the erosion of their influence generally dissented. Eric Louw, their chief spokesman, worried about the impact of such an influx on "poor whites," many of whom were Afrikaners, but was willing to make a strategic concession to admit more immigrants, as long they "were not Jews." Breathing fire, Louw argued that "the Jewish population of South Africa was already too large," a feeling that—it was reported—was "shared by members of the United Party," Smuts' presumably more enlightened party. The emboldened Louw declared that "there is a Jewish Problem in South Africa which has been largely created by the Jews themselves and by their preponderance in the professional, commercial and industrial activities of the country." The "consensus of opinion here," said Edward Groth, the U.S. envoy in Cape Town, "is that strong steps should be taken without delay to prevent the Jews from acquiring greater commercial and economic power than is now in their hands and that in no circumstances should further Jewish immigration be permitted...." The authorities were "constantly receiving complaints that Jewish immigrants who arrived even after the outbreak of the present war were already prospering to an amazing degree at the expense of South African nationals...." Louw was deluged with "hundreds of letters approaching 'fan mail'...congratulating [Louw] on his courage...." Groth dismissed the idea that this phenomenon was exclusive to the Afrikaner population; they may have been the pacesetters, but they were not alone since "the majority of those letters are reported to be from the English speaking sections of the population," which, he said, were more directly competing with Jews in professions and businesses than the heavily rural Afrikaners. Whatever the case, this "unfortunate anti-Semitic feeling appears to be widespread." Forwarded to Washington by Groth was a proviso from Louw which specifically barred "members of the Jewish race" from becoming immigrants to South Africa.[115]

Predictably, such open bigotry backfired. The CP leader Brian Bunting recalled that his party had "lots of support from Jewish business people who tended on the whole to be more progressive than non-Jewish" entrepreneurs. Similarly, he said, the pervasive racism

115. Edward Groth to Secretary of State, 11 March 1944, Box 37, *War Refugee Board Records, Franklin D. Roosevelt Presidential Library*. Attached to this correspondence is the memo from Louw, dated 29 February 1944.

in South Africa also meant the CP "raised large sums of money from the Indian community" too.[116]

There was, then, a material basis for the CP's concern with this pestilent form of bias. The party blasted the "grotesque figure of 'Hoggenheimer' representing the bloated capitalist interest of the gold mines" and portrayed as Jewish. "Apparently," said the *Guardian* this was "not menacing enough to raise alarm" since the "new figure" of derision was "no less than Moses Kotane," the African Communist.[117] This was understandable in a sense: Andimba Toivo ya Toivo, a founding father of Namibia, declared that at that time one of his "teachers," Peter Kalangula, "used to get Communist material from the Secretary General of the Communist Party in South Africa, Moses Kotane...."[118]

Kotane is, in many ways, the unheralded father of South Africa's liberation. During these dark days, this comrade upheld loftily the banner of radical transformation. His comrade Ben Turok described him as a "man of great caution, very great caution, very great earthy wisdom," who was "very profound politically and operationally...."[119] In the immediate postwar era, James Calata, Secretary General of the ANC, expressed a gathering consensus about Kotane. "I do not object to these party men as members," of the ANC, he said, "and even as leaders of Congress" since "these people have the gift of the gab"—crucially in a multilingual fashion—"and they know how to sway the audience at meetings." Though a bit wary, he added, "I welcome the leftists for they are progressive...."[120]

Later, the CP leader Brian Bunting pointed out that during the war, a CP newspaper had a circulation of 55,000, indicative of the organization's strength. "I don't think there's another country in the world," he boasted with cause, "where the relations between the Party and the national movement," meaning the ANC, "have been of the same order as we have in South Africa...." The man principally responsible for this critical linkage, he argued, was Kotane.[121]

As the U.S. was supplanting its North Atlantic neighbors as the power capable of defending an outmoded settler colonialism, Pretoria

116. Oral History, Brian Bunting, 3 October 2000, *University of Connecticut-Storrs.*

117. *Guardian*, 22 June 1944.

118. Andimba Toivo ya Toivo, *On Trial for my Country*, 45.

119. Interview with Ben Turok, 15 March 1973, Box 10, *Gwendolen Carter Papers, University of Florida-Gainesville.*

120. James Calata Statement, 4 December 1947, Reel 4, *A.B. Xuma Papers.*

121. Oral History, Brian Bunting, 3 October 2000, *University of Connecticut-Storrs.*

was insufficiently nimble to adjust its anachronistic anti-Semitism to make itself a more attractive partner. Instead, Washington was being flooded with reports about the unalloyed bigotry that stained Pretoria, which could have been downplayed or excused or rationalized if it had been limited to Africans. There was "more vicious sabotage and espionage in South Africa,'" Washington was told, "than in any other country," certainly in Africa. "The people are also anti-Jewish and frequently loud in their denunciation of the British and the Jews," while "subversive activities are common among the officials of the country. Very many believe that General Kloppen, in charge of South African troops at Tobruk," the North African site of an epochal wartime battle, "had double crossed his men," leading to a severe setback for the Allies. The labor shortage in South Africa "could easily be remedied if black people were allowed to be used for other than the most menial jobs."

This report was filed by Albert Edward Daff of Hollywood's Universal Pictures—Australian by birth, he was in the process of becoming a U.S. citizen—representing a firm desperately concerned with market penetration and part of an industry where Jewish Americans played a pivotal role. His comparative reflections on South Africa were based upon annual travels of a stunning 100,000 miles. Perhaps because of the association of cinema with the Jewish community—including I.W. Schlesinger of Johannesburg, who operated the only motion picture studio in the land—he was struck by the "bombing of motion picture theatres showing British propaganda films." There was also a "slow down in many factories and industries engaged in manufacturing war equipment," along with a "tie up of shipping...." There was also a companion effort to "evade United States export restrictions by purchasing United States goods in Argentina and Brazil," depriving the North American republic of profits rightfully theirs. Worryingly, Daff "pointed out that United States colored troops are positively not wanted in South Africa," hindering the war against Berlin, not coincidentally; overriding all else was the "fear" of these Negroes' "possible effect on these natives...."[122]

The critical role of Schlesinger was revealing of the dilemma in which the U.S. was placed when confronting anti-Semitism. The Hollywood giant 20th Century Fox was in the "strongest possible competition" with Schlesinger who, it was said, had a "complete monopoly in South Africa." Murray Schwartz, the firm's executive

122. P.S. Brown to Louis Beam, citing report by Albert Edward Daff, 14 August 1942, Box 88, *Louis Beam Papers, Franklin D. Roosevelt Presidential Library.*

who presided over foreign distribution felt this was to the "financial detriment of the American industry...." With mounting anger, he acknowledged that "our company has for a number of years fought a grim battle against the Schlesingers and we suffered terrible losses...." There was a "necessity of secrecy" in discussing this fraught matter, said Schwartz, as the Schlesinger empire was seen as veritably ubiquitous.[123]

It was not easy for Washington to turn its back on Pretoria altogether because supporters of its own Jim Crow made for a built-in constituency for the emergent apartheid. Thus, when during the war Pretoria sought to make a "bulk order for one million 12 bore shotgun cartridges and three million 22 caliber long cartridges" for "essential civilian use," it was difficult to turn this request down, though—as in Dixie—Africans would be the likely recipient of this birdshot.[124]

Washington's basic quandary was exposed when Harlan Clark of their legation visited the farm of Dr. J.F.J. Van Rensburg, a leader of the Sentinels, who also happened to have studied German intensively (in his extensive travels he met both Hitler and Goering). When Clark arrived at Rensburg's abode in November 1943, his host had just finished listening to a stem-winding speech by Hitler from Munich, transmitted by radio. Exchanging stilted pleasantries, Clark revealed that he was from Ohio. Stiffly, the pro-Nazi leader said he preferred Dixie since "the Southerners know how to keep the Nigger in his place." Turning to the war, he expressed reservation over Tokyo's ascent, then assailed Bernard Baruch and Henry Morgenthau as agents of a supposed Jewish conspiracy. But reassuringly, he told Clark that "as a matter of course, the Afrikaners will always support the United States against England." However, the loquacious speaker also revealed that the "courts" and "police force"—even Smuts' "bodyguards"—were "honeycombed" by the Sentinels he commanded. Boastfully, he concluded, "I have kept two full divisions from fighting against the Germans and thereby have weakened the British effort...."[125] The pro-Nazi leader was said to aver that "the backbone of Afrikaner republicanism is...that a German victory is

123. Murray Schwartz, Vice President, 20th Century Fox Film Corporation to Francis Colt de Wolf, Chief, Telecommunications Division of the State Department, 15 May 1944, RG 59, Decimal File, Box 5126.

124. Letter to Secretary of State, 13 May 1944, RG 59, Decimal File, Box 5125, *NARA-CP*.

125. Harlan Clark to Secretary of State, 20 November 1943, RG 59, Decimal File, Box 5121.

an obvious condition for an Afrikaner Republic to come into existence."[126] As matters evolved, he was wrong: for under the influence of the North American republic, a different republic was proclaimed a few decades after his tendentious remarks were uttered.

It was not easy for the legation to dismiss these concerning remarks as idle gossip, for the Secretary of State was told a few days earlier that "there is little doubt but that the phone conversations of American government officials are recorded" and "there is a possibility that knowledge of some of these conversations is finding its way to quarters other than ....Smuts...," suggesting they were falling into the purview of those like Van Rensburg.[127]

Even the good news for Smuts contained mixed messages. The increasingly influential Communists concurred with his critique of Tokyo, denouncing the purported Japanese cry of "out with the white man," which amounted to "anti-white hatred," converting "the British and Americans" into the "Jews' of the Far East." Instead of seeing the February 1942 fall of Singapore as a step along the path of the erosion of white supremacy, it was seen instead in apocalyptic terms, presaging an uncertain fate for South Africa itself. Of course, the fact that Smuts and the Communists were on the same side could serve to undermine his already parlous position with the Afrikaner elites who were to install apartheid within a few years.[128]

Doubtlessly, this elite was not comfortable with the left's idea that Tokyo's successes "have exploded once and for all the myth of 'Nordic' superiority" in that "the yellow skinned Asiatic is if anything superior to the 'blond Aryan'"; this meant that a "growing number of darker skinned peoples look with sympathy" to Japan, which was "based on a racial sentiment that has been developed in them by their white rulers." In response hundreds met in Cape Town and passed a resolution proclaiming that "large numbers of Africans [were] deluded into believing that the Japanese may bring them freedom from colour bars.... [and] may even wish for a Japanese victory...."[129] Their conclusion was unsettling for Pretoria: end racism to confront the threat from Tokyo. The continued chatter about Smuts arming Africans, Coloureds, and Asians in order to blunt an

126. *Guardian*, 10 September 1942.

127. Report to Secretary of State, 29 October 1943, RG 59, Decimal File, Box 5122.

128. *Guardian*, 26 February 1942.

129. *Guardian*, 13 March 1942.

expected Japanese invasion suggested that the cure might have been worse than the illness, as far as Pretoria was concerned.[130]

But the Afrikaner elite was compromised and ultimately hoisted on its own petard: how could it root for Berlin while opposing Berlin's ally in Tokyo? Should not this have been a tipoff that white supremacy was becoming too ensnarled with contradiction to be sustained? This insight was generally absent from the thinking of Dixie and Pretoria, the latter of which had convinced itself that white supremacy was not simply a miserable stage in history but an eternal verity.

The South African left enlisted the prestige of Robeson in order to rebut Tokyo's seductive appeal,[131] as well as its own Kotane.[132] Unfortunately, the left bent the truth in order to combat Japan, contending that there was "no colour bar in U.S. forces,"[133] a false claim made to distinguish the republic from the monarchy. The Communist influenced left seemed duty bound to burnish the image of U.S. imperialism, to better mobilize against fascism. Trafficking in falsehoods to do so, however, was simply self-defeating. Thus, the left also trumpeted yet another false claim that "skilled jobs for U.S. Negroes" were allocated in airplane plants. The intention was noble: if the U.S. can do it, why can't South Africa? The problem with this tactical mendacity was the long-term corrosive impact on the left's credibility.[134]

Nonetheless, Robeson's demand to "arm the Africans," proclaimed at a Manhattan rally of thousands and reported in Cape Town, was designed to unsettle complacent Europeans. Like a military strategist, Robeson determined that with Pretoria sending a good deal of its military to sites like Tobruk, while harboring a "strong fifth column," South Africa was vulnerable. Sarcastically, he opined that Malan and his ilk were declaring "rather than arm the non-Europeans, let South Africa fall."[135]

There was grave wariness in Washington about pro-Berlin sentiment in Pretoria. Robert Sherwood, the celebrated writer, was recruited for his counsel. By mid-1943, he said, there was serious contemplation of the Union leaving the war if General Erwin Rommel captured Alexandria, which had been expected. Since the route via

130. *Guardian*, 19 March 1942.
131. *Guardian*, 14 May 1942.
132. *Guardian*, 9 April 1942.
133. *Guardian*, 17 September 1942.
134. *Guardian*, 26 November 1942.
135. *Guardian*, 11 June 1942.

the Cape was the only means of supplying Allied forces in both the Middle East and the Far East, this was no minor matter. Fortunately, South Africa preferred U.S. movies and automobiles—though many among the Afrikaner masses considered the republic both godless and immoral. The goldmines were dependent upon U.S. machinery, another plus. As it had for decades, Pretoria continued to "treat the Negroes with more severity than any other white people," said this high-level Washington operative, and this would come to complicate bilateral relations postwar. But at that point, the mandate was clear: it was insisted that "we must concentrate our efforts upon the whites," and, complementarily, "we must be very careful in making any special appeal" to Africans, since the "Axis is already making effective use" of Washington's alleged squishiness on racism. This served to "arouse the color prejudice of South Africans against us…." There was the related matter of "soft-pedaling the more strident champions of India in the United States…." However, Washington was advised to find a way to erode the calcified anti-Jewish bias, as well as the "considerable anti-Catholic sentiment," while holding the line against the retreat of anti-African bias. Anticommunism was a special case given the awkwardness of sheltering the Moscow ally. "Avoid the label 'Communist' as a prefix to 'Russia'" was the advice, adding boldly, "[do] not hesitate to talk approvingly and admiringly of Russia's part in the war."[136]

This memorandum reflected a peculiar situation: Nazi saboteurs and anxieties about Japanese invasion were not the only problems endured by South Africa during the war. Anti-fascist breezes from abroad and at home probably emboldened Africans, leading to what were described as the "Pretoria Riots," leaving a European soldier slain.[137] These were followed by what were described as "serious race riots" in Johannesburg, beginning after a tramcar trampled an African. The uprising involved thousands: one African died, and six others were seriously injured, while fifty were admitted to hospital. Although only one European was hospitalized, some among this community began to arm themselves and then started a fire at a local African newspaper, the *Bantu World*.[138] These events were preceded

136. Memorandum from Robert Sherwood, Office of War Information, 3 July 1943, Box 24, *Phileo Nash Papers, Harry S. Truman Presidential Library-Independence, Missouri.*

137. *Guardian*, 28 December 1943 and 7 January 1943.

138. *Guardian*, 9 November 1944.

by what was described as an "African strike wave," adding to the overall complexity.[139]

By April 1943 internment camps were being considered in Pretoria for "non-Europeans" who were said to have abused their democratic rights. Van Rensburg was then threatening that if elections did not veer in his ultra-right direction, his Sentinels would openly resort to violence—and this, said the *Guardian*, would mean the rise of "the Fascist state."[140] Van Rensburg had reason to issue threats, for it was in August 1943 that the CP made its first appearance in Union-wide elections and netted almost 7000 votes, "11 percent of the total" as reported (of course, the overwhelming majority of the populace were barred from casting a ballot). In Cape Town, about 20% of those voting voted for the Reds.[141]

Max Yergan weighed in on these elections on behalf of the CAA, reproving the "pro-fascist record of Malan and Pirow," along with their anti-Semitism, while praising the steadfastness of the Negroes and Africans.[142]

In Cape Town, the picturesque fogbound metropolis, ringed by mountains and hugging the ocean, Communists made history with the victory of two candidates who stood for the City Council, including Betty Sacks (also known as Betty Radford), the editor of the *Guardian*, and her comrade, Sam Kahn.[143] Hilda Watts was elected as the first CP City Councilor in Johannesburg-Hillbrow.[144] The growth of the organized left, the atmosphere created by the anti-fascist war, even the idea that Africans might be armed, led to Robeson's Council on African Affairs providing "appreciative recognition" to Colonel Deneys Reitz, Minister of Native Affairs, when the decision was taken to "relax the Native Pass Laws...."[145]

But Smuts was not cowed by this electoral and political detour because, according to his detractors, he was ambitiously seeking to extend the remit of South African imperialism northward, surging beyond the Limpopo River and demanding a "Greater South African Federation," propelled by mine barons' lust for an increased supply of cheap African labour.[146] Smuts demanded the annexation

139. *Guardian*, 28 January 1943.
140. *Guardian*, 1 April 1943.
141. *Guardian*, 6 August 1943.
142. CAA Press Release, 16 July 1943, Reel 2, *A.B. Xuma Papers*.
143. *Guardian*, 9 September 1943.
144. *Guardian*, 2 November 1944.
145. Max Yergan to Colonel Reitz, 1 July 1942, Reel 2, *A.B. Xuma Papers*.
146. *Guardian*, 9 December 1943.

of Swaziland, Bechuanaland. and Basutoland, raising tensions with a London already weakened by the war, though dovetailing with Washington's strategy of twisting the tail of John Bull. A left-wing journalist thought the plan would backfire by increasing the amount of cheap labor to exploit, which would not be helpful to "a large section of the whites" already enduring "poverty and cultural degradation." These imperialistic designs were, it was said, "taking a leaf out of America's book."[147] Such a plan would bolster "the creditor country, the moneylender to the world," i.e. endorsing objectively "what American propagandists like to call the American century," a "century of Dollar Imperialism...."[148]

South African imperialism, a junior partner of the U.S. version, also sought domination through capital investments and trade. But their African policy was riddled with contradiction, since an Africa kept purposefully underdeveloped was hardly able to play the role for Pretoria that Europe was to play for Washington.[149]

His willingness to coordinate with U.S. imperialism, even while seeming to foil his patron in London, earned Smuts an invitation to San Francisco in 1945 to aid in drawing up what became the Charter of the United Nations. The hirsute general told his legislature that despite their disagreements, what united the once warring antagonists—Boer and Briton—behind his proposal was "that it is the fixed policy to maintain white supremacy." The problem here was not only that the rapidly concluding war was discrediting this moth-eaten notion, but that even its heightened articulation could not obscure the point that opposition to widespread European immigration—a position staunchly held in Pretoria—was not fortifying white supremacy when it needed it most. More to the point, as London faded and Washington stepped forward, the latter was being forced to retreat from the more egregious aspects of white supremacy, thereby impairing apartheid just as it was being conceived.[150]

Smuts should have paid closer attention to the stormy protests against Pretoria's maltreatment of South Asians at the founding of the U.N. It did not take a seer to recognize that as India and Pakistan came to independence, South Africa would come under unremitting pressure from New Delhi and Islamabad, pressure which proved to be decisive. Harry Lawrence not inaccurately referred to this as a

147. *Guardian*, 23 March 1944.
148. *Guardian*, 4 May 1944.
149. *Guardian*, 29 March 1945.
150. *Guardian*, 22 March 1945.

"difficult matter" in the founding.[151] Andimba Toiov ya Toivo was correct in asserting of India (and the Soviet Union), "those are actually the two countries that saved Namibia, otherwise we could have become South Africa's 'fifth province.'"[152]

As it became ever clearer that Washington rather than Berlin would prevail during the war, Pretoria was sufficiently agile to begin a steady shift toward the North American republic. Even visits by low-level officials from the U.S. were greeted with elation. Thus in 1944, when Hugh Bennett, a relatively insignificant official, was due to arrive, Elmer Davis, the Director of the Office of War Information in Washington, found that the "prospect" of this "visit has aroused unusual interest in South Africa where the Minister of Agriculture said that it was 'the best news we have heard in a long time'" and "would pay dividends for the United States in a distant allied country."[153] Bennett happened to be the republic's foremost expert on soil conservation.[154] He may have recognized what the *Rand Daily Mail* acknowledged: because of soil erosion the African continent was "moving slowly towards America" and this actual and figurative closeness had implications for Pretoria's future since the "average American view" of South Africa could be "summed up in the words: gold, diamonds, ostrich feathers and Zulus," along with the "idea that South Africa has a colour problem, a poor white problem, an 'Indian' problem" and other related issues. This made South Africa a "novelty" to the U.S., it was suggested, but—speaking of the European minority— "nor are we much better acquainted with the United States."[155]

This was largely but not wholly true. It was also in 1944 that the U.S. Department of Justice proposed an "equity suit against De Beers," which had a "monopoly of industrial diamonds," resulting in "monopoly prices being paid for the 13,000,000 carats imported annually" to the U.S. The cartel controlled 95% of the world's production but "refused to sell a large quantity of diamonds" to the U.S.

151. Harry Lawrence to Charles Fahy, 19 November 1947, Box 88, *Charles Fahy Papers, Franklin D. Roosevelt Presidential Library.*

152. Andimba Toivo ya Toivo, *On Trial for My Country*, 58. See also "Exchanges of Correspondence Between the Governments of India, Pakistan and the Union of South Africa, in Regard to a Round Table Conference to Discuss a Solution to the Indian Question in the Union—July 1949 to June 1950," RG 59, Decimal File, Box 2929, *NARA-CP.*

153. Elmer Davis to Marvin Jones, War Food Administrator, 6 May 1944, Folder 23, *Hugh Bennett Papers, University of North Carolina-Chapel Hill.*

154. Scrapbook, no date, Folder 45, *Hugh Bennett Papers.*

155. *Rand Daily Mail*, 17 August 1944.

even as this commodity was "vital to the war effort." De Beers was garnering huge profits, paying dividends of 40%, a humongous sum grounded in brutal exploitation of labor. Along with the Afrikaners' sympathy for Nazis, the diamond factor complicated bilateral relations.[156]

The war and its aftermath would serve to resolve this latter problem partially. Approaching his expiry, the old Boer battler Fredrick Burnham admitted that he felt "sure that these countries," meaning the Union of South Africa and the United States of America, "will be drawn closer as the years go by." "That nation," meaning the South Africa, "occupies a strategical position in the world and many of their problems are the same as those of our own."[157]

---

156. Memorandum, 28 January 1944, Box 175, WHORM CO 141 South Africa 59200 and CO 143 Namibia, *Ronald Reagan Presidential Library-Simi Valley, California.*

157. Frederick Burnham to Howell Wright, 16 May 1944, Box 3, *Frederick Burnham Papers.*

Chapter 5

Washington Midwifes Apartheid's Birth, 1945-1952

BY July 1945 Madie Hall Xuma felt sufficiently adjusted to her new South African home that she contacted a U.S. firm about publishing "some stories I had written and collated about African children...." For the previous few years she had been studying anthropology at the University of Witwatersrand, "for the purpose of learning something of the traditions and customs of the African peoples in this country." In other words, the tears she shed upon arrival in Cape Town had dried and been replaced by smiles.[1] Sadly, regressive attitudes toward Africa had not faded in her place of birth. The prominent publisher Scribner's rejected her proposal since they already had a mere "two books" about Africa on their list.[2]

At the same time, her spouse was maneuvering to attend the Pan African Congress in London hosted by W.E.B. Du Bois of the NAACP, designed to assess and plot the anti-colonial future. Unfortunately, snafus barred his departure[3], just one of several setbacks ensnared his movement in the wake of the war's end. He was even crossing swords with his long-time ally Moses Kotane. The Communist informed Xuma that he had "wrongly interpreted and accused me of plotting to overthrow you from the presidency" of the ANC. Kotane was gratified that Xuma had not "sulked" and reassured him that "I have no desire to become the leader of Congress"[4] (of course, the idea of a Communist leader becoming head of the NAACP was risible even then). Gratified but still shaken, Xuma then informed Robeson that "I have been working under great difficulties recently

1. Madie Hall Xuma to Scribner's, 11 July 1945, Reel 2, *A.B. Xuma Papers.*
2. Scribner's to Madie Hall Xuma, 12 September 1945, Reel 2. *A.B. Xuma Papers.*
3. A.B. Xuma to Dear Sir, 3 September 1945, Reel 2, *A.B. Xuma Papers.*
4. Moses Kotane to A.B. Xuma, 3 April 1946, Reel 2, *A.B. Xuma Papers.*

in my private as well as my public activities," the former a veiled reference to his spouse's ongoing difficulties in adjusting wholly to her new home.[5]

Nevertheless, until he departed unceremoniously from his post as ANC president in early 1950, Xuma was often found alongside Communists, as in the December 1948 meeting of the group's executive where he could be found huddling with Kotane and J.B. Marks.[6] In 1943, Xuma was feeling the heat generated by the Young Turks of the African National Congress Youth League. Wolfie Kodesh, a Communist, recalled later that the key figure among these rebels—Mandela— "was anticommunist and used to fight against the Communists at meetings,"[7] during a time when Xuma was close to Kotane. (Mandela was to evolve beyond this stance.) The canny Communist Edwin Mofutsanyana conceded later that despite this initial ideological twist, "even at that time Mandela, Tambo and Sisulu were quite different than other members of the [ANC] Youth League" which they helped to energize to become the vector of this tendency.[8]

Communist Hilda Bernstein encountered Mandela during this phase of his varied life. He visited her home in Johannesburg, and she described him as a "cautious young man, uneasy and distrustful of whites...." He was big, "broad and imposing" too; her children called him the "giant." Both she and her spouse Rusty had joined the CP during the wartime era and were by then well-versed in its ins and outs. "It was the only political party that had no colour bar"; eventually they were to win over the skeptical Mandela for, as she recalled later, "among the mass of people not only is there no anti-communist feeling, there is also recognition of the one political organization that sets itself inexorably against the colour bar in deeds as well as words. We were accepted by Africans because we were Communists"—though this "set you completely apart from ordinary white society...."[9]

---

5. A.B. Xuma to Paul Robeson, 4 October 1946, Reel 2, *A.B. Xuma Papers*. See also Eslanda Robeson to "My Dear Alfred," no date, Reel 7, *A.B. Xuma Papers*.

6. Minutes of Meeting of ANC Executive, Bloemfontein, 13 December 1948, Reel 4, *A.B. Xuma Papers*.

7. Oral History, Wolfie Kodesh, 4 October 2000, *University of Connecticut-Storrs*.

8. Robert Edgar interview with Edwin Mofutsanyana, 18 February 1983, Reel 6, *Oliver Tambo Papers*.

9. Hilda Bernstein, *The World that Was Ours*, London: Persephone, 2009, xii, 12,

When Communist leader J.B. Marks praised the fountainhead of this youthful tendency—Anton Lembede, who died prematurely in 1947—he stated bluntly that he represented the "embodiment of extreme African nationalism." But when the ANC Youth League sent a delegation to Prague, on the verge of a Communist seizure of power, it signaled that the organization's orientation toward the U.S.—as represented by Xuma—was lurching to a close.[10] When it was reported in Cape Town that Robeson was "popular in Prague,"[11] it further stimulated the onrush of this emerging identification with the socialist camp. By March 1950 Xuma resigned. "I do not want to be dictated to," he asserted, recalling how on 5 December 1949 Walter Sisulu, Tambo, and Mandela met him in his home on behalf of the ANCYL, averring that they would back him if "I accepted a three point programme of Africa for the Africans, African nationalism and the boycott of advisory boards, bungas and local councils." Xuma balked, then resigned.[12] Mandela and his close comrades fired back at Xuma, as the rift deepened.[13]

Ironically, while Sisulu, Mandela, and Tambo seemed to represent an emergent "African Nationalism" that would flower in the U.S. soon under the rubric "Black Power"—the three instead became among the closest allies of the Communists. Seemingly ratifying this notion, in 1950 a "small clique" was accused of wrecking an ANC conference in the Transvaal. "In the forefront" were "African Nationalists."[14] then accused of "exploiting [the] anticommunist issue" in opposing Marks.[15] Mandela, et al. were being accused of harboring the same ideological tendency for which they would contemptuously condemn their bitter rivals, the Pan Africanist Congress, a little more than a decade later. More than irony, this reversal represents something deeper: the ultra-nationalism of the Nationalists was creating an atmosphere congenial to a certain kind of "African Nationalism." More than this, the kind of "African Nationalism" exuded by the younger Mandela would have difficulty in sustaining itself in the midst of a resurgent neo-fascism in South Africa if not aligned with the socialist camp, while being shunned by more traditionally minded U.S. Negroes.

---

10. *Guardian*, 7 August 1947.
11. *Guardian*, 9 June 1949.
12. *Guardian*, 21 March 1950.
13. *Guardian*, 13 April 1950.
14. *Guardian*, 12 October 1950.
15. *Guardian*, 28 March 1951.

* * *

Xuma was not the only one enduring "difficulties" after the war. The crucial year of 1945 was a hinge moment in the torturous path to decolonization in 1994. Coming on the heels of the anti-fascist war, the Cold War helped induce Washington to retreat from the more egregious aspects of Jim Crow, in order to position itself ideologically to capture "hearts and minds" in the rapidly decolonizing Africa and Caribbean.[16] The price of the ticket for anti-Jim Crow concessions for U.S. Negroes was obeisance to the new Red Scare consensus—and shunning previous stalwarts, Robeson and Du Bois most pointedly.[17]

Though U.S. Negroes had quite a bit at stake, so did Washington. The veteran politico William Langer acknowledged portentously in 1948 that "Africa might spell the difference between our ultimate security and the loss of a new world war," since it was the repository of uranium and other vital resources. How could Moscow be fought if Africans had "learned to hate and fear us as the associates and backers of European enslavers"? This foretold Washington's ultimate attempt to undermine France in Algeria, among other such maneuvers. "The doorway to the American continent," he said in a veiled reference to Negroes, "could more easily be by way of Africa than by way of Alaska and the Bering Straits…." A Londoner "had the effrontery to call for American participation in the so-called African Development Company on the claim that part of its benefits would be that the Negroes of the United States could be sent back there," conveniently under London's jurisdiction, whereas Washington imagined Negroes as their Trojan Horse in Africa. He rejected this idea of "outright slavery" and a "great concentration camp" for Negroes—but inevitably there would be compatriots of his who would disagree.[18] In other words, another reason for the retreat of legalized racism in the U.S. was the desire to employ Negroes as stooges in Africa.

---

16. Gerald Horne, *Mau Mau in Harlem? The U.S. and the Liberation of Kenya*, New York: Palgrave, 2009; Gerald Horne, *Cold War in a Hot Zone: The U.S. Confronts Labor and Independence Struggles in the British West Indies*, Philadelphia: Temple University Press, 2007.

17. Gerald Horne, *Paul Robeson: The Artist as Revolutionary*, London: Pluto, 2016; Gerald Horne, *W.E.B. Du Bois: A Biography*, Westport: Greenwood, 2010; Gerald Horne, *Race Woman: The Lives of Shirley Graham Du Bois*, New York: New York University Press, 2001.

18. Speech by William Langer, 15 April 1948, Box 84, III, Speech/Media, *Richard Russell Collection, University of Georgia-Athens.*

Symbolic of these developments was the abrupt turnabout of Max Yergan, Robeson's comrade in the upper reaches of the Council on African Affairs. In May 1946 he joined Robeson in rebuking the newly born United Nations for acquiescing to the admission of South Africa to their elevated ranks.[19] That was followed by another demarche by the dynamic duo, pressuring the U.S. delegation at the United Nations to join a protest by emerging India against South Africa.[20] When 4500 rallied in Manhattan in condemnation of Pretoria's "Native Policy," Robeson and Yergan were the driving forces delivering this impressive assemblage.[21] In a solo effort, Yergan denounced Pretoria's "Indian Policy" and detailed the "fascist character of South African rule," which he compared—in the ultimate insult—to the retrograde activism of "poll tax Congressmen" in Dixie. In a cry that was to mount in coming years, he demanded that the United Nations take action against Pretoria.[22] It was Yergan who was the sparkplug that drove Robeson and the blooming chanteuse Lena Horne together to back fundraising efforts against famine in Africa.[23] Giving thanks, the budding passive resistance movement in the Transvaal sent a message to Robeson's Council on African Affairs as it marked its 10th anniversary.[24]

This outreach to Robeson was understandable. On the anniversary of his birth in 1978, Leslie O. Harriman, the Nigerian Ambassador to the U.N., recalled how his CAA had "sponsored lectures by Professor D.D.T. Jabavu and Dr. Alfred Xuma" of South Africa; "submitted a memorandum to the [U.N.] Commission on Human Rights as early as 1946 calling for an investigation of racism in South Africa;" and on 9 June of that same year "organized a massive rally of 15,000 people in Madison Square Garden" in Manhattan "to denounce the racist regime…." It was that same year that the CAA "hosted the first delegation of the South African liberation movement," speaking of

19. Paul Robeson and Max Yergan to Henri Laugier, Assistant Secretary for Social Affairs, United Nations, 10 May 1946, RG 59, Decimal File, Box 6190, *NARA-CP*.

20. Paul Robeson and Max Yergan to Herschel Johnson, U.S. Delegation to U.N., 28 June 1946, RG 59, Decimal File, Box 6190, *NARA-CP*.

21. *Guardian*, 14 February 1946.

22. *Guardian*, 25 April 1946.

23. *Guardian*, 20 June 1946.

24. *Guardian*, 24 April 1947. Robeson continued to be pictured frequently in this periodical, e.g. the 19 June 1947 edition, alongside Henry Wallace and the 8 July 1948 edition with the caption "Defies Senate" and the 3 March 1949 edition, pictured in London and the 28 April 1949 edition and the 29 June 1950 edition.

Xuma's visit, along with H.A. Naidoo, the Indian leader and H.M. Bassner of the Transvaal.[25] Robeson was "more than a legendary artist," said the ANC's Johnstone Makhathini at the same forum, as he detailed his "close association with our struggles." He "attended the meeting of the Co-ordinating Committee of Colonial Peoples in London in 1949—at which the [ANC] was represented—and travelled from London to Paris with Dr. Yusuf Dadoo to represent the Co-ordinating Committee at the World Peace Congress." In South Africa, he said, Robeson "is considered an outstanding champion."[26]

Robeson's organizing was not seen benignly by opponents. Under pressure, Yergan reversed field and joined the vanguard of the Cold Warriors to became one of the most avid backers of the newly birthed apartheid.[27] This elongated Cold War in the republic effectively warped ties between U.S. Negroes and Africans, as the latter moved ever closer to the CP, a relationship that had accelerated during the war, in any case. Ironically, as the decades unfolded both Negroes and Africans were to find that the retreat and eventual collapse of the socialist camp was of disastrous consequence for both—even though they had embarked on different paths as this new era unwound in 1945.

Pretoria was not left unaffected either. The pressure at the U.N. caused Smuts to become even more double-faced than he ordinarily was on the global scene, seeking to put forward a friendlier, more civilized appearance while abroad.[28] But this only served to weaken him at home, preparing the path for the 1948 proclamation of apartheid. The troubled Yergan went on to become a fierce defender of apartheid. He was a "very difficult person to deal with," says his biographer David Anthony, and "increasingly so after his 'conversion' to conservatism."[29]

Nonetheless, Du Bois, who encountered Smuts in San Francisco, responded with hostility. He "left me cold," the septuagenarian informed South African readers. For, he continued, "here was a man representing perhaps the worst case of organized denial of

25. Remarks by Leslie O. Harriman, 10 April 1978, *E.S. Reddy Collection, Schomburg Collection, New York Public Library*.

26. Remarks by Johnstone Makhathini, February 1978, *E.S. Reddy Collection*.

27. David Anthony, *Max Yergan: Race Man, Internationalist, Cold Warrior*, New York: New York University Press, 2006.

28. *Guardian*, 24 May 1945.

29. David Anthony to George Houser, 13 September 1986, Box 4, *George Houser Papers, Michigan State University-East Lansing*.

human rights in any nation today."[30] The presence of the "Father of Pan-Africanism," Du Bois, in the pages of Cape Town's premier leftist periodical served as complement to the *Guardian*'s new column—"Pan African Review"—examining news from the continent and undermining the lengthy attempt by Pretoria to detach South Africa from its immediate African neighbors, while orienting it toward the North Atlantic allies.[31]

General Smuts' reception in Washington was much less chilly, with the White House planning a "stag dinner," a slightly risqué event, to welcome him.[32] More prosaically, the White House was advised to allow Smuts to address Congress during his visit.[33]

The turn to Africa was a wise move by the South African left, since the war had ignited stirrings on the continent that would not be satisfied without independence—a wave the ANC was then able to ride, not least by appealing to the United Nations. By 1946 pictures were appearing in the South African press of Du Bois alongside Yergan and Xuma, as they pressured this body to isolate Pretoria.[34] Xuma's notorious admiration of U.S. Negroes and the presence of the United Nations not only brought the ANC leader to Manhattan in 1946, it also allowed Robeson's Council on African Affairs to exert more influence upon him. The CAA's W. Alphaeus Hunton told Xuma directly that the U.N. had "received very few expressions of protest against the annexation" of what was to become Namibia. This was a "great surprise to us," he admonished and "most alarming. We ourselves," he added, had "been active in getting organizations" in the U.S. to protest and urged the ANC leader to act similarly and forward "dated copies" to him.[35]

By October 1946 Xuma was back at his usual U.S. residence on 135th street in Harlem.[36] In November Du Bois and the future advisor to Dr. Martin Luther King, Jr. L.D. Reddick had invited "about twenty persons" to a "non-public" meeting with the ANC leader.[37]

30. *Guardian*, 4 October 1945.

31. *Guardian*, 18 October 1945.

32. Memorandum, 19 November 1946, *Papers of Harry S. Truman Official File, OF 450*, Box 1444, *Harry S. Truman Presidential Library*.

33. Memorandum, 18 June 1945, *Papers of Harry S. Truman Official File, OF 450*, Box 1444.

34. *Guardian*, 12 December 1946.

35. W. Alphaeus Hunton to A.B. Xuma, 4 October 1946, Reel 4, *A.B. Xuma Papers*.

36. Letter to Xuma, 25 October 1946, Reel 4, *A.B. Xuma Papers*.

37. Invitation from W.E.B. Du Bois and A.B. Xuma, 21 November 1946, Reel 4, *A.B. Xuma Papers*.

By December referring to himself familiarly as "Roy," the NAACP leader surnamed Wilkins, was trying to reach the man he called "Dear Xuma."[38] With committed assistance from U.S. Negroes, Xuma was able to state the case against Pretoria so forcefully that back home in Blomfontein, the Bantu Social Institute praised his "historic flight to America and the bold step you took" at the United Nations, which "will ever be remembered by the non-European community."[39]

Xuma was also friendly with Claude Barnett, the Chicago-based Negro press baron. Like Barnett, Xuma was a graduate of Tuskegee, founded by Booker T. Washington. They even lived in the same vicinity when Xuma matriculated at the medical school of Northwestern University; there, said Barnett confidentially, "he became a ward of Samuel Insull," a U.S. plutocrat "who sent him through medical school in Vienna and Scotland."[40] Barnett did not allow his pinched view of Xuma to cloud his analysis of Pretoria. The latter's communications arm sought to influence ANP coverage and Barnett hesitated to cooperate, choosing to get information from Pretoria, then commissioning a response from the U.S. Negro intellectual William Leo Hansberry "in rebuttal as it were."[41]

Pretoria retaliated by banning the star of the Negro press, the *Pittsburgh Courier*, accused, reported the ANP, of "inciting the African brothers" to resist "Herrenvolk domination."[42] In this tit-for-tat, Barnett struck back, asking Washington if the funds used to bring German farm students to the U.S. could include similar students from Southern Africa, who would thereby escape the devastation of apartheid.[43]

By 1947 Madie Hall Xuma was back in the land of her birth, augmenting her spouse's initiative and visiting Manhattan, Philadelphia, and Kansas City in a whirlwind tour.[44] The doyenne of Black

---

38. Roy Wilkins to "Dear Xuma," 10 December 1946, Reel 4, *A.B.Xuma Papers.*

39. Bantu Social Institute to A.B. Xuma, 3 April 1947, Reel 4, *A.B. Xuma Papers.*

40. Claude Barnett to Alvin White, 7 December 1946, Box 342, Folder 3, *Barnett Papers.*

41. Claude Barnett to Alice Dunnigan, 12 March 1947, Box 136, Folder 4, *Barnett Papers.*

42. Press Release, February 1949, Reel 23, #86 and #619, Part II, Organizational Files and Part III, Series K, *Barnett/ANP Papers.*

43. Memorandum from Claude Barnett, 21 September 1949, RG 59, Decimal Files, Box 33, *NARA-CP.*

44. African Academy of Arts to A.B. Xuma, 13 September 1947, Reel 4, *A.B. Xuma Papers.*

America—Mary McLeod Bethune—invited her to a conclave of her National Council of Negro Women in Washington.[45] Hall-Xuma was well placed to wield influence in Black America, having been a member of the premier Negro sorority, Alpha Kappa Alpha, for years.[46] Her spouse was no stranger to the U.S. either, having not only attended school in the republic but having served at a Negro hospital in St. Louis,[47] where the author of this book was born.

These ties of singular intimacy bound U.S. Negroes and Africans together but the gathering Red Scare was to create a chasm difficult to bridge. Some difficulties were not new, for example, Pretoria's efforts to keep U.S. Negroes far distant from South Africa. C.C. Adams, Corresponding Secretary of the Foreign Mission Board of the National Baptist Convention, in 1947 stated bluntly that "no American Negro is welcomed in the Union of South Africa.... Being held up indefinitely by immigration officers at the border was customary...." Officials "went out of their way to embarrass and intimidate" Adams and his wife on their visit there. They "threatened to fingerprint and intern" him. Thus, by the time the delegation arrived at the "beautiful and modern home" of the Xumas, they were exhausted. He was an "eminent and wealthy" physician, while she was a "former schoolmate" of his at Shaw University in North Carolina. But their travails did not cease upon walking through the door of the Xumas' commodious home. "Africans as a rule do not make much money but when they catch an American Negro they cash in for [what] they can get," Adams said, referring to taxi drivers. While "the white man does not want the American Negro with his greater enlightenment, broader and ambitious ideas of freedom to contaminate the oppressed natives...." Still, he detected a rising tide of unrest, not only in the Union but in the Rhodesias and Nyasaland too.[48]

Claude Barnett, the press maven, inquired about the persistent practice of denying U.S. Negroes visas and was informed curtly by the State Department that this was a "matter of internal administration" in Pretoria and "not appropriate" for Washington's

45. Mary McLeod Bethune to Madie Hall Xuma, 31 October 1947, Reel 4, *A.B. Xuma Papers*.

46. U.S. passport of Madie Hall Xuma and Membership data on AKA, 24 January 1948, Reel 7, *A.B. Xuma Papers*.

47. Letter to A.B. Xuma, 26 May 1926, Reel 7, *A.B. Xuma Papers*.

48. Report of C.C. Mason, April 1947, Reel 7, *A.B. Xuma Papers*.

involvement (even though U.S. citizens were facing discrimination).[49] It was Barnett who in 1948, as apartheid was being encrusted, protested directly to Secretary of State George Marshall about Pretoria's questionable occupation of the nation that became Namibia. He objected sternly to the "growing opinion" that the U.S. "in concert with Great Britain is failing to support the cause of small disadvantaged areas."[50]

Barnett was simply one of several Negro opinion molders who maintained a steady drumfire of protest against Pretoria. South Africa provided, his ANP said, an "indefinite answer" to his queries about barring U.S. Negro visitors. "Clergymen and missionaries of Negro blood who work for organizations in South Africa can now secure visas but that black travelers generally are barred."[51]

A weakened London was hardly able to restrain an emboldened Pretoria, still enmeshed in revenge seeking, payback for the defeat it had suffered decades earlier. The much-ballyhooed Marshall Plan, often portrayed as a kind of charity to a bloodied Europe, served to allow the U.S. to invade colonial precincts more effectively under the guise of "aid." This "aid" led to new roads, railways, and irrigation works in Angola, for example—and also the arrival of more U.S. personnel there, along with more U.S. investment and influence.[52] Across the continent in Mozambique, the growing U.S. presence was confronted by a growing branch of the highly surveilled Portuguese Communist Party, which was to fortify the influence of the comrades generally in the region.[53] The CP in Portugal, one of the heartiest globally, had influence that reached into Mozambique as early as the 1930s.[54]

49. John M. Patterson, Acting Chief, Division of Public Liaison, State Department to Claude Barnett, 7 July 1948, Box 208, Folder 6, *Claude Barnett Papers*.

50. Claude Barnett to Secretary of State George Marshall, 10 August 1948, Box 208, Folder 6, *Claude Barnett Papers*.

51. Press Release, November 1948, Reel 39, #254, Part I, Press Releases, *Barnett/ANP Papers*.

52. Linda Heywood, *Contested Power in Angola, 1840s to the Present*, Rochester: University of Rochester Press, 2000, 66-67.

53. Teresa Maria da Cruz e Silva, "The Clandestine Network of FRELIMO in Lourenco Marques (1960-1974), Diploma Work for Eduardo Mondlane University-Maputo, 1986, Box 4, *Herb Shore Collection, Oberlin College-Ohio*.

54. Gregory Alonso Pirio, "Race and Class in the Struggle Over Pan-Africanism: A Working Paper on the Partido Nacional Africa, the Liga Africana and the Comintern in Portuguese Africa," FA 021, RG 1, Series I, Subseries I,

Oppositely, the South African Labour Party, an extension of the Labour Party of Britain and, thus, tended toward a pro-London stance, could not survive this hothouse environment and rapidly collapsed postwar.[55] London, the prime colonial power, was also under assault by Robeson, who was unsparing in his critique of Britain's proposal to continue colonialism under the guise of a U.N. Trusteeship.[56] Meanwhile, the U.S., or at least its financial center, was under attack by the Cape Town-based left: "Wall Street Uber Alles" was the target, along with the "almighty dollar" deemed to be the "greatest menace to world peace."[57] After the war, U.S. exports to South Africa became more important to the latter's economy. Pro-London forces balked but the Nationalists applauded enthusiastically. Malan argued accurately that this "greater American trade influence would strengthen" his forces. With cunning he proclaimed that the U.S. would seek to destroy the "imperial preference" that fastened Pretoria to London from the outside, while his party would seek to do it from the inside. The proclamation of apartheid in 1948 at the behest of this Afrikaner elite was an essential part of this scheme; however, Malan was apparently unable to see that the tradeoff made in the U.S. would lead to the enhanced enfranchisement of U.S. Negroes, ultimately corroding this initial positive jolt for the Nationalists.[58]

Also, part of the creation story of apartheid was the deepening reality that after the war, Smuts' party was squeezed by Afrikaner nationalism and the ANC alike. Many Afrikaners were driven into urban areas at the same time as a result of titanic economic forces and were forced into competition with the ancient British antagonist and Africans alike. With propulsion, the political expression of Afrikaner nationalism—the appropriately named Nationalist Party—seized power in 1948 with the aim of uplifting the less wealthy Afrikaners, not least through the exercise of state power.[59]

Malan's final successor, F.W. de Klerk, knew that when the Nationalists came to power in 1948 that "most of its supporters were blue collar workers and small farmers," who had memories of the

---

Box 9, *Social Science Research Council Records, Rockefeller Archive Center, Sleepy Hollow, New York.*

55. *Guardian*, 4 April 1946.

56. *Guardian*, 6 June 1946.

57. *Guardian*, 12 September 1946.

58. Memorandum from Division of British Commonwealth Affairs of State Department, 1 January 1945, RG 59, Decimal File, Box 6189.

59. Elizabeth Schmidt, "Competing for Power: An Analysis of Conflicting Interests in South African Society, 1924-1948," Occasional Paper #11, 1982, Box 5, Folder 38, *Prexy Nesbitt Papers, Columbia College-Chicago.*

turn-of-the century war and were eager to seize the reins of power to strike back at their eternal British foes. They were also "concerned," said de Klerk, "about the threat to white workers and miners posed by competition from cheaper black labour." Part of the remedy would be to de-nationalize Africans, treating them as akin to migratory Mozambican labor in the mines: bereft of rights, foreigners in their own land. Apartheid sought to wall off the Nationalist base from competition but with the inflow of foreign capital, came foreign—particularly U.S.—influence, that faced enormous pressure to press Pretoria. This inflow of capital also created the need for more skilled workers who were African and literate, which was at odds with the thrust of apartheid.[60]

Apartheid from its inception was entrapped in racial and class contradictions. Du Bois recognized at the time that in both his homeland and South Africa, "it has been the organized white labourers who have systematically, by vote and mob, opposed the training of the black worker and the provision of decent wages for him."[61] Under unremitting global pressure, Washington was compelled to retreat from Jim Crow, which uplifted Negro workers to the consternation of many in the U.S. working class, then placed pressure on Pretoria to retreat from apartheid, which it had to do not least because of the demands of the marketplace.

To that end, it seemed that Pretoria had blundered when in an April 1945 debate the opposition in the House of Assembly refused to join in a motion of sympathy and regret in the aftermath of the death of FDR.[62] This refusal, however, was (like the call in South Africa for a local "Ku Klux Klan"[63]) merely a signal to the ascending hard-right forces in the U.S. that they had a friend in South Africa worthy of support and attention, an opportunity that the American right exploited relentlessly in coming decades. These reactionaries may have seen validation in their distaste for FDR when the *Guardian* not only lamented his passing but added the further note that his successor should have been the progressive, Henry Wallace, who had been dislodged as his vice-president in 1944, in one of the more disastrous personnel moves of the 20th century.[64]

---

60. F.W. de Klerk, *The Last Trek*, 16, 75.

61. Du Bois quoted by Dr. Ronald Walters in Remarks at the United Nations, 23 February 1978, *E.S. Reddy Collection, Schomburg Center, New York Public Library.*

62. Report, 17 April 1945, RG 59, Decimal File, Box 6189, *NARA-CP.*

63. *Guardian*, 22 November 1945.

64. *Guardian*, 19 April 1945.

Joe Matthews of the ANC was among those who mourned the passing of this president. A "great admirer" of Roosevelt and a "very strong supporter" of the U.S., Matthews—whose father spent considerable time in the U.S. too—also "worked closely with blacks in the United States," and had the temerity to have "argued" with Robeson over the role of Communists.[65]

On the other hand, the U.S. side was compelled to move more aggressively against anti-Semitism than its Union counterpart, for similar global and ideological reasons that compelled the retreat from Jim Crow. Thus, it did not go down well in Washington when a trade delegation visited South Africa only to be derided by some recalcitrant elements as "Uncle Shylock," a throwback to the defiant characterization of the FDR administration.[66]

But Washington was wedded to the idea of South Africa as a key node in their chain of anticommunist allies, as the strategy evolved of destabilizing anti-colonial movements—and blunting their U.S. backers—by tarring them as dupes of Moscow. In 1950 *Die Burger* cheered when Washington agreed to supply arms and ammunition to Pretoria because, said this Afrikaner commentator, "'our outspoken anticommunist standpoint'" was being recognized.[67] In this context, trade talks proceeded between the U.S. and the Union that were cloaked in secrecy, with even the names of U.S. delegates kept secret, as Washington acknowledged implicitly that enhancing ties with what was becoming a polecat regime stood at odds with its pretensions of being leader of the "Free World." There were other contradictions: Washington was reluctant for London to accede to anti-colonial forces though it demanded the erosion of the glue that kept the British Empire intact: imperial preference. To that end, Washington sought to flood South Africa with exports, then to overcome Pretoria's tariffs—designed to protect its own nascent manufacturing sector—by establishing more plants there.[68]

U.S. auto manufacturers had established a toehold in the Union years earlier. In 1948 the leader of a visiting U.S. delegation, Whitney Shepardson, found himself on a main street in Johannesburg: "I counted the cars parked.... forty-eight" all told. Most of them were new. Forty-three of them were made in the United States. "Almost

65. Oral History, Joe Matthews, 2 October 2000, *University of Connecticut-Storrs.*

66. Clipping, circa 1946, Box 1, *William Clark Papers, Harry S. Truman Presidential Library-Independence, Missouri.*

67. *Guardian*, 28 December 1950.

68. *Johannesburg Times*, circa 1946, Box 1, *William Clark Papers.*

everyone wants an American car," he marveled.[69] By 1950 the State Department was broadcasting the fact that Washington and Pretoria had signed "tax protocols," which would link the two nations even closer.[70]

The transatlantic reactionary bloc was confronted by a similar trans-oceanic bloc of the opposite ideological orientation. U.S. Communist patriarch William Z. Foster was beginning to appear in the pages of the *Guardian* denouncing the imperialism of his homeland.[71] Foster's appearance reflected of the fact that the CP of South Africa continued to take potshots at Foster's foe in U.S. Communist ranks, Earl Browder, who during the war had sought to liquidate the North American CP. CPSA leader George Findlay had gone as far as writing a lengthy attack on Browder, as the two parties became ever more entangled.[72]

For the U.S, per usual, was monitoring events in South Africa carefully, particularly the postwar rise of the unrepentant pro-fascist forces who had not been squelched simply by Berlin's defeat. By September 1946 ex-soldiers, said to be Communists, were clashing physically with self-styled "grey shirts" on the steps of City Hall in Johannesburg. These ultra-rightists referred contemptuously to the republic as a "Jew-ocracy" and saluted Texas, site of a recent victory for conservatives since the state had not surrendered to the "Nigger Vote." When the U.S. envoy commented that "Communist meetings" were "growing larger," it was fair to infer that he was more worried that this would mean a diminishing of pro-fascism than anything else.[73] When Paul Robeson sent a message to his South African comrades hailing the defeat of Germany,[74] it would have been fair to infer that there were those in Pretoria who disagreed adamantly.

So motivated, the pro-Nazis launched a "race riot" in Johannesburg in the late summer of 1945; "one of the worst outbreaks of racial hooliganism ever seen," said a mesmerized journalist. There were assaults on African bystanders by police, energetically aided by European civilians.[75] By early 1946 complaints had emerged about "Ku Klux Klan methods" and "hooliganism in Transvaal," that were

69. Report by Council on Foreign Relations, 25 October 1948, Box 5, *John D. Sumner Papers, Harry S. Truman Presidential Library.*

70. Press Release from State Department, 13 July 1950, Box 104, *Records of the Democratic National Committee, Harry S. Truman Presidential Library.*

71. *Guardian,* 19 July 1945.

72. *Guardian,* 10 January 1946.

73. Report, 11 September 1946, RG 59, Decimal File, Box 6190.

74. *Guardian,* 19 April 1945.

75. *Guardian,* 6 September 1945.

"entirely unprovoked," leading to "assaults by bands of European youths on Africans, Coloureds and Indians," all "encouraged by the extremist press."[76] These hooligans were receiving sustenance from their cross-border comrades in Windhoek, where Nazism may have flowered even more dramatically than in Pretoria. As was typical of both capitals, the militants were more Afrikaner chauvinists than racial chauvinists, colored with a dash of Berlin—their "fuehrer" was Louis Weichardt, who was tied to both Malan and Pirow, and could thereby be could be considered a founding father of apartheid.[77] The "grey shirts" that Weichardt led called for a united front against what it termed the "black peril," which would also comprise the Nationalists, the Sentinels, and the Broederbond.[78] Even Washington seemed concerned when Weichardt was appointed by the Nationalists as their leader in Natal, a base of support not only for the British foe but also the homeland of the Zulus, who had to be monitored closely if apartheid were to remain intact. He was a "rabid racialist and anti-Semite," said U.S. representative in Pretoria, Joseph Sweeney. He even "served in the German Army during World War I." The grey shirts, which he helped to organize, concluded their meetings in the 1930s with the Nazi salute.[79] Perhaps out of the necessity of self-preservation, the *Guardian* began covering the ascension of KKK activity in Atlanta and Georgia more generally, seeing them accurately as Weichardt's allies.[80] When an airy, well-appointed theatre was opened for "Europeans only" in South Africa and named "the Alabama,"[81] the value of tracking trends in Dixie became evident.

Anticommunism was binding South Africa and the United States in a way that racism and anti-Semitism could not. It also sharpened mutual hostility to Moscow and domestic Communists which—in the long run—would be more important in propping up both U.S. and South African imperialism. Thus, counterproductive anti-Semitic attacks on Harry Oppenheimer, scion of one of the more affluent families in the Union, were not necessarily embraced warmly in Washington.[82]

---

76. *Guardian*, 17 January 1946.
77. *Guardian*, 7 March 1946.
78. *Guardian*, 27 June 1946.
79. Joseph Sweeney to Secretary of State, 24 October 1950, RG 59, Decimal File, Box 3571, *NARA-CP*.
80. *Guardian*, 24 January 1946.
81. *Guardian*, 29 September 1949.
82. Bernard Connelly to Secretary of State, RG 59, Decimal File, Box 3571.

In short, the defeat of Germany did not lead to the repression of their wartime comrades in South Africa. Instead, they seemed to be energized, as the fracas in Johannesburg suggested. "What about SA's fascists?" the *Guardian* asked querulously, as they gazed in horror at the spectacle of "Fuehrer Van Rensburg," who hardly shrouded his support for the Nazis during the war—and the "police protection" he received as his adversaries were being beaten. "I couldn't believe my eyes," said an astounded journalist, "I thought I was back in Germany," referring to the breakup of a May Day demonstration just before the final victory in Berlin. Revealingly, the theme they pressed was "race prejudice" while the "Jewish scapegoat," the traditional target, "was largely neglected,"[83] suggesting that the defeat of Berlin may have made this impact. Still, it was evident that the continent—and the world as a whole—would pay a steep price for the failure to suppress fascism in South Africa, which led directly to the installation of apartheid in 1948, and then bloody wars that dragged in major powers. "U.S. imperialism is [the] main enemy of Africa," announced the *Guardian* with sobriety in mid-1951.[84] This fact was an outgrowth of Washington's alliance with a Pretoria, a regime deeply suffused with neo-fascist nostrums and on the precipice of launching numerous cross-border raids into neighboring nations.[85]

Washington well knew of these Nazi trends in South Africa. It was in mid-1946 that a U.S. emissary paid a visit to Van Rensburg, a leader of the wartime saboteurs, many of whom were interned. They spoke for three hours and the South African unburdened himself, "speaking quite freely," as was reported, "of the sabotage and violence committed by his followers during the war years...." There was an elite corps of "Stormjaers or Storm Troopers," Van Rensburg said, many of whom—including himself— "believed in the National Socialist Philosophy," an ideology solidified in 1936 when he visited Germany and conferred with Goebbels, "whom he admired very much...." His present plans included bringing as many as ten thousand homeless German children to South Africa, presumably widening the base for apartheid,[86] though other ultra-rightists would balk at the very idea of diluting Afrikaner supremacy.

This initiation of apartheid marked the confluence of diverse trends. The Carnegie Corporation of New York had provided the

83. *Guardian*, 11 May 1945.

84. *Guardian*, 16 August 1951.

85. Gerald Horne *From the Barrel of a Gun*, passim.

86. "Confidential" Report from T. Holcomb, 17 June 1946, RG 59, Decimal File, Box 6190, *NARA-CP*.

blueprint in the previous decade, creating a kind of "affirmative action" for Afrikaners, including the poorest among them.[87] The fascist upsurge provided the necessary momentum to push Pretoria in that direction. The same could be said of the postwar turn to the right in the U.S., which was coupled with the completion of Washington's long effort to push London aside as the major external force in South Africa. Afrikaner nationalists' changing perspective on South African Jewry also was a factor. Smuts and his United Party played a role too, creating conditions that made apartheid possible by reveling in racism[88] while bowing to the affluent, which created an opening for the Nationalists' united front of Afrikaners, expressed in apartheid.

The Associated Negro Press instantly sensed the danger apartheid presented to African Americans. Their correspondent George McCray found the Nationalist victory to be a triumph for the "doctrine of race subjugation," which "acquired new vigor in other areas in Africa and the Southern States of the United States," offering the latter justification for their own retrogression.[89] He could have added Australia too—a settler colonial friend of Washington and Pretoria alike—for the policy there, said the ANP, did "allow Negro entertainers from America to come in, but only for certain specified times," with the bulk of this community barred.[90]

The U.S.-based scholar Gwendolen Carter arrived in South Africa weeks after the critical 1948 election that led to the invention of apartheid. As she saw things, Malan—the victor—saw the so-called Communist "threat" as domestic, while Smuts saw it as global, which made him more appealing to Washington. Like other sojourners—before and since—she was taken aback by the extent of the antagonism between Boer and Briton. "In fact," she confessed, "I had never had such a strong feeling of the imminence of the past;" a "very high proportion of the English South Africans I talked to told me that they hardly knew any Afrikaners; from the other side, the answer was the same." A baffled Carter stated, "to read English and Afrikaans newspapers on the same day was often to wonder whether they could possibly be referring to the same events."[91] Likewise, C.C. Mason, a

87. Joanna Jordan, "Adapt or Leave: White Emigration as Apartheid Crumbles," Honors Thesis, University of North Carolina-Chapel Hill, 2000, 11.

88. *Guardian*, 27 March 1947.

89. Press Release, November 1948, Reel 39, #398, Part I, Press Releases, *Barnett/ANP Papers*.

90. Press Release, August 1949, Reel 41, #339, Part I, Press Releases.

91. Autobiography, Box 3, *Gwendolen Carter Papers, University of Florida-Gainesville*

Negro cleric visiting South Africa, found a yawning gap between the Afrikaners —"uncouth, abrupt and largely heartless"—and the British, who even in Rhodesia, he found to be courteous.[92] By mid-1951 Afrikaners were reportedly departing the air force because of their inability—or unwillingness—to speak English, a job requirement; this was causing, said John Birch, the U.S. envoy in Pretoria, "bitterness, frustration."[93]

It was in Washington's interest to unite the two on a common platform of anticommunism. This effort was largely successful but in the long run did not prevent white supremacy from retreating.

This was hardly the fault of Smuts, the favored South African in Washington. Speaking just after the proclamation of apartheid in 1948, he was ecstatic about the United States: "I love America and the American people. I was in your country in 1945...New York City is overwhelming...." More to the point, he asserted that "'we must be prepared for the worst" concerning "Communism and the Fifth Column." He was enthusiastic about FDR, a "great man. I knew him during the first World War when we called each other fellow Dutchmen...." Appealing to Dixie, he called Robert E. Lee, "a magnificent man." As for Truman, he knew him too and said bluntly, "I like the old boy." In his youth, Smuts had learned Dutch, English, and German, all of which proved valuable during his lengthy career.[94]

Aware of the profundity of the turn of events, a high-level U.S. delegation arrived in South Africa in the early fall of 1948. Derisively they spoke of the "vast and obscure continent, largely forgotten to the outside world" that they had visited, eliding the fact that their own nation was built on the back of African slave labor. Present for three months, they described the recent defeat of Smuts as a "shock." The "Nationalist victory," they said perceptively was "in one aspect, revenge for the defeat which the Boers suffered at the hands of the British at the beginning of the century"—this electoral triumph was not such a difficult achievement since there were an estimated 1.2 million of the former and 850,000 of the latter. They spent two days at the University of Pretoria and "did not hear one word of English spoken which was not addressed to us...." Malan, who spoke fluent English, nonetheless used Afrikaans exclusively in Parliament, even in response to questions posed in English. Now the agendas

92. Report of C.C. Mason, April 1947, Reel 7, *A.B. Xuma Papers*.

93. "Secret": John Birch to Secretary of State, 22 June 1951, RG 59, Decimal File, Box 3573.

94. Vignette on Jan Smuts, circa 1948, Box 28, *Rebecca Franklin Morehouse Family Papers, University of Georgia-Athens*.

for cabinet meetings were drawn up in Afrikaans only. The victory also meant, they found, a "Jim Crow system" was "now established on the commuting trains operating in and out of Cape Town," while "sending military officers to England for coordinated staff training" had "been stopped"—creating enormous opportunity for Washington to fill the resultant vacuum. The Nationalists were "politically supported by the strong [,] secret anti-British pro-Afrikaans societies, the Broederbond and the Ossewa Brandwag...." Fortunately, the delegation ascertained that "neither the United Party nor the Nationalist Party has any use for any aspect of communism...." Amid this reactionary upturn, they found South Africa to be a "very poor country," despite the plethora of gold and precious minerals: "two and a half million, almost all of them whites, have all the wealth there is," and all discuss the "Native Problem...over and over again...," a discourse permeated by "apprehension of physical danger...."

There was now the "magic word 'apartheid'—segregation or to be more accurate deportation," i.e. ousting Africans and sending them to barren so-called "homelands," or "Bantustans," not wholly dissimilar from the "Indian reservations" of the republic. When Smuts' party left office, "only about 18,000 native children were getting high school education out of a whole native population of 9,000,000" and "somewhat less than 600 were in college...." The delegation asked, "are there any articulate political leaders among the natives" and responded waspishly, "none at the present time who are both articulate and leaders...." Yet they were complimentary of "the Malan government," replete with fascists, which had "been [able] to gain the good opinion of the United States in every way possible;" they recognized that the "purpose" of this bonhomie was to "strengthen themselves against the British element...." Delicately acknowledging the fact that "during the war the Nationalist Party tended to be somewhat pro-Nazi," this was rationalized as being "mostly anti-British rather than pro-Nazi or indeed pro-Dutch...."[95]

A chord struck by this delegation was the lingering Boer-British conflict. This antagonism did complicate the construction of a true white supremacy since Afrikaners were wary about being outnumbered, even by other Europeans. Washington sensed an opportunity, however, in attitudes that were in some ways inimical to the white supremacist project. Thus, when Nationalist T.E. Donges was appointed Minister of the Interior, the U.S. envoy in Pretoria seemed pleased—albeit in a "confidential" missive—that he held dear an

95. Report by Council on Foreign Relations, 25 October 1948, Box 5, *John D. Sumner Papers, Harry S. Truman Presidential Library.*

"anti-British point of view that would [facilitate] association with the United States [in contrast] to affiliation in the British Commonwealth…." Donges was the "guiding genius" of the Broederbond, which carried a whiff of fascism; still, "American leaders and officials will find him co-operative and responsive…."[96] By mid-1951, tensions between the two European groups in South Africa had deteriorated so precipitously that Bernard Connelly, the U.S. delegate in Cape Town, was warning of "civil war" because of "growing bitterness between two white points of view" that could mean "trouble, even violent trouble."[97] The bitter legacy of the earlier war combined with sharp conflicts over the extent to which white supremacy should be augmented by immigration to create a combustible atmosphere.

Washington, in the midst of an agonized retreat from a state-sanctioned apartheid of its own, could more effectively unite the warring factions on the basis of a shared anticommunism. When J.G. Strydom, Minister of Lands, claimed that during World War II the U.S. foolishly destroyed Nazi Germany, a bulwark against Moscow, the U.S. emissary could hardly object since his own nation was now bent on accomplishing what Berlin did not: destroying the Soviet Union.[98] Washington found it hard to object when Pretoria sought to send a man a U.S. bureaucrat called "a very active partisan of the Nazis" to Washington; an attempt was made to invoke the gravitas of alleged liberal heroine, Eleanor Roosevelt, on behalf of Dr. Otto Du Pleassis.[99]

Similarly, in the catbird seat, Washington could appeal to the Nationalists and their competitors. A confidential report praised Phillip Alan Moore, a pro-Smuts parliamentarian from the Transvaal; he was "vehemently pro-American," it was said, having "sent his son for training in the New York Stock Exchange… [he] was sympathetic to his son's desire to remain in the U.S.;" besides, he had "two sisters living in Florida and a host of American cousins…."[100] The republic could appeal to both the Nationalists, providing a protective shield for apartheid because of Pretoria's anticommunism,

96. Bernard Connelly to Secretary of State, 11 October 1950, RG 59, Decimal File, Box 3571, *NARA-CP*.

97. Report from Bernard Connelly, 20 June 1951, RG 59, Decimal File, Box 3571.

98. Report from Bernard Connelly, 4 December 1950, RG 59, Decimal File, Box 3571.

99. Eleanor Roosevelt to John Hickerson, 7 July 1951, RG 59, Decimal File, Box 3577.

100. Report from Joseph Sweeney, 1 September 1950, RG 59, Decimal File, Box 3577.

and Smuts' party also, since the U.S. too was part of the "Anglosphere," enjoying familial and linguistic ties to the British.

Still, Washington had to straddle these often-combative European groupings. The republic's model of integrating Dutch, French Huguenot, British—in fact Europeans generally—into a synthetic whiteness was deemed worthy of emulation. Still, by 1950 Washington was told of rising Afrikaner nationalism that had leaped the border and entered Rhodesia, propelling rising fear of a South African Anschluss that would have been a gift to Africans seeking to take advantage of Europeans on both sides of the divide.[101] Washington knew that the Broederbond in Transvaal thought that "in due course" the Rhodesias would be swallowed by the Union.[102]

Southern Rhodesia was to become the chink in the armor protecting Pretoria, notably when Zimbabwe became independent in 1980. In the postwar era, the Communist Ray Alexander was apprised that the "native is driving out the white man slowly but surely" from this northern neighbor. "Have a look at the Rhodesians Railways & you will see what I mean,"[103] as they were forced to hire more Africans in a colony that had a smaller proportion of Europeans than its southern neighbor, outnumbered at times 20-1 (in South Africa, it was generally about 10-1).

Thus, the majority British population in Salisbury was pressed on all sides, assailed by Afrikaner nationalists and Africans alike, which was not a prescription for stability.

But Pretoria's policy was also rife with contradiction that proved to be undermining. There were plans to bring thousands of "Chetniks" to South Africa, remnants of defeated fascists and anticommunists in Yugoslavia,[104] but this conflicted with Afrikaners skepticism of immigration. The impending arrival, however, was a bow to Washington's advocacy for a truer, synthetic whiteness, supplementing the U.S. push to enlist South Africa in its anticommunist crusade. This is one reason among many why the South African left demanded that Nazis be deported.[105] Instead, months after the instigation of

101. Al Gray, Consul General-Salisbury to Secretary of State, 29 September 1950, RG 59, Decimal File, Box 3577. +

102. T.H. Eustace, Consul General Salisbury to Secretary of State, 12 January 1951, RG 59, Decimal File, Box 3577, *NARA-CP*.

103. Letter to Ray Alexander, 16 November 1946, C1.5, *Jack Simon and Ray Alexander Collection*.

104. *Guardian*, 23 January 1947.

105. *Guardian*, 29 May 1947.

apartheid, scores of German Nazis were inducted into South African citizenship.[106]

This move would have come as a surprise to the October 1948 delegation from the U.S.'s elite Council on Foreign Relations, which determined that the "United Party's program to increase white immigration has been abandoned, to the extent at least of turning back the immigrant ships [of] the Union Castle Line...."[107] Soon Smuts' UP would be collaborating with U.S. newsmen sniffing out tales about the Broederbond's connection with the Nationalists.[108] It is unclear if the UP was the source for the allegation that Sentinel leader Van Rensburg—a Nazi sympathizer—paid "regular monthly visits" to a psychiatrist.[109]

Some U.S. journalists were not above shaping the news in a way that the UP would find congenial. By 1950 G.H. Archambault, correspondent of the *New York Times*, was developing a profile of longtime U.S. favorite General Smuts. The journalist worried that an accurate portrayal would erode the local position of his employer, making life more difficult, giving tensions still boiling decades after the turn-of-the century war. The Nationalists already looked askance at the U.S. paper of record, seeing Arhambault as a hostile critic. Thus, in an extraordinary and flagrant example of collaboration between Washington and its supposed watchdog, the reporter sent a copy of his profile to the U.S. Embassy for vetting. "Any betrayal of Archambault's confidence," warned envoy Joseph Sweeney, "would jeopardize one of the Embassy's most valued sources." Apparently, the paper's editor demanded more positivity, which was remarkable since one of the reporter's suggestions was a call for a Hollywood epic on General Smuts (naturally, the indelicate question of maltreatment of Africans was omitted).[110]

It was not as if anti-Semitism had retreated in postwar South Africa, a supposed concern of this newspaper owned by a prominent Jewish-American family. In the face of the rising allegation that "Jews avoided combatant units" during the war, staying home and

106. *Guardian*, 10 February 1949.

107. Council on Foreign Relations Report, 25 October 1948, Box 5, *John D. Sumner Papers, Harry S. Truman Presidential Library*.

108. Confidential Report from Joseph Sweeney, 7 August 1951, RG 59, Decimal File, Box 3571.

109. Secret Report from Joseph Sweeney, 5 October 1951, RG 59, Decimal File, Box 3571.

110. Joseph Sweeney to Secretary of State, 23 May 1950, RG 59, Decimal File, Box 3577.

profiteering instead,[111] the South African left-wing press felt compelled to announce that "10,000 Jews" joined the military during the war "out of a Jewish population of 100,000, while "1175 were casualties and 307 were killed."

Thus, a few months before this outrageous claim, the fascists took to the steps of Johannesburg City Hall once more, singing lustily the Nazi hymn, "Deutschland Uber Alles" and chanting intermittently "Heil Hitler." Unbowed, a left-wing writer editorialized bluntly, "for six years while our men were fighting fascism," this bacillus was "being allowed to flourish practically without let or hindrance."[112] Hence, those who had been interned for pro-Nazi activities during the war were now being released and some were receiving promotions at the expense of anti-fascist competitors.[113]

Just after the proclamation of apartheid, the *Guardian* announced soberly, "we have our own Ku Klux Klan," who were among the "kidnappers" of a Coloured man who was then thrashed. It was true that unlike their republican counterparts, they "were not dressed in white gowns and hoods. They burnt no fiery cross on a hillside. But otherwise they were no different from United States Ku Klux Klan members...."[114] The South African press, said the U.S. envoy in Cape Town, "depicted the American scene mainly in terms of the Ku Klux Klan" and seemed to enjoy in publicizing articles on racism in the U.S., "such as the plan presented by Senator [Richard] Russell of Georgia calling for the redistribution of Negroes in the United States."[115] Repeatedly during the apartheid era, the Nationalists drew sustenance from analogous events in Dixie. "Do the Nats want a Ku Klux Klan"? it was asked rhetorically in 1950 after "their party organ" in the Transvaal "praised the Governor of Georgia...who predicted bloodshed should the court decide that European and Negro children should sit on the same school benches in Atlanta." The "frank standpoint" and brusque "colour feeling will be supported in South Africa," said the "Transvaler," who went on to claim that the "colour feeling of the Southern United States would find a sympathetic echo in South Africa, because the overwhelming majority of the whites in this country felt the same way and because South Africa appreciated an 'honest and frank attitude' towards this

111. *Guardian*, 20 September 1945.

112. *Guardian*, 28 July 1945.

113. *Guardian*, 9 August 1945.

114. *Guardian*, 25 November 1948.

115. North Winship to Secretary of State, 1 February 1949, RG 59, Decimal File, Box 6192.

matter."[116] Likewise, the *Guardian* adopted the nomenclature of the republic when it termed a medical school in Durban a "'Jim Crow' institution."[117]

The left in South Africa was not taken altogether by surprise at this turn of events. Though others may have forgotten, the *Guardian* recalled that after the victory over Berlin Pirow—soon to be the chief persecutor of Mandela—had termed the now deceased Hitler the "greatest man of his age and one of the greatest of all time" and praised Mussolini in only slightly more tempered tones.[118] Soon Pirow, Weichardt, and Malan attained a craven goal when Communist leaders—including Kotane and J.B. Marks—were put on trial for sedition,[119] the first of many trials that would rock South Africa in coming years. This was part of an attempt to blame a massive miners' strike on the CP, which did not succeed, though the failure would not stop a series of attempts to jail Communist and left-wing opponents of the regime.[120] A few months later, eight members of the Central Executive Committee of the CP were arrested, including Kotane, William Andrews, Betty Sacks, and I.O. Horvitch.[121] Such repression did not prevent the election of South Africa's first Communist MP, Sam Kahn, brought to office by a huge majority in 1948.[122]

By August 1949 Kahn returned unopposed as a Councillor in Cape Town, the first time a Communist had been reelected to a public body in South Africa without facing a challenger.[123] Weeks later one of the largest demonstrations ever seen in South Africa occurred in Cape Town.[124] The success of Kahn and his comrades was sufficiently worrisome to cause the U.S. Embassy to interview him. He apparently told them that his party had 10,000 "adherents" during the war and of this number 3000 held membership cards and 1500 paid dues.[125] (Gwendolen Carter, the visiting scholar, ascertained that there were "probably not more than about 500 Communists in South Africa" in the early 1950s, while the Broederbond—allied with

116. *Guardian*, 12 October 1950.
117. *Guardian*, 27 September 1951.
118. *Guardian*, 5 July 1945.
119. *Guardian*, 5 September 1946.
120. *Guardian*, 19 September 1946
121. *Guardian*, 19 September 1946.
122. *Guardian*, 25 November 1948.
123. *Guardian*, 11 August 1949.
124. *Guardian*, 15 September 1949.
125. Joseph Sweeney, U.S. Embassy to Secretary of State, 22 June 1950, RG 59, Decimal File, Box 3573.

the discredited Nazis—had about 5000 members: both appear to be underestimations.)[126]

Whatever the estimate of CP membership, the U.S. emissary North Winship was probably correct when he declared that "the racial policy of the present Government is doing much to turn the natives toward Communism."[127] His fellow diplomat Bernard Connelly concurred, saying that he "could never understand why…Communism had not gained more adherents in South Africa" since the CP was the "only political party an African could join."[128]

The experience of Andimba Toivo ya Toivo in Namibia bears out the basis of this assessment. While in Cape Town postwar he worked for the Communist couple Ray Alexander and Jack Simons. Every time they went on holiday, he recalled, "I would look after their house…they were the first whites with whom I was so closely associated without noticing discrimination…it was they [who] persuaded me to join the ANC" and go on to become a founder of SWAPO, the South West Africa People's Organization, still the ruling party in Windhoek. And, he recollected, "it was through the interactions with the members of the Communist Party and the South African Indian Congress and the African National Congress I got a fuller understanding of the international dimension of the Namibian issues…."[129]

It had been evident for some time that Pretoria was resting uneasily on the mouth of a volcano. Yet it was still being slated by the United States as a sturdy anticommunist partner. In early 1949 the recently born Central Intelligence Agency provided an analysis of the scene to President Truman. Their report highlighted the "strategic position" of the Union—which possessed a crucial naval base—between the sea lanes heading respectively to Suez and the riches of Asia. But "worldwide sensitivities to the racial issues" compromised Pretoria as an ally, a situation made worse by the regime's unseemly fondness for Nazis. Nevertheless, it was "the only independent state of European traditions and of substantial power and stability on the African continent." At that point it was producing 12 of the 23 strategic minerals listed by the National Security Resources Board. Then there was the influence of Pretoria on London. The United Party, it

126. Autobiography, Box 3, *Gwendolen Carter Papers, University of Florida-Gainesville.*

127. North Winship to Secretary of State, 20 October 1949, RG 59, Decimal File, Box 6192.

128. Report by Joseph Sweeney, 1950-1952, Box 4, *Joseph D. Sweeney Papers, Harry S. Truman Presidential Library.*

129. Andimba Toivo ya Toivo, *On Trial for My Country*, 60, 61.

was said, "actually received more popular votes than the Nationalist and Afrikaner parties combined" during the 1948 election that led to apartheid, "but since rural constituencies in South Africa normally contain fewer voters than urban ones, this was insufficient for parliamentary control...." Besides, a racialist regime perforce becomes heavily dependent on the most racialist constituency, and—rightly or wrongly—rural Afrikaners held that heavyweight title. The Sentinels were said to number 30,000 members even then. The overriding problem, from the CIA's vantage point, was that allying with Pretoria left a stain on Washington: "black white antagonisms are on the rise," it was said with sobriety, "not only in the Union but in colonial Africa generally and the problem is one which affects the U.S." Apartheid had "symbolic values for colored peoples in other continents as well," pointing to India. All of this provided rich fodder for "Communist agitation" and "Soviet propaganda...." That Pretoria had a "complete lack of any international alternative to alignment with the U.S. and the U.K." was indicative of Pretoria's parlous position, which, in turn, weakened the chain of alliances that linked it to Washington—meaning apartheid was weakening the North Atlantic bloc more generally.[130]

The gathering alliance with Washington did not come without cost, which Pretoria would be paying for decades. By late 1945 a visiting group of U.S. Negroes who had somehow wangled visas were in Cape Town expressing horror at the pass laws. One of these visitors, Wilson James, was sufficiently bold to term Robeson a "great American institution." A visiting U.S. warship had also arrived around the same time; soon such vessels would be sites of contention after Pretoria expressed dismay at granting non-discriminatory rights ashore to Negro sailors.[131]

The traffic was heading in both directions. By 1948 Albert Luthuli, the future Nobel Laureate and ANC leader, had arrived in Dixie. "My Negro friends were very eager to hear about South Africa," he recalled, "and their readiness to help resolved itself many times into the question, 'Can we come over there to assist you?'" His response? "The more democratic America becomes," he averred, "the better for those whom she influences," in the first instance his homeland. There were touches of home, in any case; thus, in Atlanta he wanted to go to a movie but heard of Jim Crow restrictions and stoutly refused to enter the theater. He also encountered Jim Crow in the

130. CIA Report, 31 January 1949, Box 217, *Papers of Harry S. Truman, President's Secretary's File, Harry S. Truman Presidential Library*.

131. *Guardian*, 22 November 1945.

alleged citadel of liberty, Washington, D.C. Another discordant note was struck when he preached a sermon in the U.S. and said, "I'm glad to be amongst my people," to be met by a youngster taking exception to his admiring words and telling him that she—despite displaying conspicuous melanin content—was "not of Africa," a comment reflecting the legacy of slavery that too was soon to wither in coming decades.[132]

U.S. Negroes and Africans were a kind of odd couple that had managed to forge close ties, nonetheless, as exemplified by the actual couple, the Xumas. But the postwar environment provided a stiff challenge to this union, as Washington moved contradictorily to ease Jim Crow while seeking to elbow aside London and co-opt liberation movements for the ends of anticommunism. Pretoria was supportive of the latter effort but fiercely opposed to the former. As the curious case of Yergan suggests, the U.S. Negro leadership was also willing to go along with the anticommunist project—but the ANC, which even under the Xumas was able to form close relations to the CP, was also less willing than the NAACP to go along with the state consensus. Instead, as time passed, the ANC moved closer to the socialist camp while the Negro leadership, denuded of the potent influence of Robeson and Du Bois, marched in an opposing direction.

There were contrary notes emitted from the NAACP camp, albeit inconsistently pursued. As apartheid was beginning in 1948, Claude Barnett of the Associated Negro Press conceded, "We hold no brief for Communists," while adding, "I admit that if there was [a] place where Communism might appear to be a useful weapon is in South Africa...."[133] In touch with South Africans, Barnett was aware of the relative lack of anticommunist feeling among Africans, and said he was "stirred by the strike and the happenings in South Africa."[134] Barnett was able to monetize news coverage of Africa and, thus, had

132. Albert Luthuli, *Let My People Go*, New York: McGraw, 1962, 83-84. Years later his visit still reverberated. See Morris Dembo to Secretary of State, 18 November 1952, RG 59, Decimal File, Box 3572, *NARA-CP*: In a "conversation with Chief Luthuli" the ANC leader spoke of how "he had visited the United States in 1948 under the auspices of the American Board of Commissioners for Foreign Missions to speak to church groups....he made a point of going to the South to visit Negro schools. To questions from Negro professors about what they could do in Africa to help African people, he had replied that their most profitable field of work was in the United States."

133. Claude Barnett to H. Ahmed, 10 May 1948, Box 175, Folder 1, *Claude Barnett Papers.*

134. Claude Barnett to H. Ahmed, 5 October 1946, Box 175, Folder 3, *Claude Barnett Papers.*

a material interest in learning about that region of the continent. Bobby Naidoo of South Africa, who received ANP news, wanted more information on "boxing particularly, as baseball and American football" did "not have a following here…."[135]

The Truman regime was being told by its delegate in Cape Town that Malan was battering Smuts for supposedly being soft on the CP (a claim which had the added advantage of providing cover for the resurgence of fascism). This was "gross negligence," said the Nationalist. He accused Moscow of "encouraging revolution in South Africa" while, alternatively he emphasized the supposed dangers of the "Black Menace."[136]

The arrest of the top CP leadership in Manhattan in July 1948 was greeted ecstatically in South Africa in reams of press coverage passed on to the State Department. In understated fashion the comment appended to the report was that the "general attitude of the press has been favorable…."[137] As late as November 1950, South Africans were continuing to follow the trials of various U.S. Communist officers with keen interest.[138] Unsurprisingly, this anticommunist signal was quickly followed by the electoral victory of the Nationalists, the eclipse of Smuts and the United Party, and the proclamation of apartheid.[139] By September 1948, U.S. envoy North Winship was reporting on Cape Town newspaper articles lauding "apartheid American style," in reference to the refusal by Henry Wallace—then running for president with the backing of the reviled, recently detained CP leaders—to speak before a Jim Crow audience in Birmingham, Alabama.[140] Wallace attracted further attention in Cape Town when during his ill-fated presidential run he endorsed the idea of all voting in South Africa and not just those defined as "white."[141] Because his horizon stretched further than that of others in the NAACP camp, Barnett's ANP was able to make linkages that escaped others in this ambit, noting that "There is a straight line from

135. Bobby Naidoo to Claude Barnett, 9 August 1947, Box 175, Folder 1, *Claude Barnett Papers.*

136. Report, 23 March 1948, RG 59, Decimal File, Box 6191, *NARA-CP.*

137. North Winship to Secretary of State, 11 August 1948, RG 59, Decimal File, Box 6192.

138. John Erhardt to Secretary of State, 6 November 1950, RG 59, Decimal File, Box 3573.

139. North Winship to Secretary of State, 11 August 1948, RG 59, Decimal File, Box 6192.

140. North Winship to Secretary of State, 14 September 1948, RG 59, Decimal File, Box 6192.

141. *Guardian*, 27 May 1948.

Peoria, Illinois," where Robeson had been assaulted in the spring of 1947, "to Pretoria, the capital of South Africa."[142]

As suggested earlier, a signal aspect of South African politics was the participation of the Jewish community in the ranks of the CP. But soon, Winship—in a "restricted" dispatch—spoke of the "birth of a pro-Government movement among South African Jewry—led by [Joseph] Nossel of Cape Town who was the first Jew to be admitted to the Nationalist Party in the Cape Province;" part of a trend that had swept "Johannesburg, Pretoria, Brakpan, Benoni, Bloemfontein and Kimberley…." That is, just as Washington was striding boldly to conciliation with its African American population, Pretoria was moving haltingly in a similar direction vis-à-vis its Jewish population (the African majority was much too large to conciliate at that juncture). Typically, the Transvaal was still seeking to uphold anti-Semitic barriers, and opinions on this matter went back and forth, like a seesaw, nationally until 1994. F.W. de Klerk, an architect of the 1994 dispensation, was part of a family that was then straddling the fence. His father, Chief Secretary of the Nationalists in the Transvaal, denied that there was a "softening" on this bedrock matter. Strikingly, Eric Louw, designated correctly by Winship as the "bitterest anti-Semitic personality" during the 1930s, was "conspicuously silent."[143]

Arguably to that end, South Africa was the first Dominion within the British Empire to recognize the state of Israel, inaugurating a fruitful bilateral tie between the apartheid regime and the Zionist project.[144] The *Rand Daily Mail* hailed the Smuts administration for this move while "recognizing the fact that this course would be unpopular among many of his followers."[145]

By 1951 Bernard Connelly of the U.S. legation in Pretoria weighed in, underscoring the "known anti-Semitism of many [Nationalist] leaders;" he noted it was "anomalous for all the other provincial parties to admit Jews and have the Transvaal persist in excluding them."[146]

The Nationalists were divided on the issue of South African Jewry, facing pressure from Washington to adapt to the post-1945

142. Press Release, April 1947, Reel 34, #755, Part I, Press Releases, *Claude Barnett/Associated Negro Press Papers.*

143. North Winship to Secretary of State, 18 October 1948, RG 59 Decimal File, Box 6192.

144. North Winship to Secretary of State, 7 June 1948, RG 59, Decimal File, Box 6192.

145. *Rand Daily Mail*, 27 May 1948.

146. Bernard Connelly to Secretary of State, 21 September 1951, RG 59, Decimal File, Box 3573.

consensus to ease anti-Semitism but hesitant to disrupt the party's united front that had included fascists. Jews, said Louw, were pandering to his comrades since they knew the Nationalists would be in power for a long time. Echoing this sentiment, a 1947 rally amplified demands that Indians should be sent back to India, "Kaffirs" should be kept in their place, and Jews dispatched forthwith to Palestine.[147] Malan's support of the creation of Israel, said the *Guardian*, "can only be interpreted as a thinly veiled desire to rid the country of an 'un-Christian, un-national element.'"[148] Louw and Malan were not alone. J.S. von Moltke, another Nationalist leader in Parliament was, it was reported, "one of South Africa's most eminent Jew haters" in his capacity as a militant for the "grey shirts."[149]

Washington by this juncture was pouring its bigotry into anticommunism, not anti-Semitism, and, thus, found it appropriate to pay attention to Communists on both sides of the Atlantic, filing away a revealing photograph of Kotane, Sam Kahn, and other leading comrades at a CP meeting, replete with identifying banner.[150] Washington may have heard that the *Guardian*, deeply influenced by the CP, had a circulation of only 7500 in 1938 but with the paper's revealing coverage of London's sellout in Munich, it soared to 14,000 and by July 1941 stood at 22,000[151]—and climbing higher postwar.

The South African left sensed the growing role U.S. imperialism was playing in their country. The republic was the "dog in the manger," said the *Guardian*, finding that "Dollar Imperialism means unemployed in South Africa," as exemplified by the leather industry, where exports were submerging local production. The ostensible patron, Britain, needed dollars and bought them from the U.S., rather than the Union,[152]to the latter's detriment, it was charged. There was a "U.S. Eagle" hovering over Africa, meaning an "increase in American investment in the South African investment in the South African mining industry," with mega-mogul David Rockefeller playing a crucial role.[153] His father, John D. Rockefeller, took time from his busy schedule to confer with Nationalist leader Nicolaas Havenga.[154]

147. *Guardian*, 18 September 1947.

148. *Guardian*, 6 November 1947.

149. *Guardian*, 7 June 1951.

150. "Restricted" photograph, 17 January 1949, RG 59, Decimal File, Box 6192.

151. *Guardian*, 26 February 1948.

152. *Guardian*, 12 June 1947.

153. *Guardian*, 30 October 1947.

154. *Guardian*, 7 October 1948.

The left highlighted the demand by the CAA to urge the U.S. to stop buying South African gold as a protest against apartheid. By the late 1940s U.S. exports to the Union were valued at 107,000,000 pounds, over 600% higher than in 1939 and almost four times the value of South African exports to the U.S. The imbalance was a heavy drain on South Africa's dollar and gold reserves, contributing to more borrowing from Wall Street and more U.S. influence.[155] Instead of boycotting gold U.S. experts had descended on South Africa by 1950, in search of uranium for a new generation of atomic weapons and finding a treasure trove in the nation that was to become Namibia.[156]

A delegation from the elite, Manhattan-based Council on Foreign Relations arrived in South Africa in 1948 and their report, which made its way to the White House, expressed astonishment at "how completely the economy of the Union of South Africa is based on the production of gold and upon the willingness of other countries, particularly the United States, to take all gold offered at a fixed and certain price and to give goods and services in exchange therefore…."[157] Disrupting this neat arrangement was a high priority for the emerging anti-apartheid movement, just as support for mineworkers was a sacred cause for the CAA, not only in South Africa but in Nigeria too.[158] In any case, Pretoria and Washington often clashed over the precious metal, with the Union charging that the republic was keeping the price artificially low.[159]

It was understandable why the CAA was not bound by borders. Historically there had been a major influx of cheap labor from Mozambique and the surrounding region into South African mines. Before the so-called Anglo–Boer war perhaps 60% of the Transvaal labor force was Mozambican. In 1925 Edward Ross of Wisconsin visited Angola and Mozambique and castigated the "state serfdom" that amounted to neo-slavery. Still, these workers often propelled both socialist principles and strike waves, leading in the post-1945 era to forced labor and horrific beatings which only served to generate greater militancy.[160]

155. *Guardian* , 6 January 1949.

156. *Guardian*, 24 November 1949.

157. Report of Council on Foreign Relations, 25 October 1948, Box 5, *John D. Sumner Papers*.

158. *Guardian*, 16 February 1950: Du Bois is pictured giving a check to Nnamdi Azikiwe of Nigeria for mineworkers.

159. Bernard Connelly to Secretary of State, 18 May 1951, RG 59, Decimal File, Box 3573.

160. Jeanne Marie Penvenne, *African Workers and Colonial Racism: Mozambican Strategies and Struggles in Lourenco Marques, 1877-1962*, Portsmouth,

It was not just Africans from Lisbon's colonies that were stirring concern. In a 1949 "confidential" message, Washington was apprised of "riots" in Mogadishu, Somalia, perpetrated by radicals "trained in [a] Communist school at Addis Ababa," some of whom had travelled down the coast to Durban. This school was administered by the Soviet Embassy, indicating the peril of surrendering to sovereignty on the continent, and was "training natives from all parts of Africa in Communist doctrine and methods of street fighting...."[161]

Robeson remained a hero in South Africa, even as his halo dimmed in his homeland. The *Guardian* endorsed the campaign around the Trenton 6, a group of young African American men facing trumped-up murder charges near Robeson's place of birth in Princeton. The message from Cape Town was that this was a "new Scottsboro case in the making," no less than a "legal lynching."[162] There was solidarity from the left in South Africa not only for these defendants but also in regard to similar campaigns spearheaded by their Communist allies in the U.S., including the Martinsville 7,[163] the case of Mississippi's Willie McGee,[164] the case of Edward Honeycutt,[165] and the case of John Derrick, who too was "legally lynched."[166] Likewise, when Du Bois was indicted in 1951, the South African left, despite being under siege itself, took time to object.[167]

Fed up, Pretoria banned Robeson's recordings shortly thereafter. "I can only give you one parallel to the South African radio's recent restriction on my recordings," he replied in an "exclusive interview" with the *Guardian*: "That was during the war when the Nazi gauleiter of Norway banned my records there..."[168] South African readers had the opportunity to follow Robeson's doings in the press, e.g. when he blasted "stooges," at a "jammed Rockland Palace"

New Hampshire: Heinemann, 1995, 24, 73, 82, 103, 115, 136.

161. "Confidential" report from "Acheson," 21 February 1949, RG 59, Decimal File, Box 6192.

162. *Guardian*, 14 April 1949.

163. *Guardian*, 15 February 1951.

164. *Guardian*, 17 May 1951.

165. *Guardian*, 12 June 1951. For more on the prosecution of Du Bois, see *Guardian*, 25 October 1951.

166. *Guardian*, 3 February 1951: For more on these cases, see Gerald Horne, *Communist Front? The Civil Rights Congress, 1946-1956*, London: Associated University Presses, 1988. See also protests about a Virginia case whereby "4 U.S. Negroes face death charge" with the request that protests be sent to the governor: *Guardian*, 30 August 1951.

167. *Guardian*, 5 July 1951.

168. *Guardian*, 21 April 1949.

gathering in Harlem, who had challenged his remark in Paris questioning if Negroes would rally to the growing cause of war on Moscow.[169] Referring to Marx, Robeson predicted that "Communists and Negroes ....would be in the vanguard of the struggle to regain for the American people the rights they were losing...."[170] When Robeson confronted raucous and racist demonstrators at a concert in Peekskill, New York in 1949, readers were told how he "defies U.S. fascists...."[171] Walking in Robeson's footsteps was James Phillips, a singer who performed for the left in Johannesburg; educated at Lovedale, he was proud to announce that his "favourite singer" was Robeson—"of course."[172]

The celebration of Robeson could not obscure the reality that the CPSA was under attack in the aftermath of the proclamation of apartheid. By mid-1950, in the wake of the Suppression of Communism Act, the party chose to dissolve—though this was a pro forma decision more than anything else.[173] (Becoming the South African Communist Party—SACP—simultaneously was part of the alleged dissolution). Soon the *Guardian* was facing suppression, which brought an angry rebuke from Robeson. "I recognize," he said, "the connection between events here and in the West Indies and Africa. We are all fighting for freedom."[174] As Pretoria ignored U.N. admonitions on its would-be colony of Namibia, James Moroka, a physician like Xuma, lamented in his capacity as ANC president that "for the first time since 1912 the Congress had been stopped from holding a meeting. This was because," he said with a hint of what was to come, "the Congress was no longer satisfied just to pass resolutions...."[175]

By 1951 the soon-to-be celebrated actor Sidney Poitier arrived in South Africa to film Alan Paton's novel *Cry the Beloved Country*. "Hatred and fear run like a breeze" in the land of apartheid, he said disparagingly. "The whites fear for their lives, their possessions, their social and economic position," making a "showdown... inevitable...." He was gratified that "we as somewhat privileged American Negroes lived on a farm" and managed to escape the worst excesses then obtaining. His co-star Canada Lee publicly disagreed with Poitier, stunning the anti-apartheid leader Y.M. Dadoo

169. *Guardian*, 21 July 1949.
170. *Guardian*, 28 July 1949.
171. *Guardian* , 8 September 1949.
172. *Guardian*, 10 November 1949.
173. *Guardian*, 22 June 1950.
174. *Guardian*, 22 November 1951.
175. *Guardian*, 20 July 1950.

since the thespian and former boxer had spoken with him in tones similar to Poitier's.[176] Lee may have noticed that the death of the Euro-American entertainer Al Jolson, known for his insultingly derisive "blackface" performances, was big news in South Africa, where a section of the population found his insulting act appealing.[177]

Dadoo, who was a leader of both the CP and the South African Indian Congress, was probably persuasive since by early 1952 the South African ambassador to the U.S., G.P. Jooste, was complaining to the State Department and presenting an "attached broadcast" from Lee that suggested support for "threats to picket" Pretoria's consulate and embassy. Worriedly, the South Africa wrote, "Mr. Robeson's name appeared on the letterhead of several of these [protesting] organizations."[178]

The reported production of a musical in South Africa—*Lost in the Stars*—was not greeted warmly back in the U.S. Dissenting strenuously to another Hollywood production in South Africa, it was publisher Claude Barnett who promptly arranged for a protest to reach producer Alexander Korda, directing an employee to inquire "whether it is true that the American Negro actors" who arrive in the land of apartheid "will have to be admitted as 'body servants' of Korda in order to get around the…Malan government's vicious anti-African and anti-Negro law."[179] Barnett, like others, thought the rise of Malan was ominous: "As bad as General Smuts…is, he is still much to be preferred."[180] "While Prime Minister Smuts has become a synonym among our people for all that is evil in the race question," said Barnett earlier, " in South Africa there are so many who are much worse by comparison he seems reasonably decent. Here when you say Smuts you had as well say the devil himself."[181] His Associated Negro Press found it similarly ominous that Pretoria adopted Dixie's claim that the doctrine of "states' rights"

176. *Guardian*, 14 June 1951.

177. John Erhardt to Secretary of State, 6 November 1950, RG 59, Decimal File, Box 3573, *NARA-CP*.

178. "Memorandum of Conversation" with G.P. Jooste, 28 March 1952, RG 59, Decimal File, Box 3572, *NARA-CP*.

179. Claude Barnett to Alvin White, 26 August 1950, Box 342, Folder 4, *Claude Barnett Papers*.

180. Claude Barnett to Foreign Editor, 'New York Herald Tribune,' 19 May 1948, Box 342, Folder 4, *Claude Barnett Papers*.

181. Claude Barnett to Francis Gow, 14 March 1946, Reel 8, #641, Part III, Series J, *Barnett/ANP Papers*.

barred inquiry into the propriety of apartheid—or Jim Crow for that matter.[182]

The wider point is that as relations between the U.S. and the Union tightened, more pressure was placed on Negroes, notably Negroes of the left like Canada Lee, to conform.

By 1951 it was evident that given growing capital flows and the emergence of Pretoria as a reliable anticommunist ally, the two countries had grown considerably closer. By then South Africa had received a $10 million loan and a $20 million revolving credit line from U.S. banks in addition to a $50 million World Bank loan—backed by Washington—for power and transport projects. Then there was the steady flow of military and police equipment to the Union. South Africa was one of 16 nations that joined the U.S. as part of the armed forces on the Korean peninsula. A South African air squadron had been in combat there since November 1950. There were clouds blurring this otherwise bright horizon: for example, Pretoria ignored a U.N. General Assembly resolution demanding a trusteeship for what became Namibia rather than continued South African occupation. This action was rationalized by U.S. Secretary of State Dean Acheson, who was skeptical of Reverend Michael Scott, advocate for Namibia, since a "highly reliable" source had informed him that the CP was "associated" with the cleric in the 1930s in Britain, where as a "result of the influence of Emile Burns," Scott was "drawn into actual membership" of the Communist Party.[183] Still, lassitude on this matter of decolonization was not only to complicate bilateral ties between Pretoria and Washington but would serve as a mechanism uniting anti-colonial Africa and the international community as a whole against this occupation.[184]

The South African intervention alongside the U.S. in Korea established a new level of fraternity.[185] When the U.S. envoy met with Pirow in Pretoria in August 1950, weeks after hostilities commenced, the Nazi backer told him bluntly that the "third world war has already begun" and, in any case, the air squadron sent eastward by

182. Press Release, October 1948, Reel 38, #1083, Part I, Press Releases, *Claude Barnett/Associated Negro Press Papers*.

183. Dean Acheson to Cape Town consulate, 5 June 1950, RG 59, Decimal File, Box 3573.

184. Report, 27 March 1952, Box 104, *Records of the Democratic National Committee, Harry S. Truman Presidential Library*.

185. Joseph Dougherty to Secretary of State, 19 January 1951, RG 59, Decimal File, Box 3571.

Pretoria would gain "invaluable experience" there that could pay dividends in showdowns to come with African neighbors.[186]

* * *

If Pretoria had been able to connect the dots it would have been acutely cognizant that forces were gathering which would deliver a severe challenge to apartheid. Eduardo Mondlane of Mozambique had been expelled from the University of the Witwatersrand in the immediate wake of the initiation of apartheid in 1948. He managed to study in Lisbon—reportedly the first Mozambican to matriculate there in 450 years[187]—where he encountered other revolutionaries from Angola and Guinea-Bissau, forming an important network of opposition to colonialism. There he encountered a generation that was to serve as the principal vector of opposition to Portuguese colonialism, including Agontinho Neto (founding father of modern Angola); Amilcar Cabral (founding father of modern Guinea-Bissau); Marcelino dos Santos, who worked shoulder-to-shoulder with Mondlane in liberating Mozambique; Mario Andrade, premier Angolan intellectual—and others.[188]

He then sought to matriculate in the U.S. But Julian Rea, the head of the American Methodist Mission in Mozambique, did everything he could to prevent Mondlane from studying there. There were clear tensions between the future Mozambican leader and the missionaries, which were difficult to separate from the racially chauvinistic atmosphere delivered by colonialism.[189] By 1950 Cleveland couple Darrell and Mildred Randall was lobbying on his behalf, informing friends in the area that he was a close friend of theirs and, like many of the Southern African revolutionaries, was multilingual, capable of expressing himself in various African indigenous languages along with Portuguese, French, English, and Afrikaans. He was seeking aid to further his education.[190] Reportedly, neither Angola nor Mozambique had a single college graduate then and the

186. Bernard Connelly to Secretary of State, 4 August 1950, RG 59, Decimal File, Box 3573, *NARA-CP*.

187. Ed Hawley, 'Eduardo Mondlane: A Personal Memoir," Box 4, Subgroup II, Series I, *Herb Shore Collection, Oberlin College-Ohio*.

188. Herbert Shore, "The Legacy of Eduardo Mondlane," circa 1994, Box 1, Subgroup II, Series I, *Herb Shore Collection*.

189. Robert Faris, *Liberating Mission in Mozambique: Faith and Revolution in the Life of Eduardo Mondlane*, Cambridge, U.K.: Lutterworth, 2015, 63.

190. Darrell and Mildred Randall to "Dear Friends," June 1950, Box 2, Subgroup II, Series I, *Herb Shore Collection, Oberlin College-Ohio*.

latter contained not a single high school graduate. The "average able bodied African" said an angry observer reputed to be Mondlane, was "little better than a slave," as "forced labor" was rampant.[191] By 1951, Lisbon had determined that its principal African colonies were overseas provinces, i.e. part of Portugal, though distant—just like Hawaii, far from the North American mainland, which became part of the U.S. itself in 1959.[192]

Though working underground, the Portuguese Communist Party wielded influence at home and abroad, playing a role in the strong Marxist influence that would inflect the liberation movement founded by Mondlane from its inception. As should be apparent, the Communists had a global network that allowed, for example, Communists in South Africa to exert influence across the border in Mozambique.[193]

In 1952 Mondlane participated in a major radio broadcast from the University of Chicago featuring the anthropologist Melville Herskovits and the academic Edwin Munger, who specialized in the study of Southern Africa. Herskovits lamented the "lack of knowledge" and "lack of understanding" about Africa in the U.S., an ignorance which served to uphold the tawdry alliance then developing between Washington and neo-Nazis in Pretoria. Mondlane spoke in similarly reproachful terms and reminded the audience of a point that may have eluded their attention: "I understand," he said, "that the Orange Free State gold mines are mostly owned by American corporations."[194] One of the advantages that Pretoria enjoyed in the U.S. was the abysmal ignorance of Africa, which allowed the depredations of apartheid to evade scrutiny more than once.[195]

---

191. Letter from Vincent Robertson to "New York Times", 18 August 1952, Box 3, *Herb Shore Collection*. Scribbled on this copy is the notation: "apparently written by Eduardo under pseudonym."

192. Teresa Maria da Cruz e Silva, "The Clandestine Network of FRELIMO in Lourenco Marques (1960-1974)," Diploma Work for Eduardo Mondlane University-Maputo, 1986, 41, Box 4, Subgroup II, Series I, *Herb Shore Collection*.

193. Sonia Kruks, "From Nationalism to Marxism: The Ideological History of FRELIMO, 1962-1977," Presented at Conference on Class Struggle in Angola, Mozambique and Guinea-Bissau, University of Minnesota, 25-27 May 1983, RA 021, RG 1, Series 1, Subseries 1, Box 9, *Social Science Research Council Records, Rockefeller Archive Center, Sleep Hollow, New York.*

194. Report on University of Chicago Roundtable, 6 January 1952, Box 4, Subgroup II, Series I.

195. Claude Barnett to Foreign Editor, "New York Herald-Tribune", 19 May 1948, Box 342, Folder 4: "Your selection" of a "photograph of the

However, the arrival on U.S. shores of those like Mondlane slowly began to alter this dismal picture. He received aid from NAACP leader Channing Tobias, who also helped to administer the Phelps-Stokes Fund to assist Africans arriving in the U.S. to study first, as noted, in Portugal, then at Oberlin College in Ohio. As early as 1952 one onlooker had concluded of this Mozambican that "no African now studying in the U.S. has made a greater impact in stimulating interest in Africa."[196] Negro identification with Africa was to generate activism against colonialism and apartheid.

By 1952, heading in the other direction, toward South Africa, was the U.S. national Herb Shore. He was to be hosted there by the Communist couple—Joe Slovo and Ruth First—and carried introductory letters from the North Stars of U.S. (and African American) leftism, including Du Bois, Robeson, and W. Alphaeus Hunton. There he met Chief Albert Luthuli, a future ANC leader; Yusuf Cachalia; 'Kathy' Kathrada; Ismail and Fatima Meer—leaders all, not to mention Mandela and Walter Sisulu.[197] The latter two had moved closer to the CP just as the NAACP was moving in an opposing direction. In a certain sense, the suppression of the CP in South Africa backfired because it caused a number of Communists to seek political shelter within the ANC, creating a better complementarity between the two.[198]

Chief Luthuli also became close to Communist Party leader Moses Kotane. When the latter died in 1978, his obituary stated accurately that he had a "very close association" with the ANC leader. "Whenever a difficult problem arose Chief Luthuli used to say: 'Kotane is the leader of the workers. We must hear what the leader of the workers has to say about this.'"[199]

By the early 1960s, Mondlane had returned to southeastern Africa and was the major force organizing FRELIMO, the Liberation Front of Mozambique, whose 1975 triumph over Lisbon was to provide a reliable rear base for the ANC to attack apartheid. Shore was emblematic of the scores—if not thousands—of U.S. nationals who

---

medical school in Yaba, Nigeria" used to "illustrate an article on unspeakably atrocious South Africa seemed most inappropriate. Nigeria is thousands of miles away from South Africa. You would scarcely see students in a medical school in South Africa..."

196. Darrell Randall to Dorothy Smith, Oberlin Bureau of Appointments, 2 January 1952, Box 1, Subgroup II, Series I, *Herb Shore Collection*.

197. Herb Shore to Nelson Mandela, circa 1995, Box 5, Subgroup II, Series 5, *Herb Shore Collection*.

198. Anthony Sampson, *Drum: An African Adventure and Adventure*, London: Hodder and Stoughton, 1983, 103.

199. Obituary, 25 May 1978, Reel 7, *Oliver Tambo Papers*.

began to flock to Southern Africa, often with goals hostile to those of U.S. imperialism. Mondlane and Shore were, therefore, symbols of what was soon to come, though this was barely glimpsed in 1952. Perhaps not coincidentally, Gulf Oil began prospecting for petroleum near that same time while Firestone Rubber was in the midst of augmenting its operations in Beira in the north of the nation.[200]

The U.S. and South Africa were yoked in chains of state-sanctioned racism, yet the global pretensions of U.S. imperialism were forcing Washington to move in another direction, culminating in 1954 with the high court's decision to declare Jim Crow unconstitutional. There then ensued a lengthy battle—yet to be consummated—between resistant forces eager to ally with apartheid for sustenance and progressive elements tugging the other way. The latter were to prevail in the short term but the collapse of the socialist camp by the end of 1991 compromised the long-term struggles of both U.S. Negroes, largely willing to endorse this disaster, and Africans who largely did not.

200. Eduardo Mondlane, *The Struggle for Mozambique*, London: Zed, 1983, 94, 95.

Chapter 6

"Where are the Militant Non-Communist Whites?" 1952-1956

AS should be evident by now, since the late 19th century U.S. Negroes and Africans in the southern cone of the continent had shared a mutual influence. Nelson Mandela, for example, was rhapsodic in recounting how "as a young man I idolized the Brown Bomber," the nickname of U.S. boxer Joe Louis, "who took on not only his opponents in the ring but racists outside of it."[1] Mandela also spoke respectfully of Jack Johnson, the heavyweight boxing champion at the beginning of the 20th century. U.S. Negro women, on the other hand, influenced their counterparts in South Africa to straighten their hair.[2] May Day, the worker's holiday, was made in the U.S.A. and it was on that day in South Africa in 1950 that Mandela watched agape as the police ran riot, beating and slaying celebrants, a landmark on his road to embracing the CP—he narrowly escaped being killed.[3] A few years later Philip S. Foner, the U.S. historian thought to be close to Communists, was recruited by the South African left to explain "How May Day Began."[4]

Walter Sisulu, perhaps Mandela's closest comrade during his lengthy imprisonment, fondly recalled Wellington Buthelezi from the 1920s, who "spoke in English" and sought cachet by posing as a U.S. Negro. "Because of [the] story of Black Americans," said the ANC leader, "we thought of America as a black people's continent" and held closely the "feeling that black Americans are coming" and will be "liberating us." Thus, there was "great excitement when the

1. Kelly Knauer, ed., *Nelson Mandela: A Hero's Journey*, New York: TIME, 2013, 47.

2. Amanda Denise Kemp, "'Up From Slavery' and Other Narratives: Black South African Performances of the American Negro (1920-1943)," 103, 156.

3. Ibid., Kelly Knauer, 44.

4. *New Age*, 26 April 1956.

first ever plane came in the area"; and there was reverence for the "spirit and influence of Marcus Garvey." Born in 1912, Sisulu read the writings of Booker T. Washington, who "influenced me" because he was "poor" and strived forward nonetheless and conceded that the latter's sparring partner, Du Bois, "influenced" him too. Washington's influence was "cultural" whereas Du Bois' seemed to be political.[5]

But the impact made by U.S. Negroes in Southern Africa postwar was beginning to lessen, blocked by Cold War barriers and the marginalizing of those like Du Bois. Thus, Sisulu also cited J.B. Marks and Moses Kotane as influences, bringing him closer in thinking to the now departed Xuma. Still, by 1952 he was in touch with Robeson.[6]

Ahmed Kathrada, yet another of Mandela's close prison comrades, admired Robeson's rendition of "Ol' Man River" and quoted U.S. novelist Howard Fast, cited F. Scott Fitzgerald and the abolitionist William Lloyd Garrison. Kathrada joined Sisulu at the Soviet legation for the 36th anniversary of the Russian Revolution.[7] Howard Fast, soon to repudiate his former comrades in the CP, was often celebrated by the South African left.[8]

Pretoria sough to circumscribe the effects of these artists' work. Roger Baldwin of the American Civil Liberties Union informed the U.S. delegation to UNESCO [United Nations Educational, Scientific and Cultural Organization] of his objection to the "standards established by the Union of South Africa for the denial of admission of works by American Negroes" but it is doubtful if his objection would have included the works of Robeson, who had become radioactive, even among "liberals" like James Baldwin.[9]

Negro music was also popular in South Africa, as were writers like Willard Motley. Gangsters in South Africa took their cues from Hollywood, especially the depictions by the actor Richard Widmark. One of the most popular gangs in Xuma's Sophiatown called themselves the "Americans." They wore expensive clothes associated with the

---

5. *"I Will Go Singing: Walter Sisulu Speaks of His Life and the Struggle for Freedom in South Africa in Conversation with George M. Houser and Herbert Shore,* New York: Africa Fund, circa 1995. Box 4, Subgroup II, Series I, *Herb Shore Collection, Oberlin College-Ohio.*

6. Biographical Materials on Walter Sisulu, no date, Box 3, Subgroup II, Series I, *Herb Shore Collection.*

7. Ahmed Kathrada, *Memoirs*, Cape Town: New Holland, 2004, 11, 122, 127, 199, 36.

8. *Advance* [Cape Town], 16 April 1953.

9. Roger Baldwin to Mary McCullough, 5 November 1952, Box IIA7, *NAACP Papers.*

republic, including straw hats, elegant cardigans, brown and white shoes, and narrow blue trousers called "bogarts" because Hollywood's Humphrey Bogart once wore them. They drove Buicks.[10]

This one-sided litany is revealing. U.S. Negroes, still ambivalent about their African roots considering pervasive white supremacy, were then blocked once again from currents flowing westward across the Atlantic when the ANC allied more closely with the CP as the NAACP was moving quickly to distance itself from Communists. The eclipse of Robeson, perhaps the most popular U.S. Negro in South Africa, in the United States also effectively sabotaged the effort to build bridges across the Atlantic. Refusing to endorse anticommunist ideology, the ANC built bridges to the socialist camp—especially East Berlin, Moscow, and Havana—making them complicated partners for U.S. Negroes. The celebrated South African writer Alex La Guma is illustrative in this regard. One analyst has compared him fruitfully to Robeson, Du Bois, and Langston Hughes, "not least the fact that all viewed the Soviet Union, at one time as an ally in the struggle against global racial oppression...."[11] This was true—but this stance effectively isolated all four from the U.S. Negro mainstream, which felt compelled to capitulate to the anticommunist consensus.

By May 1954, the South African left sensed the importance of the U.S. decision to move away from juridical Jim Crow. The case of *Brown v. Board of Education,* it was said, was "of the utmost significance not only for the United States but for the whole world." Why the change, mandating the formal illegality of Jim Crow? The "force of international opinion" was the answer, the same force that would help to compel elections in South Africa itself four decades later. "The colour bar is a luxury which [Washington] cannot afford," particularly given the surge toward independence in Africa. Though the "racialists will defend their privileges with increasing ferocity," it was noted accurately, *Brown vs. Board of Education* was bound to "have widespread repercussions" in Africa. It "will blow to smithereens the apartheid pretensions" which "have long tried to maintain, quoting the United States as an example, that segregation is to the benefit of all...."[12] What was striking about this analysis was that it

10. Anthony Sampson, *Drum*, 26.

11. Christopher J. Lee, "Tricontinentalism in Question: The Cold War Politics of Alex La Guma and the African National Congress," in Christopher Lee, ed., *Making a World After Empire: The Bandung Moment and its Political Afterlives*, Athens: Ohio University Press, 2010, 266-286, 280.

12. *Advance*, 27 May 1954.

was much more perceptive than much of what was being written about this case in the U.S. itself.

To be fair, the U.S. was undergoing an agonizing reappraisal of the more horrible aspects of its despicably racist record. It was also in 1954 that the preeminent newsman Edward R. Murrow, who commanded a large television audience, turned his powerful camera on apartheid, with one canny commentator suggesting that the portrait was "not unlike a return visit to darkest Nazism,"[13] which was truer than he recognized, given the continuing prominence of the likes of Oswald Pirow. Eric Louw, responsible for foreign affairs in Pretoria, continued to smart over this perceived slight. He refused to address the American Men's Luncheon Club in Johannesburg, then chose to retaliate by speaking to the group in acid terms, adding the twist that "in view of a color issue in the United States, one would have expected a more sympathetic approach." The envoy present thought that "he appears to be trying to extend to the rest of the world the domestic political battle of the Nationalist Party."[14] In fact, the Nationalists rarely seemed to grasp that global responsibilities were compelling Washington to retreat from legalized racism at a time when Pretoria took the opposing tack: this chasm was difficult to bridge.

Months later, Louw was still irritated about the Murrow report and this irksomeness found a new target in the popular author John Gunther, who turned his spotlight on apartheid. As a result, U.S. press organs including the *New York Times* and *TIME* found it difficult to gain an audience with Prime Minister J.G. Strijdom. The Smuts-era bonhomie with Pretoria was fading. Louw provided instructions on how foreign correspondents should do their jobs, telling them that they should live in Cape Town or Pretoria—rather than Johannesburg—to be closer to government, rather than the "political opposition."[15]

Just as it was more likely for Africans to be influenced by U.S. Negroes than vice versa, the South African left, members of a nation without global pretensions, was much more insightful about what was propping up apartheid externally, as opposed to African Americans who rarely dwelled on the international dimensions of Jim

13. Patrick Henry Martin, "American Views on South Africa, 1948-1972," Ph.d. dissertation, Louisiana State University, 1974, 18.

14. William L. Wright to Secretary of State, 3 October 1956, RG 59, Decimal Files, Box 3233, *NARA-CP*.

15. Report from U.S. Embassy, Pretoria, 5 January 1956, RG 59, Decimal File, Box 3230, *NARA-CP*.

Crow. Thus "bus apartheid" in South Africa was depicted unequivocally as the product of a "foreign ideology."[16]

Writing from London, Arthur Keppel-Jones realized that as the world moved away from juridical racism, by the early 1950s Pretoria would be isolated.[17] The U.S. visitors Dorothy and Douglas Steere were gob smacked to find that the author had posited that a so-called race war would be launched in South Africa by 1970, resulting in the African seizure of power—"aided by Negro batallions" from the USA. In some ways this was a throwback to Wellington Buthelezi and the 1920s notion that Negroes in planes would liberate South Africa. In other ways, it represented growing anxiety about the long-term impact of the then glacial retreat of Jim Crow.[18]

This anxiety was also reflected in the gloomy words of Douglass Reed of the National Economic Council in New York ("dedicated to the preservation of Private Enterprise and the American Way of Life and the maintenance of American Independence.") It was in 1953 that this British author, then residing in Canada, lamented that "the world press has in recent months published more about South Africa than at any time since the Anglo-Boer War of fifty years ago." With apparent disappointment he announced, "there would be no problem today had other claimants to the land been simply extirpated," referring to Africans, recuperating the tardy notion that the majority should be simply exterminated. He was sympathetic toward the "only completely cut off white nation to have evolved overseas." This contributed to intense insularity, he suggested, explaining why South Africa was "probably the only country in the world where political news" sold "more newspapers than sport, crime, sex, café society tittle or movie tattle...."[19]

Keppel-Jones did not investigate the canyons that would separate Africans from U.S. Negroes, though this would have improved his otherwise dismal analysis. It was in 1953 that Sisulu, unabashed in detailing the influence U.S. Negroes had upon him, headed to Eastern Europe. He visited Poland and Romania and the Soviet

16. *The Clarion* [Cape Town], 7 August 1952.

17. Arthur Keppel-Jones, *When Smuts Goes: A History of South Africa from 1952 to 2010...*, London: Gollancz, 1947. 130.

18. Report by Dorothy and Douglas Steeres, 12 June 1953, South Africa File, *Records of American Friends Service Committee-Philadelphia.*

19. Douglas Reed, "Unknown South Africa," 1953, Box 1, *Robert Cecil Cook Papers, University of Southern Mississippi-Hattiesburg.*

Union, then headed to China.[20] In the early stages of this journey, he passed through Israel and met with the left-leaning Naomi Shapiro but was blunt in asserting, "I did not have any admiration for those who left the Soviet Union to settle in Israel," since such departures were "probably the first cause of friction between the USSR and Israel." In a simple sentence, Sisulu had violated two articles of faith of the Cold War U.S.: don't say anything positive about the Soviet Union and don't say anything negative about Israel.[21] Sisulu won few admirers in Washington when in a talk broadcast on Peking Radio he termed China an "inspiration" that left him thoroughly "impressed."[22] His comrade Kathrada was then in Moscow, finding it similarly praiseworthy.[23] By December 1953, ANC leader Duma Nokwe had just returned from a lengthy journey to China, the Soviet Union, the Netherlands, Israel, Czechoslovakia and Poland.[24] The Communist Ruth First was to be found in China in 1954, hailing socialism.[25] By 1955 Kotane's arrival in China hardly raised an eyebrow among South African leftists.[26] Portentously, he made a stop during his lengthy journey in Bandung, Indonesia, site of an important gathering of the colonized and newly independent nations, many of which were from Africa. It was intended as the ultimate compliment when the British writer Cedric Belfrage gushed that Kotane "could be taken for [Robeson's] younger brother." All told, Kotane spent two months in "New China", three months in India, and an undetermined amount of time in Warsaw.[27]

His presence did not go unnoticed. A conversation between Prime Minister J.G. Strijdom and Edward T. Wailes, the U.S. envoy in Cape Town, led the South African to denounce Bandung, as he "mentioned the presence of Moses Kotane and Maulvi Cachalia, two… non-Europeans who are Communists…." Walies noted cogently that "he bluntly emphasized *baaskap* [white supremacy] more than apartheid [racial separation]," which could have been seen as a distinction without a difference; worse, it was insincere since Strijdom should

20. Biographical Data on Walter Sisulu, no date, Box 3, Subgroup II, Series I, *Herb Shore Collection*.
21. Ibid., Walter Sisulu, 85.
22. *Advance*, 5 November 1953.
23. *Advance*, 12 November 1953.
24. *Advance*, 10 December 1953.
25. *New Age*, 25 November 1954.
26. *New Age*, 20 October 1955.
27. *New Age*, 16 February 1956.

have spoken frankly about his real agenda: Afrikaner supremacy.[28] The Prime Minister would have been more honest if he had stressed his other ideological guide: anticommunism.

The Communist Ben Turok met Sisulu and Nokwe in Bucharest at a Communist youth festival in the early 1950s, suggestive of the magnetic appeal exerted by Eastern Europe, which was rapidly becoming a bulwark of support for the anti-apartheid movement.[29] Few should have been surprised when the ANC introduced a new uniform that bore a close resemblance to the collarless "Mao" suit still donned in certain left wing circles.[30] For assuredly Moscow and its far-flung allies served to bolster anti-apartheid forces when the situation seemed to be grim and glum.

The writer Mary Benson, who interviewed Sisulu during this time, described him as being of medium height with pale skin, "ugly with uneven teeth" and a "slightly eastern look." He joined the ANC in 1940. Contrastingly, she described Mandela as "huge" and "handsome," also with "palish skin" and "firm hands." He was "gentle" with "immense warmth and affectionate" besides. As the Suppression of Communism Act began to bite in 1950, Mandela was brought into closer contact with Reds, then seeking political sanctuary. "There are two streams of African nationalism," he said then: "one centres around Marcus Garvey," it was "extreme and ultra-revolutionary." Another stream, he contended, was reflected in his own Congress Youth League, which was left-leaning.[31]

This was not just a matter of closer personal relations, though it was that too. Mandela was also becoming better acquainted with the massive Communist bibliography, developed over decades, on methods of struggle. It was Mandela, his comrade Raymond Mhlaba recalled, who devised the fightback scheme, which reflected classic Communist doctrine: "he proposed that the branches be divided into cells based on a single street, headed by a cell steward. Seven street cells would form a zone, headed by a chief steward. Four zones would form a ward, headed by a prime steward. Wards would form a branch, headed by a secretariat that would co-ordinate the

28. Edward T. Wailes to Secretary of State, 4 May 1955, RG59, Decimal File, Box 2612, *NARA-CP*.

29. Interview with Ben Turok, 15 March 1973, Box 10, *Gwendolen Carter Papers*.

30. *Advance*, 12 August 1954.

31. Description of Walter Sisulu and Interview with Nelson Mandela, no date, Box 1, Folder 3, *Mary Benson Research Materials about the African National Congress of South Africa, University of California-Los Angeles.*

activities of the ANC within the townships. This was the strategy that became known as the Mandela Plan or M-Plan." Through this elaborate scheme, "it was easy for the ANC branches to spread the message about the Freedom Charter,"[32] the animating document from the mid-1950s that was to guide the struggle to victory by 1994.

The Communist Wolfie Kodesh, who had reproved Mandela's previous hostility to the party, agreed that anticommunist legislation had the perverse effect of driving the ANC and CP into each other's arms. The party's new name—the South African Communist Party—reflected a new orientation, in that it was one of the few multi-racial, multi-ethnic groupings; a fact that helps to account for its relative success—and "not only the philosophy of Marx and Engels."[33]

Frank S. Loescher, arriving in South Africa in 1953, also noticed this trend: "one of my disturbing findings concerning the movement for equality of opportunity" there was that "by and large the Communists, with the exception of a handful of white clergymen, have been the only white people to work shoulder to shoulder with the Africans."[34] After meeting with Mandela for an hour, Loescher seemed distressed to find that "both the Coloureds and the Africans in these groups draw no line against Communists...."[35] (Visiting on behalf of Philadelphia-based Quakers, Loescher had a "shock" when he found that "English speaking people" declare "that the only hope" for their benighted land "was intervention by Britain, the U.N. or America," so desperate were they to escape the suffocation of Afrikaner supremacy.[36] Loescher, who held among other posts a professorship at Temple University, left for Johannesburg in March 1953 with his spouse Mildred and their 11-year-old son—at the behest of the Ford Foundation,[37] whose munificence was based

32. Thembeka Mufamadi, narrator, *Raymond Mhlaba's Personal Memoirs*, Pretoria: Human Sciences Research Council, 2001, 95, 103.

33. Oral History, Wolfie Kodesh, 4 October 2000, *University of Connecticut-Storrs*.

34. Report by Frank S. Loescher, 15 September 1953, Foreign Service-1953 File, *Records of American Friends Service Committee-Philadelphia*. Hereafter denoted as AFSC.

35. Report by Frank S. Loescher, 5 May 1953, Foreign Service 1953 File, *AFSC*.

36. Report by Frank S. Loescher, 21 June 1953, South Africa File, *Records of American Friends Se Committee-Philadelphia*. Hereafter denoted as AFSC.

37. Lucretia Wood to Kirk Franken, 6 March 1953, Foreign Service 1953 File, *AFSC*.

on stock holdings in the vehicle company of the same name, which happened to be invested heavily in South Africa.)

Mandela was then rising in the ANC hierarchy but, tellingly, when the *Bantu World*[38] unveiled a preferred cabinet to rule the land in 1953, it included the recently elected ANC head Albert Luthuli as president; Z.K. Matthews as Prime Minister; Kotane as Minister of the Interior; and Kathrada as Secretary of Transportation. It was a "political fantasy," harrumphed the U.S. envoy in Pretoria,[39] but, as things turned out, the only fantasy involved was the exclusion of Mandela from this "dream team." For the authorities had their eye on the tall, imposing Mandela. By December 1952—just as Luthuli was elected as ANC president—Mandela was served with a double set of notices preventing him from attending all gatherings in the Union outside of Johannesburg.[40]

This was only the beginning. By 1956, the *New Age*, a lineal descendant of the *Guardian* of Cape Town, billed Mandela as a "prominent African attorney" who had "received perhaps more banning notices and prohibitions than any other Congress figure," the latest "prohibiting him from attending all gatherings...." The paper recalled the September 1953 notice that "ordered" Mandela to "resign" from the ANC. So, cramped, he was now "limiting his extensive legal practice in partnership with Mr. [Oliver] Tambo."[41]

Anticommunism shaped the trajectory of the movement in many ways. The SACP, for example, had a bent toward organizing in factories and mines. Yet, as Turok explained, "organizing the ANC was an awful lot easier than organizing trade unions," because "terror against trade unionists was very much fiercer" while an "ANC group could get together in a township" or "they could meet in someone's home." But "the moment you went to a factory.... always the white foreman or the manager or the boss himself" intervened. Further, seeking to "organize workers at the residential level was very difficult," even in Cape Town, which "was in a sense a little more left-wing than the rest of the country...."[42]

But, if the U.S. envoy is to be believed, there were further reasons why the ANC, as influenced by the SACP, was able to gain traction. By the summer of 1952 Joseph Dougherty envisioned "continued

38. *Bantu World*, 13 June 1953.

39. Henri E. La Tendresse, Pretoria to Secretary of State, 12 June 1953, RG 59, Decimal File, Box 3572, *NARA-CP*.

40. *Advance*, 18 December 1952.

41. *New Age*, 29 March 1956.

42. Interview, Ben Turok, 15 March 1973, Box 10, *Gwendolen Carter Papers*.

and increasing difficulty with Communism in South Africa during the next four to six years…." Yes, the so-called "'Russian' gang made up of Basutos was not Communistic" but the "civil guard made up of Zulus and Swazis was Communistic and was well organized." Certainly the "leaders were Communists" and, slyly, "had made an effort to become a part of the law enforcement…." The "danger point" for this infiltration was the "educated Native" and the "focal points for the dissemination of Communistic propaganda was the Russian Consulate General" in Pretoria, soon to be expelled. Referring to the Red leader Solly Sachs, he deduced that a "favorite trick of Communists was to say they had been kicked out of the Party and then continue with their dirty work"—for example, sheltered in the warm embrace of the ANC.[43]

Thus, by 1952 Mandela was designated as "Volunteer-in-Chief of the Defiance Campaign," a massive protest against apartheid held to mark the 300th anniversary of the European invasion of the Cape. Now he was giving an "exclusive interview" to a periodical known to be shaped by Communists. He accused the regime of saying figuratively, "why are we white men fighting against one another, on minor issues when we are all really in agreement that the African should be segregated into ghettoes, should provide a perpetual source of cheap labour and be kept in permanent political subjugation." He warned against a "European front" of Nationalists and the remnants of the United Party—now known as Liberals—that "would turn the whole movement into a racial front with disastrous consequences for all…." He objected to the "view that possession of a University degree or property entitles the possessor to different treatment," e.g. the distasteful idea that the vote be accorded to "civilized" Africans alone. Instead, Mandela insisted, "the people are demanding direct representation in Parliament and nothing [less than] this will satisfy them."[44]

This campaign was a marker laid down by the left after it was thought they had been successfully pummeled. "Today", said the campaign coalition that included the ANC and the Indian Congress, "we are [persecuted] tomorrow it may well be parliamentary opposition who dares to criticize the Nationalists. The same thing," it was said forebodingly, "happened in Nazi Germany." Mandela, concluded upliftingly: "I am however convinced that the people have heard what they can do and no power can stop their forward march

43. Memorandum of Conversations with Ministers Swart and Sauer by Joseph Dougherty, 6 August 1952, RG 59, Decimal File, Box 3572, *NARA-CP*.

44. *People's World* [Cape Town], 2 October 1952.

toward freedom."[45] Joe Matthews of the ANC was among those who found the campaign to be a rousing success, as indicated by the fact the participation of women was "fifty, fifty", a real breakthrough.[46]

African American women may have had a role in this turnout. In April 1952 Los Angeles-based editor Charlotta Bass and her comrade with Sojourners for Truth and Justice, the Harlem activist Louise Patterson, lent "full support to the launching of a national campaign of Civil Disobedience by the colored peoples of South Africa," adding "we have been inspired by the example of militant action on the part of African women," concluding with the frequently cited point that "our fight for freedom in the United States is inextricably linked to the struggle against the tyranny of the white supremacists...."[47] Suitably impressed, Du Bois also endorsed wholeheartedly the Defiance Campaign.[48]

Unimpressed were Mandela's fellow attorneys, who initiated proceedings to bar him from the profession, because of a conviction arising out of this spirited campaign.[49] They failed.[50]

Later, Quaker staffer Bill Sutherland would reflect that the "key point" is that "in terms of applied nonviolent methods and sacrifice and suffering in carrying out essentially nonviolent campaigns, Africa was far ahead of American and European pacifists...the 1952 Defiance Campaign against unjust laws" in South Africa "predates by several years the Montgomery Bus Boycott." Similarly, "the Positive Action campaign in Ghana's independence struggle, 1948-1952—was definitely inspired by India...." Continuing in that vein, the Negro activist wrote, "when I first went to Nkrumah's small house in 1954 there were two pictures on his wall: one of Marcus Garvey, the other of Gandhi...when I first met [Kenneth Kaunda, Zambian leader] in 1958 [he] had just returned from India,"[51] indicative of the cross-border waves that drove change.

---

45. "Bulletin of the Campaign for the Defiance of Unjust Laws," 8 September 1952, Box IIA7, *NAACP Papers*.

46. Oral History, Joe Matthews, 2 October 2000, *University of Connecticut-Storrs*.

47. Charlotta Bass, National President and Louise Patterson, Secretary, Sojourners for Truth and Justice to Ray Alexander, 5 April 1952, C1.5, *Jack Simons and Ray Alexander Collection, University of Cape Town*.

48. *People's World*, 11 September 1952.

49. *Advance*, 25 March 1954.

50. *Advance*, 6 March 1954.

51. Bill Sutherland to Jo Ann Robinson, 23 August 1979, PED 1979 SOUTHERN AFRICA PROGRAM, *AFSC*.

In the early 1950s Mandela was echoing Communists. In his capacity as President of the Transvaal ANC, a position which put him face-to-face with the strongest supporters apartheid had to offer, he warned of the "Danger of War in Africa," succinctly elaborating: "for years now the capitalist countries have lived on raw materials and cheap labour from Asia and Africa" but now "under the guise of defense against Communism, the [U.S.] is in fact eliminating British influence…." Addressing the left-inflected South African Peace Congress, he denounced the "mad lust for profits and markets in Africa, the war preparations of the United States and its satellite countries…."[52] By September 1953, he had published an article entitled "Africa and Peace" that reflected these newfound, Marxist-oriented notions.[53]

Meanwhile, back in the republic a group known as the "American Peace Crusade" was threatening to picket the apartheid legation. Worryingly, the ambassador "stated that Mr. Robeson's name appeared on the letterhead of several of these organizations," which also included CAA, National Council of Arts, Sciences and Professions, Americans for South African Resistance, the African Nationalist Movement—but not the NAACP.[54] Both Mandela and Robeson were being firmly targeted as a result.

Mandela's new orientation was not greeted with equanimity. The left charged there was a "little Broederbond" in the ANC, a "secret splinter organization," which Mandela renounced as "unhealthy" and Kotane called "disruptive."[55] In a sense, it was a premonition of what was to unfold in less than a decade when the nationalist Pan Africanist Congress emerged to challenge the ANC.

Naturally, the NAACP—which had purged Du Bois and waged a virulent anticommunist war[56]—sought to woo ANC leader Z.K. Matthews, after he came to the U.S. in the early 1950s. Matthews caught the eye of Washington when he lectured at the University of Cape Town and argued that Marcus Garvey—contrary to the historical

---

52. *Advance*, 3 September 1953. Despite the date on the newspaper, it might have actually been published 3 December 1953.

53. *Advance*, 10 September 1953.

54. Joseph Dougherty to Secretary of State, 6 August 1952, RG 59, Decimal File, Box 3572, *NARA-CP*.

55. *Advance*, 22 October 1953.

56. Gerald Horne, *Black and Red: W.E.B. Du Bois and the Afro-American Response to the Cold War, 1944-1963*, Albany: State University of New York, 1986.

record—"had never won a following in the Union."[57] It was in 1953 that Walter White of the NAACP told CIA official Cord Meyer[58] that Matthews and his spouse "would be most happy to hear from their friends in America...."[59] A similar letter was sent to CIA Director Allen Dulles.[60]

It is not evident if Matthews was a willing accomplice or, as often happened, White was just inflating his own importance by passing himself off to be closer to the ANC leader than he was.[61] For at the same time, it was reported by the Cape Town left that Pretoria and Washington "tried to bully Prof. Matthews" since they were "frightened of revelations before [the] United Nations" he could well deliver.[62]

On the other hand, pointing in a different direction was a "confidential security information memorandum for the files" prepared in April 1953 in which Matthews, then head of the ANC in the Cape, was cited as saying that he was "afraid that the ANC would fall under Communist control" and that "he had fought hard against Communist influence"—all while baiting the Indian population, a dangerous kind of gesture that had sparked riots in the recent past, while calling into question the strong diplomatic support rendered by New Delhi and Islamabad.[63]

White himself had earlier sought to travel to South Africa but Secretary of State Dean Acheson told him then that the "President expressed concern for your safety in the Union of South Africa" since the nation had "recently experienced some of the most serious racial riots in its history and the situation" was "extremely delicate. We have some doubts as to the feasibility of giving you an official designation," he said—which was probably a stroke of good luck for the anti-apartheid movement.[64] This idea of sending a Negro to resolve the nettlesome matter of apartheid arose repeatedly. Loescher, the Quaker representative, stressed in 1953 that a "top American Negro"

57. Report by Wilson Flake, 18 March 1955, Reel 11, *Confidential State Department Central File, South Africa-NARA-CP.*

58. Cord Meyer, *Facing Reality: From World Federalism to the CIA*, New York: Harper & Row, 1980.

59. Walter White to "Dear Cord," 21 September 1953, Box IIA7, *NAACP Papers, Library of Congress-Washington, D.C.*

60. Walter White to Allen Dulles, 24 September 1953, Box IIA7.

61. Kenneth Janken, *White: The Biography of Walter White, Mr. NAACP*, New York: New Press, 2003.

62. *Advance* [Cape Town], 20 November 1952.

63. Memorandum, 21 April 1953, RG 59, Decimal File, Box 3572. *NARA-CP.*

64. Dean Acheson to Walter White, 2 March 1950, IIA603, *NAACP Papers.*

should be dispatched forthwith to South Africa: "I recommend Charles Johnson as a Negro who is 'above the battle'" in the U.S. to pose the irrelevant query, "Should they start an 'NAACP' and Urban League"—as if the ANC was insufficient or needed to be circumvented. "America is admired by the Afrikaners," which was true. "After all," he continued, "we got our independence from the British and most Afrikaners want their independence. And, we too have a race problem,"[65] which was also true. Forgotten, however, was Pretoria's reluctance to provide visas to U.S. Negro mediators.

This magic bullet would not disappear. Secretary of State Dean Acheson was asked to "confirm" if Negro leaders including Ralph Bunche, Raymond Pace Alexander, and Horace Mann Bond would be headed to Pretoria in order to formulate a "confidential report" on apartheid and what to do about it.[66] Loescher, like generations of U.S. visitors to come, persisted in thinking that the similarities between the Union and the republic provided the latter not only with insight into the former but the responsibility to intervene there too. "Our two countries," he said, "are also alike in that the whole world is watching us. Americans who go to Europe or Asia are always asked about our treatment of the Negro. I am told the same thing happens to South Africans, when they go abroad!"[67]

Loescher, who was the Executive Director of the Commission on Human Relations in Philadelphia, met in Johannesburg with an editor at the popular publication *Drum*: one of his "buddies" there "arranged an interview for me with Dr. [Yusuf] Dadoo, head of the Transvaal Indian Congress and reported brains behind the African National Congress," a questionable—even bigoted—idea widely circulated, which vitiated the skill and intelligence of Africans. "It's harder to get an interview with Dadoo than almost any figure in South Africa," Loescher claimed further. "I felt very lucky when I had two hours with him."[68]

Rather naively, White demanded that since Washington barred "Foreign Communist, Nazi, fascist and other totalitarian parties," that members and leaders of the "Nationalist Party of the Union of

65. Report by Frank Loescher, 15 September 1953, Foreign Service 1953 File, *Records of American Friends Service Committee-Philadelphia.*

66. James Fleming to Secretary of State Acheson, 22 August 1952, RG 59, Decimal File, Box 3572.

67. Report by Frank S. Loescher, 7 August 1953, Foreign Service 1953 File.

68. Report by Frank S. Loescher, 7 August 1953, Foreign Service 1953 File, *AFSC.*

South Africa" be excluded from the republic.[69] He did not seem to realize that Pretoria's status as an anticommunist ally and anchor would prevent its leaders from being barred, the NAACP's protests to the contrary.

White, a kind of publicity hound, was reprimanded by A.J. Norval of Pretoria's Department of Commerce after he visited the NAACP leader in the U.S. "I had taken you to be 'white,'" Norval confessed, which may have caused him to be more candid than he should have been since the conversation descended into talk of the relative inabilities of African-Americans versus Africans. Norval determined that it was "sheer hypocrisy on the part of anyone in the United States to criticize [apartheid]" on "racial issues." This he knew since he traveled "very extensively" in the U.S. and left decidedly unimpressed. "I encountered conditions there which were as bad as, if not worse than, the worst" in his own homeland. Norval rejected the ascending line in the U.S. that White articulated—i.e. the "retort that all that was being cleared up and that all barriers between 'white' and 'Coloured' were crumbling…." Without reservation, Norval "replied that I had seen very little evidence of that." Instead he spoke freely of a "strong underlying current of tension between the races in the United States, particularly up North…." Thus, he found the "position of the Bantu" back home was "infinitely preferable to that of the American Negro," which was self-serving but ultimately true—but only because the "Bantu" could gain sovereignty and self-determination, something denied to Negroes. Thus, agreeing with Acheson, but for different reasons, Norval felt compelled to "retract the promise to support a visit" to South Africa for White. He had visited White at the "suggestion of the State Department" but departed with "great disappointment."[70] This conflicted episode, inter alia, revealed the difficulty that Washington would face in welding together anticommunists of various stripes.

Norval should have admitted, however, what White was told in June 1953: South African courts were drawing on U.S. jurisprudence to uphold the lineaments of apartheid. "Separate but equal," said Robert Carter of the NAACP staff, was being applied with a vengeance in South Africa, which had "moved further than American courts in the application of this doctrine," he argued.[71] Loescher concurred

---

69. Walter White to Attorney General McGrath, 26 October 1950, Box IIA7, *NAACP Papers*.

70. *Rand Daily Mail*, 5 November 1952 and A.J. Norval to Walter White, 8 November 1952, Box IIA7.

71. Robert Carter to Walter White, 5 June 1953, Box IIA7.

with Norval in comparing the racial integration of the police force in his own Philadelphia with Cape Town. But Loescher found that apartheid in 1948 had meant a leap backward by the Union. At the citadel of higher education in Afrikanerdom—Stellebosch University— "twenty years ago," he said in 1953, "the theological school occasionally had non-European speakers. I was told that such a thing was unthinkable today...."[72] Loescher also found that "some leaders of the African National Congress welcome the Nationalist victory because it helps to sharpen the issues and to heighten African solidarity."[73] Maybe. But this "victory" was hard to spin as a step forward for Africans.

Loescher also noticed similarities between the lands of Jim Crow and apartheid. By late April 1953 he had been in South Africa for only two weeks, since—typically— "our visas [were] held up for a month." Yes, he said with weariness, "the skyscrapers and traffic remind us of USA cities but in the USA cities one doesn't see dark-skinned people barefooted or women carrying babies on their backs and bundles and suitcases on their heads."[74]

The accuracy of Norval's critique of the U.S. notwithstanding, he could not obscure the bitter ironies of apartheid. It was in 1954 that the Durban Film Festival was launched, naturally on a racially segregated basis—except for a screening of *The Story of Helen Keller* open to all non-European audiences.[75] The logic of the film choice was hard to grasp but, possibly, since the story was about a blind character, it may have been an inadvertent nod to the moral blindness of apartheid .

Norval and White would have served their respective nations more effectively if they had both confronted the essential epoxy that fastened their nations tightly: the lust for profit. This vital imperative was not ignored by the U.S. Consul General in Port Elizabeth when in 1955 he reminded the State Department that "from the opening of the plant in 1926 until about 1948 the General Motors [facility] here relied upon European labor to fill virtually all skilled and semi-skilled positions." Now GM bosses and other managers of U.S. firms

72. Report by Frank S. Loescher, 21 June 1953, South Africa File,

73. Report by Frank S. Loescher, 30 April 1953, Foreign Service 1953 File, *AFSC*.

74. Report by Frank S. Loescher, 30 April 1953, Foreign Service 1953 File, *AFSC*.

75. Consul General, Durban to Secretary of State, 20 December 1954, Reel 8, *Confidential U.S. State Department Central Files, South Africa, 1955-1959, NARA-CP*.

in the vicinity of this industrial metropolis had to "admit in private discussions that much of the European labor they get fresh from the farms is less suitable for their mechanized operations than much Colored labor and second-generation Native labor." One boss was "quoted in the press as saying that if suitable European labor could be found, the plant would be ready to dismiss all non-European labor." Such a plan was infeasible, but the idea still "caused indignation and bitterness among non-Europeans,"[76] placing GM in a vise, forced to choose apartheid over raw profit. Ultimately, the former would have to yield to the latter by 1994.

David Ladin, a U.S. national of Swedish ancestry, was Managing Director of GM in Port Elizabeth. He was described as a "conservative old South African hand and enjoys the confidence and the cooperation of South African officials," a testament to his political reliability. Yet even he, it was reported, was "worried about the Native Question...."[77]

Representing the U.S. government, David Robertson spoke at length with an American executive at Firestone Rubber in Port Elizabeth, who was described as a "progressive Southerner" with 18 years' experience in South Africa. He had purchased a home and other property and had a son studying medicine at the University of Cape Town. He was then contemplating retirement in the land of apartheid. Understandably, he was "deeply concerned over the Native Problem" and specifically the "high degree of organization" demonstrated by the ANC during a recent strike.[78] Likewise, James Sappington III, the U.S. emissary in Pretoria, spoke with Professor Gwendolen Carter of Smith College in the U.S. after she had visited Port Elizabeth and neighboring New London, and she too agreed that the ANC was "spreading" in influence.[79]

On his South African trip, Loescher was stunned to find that while in "Western Europe and the USA the ratio of salaries for skilled, semi-skilled and unskilled workers is roughly 5:3:2," in the land of apartheid "the ratio is roughly 16:3:1." This unjust enrichment had benefited European labor but with the erosion of apartheid could turn it into profit for U.S. corporations. Loescher was also struck by

76. John J. Harter to Secretary of State, 15 August 1955, Reel 6, *Confidential U.S. State Department Central Files, South Africa, 1955-1959...., NARA-CP.*

77. Report, circa 1952, RG 59, Decimal File, Box 3572, *NARA-CP.*

78. Report by David Robertson, 2 December 1952, RG 59, Decimal File, Box 3572, *NARA-CP.*

79. Report by James Sappington III, 29 May 1953, RG 59, Decimal File, Box 3572.

the "positive discrimination" on behalf of Afrikaners engendered by apartheid's coming: "USA Republicans who have opposed public housing would have a fit if they could see some of the features of European public housing...." In fact, "practically every white family has one or more African servants and the government makes provision for this custom even in public housing!"[80]

This complex matter of deployment of labor was not trivial for GM, since by 1954 this giant and the fellow Michigan-based manufacturer, Ford, accounted for about 52% of all passenger vehicles and about 69% of trucks in the land of apartheid.[81] Of course, promoting African labor and raising wages concomitantly—which could happen if apartheid eroded—could simultaneously lift profits for these corporations, since rising wages would likely translate into higher sales. These misbegotten profits, like a stimulant, gave a jolt to the apartheid economy. U.S. visitors Dorothy and Douglas Steere felt that the booming South African economy gave African workers "bargaining power" since the boom meant an expansion of industry which led to increased hiring and training of African skilled workers, providing them with leverage—despite opposition from the reactionary wing of the working class.[82]

White's proposed trip to Pretoria was an extension of the wider trends bringing the Union and the republic much closer. By 1953, traditional South African methods of crime investigation, largely derived from Scotland Yard, were being replaced by the methods of the FBI. Operatives from Pretoria were being sent to study under U.S. teachers. These adoptions marked a wider embrace of the so-called "American Way of Life;" this was also seen in a resolution of the Transvaal Congress of the Nationalist Party calling for the establishment of an "Un-South African Activities Committee", a mirror image of the U.S. Committee on Un-American Activities,[83] a convergence noted by Loescher.[84]

Rather cannily, Pretoria did not bar all Negro visitors. When Marie Bryant, described as a "Negro singer," arrived in South Africa in 1953, this New Orleans based performer offered the slogan "Don't

---

80. Report by Frank S. Loescher, 21 June 1953, South Africa File, *Records of Africa Friends Service Committee-Philadelphia.*

81. Consul General-Johannesburg to Secretary of State, 8 April 1954, Reel 8, *Confidential U.S. State Department Central Files, South Africa.*

82. Report from Dorothy and Douglas Steere, 20 January 1953, South Africa File, *AFSC.*

83. *Advance*, 1 October 1953.

84. Ibid., Frank Loescher, 21 June 1953.

malign Malan," in support of the "wonderful man." "It is quite right," she crooned, "that our filthy old houses be burned down...." Yet even this Quisling was forthright in "condemning the colour bar and discrimination in America."[85] Also making the journey across the ocean was the activist Homer Jack, who was to become part of the leadership of the American Committee on Africa, organized in 1953—in part as an anticommunist counterpoint to Robeson's Council on African Affairs. With a surfeit of optimism, Jack predicted in 1952 that apartheid would be gone in a decade. Boasting to a left-wing journalist that he was "as anti-Communist as they are made in America today," he woefully conceded that "it seemed to be only 'the Communists'...who were prepared to give open support to the demand of the non-Europeans for equal rights."[86]

Thus, Pretoria may have been pleased by the perfidy of Max Yergan, Robeson's former comrade, who reversed field and endorsed apartheid at this same time; he was castigated by the South African left and in the same breath his soon-to-be-liquidated Council on African Affairs was praised.[87] Arriving in South Africa in 1952 , he was booked for an appointment with a "Cabinet Minister and other high-ups," a newspaper reported. Traveling at the behest of the munificent Ford Foundation, he warned of the supposed perniciousness of Communists. "I feel strongly that we should play some part in tackling the question of Communism in Africa," he advised.[88] Robeson, on the other hand, held strong against this reversal, which he repeated in a message sent to the Natal Indian Congress in early 1954.[89]

The overtures to Matthews and the Yergan trip to South Africa were indicative of the increasing comprehension in Washington of Pretoria's apparent inability to crush the ANC and their Communist allies. To gain indirect intelligence and improve relations with certain domestic constituencies, the U.S. began to arrange for the arrival of various academics in South Africa. But by June 1953 Pretoria sent the message that this maneuver would not necessarily be embraced when they expelled U.S. nationals Emmett and Joyce Murphy—he a scholar, she a librarian—who had been teaching at Mandela's alma mater, Fort Hare.[90] (Mandela had been asked to leave Fort Hare at

85. *Advance*, 28 May 1953.
86. *The Clarion*, 14 August 1952.
87. *Advance*, 28 May 1953.
88. *People's World*, 11 September 1952.
89. *Advance*, 11 February 1954.
90. Report from W.J. Gallman, 10 June 1953, RG 59, Decimal File, Box 3572.

the age of 19, indicative of why the U.S. paid close attention to this institution.[91]) The expulsion of the couple was surprising since one of Murphy's key tasks was reporting to Washington about the extent of radicalism on campus. The "outspoken" scholar, it was said, "felt that about twenty percent of the students were influenced…by Communist doctrines…." The "information given us with respect to Joseph Matthews and his alleged Communist affiliations [should] be kept absolutely confidential," said grateful U.S. delegate Gordon Minnigerode in reference to Murphy's report. Murphy was "greatly embittered" about his ouster and threatened to speak to "his friends in the FBI" about his disappointment.[92]

The scholar's "friends in the FBI" may have been intrigued to hear what he told Minnigerode: about "4%" of the students he met were "outright Communists" and a "good deal of [Marxist] literature in the English language as translated from the Russian is arriving in the university…." Matthews, who Minnigerode knew "very well," said the literature came mostly "from the West Coast of Africa" and some from Britain. Another questionable conclusion that the anthropologist Murphy reached was that "Without a doubt the ANC is a Communist front organization."[93] Yet despite his service to anticommunism, Murphy was expelled since Pretoria was irked by his friendliness with students—though it is doubtful if he could have obtained intelligence without at least feigning friendliness. The scholar and his spouse were seen by Pretoria as "kaffirboeties"[94]—or what might be called "nigger lovers" in Murphy's own Chicago. The inflexibility of Pretoria, unable to detect an anticommunist comrade critical for Cold War success, also pointed to why they would lose support in crucial circles in Washington.

Pretoria should have paid attention when the anthropologist reported that about "15/20%" of the students were "swayed by certain of the Communist arguments," among them Joe Matthews, "who admitted after five months of probing that he was a Communist," though it was unclear if he was among "several Africans who

91. Ibid., Kelly Knauer, 6.

92. Gordon Minnigerode to W.J. Gallman, 15 May 1953, RG 59, Decimal File, Box 3572.

93. Memorandum of Conversation with E.J. Murphy, no date, RG 59 Decimal File, Box 3572.

94. E.J. Murphy to Ambassador, 17 May 1953, RG 59, Decimal File, Box 3572.

are Moscow- trained."[95] (Ironically, Murphy had been brought to Fort Hare to substitute for Z.K. Matthews, then at the Union Theological Seminary in Manhattan.)[96] Murphy, who had spent almost a year in the Union, felt that there was "widespread Communist [work] being carried out not only among the University students but throughout the Union...."[97]

Though anticommunist, Murphy may have been too liberal for Pretoria's tastes. Other analysts seemingly were more tailored to the unique cloth from which apartheid was cut. In a 1952 racist attack, Cape Town writer Barend Jacobus submitted, almost wearily, "we must confess that the record of the negro up to the present time has not been convincing." Yes, he conceded reluctantly, "they have produced great men like Booker T. Washington, Toussaint L'Ouverture and [Marcus} Garvie[sic]"—who he added, in a burst of apparent ignorance expanding beyond the misspelling of his name, the incorrect detail that he was "of Tuskegee." Jacobus then twisted the knife, saying "as a group they have nowhere as yet proved that they are the equals of the whites." On his trip to the U.S. he managed to find those who shared a common belief of some circles: "the true African Negro has a short tail of approximately four inches but no soul." Another confidante told him "the negro entered the ark as an animal." He was distressed to find nonetheless that "one of the aims of the Soviets was to use the American Negroes as a vanguard to influence the black races of Africa." Similarly distressing was the fact that leading Negro educator Benjamin Mays—a mentor of Martin Luther King, Jr.— "makes no secret of the fact that he welcomes the pressure put on the world by Communism."[98]

White may have thought his reproaches of the ANC and the CP were vindicated when in 1953 the ANC "'mourned'" the death of Josef Stalin as a "great loss throughout the world particularly [for] the working class and oppressed colonial peoples," adding: "Our sympathies go out to the Russian people whom he has so ably led." Joe Slovo, a rising Communist, said Stalin "combined the best attributes of the scholar, the worker and the simple soldier." His passing,

95. Memorandum of Conversation with E.J. Murphy, 13 May 1953, RG 59, Decimal File, Box 3572.

96. E.J. Murphy to Ambassador, 17 May 1953, RG 59, Decimal File, Box 3572.

97. Report by W.J. Gallman, 10 June 1953, RG 59, Decimal File, Box 3572.

98. Barend Jacobus, *Colour: Unsolved Problem of the West*, Cape Town: Timming, 1952, 45, 98, 10, 230,

said, *Advance*, was a "tragedy for world's peoples."[99] Mandela's creation, the ANC Youth League, took time to praise the "noble ideals [of] Stalin," while condemning "U.S. imperialism."[100] In March 1954 the ANC co-sponsored a memorial in Durban for the late Soviet leader on the first anniversary of his passing.[101] At the same time as it beatified Stalin, the left denounced the U.S. as "heir to all the exploiters of the past."[102]

* * *

In early 1952, U.S. ambassador to South Africa W.J. Gallman paid a visit to Prime Minister Malan in order to press him about the ongoing U.N. debate concerning the nation to be known as Namibia. The Secretary of State, who received Gallman's dispatch about this encounter, may have been startled to read that "Malan then asked in [a] somewhat jocular manner what our position [would] be if American Negroes were invited to appear before GA [U.N. General Assembly] Committee to testify on how they were treated." Gallman evaded the relevant inquiry.[103] Malan twisted the shiv adroitly when he argued that there was no real difference between Dixie "segregation" and "apartheid."[104] Pretoria could sense—even if Gallman could not—the reality that the republic would have to retreat from the more terrible aspects of Jim Crow in response to domestic and global pressures.

Malan was simply too precious an ally to alienate. Gallman met with him again later that year during a disruptive strike by steelworkers in the U.S. Malan agreed to "assistance in stepping up manganese exports" and "increased shipments" did occur. An important footnote was appended to the memo: "participation of the South African air squadron in Korea has had his personal support."[105]

Subsequently, the U.S. man in Pretoria, David Robertson, dined with T.E. Donges, Minister of Interior, who upbraided him for allowing a "Communist, Michael Scott, to enter the country" to speak on

99. *Advance*, 12 March 1953.

100. *Advance*, 16 April 1953.

101. *Advance*, 18 March 1954.

102. *Advance*, 28 May 1953.

103. W.J. Gallman to Secretary of State, 14 January 1952, RG 59, Decimal File, Box 3572, *NARA-CP*.

104. James Sappington, First Secretary-Pretoria to Secretary of State, 6 March 1953, RG 59, Decimal File, Box 3574.

105. W.J. Gallman to Secretary of State, 2 March 1953, RG 59, Decimal File, Box 3572.

the matter of South Africa's colony at the U.N. Donges was unwilling to accept the excuse that the U.S. was merely bowing to U.N. protocols in providing the visa. The South African popinjay blustered that the pusillanimous republic had become a "'captive' of the creature of its creation," meaning the U.N., which was "dominated by the Arabic-Asiatic bloc" of which "India had seized the leadership."[106] This was not wholly inaccurate, particularly the important role of India, a nation which Washington had to court if it wanted to prevent its falling wholly into the outskirts of the socialist camp: a necessity which contributed to Pretoria's gathering isolation and was a problem that remained difficult to resolve in the prelude to 1994. It was also in 1952 that J.G.N. Strauss of the United Party called for a spectacular increase in the European population in South Africa: "10,000,000" was the figure floated (today's is about 5 million, by way of comparison).

But the questions concerned not only from whence they would come and what enticements would be necessary to attract them but, per usual, how would the Afrikaners react?[107] Like others before and since—especially those who blithely accepted the construction of whiteness that was precisely at issue—Gallman was stunned by the inter-European conflict. "Anglophobia," he said sounding surprised, "is very deeply seated" among Afrikaners, who were well organized via the Nationalists and the Broederbond and preserved a dedicated identity from cradle to grave.[108]

Gallman was repeatedly frustrated by what he called the "white problem": the "white standard, in a word...is low in South Africa and it is kept low by lack of competition, outside stimulation and a studied attempt to limit the further influx of whites...incompetent whites are caught up in the Government owned and run railroad system or used as elevator operators;" and many of these incompetents were supervising Africans who did not require their management. This was a massive waste of human capital, making South African increasingly uncompetitive and presenting a dreary future as a result.[109]

---

106. David Robertson to Secretary of State, 27 October 1952, RG 59, Decimal File, Box 3572.

107. *Rand Daily Mail*, 4 September 1952.

108. W.J. Gallman to Secretary of State, 17 September 1953, RG 59, Decimal File, Box 3572.

109. W.J. Gallman to Secretary of State, 20 October 1953, RG 59, Decimal File, Box 3572.

Still, Gallman was only partially perceptive. He failed to note what another envoy did: the attempt to restore citizenship to those convicted of "treason during the later war."[110] Such neo-fascism buoyed the Afrikaner nationalism he espied, while providing breathing space to the still numerous German settlers across the border in Windhoek, who had their own innovative strategies for spreading neo-fascism. He did notice the "German influence" when he arrived in Windhoek in 1954, mentioning that their language was "widely spoken" and there were "German signs everywhere." He also sensed that these settlers, probably as an outgrowth of the persistent Afrikaner nationalism, felt distant from Pretoria, on which their survival depended.[111]

* * *

In coming decades, Washington would become exceedingly nervous whenever the sticky matter arose of U.S. Negroes approaching the U.N. with their grievances, something that Robeson had managed to do as Gallman was ducking the question.[112] Providing protective cover for Washington's odious Jim Crow was the likes of Ralph Bunche. He had visited South Africa in 1937 and then returned to teaching at Howard University before joining the Office of Strategic Services—the precursor to the CIA—as an African specialist, and finally affiliated himself with the nascent United Nations. As the CP was being handcuffed in both nations, widely syndicated columnist Robert Ruark wrote approvingly of "Bunche v. Robeson," juxtaposing the latter unfavorably with the former.[113] This was a turnabout of sorts for Bunche, who had been a man of the left during his academic career[114] before this ideological affiliation became a sword of Damocles hanging over his livelihood. Nevertheless, Bunche's abandonment of the left did not deliver him from Jim Crow. When he was being heralded in 1948 for his role in helping to bring the state of Israel into being, while serving with the U.N., Grace Hudson of the Pasadena Foothill Democratic Club fumed that the nearby Wardman

110. H. Gordon Minnigerode, Consul-Port Elizabeth to Secretary of State, 19 January 1954, RG 59, Decimal File, Box 3573.

111. W.J. Gallman to Secretary of State, 6 August 1954, RG 59, Decimal File, Box 3572.

112. Gerald Horne, *Paul Robeson: The Artist as Revolutionary*.

113. Column by Robert Ruark, 3 October 1950, Box 26, Folder 5, *Brian Urquhart Collection on Ralph Bunche, University of California-Los Angeles*.

114. "Alleged Communistic Activities at Howard University, Washington, D.C., 74th Congress, 2nd Session, Senate Doc. 217," 1936, Box 10, Folder 7, *Brian Urquhart Collection on Ralph Bunche, University of California-Los Angeles*.

Park Hotel "refused to let Dr. Ralph Bunche speak in one of the hotel rooms because he is a Negro!" Irate, she continued, "what a spectacle we present to the world....Dr. Bunche was right when he said last week at a U.N. dinner in his honor that our handling of the Negro problem makes a mockery both of our Constitution and of the U.N. Charter."[115] Dr. Bunche, however, persisted in contributing to the illiberal attitude that was to ensnare him, applying an anticommunist lens in evaluating the Indian Congress and the Congress of Democrats[116]—even using the "meaning of the Communist Suppression Act of the Union of South Africa" as his filter.[117]

Robeson was not involved in this controversy but ratifying Ruark's comparison, he remained a burr under the U.S. saddle nonetheless, in light of his global reach. His comparison of the jailing of his good friend and comrade Ben Davis—the Communist leader from Harlem—and the arrest of ANC leader J.S. Moroka was highlighted in South Africa (both were viewed by Robeson as egregious examples of anticommunism).[118]

Moroka had trained as a physician in Edinburgh and practiced in Austria and Germany. Professor Gwendolen Carter, who visited his home in 1952, was nevertheless struck by the "shabbiness" of his abode. She could have added the same descriptor to some of his views, e.g. his opposition to India's appeal to the United Nations on behalf of Africans. Still, when he was put on trial, the authorities managed to find an exchange of letters between him and Communists in Russia, China, India and the United States, likely the fruit of journeys taken by Sisulu, Kathrada, Duma Nokwe, and other comrades.[119] The regime's crackdown on Moroka, a man described as "light skinned and well-dressed [and] very wealthy,"[120] was emblematic of its failure to play adroitly upon class and color contradictions among the non-European population, a praxis that would have to await the post-1994 dispensation. On the other hand, the crackdown may have "worked," since by 1982 Moroka—ousted from the ANC in the aftermath of the Mandela-led Defiance Campaign when he

115. Grace Hudson to Senator J. Howard McGrath, 23 May 1948, Box 26, Folder 4, *Brian Urquhart Collection on Ralph Bunche.*

116. Walter White to Ralph Bunche, 9 September 1954, Box IIA7, *NAACP Papers.*

117. Ralph Bunche to "Dear Walter," "personal and confidential," 14 September 1954, Box IIA7.

118. *The Clarion,* [Cape Town] 18 September 1952.

119. Interview with Dr. J.S. Moroka, 21 November 1952, Box 2, *Gwendolen Carter Papers.*

120. Anthony Sampson, *Drum,* 104.

objected to the deployment of SACP lawyers—was said to be living comfortably and owning "four farms."[121]

Robertson, the U.S. emissary, also had to grapple with the nervousness of U.S. executives, an ill-fitting match with Pretoria's awkwardness in exploiting class and color tensions among Africans. Meeting a group of them in Port Elizabeth he detected an "undercurrent of anxiety over the future," forbidding "the clear promise of profitable future activities." This was a fair assessment of the state of play in 1952: putting their ear to the ground, the corporate leaders could sense an approaching anti-apartheid stampede, but the profits then were so lush, it was difficult to consider alternatives.[122]

The attempt to suppress the CP on both sides of the Atlantic united Pretoria and Washington. The *Guardian* was reeling from the 1950 anticommunist law and in coming years was to change its name repeatedly in a futile effort to escape the snare of prosecution. Still, the left's critics, even those thought to be evenhanded, may have overstated their difficulties. Thus, by late 1952 Gwendolen Carter in communicating with Arthur Hayes Sulzberger of the *New York Times* probably undercounted the membership of the SACP, which likely contributed to an overly rosy estimate of apartheid's longevity.[123]

For despite clear weaknesses, the gathering ANC-SACP alliance continued to be buoyed by powerful global forces that enhanced the sound emitted from its still potent megaphone. It was also in 1952 that the *Guardian* charged "Washington with terrorism" after the assassination of NAACP stalwart Harry Moore in Florida.[124] "Race violence rolls on" in the U.S. the paper continued, deriding Edith Sampson, Washington's prime Negro envoy, as a "stooge."[125] The attempt by the U.S. Communist-backed Civil Rights Congress to bring cases of racist injustice to a global audience was aided materially by the South African left. This in turn aided the anti-Jim Crow struggle, which could then assist more pointedly anti-apartheid forces in a virtuous circle. The connection between the two was especially evident in shaping Robeson's effort to file a U.N. petition

---

121. *Rand Daily Mail*, 22 February 1982.

122. David Robertson to Secretary of State, 2 December 1952, RG 59, Decimal File, Box 3572.

123. Gwendolen Carter to Roger Evans and Arthur Hays Sulzberger, 1 November 1952, RG 1.2 (FA387), RF, Series 200: US. Box 552, *Rockefeller Foundation Records, Rockefeller Archive Center, Sleepy Hollow, New York.*

124. *Guardian*, 3 January 1952. See also Ben Green, *Before His Time: The Untold Story of Harry Moore, America's First Civil Rights Martyr*, New York: Free Press, 1999.

125. *Guardian*, 27 March 1952.

charging the U.S. with "genocide" against African Americans. The *Guardian* demanded "prompt and resolute international action" and added that "no person in his right senses would attach any importance" to Washington's "professed mission as protector of the free world"—which included wholly unfree South Africa. The hypocrisy, it was said knowingly, "reveals a situation which finds its parallel in South African life."[126] According to this organ, there was reciprocity on May Day 1952 in Manhattan, when "50,000"—probably an inflated figure— marched in pursuit of a raft of demands, including a "protest against the racial discrimination in South Africa…."[127]

By June 1952 this newspaper was known as *The Clarion* and was cheering on Du Bois and his Progressive Party, exclaiming "a third party or die!"[128] By August the name had changed again—it was now the *People's World*—but the tune was still the same: touting resistance efforts within the republic. This time in the spotlight was the "Sojourners for Truth and Justice," an organization which reciprocally "pledged full support of the passive resistance campaign" in South Africa. Cape Town readers were told that STJ was "inspired by the example of militant action on the part of African women. We realize that our fight for freedom in the United States is inextricably linked to the struggle against the tyranny of the white supremacists…[and this] must lead to the complete emancipation of women throughout the world."[129] Returning the favor, the paper's left-wing South African journalist saluted these "U.S. Negroes who champion[ed] [the] colonial freedom struggle" since "real freedom for the Negro people in America is linked with the liberation of Africans in Africa and with the strength of colonial peoples everywhere…."[130]

This closeness had not eluded the attention of the authorities: In a piece of "confidential security information," Washington voiced suspicions—perhaps accurate—that a CP document from South Africa was "being circulated among Communist leaders in the Chicago area."[131]

Keeping one step ahead of the posse, the paper's name had changed again by November, when *Advance* declared that the "U.S. shields Malan" from a "racism inquiry" launched by the U.N., because it

126. *Guardian*, 3 April 1952.
127. *Guardian*, 24 April 1952.
128. *The Clarion*, 26 June 1952.
129. *People's World*, 21 August 1952.
130. *Advance*, 20 August 1953.
131. Report, 18 March 1953, RG 59, Decimal File, Box 3575, *NARA-CP*.

was "tarred with [the] same brush."[132] Pretoria and Washington alike were "frightened of revelations before [the] United Nations."[133] Echoes of this flap reached Pretoria when the U.S. envoy David Robertson sadly reported to the Secretary of State that the "Afrikaans press" was "particularly critical of the U.S." Their "criticism was aimed at the U.S. request to postpone the Union's color policy debate until after the American presidential debate" to not embarrass the republic for their embrace of this questionable ally. When Washington started inching toward desegregation, it was seen as ill-timed: "responsibility for unrest among the Union's natives and the French colonials was placed at the door of the U.S." The U.S. election, which highlighted this gradual desegregation process known as "integration," "aroused great interest among South Africans. All newspapers gave excellent front page coverage to election results."[134]

While South African militants were scurrying from pillar to post,[135] seeking to avoid pillorying, a visiting U.S. delegation arrived in the region. Before arriving in Johannesburg, this Joint Congressional Committee on Atomic Energy stopped in the then Belgian Congo to examine uranium deposits, essential if Cold War threats against Moscow were to be credible. While there they counted "78,000 whites in the Congo," of which "1139" were from the U.S., mostly missionaries; fortunately, the "death rate" for this population as a whole, "was only 5.07 per 1000; less than half of what it was twenty years previously."[136] The left in Cape Town noticed that supplying uranium for atom bombs was a prime job for South African imperialism too,[137]

132. *Advance*, 20 November 1952.

133. *Advance*, 4 December 1952.

134. David Robertson to Secretary of State, 7 November 1952, RG 59, Decimal File, Box 3574.

135. Soon the South African left would run out of names for journals and run out of space to retreat and their newspapers were plunged into a death spiral as a result. This was unfortunate for many reasons, including for the needs of today's researchers. Reputedly, during the mid-19th century Crimean war, The Czar of Russia claimed to obtain all the intelligence about the British military he needed could be obtained from the press in London. The *Guardian* and its progeny as the foregoing—and subsequent--pages suggest, provided intelligence essential for an understanding of the early years of apartheid. See e.g. Stephen Wade, *Empire and Espionage: Spies in the Zulu War: The Anglo-Zulu War, 1879*, Yorkshire: Pen and Sword, 2010, 85.

136. Report on Delegation, 1-2 September 1953, Box 34, *Bourke Hickenlooper Papers, Herbert Hoover Presidential Library—West Branch, Iowa.*

137. *People's World*, 16 October 1952.

via its colony centered in Windhoek and its role as gendarme of the sub-region.

By then the U.S. had begun to pay closer attention to the Congo, as large as the eastern half of the U.S. itself. It was former president Herbert Hoover who pointed out in 1953 that Congo "is one of the world's richest mineral regions" and the "world's largest producer of industrial diamonds and cobalt," though "cotton is the chief agricultural and principal money crop." The kind of "imperial preference" in place elsewhere on the exploited continent was blunted in Congo by "both import and export duties" that were "the same for any nation trading" with this colony. The problem for the U.S. was the small number of Europeans available to play the role of overseer, with little prospect of attracting more, even if Eastern Europe were to be destabilized—as the 1956 revolt in Hungary would show. "Practically all seriously ill whites leave the Colony," Hoover lamented; there were "practically no old white persons in the Congo; in fact… less than 10 percent of the total white population has attained the age of even 50 years…." In the long run this would make problems for both settler colonialism and old-style colonialism, leaving neo-colonialism—rule through African surrogates—as the chief alternative. However, such a program was not on the agenda then. What was envisioned instead was an alliance with South Africa and its neighbors, which could supply the manpower that Belgium simply could not. This would not be easy nor simple, however. Thus, Hoover found a "certain prejudice against Americans" in Southern Rhodesia, which combined with the animosity to Afrikaners there indicated that constructing a synthetic whiteness was one of the stiffest challenges faced by U.S. imperialism and neo-colonialism.[138]

Deep down Washington knew that apartheid was a risky long-term bet, but with the opposition so heavily influenced by the CP it seemed to be the only reasonable option. Most of all they knew—as the Congo exemplified—that there were simply not enough "whites" to man battle-stations or even grow the economy. "There is such a shortage of European manpower," moaned U.S. ambassador W.J. Gallman in 1953, that the "enlarged number of young men who will have to undergo three months' continuous military training each year…will necessitate some form of revised civilian planning."[139]

---

138. Herbert Hoover to A.H. Ackerman, 17 March 1953, Pre-Commerce Correspondence, Box 1, *Herbert Hoover Papers, Herbert Hoover Presidential Library.*

139. W.J. Gallman to Secretary of State, 21 August 1953, RG 59, Decimal File, Box 3574, *NARA-CP.*

The congressional delegation bypassed Windhoek, whose surrounding territory also contained uranium, as it headed southward to confer at the University of the Witwatersrand. By 8 September 1953 its members were being regaled at a cocktail party at the Carlton Hotel given by the Uranium Technical Sub-Committee of the Chamber of Mines, as further plans were laid for securing material for the atomic bomb.[140] This otherwise mundane visit also highlighted why Washington found it difficult to quit Pretoria: besides an endless supply of cheap labor and anticommunist solidarity, South Africa controlled an ample supply of uranium.

Thus, Washington watched Pretoria as Pretoria watched the republic, since the Union was increasingly becoming a prime ally on the continent. Washington knew that senior South African military figures were keenly watching the 1952 Republican Party convention and provided "outspoken approval of the party platform," notably from the army. Officers applauded the triumph of fellow military man Dwight D. Eisenhower while voicing criticism of the "isolationism" of the now discredited Herbert Hoover, since it seemed to portend a reduced U.S. presence on the continent.[141]

The weight of anticommunism, which reached a kind of apex during the war in Korea, bore on the re-election of General Eisenhower in 1956. That same year, the Council on African Affairs, which had upheld the banner of anti-colonialism since 1937, finally collapsed under a farrago of prosecutorial inquisitions, harassment, and innuendo. Nature abhors a vacuum, however, and a successor arose just before the CAA's collapse: the American Committee on Africa, led by liberal anticommunists, symbolized by long-time leader George Houser. Houser's parents were missionaries in the Philippines and he was a comrade of Norman Thomas, the notoriously anticommunist Socialist. He was a Conscientious Objector during World War II, refusing to join the military. The ACOA leadership included Thomas, Roger Baldwin of the American Civil Liberties Union, Howard professor Rayford Logan, civil rights champion James Farmer, affluent Manhattan attorney Peter Weiss, and Walter Offutt of the NAACP.

Houser, the organization's workhorse, did seek to establish ties with diverse anti-colonial forces in the region but given Washington's growing interest in Southern Africa, this meant linking with questionable groupings, leading to charges that ACOA was collaborating

---

140. Report of South Africa delegation, 8-13 September 1953, Box 34, *Bourke Hickenlooper Papers*.

141. "Confidential," "Message Unsigned," 18 July 1952, RG 59, Decimal File, Box 3574, *NARA-CP*.

with the CIA.[142] Certainly the ACOA was, unlike the CAA, quite willing to bond with anticommunist forces in South Africa, but even on this front, it was fair to say that liberal anticommunists in South Africa were often more realistic than their U.S. counterparts. Patrick Duncan, scion of a South African political dynasty, was exemplary in this regard, in that—unlike the house organ of liberal anticommunism in the U.S., the *New York Times*—he was willing to acknowledge the facts. He informed Houser directly that this paper's claim that the ANC was "nearly moribund" by May 1954 was "sheer rubbish." In fact, he said, their "actual membership is probably 20,000," which was quite respectable. In a "by election in the African constituency of Cape Western [sic], the Communists got 3500 votes" and his own "Liberals 998," providing a fair assessment of the balance of forces.[143] Houser also received intelligence reports from South Africans tied to the U.S.-based Fellowship of Reconciliation,[144] which pioneered the use of civil disobedience to destabilize Jim Crow.

By September 1954, Houser had wangled a visa—his elite connections meant he had a helping hand from the National Broadcasting Company, a major television network[145]—and was resting in Cape Town. He passed through Angola where he found that the "white population has risen spectacularly," augmenting colonialism. It had soared "more than 75% between 1940 and 1950"; and he "saw no African taxi drivers," suggesting a European working-class base for colonialism. In the slums to which Africans were consigned, he found "no running water" and "no toilets."[146]

Kenneth Kaunda, who would become the founding father of Zambia, told Houser bluntly that he was "not surprised to hear you were not allowed into the Federation," speaking of his nation and immediate neighbors. "It is fast becoming a Police State," he said wearily, which ran contrary to Houser's own assessment of South Africa. "An iron curtain" had descended, said Kaunda, "so that people who themselves are ... or represent progressive organizations won't just be allowed in...without doubt they must be censoring

---

142. George Houser, *No One Can Stop the Rain: Glimpses of Africa's Liberation Struggle*, New York: Pilgrim, 1989, 5, 7, 63, 172.

143. Patrick Duncan to George Houser, 3 May 1954, Reel 1, Part II, #202, *American Committee on Africa Papers, Library of Congress-Washington, D.C.* Hereafter ACOA Papers.

144. Arthur to George Houser, 13 September 1954, Reel 1, Part II, #223, *ACOA*.

145. Report by George Houser, 1 October 1954, Reel 1, Part II, #233.

146. Report by George Houser, 23 September 1954, Reel 1, Part II, #233, *ACOA*.

our correspondence—I mean from you to us and vice versa,"[147] a dire reflection on the final decade of London's forced retreat from colonialism.

Like Loescher, Houser found South African cities to be "quite American—even more American than they are European," which was "especially true of Johannesburg." This included dedicated interest in events in the U.S.: "we can't keep our dirty linen from being washed in public," he opined, referring to news that leaked throughout the region, aiding the anti-Jim Crow movement. From his viewpoint, the land of apartheid was "not a police state," a conclusion that may have surprised some of his interlocutors, among them Duncan and Z.K. Matthews. He had met the ANC leader in Manhattan during his stay at the Union Theological Seminary. Despite his appraisal, Houser was followed by plainclothes police, who were "shadowing" him relentlessly during his stay in South Africa. He "didn't see the last of the police until my ship sailed away from the dock in the Cape Town harbor," though the surveillance was felt "most acutely in Pretoria." He too, like so many other visitors previously, sensed the persistent "bitterness of the Boer War," contributing to and propelled by the unremitting reality that the "English have an uneasy sense of superiority over the Afrikaner." He sensed instinctively that these combatants' joint fear of the African majority kept them from waging war again. "The one thing," he noted sagely, "which keeps as much union as does exist among the European population is the insecurity in the face of an actively growing non-white organizational program...." He anticipated, nonetheless, what was to happen in less than a decade: "creating a South African Republic probably outside the British Commonwealth," a direct response to London's perceived unsteadiness in the face of "winds of change."

He sensed the storm that was to come: "one of the first Africans I met was wearing a button" of the ANC and "in non-European movies any illegal act is created with cheers...." He accepted the figure proffered by Duncan that the ANC's membership was 20,000 and—ever the liberal anticommunist—averred that "no doubt that the Communists are exploiting the situation for all it is worth;" the fact that they tended to "work quite efficiently" meant they held sway "in various organizations." Also, like others, he noticed that "there are practically no militant non-Communist whites," which as apartheid deepened meant the SACP was bound to grow.

147. Kenneth Kaunda to George Houser, 24 December 1954, Series III, Box 149, *American Committee on Africa Papers, Tulane University-New Orleans.*

He was premature in his critique of Washington, writing in astonishment, "I never realized before how really bad United States foreign policy vis-à-vis Africa looks from an African point of view. The so-called world democratic forces haven't a chance of influencing the people of Africa as long as their influence is on the side of the status quo. White Communists in South Africa, by their active participation in the movement, help to keep the movement of the non-Europeans from being just anti-white."[148]

This latter point helped to explain the evolution of Nelson Mandela and others like him, who after Communists sought shelter within the ANC in the aftermath of the Suppression of Communism Act of 1950, came to work closely with the SACP. This was also a reflection of the prestige of Robeson, yet to decline in South Africa even as it was receding in certain U.S. precincts. It also sent a message to the U.S., where the presence of "militant Communist whites" was becoming a distant historical mystery, creating fertile conditions for the kind of Black Nationalism that Mandela had abjured, and which sunk deeper roots within the republic just as Jim Crow was loosening. Houser was also to find that this rise of Black Nationalism was to wrack his own organization.

148. Report by George Houser, 1 October 1954, Reel 1, Part II, #233.

Chapter 7

Emboldened Africans and Negroes, 1955-1957

IN July 1955 the U.S. emissary in Pretoria filed what appeared to be a typical report on doings in this beleaguered nation but which turned out to contain many more layers of significance than initially realized. The "Congress of the People" had just met with 2884 delegates, including "112 whites." Messages of support were received from the usual suspects: Robeson, Howard Fast, Chou en-Lai of China, the World Federation of Democratic Youth, the World Federation of Trade Unions, etc.[1] Dispatching 50,000 organizers into the teeming slums and sedate suburbs, the ANC and their allies returned with concrete proposals concerning land and wages and education.[2] Washington did not appear to be overly perturbed when documents were seized at this historic gathering as part of the pursuit to press a "case of high treason."[3] Beforehand, the U.S. envoy, William Wright, downplayed its significance, expecting it be "disorganized and poorly attended" and weighted down with Communist influence besides.[4]

Washington should have been paying more attention to the international solidarity that was extended for this crucial gathering. Months later, the South African Congress of Trade Unions, influenced by the ANC and SACP and comprised heavily of African workers in mass production industries, held its initial convention and messages poured in from—again—the World Federation of Trade Unions,

1. William L. Wright, Jr. to Secretary of State, 8 July 1955, RG 59, Decimal File, Box 3233, *NARA-CP*.

2. Hilda Bernstein, "The Freedom Charter," **Third World Quarterly**, 9(Number 2, April 1987): 672-677.

3. "Monthly Digest of South African Affairs," August 1955, Reel 1, *Confidential U.S. State Department Files, Internal Affairs....Foreign Affairs...South Africa...NARA-CP*.

4. Report, 2 June 1955, RG 59, Decimal File, Box 3233, *NARA-CP*.

thought in the North Atlantic nations to be a despised "Communist Front," and left-leaning U.S. unions like the International Union of Mine Mill and Smelter Workers.[5]

It was a "Communist controlled organization," a U.S. observer expectorated, that assembled at the Salt River Hall in Cape Town; there were almost 700 present, conferring in English with "on the spot" translations into Zulu and Xhosa.[6] It was this international solidarity that was to prove decisive in determining the pace of apartheid's retreat, which is why the anticommunist, U.S.-dominated International Confederation of Free Trade Unions descended on South Africa in 1957, at the behest of the Trade Union Council of South Africa, dominated by European labor.[7]

This relative indifference to what amounted to a critical gathering was fostered in part by the news emerging in early 1956 from Pretoria: it had "become more and more apparent," the Embassy chortled, that it is the "intention of [South Africa] to concentrate…on the purchasing of military equipment from North America." Even the reported purge of English speakers in favor of their Afrikaner brethren left the envoy unruffled,[8] as the long-term trend of the move away from London and towards Washington accelerated, especially in the wake of the Suez debacle which sounded the tocsin for the British Empire. "The Union is willing and anxious to cooperate with the United States," it was announced ecstatically in August 1955. The union "would do more for us than they are willing to do for the British. The top military men here, particularly, seem anxious to draw away from the British and align themselves with" Washington, notably in supposed "defense" of Africa and the regions due east.[9]

In December 1955 Minister of Defense F.C. Erasmus sped to Washington for urgent consultations on "Communist Infiltration" into "Africa's Black Defense Organizations."[10] Repeatedly, Minister Erasmus expressed frightened concern over Moscow's purported

5. Report by John Stone, Cape Town, 8 March 1956, RG 59, Decimal File, Box 4497.

6. Report, 8 March 1956, Reel 7, *Confidential U.S. State Department Central Files, South Africa……Internal Affairs….and Foreign Affairs, NARA-CP.*

7. Benjamin Pogrund, *How Can Man Die Better: Sobukwe and Apartheid*, London: Peter Halban, 1990, 111.

8. Report, U.S. Embassy, 27 January 1956, Reel 1, *Confidential U.S. State Department Files, Internal Affairs.*

9. Edward Waites to R.G. Miner, 31 August 1955, Reel 4, *U.S. Confidential U.S. State Department Files, Internal Affairs…and Foreign Affairs.*

10. Report, 8 December 1955, Reel 4, *Confidential U.S. State Department Files, Internal Affairs….and Foreign Affairs.*

"scheme to arm Black Africa"[11]—but the logic of racism thwarted the thrust of anticommunism, for on the cusp of independence Africa wanted no part of an apartheid regime, effectively nullifying this ambitious scheme.

However, the bonanza was just too large, and the anticommunist advance too significant to take a balanced viewpoint. Thus, when Moses Kotane was detained in May 1956 after a long journey that took him to Bandung--he was said to be "traveling extensively in Communist and satellite countries"--the legation seemed pleased by this handcuffing of "probably the best known local Native Communist."[12] The plans by Pretoria to float a dollar loan on the New York market sent pulses racing on Wall Street at the prospect of hefty fees. Wisely, Pretoria was considering the politically connected investment banking firm, Dillon Read for this dollar bond issue.[13]

Relations between the Union and the republic were not entirely smooth; the price of gold was causing friction, with the U.S. issuing firm "objections" to rising prices and South Africa rejecting same. Washington thought that Moscow would be a "substantial beneficiary" if prices rose, being a major producer (though smaller than South Africa). So, Pretoria, cloaking itself in the current verbiage, argued strenuously—and with typical self-interest—that the "free world as a whole would benefit far more than the Soviet Union" from a price rise.[14]

Also on the business front, the legation in Cape Town was pleased to observe that the "dean in shipping circles" in this busy port, "an American, Captain C.W. Schmidt of the Farrell Lines," was bound to see even more business as bilateral relations became ever closer.[15] This was a savior for this carrier, since it was encountering problems otherwise in Africa, particularly in French-dominated territories. The "French merchant is penalized for shipping on American flag vessels," it was noted sadly by a vice president of Farrell in 1955. In Portuguese colonies then the colonizer's vessels received "preferential berthing," disadvantaging Farrell too. Ditto for the Belgian Congo and British East Africa. Even Pretoria discriminated in favor

11. Report, 15 December 1955, Reel 4, *U.S. Confidential U.S. State Department Files, Internal Affairs…and Foreign Affairs.*

12. Report, U.S. Embassy, 18 May 1956, Reel 1, *Confidential U.S. State Department Files, Internal Affairs.*

13. Edward T. Wailes to Secretary of State, 26 August 1955, RG 59, Decimal File, Box 4498.

14. Report, 26 October 1955, Reel 7, *Confidential U.S. State Department Central Files….Internal Affairs…and Foreign Affairs.*

15. Report, 3 May 1956, RG 59, Decimal File, Box 4500,

of South African vessels; this meant, he said, "an actual financial loss to us."[16]

Similarly, it was in mid-1955 that the fabulously wealthy U.S. national H. Smith Richardson arrived in the region. "I was fascinated with South Africa," he said at the time, "the climate and the people." He "met the top men in government (both the Party-in-Power and the Party-in-Opposition,)" meaning Europeans, of course. "These people are thinking exactly" like he was, he confessed. "I sympathize with them because world opinion is against them—and they are getting a very bad international press" though "Cape Town, Port Elizabeth, East London and Durban—and Johannesburg" were "booming." Indeed, he exulted, "more new building is going up in South Africa than in any of the 25 countries I have visited in the last 3 years…except possibly Sweden. Port Elizabeth especially has grown rapidly recently—with a great many American companies putting in new plants there…." He found the time to visit Dr. Xuma's Sophiatown, "which would be like Harlem in New York …. except for a few agitators," he said misleadingly, "no one would ever think this slum-clearance project"—i.e. the massively wrenching plan to "relocate these natives"— "was not a most commendable undertaking."[17]

Like Richardson, the consul in Port Elizabeth, H. Gordon Minnigerode, was "impressed" by the "degree of American influence on South Africa"—a trend shaped by the overbearing presence of General Motors, Goodyear and Firestone, among others.[18] Business for these tire giants was booming by the mid-1950s; they had opened for business years earlier and now had begun receiving rubber from the Malay peninsula, Ceylon (Sri Lanka) and Firestone's own plantations in Liberia. Production was less mechanized than in the U.S., which meant a greater reliance upon cheap African labor—the hallmark of U.S. corporations in Africa generally. "Machinery is relatively expensive and labor relatively cheap," said Minnigerode. Seemingly drooling, he said that "unlimited amounts of Native labor are available" for cruel exploitation. Apartheid was a fetter, however, since "some of the natives…do become quite proficient but plant managers prefer not to antagonize the skilled workers"—most

16. Report by G.M. Wauchope, Executive Vice President, Farrell Lines, 17 October 1955, Box 14, *International Affairs Department, AFL-CIO Papers, University of Maryland-College Park.*

17. H. Smith Richardson to Captain Greer A. Duncan, 7 June 1955, Box 1, *H. Smith Richardson Papers, University of North Carolina-Chapel Hill.*

18. Report by Consul-General, H. Gordon Minnigerode, 29 March 1956, RG 59, Decimal File, Box 4501.

of whom were Afrikaners. The stars had aligned for these companies since roads were "quite rough," as he put it, meaning more wear and tear and bl[illegible]outs, meaning more sales.[19] Dunlop of the U.K. was the only co[illegible] to the U.S. giants but as the Empire faded, it could hardl[illegible]kee encroachment. As Uitenhage benefited from tire pro[illegible]kron, Ohio began traversing a slippery slope of decline.[20]

The sam[illegible] said for Port Elizabeth and Detroit. By October 1955 [illegible] journalist found the former city was booming: it "can't [illegible] products fast enough" and there was "an air of optimis[illegible]where...." General Motors had 3500 workers there and as [illegible]tariat grew, so did their capacity to organize politically. [illegible]y, they could churn out 90 to 100 cars and trucks, plus [illegible]ors, ranges, freezers and automotive battery cases daily. Ford, established there in 1924, produced an average of 120 units daily with an employee roll numbering 1500; Firestone was producing 2500 tires per day. As for Goodyear, approximately half of their 1500 workers were African—in 1951 there had been less than 100. And, still, jobs reserved for Europeans often went unfilled. Since Goodyear served an area stretching into Kenya and Uganda, and General Tire reached into the Belgian Congo, and since decolonization was on the horizon, opening new vistas for profiteering, it was vital for these corporations to adjust to new realities that apartheid resisted. There were other considerations: a Studebaker car could be produced in the U.S. and shipped to this country at about the same price that one could be assembled in Uitenhage—though shipping costs and import taxes could drive the price up (but U.S. lobbying and influence peddling could just as soon drive this cost downward).[21]

The combination of cheap labor and resources was a magnet for U.S. manufacturers, inducing them to abandon their homeland. By 1957, Burlington Industries of the Carolinas had a hosiery interest in South Africa.[22]

---

19. H. Gordon Minnigerode to Secretary of State, 28 February 1955, RG 59, Decimal File, Box 4502.

20. Report from Consul-General, Port Elizabeth, 28 February 1955, *Confidential U.S. State Department Files, South Africa....Internal Affairs...and Foreign Affairs.*

21. Consul General, Port Elizabeth, 12 October 1955, Reel 9, *Confidential State Department Central Files, South Africa....Internal Affairs...and Foreign Affairs.*

22. Clipping, 12 September 1977, Box 25, *Burlington Industries Papers, University of North Carolina-Chapel Hill.*

By mid-1955, 20th Century Fox of the U.S. was negotiating with John Schlesinger of South Africa for the purchase of African Consolidated Theatres, established by U.S.-born Isadore Schlesinger, who arrived in Johannesburg in the early 1900s, as the war was expiring, and reconstruction was the order of the day. The Schlesingers had a practical monopoly on film distribution but just before World War II, Fox and MGM began to undercut ACT. Now Fox lusted for ACT's 350 theatre outlets in South Africa and 762 on the continent, then purchased them in an eight-figure deal in South African currency payable in the U.S., described as the "largest foreign deal ever made" by Fox "or any other American film company." The deal would have provided Fox virtual monopoly in the distribution of movies in South Africa—with its only serious competitor being MGM. Unfortunately for the status quo, both were bent on exploiting the "non-European market",[23] which would mean more money to be poured in the pockets of Africans and Coloureds and Indians and more images designed to appeal to them. Both goals were arguably inimical to the future of apartheid. Thus, like a visiting potentate, Spyros Skouras of Fox conferred with Prime Minister Strijdom in a meeting judged "highly satisfactory" by the legation: "I have rarely seen an American businessman as enthusiastic over a twenty to thirty-minute talk" said one U.S. official. There was a hidden U.S. agenda too since the Fox deal would mean more newsreels arriving in South Africa which would undercut the South African Press Association—thought to operate as an adjunct of Reuters of London, increasingly viewed with disdain in Washington.[24]

So prompted, arriving in Johannesburg in pursuit of the gold rush were U.S. newspaper executives. John McDermott of the *Miami Herald*, who was also representing the soon to be defunct *Chicago Daily News*, was enthusiastic after a brief stay. Previously he thought of the country as a "police state" but had softened considerably, now seeing draconian measures as—the Consul General put it—"necessary in view of existing problems;" he "felt that the police were well-advised to watch closely those elements considered leftist as he feared for the future if those [forces] took hold of the Native population...." Like others, in a growing consensus about the simultaneous decline of Jim Crow and rise of apartheid, he dissented from the "preconceived notion" that the "Native was like the American

23. Charles S. Reed II to Secretary of State, 20 June 1955, RG 59, Decimal File, Box 4504.

24. Report, 29 June 1955, RG 59, Decimal File, Box 4504. See also *Rand Daily Mail*, 3 November 1955.

Negro" since "in the long run, the Native problems seemed to be an insoluble one…." McDermott also discussed "immigration" with Pretoria, but it was unclear if this was a personal inquiry or on behalf of Euro-Americans generally.[25]

U.S. rivals in the North Atlantic bloc had yet to recover from the ravages of war, while the republic was not affected to a similar degree. Thus, investors from the U.S. descended upon Southern Africa like a band of rapacious locusts. One unnamed "prospective American investor" conducted an "extensive survey of the economic potentialities of South Africa" and had "long consultations with Sir Ernest Oppenheimer," the Chair of Anglo-American, vanguard of the Union's own imperialism. He was interrogated about rumors that he was moving assets into Rhodesia and what is now Malawi, which were denied. He was "one of the world's shrewdest businessmen," conceded the U.S. emissary.[26] Though he converted to Anglicism, many of the Nationalists found it hard to swallow that he was still widely considered to be Jewish, necessitating his snuggling ever closer to Washington.

U.S. private investment in South Africa leapfrogged from $6 million in 1943 to $194 million by 1954 and $257 million by the end of 1956. "U.S. businessmen don't mind apartheid" was the headline that captured the moment.[27] This tsunami of dollars meant apartheid found it harder to ignore the republic's own painful retreat from state-sanctioned racism, creating an unstable relationship of dependency and fury simultaneously.

The flood of Marshall Plan "aid" carried U.S. capital into the region and was creating waves of wealth and U.S. influence—and regional change. Douglas and Dorothy Steere, seconded to South Africa by the Quakers, found by mid-1955 "one tendency" that was "unmistakable in the Johannesburg region": "if industry and mining and finance were at one time almost entirely in British and Jewish hands in South Africa, this is being changed," a fruit of the 1948 implantation of apartheid. "Each year," they said, "shows a steady increase in Afrikaner influence," as "Afrikaner banks are swelling their assets enormously and their share of business holdings is mounting steadily…." Chillingly, the couple "had been in Germany for a year from

25. Report by Charles Reed II, 6 December 1956, Reel 1, *Confidential U.S. State Department Files, Internal Affairs….and Foreign Affairs.*

26. Charles Reed II to Secretary of State, 23 November 1956, Reel 7, *Confidential U.S. State Department Central Files….Internal Affairs…and Foreign Affairs.*

27. *New Age*, 7 November 1957.

1933-34, the first Hitler year," and again in 1937, and observed that "success after success seemed to the unperceiving to justify the way that was being taken"—"this same mood," they noted unsettlingly "was repeating itself in the attitudes of those we saw in...South Africa."[28]

* * *

The pivotal year of 1956 delivered major convulsions that were to rock both Pretoria and its North Atlantic allies: the botched attack on Egypt accentuated the anticommunist stability of South Africa while it delivered a withering blow to London, driving Pretoria closer to Washington. The devaluation of Stalin's past rule in Moscow rocked U.S. Communists—and the SACP to a degree—while the Hungarian revolt sent refugees fleeing to the Union, augmenting the European population. The victory against Jim Crow in Montgomery and a contemporaneous bus boycott in Cape Town reinforced each other: the symbol of the former, Dr. Martin Luther King, Jr., was to adopt opposition to apartheid as a holy cause. Thus, by November 1956 Cape Town was hit by "congestion and delay" according to the legation, which was "highly serious,"[29] with ships descending upon this port since they were unable to reach Asia via Egypt as before. Durban, it was reported, "has taken on a new significance in the field of international shipping" as a direct result.[30]

This year of rapid change—1956—delivered momentous ramifications. The wheels of cogitation were whirring furiously in the Pretoria embassy as a result of these far-reaching political convulsions. "Relations" between the two racist states "continue to be good," it was said happily, though "South Africans seem anxious that they should become closer"—probably because they had assessed the growing strength of the ANC and desired backup. Deepening connections to the United States would also offer "compensation for weakening of ties with England and, after all, the American colonies were the first to throw off the British yoke...." Revealingly, there was clear "interest in military cooperation" while "American investments and

---

28. Report by Douglas and Dorothy Steere, 15 June 1955, South Africa File, *AFSC*.

29. Report from Consul General, Cape Town, 5 November 1956, Reel 14, *Confidential U.S. State Department Central Files, South Africa....Internal Affairs...and Foreign Affairs-NARA-CP*.

30. Report from Consul General, Durban, 15 November 1956, Reel 14, *Confidential U.S. State Department Central Files, South Africa...*

American industries appear generally to find favor...." With more than a little satisfaction, it was remarked that Washington "undoubtedly enjoys great prestige in South Africa," especially considering growing "concern over Soviet penetration into Africa and the Middle East;" thus, in February 1956 South Africa "compelled the Soviets to close down their consulates in Pretoria and Cape Town and to withdraw all personnel from the Union...." The "immediate motivation" was the "fact that the Soviet Consul General held an inter-racial party on the anniversary of the October Revolution," while reports to come would suggest that Soviet submarines were ferrying African militants abroad or to regional bases. (These vessels were detected off the coast of Port Elizabeth: "the Russians were establishing contacts with Native Communist leaders," it was said despondently by the Consul, including "introducing Communist literature.")

There were "cleavages of opinion" within the ruling Nationalists. There was a "school of thought in the Embassy which feels that we should search for ways of exploiting these cleavages or stimulating their development." It was "desirable" that "an open split should take place" in their ranks for it was "inevitable in the long run that the political power in South Africa will pass, at least in some measure, to the hands of the Africans"—a devastating conclusion for Pretoria, if ventilated. So, in addition to splitting the Nationalists, an attempt should be made to "unseat the present pro-Communist leadership" of the ANC and "replace it with a neutralist or possibly pro-Western group." This gross interference in sovereign affairs, it was said with understatement, would require "the most imaginative and constructive thinking on our part...."[31] Given the high-level participation of Jewish South Africans in the SACP, perhaps not surprisingly Washington's Joseph Neubert began working with certain Israelis and South African businessman Lionel Schwartz in an attempt to forge an "anticommunist movement" in the land of apartheid and continent wide.[32]

* * *

31. On submarines, see Consul General-Port Elizabeth to Secretary of State, 14 May 1957, Reel 4, *Confidential U.S. State Department Files, Internal Affairs....and Foreign* Affairs. For other sources for this and the preceding paragraph see Report, 6 August 1956, Reel 1, *Confidential U.S. State Department Files, Internal Affairs. ....and Foreign Affairs.*

32. Memorandum of Conversation, 19 March 1957, Reel 3, *Confidential U.S. State Department Files, Internal Affairs...and Foreign Affairs.*

The multi-racial, multi-ethnic, multi-class, multi-generational gathering in Kliptown noted at the start of this chapter marked a turning point in the centuries long struggle against settler colonialism and a key moment in the battle against white supremacy. In proclaiming that the nation belonged to all, the Freedom Charter adopted in Kliptown also bore more than a hint of socialism, which was bound to enrage Pretoria and Washington alike. Tellingly, some of the document's most resonant verbiage was crafted by the Communist Rusty Bernstein. "I wrestled with it," he recalled later, "until a slogan which seemed to crystallize the essence of the COP came to mind: 'Let Us Speak of Freedom'."[33] According to the Communist Bawo Andrew Mlangeni, however, who shared a Communist cell with the heralded Ruth First and a prison block with Mandela, it was Z.K. Matthews who should be given credit for the idea of the fabled "Freedom Charter." It was "nonsense," he scoffed, "for people to say this was an idea of Joe Slovo and the Communists," a tale spread by their ideological opponents. So moved, the ANC sent a battalion of canvassers to solicit opinion of the populace as to what future they sought and were given all manner of notions; some said, "I want a golf course" or "proper clinics" or "football grounds."[34]

Unimpressed, the U.S. delegate dismissed this massive organizing effort—even before it took place—as merely "Communist dominated."[35]

Those like this delegate who were influenced by the U.S. press were hardly able to evaluate this breakthrough. Even Wilson Flake of the U.S. legation peremptorily dismissed the correspondent of the *New York Times*, Albion Ross, as a "frequent visitor to the Embassy, usually to seek our agreement with what he was reporting…he was most unhappy here" and was "constantly seeking something bordering on the sensational to make sure his byline would appear" in the self-proclaimed "paper of record."[36]

The U.S. Embassy was more measured about the works of other writers, noting that "American and British books appear in South Africa in quite some abundance and remarkably soon after publication…. I find that Brentano's in Washington," a popular bookstore,

---

33. Rusty Bernstein, *Memory Against Forgetting*, 147.

34. Oral History, Bawo Andrew Mlangeni, 5 November 2003, *University of Connecticut-Storrs*.

35. Report by C.H. Hall, 23 November 1954, RG 59, Decimal File, Box 3572.

36. Wilson Flake to Musedorah W. Thoreson, Office of British Commonwealth and North European Affairs, 5 October 1954, RG 59, Decimal File, Box 3573.

said W.J. Gallman, "can rarely compete with the bookshops of Cape Town and Pretoria...."[37]

Journalistic and writerly malfeasance aside, even before the rise of the PAC there was another competitor to what became known as the "Congress Alliance"—featuring the leadership of the ANC and the CP, but including affiliated groupings of Coloureds, Indians, Europeans, and trade unions respectively (at this point, only the SACP was broad enough to encompass all of the above, providing this organization with untold leverage among anti-apartheid forces). There was the Non-European Unity Movement, formed during World War II: it originally included the ANC too, but the party withdrew early on. The greatest following reportedly came from teachers in the Cape and in the Transkei, where they called the ANC "quislings" and deemed the SACP to be "Moscow Imperialists," phrases suggestive of their Trotskyist influence. It also, however, suggested why the split between Moscow and Beijing just over the horizon was to resonate in Southern Africa.[38] In a presentiment of the emergence of the PAC a few years later, Potlako Leballo, who had been expelled from the Congress Youth League once headed by Mandela and who had formed his own rebel youth movement, was present at a gathering of the Transvaal ANC in the fall of 1955. He claimed that the struggle was being "deflected by foreign ideologies...by cooperation with Europeans, Coloured and Indians."[39]

Once more those described as "Africanists" were routed at a Special Congress of the ANC, which adopted their now renowned "Freedom Charter." Ruth First, Communist leader, detailed that "the only opposition" came from a "tiny group of 16 'Africanists.'"[40] In a like vein it was First who edited a left-leaning publication that reprimanded the veteran Pan-Africanist George Padmore after he published a book-length study juxtaposing what he thought to be opposites: "Pan Africanism or Communism."[41]

Also contributing to the anticommunist atmosphere was the air wafting from Pretoria's colony that would be known as Namibia. Months before the Kliptown gathering, Ambassador W.J. Gallman visited this disputed territory and despite the ideological compatibility he found that Pretoria was "disturbed by the number of German

37. Report by W.J. Gallman, 6 August 1954, RG 59, Decimal File, Box 3573.

38. Wilson Flake to Secretary of State, 21 April 1954, RG 59, Decimal File, Box 3573, *NARA-CP*.

39. *New Age*, 20 October 1955.

40. *New Age*, 5 April 1956.

41. *Fighting Talk*, November 1956.

immigrants who had been" arriving of late, particularly after the initiation of the socialist German Democratic Republic and the failed rebellion against this new state. Yet despite the difficulty that this colony would face in standing alone, he found a desire to cut all ties with Pretoria. Still, the anticommunism of this colony buttressed the like trend across the border.[42]

Though Chief Luthuli had downplayed SACP sway within his ranks,[43] U.S. envoy Wilson Flake begged to differ: "contrary to impressions left" by this leader, he said, "Communists are currently exercising a growing influence over ANC affairs, especially in the Johannesburg office,"[44] where Mandela and Tambo had made impact. A "confidential" analysis uncovered extensive "Communist influence" within the ANC, as the organization was accused of following the "Communist line on both South African and international issues…." Tambo denied membership though he was accused of having "never failed to support the Communist line within the ANC," The same held true for Luthuli too. Signaling its importance, copies of this analysis were sent to major South African and African cities including Lourenco Marques, Leopoldville, Durban, Salisbury, Johannesburg, and Cape Town, among others.[45] It was in July 1956 that the Pretoria legation was grappling with a "confidential" CIA "request"—a "need" in fact—for "characterization of nature, degree and locus within the African National Congress of Communist influence," an obsession of U.S. policy for decades to come.[46] Weeks later, the State Department was informed that Chief Luthuli "and the other non-Transvaal members" of the leadership "support the policies of the Communist majority" within the executive. This widely circulated report characterized the ANC bluntly as "Communist dominated."[47] In that light, Washington was displeased when it appeared that "Communist propaganda in South Africa" seemed to be targeting invective at U.S. Secretary of State John Dulles.[48]

---

42. Report by W.J. Gallman, 6 August 1954, RG 59, Decimal File, Box 3573.

43. *Drum* [South Africa], January 1955.

44. Report by Wilson Flake, 8 March 1955, Reel 11, *Confidential State Department Central Files, South Africa-NARA-CP.*

45. Report, 24 August 1956, Reel 1, *Confidential U.S. State Department Files, Internal Affairs.*

46. Report, 31 July 1956, Reel 3, *Confidential U.S. State Department Files, Internal Affairs….and Foreign Affairs.*

47. Report, 24 August 1956, Reel 3, *Confidential U.S. State Department Files, Internal Affairs…and Foreign Affairs.*

48. Report, 19 August 1955, Reel 3, *Confidential U.S. State Department Files, Internal Files….and Foreign Affairs.*

Apparently, it was Joe Matthews—Z.K.' s son—who told the legation that "virtually all Native intellectuals were being absolutely 'inundated' by vast quantities of Communist publications sent to them by mail from Russia, China, Poland, Czechoslovakia" and elsewhere in the socialist bloc. Evidently this effort "had succeeded in penetrating the Native mind and was definitely having an effect," especially since "American periodicals were relatively expensive and difficult to obtain." Supposedly, father and son— "both Matthews"—had "offered to be of assistance in finishing a mailing list of names of key Native intellectuals" who could be counter-programmed.[49]

Months before Kliptown an attempt to disbar Mandela failed but he was then "banned," as a result of a conviction arising out of the Defiance Campaign. He was sentenced to a suspended sentence of nine months' imprisonment under the—yes—Suppression of Communism Act.[50] By the Spring of 1956 Mandela, who was described as having "received perhaps more banning notices and prohibitions than any other Congress figure" was barred from all gatherings; in November 1953 he had been confined to Johannesburg and in September 1953 he was ordered to resign from the ANC. This latest order was seen as "limiting his extensive legal practice" but it did more than that: it was a shot over the bow, warning Mandela that sterner measures were en route.[51]

If the legation simply read *Advance*, the journal known to be close to the SACP, they would have been even more concerned if they had noticed that the ANC called on "Africans to support" this publication, which was then aiming ambitiously for a healthy circulation of 100,000 in the Cape alone.[52] Mandela's comrade Walter Sisulu actually sold this paper's successor—*New Age*—in the streets of Johannesburg.[53] It was this paper that focused on a U.S. battleship that was mocked by "peace pickets" when it docked in Cape Town.[54]

The U.S. legation noticed that the mainstream press reported the reproving words of Senators Hubert Humphrey of Minnesota—a future Vice-President—and Herbert Lehman of New York, scion of a major fortune, who objected to segregation of Negro crew members, more evidence that the republic's turn away from Jim Crow

49. Report, 1 March 1957, Reel 1, *Confidential U.S. State Department Files, Internal Affairs....and Foreign Affairs.*

50. *Advance*, 6 May 1954.

51. *New Age*, 29 March 1956.

52. *Advance*, 1 April 1954.

53. *New Age*, 30 December 1954.

54. *Advance*, 20 January 1955.

was now hampering its alliance with apartheid.[55] Worryingly—for Washington—the *New Age* then cited a report from the U.S. Negro press on this protest. James Hicks castigated the "bigoted harbour" that was Cape Town, where "Negro members of the Midway's crew…were required to carry special passes" ashore. Contemptuously, it was concluded that when the U.S. Navy speaks of "integration it was like hearing 'a prostitute speaking of love.'"[56] The NAACP was horrified to find that the "Navy made no protest" about these "400 colored crew members" subjected to apartheid while ashore.[57] The Chicago-based Associated Negro Press blared this story far and wide.[58]

There were other reasons the legation was becoming increasingly concerned with the turn of events in South Africa. Another journal in the orbit of the SACP, *Fighting Talk*, the organ of the Springbok Legion,[59] progressive veterans that included First's spouse, Joe Slovo, was still praising Stalin months after his passing, calling him a "leader of a new type."[60] Naturally, Mandela contributed to this militant periodical[61] edited by First.[62]

While the Pentagon was being flayed, Robeson was being hailed for conducting a spirited campaign to restore his passport.[63] *Fighting Talk* too featured Robeson, praising his anti-imperialist views of Africa.[64] His message to the ANC was highlighted: "there should be and must be," he insisted, "much closer and stronger bonds between us because of the very nature of our common struggle for human decency and dignity."[65] When a Soviet filmmaker invited Robeson to star in a production in his signature role as "Othello," the South African left seemed as gleeful as some of his U.S. comrades.[66] He was again saluted when he stared down an inquisitorial congressional

55. Edward T. Wailes to Secretary of State, 17 January 1955, Reel 1, *Confidential U.S. State Department Files, Internal Affairs….Foreign Affairs….South Africa, NARA-CP*.

56. *Advance*, 17 February 1955.

57. "Cross Reference Sheet," January 1955, Box IIA7, *NAACP Papers*.

58. Release, January 1955, Reel 56, #382, Part I. Press Releases, *Barnett/ANP Papers*.

59. *Fighting Talk*, January 1954.

60. *Fighting Talk*, March 1954.

61. *Fighting Talk*, July 1955.

62. *Fighting Talk*, November 1956.

63. *New Age*, 23 December 1954 and 10 March 1955.

64. *Fighting Talk*, April 1955.

65. *New Age*, 23 December 1954.

66. *New Age*, 14 July 1955.

panel he described boldly as "murderers of my people" and entertained the distinct possibility of a "prison sentence."[67] His comrade Du Bois—quite generously--was given credit for proposing what became the famous "Freedom Charter," which was to guide South Africa until independence.[68]

Their comrade, the Afro-Guyanese-American writer Louis Burnham was a frequent presence in the press of the South African left.[69] Another young Negro writer, John Oliver Killens, was praised when he published the riveting novel, *Youngblood,* characterized as an "indictment of the Southern way of life."[70] The pre-eminent Negro writer Langston Hughes was in touch with Richard Rive of South Africa.[71] Yet another young Negro writer—in what was becoming a trend—took to the pages of *New Age*: Mason Roberson of San Francisco denounced the U.S. role in Africa.[72] While the "American grip on South Africa" was riddled with criticism,[73] presciently it was seen in 1955 that "Afghanistan on Soviet border is now U.S. target."[74]

It was evident that the post-Montgomery scene had emboldened U.S. Negroes. It was also in 1956 that yet another Negro writer—William Worthy—was detained by Pretoria after attempting to enter South Africa without a valid visa.[75] Perhaps he should not have taken this as a slap since even U.S. missionaries by this point were being refused visas.[76] (U.S. missionaries as a rule were seen as much too liberal, ancestry aside, while missionaries of German and Dutch origin were smiled upon—except that Louw, the apartheid don, confided "confidentially" that the Union generally disfavored Catholic missionaries because of their supposed liberally racial attitudes.)[77]

---

67. *New Age*, 28 June 1956.
68. *New Age*, 19 May 1955.
69. *New Age*, 22 March 1956.
70. *New Age*, 10 January 1957.
71. Stephanie Pierre Raymond Robolin, *Grounds of Engagement: Apartheid Era African American and South African Writing*, Urbana: University of Illinois Press, 2015, 1.
72. *New Age*, 31 March 1955.
73. *New Age*, 14 May 1955.
74. *New Age*, 12 May 1955.
75. H. Timothy Lovelace, "William Worthy's Passport: Travel Restrictions and the Cold War Struggle for Civil and Human Rights," *Journal of American History*, 103(Number 1, June 2016): 107-133, 108.
76. Report, 11 January 1956, RG 59, Decimal File, Box 4499, *NARA-CP*.
77. Report, 27 April 1956, Reel 8, *Confidential U.S. State Department Central Files, South Africa....Internal Affairs...and Foreign Affairs.*

Claude Barnett of the Associated Negro Press knew about this all too well. He recounted the experiences of Bishop Frederick D. Jordan of the African Methodist Episcopal, a U.S. Negro denomination with deep roots in the region. He had been assigned to South Africa in an area where the AME had for years been active in missionary work. An application was peremptorily denied for months on end, a continuation of the trend blocking visits by U.S. Negroes of whatever stripe. After landing in what is now Zambia, he was placed in custody and then shipped back to Rome.[78] (Possibly word had reached Lusaka that Harry Nkumbula, the premier African leader there, had asked Barnett whether it was "possible that we could raise money in America through the ANP").[79] The ANP had readers in what became Tanzania, one of whom recalled that "Mrs. [Marcus] Garvey…used to send me some [copies of] 'Negro World'" and now he wanted "Negro news" from the ANP.[80] Jacob Mnemba of the nation that became Zimbabwe was also "very fond of reading Negro papers" and desired a complete list of them to that end.[81] (Perhaps not coincidentally, as the kerfuffle over the visiting U.S. naval vessel captured headlines, Z.K. Matthews was in Barnett's Chicago.)[82] After much arm twisting Pretoria informed Barnett baldly that there was "no specific prohibitions on Americans of African descent as such…[they are] dealt with strictly on their merits like…all other aliens…."[83]

It was understandable why the South African left paid so much attention to U.S. imperialism for even events that did not grab front page headlines captured the imagination on the beset continent. In 1955 when the boxer Rocky Marciano—an Italian-American—defeated Jersey Joe Walcott, an African-American, "the pure-blooded Southerners and their brothers-in-law in South Africa rejoiced," said the *New Age*, as if this were a replay of Rome's conquest of Addis Ababa in the 1930s. "The Nationalist press in [Johannesburg]

78. *Chicago Daily News*, 7 May 1953 and Claude Barnett to Basil Walters, circa 1953, Box 143, Folder 3, *Claude Barnett Papers*.

79. Harry Nkumbula to Claude Barnett, no date, Box 174, Folder 6, *Claude Barnett Papers*.

80. R.K. Kanakuyla to Claude Barnett, 22 July 1953, Box 173, Folder 1, *Barnett Papers*.

81. Jacob Mnemba to Claude Barnett, 28 November 1955, Box 174, Folder 6, *Barnett Papers*.

82. Claude Barnett to St. Clair Drake, 23 May 1955, Box 175, Folder 1, *Barnett Papers*.

83. Secretary for the Department of Interior-Pretoria to ANP, 22 September 1948, Box 175, Folder 1, *Barnett Papers*.

splashed the news all over its front pages with unconcealed glee."[84] When the black teenager Emmett Till was lynched in Mississippi by racists, this same paper charged that the republic itself was "on trial" as "lynch law strikes Negroes."[85] A detailed report on the case referred angrily to "apartheid in America," after "lynchers" were allowed to "go free."[86]

When the Montgomery Bus Boycott erupted in late 1955, a casual reader might have thought that it had occurred in the Union, particularly in the reference to "apartheid buses." The role of the sterling heroine Rosa Parks was spotlighted.[87] When simultaneously Autherine Lucy sought to desegregate the University of Alabama, one might have thought that the "Negro girl" who "fights against U.S. apartheid" in confronting "mob terror" could just as well have been in Johannesburg.[88] Coincidentally enough, it was also in 1956 that it was reported breathlessly from Cape Town that a "bus boycott gathers momentum."[89] "We are not prepared to let apartheid on the buses go unchallenged," said Alex La Guma.[90] Then a French cartoonist was recruited to create an image suitable for both protests as Africans/Negroes hung like lynch victims from straps on a bus as corpulent Europeans/white men in Texas cowboy hats sat silently.[91]

A "great victory for U.S. bus boycotters" was celebrated in December 1956 as if South Africa could claim alongside Dr. Martin Luther King, Jr. that "old man segregation is on the death bed."[92] Yet another "victory over U.S. racialism"[93] was honored, while a companion analysis concluded that "anti-Semitism is widespread" in the republic.[94] When the Negro Congressman Charles Diggs of Detroit moved for "exclusion" of Mississippi delegates in Washington, his maneuver to oust these "apartheid representatives" was backed enthusiastically.[95]

Lionel Forman, editor of the *New Age*, was sufficiently bold to contact the officially anticommunist NAACP leadership, remarking that his office had "been receiving regularly copies of U.S. Negro

84. *New Age*, 15 September 1955.
85. *New Age*, 13 October 1955.
86. *New Age*, 10 November 1955.
87. *New Age*, 26 January 1956.
88. *New Age*, 4 March 1956.
89. *New Age*, 26 April 1956.
90. *New Age*, 15 December 1955.
91. *New Age*, 24 April 1956 and 24 May 1956..
92. *New Age*, 6 December 1956.
93. *New Age*, 7 April 1955.
94. *New Age*, 14 April 1955.
95. *New Age*, 8 December 1955.

newspapers carrying reports on the fight for civil liberties in your country," leaving all who read these accounts heartened. "The news of the Alabama boycott has been of very great interest and I enclose a copy of our latest issue with a report of our own boycott with the same aims here. Please convey the greetings of the Cape Town boycotters," he ended with misplaced concord, "to the people of Alabama."[96] Forman did not seem to recognize that the NAACP would hardly be enthusiastic about bonding with those thought to be Communist, even those on the frontlines against white supremacy. Similarly, no response survives to the query from Cape Town's Ronald Segal to Alabama's Fred Shuttlesworth, reminding him that "the Johannesburg boycott is in many respects similar to the great Birmingham boycott" and requesting a publishable reply.[97]

The recently formed American Committee on Africa would have been a bit more forthcoming in response to such an overture. Their leader, George Houser, was joined by Howard University's Rayford Logan in conferring with the State Department in December 1955 about U.S. policy; the fact that it was a "friendly" talk, may have unnerved anti-apartheid combatants given Pretoria's dependence upon Washington.[98] It was shortly thereafter, in 1956, that NAACP leaders Roy Wilkins and Channing Tobias joined famed South African writer Alan Paton—not thought to be part of the SACP circle—in a conversation on "the long shadow of Lincoln" that was broadcast nationally in the U.S.[99]

The U.S. Communist journalist Abner Berry enthused, in words that would gain in velocity and profundity in coming years, that a "common struggle unites people of Cape Town and Montgomery, USA" because of the dual bus boycotts.[100] Contemporaneous strugglers in the U.S. would have benefited immensely if they had read South African analyses. It was in December 1955, just as the Montgomery offensive was launched, that *Fighting Talk* highlighted Du Bois' 1947 petition to the U.N. on behalf of Negroes as a turning point against Jim Crow. In some ways, it was argued, the status of Negroes had fallen since 1865, since in the previous era "the Negroes in the

---

96. Lionel Forman to NAACP, 24 April 1956, Box IIA603, *NAACP Papers.*

97. Ronald Segal to the Reverend F.L. Shuttlesworth, Box IIA603, *NAACP Papers.*

98. Memorandum of Conversation, 20 December 1955, Reel 14, *Confidential U.S. State Department Files, South Africa...Internal Affairs....and Foreign Affairs.*

99. Press Release, 2 February 1956, Box IIA603, *NAACP Papers.*

100. *New Age*, 19 April 1956.

South had practically a monopoly of skilled jobs (just like slaves at the Cape)". The paper castigated anti-Jewish quotas in the U.S., citing progressive Jewish-Americans, and concluding with the coda: "one can only wish that certain South African-Jewish leaders might show a similar clarity of vision…."[101]

"The tide of history has undoubtedly turned in favour of the Negroes," was the wise judgment of the *New Age*, speaking of the U.S. And "with them in spirit are the overwhelming majority of mankind marching towards similar goals in Asia, Africa, the Middle East and Latin America…." These anti-apartheid strugglers were also capable of ferreting out contrary trends, observing that "McCarthyism has been given a new lease on life by the recent increase of international tension," a veiled reference to the escalation of war in Algeria in 1957.[102]

Another countervailing trend was the increasing U.S. interest in South Africa. It was in 1957 that Adlai Stevenson, a two-time failed candidate for the White House, arrived in the country. As he was deplaning, said the *New Age*, the Nationalists had adroitly "done everything in its power to encourage [U.S.] interests to entrench themselves in the South African economy," as U.S. "surplus products" had "flooded" the nation, leading to "dollar shortages," entailing "borrowing money to meet the deficit," meaning more Yankee control. Pretoria would then wind up "becoming mere economic dependencies of the American monopolists," but it would also "lead directly to the strengthening of the Nationalist regime," bailed out by Washington and Wall Street. Thus, it was a "serious mistake," to think in examining the anti-Jim Crow measures, "that the Americans will help free South Africa from the domination of the Nationalists."[103] But Governor Stevenson's arrival was not appreciated by the right wing either. Across the border in Salisbury, Rhodesia, the League of Empire Loyalists, whose principles included "racial superiority of the white…anti-Americanism…[and] anti-Zionism," also joined in opposition to the failed presidential candidate.[104]

Similarly, anti-Jim Crow crusaders often dimly realized that backing apartheid was inimical to their holy cause. In contrast, anti-apartheid militants saw a deadly parallel between Strijdom's naked racism and Dulles' wicked anticommunism.[105]

101. *Fighting Talk*, December 1955.
102. *New Age*, 4 April 1957.
103. *New Age*, 13 June 1957.
104. Report, 10 July 1957, RG 59, Decimal Files, Box 3233, *NARA-CP*.
105. *New Age*, 15 August 1957.

Even Z.K. Matthews took to the pages of the left press to analyze civil liberties in the U.S. while chiding the republic for Jim Crow[106]—a disturbing sign given the energy spent on introducing him to CIA leaders for anticommunist purposes. The leaders of apartheid sought to explain their lagging behind the tepid desegregation initiatives in Washington by invidiously comparing the "Bantu" to the Negro: even the U.S. Consul General in Johannesburg found the former to be "much different from the American Negro, who has been assimilated into the population"[107]—which would have come as a surprise to many of those described.

From another shore, a speaker at the "American Businessmen's Club" in South Africa found that "living conditions of the Bantu on the Witwatersrand were far superior to those prevailing on the outskirts of large [U.S.] cities…even the 'shanty towns' near Johannesburg appeared to be less unhealthy and undesirable than the Negro shacks on the outskirts of almost city in the Deep South."[108]

This dual anti-Jim Crow, anti-apartheid barrage should not be seen as the norm. Pretoria featured an item quoting A.E. England of the Hollywood Chamber of Commerce, who demanded, "you must not make the same mistake as was made in America by granting equality to the Non-Whites," for if this tack was taken, "you can expect to be slaves within a very short time and they will be free."[109]

Besides, Washington was not pleased by the reports of mainstream apartheid opinion as anti-Jim Crow unrest surged. "Considerable prominence to racial disturbances in the United States connected with school integration" was reported about the South African press. The legation was miffed that many Europeans there had "taken some satisfaction" in the republic's instability, since such feelings could cause a backlash against desegregation and more support for Pretoria, as England's comment suggested. A South African visitor to the republic "found sympathy" there "for the Union's racial problems," but "he sensed racial tension in the Southern United States which did not exist in South Africa."[110] This was part of the disappointment

106. *Fighting Talk*, November 1956.

107. Report by Charles Reed II, 4 September 1956, Reel 1, *Confidential U.S. State Department Files, Internal Affairs….and Foreign Affairs, NARA-CP*.

108. Charles Reed II to Secretary of State, 26 April 1956, RG 59, Decimal File, Box 3230.

109. "Monthly Digest of South African Affairs," 7 June 1955, Reel 1, *Confidential U.S. State Department File, Internal Affairs….*

110. Report from Pretoria Embassy, 18 September 1956, Reel 1, *Confidential U.S. State Department File, Internal Affairs.*

in wide South African circles with the violence unleashed against angelic protesters against the status quo in Dixie, which carried clear implications for apartheid. The SACP leader, Ray Alexander, was queried if she had "been able to follow the disgraceful events in Arkansas" in 1957. The lesson? "It goes far toward demonstrating the fruitlessness of timidity and gradualism…."[111]

Apartheid and Jim Crow were becoming a burden for the North Atlantic powers generally. A U.S. missionary, Ralph Galloway, found in 1956 that "growing anti-white sentiment in French Cameroons can be traced to the tense racial situation" in Dixie and South Africa.[112]

Rather than extend solidarity, the South African press gloated about the Arkansas school desegregation crisis. "The Afrikaans press derived some consolation from the American predicament," said the legation balefully.[113]

* * *

The Nationalists and the remnants of the United Party were still at each other's throats, with the legation reporting that the British on the east coast heading outward from Durban wanted "cheaper labor for work now performed by whites; others saw the Native as a political ally…." It was Dr. L.J.E. de B. Beyers, head of the Department of Mercantile Law at the University of South Africa, who uttered these heretical words, and he went further, arguing that London "looked upon the Natives as potential armed divisions fighting under the Union Jack…." This academic, a skeptical envoy averred, was "still fighting the Boer War." Nonetheless, one straw in the wind was that the *Bantu World* was "now printing the entire paper in English," and there was, likewise, a "great desire of Natives to learn and use English"—countered by an attempt to instruct them in Afrikaans, an understandable but disastrous maneuver that led to the Soweto Uprising of June 1976, marking the beginning of the end of apartheid.[114]

111. Lars Lawrence to Ray Alexander, 30 September 1957, C1.7, *Jack Simons and Ray Alexander Collection, University of Cape Town.*

112. Release, February 1956, Reel 59, #318, Part I, Press Releases, *Barnett/ANP Papers*

113. Report, 4 October 1957, Reel 1, *Confidential U.S. State Department Files, Internal Files….and Foreign Affairs.*

114. Report, 2 November 1955, Reel 13, *Confidential U.S. State Department Central Files, South Africa, Internal Affairs….and Foreign Affairs, -NARA-CP.*

As Beyers' remarks suggested, there were those among the Afrikaners who felt increasingly isolated as the U.S. moved away from Jim Crow and the U.K.'s global role diminished. Johannes de Klerk, father of apartheid's final ruler, claimed at a Nationalist rally in Cape Town in 1955 that the "white labor shortage had become so critical that the whole future of the European race and its ability to maintain *baaskap*," Afrikaner supremacy in the guise of white supremacy, was threatened. Raising the retirement age was one suggestion.[115] Immigration should have been on that checklist (and the Hungarian crisis forced its way on to this agenda), but, generally, Afrikaner apprehension about being outnumbered, even by other Europeans, put a damper on this too.

In March 1955, months before the Hungarian crisis, the fading United Party encouraged immigration of all types (of course, they meant all European types). Earlier, in 1948, there had been a large influx from a Britain, still battered by war—more than 46,000 all told—but the Nationalists objected vociferously, arguing that this was little more than a plot to increase the UP vote. The Nationalists said that immigrants from Holland or Germany would be acceptable—but even the latter might be frowned up given the possibility they might only come to spearhead a lurch toward an ersatz Namibian independence.[116]

While complaining about the European minority, the legation was busy—as planned—with deepening "cleavages" among them. Sir de Villiers Graaf, a leader of the weakened United Party, was described disdainfully as possessing a "swarthy complexion" with a "general appearance" that "lends some credence to the allegation often heard that he has Colored blood;" this could be a political—if not literal—death sentence, if exposed. But luckily he was "friendly toward the United States" though the "Nationalists have started a whispering campaign against him," that did not seem terribly upsetting to the legation.[117] Close tabs were also kept on Dr. Willem Christiaan Naude, apartheid's envoy to Switzerland, who had been posted in Washington at the time of the crucial Bretton Woods talks that formed the postwar global financial architecture a decade or so earlier. He was also part of the Broederbond and thus within the bounds set by the mainstream Nationalists, meaning he could be pushed forward

115. Report by Wilson Flake, 10 March 1955, RG 59, Decimal File, Box 3230, *NARA-CP*.

116. William Wright, Jr. to Secretary of State, 3 March 1955, RG 59, Decimal File, Box 4499.

117. Report, 6 December 1956, RG 59, Decimal File, Box 3233, *NARA-CP*.

as a Prime Minister. He was influenced by his wife. The poetically named Maude Naude was considered "friendly and impetuous," ergo subject to manipulation; that she "occasionally over indulges in alcohol" was also relevant here.[118] Another Nationalist leader, Dr. Carel de Wet, descendant of a legendary Boer commander during the anti-London war, was described as being "very friendly to Americans" and "an admirer of the United States.....he feels at home with Americans and....appreciates their frankness and honesty" and "would very much like to visit the United States."[119]

It was felt in Washington that Pretoria's envoy in Switzerland, John Kenneth Christies, could be co-opted effectively. He was "well known to most of the American embassy staff" there and "was especially friendly to the reporting officer. He apparently likes Americans and admires the United States" and "would be more than pleased to exchange information and to cooperate with American representatives in Bern."[120] A similar sunny view was held about the United Party's Robert Badenhorst Durrant, who too was "very friendly to Americans and a great admirer of the United States." He "frequently invited members of the American embassy to his weekend cottage on the Cape." The legation, in fact, had numerous reports on numerous South African officials who were seen as potential agents for Washington.[121]

As for the ANC, the consulate in Durban engaged with Jordan Ngubane, who was unsympathetic to the SACP and therefore a prized contact. They were pleased to have confirmed their presupposition that the "internal struggle" in the ANC meant that it would not "play as important a role as it might in the solution of the interracial problems of this country."[122]

Some of the leading members of the SACP were of Indian descent and it was from Madras that Henry Ramsey brought to the urgent attention of his colleagues "the lead editorial" of the influential *Swantantra* which declared that "the battle between Communism and the Western democracies will be determined in South

118. "Confidential" Report, 1 November 1956, RG 59, Decimal File, Box 3233.

119. Report, 29 May 1957, Reel 4, *Confidential U.S. State Department Files, Internal Affairs...and Foreign Affairs.*

120. Report, 5 June 1957, Reel 4, *Confidential U.S. State Department Files, Internal Affairs...and Foreign Affairs.*

121. Report, 6 June 1957, Reel 4, *Confidential U.S. State Department Files, Internal Affairs....and Foreign Affairs.*

122. Report by C.H. Hall, Consul General-Durban, 4 March 1955, RG59, Decimal File, Box 3230.

Africa"—concluding that if London and Washington wanted to prevail "they must not allow the Communists to pre-empt the issue of racialism as they have the issue of colonialism." This would prove a difficult assignment to fulfill if Pretoria relied upon a European elite that favored both racialism and colonialism,[123] while virtually conceding almost 90% of the population to the Communists without a struggle. Actually, it was worse than it appeared: a different newspaper in Madras, described as "South India's most influential conservative" periodical, was irate about a well-publicized incident involving segregation of the (dark-skinned) Indian Ambassador in Houston because of Jim Crow. New Delhi was needed to better confront the Soviets and China, but state-sanctioned racism was hampering this strategic objective.[124]

A decisive force in battering apartheid into submission was the international community. An Afrikaner elite reluctant to retreat an inch from racialism—when their chief ally in Washington moved otherwise—was not a sustainable proposition. Empowered U.S. Negroes had extended solidarity across the ocean even during the darkest days of Jim Crow; these efforts would only grow stronger as Jim Crow began to crumble. There were other examples of the impact of global events on apartheid, the Suez debacle in particular: the war against Nasser's Egypt for control of the canal by a joint brigand of France, the U.K., and Israel. The results were predictable: Moscow backed Cairo and forced the aggressors to stand down, increasing the prestige of the Soviets in Africa. As in the aftermath of the Haitian Revolution in the early 19th century, London recognized the jig was up and began the agonizing retreat from power—while Paris, upset with Washington's decision not to back this aggression, decided that the North Atlantic Treaty Organization, dominated by the U.S., was inconsistent with France's grander ambitions and began to try to develop its own military arm. This was unrealistic and soon France was compelled to withdraw from Algeria, not least because of Egyptian support for the rebels. Indeed, this fiasco was driven in no small measure by Paris' desire to end Cairo's support for Algerian independence.[125]

---

123. Report by Henry Ramsey, 21 December 1954, RG 59, Decimal File, Box 4503.

124. Report from Consul General, Madras, 6 November 1955, Reel 11, *Confidential State Department Central Files on South Africa....Internal Affairs....and Foreign Affairs.*

125. Jeffrey James Byrne, *Mecca of Revolution: Algeria, Decolonization and the Third World Order*, New York: Oxford University Press, 2016, 50.

Eventually, Washington would seek to undermine France's position in Africa in the guise of anti-colonialism. But as of 1956 the U.S. was sending advanced aircraft for combat in Algeria by French forces, just as it had sought to bail out France in Indochina.[126]

As for South Africa, this abortive war initially seemed to work in Pretoria's favor. In August 1956, the U.S. legation described Pretoria's initial reaction to this conflict as "very disappointing," since the Nationalists seemed to be hedging their bets. "One account," it was reported, "states that South Africa will be restored to its wartime prosperity since so many additional ships will now be using the Cape Town route," which was generally accurate. More rifts were introduced internally, as once again the Afrikaner elite seemed to be reliving the turn-of-the century war, denouncing their British counterparts for "slavishly and unpatriotically supporting [London]," as if the national interest could only be served by aping the Nationalists. Yet, simultaneously, the Nationalists were also concerned about what should have been seen as the long-term threat: they "expressed worry over Egyptian propaganda broadcasts urging the Blacks to unite to throw off colonial oppression."[127] Soon a profusion of anti-apartheid fighters would be found in Cairo, backed to the hilt by Nasser. Zenzile Ngalo, who was to serve as ANC delegate in Cairo, recalled rubbing shoulders with freedom fighters from Zimbabwe, Mozambique, and elsewhere: "we were all together there…. I was broadcasting in Xhosa daily….I was broadcasting in English…."[128]

Also, on the African front, Ghana's surge to independence in 1957 was of incalculable consequence for the anti-apartheid movement, marking the imminent retreat of colonialism generally, not least because of the diplomatic and military support that would be rendered by Accra. This "inspired all of us," said SACP leader Billy Nair.[129] Oswald Pirow said that diplomatic relations with Ghana "would mark the beginning of the fall of *apartheid*." [emphasis in the original] Of all things, the "Black Minister on official occasions would sit next to a white woman" and "Black clerks would be placed over white typists and the embassy would become a propaganda

126. John P. Cann, *Flight Plan Africa: Portuguese Airpower in Counterinsurgency, 1961-1974*, West Midlands: Helion, 2015.

127. Report, 2 August 1956, Reel 1, *Confidential U.S. State Department Files, Internal Affairs….and Foreign Affairs.*

128. Oral History, Zenzile Ngalo, 5 July 2001, *University of Connecticut-Storrs.*

129. Oral History, Billy Nair, 10 February 2000, Billy Nair, *University of Connecticut-Storrs.*

center for anti-white agitation." Such obstinacy only underscored that Pretoria was, at best, a problematic ally for the republic.[130]

Pirow may have had in mind the betrothal of Eduardo Mondlane, founding father of modern Mozambique, and Janet Johnson, a Euro-American. Mondlane had been infamously ousted from South Africa in 1948 and made his way to the United States, where he enrolled in college. Their relationship was difficult. They first met when she invited him to speak at her Indiana church; to save money, she suggested he stay at her father's home, but he replied stiffly, "I will not allow any black man in this home and I don't want anything to do with any black man." A shaken Mondlane attributed a great deal of the problem to the deep-seated racism in the U.S., which was reflected in the U.S. missionaries he encountered in Mozambique as well as in the parents of the woman who was to become his spouse—who were threatening to cut off her financial support if she did not end the relationship with him. When he was asked to depart a Nashville church on Jim Crow grounds, his sour view of the republic deepened further.[131]

Oppositely--and understandably--Pirow was fixated on Accra. Ghana was massively emboldening to Africans. An Associated Negro Press columnist, A.J. Siggins, sardonically referred to Pretoria as "Genocidia" and demanded, ala Bandung—the profound confab attended by Kotane—that a "Pacific and Indian Ocean People's Federation" be consummated to confront both Pretoria and its sidekick in Washington. He reprimanded both Harlem Congressman Adam Clayton Powell—sent to Bandung by the U.S.—and Ralph Bunche for not being more passionate in confronting U.S. imperialism, citing particularly the former's backing of "NATO and SEATO [Southeast Asian Treaty Organization]," the two major anticommunist formations. Both men should know, he insisted, that "their problem," meaning Jim Crow, "is part of a world problem and therefore needs world action to arrive at solution...." Thus, he veritably shouted, the two polecats of racism should be forced to "JOIN THE WORLD MOVEMENT FOR THE ABOLITION OF COLOR DISCRIMINATION AND COLONIALISM."[132]

Once again, the Afrikaners were so blinded by their distaste for their fellow Europeans and their racist underestimation of the

---

130. Report, 4 October 1957, Reel 1, *Confidential U.S. State Department Files, Internal Affairs....and Foreign Affairs.*

131. Robert Faris, *Liberating Mission in Mozambique: Faith and Revolution in the Life of Eduardo Mondlane*, Cambridge, U.K.: Lutterworth, 2015, 80, 82, 100.

132. Release, March 1956, Reel 59, #631, Part I, Press Releases.

capabilities of Africans that they could not divine their true colonial interests. (Of course, Pretoria's inability to see itself as a settler colonial occupier also shrouded its vision.) And, yes, Pretoria was emulating its patron in Washington, which was also ambivalent about anti-colonial intervention in Africa: gleeful about undermining of European rivals but fretful about the rise to power of unruly Africans.

There was no such hesitation in Pretoria about the Fall 1956 revolt in Budapest. Perhaps because the resultant refugees were not perceived as allies of the British, the Nationalists acceded to earmarks being accorded to these newcomers, though this effort was focused on importing skilled artisans most of all. In a burst of anticommunist zeal, Union students from Stellenbosch—the citadel of the Afrikaner elite—volunteered to become "freedom fighters" in Hungary; and student protests about this crisis were almost exclusively limited to Afrikaner universities.[133] Right after the revolt was squashed, Hungarian refugees started streaming into South Africa. The "response from employers had been terrific," beamed the U.S. legation. So impressed was Pretoria that it decided to raise the quota of refugees by 100%, from 500 to 1000[134]—not much in the larger scheme of things but a breakthrough considering Afrikaner hardliners. The South African left did not win many friends in Pretoria when it lambasted the arrival of Hungarian refugees; and the new arrivals alienated many Africans by praising the purported freedom they found under apartheid.[135]

In short, apartheid was facing a crisis that the arrival of hordes of anticommunists from Hungary could not conceal. Its chief ally, the U.S., was moving slowly away from the bedrock matter of state-sanctioned racism, undermining bilateral ties. Africans in turn were emboldened by the inspiration and support they received from U.S. Negroes. Both factors weakened Pretoria as a mainstay of anticommunism. Thus, by 1956 there were fewer immigrants arriving, notably those who could be defined as "white"; more from this group emigrated and the net population gain in "whites" that year was the smallest since 1952. It would have been even lower without the arrival of a few hundred Hungarian refugees in December 1956, the first of some 1000 that South Africa had agreed to accept—though

133. Report, 21 November 1956, RG 59, Decimal File, Box 3230, *NARA-CP*.

134. Report, 3 January 1957, Reel 1, *Confidential U.S. State Department Files, Internal Affairs….and Foreign Affairs.*

135. *New Age*, 17 January 1957.

some Nationalist outliers were nervous about the staunch Catholicism of some of them.[136]

Skepticism about this Hungarian influx came from a different corner too. Roy Wilkins of the NAACP received a copy of a letter about an advertisement seeking hundreds of U.S. emigrants to Southern Rhodesia; this NAACP member, a self-described "qualified Negro farmer" wondered if this would include a "welcome" to "skilled Americans of African ancestry."[137] The answer from the apartheid ally was not favorable.

A frustrated U.S. envoy, Edward T. Wailes, summed up the dilemma of the Nationalists as they sought to fortify apartheid while shunning anyone who might conceivably stand in their way. "We don't want British because we have too many; we don't want Dutch or German because they join the United Party; we don't want Italians because they are Catholic"—like many of the Hungarians he could have added—and "we would like some skilled American or other workers but can't afford to pay their wages."[138] Apartheid could not adapt and was therefore doomed to die, like the prehistoric creatures it so resembled.

Unfortunately for anti-apartheid fighters, their bulwark of support was also having difficulty adapting. SACP leader Brian Bunting recalled with dismay the third global shock of 1956, after Suez and Hungary. The report from Moscow that devalued Stalin's legacy, Bunting said, was a "shock, a terrible shock," leading to "many discussions here in Cape Town" though his comrades—like many worldwide and particularly in the land of apartheid— "concluded that the pluses of the Soviet Union outweighed the minuses...." Bunting was not repulsed by the Stalin revelations, in that a few years later Bunting was serving as South African correspondent for Tass, the Soviet news agency;[139] actually, revulsion at the crimes committed in the name of socialism shook the comrades to the same

136. Edward Holmes to Secretary of State, 7 March 1957, RG 59, Decimal File, Box 4497.

137. Anton Nelson to Kenneth Ledbetter, Intergovernmental Committee for European Migration, Salisbury, Southern Rhodesia, 17 August 1956, Box IIA603, *NAACP Papers*.

138. Edward T. Wailes to Secretary of State, 27 January 1956, RG 59, Decimal File, Box 3230.

139. Oral History, Brian Bunting, 3 October 2000, *University of Connecticut-Storrs*.

extent that crimes committed in the name of capitalism shook North America.[140]

Finally, Pretoria had had enough. In late 1956 Mandela answered the door at his home and was confronted by a squad of police officers holding a warrant for his arrest. That year he and scores of ANC leaders and their allies were detained and then put on trial for treason, in a laborious procedure that would tie up the defendants until 1961.[141] But just as the Suppression of Communism Act of 1950 had the paradoxical impact of driving Reds to seek shelter within the ANC ranks, Rusty Bernstein argues that this particular trial "made things better by bringing many leaders together in one place." Previously "despite widespread popular support," the ANC was "in truth, much more of a mass frame of mind than a centralized modern political body." The arrests "could have made matters worse," but "in this new setting [leaders] were able to overcome many of [the movement's] structural and organizational weaknesses. For the first time the leaders are concentrated in one place, always available for meetings and accessible to ordinary members," meaning "quality of the leadership is transformed and brought closer to their members and supporters than ever before…."[142]

Dramatically, Oswald Pirow, the neo-Nazi warhorse, was drafted to lead the prosecution. As recently as 1946 he had gushed that Hitler was not just "the greatest man of his age," he was "perhaps the greatest of the last 1000 years;" and a year before, said of the Jewish community, "I firmly believe that if every Jew could vanish from the earth, the world as a whole would be a better place." As for "Non-Europeans," they were worthy of little more than "compulsory labour service." During the war, his numerous supporters greeted him with the cry, "Heil Pirow."[143]

Ironically, perhaps perversely, the trial was to be conducted in a former synagogue, with public and press galleries rigidly segregated, as noted by Harvard's eminent Erwin Griswold,[144] an observer whose presence indicated the importance of the trial—and the nation where it was held.

---

140. Gerald Horne, *The Apocalypse of Settler Colonialism: The Roots of Slavery, White Supremacy and Capitalism in 17th Century North America and the Caribbean*, New York: Monthly Review Press, 2018.

141. Kelly Knauer, ed., *Nelson Mandela*, 34, 56.

142. Rusty Bernstein, *Memory Against Forgetting*, 178.

143. *New Age*, 11 July 1956.

144. Report by Erwin Griswold, no date, Box 139, *Allard Lowenstein Papers, University of North Carolina-Chapel Hill.*

Chapter 8

Turning Point, 1957-1959

THOUGH only faintly recognized in Pretoria, by 1957 the countdown to the demise of apartheid had sped up. The decolonization of Ghana and the desegregation crisis in Little Rock, Arkansas were the most dramatic examples of how external events were driving matters domestically. Pretoria's chief ally in Washington would be forced to choose between cavorting with apartheid or cutting deals with independent Africa and, in any case, an increasingly empowered U.S. Negro population was narrowing republican options too. The South African memoirist Bloke Modisane, who wrote at length about the fascination with all things U.S. in his homeland, from Florsheim shoes to Hollywood, also saw a general turning point in South African culture in 1957-1958, when U.S. musicians Tony Scott and Bud Shank toured and sought to play with African musicians before desegregated audiences.[1] This was perceived as a breach in the wall of apartheid, a harbinger of others to come. Symptomatic of the changing times was the breathless announcement in April 1958 in the pages of the left-leaning *New Age* that "in South Africa a long-playing record of songs by [Robeson] is now available for the first time in many years."[2] These trends in music were simply aping trends in politics.

As the manacles of Jim Crow began to loosen, Negroes were then able to intervene more forcefully on the complex matter of colonialism in Africa. A columnist for the Associated Negro Press implored Negroes to become more involved in global affairs, as this would serve to solidify their recent hard-won gains.[3] Congressman Charles Diggs of Detroit needed no convincing. The portly, light-skinned

1. Bloke Modisane, *Blame Me on History*, New York: Simon & Schuster, 1986, 50.

2. *New Age*, 10 April 1958.

3. Release, October 1958, Reel 65, #494, Part I, Press Releases.

Negro with rapidly thinned straightened hair was becoming a one-man anti-apartheid lobby. After returning from a journey to Ghana, he inquired about a South African who was a substantial property owner who had perished while in Ghana. The State Department seemed surprised that Diggs "has manifested an active interest in African affairs" but such inquiries would soon become constant.[4] As the following suggests, ferment in Africa and involving Africa accelerated after 1957.

Pretoria thought it had executed a coup when it placed the anti-apartheid forces on the defensive in the Treason Trial, which—at the very least—would tie up opponents in court proceedings for years to come. What they could not account for was the growing activism of U.S. Negroes whose interest in Southern Africa had not waned. This interest was facilitated—as it had been for decades—by Africans escaping to North America for higher education. In 1959 the man who was to become the founding father of what became Malawi, Hastings Banda, sent effusive greetings to the ANP from his dank prison cell after the news organization sent him a box of books he had requested. Banda, recalled the ANP, ran away from home as a young teenager, winding up like so many of his compatriots as a laborer in a South African gold mine. In that nation he met Bishop William Tecumseh Vernon of the AME denomination, who brought him to the U.S. and enrolled him at the historically black Central State University in Wilberforce, Ohio, then the Meharry Medical College in Nashville, and finally the University of Chicago, where he apparently became conversant with the ANP.[5] To Claude Barnett, the agency founder, Banda was an "old and personal friend."[6] Reciprocating, Banda found it "extremely pleasing" to "see that friends in the United States, both colored an white, have not forgotten me, over all these long years I was there;" nor had they forgotten his "arrest and detention." He was heartened to have received "letters and books and gifts from both colored and white people" and "my former teachers at the University of Chicago."[7] (If his correspondents had been paying acutely close attention, they might have noticed

---

4. Memorandum, 15 January 1959, *Confidential U.S. State Department Files. Internal Affairs....and Foreign Affairs.*

5. Release, December 1959, Reel 69, #227, Part, Press Releases. See also interview with Banda in Blantyre: Release, December 1961, Reel 75, #470, Part I, Press Releases.

6. Claude Barnett to Nicholas Mbicholo, 29 May 1963, Box 174, Folder 9, *Claude Barnett Papers.*

7. [Hastings] Kamuzu Banda to Claude Barnett, 21 January 1960, Box 174, Folder 6.

that that Dr. Banda's ideology contained the seeds of the tyranny that he proceeded to foist upon his homeland for decades to come.[8] The fact remained, however, that intense repression may have driven Dr. Banda over the cliff.) The Philadelphia Quakers had contact with both Banda and Kenneth Kaunda of Northern Rhodesia while both were jailed by the colonizer.[9]

Banda's matriculation in the republic was—in a sense—contrary to a coming trend, as more and more Africans had begun to study in the Soviet Union. When the Quaker representative in the region visited Nyasaland—Malawi—in 1958, he was told by delegates from Britain's Xaverian Brothers that "Communist influence is at work in Africa because of the questions he is being asked by his students," e.g. "why is Russia willing to give us full-paid scholarships and Britain not?"[10] Washington was being compared to Moscow invidiously too, placing pressure on the former. In 1958, the *New Age* chastised the republic for having the gall to not "invite a single African, Indian or Coloured to join with the white guests" in their Independence Day festivities. Yet, "when the Soviet Consul General was here, he always invited Non-European guests to his functions."[11]

Meanwhile, back in Rhodesia, George Loft—the Quaker envoy—was stunned by a manifestation of bigotry towards Africans at a social function held by a major U.S. corporation that, after all, was common in the republic, making it all the more difficult to uproot.[12] It may not have been coincidental when soon the legislature in

8. Nicholas Mbicholo, Malawi Press Ltd. To ANP, 19 February 1963, Box 174, Folder 9: "Will you note that Dr. Banda should be accorded with honour and respect by using the official titles conferred on him by his party? The most effective title is 'NGWAZI' which means 'CHAMPION OR THE CONQUEROR.' This title is equivalent to the title 'OSAGYEFO' which Nkrumah in Ghana carries."

9. George Loft to Father Peter J. Walsh, 27 November 1959, Box Foreign Service 1958, Country-Africa.... *AFSC*. In the same box, see also George Loft to Father Peter J. Walsh, 21 December 1959: "I have been visiting Kenneth fairly regularly in Salisbury Prison, and have been impressed by the desire he had to feel a sense of God's guidance in his life. I hope that this aspect can be reinforced in Kenneth and that Government can be encouraged to deal with him creatively and constructively, in light of these sentiments which Kenneth has."

10. George Loft to "Dear Allen," 28 May 1958, Box Foreign Service 1958, Country-Africa.... *AFSC*.

11. *New Age*, 17 July 1958..

12. George Loft to "Dear Allen," 28 February 1958, Box Foreign Service 1958: "The Central African branch of a large American drug company this

Northern Rhodesia was debating a bill banning discrimination in public places, with one of the legislators—described as "liberal"—contacting the Quaker envoy for "related legislation from the States," which he happily provided.[13]

The Quakers in what is now Zambia thought they had spotted a trend when a local European clergyman noted that he had just read the latest book by Dr. Martin Luther King, Jr. and now wanted "any literature about the Montgomery situation or about King himself."[14] Days later, the Quakers were mulling over the possibility of circulating in Southern Africa the anti-Jim Crow suggestions of the writer Harry Golden: that is, "put signs on all of the white washrooms reading 'out of order.' And to put signs on certain trees, reading 'for white dogs only.'" The Southern African visitors took notes and "appeared to greatly appreciate this kind of humor."[15]

By late 1959 arriving in the U.S. was another journalist, Laurence Gandar of the *Rand Daily Mail*, a publication viewed as "liberal" on the narrow spectrum of pro- apartheid opinion. His brief included studying desegregation and he was less than impressed. He was taken by the widespread evidence of racism, particularly in Dixie. Remarkably—albeit in a "confidential" missive—the U.S. envoy in South Africa found that "newspaper editors in the Union are not confronted with such marked economic pressure as is seen" in Dixie, where informal economic sanctions were applied to those who refused to toe the racist line. Dixie publishers were "under considerable economic pressure and run the danger of losing advertising accounts if they become too liberal."[16] No explanation was provided

---

week had a 'sundowner' (cocktail party) in one of Salisbury's leading restaurants for the press and other bigwigs. Among those invited were Lawrence Vambe and Nathan Shamuyarira.... Nathan was already in the restaurant when he was asked to leave by the management because a group of Europeans in another corner of the lounge had objected to his presence. When Lawrence arrived, he was told at the reception that he could not go in, and he met Nathan coming out. The two men said that this was the first time that they had been turned out of an establishment in the course of their professional duties;" both men were among the "better known African journalists here."

13. George Loft to "Dear Stewart," 3 December 1959, Box Foreign Service 1958, Country-Africa.... *AFSC.*

14. George Loft to "Dear Allen," 8 March 1959, Box Foreign Service 1958.

15. Allen White to George Loft, 15 May 1959, Box Foreign Service 1958.

16. "Confidential" Report, 12 November 1959, Reel 13, *Confidential U.S. State Department Central Files. South Africa...Internal Affairs...and Foreign Affairs.*

to explain why Jim Crow might be to the right of apartheid. On the other hand, apartheid publishers had the "luxury" of being able to criticize Dixie because of elite distaste for U.S. pressure while Dixie publishers felt they had to defend racism relentlessly, everywhere it existed—including an increasingly critical Pretoria.

Few on either side of the barricades found any humor in the events of January 1959 in the Congo. A giant of the southern cone, Congo also harbored a goodly number of European settlers and, as such, the steadying drumbeat of unrest was framed as troubling "riots" in the apartheid press, which viewed these events with a "grave and pessimistic" manner, said the Pretoria legation. The Afrikaner press, quite sensitive to any challenges to the continental status quo, pointed to Africans' "immeasurable thirst" for power.[17] Complicating things for the colonizers was the point that California sardines—a notoriously cheap and nutritious food and, thus, ideal for dirt poor Congo—were competing with sardines from South African and Portuguese territories. There was fear in Luanda and Pretoria that since there were only about 150 U.S. residents in Leopoldville—including children— (presumably an insufficient number to lean toward the colonizers) that this would make Washington prone to tip the balance in favor of California exporters, harming the overall interests of white supremacy.[18]

This did not prove to be the case and California's fishing industry entered a long-term decline, victimized by Southern Africa. Before 1950 Los Angeles was recognized as the fishing capital of the world, producing some 940 million pounds valued at $45.5 million but then was devastated by overfishing before what became Namibia eroded the Golden State's influence further. The U.S. had been whaling in the vicinity of Walvis Bay since 1784 and South African lobster had been arriving in Philadelphia since 1876. Then the U.S. firm Del Monte shifted from California to Africa, further sinking the industry, as Congolese began to be fed from sources closer to home.[19]

W. Clifford Shields, Vice President of Farrell Lines in New York City, also found that "our major obstacle" was in the Congo. "The Societe Generale de Belgique does about 85% of the banking, trading,

17. Report, 9 January 1959, Reel 1, *Confidential U.S. State Department Files. Internal Affairs….and Foreign Affairs.*

18. Jerome R. Lavallee, Consul General-Leopoldville to Secretary of State, 4 May 1959, RG 59, Decimal File, Box 4501.

19. "The Rise and Fall of the California Fishing Industry," no date, Box 94, Series III, *American Committee on Africa Records Addendum.* See also Leaflets on Campaign Against Del Monte, no date, Box 1, *Carol Thompson/Bud Day Papers on South Africa, Michigan State University-East Lansing.*

mining and manufacturing" in the Congo. The "Belgian Flag Line" thus "competes with us severely," "despite the fact that the [U.S.] buys twice as much from the Belgian Congo as it ships to the Congo," meaning "American shipping is practically excluded…."[20] There was therefore a basis for Washington to back the ouster of the Belgian colonizers, though this realization would be unsettling in Salisbury, Pretoria, and points southward.

Pretoria was not reclining recumbent as Africans and U.S. Negroes were launching fusillades in apartheid's direction.[21] There was growing and stinging Afrikaner criticism of U.S. influence as the 1950s unwound: this was not the ideal manner in which to forge a fruitful bilateral relationship. One cabinet member in Pretoria, Paul Sauer, startlingly denounced "American Economic Imperialism" in 1958,[22] as if he were a covert SACP member. The *South African Observer* even denounced the U.S. Information Service as "anti-white" as the paper executed what William P. Maddox of the legation termed furiously an "editorial vendetta" against his homeland.[23] This crusade included discrediting U.S. heroes like Lincoln and Jefferson by citing their racist words, an act which "fosters a certain amount of cynicism about American policy,"[24] Maddox moaned. By late 1959 the legation had determined that the remnants of the old Smuts' party were "even more British than the British" in harboring a "deep resentment at America having assumed the leadership in world affairs once held by Britain and tend to seize eagerly upon any opportunity to criticize Americans…." There were outliers, e.g. the rand titan Harry Oppenheimer, who seemed to foresee the unraveling of apartheid and was not as hostile to Washington. But this could hardly counterbalance the contrary opinions of the two major European forces: the Nationalists and their electoral opponents.[25]

---

20. Report by W. Clifford Shields, 17 March 1958, Box 3, *U.S. Council on Foreign Economic Policy, Office of the Chairman, Records, Randall Series, Trips Subseries, Eisenhower Library*.

21. Professor Edwin Munger on South African Bureau of Racial Affairs, 14 April 1959, Reel 16, #416, *American Committee on Africa Papers*.

22. Report, 8 May 1958, *Confidential U.S. State Department Central Files. South Africa…. Internal Files….and Foreign Affairs*.

23. Report, 11 February 1959, Reel 13, *Confidential U.S. State Department Central Files. South Africa…. Internal Files…and Foreign Affairs*.

24. Report, 12 March 1959, Reel 13, *Confidential U.S. State Department Central Files. South Africa…. Internal Affairs…and Foreign Affairs*.

25. Consul General-Johannesburg to Secretary of State, 9 October 1959, Reel 14, *Confidential U.S. State Department Central Files. South Africa…. Internal Affairs….and Foreign Affairs*.

The wider point was that anti-Washington viewpoints were escalating from virtually every point on the South African political spectrum. Most strident—and sophisticated—of all were those within the orbit of the SACP. Unlike others in the Union, they paid carefully close attention to developments among U.S. Negroes. The analysis in *Fighting Talk* of Richard Wright's novel *The Long Dream* was more incisive than most reviews in this expatriate's homeland; the plight of the Negro, said the reviewer, should have led to the work being titled a "nightmare" instead of a dream.[26] *New Age* reprinted a lengthy speech by Langston Hughes, the Harlem Bard, that concluded sagaciously of Negroes that "we have been blacklisted all our lives."[27] In their pages could also be found a sharp attack on Eisenhower after he severely weakened a civil rights bill, a maneuver which *Die Burger* yelped was a "blow struck for apartheid in America."[28] Little Rock was not spared in their pages either and U.S. Negroes were said to be "determined and triumphant backed by the rising world anti-Colonialist and anti-apartheid tide...,"[29] while their editorialist deplored the reality that "Negro children [were] persecuted."[30] *New Age*'s solidarity with U.S. Negroes was rewarded when the editor of mainstream Negro periodical, the *Atlanta Daily World*, paid a visit to their Johannesburg office.[31]

The U.S. was simply trying to "capture Africa's vast resources for American Big Business" was the crux of their argument.[32] Washington was portrayed as Pretoria's staunchest comrade, providing support for "Africa's most hated government" and seeking to save the Union "from economic and political disaster" by way of "direct assistance." Citing a book by Robeson's ally W. Alphaeus Hunton, who was shortly to choose exile first in Guinea-Conakry and then Zambia, the paper drove home the point that postwar South Africa was buying more goods from the U.S. as their foreign currency reserves dropped, with the shortfall made up by turning over uranium to the republic. The verdict? Hunton's book was a "must."[33] Thus, the republic was "prepared to play ball" with the Union, a

26. *Fighting Talk*, August 1959.
27. *New Age*, 18 July 1957.
28. *New Age*, 15 August 1957.
29. *New Age*, 12 September 1957.
30. *New Age*, 3 April 1958.
31. *New Age*, 22 January 1959.
32. *New Age*, 7 November 1957.
33. *New Age*, 28 November 1957.

reality driven by "increasing interest of American investors,"[34] notably in what was to become Namibia.

The revolt against the gains of anti-racism mounted in the U.S., however, as the Ku Klux Klan and their sordid comrades began to flourish and then to provide ample support for apartheid.[35] These efforts vitiated and countervailed even wishy-washy and mealy-mouthed critiques of apartheid, the latter rapidly becoming Washington's specialty.

U.S. solidarity with apartheid was not just a product of Washington's maneuvers. By 1959, Hodding Carter, editor of a racially regressive periodical in Greenville, Mississippi, was to be found in South Africa—"with a fairly heavy schedule," said a Quaker agent, suggestive of the demands on his time.[36] The Quakers found that some of their co-religionists in Rhodesia—those that were European—"objected to anyone coming from the U.S. or the United Kingdom to tell those in Central Africa what to do" about racism. George Loft, the Quaker emissary, was "asked how I would like it" if this skeptic "were to go to Little Rock" to consult.[37]

By the same token, by August 1958 the left-wing South African press found it necessary to editorialize that "We don't want the Ku Klux Klan here," indicative of its transatlantic spread. Reference was made to thuggish attacks on Chief Luthuli, with assailants "claiming to represent the Afrikaner people."[38] The KKK was to be found in Cape Town too.[39] *New Age*'s editorial cry responded to "hooliganism" run amok. "Now a trade union office is ransacked, and obscene Ku Klux Klan slogans are scribbled on the walls;" sadly, "a new element is creeping into our national life."[40] As Dixie's racist institutions came under assault, it responded by seeking to spread its influence more extensively abroad—particularly in Southern Africa.

---

34. *New Age*, 12 June 1958.

35. Jennifer Sutton, "Resisting the Winds of Change: The Citizens' Councils and European Decolonization," in Manfred Berg, et.al., eds., *The U.S. South and Europe: Transatlantic Relations in the Nineteenth and Twentieth Centuries*, Lexington: University Press of Kentucky, 2013, 265-282. See also Stephanie R. Rolph, "The Citizens' Council and Africa: White Supremacy in Global Perspective," *Journal of Southern History*, 82(Number 3, August 2016): 617-650.

36. Report by George Loft, 14 June 1959, Box Foreign Service 1958.

37. George Loft to Dear Stewart, 17 November 1959, Box Foreign Service 1958, Country-Africa.... *AFSC*.

38. *New Age*, 28 November 1958.

39. *New Age*, 12 February 1959.

40. *New Age*, 30 April 1959.

In 1959 *New Age* claimed that U.S. envoy Henry Byroade had been sacked because of his less than firm adherence to the colour bar,[41] indicating the raging battle underway as Washington was tugged by apartheid and anti-Jim Crow simultaneously. Pretoria probably celebrated, since it was this envoy who during the latter Eisenhower years claimed that the "boom is over" in South Africa and the "economy cannot progress under apartheid...."[42] David Post, yet another U.S. representative, blamed apartheid for the narrow size of the local market, meaning "low purchasing power of most of the people"[43] and concomitant economic gridlock.

Also providing ample support for apartheid was Wall Street. "One of the major financial developments of the Fourth Quarter," said the Pretoria legation, "was the announcement on December 2, 1958 of a [loan of] 17.85 [pounds] ($50 million) to [South Africa] by Dillon Read...and the World Bank." Chase Manhattan Bank was slated to expand in the Union too. There was "much speculation" as to the reasons for the "'sudden' interest" in the land of apartheid. "Many people feel that it must have something to do with a coming increase in the price of gold [in] response to an awakening interest in South Africa on the part of American industry and commerce...."[44] Soon Chase followed up with a $9-10 million loan to Pretoria, sending additional millions to the Industrial Development Corporation. Understandably, in Pretoria it was interpreted widely as a vote of confidence in apartheid.[45]

In that vein, Frank Carlucci, a Vice Consul General in Johannesburg who was soon to play a leading role in both Congo and the Pentagon, enthused that "Africa and South Africa," specifically, "offer perhaps the greatest opportunity for development in the world today, outside of the 'closed areas' dominated by Communism...."[46] There were downsides to investment expansion. There was the perception

---

41. *New Age*, 8 January 1959.

42. Memorandum by Henry Byroade, no date, Box 7, *Clarence Randall Journals, Dwight D. Eisenhower Presidential Library- Abilene, Kansas.*

43. Briefing by David Post, Economics Officer, U.S. Embassy-Pretoria, 27 March 1958, Box 1, U.S. *Council on Foreign Economic Policy Records, Reports Series, Eisenhower Library.*

44. Report, 19 January 1959, Reel 5, *Confidential U.S. State Department Central Files, South Africa.... Internal Affairs...and Foreign Affairs.*

45. Report, 16 July 1959, *Confidential U.S. State Department Central Files, South Africa.... Internal Affairs...and Foreign Affairs.*

46. Frank Carlucci to Secretary of State, 26 January 1959, Reel 5, *Confidential U.S. State Department Central Files, South Africa.... Internal Affairs...and Foreign Affairs.*

of a dearth of navigable rivers in South Africa, for one. And the country offered a relatively small domestic market, meaning a disproportionate percentage of U.S. investment was in mining, dependent upon a labor force that was becoming ever more militant.[47]

Adding to the mass of contradictions besetting U.S. policy in the region, France was skeptical of Washington, given the latter's slow but steady creep toward opposing the war in Algeria, while Britain understood that the republic was seeking to replace the monarchy as the preeminent power in the southern cone. Or so said Lord Malvern, who in 1958 informed a representative of the Quakers that the "sole concern" of Washington was "to push the European powers from their spheres of influence," which would only create a "vacuum" for the ubiquitous Communists, at which point the U.S. would be the "first to complain" about the result they engineered. "I am told," said the Quaker representative speaking from Salisbury, Rhodesia, "that his reply aroused an ovation among those present."[48]

The U.S. was trying to ride two horses heading in different directions simultaneously: one path led toward a closer embrace with apartheid while the other pointed to the erosion of the state-sanctioned racism that had given this policy sustenance. Eventually, the former would be abandoned for the latter, but this would take decades.

As for Little Rock, it continued to receive massive press coverage in South Africa that then ricocheted back to Washington. The *Cape Times* feigned commiseration with Negro pupils, terming them "human guinea pigs" in what was considered an ill-advised experiment.[49] The *Pretoria News* was candid in admitting that African and Asian nations saw Little Rock as a test of U.S. sincerity, though it too lamented the "attempt to enforce racial integration...on an unwilling people."[50] Both the *Rand Daily Mail*[51] and *Die Vaderland*[52] provided pessimistic front-page coverage of the sharp clashes in Arkansas, a not atypical concurrence between British and Boer. Similarly, the *Pretoria News* gave extensive coverage to related fights between and

---

47. Consul General, Johannesburg to Secretary of State, 17 June 1959, Reel 5, *Confidential U.S. State Department Central Files, South Africa.... Internal Affairs...and Foreign Affairs.*

48. George Loft to "Dear Allen," 26 May 1958, Box Foreign Service 1958, Country-Africa.... *AFSC.*

49. *Cape Times*, 1 September 1957.

50. *Pretoria News*, 20 August 1958. See also Report by William P. Maddox, 4 November 1958, RG 59, Decimal File, Box 3231.

51. *Rand Daily Mail*, 1 October 1957

52. *Die Vaderland*, 1 October 1957.

among hundreds of Negro and Euro-American students in Chicago under the imposing headline: "Children fight it out in U.S. over Integration."[53] Generally, it was the Afrikaner press that gloated with a kind of schadenfreude about the growing pains of U.S. desegregation, seeing every difficulty as a tacit endorsement of apartheid.[54] Eric Louw, who along with Pirow epitomized the apartheid hardline, was also emblematic of how Pretoria kept Washington at a distance just as it became more dependent upon its chief ally. Minister of External Affairs by 1957, he denounced the American Committee on Africa, the functional replacement for Robeson's CAA, in the same radio address in which he signaled a shift in Afrikaner hostility to migration by praising the Union's absorption of 1300 Hungarian refugees.[55] The combination of the two subjects, hostility to liberalism and the embrace of anticommunism, could be seen as congruent with the zeitgeist of the capitalist world.

This brusqueness toward ACOA came in apparent response to a letter from the group, co-signed by Dr. Martin Luther King, Jr., directed toward President Eisenhower in protest of U.S. policy toward Pretoria.[56] It may also have been a reaction to ACOA's hefty $75,000 donation to the defense during the Treason Trial.[57]

ACOA was not singular in providing material aid. The popular bandleader Lionel Hampton held a fund raising concert in London for the defendants,[58] and in Berkeley there was a benefit production of the play *Lost in the Stars*.[59] It was also in 1957 that 134 self-described "leaders of the Free World"—including novelist James Michener; the politico Edmund Muskie; labor leader Walter Reuther; writer William Carlos Williams; philosopher Eric Fromm; theologian Reinhold Niebuhr; and NAACP attorney Thurgood Marshall—took out a full page advertisement in the *New York Times* denouncing apartheid.[60] That same year, Secretary General of the ANC Tambo thanked

53. *Pretoria News*, 25 September 1957.

54. Report, 4 October 1957, *Confidential U.S. State Department Central Files, South Africa.... Internal Affairs...and Foreign Affairs.*

55. Text of Radio Address by Eric Louw, 12 December 1957, Reel 12, *Confidential U.S. State Department Central Files, South Africa.... Internal Affairs... and Foreign Affairs.*

56. Dr. Martin Luther King, Jr., et.al. to President Eisenhower, 15 August 1957, Reel 12, *Confidential U.S. State Department Central Files, South Africa.... Internal Affairs....and Foreign Affairs.*

57. George Houser, *No One Can Stop the Rain*, 121.

58. *New Age*, 26 September 1957.

59. Program, 5 September 1959, Box 2, *Mary Louise Hooper Papers.*

60. *New York Times*, 8 December 1957 in Box IIIA35, *NAACP Papers.*

the NAACP "with gratitude" for their initiatives in this conflicted realm.[61]

Sensing a change in the political winds, the ever-opportunistic Congressman Adam Clayton Powell, Jr. of Harlem, evidently dissatisfied with the payoff for his lobbying for Washington at Bandung, reversed field and criticized U.S. policy in South Africa.[62]

The NAACP—and Black America—were monitoring the Treason Trial, highlighting another way in which this spectacle backfired. The legation marveled at the reality that this event "became one of South Africa's attractions for Americans on study tours or just traveling. New York City Municipal Judge Bertha Schwartz and a traveling companion," were among those who "attended the trial's second session." Other visitors from the U.S. included a group from San Francisco State College, soon to erupt in fiery student protests: their pictures from South Africa ran on the front pages of newspapers. It appeared that some of the visitors had met some of the defendants overseas.[63] Henry Lee Moon, longtime NAACP executive, told Ronald Segal of Cape Town that "all of us here are greatly distressed about what is happening in South Africa and especially about the 'Treason Trial'. I personally have a sense of frustration," he confided, "because I do not know a single helpful thing I can do. I doubt very much," he concluded pessimistically, "that even organized protest in this country, unless it is massive and overwhelming, could stay the hand of the Nationalist government...."[64] Yet, an assistant to the group's leader, Roy Wilkins, spoke for many within the ranks when he said they were all "intensely sympathetic" to the trial defendants; however, he noted, "we simply operate most of the time at the utmost limit of our resources of time and personnel...."[65]

The winds of change blowing through South Africa were elsewhere registered when Roger Baldwin, a stalwart of Cold War liberalism, joined about a dozen other U.S. nationals in sponsoring a magazine published in the Cape Town, edited by Segal and designed to "oppose the race policies" of Pretoria.[66]

61. O.R. Tambo to NAACP, 18 November 1957, Box IIIA35, *NAACP Papers*.

62. Congressman Adam Clayton Powell to Secretary of State John Foster Dulles, 8 January 1957, RG 59, Decimal File, Box 3230, *NARA-CP*.

63. Report by William P. Maddox, 9 August 1958, Reel 2, *Confidential U.S. State Department Files, Internal Affairs....and Foreign Affairs*.

64. Henry Lee Moon to Ronald Segal, 30 January 1957, Box IIIA35, *NAACP Papers*.

65. John A. Morsel to Harold Isaaces, 9 January 1957, Box IIIA35

66. Roger Baldwin to George Meany, 17 June 1957, Box 14, *AFL-CIO International Affairs Department Papers, University of Maryland-College Park*.

There was, in any case, an operative division of labor that consigned a good deal of African solidarity work to the ACOA. By his own admission, however, the organization's leader, George Houser, was enduring "travel difficulties in Africa" and was—he thought—banned from South Africa.[67] Still, it was Houser who reached out to Z.K. Matthews—increasingly the republic's favored interlocutor—reminding him that "very little is coming through to us these days about the Treason Trial," and, requesting a report, he also asked about the growing "Africanist" trend.[68] Signaling increasingly close ties, it was Patrick Duncan, an ally of the "Africanist trend," who—quite suspiciously—wrote Houser to hail Z.K. Matthews, whose ANC was the chief organizational opponent of this trend.[69] And it was Houser who expressed directly to the Reverend J.J. Skomolo of South Africa his concern about SACP influence in South Africa.[70] A displeased *New Age* admonished "liberals and Coloured 'Africanists'" who had chosen to "join hands against" the "Charterists," code for the ANC-SACP dyad.[71] All of this indicated that the liberal anticommunist bloc had sensed that the ANC-SACP alliance was gaining strength and that it would be a top priority to split them.

When the State Department pressed the White House to reply to the ACOA anti-apartheid demarche, this protest became harder to ignore.[72] With cogency, the U.N. Mission of the republic interjected that it was "increasingly difficult [to] justify" the United States' continual "abstention" on votes concerning apartheid. These actions were "confirming suspicion," it was said disconsolately, among "many African and Asian members" that on "Racial and Colonial Issues we have different standards in judging problems white and non-white...." This "will not help us," it was asserted with crystalline accuracy, "when next we seek Afro-Asian support on U.S.-Soviet issues...." Ambassador Henry Cabot Lodge, scion of a venerated

67. Report by George Houser, 30 July 1957, Series III, Box 142, *American Committee on Africa Papers-Tulane University*.

68. George Houser to Z.K. Matthews, 30 September 1959, Reel 2, #23, Part II, *American Committee on Africa Papers*.

69. Patrick Duncan to George Houser, no date, Reel 2, #113, Part II, *ACOA Papers*.

70. George Houser to the Reverend J.J. Skomolo, no date, Reel 2, #411, *ACOA Papers*.

71. *New Age*, 21 August 1958.

72. Letter from U.S. State Department, 19 September 1957 in Ibid., 19 September 1957, Reel 12.

New England political dynasty, urged "reconsideration at [the] highest level of our present position on apartheid...."[73]

It was slowly being grasped that media attention to the horrors of apartheid was opening the door to a wider scrutiny of racism generally, bringing the U.S. itself into disrepute. In May 1958 Thomas Mann, Assistant Secretary of State, declared that "discrimination by American companies on the grounds of race" was a "problem different...only in degree" compared to what "exists in Latin America" for U.S. firms, which would inevitably bring pressure for change there too.[74]

When Lodge's advice was accepted, it brought indignation from South Africa. The hardline Afrikaner organ *Die Transvaler* inflamed the ire of the legation when—after the U.S. declined to veto a U.N. resolution—the newspaper sarcastically denounced "this great country with its unenviable history of slavery, civil war, court edicts, Little Rock and bayonets" that now recoils in "horror over South Africa's 'savage' apartheid.'"[75] These eruptions were becoming normal. William P. Maddox of the legation was stunned when he met with Piet Meiring, South Africa's Director of State Information, who "exploded more violently than anyone I have heard in South Africa about America" and its sour view of apartheid, while Maddox himself complained of the "prominent publicizing" of the sensitive matter of "lynching" in Dixie.[76]

The compelled retreat from Jim Crow was not accepted with equanimity by U.S. allies who had less room for maneuver, given how badly they were outnumbered. The Eisenhower administration was informed that in Mozambique, the "Portuguese are as suspicious locally of the United States and its motives as they are of the Russians...." The U.S. agent fired back, changing that "forced labor

---

73. Henry Cabot Lodge to State Department, 20 November 1957, *Confidential U.S. State Department Central Files, South Africa.*

74. Thomas Mann to Clarence Randall, 7 May 1958, Box 13, *U.S. Council on Foreign Economic Policy Records.... Policy Papers Series, Eisenhower Presidential Library.*

75. Report, 28 October 1958, Reel 1, *Confidential U.S. State Department Files, Internal Affairs....and Foreign Affairs.* See also Patrick Henry Martin, "American Views on South Africa, 1948-1972," Ph.d. dissertation, Louisiana State University, 1974, 120: Prior to 1958 the U.S. avoided castigating the Union at the United Nations.

76. William P. Maddox to Secretary of State, no date, RG 59, Decimal File, Box 2505.

is a reality" in this colony;[77] hardly a revelation but indicative of a fraying tie.

Ambassador Lodge was facing a dual barrage from U.S. Negroes and Africans alike. But the articulation of U.S. interests left little room for maneuver. South Africa was now paired with the Suez Canal as a vital chokepoint and strategic minerals from the region were seen as vital to the U.S. economy. Both interests led to an entente with Pretoria that could enrage U.S. nationals. Envoy William P. Maddox observed that there was a lurking fear that there would be "explosive repercussions of a local debacle in race relations" that might soar "beyond" the Union and "could become a cardinal threat to American security…."[78]

Just before the riveting episode that was Little Rock, Pretoria was shaken when a young Euro-American woman, Mary Louise Hooper, described not falsely as a "wealthy American," was accorded a "'secret' departure" from the Union after it was revealed she had become a top aide to Chief Luthuli.[79] By early 1956 the ANC leader informed George Houser that she had been working satisfactorily with the ANC "since August of last year…."[80] A Quaker and Phi Beta Kappa at Stanford, she was billed as "the only white [American] person ever to work inside" the ANC. Her family had been missionaries in the region and she moved near Durban in 1955, working for two tension-filled years at Chief Luthuli's side, before being jailed in 1957. Her comrades did not forget her: she was "elected the first Caucasian member in 1959" of the ANC, it was said, and went on to represent the group abroad, in Ghana in 1958, Tunis in 1960, and Cairo in 1961.[81] Her ouster led to a lawsuit in which Pretoria was dunned for $3500. She had spent five uncomfortable days incarcerated. Depicted as an "American Dollar Millionairess," she won a kind of celebrity status in South Africa. Speaking modestly about her role with the

---

77. Memorandum to Council on Foreign Economic Policy, circa Spring 1958, Box 7, *Clarence Randall Journals, Dwight D. Eisenhower Presidential Library, Abilene, Kansas.*

78. Report by William P. Maddox, 11 April 1957, RG 59, Decimal File, Box 4214, *NARA-CP*

79. See *Rand Daily Mail*, 6 June 1957 and C.T. Wright to Secretary of State, 18 June 1957, Reel 12, *Confidential U.S. State Department Central Files, South Africa…. Internal Affairs…and Foreign Affairs.*

80. Albert Luthuli to George Houser, 29 March 1956, Reel 5, #406, Part II, *ACOA Papers.*

81. Information Sheet, 1961, Box 5, *Mary Louise Hooper Papers, Michigan State University-East Lansing.*

ANC, she said, "I just ran errands and took notes...."[82] The U.S. legation monitored her case[83] and the English-language press went into overdrive with coverage.[84] She was deported, it was said later, after the authorities found a report in Chief Luthuli's home describing her as an ANC "agent."[85] Soon Mandela and Tambo were telling her bluntly, "we are missing you badly" since "your coming to South Africa contributed a lot to the effective political changes that shall take place" and "your name shall be amongst those who shall have suffered and sacrificed for this country."[86]

Hooper's deportation did not put a stop to her work on behalf of the ANC. A few years later, then ensconced back home, she happily told Tambo—her closest friend in the group after Luthuli died tragically—"this work for South Africa has become my whole life....I work often 16 hours a day and usually seven days a week on it...."[87] She often considered returning. "I am a skilled and very enthusiastic horseback rider," she told Tambo later, and could land in Lesotho and ride into the Union; to "go through the mountains...would be quite safe," she assured him, and it would be "my idea of a wonderful holiday."[88]

She had conducted her work in South Africa with a similar level of manic enthusiasm, making her departure yet another blow to the ANC. "I worked almost daily with Chief Luthuli during my two-year stay," she admitted later. Their missionary backgrounds were not dissimilar, she said: he was born in what is now Zimbabwe to "South African parents who accompanied American missionaries there...." He then studied—and eventually taught—at Adams College in the Union, administered by "American missionaries" before

---

82. *San Francisco Chronicle*, 12 August 1957, Box 2, *Mary Louise Hooper Papers*.

83. C.T. Wright to Secretary of State, 18 June 1957, RG 59, Decimal File, Box 3230.

84. *Rand Daily Mail*, 6 June 1957.

85. Thomas Karis to Secretary of State, 14 February 1958, RG 59, Decimal File, Box 3231. See also "Applicant's Replying Affidavit" in the Supreme Court of South Africa, Witwatersrand Local Division in the Matter of Mary Louise Hooper (born Fitkin) ...." Circa 1957, Box 5, *Mary Louise Hooper Papers*.

86. Mandela and Tambo to Mary Louise Hooper, no date, Box 1, *Mary Louise Hooper Papers*.

87. Mary Louise Hooper to Oliver R. Tambo, 3 August 1960, Box 2, *Mary Louise Hooper Papers*.

88. Mary Louise Hooper to Oliver R. Tambo, 2 February 1961, Box 2, *Mary Louise Hooper Papers*.

being shut down by the regime in 1956.[89] "I know how dear and close the Chief was to you," she was told by Duma Nokwe.[90]

Before landing in Durban in 1955 she pondered moving to Swaziland, where her family had "financial...interest" in "a hospital there." She also considered Ghana[91] but South Africa won out.

She was later described as a "gentle American woman who has won the title of South Africa's public enemy Number One." Her relative affluence had allowed her to buy a home in a fashionable European district and to acquire a car and chauffeur. Because of her melanin deficiency, she had a certain freedom of movement that she mobilized on behalf of the ANC.[92]

Described widely as attractive, with black hair, spectacles, and a short bob[93] she was not close to only Chief Luthuli. She was also friendly with the future famed writer Ezekiel Mphahlele. He used to show her around Johannesburg and during their travels they would debate. He had a "very odd idea of the ANC and one with which I heartily disagree," she said later: "the notion that we [in the ANC] are becoming 'tribalistic,' with favor going heavily to the Zulus." This was utter rubbish, she thought, mentioning Tambo, Duma Nokwe, Reg September, many more. "I tried to talk him out of it when he was in my home."[94]

Hooper apparently executed tasks across the continent for the ANC. By the summer of 1956 she was in the nation that was soon to become Ghana, where Kwame Nkrumah praised her as "revolutionary." She "had letters to him [from] Du Bois, his old 'mentor'" and also from George Padmore, the Trinidadian former Communist, who she met in London. She "never expected that the busy Prime Minister would spend so much time with me!" He seemed "lonely" and was appreciative of "the American woman"— "he gets tired of the provincial G[old] C[oast] girls...." And so, she was "invited to his office...within an hour of my arrival." She "hardly had time to bathe" before they "talked for nearly an hour" as a "Cabinet Minister

89. Mary Louise Hooper to Chief Luthuli, 17 November 1961, Box 5, *Mary Louise Hooper Papers*.

90. Duma Nokwe to Mary Louise Hooper, 8 August 1967, Box 5, *Mary Louise Hooper Papers*.

91. Mary Louise Hooper to Canon John Collins, 15 December 1957, Box 2, *Mary Louise Hooper Papers*.

92. *Washington Post*, 30 March 1965, Box 1, *Mary Louise Hooper Papers*.

93. Picture of Hooper on ANC stationery, February 1960, Box 1, *May Louise Hooper Papers*.

94. Mary Louise Hooper to Sam, 26 February 1975, Box 2, *Mary Louise Hooper Papers*.

cooled his heels outside" while they discussed South Africa. He shared with her his plan to begin radio broadcasts throughout the continent, including South Africa, which was to have an electrifying impact on decolonization. "He has not been 'spoiled' by fame (although quite a bit by women)," she mysteriously concluded.[95]

Hooper's appearance on the continent was not always applauded, even within the movement. She informed Tambo that ANC veteran Duma Nokwe was "telling people" for a "long time now" that she was a "CIA agent." He even sought to "turn Moses [Kotane] against me. He didn't succeed...."[96] Kotane's support for her was a shield. They met during the Treason Trial, where she found him to be eerily quiet. He told her that he "'knew Americans disliked Communists' and he didn't want to disturb my affection for the ANC.... I liked him at once."[97]

Representing the ANC at various global gatherings, Hooper was bound to attract unwanted attention. She was recruited for the important trip to Ghana after Govan Mbeki, SACP stalwart and writer for *New Age* in Port Elizabeth, was refused a passport.[98] The Accra confab of late 1958 may have been the highlight of her globe-trotting for the ANC since it was presided over by Nkrumah, the reigning symbol of African freedom. Nokwe—no longer betraying any suspicions about her, reported to "Dear Louise," that "we too are missing you," as he—and his co-defendants in the Treason Trial—were "bored stiff" since the prosecution (as in the notorious anti-communist Smith Act trials in the U.S.) featured laborious readings of dusty tomes penned by Stalin and Lenin in order to impute their motives to unwitting activists. But Nokwe's primary reason for writing her was Accra. He was "thrilled by your report," he jubilated: "in fact, it is the only report we have received so far," a dramatic commentary on her importance to the organization. "The Executive" of the ANC "has asked me to express its deep appreciation of the manner in which you...represented the ANC. We are really proud of you" and "your sincere devotion to our organization...." It was a "great honor," he said, "to be the Secretary General of so mighty an

95. Mary Louise Hooper to Ethel Ray Nance, 21 August 1956, Box 2, *Mary Louise Hooper Papers*.

96. Mary Louise Hooper to O.R. Tambo, 7 March 1975, Box 2, *Mary Louise Hooper Papers*.

97. Mary Louise Hooper to "Dear Sam," 10 February 1975, Box 2, *Mary Louise Hooper Papers*.

98. *New Age*, 18 December 1958.

organization as the ANC"—and apparently an "honor" to work with Hooper too.[99]

Nokwe's commendation was understandable. She found the Accra gathering to be a "wonderful" experience: "we were busy from dawn to dusk and then 'partied' until 2 or 3 in the morning." Her prestige was ratified when she "had breakfast" with Nkrumah, "just the two of us," and so impressed was he with her performance that "he offered me a job," though she was unable "to accept" since, referring to South Africa, she said "you are my country and my people...." "I am wedded to South Africa" she insisted. Unlike many delegates, she noticed "not many women at the conference," as "men still run the national movements of Africa...." Gender notwithstanding, she said, "I was received with great friendship and respect everywhere, although with a bit of curiosity at first...."[100]

It is likely that Irving Brown,[101] a renowned U.S. labor liaison to the CIA, was among those exhibiting "curiosity" about her in Accra. He told his fellow intelligence conspirator, Jay Lovestone, that there was disappointingly "not even the remotest reference to the dangers of Communism" in Ghana. Tom Mboya of Kenya "specifically mentioned" ACOA and "their work on the Treason Trial": the praise of Houser seemed to delight him. The "biggest reception was given" to the "delegation" from Egypt, not a good sign as he saw it. "They invited one and all to come to Cairo and promised all sorts of financial aid and moral assistance." Brown was unimpressed: "their policies and statements at this conference coincided with the major line of the Communists," meaning "Cairo is a definite threat...."[102]

Houser was "effective in Accra," reported Brown. His "quiet but effective manner" was impressive. He was less impressed by the "many American Negroes in and around the conference," but fortunately—in his opinion—they did "not have the kind of influence and prestige which American trade unionists," more likely to be swayed by the CIA, "could have" mobilized. As for the ACOA,

---

99. Duma Nokwe to "Dear Louise," 29 January 1959. Box 5, *Mary Louise Hooper Papers*.

100. Mary Louise Hooper to "Dearest Shiemie," 8 February 1959, Box 2, *Mary Louise Hooper Papers*.

101. Ben Rathbun, *The Point Man: Irving Brown and the Deadly Post-1945 Struggle for Europe and Africa*, New York: Minerva Press, 1996.

102. Letter from Irving Brown, 26 December 1958, Box 1, *Jay Lovestone Papers, University of Maryland-College Park*.

"they deserve some support and they certainly have good contacts in Africa, especially in Kenya" worthy of exploitation.[103]

In that same category were the U.S. Negroes Maida Springer and George McCray, who "should be spending more time in Africa" (which they proceeded to do), since "they could especially be of value in a country like Nigeria," then "moving in a most dangerous direction."[104] Soon Houser was inviting Springer to join the top leadership of ACOA.[105] Nevertheless, reflecting the new moment, the top leadership of the AFL-CIO chose—even before the Accra gathering—to "condemn this racist course" pursued by apartheid, not least "because we have outspokenly opposed anything similar in our own country." They also condemned the Treason Trial since Pretoria was simply "playing into the hands of the Communists," something it was necessary to avoid.[106] Brown was apparently unfazed by the fact that the ACOA was continuing to send funds to the Treason Trial defendants—$2000 more by late 1959.[107]

Brown and others of his ilk were unsure as to how to approach Houser and his organization. After Togo—apparently with Houser's backing—sought to ask the U.N. to provide security and forego military spending, the Quakers were informed that the ACOA "approach is sometimes sensational and not too sound.... Some of their tactics and methods would grate on us," while the State Department remained "quite hostile" to ACOA.[108]

This "hostility" was a reflection of the reality that Washington was seeking to cater to both anti-racist and pro-apartheid forces and ACOA found it difficult to execute the latter trick, which inexorably brought criticism to their doorstep.

As for Brown's boss, George Meany—head of the American Federation of Labor and Congress of Industrial Organizations (AFL-CIO)—he agreed with his subordinate, adding the gloss that there was a "hard choice between the milder Black Nationalism of

103. Letter from Irving Brown, 24 December 1958, Box 1, *Jay Lovestone Papers.*

104. Irving Brown to George Meany, 24 December 1958, Box 1, *Jay Lovestone Papers.*

105. George Houser to Maida Springer, 20 July 1960, Box 14, *AFL-CIO International Department Papers, University of Maryland-College Park.* Hereinafter denoted as IAD.

106. Statement by AFL-CIO Executive Council, 1 May 1958, Box 14, *IAD.*

107. Ann Morrissett of ACOA to Reverend Ambrose Reeves in Johannesburg, 18 November 1959, Reel 2, #65, Part II, *ACOA Papers.*

108. "Dear Allen" from unclear, likely George Loft, 21 December 1958, Box Foreign Service 1958, Country-Africa.... *AFSC.*

Nkrumah" on one hand and "the Communists and Nasser on the other"—regarding the former as the "lesser evil."[109] This realization led to a fateful decision. In August 1959 Holden Roberto of Angola visited the U.S. and was given the red-carpet treatment by the State Department, the CIA, Eleanor Roosevelt—and the AFL-CIO. Houser also developed a relationship with him that would return to haunt him when the Angolan's extensive ties to U.S. intelligence were exposed in the midst of the 1975-1976 crisis.[110]

Given the general role of Euro-Americans in the region, doubts about the reliability of allies like Hooper were understandable. While Hooper was being ousted from South Africa, the U.S. legation was conferring—again—with Z.K. and Joe Matthews. In a "confidential" report, William Matthews (no evident relation) found the latter "probably sincere in his offer to provide Native mailing lists for USIS [United States Information Service] to combat Communism and promote goodwill toward the United States," while the elder Matthews wanted to know if anything could be done to rescue Hooper. She had purchased property near Durban and had become a fixture there. The son "knew her well," it was reported, but conceded she had been "most indiscreet" in "flaunting the color bar." "She is definitely anti-Communist," he insisted, music to Matthews' ears that would have been discordant to Nokwe's. Contrarily, Matthews would have frowned at the son's words that there had been an "influx of Communist literature" into the Union that had "inundated" Africans and had "succeeded in penetrating the Native mind."[111] Also reported to be anticommunist—though perhaps not accurately—was former ANC leader A.B. Xuma. By 1958 the Consul General in Johannesburg was depicting him as a "respectable anti-Communist," while P.Q. Vundla, a former Communist, was now "identified with the Moral Rearmament Association," a group of fanatical anticommunists.[112] Reputedly, Madie Hall Xuma was "eager to meet" with these envoys. Henry Byroade was exhilarated: "if only Americans could produce more Negroes like that!"[113] Soon, A.B. Xuma was speaking

109. Report by George Meany, December 1958, Box 1, *Jay Lovestone Papers*.

110. Nathaniel Weyl, *Traitor's End: The Rise and Fall of the Communist Movement in Southern Africa*, New Rochelle: Arlington House, 1970, 152.

111. William Matthews to Secretary of State, 18 March 1957, "confidential," RG 59, Decimal File, Box 3230, *NARA-CP*.

112. Consul General, Johannesburg to Secretary of State, 9 September 1958, Reel 6, *Confidential U.S. State Department Central Files, South Africa... Internal Affairs...and Foreign Affairs*.

113. "Confidential" Report by Henry Byroade, 4 December 1958, RG 59, Decimal File, Box 2505,

at the University of Potchefstroom, a bastion of Afrikaner dominance, an event which Thomas Karis of the U.S. justifiably called "unprecedented." This was reportedly after his wife had encouraged him to stay in the U.S., but he insisted on returning.[114]

In mid-1959 the envoys were admitted to what they described as a "pleasant living room by Mrs. Xuma, the North Carolina born wife" and her spouse, a "small man with flashing eyes and quick nervous gestures...." They carefully considered their own conclusion that he was "expelled [from the ANC] for being too moderate." What brought these diplomats to his comfortable home was their feeling that "moderates such as himself are going to have an increasingly hard time keeping their people from falling for the red line...."[115] Soon the legation was arranging a "dinner party" featuring Dr. Xuma and the emerging "Africanist" and anti-ANC leader Potlako Leballo, as if the envoys sought to forge a bloc opposed to Luthuli, Mandela, et al.[116] (When Kenyan leader Tom Mboya was invited to a meeting of the ANC-affiliated South African Congress of Trade Unions, the U.S. legation fretted that it was "attracting front page publicity" in the land of apartheid, a fact of no small concern.[117])

The evident inundation of South Africa with left-wing literature and the arrival—then departure—of the likes of Hooper were indicative of the closer (though often conflicted) ties between the Union and the republic that grew as the Cold War deepened and Pretoria was perceived as a reliable anticommunist ally. The problem was that the United States' global responsibilities were forcing it to retreat from the more egregious aspects of Jim Crow while Pretoria saw no reason to budge. By late 1957 the Consul General in Durban met with the "Non-European Affairs Committee of the Federated Chamber of Industries" and was "particularly struck" by the "increasing anti-White solidarity between political organizations representing the three non-European groups"—African, Coloured, and Asian—and a "growing tendency toward Communist sympathies within these organizations...." This path was lubricated by the reality that "International Communism openly deplores distinctions

114. Thomas Karis to Secretary of State, 19 August 1958, RG 59, Decimal File, Box 3231.

115. Report, 18 June 1959, Reel 1, *Confidential U.S. State Department Files, Internal Affairs....and Foreign Affairs.*

116. Report, 23 January 1959, Reel 1, *Confidential U.S. State Department Files. Internal Affairs...and Foreign Affairs.*

117. Report, 6 March 1959, Reel 7, *Confidential U.S. State Department Central Files.... Internal Affairs....and Foreign Affairs.*

based upon race and as such must commend itself very strongly to the non-European communities of South Africa...."[118] Pretoria, with its rigid racism, blocked the usual U.S. neo-colonial effort of making overtures to these groups, thus jeopardizing the larger project of anticommunism. An African told Anthony Sampson in South Africa that he thought the definition of Communist was being seen as "a friend of the Africans," a heavy burden for Washington to meet.[119]

In 1957 Nguhwo Jepongo of the region known as Ovamboland, the centerpiece of what became Namibia, petitioned the U.N. while seeking to neutralize the chief ideological weapon wielded against his movement: "we are aware of the fact," he asserted, "that every Native, whoever disagrees with apartheid is regarded a 'Communist' by apartheid followers...."[120] The next year Andimba Toivo ya Toivo smuggled a tape to ACOA depicting the horrors that reigned in South Africa's colony to the immediate north. It was transported in the pages of a hollowed-out novel, Robert Louis Stevenson's *Treasure Island*. Music occupied most of the tape and the ten-minute message was found in the middle of the recording.[121]

The sprouting discontent in what became Namibia opened another front against apartheid's very legitimacy. After conferring with Herero leaders, a U.S. diplomat recalled with awe their "history of intransigence." Following the early 20th century war with the Germans, the "Herero women swore they would never bear children [un]til the Germans ceased to rule [South West Africa] and kept their oath for seven years until World War I ousted the Huns."[122]

It was harder still to defend Pretoria's colonial occupation of this vast region. By 1959, Negro hero and baseball star Jackie Robinson was vehemently saying that Pretoria "actually has no business in SouthWest Africa in the first place," and that Washington's "wishy washy" stance on the matter was "probably...a result of its own dirty backyard in Mississippi...."[123] So moved, Andimba Toivo ya Toivo, writing from Windhoek, thanked Houser and "your organization" for their fruitful solidarity with his group, which became known as

118. Consul General, Durban to Secretary of State, 17 December 1957, Reel 8, *Confidential U.S. State Department Central Files, South Africa.... Internal Affairs...and Foreign* Affairs. r

119. Anthony Sampson, *Drum*, 113.

120. Andimba Toivo ya Toivo, *On Trial for My Country*, 86.

121. Press Release, 7 October 1958, Box 94, Series III, *American Committee on Africa Records Addendum, Tulane University-New Orleans.*

122. Report, 28 October 1958, RG 59, Central Decimal File, Box 3231, *NARA-CP.*

123. *New York Post*, 28 December 1959.

SWAPO [South West Africa People's Organization].[124] The ACOA, as Toivo ya Toivo noted, was instrumental in securing a visa for their comrade, the Reverend Michael Scott.[125] The ACOA was also "invaluable" in bringing Namibian representatives to the attention of the U.N., a point made by the trio of Sam Nujoma of the then Ovamobland People's Congress, Chief Hosea Kutako, and Chief Samuel Witbooi. It was the ACOA, said these three, that helped "in placing your legal experts at the disposal" of these African leaders and "it was through your assistance that the question of SouthWest Africa will now be referred to the [International Court of Justice]."[126]

This newfound U.S. activism was partially the fruit of aggressive African campaigns for decolonization, which then spurred U.S. Negroes to push even harder on their behalf. As Ghana was being propelled to decolonization, Black Nationalist James Lawson of Harlem hosted an event featuring "the ambassadors of the three newly freed nations of the Sudan, Morocco and Tunisia."[127] In 1957 Julius Nyerere wrote to Houser, "Thank you for all that you did for me while I was in the States" on behalf of what became Tanzania.[128]

It was not clear if financial relations would serve as a bridge over the troubled waters of anti-racism. By 1958 U.S. envoy Henry Byroade was describing bilateral ties as "tensing up" in a "confidential" message. Later that year the major U.S. investor and mineral magnate Charles Engelhard hosted a dinner for officials of the National City Bank and the Chase Manhattan Bank. Pretoria's newly installed Finance Minister, Eben Donges, suggested that Engelhard talk to Byroade about Pretoria's concern with U.S. press attacks on apartheid, which Nationalists found to be malicious. The problem had been discussed in recent cabinet meetings, suggesting the importance it was given in South Africa.[129] This tension had to trouble Engelhard—at times referred to as "Goldfinger," after the fictional baron who crossed swords with Ian Fleming's James Bond: he

124. Andimba Toivo ya Toivo to George Houser, 8 September 1958, Box 94, Series III, *American Committee on Africa Records Addendum, Tulane University.*

125. Andimba Toivo ya Tovio, 10 August 1959, Box 94, Series III.

126. Sam Nujoma, Chief Hosea Kutako and Chief Samuel Witbooi to ACOA, 19 November 1959, Box 94, Series III, *American Committee on Africa Records Addendum.*

127. Leaflet, 8 February 1957, Box 55, Series II, *American Committee on Africa Records Addendum, Tulane University-New Orleans.*

128. Julius Nyerere to George Houser, 11 April 1957, Box 94, Box III, *American Committee on Africa Records Addendum, Tulane University.*

129. Ambassador Henry Byroade to Secretary of State, 5 December 1958, RG 59, Decimal File, Box 3230, *NARA-CP.*

also lunched with Philip K. Crowe of the legation, who referred to him as the "Platinum King," a major export from the Union. He also controlled mines, newspapers, forestries, and other "extraordinary concessions" from Pretoria that could be jeopardized if bilateral relations plummeted.[130] Born in 1917, Engelhard was educated at Princeton and had been described by a U.S. delegate as "one of the most influential men in Africa...."[131] This view was ratified when 3 cabinet members, prominent bankers, and 80 of the most influential businessmen of the Union attended a dinner in his honor.[132] The legation found his spouse to be "an extremely attractive girl": husband and wife were both interested in race horses, which they maintained on their plush estate in New Jersey. "But from the state of his tummy," it was said sarcastically, he "does not ride them or take much other exercise."[133]

As Engelhard's ramified investments indicated, the U.S. was becoming the lifeline for apartheid, a reflection of its staggering importance in the capitalist world generally. As Byroade was conferring with Engelhard, he was made aware that in relatively small Brakpan, South Africa alone, a gold and uranium center, there had been three recent inquiries from U.S. nationals concerning the availability of industrial land, as the phenomenon of "runaway shops"—opened by U.S. corporations fleeing to low-wage havens—proceeded apace.[134] Complementarily, by 1958 the Chairman of the South African Tourist Board announced that the number of visitors from the U.S. to the Union had increased 25% in recent months. This would have knock-on effects benefiting airlines, hotels—and, it was hoped—solidarity too.[135] Thus, by 1959 a hotel described as "American in style" was erected in Beaufort West by a U.S. national. The U.S. was then considered the largest purchaser of diamonds in Kimberley and these economic bonds contributed, said U.S. representative

---

130. Philip K. Crowe to Secretary of State, 4 April 1959, RG 59, Decimal File, Box 2505, *NARA-CP*.

131. Report, 2 September 1959, Reel 1, *Confidential U.S. State Department Files. Internal Affairs...and Foreign Affairs.*

132. Report, 5 December 1958, Reel 14, *Confidential U.S. State Department Central Files. South Africa.... Internal Affairs....and Foreign Affairs.*

133. Memorandum of Conversation, 4 September 1959, Reel 14, *Confidential U.S. State Department Central Files. South Africa...Internal Affairs...and Foreign Affairs.*

134. Henry Byroade to Secretary of State, 12 December 1956, RG 59, Decimal File, Box 4498.

135. Report to State Department, 26 August 1958, Reel 5, *Confidential U.S. State Department Files on South Africa.... Internal Affairs...and Foreign Affairs.*

S.D. Boykin, to a "great feeling of friendship for the United States,"[136] counteracting the backwash of anti-Jim Crow initiatives.

The visibility of Wall Street banks and mega-investors like Engelhard was emblematic of the closer financial links between the Union and the republic. In order to enter U.S. markets, South Africa had to open the kimono and provide the U.S. with useful information on budgeting, spending, investment choices, etc., which was a force multiplier allowing Washington and Wall Street alike to magnify their already burgeoning interests. The heady scent of profit seemed to hypnotize both. When Pretoria sought loans in the U.S. in 1957, C. Vaughan Ferguson of the State Department found their detailed "prospectus" to be "accurate," then added with a soupçon of delusion that "there is no clear indication of non-White opposition to Government policy" and "certainly no adequate indication of racial tension in the Union."[137] First National City Bank of Manhattan was opening offices in Johannesburg by 1958, which had the Consul General giddy: "the stock of everything American is very high indeed," he exulted. "One frequently found a preference for American products, all things being equal...."[138] Not far behind was Eugene Black, who led the U.S.-dominated World Bank; that same year he could be found at the posh Pretoria Country Club, visiting at the invitation of the Ministry of Finance.[139]

But by 1959 Pretoria was dissatisfied. Dr. H.J. Van Eck was among those critical of the U.S. Though substantial flows of private capital had been arriving in South Africa, he derided much of it as "paper investment." He wanted more U.S. dollars flowing into in chrome and manufacturing. Deemed "one of [South Africa's] leading industrial figures," his complaint had to be taken seriously.[140] Dr. Van

---

136. S.D. Boykin, Consul General-Cape Town to Secretary of State, 18 March 1959, RG 59, Decimal File, Box 3233, *NARA-CP*.

137. Report by C. Vaughan Ferguson, 20 September 1957, Reel 7, *Confidential U.S. State Department Files on South Africa.... Internal Affairs...and Foreign Affairs.*

138. Victor von Lossberg to Secretary of State, 12 May 1958, Reel 7, *Confidential U.S. State Department Files on South Africa.... Internal Affairs...and Foreign Affairs.*

139. Engraved Invitation, 17 March 1958, Box 5, *Eugene Black Papers, University of Georgia-Athens.*

140. Consul General-Johannesburg to Secretary of State, 1 April 1959, Reel 8, *Confidential U.S. State Department Central Files, South Africa.... Internal Affairs....and Foreign Affairs.*

Eck was probably pleased when the U.S. expressed interest in more nuclear cooperation with South Africa.[141]

The "tensing" reached Washington when Pretoria's representative complained bitterly about prominent Republican official Mason Sears' address to the National Council of Negro Women, which was critical of apartheid. Why do this, it was asked, when South Africa was displaying its anticommunist resolve with the ongoing Treason Trial?[142] By 1958 the U.S. legation was carping about tariffs. "North American cars would be still more heavily hit as a result of these measures, although the market for Chevrolets and Fords as well as heavier vehicles have been declining"—a reflection of the rapid recovery of Japan's Toyota. Thus, "American cars would command only 10% of the market in 1958 as against 19% in 1957," and it was feared that the trend was headed further downward.[143]

Pretoria did not seem to realize that as newly enfranchised U.S. Negroes formed a united voting bloc, the political parties would have to contend for their favor. Nor did they seem to realize that more and more "non-Europeans" were bonding with U.S. Negroes, providing momentum to anti-apartheid. It was in late 1957 that members of the AME denomination, whose roots in South Africa extended to the late 19th century, met in the Transvaal under the guidance of Bishop F.H. Gow, a "Cape Coloured" who had lived for thirty years in the U.S.[144] It was later acknowledged by the legation that Gow's spouse was a "Colored American."[145] Gow served in the U.S. military during wartime and was described—suspiciously-- by the Cape Town legation as being of "rather dark skin...."[146] By the Spring of 1958 eleven Negroes led by Bishop R.R. Wright arrived to mark the 60th anniversary of the AME, and, said the legation, following a trend that would soon cease, received "routine news treatment."[147]

---

141. *Cape Times*, 19 September 1959.

142. Memorandum of Conversation, 3 January 1957, RG 59, Decimal File, Box 4503.

143. U.S. Embassy-Pretoria to Secretary of State, 31 July 1958, Reel 7, *Confidential U.S. State Department Files on South Africa.... Internal Affairs...and Foreign Affairs.*

144. Arthur Beach to Secretary of State, 17 December 1957, RG 59, Decimal File, Box 4504.

145. J.C. Satterhwaite to Secretary of State, 16 May 1963, RG 59, Central Foreign Policy Files, Box 4031, *NARA-CP.*

146. Memorandum of Conversation, 23 March 1963, RG 59, Central Foreign Policy Files, Box 4213, *NARA-CP.*

147. Report by Embassy-Pretoria, 3 April 1958, RG 59, Decimal File, Box 3231.

There was also a countervailing development. The bus boycott in Johannesburg helped to spotlight the presence of Hyman Miller, who was born in Altoona, Pennsylvania in 1907 and arrived in South Africa in 1910. He had rocketed to eminence, serving as a Johannesburg City Councilor and a member of Parliament—and in 1952 was elected Mayor. He was also, importantly, Vice Chair of the South Africa Board of Jewish Education.[148] Though pleasing to Washington, it was not evident that a similar reaction to Miller's ascension would be evinced by Pirow, Louw and the neo-fascist caucus in the land of apartheid: more likely than not, it was bound to heighten tension between Pretoria and Washington, illustrating the utter instability of their exceedingly intimate relationship of unalloyed sin.

For the rise of the Nationalists was continuously corrosive to the ambitions of the Jewish population. It was in 1959 that Helen Suzman, a liberal legislator who proved to be friendly to an imprisoned Mandela, was subjected to an "outburst" a U.S. observer described as an the "most vicious demonstration of anti-Semitism in the House since the war…." Nationalists and their allies "clamored that Jewish landowners and not Afrikaners were brutalizing native labor. It would be laughable," it was added mournfully, "were not this type of thinking so typical of the fascist mind"[149]—then on full display at the Treason Trial featuring Oswald Pirow. While the U.S. was steadily tamping down the more overt aspects of anti-Semitism, this kind of misbehavior targeting Suzman only deepened the impression that South Africa was an awkward ally. In 1959 the chair of the powerful South African Broadcasting Corporation was Dr. P. J. Meyer, a leading Broederbonder and once an admirer of fascist Berlin. He was close to Prime Minister Hendrik Verwoerd,[150] who could be described in similar terms. So, charged *New Age*, which contended that this leader's newspaper spouted Nazi propaganda during the recent world war.[151]

In April 1959 a U.S. diplomat conferred with Verwoerd. The unflattering description forwarded to Washington painted him as middle aged, with white hair and a tendency to pudginess. It also called

148. Report from Consul-General, Johannesburg, 9 September 1958, Reel 6, *Confidential U.S. State Department Central Files…. Internal Affairs….and Foreign Affairs.*

149. Report, 22 June 1959, Reel 1, *Confidential U.S. State Department Files. Internal Affairs…and Foreign Affairs.*

150. Report, 4 August 1959, Reel 4, *Confidential U.S. State Department Files. Internal Affairs….and Foreign Affairs.*

151. *New Age*, 11 September 1958.

him a "fanatic" with "considerable personal charm." "His manner was extremely friendly," and the envoy was pleased to "have established [a] working relationship that might someday pay moderate dividends." Still, he hinted strongly that his plans included aggression: seizing the BLS states—what became Botswana, then Lesotho, then Swaziland—at the appropriate moment, while London's influence waned in all three. Independence for these mini-states would mean a "black man treated as white man" in Pretoria and "leaders of local Bantu would want similar treatment," an intolerable situation. He had a "low opinion" of the U.S. press, saying he "used to like *TIME*...until it published lies about [the] Union."[152]

As would remain the case virtually until the first democratic elections of 1994, the Afrikaner elite was still overly ethnocentric and even chauvinist. The "Nationalists are still scared of immigration," complained Sir de Villiers Graaf, a leader of the opposition in 1959. He was not wrong.[153] More from the European minority were departing, leading to an acute shortage of engineers and a broader shortage of skilled workers, artisans, and mechanics at a time when apartheid hamstrung attempts to fill these posts with Africans. Even members of the military were heading to Rhodesia, since wages were often higher there. And the improving economy in Western Europe would be a hindrance to migration in any case.[154]

Washington was continually exasperated by the Afrikaners' shortsightedness (and, to be fair, that of other European colonizers too). The Consul General in what was to become Maputo found "considerable personal dislike and distrust...between individuals of both countries," Mozambique and South Africa. Nationals of the latter were "often heard to speak disparagingly of the Portuguese: many racially

---

152. "Confidential" Report, 28 April 1959, Reel 14, *Confidential U.S. State Department Central Files.... Internal Affairs...and Foreign Affairs.*

153. Transcript of Speech of Sir de Villiers de Graaf, 8 October 1959, Reel 3, *Confidential U.S. State Department Files. Internal Affairs...and Foreign Affairs:* "We have the supreme example of successful immigration in the history of the [USA].... even today the USA welcomes an average of approximately 500 immigrants every day." [emphasis-original] "The state of California which in many ways resembles South Africa, increased its population from 7 to 12 million in 10 years between 1946 and 1956......we white South Africans want—the security of the presence of larger numbers of our fellow Europeans; we want the security of the knowledge that the skills of our white population can hold their own...."

154. Embassy Pretoria to Secretary of State, circa 1958, Reel 8, *Confidential U.S. State Department Central Files, South Africa.... Internal Affairs...and Foreign Affairs.*

arrogant persons consider that all Portuguese are 'half breeds,'" a damning indictment in Pretoria.[155] By 1959 the Secretary of State was told that "many American businessmen in South Africa claim that if the English press as well as the Afrikaans press would let their white readers forget their past differences stemming from the South African War instead of attempting to make political capital out of every conceivable incident, the Union would be a better place in which to live."[156]

Then there were U.S. scholars like Edwin S. Munger. According to *New Age*, he represented the liberal anticommunist wing of the U.S. ruling elite, backed avidly by the Ford Foundation.[157] As a liberal, he focused intently on how to refer to the Union's majority: "he dismissed 'kaffirs'" and "natives," Bantu too. Since he said that use of "African" was "bordering on 'Communistic,'" it was unclear what term he preferred.[158] He was also tied to Harold Hochschild, the U.S. national with vast investments in African minerals.[159] Munger taught at the elite California Institute of Technology in Pasadena, where he had moved from the University of Chicago. He arrived in Johannesburg in 1958 with a keen interest in "Communist Activity in South Africa." The Treason Trial captured his attention when he found that 16 of the 91 defendants are "card carrying" Communists. The ANC, he thought, was "dominated at the national and for most the part at the provincial level by white Communists" and had in 1949 gained the "upper hand" in the Congress. *New Age*, seen as the journalistic embodiment of this alliance, had a mostly African circulation of 30,000, though "readership" may have been more than three times as high. He was displeased to read regularly in these pages how, for example, an ANC politician hammered "American Imperialism: A New Menace in Africa" or the "swipes" taken at the Little Rock crisis and the House Un-American Activities Committee. *Fighting Talk*, the cousin of *New Age*, featured regular articles by Louis Burnham, who was quite close to U.S. Communists. Communist publications from Hong Kong were also readily available in South Africa. At the time

155. Consul General-Lourenco Marques to Secretary of State, 10 August 1959, Reel 14, *Confidential U.S> State Department Central Files. South Africa.... Internal Affairs...and Foreign Affairs.*

156. Consul General, Johannesburg to Secretary of State, 3 June 1959, Reel 7, *Confidential U.S. State Department Central Files, South Africa.... Internal Affairs....and Foreign Affairs.*

157. *New Age*, 13 November 1958.

158. Report by Edwin Munger, 27 March 1959, Reel 16, #416, Part II, *ACOA Papers.*

159. *New Age*, 12 March 1959.

of the Suppression of Communism Act in 1950, he believed that the CP had 1200 African members, 900 of whom were Europeans, 250 Asians, 150 Coloureds. The "two ablest Communists," in his estimation, were Ruth First and her spouse Joe Slovo. Slovo was "rising steadily in the Johannesburg legal profession and moving into the upper income brackets and either or both had travelled to both the Soviet Union and China". He met them at a "small dinner party" and "found them personally charming," especially since they seemed to "share the South African tradition of knowing relatively little about the rest of Africa...." Still, his main takeaway was that "I have no doubt of their willingness to accept orders from Moscow," though the "definition of 'Communist' is not as strict as that applied in the United States." He noted that First shared with him remembrances of "some gay parties thrown by the Russians" in South Africa. As for Z.K. Matthews, Munger was elated to see that he "held himself somewhat apart from the Communist Party members among the accused" during the Treason Trial and, moreover, he was "surprised that he wasn't released," adding "I thought they would let go all except the hard-core Communists."[160]

Professor Munger's view was not his alone. Then U.S. emissary and future scholar Thomas Karis, who was not fond of the California researcher, concurred that *New Age*, which attacked Washington regularly, was "widely read among non-Whites in the Union...."[161] Apparently surveilling Slovo and First, he added, "Munger had a convivial dinner with Joe Slovo and his wife, Ruth First" and Al Friendly of the *Washington Post* also of late "had dinner with the Slovos...."[162]

That elite academics and journalists were rubbing shoulders with Communists was not a positive sign for Pretoria. That some of these figures were also Jewish was also potentially irritating to the Nationalists. As "the Slovos" were breaking bread with Munger, the heralded Kruger Festival Committee refused to lend the late President Kruger's state coach for the Krugersdorp 70th birthday celebration unless the application was made in writing "in decent Afrikaans'"—a real sticking point—and also "that no Jew would be allowed to travel in the coach."[163]

---

160. "A Letter from Edwin S. Munger," 8 June 1958, Reel 16, #416, Part II, *American Committee on Africa Papers-Library of Congress.*

161. Report by Thomas Karis, 17 March 1959, RG 59, Decimal File, Box 3230.

162. Thomas Karis to Secretary of State, 17 March 1959, RG 59, Decimal File, Box 2505.

163. Waldemar Campbell to Secretary of State, 5 September 1957, RG 59, Decimal File, Box 3230.

Given the proclivity of "non-Whites in the Union" to gravitate toward the SACP and their ANC comrades (referred to as "Charterists" in light of the Freedom Charter), who in turn were seen as a Trojan Horse for Moscow, it should not be surprising that the U.S. welcomed the development of other ideological trends. By 1958 the legation was eyeing "rivalry between Charterists and Africanists"—who were soon to form the Pan-Africanist Congress—roaring in "the Cape and Transvaal African National Congress." This very same report also exposed—in part—why Washington was so maniacal in its opposition to Communists, for their internationalism impelled them to comment on the sore point that was Jim Crow. Alex La Guma, for example, had praised the Alabama governor's commutation of Jimmy Wilson's sentence, an action, the "Coloured Communist" said, was "due to the protest of thousands of civilized people in and outside the U.S."[164]

It was *New Age*, known to be within the ambit of the SACP, that warned of the spread of the KKK to Britain, as migration from the Caribbean and Africa grew.[165] *New Age* saluted Robeson—still—along with the "27,000 Negroes" who marched in Washington in an important "Pilgrimage for Freedom." The demonstration's "weakness," it was reported presciently, was "inadequate 'white support'...as if the fight for Negro rights was simply a 'Negro problem'...."[166] "10,000 Americans march in protest against colour bar" was *New Age*'s 1958 headline to an article that highlighted the role of Dr. King and his comrade, the entertainer Harry Belafonte.[167] *Fighting Talk*, the companion left-wing periodical, hailed Robeson on his 60th birthday in 1958.[168] *New Age* reprimanded the authorities in Little Rock and publicized those, like the popular entertainers Louis Armstrong and Eartha Kitt, who publicly voiced similar criticism.[169] *Fighting Talk* lavished praise upon Du Bois after he managed to leave the republic for London, where he was embraced warmly by Doris Lessing, Basil Davidson, and Amy Jacques Garvey. He was a "humble but Great Old Man" it was said of the Negro Patriarch who with his spouse, Shirley Graham, had just returned from China with words of

164. Report, 17 October 1958, Reel 1, *Confidential U.S. State Department Files. Internal Affairs....and Foreign Affairs*. See also *New Age*, 9 October 1958.

165. *New Age*, 16 May 1957.

166. *New Age*, 13 June 1957.

167. *New Age*, 18 December 1958.

168. *Fighting Talk*, June-July 1958.

169. *New Age*, 3 October 1957.

praise.[170] *New Age* cited Du Bois for the stark proposition: "Socialism or Capitalism—Africa must choose."[171]

The SACP used the CPUSA as a kind of touchstone, citing critiques of the latter by French Communist leader Jacques Duclos as an implicit warning to radicals in the Union.[172] The references to Duclos came by way of rebuke to the once favored novelist Howard Fast, whose voluminous works were celebrated until he reversed field in the wake of the 1956 revelations about Stalin and admonished the CPUSA. His books, it was said, "have for a long time enjoyed great popularity within the ranks of the progressive movement...even as his literary position declined during the Cold War years in America...his books were selling in [the] hundreds of thousands abroad... his collected works have had a world sale of 20,000,000," but now his career "suddenly took on a new turn."[173]

When the conviction of a number of U.S. Communists was squashed, *New Age* compared the case against them with the Treason Trial: "the story which the [U.S.] government was forced to admit to be false is almost identical with the allegations that have been made by Minister Swart against 'Communists in South Africa,'" especially concerning allegations of sabotage.[174] This concern for U.S. Communists was yoked to fierce denunciations of the "Eisenhower Doctrine for Africa," which meant increased investment in mining, encouraged by the Nationalists even as they continued to reproach Washington's official anti-Jim Crow policy. The left recognized that this enhanced investment would mean that "'Communists' and other 'agitators' must be put down" at all costs; thus, it was a "mistake to think that the Americans will help free South Africa from the domination of the Nationalists," the rhetorical posturing of the former aside.[175]

Thus, by late 1958 the legation did not seem terribly displeased when reports emerged of a breakaway from the ANC led by Potlako Leballo, who happened to be employed by the United States Information Service in Johannesburg—performing "mimeographing, film maintenance, etc.," said the embassy. "He is a good workman," it was observed assuredly, "a useful person to have around." This "good workman" was among a "hundred Africanists [who] attended [a tense meeting] in a group and many were armed with

170. *Fighting Talk*, October 1959. See also *New Age*, 23 July 1959.
171. *New Age*, 25 December 1958.
172. *New Age*, 28 February 1957.
173. *New Age*, 30 January 1958.
174. *New Age*, 29 November 1956.
175. *New Age*, 13 June 1957.

sticks and batons," though "violence was avoided"—barely. Leballo, it was said, emphasizes "nationalism and deprecates the class struggle." His leader was Robert Sobukwe, who taught African languages at the University of Witwatersrand. In a throwback to Marcus Garvey, they proclaimed "Africa for the Africans," a phrase that would also find willing ears among U.S. Negroes. Importantly, their cry had "frequent emphasis on hatred of the Indians and Whites," though this dictum was applied inconsistently, as people from these groups often served the resultant PAC.[176] (Patrick Duncan, for example, a member of the European elite, collaborated with the PAC and was viewed by Adam Hochschild, U.S. heir to a fortune based on mining investments in the region, as "wildly, exuberantly pro-American...."[177]) According to Sobukwe's biographer, there were "rumours" that Leballo worked for the CIA with the USIS's David Du Bois as his handler. "It is possible but not certain," said Benjamin Pogrund, "that Du Bois was aware of what Leballo was doing for the PAC on the side and that he chose to ignore it."[178] This negative evaluation of the "Africanist" trend was shared by Dan Tloome, a so-called "Charterist" who was unsparing in his criticism.[179] *New Age* was pleased when in 1957 the Africanists were "routed" at a Durban conference of the ANC Youth League.[180] At the same time the legation was monitoring the *New Age*, taking note when this journal "remained silent" about controversial aspects of Leballo's and Sobukwe's activities. They did notice, however, when this periodical reported on talks between "Africanists" and the South African Bureau for Racial Affairs on U.S. premises. In that coverage, the paper's leftist journalist termed Leballo, et al. a "lunatic fringe."[181]

In early 1959 Leballo was conferring with leading Afrikaners and was said to have told them that "the Afrikaner and the African were the only ones who had a real stake in South Africa. He urged them to share the country...and to forget about the English and the Indians, who really had no business in South Africa...."[182]

176. Report, 4 November 1958, Reel 1, *Confidential U.S. State Department Files. Internal Affairs....and Foreign Affairs.*

177. Adam Hochschild, *Half the Way Home: A Memoir of Father and Son*, New York: Viking, 1986, 113.

178. Benjamin Pogrund *How Can Man Die Better*, 118.

179. *Fighting Talk*, August 1958.

180. *New Age*, 4 April 1957.

181. William Maddox, Cape Town Legation to Secretary of State, 10 January 1959, RG 59, Decimal File, Box 4504 and *New Age*, 29 January 1959.

182. Arthur E. Beach, Consul General-Johannesburg to Secretary of State, 23 January 1959, RG 59, Decimal File, Box 3231, *NARA-CP*.

New Age was less forgiving of the Africanists. They were accused of deploying "violence" that "ended in chaos." "Gangster tactics" abounded, along with "roughhouse" methods, as "fights broke out." The Africanists were "dressed in black shirts" and "wielding knives and batons" as they made a "determined effort to smash up" an ANC confab. The author of this denunciation, Govan Mbeki, charged that the "Africanists" accused the ANC of "associating with Jews," one in a "regular flow of anti-Semitic and anti-Communist cries."[183] These attacks had begun with the Mandela-led Defiance campaign of 1952 and had gotten worse with every passing day.[184] "Good riddance" was the paper's premature salutation after the "Africanists" were routed in 1958.[185]

It was a tumultuous time. In the prelude to this uproar, Africanists were supposedly considering the desperate stratagem of kidnapping ANC leaders. Their list of victims included Mandela, Tambo and Luthuli.[186] The International Confederation of Free Trade Unions was similarly busy. Allegedly seeking to promote African trade unions, soon the ICFTU played a role in the formation of the Federation of Free African Trade Unions, which was close to the emerging PAC and designed to blunt the ANC tied South African Congress of Trade Unions.[187]

But the ultimate target of these strenuous efforts—it was said—was the SACP. Certainly, this group was unsparing in its critique of U.S. imperialism and its allies, observing that "at one time they captured millions of our people and deported them to Europe and America as slaves. Afterwards, they enslaved Africans in their own continent, through forced labour on European-owned plantations, farms and mines in starvation wages." Now—in 1959— "American officials are running all over the continent of Africa offering dollars—if only the people will help them against Communism," amply aided by the Nationalists, who took immense pride in their mutually constitutive staunch anticommunism.[188]

183. *New Age*, 27 February 1958.

184. *New Age*, 14 August 1958.

185. *New Age*, 6 November 1958.

186. Luli Callinicos, *Oliver Tambo: Beyond the Engeli Mountains*, Claremont, South Africa: David Philip, 2005, 237.

187. Benjamin Pogrund *How Can Man Die Better*, 111.

188. Editorial, "The New Africa—Capitalist or Socialist," *African Communist*, (Number 1, October 1959) in *South African Communists Speak: Documents from the History of the South African Communist Party, 1915-1980*, London: Inkululekp, 1981, 248-254, 249.

Chapter 9

In the Shadow of Sharpeville, 1960-1962

THE election of John F. Kennedy as U.S. president in 1960, backed avidly by U.S. Negroes, seemed to suggest that the tug-of-war between anti-Jim Crow and pro-apartheid forces would be resolved on behalf of the former. The problem remained that Pretoria was too appealing an anticommunist bulwark for Washington to ignore, especially as a beleaguered Africa strode toward decolonization, often with the backing of Moscow. The Sharpeville Massacre of March 1960 further unmasked Pretoria as the heir to Nazi barbarism and placed further pressure on Washington to rein in its recalcitrant ally. Within hours of Sharpeville, Roy Wilkins of the NAACP had implored Secretary of State Christian Herter to denounce Pretoria: "diving jet planes were also employed" against protesters, he said with astonishment, "purchased with funds made available" to Pretoria via the U.S., he added in implicit condemnation.[1] On 29 March 1960, days after this outrage, a delegation from the U.S. National War College arrived in South Africa, at what Philip K. Crowe of the legation in Cape Town contradictorily termed "a most propitious but difficult time...."[2] A few weeks later, in seeming response, Wilkins invited Oliver Tambo of the ANC to their convention in his hometown of St. Paul, Minnesota.[3]

The backdrop to Sharpeville was raging conflict between the ANC and those who were to form the rival "Africanist" faction. The astringent critic of the SACP, U.S. Negro Richard Gibson, spoke of a "vast

---

1. Roy Wilkins to Secretary of State Christian Herter, 22 March 1960, Box IIIA35, *NAACP Papers*.

2. Philip K. Crowe to Secretary of State, 29 March 1960, RG 59, Decimal File, Box 1690.

3. Roy Wilkins to Oliver Tambo, 13 May 1960, Box IIIA35, *NAACP Papers*.

purge" of "Africanists" that had "begun under Nelson Mandela" in 1958.[4]

While Washington was being pummeled from the right for being supposedly too vigorous in pursuing anti-racism, more insistent blows were coming from the left: The *Panama Tribune* was among the periodicals raking the republic over the burning coals for being too friendly to apartheid. Their editorial was penned by George Westerman, characterized by a U.S. bureaucrat as being "of West Indian Negro descent," which only partially explained his chastisement, since similar reproaches were pouring in from the four corners of the planet.[5] Retained in the same files was a cartoon from a popular journal in Mexico City that compared South Africa and Arkansas; atop a heap of bodies stood a "Boer type" with a smoking machine gun and a comrade wearing a hood and holding a lash, with the caption: "don't be so barbaric!" and the retort: "look who's talking."[6] Such was the condemnation raining down after South African authorities systematically mowed down peaceful protesters at Sharpeville.

Just after this *New Age* reported that South Africa was "not the only country in which a bitter anti-apartheid struggle is being waged," pointing to Dixie. The recently launched sit-ins by Negro college students in Greensboro, North Carolina—the opening shot in a youth offensive that was to march relentlessly through the South—were saluted, while the paper bluntly asked, "Where is the voice of President Eisenhower"?[7] They invoked the historic 1952 campaign led by Mandela, stating that "a defiance campaign has been started" in Dixie, meaning a "battle inside and outside of Congress for civil rights for American Negroes…is being stepped up…."[8] The coverage was followed by an admiring profile of Dr. Martin Luther King, Jr.[9]

Pretoria continued to be unnerved by the mild anti-apartheid resolution the U.S. backed at the U.N. in 1958, assuming correctly that it was simply a premonition of more to come.[10] The reaction

---

4. Richard Gibson, *African Liberation Movements: Contemporary Struggles Against White Minority Rule,* New York: Oxford University Press, 1972, 55. In turn, the SACP journal was harshly critical of Gibson's handiwork: see review of his book in *African Communist,* 51(Fourth Quarter, 1972): 117-121.

5. U.S. Embassy-Panama to Secretary of State, RG 59, Decimal File, Box 1688.

6. Report from Mexico City, 28 March 1960, RG 59, Decimal File, Box 1688.

7. *New Age,* 31 March 1960.

8. *New Age,* 17 March 1960.

9. *New Age,* 6 July 1961.

10. Daniel Massey, *Under Protest: The Rise of Student Resistance at the University of Fort Hare,* Pretoria: UNISA Press, 2010, 124.

to Sharpeville only reinforced this uneasiness. Senator—soon to be President—John F. Kennedy spoke critically of Pretoria, as did the prominent Negro educator Frederick Douglass Patterson. When Dr. Martin Luther King, Jr. remarked that the slaughter "should serve as a warning signal" to the U.S. itself,[11] it provided further confirmation of Pretoria's deteriorating value as an ally. When the increasingly vocal Congressman Charles Diggs of Detroit echoed Dr. King,[12] it was evident that a political Rubicon had been crossed. Sharpeville, said the Associated Negro Press, mimicking King and Diggs, was a "grim reminder that the same thing could happen here. For there are thousands and thousands, if not millions and millions of whites in this country, who feel toward us Negro citizens as the whites feel toward the Negroes of South Africa;" in fact, events in Sharpeville were eerily similar to "what they feel like doing in Mississippi and for the same reason—white supremacy."[13] Sufficiently inspired, by October 1962 Dr. King was conferring with Ben Bella of independent Algeria—soon to back the ANC militarily—and finding a point of agreement in the idea that the U.S. risked losing ground globally unless Jim Crow was subdued.[14] His global profile rising, King also conferred with Adelaide Tambo—spouse of the ANC leader—when he passed through London. At Chief Luthuli's request, Dr. King sent him a copy of his book *Stride Toward Freedom*.[15]

Not propitious for apartheid was the decision months before Sharpeville by African and Caribbean nations—including Ghana and Jamaica—to discontinue trade with South Africa and/or to refuse to unload goods from there. Soaring to independence, they were joined by Barbados, Grenada, Dominica, Trinidad, and British Guiana—and could soon count independent Africa in the agreement.[16] Until 1994, it would be fair to suggest that Pretoria was laboring in the unforgiving shadow of Sharpeville.

Likewise, grave for apartheid was the liberalizing atmosphere created by anti-Jim Crow measures that led to passports being returned

---

11. Release, March 1960, Reel 69, #1094, Part I, Press Releases.

12. Release, March 1960, Reel 69, #1094, Press Releases.

13. Release, April 1960, Reel 70, #137, Part I, Press Releases, *ANP/Barnett Papers*.

14. Jeffrey James Byrne, *Mecca of Revolution*, 141.

15. Adelaide Tambo to Dr. King, 17 May 1962, in Clayborne Carson, et.al., eds., *The Papers of Martin Luther King, Jr.: To Save the Soul of America, Volume VII, January 1961-August 1962*, Berkeley: University of California Press, 2014, 462-463, 508.

16. David Post, Pretoria Embassy to Secretary of State, 16 July 1959, RG 59, Decimal File, Box 4496.

to the likes of Robeson. On the first anniversary of the massacre, he was to be found in his new home in London singing on behalf of *New Age*, alongside Dr. Yusuf Dadoo of the SACP and the Indian Congress. Hundreds were present as he spoke movingly of his deep feeling for South Africa, while a number of exiles from there looked on. Like others in decades previous, he observed that this faraway nation reminded him of his own homeland; though in that part of Africa, he was struck by how much more easily those of varying ancestries—African, Indian, European, Coloured—mixed than in the U.S. Hundreds of pounds were raised for the anti-apartheid cause and the journal that received this largesse felt compelled to ask, "When are you coming to Africa, Paul"—with both question and answer sending a shudder through Pretoria.[17] Robeson was repaying a debt: when his passport had been denied, ANC leader Mac Maharaj, then in London, was among the South Africans who helped to organize a transatlantic concert with him singing via telephone lines.[18]

Predictably, at this moment allegedly scholarly nostrums began to appear claiming—like conservative Russell Warren Howe— "Africans did not like American Negroes and American Negroes did not like Africans."[19] As the movements against Jim Crow and apartheid not only accelerated but became more closely linked, this line was pushed ever more insistently. By way of contrast, it was in November 1961 that Putuse Appolus of the nascent South West Africa People's Organization [SWAPO]—writing from Dar es Salaam—thanked the African American Reverend James Robinson, who collaborated with ACOA, for "your most encouraging letter" which "brought a ray of hope to frustrated souls. I have circulated it to all the refugees from South Africa and South West Africa."[20]

On the other hand, it remained true—and would become truer with every passing day—that as U.S. Negroes climbed the class ladder, propelled by powerful anti-Jim Crow gusts, some would feel compelled to express solidarity with Africa's foes. Thus, it was also in 1961 that the youthful attorney Roger Wilkins—nephew of the

17. *New Age*, 30 March 1961.

18. Padraig O'Malley, *Shades of Difference: Mac Maharaj and the Struggle for South Africa*, New York: Viking, 2007, 82.

19. Horace Mann Bond, "Howe and Isaacs in the Bush: The Ram in the Thicket," 1961m Box 71, Series II, *American Committee on Africa Records Addendum, Tulane University*. Hereafter ACOARA.

20. Putus Appolus to Reverend James Robinson, 23 November 1961, Box 94, Series III, *ACOARA*

NAACP leader—threatened to sue ACOA after the group unleashed a bitter assault on Portuguese colonialism.[21] As if on cue, the conservative Republican Senator John Tower of Texas assailed the ACOA's stance on Angola.[22] Similarly, the anticommunist onslaught had a devastating impact on the ideology of African Americans. It was also in 1961 that Joshua Nkomo, a founding father of Zimbabwe, writing from the Jamesson Hotel in Salisbury (soon to be Harare), complained to "Dear George" Houser of ACOA about a recent book by the popular Negro journalist Louis Lomax, which he found "damaging" and "unfounded" because it opened the door for enhanced red-baiting. "I know he was not serious when he wrote this thing," said the former union leader, "but it is being used here...."[23]

Washington was in the same bind in which it had been ensnared for years: eager to take advantage of the vast mineral wealth and cheap labor of Southern Africa but reluctant to be left holding the apartheid tar-baby. Then there was the vise in which U.S. imperialism found itself when it was compelled to back away from centuries of encrusted anti-Negro racism. It was in 1960 that presidential aspirant Richard M. Nixon declared ingloriously that "some of the peoples of Africa have been out of the trees for only about fifty years." These remarks were followed by another official who spoke acerbically of JFK's comrades G. Mennen Williams and Chester Bowles: "when they saw a handful of black baboons beating tom-toms they saw George Washington." A 1962 State Department policy paper cast Africans as barbarians in a sea of whiteness. Yet it was Williams—JFK's point man on Africa—who acknowledged that unless Washington moved more forcefully against apartheid it might lose military bases in Libya and Ethiopia, scientific bases in Nigeria and Zanzibar, and communications facilities in Liberia and Nigeria.[24]

Ideological squishiness was not only a problem for Negroes. In mid-1961, Ralph Dodge of the United Methodist Church in Salisbury also wrote "Dear George" Houser about his meetings with the recently born MPLA [Popular Movement for the Liberation of Angola] and with their combative foe Holden Roberto, who was to collaborate with the CIA. He sought an invitation to the U.S. for the Angolan intellectual Mario Andrade, known to be close to the

---

21. Roger Wilkins of Delson, Levin and Gordon, New York City to Collin Gonze, 12 December 1961`, Box 149, *ACOARA*.

22. George Houser, *No One Can Stop the Rain*, 121.

23. Joshua Nkomo to "Dear George," 3 February 1961, Box 149, *ACOARA*.

24. Ryan N. Irwin, *Gordian Knot: Apartheid and the Unmaking of the Liberal World Order*, New York: Oxford University Press, 2012, 76, 82, 83, 87.

MPLA, while cautioning, "this does not mean that in any sense, we should [lessen] our support for Holden Roberto…."[25]

Houser was also in touch with Agostinho Neto, founding father of modern Angola, which was suggestive of ACOA's ecumenism—or, as critics would have it, its ability to leverage ties to legitimate leaders on behalf of the illegitimate, e.g. Roberto. Still, speaking from the city then known as Leopoldville in 1961, Neto said that he was "sorry I did not see" Houser when the Euro-American passed through. "I did want to see you very much" since "we need aid." He did not necessarily discourage Houser's outreach to Roberto: "the cause of unity is a problem that we must solve…perhaps it may be that on American soil that the first visible sign of unity can be established,"[26] words that impelled Houser further. For the balding and diminutive Houser had become a kind of powerbroker by supplanting the CAA, in 1962 addressing the third figure of the triumvirate representing the three-way split in Angolan politics as "Dear Jonas,"[27] i.e. Savimbi, who also became a darling of the CIA in subsequent years.

As the Kennedys moved into the White House, the southern cone of the continent was aflame. It was not just the unrest in the Congo that led to the murder of Patrice Lumumba and decades of instability. By August 1960, even Julius Nyerere from Dar es Salaam was telling "My Dear Maida" Springer, the anticommunist labor leader, that "happenings in the Congo have caused a few jitters here among members of the immigrant communities."[28] By mid-1961 the Quaker delegate in the region was referring worriedly to "horrible atrocities" in Angola after a reported attack by the newly minted Popular Movement for the Liberation of Angola [MPLA], which would come to power about a decade and a half later. The "Portuguese are attempting to systematically eliminate all adult male Africans from a large area of the country," said Lyle Tatum, while "white civilians [were] hunting Africans like wild game," a virtual call for even angrier retaliation against this vulnerable minority.[29] This outrage did not escape the intense gaze of Dr. King. "I know of no situation in the world," he told Houser, "that concerns me more than the

25. Ralph Dodge to "Dear George," 19 July 1961, Box 149, *ACOARA*.

26. Agostinho Neto to George Houser, 18 September 1962, Box 79, *ACOARA*.

27. George Houser to "Dear Jonas," 3 December 1962, Box 94, *ACOARA*.

28. Julius Nyerere to "My Dear Maida," 18 August 1960, Box 13, *International Affairs Division, Country Files, AFL-CIO, University of Maryland-College Park*.

29. Lyle Tatum to George Loft, 5 July 1961, International Service Division 1960…. *Africa Program, AFSC*.

brutality and barbarity taking place in Angola today." Writing in July 1961, he announced, "I would like to be part of such a commission" to go to Luanda for an investigation since "I am always interested in what is taking place in Africa...."[30]

From February 1961 until liberation in November 1975 Angola was rocked by an anti-colonial war spearheaded by the MPLA, then was beset and bedeviled by an internal revolt led by Savimbi and sponsored by Washington and Pretoria. Claude Barnett of the Associated Negro Press saw Portugal as "one of the worst of the colonizing nations" and, thus, he "would like to send a competent reporter" to Luanda.[31] As with Roger Wilkins, Barnett's public relations comrade Sam Bledsoe had a contract with Lisbon to deodorize their smelling image. "We have a man in Angola," he told Barnett in May 1961. Yes, "Portugal has made mistakes," he conceded guilefully of a nation that had countenanced the slave trade and the vast looting of a potpourri of minerals. "There is no racial prejudice in the ordinary sense in Angola," he parsed slyly, which was "not the true case in the United States," which he condemned in comparison.[32]

Angola was "not a simple...problem," he insisted wanly, since it was in a "primitive state", for reasons presumably unconnected to centuries of colonialism and was therefore susceptible to "chaos and Communist dictatorship..." The U.S. "world position has deteriorated rapidly," he said accurately, and "if this trend continues our survival as an independent nation is greatly in doubt" because of the advantage to be gained by "Russians and the Chinese," necessitating solidarity with Portuguese, not Angolans.[33]

Taking up the cudgel on behalf of Lisbon was the Father of Black Conservatism, George Schuyler. He journeyed to Angola and Mozambique but said it was a "lie" that he was biased in favor of Lisbon. Instead, he excoriated the "murderous Communist controlled racket" presumably behind this supposed falsehood.[34] He insisted that there was "no racial or colour discrimination" in these colonies

30. Dr. King to George Houser, 19 July 1961, Box 5, *George Houser Papers, Michigan State University*.

31. Release, August 1960, Reel 71, #434, Part I, Press Releases.

32. Sam Bledsoe to Claude Barnett, 29 May 1961, Reel 4, #425, Part II, Organizational Files, *ANP/Barnett Papers*.

33. Sam Bledsoe to Claude Barnett, 31 May 1961, Reel 4, #426, Part II, Organizational Files.

34. George Schuyler to Carlos Goncalves, Director-UPA Information Service, 13 March 1962, Reel 23, #17, Part II, Organizational Files.

then tied to the apron strings of Pretoria.[35] Even Holden Roberto, thought to be a CIA asset, was dissatisfied by Schuyler's reportage. He also denounced Max Yergan, Robeson's former comrade now in the pocket of Pretoria.[36] Even Barnett, to his credit, sought to generate attacks on Schuyler's reporting on Angola.[37]

To this end Barnett contacted Roberto, informing him that "we are not hearing enough from your headquarters about what is going on in Angola."[38] Sufficiently prodded, Portugal's U.S. legation then told Barnett that they wanted "American Negroes to be fully informed about the multiracial policy" supposedly pursued in Angola and sought aid in disseminating this meretricious view.[39]

Moscow's launch of Sputnik added another wrinkle to this complicated picture. Negroes charged that this Soviet victory was due in no small part to the fact that the U.S. was more interested in the "race race" than the "space race."[40] This charge also created momentum against apartheid. As ever, there were tugs in the other direction. The newly formed National Aeronautics and Space Administration in Washington desperately desired a tracking station in the Union, which Moscow characterized as a "military base."[41] Pretoria did not help its case when it insisted on a kind of racial cleansing for a visiting NASA delegation. "To the best of my knowledge," cautioned U.S. official Philip K. Crowe, Pretoria's Eric Louw was misguided in the request, since "no one of mixed blood was included" in this important deputation—nor was there a "Chinese American" either, to be precise.[42] The U.S. conservative leader Russell Kirk—a comrade of William F. Buckley, intellectual godfather of this resurgent movement—agreed with Louw. Well, Kirk huffed, since the U.S. does not object to Saudi Arabia's refusal to admit Jewish-Americans

---

35. Column by George Schuyler, 1 July 1961, Reel 23, #47, Part II, Organizational Files.

36. Release, December 1961, Reel 75, #730, Part I, Press Releases.

37. Claude Barnett to Howard Embrey, 12 December 1961, Box 174, Folder 5, *Claude Barnett Papers, Chicago History Museum.*

38. Claude Barnett to Holden Roberto, 2 December 1961, Box 174, Folder 5, *Claude Barnett Papers.*

39. B. Teixeira, Portuguese Embassy to Claude Barnett, 13 September 1961, Box 174, Folder 5.

40. Gerald Horne, *Storming the Heavens: African Americans and the Early Struggle for the Right to Fly*, Baltimore: Black Classics Press, 2017.

41. Glenn G. Wolfe, Counselor of U.S. Embassy to Olcott H. Deming, State Department, 12 October 1960, RG 59, Decimal File, Box 1249, *NARA-CP.*

42. Philip K. Crowe, U.S. Embassy Pretoria to Secretary of State, 12 November 1959, RG 59, Decimal File, Box 4504.

why go after Pretoria? The U.S. does not rule the world, he blustered: Pretoria is sovereign.[43]

Yet the military fright delivered by Sputnik allowed little room for maneuver. "I remember staring at the directory board in the foyer of the U.S. Embassy" in South Africa, said the writer and heir to a huge fortune based on debasement of Africans, i.e. Adam Hochschild, speaking of the early 1960s, "and being astonished by the long list of military attachés we had there."[44]

As Moscow marched from triumph to triumph, *New Age* provocatively published an article with the sub-headline: "an American Negro editor gives one reason why the United States is way behind in the Race for Space...." James Hicks declaimed passionately, "let the record...show that as the Russian engineers made mankind's greatest history there was not a single Negro engineering school south of Washington, D.C.," where most of his people resided—and continue to reside. Worse, the "U.S. Navy had just finished permitting South Africa to humiliate Negro American sailors" in Cape Town. With emphasis he observed that if the U.S. "had spent as much time PUSHING AHEAD in the race for space with Russia as it did HOLDING BACK the Negro BECAUSE of his race—America and not Russia would be accepting the congratulations of the world today—instead of arguing about who won the Civil War one hundred years ago...."[45]

This was a message that was bound to resonate in South Africa, where apartheid's inability to deploy human capital had long hamstrung the economy. Moreover, arguments about who won—or more precisely, who suffered most during the war at the turn of the century—were as fierce, if not fiercer, in Pretoria; a diversion from the larger goal of maintaining white supremacy.

This battering of Washington provided Pretoria and its regional allies with more leverage to use against the republic. This, along with an overestimation of their weakening position and their racist underestimation of Africans, combined to augment a pre-existing colonial arrogance. The so-called federation that was to include, inter alia, the emerging nations of Zambia, Zimbabwe, and Malawi, was exuding "anti-Americanism," or so thought the U.S. emissary in

43. Undated clipping, Box 120, *William Rusher Papers, Library of Congress, Washington, D.C.*

44. Adam Hochschild, "Revolutionary Aristocrat," *Mother Jones*, April 1985, Box 151, *Leroy Walker Africa News Service Archive, Duke University, Durham, North Carolina.*

45. *New Age*, 27 July 1961.

Southern Rhodesia. It was a "wave" that was "engulfing the European population."[46] Simultaneously, anti-colonialism was engulfing the ANC. At their leadership meeting in Durban on the cusp of 1960, maximum attention was paid to decolonization of Africa on a granular, country-by-country level.[47] According to Rusty Bernstein, the group then counted a hefty membership of 120,000.[48]

In a sense, it was understandable why Rhodesians were so upset with Washington. Through the latter's aegis, Luther Foster of Tuskegee— the capstone of Negro education founded by the legendary Booker T. Washington—was making his way to Salisbury. In 1962 he was invited by the State Department to participate in the opening exercises for Nyatsime College in Southern Rhodesia, an institution patterned after his own Tuskegee. The granting of this passage could allow an outsider—a Negro outsider at that—to monitor and expose the horrific conditions inflicted upon Africans there.[49]

It also brought the Negro experience closer to Southern Africa, which had been perceived for some time as a subversive development. When the African Stan Samkange read Booker T. Washington's autobiography at the age of 16, he found inspiration that shaped his activism in Southern Rhodesia. Then he traveled to the U.S. to study and returned by 1958 with a degree from Indiana University and an African-American spouse with a doctorate in psychology, the former Tommie Anderson of Jackson, Mississippi. He raised money from the Rockefellers for his various projects, and the trumpeter Louis Armstrong performed a benefit concert on his behalf. His spouse was unsparing in her criticism of her new home in Africa. It was "worse" than Jackson, she argued, since in Dixie there were Jim Crow buses, but in Salisbury there were entirely "separate buses for whites and blacks"; and in Rhodesia the government made "no provision for the education of Africans, while it provides excellent schools for whites."[50]

This steady stream of African Americans was ruffling. When the choreographer Pearl Primus arrived in Salisbury in 1962 she became enmeshed in a dispute that led to her forced removal from

46. Consul General-Salisbury to Secretary of State, 14 April 1960, RG 59, Decimal File, Box 1249.

47. Minutes of ANC Executive, December 1959, *Albert Luthuli Papers.*

48. Rusty Bernstein, *Memory Against Forgetting,* 312.

49. Luther Foster to Claude Barnett, 5 October 1962, Reel 9, #759, Part III, Series B, *ANP/Barnett Papers, Chicago History Museum.*

50. Release, November 1961, Reel 75, #@401, Part I, Press Releases, *ANP/Barnett Papers.*

a restaurant—not the ideal example for Africans from Rhodesia's viewpoint.[51]

By the time segregationist Senator Allen Ellender of Louisiana showed up in Salisbury to garland the regime with praise, the damage had been done.[52] The legislator insisted nonetheless that "I have yet to meet any Africans who have the capacity to run their own affairs." His ideological soulmate, Republican Party ideologist William F. Buckley, then approvingly quoted Ellender's "sensitive truths."[53] One analyst found that "white Southerners, even those who did not support segregation in the South, tended to be favorable to South Africa and to sympathize with its problems...." Those defined as "white" in Dixie, says Patrick Henry Martin, "were more inclined to support colonialism than were other Americans," while "Southern newspapers did not give Sharpeville the prominence that many newspapers in other parts of the country gave it...." Some of these journals endorsed the massacre. The Mississippi state legislature passed a resolution praising apartheid in the Sharpeville's aftermath: the vote was 45-0 in the upper chamber.[54] The Minister of Justice in South Africa welcomed warmly this pro-apartheid resolution passed by the similarly beleaguered Mississippi legislature, with support premised on the notion that both sites were confronting the "dangers of Communist activity."[55]

As the crisis of colonialism—a major moment in world history—was unfolding, Washington too had to contemplate what was to come. Yes, U.S. imperialism was not terribly upset up as its European allies *cum* competitors packed their bags and exited the scene, taking with them the noxious "imperial preference" that locked African nations into one-sided trade agreements, often shutting the door on Washington and Wall Street. Still, there was fear that Bandung 1955 provided the foretaste of a militant "Third World" allied with the socialist camp. Harlan Cleveland, high-level State Department official during the JFK regime, recalled subsequently how their worry about "dominance of the Third World in U.N. Matters" led to consideration of "weighted voting" in the General Assembly of the

51. Release, July 1962, Reel 76, #1180, Part I, Press Releases.

52. Release, December 1962, Reel 78, #178, Part I, Press Releases.

53. Thomas A. Becnel, *Senator Allen Ellender of Louisiana*, Baton Rouge: Louisiana State University Press, 1995, 209, 210.

54. Patrick Henry Martin, "American Views on South Africa, 1948-1972," 48, 234, 237, 239.

55. U.S. Embassy, Cape Town to Secretary of State, 8 March 1961, RG 59, Decimal File, Box 1689.

United Nations—extending the hegemony of the Security Council to this universal body. He also validated the rift with Europe when discussion of the 1961 resolution on Angola found Washington seeking to distinguish itself from its colonial ally in Lisbon.[56]

As anti-racism was propelled by the mass action of Negroes and the avid support of national liberation forces and the socialist camp, Washington reacted by tarring the most militant activists on behalf of the Negroes and Africans—Robeson, Mandela, Neto, Nkomo, Nkrumah, Lumumba, et al.—as unrepentant Communists in the mold of the then reviled Stalin, in a bald attempt to sway unsteady public opinion (of course, some of these men were actual Communists). The European minority in Southern Africa—according to the U.S. man in Southern Rhodesia—felt that "official American activity in Africa is a cover for our preparations to fight the next war on this continent;" thus, the U.S. "threat" was coupled with that said to be emerging from Moscow.[57]

This red baiting was misleading in fundamental ways. It was in 1962 that the Quaker activist—and Negro—Bill Sutherland asked Lyle Tatum, "how well do you really know Kaunda…he was my guest in 1958 soon after he came back from India…he took a good many of my books on Gandhi and nonviolence."[58] History shows that Kaunda was not the only liberation leader who was not a Marxist, though he was said to be otherwise pre-independence.

There was a tendency in what became Zimbabwe to blame Washington for various dramatic developments. Thus, there was "vituperative" "abuse" of the U.S. in the *Sunday Mail*—which enjoyed the "largest circulation in the Federation"—after Pretoria withdrew from the British Commonwealth. The paper combined these complaints with a castigation of lynchings in the U.S., adding with scalding intensity that "nowhere in the world is human dignity affronted more frequently and more viciously than in the great American democracy." Though the words came from Salisbury, the impulse was thought to be embedded in South Africa.[59] The day after the Sharpeville Massacre the Salisbury consulate reported that "racial

56. Harlan Cleveland, Oral History, 30 November 1978, *John F. Kennedy Presidential Library-Boston.*

57. Edward Mulcahy to Secretary of State, 1 June 1960, RG 59, Decimal File, Box 1249.

58. Bill Sutherland to Lyle Tatum, 18 September 1962, Administration Africa Program Daily Planning Prog….1962, *AFSC.*

59. Consul General-Salisbury to Secretary of State, 24 March 1961, RG 59, Decimal File, Box 1249.

problems in U.S. receiving wide press, radio play here and providing grist [for] current anti-American outbreak,"[60] as if the message was that racism was not unique to Southern Africa, so why complain about it?

Contrarily, writing from Johannesburg, the Student Representative Council, expressed their "full support" for the Negro student James Meredith, then seeking to desegregate the oaked and blood-soaked campus of the University of Mississippi-Oxford. They saw the conflict as a "fight for academic freedom and [an] open university" with "academic merit" being the "only criterion for admission"—and not European ancestry.[61] "How much I admire your firm stand," chimed in Barbara Harmel from Johannesburg. "There are many of us who support you," she reassured, speaking of her own University of Witwatersrand. Same struggle, same fight was her pithy analysis of the dual battles against Jim Crow and apartheid. "Nonwhite students are no longer allowed to attend the same universities, nor lectures, nor play sports," she said of South Africa. "Segregation—or apartheid as it is known here—is legally enforced," which was an implicit call for an ANC led armed struggle, then already on the verge of erupting.[62]

The Southern African right could have footnoted their anti-U.S. screed with sources from the left. The brutal 1959 lynching of Mack Parker in Dixie on typically specious grounds was detailed in *New Age* by the veteran U.S. Communist journalist Art Shields.[63] Dr. Martin Luther King, Jr. was quoted on the "hypocrisy and chicanery" that permeated the U.S. when it came to Negroes.[64] When Robeson termed "U.S. imperialism" the "worst enemy of mankind today," his simultaneous commendation of the socialist camp kept the right from lifting the remark from the pages of the left.[65] When Robeson's comrade W. Alphaeus Hunton was calling for "resisting

---

60. "Joint Consulate General-USIS Dispatch", 22 March 1960, RG 59, Decimal File, Box 1688.

61. Resolution, 3 October 1962, *James Meredith Papers, University of Mississippi-Oxford*.

62. Barbara Harmel to James Meredith, 3 October 1962, *James Meredith Papers*.

63. *New Age*, 25 June 1959.

64. *New Age*, 22 September 1960. Lewis V. Baldwin, *Toward the Beloved Community: Martin Luther King, Jr. and South Africa*, Cleveland: Pilgrim Press, 1995.

65. *New Age*, 22 December 1960.

neo-colonialism," only the recent vintage of this neologism might have prevented it from being echoed in Salisbury and Pretoria.[66]

At times it seemed that Salisbury and Pretoria were blinded by their one-sided dislike of Washington and insensitive to this power's difficult position, under siege by anti-racist forces. Though the pro-apartheid force could at times echo Dr. King, they would be hard-pressed to ape the demand sent by powerful labor leader Walter Reuther of the United Auto Workers in Detroit to Secretary of State Christian Herter on behalf of the AFL-CIO Executive Council, expressing "outrage" at negative trends in Southern African and Washington's complicity therein, demanding the recall of the Ambassador and the suspension of gold purchases.[67]

By May 1960 in Bulawayo there was formed an "African Committee on America"—a clear rebuke of the American Committee on Africa—to counteract anti-racist initiatives from the U.S. and publish details on maltreatment of Negroes. The *Bulawayo Citizen* asserted that the Negro was treated far more harshly than the African in Africa and that the U.S. must "set its own house in order before interfering with the internal position of countries outside its borders."[68] These stinging critiques reflected the gathering sentiment among the European minority that a major political party—the Democrats—was becoming too dependent on Negro votes, which jeopardized apartheid and its progeny. They remembered the visits of Adlai Stevenson in 1955 and 1957 and the perception that he was not supportive of apartheid and, moreover, was close to the Oppenheimer family, a potent and fabulously wealthy outfit. The combination of the ascendant Democrats allying with sub-regional and domestic capital was viewed with hostility by those who held apartheid dear.[69]

It was debatable whether Negroes were treated worse than Africans. The admonishment from Bulawayo was one more pressure point compelling Washington to improve its horrendous domestic record. But it had classic boomerang effect: bolstering the Negro struggle allowed African Americans to more effectively confront apartheid. Yet near that same time, Brian Bunting, a prominent SACP leader, spoke at the University of Cape Town, during an era

66. *New Age*, 13 July 1961.

67. Walter Reuther to Christian Herter, 9 March 1960, Box IIIA35, *NAACP Papers*.

68. *Bulawayo Citizen*, 29 April 1960 and Edward Mulcahy, Consul General-Salisbury to Secretary of State, 3 May 1960, RG 59, Decimal File, Box 1690.

69. Victor von Lossberg, Consul General-Johannesburg to Secretary of State, 8 September 1959, RG 59, Decimal File, Box 3231.

when it would have been difficult—at best—for a U.S. counterpart to speak at, e.g. the University of Mississippi.[70] In other words, as of—roughly—1960 it was unclear if South Africa were more anti-communist and more racist than the U.S.

The attack on the federal government in Washington launched from Salisbury and Pretoria was a mirror image of a similar assault launched from Richmond and Raleigh and Atlanta. In the first issue of its newsletter, the notorious Citizens' Council of Dixie printed two articles favorable to apartheid written by S.E.D. Brown, editor and publisher of the *South African Observer*. Brown was a key man: he also contributed to the mouthpiece of the zealously anticommunist U.S. grouping, the John Birch Society,[71] and he was a boon comrade of the fanatically racist Senator James Eastland of Mississippi.[72] This periodical also reprinted a 1959 article from the *American Mercury* tormenting the Negro who now served at the highest level of the U.N., making him an object of derision on more than one count: "Who or what is Ralph Bunche?" They accused him of being a dumb Communist who happened to pick the "winning side." By January 1960 there was a pen pal matching service between the land of apartheid and the land of Jim Crow: it was initiated by the curiously named "Society of the Two Souths" formed in Germiston, Transvaal, this province containing some of the hardest of hardliners.[73]

It was difficult to ignore Rhodesia in Washington. The common language and Anglo-centrism tended to unite the two in a way that was hard to maintain in Pretoria. At the 375th meeting of the National Security Council in Washington in the latter days of the Eisenhower Administration, the minutes reflect the statement that "Africa was usually thought of in terms of the black man but that one area in Africa—Rhodesia—was eminently suitable for white settlement and development. The Prime Minister of Rhodesia...was ready to open the country to immigration from all sources," including the U.S., a variation from Pretoria's rigid policy. But then the conversation took a turn, revealing how the rise of Africa both opened new doors

70. Embassy, Cape Town to Secretary of State, 13 March 1961, RG 59, Decimal File, Box 1689.

71. Allen Drury, *A Very Strange Society: A Journey to the Heart of South Africa*, New York: Trident, 1967, 369.

72. Patrick Henry Martin, "American Views on South Africa, 1948-1972," Ph.d. dissertation, Louisiana State University, 1974, 242.

73. Zoe Hyman, "American Segregationist Ideology and White Southern Africa, 1948-1975," Ph.d. dissertation, University of Sussex, 2011, 114, 115, 125, 139

for Washington and raised new problems. President Eisenhower "remarked parenthetically that he was having a continuing protocol discussion with the State Department, which insisted that he invite half a dozen American Negroes to any White House reception of a distinguished African visitor."[74] This gesture could only engender heartburn in Salisbury and Pretoria.

Thus, it was during this troubled era that during a briefing for U.S. officials in Nairobi, the opinion was uttered that "people of tropical Africa, potential slaves until a few decades ago" were "still ill fitted psychologically, sociologically, economically and by education to undertake the country's responsibilities." The only cloud spotted on the blue horizon was the symbolism of Nkrumah,[75] which turned out to undermine such unsavory views of African potential.

Previously Black guests in the White House were few and far between, but in this new era they were invited to inner sanctums, confines which provided an opportunity for more adept lobbying—on behalf of themselves and Africa too. Eisenhower was, in any case, an imperfect instrument of desegregation. His grandchildren were sent to a private all-white school miles away from their army base home after the base's school was desegregated in accordance with law.[76]

To be sure, there was resistance to the heightened role of U.S. Negroes from domestic and international quarters alike. It was also during the Eisenhower Administration that discussions unfolded concerning the "widespread suspicion of the U.S." by the colonizers since anti-Jim Crow measures were undermining white supremacy itself. As Negroes were allowed to climb the class ladder, how could Southern Africa resist the same trend? The U.S., which contained a Negro minority, had more flexibility in this regard than ferociously outnumbered colonizers. "Portuguese are most bitter and outspoken on their resentment of what they regard as American anti-colonialism," it was reported. As they saw things, this dangerous leveling movement simply meant that the "African National Communists [sic]" would continue to "exercise potent influence in

74. Minutes of 375th Meeting of the National Security Council, 7 August 1958, Box 10, *Papers as President, Ann Whitman File, NSC Series, Eisenhower Library.*

75. Briefing, 25 March 1958, Box 1, *U.S. Council on Foreign Economic Policy Records, Reports Series, Eisenhower Library.*

76. Zoe Hyman, "American Segregationist Ideology and White Southern Africa, 1948-1975," Ph.d. dissertation, University of Sussex, 2011, 45.

the Union of South Africa,"[77] with the misnomer for the ANC likely being intentional and exposing a deeper fear.

An eye-opening aspect of this mixture of resistance and acquiescence was exposed when in early 1960, as the Eisenhower Administration was being ushered out of power, its primary Negro aide—Fred Morrow—was ousted from a State Department flight to Liberia by rudely denying his spouse a seat; yet at the same time officialdom was hailing the work of another Negro, Reverend James Robinson and his Operation Crossroads Africa—a kind of precursor of Kennedy's Peace Corps in dispatching well-meaning U.S. volunteers to Africa.[78]

The Quakers in the region often found themselves targeted by the colonizers as a direct result. In late 1960 in Salisbury, Lyle Tatum of the "Friends" was upbraided by a neighbor. The neighbor had just visited Tatum's homeland and informed him pointedly that "there is much work for your society to do there before branching out to other countries"—Rhodesia, for example. "I object," he said angrily, "to Africans being asked to tea or other social gatherings in my neighbourhood" and "when the riots" then erupting "in the Congo get worse I hope your African friends will protect you."[79] The Quaker delegate was asked to abandon his home in Salisbury because he entertained an Africa with tea there.[80]

Recollecting later, Tatum reflected that the "Salisbury Meeting," i.e. the assemblage of Quakers, during this era "consisted of about 20 persons with widely divergent political opinions.... there were three civil servants of the Southern Rhodesia government and there was a heavy weighting on the reactionary side of any social or political issue...." His mistake came after he rented a house, "moved in and invited an African guest to dinner"—soon the "owner of the house said the neighbors complained. And we'd have to move."[81]

---

77. Report, 1 April 1958, Box, *White House Office of Special Assistant for National Security Affairs, Records, OCB Series, Administrative Subseries, Eisenhower Library.*

78. Frederick Fox to Karl Harr, 15 January 1960, Box 1, *White House Office of Special Assistant for National Security Affairs Records OCB Series Subject Subseries, Eisenhower Library.*

79. Lyle Tatum to AFSC, 1 November 1960, *International Service Division 1960, Latin American Program, Africa Program,* AFSC.

80. Clipping, *Evening Standard,* November 1960, *International Service Division 1960......AFSC.*

81. Lyle Tatum to Mary Massaro, 5 January 1994, Box: ID Administration, Africa, *AFSC.*

The Quakers were not welcomed with open arms by the settlers in Rhodesia. They thought the U.S. was meddling officiously, hoping to take over from a fading London and other departing metropolitan powers. The U.S. was requested to solve its own problem of racism before departing for overseas ventures.[82] Again, this line could also be found in the playbook of the left: U.S. imperialism, said *New Age*, hoped to benefit from the missteps of the colonizers by simultaneously undermining them—flaunting anti-Jim Crow measures easier to pursue where Africans were a minority—and selectively backing independence struggles, e.g. the belated turn toward the Algerian rebels.[83]

* * *

The crisis in Congo staggered backers of Jim Crow. A full-page advertisement in the *New York Times* bellowed that "Katanga", a mineral rich province where the crisis was sharpest, "is the Hungary of 1961!"—i.e. a holy cause for the ultra-right.[84] A Belgian analysis that made its way to Oxford, Mississippi, site of a fierce anti-racist fracas, bemoaned the "atrocities committed by the Congolese army against the white population...." Well aware of their target audience, Brussels stressed the "real savagery of which the whites in the Congo were the victims"; there was much focus on rapes, less on murder for, it was said, "the number of persons killed seems to have been relatively small."[85] "Congo riots were worse than reports

82. George Loft to Colgate Prentice, 27 August 1960, International Service Division 1960, *AFSC*.

83. *New Age*, 10 March 1960.

84. *New York Times*, 14 December 1961. See also the cartoon in the *Los Angeles Times*, 26 December 1961, featuring an African with a rifle slung over his shoulder in Congo encountering a pudgy visitor in a pith helmet chewing on a cigar and carrying a satchel with the inscription, "Friends of Tshombe Committee" (a reference to a favorite of the ultra-right) with the caption reading: "Senator Eastland, I presume!": a reference to the Mississippi legislator.

85. "A Preliminary Report on the Atrocities Committed by the Congolese Army Against the White Population of the .... Congo...." no date, Box 4, *Race Relations Collection-University of Mississippi-Oxford*. At the same site, see also Dana Brown to Senator Eastland, 13 December 1962, FS 3 SS1, Box 83, *James Eastland Papers*: Claimed were "more than one thousand rapes of European women in the Congo plus scores of murders.......I personally have travelled thousands of miles within the Belgian Congo and have spent many months in that country and ....Ruanda-Urundi [sic]...."

disclosed," said the *Johannesburg Star*, as "whites are uneasy," with many fleeing in all directions.[86] Substantiating their polemic was an analysis from the *Baltimore Afro-American* on the Congo and Lumumba,[87] and another from Dr. Du Bois, "the Grand Old Man of African Liberation."[88]

Also unsettling for Jim Crow was the vehement reaction in Black America to the murder of Lumumba. In February 1961 U.S. Negroes invaded the floor of the U.N. and became embroiled in a vociferous protest against this slaying, overwhelming security forces. "FBI and CIA agents lounged conspicuously," said one observer, "clicking their cameras as we approached...." They had come to confront Ambassador Adlai Stevenson, no stranger in Southern Africa. A "heated conference" ensued, which proved to be "unproductive" said the observer William Worthy. But it was the fracas that garnered global headlines, not to mention extensive coverage in the U.S. bourgeois press, including the ABC television network, the Associated Press, and the *New York Times*. These various organs, said Worthy, a journalist and activist, "carried news of the protest to every corner of the earth." From that point forward, said Worthy proudly, Stevenson would "have to look over his shoulder to see if dissenters from Harlem, poised to demonstrate, are sitting in the gallery," as he mounted the rostrum to defend Lisbon and Pretoria.[89] Tragically and counterproductively, the protesters at the U.N. sought to bar African-American Communist leader Ben Davis—a close comrade of Robeson—on anticommunist grounds, a troubling sign of disturbing trends to follow after many of these same forces became strident critics of the ANC-SACP alliance.[90]

In the prelude to Sharpeville, Nkrumah loomed in Pretoria and Washington as a forbidding figure, even more than Nasser in Egypt. His formidability was manifested in a site where U.S. interests flourished: Ethiopia, also the home of a military base that monitored oil-rich Saudi Arabia and points east. This Nkrumah factor did not only potentially constrict access to African resources but it also meant, as one U.S. official put it, while "formerly Africa was the dumping ground for the misfits, the alcoholic and the neer-do-wells," now a

86. *Johannesburg Star*, 12 January 1959, Reel 7, *Xuma Papers*.

87. *New Age*, 6 October 1960.

88. *New Age*, 22 December 1960.

89. William Worthy, "Anatomy of as Sit-In," circa 1961, Box 340, *Adlai Stevenson Papers, Princeton University-New Jersey. i*

90. See e.g. Gerald Horne, *Black Liberation/Red Scare*, passim.

sovereign Africa was placing this ugly process in jeopardy,[91] meaning the deployment of more competent cadre to Africa meaning fewer to be sent to e.g. Latin America, Asia and Europe: this was debilitating imperialism overall.

This was part of the contradiction hardly confronted at the time. It was not only East Africa where miscreants were dumped: Pretoria was infested with Nazis and other anti-Semites while they were being sidelined in Washington, which was much more capacious in its definition of "whiteness." Both nations were anticommunist, but Pretoria was less successful in routing the enemy compared to the reputedly more "liberal" Washington. The U.S. was moving hesitantly in an anti-racist direction, while Sharpeville showed that Pretoria was not similarly inclined. Thus, when a U.S. emissary met with Sarah Gertrude Millin—described as South Africa's "most distinguished writer"—he seemed bewildered by her words. She was reliably anticommunist, blasting the ANC as Communist-dominated and enthusiastically opposing independence for what became Namibia. So, when she said that Prime Minister Verwoerd was a "Nazi," she was hard to dismiss. Her spouse, the late Mr. Justice Philip Millin, was the presiding judge at the trial in which Verwoerd sued the *Johannesburg Star* for libel because it had accused him of being pro-Nazi during the late war. In her opinion, Verwoerd continued to possess strong fascist leanings and was both "anti-Semitic and strongly authoritarian," which did not seem to discredit him in the eyes of Washington.[92]

As the anti-Jim Crow and anti-apartheid movements bonded, so did their opponents. Again, news was reported of the rise of terrorist tactics thought to be native to the U.S. By 1959 Assistant Secretary of State William Macomber, Jr. told Senator Philip Hart of Michigan about the troubling "establishment of the Ku Klux Klan in the Union of South Africa…."[93]

It is not as if Verwoerd were alone in his distasteful sympathies. By 1960, Johannes de Klerk, scion of a family that would emblazon their name in the apartheid pantheon, had become Minister of Labour and was waiting in the wings. He was a "rigid apostle of

---

91. C. Vaughan Ferguson to Clarence Randall, 1 April 1958, Box 3, *U.S. Council on Foreign Economic Policy, Office of the Chairman, Records, Randall Series: Trip Subseries, Eisenhower Library.*

92. Legation, Pretoria to Secretary of State, 16 June 1960, RG 59, Decimal File, Box 1689.

93. William Macomber, Jr. to Senator Hart, 11 August 1959, RG 59, Decimal File, Box 2505, *NARA-CP.*

white supremacy," said the legation, though he "hides his extreme views in his social contacts," which stretched across the "respectable" spectrum of opinion in Pretoria. Paunchy and described as "rather kindly looking," his sister had married the late Prime Minister Strijdom; yet despite this pedigree he was considered "less ferociously anti-British than many," which purportedly placed him in an advantageous position to succeed Verwoerd, especially since he abjured the U.N.—a view "colored by his fears that the white nations would soon be swamped by the blacks, browns and yellows...."[94] Ironically, his son—the last apartheid ruler—was left to confront the awkward reality bequeathed to him by the maladroitness of his father and those in that circle, who could not maneuver beyond the "color" of their fears.

As these important events were unfolding, the legation in Cape Town was conferring with Patrick Duncan, totemic of the liberal anticommunist, "Africanist" bloc, united against the alliance of the SACP, ANC, and South African Congress of Trade Unions. Duncan's Liberal Party was said to have 3500 members, including the famed writer Alan Paton, one of the better-known South Africans globally. Oblivious to the disaster that Sharpeville would become, it was blandly reported that the "Africanists" and their allies were planning a "mass movement against the pass system", while perking the envoy's interest was the organizers' view that the ANC was "dominated by Communists." Stanley Uys of the Johannesburg *Sunday Times* was deemed to be a "fellow traveler" alongside Duncan, i.e. "certainly dead [set] against any Communist influence...."[95]

Anticommunism was at the heart of the Treason Trial, still in motion in 1960, though the focus was sharpening on Mandela and Duma Nokwe.[96] In this context, Duncan played a critical role.

These anticommunist voices were important since they substantiated the hegemonic view that prioritized the alleged "Red Menace," as the interminable Treason Trial suggested. The Secretary of State was informed that Duncan "told me that he is convinced that the Russians are landing agents and guns off the coast of Natal, ostensibly from submarines...."[97] Duncan was frequently flayed by *New*

94. Report by Embassy-Pretoria, 15 August 1960, RG 59, Decimal File, Box 1690.

95. U.S. Embassy, Cape Town to Secretary of State, 9 February 1960, Box 1688.

96. *New Age*, 8 September 1960.

97. Embassy-Pretoria to Secretary of State, 17 November 1960, RG 59, Decimal File, Box 1690.

Age because of his "rabid anticommunism" that "closely resembles the late and unlamented Senator Joseph McCarthy," a twist that led to his attacking Patrice Lumumba, then under siege in the Congo, while backing his successor, the eventual dictator then known as Joseph Mobutu.[98] Yet the liberal U.S. anticommunist Adam Hochschild, who happened to be heir to a fortune based on malicious exploitation of African mines, praised Duncan, not least since he saw U.S. intervention in Pretoria as the "best hope for South Africa." His Liberal Party was "coupled with an extraordinarily vigorous anticommunism." Duncan, he said proudly, "attacks…the Russians" at every opportunity, though Hochschild dismissed peremptorily the "rumors" that he enjoyed "CIA funding…." Despite the Africanists' purported disdain for the ANC's ties to Europeans, Duncan—"enthusiastically" pro-U.S.—joined the Pan Africanist Congress, becoming the "organization's only white member," an analogue to Mary Louise Hooper of the ANC.[99]

Duncan and the Africanists were often joined by the Zulu chauvinist Gatsha Buthelezi. By the 1990s he was in the forefront of a bloodbath targeting ANC and SACP cadre. Nonetheless, he was embraced by Leballo and by the official U.S. labor groupings, which awarded him the George Meany award for—risibly—human rights. He was eventually to attend Prayer Breakfasts with Ronald Reagan. Strikingly, the PAC's Sobukwe was Buthelezi's mentor at Fort Hare, and the Zulu kingmaker was utterly sympathetic to the explosive charge that the ANC was too much in thrall to Europeans, Indians, and Communists.[100] According to Quaker Lyle Tatum, speaking in 1962, there was reason to think that Leballo was "almost psychopathic," which did not bode well for stable ties to the ANC.[101]

Ironically contributing to the anti-Soviet consensus was a force whose rise has yet to be fully digested to this very day. By 1960, the SACP and ANC were being "squeezed," according to the party's Rusty Bernstein, by what was termed the Sino-Soviet split. The issue first arose at a gathering in Johannesburg, where Bernstein found "there was little enthusiasm amongst us for the recent theoretical

---

98. *New Age*, 22 December 1960.

99. Adam Hochschild, "Revolutionary Aristocrat," *Mother Jones*, April 1985, Box 151, *Leroy Walker Africa News Service Archive-Duke University, Durham, North Carolina.*

100. Ben Temkin, *Buthelezi: A Biography*, London: Cass, 2003, 190, 214, 218, 72.

101. Lyle Tatum to Leslie Smith, 14 November 1962, Box: Administrator, Africa Program Family Planning, Prog Administrator, *AFSC.*

pronouncements of Chairman Mao" since "most of us favored the Soviet position," though "our members distributed both country's publications illegally and at some risk…."[102] As matters evolved, members of the Pan Africanist Congress were to find a hearing in China, bedeviling the SACP-ANC alliance for years to come. The same could be said for the Zimbabwe African National Union across the border, the only China-backed liberation movement that managed to seize power.[103]

This Chinese contretemps arrived at an inopportune moment; by 1959 Moscow and its allies had become the main source of ordnance and ideology alike for liberation forces in Algeria.[104] Then China began to accuse the Soviet Union of selling out to U.S. imperialism because of its peaceful coexistence policy—the precursor to China itself cutting a deal with Washington in the early 1970s, leading to massive direct foreign investment as the payoff, creating a juggernaut that today bids to leave U.S. imperialism in the dust.[105]

New Age betrayed the anxiety about this rupture when it claimed—prematurely—in 1960, "there is no 'split' between Russia and China."[106] This was an understandable stance since thwarting either rival was not in the interest of the anti-apartheid movement. Shortly after these words were published, Raymond Mhlaba headed to China. Mao Zedong himself "met and welcomed us", he said of his small delegation. He wanted a view of the split. "I indicated to him," said this wily African, "that we did not want to take sides," a viewpoint that did not withstand the test of time. This was fortunate since in China "we received specialized training in guerilla warfare" and were "taught…how to manufacture and use indigenous weapons," along with "hit-and-run techniques. We learnt to make and use light weapons for these techniques…. most of our training took place in Southern China…."[107]

It took a while for the SACP and ANC to understand what was occurring on this front. The impact of China's veering off course was not instantly evident. But the Africanist prodding, chiding the ANC for being overly sympathetic to Indians and European Communists,

---

102. Rusty Bernstein, *Memory Against Forgetting*, 225, 226.

103. Gerald Horne, *From the Barrel of a Gun: The U.S. and the War Against Zimbabwe, 1965-1980*, Chapel Hill: University of North Carolina Press, 2001.

104. Jeffrey James Byrne, *Mecca of Revolution*, 54.

105. Gerald Horne, *Blows Against the Empire: U.S. Imperialism in Crisis*, New York: International Publishers, 2008.

106. *New Age*, 15 September 1960.

107. *Raymond Mhlaba's Personal Memoirs*, 115.

probably sheds light on why the future president Thabo Mbeki argued in mid-1959 from his Eastern Cape birthplace, Idutywa, that it was "not [the] time to form [a] multi-racial Congress,"[108] which would emerge years later.

This ideological warfare had erupted at an inopportune moment. In April 1961 Mandela was at a Pietermaritzburg conference, where inevitably the ongoing conflict with the PAC would arise.[109] In May 1961 Mandela was on the attack against the Pan Africanist Congress after they rebuked the ANC's plan to stage demonstrations at the end of the month marking rejection of the formation of the so-called Republic of South Africa, an abandonment of the Union and the British Commonwealth alike. A general strike was also planned as Mandela warned that Pretoria was threatening to crush the protests by violence, à la Sharpeville.[110] Perhaps not accidentally, the battle on the PAC front detracted from the campaign's focus on Pretoria.

This moment was also inopportune since the ANC and SACP were taking on new battles. By April 1961 Mandela was designated as Secretary of the "National Action Council," a harbinger of his leadership of the ANC's armed wing, Umkhonto we Sizwe (Spear of the Nation). Tellingly, his picture in this newly minted capacity was placed in *New Age* alongside another of university students demonstrating at the U.S. Embassy in Cape Town, protesting the attempt to destabilize Cuba, whose 1959 revolution was to be of maximum consequence for Southern Africa.[111] Then the words of Raul Rao, the well-known Cuban diplomat, found their way to South Africa when he quoted a message from the anti-Jim Crow activist Robert F. Williams, who declared that since Washington was purportedly "desirous of repelling aggression," their wrongheaded view of Cuba's alleged hemispheric role, "the oppressed Negroes of the South officially request tanks, artillery, [and] bombs" in order to assault "racial tyrants" in Dixie.[112] Williams was bold, but Ray Alexander of the SACP was told by a U.S. national that, sadly, "the mass of people in this country are behind the administration on Cuba."[113]

In short, the battle against racism was heating up on both fronts.

---

108. *New Age*, 18 June 1959.

109. *Fighting Talk*, April 1961.

110. *New Age*, 18 May 1961.

111. *New Age*, 27 April 1961.

112. *New Age*, 4 May 1961.

113. Alice Citron to Ray Alexander, 25 April 1961, C1.5, *Papers of Jack Simons and Ray Alexander, University of Cape Town.*

By June 1961, however, Mandela was lamenting the failure of an ANC initiative: "it was not the national success I had hoped for," he announced regretfully. For Pretoria had imposed a tight and brutal military and police occupation with 10,000 at minimum arrested, as helicopters flashed searchlights from on high. "Never before in our history," said *New Age* "has the demand of the people for an equal share...been voiced so insistently...."[114] In response later that month, Mandela called for non-cooperation with apartheid and announced that he would remain living underground to lead a full-scale campaign aimed toward this goal. He would separate himself from his spouse and children, shutter his law firm and abandon his profession to "live as an outlaw in the land of my birth" in order to fight the regime "inch by inch and mile by mile, until victory is won...." Then in a cry that would resonate in the U.S. he chose to "call on the nations of the world to sever connections and diplomatic relations with South Africa."[115]

His spouse, Winnie Mandela, was said to display "acceptance of Nelson's decision." He was depicted in turn as a man "alive with energy" in "well cut suits" that "fail to hide the broad chest and strong arms" that marked his physiognomy. In 1952 he was one of the first to go to jail, receiving a suspended sentence, then a ban. For several years he was unable to address a meeting or leave Johannesburg. "But all the time his stature grew," it was said knowingly. Now he has "taken the brave decision to go underground." When a reporter journeyed to the Mandela home in Westcliff, Orlando, his spouse laughed when asked about her present unsettled life. Their child Zenani cried for him at times, she confessed, but she added quickly that they had never had a settled life.[116]

By December 1961, Mandela was pictured as "leading the freedom struggle from underground."[117] By August 1962, Houser told "Dear Oliver" Tambo that he had "heard about the arrest of Nelson Mandela and was greatly concerned....we might be able to send $200," though "the demands upon us have been very great with the happenings in Angola, refugee problems, etc."[118] By October Mandela entered the courtroom in Pretoria as most present stood. He appeared wearing what a British observer termed "largely tribal

114. *New Age*, 1 June 1961.

115. *New Age*, 29 June 1961.

116. *New Age*, 13 July 1961.

117. *New Age*, 28 December 1961.

118. George Houser to "Dear Oliver", 17 August 1962, Reel 3, *Oliver Tambo Papers*, University of Witwatersrand-Johannesburg.

dress with the traditional jackal skin," a nod to the percolating Africanist sentiment. He wanted the case remanded since his attorney, the Communist activist Joe Slovo had been confined by the Minister of Justice to Johannesburg and was therefore unable to be present. Though portrayed as "tense," Mandela spoke clearly and presented his case "effectively." The mostly African crowd stood and shouted greetings at him when he left the courtroom. He managed to speak to the Communist Hilda Bernstein cordially as he departed, which upset the British emissary present. "Though we had an amusing talk and much merry laughter," he began, "I came away faintly depressed that it is to these fellow travelers that the defense of such prominent African leaders as Mandela and [Walter] Sisulu is entrusted, who whatever their relationship with Communism (and it is admittedly fairly close), cannot but become progressively indebted to their legal champions and the political allegiances which motivates them."[119]

Just as the Treason Trial backfired to the extent that it drove SACP and ANC leaders closer together, the representation of Mandela by Slovo attained a similar purpose. Born in Lithuania of Jewish heritage, Slovo joined the Communist Party in 1942 and by 1949 married fellow Communist, Ruth First, who was the daughter of party treasurer Julius First. By 1963 he was driven into an exile that meant circuitous stays in London, Angola, Mozambique, and Zambia before returning in triumph by the early 1990s.[120] Mandela himself had served as an apprentice attorney with a firm that included Jewish lawyers. His experience with those like Ruth First helped to disabuse him of his early anticommunism. "Anyone meeting Mandela for the first time," it was reported in 1962, "might have been forgiven for writing him off as a handsome rather superficial but likeable well-dressed young man. They could not have known that he conceived the M Plan—the basis for political organizing" in the country—then there was his "acknowledged work…in the legal field."[121]

This arrest of Mandela was the beginning of a difficult stretch for the ANC, as leaders were driven underground, into exile or prison by the sledgehammer blows of the regime. By mid-1963, Mandela was reported by the U.S. legation as having been moved to Robben Island; it was surmised that his "presence might have agitated the

---

119. Report, 16 October 1962, FO371/161901, National *Archives of United Kingdom -London*.

120. Memorial For Joe Slovo, 18 February 1995, Box 2, Folder 11, *Prexy Nesbitt Papers, Columbia College-Chicago*.

121. *Fighting Talk*, September 1962.

many [PAC] prisoners on the island and that his life might have been endangered thereby…."[122]

Subsequently, Adelaide Tambo, the leader's spouse, recalled that her husband was deflated after Mandela had been detained: "that's when I saw him hurt," she said. "He sat down, and I brought him some tea—I don't think he knew what he was drinking, because his mind was not on the tea…."[123]

But he was not sufficiently deflated to neglect organizing for Mandela's release. Writing from Dar es Salaam in August 1962 he told Houser that the detention of his comrade, this "powerful underground leader in South Africa has increased our traveling and related expenses beyond our means," and making necessary an "appeal" to the ACOA for "substantial aid pending [a] speaking tour in U.S."[124]

This was the beginning of an organized ANC exile presence. By 1961 Mac Maharaj, one of Mandela's closest comrades, was in East Germany for military training. Linkages with Prague via the World Federation of Trade Unions also proved helpful to the ANC and SACP, he recalled; ditto for the Berlin-based World Federation of Democratic Women and the Budapest-headquartered International Union of Students. Since Maharaj worked at a quarry as a youth, he had already learned the use of dynamite—though "shooting practice" proved quite helpful.[125] The German Democratic Republic, he said, was "almost as generous" as Moscow toward the ANC. On a personal level it was there "for the first time" that his "color was not at issue, at least not overtly. He discovered his dignity as a human being." Other cadre were sent for similar training to other Eastern European nations and China. The ANC's Communist ties proved crucial here, for at one time or another, says Maharaj, party members included Walter Sisulu, Thomas Nkobi, Alfred Nzo "and most likely for a brief period, Nelson Mandela…." "Comrades were going for training in the socialist countries," says Maharaj, "and were coming back well disposed toward Communism. So most trained members of MK [ANC's armed wing] were Communists."[126] Tim

122. Report, 21 June 1963, RG 59, Central Foreign Policy Files, Box 4032, *NARA-CP.*

123. Undated Interview with Adelaide Tambo, Reel 4, *Tambo Papers.*

124. Oliver Tambo to ACOA, 10 August 1962, Box 94, Series III, *ACOARA.*

125. Oral History, Mac Maharaj, 9 October 2000, *University of Connecticut-Storrs.*

126. Padraig O'Malley, *Shades of Difference: Mac Maharaj and the Struggle for South Africa*, New York: Viking, 2007, 88, 90, 63, 363.

Jenkin, born in 1948, also was trained in the GDR. There he learned, as he recalled later, "how to plant a mine, how to create a hand grenade...how to create an explosive device...how to mix your own chemicals...."[127]

By 1964, the SACP noted that it was "keenly conscious of the solidarity of the support both moral and practical, rendered to our struggle by the Soviet Union and other socialist countries."[128]

It had been a serpentine path for Mandela. After the 1960 vote remaking the Union as a republic, he chaired a conference designed to respond. He was the commander when the ANC's newly formed military wing, colloquially known as MK, conducted its first operation on 16 December 1961, an attack on government buildings in Johannesburg, Pretoria, and Port Elizabeth. Since the nation was so heavily dependent on foreign capital, such sabotage was aimed toward frightening it away, weakening apartheid. By 1962 Mandela was in Ethiopia seeking support: "my tour was a success," he said, "I started to make a study of the art of war and revolution and whilst abroad, underwent a course in military training...."[129] Joe Matthews claims that he aided Mandela's journey abroad due to his ties to Botswana, arranging an Ethiopian passport for the ANC leader, and that ties to the SACP—Matthews says he was recruited by Kotane in 1958—also proved helpful.[130]

Mandela's comrades were likewise on the run. By January 1962 Albert Xuma had expired and his widow departed for North Carolina. "You leave as quickly as you can" after his death, he had advised. "I did get telephone calls after he died," Madie Hall Xuma said, "telling me to get out of South Africa. I was glad to get back," she added with relief. "I felt safer in America," where she would live for the last two decades of her life.[131]

"I read of your escape to Bechuanaland," said Mary Louise Hooper to Tambo in May 1960. She was writing from San Francisco, working

---

127. Oral History, Tim Jenkin, 6 October 2000, *University of Connecticut-Storrs.*

128. "Strive for World Communist Unity," Statement by the Central Committee of [SACP]," *African Communist*, January 1964, in *South African Communists Speak: Documents from the History of the South African Communist Party, 1915-1980* London: Inkululeko, 1981, 335-341, 337

129. Nelson Mandela, *Let Freedom Reign: The Words of Nelson Mandela*, Northampton, Massachusetts: Interlink, 2010, 39, 44, 47

130. Oral History, Joe Matthews, 2 October 2000, *University of Connecticut-Storrs.* Cf. 1964 Notes, Box 1, Folder 2, *Mary Benson Research Materials about the African National Congress of South Africa, UCLA*: "Luthuli said of Joe Matthews—wouldn't trust him."

131. Emily Herring Wilson, *Hope and Dignity*, 148.

with the Manhattan-based "South Africa Defense Fund" and eager to arrange engagements for him. One was at a Los Angeles synagogue. Her financial backing could not be discounted either given the straits in which the organization found itself. "It has been my custom," she said, "to send regular support for an organizer (30 pounds a month) and an additional 15 pounds a month to assist with those of the ANC who have been banished;" addressing the money to Duma Nokwe, "as he instructed...." She also made an offhand comment bound to raise tension with the "Africanists." "This is the strange thing," she began. "Ghana has helped many other countries, including Nyasaland, Southern Rhodesia and Angola but it never has given a penny to South Africa. I never could figure out why...." Perhaps naïveté prevented her from recognizing that in Accra there was more enthusiasm about the "Africanists."[132] Bawo Andrew Mlangeni of the ANC and SACP admitted later that Ghana was a PAC "stronghold."[133] Officially, Adelaide Tambo agreed with Hooper. She was asked about Nkrumah, "Why was he pro-PAC?" She disagreed though she noted revealingly that while in Accra, she was asked repeatedly why were there so many "whites" involved in the struggle, with so many seduced by the very name "Pan Africanist."[134]

Hooper knew, for example, that "especially among American Negroes one hears quite frequently lately criticism of Chief [Luthuli] as a 'moderate'," a bad word then in Black America. "I was foolish enough to fear for a moment that you might be influenced by criticism of this kind," she told Tambo, though it was unavoidably true that the rise of "Black Power" would serve to make the PAC ever more popular in Black America—perhaps even more popular there than in South Africa. Again, ever faithful, she continued "sending... money" to Johannesburg.[135] (Fortunately, she was not alone in donating. In 1962 Hosea Kutako and Samuel Witbooi, writing from Windhoek, successfully importuned Houser for "funds for a case against me and Chief...Witbooi....")[136]

---

132. Mary Louise Hooper to Oliver Tambo, 3 May 1960, Reel 3, *Oliver Tambo Papers, University of Witwatersrand-Johannesburg*.

133. Oral History, Bawo Andrew Mlangeni, 5 November 2003, *University of Connecticut-Storrs*.

134. Undated Interview with Adelaide Tambo.

135. Mary Louise Hooper to "Dear Oliver," 14 July 1960, Box 2, *Mary Louise Hooper Papers*.

136. Hosea Kutako and Samuel Witbooi to George Houser, 28 June 1962, Box 94, Series III, *American Committee on Africa Records Addendum*.

But funds were not offered to all. "I really wonder how much longer we will be able to pretend to get along with them," she said irritably about the PAC in mid-1961.[137]

By 1960 Tambo's effort to obtain a U.S. visa at the embassy in Cairo was refused,[138] as Washington continued to bank on splitting the ANC-SACP alliance, not least through the anticommunism of "Africanists" and the likes of Patrick Duncan. Eventually, however, Tambo was granted entry to the U.S. He was not deflated by the ideological divide, engaging in a round-robin of meetings in Manhattan with a stellar cast of affluent donors, including Cora and Peter Weiss and Peggy Dulany of the Rockefeller family.[139] The chasm between the PAC and the ANC had been growing since February 1962, when the attempted united front crumbled, creating more problems for the ANC and necessitating more energetic fund-raising and lobbying, notably in the U.S. where the PAC maintained one of their strongest bases of support.[140]

Subsequently, Vus Make—better known in the U.S. as a former intimate partner of artist, Maya Angelou—told an inquiring scholar that it was "at the instigation of Kwame Nkrumah" that a united front was formed in 1961 between the ANC and PAC. "It lasted only about two years," said this PAC cadre, who acknowledged the obvious: "Africanist ideological affinities with many African Americans" meant "close ties" between them and his PAC. Ghana, said Make, was the "ideological inspiration of the PAC", confirming Hooper's suppositions.[141]

---

137. Mary Louise Hooper to Oliver Tambo, 6 June 1961, Box 2, *Mary Louise Hooper Papers.*

138. Homer Jack to Dear Friend, 7 June 1960, Box 14, *International Affairs Division, Country Files, AFL-CIO, University of Maryland-College Park.*

139. Luli Callinicos, *Oliver Tambo*, 274.

140. Luli Callinicos, *Oliver Tambo*, 327.

141. Vus Make to Kevin Gaines, circa 18 August 2002, Box 18, *Richard Gibson Papers.* Make added: "I had no working relationship with *Freedomways*", a popular journal of the era in the U.S. where Communists wielded influence (full disclosure: I was a frequent contributor to their pages). Make "had a good friendly relationship with Malcolm X until his death," as for "Rob[ert] F. Williams," a noted proponent of "Black Power", "I knew him well and with my PAC comrade David Sibeko, actively worked with Milton Henry and Richard Gibson in London to get the U.S. government to honor the agreement for his return to the States," which occurred. Despite the felonious charges that had sent Williams fleeing from Jim Crow North Carolina to exile in Cuba, then China, he managed to escape imprisonment upon his return, possibly because of his closeness to China at a time when an entente

For its part, the SACP was relentless in assailing the U.S. and its role in bolstering the PAC—a critique that was reciprocated in kind[142] –dooming this brief alliance to an ineluctable failure.

"Nothing makes greater nonsense of America's claim to the 'leader of the free world' and the home of democracy and liberty than the outrageous treatment of our brothers and sisters in the United States." Such was the conclusion of the *African Communist*, the SACP journal, in mid-1962. "Lynchings and Jim Crow laws" were rampant. "Many of the worst practices of Verwoerd and other white supremacists in Africa are paralleled by the treatment of those whom the Americans call Negroes," the periodical said in an implicit attempt to embrace this persecuted group of U.S. citizens as Africans. In a typical display of insight, this journal observed "the white 'planters' of the South, the colons of Algeria, the 'white highlanders' [in Kenya] and the white supremacists of South Africa have an essential unity of outlook and purpose." This class *cum* race solidarity by oppressors, it was said, served to "provoke bitter indignation on the part of the African people," meaning the "time" had arrived "for us to take practical steps to assist" their brethren in the U.S., a conclusion reached by citing the Black Communist William Patterson.[143]

By early 1962 Hooper had connected with Tambo in Oslo, where Chief Luthuli was to be awarded the Nobel Prize. She "enjoyed particularly working with Oliver," as "we worked just as hard as I have ever worked in my life," and they "did not sleep more than 3 or 4 hours several nights." "Everyone from ambassadors on down [were] phoning me frantically for appointments...my suite was a regular mad-house...." There were "quite a few letters in French and German which I was glad to be able to translate for Chief," she said

---

with U.S. imperialism was being brokered. When Williams was stuck in London in an effort to return home, Gibson was identified as his "friend" who had "known him for 10 years...." See *New York Times*, 9 September 1969 and *London Evening Standard*, 9 September 1969.

142. Richard Gibson, *African Liberation Movements: Contemporary Struggles Against White Minority Rule*, New York: Oxford University Press, 1972, 55. Gibson, and thought to be close to U.S. intelligence, was born in Los Angeles in 1931 and educated at Kenyon College in Ohio. He claimed to be related to famed Negro painter, Henry Tanner and also asserted that "in September 1961 I next saw Malcolm [X] again," after encountering him earlier at "Harlem's Hotel Theresa as I led Fidel Castro and his delegation into the building...." He says that he introduced the two: See Biography and undated report, Box 18, *Richard Gibson Papers*.

143. B. Pela, "Apartheid in America," *African Communist*, (Number 10, July-August 1962): 39-44, 39.

modestly. But already she was exhibiting signs of a melancholy that would ultimately sideline her: "[I was] more lonely than usual after my return from Oslo," she confided. "Things do not go well in my personal life...."[144] Yet, she confessed, "this work for South Africa has become my whole life.... I work often 16 hours a day and usually seven days a week on it...."[145]

Her presence in Oslo was not as unusual as it may first appear. The liberal U.S.-born anticommunist Allard Lowenstein was there too. Tambo—who was designated "Chief Luthuli's right-hand man" at the Nobel Laureate ceremony[146]—told Lowenstein that he was "personally keen that as many of our friends in America as possible should join our group at Oslo...."[147]

Hooper was an effective advocate for the ANC. It was unclear if she included in her 16-hour days her appearance at the aforementioned benefit for the Treason Trial defendants in Berkeley, a performance of the play, *Lost in the Stars*. The star of the production, a local firefighter, was supposed to make a speech about the accused but, she said feelingly, "all he could do was weep, so he called me to the stage—quite unexpectedly—and asked me to say something....I had been weeping all through the performance," she recollected, and through a vale of tears, "all I could think of to say was 'Afrika'!" It was a "strange experience,"[148] but also affecting.

Hooper may have been working too hard, setting aside the depth and profundity of the problem of apartheid. Even before Oslo she admitted to being "close to the verge of what we call a 'nervous breakdown.' I could not even concentrate on driving the car safely...."[149]

For his part, Tambo referred to her movingly as "My Dear Louisa" as she was "one so close & so dear to me as you are," then adding cryptically, "I do not keep copies of my handwritten letters...."[150]

144. Mary Louise Hooper to "Dear Friend," 3 February 1962, Box 1, *Mary Louise Hooper Papers.*

145. Mary Louise Hooper to Oliver Tambo, 3 Augsut 1960, Box 2, *Mary Louise Hooper Papers.*

146. Letter to "Dear Helen," no date, Box 141, *Allard Lowenstein Papers, University of North Carolina-Chapel Hill.*

147. O.R. Tambo to Allard Lowenstein, 20 November 1961, Box 141, *Allard Lowenstein Papers.*

148. Mary Louise Hooper to W.Z. Conco, 17 September 1959, Box 2, *Mary Louise Hooper Papers.*

149. Mary Louise Hooper to "My Dearest Sister", 27 February 1958, Box 2, *Mary Louise Hooper Papers.*

150. Oliver Tambo to "My Dear Louisa," 7 July 1960, Box 2, *Mary Louise Hooper Papers.*

This was probably a wise choice since their correspondence was surveilled. "What happened to your letter is quite mysterious to me," Tambo related in mid-1960, "and I am suspecting foul play."[151] "Looks as if Joe's mail is tapped," said Hooper in early 1961, referring to the younger Matthews. His letters had been "intercepted," meaning his "correspondence is no longer safe from being opened...."[152]

Hooper's correspondence was worthy of snooping from imperialism's viewpoint. When Nkrumah advisor George Padmore expired, she was in the elite company of Jomo Kenyatta of Kenya and Nnamdi Azikiwe of Nigeria—founding fathers both—and both among the select few to receive cablegrams.[153]

Increasingly, Africans were making their way to reside in the U.S., which could reduce the viability of Hooper's role as a trusted intermediary. By February 1962, Ezekiel Mphahlele was in Boston. He was unimpressed, terming it a "hideous city": "the town is full of itself with the history of the American Revolution," he said contemptuously but not inaccurately. At the campus of the Massachusetts Institute of Technology, he encountered fellow writer Lewis Nkosi, who was similarly "miserable" and "how very eager to run out of the U.S." But he remained. "At least England has something to offer intellectually," unlike the U.S. They spent "long hours together talking about Americans who look like people in a nasty hole without knowing it...." He was disappointed that some "American Negroes" were "ashamed to speak of such great Negroes as W.E.B. Du Bois and Paul Robeson...." The Communist Party there was "getting hell...." U.S. nationals were generally "very easy to make friends with," and they "also make enemies easily...." Racism "embarrasses them very much and yet they don't exert as much effort as they are capable of towards uprooting this plague...." He slammed anticommunism and the general ignorance of Africa, both of which were pervasive. Mphahlele knew James Baldwin, the celebrated Negro writer, who he conversed with in Paris and may have inherited his sourness about Jim Crow.[154] He also knew the SACP member Ray Alexander,

151. Oliver Tambo to Mary Louise Hooper, 26 July 1960, Box 2, *Mary Louise Hooper Papers*.

152. Mary Louise Hooper to Oliver Tambo, 2 February 1961, Box 2,

153. Leslie James, "What We Put in Black and White: George Padmore and the Practice of Imperial Politics," Ph.d. dissertation, London School of Economics, 2012, 237.

154. *Fighting Talk*, February 1962.

who helped to publicize his fiction and who he told, "let us hope that one day evil will disappear from our bleeding land...."[155]

During this period, there was also the specter of Moscow looming over the ANC's bilateral relations, as those with any tie there were immediately scorned as "puppets" of the despised Reds. Even the NAACP, which had relations of sorts to the ANC, covered its right flank by cooperating with a program that was seeking to bring to the U.S., Cape Town's George Andrew Manuel, author of "The Communist Threat to the Coloured People."[156] Even ACOA, whose liberal anticommunist credentials were unassailable, was so accused. Hooper, who toiled on their behalf for years, met a woman who had donated to the group until she "discovered that there was so much Communistic activity in the ACOA that the church had been compelled to withdraw its support. I was simply open-mouthed."[157] Conservatives found it hard to understand why the ACOA was in close touch with alleged "Communist fronts" e.g. the ANC and MPLA. One pro-Portuguese colonial sympathizer red-baited Houser and ACOA, and then went a step further to denounce Holden Roberto—CIA asset—as "pro-Communist."[158] The Negro writer Richard Gibson—subsequently thought to be close to U.S. intelligence services and "Black Power" advocates and "Maoists" alike-- accused the ANC of being captured by "the Russians."[159] (The activist Prexy Nesbitt was outraged by Gibson's misleading analysis: "it can only confuse," he asserted, scorning Gibson's "Maoist pose," a stance that became a left-wing cover for collaborating with U.S. imperialism.)[160]

Gibson's reproach was indicative of the siege endured by the ANC. London maintained a detailed record of real and imagined Communist activity in Africa, including radio broadcasts, diplomatic missions,

155. Ezekiel Mphahlele, 15 October 1959, C1.5, *Papers of Jack Simons and Ray Alexander, University of Cape Town.*

156. Material on George Andrew Manuel, 1 September 1960, Box !!!A35, *NAACP Papers.*

157. Mary Louise Hooper to Houser, 15 October 1959, Box 2, *Mary Louise Hooper Papers.*

158. Portuguese American Committee on Foreign Affairs, "The Communists and Angola," circa 1961, *University of Kansas-Lawrence.*

159. Richard Gibson, *African Liberation Movements*, 1972, 75.

160. Prexy Nesbitt, "Toward Understanding National Liberation Movements," *Africa Today*, 19 (Number 4, Autumn 1972): 83-88, 85.

technical aid, and the like.[161] With barely disguised contempt, apartheid leader Niel Barnard, called Mandela a "crypto-Communist."[162]

Intelligence agencies played this angle promiscuously. After Mandela was arrested in 1962 a "secret" message from the British embassy in Pretoria opined that the "theory most widely held" concerning this setback, "is that the Communist wing of the ANC betrayed Mandela as part of their plan to dominate the ANC…." Then after mulling this over, the idea was reached that the "in view [of the] known co-operation between Mandela and the Communist sympathizers, this theory does not seem altogether likely…." Brightening, the analysis concluded that more worthy of exploitation was the "feud between the PAC and the ANC," which "may have had more to do" with Mandela's detention.[163]

161. Report, 1960-1963, DO154/51, *National Archives of United Kingdom-London*.

162. Niel Barnard as told to Tobie Wiese, *Secret Revolution: Memoirs of a Spy Boss*, Cape Town: Tafelberg, 2015, 201.

163. Report, 18 August 1962, FO371/161901, *National Archives of United Kingdom-London*.

Chapter 10

Pivotal Years, 1963-1964

1963 and 1964 were pivotal years in the transatlantic struggle against Jim Crow and apartheid. With his remarkable address in Washington, D.C. in August 1963, Dr. King soared to the forefront of the U.S. movement. Given his less than rigid adherence to the gospel of anticommunism, this augured well for the ANC and it could certainly be anticipated that—contrary to the NAACP—the cleric would not seek to promote ties between "moderate" Africans and the CIA. This was also the year that JFK was assassinated, thereby inaugurating a period of instability in the U.S. that saw escalating anti-Jim Crow and antiwar unrest, boding well for anti-apartheid too.

Dr. King was cooperating more closely with the ACOA, however. Weeks after his trailblazing speech, Houser archly told him, "I had a dream, just like you did," a reference to his eloquent words. "I dreamed that [King] appeared before the U.N. Committee on Apartheid and made a tremendous impact on the international level," a nightmare for the White House.[1] By December 1964 Dr. King was to be found in London: "I understand there are South Africans here, tonight," he said welcomingly. "We feel a powerful sense of identification with those in far deadlier struggle for freedom in South Africa," he continued. "We have honored Chief Luthuli for his leadership," since "clearly there is much in Mississippi and Alabama to remind South Africans of their own country…." Ecumenically, he praised "today's great leaders—Nelson Mandela and Robert Sobukwe…." Because there was a "danger of a race war," he continued, "we in America and Britain have a unique responsibility…." Hence, "if the UK and the US decided tomorrow morning not to buy South African goods, not to buy South African gold, to put an embargo on oil; if

1. George Houser to Dr. King, 4 September 1963, Box 5, *George Houser Papers, Michigan State University-East Lansing*.

our investors and capitalists would withdraw their support for that racial tyranny, then apartheid would be brought to an end."[2]

This was an essential matter. By early 1964, South African gold and foreign assets totaled the highest level in history—three-quarters of a billion U.S. dollars. By 1963, one account had U.S. companies in South African industry averaging a 27% profit. Foreign investment was cascading into the nation as a result. Both General Motors and Ford were jostling to see which would be the leading investor in auto production, spending hundreds of millions in the process. U.S. investment, according to this source, was over $600 million.[3]

Writing from Dar es Salaam, the capital of the regional movement, Bill Sutherland of the Quakers, was thinking about how to intervene in this disturbing pattern, requesting a "tried and able group of Afro-Americans from the Birmingham scene," site of racist tumult in Alabama that captured global headlines, to come to Tanzania—though he quickly clarified he actually meant "the whole movement" in Dixie; they should be "brought over here with strategists like Bayard [Rustin]," Dr. King's troubleshooter. He referred to recent remarks by Uganda's leader, Milton Obote, and Kenya's Jomo Kenyatta, both of whom "have been trying to push for the struggle in the South." This could mean a "realistic driving project with snowball potential." He was sure that the Namibians and Mondlane – "even Nkomo" of Zimbabwe—"would listen." Unfortunately, it seemed like an aim of this otherwise laudable project was to divert the region from armed struggle into a "nonviolence programme" palatable in Washington and of questionable relevance.[4]

Nonetheless, Sutherland was responding to real trends. "Many Americans have passed through Dar," as of 1964 said Janet Mondlane, the U.S.-born wife of the Mozambican leader, which augured well for a budding alliance between U.S. Negroes and Africans.[5]

Sutherland's colleague A.J. Muste was simultaneously seeking to establish a non-violent center in Northern Rhodesia (now Zambia).[6]

2. Remarks by Dr. King, 7 December 1964, Box 71, Series II, *ACOA Papers.*

3. James Brewer to Richard Nolte, 25 January 1964, Box 52, *Records of Institute of Current and World Affairs, Columbia University.*

4. "Bill" to ACOA, 31 May 1963, Box 142, Series III, *ACOARA.*

5. Janet Mondlane to George Houser, 3 April 1964, Box 142, Series III, *ACOA Papers.*

6. A.J. Muste to Lyle Tatum, 13 June 1963, Box 149, Series III, *ACOARA*: Sutherland, said Muste, continually hectored Julius Nyerere, the Tanzanian leader, about reputed violations of civil liberties' deprivations. See also A, J, Muste to Lyle Tatum, 13 June 1963, ISD, Africa Program, *AFSC*: Sutherland "had written letters to Julius" Nyerere "about restrictions on civil liberties

Still, associating anti-Jim Crow with anti-colonialism—in Dar es Salaam no less—was a path-breaking course to propose.

Fleeing apartheid repression and arriving in the U.S. because of the perception that the easing of Jim Crow allowed for more opportunity, more Africans were arriving in the U.S. steadily, which had the added benefit of influencing U.S. Negroes. By 1964 the poet and writer then known as William Kgositsile was residing in Manhattan (he would eventually wed an African American, Melba Johnson). "For the past two years," he said, "South African students in the [U.S.] have addressed various groups of Americans. Thousands of these Americans were shocked," he declared, "not only by apartheid practices but also by learning that America has done a great deal to assist the Verwoerd regime." He was part of the recently formed "Student Aid Association of South African Abroad," which included the famed musicians Hugh Masekela as Vice President and Jonas Gwangwa as Treasurer. Singer Miriam Makeba was Honorary Patron, and indicative of the resonance of apartheid was the presence as Patrons of Hollywood celebrities, e.g. Harry Belafonte, Marlon Brando, Diahann Carroll, Sidney Poitier, and Pernell Roberts.[7] Kgositsile's arrival accelerated an ongoing alliance between and among African and U.S. Negro writers that came to include Richard Rive, Langston Hughes, Lewis Nkosi, Bessie Head, James Baldwin, Gil Scott Heron, Toni Morrison, Alice Walker, Richard Wright, and others of prominence.[8]

By 1964 Stanislaus Sangwene was studying at Cornell University in Ithaca, New York. There he encountered Dennis Worrall, who eventually became a parliamentarian in South Africa. "I found him very much liberal," said the African, "but very patronizing of course," so "we clashed a great deal"[9]—and New Yorkers learned directly that there was no unanimity of viewpoint about apartheid. The Pretoria legation thought more highly of Worrall; he spent "five

---

and such things. Bayard [Rustin] was apprehensive that this had offended Julius. Julius brought up the subject himself and said it was a good thing for him and others in his position to have people like Bill around......now Bill has a job working with refugees...."

7. William Kgositsile in "The South African Students Journal," September 1964, Reel 36, *ACOA Papers.*

8. Stephanie Pierre Raymond Robolin, *Grounds of Engagement: Apartheid-Era African American and South African Writing*, Urbana: University of Illinois Press, 2015, 1, 24-25, 37, 91, 94, 117, 126.

9. Oral History, Stanislaus Sangweni, 6 July 2001, *University of Connecticut-Storrs.*

years in the U.S. as a graduate student," it was reported, which had "given him an understanding of American life."[10]

This increased presence of exiles was quite helpful in eroding ignorance. By early 1964 Mary Louise Hooper, the anti-apartheid leader, "had not been able to work because of illness during most of 1963" but what was preoccupying her was "how ignorant most Americans" were about apartheid, as most "know next to nothing" about this system.[11]

Suggestive of the renewed anti-apartheid atmosphere was a May 1964 demonstration at the South African consulate in Manhattan at 60th Street and Madison Avenue, where the NAACP joined local activists in protest.[12] Also suggestive and intimidatingly designed to forestall such activism was the visit to the NAACP office by an FBI agent Melvin Flohr after a Soviet youth official had visited the same office.[13]

At this point, it seemed as though an unstoppable confluence of mighty waves were flowing from North America and Africa. By 1964, John Lewis—a future Congressman from Atlanta, then a militant with the shock troops known as the Student Non-Violent Coordinating Committee [SNCC]—was headed to Accra, where he and his fellow traveler Donald Harris conferred with Shirley Graham Du Bois. "For some three hours," they reported, "we discussed the possibilities of a strong link between the Rights Movement in the States and a direct contact with the African countries...." Their plan was to "keep Ghana people informed about what was going on in the States...." There they also spent time with the PAC: they were "received warmly and enthusiastically and barely could escape within two hours of our arrival...." Julian Mayfield, the writer then exiled from the U.S. in Ghana, suggested that they travel to Cairo, "the most important single center on the continent...." Malcolm X had just departed Accra a few days before their arrival and "had made fantastic impressions...." Then it was southward to Lusaka: "everyone was quite pleased to meet us," they said, "and were especially happy that that the U.S. Rights Struggle would be represented at the Zambian independence" soon to be launched. At the office

10. Embassy-Pretoria to Secretary of State, RG 59, Central Foreign Policy Files: Political and Defense, Box 2463, *NARA-CP*.

11. Mary Louise Hooper to Mindy Msimang, 2 January 1964, Box 2, *Mary Louise Hooper Papers*.

12. Press Release, 21 May 1964, Box IIIA35, *NAACP Papers*.

13. Maurice White to Roy Wilkins, 11 August 1964, Box IIIA32, *NAACP Papers*.

of the party of Kenneth Kaunda, they "spent many hours smoking many cigarettes in heated discussions...." These exchanges took place among exiles from "South Africa, Mozambique, Rhodesia, Angola [and] Basutoland," and there was much "joking about the kind of white man that angered us most," a shared transatlantic concern. These "intense nervous people...knew the inside of many jails and the loneliness of being separated from family and friends...." They were convinced that "SNCC will not be forgotten very soon in Zambia...." Then they hopped on Kaunda's plane and headed northward to Nairobi and Cairo. In the former city, "the first person we saw on arrival at our hotel was Malcolm X," who had just jetted in from Dar es Salaam.

They held a "very important meeting," said Lewis and Harris. At that point, the former Nation of Islam leader had been to 11 nations, conferring with heads of state and addressing parliaments. The discussion centered on Malcolm's proposal to bring the case of African Americans before the U.N., a replay of Robeson's earlier initiative, though that was little recognized at the time. Unfortunately, there was little "support from the civil rights voices" back home, who were certain that there had been a decisive shift toward Negro freedom, a misplaced notion in retrospect.

In Cairo they met with the PAC again for three hours. One of the first questions they received from those across the table was their "organization's relationship to Malcolm X," the new touchstone. Then David Du Bois, Shirley Graham Du Bois' son, arranged for them to meet with the "American Muslim Student Union," which was "composed of all Afro-Americans" (or "former Afro-Americans") as "many of their members were former Black Muslims," now integrating into Egyptian society. Cairo proved to be "the most important stop we made" and David Du Bois was "our best single contact." They learned that on the occasion of Dr. King's trailblazing speech of 28 August 1963, 1700 marched in Cairo to the U.S. embassy, with marchers from 19 different nations, where they delivered a protest to the ambassador. "A great lack in the Rights Movement," they concluded "has been the complete failure to utilize the great number of African diplomats that are constantly in this country," meaning the U.S.[14]

This opinion was a source of sleepless nights in Washington. In the early Cold War era, there was a real fear of international pressure on Jim Crow, one of the impetuses for the so-called "Bricker

14. Report by John Lewis and Donald Harris, 14 December 1964, Box 55, Series II, *ACOA Papers*.

Amendment," meant to insulate the U.S. from U.N. and other supposed interference in the nation's internal affairs. The "Bricker Amendment," said conservative legal icon Clarence Manion, was the "hottest issue since the Civil War."[15] Seemingly hyperbolic, this assessment was common in Dixie.[16] The sidelining of Robeson, who famously had sought to drag Washington into the global dock for perpetrating "genocide" against U.S. Negroes, was thought to have eliminated this global threat.[17] By 1970 Manion was still seeking to "prevent the resurrection of the Genocide Treaty"; a close colleague was "confident that we had had that one dead and buried but the internationalists never give up"[18]—which was (and is still) true. Manion then marched to Congress and told the Senate Foreign Relations Committee that this treaty meant that the "mere charge of 'racism'... would subject Americans to trial in an international court without the protections of the United States Constitution," and potentially criminalized cozying up to Pretoria.[19]

* * *

Back in the U.S. Mary Louise Hooper continued to be a chief liaison for the ANC, at variance with SNCC's budding tie to PAC. "Oliver Tambo of South Africa always stays at her house when he is here for work at the United Nations," said Houser. He was unsure if "Holden [Roberto] has met her or not"—probably not given the ANC's standoffish attitude toward him, though "she was at a meeting we arranged for him [Roberto] when he was here" in the U.S.[20] Roberto was the CIA's man in Angola and, coincidentally, a friend of Houser, a relationship that would come to haunt him. Subsequently, this Angolan whose dark glasses routinely shaded his shifty eyes later told his friends in the U.S. Congress that, "I was privileged to spend my younger years under the guidance of American and British missionaries. In 1957 through my contact with an American missionary,

---

15. *Denver Post*, 7 November 1953, Box 62, *Clarence Manion Papers, Chicago History Museum.*

16. See 1956 mail, Box 83, FS 3 SS1, *James Eastland Papers*, University of Mississippi-Oxford.

17. Frank E. Holman, "Story of the Bricker Amendment", New York: Committee for Constitutional Government, 1954, Box 62, *Clarence Manion Papers.*

18. Clarence Manion to Alfred J. Schweppe, 17 February 1970, Box 68, *Clarence Manion Papers.*

19. Testimony of Clarence Manion, Senate Foreign Relations Committee, 24 April 1970, Box 68, *Clarence Manion Papers.*

20. George Houser to Ian Gilchrist, 10 February 1964, Box 79, *ACOA Papers.*

I was introduced to an American diplomat"—Roger Bearce; and it was he who "arranged for me to come to the United States in 1959,"[21] where he made contacts that were to benefit him handsomely while bedeviling Angolans.

Then serving at the U.N., Adlai Stevenson—who had also expressed concern about Dr. King addressing the U.N. on apartheid[22]—was forwarded a memo reflecting these cross-currents. Prepared shortly after the May 1963 conflagration in Alabama, this ambassador was apprised that "reports from Ethiopia and Camerouns [sic] suggest that regular press and radio coverage have left a negative impression of United States' race relations...." A Nigerian commentator says the U.S. was now "exposed" as "a striking bundle of contradictions, pretenses and hooliganism," not to mention "brigandry and gangsterism [sic]." The consensus from the continent was that "even Verwoerd, with all his inhumanity would find it hard to break the record...of God's own country."[23]

The apprehension about Dr. King addressing the U.N. and linking Jim Crow and apartheid then shifted by 1964 to worries he would do the same thing in Scandinavia, where he was to become a Nobel Laureate. President Johnson was instructed nervously by aide Lee White about "statements" made by Dr. King "abroad about an economic blockade of the Union of South Africa [sic] and a perhaps unfortunate linkage of Mississippi and South Africa...."[24]

The State Department was panicking. Citing the hysterical reports of the *Cape Times* and the *Johannesburg Sunday Times*, the legation in Cape Town concluded that there was a deal just brokered "in which American Negroes will use their balance of power position in American elections to pressure [Washington] for more active steps against apartheid in return for moral support by the African states for the

21. Testimony of Holden Roberto, "The Struggle for Freedom in Angola," Hearing Before the Task Force on Foreign Affairs, Republican Study Committee, U.S. House of Representatives, 10 April 1986, Box 11, OA 26258 16591, *Carl Anderson Files, Ronald Reagan Presidential Library, Simi Valley, California.*

22. Adlai Stevenson to State Department, 3 June 1963, Box 159, *Papers of President Kennedy, National Security Files.*

23. Memorandum Prepared by IRS/USIA, 16 May 1963, Box 340, *Adlai Stevenson Papers, Princeton University*. See also **Times** of Nigeria, 15 May 1963

24. Lee White to President Johnson, 18 December 1964, Box 71, *Papers of Lyndon B. Johnson, White House Central File, Subject Files Gen Co 296, Lyndon B. Johnson Presidential Library.*

civil rights struggle in the U.S., through needling statements and diplomacy."[25]

Washington, in sum, was fearful of enhanced exposure of the obvious confluence between Jim Crow and apartheid. In June 1963 the National Security Council was apoplectic in contemplating the prospect that Dr. King would appear at the U.N. to denounce apartheid, leaving in its wake an implicit condemnation of Dixie (or worse, an explicit one).[26] For Washington, this was a nightmare scenario: being draped in the ragged racism of apartheid, while being flayed by the whip of Jim Crow—all before a global audience.

This matter was sufficiently weighty for the Secretary of State Dean Rusk to contact, in "confidential" terms, the president himself. Fortunately, the relevant politico at the U.N. who would have a say on King's appearance was a Costa Rican who "cooperated with" the U.S. and would instruct Dr. King to "confine his public testimony entirely to South Africa," though—unmistakably—there were "previous instances in which Americans appearing before the Committee have veered into criticism of the domestic United States racial situation" and inexorably, some uncooperative "members of the Committee" would "make it difficult for Dr. King to avoid being drawn into a discussion of United States racial problems...." Secretary Rusk was adamant: "I have serious reservations about the desirability of Dr. King's appearing before the U.N. Committee in view of the danger that our domestic racial policies will be made the focus." This "would be unfortunate," he said, if it seemed that Dr. King was "in some sense appealing to the United Nations for assistance. You may wish to take this up with Dr. King," he informed the president. "Mention to him the serious implications of his appearance"[27]—a replay of U.S. Communists dragging Washington before the U.N. on charges of genocide against African Americans a little more than a decade earlier.

As Dr. King was preparing his epochal remarks in early August 1963, the JFK regime was in a familiar bind: how to craft a U.N. resolution that would satisfy Pretoria and Accra alike. In a "confidential" "memorandum for the President," Harlan Cleveland was

25. William Witt to Secretary of State, 10 June 1963, RG 59, Central Foreign Policy File, Box 4029, *NARA-CP*. See also *Cape Times*, 3 June, 4 June and 6 June 1963 and *Johannesburg Sunday Times*, 2 June 1963.

26. Adlai Stevenson to State Department, 3 June 1963, Box 159, *Papers of President Kennedy, National Security Files, John F. Kennedy Presidential Library*.

27. Dean Rusk to John F. Kennedy, 21 June 1963, Box 159, *Papers of President Kennedy, National Security Files, Joohn F. Kennedy Presidential Library*.

twisting into a pretzel by efforts to assuage Ghana, Morocco, and the Philippines and their stringent anti-apartheid resolution. "The boycott language is quite unacceptable," he sniffed, though premature might have been a more precise term, since boycotts aimed toward apartheid were to sweep like wildfire through the international community in coming years. The U.S. would "abstain" if "economic sanctions" were included in the resolution, he insisted. With typical U.S. arrogance he announced that "we could live with" a ban on "strategic minerals of direct military value," a loophole that swallowed the supposed reservation. This ban, in any case, would be inapplicable to machine tools and civilian vehicles, among other items. As of that moment, there were only six votes for the Accra demarche—Ghana itself, Morocco, USSR, China, the Philippines, and Venezuela while coordination with the colonial behemoths, London and Paris, left Cleveland assured that Pretoria again would be protected.[28]

Washington was not wholly unaware of the forces shaping their amoral policy toward apartheid. In October 1963, Secretary of State Dean Rusk was told in a "secret" message that "one of the most anomalous aspects of our current policy is that [the] rate of U.S. investment in South Africa is growing as apartheid gets worse and as we increasingly oppose South Africa politically." The problem was how to maintain the "proper image"—as opposed to substance—of the U.S. in "world public opinion…."[29]

This was not an easy circle to square since the cheap labor and ample minerals of South Africa were so substantial that the U.S. regime found it difficult to envision an alternative to the unsustainable status quo. By the end of 1962 U.S. direct investment in South Africa was reported to be a mighty $353,000,000—and if private bank deposit portfolio investments were added, total U.S. private investment soared to about $600,000,000. A key metric—return on U.S. capital—was high: about 16% in the mining industry and almost 20% in the manufacturing and commercial fields. More than 150 U.S. firms had holdings in the land of apartheid, creating a mighty lobby for their continued presence. Of these, 12 were in the automotive field, 12 in drugs and cosmetics, 12 in the electrical equipment and appliance trade, and 10 in food processing. The giants included an all-star team of transnational capital: General Motors, Ford, Studebaker, Chrysler, Firestone, Goodyear, General Electric,

28. Memorandum, 8 August 1963, Box 98, *Harlan Cleveland Papers, John F. Kennedy Presidential Library*.

29. Office of U.N. Political Affairs to Secretary of State, 25 October 1963, Box 99, *Harlan Cleveland Papers*.

Westinghouse, Cal-Tex, (i.e. ESSO), International Harvester, American Cyanamide, Kellogg, and Procter and Gamble. Even beyond the obvious effect of bolstering apartheid, their presence was hardly neutral. These firms were under pressure to make their investment conform to Pretoria's dicta, including the production of bulletproof tires in the case of Firestone, designed to make police and military vehicles more impregnable to militants.[30] Thus, the strong aroma of profit overwhelmed any trepidation about being tied to apartheid. The average rate of return on investment after 1964 was among the highest, if not the highest, in the world. Even in 1994, when apartheid was being escorted forcibly from the world stage, U.S. corporations received an 18% return on South African investment compared with, say, 8% in Britain.[31]

Pretoria had good reason to think that these handsome profits would bind the U.S. to apartheid indefinitely. This relationship was heightened when the perception arose that the same could not be said for all allies. By 1964, J. Wayne Fredericks of the U.S. legation had spoken to an apartheid envoy who had just returned from Japan, where he was told that it would be difficult to maintain trade ties with South Africa unless racial policies were altered. This Asian giant was the third largest market overseas for South African goods and the fourth largest source of South African imports.[32]

Like a seesaw, as U.S. corporations flourished, African labor was driven down relentlessly. Adam Hochschild recalled that "at the time I was growing up, for example, black miners at the [Hochschild's] vast Tsumeb mine in Namibia earned less than a dollar a day."[33] The anticommunist liberal Allard Lowenstein managed to enter what became Namibia and penned an exposé of what he called Pretoria's "Brutal Mandate" there. He tried to interest Hollywood in his derring-do but conceded defeat by 1963, serving to ensure that miners would continue to be exploited shamelessly.[34]

But it was more than just mines and tires and failed film productions. Carl Kaysen, the M.I.T. scholar and policy analyst, told the State Department's George Ball brusquely that there was little rationale—beyond profiteering and backing apartheid—for selling

30. Memorandum, 30 October 1963, Box 99, *Harlan Cleveland Papers.*

31. Padraig O'Malley, *Shades of Difference*, 551.

32. J. Wayne Fredericks to George Ball, 27 May 1964, RG 59, Central Foreign Policy Files, Box 3238.

33. Adam Hochschild, *Half the Way Home*, 172.

34. Report by Bernie Sindell, Sindell Agency, 29 April 1963, Box 132, *Allard Lowenstein Papers, University of North Carolina-Chapel Hill.*

Pretoria submarines since "you don't chase Africans with submarines." The adroit Ball flipped the argument and countered that this was a reason to sell this item since it was akin to a useless toy to sate the voracious appetite of the apartheid military. Washington would "pay the political cost" either way, it was thought.[35] So after consulting with the legal advisor Abram Chayes, Ball arrived at the agreement "to continue selling them arms for external defense as a specific *quid pro quo* for the tracking station" on their soil to monitor satellites and space vehicles.[36] [emphasis original]

Fortunately, Washington was not driving events in Southern Africa, meaning that this purported superpower was becoming more reactive in responding. The main shaper of Washington's policy toward Africa, the Michigander G. Mennen "Soapy" Williams, was among those who fretted incessantly about the despised Communists—at home and abroad—taking advantage of the U.S.'s pro-apartheid policy unartfully disguised as something else.[37]

There was little doubt that fear of Communist—especially SACP—advance was shaping U.S. policy in the region. Five days before Dr. King's important speech, George Ball spoke with White House aide McGeorge Bundy, a future president of the Ford Foundation. The words exchanged, said Ball, "make my hair stand on end." "What this may come to," it was said, "is an African invasion of South Africa in which ...the whites can be captured by the Communists...." Then, as this tale was spun, Ball implored, "you don't seriously think that when the chips were down that we're going to be a party to a black invasion of South Africa in order to drive out South Africans." Williams then said, "let's not make that decision now," while Bundy offered his view that "the notion of anybody invading South Africa is preposterous." This latter point may have been accurate but the fact that it was weighing on the minds of policymakers was suggestive of the unsustainability of U.S. policy.[38]

A problem for shaping a more realistic policy in Washington was that anticommunism had taken a huge toll, pushing the body politic so far to the right that it was hard to veer toward anti-apartheid. The

35. Memorandum of Conversation between George Ball and Carl Kaysen, 18 March 1963, Box 7, *George Ball Papers, John F. Kennedy Presidential Library.*

36. Memorandum of Conversation between George Ball and Abram Chayes, 12 July 1963, Box 7, *George Ball Papers.*

37. G. Mennen Williams to Secretary of State, 30 October 1963, Box 99, *Harlan Cleveland Papers.*

38. Memorandum of Conversation between George Bundy and McGeorge Bundy, 22 August 1963, Box 7, *George Ball Papers.*

State Department's Harlan Cleveland had a "long discussion" with labor leader George Meany, who "agreed that we should...restrain the ILO [International Labor Organization] from going any further in the direction of discriminating against the South Africans."[39] That is, shield Pretoria from assailment.

Then the U.S. had to consider how South Africa would retaliate if cornered. Bundy was informed that "economic reprisal" was not a one-way street; in fact, it was argued, "they would have much the best" of such a tit-for-tat. For they could engage in "manipulation of its sales on the London gold market," which would mean "massive sales of U.S. and U.K. monetary gold" in order to "restore the normal price," thereby shocking capitalist economies globally.[40] South Africa, warned U.S. intelligence officer Thomas Hughes, possessed a "potential grasp on more U.S. assets than the U.S. has on South African assets" and "could squeeze U.S. assets selectively for deterrence or retaliation."[41] He did not add that a regime that bars the majority from voting and intentionally plunges them into economic depression enjoys extraordinary flexibility—at least until the majority begins to upset this applecart.

So armed, Pretoria was heartened. By November 1963 the apartheid rulers were upset since Washington had dispatched Ulric Haynes, a Negro and desk officer for South West Africa, but he needed a visa. The "appointment of a Negro might be regarded in Pretoria as a 'deliberate provocation,'" causing some "heartburn." Verwoerd "himself had cabled that he considers the matter 'in a very, very serious light.'"[42] McGeorge Bundy was told that Washington was "getting into a first-class fight" over Haynes since Secretary Rusk demanded "normal diplomatic treatment of Negro officers," a clear violation of apartheid law.[43]

Just as anti-apartheid forces were buttressed by anti-Jim Crow forces, the same held true for their enemies: Pretoria's reactionaries

39. Harlan Cleveland to Francis Plimpton, 30 October 1963, Box 99, *Harlan Cleveland Papers.*

40. William Brubeck to McGeorge Bundy, 12 September 1963, Box 159, *Papers of President Kennedy, National Security Files, John F. Kennedy Presidential Library.*

41. Thomas L. Hughes, State Department Bureau of Intelligence and Research to Secretary of State, 12 Augsut 1963, Box 159, *Papers of President Kennedy, National Security Files.*

42. Memorandum of Conversation- "Confidential", 30 November 1963, RG 59, Central Foreign Policy Files, Box 4031.

43. William Brubeck to McGeorge Bundy, 5 December 1963, *National Security File, Country File,* Box 78, *Lyndon B. Johnson Presidential Library.*

relied heavily upon their U.S. peers, often printing screeds from the John Birch Society, one of which--preposterously--accused the U.S. ambassador of being a "revolutionary" in league with the SACP,[44] an indication of the hysteria and utter dearth of realism that gripped Pretoria, which inexorably led to making bad choices. The supposedly respectable face of U.S. conservatism William F. Buckley saw apartheid sympathetically as a sincere response to racial complexity.[45] His widely read journal *National Review* was a reliable friend of apartheid.[46]

Strengthened sufficiently, by 1964 Pretoria sought to boycott Ford, barring purchase of their vehicles by the government, since the company refused to bid on military truck tenders.[47] The pro-apartheid cabal also included Anthony Harrigan of the *News and Courier* of Jim Crow Charleston, South Carolina. He was a "well known admirer of South Africa" and "apartheid," said the legation in late 1964, who was "on intimate terms" with Pretoria. He was a "professional anti-communist" whose most recent book was published to sustained applause by apartheid backers and "prominently displayed in bookstores throughout" the country.[48]

Washington was trapped between an unyielding ally in Pretoria bent on maintaining a racially obdurate regime and a rising Africa backed by a more aggressive U.S. Negro lobby that was determined to alter the status quo. Thus, in 1964 McGeorge Bundy was told that "if there is public disclosure of Lockheed sale to [South Africa] before or during the [U.N.] General Assembly the reactions there will be pretty messy" since "this sale associates us with the British, French and Portuguese as helping the South Africans…."[49]

In a closely held intelligence assessment by the U.S. authorities in 1964, it was determined that Pretoria "certainly regards its willingness to permit U.S. missile and space vehicle tracking facilities and

---

44. Pretoria legation to Secretary of State, 17 August 1963, RG 59, Central Foreign Policy File, Box 4032.

45. William F. Buckley, "South African Fortnight," *National Review,* 14(Number 2, 15 January 1963): 17-23.

46. See Patrick Henry Martin, "American Views on South Africa, 1948-1972," Ph.d. dissertation, Louisiana State University, 1974, 220.

47. Confidential Report to George Ball, 9 November 1964, RG 59, Central Foreign Policy Files, Box 2639, *NARA-CP.*

48. J.C. Satterthwaite to Secretary of State, 24 December 1964, RG 59, Subject Numeric Files, Box 1694, *NARA-CP.*

49. William Brubeck to McGeorge Bundy, 23 September 1964, *National Security File Country File,* Box 78, *Lyndon B. Johnson Presidential Library.*

U.S. use of other installations on its territory" as a "source of considerable leverage upon the U.S."[50]

Faced with such stubbornness, Washington was reduced to seeking to manipulate personalities.[51]

This attempt to manipulate marriages was a constant preoccupation of Washington. Keen attention was paid in 1964 when it was discovered that the daughter of A. Gardner Dunn, Deputy Chief of Mission in Washington for South Africa, was "marrying an American next June…."[52]

Still, Pretoria may have overplayed its hand, not fully aware of how postwar currents had pushed the U.S. toward a rethinking of routine bigotry. The Nationalists continued to adhere to a toxic anti-Semitism that was becoming less popular in Washington. The presence of those like Joe Slovo, the SACP leader of Jewish descent, continued to impel some within South African Jewry to show that they were utterly unsympathetic to his ideology, lest they be tarred via guilt by shared ethno-religiosity. "South African Jewish opinion is toward a more conservative and essentially Nationalist viewpoint," was the opinion of U.S. diplomat William Witt in 1964. The Nats in turn praised Israeli law "forbidding Arab-Jewish marriage" as a rationale for similar anti-miscegenation laws emanating from Pretoria. The "heavily business oriented Jewish community," he said, "is profiting substantially from the current economic boom," though this community tried to ignore the "undoubtedly latent anti-Semitism in the Nationalist Party." "Latent" was a misnomer. Helen Suzman continued to be frequently interrupted in Parliament with the insulting cry, "There go the Jews again" or "why don't you go to Israel."[53] After conversing with a South African emissary in Washington, the conclusion was reached that Pretoria's "prevailing view" was that the U.S. was "entangled in a 'conspiratorial Negro-Jewish-Communist web.'"[54]

For obvious reasons this was terribly short-sighted. Suzman's fellow parliamentarians may not have known—but Washington surely

50. Report, 20 May 1964, Box 8, *National Security File, National Intelligence Estimates, Lyndon B. Johnson Presidential Library-Austin, Texas.*

51. G. Mennen Williams to "Mr. Johnson," 8 March 1963, RG 59, Central Foreign Policy Files, Box 4031.

52. Memorandum of Conversation, 23 March 1964, RG 59, Central Foreign Policy Files, Box 2637.

53. William Witt to Secretary of State, 7 April 1964, RG 59, Central Foreign Policy Files, Box 2633, *NARA-CPI.*

54. Memorandum of Conversation, 23 March 1964RG 59, Central Foreign Policy Files, Box 2637.

did—that her brother-in-law, Arthur Suzman, had numerous U.S. firms among his clients, including General Tire and General Electric, and had studied at Harvard in the 1930s. Yet, these South Africans were being alienated systematically.[55] Thus, pro-apartheid writers claimed that "Lenin's parents were Jews and that he was reared in a Jewish foster home" and that "Jews organized, directed and financed Russian Bolshevism…."[56]

It was not as if the U.S. was moving wholly away from bigotry, and this failure only gave added sustenance to Pretoria. Lawrence Marshall of Cambridge, Massachusetts founded Raytheon in 1920: by 1964 it was a major Pentagon contractor. He had a massive farm 70 miles south of Windhoek and was "concerned," said his State Department interlocutor, "that the U.N. attempt to bring about independence" of this colony would compromise his interests; thus, he wanted Pretoria to "continue as administrator." After all, his privileged position had allowed his daughter to write at length about the indigenous "Bushmen" there and his son had produced a documentary about them.[57] Then there was Samuel Collins, a U.S. national but a leading pioneer in the quest for diamonds in the coastal waters separating South Africa from its northern colony. He was a firm backer of the Nationalists, donating substantially to the Cape Town branch. His roots were in Ireland with relatives in Texas, the latter helping to explain his staunch opposition to desegregation and endorsement of apartheid.[58]

There were also "white" South Africans who made frequent visits to the U.S. like Dr. Abraham Van Zyl. This Broederbond member with a doctorate from Columbia toured the U.S. regularly. In 1963, traveling in league with the Carnegie Corporation of New York, he found more sympathy to apartheid than opposition. This discovery was particularly revealing since he and his spouse stayed at the home of the U.S. envoy's father in Buffalo; he had known this

55. Memorandum of Conversation, 24 June 1964, RG 59, Central Foreign Policy Files, Box 2628.

56. William Witt to Secretary of State, 15 October 1964, RG 59, Central Foreign Policy Files, Box 3236. *Sunday Times* of Johannesburg, 11 October 1964.

57. Memorandum of Conversation, 3 September 1964, RG 59, Central Foreign Policy Files, Box 2640.

58. Charles Manning to Secretary of State, 15 July 1964, RG 56, Central Foreign Policy Files, Box 2629. See also Consul General-Durban to Secretary of State, 19 December 1968, RG 59 Subject Numeric Files: Political and Defense, Box 2468, *NARA-CP* Former elected official, Cyril Milne, convicted and sentenced for bribing U.S. national Samuel Collins, favoring him in a sewage pipeline contract, causing Collins to flee.

ambassador fairly intimately over the years, as they were frequent tennis partners and shared home visits. But in contrast to the people with whom he spoke, the only unbiased U.S. periodical, said Van Zyl, was the conservative *U.S. News and World Report* and he strived to bar the rest from South African schools.[59]

The bold Nationalists sought to foil U.S. policy to distinguish the ANC and the PAC based on the latter's hostility to the SACP.[60] *Die Burger* rejected this distinction, complicating U.S. foreign policy[61] and further indicating how confident Pretoria felt in confronting Washington.

Feeling such strains, Washington retreated into fantasy, repeating the canard that would be cited incessantly in coming decades: Pretoria was a "valuable ally in three [wars]," eliding the Nazi sympathies of the ruling Nationalists. "Are we prepared to abandon all efforts to block direct Soviet and CHICOM [Chinese] penetration" into the region? Referring to the fiery anti-Jim Crow battles in Birmingham, the Pretoria legation—acting as if it were a client of the South African government—asked imploringly "in view [of] recent events in Alabama, perhaps we should be a little less enthusiastic in condemning" South Africa.[62]

The Kennedy team then considered blocking a U.N. challenge to South Africa's membership there since, said the State Department, the move "should be viewed from a standpoint of protecting our overriding interests on Chinese representation," i.e. blocking "CHICOM" recognition and membership at this body. There was a "possible linkage of these two by Africans," increasingly active in the wake of anti-colonial independence "as a means of applying leverage on us."[63]

It was hard to find a way to embrace both apartheid and liberation forces, Pretoria and Accra. By September 1963 Mozambique's Eduardo Mondlane was among those sharing "great disappointment" with Washington "in relation to Portugal"; it "shocked me," he confided to George Houser. Why, he cried, "at this late hour of African Nationalism," the U.S. "would still insist on declaring that she is not

59. Argus Tressider to U.S. Ambassador, 11 December 1964, RG 59, Central Foreign Policy Files, Box 2629.

60. Cape Town Legation to Secretary of State, 1 April 1964, RG 59, Central Foreign Policy Files, Box 2635.

61. *Die Burger*, 1 April 1964.

62. Pretoria legation to Secretary of State, 18 September 1963, Box 159, *Papers of President Kennedy, National Security Files*.

63. State Department to Pretoria legation, 20 September 1963, Box 159.

in favour of seeing Portugal out of Africa" was a concept that eluded his understanding. Nor did he accept this threadbare rationale that ousting Lisbon would be a gain for the despised Reds.[64]

Also, in September 1963 the Pretoria legation was involved in urgent consultations with Progressive Party leaders Jan Steytler, John Cope (a former MP), and Lawrence Robertson. They were given the bracing news that the "majority [of] South Africans"—meaning Europeans—"believe American people" and Washington both "advocate early introduction of 'one man, one vote,'" then deemed a bridge much too far: this was a belief that "plays directly into [the] hands of Doctor Verwoerd," the Nationalist firebrand leader. The PP delegation wanted Ambassador Adlai Stevenson to repudiate the idea of "one man, one vote," a reversal of Washington's pro-democracy rhetoric, already difficult to articulate considering Jim Crow voting restrictions. "Political problems" were "involved" if the U.S. were to move in this problematic direction, the legation said understatedly, "because of [the] strong appeal of this slogan"—one man, one vote— "in all independent African states." Stetyler, like his interlocutors, was deathly concerned about "Commie influence in ANC and PAC," and prompted a discussion of "partition" of South Africa, a process already unfolding via the creation of illegitimate Bantustans.[65]

Meanwhile, refugees were pouring out of South Africa, fleeing intensified repression. The message to Houser in October 1963 said matters behind the "Iron Curtain"—the anticommunist term appropriated for Southern Africa—were terrible: there was "terror for all political activists."[66] Ian Gilchrist encountered many refugees from his perch on the Congo-Angola border and by early 1963 noticed a profusion of "bona fide Communist literature," i.e. "hard covered books in English and French mostly on economics, exploiting the anti-colonialist theme and rabidly anti-American." One reader of such literature spotted by Gilchrist, among those who the colonizers insisted to be illiterate and impotent, was also among those with a "tendency to mistrust Americans because of a fear of their 'imperialism.'" He told Houser that there was "definitely a need for literature presenting the opposite view without blowing the American horn too much," a difficult tightrope to tread.[67] Rather than discouraging

64. Eduardo Mondlane to George Houser, 3 September 1963, Box 142, Series III.

65. Pretoria legation to Secretary of State, 30 September 1963, Box 159.

66. "Zami" to George Houser, 20 October 1963, Box 142, Series III.

67. Ian Gilchrist to George Houser, 19 February 1963, Box 94, Series III.

the attempt to sanitize the odoriferous U.S. image, Houser instead commiserated with Gilchrist, who was then being described "as a representative of American imperialism." "One has to develop a pretty thick skin when one is working in Africa," he said.[68]

Bundy was informed weeks before the Kennedy assassination that "Soviet exploitation of the refugee situation in Southern Africa has created a serious problem"—for the U.S., of course. "The Communists have a much [better] program than the West"—the "ratio of scholarships is now at least eight to one in favor of the Communists" versus the U.S. and its allies. The latter would have to educate more Africans if they wanted to compete, meaning the creation of more critical thinkers, inimical to apartheid. ANC camps were being larded with Communist aid, it was said, while the PAC was resorting to the begging bowl. "In despair PAC recruits and members are then forced to ask the ANC for help." Because "this weakens non-Communist elements," the U.S. had an objective interest in coming to the rescue of the PAC.[69] Thus, Bundy was told that regrettably, the U.S. was not doing enough to "help the anticommunist PAC."[70] This was worrisome, said the CIA, because "since World War II the number of African members has increased" in the SACP "and the party has become identified with nonwhite nationalism."[71]

But rather than engage with this force, the U.S. sought to turn a cold shoulder to them. When the South African Peace Council rebuked U.S. policy in Cuba, Panama, and China, the legation responded coldly that "in light of the obvious Communist character of the Council's letter, the Embassy does not intend to reply."[72]

In December 1963, L.T. Mgweba of the PAC office in Cairo paid a visit to the U.S. envoy there, Donald Bergus. He wanted aid from the U.S. and dialogue too, which was viewed favorably since, said Bergus, "it must be presumed he is being approached by Bloc missions here," meaning Moscow and its allies.[73] Nana Mahomo, Secretary of

68. George Houser to Ian Gilchrist, 26 February 1963, Box 94, Series III.

69. Bureau of African Affairs to McGeorge Bundy, 6 November 1963, Box 159.

70. William Brubeck to McGeorge Bundy, 29 October 1963, Box 387a, *William Brubeck Papers, John F. Kennedy Presidential Library.*

71. "Special Report" from CIA on "Subversive Movements in South Africa," 10 May 1963, Box 387, *William Brubeck Papers, John F. Kennedy Presidential Library.*

72. Willliam Witt to Secretary of State, 10 March 1964, RG 59, Central Foreign Policy Files, Box 2635, *NARA-CP.*

73. Donald Bergus, U.S. Embassy-Cairo to Secretary of State, 4 December 1963, RG 59, Central Foreign Policy Files, *NARA-CP.*

Foreign Affairs for the PAC, met with U.S. labor leaders, including George Meany, Maida Springer, and others about assistance. It was demoralizing, said Mahomo, to see aid flowing from Moscow to the ANC while the PAC languished. "We got more out of the visit than Mahomo did," said U.S. delegate Wendell Coote. "We wanted information" and he gave it; he wanted "money and vehicles" and got neither.[74] This was even more disappointing to the PAC since their leader, the jailed Sobukwe, reportedly admired President Johnson,[75] successor to the slain Kennedy.

Nonetheless, by early 1964 Mahomo was in Washington, D.C. preparing for a "completely off the record" briefing to which powerbroker McGeorge Bundy was invited. Then it was off to Manhattan for another session with the AFL-CIO, and a meeting with the Council on Foreign Relations, then on to Stanford for more briefings.[76] When Bundy—in a rare gesture, not yet accorded to the ANC—chose to meet with Mahomo, he revealingly informed Irving Brown, then asked him to call.[77] The ACOA too was part of this setup. Joshua Nkomo, a founder of Zimbabwe, reminded Michael Ross of the AFL-CIO that when they met, "Mr. George Houser made the introduction in your office...."[78] Ross' colleague Maida Springer peppered Nkomo's comrade Reuben Jamala with books by Thomas Jefferson, Woodrow Wilson, and various anticommunist ideologues.[79]

The prominent scholar of Angola John Marcum was "very friendly with PAC leadership and especially with Nana Mahomo," said Houser, recalling the time "back in 1962" when he and Marcus "walked together with the Angolan rebels from the Congo into the northern part of Angola when the revolt there was at its height."[80]

---

74. Wednell Coote to Jesse McKnight, 22 October 1963, RG 59, Central Foreign Policy Files, Box 4029, *NARA-CP*.

75. Benjamin Pogrund *How Can Man Die Better*, 231.

76. Thomas Schroth, Congressional Quarterly Service to McGeorge Bundy, 2 March 1964, White House Central File, Subject Files, Gen Co 296, Box 71, *Lyndon B. Johnson Papers, Lyndon B., Johnson Presidential Library, Austin, Texas.*

77. McGeorge Bundy to Irving Brown, 16 February 1964, White House Central File, Subject Files, Gen Co 296, Box 71.

78. Joshua Nkomo to Michael Ross, 24 October 1960, Box 12, *International Affairs Department Country Files-AFL-CIO, University of Maryland-College Park.*

79. Maida Springer to Reuben Jamala, 4 April 1961, Box 12, *International Affairs Division Country Files-AFL-CIO*

80. George Houser to "Dear Oliver" Tambo, 11 May 1965, Box 142, Series III, *ACOARA*.

Then in Dar es Salaam there was another reported conversation with PAC leadership in which it was stated that the ANC was an "instrument of International Communism." While PAC rule in Pretoria would be "neutral," the ANC would form instead a "Communist People's Republic."[81] Just before Dr. King mounted the rostrum to address hundreds of thousands in D.C., "Soapy" Williams was told that that the PAC was "in danger of collapsing because of a woeful lack of funds," which would be a "calamity to the West," given "evidence of increasing Communist infiltration of the ANC."[82] Obviously, when the Soviet Union disappeared the leverage of Africans of diverse ideological persuasions disappeared along with it.

Mandela was among those who charged that PAC leader Leballo had somehow left a list of thousands of members at headquarters though he knew a raid was imminent—just before Sobukwe was about to be released from prison, which led to his further detention. Leballo was said to have sold Duncan sensitive PAC material in exchange for various material possessions. This secret information was divulged by Leballo at a press conference in Maseru.[83] Duncan came to represent the PAC in Algeria, a crucial posting, despite the group's supposed objections to the ANC's working alongside those defined as "white."[84]

These were the swirling waters that George Houser and the ACOA had to navigate. The CAA was long gone, and Robeson was in terminal decline, having fled the U.S. after being granted a passport.[85] The nation's ruling elite was sufficiently agile to allow ACOA and Houser ideological leeway and, in return, it did seem that they shared insights with questionable characters, e.g. Irving Brown, the CIA's liaison to labor. "Irving Brown brought the five hundred dollars from you yesterday,"[86] was the message Ian Gilchrist sent from the Congo-Angola border to Houser in early 1963, a donation presumably for charitable purposes, the loathsomeness of the intermediary notwithstanding. By the summer of 1963 the Pentagon's William

81. Memorandum from Jesse McKnight, 8 November 1963, RG 59, Central Foreign Policy Files, Box 4029.

82. Jesse McKnight to G. Mennen Williams, 26 August 1963, RG 59, Central Foreign Policy Files, Box 4031.

83. Memorandum of Conversation, 9 September 1964, RG 59, Central Foreign Policy Files, Box 2630. See also Luli Calolinicos, *Oliver Tambo*, 328.

84. Benjamin Pogrund *How Can Man Die Better*, 276.

85. Gerald Horne, *Paul Robeson: The Artist as Revolutionary*, London: Pluto, 2016.

86. Ian Gilchrist to George Houser, 19 February 1963, Box 94, Series III, *ACOARA*.

Bundy was meeting with Patrick Duncan, the anticommunist liberal from South Africa, summarizing that "he was trying to develop a strong relationship with the [anticommunist] ICFTU [International Confederation of Free Trade Unions] and happened to be occupying Irving Brown's New York apartment at the present time,"[87] within hailing distance of the ACOA office. Naturally, when Duncan met with the president's brother, Attorney General Robert F. Kennedy, he was billed as the "only white member" of the PAC, for which he was raising funds.[88] For his part, in 1964 Houser could be found conferring with the Israeli ambassador in Dar es Salaam,[89] an essential component of the anticommunist cabal.

Duncan, an acolyte of the liberal anticommunism that characterized the ACOA, also sought to raise funds from Maurice Tempelsman, soon to be notorious as the consort of Jacqueline Kennedy, the murdered president's widow, and billed by the Pretoria legation as an "industrial diamond merchant." He said that Duncan requested a "substantial contribution" to the PAC in aid of his effort to raise one million pounds in the U.S. Tempelsman was the proper person to ask since he was advertised as a "businessman with substantial interests in South Africa"; thus, his "business would be protected when Africans seize power if he contributed...." Despite the rationality of this analysis, the novelist Paton was among those who felt Duncan was afflicted with a "growing psychological imbalance...."[90] As for Tempelsman, he had ties to the Oppenheimers of South Africa (as well as the Kennedys); by 1980, the slain president's only son was touring South Africa and through Tempelsman's good offices was given a tour of mines and, said the ACOA, "special treatment by the De Beers people."[91]

Still, Washington jerked the ACOA's chain from time to time. In September 1963, for example, the U.S. Department of Justice asked if the ACOA should be required to register as a foreign agent, a potentially disastrous move. "Portuguese pressure is really at work here," said Houser and he could have added conservative anticommunist

87. William Bundy to J. Wayne Frederick, 22 June 1963, RG 59, Central Foreign Policy Files, Box 4029.

88. G. Mennen Williams to "the Secretary," 24 August 1963, RG 59, Central Foreign Policy Files, Box 4031.

89. George Houser to Eduardo Mondlane, 14 September 1964, Box 142, Series III, *ACOARA*.

90. Pretoria legation to Secretary of State, 14 September 1963, RG 59, Central Foreign Policy Files, Box 4032.

91. Richard Knight of ACOA to "Dear Thabo," 13 May 1982, Reel 6, *Oliver Tambo Papers*.

pressure too. The goateed Houser "did not feel very encouraged by conversations" with officialdom there, which convinced him—correctly—that "events in Africa alone will change this situation."[92]

A sector of the U.S. political elite had reason to look askance at Houser. It was also in 1963 that a future leader of Zimbabwe told "Dear George" about the "crisis regarding the activities of the American Consul in Salisbury," who was close to the racist "Rhodesian Front" rulers. Indeed, the RF's so-called "'self-development' program," a warmed-over version of apartheid, was "fathered" by this U.S. envoy, who was also a "personal friend of the Front Cabinet members." The only wrong note in this alarming report was the notion that this flap "threatens to ruin [the] American reputation here," which was probably beyond saving by then.[93] The wider point was that those in Washington still enamored of the idea of allying with the odious RF could now be undermined by Houser's intelligence sources.

Still, Houser was well integrated into African leadership. Thus, Houser boasted—not falsely—that Mondlane of Mozambique was "an old friend of mine."[94] The Mozambican told the ACOA leader that he "realize[d] the value of an occasional $25, $50 or $100 check.... we can make use of any amount," he joked, "one million included!"[95] (Unfortunately, by early 1964 Stanley Levison of the ACOA, who was also close to Dr. King and suspected of past Communist ties, was asserting that the renewed interest in domestic civil rights exerted an "adverse effect on our fund raising" in the ACOA.)[96]

By 1964, Mondlane was expecting ACOA to offer a "medical unit like one maintained by your organization in the Congo" for Holden Roberto's forces.[97] To Houser, he was "Eduardo" and his spouse was "Janet."[98] Houser also remained close to Chief Luthuli,[99] a relationship lubricated by the fact that Mary Louise Hooper was part

92. George Houser to Eduardo Mondlane, 23 September 1963, Box 142, Series III.

93. Eddison Zvobgo to George Houser, 11 March 1963, Box 149, Series III, *ACOARA*.

94. George Houser to A.P. Zwane, 10 July 1962, Box 142, Series III, *ACOARA*.

95. Eduardo Mondlane to George Houser, 16 January 1964, Box 142, Series III, *ACOARA*.

96. Minutes of Meeting, 29 January 1964, Reel 6, #0024, *ACOA Papers*.

97. Eduardo Mondlane to George Houser,

98. George Houser to "Dear Eduardo," 18 March 1963, Box 142, Series III.

99. George Houser to W.Z. Conco, 19 April 1963, Box 142, Series III, *ACOARA*.

of ACOA too. "Again, I am enclosing a note for Chief Luthuli," he said to their Swazi intermediary, while mock complaining that it was "difficult, if not impossible, to keep up a correspondence with one's many friends" in the region.[100] By September 1963 he had just met with Tambo and Duma Nokwe in Addis Ababa in an important Pan-African gathering. "Our own civil rights struggle," he told W.Z. Conco of Swaziland, "has reached a stage of intensity that it has never known before," the downside being—he thought— "it does sap some of the energy in the interest of the liberal American public in events in Africa"[101] . Sam Nujoma, founding father of Namibia, found time to express "deep gratitude for the [ACOA] for the generosity [of] support" rendered to SWAPO.[102] Weeks before Dr. King's impassioned remarks in Washington, Houser was informing Mondlane that he had just spent "two weeks in the Congo" and "went down to the Angola border" where he "did see Dr. Neto," top MPLA leader, "and had a pretty good talk."[103] It was unclear if Dr. Neto was aware that Houser was also conferring in Leopoldville with Ian Gilchrist, who repeatedly was bombarded with "charges of American imperialism. "Most of this propaganda," he charged, "seems to originate with MPLA."[104]

Understandably, liberation movements saw ACOA as a resource. It was not just the funds raised and the doors opened in the corridors of power. In 1963 an ANC leader in Dar es Salaam asked ACOA for a copy of a recent U.S. television broadcast on sabotage in South Africa for their use, though their "London office" already had a copy;[105] inexorably the group would reply positively. It was the ACOA that paid for Mondlane's subscription to the *New York Times*. "The paper goes first to the FRELIMO office," speaking of the liberation movement, "where it is read, then to our home," said his spouse, "and then to my office where it is clipped for pertinent articles;" thus, "it was well used," thanks to ACOA.[106]

This was an auspicious moment. By 25 September 1964, Mondlane's organization, FRELIMO, had launched armed struggle,

100. George Houser to W.Z. Conco, 6 September 1963, Box 142, Series III.

101. George Houser to W.Z. Conco, 6 September 1963, Box 142, Series III.

102. Sam Nujoma to ACOA, 19 February 1963, Box 142, Series III.

103. George Houser to Eduardo Mondlane, 1 July 1963, Box 142, Series III.

104. Ian Gilchrist to George Houser, 27 April 1963, Box 94, Series III.

105. J.J. Hadebe to Deborah Kallen of ACOA, 2 August 1963, Box 142, Series III.

106. Janet Mondlane to George Houser, 28 February 1964 and Zolata Havas, Circulation Director of "New York Times" to Eduardo Mondlane, 20 January 1964, Box 142, Series III.

hastening the countdown to apartheid's ultimate retreat—a date he regarded as "one of the most important dates not only in the history of Mozambique but in the history of the African continent;" no puffery in retrospect. By March Pretoria had been sucked into this conflict, draining funds and soldiers alike, as they roused enmity toward apartheid by Mozambicans generally.[107] According to Professor Marvin Harris of Columbia University, apartheid praxis was worse in Mozambique than South Africa, suggesting that as this system of iniquity came under attack to the east, it was bound to be amplified in Pretoria.[108] As the struggle in Mozambique heated up, anti-FRELIMO elements began cropping up in the U.S. This nation became a destination for Mozambican Catholic ex-seminarians who had split from FRELIMO, to the point where Samora Machel, Mondlane's comrade, called them insultingly "janitors in the toilets of white Americans."[109]

Shortly after the initiation of armed struggle, the U.S. Negro Charles R. Swift was with Mondlane in his living room in Dar es Sallam. "I was startled to see," he said later, "automatic guns strewn about the floor and furniture," all captured from the Portuguese military. "He showed me manufacturers' markings, proving that NATO [North Atlantic Treaty Organization] arms from the United States were being used by the Portuguese in Mozambique....I wondered to myself that Eduardo would discuss such matters so casually with an American he had first met only an hour before," a sign of lax security for which FRELIMO would pay a high price. The Mozambican leader, said Swift, "seemed more American than Mozambican. He used American slang freely," betraying his school years at Oberlin.[110]

Houser was in the advantageous position of mediating between and among African leaders. Mondlane felt that Holden Roberto of Angola was allied with his "opponents in Leopoldville" and his "attitude toward me is a consistently negative one," which was nothing to dismiss, given the murderously sectarian impulses that often operated in Congo. Why this was occurring eluded the Mozambican in his assessment of this "frightened man." Roberto, he said, "wants me to be his East African agent," which was unacceptable to him. Mondlane had "still scars in my character from bruises inflicted by

107. Iain Christie, *Samora Machel: A Biography*, London: Zed, 1989, 33, 42.

108. *Sunday Times* of Johannesburg, no date, Reel 7, *Xuma Papers*.

109. Alex Vines, *RENAMO: From Terrorism to Democracy in Mozambique?* London: James Currey, 1991, 42.

110. Charles R. Swift, *Dar Days: The Early Years of Tanzania*, Lanham, Maryland: University Press of America, 2002, 43.

his opponents" in their "campaign against me." This was inadequate payback since the cosmopolitan Mondlane continued to "insist on defending him against those who consider him a capitalist mercenary…." Then Mondlane began to question Houser, wondering—appropriately— "why you people are concentrating on Leopoldville and completely neglecting Dar," favored by liberation movements. With Lumumba now gone, Washington preferred Congo given the intelligence and other aid available from the regime, largely absent in Tanzania.[111]

It was under the imprimatur of the ACOA that Mondlane joined Roberto in a 1963 forum in Manhattan at the Community Church at 35th Street and Park Avenue.[112] Since the AFL-CIO backed Roberto and ACOA was determined to appeal to them and keep a toehold on the mainstream, it was difficult for Houser to act otherwise. Labor's George Meany told the White House that Roberto was worthy of support since he was "anticommunist" and "anti-Soviet," while MPLA was "penetrated by pro-communist elements."[113] Nonetheless, Meany was informed by Lisbon lobbyists that—contrary to popular opinion—ACOA "backs the terrorist activities in Angola," meaning precisely MPLA.[114]

Meany's colleague George McCray praised a Nigerian labor leader since he was likewise "holding the dike against communism in the African trade union movement."[115] Across the continent in Dar es Salaam, P.P. Mandawa had just been ousted from the Tanganyika Federation of Labour and, he said, "the plot against me and most of the hatred came out of the AFL-CIO programme," with others being purged.[116] By 1964 there was a "military mutiny" in the then Tanganyika and "a great number of trade union leaders were arrested," about 200 altogether—though it was unclear if the AFL-CIO had a hand in this unrest.[117] Yet Houser felt compelled to ask Meany to provide a keynote at an important ACOA gathering.[118]

---

111. Eduardo Mondlane to George Houser, 3 September 1963, Box 142, Series III.

112. Announcement, 16 April 1963, Reel 6, #0011, *ACOA Papers*.

113. George Meany to President Kennedy, 17 December 1962, Box 12, *International Affairs Division Country Files-AFL-CIO*. Hereafter IAD-AFL-CIO.

114. Martin Camacho of Portuguese American Committee on Foreign Affairs—Boston to George Meany, 23 October 1961, Box 12, *IAD-AFL-CIO*.

115. George McCray to "Dear Mike," 9 August 1960, Box 13, *IAD-AFL-CIO*.

116. P.P. Mandawa to "Dear Maida," 17 May 1960, Box 13, *IAD-AFL-CIO*.

117. National Catholic Welfare Conference to "Gentlemen", 7 February 1964, Box 13, *IAD-AFL-CIO*.

118. George Houser to Michael Ross, 1 May 1960, Box 14, *IAD-AFL-CIO*.

ACOA maintained curious contact with Holden Roberto for years, though Houser knew this Angolan had "several bank accounts in Switzerland and he's sending his wife to Switzerland" regularly,[119] not normal behavior for a leader of a national liberation movement. Besides, Houser knew as early as 1964 that Roberto was collaborating with the Portuguese authorities against his rivals, principally MPLA. "The South Africans too now have many Special Branch people here," said ACOA liaison Ian Gilchrist, "and I have learned that they too are keeping a file on me."[120] Houser was also in touch with "Dear Jonas" Savimbi, a subsequent U.S. conservative favorite.[121]

By his own admission, Gilchrist was "no novice" to "Angola or Africa...having been pretty associated with the continent since 1935..."—the year he was born to missionary parents in Halifax, Canada; his father was still in Angola as of 1964.[122] He fit nicely with the ACOA in that he was opposed to both "tribalism" and "communism." "I could not continue without your support," was his confession to Houser. Yet he too was concerned about this organizational tie to a questionable Roberto: "My question, which has remained unanswered, is whether your support of me up to this point has been for HR [Roberto] or for the Angolan people," since "HR's present attitude can only lead to fratricidal strife and perhaps the ultimate impossibility of ever seeing the Angolan objective, at the same time allowing the recrudescence of the MPLA in a more-than-ever militantly Communist tradition. If this is what you would wish then I must withdraw,"[123] he confided. Yet, for whatever reason, Houser and the ACOA continued this problematic relationship with Roberto, which was to raise searching questions about Houser and the ACOA by independence in 1975.

But Mondlane too was not necessarily au courant with the complexity of issues then whirling. He was "very pleased to note" that Roberto was "making arrangements to visit China and was ready to accept help from Communist countries. Probably my trip to China,"

119. Ian Gilchrist to George Houser, 25 February 1964, box 79, *ACOA Papers*.

120. Ian Gilchrist to George Houser, 15 September 1964, Box 79, *ACOA Papers*.

121. George Houser to "Dear Jonas", 11 August 1965, Box 142, Series III, *ACOARA:* "Very good to hear from you after so long a time."

122. James Robinson to Maida Springer, 26 March 1964, Box 12, *IAD-AFL-CIO*.

123. Ian Gilchrist to George Houser, November 1964, Box 79, *ACOA Papers*.

he suggested, "helped him a little."[124] Apparently, Mondlane did not realize that China, then speeding toward full-blown anti-Sovietism, was on a glide path to direct collaboration with U.S. imperialism in Southern Africa, a trajectory that would complicate Angolan independence in 1975.

It was already complicating matters in mid-1963, when Houser was informed of a "MPLA split," that was considered a "manifestation of the Moscow-Peking split." Though the supposed "pro-Moscow" faction was more forthcoming to Europeans than their counterparts—who were akin to the PAC—Washington was friendlier to the purported "pro-Peking" faction, given their obsession with the Soviet Union. "One of the first things" the PAC-aligned grouping did "was to prohibit those with Portuguese wives from holding office." Thus, "Veriato Cruz has been the moving force in the split-off and he has just returned from Indonesia where he had extensive contacts with the Chinese."[125] By 1965, says one scholar, "political elites in many of the smaller Third World countries were of the view that the Sino-Soviet rivalry had become an almighty pain,"[126] though the sources of that pain predated this year. Given China's role as a close ally of Dar es Salaam, the emerging headquarters of liberation movements, this "rivalry" resonated ever more loudly.[127]

By the early 1960s, ANC leader and SACP member Kader Asmal recalled in 2001, "the position of the Chinese comrades toward us was ambiguous," the training of their cadre notwithstanding, "and the Soviet Union gave us much more assistance than China did…."[128] As China got closer to the U.S. and was wooed by the PAC, the ANC found itself placed deeper in a disadvantageous position vis-à-vis the Sino-Soviet "rivalry." Sindiso Gregory Mfenyana, who fled to Moscow in January 1962 for Kiev, where he learned Russian, recalled that "we used to refer to the PAC as political chameleons, they took the cover of whatever environment they happened to be in. So, when PAC people went to America, they were against Communism. When the PAC people went to China, they were against revisionism"—code

124. Eduardo Mondlane to George Houser, 16 January 1964, Box 142, Series III.

125. Ian Gilchrist to George Houser, 21 July 1963, Box 94, Series III.

126. Jeffrey James Byrne, *Mecca of the Revolution*, 270.

127. Gregg A. Brazinsky, *Winning the Third World: Sino-American Rivalry During the Cold War*, Chapel Hill: University of North Carolina Press, 2017; Jeremy Friedman, *Shadow Cold War: The Sino-Soviet Competition for the Third World*, Chapel Hill: University of North Carolina Press, 2015.

128. Oral History, Kader Asmal, 5 July 2001, *University of Connecticut-Storrs.*

for anti-Sovietism— "and when PAC people went to Africa, they were Pan Africanists. So we had absolutely no respect for them intellectually....they were opportunists...," he conceded in early 2001.[129] Alven Bennie Pemba—who "was in the group which went to the Soviet Union, with Joe Modise and Ronnie Kasrils, [and] trained in Odessa"—also saw the PAC as opportunist: "they said the ANC... had Jews in their organization, Jews who were oppressing the Arabs in Palestine," their counter to the ANC attempt to organize in Arab countries.[130]

The Sino-Soviet dispute—or China's dispute with the worldwide movement of Communists—manifested throughout the region. Moscow and its allies designated certain liberation movements to be "authentic" and, reactively, China then sought to back any not so designated. As matters evolved, the only "non-authentic" grouping that prevailed was Robert Mugabe's Zimbabwe African National Union. The biographer of Samora Machel, a founding father of independent Mozambique, observes sardonically that this meant that CIA and Portuguese police agents "miraculously transformed themselves into Maoists" in order to gain Chinese funding, wreaking havoc nationwide.[131] One of FRELIMO's staunchest foes domestically, the so-called Revolutionary Committee of Mozambique [COREMO], had a leader—Paulo Gumane—who strangely enough for a representative of a liberation movement, spent months on end in the U.S., Portugal's prime ally.[132]

The PAC "flexibility," however, eventually proved to be quite useful in raising funds—particularly in China. With a finite amount available, this meant less money for the ANC. Nonetheless, China did train ANC cadre too, including Wilton Mkwayi—who also worked for the WFTU in Prague and received further assistance from Mongolia and the Soviet Union.[133] Bawo Andrew Mlangeni of the ANC and SACP acknowledged the "great influence of Marcus Garvey" on the PAC but blamed this group for the "mismanagement, the mishandling of the whole issue" that eventuated in Sharpeville.

129. Oral History, Sindiso Gregory Mfenyana, 28 January 2001, *University of Connecticut-Storrs.*

130. Oral History, Alven Bennie Pemba, 10 June 2002, *University of Connecticut-Storrs.*

131. Iain Christie, *Samora Machel*, 72.

132. Embassy-Lusaka to State Department, 9 August 1968, RG 59, Central Foreign Policy Files: Political and Defense, Box 2464, *NARA-CP*.

133. Oral History, Wilton Mkwayi, 6 October 2000, *University of Connecticut-Storrs.*

But he too was trained in China from 1961-1963; the comrades there were not satisfied with their presence, however—because "the number was too small. That is what made them unhappy, they said you must send a huge delegation, comrade," after only 6 had arrived. There, sited near the border with North Korea, he "specialized in radio communication," i.e. "how to make a military transmitter and a receiver," along with "Morse Code," He learned that "without communicating you are doomed...." Perhaps as a result of this experience, his son was trained in the Soviet Union and GDR before decamping to Angola.[134]

By 1964 Cletus Mzimela was being trained in China. "We ate a lot...we got so fat.... For the first time I carried a gun in my hands. They showed us how to operate it. I saw a hand grenade for the first time." There were classes in "military tactics," e.g. "how you attack and retreat," all of which left him "grateful to the Chinese."[135]

David Sibeko of the PAC was thought by the U.S. envoy in Dar es Salaam to "have taken a more pro-Chicom [Chinese Communist] line," though he had "maintained good personal relations" with this diplomat. In fact, he said, the PAC had "constantly presented themselves as being friendly to the United States and [A.B.] Ngcobo [of the PAC] on several occasions has asked for U.S. Government assistance," which proved to be a request not inconsistent with China's aims.[136]

The Sino-Soviet "rivalry" proved to be a gift to U.S. corporations that could have faced a formidable bloc of national liberation movements backed by united Communists. Instead, by 1964 Kenneth Kaunda was dining in Manhattan alongside Negro publisher Claude Barnett and his spouse, the singer and actor Etta Moten. Presiding was Harold Hochschild, a major investor in Southern Africa's storehouse of mineral wealth, copper in Zambia's case.[137] Left disunity

---

134. Oral History, Bawo Andrew Mlangeni, 5 November 2003, *University of Connecticut-Storrs.*

135. Oral History, Cletus Mzimela, 12 August 2003, *University of Connecticut-Storrs.*

136. Report from Embassy-Dar es Salaam, 28 July 1967, RG 59, Central Foreign Policy Files: Political and Defense, Box 2464.

137. *Chicago Defender*, 9 December 1964. See also A.J. Muste to Lyle Tatum, 13 June 1963, ISD African Program, *AFSC*: The writer was irked because despite their liberal anticommunist credentials, the State Department kept ACOA and those like himself away from Kaunda during his U.S. visit. Perhaps relatedly it was in 1964 that Vice President elect Hubert H. Humphrey resigned from his post with the ACOA: Minutes, 7 December 1964, Reel 6, #0024, *ACOA Papers.*

also made it easier for those like Barnett to rationalize sidling beside Hochschild, with whom he communed at the latter's "beautiful estate."[138]

This disunity came at an inopportune moment. Mandela had been arrested on 5 August 1962 and by December was given a five-year prison term. By July 1963 there was the now renowned "Rivonia" raid that led to the detention and trial of top ANC and SACP Leaders. The trial began in October, and there Mandela denounced as "wholly incorrect" the gravamen of the indictment—i.e. that the ANC was a mere tool of the SACP and, by implication, Moscow. Mandela later placed this resistance in the context of that of S.M.M. Masabalala, whose 1920 imprisonment in Port Elizabeth prison was met by protest from amassed Africans who were then slaughtered by the authorities. More Africans were killed the next year, 1921, in the Bulhoek affair. In 1924 hundreds were killed protesting in the colony that was Namibia. And there was Sharpeville too, never to be forgotten.[139]

---

138. Claude Barnett to Harold Hochschild, 11 November 1 and 1964, Box 174, folder 7, *Barnett Papers*.

139. Nelson Mandela, *Let Freedom Reign: The Words of Nelson Mandela*, Northampton: Interlink, 2000, 32, 33, 45, 50: As noted in these pages, Mandela did not shrink from defending his alliance with the SACP, unlike leaders of the NAACP, who too once had collaborated with Communists: "There has often been close cooperation between the ANC and the Communist Party....perhaps the most striking illustration is to be found in the cooperation between Great Britain, the United States of America and the Soviet Union" during the world war. Thus, "theoretical differences amongst those fighting against oppression is a luxury we cannot afford at this stage...for many decades Communists were the only political group in South Africa who were prepared to treat Africans as human beings and their equals.... Africans who, today, tend to equate freedom with Communism...we count Communists as amongst those who support our cause. In the international field, Communist countries have always come to our aid....the Communist bloc speaks out against it [apartheid] with a louder voice than most of the white world....today I am attracted by the idea of a classless society, an attraction which springs in part from Marxist reading....I have been influenced by Marxist thought" but this is "also true" of Nehru, Nkrumah, Nasser, et.al. See also Robin Malan, compiler, *The Essential Nelson Mandela*, Cape Town: Mayibuye, 1997. "Through highly sensitive channels," the U.S. legation obtained a copy of Mandela's statement "used in his own defense." Mandela was cited as saying, "I, personally am a socialist....I have never been a member of the Communist Party....We were heavily defeated" in 1948-1949 when "we of the ANC Youth League started a move for the expulsion of Communists....I was eventually won over to [the] point of view"

The timing was made worse by the fact that Mandela had been quite effective in the many months he had been on the lam. His activism came to a crushing halt when he was arrested, reputedly with the direct aid of the CIA.[140] Via an underground transmitter, he had been broadcasting on radio. Like a "Black Pimpernel" he had been popping in and out of meetings in Johannesburg, visiting Bechuanaland, London, and Africa generally. Then he was arrested. Perhaps reacting to the "Africanist" thrust, Winnie Mandela arrived in court dressed in Tembu garb with a little clay pipe. Africans were singing; hundreds of spectators materialized for Mandela's court appearance. "I challenge the right of this court to hear my case," he exhorted, an abrupt confrontation with apartheid's legitimacy.

At the Rivonia trial, Mandela was noticeably thinner, incarceration having exacted a toll. Even his skin had a greenish gray pallor. Still, he did not flinch from acknowledging his debt to Communists, speaking hour after hour after hour. At that juncture, the ANC had a reputed 120,000 members, which underscored why he was then in the dock.[141]

During his testimony, Raymond Mhlaba refused to confirm that he had been in East Germany and the Soviet Union in December 1961, despite an offer of indemnity from prosecution, a testament to the steadfastness of the accused.[142]

Even as the trial was unfolding, President Johnson was being pressured to intervene. James Farmer, one of the "Big Six" leaders of the anti-Jim Crow movement, urged him to "take action to

---

of the ANC as "parliament of the African people" that should not exclude Communists. He compared China and the KMT under Sun Yat-sen which did not exclude the CP either or Malaya for that matter. Then there was the previous world war where "Britain, the USA and France formed the Grand Alliance with the Soviet Union." He had special praise for Kotane and Marks, adding "I have no doubt been influenced in my ideas by Marxism…" See G. Edward Clark to Secretary of State, 25 March 1964, RG 59, Central Foreign Policy Files, Box 2635.

140. Nicholas Grant, *Winning our Freedoms Together: African Americans and Apartheid, 1945-1960*, Chapel Hill: University of North Carolina Press, 2017, 11: The CIA culprit here is reported to be Donald Rickard.

141. Hilda Bernstein, *The World that was Ours*, 61, 62, 65, 66, 173, 243, 244. See also Kenneth S. Broun, *Saving Nelson Mandela: The Rivonia Trial and the Fate of South Africa*, New York: Oxford University Press, 2012.

142. Report from Pretoria legation, 27 July 1964, RG 59, Central Foreign Policy Files, Box 2636.

secure release of South African political prisoners."[143] Fourteen distinguished leaders of churches from across the world joined with an equal number of Negro leaders of U.S. churches in Atlanta, demanding that the White House "intervene" in the "death trial of Nelson Mandela", et al. "These are men of character and integrity," it was said insistently.[144] "There is [a] rising wave of protest abroad," noted the Director of U.S. Central Intelligence, "against the possible imposition of death sentences or long prison terms on the defendants...in the 'Rivonia' trial."[145]

Mandela and Sisulu, McGeorge Bundy was told, "are particularly well known abroad. This trial has received worldwide publicity," and the death penalty "would be ominous." The previous October at the U.N. the U.S. "voted for a General Assembly resolution directed at the Rivonia trials," though the representative "abstained on the principal operative paragraph of that resolution" since Pretoria has a "right to defend itself." An official observer had also been sent to the trial.[146] In Nigeria the Foreign Minister summoned a U.S. envoy since he did not have a proper channel to Pretoria; the message he wanted transmitted to South Africa was to avoid the death penalty since, he warned it "might result in incidents much worse than Sharpeville," which would place Lagos in an "impossible situation" with its populace demanding retaliation.[147] This dire warning was echoed by journalist Colin Legum who warned, in words the U.S. legation in London considered "confidential," that if Mandela, et al. were executed, it "could easily lead to attacks on U.K. and U.S. embassies."[148]

Ironically, as Kathrada later pointed out, on the day in 1964 the defendants were found guilty, Dr. King was arrested in St. Augustine, Florida—almost 400 years after European settlement had

143. James Farmer to President Johnson, 12 June 1964, Box 72, *Papers of Lyndon B. Johnson, White House Central Files, Gen Co 302.*

144. Protest, 9 May 1964, Box 72, *Papers of Lyndon B. Johnson, White House Central Files.*

145. Report by Director of Central Intelligence, 20 May 1964, Special National Intelligence Estimate, Short Term Prospects for South Africa, Box 8, *National Security File, National Intelligence Estimates, Lyndon B. Johnson Presidential Library.*

146. Benjamin Read to McGeorge Bundy, 20 May 1964, Box 78, *National Security File, Country File, Lyndon B. Johnson Presidential Library.*

147. Report from Lagos, 9 April 1964, RG 59, Central Foreign Policy Files, Box 2635.

148. Report from U.S. legation-London, 7 May 1964, Central Foreign Policy Files, Box 2636.

commenced.[149] This irony did not seem to move the prosecutor, Percy Yutar, who Rusty Bernstein called a "St. George slaying the Communist dragon single handed and a prophet—or perhaps a clown."[150] The anomalous Yutar was a Jewish man defending an anti-Jewish regime. He seemed to take umbrage when the visiting North American academic Gwendolen Carter greeted Mandela in court from the V.I.P. box.[151] Mandela waved back at her, infuriating Yutar. The official U.S. observer, John Miles, found the prosecutor to be "weak and ineffectual," which was not adequately portrayed since there was "no international press represented at the trial and only U.S., U.K. and Dutch diplomatic observers."[152]

Miles of the Pretoria legation considered the trial to be "fair" and the "sentences justified." Though he objected to Yutar's cross-examination of the writer Alan Paton. When the judge did not impose the death penalty, it saved Pretoria from the "difficult political decision of whether to commute the sentences in the face of overseas pressures," which were enormous. Miles was struck by the "impressive and important recitations by Kathrada and Mbeki of the social, political and economic conditions facing the Indian and African people respectively." It appeared that the otherwise angelic Chief Luthuli "was in fact consulted and approved the formation of the MK," the armed wing of the ANC, which was at the heart of the prosecution. Ironically, days after the sentencing, the wife of the defendants' lawyer Bram Fischer—a daughter of Jan Smuts' niece—was killed.[153]

Fischer had been a Rhodes Scholar serving alongside Secretary of State Dean Rusk at Oxford. After the trial he told Rusk why he had joined the SACP and gave as a reference Dean Erwin Griswold of the Harvard Law School and Professor Gwendolen Carter, who "would be prepared to vouch for my bona fides"—and for good measure attached an article wherein apartheid's Eric Louw assailed Rusk.[154]

Mandela's opponents disagreed vociferously with those in the dock. One alleged that the future president was actually "a member

149. Ahmed Kathrada, *Memoirs*, 188.

150. Rusty Bernstein, *Memory Against Forgetting*, 322.

151. Joel Joffe, *The Rivonia Story*: Bellville: Mayibuye, 1996, 181

152. John Miles to Secretary of State, 10 March 1964, RG 59, Central Foreign Files, Box 2635.

153. John Miles to Secretary of State, 25 June 1964, RG 59, Central Foreign Policy Files, Box 2635.

154. G. Mennen Williams to Secretary of State, 14 December 1964, RG 59, Central Foreign Policy Files, Box 2636.

of the Center of the outlawed Communist Party" and a "tendentious document in his handwriting was produced at the Rivonia trial entitled 'How to be a Good Communist';" hence, it was said the SACP leader "was not [Joe] Slovo" but Nelson Mandela.[155] Pretoria highlighted this Communist document, purportedly in his handwriting, billed as a 62-page monograph consisting of the three chapters.[156]

Left disunity was invoked during the tempestuous Rivonia trial when defendant Ahmed Kathrada was asked by the prosecutor if he followed the Soviets or China.[157] Apparently, this division did not curb the enthusiasm of protesters who gathered at apartheid's U.N. mission in Manhattan. Almost a dozen were arrested after staging a sit-in there.[158]

Robben Island would not be denied. A Houser correspondent lengthened the historical analogy, pointing to 1819 when Makana (also known as Makhanda), described as "the prophet soldier" and a "nationalist leader...perhaps the first nationalist leader on record who strove for Xhosa chiefs' unity against the colonists," drowned while trying to escape Robben Island, which was to house Mandela and his comrades for more than two decades.[159] The island had a lengthy history as a site of African resistance.

The island was a difficult site—beyond the obvious reasons—for Mandela and his imprisoned comrades. James Wongama Ngqondela, born in 1928, joined the ANC in his mid-twenties and became part of the group's armed wing in the 1960s, which contributed to his imprisonment on the island. "The majority" of those housed there then were "members of the PAC," he recalled. "The PAC had in fact more members than the ANC. They were the majority in that island." In one section of the prison holding 50 inmates, only five were ANC cadre—at least early on, but this would change after 1975.[160]

The ideological opponents coexisted on this small island—3.2 by 1.6 kilometers—buffeted by icy winds and strong currents, virtually

155. Nathaniel Weyl, *Traitor's End: The Rise and Fall of the Communist Movement in Southern Africa*, New Rochelle, New York: Arlington House, 1970, 180.

156. *American Intelligence Digest*, Phoenix: Council on Southern Africa, 1983, *University of Kansas-Lawrence*.

157. Ahmed Kathrada, *Memoirs*, 187.

158. George Houser to W.Z. Conco, 6 July 1964, Box 142, Series III, *ACOARA*.

159. "Zami" to George Houser, 26 September 1964, Box 142, Series III, *ACOARA*.

160. Oral History, James Wongama Ngqondela, 8 July 2001, *University of Connecticut-Storrs*.

designed to foil the strongest swimmer seeking escape to the mainland, a mere eight kilometers distant. Rocky shores made access by boat to this oval-shaped real estate impractical. The island was nearly flat and low-lying, the highest point twenty meters above sea level, with scrub being the most distinctive topographical feature.[161] There Mandela—and many of his comrades—would be stuck for decades.

Locking up Mandela and his comrades did not remove Pretoria's problem altogether, suggesting the breadth of apartheid's dilemma. For other events then unfolding made Pretoria more nervous than usual. David Plotz, a Johannesburg executive traveling abroad, met Sheila Jo Glover of the U.S., who had resided in Cape Town. She had been asked by a former "boyfriend" Robert Watson of the "African Resistance Movement," who had fled South Africa to act as a "secret postbox" in the U.S. to redirect coded letters to Cape Town. Plotz, in coordination with the South African legation in London, infiltrated the group, thereby disrupting this plan.[162] Washington was informed that the ARM was directed by the London office of the SACP, though some of its leaders were associated with the Liberal Party and organized student groups.[163] Almost effortlessly, apartheid generated a ceaseless procession of antagonists.

161. Benjamin Pogrund *How Can Man Die Better*, 188.

162. G. Edward Clark to Secretary of State, 18 December 1964, RG 59, Central Foreign Policy Files, Box 2635. See also *Sunday Times* [Johannesburg], 6 December 1964.

163. "Confidential" report from U.S. legation-Pretoria to Secretary of State, 17 July 1964, RG 59, Central Foreign Policy Files, Box 2636.

Chapter 11

Washington and Pretoria: Can This Marriage be Saved? 1965-1967

ROBBEN Island was a grueling experience, featuring meals almost designed to induce malnutrition and uniforms with short pants tailored to engender subordination. The warder at the prison, Van Rensburg, had a swastika tattooed on his wrist, indicative of his leanings—and those of the regime he served. The shrewd Mandela took an interest in every prisoner, which helped to defang ideological differences among the imprisoned, which the regime would have preferred to see exacerbated. Following suit, ANC and SACP leader Ahmed Kathrada also became close to PAC leaders.[1]

For our purposes here, what is remarkable is how U.S. culture seeped into prison cells. The music of Louis Armstrong, Ella Fitzgerald, Nat "King' Cole, Harry Belafonte, and Joan Baez were staples.[2] The writings of Noam Chomsky were part of the prisoners' syllabus[3]—alongside works by Howard Fast, F. Scott Fitzgerald, and John Steinbeck. Later the prisoners watched movies like *The Godfather*, and, intriguingly, *The Great Escape*.[4] Harry Gwala, one of the hardest of the hardliners in the CP and ANC spoke of Robeson fondly. On the other hand, Robert Sobukwe, PAC leader, was a fan of the anticommunist writer, Arthur Koestler, and wielded this novelist's anti-Moscow strictures like a cudgel in his spirited debates with the ANC, much of which revolved around the nature of the Soviet Union.[5]

---

1. Ahmed Kathrada, *Memoirs*, 228.
2. Padraig O'Malley, *Shades of Difference*, 162, 168.
3. Luli Callinicos, *Oliver Tambo*, 402.
4. Ahmed Kathrada, *Memoirs*, 236, 236, 263, 281. See also Neville Alexander, *Robben Island Prison Dossier, 1964-1974*, Rondenbosch: University of Cape Town Press, 1994.
5. Ashwin Desai, *Reading Revolution: Shakespeare on Robben Island*, Chicago: Haymarket, 2012, 57, ix.

What electrified the atmosphere in the region was the Unilateral Declaration of Independence pronounced by the minority regime in Salisbury in November 1965. The renegade Rhodesian leadership captured the imagination of many Euro-Americans and ultra-rightists generally.[6] Salisbury's man in Washington, Kenneth Towsey, was exhilarated to report by late December that "White House mail [is] currently running seven to one in our favor...."[7] Executives of the First National City Bank in Manhattan were among those who thought that this settler revolt would prevail, a viewpoint endorsed by J.A. Johnson of Allis-Chalmers, the U.S. machinery giant with facilities in South Africa. "All the businessmen he has been in contact with," it was said of Johnson, "are in favor" of the revolt.[8]

U.S. settlers could relate more effectively with the English-speaking elite (as opposed to the Afrikaans-elite in Pretoria) and their rebellion against London because the drift toward African majority rule in this colony resonated with those who had rebelled against the drift toward abolitionism.[9] For Senator James Eastland of Mississippi, Ian Smith—the Rhodesian leader—resembled George Washington, calling Rhodesians "latter day Americans sacrificing for their freedom." The rebel colony, he said, reminded him of "our native Mississippi." Shortly after UDI, about 180 chapters of "American Friends of Rhodesia" had been formed, which was followed by a steady stream of Euro-American mercenaries arriving to fight for neo-apartheid.[10] The Atlanta chapter was typical. The leader, A. Rivers-Bulkeley, was an executive at Citizens and Southern Bank, one of the largest in Dixie. In a "confidential" message, Towsey conceded frankly that the "kind of people who were prepared to work actively in Rhodesia's cause were avowed racists." This banker had a kind of private intelligence service: "[his] collection of reference files on Rhodesia and Africa are the comprehensive I have seen," marveled Towsey to his supervisor in Salisbury. In San Diego Towsey worked closely

6. Gerald Horne, *From the Barrel of a Gun: The United States and the War Against Zimbabwe, 1965-1980*, Chapel Hill: University of North Carolina Press, 2001 and Harare: SAPES, 2002.

7. Kenneth Towsey to R.B.N. Wetmore, 30 December 1965, Box 1, *Kenneth Towsey Papers*.

8. Consul General-Johannesburg to Secretary of State, 25 November 1965, RG 59, Central Foreign Policy, Box 2631.

9. See Gerald Horne, *The Counter-Revolution of 1776: Slave Resistance and the Origins of the United States of America*, New York: New York University Press, 2014.

10. Zoe L. Hyman, "American Segregationist Ideology and White Southern Africa, 1948-1975," 170, 196.

with the prominent Journalist, Michael Newman— "formerly our own Information Officer", who was "in tremendous demand as a speaker" besides.[11]

By May 1966 Towsey claimed that "total membership of the 'Friends' group including the well-disposed but inactive probably amounts to about 10, 000;" he knew that "politics in America tends to extremism at the grassroots level" and "to segregationist groups we represent the white man's struggle for survival," i.e. a "courageous anticommunist bastion of the free world". Thus, he was invited, alongside Republican Party titan, Barry Goldwater, to address the influential Young Americans for Freedom, a sparkplug for the potent right wing.[12] Towsey was optimistic since in the citadel of extremism that was Mississippi, Senator Eastland had told him in 1966 that there were "three dominant issues in Mississippi politics—Vietnam, Civil Rights and Rhodesia."[13]

Soon there was a "new bunch of Americans," Houser was told, who were "sponsored" by the "Friends of Rhodesia" said to be "occupying" the recently abandoned "former offices of the U.S.... Consul General" in Salisbury.[14] Their presence made the residence in Salisbury of those not as favorable to UDI, like the Quakers, increasingly untenable. Weeks before UDI, Lyle Tatum of the Quakers was declared to be a "prohibited immigrant." He had lived there since August 1960 and survived when his wife and son died a car crash and his vital papers were lost; he requested duplicates of the papers attesting to his status as a permanent resident—but instead was ousted.[15]

Yet Frank Loescher, who also had toiled on behalf of the AFSC, had apparently become acclimated since he was reported to have endorsed Pretoria's illegitimate occupation of Namibia.[16] As the pivotal 1966 International Court of Justice ruling on Pretoria's occupation approached, Washington seemed to be nudging ever closer to

---

11. Kenneth Towsey to Secretary for External Affairs, 11 March 1966, Box 1, *Kenneth Towsey Papers.*

12. Kenneth Towsey to N.R. Heathcote, 12 May 1966, Box 1, *Kenneth Towsey Papers.*

13. Kenneth Towsey to R.B.N. Wetmore, 21 July 1966, Box 2, *Kenneth Towsey Papers.*

14. G.C. "Jack" Grant to George Houser, no date, Box 149, Series III,

15. Lyle Tatum to AFSC, 16 August 1965 and Memo from Tatum, 15 July 1965, ISD, 1965, Administration Africa Program .... *AFSC.*

16. "Confidential" Report from Colin Bell and Mike Yarrow on conversation with Lyle Tatum, 6 November 1967, IAD, 1967, Conferences & Seminars, *AFSC.*

apartheid. Exhibit A in this regard was Professor Richard Logan of UCLA, who—said envoy William Witt—was "on excellent terms" with the occupation administration, giving him "ready access" to Ovamboland. His popularity in Pretoria soared when he travelled to The Hague to testify in favor of the occupation, insisting that Africans in Katatura, the rancid Windhoek slum, enjoyed "housing as good as that of the student body at UCLA" in the posh Westwood section of Los Angeles. His spouse thought that Windhoek was a "lot safer to walk around in than Los Angeles." The revolt in the Watts neighborhood of L.A. had just concluded during Witt's talk with Professor Logan, which prompted the academic to aver tritely that "some of my best friends are Negroes."[17]

Like Ghana's independence in 1957, the 1960 "year of African independence," the founding of the Organization of African Unity in 1963; and UDI in 1965, the ICJ case was an inflection point on the road to decolonization of Southern Africa. In a confidential conversation with Ernest Gross, lawyer for Ethiopia and Liberia, parties to the case against Pretoria apparently provided detail about the inner workings of the matter. Sir Percy Spender, who headed the court, moved to disqualify the newest member, Zafrullah Khan, virtually on his own, leaving Khan embittered and potentially bringing further disrepute to the court.[18] Because of the growing opposition to the occupation, which only increased after the ICJ opinion, the idea arose in Pretoria that "Red Yanks were behind invasion plans" of the region, with the finger of accusation pointed at Arthur Goldberg, who was said to have links to U.S. Communists.[19] These charges came after G. Mennen "Soapy" Williams resigned from the State Department, which was said to be a "direct result" of Pretoria's "explosive reaction to the TV broadcast" in which the Michigander "is alleged to have said the United States policy is to 'bring South Africa to its knees.'"[20]

Official Washington was not as enthusiastic about UDI as their paymasters in the business community, signaling a rift that would be exploited by the Republican Party during the 1968 elections.

17. Report by William Witt, 21 September 1965, RG 59, Central Foreign Policy Files, Box 2640. See Gerald Horne, *Fire This Time: The Watts Uprising and the 1960s*, Charlottesville: University Press of Virginia, 1995.

18. Memorandum of Conversation, 20 July 1966, RG 59, Central Foreign Policy Files, Box 2641.

19. "Confidential Telegram" from Pretoria, 20 July 1966

20. H.F. Byrne, Consul General-Pretoria to Secretary of State, 18 March 1966, RG 59, Central Foreign Policy Files, Box 2638.

After conversing with the Republican leader, Senator Everett Dirksen, Towsey found that the avuncular legislator "confirmed my suspicion that we are too much of a risk as far as the Negro vote is concerned," which President Johnson's Democrats had to rely upon, given the defection of their racist backers in Dixie considering anti-Jim Crow measures pushed by the White House.[21] Towsey was happy to report that this "'White Backlash' might be influencing foreign policy judgments" in Washington relevant to the "Southern Africa area", which "ought to work to our advantage"—which was not inaccurate, at least by 1968.[22]

The criticism of UDI by Arthur Goldberg of the U.N. mission fed what was termed a "growing anti-Americanism" among the European minority in the region.[23] This perception was confirmed at a cocktail party in Pretoria in a candid conversation between Argus Tressider of the U.S. and A.G. Dunn of Pretoria's Foreign Affairs Department. Dunn acknowledged that at the "top level the anti-Americanism is very strong." On the other hand, this admission came after the South African had been plied with a "discreet number of drinks (and he had three more during this conversation," which may have influenced why he "seemed anxious to stress his personal pro-Americanism."[24]

One correspondent of George Houser wrote that UDI was "no different from the American Declaration of Independence in 1776," adding that "if it was the missionaries who were troublesome in the 19th century, then it is Afro-Asians, Communists & [the U.N.] who spread wrong ideas in the present."[25]

As for Houser himself, he was largely correct in asserting after UDI that "the political scene has changed so much over the last ten years in Africa that unless one has been close to it, he may not recognize what new forces are at work...."[26]

Jim Crow and apartheid were intimate partners, a point implicitly recognized by G. Mennen "Soapy" Williams, who described the

---

21. Kenneth Towsey to R.B.N. Wetmore, 18 March 1966, Box 1, *Kenneth Towsey Papers*.

22. Kenneth Towsey to R.B.N. Wetmore, 7 October 1966, 2, *Kenneth Towsey Papers*.

23. Livingston Watrous, Consul General Cape Town to Secretary of State, 10 December 1965, RG 59, Central Foreign Policy Files, Box 2634.

24. Argus Tressider, U.S. Legation-Pretoria to Secretary of State, 24 March 1966, RG 59, Central Foreign Policy File, Box 2638.

25. "Zami" to George Houser, 18 November 1965, Box 142, Series III.

26. George Houser to James Bristol, 11 July 1966, Box 150, Series III.

regime in Salisbury as being of the "Governor Wallace type."[27] The rise of Rhodesia simultaneously boosted interest in the region generally in the U.S. and gave a jolt of pure adrenalin to the pro-apartheid bloc. The Salisbury-Pretoria relationship was buoyed by the reality that a high percentage of the settlers north of the Limpopo River had either resided previously in South Africa or were of old Afrikaner stock.[28]

The influx of Euro-Americans to Rhodesia, post 1965, was eased by the fact that they were not required to obtain a visa for entry, whereas difficulties were strewn in the path of British visitors seeking to get to Salisbury.[29] Simultaneously, those thought to be hostile or indifferent to UDI or apartheid were barred routinely by Salisbury and Pretoria. The reluctance to admit Ulric Haynes has been noted. But even the Harlem Globetrotters, the farcical basketball team comprised mostly of U.S. Negroes, were barred. When Averill Harriman, at the apex of the U.S. elite, considered a visit, he was instructed not to bring a "non-white special assistant." Henry Morgenthau, son of a former Treasury Secretary, was barred too. U.S. military officers were barred since their delegation included two Negroes. Yet Adolf Hitler's former bodyguard, Otto Skorzeny, who rescued Benito Mussolini from Allied imprisonment, was welcomed with open arms.[30] (The odious Skorzeny—according to Salisbury—was embraced since he was "often invited by the Pentagon to go to the U.S.", his "Nazi antecedents" notwithstanding.[31]) A Negro cleric was blocked from obtaining a visa; then it was proposed that a "trade" be effectuated whereby a Pretoria military man who refused to fight during World War II be allowed into the U.S. in exchange for a visa for the cleric.[32]

As U.S. interest in Rhodesia rose, so did new waves of U.S. investment in neighboring Mozambique, then the site of an increasingly bloody war.[33] Mozambique had historically been linked to the economy of South Africa, in any case. Thus, the father of Samora

27. Ryan M. Irwin, *Gordian Knot*, 98.

28. James Brewer to Richard Nolte, Box 52, Records of *Institute of Current and World Affairs, Columbia University-New York City.*

29. Winifred Armstrong to Harold Hochschild, 26 October 1966, Box 6, *Winifred Armstrong Papers, Stanford University-Palo Alto, California.*

30. J. Wayne Fredericks to Governor Averill Harriman, 6 May 1965, RG 59, Central Foreign Policy Files, Box 2635.

31. Secretary for External Affairs to Rhodesian envoy in Lisbon, 30 November 1966, Box 2, *Kenneth Towsey Papers.*

32. "Secret" Report, 15 April 1965, RG 59, Central Foreign Policy Files, Box 2638.

33. Eduardo Mondlane, *The Struggle for Mozambique*, 94.

Machel, a founder of the liberation movement that came to rule in Maputo, began working in South African mines in 1912. As in Pretoria, Africans faced apartheid restrictions—even before 1948—e.g. being barred from boxing Europeans.[34] The U.S. was also part of this inflamed circle of iniquity. During one of Mondlane's lengthy absences from the region, somehow a U.S. Negro, masquerading as an African, was able to worm his way into the top ranks of the FRELIMO leadership, causing havoc. A leading Portuguese military man in Mozambique, General Kaulza de Arriaga, who arranged to send military officers to the U.S. to be trained and was friendly with prominent U.S. commanders in Vietnam, also happened to be among the stubbornest of the hardliners during the African war.[35]

He was not singular. Perhaps the leading military figure during the reign of apartheid was Magnus Malan. He travelled to the U.S. in 1962 to study military science in Leavenworth, Kansas. He was photographed then alongside Robert Kennedy, indicative of the high-level ties that also allowed him to meet and talk with his brother, the president.[36]

Rhodesians also weighed in on this war. Their envoy in Washington, knew that his rebel regime's crisis was a minor "conflict compared with Vietnam and we cannot emphasize too strongly how valuable it could be for us to make some loud and clear demonstration of support for the president's policies [there]."[37] In 1967 a strong rumor was percolating that Rhodesia was on the verge of dispatching troops to Vietnam; it was likely that this rumor was false, but its dissemination led to an aide to Senator Eastland conferring in the White House about a "personal & secret" visit to Washington by Prime Minister Ian Smith.[38] The envoy, Towsey, who should have been expelled from the U.S. because of his representation of an illegal regime, instead was embraced. By mid-1966 he was conferring with Congressman Edward Derwinski of Illinois who confirmed what he already knew: "sharpening of the conflict in Vietnam would work to

34. Iain Christie, *Samora Machel*, 3, 13.

35. Malyn Newitt, *A History of Mozambique*, 522. On the curious case of the poseur, Leo Milas, see George Houser, *No One Can Stop the Rain*, 184.

36. Magnus Malan, *My Life with the South African Defense Force*, Pretoria: Protea, 2006, 42.

37. Kenneth Towsey to R.B.N. Wetmore, 2 December 1965, Box 1, *Kenneth Towsey Papers*.

38. Kenneth Towsey to G.B. Clarke, 24 May 1967, Box 2, *Kenneth Towsey Papers*.

our advantage" as it would "make the American public more belligerent in its attitude to the Communist world."[39]

These military connections between Pretoria and Washington were especially significant. A.Z. Berman was a parliamentarian in Cape Town, but as he told President Johnson's key aide Marvin Watson, he had a "special link" with the U.S., having "served with the United States Fifth Army" during the World War; "and I was attached to Army Headquarters and served both under General Mark Clark and General Lucian K. Truscott, Jr., I was the first South African officer and for a long time the only one to serve with the American Fifth Army Headquarters"—a position hardly available to Africans, not to mention U.S. Negroes.[40]

Lisbon was amply supported by the U.S. and its North Atlantic allies. Hundreds of combat aircraft formed the core of the Portuguese air fleet, thanks to Washington. Warships, jeeps, and light weapons were all part of the armory the U.S. contributed for the Mozambican war.[41]

FRELIMO had been established on 25 June 1962 and many of its earliest armed militants had been trained in Algeria. By November 1967 Mondlane claimed that there were 8000 within their guerilla army, with 20% of the nation under their control. "We work with MPLA," said Mondlane then, "not GRAE" or Holden Roberto's forces. Aid was being received from the Soviet Union, China, India—even Japan and Indonesia. He accused President Kennedy of "equivocation" in backing his forces, while his successor, Johnson, was even worse: "equivocation without direction," then "support for the status quo." Mondlane gave high praise to neighboring Tanzania and expressed his support for a "socialist state." Also displeasing to U.S. imperialism was his support for the Vietnamese, then being attacked by Washington: he believed the conclusion of this conflict would aid in the resolution of the war in Mozambique.[42]

---

39. Kenneth Towsey to R.B.N. Wetmore, 29 June 1966, Box 1, *Kenneth Towsey Papers.*

40. A.Z. Berman to Marvin Watson, 5 March 1965, RG 59, Central Foreign Policy Files, Box 2628.

41. Allen Isaacman and Jennifer Davis, "Lost Opportunities—U.S. Policy Toward Mozambique: The Myth of Self Determination in Support of Western Imperialism," no date, Box 83, Series III, *ACOARA.*

42. Interview with Eduardo Mondlane, *Africa Report*, November 1967, Box 4, Subgroup II, Series R, *Herb Shore Collection, Oberlin College-Ohio.* Key leader, Samora Machel, was trained in Algeria, for example. See Report, 10 August 1973, Box 1, *George Houser Papers, Michigan State University-East Lansing.*

European allies, e.g. France, were also becoming more concerned with U.S. policy in the region. The French diplomat Hubert Dubois queried his U.S. counterpart Peter Hooper about the nature of U.S. policy toward apartheid. In particular he wanted to know "how much of a factor domestic consideration"—meaning the surging anti-Jim Crow movement—would play in shaping policy.[43] This was a question that would be answered decisively in the coming decade.

Mondlane was uniquely positioned to answer this query and his words were all the more biting given his familiarity with the U.S., where he had spent a dozen years. His friend Ed Hawley argued accurately that during that time "literally thousands of Americans… first became aware of the aspirations to independence of colonial Africa" because of his many public appearances; likewise, African-Americans "first became aware of black pride" and consciousness of Africa because of Mondlane. In turn Mondlane's awareness of the inequality imbedded in U.S. imperialism was sharpened during his years overseas. It was not just being turned away from a Methodist church in Nashville on racist grounds, a shaping experience for him, it was also his difficulty in securing a residence in Oberlin, Ohio. (Interestingly, after buying a shortwave radio the first thing he heard was Louis Armstrong playing in Budapest.)[44]

Mondlane was familiar with missionaries from Mozambique and his continued ties to clerics in the U.S. did not improve his opinion of this group. The "Christian church," he emphasized, "used to be the major instrument of both *change* and *control,*" but now, he said, a few years before the founding of FRELIMO, "it has relinquished its function as an instrument of *change* in favor of *social control.*" This was "very much the case," he said, in the U.S. and South Africa—and, he could have added, Mozambique. "I consider opposition to interracial marriage as a symptom of something not quite right in human relations,"[45] a reference to the staunch opposition he faced when he wed.

* * *

43. Memorandum of Conversation, 16 August 1965, RG 59, Central Foreign Policy Files, Box 2638.

44. Eduardo Mondlane, *A Personal Memoir*, no date, Box 4, Subgroup II, Series R, *Herb Shore Collection.*

45. Eduardo Mondlane to George Carpenter, 29 August 1956, Box 2, *Herb Shore Collection.*

Tactics of terror were becoming more prevalent during the war in Angola.[46] The same held true in neighboring Namibia. By 1967 Andimba Toivo ya Toivo was on trial in Pretoria because of his staunch opposition to occupation. The presence of the legal observer from the U.S.—Richard Falk—did not prevent his conviction; the authorities seemed to be moved by the evidence that suggested the defendants had received aid from Moscow.[47] Joining Falk in protest were Robert Carter of the NAACP and about 200 other U.S. lawyers contesting the prosecution of Toivo and 34 other Namibians.[48] Placing dozens of Namibians on trial did not squash dissent. As this trial was being launched, the U.S. firm Navarro Mining opened for business in Windhoek and hired Theobald Mengo, of Herero ancestry, as chief geologist—and then promptly sacked him when it was ascertained that he was a comrade of Toivo in SWAPO.[49]

The pro-colonial sentiment in the U.S. was infectious, however. Shortly after the conviction of the Namibian patriots, Professor John Marshall of Johns Hopkins University arrived at Fort Hare University in order to argue in favor of Pretoria's occupation of the colony.[50] The Pretoria legation also had a "long conversation" with U.S. national Father Shannon Mallory—Director for five years of the Anglican Mission in "Ovamboland" in the far north of the colony—which proved to be consequential.[51]

As powerful U.S. elites placed their thumb on the scale in favor of apartheid and colonialism, there were wider shifts in favor of these ogres. There was a split between the State Department, which harbored at least rhetorical critics of apartheid, while the potent troika that was the CIA, the Pentagon, and the Joint Chiefs of Staff, were much more favorable toward apartheid on fierce anticommunist grounds. Neither force objected as the framework dramatically shifted from judging Pretoria's occupation of Namibia to be determined along the lines of the Nuremberg war crimes adjudication to one—more amenable to apartheid—in which it was treated akin

46. Bernardo Teixeira, *The Fabric of Terror: Three Days in Angola*, New York: Devin-Adair, 1963.

47. Andimba Toivo ya Toivo, *On Trial for my Country*, 156, 160.

48. Protest by Robert Carter, et.al., 11 December 1967, Box 3, *Files of Edward K. Hamilton, Lyndon B. Johnson Presidential Library*.

49. Consul General-Johannesburg to Secretary of State, 1 February 1967, RG 59, *Central Foreign Policy Files, Political and* Defense, Box 2461, *NARA-CP*.

50. Daniel Massey, *Under Protest: The Rise of Student Resistance at the University of Fort Hare*, 192.

51. Embassy-Pretoria to Secretary of State, 8 September 1967, RG 59, Central Foreign Policy Files: Political and Defense, Box 2461.

to the U.S.'s own *Brown v. Board of Education* decision in 1954 (yet to be enforced fully to this day). That the man at the head of the State Department—Dean Rusk, a son of segregationist Georgia—declared undiplomatically that the "'white race in the world is in the same position as it is in South Africa,'" i.e. a "'minority,'" tended to vitiate any meaningful distinction between Foggy Bottom and its counterparts. In seeming unison with Rusk, Harold Taswell, Pretoria's chief envoy in the U.S., declared that his illegitimate regime was a force for "law and order," not unlike the government in Washington then facing a series of what were called "long hot summers," i.e. rebelliousness in Black America.[52]

Investment seemed to follow repression. And the itinerary of investment was conversely indicative of political trends in the region. By 1966, the uber-banker David Rockefeller of Chase Manhattan was told that whereas his nation's investment in South Africa was $87 million in 1953, by 1966 it had soared to well over $700 million.[53] Propelled by a flood of foreign capital, the number of Europeans migrating to South Africa rose. Since 1952 the Intergovernmental Committee for European Migration in Pretoria had helped to deliver 25,000 Europeans to the land of apartheid, more than half of whom arrived during the period from 1962 to 1965—and some 4300 in 1965 alone, many of whom were skilled workers, thereby curtailing the necessity of hiring Africans for these posts.[54]

Financial interest in Pretoria's colony to the north was also growing. By 1965, U.S. General S.L.A. Marshall arrived at the massive Tsumeb mine controlled by U.S. nationals. He provided full-throated support for the occupation of Namibia and denounced U.S. diplomats Arthur Goldberg and G. Mennen "Soapy" Williams for purportedly "letting the least civilized states of Africa…shape American foreign policy," and in the process had "loosed the Simbas." Like others, he compared UDI to 1776.[55] The peripatetic general visited the colony twice in 1965 and, remarkably, had not seen any military bases. Indeed, he denied the presence of nuclear and military bases in this

52. Ryan Irwin, *Gordian Knot*, 117, 152, 165.

53. University of Virginia Chapter of Southern Student Organizing Committee, "An Open Letter to David Rockefeller on Apartheid and the Chase Manhattan Bank, Circa 1966, *University of Kansas-Lawrence*.

54. John Marcum, "Southern Africa and United States Policy: A Consideration of Alternatives," October 1967, *University of Kansas*.

55. Report, 10 October 1965, Box 57, Folder 480, *S.L.A. Marshall Papers, University of Texas-El Paso*.

uranium-rich region. He found instead "unguarded premises."[56] The feisty military man found it necessary to testify on Pretoria's behalf before the International Court of Justice in the case against the occupation of what became Namibia. He was joined by Ernest van der Haag of New York University, who also saw fit to justify Jim Crow to bolster his testimony. They were part of an intellectual tendency that promulgated "scientific racism;" a cabal which included Nathaniel Weyl and Stefan Possony and argued that so-called intellectually inferior races were reproducing at a faster rate than were purported intellectually superior races. Hodding Carter of Mississippi, a newspaperman, agreed that suffrage in South Africa should be limited severely, as he compared his fellow Dixiecrats to the Boers.[57]

By the fall of 1966 Possony was presiding at an anticommunist symposium in Pretoria. Pandering to Afrikaner chauvinism, nearly all the English-language journalists were ejected from the hall.[58] Also present was Ruth Matthews, spouse of J.B. Matthews, a hero of the Radical Right and former assistant to Senator Joseph McCarthy, whose surname defined an era of reaction. Also, present was Luis Manrara, a political refugee from Castro's Cuba.[59] They were preceded by William Strube of the Christian Anticommunist Crusade, who happened to spend a "holiday" in South Africa and wound up addressing the police in Durban.[60]

Perhaps to blunt the popularity of left-leaning clerics, their right-wing antipodes began flocking to South Africa. This lengthening list included Dr. Howard Eldred Kershner, President of the Christian Freedom Foundation in New York City, who promptly upon arrival endorsed Bantustans.[61] Major Edgar Bundy of the Church League of America also appeared in South Africa at the "Council to Combat Communism" meeting in Pretoria. B.J. Vorster, a leader in Pretoria, chaired the gathering, his political preeminence guaranteeing a kind of gravitas. H. Stanton Evans, who had ties to the John Birch Society,

56. "Ethiopia and Liberia versus South Africa," in "Newsletter: South Africa Scope" April 1966, Box 155, *Burke Hickenlooper Papers, Herbert Hoover Presidential Library.*

57. Patrick Henry Martin, "American Views on South Africa, 1948-1972," Ph.d., Louisiana State University, 1974, 220.

58. *Washington Post*, 13 October 1966.

59. Consul General-Johannesburg to Secretary of State, 29 September 1966, RG 59, Central Foreign Policy Files, Box 3236, *NARA-CP*.

60. Consul General-Johannesburg to Secretary of State, 16 December 1965, RG 59, Central Foreign Policy Files, Box 3236.

61. H, F. Byrne, Consul General-Port Elizabeth to Secretary of State, 15 October 1965, RG 59, Central Foreign Policy Files, Box 3237.

was there, along with Carl Baarschlag, a close comrade of Bundy.[62] Returning the favor, the Reverend J.H.P. van Royen of South Africa made an official—and partially subsidized—trip to the U.S., where he conferred with the stars of the religious ultra-right including Fred Schwartz and Carl McIntire.[63] At this juncture, it was not easy to separate the strands of the religious right from the political right.

Perhaps because of the strength of the anti-Jim Crow movement, Pretoria's self-reassuring words that "peace and calm" prevailed in the land of apartheid were contradicted by other actions. It was in 1966 that the Natal Branch of the South African Bureau of Racial Affairs demanded "nonwhite racial brainwashing," to respond to militancy. "Laws and weapons" were insufficient to maintain hegemony, for Africans could not be relied upon in the event of a foreign attack. The use of radio as a tool of propaganda was the key recommendation.[64]

It would be mistaken to see the views of General Marshall and those like him as outside the boundaries of elite opinion in the U.S. George Kennan, architect of the Cold War and considered a highly respectable voice in oak-paneled boardrooms, saw fit during this conflicted era "to question" the "wisdom" and "propriety" of the Johannesburg consulate holding "inter-racial reception[s]." He did not shrink from giving the "appearance" of being "an apologist" for apartheid.[65] Another U.S. grandee who was present at the creation of the Cold War was not registered as a foreign agent for South Africa. However, the law firm of former Secretary of State Dean Acheson—Covington and Burling—had a lucrative retainer fee from Pretoria, though it was unclear if it was only this money behind his sympathy for minority regimes in Southern Africa.[66]

Throughout the continent, Africans were not necessarily swallowing the bromide that they should back colonialism and apartheid to better fight Communists. To many this seemed to be a threadbare rationalization justifying the brutal exploitation of cheap labor and natural resources. Weeks before UDI, Curtis Joseph of the Nigerian

62. Report, 1 September 1966, RG 59, Central Foreign Policy Files, Box 2630. See also *Newsweek*, 29 August 1966.

63. Memorandum of Conversation, 27 April 1966, RG 59, Central Foreign Policy Files, Box 2627.

64. Consul General-Durban to Secretary of State, 2 September 1966, RG 59, Central; Foreign Policy Files, Box 3237.

65. Entries, 12 May 1967 in Frank Costigliola, ed., *The Kennan Diaries*, New York: Norton, 2014, 441,

66. Murray Bellman to Mr. Fredericks, 6 February 1967, RG 59, Central and Foreign Policy Files: Political and Defense, Box 2467.

Council for Peace told U.S. Senator Frank Church as much, when he denounced the "pretense of fighting Communism," notably since he espied "many things seriously wrong with the practical interpretation of American democracy."[67] He may have read the widely circulated story concerning Berhanou Dinke, a former Ethiopian Ambassador to the U.S., who then turned against the regime (which was to be overthrown in the following decade), and was angered when refused a haircut on racist grounds by a U.S. barber.[68]

These Africans were doubtlessly aware of Pretoria's self-assurance, despite the signals given by decolonization of the continent. A commentator for the South African Broadcasting Corporation called for a "Monroe Doctrine" by Pretoria, justifying intervention continent-wide. By that point, he said, South Africa was 57-years old, the same age as than the "strapping American giant" in 1823. This maneuver would evict "foreign guns and ideology [from] the southern sector of the continent," minimally, and provide a signal Moscow could not ignore.[69]

Washington was not so obtuse that it failed to recognize that it too was a potential target of this so-called new "Monroe Doctrine." Pretoria thought that Washington was gaining outsized influence in the nations that were to emerge independently as Botswana, Lesotho, and Swaziland. "There is a basic element of truth in the Afrikaner position," said the U.S. emissary in Gaberone, that the U.S. "does tend to draw these territories [sic] away" from Pretoria[70]—dangerous for apartheid, given the U.S.'s movement away from Jim Crow. Herbert Reiner, Jr. of the U.S. legation, on the other hand, feared that Lesotho was being subjected to "Communist Control," which bode ill for Pretoria and Washington alike.[71]

Apartheid's existence was at cross-purposes with the stated U.S. goal of anti-racism. This dilemma led to a massive propaganda offensive by Pretoria. The U.S. was inundated with slick and glossy publications from South Africa of various types, as the budget for

---

67. Curtis Joseph to Senator Church, 20 August 1965, Box 23, *Frank Church Papers, Boise State University-Idaho*.

68. *Washington Post*, 17 June 1965. See also Berhanou Dinke, "I Stand Alone," no date, Box 23, *Frank Church Papers*.

69. Consul General-Johannesburg to Secretary of State, 13 September 1967, RG 59, Central Foreign Policy Files: Political and Defense, Box 2461, *NARA-CP*.

70. Embassy-Gaberone to Secretary of State, 1 August 1967, RG 59, Central Foreign Policy Files: Political and Defense, Box 2461.

71. Herbert Reiner, Jr., Consul General-Cape Town to Secretary of State, 15 April 1965, RG 59, Central Foreign Policy Files, Box 2634.

such propaganda rose from about $146,000 in 1949-1950 to $4.5 million by 1965. Apartheid sympathizers, like General Marshall, were quoted frequently in these pages.[72]

Pretoria was aided immeasurably by a comparable propaganda offensive within the U.S. itself, targeting U.S. citizens. By 1966 Max Yergan, long since departed from Robeson's Council on African Affairs, joined with conservative intellectual William Rusher in forming the "American-African Affairs Association," which published a whopping 150,000 copies of a pro-Salisbury journal that received wide circulation, including within the august pages of the *Congressional Record*.[73] Apparently, there was an equivalence between the AAAA and the preeminent journal of conservative opinion, the *National Review*, which included Rusher and his close colleague William F. Buckley, all of whom had collaborated in the failed secession of Katanga from the Congo during the same period.[74]

Perhaps heeding the likes of Buckley, Pretoria's relations with Washington were on a seesaw. There was a "deterioration" and "estrangement," said the *Rand Daily Mail* in 1966, along with an "increasing coolness." This was occurring even though "South Africans identify with Americans more readily than with the peoples of Europe," given their mutual identity as settler colonial regimes.[75] The problem was that the global pressure impelling the U.S. on a pell mell retreat from state-sanctioned racism left South Africa dangerously exposed.

There was, however, a contrasting trend in the U.S., propelled by the strength of the then rising anti-Jim Crow movement, which in turn was buoyed by the fact that Washington found it difficult to win hearts and minds abroad if its escutcheon carried the stain of official bigotry. Yet there was a cognitive dissonance about U.S. policy, which was neither fish nor fowl—supposedly anti-apartheid and anti-Jim Crow, while harboring at the highest levels those who vociferously disagreed. This was a "Dr. Jekyll and Mr. Hyde approach," often leaving all sides immensely dissatisfied. It was "schizophrenic," said a Houser correspondent, leaving Washington "bound to lose the

---

72. Vernon McKay, "South African Propaganda on the International Court Decision," *African Forum: A Quarterly journal of Contemporary Affairs*, 2(Number 2, Fall 1966): 51-64, 51-52, 56, *Group Research Archives, Columbia University*.

73. William Rusher and Max Yergan to All, 20 May 1966, Box 130, *William Rusher Papers, Library of Congress-Washington, D.C.*

74. F. Botha, South African Embassy to William Rusher, 5 May 1966, Box 127, *William Rusher Papers*.

75. *Rand Daily Mail*, 23 September 1966.

game in the long run together with their satellites....it is a simple law of contradiction: 'nothing can both be [and] not be for apartheid'."[76]

This tendency was sensed by Hans Ries, Vice President of the Continental Ore Corporation who visited South Africa in 1964. He was disappointed that the legation had weak contacts with Afrikaner nationalists. Apparently, his contacts were confident to the point of cocksureness about maintaining hegemony when he was there months earlier. But now he found them to be worried because of the changing posture of the U.S., buffeted by anti-Jim Crow forces. "They realized that the U.S. position was more important to them than that of any other country," it was reported.[77] The U.S. legation paid attention when the South African Broadcasting Corporation attacked U.S. domestic policy on racism, while adding that the U.S. actually agreed with Pretoria's policies but had to "cater verbally" to the international community.[78]

This bifurcated tendency was manifested dramatically when Robert Kennedy, brother of the slain president and a formidable politico in his own right—thought to have presidential ambitions—arrived in South Africa. On the auspicious date of 6 June 1966, he addressed an attentive audience at the University of Cape Town and—like so many before and since—drew striking analogies between the histories of his homeland and the site of his remarks. Though his impassioned commentary struck a chord in liberal circles, the reality was that hardline Jim Crow and apartheid supporters had yet to be defeated. Even after their obituaries had been written, these forces retained credibility of a kind, not least regarding the basic agreement between liberals and conservatives that Kennedy represented.

"I am unalterably opposed to communism," he told those assembled—and since he could not outdo conservatives in this regard, he was granting them—perhaps unintentionally—an honored mantle. For the most part, Kennedy's turgid remarks observed the vaporous lineaments of what used to be called BOMFOG (Brotherhood of Man, Fatherhood of God), peppered with personal

76. W.Z. Conco to George Houser, 7 December 1967, Box 142, Series III, *ACOARA*.

77. "Confidential" Memorandum of Conversation, 27 March 1964, RG 59, Central Foreign Policy Files, Box 2637.

78. Consul General-Johannesburg to Secretary of State, 20 October 1966, RG 59, Central Foreign Policy Files, Box 2627, *NARA-CP*.

reflections: "as my father grew up in Boston, signs told him that 'no Irish need apply.'"[79]

Reportedly Kennedy was frustrated with the anti-Semitism he sensed in South Africa, wondering why Pretoria thought the Jewish community to be "the enemies of South Africa," with their responses leaving him frustrated—though he was unwilling to antagonize the Afrikaner elite, the locus of this sentiment. In Durban, however, he managed to mouth the quip that "You are going to be in a damn lot of trouble if God turns out to be black." His speechwriter, Adam Walinsky, perhaps responsible for this offhand remark, concluded that if the trip had "lasted another couple of weeks [they] would damn near have turned into an effort to overturn the government." This was rhetorical excess at best; more incisive was the point made by a one analyst that the European minority's "fear" of "black militancy in the American South spreading to South Africa" was "being used to justify their own policies of racial segregation."[80]

George Houser said the Kennedy trip "undoubtedly did some good" but expressed "disappointment" in his shakiness advocating for "sanctions" and his support of corporate responsibility principles for U.S. businesses in South Africa, later to be codified in what became known as the "Sullivan Principles."[81] His correspondent felt that the visit "did bring a different tone to the political landscape (white) and all Africans did was to give him a resounding ovation."[82]

Harold Taswell, South Africa's ambassador in Washington, sought to hoist Kennedy on this petard. He spoke sarcastically of the politician's "glowing praise" for Chief Luthuli, while ignoring the ANC leader's support for "Fidel Castro" and Cuba during its standoff with Washington in 1962. The Chief, he reminded, "repeatedly inveighed against the United States for a capitalist war-mongering and identified himself with the Soviet Union's and Red China's aims...."[83] In coming years, Washington would seek to pressure the ANC to move away from its Communist backers in return for uncertain support from the U.S. The collapse of the Soviet Union pushed

79. Speech by Robert F. Kennedy, 6 June 1966, Box 181, *John Kenneth Galbraith Papers, John F. Kennedy Presidential Library*. See also Kennedy remarks, 8 June 1966, Box 12, *Peter Edelman Papers, John F. Kennedy Presidential Library*.

80. Dommie Sandbrook, "Robert Kennedy and South Africa," M. Litt. University of St. Andrew's, 1998, 36, 51, 72, 16.

81. "George Houser to W.Z. Conco, 24 August 1966, Box 142, Series III, *ACOARA*.

82. W.Z. Conco to George Houser, 8 July 1966, Box 142, Series III, *ACOARA*

83. Harold Taswell to Robert F. Kennedy, 25 August 1966, Box 155, *Burke Hickenlooper Papers, Herbert Hoover Presidential Library, West Branch, Iowa*.

the ANC unavoidably in this unpromising direction. Congressman Burke Hickenlooper encouraged this approach, and after receiving a copy of this correspondence congratulated Pretoria's representative and assailed Kennedy's "propaganda."[84]

Clarence Crowther, a U.S. national who served as Anglican Bishop at Kimberley, was trying to reach Kennedy when he was arrested by two armed police officers who assaulted him with rifle butts. He managed to meet the visiting politico though both parties were tipped off that the encounter would be bugged, so they strolled away from the airport building where they had met. Apparently, Crowther had been under surveillance by the authorities, indicative of how seriously—and nervously—this visit was taken.[85] The tall and broad-shouldered cleric had an engaging personality, which did not seem to win over his harassers. The "Special Branch" interrogated him about "American politics" and the "U.S. civil rights movement" and told him that they had detailed files on his anti-racist activities at the UCLA campus. They eyed suspiciously the books on his shelves, notably *Das Kapital* and books by writer James Baldwin, though they curiously ignored *Mein Kampf*.[86]

The rise of progressive clerics like Dr. King and the companion ascension of the Latin American doctrine of "Liberation Theology" did not leave Southern Africa unaffected. Somehow the Cape Town legation thought that the Atlanta pastor would speak in Durban in November 1965, though the chances of his getting a visa were slim.[87] There was a kind of panic over the apparent ubiquity of Dr. King, with hysteria mounting when a report emerged that 1200 copies of a recording of his speeches was sent to clergymen of all denominations in South Africa. "We have listened to the record," stressed the U.S. Consul, "and find it a STRAIGHTFORWARD defense of non-violence in the American Negro Revolution;" true, there was "no mention of South Africa"—though "the parallels are there, and it could be interpreted as incitement to a non-violent revolution here...."[88]

---

84. Burke Hickenlooper to Ambassador Taswell, 29 August 1966, Box 155, *Burke Hickenlooper Papers*.

85. Consul General-Johannesburg to Secretary of State, 21 July 1966, RG 59, Central Foreign Policy Files, Box 3236, *NARA-CP*.

86. Memorandum of Conversation with Clarence Crowther, 10 June 1966, RG 59, Central Foreign Policy Files, Box 3236, *NARA-CP*.

87. Allen McNeill, Jr., Consul General-Cape Town to Secretary of State, 5 November 1965, RG 59, Central Foreign Policy Files, Box 2631.

88. Herbert Reiner, Jr., Consul General to Secretary of State, 21 July 1966, RG 59, Central Foreign Policy Files, Box 2635.

The impact of progressive clerics dawned on the U.S. legation when they queried R.H. Mize, the Anglican Archbishop of Damaraland in Namibia. He was the leader of the 17,000-member congregation for five years. Speaking in what was described as a "noticeable mid-western accent" when confronted at the Nelson Hotel in Cape Town, he had irked Pretoria because of his work with the Hereros, whose language he had learned and for whom he had begun English-language instruction. This ethnic group, it was said, was "the main group offering resistance to the white Nationalists." Tellingly, of the 25 odd Anglican clergy in the colony, at least eight were from the U.S., including those stationed in strategic "Ovamboland".[89] By 1968 the tormented case of Mize continued to be "foremost in our bilateral relations," according to the Pretoria legation, as the authorities sought to "terminate the residence in SWA of the Bishop."[90]

A Cape Town journalist challenged President B.J. Vorster to "show proof" for his oft cited assertion that Dr. King was a Communist, a viewpoint imported from likeminded figures in the U.S. itself.[91] Vorster was smarting since Dr. King had made apartheid a whipping boy, calling for an "international boycott" of the nation while speaking at Hunter College in Manhattan in December 1965. The human rights crusader wondered querulously why the U.S. invaded the Dominican Republic earlier that year but not South Africa. With a final flourish unsettling to Pretoria, he added, "for the American Negro there is a special relationship with Africa. It is the land of his origin."[92]

Many of these clerics—even the progressive ones—were not comfortable with the idea of armed struggle, but it was Houser, who had a background in mission work, who cautioned that "the [African] nationalists are very negative in their attitudes toward non-violence."[93]

Practically, however, the regime may have been involved—at least indirectly—in seeking to push the idea of non-violence as a route to discrediting armed struggle. It was in 1967 that anti-Jim Crow leader

89. Memorandum of Conversation with R.H. Mize, 24 November 1965, RG 59, Central Foreign Policy Files, Box 3237.

90. Pretoria legation to Secretary of State, 6 September 1968, RG 59, Central Foreign Policy Files: Political and Defense, Box 2462.

91. Livingston Watrous, Consul General-Cape Town to Secretary of State, 24 November 1965, RG 59, Central Foreign Policy Files, Box 3237.

92. Speech by Dr. King, 10 December 1965, Box 71, Series II, *ACOARA*.

93. George Houser to James Bristol, 11 July 1966, Box 150, Series III, *ACOARA*.

Diane Bevel and her spouse and fellow leader Jim Bevel considered the idea of exporting their non-violent approach to Southern Africa. "I did not see how Jim Bevel who came here in June of this year," said Jim Bristol from Lusaka in October 1967, "could work effectively in Africa…." He had been asked, "would a man like [Angolan leader] Dr. [Jonas] Savimbi & people…in SWAPO welcome having a person like Bevel moving about in Africa…'linking'…their movements with the American Freedom Movement & in other ways contributing toward the emergence of new concept for struggles of liberation which would not be finally limited to the harsh choices of violent struggle?" Apparently Savimbi, who was to collaborate with apartheid and U.S. imperialism alike, was poring over the writings of Dr. King, which may have won over the naïve in the U.S. but belied his subsequent bloody history.[94] The Quakers were then considering establishing a center for non-violence in Zambia but beyond the mind of Kenneth Kaunda, the leader already in power there, it did not generate much interest, in part because of what Bristol termed the "anti-American attitude that seems to be increasing in some Zambian circles."[95] This episode also illustrates the folly of seeking to export U.S. theories based on confronting tear gas and dogs to Southern Africa where tanks, fighter jets, missiles and armored personnel carriers were normative. Besides, the anti-Jim Crow crusaders had difficulty acknowledging that—in any case—the influence of the socialist camp and decolonizing Africa on Washington was a condition precedent for the "success" of their non-violence.

Kaunda may have been the Southern Africa leader most influenced by U.S. activists, particularly those who preached the gospel of non-violence. When he was jailed in 1959, a Quaker delegate visited him, finding him to be "in good condition, physically and mentally."[96] Kaunda had known the Quakers' Bill Sutherland for years. Sutherland had been active with this group since the 1930s and when the important December 1958 convention took place in Accra, Sutherland was one of those present familiar with the widest

---

94. James Bristol to Stewart Meacham, 27 October 1966, Box 150, Series III, *ACOARA*.

95. "Confidential" Report by James Bristol, no date, Box 150, Series III, *ACOARA*.

96. George Loft to Father Peter J. Walsh, 27 November 1959, Box Foreign Service 1958 Country-Africa to Country-Holland, *AFSC*.

range of delegates. And he was uniquely placed to spread the gospel of non-violence.[97]

In other words, an open marriage existed between the anti-Jim Crow and anti-colonial movements, with the latter disregarding the former's vow of non-violence. Shortly after UDI, Mary Louise Hooper was informing "Dear Oliver" Tambo about the protocol of a planned U.S. rally. Houser "briefed" Dr. King "on the subject of non-violence" as it pertained to Southern Africa. "We thought we had to do this," she said, "or he might possibly say something in good faith but through ignorance (or 'wishful thinking') that would offend Africans. Of course, in the last analysis he will say what he wants to, but at least we tried!"[98]

Nonetheless, Dr. King, particularly after he was crowned Nobel Laureate, became a kind of *bête noire* in Pretoria. This was after a 1965 report emerged showing that pressure from U.S. Negroes had led to cancellation of a visit by a U.S. carrier. Pretoria was worried, it was said, "disturbed by this trend because Dr. Martin Luther King has managed to identify [South Africa] problem with racial crisis in American Deep South" to the detriment of both.[99] But Dr. King was just a stand-in for a larger justified fear about the danger to apartheid presented by a newly enfranchised Negro community within the bosom of their chief ally, the U.S. It was also in 1965 that visiting U.S. Negro seaman Clarence Smith and 9 members of his crew vehemently protested discrimination against African Americans in South Africa. He told Consul General H.F. Byrne in Cape Town that "a Negro boycott of Ford and General Motors products" in the U.S. was contemplated, along with a publicity campaign in the Negro press.[100]

The growing hysteria about U.S. Negroes was also reflected when the Reverend David Botha, who had traveled to the U.S. on behalf of the United Presbyterians, declared that the anti-Jim Crow movement was undermining apartheid, comparing U.S. Negroes to South

97. Report by George Loft, December 1958, Box Foreign Service 1958 Country-Africa to Country-Holland, *AFSC*.

98. "Louise" to "Dear Oliver" Tambo, 24 November 1965, Box 149, Series III,

99. Joseph Satterthwaite to Secretary of State, 14 May 1965, RG 59, Central Foreign Policy Files, Box 3238. *Rand Daily Mail*, 14 May 1965.

100. H.F. Byrne to Secretary of State, 7 May 1965, RG 59, Central Foreign Policy Files, Box 3238.

Africa's "Coloured" population, which was now being inspired by events in North America.[101]

As Kennedy was packing his bags to return home, the popular writer Allen Drury, known for his potboiler novels about Washington, was arriving in South Africa, He was stunned by the feeling of betrayal he sensed from the European minority as the U.S. was accused of abandoning state-sanctioned racism. Worse, there was a real fear of U.S. military intervention, as they anxiously watched a U.S. fleet off Plettenberg Bay. The British-Boer divide evaporated when this topic arose. What about "Mexican labor camps in Texas," he was asked, what about exploitation there? The European assertion that "the only good Kaffir is a dead Kaffir" was seen as comparable to the 19th-century U.S. slogan that likewise targeted the indigenous. Even after returning Drury continued to receive a steady stream of newspaper cuttings with scribblings, e.g. "RACE RIOTS ROCK SAN FRANCISCO" or "GUARDS CALLED OUT IN DETROIT." The chastened Drury reported that during his lengthy stay "we went to the farm and sat in the sun, watched an American tractor, ate American peanuts and smoked American cigarettes but we didn't hear any rifle shots or see any demonstrations…." Disturbing to his U.S. audience, which was also retreating from the most egregious forms of anti-Semitism, was the "resentment" of the Jewish people he met in Johannesburg. "Most of the proved Communists who have been caught plotting to overthrow the government have been Jewish," he said. Even mild opponents of apartheid, like Helen Suzman, were also Jewish. Religious bigotry was multifaceted; he even found a number of Protestants nervous about the arrival of Catholic immigrants. This was occurring as South Africa "lost more people to Canada, the United States, Finland and Malaysia than she gained from these countries" in recent months.

Then there was the affluence. He spotted more swimming pools in Johannesburg than he'd ever seen in Dallas. The hotels were more modern than those he knew in Florida, and Durban had twice as many as Miami Beach. He also found "well fed complacent Americans" in Port Elizabeth, the industrial center, replete with U.S. manufacturers like General Motors; they "have never had it so good in terms of soft living, multitudinous cheap servants, low prices, the good life."[102]

---

101. Livingston Watrous, Consul General-Cape Town to Secretary of State, 12 January 1965,

102. Allen Drury. *A Very Strange Society: A Journey to the Heart of South Africa*, New York: Trident, 1967, 28, 63, 88, 98, 101, 162, 214, 236, 279, 280, 283.

By 1964 GM and Ford, on the verge of downsizing in Detroit, were considering spending $45 million to expand in South Africa. By then U.S. investment was in the hundreds of millions of dollars there, while South African gold and foreign assets were above $720 million and the return on investment for U.S. companies in this lush market was at an eye-watering 27%.[103] This influx of capital was buoying the good life for Europeans that startled Drury.

As Kennedy returned to the U.S., events were unfolding back in South Africa that would stir the political waters for years to come. Prime Minister Verwoerd was assassinated by a 48-year old Portuguese national from Mozambique, Demetrios Tsafendas. In November 1965 Tsafendakis had visited the U.S. legation in Cape Town with a story about his forced repatriation from New York to Greece in 1947; he had been a foreign seaman employed by the U.S. Merchant Marine at Cape Town during World War II. The fact that an official said he "appeared to be slightly mentally disturbed" did not erode the fear that given increasingly strident attacks on apartheid, the suspicion would arise in Pretoria that the long hand of Washington was somehow involved in a political murder.[104] (Later the cruelly right-wing Senator Herman Talmadge of Georgia, was told of the "similarity of the assassination of Prime Minister Hendrik Verwoerd to that of John Kennedy and the peculiar role played in the crime by then Justice Minister Vorster, who claimed Verwoerd's job"—deeming both Vorster and Ian Smith to be "treasonous."[105])

The accused was born in Mozambique and, suspiciously—from apartheid's vantage point—his mother was "colored," according to LBJ aide Edward K. Hamilton. In 1962 he offered to spy for the U.S., which led to much fretting about what Pretoria should be told about this.[106]

The elliptical remarks of President Johnson's key advisor Walt Whitman Rostow would not have been reassuring to Pretoria if they had had an opportunity to skim them. "I am afraid that our cat is out of the bag," he told the president, since "South African Security people have now asked for an interview with our Consul in Cape

103. James Brewer to Richard Nolte, 25 January 1964, Box 52, *Records of Institute of Current and World Affairs, Columbia University-New York City.*

104. Cape Town legation to State Department, 9 September 1966, Box 3, *Files of Edward K. Hamilton, Lyndon B. Johnson Presidential Library.*

105. Mildred G. Seiler to Senator Talmadge, 19 February 1976, Box 264, *Herman Talmadge Papers, University of Georgia-Athens.*

106. Edward K. Hamilton to Walt W. Rostow, 7 September 1966, Box 3, *Files of Edward K. Hamilton.*

Town." Compliance was recommended, though it was planned that the envoy would be "saying nothing inconsistent with—the Robert Kennedy episode," i.e. boilerplate anti-apartheid verbiage.[107] Subsequently, the *Rand Daily Mail* declared that the CIA was "probably responsible for the assassination" and cited the words of Louis Stofberg, Cape leader of the Herstigte Nationale Party, who in 1977 said agency agents "should be thrown out of South Africa by the scruff of their necks."[108]

Revealingly, Washington had kept a close eye on possible replacements, including Balthazar Johannes "John" Vorster, apartheid's top leader from 1966-1978. Of medium height and solid build with thinning dark hair and bushy eyebrows, Vorster suffered from chronic low blood pressure—at times as low as 80—which limited his energy and induced periodic blackouts. Falling asleep in his seat was not uncommon—particularly when the subject turned away from his priority: security. He never apologized for his pro-Nazi stance during the World War. But subsequently he then felt that apartheid's future depended on strengthening ties to Washington. Unlike the man he was to replace, it was noted before that leader's murder, "he does not express the criticisms of the United States frequently engaged in by Verwoerd." Thus, Vorster was seen as an "improvement," despite the caricature of him as a "Jack booted Nazi." The fact that Verwoerd was born in the Netherlands was seen to indicate how out of touch he was, while Vorster's reputed knowledge of Xhosa was considered a plus.[109] Vorster's presumed friendliness to Washington gave impetus to the idea that the slaying of his predecessor was hardly coincidental.

Part of the problem with Verwoerd turned on personnel, specifically Ulric Haynes, the U.S. Negro who was helping to shape U.S. policy toward apartheid, and whose very presence seemed like a deliberate affront to Pretoria. By mid-1965 he detected a conflict between the White House's "progressive position on domestic race relations" and apartheid itself: "in order to prevent the Communists from seizing the initiative in Southern Africa," he intoned portentously, Washington had "no choice but to stand on principle" against

107. Walt W. Rostow to President Johnson, 7 September 1966, Box 3, *Files of Edward K. Hamilton*.

108. *Rand Daily Mail*, 5 November 1977.

109. Profile of B Vorster by William Witt, 30 December 1964, RG 59, Central Foreign Policy Files, Box 2638.

apartheid.[110] "Our greatest problem in South Africa," said Haynes, "is convincing the increasing number of [Nationalist] supporters" that Washington is "'sincere' in its opposition to apartheid....at some point" : he emphasized that at some point "the U.S. will have to abandon its long-standing internationally embarrassing policy of quiet acceptance of whatever [Pretoria] may dish out."[111]

As if Haynes' presence was insufficient to insult the Nationalists, this Negro diplomat was also praising their opposition, specifically Helen Suzman, whose party—the "Progressives"—was "financed" by Harry Oppenheimer: "the 'progs'," said Haynes, "are the group in South Africa whose program most closely coincides with U.S. objectives" and, thus, "deserves a boost."[112]

Washington was seeking to export liberal anticommunism to South Africa, which would prove more difficult than implementing it at home. Youthful "progs" were "American influenced," according to a U.S. emissary. "Continually throughout the meeting" he attended "there were quotes tossed in from every imaginable American source from Thomas Jefferson and Adlai Stevenson to Wendell Wilkie." The Kennedy brothers were "given special prominence" (Suzman praised his recent visit). All were upset by the banning of a recording of speeches by Dr. King and music of the Beatles, who were to ascend globally after their U.S. debut.[113]

Supposedly it was Suzman who, in a conversation with top U.S. official Nicholas Katzenbach, said that the way to think of South Africa was to imagine Washington under the total control of Alabama and Mississippi.[114] Since Suzman had a married daughter living in Cambridge, Massachusetts, it seemed that her words were taken quite seriously.[115]

Sensing that the gravy train was leaving the station, the United Party too wanted to get closer to the U.S. so as to solicit campaign

---

110. Memorandum by Ulric Haynes, 28 June 1965, Box 3, *Files of Edward K. Hamilton*.

111. Memorandum, 30 July 1965, Box 3, *Files of Edward K. Hamilton*.

112. Memorandum by Ulric Haynes, 30 September 1965, Box 3, *Files of Edward K. Hamilton*.

113. Livingston Watrous, Consul General-Cape Town to Secretary of State, 23 September 1966, RG 59, Central Foreign Policy Files, Box 2630.

114. Memorandum of Conversation, 14 December 1966, RG 59, Central Foreign Policy Files, Box 2628.

115. J. Wayne Fredericks to Secretary of State, 12 December 1966, RG 59, Central Foreign Policy Files, Box 2628.

donations.[116] Theo Aronson of the UP wanted U.S. businesses to donate to his coffers and for the U.S. representative to introduce him to executives at Ford and General Motors, particularly "in light of [Pretoria's] boycott of Ford...products;" hence, Ford should donate to the party via "some sort of third party arrangements," circumventing the law and/or regulations.[117]

But the Nationalists were sufficiently sophisticated—Vorster notwithstanding—to sense that overtures to those like Suzman and the UP were not in their interest, given the fact that the patrons of these "progs" in Washington were being influenced by anti-apartheid Negroes.[118] A U.S. diplomat noted that the Afrikaans press was rampaging against "local Jewry—charging Zionism weakens loyalty to South Africa," yet another brickbat aimed at Suzman. This allegation was echoed by a visiting U.S. rabbi who in a sermon on the eve of the Day of Atonement averred that the "local Jewish element suffered from too much Zionitis [sic]."[119] Haynes could also have mentioned that it was not unusual when there was a celebration of Hitler's birthday in the Hillbrow neighborhood of Johannesburg, which was wildly inconsistent with overtures to Suzman.[120] Someone daubed swastikas on two synagogues in Johannesburg on the same day, to the consternation of the U.S.-born rabbi Solomon Poupko, infamous for his conservatism, who had only arrived in the nation in 1965. Contrarily, his fellow U.S.-born rabbi Norman Bernhard of the Oxford Synagogue in Houghton urged his congregation to not be afraid of backing Suzman.[121] Before the assassination, Bernard Sachs of Johannesburg found growing support for Verwoerd among South African Jewry but that this was "dictated more by fear than by conviction," i.e. fear of what would follow his departure.[122]

Nevertheless, even the Jewish-American scholar Robert Weisbord was stunned to discover that "possibly for the first time in history,

---

116. H.F. Byrne, Consul General-Port Elizabeth to Secretary of State, "Confidential", 18 October 1965, RG 59, Central Foreign Policy Files, Box 2634.

117. H.F. Byrne, Consul General-Port Elizabeth to Secretary of State, 13 October 1965, RG 59, Central Foreign Policy Files, Box 2930.

118. *New York Times*, 10 March 1965.

119. Consul General-Johannesburg to Secretary of State, 18 November 1965, RG 59, Central Foreign Policy Files, Box 3236.

120. Embassy-Cape Town to Secretary of State, 11 May 1967, RG 59, Central Foreign Policy Files: Political and Defense, Box 2464, *NARA-CP*.

121. Herbert Reisman, Consul General-Johannesburg to Secretary of State, RG 59, Central Foreign Policy Files, Box 3236.

122. G. Edward Clark to Secretary of State, 12 February 1965, RG 59, Central Foreign Policy Files, Box 3238.

large numbers of Jews paid homage to a man with a notorious anti-Semitic past," referring to Verwoerd. It was not necessarily seen as contradictory that while "Nazism flourished in South Africa," the country had "been a hotbed of militant Zionist activity"—and elements from the Jewish community were now mourning a bigot. Zionists there were among "the most ardent in the world" and yet, beginning in the 1930s and continuing thereafter, "Jewish financial support for the Nationalists increased."[123]

Visiting Cape Town from his native Germany in 1965, Hubertus zu Lowenstein was sufficiently concerned by this trend to tell the *Cape Times* how much he was disturbed by the "activities of certain German radical groups who are making pilgrimages" to South Africa, including "Neo-Nazis,"[124] doubtlessly attracted by the echoes of the 1930s audible in Namibia. But these noxious forces were also fed by Jim Crow. It was in 1965 that six busloads of sheeted, hooded, and masked "Klansmen" marched from the U.S. legation in Cape Town through the winding streets. They were from the "Stellenbosch Klan,", i.e. the local university.[125] Similarly, the U.S. Consul in Johannesburg described a "recent flood of Nazi literature into South Africa—from Lincoln Rockwell's American Nazi Party," then "bannered in all local newspapers."[126]

Harsh reality was catching up with Pretoria. As anti-Semitism was raging, the South Korean trade representative requested "White Status," like that already accorded to Japanese. "Honorary Member of the White Race" was a gaping loophole in the edifice of white supremacy,[127] rendering the concept more ludicrous that it already appeared. In a conversation with a South African official just back from Japan, J. Wayne Fredericks of the U.S. was told that Tokyo was becoming increasingly frustrated by apartheid. By 1964 Japan was the third largest overseas market for South African goods and the fourth largest source of apartheid's imports. But Tokyo was coming under pressure not only from African nations but from the Philippines, Malaysia, and Indonesia to change course, and these

123. Robert G. Weisbord, "The Dilemma of South African Jewry," *Journal of Modern African Studies*, 5(Number 2, 1967): 233-241, 233.

124. Report from Embassy-Cape Town, 7 April 1965, RG 59, Central Foreign Policy Files, Box 3238. *Cape Times*, 31 March 1965.

125. Edward Clark, Consul General-Cape Town to Secretary of State, 5 May 1965, RG 59, Central Foreign Policy Files, Box 2635.

126. Consul General-Johannesburg to Secretary of State, 23 March 1967, RG 59, Central Foreign Policy Files: Political and Defense, Box 2463, *NARA-CP*.

127. Robert Eisenberg, Embassy-Pretoria to Secretary of State, 31 March 1966, RG 59, Central Foreign Policy Files, Box 3236.

markets—especially the one centered in Jakarta—were simply too important to ignore.[128] At the same time, Sewsunker "Papwa" Sewgolum, the South African golfer of Indian descent considered the equal of Gary Player, was barred from a Cape Town tournament on racist grounds.[129]

Haynes was on the verge of being declared persona non grata by South Africa, instructed to make only the "briefest appearance" at a reception at their Washington embassy.[130] In South Africa, U.S. delegate Joseph Satterhwaite was holding multiracial receptions in line with the newly minted policy, which had been instituted in 1963 on instruction by the State Department but these extravaganzas were boycotted by the U.S. business community, much more concerned about entente with Pretoria.[131]

Moving aggressively, Haynes recommended that President Johnson buttonhole Charles Engelhard, "the largest single investor in South Africa and an active Democrat to express his concern" about his businesses there and move the important U.S. tracking station eastward to Madagascar.[132] Engelhard was displeased with this maneuver, contacting top White House aide, Texas's Jack Valenti, to tell him that at a recent dinner with a South African diplomat, "he mentioned with some bitterness" his inability to gain an audience with President Johnson or his slain predecessor. "American business has something in excess of seven hundred million dollars invested" in South Africa and there was a "certain growing feeling of bitterness" about this cold shoulder.[133]

Engelhard had other worries. At a 1965 ACOA confab in Washington he came in for special attention because, said a State Department observer, of his "asserted influence on U.S. policy"; thus, "he could

128. J. Wayne Fredericks to George Ball, 27 May 1964, RG 59, Central Foreign Policy Files, Box 3238.

129. *Rand Daily Mail*, 10 January 1966; Consul General-Johannesburg to Secretary of State, 13 January 1966, RG 59, Central Foreign Policy Files, Box 3236.

130. Memorandum by Ulric Haynes, 8 September 1965, Box 3, *Files of Edward K. Hamilton*.

131. Report, 12 March 1965, Box 78, *National Security File, Country File, Lyndon B. Johnson Presidential Library*.

132. Memorandum by Ulrich Haynes, 28 June 1965, Box 3, *Files of Edward K. Hamilton*.

133. Charles Engelhard to "Dear Jack" Valenti, 13 January 1965, Box 71, Gen Co 296, *Papers of Lyndon B. Johnson, White House Central Files*.

be reached by pressure on the White House itself,"[134] with the ruling Democratic Party already more dependent on Negro votes to hold power.

Engelhard was increasingly under fire in his native New Jersey. ACOA questioned Washington's decision to sell stockpiled platinum to him for "less than the open market price," which boosted his position globally. "What are the hiring practices in Engelhard mines in Attapulgus, Georgia and its plant in Berger, Arkansas, its facilities in Wilkinson and Washington counties, Georgia"—and Southern Africa?[135]

Engelhard may have heard that Arthur Goldberg, the U.S. Ambassador to the United Nations, wanted to publicly announce a voluntary program to curb U.S. investment in South Africa but was met with "reservations" in deliberations. Backed by "Soapy" Williams, Goldberg "rebutted" by declaring "we simply must square our position on this issue with our efforts in this area in our own country."[136] But this was easier said than done. In the aftermath of Sharpeville, President Johnson was told, "investors began deserting" South African and the economy there seemed to be "on the verge of collapse" but then Chase Manhattan Bank extended credit, followed by hundreds of U.S. corporations and the Atomic Energy Commission of the U.S., bailing out apartheid. Goldberg sought to capitalize on this immediate post-Sharpeville sentiment.[137]

Pretoria had a point in objecting to Washington's inconsistent policy: embracing the land of apartheid on grounds of anticommunism and national security while distancing itself for reasons of image and political propriety. The former needs provided leverage that the latter ones found difficult to overcome. It was Haynes who objected to Pretoria's "effort to dictate the racial composition of the crews on U.S. planes operating from a U.S. naval vessel." "The lack of an immediate and firm negative response by our Embassy officer," he said, "is typical of the pussy-footing which characterizes our official approach in the field" toward Pretoria. Haynes was responding to

---

134. State Department to Cape Town Legation, 1 April 1965, RG 59, Central Foreign Policy Files, Box 3238.

135. "May Day" Demonstration in Newark, New Jersey, no date, *Anti-Apartheid Movements: File of Clippings and Miscellanea, Michigan State University-East Lansing.*

136. Gordon Chase to McGeorge Bundy, 13 September 1965, Box 78, *National Security File, Country File, Lyndon B. Johnson Presidential Library.*

137. Michael Agranoff to President Johnson, 1 December 1965, Box 72, *Papers of Lyndon B. Johnson, White House Central Files, Gen Co 302.*

a message from Pretoria that said, "it would be appreciated if only white U.S. crew members are used for aircraft flights to and from Ysterplaat and D.F. Malan airport."[138]

Yet Thomas Nyquist, a U.S. scholar then studying at Rhodes University in South Africa, told a U.S. diplomat at Port Elizabeth about "'bloody disorders'" then occurring at the "African location in Grahamstown." But "not a word appeared in the South African press. Detroit received pages of news coverage" in the local press in contrast. "How many other riots," it was asked reasonably, "take place in South Africa" that are "unknown except to those who weep for loved ones"? U.S. envoys may have been more informed than some in Pretoria since they received a constant stream of reports from U.S. nationals honeycombed throughout South Africa.[139]

The U.S. Director of Central Intelligence announced in 1964 that Pretoria "almost certainly regards its willingness to permit U.S. missile and space vehicle tracking facilities and U.S. use of other installations on its territory [as] a source of considerable leverage upon the U.S."[140] Pretoria agreed with this assessment and made it clear that it would not tolerate the presence of any Negroes on either space or Pentagon missions.[141] Undeterred, yet another U.S. Negro official—Clifford Alexander—inquired querulously, "are we examining the possibility of moving our tracking stations out of South Africa?"[142]

Moving this facility would not be simple; Pretoria might interpret a move as a slap in the face, encouraging retaliation. Then there was the related issue of Cape Town's role as a transit facility for U.S. vessels headed to the ongoing war in Vietnam, a site that became even more important as the Suez Canal was under the aegis of Egypt—not a balmy companion of Uncle Sam.[143]

---

138. Memorandum by Ulric Haynes, 8 April 1965, Box 3, *Files of Edward K. Hamilton*.

139. Consul General-Port Elizabeth to Secretary of State, 17 November 1967, RG 59, Central Foreign Policy Files: Political and Defense, Box 2467.

140. Report by Director of Central Intelligence, 20 May 1964, Box 8, National *Security File, National Intelligence Estimates, Lyndon B. Johnson Presidential Library*.

141. State Department to Pretoria Embassy, 6 July 1965, RG 59, Central Foreign Policy Files, Box 2638, *NARA-CP*. See also *New York Herald Tribune*, 5 July 1965 and 2 July 1965.

142. Clifford Alexander to Edward Hamilton, 20 February 1967, Box 3, *Files of Edward Hamilton*.

143. Embassy-Pretoria to Secretary of State, 20 July 1967, RG 59, Central Foreign Policy Files: Political and Defense, Box 2461, *NARA-CP*.

As ever, Pretoria knew that anti-apartheid sentiment was far from unanimously held at the highest levels in Washington. It was Haynes who informed McGeorge Bundy that Pretoria had leaked to the press a story about a U.S. vessel cancelling a port visit in South Africa in objection to an attempt to dictate the racial composition of visiting U.S. personnel. This was done, said Haynes, since "arch conservatives" in the U.S. could then use this story to bash the White House, a notably effective demarche in Dixie.[144]

Unfortunately for Pretoria, "arch radicals" and liberals were also active on the anti-apartheid front. Late on the morning of 25 March 1966, about a dozen protesters from the Student Non-Violent Coordinating Committee [SNCC] arrived at the South African Mission to the U.N. at 300 East 42nd Street. They shouted anti-apartheid slogans loudly as they banged raucously on the doors of the office. Police arrived but were described as "ineffectual" in "attempts to contain the demonstrators." By 2 PM the protesters sought to barge into the inner sanctum and in the process allegedly slammed the head of an official against the wall. The uninvited delegation was comprised of roughly equal parts men and women; and as "resistance" to their protest mounted, they eventually had to be carried out bodily. Their attorney, Leonard Boudin, was a well-known litigator, who over the years had represented many radicals, including Robeson. That this protest was reported directly to Haynes was indicative of its importance.[145] Unbowed, SNCC leader James Forman announced that demonstrations would continue until South African envoys were ousted from the U.S. This demand was punctuated by epithets hurled at the envoys, as the demonstrators rattled doors to create maximum disturbance.[146] True to his word, a few days later SNCC militants again were to be found staging a sit-in at the South African embassy in Washington: "this is only the beginning," Haynes noted accurately.[147]

There was growing resentment in official circles because of the escalating rambunctiousness of anti-apartheid protesters. The State Department sent an unimpressed observer to an ACOA confab in

144. Ulric Haynes to McGeorge Bundy, 13 May 1965, Box 78, *National Security File, Country File, Lyndon B. Johnson Presidential Library.*

145. Stephen Schwebel to Ulric Haynes, 25 March 1966, Box 3, *Files of Edward K. Hamilton.*

146. U.S. Mission to U.N. to State Department, 24 March 1966, Box 3, *Files of Edward K. Hamilton.*

147. Memorandum from Ulric Haynes, 29 March 1966, Box 72, *Papers of Lyndon B. Johnson, White House Central Files, Gen Co 302.*

Washington's plush Willard Hotel in March 1965. Speakers included Nat Nakasa of South Africa, along with Victor Reuther of the United Auto Workers and James Farmer. The liberal anticommunist Allard Lowenstein was assailed for his supposedly overwrought presentation (apparently his harrowing journey to Namibia had left a deep imprint upon him). Farmer, it was reported, "left the meeting in overalls to join the march in Montgomery" against Jim Crow; "civil rights demonstrations, said this eloquent leader who spoke in stentorian tones, should always include references to "Sharpeville and apartheid." Contrastingly, the NAACP's Gloster Current thought it "unwise to plan a demonstration at the South African Embassy...when American embassies around the world were being splattered...." His colleague Clarence Mitchell thought that "Maine lobster tails should be promoted in preference to South African imports."[148]

Subsequent events would show that meshing the anti-Jim Crow and anti-apartheid forces in the U.S. would not be as simple as it appeared. It was Houser who told a colleague in Lusaka that "there are some elements of the civil rights movement here that think that simply because they have been involved here, they can step into the African scene as if they owned it. Those forces will find out very quickly that in the long run they have about as much leverage there as another generally liberal force in this country."[149]

This skepticism about domestic forces may ironically have pushed the ACOA to the left, as they moved to display their own militant mettle. Deeply influenced by the onrushing tide of anti-Jim Crow protest across the U.S., the ACOA accelerated its own activism, often in innovative ways. With a delegation that included Houser, Flemmie P. Kittrell of Howard University, the theologian Gayraud Wilmore, and Dr. John Holloman of Manhattan, they sought to fly like aerial "Freedom Riders" into Namibia without authorization, challenging Pretoria's illegitimate occupation.[150] "We deliberately have not sought visas from the government of South Africa" in order to enter the colony, said the feisty Houser.[151] It was a dangerous mission. They penetrated the airspace of the colony but were not allowed to

148. State Department to Cape Town Legation, 1 April 1965, RG 59, Central Foreign Policy Files, Box 3238.

149. George Houser to James Bristol, 11 July 1966, Box 150, Series III, *ACOARA*.

150. *Rand Daily Mail*, 7 December 1967; *Times of Zambia*, 7 December 1967. *Zambia Mail*, 8 December 1967.

151. *Windhoek Advertiser*, 7 December 1967.

land and barely made it to Botswana.[152] That was not the end of their challenge to the occupation. They also sought to organize an expedition via sailboat from the south of the Congo River to Luderitz, a 1500 mile journey—again without visas.[153] Apparently, this bold initiative was cooked up with the aid of SWAPO's Sam Nujoma.[154] Another co-conspirator was Julius Nyerere of Tanzania, along with Kenneth Kaunda of Zambia, the United Auto Workers of the U.S., and recently elected Congressman John Conyers of Detroit.[155] V.J. Mwaanga, the Zambian diplomat, was also "glad to help" with this venture," particularly since the "publicity" was enormous and disseminated "all over world," which "undoubtedly left a tremendous impression."[156] Pretoria was utterly displeased. Coincidentally enough the experienced pilot of this adventure, David Bohman, was killed in a crash near Lusaka shortly after accolades began to arrive.[157]

South African envoy in Washington, Harold Taswell was terribly upset by this adventure, warning that it was a "forerunner of further efforts to create incidents," while adding ominously that the "activities of the group bear watching closely."[158] Taswell, who also spoke German and Portuguese and had served in Berlin, was well positioned to reflect the views of the Pretoria elite.[159] Linguistic facility aside, Taswell's ties to the U.S. were remarkable: two of his daughters were U.S. nationals and a third was married to one.[160]

Militancy in Southern Africa clashed oddly with what befell the ACOA back home: it was accused of collaborating with the CIA. Cold War anticommunism was taken quite seriously among liberals, and some among this cohort saw fit to undermine Communists by any means necessary. This partly explains why NAACP leader Walter White would seek to forge a connection between the ANC's Z.K. Matthews and the CIA. Other U.S. entities involved with Africa,

---

152. *Southern Africa Bulletin*, March 1968, Box 94, Series III, *ACOARA*.

153. "Confidential South West Africa Project," no date, Box 94, Series III.

154. George Houser to "Dear Sam" Nujoma, 13 September 1967, Box 142, Series III, *ACOARA*.

155. George Houser to Julius Nyerere, 18 October 1967, Box 142, Series III.

156. V.J. Mwaanga to George Houser, 25 January 1968, Box 142, Series III.

157. George Houser to Thomas Karis, 31 December 1968, Box 142, Series III, *ACOARA*.

158. Harold Taswell to Thomas Mann, 11 December 1967, Box 3, *Files of Edward K. Hamilton*. See also *New York Times*, 7 December 1967.

159. Biographical Details on Harold Taswell, 13 November 1964, RG 59, Central Foreign Policy Files, Box 2639.

160. Joseph Palmer to Secretary of State, 19 March 1969, RG 59, Subject Numeric Files: Political and Defense, Box 2469.

including the African American Institute and the American Society of African Culture were recipients of CIA funds. The sympathetic biographer of Horace Mann Bond, the Negro leader who had similar connections, declared that "if Bond did not know of the links between his own groups and the CIA, he should have known."[161] Houser sought to rebut these allegations, which dogged him repeatedly—though, as suggested earlier, his past ties to the discreditable Irving Brown did little to undermine these assertions.[162] Even the pro-Rhodesia lobby, no stranger to U.S. intelligence, blared "CIA finances Leftists" in reference to the ACOA.[163]

The revelations about possible CIA ties to the ACOA instigated anguished debate within the higher councils of the organization and gimlet-eyed skepticism of the group in Africa itself. In March 1967 Houser informed Mondlane that it was "hard for me to estimate the effect overseas" of these bombshell revelations. It could "hurt the fund-raising efforts of AAI [African American Institute]" and the "suspicions overseas that any African office established with African funds...really assumes that the CIA is somehow or other involved...."[164] Mondlane countered that "we were already accused of being financed by [Washington] for the simple reason that American organizations such as ACOA were favourable to us."[165] Houser informed a skeptical Tanzanian audience of his group's "decided embarrassment" about purported CIA ties, but this stain would prove difficult to eradicate and was not assuaged because of ACOA's friendliness toward the compromised U.S. labor movement.[166]

The controversy had wide repercussions, leading Houser to ask Mondlane, "will there be undue suspicion cast upon you if a FRELIMO office opens up within the next few months" in the U.S.[167]

---

161. Wayne J. Urban, *Black Scholar: Horace Mann Bond, 1904-1972*, Athens: University of Georgia Press, 1992, 168. See also *Newsweek*, 6 March 1967.

162. George Houser, *No One Can Stop the Rain: Glimpses of Africa's Liberation Struggle*, New York: Pilgrim, 1989, 172.

163. See "American Southern African Review.... incorporating Friends of Rhodesia Independence" February-March 1967, Box 1, *George Houser Papers, Michigan State University-East Lansing*.

164. George Houser to Eduardo Mondlane, 9 March 1967, Box 142, Series III, *ACOARA*.

165. Eduardo Mondlane to George Houser, 10 April 1967, Box 142, Series III, *ACOARA*.

166. George Houser to "Spotlight on Africa,' 5 May 1967, Box 142, Series III.

167. George Houser to Eduardo Mondlane, 9 March 1967, Box 2, Subgroup II, Series 1, *Herb Shore Collection*. In this same collection, same Box

The U.S. activist Arthur Waskow was among those who asked that ACOA open the kimono and reveal all sources of funding. Houser replied that the group received "in the neighborhood of 10,000 contributions a year most of them below $10."[168] The scandal gripped ACOA for months and was repeatedly discussed at length. "The disclosures about the CIA," it was reported in April 1967 "have revealed that organizations working in the African field have been involved... every organization dealing with foreign affairs will be looked upon suspiciously.... casting suspicion on our real aim of influencing the direction of U.S. policy to Africa...." This assessment was accurate, but it begged the question of the ACOA's complicity with and failure to confront the anticommunist predicates of U.S. policy, positions which some among the leadership shared.[169]

As this flap was unfolding, Houser guilelessly continued to make moves that whipped up the flames of a contretemps. After departing battered from an ACOA leadership meeting, Houser got in touch with Jonas Savimbi—soon to be revealed as a CIA favorite in Angola—informing the bearded fighter that it had been "quite some time since we have been in touch;" it would be "good to see you and have a chance to talk" during his forthcoming trip to Zambia. "Messages can be left for me," he instructed, "c/o American Embassy in Lusaka," a curious site given this legation's well-known reputation for intrigue and destabilization of African initiatives.[170]

Earlier, Ian Gilchrist had informed Houser that his other Angolan contact—Holden Roberto—could "indeed" be "in the pay of the Portuguese;" there were "many political and military reasons for not rejecting the possibility completely...." Angola was studded

---

and Series, see the handwritten and undated note from former State Department and Ford Foundation official, Wayne Fredericks: Mondlane and the Mozambique Institute for which his spouse toiled, had a "relationship with the CIA," covering "all matters except military support." Robert Kennedy "prevailed upon the CIA to develop a FRELIMO fund" against the wishes of other leaders. Nyerere, it was said, "knew full well about the CIA involvement with FRELIMO.'

168. George Houser to Arthur Waskow, 8 March 1967, Box 1, *George Houser Papers*. See also Minutes of Steering Committee, 23 February 1967, Reel 6, Part I, #0004, *ACOA Papers, Library of Congress*: On the "CIA controversy.... Board member Arthur Waskow" wants "list of those who have contributed to support the work" of ACOA. See also same reel, #114.

169. Minutes of Executive Board, 3 April 1967, Reel 5, Part I, #258, *ACOA Papers* On the same reel, see also #258.

170. George Houser to Jonas Savimbi, 5 May 1967, Box 150, Series III, *ACOARA*.

with faux liberation movements and given ACOA's ecumenical approach—seeking to deal with one and all—Gilchrist felt compelled to ask, "can it be that [Roberto] is indeed in the pay of the Portuguese Embassy also"?[171]

Undaunted, Houser continued to gush to Roberto about the "friendship which we have had over so many years," which would remain unaffected by the Angolan's rift with Gilchrist. Allard Lowenstein, the epitome of anticommunist liberalism who also had travelled to the region, was a "good friend of mine," Houser told Roberto. The ACOA leader was headed to Leopoldville, and desired to "see and talk with" Roberto.[172]

Houser was in a difficult position: straining for enough respectability to maintain entrée into the White House while keeping credibility with diverse forces in Africa, many of which Washington deemed to be perilously left wing.

Still, Houser and his cohort continued to press Washington, perhaps even more insistently, in order to deflect these pesky stories about CIA ties. Donald Harrington and A. Philip Randolph, liberal anticommunists speaking for ACOA, were among those raising their voices against the "treatment of Negro crew members in South Africa" and demanding the removal of the tracking station.[173] With insistent emphasis, the ACOA told the White House bluntly: "TO DATE NO AMERICAN NEGRO IS EMPLOYED AT THE TRACKING STATION AND THE UNITED STATES SILL SUPPORTS THE EXISTENCE OF SEGREGATED FACILITIES FOR NON-WHITES IN MENIAL OCCUPATIONS AT THE STATION."[174]

Yet, ACOA was not alone in snuggling closely to the questionable Roberto. When Baptist missionaries in the Congo, Britons David and Margaret Grenfell, were departing in 1967 after 34 years of service—six of them in Congo—Roberto and his closest comrades attended their farewell party. The couple was also quite close to the Quakers.[175] The Baird Foundation, which funded the Quakers' efforts in Africa, "assured" the group "that no CIA funds were involved" in

171. Ian Gilchrist to George Houser, 7 June 1965, Box 79, Series III, *ACOARA*.

172. George Houser to Holden Roberto, 1 June 1966, Box 79, Series III, *ACOARA*.

173. Donald Harrington and A. Philip Randolph to President Johnson, 15 February 1967, Box 3, *Files of Edward K. Hamilton*.

174. ACOA Memorandum, 15 February 1967, Box 3, *Files of Edward K. Hamilton*.

175. Memorandum from Baptist Missionary Society, 3 October 1967, ISD, 1965, Administration, Africa.... *AFSC*.

the disbursement, though one Quaker operative acknowledged that "it is difficult if not impossible to know for sure what the original source of funds may be," adding inconclusively, "so far as we know we have never received CIA funds."[176]

There were cascading consequences flowing from this dispute. Zambia chose to bar the Peace Corps, the U.S.-based entity providing foreign aid, after the Corps in Tanzania was accused of working for the CIA. The question was raised in Parliament there. This led to a "lot of hostility to America" in Lusaka, said one informant, with one Zambian declaring that "he hated all Americans," listing "Korea, Vietnam, Santo Domingo, the CIA in Indonesia," the latter a reference to a recent bloodbath in the midst of a military coup,[177] which illustrated the length to which Washington would go in pursuit of its maniacal anticommunist obsession.[178]

Many in Dar es Salaam, says one scholar, "assumed most Americans were CIA agents until proven to be otherwise." Apparently, says Lessie B. Tate, there were a number of U.S. Negroes in this important site who were "strategically placed CIA agents."[179]

Even the most well-intentioned U.S. national was burdened by the fact that the government to which they paid taxes was often involved in deviltry in Africa. Washington refused to fund armed struggle against minority and colonial regimes in Southern Africa and excoriated the militants who then turned to the socialist bloc for aid, castigating them as "dupes" of the Communists; this purported stain was often transferred to those in the U.S. who backed these militants. Of course, the anticommunist consensus which was strictly enforced—see Robeson—restricted and constrained those who may have ordinarily been sympathetic to liberation movements compelled to seek aid from Moscow. In sum, U.S. policy was as entangled as a bowl of spaghetti and internally contradictory besides.

Like the 1956 Suez crisis, the June 1967 war against Egypt provided an opportunity for Pretoria to attempt to parlay its strategic importance. The "American racial difficulties," then unfolding in

176. Harry Passmore to Bard McAllister, 10 March 1967, ISD, Social & Technical Assistance, Administration Mexico Africa, Administration Zambia….1967, *AFSC*.

177. Letter to "Dear Henry" from unclear correspondent, 16 March 1967, ISD, Social & Technical Assistance, Administration, Mexico, Africa…. *AFSC*.

178. See Geoffrey Robinson, *The Killing Season: A History of the Indonesian Massacres, 1965-1966*, Princeton: Princeton University Press, 2018.

179. Lessie B. Tate, "The Power of Pan-Africanism: Tanzania/African-American Linkages, 1947-1997," Ph.d. dissertation, University of Illinois, 2015, 79, 164.

global headlines, tended to provide "obvious delight to many South Africans," making apartheid appear to be rational in their estimation. One Pretoria cabinet member was so energized by these developments that he stooped to referring to Negroes as "Kaffirs."[180] The 1967 rebellion in Detroit involving mostly Negroes in combat with the authorities drew heavy press coverage in South Africa. It "provoked intense interest" said a U.S. delegate, ranging "from sympathy to thinly disguised gloating" by those who celebrated it as a "failure of integration" and justification for the essence of apartheid: "separate development" or "Bantustans." South Africa's "peace and calm" were compared with the "anarchy and chaos" of the U.S.[181]

Israel gained more support from an increasingly potent Jewish-American community, as it lost support in Africa—and from radical U.S. Negroes—which brought it closer to Pretoria. Washington bristled at Pretoria's incessant nagging about urban rebellions and other examples of U.S. failure to repress—or satisfy—Negroes: this drove a further wedge between Pretoria and Washington. Yet Negroes had been ideologically disarmed by the sidelining of Robeson and his comrades, leaving this beleaguered group ill-equipped to navigate tricky global currents.

---

180. Embassy-Pretoria to Secretary of State, 21 September 1967, RG 59, Central Foreign Policy Files: Political and Defense, Box 2461, *NARA-CP*.

181. Embassy-Pretoria to Secretary of State, 16 August 1967, RG 59, Central Foreign Policy Files: Political and Defense, Box 2461.

Chapter 12

Back to Black, 1967-1968

THE bludgeoning of those like Paul Robeson in the U.S. left an ideological vacuum that was eventually filled with the rise of what was called "Black Power." This tendency was multifaceted but was generally not sympathetic to those who seemed to be Moscow-oriented, which made it skeptical toward the African National Congress since it was allied with the SACP and favorable toward the PAC and the ZANU of Robert Mugabe. The writings of those like Eldridge Cleaver and the activist then known as Stokely Carmichael, avatars of "Black Power" both, in turn influenced activists in Southern Africa—and not always for the better.[1] Joe Matthews of the ANC thought this trend meant enhanced alienation from those defined as "white." It was in mid-1968 that he told the ACOA's Mary Louise Hooper that "in the U.S. the attitude of Afro-Americans is very bitter. I have been quite alarmed at some of [the] things said and done there...."[2] Still, the enhanced alienation from Washington delivered by this ideological trend may have propelled further skepticism toward the homeland of Negroes—make that: Black Americans. When African Americans in Tanzania in 1966 boycotted the iconic July 4th U.S. national holiday, a message was sent to Africans that this superpower was not worthy of respect.[3] Still, "Black Power" opened the door for more influence by shady characters, e.g. Richard Gibson and contributed to Black American skepticism of the ANC-SACP alliance when it was under assault by Washington.

---

1. Gail M. Gerhart, *Black Power in South Africa: The Evolution of an Ideology*, Berkeley: University of California Press, 1978, 275, 276, 279.

2. Joe Matthews to Mary Louise Hooper, 12 July 1968, Box 2, *Mary Louise Hooper Papers*.

3. Bill Sutherland and Matt Meyer, *Guns and Gandhi in Africa: Pan-African Insights on Nonviolence, Armed Struggle and Liberation in Africa*, Trenton: Africa World Press, 2000, 68.

Serendipitously arriving in Tanzania in 1965 was the young African American student known as Prexy Nesbitt, who was to be a pioneer in constructing solidarity with liberation movements, especially FRELIMO. Upon arrival in Dar he immediately immersed himself in the ANC exile community, though he intended to join FRELIMO as a militant. Eduardo Mondlane was a good friend of his uncle. He also found a heterogeneous U.S. Negro community that came to include Calvin Cobb, a disbarred attorney who fled various offenses back home in favor of expatriation. Eventually, others fleeing the U.S. for political reasons—e.g. Black Panther Party cadre—were to find a home in Tanzania, to the consternation of Washington.[4] Like so many others—including the present writer—Nesbitt was seized with interest in the liberation wars. He had left Antioch College in Ohio for Dar, then went to London where he worked alongside historian Basil Davidson. His father and uncles were part of the Marcus Garvey movement and sparked his interest in the continent, leading him to write a paper when he was about 12 years old on Paton's novel *Cry the Beloved Country*.[5]

Traveling in the other direction was Walter Bagoya of Tanzania, who spent four years in Kansas from 1960 to 1964. U.S. Negroes rescued him from a potential lynch mob after he was seen driving a car with a Euro-American woman, though—on the positive side—this helped to forge his understanding of the U.S. and the sorry plight of those who saved him.[6]

Also present in Tanzania in 1965 was the mercurial Joe Matthews, then an ANC member. There he met the visiting Che Guevara, then sizing up the anti-imperialist future of the region, and Jonas Savimbi, who was doing the same, albeit for a different purpose.[7]

Dar es Salaam was a site where many of these trends converged since it had become a favored place of expatriation for U.S. Negroes fleeing repression and alienation alike. There were also ANC and PAC militants, FRELIMO leaders, Zimbabwean patriots, Namibian fighters, Angolan rebels—and more. SACP member Ray Alexander was taken aback to find that by 1966-1967 the Nyerere government "was siding with the PAC." Alexander also said that the SACP received a

---

4. Lessie B. Tate, "The Power of Pan-Africanism: Tanzania/African American Linkages, 1947-1997," Ph.d. dissertation, University of Illinois-Urbana, 2015, 162, 164.

5. Oral History, Prexy Nesbitt, 1 April 2009i, *Columbia College-Chicago.*

6. Ibid., Seth Markle, dissertation, 179.

7. Oral History, Joe Matthews, 2 October 2000, *University of Connecticut-Storrs.*

"lot of money from the Soviet Party," and perhaps expected something similar from Tanzania.[8]

Aid to the SACP trickled down to the ANC. By 1971, for example, an ANC youth and students summer school was held in East Germany where—according to Thabo Mbeki, son of the jailed Govan Mbeki of the SACP and ANC—there were lecturers from the SACP.[9] Alfred Nzo, Secretary General of the ANC, in 1971 echoed his comrades when he expressed "deepest gratitude" for the "fraternal ties that link the ANC" and the GDR.[10] Thus, Radio Berlin in the German Democratic Republic proved to be of maximum assistance to both SACP and ANC.[11] Typically, Alfred Kgokong of the ANC in Tanzania made "arrangements" for his "medical check-up in the GDR" in 1971.[12]

It may have been fairer to say that Dar was ecumenical, welcoming the PAC and the ANC alike. Thus, Siegfried Bengu (also known as Bengu Siegfried) who received military training in Nanking, also was posted to an ANC facility in Dar.[13] Donald Sifiso Mathengela pled guilty in 1969 in Pietermaritzburg after conceding that he had received military training from 1962-1966 in China, Tanzania, Egypt, and Odessa in the art and science of blowing up buildings, bridges, and electric pylons.[14] These two were hardly singular.

According to one U.S. source, by 1967 there were 200 militants from South Africa receiving military training in China, who would then make their way to 13 guerilla bases in Tanzania and 3 in Zambia, all

---

8. Transcripts of Interview for an Autobiography, 22 November 1997, A.28, *Jack Simons and Ray Alexander Simons Collection, University of Cape Town.* See also "Report of National Executive Committee" of PAC, 19-22 September 1967, Moshi, Tanzania, RG 59, Central Foreign Political Files: Political and Defense, Box 2463.

9. "Short Report" by Thabo Mbeki, 8 September 1971, Box 16, Folder 78, Part I, *Lusaka Mission Records, ANC Records, Fort Hare University.*

10. Alfred Nzo to Afro-Asian Solidarity Committee of GDR-Berlin, 20 October 1971, Box 16, Folder 69, Part I, *Lusaka Mission Records, ANC Records.*

11. Arnold Selby, Radio Berlin International to "Dear Comrade" Nzo, 6 October 1972, Box 13, Folder 35, *Lusaka Mission Records, ANC Records.*

12. M. Msimang to Alfred Kgokong, 14 October 1971, Box 13, Folder 43, *Lusaka Mission Records, ANC Records.*

13. Report from Durban, 15 September 1965, RG 59, Central Foreign Policy Files, Box 2637.

14. *Natal Witness*, 9 December 1969 in RG 59, Subject Numeric Files, Box 2468.

armed by Soviet and Czech weapons,[15] suggesting that at this stage there was de facto collaboration on both sides of the Sino-Soviet divide—which was to change in Angola by 1975.

Other signs were unmistakable. In 1965 A.B. Ngcobo of the PAC visited the U.S. Embassy in Tanzania. It was time, said the U.S. official who spoke with him, to arrest the "leftward drift" of the party and "offer assistance" to them. It "could be clandestine," said John Millar, so as not to compromise their purported radicalism; it could be "secretly given" in the form of "radio transmitters and receivers" and "scholarships for PAC personnel" and "expense paid tours to lecture" in the U.S. through the good offices of the Council on Foreign Relations and the African American Institute, both of Manhattan.[16] By 1967 an internal PAC report pointed to stealing by leaders, including the mysterious disappearance of funds from Chinese sources. The report was signed by A.B. Ngcobo in his capacity as Treasurer-General of the PAC, writing from Tanzania.[17]

It was reportedly after the so-called Six Day War between Israel and its antagonists in 1967 that Leballo did the unthinkable, secretly flying to Tel Aviv where he was given a large sum of money, whereupon he sneaked back into Dar. This illicit affair immediately chilled ties between the PAC and Algeria. David Sibeko, a portly PAC operative—soon to be murdered by his erstwhile comrades—was described by his harsher critics as a "man who excels in taking care of his stomach by way of great food and fine drinks" by dint of "drawing a guaranteed monthly subsistence allowance" from these very same "Zionists." This allowed him to drink "exclusively whiskey." Like others, he was said to have "relayed information about the movements and position of his fellow refugees in Botswana back to racist South Africa...." He was said to have "close relations with Andrew Young," soon to be shaping U.S. policy toward the region, and future U.S. spokesman Jody Powell, and to possess "similar American big-shot connections...." There was "little wonder that he has so much to spend on himself and his family for globetrotting...."

---

15. *U.S. News & World Report*, 25 September 1967; *Washington Post*, 27 September 1967; *Baltimore Sun*, 27 September 1967. See Brochure from "Rhodesia Information Office" 29 September 1967 box 23, *Frank Church Papers, Boise State University.*

16. John Millar to Secretary of State, 2 October 1965, RG 59, Central Foreign Policy File, Box 2930.

17. Report of the Treasurer General of the Commission of Inquiry set up by Moshi Meeting (19-21 September 1967) of the National Executive Committee of the Pan-Africanist Congress of Azania, Reel 18, *Oliver Tambo Papers.*

He had a "long standing friendship with one Black American called Richard Gibson, who lives in London" and was "known to have CIA connections but Sibeko defends him with passion…." (Gibson was also close to "Black Power" stalwarts: Amiri Baraka and Robert F. Williams.) By the late 1960s the PAC sought to send him to Tirana, Albania, then China's chief European ally, but he balked and wound up in Manhattan.[18]

By 1968 the PAC was banned in Zambia, with 15 members arrested, including Leballo. The organization was described as "Peking oriented," with links to ZANU; and the OAU had withdrawn financial support.[19] By early 1969 T.T. Letlaka and A.B. Ngcobo of the PAC were requesting aid from Washington. They made their way from Kinshasa to Addis Ababa on tickets supplied by Holden Roberto. Upon arrival in Ethiopia, Ngcobo told U.S. officialdom that in June 1968 Leballo had been ousted since he was reputedly "actively serving the interests of Communist China," but Tanzania and the Organization of African Unity both objected. According to R.L. Yost of the U.S., Nyerere wanted him reinstated since he was interested in "destroying the anti-Maoist leadership of the PAC and ensuring Chicom [Chinese] control…." Tanzania, it was reported, was "constantly pushing the interests of Chinese influence in the liberation movements," amidst claims that PAC "executives" were deemed to be "CIA agents."[20] Tellingly, Herman Cohen, who was to attain infamy as the chief henchman of U.S. policy in Africa, reported from the cloak-and-dagger capital of Kinshasa that he was "impressed" with both Letlaka and Ngcobo, who were "strongly committed to retaining and strengthening PAC's pro-western orientation;" thus, the wily Cohn would "attempt to maintain discreet contact with the PAC leaders…."[21] (Surely, their questionable ties to Roberto were bound to raise eyebrows. As early as 1961, the Angolan leader was reportedly receiving $1000 monthly from the CIA and $10,000 monthly a few years later.[22])

---

18. "The Profiles of Leballo's Gang," 5 May 1978, Box 4, Folder 15, *Prexy Nesbitt Papers, Columbia College-Chicago.*

19. *The Economist*, 31 August 1968, Box 144, *Leroy Walker Africa News Service Archive, Duke University.*

20. R.L. Yost, U.S. Embassy, Ethiopia to Secretary of State, 27 February 1969, RG 59, Subject Numeric Files: Political and Defense, Box 2468.

21. Herman Cohen to Secretary of State, 13 February 1969, RG 59, Subject Numeric Files: Political and Defense, Box 2468.

22. Andy De Roche, *Kenneth Kaunda, the United States and Southern Africa*, London: Bloomsbury, 2016, 17.

Nyerere was quite familiar with the U.S., having traveled there as early as 1955 to address the United Nations. By 1963 he was in the vanguard of those comparing Jim Crow and apartheid.[23] He conferred with Dr. King just before his epochal remarks in Washington in August 1963 where he expressed fervent solidarity.[24] When Malcolm X arrived in Dar, he was received warmly.[25] Fatefully, on 13 October 1964 at 7 PM, Malcolm and the Tanzanian leader met as news emerged that China—which they both admired—had developed an atomic weapon, leaving them both overjoyed. Portentously, the visitor announced that "for the first time today in recorded history, a former colonial country has been able to develop weapons at par with any colonial power. This is the end of colonialism through and through." A few months later, Malcolm X and the Zanzibar leader A.M. Babu met for half a day in Manhattan, discussing the formation of a "global black united front against colonialism." A few weeks later, Tanzanians joined the ANC, PAC, and SWAPO in mourning his tragic murder, a result of bitterly internecine conflict.[26]

His passing did not obliterate Tanzania's dedicated interest in a Pan-Africanism that did not exclude the African diaspora. By May 1967 Tanzanian leader John Malecela was drafting a proposal for the U.N. calling for seminars on apartheid, racism, and colonialism in Southern Africa. His initiative was accepted by the General Assembly and a meeting was planned for Zambia in July and August. The leading anti-Jim Crow groups were invited but the NAACP and the Southern Christian Leadership Conference chose not to attend,[27] to their detriment and, worse, that of the community which they purported to represent.

James Forman, a leader of the Student Non-Violent Coordinating Committee, came to Kitwe, Zambia to address those assembled. He praised Guinea-Conakry and Tanzania, the dual lodestars of African liberation, particularly after the dislodging of Nkrumah in Ghana. This gathering, he exulted, "marked another milestone in the liberation of Black people in the United States," and he now demanded that the plight of the Negro be "fully debated in the United Nations

23. *Washington Post*, 16 July 1963.

24. *Washington Post*, 22 July 1963.

25. Seth Markle, "'We Are Not Tourists': The Black Power Movement and the Making of Socialist Tanzania, 1960-1974," Ph.d. dissertation, New York University, 2010. 55:

26. Ibid., Seth Markle dissertation, 58, 63, 65. On the assassination, see *Tanganyika Standard*, 25 February 1965.

27. Ibid., Seth Markle dissertation, 96.

as a Human Rights problem" akin to apartheid. "Our own experiences" in the U.S., he insisted, "have prepared us to understand the emotional and psychological ordeal of a colonized people;" it was a mere "accident of history that we were not left in Africa where there are now independent Black nations…." He sought assiduously to link the struggles against Jim Crow and apartheid, pointing to the protest against U.S. naval vessels docking in Cape Town as a harbinger of what was to come. Washington, he exhorted, was "willing to let Black sailors who had been fighting in Vietnam to protect the security of white Americans subject themselves to apartheid racism." This outrageous "visit was cancelled after much protest."[28]

Black Power theoretician Carmichael was in and out of Dar intermittently, before finally settling across the continent in Conakry. He had raised the question of African American volunteers fighting in neighboring Guinea-Bissau, though it seemed that the PAC was closest to his heart. He was no fan of multiracialism and what he deemed to be Marxism's limitations, a point that he raised during a stay in Dar. Thus, he was critical of the ANC, FRELIMO, and Joshua Nkomo's ZAPU, which he saw as akin to U.S. civil rights groupings—like the NAACP—that were dependent upon white patronage (with aid from the socialist bloc considered to be in this unfavorable category). As this cry was raised, Tanzania's relations with the U.S. were deteriorating. There were expulsions of diplomats and Peace Corps workers, charges of involvement in coup plots and general mudslinging. Even Bill Sutherland, the Quaker functionary, was suspected since he played tennis at the U.S. Embassy.[29]

Back in South Africa, weeks before the murder of Dr. King in Memphis, the U.S. delegate in Johannesburg found that "the racial tension in the United States is not a liability with these people," his offhanded, perhaps contemptuous reference to Africans. "They identify with Martin Luther King and not Stokely Carmichael," he reassured the Secretary of State. Besides, he continued, "American history is taught in non-white as well as white schools (showing the British being beaten by a hardy frontier people on an independent continent)," of maximum importance to the Afrikaner elite. As for the African "elite," "as it watches Greek, Italian and Portuguese immigrants, many with little or no skills, entering the country and being awarded better jobs, homes and futures than blacks," it was "very galling" to see "the immigrants get theirs back by behaving as

28. "James Forman of SNCC Addresses the United Nations," *Liberator*, 7(Number 12, December 1967): 8-9, Box 54, Series II, *ACOA Papers*.

29. Ibid., Seth Markle dissertation, 105, 134.

the rudest white group." He could have added that absent the class radicalism espoused by the ANC-SACP alliance, this was simply a recipe for the kind of Black Power that the envoy, Herbert Reiner, was pooh-poohing.[30]

Still, Dixiecrats like Senator J. Strom Thurmond of South Carolina, took to the floor of the Senate in 1967 to announce that the despised "Communists" planned "to use the American Negro as the fulcrum for fomenting a hot revolution, a bloody revolution in America."[31] It would be an error to see those like Thurmond as outliers; instead, they should be seen to represent a considerable body of opinion among Euro-Americans. President Johnson thought so, for by 1967 he became concerned that pro-Salisbury sentiment in Congress would handcuff him politically.[32]

Thurmond's invocation of monolithic Communists came as Soviet-Chinese relations were deteriorating, which came as a shock to those who had been closely following this star-crossed relationship. When Ray Alexander left South Africa in 1965, she did not know there was "friction" between the two, declaring that it was "kept away from us" (by whom she did not say). She "cried," she confessed unashamedly, after witnessing a vitriolic Chinese attack on a Soviet comrade at an international confab.[33]

There were various grounds for China's proliferating hostility to the Soviet Union, but part of their complaint was the claim that "peaceful coexistence" between socialism and capitalism—a means of avoiding nuclear war, which obviously did not mean acceptance of the colonial status quo, as evidenced by growing aid to national liberation movements and Vietnamese comrades alike—was a sell-out. Ironically, after President Nixon's trailblazing journey to China, it was the latter nation that went on to wage war against a struggling Vietnam—but that was to come later. As of the 1960s—as pointed out by Waldemar A. Nielsen of the African American Institute, known to be a recipient of CIA funding—China was hammering "incessantly and everywhere on the theme of color." The U.N.'s U Thant was among those who felt that "racial conflict, if we cannot curb and finally eliminate it, will grow into a destructive monster compared to

---

30. Herbert Reiner, Consul General-Johannesburg to Secretary of State, 17 January 1968, RG 59, Central Foreign Policy Files: Social, Box 3094.

31. Speech, 18 April 1967, Box 25, Series II, *J. Strom Thurmond Papers, Clemson University*.

32. *New York Times*, 13 January 1967; Ibid. Zoe Hyman, 214.

33. Transcripts of Interviews for an Autobiography, A. 28, *Jack Simons and Ray Alexander Collection*.

which the religious and ideological conflicts of the past and present will seem like small family quarrels."[34]

Hammering on the theme of "color" was immensely attractive to Black Power advocates who were involved in a likeminded campaign—though strikingly Steve Biko, a founder of "Black Consciousness" in South Africa, seen as an analogue to Black Power, was not sympathetic to the U.S. counterpart. It was a "minority philosophy in the United States," he scoffed, whereas Africans were a majority in South Africa. Plus, overseas they were "talking within the American context of using the ballot box," whereas armed struggle was operative in Biko's backyard. And unlike an influential wing of the U.S. tendency, Biko confirmed that it is "not our intention to generate a feeling of anti-White-ism amongst our members."[35]

Despite his valiant attempt to distance Black Consciousness from Black Power, Mandela found this argument wanting. He cited unnamed "critics"— seemingly including himself—who were "suspicious of the support the movement enjoys from the imperialist countries, particularly the USA, as well as the movement's alleged hostility to Marxism"—though, to be fair, this latter description was more fitting for Black Power. Unmoved, Mandela contended that "some of the critics" of Black Consciousness "dismiss the movement as the brainchild of the American Central Intelligence Agency…." BCM, he said, exuded a "dogmatism" which "flows from the fact that the concept of Black Consciousness advocated by the BCM is imported from America and swallowed in a lump without regard to our concrete situation, to which progressive whites, including Marxists…form part of the liberation movement…." This trend was "in essence a rehash of Garveyism…." Mandela also rebuked *Black Power*, the foundational text of the U.S. movement co-authored by Carmichael and added that "the history of our country bears out Marxist theory"—a difficult proposition to mount in the U.S. given the inability of Marxists to comprehend "settler colonialism" and the rebellion against it that initiated the republic. Mandela was skeptical of BCM's "hostility to the Soviet Union," upon which the ANC-SACP alliance then relied. Thus, he found BCM's "position similar to that of the PAC." After all, "PAC and BCM members have been equally critical of the close cooperation between the ANC and SACP

34. Statement by Waldemar A. Nielsen to Subcommittee on Africa of House Foreign Affairs Committee, 3 March 1966, Box 127, *William Rusher Papers, Library of Congress.*

35. Millard Arnold, ed., *Steve Biko: Black Consciousness in South Africa*, New York: Random House, 1978, 99, 42.

as well as the help the ANC receives from the Soviet Union. They have joined Western spokesmen and conservatives in accusing us of being a Communist front and the tool...of the Soviet Union."[36]

Mandela notwithstanding, the focus on color by BCM and PAC was unsettling to regimes in Africa that wallowed in color bias and pointed to the dilemma faced by Pretoria and Salisbury, which were compelled to disdain forces that merely demanded wealth redistribution and abjured race baiting: race-baiting being a forte of the PAC. This point came up during a conversation between the US.'s William Witt and W.C. du Plessis, former South African Ambassador to the U.S., who spoke at length of the "Red Chinese exploitation of color bonds with Africans," which led him to "visions of the 'Chinese and Indians' spilling out over Southeast Asia, Australia and Africa...." In this overheated context, du Plessis "felt it necessary to raise the subject of America's race problems," which was of concern to him since—he thought— "we are taking a wrong line" in response to a "frustration which affects our Negro population." In contrast he declared "no one could expect the whites in South Africa...to 'commit race suicide' and averted to cautions over race war which he said John Foster Dulles had set forth in one of his books."[37]

Suicide was the policy Pretoria thought it was being offered when the Central Chinese Association of South Africa, representing a purported 8000, wanted the government to admit 400 refugees fleeing China. They denied they were spies in waiting, though the apartheid authorities were not as sure.[38] The former Taiwanese envoy in Johannesburg, Y.Y. Chen, was "outspoken" from his new posting in Blantyre, "about the unpleasant and unhappy experiences" he endured in South Africa, where he was viewed contemptuously as "nonwhite."[39] If Pretoria could not win over anticommunist Taiwanese and felt compelled to mistreat them too on racist grounds, then the situation for apartheid was more dire than it appeared.

Sharp lines of demarcation were drawn as a result, with China and PAC and ZANU on one side and the ANC and ZAPU on the other,

---

36. Nelson Mandela, "Whither the Black Consciousness Movement: An Assessment," in Mac Maharaj, ed., *Reflections in Prison: Voices from the South African Liberation Struggle*, Amherst: University of Massachusetts Press, 2001, 21-64, 21, 39, 40, 43, 45, 47, (published initially in 1976).

37. Report by William Witt, 22 July 1965, RG 59, Central Foreign Policy Files, Box 2642.

38. Embassy-Cape Town to Secretary of State, 5 June 1967, RG 59, Central Foreign Policy Files: Political and Defense, Box 2464.

39. U.S. Embassy-Blantyre to Secretary of State, 29 July 1969, RG 59, Central Foreign Policy Files, Political and Defense, Box 2462.

while others sought to avoid the resultant flack. In 1966 a PAC official in Dar informed a U.S. emissary that his group was getting aid from China.[40] Apparently, this funding was insufficient since soon the legation in Dar found the PAC to be in "grave financial difficulty" due to its "unwillingness to cooperate with Communist countries," apart from China—though this may have just been a ploy by the PAC tailored to extract aid from Washington.[41] In a "confidential" 1965 report, a U.S. official described a meeting with Duma Nokwe of the ANC leadership, a "cherub with a frown." He said that there had been a kind of "unity" with the PAC until 1962 but the latter "broke it over ostensible issue of Communist influence in [the] ANC," though the PAC itself was "tying up with Chinese Communists."[42]

PAC became an astringent critic of Moscow and what it called the "counter-revolutionary role" of the South African Communist Party, particularly their leader Bram Fischer. "Their retreat from Marxism under the cover of Marxism" was matched only by "their concern over the fate of the privileged whites;" the Communists, it was said inaccurately, "rule out force completely" in overthrowing apartheid.[43] This denunciation was mirrored by the words of Black Power icon Robert F. Williams of the U.S., who had fled Jim Crow for exile in Cuba, then China, and by early 1967 was rebuking "Moscow Communists," deriding them as "revisionists" while praising the "Great Proletarian Revolution then occurring in China. It was "the greatest event in the history of mankind," he said of a process that was eventually condemned in China itself. He had left Cuba—a Soviet ally—in a huff, then sent a 16-page, 8550-word rebuking letter to Fidel Castro explaining why. All of this was reported by another U.S. Negro, Richard Gibson, who was a similarly sharp critic of the ANC and their Eastern European allies.[44] Williams was unsparing in his condemnation of Cuba at a time when it was under siege by U.S. imperialism.[45] Gibson fanned the flames, rebuking "South African Toms," a derisive description of the ANC, after they were involved

---

40. Francis McNamara, Second Secretary-U.S. Embassy, Dar es Salaam to Secretary of State, 25 April 1966, RG 59, Central Foreign Policy Files, Box 2630.

41. John Millar, U.S. Embassy-Dar es Salaam to Secretary of State, 9 November 1966, Central Foreign Policy Files, Box 2630.

42. Report, 9 February 1965, RG 59, Central Foreign Policy Files, Box 2637.

43. *Azania News*, 1 (Number 21-22): 10-11, Box 142, *Allard Lowenstein Papers, University of North Carolina-Chapel Hill.*

44. "Richard Gibson Reports: International News and Features," March 1967, Box 55, Series II, *ACOA Papers.*

45. "Richard Gibson Report," May 1967, Box 55, Series II, *ACOA Papers.*

in a reported tiff with Carmichael; he congratulated the "black revolutionary PAC" and ZANU.[46]

Reprimanded, the ANC responded in kind, but Tambo dissented, telling Houser that "none of the circumstances merited an editorial on Stokely Carmichael in spite of the fact that he appears to have said a number of things which were critical of or may even have [been] interpreted as an attack on the liberation movements generally." After all, said the parsing ANC leader, "he made no specific reference to the ANC...." This was even more unfortunate since "some people took the statement in our editorial as indicating our disapproval of the 'Black Power' movement in America." "Nothing could be further from the truth of course," said the diplomatic leader.[47] He was echoed by Thabo Mbeki, a future South African president, who spoke of a seminar in East Germany in 1971 that engaged this topic: "we must adopt the progressive aspects of Black Power," he advised, "and seek to guide this 'movement' into the proper directions."[48]

Contrastingly, the SACP more than once expressed how the organization was "keenly conscious of the solidarity, the support, both moral and practical, rendered to our struggle by the Soviet Union and other socialist countries,"[49] and seemed less prone to rationalize "Black Power" excess.

According to Negro exile Charles R. Swift, many of his fellow exiles were "anti-white," an outgrowth in part of the mass support over the centuries for slavery, and then Jim Crow, among Euro-Americans, coupled with the suppression of the radical left which was not so inclined. This dynamic created conditions for these Negroes to be swayed by the PAC and China too. Tanzania's complicated relations with Moscow fueled such feelings too, a point which became clear after Nyerere criticized the Soviet intervention in Prague in 1968.[50] In contrast, Tambo backed Duma Nokwe's

---

46. Richard Gibson, "South African Tomes Denounced Stokely," no date, Box 54, Series II, *ACOA Papers*.

47. Oliver Tambo to George Houser, 2 January 1968, Box 142, Series III, *ACOARA*.

48. Comment by Thabo Mbeki, 14 October 1971, Box 16, Folder 78, Part I, *Lusaka Mission Records, ANC Records, Fort Hare University-South Africa*.

49. "Strive for World Communist Unity," Statement by the Central Committee of the South African Communist Party, *African Communist*, January-March 1964, 337, in *South African Communists Speak: Documents from the History of the South African Communist Party, 1915-1980*, London: Inkululeko, 1981, 335.

50. Charles R. Swift, *Dar Days*, 43, 108.

statement of support for the intervention.[51] And the Central Committee of the SACP, which had an interlocking directorate with the ANC leadership, "fully understood the concern of the Marxist-Leninist Parties of the Soviet Union and other neighboring socialist countries and appreciated their efforts to strengthen socialism in Czechoslovakia and rebuff the forces of counter-revolution."[52]

In the bipolar world that existed then, it was folly to expect the North Atlantic bloc to back the overthrow of the apartheid regime. For liberation fighters this left the alternative of turning toward Moscow and its allies. And even then, the spigot of aid did not seem to be turned on until after 1976, with the overthrow of colonialism in Angola and Mozambique and the Soweto uprising.[53]

Naturally, this meant that Pretoria and Washington would view Moscow as a mortal foe and would propagandize accordingly.

It was in 1966 that SACP lawyer Bram Fischer explained that the armed wing of the ANC—known as MK—was "not only to be secret but was to self-controlled by men selected by Mandela but was to finance its own affairs and was to [be] kept entirely separate and distinct from the Congresses and the Communist Party."[54] But after Mandela was jailed and tumult beset erstwhile allies in Africa, e.g. Egypt, and liberation movements came to power in places like Angola (which too was dependent upon aid from Havana and Moscow), MK also came to rely heavily on these latter two capitals. This de facto alliance was facilitated by the reality that the SACP was close to both Havana and Moscow and—unlike Black America—Africans were able to withstand the ideological onslaught of anticommunism. Born in 1958, anti-apartheid activist Wendy Majala was not alone in his assertion that "I read quite extensively on people like Marx, Engels...."[55] Born in 1927, ANC and SACP member Maxwell Bonisile Mayekiso was among those who received military training

51. Luli Callinicos, *Oliver Tambo*, 357.

52. Statement on the Czech Crisis, 23 August 1968 in *South African Communists Speak*, 365.

53. Christopher J. Lee, "Tricontinentalism in Question: The Cold War Politics of Alex La Guma and the African National Congress," in Christopher J. Lee, ed., *Making a World After Empire: the Bandung Moment and its Political Aftermath*, Athens: Ohio University Press, 2010, 266-286, 280.

54. "Extracts from Court Speech of Bram Fischer on March 28, 1967," in *South African Communists Speak*, 346-356, 354.

55. Oral History, Wendy Majala, 14 August 2004, *University of Connecticut-Storrs*.

in Ethiopia, where a Marxist-oriented regime came to power in the 1970s.[56]

In the late 1960s Slovo recalled "sitting in Moscow with admirals and generals from the Soviet armed forces who were helping us," notably in infiltrating South Africa from the sea. It was "really a very sophisticated project."[57] According to the politicized South African miner Zanemvula Pat Matosa, Slovo "understood the art of military science"[58]—and to the extent that was true, his experience with comrades in Eastern Europe was a major factor explaining why.

Wolfie Kodesh of the SACP observed in 2000 that "we got everything we wanted, sometimes more, surplus" and the like from Moscow (and Sweden and "also Holland").[59] Schloho Azariel Lebona said in 2003 that "some people said that the Russians would not come and fix our country"—though "it is a matter of going there. They would support us by prov[id]ing us with arms...." The anti-apartheid forces, it was said, "had problems especially in the West. They were the people who did not understand what the struggle was all about. But in Russia, the Soviet Union they understood," the same was true for "Cuba and East Germany...."[60]

In the 1960s Sindiso Gregory Mfenyana was conferring with Mandela and Thabo Mbeki in Johannesburg and Durban about the plan for him to study economics and engineering in Eastern Europe. He also happened to meet Jose Eduardo dos Santos, who became president of Angola years later. After that consultation Tambo informed Mfenyana, "you are going to fly to Moscow...you don't need money there, everything will be taken care of...." Thus, with nine others he found himself at Heathrow airport in London: "transit passengers.... were staring at these Africans, all nine of them, going to the plane to Moscow." They boarded "an empty plane "and wound up in Kiev, where they studied Russian and were trained otherwise: "at no stage," he insisted, "did we feel racial discrimination...people were friendly, really friendly...." Though he was "ecstatic" about residing

56. Oral History, Maxwell Bonisile Mayekiso, 24 May 2002, *University of Connecticut-Storrs.*

57. Luli Callinicos, *Oliver Tambo*, 367.

58. Oral History, Zanemvula Pat Matosa, no date, *University of Connecticut-Storrs.*

59. Oral History, Wolfie Kodesh, 4 October 2000, *University of Connecticut-Storrs.*

60. Oral History, Schloho Azariel Lebona, 15 September 2003, *University of Connecticut-Storrs.*

there, he departed by 1967. Even in 2001 he confided, "we thought it was a wonderful system."[61]

Cletus Mzimela was in China at the time of the Rivonia trial, then it was on to Dar via Burma and India and Yemen. Then it was to the Soviet Union for more training via Kenya and a "special flight" from Somalia to Odessa. He "started with Military Science" where he learned to "dislodge and rejoin" an AK47 weapon in "darkness." They'd "blindfold your eyes...." Some of his comrades decried "the manner in which they were trained in Egypt where they were sometimes made to walk on an area of feces" but there were no such complaints from trainees in Odessa where they were schooled by war heroes: as a result, "we could read in Russian...."[62]

Peter Peyise was also trained in Odessa. "It was cold, the place was cold," and he was "sick for two weeks." He was in Mozambique by 1967, where "military camps were on the banks of the Ruvuma River" on the Tanzanian border. He was addressed there by Samora Machel—and bombed by the Portuguese. "We were helped by the Russians, because we had political lessons in Russia...." After instability in Dar, induced in part by rumors floated by the PAC of a coup to be perpetrated by the ANC, he said, it was back to the Soviet Union—Tashkent precisely. Then to Algeria for more training, where cadre were "very friendly" and there were trainees too from SWAPO and MPLA.[63] His experience—born in South Africa but winding up in a military camp on the Tanzanian-Mozambican border—was not unusual. James April of the ANC, who received military training in East Germany, fought in Rhodesia.[64] When Eduardo Mondlane bumped into Houser in the 1960s on a flight from Cairo to Nairobi, the Mozambican told him that East German comrades had provided FRELIMO with "hundreds of cameras," quite useful in presenting a more accurate picture of events in southeastern Africa. Even though the ACOA too had provided aid in the form of a Land Rover, Mondlane did not hesitate to tell him that he felt safest in Eastern

61. Oral History, Sindiso Gregory Mfenyana, 28 January 2001, *University of Connecticut-Storrs.*

62. Oral History, Cletus Mzimela, 12 August 2003, *University of Connecticut-Storrs.*

63. Oral History, Peter Peyise, 23 February 2001, *University of Connecticut-Storrs.*

64. Ahmed Kathrada, *Memoirs,* 248.

Europe—an understandable judgment, particularly later considering his assassination in Tanzania.[65]

While the PAC and many Black Power adherents were highly supportive of China, SACP Chairman J.B. Marks mounted the rostrum at a gathering of Communists in Moscow and took an opposing tack, as he repudiated the "sidetracking and disruption of various international solidarity organizations by Chinese delegations who persisted in dragging into gatherings of non-Communists their alleged 'ideological' campaigns against the CPSU [Soviet Communists] and the World Communist Movement...." In a thinly veiled reference to the PAC, Marks caustically derided how "the Maoists" have been "subsidizing and actually preserving from complete collapse a group of right-wing renegades from our struggle whose documentary evidence now proves to have been started at the instance and with the support of the CIA."[66]

Sindiso Gregory Mfenyana, educated in the Soviet Union, mourned the ascension of the "Sino-Soviet dispute," observing that "in Zimbabwe, this division took a serious turn." "Our allies were ZAPU [Zimbabwe African Peoples Union] and they didn't even want to speak to ZANU [Zimbabwe African National Union] and they didn't want their allies, us, to be seen speaking to a ZANU person...." He found this "very strange" since "we had families that had members of ANC and PAC." Studying in the Soviet Union fed Pan-Africanism, he thought, since ANC cadre had "weekly meetings" with other Africans, in which among things they imbibed the lesson from Kenyans that "Mau Mau...lost because they didn't consolidate their nationalism" and his comrades' "belief was that you could only be a good socialist if you were a good nationalist...." The comrades also "admired, if not worshipped the Vietnamese," which did not endear him to Washington, because of "their ability to take on a superpower."[67]

As the ANC noted repeatedly, the PAC was like a chameleon, appearing to be "Maoists" in China, Pan Africanists in Africa and

65. Houser on Mozambique, no date, Box 4, *George Houser Papers*. See Eduardo Mondlane to George Houser, 24 January 1966, Box 142, Series III, *ACOARA*: "We have finally received the long-awaited twelve-seater Land Rover which [ACOA] has kindly given us;" it was already being used "to pick up a number of refugees who are sick" in Tanzania.

66. J.B. Marks, "South Africa and the World Communist Movement," in A. Lerumo, ed., *Fifty Fighting Years: The Communist Party of South Africa, 1921-1971*, London: Inkululelo, 1987, 162.

67. Oral History, Sindiso Gregory Mfenyana, 28 January 2001, *University of Connecticut-Storrs*.

anticommunists—or Black Power advocates, depending on the audience—in the U.S. Their leader Sobukwe admired President Johnson and was unhappy to hear that Senator Robert Kennedy was gearing up to challenge him for the White House in 1968. "My greatest hope," he confided then, "is to land up in a U.S. university." Historically Black Lincoln University wanted to give him an honorary degree and the NAACP offered him a job—this at a time when the ANC was considered radioactive because of its Moscow connections. "I have already read 'Darkness at Noon' twice," said the PAC leader, referring to a renowned anticommunist tome, "and have read it again.... It was [the author, Arthur] Koestler who provided me with ammunition to fight the Reds." He was also a fan of another anticommunist classic, *The God that Failed*, an opinion which was bound to win him adherents in the fanatically anticommunist U.S.[68] Possibly it was this literary bent that led the Southern African poet Dennis Brutus to confer with the U.S. legation in London about plans to settle Sobukwe in the U.S.[69] Perhaps unbeknownst to Sobukwe, his brother-in-law, Dr. Fabian Ribeiro, was sharing "personal letters" from the jailed PAC leader, including details that the Pretoria legation found informative.[70]

In turn Moscow began stepping up aid to the ANC and the other so-called "authentic" liberation movements, including FRELIMO, MPLA, and SWAPO. Thus, in early 1969 Thomas Nkobi of the ANC found happily that his "request to grant 5 scholarships" to students by the Soviet Afro-Asian Solidarity Committee was met.[71] At the same time Houser was finding that he could hardly get visas for those tied to the ANC, let alone scholarships. Leaders like Tambo, Robert Reesha, and Dennis Brutus had been listed as Communists under Pretoria's Suppression of Communism Act and, said Houser lamentably, this outlook "had just been taken over by the U.S. lock, stock and barrel as a definition of what a Communist is." This was "something which burns our African visitors up," he said resignedly.

---

68. Benjamin Pogrund *How Can Man Die Better*, 218, 231, 247, 253.

69. Ronald Spiers, Embassy-London to Secretary of State, 7 August 1968, RG 59, Subject Numeric Files: Political and Defense, Box 2468.

70. William Witt to Secretary of State, 19 November 1964, RG 59, Central Foreign Policy Files, Box 2636, *NARA-CP*.

71. A. Ozasokhov to Thomas Nkobi, 25 February 1969, Reel 8, *Oliver Tambo Papers*.

He could have added that it also put the torch to any U.S. efforts toward building a sturdy bridge to the anti-apartheid cause.[72]

While Washington was seeking to block anti-apartheid visitors, favorites of Pretoria were flocking to the U.S. Sugar exports from South Africa, along with corpulent executives, were arriving at U.S. docks, just as South African Airways planes were landing. "These are all factors which support the status quo," claimed Joel Nordby of the United Methodist Church with some justification.[73]

Yet to aid non-communist and anticommunist unions, the AFL-CIO, with U.S. assistance, dispatched functionaries to South Africa to lend a hand. "Much of the criticism directed against South Africa," explained one official, "is based on faulty information or a distortion of facts" since "our countries are so similar."[74]

The ANC's difficulty in obtaining visas was garnished with concomitant harassment—particularly that directed at Mandela's spouse. With barely concealed lasciviousness, the U.S. emissary in Johannesburg reported on alleged bedmates of Ms. Mandela, using Eric Louw—apartheid's embodiment—as his source.[75] "In her personal life," said Consul General Reiner, speaking of Winnie Madikizela Mandela, she was "something less than a Penelope waiting for the conquering hero due back from the Trojan War." He also

---

72. George Houser to Mary Louise Hooper, 7 February 1967, Reel 2, Part I, #409, *ACOA Papers*.

73. Joel Nordby to Congressman Allard Lowenstein, 15 August 1969, Box 88, *Allard Lowenstein Papers, University of North Carolina-Chapel Hill*.

74. Report by E.H. Splain of U.S. Embassy-Pretoria, May 1967, Box 12, IAD Country Files, *International Affairs Department, AFL-CIO, University of Maryland-College Park:* Gene Weishan of the Retail Clerks union was sent there.

75. Joseph L. Dougherty, Consul General-Johannesburg to Secretary of State, 25 February 1965, RG 59, Central Foreign Policy Files, Box 4215: "[Eric] Louw said that Mrs. Mandela candidly admitted to sleeping with both [Brian] Somana and Vutela," librarian at the University of Witwatersrand who then got into a fracas "over her 'favours'....Somana had caught her in bed with Vutela. A furious argument ensued after which she 'kicked' Somana out of her home.... Mrs. Mandela's amoral activities are not out of character if local rumors are to be believed. She is a decidedly attractive young lady who, even before her husband was sentenced to Robben Island, was reported to be 'sleeping around'." See also Oral History, Joyce Mohammed, 21 December 2001, *University of Connecticut-Storrs*: "I never trusted Winnie......[she] had an affair with Brian Somana.... every now and then Winnie was arrested for nothing, just to get information" because she was so compromised. "She has been working with the government...."

seemed concerned that her periodic court appearances involved, "an unnamed American lawyer."[76]

As ANC cadre were subjected to spying and finding it difficult to get visas to the U.S., the PAC faced different challenges. Willard De Press of the U.S. embassy in Accra talked with Potlako Leballo, who termed the recently deposed Nkrumah "one of our best supporters"—but now they were being forced to depart from Ghana as a result of the pro-U.S. coup. The PAC leader was described as "very bitter about Soviet opposition to PAC participation" at the all-important Tri-Continental Conference in Havana and the sidelining of PAC within the Afro-Asian Peoples Solidarity Organization, known to be influenced by Moscow. A sign of the times was the imminent opening of a PAC office in Manhattan—thanks to ACOA—and the shuttering of their facility in Jakarta in the aftermath of the anti-Sukarno coup.[77] The PAC did not seem to recognize that consorting with Washington while the CIA was deposing governments friendly to the group was the essence of an incoherent policy.

To be fair to ACOA, it was continuing its ecumenical approach, seeking to aid PAC and ANC alike. The problem was that the latter was perceived as being aligned with Moscow, making it difficult to maintain contact with the ANC, especially when its leaders were denied visas. Writing in his capacity as an ANC leader, Moses Kotane of the SACP in Tanzania told Mary Louise Hooper that "a period of two years in the USA for a fund raiser would be a bit of a hardship," even assuming a visa was available—and likely it was not. The group, he said accurately, "may not be able to afford the expenses involved!" He was, in any case, "practically alone here in Morogoro," Tanzania where he was "not only in charge of the organization's finances" but also "personnel and its everyday political and administrative affairs…."[78] This reflected the ever closer alliance between the SACP and ANC but it also indicated whey it was so difficult for the party of Mandela to effectuate an entente with Washington, the citadel of anticommunism. At this juncture, Kotane's proximity to Moscow did not seem to be delivering dividends to the ANC, who he was serving as Treasurer-General. "Our scales of

76. Herbert Reiner, Consul General-Johannesburg to Secretary of State, 15 November 1967, Central Foreign Policy Files: Social, Box 3094.

77. Memorandum of Conversation with Potlako Leballo with Willard De Pree, First Secretary, Accra Embassy, 11 March 1966, RG 59, Central Foreign Policy Files, Box 2630.

78. Moses Kotane to Mary Louise Hooper, 22 January 1968, Box 142, Series III, *ACOARA*.

value are not the same," he told Houser in early 1968. "Large sums of money in the United States means billions of dollars. To us," he lamented, "it merely means thousands;" thus, he concluded, "we want you not merely as advisors but as the leaders of our fund raising campaign in the United States."[79] For obvious reasons, Kotane and the ANC were willing to overlook ACOA's ties to the PAC, not to mention regnant suspicions about the group's ties to unsavory elements in Washington: the "problem of money is becoming acute," said Kotane in April 1968.[80]

Though the ANC was hardly able to secure visas, Houser valiantly sought to aid the group, even filling optometry prescriptions for Tambo. "I keep them in my desk drawer," he told the ANC leader in mid-1968, "so that I can take action just as soon as I have some word from you."[81] "We have a chronic problem in sending anyone to the U.S. or indeed any other part of the world," Tambo told Houser in late 1965. "Friends in the U.S. have urged upon us the importance of a top leader of the ANC visiting the U.S. and helping to revive the image of the ANC which seems to have been blurred somewhat by the activities of a wide variety of self-seeking careerists…." This latter point was upsetting but the wider point was crudely simple: "we are in a financial mess."[82] The ever-helpful Houser found time to make his way to the ANC's obscure base in Tanzania. "It was wonderful meeting you in this very remote little corner of the world," Tambo wrote from Morogoro in 1967, which conveniently was "concealed in the foot of an imposing mountain," presumably hidden from the prying eyes of Pretoria's military. "You are the only visitor from abroad—the only one among our friends who has been out here."[83] Houser and Tambo met first in Johannesburg in 1954 and encountered each other in Morogoro as early as 1967; the "elevation" there, said Houser, "made it easier to keep his asthma under control."[84]

Houser also remained close to Joshua Nkomo in war-torn Zimbabwe, terming him "My Dear George," whose "work…we have been

79. Moses Kotane to George Houser, 22 January 1968, Box 142, Series III, *ACOARA*.

80. Moses Kotane to George Houser, 30 April 1968, Box 142, Series III, *ACOARA*.

81. George Houser to Oliver Tambo, 24 June 1968, Box 142, Series III, *ACOARA*.

82. Oliver Tambo to "Dear George" Houser, 25 November 1965, Box 142, Series III, *ACOARA*.

83. Oliver Tambo to George Houser, 7 June 1967, Box 142, Series III.

84. Report by George Houser, no date, Box 4, *George Houser Papers*.

following...from this remote area of the world. We listened to your interview on Voice of America about some of your companies that continue to buy from here," at least until he and his comrades were "relieved of our radio receivers...." He was reading "Advanced Economics" while jailed, an optimistic course that could be of use after independence.[85]

The news got worse. Houser was saddened to report a few months later that Hooper "had a breakdown" while travelling in Yugoslavia and had to be airlifted to the U.S., where she was placed in "complete isolation in a private mental hospital." Her family was "very much opposed to her activities as they related to ACOA and to South Africa," which "caused her mental anguish," meaning she was "working under great tension" and now was "not able to act on her own."[86] Like so many others globally, she was deeply moved by the death of Chief Luthuli, run down by a freight train in 1967. "I know how dear and close the Chief was to you," was the message to her from Duma Nokwe.[87] Tirelessly, she had been working overtime on behalf of the anti-apartheid cause, with her latest project joining Nyerere, Kanunda, Trevor Huddleston, and His Imperial Majesty, Haile Selassie, in organizing the Luthuli Memorial Foundation in honor of the late ANC leader after his untimely passing.[88]

(The SACP was not as forgiving about the ANC leader's reportedly accidental death: "[The] white imperialistic establishment in the USA killed [Dr. King] just as surely as apartheid South Africa killed Chief Albert Luthuli.)[89]

Yet, she had to retreat from the frontlines and by April 1968 was residing on what she called a "big ranch (800 acres) in Southern Oregon" with her daughter and grandson. There had been "lots of pressure on me," she told Nkomo freely,[90] who in response said, "we cannot [afford] losing people like you...."[91] Kotane told "Dear

---

85. Joshua Nkomo to George Houser, 16 February 1966, Box 142, Series III. *ACOARA*.

86. George Houser to Moses Kotane, 17 September 1968, Box 142, Series III, *ACOARA*.

87. Duma Nokwe to Mary Louise Hooper, 8 August 1967, Box 5, *Mary Louise Hooper Papers*.

88. Brochure, no date, Box 5, *Mary Louise Hooper Papers*.

89. Lerumo, "Our People in the USA," *African Communist*, (Number 33, Second Quarter, 1968): 12-25, 12.

90. Mary Louise Hooper to Joshua Nkomo, 25 April 1968, Box 5, *Mary Louise Hooper Papers*.

91. Joshua Nkomo to Mary Louise Hooper, 6 March 1968, Box 5, *Mary Louise Hooper Papers*.

Louisa" that he was so "sorry to hear that you are not quite well and had been forced to enter a 'rest home'"; yet "large sums of money" were still needed and he wondered if she had any ideas in that regard.[92] Even Nkrumah, now on the sidelines, exiled in Conakry, found time to tell her, "I admire you so much for this wonderful devotion to the African cause," a testament to an unsung soldier.[93] Joe Matthews told her that "you were always a part of the ANC family and are not 'white' as far as we are concerned,"[94] an intended compliment.

* * *

U.S. overtures to the PAC may have been driven by a misleading underestimate of the popularity of the ANC, then subject to fierce repression. Mandela, it was reported from Cape Town in 1969, "continues to have some influence among Africans in South Africa but it is obviously waning...."[95] The SACP was said to have "approximately 600" members in late 1968, though "none of them are openly active"—which would have been unwise given the trenchancy of anticommunism.[96] This the U.S. knew instinctively, for when envoys reported on a special conference of the ANC at Morogoro, Tanzania, they detected a "strong degree of Communist influence" and a naked "pro-Moscow orientation."[97]

Likewise on the decline, it was thought, was the Liberal Party of Alan Paton, which once had 8000 members but by early 1968 had shrunk to 2000—"of whom only 1000" were "truly active" with "principal financing," according to the writer's son Jonathan Paton, coming from the pocket of his father.[98] A few months later in Durban, the party was said to be disbanding altogether, with the elder

92. Moses Kotane to Mary Louise Hooper, 12 October 1967, Box 2, *Mary Louise Hooper Papers*.

93. Kwame Nkrumah to Mary Louise Hooper, 6 April 1968, Box 2, *Mary Louise Hooper Papers*.

94. Joe Matthews to Mary Louise Hooper, 12 July 1968, Box 1, *Mary Louise Hooper Papers*.

95. Cape Town legation to Secretary of State, 24 April 1969, RG 59, Central Foreign Policy Files: Political and Defense, Box 2462.

96. Pretoria Embassy to Secretary of State, 4 November 1968, RG 59, Central Foreign Policy Files: Political and Defense, Box 2463.

97. Report from Embassy-Lusaka, 5 August 1969, RG 59, RG 59, Subject Numeric Files: Political and Defense, Box 2463.

98. Consul General-Durban to Secretary of State, 19 January 1968, RG 59, Central Foreign Policy Files: Political and Defense, Box 2462.

Paton joining in the dirge of the anti-Jim Crow movement: "We Shall Overcome."[99]

Just as the NAACP had sought to bond Z.K. Matthews to the CIA, the U.S. authorities did not give up seeking to woo certain ANC leaders. This included Robert Resha[100] and Tennyson Makiwane, who was reported to have said that the underlying reason behind the virulence of the ANC's assault on U.S. imperialism was its dependence upon Moscow and the SACP—and that more U.S. aid would serve as an antidote to this propaganda.[101] W.R. Duggan, U.S. Consul General in Durban, claimed that Thulani Gcabashe, Chief Luthuli's son-in-law, was a "close personal friend."[102]

Pretoria was doing its own wooing, entertaining a steady stream of U.S. visitors, including Admiral Arthur Radford, a former Chairman of the Joint Chiefs of Staff, the premier military body, who hailed the land of apartheid.[103] In return, a leading apartheid military commander was taking a correspondence course with the U.S. military, gathering skills need to combat Mandela's MK.[104] It was understandable why a correspondence course was taken, as opposed to showing up in person. For when apartheid mavens Piet Koornhoff, Marais Steyn, and Paul van der Merwe appeared at Johns Hopkins University in 1968 to study, their reception was rowdy with Koornhoff called a "dirty lying pig." This rowdiness did not deter Jack Steyn, Secretary General of the Nationalists in the Transvaal, who headed to the U.S. to study "American...propaganda techniques."[105] Similarly undeterred, Koornhoff expressed a "strong desire" to visit Puerto Rico in order to scrutinize "Operation Bootstrap," a model of

---

99. Consul Geenral-Durban to Secretary of State, 10 May 1968, RG 59, Central Foreign Policy Files: Political and Defense, Box 2463.

100. Memorandum of Conversation with Robert Resha, 21 March 1966, RG 59, Central Foreign Policy Files, Box 2638.

101. Memorandum of Conversation, 2 March 1968, RG 59, Central Foreign Policy Files: Political and Defense, Box 2461.

102. W.R. Duggan, Consul General-Durban to Secretary of State, 19 January 1968, RG 59, Central Foreign Policy Files: Political and Defense, Box 2462.

103. Consul General-Johannesburg to Secretary of State, 25 July 1968, RG 59, Central Foreign Policy Files: Political and Defense, Box 2461.

104. Consul General Cape Town to Secretary of State, 25 July 1968, RG 59, Central Foreign Policy Files: Political and Defense, Box 2461.

105. Consul General-Johannesburg to Secretary of State, 18 October 1968, RG 59, Central Foreign Policy Files: Political and Defense, Box 2462.

neo-colonialism with lessons applicable to colonized neighbors and Bantustans alike.[106]

Also coming to pay respects to apartheid were a former presidential candidate, Arizona's Barry Goldwater; *New York Times* columnist, C.L. Sulzberger; and Stanley Meisler of the *Los Angeles Times*. Goldwater, it was reported, "favored the airwaves with some comments...sympathetic to apartheid and fully acceptable to the apostles of separate development." As for the journalists, Pretoria was overjoyed by the positive press reception given in the U.S. to heart transplant doctor Christian Barnard.[107] Senator James Eastland of Mississippi also arrived, on a trip aided by the Foreign Ministry, and he too—according to a U.S. observer—"found himself in agreement with apartheid."[108] Eastland also managed to visit Rhodesia and found that the rebel state "bears the earmarks of the same situation we in Mississippi face...." While "standing in the midst of giant blooming cotton fields," the sympathetic Senator "felt very close to Mississippi...." Then he noticed that the "dark cloud of Rhodesia's future.... lies to the north," for there "lies the menace," i.e. "Communist Conspiracy."[109] The *Johannesburg Star* was not far wrong in terming the Mississippian as Pretoria's and Salisbury's "most influential friend" in Congress.[110]

Senator Eastland, who sensed instinctively that a retreat of colonialism in Africa spelled doom for Jim Crow, was quite active on this front. One supporter in Vicksburg during the Congo crisis a few years earlier, was outraged by the "atrocities" said to be perpetrated by the military there, targeting the "white population". These "very barbaric monsters" were an indicator that a "day might come—and God forbid it—when another Oxford case in Mississippi will find us facing United Nations Congolese troops." A pleased Eastland replied enthusiastically that "you and I have the same views. Come and see me!"[111]

---

106. "Confidential" Report from Pretoria-Embassy to Secretary of State, 2 October 1968, RG 59, Central Foreign Policy Files: Political and Defense, Box 2462.

107. U.S. Embassy-Pretoria to Secretary of State, 18 January 1968, RG 59, Central Foreign Policy Files: Political and Defense, box 2461.

108. "Confidential" Report from Embassy-Cape Town to Secretary of State, RG 59, Central Foreign Policy Files: Political and Defense, Box 2462.

109. Article by Senator Eastland, no date, Box 1, File 1, Subseries 14, *James O. Eastland Collection, University of Mississippi-Oxford*.

110. *Johannesburg Star*, 30 July 1968.

111. O.J. Bori to Senator Eastland, 2 January 1963, FS3 SS1 Box 84, *James Eastland Papers*.

The U.S. legation continued to be pleased by U.S. investment in South Africa and the apparent flourishing of Ford auto plants near Port Elizabeth, where the company had sunk roots in the 1920s. Yes, there was a "labor scarcity," due to apartheid barriers that hindered the training of Africans but generally, it was reported enthusiastically, "American businessmen seem content with their lot."[112] An Eastland supporter, W.C. Watson of the local segregationist "Citizens' Council" was "very much disturbed by an attempted embargo on arms sales to South Africa, "the only nation in the world that is acting like the southern United States in trying to keep the race pure and separated like God intended;" it was "embarrassing that our government is licking the niggers [sic] foot" since "we as white people ...are very apprehensive about our future under the rule of the black man"—not unlike his comrades in Pretoria.[113]

* * *

The escalating fightback against Jim Crow continued to open doors for U.S. Negroes, which almost unavoidability brought this group to the doorstep of South Africa. One such visitor in mid-1968 was boxer Curtis Cokes, who—said Herbert Reiner, U.S. envoy—was "winning friends as well as fights in the townships." As for Cokes, he opined that "our slums at home make your townships look like graveyards in comparison."[114] In an interconnected world, Pretoria had difficulty shielding its citizens from the newer racial realities, for example, allowing their athletes to run the risk of defeat by their Negro betters. Such was the case in 1967 for Paul Nash, the South African sprinter, whose defeat at the hands of superior Negro runners was reported without comment in the local press—though no comment was required for a loud statement to be made.[115]

His candor did not necessarily endear Cokes to Pretoria; nor did he win many fans among the apartheid elite when he defeated their favorite, Willie Ludick, a member of the European minority. "Cassius Clay has been quite a hero over here," said Reiner, referring to

---

112. Consul General Cape Town to Secretary of State, 18 January 1968, RG 59, Central Foreign Policy Files, Political and Defense, Box 2461.

113. W.C. Watson to Senator Eastland, 18 August 1961, FS 3 SS1 Box 83, *James Eastland Papers*.

114. Herbert Reiner, Consul-General, Johannesburg to Curtis Cokes, 20 June 1968, RG 59, Subject Numeric Files: Political and Defense, Box 2466.

115. U.S. Embassy-Pretoria to Secretary of State, 20 July 1967, RG 59, Central Foreign Policy Files: Political and Defense, Box 2461.

the boxer known even then as Muhammad Ali, well on his way to staunch opposition to U.S. foreign policy. "A number of American Negro boxers come to Soweto and enjoy an idyllic life with their hero-worshippers," a list that was to include Ali.[116]

But it was not just Negro boxers who were admired in the townships. Africans, said Reiner, were "stunned" by the assassination of Dr. King in 1968, sensing that this blow would simultaneously afflict the anti-apartheid movement. "Many Africans," he said, "have had a deep feeling for King and a number of the current township elite had met him in America."[117] This elongated list doubtlessly included the family of Chief Luthuli: his granddaughter was given the name Coretta Nganya, the Zulu surname meaning "morning light" or "dawn," and the former name in honor of King's widow.[118]

Africans were capable of comparing other Negro clerics invidiously to Dr. King. For example, Pretoria forced Dr. Harrison L. Bryant of the AME denomination to leave the country, though he had refused to attack apartheid while in South Africa, and then went a step further to demand that a "white man...be sent as Dr. Bryant's replacement."[119] The inaction of those like Bryant may have inspired the U.S. academic Edwin Munger of the California Institute of Technology in Pasadena, who claimed while speaking at the University of Witwatersrand in 1968 that U.S. Negroes had brought little pressure on apartheid, isolated instances such as the port call of U.S. vessels in Cape Town aside, and even here, he argued, there was no unanimity within the preeminent NAACP.[120]

The rising tide of 1968, featuring not only assassinations but stormy marches and protests in the U.S., did not seemingly cause the Vorster regime to retreat. An emblem of Pretoria for decades had been the flourishing of anti-Semitism and the challenged regime did not back down in this regard. In 1968 one of Vorster's Cabinet members issued a stern admonition to the Jewish community "to curb the irresponsibility of their youths on South Africa's English-speaking

116. Herbert Reiner to Secretary of State, 25 April 1968, RG 59, Subject Numeric Files, Box 2466.

117. Herbert Reiner to Secretary of State, 11 April 1968, RG 59, Subject Numeric Files, Box 2466.

118. W.R. Duggan to Secretary of State, 8 November 1968, RG 59, Central Foreign Policy Files: Social, Box 3092.

119. Herbert Reiner to Secretary of State, 11 January 1968, RG 59, Subject Numeric Files, Box 2466.

120. Herbert Reiner, Consul General-Johannesburg to Secretary of State, 6 September 1968, RG 59, Subject Numeric Files: Political and Defense, Box 2469.

campuses." After fierce objection to Hilgard Muller's condescending remark that some of his "best friends are Jews," Vorster exacerbated the injury by instructing those offended to be "less hypersensitive."[121] The Afrikaner elite's endemic chauvinism, a weakness that led to their fall from power in 1994, continued through the 1960s. Unlike their comrades in Washington, the Pretoria elite found it difficult to sincerely incorporate the Jewish community into the edifice of "whiteness." And it was worse than this, since this elite still found it difficult to embrace migrants from Britain or Southern Europe or South America and even France, as they were still ceaselessly refighting the turn-of-the century war and feared that these new arrivals would gravitate to the English-speaking community. In 1967, some among the Boers feared that within two decades they would be a minority within the wider European-derived community. This fear was so resonant that even migrants from Holland often were disparaged since some of them were Catholic.[122]

Even good news on migration was clouded by chauvinism. Thus, as the war in Rhodesia heated up, more Europeans headed southward—but many of these were English-speaking, making their arrival bittersweet.[123] In any case, it was not as if Euro-Americans were being welcomed with warm embraces upon arriving in Salisbury, a logical point of entry for this group. In 1968, 9 Africans were sentenced after attacks on elderly U.S. tourists,[124] one of a spate of such incidents.[125] Still, the so-called "Anglo-Rhodesian Society" strained to overcome this sharp deterrent to migration.[126] They may have been helped by Vorster's brother, who was a frequent visitor to the U.S. and was received favorably there—particularly in religious circles, notably by Catholic clergymen and media.[127]

Benjamin Pogrund, a South African writer of Jewish descent who was close to the PAC, sued Percy Yutar, the prosecutor of the Rivonia

---

121. Consul General-Johannesburg to Secretary of State, 3 September 1968, RG 59, Subject Numeric Files: Political and Defense, Box 2467.

122. Herbert Reiner to Secretary of State, 16 March 1967, RG 59, Subject Numeric Files: Political and Defense, Box 2467.

123. W. Paul O'Neill, Jr., Consul-General-Salisbury to Secretary of State, 26 September 1969, RG 59, Central Foreign Policy Files: Social, Box 3092.

124. W. Paul O'Neill, Consul-General-Salisbury to Secretary of State, 15 November 1968, RG 59, Central Foreign Policy Files: Social, Box 3092.

125. Gerald Horne, *From the Barrel of a Gun*, passim.

126. W.O. Toomey, Consul-General, Durban to Secretary of State, 10 February 1967, RG 59, Central Foreign Policy Files: Social, Box 3093.

127. D.S. Spigler, Embassy-Pretoria to Secretary of State, 9 May 1967, RG 59, Central Foreign Policy Files: Social, Box 3093.

defendants and of the same religious heritage, on grounds of defamation. Revealingly, Pogrund prevailed before a predominantly Afrikaner panel, which the writer instinctively saw as anti-Semitic, not only because Yutar was disliked intensely by the elite but also because their bigotry did not allow them to treat him with anything but contempt, despite his clear service to the state.[128] In addition to Yutar, the Nationalist Party was served faithfully by Mendel Levin, who also happened to be Jewish—though Joel Carlson, the attorney who formerly employed her, was puzzled by Winnie Mandela's attempt to hire Levin as her attorney. Ultimately, Carlson himself was red-baited and subjected to anti-Semitic slurs.[129]

Carlson was also accused of profiting handsomely from his legal defense of a proliferating number of political prisoners—and squabbled over this to the point of "mutual antipathy" with Benjamin Pogrund, known to be close to the PAC.[130] Carlson was affiliated with the Lawyers Committee for Civil Rights' Southern Africa Project. The LC itself had been initiated by liberal attorneys after the bombing of a church in a Birmingham, Alabama in 1963. Arthur Goldberg, who was to serve on the U.S. Supreme Court and as U.S. Ambassador to the U.N., was a sponsor. By 1967 Carlson was defending SWAPO members.[131]

It was Levin who claimed that "more Jews than ever before were coming out in support of the Nationalist Party," according to an observant journalist. Levin, he continued, "lashed out at the Herstigte Nasionale Party which has barred Jews and Catholics from joining...." There were, Levin continued, "hundreds of well-known Jewish businessmen, industrialists and professional men'" flocking to the Nationalist Party.[132]

In 1967 familiar incidents erupted in the Hillbrow neighborhood of Johannesburg: Neo-Nazi celebrations of Hitler's birthday accompanied by ugly songs and slogans that led to anti-Jewish incidents.[133]

---

128. Consul General-Johannesburg to Secretary of State, 15 November 1967, Subject Numeric Files: Political and Defense, Box 2467.

129. Joel Carlson, *No Neutral Ground*, New York: Crowell, 1973, 267, 294.

130. La Rue Lutkins, Consul-General, Johannesburg to Charles Runyon State Department, 1 July 1971, RG 59, Subject Numeric Files: Political and Defense, Box 2582.

131. David Sogge to Southern African Project, 10 December 1978, ID 1978 AFRICA PROGRAM-CON'T SOUTHERN......*AFSC*.

132. *Sunday Express*, 22 March 1970, Box 117, *Allard Lowenstein Papers, University of North Carolina-Chapel Hill*.

133. Report from Johannesburg, 9 May 1967, RG 59, Central Foreign Policy Files: Social, Box 3093,

By the end of the year the South African Jewish Board of Deputies was in an uproar, forced to defend their loyalty, distressed that a relatively anodyne criticism of apartheid from Israel at the U.N. was ascribed to their influence. There was "quiet fear" in the community, said Reiner, as this incident was conflated with the pre-existing concern about how the Jewishness of those like Slovo, First, and a raft of other Communists was being interpreted—or misinterpreted. The community, said Reiner, was opposed to the status quo, which was understandable, but this only served to enrage the elite who felt uncomfortable pressure to change. Thus, simultaneously, the community tended to "dislike anyone who is rocking the boat." This reticence meant that "many incidents" of bigotry "go unpublicized" since "Jewish leaders themselves want to play the incidents down."[134]

The Israeli criticism of apartheid at the U.N., made in accord with its outreach to newly independent Africa and designed to outflank Egypt, Algeria, and the North African supporters of the Palestinians, had left South African Jewry "confused," according to Reiner. Pretoria identified with plucky Israel after its June 1967 victory over Egypt and its allies and allowed huge sums of money to flow northward to Tel Aviv from the local Jewish community, ostensibly for charity. The amount suspected was 20 million rand. But the U.N. episode led Pretoria to conclude that Jewry "could never be 'true citizens'" and this, said Reiner, "opened the gates for torrents of anti-Semitism."[135]

By May 1968, Reiner was reportedly excited about "underground cells" based on "anti-Semitic" and "anti-black" ideology with an estimated membership of 1200 engaged in military drills. They were called the "New Mounted Guard" ("Nuwe Ruiterwag").[136]

The suspicions of the Afrikaner elite even extended to their lifeline in Washington. U.S. envoy William Witt felt that "Anti-Americanism" was "always residual in the extreme right wing of the Nationalist Party."[137] In 1967 an Afrikaner periodical published a purported secret document detailing U.S. policy toward Pretoria, forwarded by a U.S. national who occupied a high post in the U.S. hierarchy.

134. Herbert Reiner, Consul-General, Johannesburg, 30 November 1967, RG 59, Central Foreign Policy Files: Social, Box 3094.

135. Herbert Reiner, Consul General, Johannesburg to Secretary of State, 15 November 1967, RG 59, Central Foreign Policy Files: Social, Box 3094.

136. Herbert Reiner, Consul General-Johannesburg to Secretary of State, 8 May 1968, RG 59, Central Foreign Policy Files: Political and Defense, Box 2463.

137. William Witt to Secretary of State, 3 September 1965, RG 59, Central Foreign Policy Files, Box 2930.

The supposed bombshell only served to reveal what was evident to whoever read newspapers carefully; Washington was torn by the competing demands of apartheid and anti-apartheid. The upshot, however, was the scorn from Pretoria toward the U.S. that this episode generated, which was not the best way to maintain a lifeline.[138]

The scorn was justified, according to Douglas Reed of Durban. He demanded that Senator Richard Russell of Georgia confirm or deny "published reports that American officers and officials are being taught Afrikaans for use on The Day" of invasion of South Africa—and since he was "unreassured [sic]" by denials, seemingly only a confirmation would suffice.[139] Jim Crow advocates were so stunned by the putative turnabout in U.S. policy that they convinced themselves that the logical next step was an invasion of Southern Africa by the U.S. Rose Marie Sorenson of the "Friends of Southern Africa of Anderson Country," South Carolina, was not alone in believing fervently that "a poll of the Senate indicates that over 80% of those questioned feel that Congress can do nothing to prevent our men from being called for service in South Africa and/or Rhodesia if the Security Council of the United Nations should do so."[140] C.C. Moseley of Grand Central Industrial Centre in Glendale, California warned tremblingly of a "United Nations war in Rhodesia or South Africa...."[141] In 1967 a Salisbury official proclaimed that it was "abundantly clear that to squeeze Rhodesia to economic death it will be consequent to a blockade involving the South African and Portuguese territories" which could only be accomplished by "the U.S. Navy."[142] J.D. Crump from segregationist Macon, Georgia, simply asked Senator Herman Talmadge, "can you tell me why we are supporting the Negroes against the white people in South Africa?"[143]

---

138. Translation of document from *Die Landstem*, 3 May 1967, RG 59, Subject Numeric Files: Political and Defense, Box 2469.

139. Douglas Reed to Senator Russell, 30 March 1967, Box 24, Subgroup C, Congressional XVI, Subject Files, *Richard Russell Papers, University of Georgia-Athens.*

140. Rose Marie Sorenson to W.J.B. Dorn, 18 May 1967, Box 86, *William Jennings Bryan Dorn Papers, University of South Carolina-Columbia.*

141. C.C. Moseley to W.J.B. Dorn, 2 May 1967, Box 86, *William Jennings Bryan Dorn Papers.*

142. D. Garner, Under Secretary, External Services, Ministry of Information and Tourism, Salisbury to Gerhard Gellermann, 14 January 1967, Subject Correspondence, Box 14, *J. Strom Thurmond Papers, Clemson University.*

143. J.D. Crump to Senator Talmadge, 12 June 1967, Box 48, V, Category Files, *Herman Talmadge Papers, University of Georgia-Athens.*

True to its historic role as a bastion of reaction, Dixie's Louis Harris, Vice President of a newspaper chain, writing from Augusta, Georgia, informed the Secretary of State that Pretoria was "more tolerant" than Washington, since Robert Kennedy was offered a visa but Ian Smith of Rhodesia was not.[144] Thoughtfully, Senator J. Strom Thurmond of South Carolina, Senator James Eastland of Mississippi, and Senator Paul Fannin of Arizona sent "best regards" to Smith on "your National Holiday."[145] The muscular "Friends of Southern Africa of Anderson County" was indignant about the "very idea!" of sanctioning Salisbury.[146] Senator J. Strom Thurmond of the Palmetto State concurred. It was in mid-1968 that he condemned U.N. sanctions against Salisbury as "the most sweeping of its kind in the history of the U.N." It was a "sad moment in the history of U.S. international affairs" besides; "one might as well proclaim the U.S. Declaration was also illegal," as like others he drew a parallel between 1776 and 1965.[147]

At the National Security Council at the White House, Ambassador Arthur Goldberg conceded that "the Rhodesian problem causes us difficulties with domestic public opinion;" for there was a "very active Rhodesian lobby" at odds with a rising anti-Jim Crow movement. "We were obliged to vote in the U.N. as we did because to do otherwise would have caused us domestic racial difficulties and hurt our business interests in every African country…." The price was alienating Salisbury and the potent pro-Rhodesian bloc in Dixie.[148]

Still, there were powerful U.S. interests in Salisbury that could not be ignored easily. By 1968 popular U.S. magazines were conspicuous on newsstands in Salisbury. U.S. music was ubiquitous on the airwaves and U.S. textbooks were to be found in schools. The U.S. observer John Montgomery also found time to huddle with Major General H.J. van den Bergh, Deputy Commissioner of Police in South Africa who was not secretive in confessing, "Yes, we cooperate with the FBI…. we have liaison with the FBI and CIA, which has agents in South Africa." Yes, the Pentagon was "teaching about 100 officers to

---

144. Louis Harris to Dean Rusk, 6 March 1968, Box 86, *William Jennings Bryan Dorn Papers, University of South Carolina-Columbia.*

145. Memorial to Ian Smith, 9 November 1967, Subject Correspondence, Box 14, *J. Strom Thurmond Papers, Clemons University-South Carolina.*

146. Eloise Cardwell to WJ.B. Dorn, 14 August 1967, Box 86, *William Jennings Bryan Dorn Papers.*

147. Speech, 4 June 1968, Box 11, Speeches, Subseries B, *J. Strom Thurmond Papers.*

148. Summary Notes of 567th NSC Meeting, 25 January 1967, 12:10 to 12:45 p.m., Box 36, *Dean Rusk Collection, University of Georgia-Athens.*

speak Afrikaans"—not for the purposes of a U.S. invasion, but closer collaboration. Montgomery was elated to find that "more than 40 of the 100 U.S. Senators have either expressed pro-Rhodesian opinions or delivered pro-Rhodesian speeches." He was pleased to bump into a trade delegation from New Orleans in Cape Town, not to mention a Chamber of Commerce delegation from Phoenix in Salisbury, and a touring party from Houston at Victoria Falls. He was overwhelmed to notice that in dining rooms from Salisbury to Pretoria "we could spot Americans by the way they ate, holding forks in their right hands and we could spot American voices in lobbies and on the streets...." Importantly, "the newspapers devote considerable space to American affairs." The buildings were familiar too since "their architecture is American. Their music is American. They wear American clothes, use American appliances and ride in American automobiles. A dollar spends as readily as a rand," useful when the time arrived to "drink the same cold drinks that are popular in the U.S." "Many of the political, business and educational leaders have visited the United States." A leader of the fading United Party in South Africa, J.O. Newton Thompson, provided sustenance when he announced that "your action in Vietnam is a shield to us and a tremendous action for the West as a whole." Thus, both Salisbury and Pretoria offered to send troops to Indo-China though this would have weakened defense on the home front. In blood chilling words, one Pretorian told Montgomery, "if we had settled our problems with the Bantu the way Americans settled theirs with the Indians, we wouldn't have a black majority now."[149]

The dominant trend of the era would also beset Salisbury: as the U.S. worked haltingly to end the most horrid aspects of Jim Crow, it became evident to this capital as well as Pretoria that unalloyed support would not emerge from the presumed backstop for white supremacy. Salisbury's delegate in Washington was startled to arrive at the conclusion that the praxis of racism in his new home was worse than in Southern Africa. He was shocked to find that his landlord on the banks of the Potomac River demanded that he sign a lease agreeing not to entertain Negroes in his apartment (of course, in Pretoria or Salisbury a lease would not be needed to ensure agreement on this fundamental point).[150] After his 1967 trip to Rhodesia,

149. John A. Montgomery, "The Bright Side of Dark Africa: Republic of South Africa, Independent Rhodesia, A Series of Articles from the *Columbia Record*," 1968, *University of South Carolina-Columbia.*

150. Report, 10 February 1967, RG 59, Central Foreign Policy Files: Social, Box 3093.

California Assemblyman E. Richard Barnes confirmed the alleged "total absence of racial discrimination in public places." This rebel state, he said, was the "spearhead of sanity and order" in Africa, a continent "torn with irrationality. Chaos and wide open to Communist manipulation and Communist takeover." "The time has come," he brayed, "for Western leaders to betray our enemies for a change, not our friends."[151]

Those lining up to berate Washington included Hans Abraham, apartheid's "Commissioner General of the Xhosas." He grouped the local English language press with that of the U.S., saying both "propagated integration." Like others he highlighted the urban rebellions breaking out in major U.S. cities as evidence for the proposition that "multi-racial 'Utopia'" was fraudulent; "after all," said Reiner, an "attack on U.S. racial integration before African audiences," Abraham's specialty, "is really bearding the lion in his den."[152] It was Abraham who argued that Washington would be well-advised to pursue a Bantustan policy all its own.[153]

Fred Staples of Pietermaritzburg was able to get a report to the aging U.S. Senator Richard Russell of Georgia, a bulwark of Jim Crow. He had "read with great interest of the black vs. white disturbances" in the U.S. and, unremarkably, his "sympathy" was extended to those who believed in the "utter impracticability of the complete integration which your Government is trying to force, not only on its own country" but "on others as well." He was elated to see that "some of your Negro leaders are now demanding that the USA be apportioned between White and Black." "What is the difference between our apartheid and theirs," he asked irritably, "except that we are trying to do things gradually and without violence...." He also was "wondering what the signatories of your Declaration of Independence would think of things today...."[154]

Thus, when in 1968 a Dallas hotel refused to serve the First Secretary of the Lesotho legation in the U.S.—M. Vitus Malapo—the South African press felt vindicated, while a U.S. official feared the

151. *San Diego Evening Tribune*, 17 November 1967, Box 105, *William Jennings Bryan Dorn Papers, University of South Carolina-Columbia*.

152. Herbert Reiner, Consul-General, Johannesburg to Secretary of State, 21 March 1968, RG 59, Central Foreign Policy Files: Social, Box 3094.

153. W.R. Duggan to Secretary of State, 23 August 1968, RG 59, Central Foreign Policy Files: Social, Box 3094.

154. Fred Staples to Charles Heinemann, Jr. and Senator Russell, 9 July 1967, Box 24, Subgroup C, Congressional XVI, Subject Files, *Richard Russell Collection, University of Georgia-Athens*.

incident "could lead to an international crisis," just one more bit of evidence of the chasm separating the erstwhile allies.[155]

There was a formidable bloc in the U.S. Congress that would have congratulated the hotelier for refusing to bend to the current fashion of desegregation. This would have included Senator J. Strom Thurmond of South Carolina, in the midst of a departure from the Democratic Party—which he had challenged from the right in the 1948 presidential race on a fierce Jim Crow platform—to the GOP, which was becoming the party of "whiteness" in light of President Johnson's push for Negro voting rights. In 1967 he hailed a local periodical after it rapped Nigeria, whose "tribal conflict is further proof to the world that many of the new African states are incapable of efficient, harmonious self-government." In contrast he hailed Pretoria, which was supposedly "vigorously illustrating its ability to unite its country in a sensible cooperative way…." "South Africa," he claimed, "is not calling for race war but instead is promoting economic cooperation between its country and the new Republic of Biafra."[156]

The buoyant Kenneth Towsey of the Rhodesia Information Office happily informed Thurmond that he did "appreciate the support you are giving our country." Attached to his note were the words of Congressman J. Arthur Younger of California, just back from South Africa, who "found only one U.S. government employee who was in sympathy with the action taken against Rhodesia," the imposition of sanctions. "Mr. Frank Johnson, Foreign Editor of the American Security Council's 'Washington Report' had a similar experience on a recent visit to South Africa and Rhodesia."[157]

Many in the U.S. saw in the Rhodesian revolt a replay of 1776. Such was the case for Thomas J. Clark of Rockford, Illinois, who thought Salisbury was "following the same course we took in 1776 and," he added ominously, "if I were twenty years younger, I'd be following the footsteps of General Lafayette and fight for them."[158]

In certain circles of the right, the only debate was whether emphasis should be placed on rescuing Rhodesia or South Africa. Senator Thurmond was informed in late 1966 that "South Africa rather

155. P. Hooper, Jr., Embassy-Pretoria to Secretary of State, RG 59, Central Foreign Policy Files: Social, Box 3094.

156. Speech, 8 June 1967, Box 25, Series II, *J. Strom Thurmond Papers*.

157. K.H. Towsey to Senator Thurmond, 6 April 1967, Box 25, Series II, *J. Strom Thurmond Papers*.

158. Thomas J. Clark to J. Strom Thurmond, 11 April 1967, Box 25, Series II, *J. Strom Thurmond Papers*.

than Rhodesia is the key to the 'Rhodesian Problem'" since Pretoria was the "real target of U.N. action...." A "U.N. invasion of South Africa" was more likely, for example. The prod here would be newly empowered U.S. Negroes and the distinct possibility that they could be "persuaded to identify themselves with foreign Negroes to bring about political pressures from America." The Carnegie Endowment was cited for the proposition that "if American Negroes increasingly identify the struggle against apartheid with their domestic civil rights struggle they could bring interest in...South African policy to a level seldom achieved by any foreign policy issue."[159] Indicating the grave concern with this point from the ultra-right was the fact that it was echoed by their tribune, Dan Smoot.[160]

Carnegie and Dixie may have been paying attention to a blossoming anti-apartheid movement that was soaring far beyond the efforts of ACOA and its more militant predecessor, Robeson's Council on African Affairs. By 1968 the leafy campus of Princeton University in New Jersey was exploding in protest because of the failure to divest the campus endowment from corporations invested in South Africa—a protest that included the present writer, then a teenager. Our leader, Paul Williams of Chicago, informed the university that "one cannot really separate the movement of black people in this country from that of black and 'colored' people all over the world," an intervention validated by the co-signature of Mohamadou Dip of the Pan African Students Organization.[161] William Scott, yet another activist, reminded the university that Pretoria refused to accept "Black Americans at the NASA tracking station," though training such technicians was now part of the school's mission. Apartheid meant barring "American Negroes from working in South Africa with American businesses," also contrary to the university's recently stated mission. State-sanctioned racism also prevented "American Blacks from serving in what constitutes the United States' largest African diplomatic mission," another policy contrary to the school's stated positions.[162]

---

159. "Canadian Intelligence Service, Supplementary Section," December 1966, Box 14, Subject Correspondence, *J. Strom Thurmond Papers.*

160. "Dan Smoot Report," 6 March 1967, Box 86, *William Jennings Bryan Dorn Papers.*

161. Paul Williams for the Association of Black Collegians to Harold Helm, Chairman of the Committee on Finance, 29 April 1968k, Box 278, *Office of the President, Robert F. Goheen, Princeton University-New Jersey.* Hereafter Goheen Papers.

162. William Scott, Co-Chair of New Jersey Committee on Southern Africa; Homer Ashby, Jr. of the Association of Black Collegians and Robert

More athletic African American students—and others—were also demanding a U.S. boycott of the Mexico City Olympics because of the participation of South Africa. The protesters also included star professional athletes like Oscar Robertson, the retired baseball infielder, Jackie Robinson, and many more, a sign of things to come.[163]

Blockum of Committee on Black Awareness to Harold Helm, no date, circa 1968, *Goheen Papers*.

163. Letter from Oscar Robertson, Jackie Robinson, Bob Boozer, Ruben Amara, Arthur Ashe, Dick Barnett, Nate Bowman, Walt Bellamy, Dave Bing, Jim Bouton, Roy Campanella, John Carlos, Lee Evans, Bob Gibson, Hal Greer, Walt Hazzard, Larry James, K.C. Jones, Sam Jones, Cazzie Russell, Tommie Smith, Chet Walker, Jerry West, et.al., 27 February 1968, Box 155, *Leroy Walker Africa News Service Archive, Duke University-North Carolina.*

Chapter 13

Contradictions, 1968-1974

AS anti-Jim Crow protests rose in the U.S., defenders of this despicable and beleaguered system seemed to be fleeing en masse to Southern Africa for succor and, for various reasons, this exodus provided propulsion to state-sanctioned racism in both places. "My trip to South Africa and Rhodesia was very rewarding," said the attorney Clarence Manion in early 1968. "We recorded a radio and television interview with Prime Minister Smith" soon to be aired in the U.S.[1] This Dean of the Law School at Notre Dame University was told he had "rendered a *tremendous* service in getting the voice of Ian Smith on the American airways," critical since Washington "refuse[d] to give him a visa to enter the USA."[2] [emphasis original] Providing a venue for Smith's poisonous voice gave a boost for Jim Crow too. "I hope you enjoyed your trip to Rhodesia and South Africa," said the fanatically racist and anticommunist Billy James Hargis: "I certainly enjoyed mine."[3] Dean Manion's African reverie may have been dimmed by the fact that his credit card was "stolen" with his "wallet in Phalaborwa, South Africa" during his stay.[4]

In any case, Manion's expectations were not elevated. While in South Africa, he bumped into Lee Anderson of the *Chattanooga News-Free Press* and the journalist warned him to take "precautions not to fall into the pot of cannibals," since "there is an extremely primitive side of Africa that cannot be overlooked...." In contradiction to his experience, Manion dismissed the notion that Africans were residing in dire conditions: "I tried to find some slums," he

1. Clarence Manion to Anthony Kubek, 8 March 1968, Box 30, *Clarence Manion Papers, Chicago History Museum.*

2. John S. Howe to Clarence Manion, 26 March 1968, Box 30, *Clarence Manion Papers.*

3. Letter from Billy James Hargis, no date Box 30, *Clarence Manion Papers.*

4. Clarence Manion to Carte Blanche, 8 March 1968, Box 29, *Clarence Manion Papers.*

said unconvincingly, but "most of the people I asked seemed not to know where any could be…there simply are not many slums in South Africa."[5]

As the throwaway comment about "cannibals" indicates, many Euro-American visitors to Africa could not resist descending into racist stereotyping. On a nearly contemporaneous visit to East Africa, the major investor Harold Hochschild remarked casually that "one of our party…was bit in the lip by a monkey in Tsavo National Park…we're not sure whether the monkey was a Masai or Kikuyu no disrespect intended."[6]

Ian Smith surely enjoyed his exposure to Manion's audience on his popular U.S. radio program. The attorney began by lambasting the U.N. since "it would [have] suspended our Declaration of Independence until we had conditionally enfranchised all of the American Indians." Smith reminded listeners that "some of our big…mines in Rhodesia are financed by American capital and we have American investment in big mining industry in Rhodesia which has been here for, I think, as long as thirty to forty years." "These companies are still operating," he said triumphantly, though with glumness he added that the minerals were not flowing to the U.S. because of sanctions. Like Manion, he blamed malevolent Communists.[7]

In January 1968 it was reported that former presidential candidate Barry Goldwater was arriving in Salisbury. "I am neither pro or anti-Negro," he said, as he exemplified the emerging trend of "color blindness" and opposition to "reverse racism." It was "indefensibly wrong," he implored to launch a "boycott against Rhodesia."[8]

Goldwater was merely one among many from Capitol Hill making their way to Southern Africa. Congressman John Ashbrook was there by early 1967, finding "tranquility"—he "never heard a siren." Sure, there was racial segregation, but the U.S. had the same. The "disadvantaged Negro" was part of the landscape in the U.S., so how could Washington complain about Salisbury? Anyway, there was "great white support" for Salisbury.[9] By late 1967, the right-wing editorialist James J. Kilpatrick was making his way to Angola and

5. "Manion Forum," 14 April 1968, Box 83, *Clarence Manion Papers*.

6. Harold Hochschild to Winifred Armstrong, circa 1968, Box 6, *Winifred Armstrong Papers, Stanford University*.

7. "Manion Forum", 17 and 24 March 1968, Box 83, *Clarence Manion Papers*.

8. *American Southern Africa Review*, January 1968, *University of Kansas-Lawrence*.

9. *Congressional Record*, April 1967, Box 12, *International Affairs Department, AFL-CIO*.

Mozambique. He compared the "pioneer" experience of the settlers to the process that had established white rule in his homeland.[10] Kilpatrick, a popular journalist, who appeared regularly on the highly rated CBS television program, "60 Minutes", was a cheerleader for Salisbury and Pretoria alike to the point where Congressman Diggs lamented that he newsman "has attacked as 'fascism' my [anti-apartheid] efforts...to investigate the Rhodesian Information Office," whose presence in Washington was a putative violation of accords to which the U.S. was a signatory. Diggs stridently assailed his support of "chrome plated racists" who sought to "promote trade with Rhodesia in violation of U.S. law."[11] Unsurprisingly, Salisbury kept a close eye on Diggs and other Black Congresspersons,[12] as well as "Negro Civil Rights organizations, militant churchmen (primarily United Methodist and United Church of Christ), liberal academics and the storm troopers [sic] that they command...."[13]

As Diggs impassioned words suggested, these junkets to Southern Africa—often subsidized by the outlaw regimes—had policy consequences. Congressman John Rarick of Louisiana was hailed by one Johannesburg resident since during his jaunt there he "'conjured up images of gang rape, cannibalism and general butchery on whites in Black Africa,"[14] all as a result of what he saw as a wrongheaded U.S. policy toward the region.

Pretoria too thought that its vast mineral wealth provided leverage that could move Washington, even in the face of a surging anti-Jim Crow movement. This idea had occurred to Nico Diedrichs, Minister of Finance, who in 1968 wondered if the U.S. "might proceed wholly to demonetize gold...wholly to detach the dollar from gold or wholly to detach gold from the dollar," a prescient prediction that would be implemented shortly. "This would pose a mighty threat to gold," he said. "I cannot imagine that the United States would ever take such a thoughtless measure," he added guilelessly. Such a move would "wholly destroy confidence in paper money," he said, perhaps prematurely. With a failure of imagination that characterized

---

10. James J. Kilpatrick, "A Special Study of the Portuguese Provinces," Box 14, *International Affairs Department Country Files, AFL-CIO.*

11. Statement of Congressman Charles Diggs, 22 May 1973, FS 3 SS 1 Box 85, *James Eastland Papers.*

12. Kenneth Towsey to L.S. Hawkins, 27 May 1971, Box 2, *Kenneth Towsey Papers.*

13. Kenneth Towsey to S.D. O'Donnell, 28 May 1972, Box 4, *Kenneth Towsey Papers.*

14. M. Gold to Congressman Rarick, 16 March 1970, FS 3 SS1, Box 95, *James Eastland Papers.*

the class he represented, he concluded, "I cannot imagine that under present circumstances another currency, for instance, the dollar, could become the criterion of the world's monetary units."[15]

Appropriately enough, it was not long before President Richard M. Nixon and his national security aide Henry Kissinger were debating what to do about South Africa and gold, as they contemplated manipulating the value of the dollar.[16]

Govan Mbeki has stated accurately that "the concern felt in the U.S. that Communists were behind the liberation struggle in South Africa completely distorted the U.S. perspective." This was reflected in National Security Study Memorandum 39, drafted by Kissinger in 1969, as U.S. investment in apartheid rose from 35.8% of all investments in Africa to 40% by 1974. Not coincidentally, the uptick occurred as the oil embargo by mostly Arab nations began to bite in 1973, heightening the importance of the uranium controlled by Pretoria—30% of global supply. The U.S., Mbeki writes, was trapped between anticommunism and Pretoria's racism. Kissinger was acquainted with fascism in Germany, born not far from East Germany and forced to flee his Bavarian home because of ascendant anti-Semitism in the 1930s, making all the more curious his countenancing of the fascist trends that inhered in apartheid.[17] On the other hand, the attempt to escape the snare that was gold could be seen as a recognition of the frailty of Pretoria.

Kissinger had been informed earlier that Senator John Tower of Texas had a "highly confidential meeting with the Finance Minister" from Pretoria and consequently, that it was "important for a close liaison to be established between our own finance people and South African leaders." Tower thought "we need to 'soften our bigoted attitude'" toward Pretoria and stare down the anti-Jim Crow and anti-apartheid movement; this should be done, said the Texan, "if for no other reason than South African powerful leverage through

---

15. Speech by Nico Diederichs, 8 April 1968, Box 155, *Burke Hickenlooper Papers, Hoover Presidential Library, West Branch, Iowa.*

16. Henry Kissinger to President Nixon, 23 December 1969, Box 744, *National Security Council Files, Country Files-Africa, Richard M. Nixon Presidential Library-Yorba Linda, California.*

17. Govan Mbeki, *Sunset at Midday: Katsgib'ilang'emmi!* Braamfontein: Nolwazi, 1996, 75. On Kissinger and NSSM 39 see also Luis Mesa Delmonte, "The Policy of the U.S. in Southern Africa," in Delmonte, ed., *Change and Counter-Revolution in Southern Africa,* Havana: Jose Marti Publishing House, 1987, 189-222.

her gold production."[18] Ultimately, Washington was unable to comply with the Senator's counsel. This was one more disappointment delivered by Nixon, a Republican Party leader, whose 1968 election was cheered in Pretoria and Salisbury.

Retrospectively, it is unclear what role Pretoria's "powerful leverage" played in Nixon's 1971 departure from the gold standard. Reputedly, the White House was comfortable with the idea that the minority regime was solidly implanted and, thus, there was little fear of winding up dependent upon an ANC-SACP regime. Still, by September 1970 Winifred Armstrong, who worked at the highest level with AMAX—or American Metal Climax, a major force in exploitation of Southern Africa's vast mineral wealth—was mulling over Washington's "new policy of discouraging U.S. investment" in what was to become Namibia. The basis of U.S. policy toward this colony was the view that it was "illegally occupied," and U.S. personnel in South Africa did "not any longer visit" there. This "new policy," Armstrong was made aware, "was specifically approved by President Nixon personally...."[19]

It was also in 1970 that Taylor Ostrander of AMAX expressed severe disappointment with post-colonial Zambia, which was not only housing liberation movements but was also a major repository of the standard-setting mineral that was copper. Writing "entirely anonymously," he did not hesitate to express "considerable disillusionment" and "disenchantment" with Kaunda, wailing that the leader "broke his word with respect to the continued private ownership of the copper mines...." He "suddenly changed his position in mid-1969," perhaps motivated by the global rise of radicalism. Worse, said Ostrander, Kaunda was "breaking a few hearts in the process" by allowing supposedly disreputable people into venues where they should be barred. Thus, the "guest list" for a Zambian reception in Manhattan was a "shambles," redolent of the recent past when "Harlem and other parts of town found they could gatecrash almost any African reception at the U.N." Yes, the "contents of this letter are dynamite," he conceded, if only because of his evident distaste for increasing ties between Afro-Americans and Africans, which could potentially turn the tables against imperialism

18. Bryce Harlow to Henry Kissinger, 12 June 1969, Box 744, *National Security Files, Country Files-Africa, Richard M. Nixon Presidential Library.*

19. Letter to "I.K.M." from unknown, 29 September 1970, Box 41, *Winifred Armstrong Papers, Stanford University.*

and neo-colonialism alike.[20] But it was not just growing bilateral ties that were upsetting to those like Ostrander. The SACP intellectual Jack Simons was holding classes—according to his spouse, Ray Alexander—"in Kaunda's house" that included "governors... cabinet...military intelligence" up to and encompassing "the Military High Command"; the purpose, she said, was "explaining imperialism, explaining colonialism,"[21] i.e. explaining the routine devastation inflicted on Africa by companies like AMAX.

Harold Hochschild, who had made a fortune investing in the minerals of Africa—principally through AMAX—was also nervously surveying the scene in Southern Africa. He was comfortingly told in 1967 that the "Rhodesian situation is not going to be changed by British action," entailing the "need to live with that situation for a period of years," and resulting in the opportunity to profit handsomely.[22]

But it was not just gold and minerals that yoked the U.S. and South Africa. The latter did not export sugar to the U.S. until 1962, when a substitute for the Cuban variety was sought in the wake of sharply declining relations. On an upward swing, the export of sugar rose from 8325 tons in 1962 to 21,823 tons by 1963 and 20,326 by 1964. Similarly, South African sugar was seeking to replace Cuban sugar in global markets, which brought praise in Washington too since the effort was weakening Havana.[23] Southern Africa's production of agricultural commodities was also part of the calculus in Washington. In early 1969 Senator James O. Eastland of Mississippi bluntly informed Herbert Jack Quenton of the Sabi Limpopo Authority in Salisbury, "I was most interested" during my tour there "in the growing of cotton...."[24] "Our six days in Rhodesia," effused Larry Speakes, Senator Eastland's press secretary (and soon to play the

---

20. Taylor Ostrander to Dr. Edwin S. Munger, 10 November 1970, Box 7, *Winifred Armstrong Papers.*

21. Transcripts of Interviews for Ray Alexander's Autobiography, 22 November 1997, A.28, *Jack Simons and Ray Alexander Collection, University of Cape Town.*

22. George Loft to Harold Hochschild, 14 January 1967, Box 6, *Winifred Armstrong Papers, Stanford University.*

23. Statement of Tom O. Murphy, Director, Sugar Policy Staff, U.S. Department of Agriculture before Subcommittee on African Affairs, 15 April 1969, Box 287, *Thomas Abernethy Papers, University of Mississippi-Oxford.*

24. Senator Eastland to Herbert Jack Quenton, 26 March 1969, Box 1, File 1, Subseries 14, *James O. Eastland Collection, University of Mississippi-Oxford.*

same role for President Ronald Reagan), "were the most enjoyable that I have ever spent anywhere."[25]

Arriving for an 11-day holiday in the Kruger Park in South Africa was Henry Ford II, head of the eponymous auto manufacturer, who probably found the time to check on his massive plant in Port Elizabeth.[26] Charles Engelhard remained the largest individual investor in apartheid (though Ford might have thought otherwise).[27] But by 1969, as the anti-apartheid movement made waves at Princeton University, this titan of industry who maintained a residence in a neighboring New Jersey town, called on his fellow captain of industry, Harry Oppenheimer of South Africa, for a discussion designed to block campus divestment from apartheid-related companies.[28]

Houser was heartened by the outbursts at these ivy-fringed institutions; these protests, he said, were "developing increasingly" and "we try to encourage" same.[29] The former State Department official turned scholar Thomas Karis was not as sure. He found it "discouraging" to "read about a young Black student yanking" a Cornell University administrator "by the scruff of the neck" during a discordant protest. But even Karis had to admit that "there's great potential on the campuses" insofar as the attack on apartheid was concerned.[30]

Nevertheless, those who made up the apartheid bloc were like characters in a drama unable to imagine they would soon be swept from center stage. Writing from Cape Town, Dean Manion observed that those with whom he conferred "are worried about our reverses in Vietnam, as we are, because they are convinced that if we lose to the Reds in Vietnam, [South Africa] will be the next target."[31] Manion also blamed these impending reversals on a U.S. policy "based on an appeal to domestic racial agitators and their international counterparts in the U.N.'s Afro-Asian bloc…."[32]

The specter of Vietnam was haunting apartheid, with its firmest defenders sensing that if the dikes were breached in Southeast Asia

25. Larry Speakes to Gosta Jan Kingma, 12 March 1969, Box 1, File 1, Subseries 14, *James O. Eastland Papers University of Mississippi-Oxford*.

26. "News from South Africa", "Produced by the Information Service of South Africa," 15 March 1967, Box 301, *Group Research Archives*.

27. Ramparts Release, 25 October 1966, Box 301, *Group Research Archives*.

28. Rogert Goheen to Harold Helm, 21 May 1969, Box 278, *Goheen Papers, Princeton University*.

29. George Houser to Thomas Karis, 19 March 1969, Box 150, Series III, *ACOARA*.

30. Thomas Karis to George Houser, 11 April 1969, Box 150, Series III.

31. Clarence Manion to W.L. McGrath, 10 February 1968, Box 83.

32. "Manion Forum," 14 April 1968, Box 83.

it would not be long before Pretoria would be inundated. The economist and intellectual John Kenneth Galbraith was informed in 1968 by Andrew Duncan of the University of Witwatersrand that "most of us here...are watching the American political scene with deep interest and a certain amount of anguish due to the circumstances surrounding the election" and "Vietnam."[33] Heightening the anxiety over Vietnam was the idea that it represented a Cold War showdown between the U.S. and Soviet Union—and if the former could not prevail here, ineluctably capitalism—and apartheid—would be destined for the dung heap of history. The SACP contributed to the anxiety in 1970 when it castigated the "most cruel and murderous war to subdue the people of Vietnam." Twisting the dagger, the party spokesman added without gratuity that this war was of a piece with U.S. "[mal]treatment of the black people in their own country," which was a "disgrace."[34]

As with so many sojourners in the land of apartheid, Manion returned energized, ready for renewed battle against "domestic racial agitators." One of his guests on his popular radio show was the doyen of black conservatism, George Schuyler, notorious for his whitewashing of Portuguese colonialism in Angola. Apartheid, said Schuyler, was "their business," meaning Pretoria's, of no concern to anyone else. South Africa was "doing pretty well" compared to the rest of the beset continent. "I don't hear anybody objecting to the Indians having the Navajo Reservation and other reservations out west and so I don't see why they should object to the South Africans having reservations for the various groups there...." He also raised an alarm about a nation with which U.S. was to effectuate an entente. "Tanzania now has thousands of Chinese—so-called engineers" who were "training and directing the military campaign against Rhodesia"—though the "target" was "South Africa generally."[35]

Manion and his minions were reacting to obvious political currents. By 1968 a high-level delegation from London was consulting with their counterparts in Washington and the message was bracing. Joseph Sisco of the U.S. conceded that the State Department was "under attack domestically for supporting sanctions" against Salisbury. "The business community in particular was criticizing

33. Andrew Duncan to Professor Galbraith, 27 March 1968, Box 181, *John Kenneth Galbraith Papers, John F. Kennedy Presidential Library-Boston.*

34. Statement by the Central Committee of the SACP, 1970, in *South African Communists Speak: Documents from the History of the South African Communist Party, 1915-1980*, London: Inkululeko, 1981, 367-384, 367.

35. "Manion Forum," 14 July 1968, Box 83.

the Administration strongly...." Worrisome was the fact that Dixiecrats had begun to "attack U.S. policy in Rhodesia and to relate this to current internal American problems," i.e. the anti-Jim Crow movement.[36]

A constrained London recognized as early as 1968 that U.S. "support for the U.N. Resolution on Rhodesia is not very popular in Washington outside the State Department and even outside the African section of the State Department." A key defector in this regard was former Secretary of State Dean Acheson—present at the creation of the Cold War—who emerged as Salisbury's chief defender; London found it revealing that despite this viewpoint, "he was recently provided with an office in the State Department when he had asked to advise about NATO [North Atlantic Treaty Organization],"[37] a prime backer of colonial Portugal.

It was Acheson who told Henry Kissinger in the White House that sanctions against Salisbury were "having adverse effects on American interests," particularly the bar on chrome imports, which he thought was only benefiting Moscow.[38] Salisbury's envoy in the U.S. spoke at length about the "friendship" he shared with Acheson, while saluting his "support for Rhodesia" which "was, of course, invaluable."[39] Acheson was not the only U.S. envoy praised by Salisbury. Their emissary in Washington took his cue from George Kennan, the Cold War's architect, in denouncing the "Afro/Asian" bloc that was continuing to flex its muscles at the United Nations. When Kenneth Towsey met with George H.W. Bush, then U.S. Ambassador at the United Nations, he found the future U.S. president to be uncommonly cordial.[40]

Despite the support of the likes of Acheson, Salisbury was passionately concerned about U.S. activists' "attempts to block the unloading of chrome imports, demonstrations against this office"—meaning the Rhodesian legation in Washington—and protests against "the chrome companies," accompanied by "infiltration of stockholders' meetings...." Viewed with trepidation were "major demonstrations

---

36. Report, 16 May 1968, FO7/813, *National Archives of United Kingdom-London*. Hereafter NAUK

37. Report, 27 May 1968, FO7/813, *NAUK*.

38. Dean Acheson to Henry Kissinger, 31 October 1969, Box 65, *Nixon Presidential Materials Project, White House Central Files, Subject Files, Richard M. Nixon Presidential Library*.

39. Statement by Kenneth Towsey, 22 October 1971, Box 2, *Kenneth Towsey Papers*.

40. Kenneth Towsey to L.S. Hawkins, 15 January 1971, Box 2, *Kenneth Towsey Papers*.

scheduled for 'African Liberation Day'", which turned out to be as formidable as feared. Indeed, so shaken was Rhodesia was shaken by the gathering storm of protest against their outlaw regime; thus, Towsey—the emissary in Washington—"with a view to knowing as much as possible about the plans of the fuzzy-wuzzies (of all races) [had] spoken to friends in the area of government concerned with internal security" about these protesters and wanted to go further and hire a "reliable private operator" to "do an investigative job for us."[41] Apparently, this shadowing paid dividends when the U.S. national, Marshall Soghoian, was arrested for aiding Zambia, then under siege by Pretoria. "About three years ago," said Towsey, "I furnished to the CIO [Central Intelligence Organization in Salisbury] a large dossier of Soghoian's activities in Zambia" involving the shipping of "very sophisticated electronics equipment that Soghoian has been buying in the United States for [Lusaka]."[42] Salisbury also expressed interest in passing on to conservative sources in Washington material to rebut a story by columnist, Jack Anderson.[43]

How could London buck Washington on Rhodesia and maintain the vaunted "special relationship" when the potent right wing in the republic was pro-Salisbury and pro-Pretoria. As early as 1966 the *Rand Daily Mail* noticed a "deterioration in relations" between Pretoria and Washington and "estrangement" over South West Africa. This was occurring while "in most respects South Africans identify with Americans more readily than with the peoples of Europe," though the "Americans" referred to did not include the bulk of U.S. Negroes,[44] while the reference "peoples of Europe" was a blunt signal to London. Rhodesians, in any case, had a special animus toward London, predicated on the premise that this once mighty power was insufficiently supportive of their secession. Towsey, Salisbury's man in the U.S., was born in Notthinghamshire, England in 1920 and had been dispatched to Salisbury—like so many Britons—in 1947 but by 1964 was posted to Washington.[45] He quickly defected to Rhodesia in 1965, turning his back on his erstwhile homeland, yet continuing to bear an uncommon animosity toward it.[46]

41. Kenneth Towsey to S.D. O'Donnell, 28 April 1972, Box 4, *Kenneth Towsey Papers.*

42. *Washington Post*, 3 August 1973; see also Kenneth Towsey to K.H. Standring, no date, circa 1973, Box 2, *Kenneth Towsey Papers.*

43. Kenneth Towsey to S.D. O'Donnell, 3 December 1974, Box 2, *Kenneth Towsey Papers.*

44. *Rand Daily Mail*, 23 September 1966.

45. Curriculum Vitae of Towsey, no date, Box 3, *Kenneth Towsey Papers.*

46. Memoirs, no date, Box 6, *Kenneth Towsey Papers.*

Still, Washington found it difficult to quit Pretoria. Despite the continuing brouhaha about U.S. naval vessels docking in South Africa, in 1967 an aircraft carrier officer was effusive in hailing Cape Town's "true and sincere warmth."[47]

Manion was part of a conservative network that was to attain a milestone when they boosted the veteran anticommunist Richard M. Nixon into the White House in 1968 and then his fellow Californian, Ronald W. Reagan, into the same perch in 1980. In February 1968 Manion received a copy of a "confidential memorandum" forwarded to the conservative intellectual William F. Buckley. Michael Struelens of "Eur Africa...Consultants on Foreign Affairs," had made a recent trip to Europe "on behalf of [Moise] Tshombe," the Congolese freebooting leader. While in fascist Spain, Struelens had "lengthy conversations with two senior officers of the U.S. Embassy" and found that Washington was "intervening actively on behalf of Tshombe" and against his left-wing opponents, many of whom were close to the MPLA in Angola. There was worry about the "Simba movement which is now supported by a strong Communist infiltration at all levels of government" in Congo. The neo-colonial power Belgium realized that it did not have the strength to withstand this left-wing push and thus was "becoming used to the idea of having the U.S. influencing things in the Congo and sometimes running them in a manner which is prejudicial to Belgian interests and which even courts the risk of eliminating the Belgian presence in the Congo." This became the theme throughout post-1960s Africa, with European powers retreating and seeking to turn over the reins of power to the neo-colonial master, the nation built on the African Slave Trade: the U.S.A.[48]

Buckley himself was no stranger to apartheid. In 1969 the advertising director of his journal, *National Review*, beamed proudly that the magazine had been a "staunch ally" of Pretoria and "probably has more readers favorably disposed to this country than any other American publication." Though competition for this title was stiff, the claim was likely accurate. It was also true that a "very high density of prospective SAA [South African Airways] travelers" read this

---

47. "News from South Africa," Produced by "Information Service of South Africa", 20 September 1967, Box 301, *Group Research Archives, Columbia University-New York City*.

48. Michael Struelens to William F. Buckley, 16 February 1968, Box 32, *Clarence Manion Papers*. See also undated Memoir, Box 5, *Kenneth Towsey Papers*: The Rhodesian leader called Tshombe "one of my favourite African politicans," a tie buttressed by their meetings in congo.

journal religiously.[49] Buckley was also the host of a widely syndicated television program, broadcast on 198 television stations with an audience estimated at 2 million. He and Rusher offered this platform to Helen Suzman in 1970, an invitation which included the perquisite of a flight to Boston—where she had close relatives—at the program's expense if she would consent to disparage the onrushing boycott against apartheid.[50] A similar deal was offered Hastings Banda of Malawi—Pretoria's good friend.[51] Continuing the television offensive, William Rusher (Buckley's comrade) appeared with various Pretoria officials on a nationwide broadcast in 1970, pontificating on an ugly issue: "Is Grand Apartheid a Policy Worthy of U.S. Support?" (Of course, the answer was a firm "yes.")[52]

Suggestive of how transatlantic relations with apartheid were reinforcing the worst impulses in the U.S. was the idea bruited by William Rusher of the *National Review* in 1969. He sought to "advocate a dramatic *demarche*: the abandonment of all out integration as America's national policy," a "classic example of an 'idea whose time has come.'" He said he was only echoing the boxer once known as "Cassius Clay" and "his forceful argument for economic as well as social segregation...."[53] [emphasis-original] (Yet Rusher's co-thinkers denounced the Republic of New Africa, proclaimed by African-Americans, and designed to establish a Black homeland in Dixie, when it was proclaimed in the 1960s, with one journal averring "Communists plan a Black Soviet Empire in Dixie." Presumably, Dixie was only in favor of a Negro homeland formed by Europeans—i.e. "Bantustans".)[54]

---

49. Patrick D. Maines to Paul Andrews, 4 March 1969, Box 150, *William Rusher Papers, Library of Congress.*

50. William Rusher to Helen Suzman, 25 November 1970, Box 221, *William Rusher Papers.*

51. William Rusher to Hastings Banda, 25 November 1970, Box 221, *William Rusher Papers.*

52. Transcript of "The Advocates," 22 December 1970, Box 71, Series II, *ACOA Papers*: Other panelists included John Chettle of the South Africa Foundation; Francis Mncube of the Bantu Urban Council of Johannesburg and George Matanzima, Minister of Justice in the Transkei.

53. William Rusher to "The Editors," 1969, Box 150, *William Rusher Papers.* Rusher's thinking may have been impaired by the haze of alcohol that seemed to follow him. See e.g. Carl A.J. Gaiano, Manager, North America, of South African Airways, 8 July 1976, Box 84, *William Rusher Papers*: "I really don't know where you would KWV Ten-Year-Old Brandy, but it will be my pleasure to give you a couple of bottles from my stock."

54. *Jackson Daily News*, 23 February 1968.

A key force in this conservative network was Lake E. High. By 1969 he was appointed Executive Director of the American Southern Africa Council, the major lobbying arm for apartheid. A native of Columbia, South Carolina, he was a 1964 graduate of the state university there and a leader in conservative and Republican politics, which were becoming coterminous. His appointment signaled a new aggressiveness from proponents of Salisbury and Pretoria.[55] As so often happened, his appointment ratified trends already in motion. As early as 1967, Arizona's governor signed a resolution barring sanctions against Rhodesia and recognizing the regime (which it was not authorized to do). Still, this act mirrored similar resolutions then debated in California, Utah, Montana, Alabama, and Tennessee.[56]

Rhodesia was a sacred cause for these forces. Thomas Abernethy in Mississippi offered to do whatever he could in this regard but was afraid that one like himself would complicate matters—i.e. an "'ole white bigot' like me from Mississippi...would probably serve to make matters worse" given the "civil rights background of the Congress."[57]

These retrograde elements were being objectively aided by the U.S. labor movement, intoxicated with anticommunism and oblivious to the reality that by doing so, they were only making it more profitable for U.S. jobs to flee to low-wage havens. In 1967 U.S. labor boss George Meany, who touted the global imperative of "out-maneuvering the Communists," spoke of "Eastern Nigeria," where the left's influence had "increased dangerously" and where opposition to colonialism was rising.[58] Still, there were opposing trends that were to become dominant in coming decades. As early as 1966 Meany's sworn foe, the United Auto Workers, backed sanctions against apartheid.[59]

More sophisticated elements among the U.S. ruling elite had long since begun hedging their bets, aware that pursuing anti-Jim Crow

---

55. *American Southern Africa Review*, October-November 1969, *University of Kansas-Lawrence.*

56. *American Southern Africa Review*, April-May 1967, *University of Kansas-Lawrence.*

57. Thomas Abernethy to John Accord, Chairman, American Southern African Council, Box 295, *Thomas Abernethy Papers, University of Mississippi-Oxford.*

58. George Meany to Irving Brown, 14 April 1967, Box 1, *International Affairs Department, African American Labor Center Regional Activity, West Africa, University of Maryland-College Park.*

59. Press Release, 10 March 1966, Box 12, *International Affairs Department Country Files.*

and pro-apartheid policies was like trying to swallow poison and an antidote simultaneously. By early 1969 David Smock was in South Africa on behalf of the Ford Foundation and sought to rebut the "silver linings" that Edwin Munger had seen there for years. These ruminations, he said caustically, were a "figment of Munger's imagination." Instead, he saw a regime under siege: "people in sensitive positions including American diplomats have their telephones tapped and their mail opened. An American consul recently discovered that his chauffeur is a government informer." Smock's room at the Savoy Hotel in Umtata "was specially bugged for visitors" like himself. Only the SACP "espouses one-man-one vote...which operates underground." He saw a similarity between the "black power credo being preached quietly in South Africa" and its U.S. peer. Morosely, he asserted, "I would not predict a race war within the next few years but only because the whites are so strong that they can put down any African uprising...." He thought that "extended visits to the U.S. by conservative South African[s]" had "helped broaden the horizons of many," which was probably mistaken since these journeys may also have reinforced the idea that they had mass support in the U.S. that would help them to cling to power. He conceded that "the weakest part" of the officially sponsored "Leader Exchange" program was on "the U.S. side with too many conservative and uninformed participants" who gave extraordinary "attention...to keeping their hosts happy and unruffled...." Since Pretoria was still loath to give visas to Negroes, Smock had to wonder if a potential visitor to South Africa with a "light complexioned wife" could slip through the mesh. He was reluctant to recommend that Ford back Joel Carlson and other U.S.-based attorneys who had become active in South African political trials—though the wealthy foundation "might consider projects to build bridges between the black communities of the U.S. and South Africa. Black American writers and civil rights activists are well-known and emulated by the African and Coloured elites in South Africa."[60]

This was an update of the old idea of seeking to co-opt Z.K. Matthews by introducing him to CIA leaders. The effort to deploy U.S. Negroes as a Trojan Horse in Africa clashed with mossback racist notions that this minority should be forever bludgeoned and certainly not accorded a cut of the riches exploited from the continent.

Thus, the idea arose of dispatching liberal stalwarts like the Harvard professor John Kenneth Galbraith to Southern Africa. From

---

60. David Smock to Wayne Fredericks, 10 March 1969, FA 739b, 3255-6261, 004 194, Box 190, *Ford Foundation Records, Rockefeller Archives Center.*

Salisbury, John Staub reminded the tall, thin, and droll intellectual that Robert Kennedy's visit to Cape Town "did his image a great deal of good. There are no U.S. bars on travel to Rhodesia," he insisted, "and I feel sure that [the] U.S. image would be enhanced with your visit."[61] "I had not envisioned a talk on race relations," said the careful Staub—who "lived in the U.S. from 1966 to 1967"—"because I fully appreciate and support your view that it would be awkward for you to speak on such a subject outside of the U.S.,"[62] not to mention the fact that Galbraith hardly discussed this fraught matter at home. The diplomatic scholar was a "trifle uncertain about the political wisdom of the visit at this time,"[63] underscoring Smock's assertion that only conservatives were sufficiently audacious to journey to a war zone.

Then it was apartheid's turn to woo Galbraith, as he was told that a "large mining firm," Union Corporation Limited, "has offered an apartment for you, your wife" and others.[64] "I have always wanted to come to South Africa," he told Professor Meyer Feldberg of the University of Cape Town but he was concerned about the reaction from the "black community here," which "not unnaturally" tended to "look askance on anyone who seems to be violating the general bar imposed against the South African regime...."[65] Feldberg, who wound up migrating to Manhattan himself, would not relent: "who should follow [Henry] Kissinger but Galbraith" he implored in a bald appeal to ego. Seemingly distancing himself and his homeland from events, he declared that "we seem to be pawns in a giant East West assessment of the importance of Southern Africa." "The atmosphere is tense and uncertain. We seem to be spectators to some historical developments."[66]

From his sanctum in the most fashionable precinct of Cape Town Feldberg may have been a spectator, but others had decided to shape events in South Africa. By late 1968 Daniel Brigham had made his way to Southern Africa on behalf of the American African Affairs Association, a conservative group chaired by William Rusher and

---

61. John Staub to Professor Galbraith, 3 June 1969, Box 181, *John Kenneth Galbraith Papers*.

62. John Staub to Professor Galbraith, 9 October 1968, Box 181.

63. Professor Galbraith to John Staub, 21 February 1969, Box 181.

64. Robert Greig, Chairman Academic Freedom Committee, University of Witwatersrand to Professor Galbraith, circa 1969, Box 181.

65. Professor Galbraith to Professor Feldberg, circa 1969, Box 1046, *John Kenneth Galbraith Papers*.

66. Professor Feldberg to John Kenneth Galbraith, 20 September 1976, Box 1046.

assisted by the renegade Max Yergan and the popular novelist John dos Passos. A Cambridge graduate and former contributor to the *New York Times* and *New York Journal-American*, Brigham spent six weeks in the region and returned with hyperbolically exaggerated news. He counted 40,000 guerrillas within their ranks mushrooming, as their training continued in China, Eastern Europe, and Africa (especially Algeria and Ethiopia). Some of his claims were especially alarming to Pretoria and Salisbury: "an estimated 125 recruits recently traveled to Cuba via an underground railway through New York…." These militants "gloated over 'the support given us by American volunteers working with our Air Force.'" Indeed, "American sources in Southern Africa confirmed there were a number of American Negroes working with the insurgent forces, but they claimed to have confirmation that only eleven of them were pilots and that none was allowed to fly the Communists' planes without Red co-pilots…." All of these "Americans were said to be members of a black so-called 'Republic of New Afrika' proclaimed in Dar-es-Salaam in August of 1968," with their leader being Robert F. Williams, recently headquartered in Cuba and China. "Among his aides and cohorts are some familiar ones: Brother Imari [Obadele], Monroe Sharp and a woman 'Commisar' Mae Mallory. These Negro Americans have repeatedly turned up frequently at the American consulate [in Tanzania] and allegedly they joined a retinue of United States and other officials in January of 1968 when [Vice President Humbert H. Humphrey] visited Zambia…."[67]

What Brigham neglected to note was that Williams was in the midst of a journey—ideological and otherwise—generally unnoticed, though obvious in plain sight. Bill Sutherland, the Negro activist who knew him, observed that this bearded man "actually served as an emissary of the Chinese government to the U.S. government." He "brought some key messages to the U.S. government from the Chinese leadership,"[68] as Washington effectuated a game-changing entente with China on an anti-Soviet basis, placing inordinate pressure on Moscow that ultimately forced it to dial back its support for liberation movements and eventually played a role in collapse of the regime in 1991. In the short term this move turbo-charged U.S. imperialism, since Washington thought that China would become

67. Daniel L. Brigham, "Blueprint for Conflict," February 1969, Box 23 *Frank Church Papers Boise State University-Idaho.*

68. Bill Sutherland and Matt Meyer, *Guns and Gandhi in Africa: Pan African Insights on Nonviolence, Armed Struggle and Liberation in Africa*, Trenton: Africa World Press 2000, 228.

a cheap labor source forevermore. Assuredly, Nixon's trip to China in the early 1970s did bring immediate dividends, e.g. China's war on a Vietnam that U.S. imperialism could not subdue.[69] In the long term, however, Washington miscalculated wildly, as the payoff to China included massive foreign direct investment from the U.S. and its allies, which has created a juggernaut that bids fair to leave U.S. imperialism sprawling in the dust.[70] Strangely, Williams, who was facing the serious criminal charges that led him into extended exile in the first place, was not prosecuted—unlike other similarly situated Afro-American militants—and wound up with a sinecure at the prestigious University of Michigan-Ann Arbor.[71] There were "funny shenanigans going on around and about Robert F. Williams," Janet Mondlane was told in early 1969, "but we can't make sense out of them yet." Perhaps after the failure to prosecute him upon his return from exile, and the dispatching of his friend Richard Gibson—a sworn foe of the ANC—to report for the mainstream U.S. press, Mondlane might have been able to figure out what was going on: with sarcasm, her correspondent termed Gibson's arrival in East Africa "great advancement for a 'revolutionary', yes?"[72]

By October 1970, a fulsome Nyerere was to be found inaugurating the much-awaited Tan-Zam railway, providing an outlet to the sea for valuable Zambian copper via a Tanzanian port. There had been discussion of this expensive project since at least 1942 but now it was completed and Nyerere was congratulatory. "The Chinese have no colonies in Africa," he asserted, "or anywhere else in the world." "It will not be a Chinese railway," though the country had funded it with "an interest free loan" and "we only begin repayment in 1983" to be finished "in the year 2012": such "terms," he said, "are more than generous." There would be "about 7000 Chinese technicians working in either Tanzania or Zambia," with "more than 4000" already present. This was the culmination of an accord with China signed in February 1967, leading to Nyerere providing "our very

69. Xiaoming Zhang, *Deng Xiaoping's Long War: The Military Conflict Between China and Vietnam*, Chapel Hill: University of North Carolina Press, 2015.

70. Gerald Horne, *Blows Against the Empire: U.S. Imperialism in Crisis*, New York: International, 2008.

71. Ibid., Bill Sutherland, *Guns and Gandhi*, 228.

72. Letter to Janet Mondlane, 18 January 1969, Box 2, Subgroup 1, Series 1, *Herb Shore Collection*.

warm gratitude to Chairman Mao...."[73] China, in short, was playing a contradictory role.

The ANC strained to maintain good relations with China but its ramified ties to Moscow made this a difficult task. In 1972 ANC leaders circulated a report on a meeting in Cairo of the Afro-Asian Peoples Solidarity Organization [AAPSO], which was known to be backed avidly by the Soviet Union. Tersely, the ANC told "all units" that "difficulties led to the withdrawal of the Chinese chapter", including the matter of whether the secession of what became Bangladesh from Pakistan should be supported.[74] ANC diplomacy soldiered on, seeking to walk a tightrope between and among warring factions, even bonding with Vietnam, increasingly resented by China. It was also in 1972 that the U.S. legation in Lusaka noticed that "after several years of animosity," China and the ANC "have become friendlier, "with the Asian giant having "recently offered the ANC scholarships...."[75]

It was not only Williams: there was no denying that as the anti-Jim Crow movement swept forward, more U.S. Negroes—now designated as "Afro-Americans"—made their way to the continent of their ancestors. By the early 1970s—after the 1966 overthrow of Nkrumah—no country in Africa attracted as many Black American militants and self-styled revolutionaries from the Caribbean as did Tanzania. David Du Bois, who aligned with the Black Panther Party and resided part-time in Cairo, was critical of the "highly developed and successful use of Black Americans as CIA agents and dupes" in Dar and elsewhere in the region. One scholar has opined that "concerns about 'reactionary elements' within the African-American community in Tanzania was not unfounded or far-fetched." Many tied to Black Power found it "a shock to meet white cadres of the black liberation movement," e.g. the Communists tied to the ANC, FRELIMO, and MPLA. This opened up those who were dismayed to manipulation by Washington as they then objected to aid from

73. Speech by Julius Nyerere, 28 October 1970, Box 9, *Gwendolen Carter Papers, University of Florida-Gainesville.*

74. "Circular to All Units" from ANC Provisional Headquarters in Morogoro, 9-13 January 1972, Box 16, Part I, Folder 78, *Lusaka Mission Records, ANC Records, Fort Hare University-South Africa.*

75. Report from Lusaka legation to Secretary of State, 14 January 1972, RG 59, Subject and Numeric Files: Politics & Defense, Box 2576, *NARA-CP.*

the socialist bloc to liberation movements on grounds of "race,"[76] though this skepticism often was not extended to China.

On the other hand, some who were motivated by the ideology of Black Power had a sincere and fruitful relationship to Tanzania. This included the Afro-American workers at the camera company Polaroid, who in 1971 contributed $10,000 to Tanzania for anti-apartheid purposes.[77] This activity was duly noted in the South African press,[78] particularly after the workers clamored for a global boycott of apartheid.[79]

Though Mandela had been critical of Black Power insofar as it tended to influence South Africa's Black Consciousness Movement, this view was hardly unanimous within the highest levels of the ANC. Secretary General Alfred Nzo, for example, said in 1970 that it was "only natural that a political consciousness grows among the Afro-American people, various political trends will emerge which on the surface may appear to be diametrically opposed to our own accepted political programme." The ANC's "task," he argued, was to "explain patiently to the various Black groups in America otherwise we might find ourselves pursuing a course contradictory to the mainstream of the movement. This may affect not only the prestige but the credibility of ANC...."[80]

Thus, between 1970 and 1974 the Pan African Skills Project, based in Manhattan, and for which the present writer once toiled before being ousted on grounds of being a Communist, sent almost 400 Afro-Americans to work in Tanzania,[81] by one estimate. A list of potential recruits for Tanzania included a librarian, an engineer, a math teacher, an electrician, and an aircraft engineer, critical posts all, though there was little comprehension of how their arrival might create tensions with their local peers.[82] Like many immersed in Black Power, the founders of this project looked askance at reputed Communists of various stripes, as did their ostensible foes in

76. Fanon Che Wilkins, "'In the Belly of the Beast': Black Power, Anti-Imperialism and the African Liberation Solidarity Committee," Ph.d. dissertation, New York University, 2001, 59, 76, 110-111, 140.

77. *New York Times*, 26 January 1971.

78. *Rand Daily Mail*, 15 February 1971.

79. *Boston Globe*, 27 October 1970.

80. Alfred Nzo to Thambi Mhlambiso, 1 July 1971, Box 13, Folder 35, Part I, *Lusaka Mission Records, ANC Records.*

81. Ibid. Seth Markle, 232. See PASP brochure listing Horne, circa 1974, Box 182, *Gerald Horne Papers, Schomburg Center, New York Public Library.*

82. List, circa 1973, Box 14, *DJB Foundation Records, Indiana University Purdue University Indianapolis.*

Washington—contrary to many of the liberation movements they supported.

Intriguingly, PASP was funded in part by the foundation of Daniel Bernstein, whose political background on the left was not dissimilar to mine.[83] By July 1973, PASP's Irving Davis had identified "20 potential candidates" for work in Zambia, and a contract with Lesotho was allegedly in the offing since Maseru had just "expelled all the white racist South African technicians from their country, as they issued an appeal...for Black Americans to come and replace them," which he considered a "courageous act."[84] Bernstein's foundation also financially supported the Institute of the Black World[85] and the Congress of African People,[86] yet another Black Power formation. It would not be far-fetched to infer that some within Black Power circles were more accepting of Euro-Americans of the left than Afro-Americans of the left, with the latter perhaps perceived as stiff competition for the favors of the wider African community.

Unfortunately, these voluntary exiles in Tanzania were not always embraced like returning prodigal sons and daughters. According to Bill Sutherland, there were those in the country who felt that this group "represented a threat to the domestic power structure," fearing that "highly skilled and capable African Americans would work themselves into powerful positions within Tanzania society and that their African ancestry would make them difficult to dislodge...."[87]

83. DJB Foundation to Irving Davis of PASP, 10 October 1973, Box 14, *DJB Foundation Records, Indiana University Purdue University Indianapolis.* He was wealthy as a result of being born into a family that made money in Hollywood. See e.g. Gerald Horne, *Class Struggle in Hollywood, 1930-1950: Moguls, Mobsters Stars, Reds and Trade Unionists,* Austin: University of Texas Press, 2000 and *The Final Victim of the Blacklist: John Howard Lawson, Dean of the Hollywood Ten,* Berkeley: University of California Press, 2008. According to his widow, he felt "terribly strongly...about race....one of the seminal horrors ...that the country really had never gotten over slavery in any decent way at all..." The turning point for him came in 1960 when he travelled to Cuba and as a result of his consorting with Communists "developed farther and farther to the left." See Oral History, Carol Bernstein Ferry, 12 October 1994, Box 23, *Carol Bernstein Ferry and Ping Ferry Papers, Indiana University Purdue University Indianapolis.*

84. Memorandum from Irving Davis, 31 July 1973, Box 14, *DUB Foundation Records.*

85. Bill Strickland to Robert Browne, 11 September 1971, Box 11, *DJB Foundation Records.*

86. DJB to Black Affairs Council of Unitarian Universalist Church in Philadelphia, circa 1972, Box 5, *DJB Foundation Records.*

87. Bill Sutherland and Matt Meyer, *Guns and Gandhi,* 229.

Even before this effort, the *Congressional Record* of March 1969 noted it "significant" that so many Afro-Americans were arriving in Tanzania as "part of a growing effort by radical blacks in the U.S. to try and establish links and exchange information with their counterparts in Africa...." Frighteningly, Robert F. Williams—soon to cut a deal with Washington and escape prosecution back home—said that "Africans had already asked him if it would be possible to have Afro-Americans with recent military experience come over to help them in their guerilla activities." The "[OAU] Liberation Committee people do feel a close kinship with the Black Power movement," he said.[88] Still, because of the negative consequences often attached to the influence of U.S. trends, the Association for the Education and Cultural Advancement of Africans and the South Africans Student Association both denied being in touch with their counterparts in the U.S. when Pretoria's Minister of Interior Theo Gerdener claimed otherwise.[89] Gatsha Buthelezi, the Zulu leader, soon to be scorned as a friend of apartheid, had no such reservations. He opened a labor meeting in South Africa by quoting liberally from Frederick Douglass,[90] the celebrated opponent of U.S. slavery.

By 1971, the Tanzanian government made official what had been implicit: a resolution was passed to "establish fraternal revolutionary relations with those (black) American citizens fighting for justice and human equality." A formal directive was issued to the effect that "Afro-Americans were welcome who wanted to help the country in the struggle for self-determination, self-reliance and a better life for Africans the world over."[91]

By this point, the memory of Robeson and his ideological orientation had faded, notably in the land of his birth. By early 1967 his old comrade W. Alphaeus Hunton had been invited to reside in Lusaka, with the mission of drafting a history of the liberation movement there and writing a column for the ANC. By 1970, however, he had expired and passing with him was a kind of anti-imperialism that had been squashed during the Red Scare of the 1950s.[92] Yet Hunton was not allowed to die in peace. Shortly after his death, an official of

88. *Congressional Record*, 13 March 1969, and *Saga*, December 1969 in Box 4, Subgroup 1, Series R, *Herb Shore Collection, Oberlin College-Ohio*.

89. R.P. Smith of Embassy-Pretoria to Secretary of State, 19 October 1971, RG 59, Subject Numeric Files: Politics & Defense, Box 2576, *NARA-CP*.

90. Edward Holmes, Consul General-Durban to Secretary of State, RG 59, Subject Numeric Files: Politics & Defense, Box 2576, *NARA-CP*.

91. Ibid., Lessie Tate, 170.

92. Dorothy Hunton, *Alphaeus Hunton: The Unsung Valiant*, New York: Hunton, 1986.

AMAX, the U.S. mineral giant that sought to dominate the Southern African commodity market, barked that there were "few places in Africa [besides Lusaka] where economic and ideological carpetbaggers seem to have such success in finding lodgings near the mighty." The prime example cited was "the American Negro Communist Hunton who lived on [Zambia's] State House grounds for a year or two before his death...."[93]

Though it was hardly recognized at the time, the weakening of the ideology represented by Hunton and Robeson had untoward consequences for the U.S. movement in solidarity with African liberation. In the resultant vacuum, Black Power was strengthened, and militant inter-racialism appeared to be an oxymoron. This was the backdrop to an ideological dustup in the American Committee on Africa, which had taken the place of Robeson's CAA, which had disappeared in 1956. In September 1970 Prexy Nesbitt, who had studied in Tanzania beginning in 1965 before conducting solidarity work in London and then joining the staff of the ACOA, was enmeshed in an internal controversy with his new employer. He objected to ACOA joining "Black Americans in Support of Israel," a perfectly acceptable tie for liberal anticommunists, but not for those, like Nesbitt, who did not fit comfortably in that ideological straitjacket. He was also upset by ACOA's continuing relationship with Holden Roberto of Angola, whose ties to the CIA were now old news. The minutes of the stormy meeting stated blandly that "lack of clear policies made work in the field very difficult," and more stormily, that this contributed to "ACOA having a white and racist image." There was "disagreement with Prexy's critique" it was summarized in more measured tones.[94]

Stung, Houser replied that he was "all for supporting MPLA"— Nesbitt's preferred option— "but not for assuming the non-legitimacy of UNITA" or Roberto either. He was "bothered by the innuendo in Prexy's report that there is something secret or mysterious about ACOA's role," i.e. the "image of ACOA as 'CIA or AAI [African American Institute] or something.'" Parsing his words, he added, "we have been charged with being...pro-Israel...pro-PAC," and then hit back hard: "Prexy might be surprised that after his first trip to London on his way to work in Tanzania, some of the liberation people asked me who he was, wondering what he was doing. CIA was the question." This was all "pure nonsense to me," he said

93. Taylor Ostrander to Dr. Edwin S. Munger, 10 November 1970, Box 7, *Winifred Armstrong Papers.*

94. Minutes, 14 September 1970, Reel 5, Part Im #584, *ACOA Papers.*

scoffing.[95] What he did not say was that the charges of ACOA and AAI collusion with the CIA, first lodged in 1967, had not abated, nor could they as long as the groups maintained relations with the politically compromised U.S. labor movement—figures like Irving Brown, for example.

Thus, as long as ACOA was somehow grouped with AAI, it would be difficult for the organization to escape the resultant taint. Thus, in 1972 Thabo Mbeki of the ANC looked askance at an AAI gathering in Lusaka. Many U.S. officials were present, but the ANC was not invited; nor were FRELIMO or MPLA or the PAIGC of Guinea-Bissau. Congressman Charles Diggs of Black Detroit "wanted to meet with us," said the future South African president, "in order to disassociate himself from the AAI 'mistake' of not inviting us, in what is obviously his attempt to build himself up as a progressive politician...while in Lusaka he came out publicly in support of armed struggle in South Africa...."[96] The wider point was that liberal anticommunism, in which ACOA was complicit, found it difficult to even talk with those liberation movements receiving aid from Moscow.

Moreover, the sensitive matter of Israel brought into sharp relief a widening chasm between African-Americans and their Jewish American counterparts. In 1970 a news item detailed that the "fragile alliance of anti-apartheid forces" was "blown apart by an intemperate attack on six Negro Congressmen for their support of Israel...." Black militants found it difficult to accept Israel's occupation of Palestinian territory, attacks on Egypt and general collaboration with both U.S. imperialism and apartheid.[97] Charles Hightower of the Washington Office on Africa, which was tied to the ACOA, was responsible for this verbal assault.[98]

Hightower and those of his persuasion were responding to wider trends in the international community, especially as an increasingly isolated Israel moved closer to a Pretoria, notorious for its anti-Semitism. By 1972 Pretoria had opened a consulate in Tel Aviv and was enjoying increased trade and travel between the two outlaw regimes. There was a concomitant decline in Israel's relations with

95. Memorandum, 25 September 1970, Reel 5, Part III, #584, *ACOA Papers*.

96. Report by Thabo Mbeki, 24 January 1972, Box 16, Folder 78, Part I, *Lusaka Mission Records, ANC Records-Fort Hare University*.

97. *Washington Star*, 18 July 1970.

98. Minutes of ACOA Steering Committee, 6 August 1970, Box 71, Series II, *ACOA Papers*.

African nations and the 120,000 strong Jewish community in South Africa continued to be harassed nonetheless.[99]

Hightower had earned credibility by working assiduously to obtain a visa for Shirley Graham Du Bois, who had renounced her U.S. nationality years earlier but was still respected in Black America.[100] There was a "growing cleavage" among African Americans, said one astute analyst, with some having a "'Third World' identification" more favorable to armed struggle—anathema to liberal anticommunism, the taproot from which the ACOA grew and the dominant tendency within the NAACP leadership too.[101]

There was also a growing cleavage separating Hightower from Houser. Hightower objected to the expense involved in ACOA's Euro-American leader traveling to an OAU meeting in Ethiopia when his own work hours had been cut. More than this, he found it galling that "these Brothers"—meaning the OAU— "obviously trust GH." Hightower was blunt: "I do not trust" Houser. It was "incredulous to me that he is so highly regarded by the OAU."[102] In the midst of Hightower's complaints, the ACOA acknowledged that it had endured a "difficult year financially" in 1970 and that "next year can be even worse."[103] For his part, Houser attributed some of these tribulations to the "pressures of race and of political alignments" bearing on ACOA, which was not far wrong.[104] "We are not a black organization," Houser exhorted, prompting the question of why this had to be said at this juncture. As for UNITA, soon to be exposed as a friend of apartheid, he found the group "very appealing." Yes, he had a "long association" with Holden Roberto but, then again, he countered, "Roberto had [Patrice] Lumumba's support" too. Besides he was "aided greatly by George Padmore" and Nkrumah too.[105]

Then in October 1970 there was a special meeting which saw Mary Louise Hooper reappearing, alongside Houser and the affluent

99. Report from Cape Town legation, 27 March 1972, RG 59, Subject Numeric Files: Political and Defense, Box 2583.

100. Gerald Horne, *Race Woman: The Lives of Shirley Graham Du Bois*, New York: New York University Press, 2001.

101. Richard Stevens to ACOA, 27 September 1970, Box 71, Series II, *ACOA Papers.*

102. Charles Hightower to Van Lierop, 19 November 1970, Box 3, *Robert Van Lierop Papers, Schomburg Center, New York Public Library.*

103. Report by Special Finance Committee of ACOA, 28 September 1970, Box 3, *Robert Van Lierop Papers.*

104. Letter from George Houser, April 1970, Box 3, *Robert Van Lierop Papers.*

105. Letter from George Houser, 29 September 1970, Box 3, *Robert Van Lierop Papers.*

funder of the group, the Manhattan attorney Peter Weiss. Also, present were the Afro-American intellectual Robert Van Lierop, whose roots were in Surinam, and the economist Robert Browne. The charge was made that the ACOA was of late cast as "a white liberal organization, paternalistic toward the black community;" moreover, "aid to Holden Roberto" was at issue, notably due to his "CIA ties" and "CIA links." Without elaboration the point was bruited that "there was even the threat of violence over the problem...." Blyden Jackson, a well-known Afro-American writer, said that "the heart of the problem" was that the group "has a radical and black staff"—e.g. Nesbitt— "working for a white liberal organization." "But the staff has little role in the formation of policy...." Hence, it was suggested that a "black co-director for ACOA" be considered, along with a reconsideration of its view of the "Middle East." Houser responded that he had "personal contact" with Roberto and his confederates "even before ACOA was started," which added another layer of complexity to the debate. Van Lierop attacked Israel as a "settler colony" not unlike Rhodesia. He was irate that some who signed the pro-Israel advertisement "refused to be publicly involved in South African issues and yet will support Israel," meaning that ACOA was risking "never [to] be taken seriously."[106] The result was predictable: Houser survived, Nebitt did not.

For his part, Weiss had just met with the State Department on the ACOA's behalf and left the important message there that "black militants generally took the position that until human rights problems were solved in Africa, it would be impossible to win their goals in the United States," an incentive for Washington to resolve both fraught matters.[107]

Houser maintained friendly contacts with Roberto; by 1975, however, with the eruption of the crisis over Angolan independence, Roberto's relationship with U.S. intelligence was revealed to a wider audience, further embarrassing ACOA and vindicating Nesbitt. Yet Houser wrote a long letter to Agostinho Neto of MPLA denying—albeit ambiguously—aiding Roberto substantially, noting "we have never given any large-scale massive assistance at all" to Roberto, leaving room to conclude that there was merely "large scale" aid to this renegade.[108]

---

106. Minutes, 8 October 1970, Reel 5, Part I, #592, *ACOA Papers*.

107. Memorandum of Conversation with ACOA, 23 September 1969, RG 59, Subject Numeric Files: Political and Defense, Box 2469.

108. George Houser to Agostinho Neto, 11 June 1969, Box 79, Part III, *ACOARA*.

Houser continued his globetrotting, just before the dustup with Nesbitt meeting in Rabat with Roberto, while broadening his scope of questionable connections by breaking bread with Shelton Siwela, who had studied in the USA and was now associated with FROLIZI of Rhodesia—the Front for the Liberation of Zimbabwe—and Nathan Shamuyarira, "formerly of ZANU and now in charge of Foreign Affairs for FROLIZI" before returning to ZANU.[109] Undeterred, ACOA had tightened ties to UNITA too: Jorge Sangumba was in the USA under the auspices of the United Church of Christ and met visitors at the ACOA office.[110] Yet despite such relationships, Houser continued to be surprised by negative coverage of the ACOA in the African press, expressing disdain for a "smear article about me and ACOA which appeared in the 'Sunday News'" in Dar. "How patently untrue it," he huffed, "that I brief [Washington] after every trip to Africa...."[111] Houser was irate about one article in particular, which blared "How ACOA serves Washington," suggesting it was a spy group, pointing to its undeniable ties with the International Confederation of Free Trade Unions and the AFL-CIO.[112]

Tanzania, the site of many of these flip-flops and ideological acrobatics, paid a steep price as it opened its doors widely to exiles of various types. By 1968 Oscar Kambona was accused of seeking a coup against Nyerere and had supposedly solicited the aid of ANC and PAC militants, a number of whom were armed or at least trained in military science. Reportedly, PAC leader Leballo agreed with this harebrained scheme, while Tambo refused to testify against Kambona, leading to the expulsion of many ANC leaders, who then decamped to Zambia. This alleged cross-border collaboration may have been mythical, but Salisbury would have agreed that this kind of alliance was hardly mythological: it was in 1967 that Dumiso Dabengwa of ZAPU and Chris Hani of the ANC and SACP worked shoulder to shoulder to fight Rhodesian troops north of the Limpopo River.[113]

109. Report by George Houser, 5 September 1970k Reel 4, Part I, #0048, *ACOA Papers*.

110. Dick Leonard of ACOA to "Eileen", 5 September 1972, Reel 4 Part I #43, *ACOA Papers*.

111. George Houser to Elias Ntloedibe, 8 August 1972, Box 142, Series III, *ACOARA*.

112. *Sunday News* [Tanzania], 16 June 1972.

113. Stephen Ellis and Tsepo Sechaba, *Comrades Against Apartheid: The ANC & the South African Communist Party in Exile*, Bloomington: Indiana University Press, 1992, 54, 59, 104. Salisbury was monitoring busily "ZAPU's active man in the United States", Sanders Bepura, because of aid from "FBI friends".

Another version of Pan-Africanism also stirred in Brooklyn, New York in March 1970 when Tchaiko Kwayana of Guyana, formerly known as Ann Cook of the U.S., conferred with L.N. Masimini of the PAC.[114] The PAC also had apparent support in Libya too. Cassius Make and Alfred Kgokong of the ANC noted in their report on the OAU gathering in Benghazi in 1972 that in the "*Libyan Times*", "South Africa is referred to as Azania," a name preferred by the PAC but rejected by the ANC.[115]

By 1971, a delegation from what was described as the "Black Liberation Army" of the U.S. had made its way to Brazzaville in the Peoples Republic of Congo, where they were hosted by the ruling Workers' Party. The U.S. side was led by Eldridge and Kathleen Cleaver, who had been identified with the Black Panther Party. The "struggle being waged by our Afro-American brothers," said the Congolese hosts, "is very important to us"; the blows inflicted by these "brothers"—and "sisters"—in the U.S., it was said, were more damaging to imperialism than those inflicted in Indo-China or Latin America. Cleaver and his comrade Michael Cetewayo Tabor both heaped high praise on China, while the former leader remarked that "returning to Africa in the Congo will help unite the Afro-American liberation struggle," then torn by ideological and other disputes. Cleaver went on to say that "what the Soviet Union meant to Europe, what China meant to Asia and what Cuba meant to Latin America," Brazzaville would mean for Africa. He contrasted the "thousands of American troops stationed" across the Congo River in Kinshasa, including "specially recruited black soldiers."[116] Radio Brazzaville proved to be quite valuable in bringing news to liberated

---

This was not shared with the CIA, however, though these malign forces knew that "Miss Janet Williams" of the "Black Liberation Front" at Cornell University and the Black Panther Party was close to Bepura: See K.D. Leaver to Kenneth Towsey, 22 August 1969, Box 4, *Kenneth Towsey Papers*. Towsey, Rhodesia's envoy in the U.S., realized that the "specially interested people here are FBI rather than CIA" and the "good deal of jealousy" between the two, created an opening for his manipulation of both: Kenneth Towsey to K.D. Leaver, 29 January 1969, Box 4, *Kenneth Towsey Papers*.

114. *Black News* [Brooklyn], 21 March 1970.

115. Report by Cassius Make and Alfred Kgokong, 17 February 1972, Box 16, Folder 78, Part I, *Lusaka Mission Records, ANC Records, Fort Hare University-South Africa*.

116. "Message to the Afro-American People from the Peoples' Republic of the Congo," May 1971, *Michigan State University-East Lansing*.

zones in Mozambique in particular.[117] White House aide Jon Howe later recounted how the radical left came to power in Brazzaville in 1968 and "proclaimed the Communist oriented regime" in December 1969—though sensing what was to come, the U.S. embassy had been closed since 1965.[118]

At the same time FRELIMO was forging close links with the organ of the Black Panther Party. "That will help bring FRELIMO into much closer contact with progressive organizations generally in the U.S. and Black organizations specifically," was the accurate assessment by a correspondent of Janet Mondlane.[119] The ANC was thinking along parallel lines. Writing from Atlanta in 1970, their U.S. representative, Thambi Mhlambiso, found that the BPP was "going to be holding a national conference" there and "for that reason," he advised, "I am going to be in Atlanta for a longish period. I have just been with some of them and they expressed a desire that I attend."[120]

By then, the ANC delegate had settled in Harlem. A few months later he spoke to the Black Studies Department at Lake Forest College and at Northwestern University too—both in the Chicago vicinity, which like Harlem and Atlanta had a complement of BPP cadre. His speech in Chicago, he said, was at the "biggest rally I have addressed in years, militant, revolutionary and what have you."[121] As the BPP grew in influence, so did the ANC. Mozambique, however, may have been the biggest beneficiary of this intensified focus on liberation wars in Africa. By late 1972, the ANC emissary in the U.S. thought his group was "perhaps the least important of all...in the estimation of some people. FRELIMO and PAIGC" of Guinea Bissau "are the most important, especially FRELIMO."[122]

But by 1972 the hammer blows of state repression rained down on the BPP were taking an ideological toll. By then Mhlambiso had

---

117. Teresa Maria de Cruz e Silva, "The Clandestine Network of FRELIMO in Lourenco Marques (1960-1974)", Box 4, *Herb Shore Collection, Oberlin College.*

118. Jon Howe to Vice President Ngoubai, 28 March 1975, Box 9, Series 19, FA 385, *Nelson A. Rockefeller Foreign Affairs and National Security Records, Rockefeller Archive Center, Sleepy Hollow, New York.*

119. Letter to Janet Mondlane, 18 January 1969, Box 2, Subgroup 1, Series 1, *Herb Shore Collection.*

120. Thambi Mhlambiso to "Comrade Alf," 27 August 1970, Box 13, Folder 35, Part I, *Lusaka Mission Records, ANC Records.*

121. Thambi Mhlambiso to Alfred Nzo, 20 October 1970, Box 13, Folder 35, Part I, *Lusaka Mission Records, ANC Records.*

122. Thambi Mhlambiso to Mendi Msimang, 29 November 1972, Box 13, Folder 35.

moved to another Harlem address and the BPP had also moved, at least politically. Mendi Msimang told him to contact Harold Rogers, an Afro-American radical in Chicago known to be close to the Communist Party: "we need to strengthen our relations with them," it was said of the team producing his important newsletter, *African Agenda*. For Rogers and his comrades thought that "splinter reactionary groups like PAC, UNITA and COREMO" had dug "strong roots in Chicago...." "This may be correct," he concluded, "because of the political confusion abounding in the Afro-American organizations. In fact, they report that the PAC recently concluded an alliance with the Black Panther Party."[123] (COREMO, the so-called Revolutionary Committee of Mozambique, was in a shambles, and by 1969 they were forced to flee Rhodesia for a sanctuary in Zambia.)[124] Though the U.S. Communists had been battered mercilessly, they still had more resources—at least in the U.S. itself—than the ANC. Thus, it did not come as a surprise when the ANC's Women's Section requested their New York City youth affiliate for assistance in "printing on our behalf a few thousand stickers, posters" and the like concerning political prisoners.[125]

Mhlambiso responded, this time from his office at 28 East 35th Street, walking distance from the U.N. He was "very fortunate" to find this site since he knew of "comrades from other [movements] who for years have been struggling to get office space without success...." Yes, he knew "Rogers and his group" and had "worked closely with some of his colleagues" but he cautioned Msimang since "we enjoy more respect and support...than any of them in Chicago," speaking of the PAC, et al. Even the "question of the alliance between the PAC & the Panther Party" was "exaggerated." Yes, David Sibeko of the PAC was in California and "met with Huey Newton," Panther leader. It was "true they gave [Sibeko] a lot of publicity." Unfortunately, the journal of the SACP had written about the BPP "unfairly," meaning they had to "work hard to soften the Panthers." He was more worried about the U.S. government, specifically the Department of Justice and their "registration forms," which

123. M. Msimang to Thambi Mhlambiso, 20 April 1972, Box 13, Folder 35, Part I, *Lusaka Mission Records, ANC Records*.

124. Report from Lusaka legation to Secretary of State, 7 January 1969, RG 59, Central Foreign Policy Files: Political and Defense, Box 2466, *NARA-CP*.

125. Sophia De Bruyn to Jeffrey Schwartz of Young Workers' Liberation League, 27 June 1974, Reel 12, *Oliver Tambo Papers*.

required "guidance & approval before I commit the movement to a step, we may regret…."[126]

Part of the problem was the distinction to be drawn between the ANC and SACP. This required "serious attention" said Mhlambiso since there was an understandable conflation between positions of the two: "point out to me," he said, "a member of the CP who is not a member of the ANC." This created "problems and sometimes what some of us mistakenly dismiss as nonsensical and naivety on the part of Black America…."[127] Mhlambiso—who the present writer knew and worked with—did not find "the question of our approach to the Blacks should be treated lightly. Any political organization that is hoping to make an impact in the U.S. must accept the fact that they are not fully conversant with our struggle. But how far do we understand their struggle?" he asked sagely.[128]

In sum, it was not just Congolese who were concerned about the Panthers. "Eduardo was very right," Janet Mondlane was told by an apparent Mozambican exile in the U.S.; "struggles without genuine progress, without an understanding of the political forces involved and the aims of the struggle are doomed from the outset," which could not be said of liberation movements but was applied to an earlier version of the BPP. Ms. Mondlane's unnamed 1969 correspondent found the "attack on the Black Panthers" to be "increasing in tempo and violence," for "as long as they were romantically black power and vaguely militant," they were "little or no threat" but with their internationalism, they were now viewed much differently. "Things have changed" and the group had "developed more and more political maturity," as they began "forming alliances" with diverse forces. "And now they are under fierce, violent attack. If the flower generation still thinks that the Age of Aquarius is underway, they are really high on pot," since it "might well become the age of American fascism, the most powerful and most dangerous brand that the world has ever produced…." Thus, it was in FRELIMO's interest, given the aid to Lisbon provided by Washington, to carefully monitor the U.S. scene and, when possible, intervene to aid the besieged Panthers. "We should have constant contact with the Black Panther paper, with 'Negro Digest,' 'Ebony', 'Sepia', 'Freedomways'…the 'Daily World', the progressive press generally…."

---

126. Thambi Mhlambiso to Mendi Msimang, 29 April 1972, Box 13, Folder 35, Part I, *Lusaka Mission Records, ANC Records.*

127. Thambi Mhlambiso to Mendi Msimang, 16 May 1972, Box 13, Folder 35.

128. Thambi Mhlambiso to Alfred Nzo, 8 July 1971, Box 13, Folder 35.

Unfortunately, this was "something that ACOA is not geared to;" an accurate assessment—the latter two organs were within the ambit of U.S. Communists and, thus, anathema to liberal anticommunism, necessitating the rise of both the African Liberation Support Committee [ALSC] and the National Anti-Imperialist Movement in Solidarity with African Liberation [NAIMSAL]. "We should have contact with the SDS [Students for a Democratic Society], Black Panthers, women's organizations, student and youth organizations, the Mexican American groups"[129] were the concluding words to Mondlane.

As the Cleavers were winging their way to Brazzaville, South Africa's ambassador in the U.S., Harold Taswell, was informed in a "confidential" missive that he might want to reconsider his plan to fly to Santa Barbara, California. For the State Department had received an "anonymous threat" that he was scheduled to be kidnapped and held hostage until Black Panther leader Bobby Seale was released. A bomb threat had been forwarded to the Channel City Club that he was poised to address. Leaflets were being distributed in the ocean-bound city of Santa Barbara calling for a raucous demonstration against his presence.[130] This threat had to be taken seriously since on 20 March 1969 at 11:45 PM the South African embassy was bombed. The State Department found that the "bomb was a machined type used by the army for training purposes," adding to the taut unease: this was, it was reported nervously, "an obvious act of commemoration of the Sharpeville incident...."[131] By 1970 it was the turn of the Portuguese embassy and the Rhodesia Information Office to be targeted: explosions at each were ascribed to the "Revolutionary Action Party."[132]

Similarly explosive were the eruptions taking place in the field of the academic study of Africa, as the mainline African Studies Association was charged with complicity with the worst aspects of U.S. policy, up to and including complicity with racism.[133] Jennifer Davis

129. Letter to Janet Mondlane, 18 January 1969, Subgroup II, Series I, Box 3, *Herb Shore Collection, Oberlin College-Ohio.*

130. Report, 23 April 1970, RG 59, Subject Numeric Files: Political and Defense, Box 2583, *NARA-CP.*

131. Memorandum to files from W.B. Campbell, 21 March 1969, RG 59, Subject Numeric Files: Political and Defense, Box 2467.

132. *Washington Post*, 2 September 1970; *Southern Africa: A Monthly Magazine of News and Opinion*, September 1970, Box 55, Series III, *ACORAA Papers, Tulane University.*

133. "A Black Paper: Institutional Racism in African Studies and U.S.-African Relations," 1969, Paper Number 1, Washington Task Force on African Affairs, Box 71, Series II, *ACOARA.*

and Susan Rogers of ACOA accused Victor Uchendu, a leader of this group, of taking subsidized trips to South Africa, which "showed a marked disregard for his responsibility as President-elect of the ASA…."[134]

This serious threat may have motivated Taswell's transfer to the calmer clime of Geneva, depriving Pretoria of one of its most experienced diplomats in one of the nation's most important postings; this transfer also hampered the ability of his daughter, married to a U.S. naval officer, to maintain contact with her far-flung family.[135] Before his departure, U.S. Vice President Spiro Agnew found the time to meet with him and Petrus "Connie" Mulder, one of the most powerful men in Pretoria (and coincidentally, a former teacher of German). Dogged by numerous scandals that would soon bounce him from office, Agnew knew more than most, or so it was said, about the pain of having "views…frequently misconstrued" and "taken out of context and then criticized by the media…." Mulder rehashed a frequent talking point in Pretoria, pointing out that "there is a tremendous difference between African blacks and American Negroes…."[136]

But with the rising militancy of the anti-Jim Crow movement, adherents were loath to benignly accept the presence of apartheid delegates on North American soil As Taswell was preparing to depart for Switzerland, bomb threats "from an unknown male," according to the State Department, were transmitted to the South African consulate in Manhattan.[137] Increasingly, apartheid entities in the U.S. were under fire. By 1969 Duma Nokwe was congratulating Houser for ACOA-organized demonstrations against South African Airways. These protests were "well publicized" in South Africa itself, he stressed, landing a mighty blow in aid of "our common struggle against the South African fascists and the U.S. involvement in the support of them."[138] So buoyed, Houser replied that the "South African press has been giving our campaign quite a bit of publicity." Thus, "in the demonstration at the airport when the first flight came in…the police, both in uniform and in plain clothes, were all over

134. Jennifer Davis and Susan Rogers to ACOA, 14 March 1975, Box 26, *Washington Office on Africa Papers, Yale University-New Haven, Connecticut.*

135. State Department to Cape Town legation, 25 May 1971, RG 59, Subject Numeric Files: Political and Defense Box 2583.

136. Report, 24 May 1971, RG 59, Subject Numeric Files: Political and Defense, Box 2583.

137. Report, 27 April 1971, RG 59, Subject Numeric Files: Political and Defense, Box 2584.

138. Duma Nokwe to George Houser, 26 February 1969, Box 142, Series III, *ACOARA*.

the place...." Presumably the protests were having the desired effect since there were "only 19 passengers and a crew of 12 on a plane that holds 139"[139]—a rate that did not bode well for the future health of the airline. T.X. Makiwane, speaking for the ANC, found this trend "encouraging," an "inspiration," instructing ACOA: "please keep home fires burning."[140]

Reverberations of this militancy may have led to the extraordinary decision by Washington in 1970 to turn down a South African request to visit the office of Motorola for consul on "riot control equipment." This consultation was deemed to be "not feasible." RCA had also expressed interest in this increasingly lucrative business.[141] Coincidentally enough, this newfound reticence in consorting with apartheid emerged as the anti-apartheid movement was beginning to bloom, as could be seen in Madison, Wisconsin in the early 1970s.[142] That this town hosted a major university campus was not coincidental for increasingly, as colleges began to throw open their doors under pressure from the anti-Jim Crow movement, African students were also admitted—as was the case at Lincoln University in Pennsylvania, where future SWAPO leader Hidipo Hamuntenya was matriculating by 1969.[143] And the presence of more African students was a co-factor in the rise of anti-apartheid protests on campuses.

As ever, what was driving the outreach to African students—in addition to anti-Jim Crow protest—was the real apprehension that failure to recruit would result in these students studying en masse in Eastern Europe; a Cold War setback. Thus, FRELIMO leaders, including Samora Machel, thought that Eduardo Mondlane's son should go to East Germany for schooling, "for education and for security reasons," said Janet Mondlane.[144] There he could be assisted, she was told, by Gottfried Lessing, the former spouse of the London writer Doris Lessing, who then was residing in East Germany. "Old

139. George Houser to Duma Nokwe 17 March 1969, Box 142, Series III, *ACOARA*.

140. T.X. Makiwane to ACOA, 3 June 1969, Box 150, Series III, *ACOARA*.

141. David Newsom to Under Secretary, 2 October 1970, RG 59, Subject Numeric Files: Political and Defense, Box 2575.

142. See voluminous files, Box 54, *ACOARA Papers*. m

143. George Houser to Bishop R.H. Mize, 19 December 1969, Box 94, Series III, *RA*.

144. Janet Mondlane to Herb Shore, 31 July 1969, Box 1, Sub group I, Series 1, *Herb Shore Collection*.

friends," e.g. Slovo and Ruth First, were in an out of Berlin too, and also could lend a hand.[145]

In 1973, Eastern European aid to the liberation movements continued to flow. It was then that Oliver Tambo profusely thanked the leadership of the Communist Party in Bucharest for donations of "Land Rovers, bicycles, funds, watches, blankets, foodstuffs," not to mention an "offer of six places for rest and treatment for our members" and the possible "supply of military equipment."[146] That same year Mendi Msimang reported that the ANC was "expecting two jeeps from Rumania," while the "six long carriage and six portable typewriters from the GDR [East Germany] have been delivered...." The ruling "Socialist Unity Party of Germany is offering a two-week holiday to two of our people" too, he said.[147] This aid upset Washington terribly, contributing to a pre-existing antagonistic anticommunism and a major push that led to the dissolution of the Soviet Union by 1991.

Though carefully monitoring the Afro-American presence in Southern Africa, Washington somehow neglected to notice a steady influx of Euro-American mercenaries—and their spouses—bent on rescuing Rhodesia and bolstering apartheid. This growing roster included Lieutenant Nick J. Smith of the Rhodesian African Rifles, slain by August 1967, who was engaged to marry Mary Ann Martin of New Jersey, teaching in Bulawayo.[148] Also to be found in Bulawayo was Bob Cooke of the College of Idaho, a frequent guest on local television, who spoke before local clubs, and conferred with the mayor.[149] By 1972 Robert Mackey—described as a "blustering, overweight, cigar chewing American who tried to bulldoze his way into a $1 [million] hotel deal at the Victoria Falls, was deported from Rhodesia"[150]—i.e. this regime continued to be a sunny site for shady people.

Perhaps unsurprisingly, U.S. envoys who had served in Rhodesia proved to be friendly to pro-Salisbury forces at home. This included

145. Letter to Janet Mondlane, 8 June 1970, Box 2, Subgroup1 Series 1, *Herb Shore Collection*.

146. Oliver Tambo to Central Committee of Communist Party of Rumania, 25 April 1973, Reel 15, *Oliver Tambo Papers*.

147. Mendi Msimag to Alfred Nzo, 2 April 1973, Box 148, Folder 21, Part II, *Lusaka Mission Records, ANC Records-Fort Hare University, South Africa*.

148. *Manchester Union Leader*, 26 August 1967, *Herald* [Rhodesia], 26 August 1967.

149. Bob Cooke to Frank Church, 11 April 1973, Box 23, *Frank Church Papers*.

150. *Sunday Mail*, [Salisbury] 6 August 1972, Box 6, *Kenneth Towsey Papers*.

Paul Springer of Aiken, South Carolina, who had served in that benighted nation from 1966-1968. Upon returning he chose to "heartily endorse" Senator Thurmond's enthusiasm for white supremacy in Africa. After complimenting the legislator's "charming wife," Springer told the balding leader that he should "be assured of my support here at the local level...."[151] Springer may have known that as of 1969 the U.S. staff in Rhodesia had been reduced from 23 to 8, while some 1100 U.S. nationals continued to reside in this rogue state.[152]

As noted, the turning point in the war for Southern Africa took place with the overthrow of fascism in Portugal in April 1974—which was followed by Mozambican independence in 1975, and then the Soweto uprising in 1976. Yet even before the crucial 1974, the flames of war were leaping. At its 16th session in Addis Ababa, the Council of Ministers of the Organization of African Unity provided precisely nothing to ZANU and ZAPU but the ANC received $35,000 and PAC, $10,000 (SWAPO got $42,000; FRELIMO, $145,000; MPLA, $82,000; and the PAIGC received $145, 000).[153] That the forces fighting Portuguese colonialism received the most was not accidental, since they were closer to the goal line of liberation, but as Lisbon was weakened, so were Pretoria and Salisbury.

Still, these OAU funds were minor compared to what Washington was supplying Lisbon alone. In 1971, this relatively small European member of the U.S.-dominated North Atlantic Treaty Organization—the primary bulwark of anticommunism—received a $435 million export-import credit, more than had been supplied to all of Africa from 1946 to 1970. As in South Africa, leading Portuguese military men had been pro-fascist during the Second World War. Antonio de Spinola, for example, fought for Hitler on the Russian front, before becoming the mastermind against FRELIMO in Mozambique.[154] Almost to the day of liberation in Mozambique—and afterwards by covert means—there were copious amounts of U.S. material aid delivered to the anticommunist forces in southeastern Africa. This was a continuation of President Eisenhower's tribute to Spinola's predecessor, Antonio Salazar, and his administration's abstention

151. Paul Springer to Senator Thurmond, 17 March 1970, Box 9, Subject Correspondence, J. *Strom Thurmond Papers.*

152. Memorandum of Conversation with ACOA, 23 September 1969, RG 59, Subject Numeric Files: Political and Defense, Box 2469.

153. Report by OAU Council of Ministers, 1971, Reel 18, *Oliver Tambo Papers.*

154. Ian Chirstie, *Samora Machel*, 75, 82.

at the U.N. on a vote authorizing an inquiry into the African colonies of Lisbon. There was an attempt by President Kennedy to change course, but he was reluctant to jeopardize the U.S. base in the Azores. Thus, a steady stream of military transport jets manufactured by Boeing, as well as defoliation chemicals and napalm, continued to flow into Mozambique.[155] The activist Prexy Nesbitt said that as late as December 1971, Washington was supplying Lisbon with "$436,000,000" in aid "in what was called the Azores Package, so that we could continue to use the Azores Islands as a base…."[156]

Washington was seemingly more concerned about reports of this collaboration than its reality. When U.S. reporter Jim Hoagland spent 3 weeks in Angola in 1971 and reported that he had seen napalm bombs with English markings, a frantic message was sent by the State Department to "all African diplomatic missions" with talking points designed to rationalize and explain away this misdeed.[157]

Increasingly, hawks in Washington were becoming ever more personally hostile to Mondlane. Segregationist Congressman John Rarick assailed the "angelic public image" of the FRELIMO leader. It was thought that Washington was favoring Mondlane as a typically least bad option in that "members of the Communist Party" were thought poised to replace him and what was described as his "light skinned American" spouse, meaning Janet Mondlane.[158] This Euro-American woman was demonized harshly by pro-colonial forces. She recalled being denounced as a "traitor, a great traitor," and "received many ugly letters, very ugly. There was a great hatred against me," she said.[159] She was even accused of murder plots by Uria Simango, an early leader of FRELIMO, eventually ousted. Simango, said Janet Mondlane, "distributed a libelous 13-page pamphlet throughout the world. I myself was included in his accusations," she reiterated. "I think Simango is slightly mentally unbalanced."[160]

155. "Portugal and NATO," Amsterdam: Angola Committee, 1971, in American Radicalism Vertical File: Angola, *Michigan State University-East Lansing*.

156. Oral History, Prexy Nesbitt, 1 April 2009, *Columbia College-Chicago*.

157. Letter "to all African Diplomatic Missions," 1 March 1971, RG 59, Subject Numeric Files: Political and Defense, Box 2584, *NARA-CP*.

158. *Congressional Record*, 13 March 1969 and *Saga*, December 1969, Box 4, Subgroup I, Series R, *Herb Shore Collection*.

159. Undated Interview with Janet Mondlane, Box 1, Series 1, Subgroup II, *Herb Shore Collection*.

160. Janet Mondlane to George Houser, 10 December 1969, Box 142, Series III, *ACOARA*.

He was aided by Miguel Murupa, who had—coincidentally enough—studied in the U.S.[161] By 1971 Murupa was in Portugal, working for the military against his former comrades.[162] Born in Mozambique in 1939, by 1962 he was working for Nkrumah's Ghana Broadcasting and by 1963 was studying in the U.S.[163] Later, Murupa wrote his "dear friend," the fabled U.S. reactionary William Rusher after he escaped into exile in Rhodesia. In reply Rusher wrote the Rhodesian official "Dear Ken" Towsey informing him that this impertinent renegade was "on the side of the angels" and should be "sent along to South Africa" in order to wreak more havoc.[164] It was also from the U.S. that one of the fiercest opponents of Mondlane emerged: Marcos Namashulua of Bridgeport, Connecticut, who accused the FRELIMO founder of being the man who "betrayed" the "Mozambican Revolution."[165] Weeks after this provocation was published, Mondlane was assassinated in Tanzania.

The day Mondlane was killed, Prexy Nesbitt was slated to meet with him that very morning, yet another ineffable connection between the U.S. and the struggle in Southern Africa.[166]

Typically, the PAC had something to say about this tragedy. One of their leaders conversed with U.S. envoys, who reported that he desperately wanted to exit Ethiopia, where he was then sited, fearing "bodily harm." Mondlane's assassination frightened him since he was "virtually certain he was murdered by pro-Chicom elements in FRELIMO, probably with the knowledge of the Tanzanian government," a report that conveniently elided possible U.S. complicity.[167] Mondlane had been killed by a mail bomb sent to him in Tanzania, which he opened at the house of a U.S. friend: the assassination remains unsolved.[168]

---

161. Janet Mondlane to George Houser, 10 December 1969, Box 2, Series I, Subgroup I, *Herb Shore Collection*.

162. Janet Mondlane to George Houser, 22 March 1971, Box 2, Series I, Subgroup 1.

163. Kenneth Towsey to "Dear Bill," 23 April 1975, Box 76, *William Rusher Papers*.

164. Miguel Murupa to "Dear Friend," 9 January 1974 and William Rusher to "Dear Ken" Towsey, 29 February 1975, Box 76, *William Rusher Papers*.

165. Marcos G. Namashulua to George Houser, 3 November 1968, Box 2, Series I, Subgroup 1.

166. Oral History, Prexy Nesbitt, 1 April 2009, *Columbia College-Chicago*.

167. Memorandum of Conversation with T.T. Letlako, 22 February 1969, RG 59, Subject Numeric Files: Political and Defense, Box 2468.

168. George Roberts, "The Assassination of Eduardo Mondlane: FRELIMO, Tanzania and the Politics of Exile in Dar es Salaam," *Cold War History*,

Mondlane's daughter, Chude, who spent considerable time in her mother's homeland, came to recognize how unfriendly the U.S. could be to anyone perceived to be of African descent. This republic was "an eye opener for her," said Houser in 1970. "I explained to her," he said in a manner familiar to parents of children perceived as Negro stretching back centuries, "that she can expect protection from" her fellow Negroes "but not from any whites." "Chude," he said, "has never been aware of this behavior because of Dar" and her upbringing there.[169]

17(Number 1, February 2017): 1-19.

169. George Houser to Janet Mondlane, 8 June 1970, Box 1, Subgroup 1, Series 1, *Herb Shore Collection*.

Chapter 14

Copernican Changes in Portugal, 1973-1974

THERE were many turning points on the road to liberation of Southern Africa: the Bandung conference of 1955, which pointed to a new direction for the formerly colonized; the Suez Crisis of 1956, which was not only an attack on independent Africa but the stern pushback against it by Moscow, indicating things to come; the rise of Ghana in 1957, which established a new stage in Pan-African solidarity; Sharpeville in 1960 and the crisis it represented for Pretoria; Rivonia in 1964, which was an apparent setback for the anti-apartheid movement but helped to spark a worldwide movement that was to make Mandela a global symbol of resistance; the U.S. Voting Rights Act of 1965, which politically empowered the Negro population, teeing up a new wave of anti-apartheid activism on their part.

Yet of all these landmarks, it is difficult to overstate the importance of the overthrow of fascism in Portugal in April 1974 as a factor in laying the groundwork for democratic elections in South Africa two decades later. The ascendance of Communists and Social Democrats in Lisbon led directly to independence for Mozambique and Angola in 1975 and proved inspirational in South Africa, leading to the Soweto uprising of 1976 and an acceleration of militancy that made the nation ungovernable. Thus, U.S. Deputy Assistant Secretary for Africa Edward Mulcahy confessed in 1974 that his nation trained "counter-insurgency forces within this country to fight against the guerillas" in Mozambique and Angola: "we provided training for Portuguese officers" too, he conceded, "about 60 or 70 at Fort Bragg," North Carolina and "all of them probably served in Mozambique".[1] But regime change in Lisbon would alter this noxious collaboration.

1. Edward Mulcahy, "United States Foreign Policy Towards Southern Africa," Remarks at Indiana University-Bloomington, December 1974, Box 10, *Gwendolen Carter Papers, University of Florida-Gainesville.*

In the prelude to April 1974 poorer Portuguese had been arriving in Luanda. The European population rose in Angola from 44,000 in 1940 to 180,000 by 1960 to over 300,000 by 1974. Their arrival reinforced an increasingly fearful racial stratum determined to fend off competition from Africans, which was rising as continental decolonization opened doors of education, previously shut tight. The "Partido Communista Angola" was founded in 1955, after it was thought that Portuguese Communists had lagged on the Algeria Question, and then formed the core of the MPLA.[2]

Fortunately, it was not just the U.S. that intervened in the prime Portuguese colony of Mozambique. A Quaker delegation in 1977 was able to meet with President Nyerere privately at his Indian Ocean beach house, where he told them, "we were ready to destroy that [Cabora Bassa] dam" in Mozambique in 1974, a hammer blow against Lisbon. "We could have destroyed it," he insisted, "then the revolution took place."[3]

A similar fate could have awaited Gulf Oil's operation in Angola, a collaboration with Lisbon that came under increased scrutiny post-1974. A report by the OAU found "living conditions" for workers there "unbearable", referring to the U.S. firm's operations in Cabinda in the far north of the nation, eyed by revanchists in Kinshasa. "A Gulf stockholder who was recently invited to visit the operation has reported that the U.S. technical personnel are 'rednecks' or racists that facilities on the drilling rigs are segregated...." It was not just Gulf, however, since their fellow giant Mobil Oil controlled approximately 44% of the South African market and had the dishonor of building the first refinery there. Caltex—a mash-up of California's Standard Oil and The Texas Company—had arrived in South Africa in 1911 and remained there too. It claimed 20% of the market and was "very closely identified with South African interests," known for its "intensive advertising campaign[s] carried out in Johannesburg papers...." Esso arrived belatedly in 1963 but was catching up steadily. Still, it only had about 65 service and filling stations, compared with over 1000 each for Mobil and Caltex. Esso made its biggest impact on the agricultural sector, though they were prospecting in what is now Namibia, a project potentially compromised by impending decolonization in neighboring Angola. The company

2. John Marcum, "Class, Race and Ethnicity: The Angolan Revolution Revisited," Box 9, FA 021k RG 1, Series 1, Subseries 1, *Social Science Research Council Records, Rockefeller Archive Center.*

3. Transcript of AFSC Study Tour Interview with President Julius Nyerere, October 1977, South Africa File, *AFSC.*

had been joined there by Tesoro of San Antonio. The same dim prospects now held true for Hunt Oil of Dallas, which was prospecting in Mozambique. Their prospects all seemed dimmer still after April 1974.[4]

All this may have occurred to the top military leaders of Pretoria and Washington who conferred in early May 1974 in the aftermath of the shock delivered to the political landscape in Lisbon.[5]

The focus on oil came as these corporations were being sieged in producing nations, especially the Arab countries. Moreover, Esso was charged with anti-Semitism in South Africa. Capitulating to prevailing sentiments in Afrikanerdom, one of its employees had taken it upon herself "to let no Jews get any further" on the corporate ladder. Initially she was fired but then the company surrendered and transferred her instead.[6]

In the prelude to April 1974, Afro-American activists placed enormous pressure on U.S. oil giants because of their varied operations in Africa. This pressure was arguably a co-factor in igniting the retreat of colonialism in what had been called "Portuguese Africa." In 1972 the Pan African Liberation Committee in Boston protested Harvard University's holdings in Gulf Oil because of its exploitation of Angolan petroleum.[7] The "Gulf issue is a terribly difficult one for us," groaned Harvard's president Derek Bok.[8] The veteran activist Prexy Nesbitt contributed to Bok's angst for he attended "shareholder meetings at their headquarters…then in Pittsburgh… and we demonstrated….There was a threat against our lives," and his delegation "had to be escorted out by the police and I remember being escorted to the bus station and put on a Greyhound bus by the police."[9]

Nonetheless, Bok's "Special Assistant," the Negro Walter Leonard, rebuked a leader of this group—Randall Robinson, who went on to become a premier anti-apartheid organizer—in a manner that was often used to discredit critics of U.S. imperialism. Leonard did

4. Report of the Administrative Secretary General to the Council of Ministers on Oil as a Weapon Against the Southern Africa Regimes, June 1974, Reel 18, *Oliver Tambo Papers*.

5. *Christian Science Monitor*, 10 May 1974.

6. *Rand Daily Mail*, 7 February 1972 and La Rue Lutkins to Secretary of State, 18 February 1972, RG 59, Subject Numeric Files: Social, Box 3094, *NARA-CP*.

7. Pan African Liberation Committee to Derek Bok, 28 April 1972, Box 1, *Brenda Randolph Papers, Michigan State University-East Lansing*.

8. Derek Bok to George Houser, 23 May 1972, Box 80, *ACOARA*.

9. Oral History, Prexy Nesbitt, 1 April 2009, *Columbia College-Chicago*.

not understand why the group did not "focus some of their concern on the problems in Cambridge, Boston and other American cities."[10] Leonard ignored the dialectical connection between right-wing momentum abroad and its beneficiaries on North American shores, which had propelled the synergy between apartheid and Jim Crow in the first instance.

Leonard had targeted a notably effective group. In 1973 Robinson said that this "Gulf boycott effort" had "organized local committees in twenty-two cities in seventeen states," producing "fifty thousand...photo posters" highlighting the corporation's problematic role in Angola. This was "followed by 20,000 bumper stickers and 200,000 brochures," to be followed by even larger posters that "will line the streets of every major city", accompanied by "organized concentrated picketing...."[11]

Perhaps affected by this critique, the Boston group went to some length to "relate to black Gulf dealers." In response to anti-Jim Crow protests, Gulf Oil had tossed crumbs to some Afro-Americans, installing them as operators of service stations. Direct no "hostility" toward them was the advice rendered by activists; instead, "direct all of our responses to the white folks who manage the corporation" and "own the stock" and "control the Board of Directors." The organizers were alert to the "growing desire among many companies to increase their Black franchise holders to the place where the majority of franchise owners in the Black community will be Black,"[12] which would presumably lessen pressure to cease exploitation of Africa.

This defensiveness about Gulf's ability to win over a middle stratum of Negroes did not deter activists from continuing to raise sizeable amounts for liberation movements. In 1973, in one example among many, the African Liberation Support Committee—which had leapt onto the national stage in previous months by organizing marches nationally in favor of wars of national liberation in Southern Africa—turned over $32,000 to what the *Johannesburg Star* contemptuously termed "five terrorist groups."[13] Sufficiently inspired, a few weeks later, New York stevedores—who unlike their West Coast

---

10. Walter Leonard to Randall Robinson, 6 March 1972, Box 1, *Brenda Randolph Papers.*

11. Randall Robinson to Ping Ferry, 9 April 1973, Box 16, *Carol Bernstein Ferry and Ping Ferry Papers, Indiana University Purdue University, Indianapolis.*

12. Pan African Liberation Committee to State and Local Organizers, 20 May 1973, Box 1, *Brenda Randolph Papers.*

13. *Johannesburg Star*, 21 July 1973.

peers were not known for their militancy—refused to unload a vessel stocked with chrome from Rhodesia.[14]

In apparent response to the rising pressure against apartheid and colonialism, Roy Wilkins of the NAACP, awakening from its slumber over these dual evils, took time to obtain a visa—often denied to Afro-Americans—for travel to the land of apartheid. In an increasingly favored tactic, he equated and said he opposed both apartheid and "black separatism" in the U.S., though the latter hardly had the force of state power.[15] His usually reliable liberal ally, the ACOA, joined many when it said it was "appalled" at his declaration that the plight of Africans would worsen if U.S. corporations were compelled to withdraw from the land of apartheid.[16] An appreciative Eschel Rhoodie, a premier propagandist for Pretoria, may have had Wilkins in mind when he argued that he found more understanding of Afrikaner dilemmas within the NAACP than among ordinary Euro-Americans.[17] Oscar Shade of the NAACP branch in Madison, Wisconsin—a city with a thriving anti-colonial movement—was unimpressed. He and the branch "experienced some backlash" as a result of this ill-advised trip, telling Wilkins that "several people did not buy tickets" to their fundraiser "because they felt that you defended the practices of United States businesses" in South Africa.[18] It was unclear if the leader of "Colored People" had been declared an "honorary white" to gain entry to South Africa though—apparently—Pretoria had proposed as much.[19]

Though Wilkins was able to obtain a visa, the same was denied, for example, to AME Bishop Fred C. James in 1973 when he sought to travel to South Africa, South West Africa, and neighboring nations.[20] A similar fate befell Anglican Bishop Charles Shannon Mallory, a

---

14. Press Release, African Liberation Support Committee, 24 September 1973, Box 275, *Leroy Walker Africa News Service Archive, Duke University-North Carolina*. For more on activism concerning chrome and the like see Gerald Horne, *From the Barrel of a Gun: The U.S. and the War Against Zimbabwe, 1965-1980*, Chapel Hill: University of North Carolina Press, 2001.

15. Press Release, 1972, Box VIA53, *NAACP Papers, Library of Congress-Washington, D.C.*

16. *New York Times*, 30 March 1972.

17. Mervyn Rees and Chris Day, *Muldergate: The Story of the Info Scandal*, Johannesburg: Macmillan, 1980, 163.

18. Oscar Shade to Roy Wilkins, 12 June 1972, Box VIA53, *NAACP Papers*.

19. David Abshire, Assistant Secretary of State to Congressman Ronald V. Dellums, 4 November 1971, RG 59, Subject Numeric Files: Social, Box 3094.

20. Consul General-Cape Town to Secretary of State, 2 February 1973, Subject Numeric Files: Political and Defense, Box 2581, *NARA-CP*

U.S. national, who was refused a visa by Pretoria, despite having served previously in South West Africa.[21] Wilkins aside, by early 1971 Pretoria had compelled the departure of a number of U.S. nationals, including five missionaries, two students, and two clerics whose presence was deemed to be inimical to apartheid.[22] In mid-1972 it barred admission to Professor Robert Williams of Union Theological Seminary in Manhattan. He was slated to be keynote speaker at a students' meeting in the midst of an internal controversy involving the heralded Steve Biko and Tema Sono, who advised cooperation with Bantustan leaders.[23] The ACOA continued to try to send representatives to illegally occupied South West Africa, smartly seeking to make use of visas from the U.N. Council on Namibia. In Kinshasa the befuddled representative of the U.S. airline Pan American said to the ACOA visitor, "You don't have a South African visa," before being met with the deft reply, "but I'm not going to South Africa."[24]

Perhaps because of the experience with Dr. King, U.S. emissaries seemed taken with the idea that clerics could challenge the status quo. Attention was paid to John Gogotya's claim that his church was supposedly using funds from U.S. churches to "prop up an ideology which is not part of their (the Americans') beliefs."[25]

In U.S. reaction to the profound significance of 1974 particularly striking was the response from ACOA allies in the U.S. labor movement. In some ways, the AFL-CIO was more distraught than official Washington at this weighty turn of events. The day of liberation in Lisbon was 25 April and by 9 May at 4:30 PM, Irving Brown and his retinue had arrived in the country. Naturally the CIA-friendly labor operative was met by members of the frazzled U.S. legation and then sped to a union meeting. They walked into a "very fluid situation absolutely cold," said a confederate, Mike Boggs. "Disorder is the order of the day," was his baleful message, as hope rose in Luanda and the city that was to become Maputo. Their influence was apparent as the Brown-led team met with future Prime Minister

21. U.S. Legaation-Gabarone to Secretary of State, 18 January 1973, RG 59, Subject Numeric Files: Social, Box 3095.

22. Memorandum to Henry Kissinger, 26 February 1971, RG 59, Subject Numeric Files: Political and Defense, Box 2481.

23. R.P. Smith, Embassy-Pretoria to Secretary of State, 7 July 1972, RG 59, Subject Numeric Files: Politics & Defense, Box 2577.

24. Report by George Houser, 1 August 1972, Box 94, Series III, *ACOARA*. In the same box, see the Report by William Booth on Trip to Namibia, March 1972,

25. John Hurd to Secretary of State, 5 October 1971, RG 59, Subject Numeric Files: Social, Box 3092, *NAFA-CP*.

Mario Soares before embassy personnel did. They fretted about the strength of the World Federation of Trade Unions, which was a boulder of support for emerging left-leaning unions in South Africa. The WFTU, it was said disconsolately, was "clearly the most firmly entrenched and best organized" of the various labor groupings. Even Raul Rêgo of the Socialist Party—who "called Holden Roberto 'an American'"— "stressed his preference [for] Agostinho Neto, with whom he had been jailed in recent years." (Neto was allied with the MPLA, which was to emerge triumphant in Angola the following year.)[26]

Brown reported that "we met with General Spinola," the man who it was hoped would turn back the left-wing tide.[27] Tellingly, the U.S. legation was dismissed by these hardline labor leaders as much too liberal for their tastes. "We deserve better" was their caustic evaluation. "Spinola is not the master of his realm" they said of the military man said to be in charge. "We were left with the feeling that he is in a balancing act, following the directions of the Captains" of the left-dominated Armed Forces Movement, whose misery in serving in losing wars in Africa had led directly to regime change. It was they, it was said, who "run the show from the wings." Despite avid support for the right wing in Lisbon, Washington now faced the enervating reality that the "obvious advantage [was] held at this moment by the Communist Party" in a NATO member state. Revealingly, after "twenty-seven years of clandestinity [sic]," the CP periodical *Avante* had just emerged to a rhapsodic reception: "it dedicated its first edition to Africa and Portuguese labor."[28]

"Irving wouldn't trust the mails" was the message from one of his comrades in France working alongside the anticommunist Force Ourvriere, a labor confederation in the image of the AFL-CIO. Though union membership was lagging in the U.S., the AFL-CIO maintained numerous offices in France, as they forged links with "military" forces that were "anticommunist,"[29] who had only been defeated soundly in Algeria a few years earlier. The idea was to use this force as a beachhead against radicalism in Portugal.

---

26. Letter from Mike Boggs, "Lisbon Trip Report," 8-10 May 1974, Box 4, *International Affairs Department, Country Files, AFL-CIO, University of Maryland-College Park.*

27. Letter from Irving Brown 20 May 1974, Box 4, *International Affairs Department, Country Files, AFL-CIO, University of Maryland-College Park.*

28. Letter from Mike Boggs, "Lisbon Trip Report," 8-10 May 1974, Box 4.

29. "Rosy" to "Ernie", 3 September 1974, Box 4, *International Affairs Department, Country Files.*

Days after liberation in Lisbon, a representative of U.S. labor was not celebrating the downfall of a regime that repressed labor shamelessly, instead he was fretting "about the future of the colonies in Africa…." It was a "necessity" it was said "for the AALC to step up activities"—a reference to the African American Labor Center, a CIA front which had been involved in South Africa for years. There was the "growing importance of the off-shore oil discoveries of Angola," which were to fill Luanda's coffers after 1975. This nation in southwestern Africa was destined to be a "new Kuwait." It was noted with acuity that it was "not the best time for the USA to deal with this kind of a new revolutionary situation while Nixon with his low profile, sinks more and more below sea level,"[30] an accurate perception of the political troubles facing a president who would soon be forced to resign.

Indeed, in explicating the veritable burst of anti-colonial and anti-apartheid activism in the U.S. in the early 1970s, it cannot be untied from the simultaneous weakening of Nixon, which was in turn connected to the culmination of anti-Jim Crow activism unleashed in the previous decade. Another factor was the shakeup in the global economy rendered by the oil embargo from Arab nations that sent the U.S. into a tailspin and eroded North Atlantic hegemony in a strategically important area. By the end of the decade, another shock was administered by the Shah's overthrow in Iran, which hurt Pretoria since Tehran was a major supplier of oil to apartheid. The Shah had been especially close to Pretoria; his father had lived in a mansion in the Houghton neighborhood of Johannesburg during the previous World War. He died there in 1944, and—in a telling move monitored carefully by Washington—the Iranian Consul General bought the same house in 1971 in seeming anticipation of his ruler's eventual exile.[31] Predictably the 1970s saw an increase in the number of Iranian workers involved in South Africa's oil industry, notably refineries.[32]

Worried about perceived losses, a few months after April 1974 U.S. labor sent a representative to Luanda to check on matters and the findings were not encouraging. The local delegate from the Armed Forces Movement seemed to be in the corner of the MPLA, thought

---

30. Report on "Visit to Lisbon," 13 May 1974, Box 4, *International Affairs Department, Country Files*.

31. Cape Town legation to Secretary of State, 19 March 1971, RG 59, Subject Numeric Files: Political and Defense, Box 2584.

32. Cape Town legation to Secretary of State, 6 March 1970, RG 59, Subject Numeric Files: Political and Defense, 2584.

to be close to Communists. Luanda was said to be "much safer than Kinshasa," where U.S. influence reigned. But typically, this envoy's focused sympathy concerned a "great fear...among the white lower and middle income groups in government offices and for instance, the taxi drivers (all but two in Luanda are white) as they are afraid to be pushed out by blacks...." Warm words were extended to Holden Roberto's comrades, then holed up in Kinshasa.[33]

U.S. labor leaders envisioned the Copernican change initiated by April 1974 as contrary to the course they had been pursuing. True to its origins as the representative of not labor generally but "white" labor, the AFL-CIO was in close touch with the similarly oriented Trade Union Council of South Africa. It was in 1969 that top U.S. labor boss George Meany sent a warm message to their annual conference. Irving Brown was told that TUCSA was "in a terrible spot and are worried that their action barring Black worker unions will not be very well received outside"[34]—except, of course, at AFL-CIO headquarters. On the verge of being overtaken by events, the U.S. labor center then sought to cultivate certain African labor figures in South Africa, including Lucy Mvubelo, General Secretary of the National Union of Clothing Workers. In 1971 she told a representative of the AFL-CIO that she attended missionary school "established by Americans"; interestingly, her mother spoke German "fluently," a language with which she was not unfamiliar. Because there had been a "shortage of white labor" during the previous World War—due not least to the conscription of Europeans—she got a job making a mere $5 for a 46-hour week. She hedged in discussing the South African Congress of Trade Unions, thought to be within the orbit of the SACP, though she was asked pointedly if it could be counted among "Communist organizations." She expressed appreciation for Polaroid—the U.S. camera company then under fire from Afro-American employees because of its relations with apartheid—saying the company "has done something very good." Speaking from Johannesburg, she was also "happy at this juncture [that] the United States Department of Labor and the United States Department have been able to invite me to visit their country."[35]

---

33. Peter Loebarth to Patrick O'Farrell, 17 October 1974, Box 9, *International Affairs Department, Country Files.*

34. Edward McHale to "Dear Irving," 17 March 1969, Box 12, *International Affairs Department, Country Files.*

35. Interview with Lucy Mvubelo, 10 June 1971, Box 1, *African American Labor Center, African Labor History Center, AFL-CIO, University of Maryland-College Park.*

As Nixon was inundated by a tidal wave of protest against the abominable wars in Indochina and the proliferating investigations into his various domestic misdeeds, the White House was less able to protect its ally in Pretoria. By early 1973 South African Broadcasting, the megaphone of apartheid, reported that "commentators in the Republic and abroad regard the ending of the Vietnam War as ominous for Southern Africa" because "as world attention is released from the massive Vietnam preoccupation, it will have more time and inclination to consider other problem areas—including ours." Forebodingly, it was said, "this will facilitate the expansion of Communist influence in the Indian Ocean and East Africa…."[36]

Then Henry Kissinger announced that the U.S. was "neither encouraging nor discouraging any U.S. investment in South Africa",[37] contradicting the previous spurious line that such investment facilitated democracy. By September 1973 he was slated to visit—in a single day—Pretoria, Lusaka, Dar, and Kinshasa, scurrying hither and yon as the liberation movements ascended and the colonizers declined slowly.[38] By June 1974, as imperialism was busily backpedaling in the aftermath of what was called the Portuguese Revolution, Senator Walter Mondale—who would become U.S Vice-President-elect by 1976—introduced legislation to deny U.S. companies operating in what is now Namibia the right to receive credits for taxes paid to Pretoria; this would have reduced dividends of AMAX (formerly American Metal Climax) at the highly profitable Tsumeb mine, heavily dependent upon cheap African labor, by nearly 40%.[39] Still, by 1970 a regional journal happily proclaimed "four American mine compounds open offices in South Africa."[40] Four years later, on the eve of the tumult in Lisbon, U.S.-born magnate Leonard Mallen struck it rich with Redbark Mines Ltd. of South Africa.[41]

Mondale's effort sought to keep up with global trends as the U.N. Council on Namibia, which challenged Pretoria's jurisdiction, was

---

36. SABC Commentary, 27 January 1973, Box 120, *Leroy Walker Africa News Service, Duke University.*

37. Henry Kissinger to Peter Flanigan, 14 July 1973, Box 744, *National Security Council Country Files-Africa, Richard M. Nixon Presidential Library-Yorba Linda, California.* .

38. Memorandum, 16 September 1973, Box 43, National *Security Adviser Trip Briefing Books and Cables for Henry Kissinger, Kissinger Trip File, Gerald Ford Presidential Library, Ann Arbor, Michigan.*

39. Letter from Senator Walter Mondale, 6 June 1974, Box 6, *Winifred Armstrong Papers, Stanford University-California.*

40. *Financial Gazette* [South Africa], 31 July 1970.

41. *Sunday Times* [South Africa], 6 January 1974.

on the verge of filing a complaint that would result in the seizure of a ship carrying exports from South West Africa. It was likely that this would be a U.S. ship sailing home from Walvis Bay, putting the nation in an uncomfortable global spotlight.[42] Arnold Miller of the U.S United Mine Workers Union broke with the line of the AFL-CIO when he understandably condemned the gross exploitation of African miners in southwestern Africa by AMAX and Newmont Mining, another U.S. giant. This was "a terrible crime," he charged.[43] Culpable, AMAX well knew that in this part of Africa "only employees are permitted to organize unions and Africans are not regarded as employees under the law"—law constructed by Pretoria and its German predecessor.[44]

While various U.S. interests jockeyed over the Tsumeb mine, SWAPO leader Sam Nujoma was rallying "solidarity" with "exploited Black Americans" at a rally in Dar, pointing out that U.S. imperialist acolytes owned "the mining complex at Tsumeb which according to the State Department spokesman is the most important single mining complex of its kind in the hands of the so-called free world." Seeking to wrest control from these interests, Nujoma sent "our warm and brotherly support to the exploited Black Americans who have been reduced to the same status as any other colonial people."[45]

Old habits die hard, however, and in 1972 the U.S. ambassador in Pretoria, John Hurd, was "objecting to the assignment of a black Foreign Service Officer to his Embassy." This emissary thought that "bilateral relations with South Africa would suffer" and, besides, "our domestic conservative opinion might attack the move."[46] Unembarrassed, Hurd confirmed the accuracy of this assessment.[47]

But Kissinger found that this intervention had created a "rising tide of criticism" of Hurd's "performance," yielding "three separate

---

42. Inter-Office Memorandum, 11 November 1974, Box 6, *Winifred Armstrong Papers*.

43. Arnold Miller to Tim Smith, Inter-Faith Center for Corporate Responsibility, 14 May 1974, Box 6, *Winifred Armstrong Papers*.

44. Inter-Office Memorandum, 4 April 1974, Box 6, *Winifred Armstrong Papers*.

45. P.H. Kreisberg of Dar es Salaam legation to Secretary of State, 25 August 1970, Box 2576, Subject Numeric Files: Politics and Defense, Box 2576: Nujoma remarks appended.

46. R.T. Kennedy to Henry Kissinger, 6 July 1972, Box 744, *National Security Council Country Files-Africa*.

47. John Hurd to Peter Flanigan, 4 June 1972, Box 744, *NSC Country Files-Africa*.

letters from Charles Diggs alone," as Detroit's Afro-American Congressman sprang into action. The Republican Senator Jacob Javits of New York also found time to protest that "large white reception[s]" continued to be held at the Embassy.[48] But it was Diggs who had become the real impediment to Pretoria-Washington engagement. By late 1973 he was in Ethiopia at an AAI meeting informing one and all that it was "shameful for self-respecting American Negroes to serve on the U.S. delegation at the General Assembly" given this relationship.[49] He may have had in mind the London-Washington veto of U.N. Security Council sanctions against Pretoria earlier that year.[50] It was also Diggs who spurred litigation against Union Carbide—a stockholders' derivative action brought because of the company's putative violation of the economic embargo imposed on Salisbury.[51]

To the chagrin of legation officials in Cape Town, Hurd, who had donated a small fortune to the ruling Republican Party, visited Robben Island—not to visit Mandela and other prisoners but for a pheasant hunting holiday. This was after former U.S. Attorney General turned dissident Ramsey Clark had been refused entrance. The obtuse Texan invaded the small island with a pack of beagles leading the way and two prisoners dragooned to pick up the dead birds for Hurd's entourage. He was accompanied by leading apartheid official Ben Schoeman. Hurd fit in well in that circle since he often referred to his darker fellow citizens as "Nigras," a corruption of the epithet deployed against Afro-Americans. He fought unsuccessfully against the policy of sending Negro diplomats to South Africa. Even some within the often soporific European minority in South Africa outdid Hurd and were stirred when taxes levied against the African majority (among others) were used to build a fabulous opera house for those defined as "white" alone.[52] But Hurd's recalcitrance was out of step with the official consensus in Washington and was much more aligned with sentiments in Pretoria. By 1973, a Negro diplomat

48. Frank Marshall Wright to Henry Kissinger, 21 July 1971, Box 744, *NSC Country Files.*

49. *Sydney Morning Herald*, 8 December 1973.

50. Clipping, 23 May 1973, Box 62, Folder 108, *Lusaka Mission, ANC Records, Fort Hare University.*

51. Bert Lockwood, Jr. to Carol Bernstein Ferry, 31 May 1973, Box 6, *Carol Bernstein Ferry and Ping Ferry Papers.*

52. State Department to South African legation, 19 September 1972, RG 59, Subject Numeric Files: Political and Defense, Box 2582, *NARA-CP.*

who spoke Afrikaans—James Baker—was en route to his posting in South Africa, a development noted by Tambo.[53]

The protests were having impact. A "secret" debate erupted at the White House as to whether Joel Carlson, the lawyer for numerous anti-apartheid defendants, should be offered asylum at the embassy or various consulates. But the fact that the policy of outgoing President Johnson concerning Carlson was not reflexively overturned indicated the changing correlation of forces domestically and globally whereby Pretoria could not be embraced without reservation.[54]

---

53. *Southern Africa: A Monthly Survey of News and Opinions*, April 1973, April 1973, Reel 19, *Oliver Tambo Papers*.

54. Report, circa 1971, Box 744, *NSC Country Files*. See also Memorandum of Conversation, 11 May 1971, RG 59, Subject Numeric Files: Political and Defense, Box 2582, *NARA-CP*: The U.S. envoy Edward McHale conversed with Benjamin Pogrund, then with the *Rand Daily Mail*, who claimed that Carlson was "guilty of the misuse of funds" from his anti-apartheid lawyering. Carlson, it was said, was "a man obsessed with the idea of personal publicity to the point where he…had placed his clients in positions of personal jeopardy in order to make 'martyrs of them.'" He was the attorney for Norma Kitson, spouse of David Kitson who was jailed in a stunning example of conflict of interest, said Pogrund, since Carlson was an "unsuccessful rival to Pogrund for her affection." Winnie Mandela "has frequently complained to Pogrund," who happened to be close to the PAC, about "money… sent for her to Carlson. He admitted he had received [such] but refused to give her these sums" and "issued statements in her name without her permission…." Carlson was portrayed as a loose cannon, charging the famed photographer Peter Magubane with being a "spy." The divisiveness and backbiting of the domestic movement, it was reported, was ascribed to the "exile syndrome" whereby those marooned abroad often felt alienated and turned on those similarly situated: anti-apartheid activists were analogized to exiles at home who were subject to the same syndrome. Carlson may have been the target of dirty tricks, however, a specialty in Pretoria. See La Rue Lutkins to Charles Runyon, 6 May 1971, RG 59, Subject Numeric Files: Political and Defense, Box 2582: A "copy of a poison pen letter on Carlson" was "sent to various foreign newspapers…." This was "presumably…the work of the Security Police…" Carlson's spouse quite curiously "unloaded five cartons of additional files ….to hold" doubtlessly containing sensitive materials. In this "confidential" missive, Carlson was derided as a "Jew" and "agnostic" besides. See also La Rue Lutkins to Charles Runyon, 11 March 1971, RG 59, Subject and Numeric Files: Political and Defense, Box 2582: After Carlson arranged to bail out Ms. Mandela from her latest scrap with the state, "she was very rude to him", according to the attorney. "He commented that he was fed up with her ungrateful and irresponsible attitude." Magubane, he said, was "emotionally involved" with her. See also La Rue Lutkins to Charles Runyon, 18 January 1971, RG 59, Subject Numeric Files:

In the highest councils in Washington it was recognized that as a result of decolonization, there was a "large African membership and disproportionate African voting power" at the United Nations and other multilateral agencies, a strength magnified by Moscow's appeal to this bloc. Yet U.S. Ambassador to the United Nations Charles Yost took an opposing tack and raised the "political viability of the United Nations and our position [there]." This "adverse trend," he cautioned in "secret" remarks, "could in large measure be counteracted by a most vigorous U.S. effort to influence—or, failing that to stand aside from—the unregenerate white minority regimes in Southern Africa."[55] The domestic conservatism on which the Nixon regime relied would not tolerate the latter approach, leaving Nixon with the unappetizing option of seeking to influence these admittedly "unregenerate" regimes in Pretoria and Salisbury most notably.

Political and Defense, Box 2582: Carlson, who apparently was much too garrulous in speaking with the U.S. authorities, "expressed a great concern about [Winnie Mandela's] situation in the future.....[she] had been virtually camping out in his office and obviously would like to get a job with him....[he] has concluded that he cannot help her and must tell her to stay away from the office, since her presence provides the Security Police with dangerous ammunition against him...." See also "Confidential Telegram" from Consul General-Johannesburg to Secretary of State, 9 March 1971, RG 59, Subject Numeric Files: Political and Defense, Box 2581: W.M. Magubane "forced his way" into Carlson's office and "angrily accused him of being friendly with [apartheid enforcer Theunis] Swanepoel and threatened to 'get him.'" Carlson was apparently a major source of intelligence on the doings of the Mandelas: La Rue Lutkins to Charles Runyonm 20 November 1970, RG 59, Subject Numeric Files: Political and Defense, Box 2581. Carlson reports that Winnie Mandela has endured a heart attack after being confined to a "small ill-ventilated lower hold" while visiting her spouse on Robben Island. La Rue Lutkins to Charles Runyon, 30 October 1970, RG 59, Subject Numeric Files: Political and Defense, Box 2581: Carlson "reports that Winnie is frustrated and depressed...he has given her 100 [rand] to send to Nelson to help him continue his studies." La Rue Lutkins to Charles Runyon, 3 February 1970, RG 59, Subject Numeric Files: Political and Defense, Box 2581: "Shotgun pellets" fired at Carlson's home; 'suspicion that the Security Police were responsible" for an accompanying "fire bomb attack.... use of benzene rather gasoline indicates considerable knowledge and expertise...." Interestingly, Carlson "did not appear outwardly upset or more nervous" afterwards; ditto for his spouse and "the same was true" for an earlier attack. Carlson ultimately fled to the U.S. by 1971: *New York Times*, 4 December 2001

55. Charles Yost to Secretary of State, no date, Box 744, *NSC Country Files*.

Then there was the nonsense being transmitted to Washington from London. "We had to remember," said an official of the Foreign and Commonwealth Office, "that the black African states were ruled by emotion to a greater extent than most other countries. So far in human history," it was said falsely, "there had been no genuine black civilization...." Hence, "there was no point in refusing to recognize that the black States were different than the white States and were going to continue to be so for a long time to come," a view which mirrored contemporaneous opinion in Washington. What was restraining the North Atlantic bloc was the fact that "if we rebuffed the Black African states too lightly, they might fall under Soviet influence."[56]

Though hardly recognized at the time, London's policy was in some ways more retrograde than Washington's, a difficult feat. In yet another "secret" report it was noted in London that "our countries' public policies are perhaps further apart" on what came to be called the Namibia Question. "We have doubts (which have not been expressed by the United States) about the competence of the [U.N.] formally to terminate [Pretoria's] Mandate" there and "our frequently stated inability to contemplate an economic confrontation with South Africa." It was observed revealingly "our attitude to Southern African problems is necessarily different from that of the Americans" since "their own domestic colour problem is an important factor which we do not share. Thus, American policies inevitably differ from our own...."[57]

The problem for Nixon and his cohorts—as even an ill-informed London recognized—was that Afro-Americans were becoming ever more involved with liberation fighters to the detriment of U.S. imperialism and neo-colonialism, exerting significant pressure. By 1971, Robert Van Lierop, a youthful Afro-American attorney turned filmmaker, was en route to southeastern Africa with the aim of making a documentary about the liberation war in Mozambique, a colony that he analogized to Mississippi. By September his crew came under direct attack by the Portuguese colonial military. The film was completed nonetheless and its title, *A Luta Continua*—The Struggle Continues—became a byword for U.S. strugglers as a direct result. I recall watching it shortly after it was completed and was impressed by the footage of events in liberated zones and the soon to be decolonized Mozambique. The film was an activist tool, aiding in the mobilization of tens of thousands of protesters in North American—particularly Washington, D.C. and San Francisco—in coming years

56. "Secret" Report, 4 January 1971, FCO36/629, *NAUK-London*.
57. "Secret" Report, 5 October 1970, FCO36/629, *NAUK-London*.

on "African Liberation Day," 25 May, the date of the founding of the Organization of African Unity. The mass marches centered on disrupting the alliance between the U.S. and apartheid and colonialism, which reached an apogee by April 1974. Still, Howard Fuller, who traveled with Van Lierop, found that "several of the Black elected politicians that we approached" upon returning home "seemed scared to associate with the African liberation movement.... They didn't want to hear nothing about the African liberation leaders," e.g. Mandela, because of the ANC's alliance with the SACP and the fear of angering anticommunists. Yet when Mandela arrived in the U.S. in 1990 some of these same politicians, responding to their constituents' enthusiasm for the ANC leader, rushed to embrace him; a hypocritical spectacle which made Fuller "want to puke."[58] Fuller had a point: according to one estimate, by 1973 about 25% of ANC leaders were simultaneously members of the SACP[59] and given the allergy to Communists in the U.S., this hampered the ability to build solidarity around Mandela and other Southern Africa political prisoners.

Fuller's reservations notwithstanding, there was little doubt that his collaboration with Van Lierop paid multiple dividends. They had travelled six weeks in liberated zones in Mozambique where they filmed, recorded, and photographed, taking advantage of the latest technology. Van Lierop was correct in terming the resultant documentary "widely viewed and critically acclaimed" in that it "played a major role in organizing substantial support in North America and Europe for the liberation struggle." Then, from "June until November 1975," his crew was back in a decolonized Mozambique to produce a follow-up film.[60]

Taking advantage of the postwar expansion of transcontinental travel, more and more Afro-Americans were making their way to Africa, particularly Tanzania, which had replaced Nkrumah's Ghana as a Pan-African North Star and a headquarters for liberation movements. This sojourning, according to prize-winning journalist Seymour Hersh, was becoming a "preoccupation" for Washington, which perceived foreign influence on Afro-Americans as a threat to

58. Howard Fuller, *No Struggle, No Progress: A Warrior's Life from Black Power to Education Reform*, Milwaukee: Marquette University Press, 2014, 126, 128-129, 135, 139, 151,.

59. Stephen Ellis and Tsepo Sechaba, *Comrades Against Apartheid*, 61.

60. Bob Van Lierop to Carol Bernstein Ferry and Ping Ferry, 20 February 1976, Box 13, *Carol Bernstein Ferry and Ping Ferry Papers.*

U.S. national security.[61] Dar es Salaam, which had become a kind of update of wartime Casablanca, crawling with operatives and espionage experts of varying persuasions, was also the site for the Sixth Pan-African Congress of 1974, weeks after the transformational events in Portugal—continuing a forum initiated by W.E.B. Du Bois earlier in a colonized century that was rapidly fading from memory.

Du Bois' role was marked at the Tenth Anniversary Summit of the OAU in Addis Ababa, highlighted along with those of Marcus Garvey of Jamaica, George Padmore and Sylvester Williams of Trinidad, Jomo Kenyatta of Kenya, and Kwame Nkrumah of Ghana. On the negative side, there was discussion of the impact of the devaluation of the dollar on contributions to liberation movements,[62] which only served to underscore the importance of the kind of solidarity expressed by Afro-Americans who chose to travel to Tanzania in 1974.

In that spirit, African leaders were paying more attention to their Afro-American brothers and sisters. As early as 1971 in Lagos there was the Third Annual Conference of the African-American Dialogue. Remarks there by the President of Botswana, Sir Seretse Khama, caught the eye of Oliver Tambo. The ferment among Afro-Americans, Khama said, was "an internal problem of considerable dimensions" and "complicated by the issue of race…." There were "cynics who say that it is only the racial factor which makes it necessary for America, in its present mood of introspection, to have an African policy at all…." But this need for "an African policy" was actually being driven by the increased activism of Afro-Americans. As a result, Africa reciprocated and "was watching with sympathy the efforts of Black Americans to assert their identity and to win themselves their rightful place in U.S. Society."[63] Sir Seretse's forthrightness was bad news for his neighbor in Pretoria. Gaborone established diplomatic relations with Moscow in 1970[64] and with China in 1974.[65] He also thought that the U.S. and its allies were willing to arm Pretoria with nuclear weapons to "enable that country to silence the voices of change in Africa."[66] The Sixth Pan African Congress in

61. *New York Times*, 25 May 1973.

62. Material and Reports on OAU, May 1973, Reel 18, *Oliver Tambo Papers*.

63. Address by Sir Seretse Khama, March 1971, Reel 14, *Oliver Tambo Papers*.

64. *Rand Daily Mail*, 11 March 1970.

65. *Washington Post*, 26 March 1974.

66. Clipping, undated, Box 38, *Leroy Walker Africa News Service Archive, Duke University*.

Tanzania was then seen as an opportunity to solidify these growing bonds between Africans and Afro-Americans.

It was appropriate that this gathering took place in Nigeria, since by 1973 a U.S. official had noticed that in this most populous of African nations a "critical view of the U.S. stance on Southern Africa issues is as strong as ever and has an inevitable adverse effect on our overall relationship." Mournfully, the official said" we pay a price every day in U.S.-Nigerian relations for voting with Portugal and South Africa" and observed "we have certainly not yet reaped the full harvest."[67]

Lagos' growing importance gave an added significance to the confab in Dar. On the flight to the "6PAC" from the U.S., the activist Howard Fuller recalled disconsolately that "Black Americans on the plane argued all night long over…Black Nationalism versus Marxism," a debate they continued in Tanzania, to the dismay of many Africans.[68] Otis Cunningham, born in 1949 and residing then in Black Chicago, recalled that these tensions came to a head in Dar: "there was a huge clash" since "a lot of movements in the African diaspora were anticommunist," along with "people in the U.S. delegation saying, well, Algeria, shouldn't be there because they ain't Africans. Kick the Algerians out of the Congress…kick out the Cubans." There were "real ideological clashes between the African liberation movements and a lot of the African American folks from here…." The source of this "major clash," he thought, could be attributed to the fact that "lot [of] African American movements and individuals" were "tied to the South African government." Ultimately, the once vibrant African Liberation Solidarity Committee "dissolved because of the splits within it."[69]

Cunningham could have pointed to the continuing baneful role of Richard Gibson, who simultaneously was quite close to Amiri Baraka, the writer once known as Le Roi Jones and an inspiration for many of the PAC delegates, not to mention Robert F. Williams, who had resided only recently in China and harbored unremitting hostility to Moscow. For his part, Gibson was an organizer of "American Friends of China in Europe" from his perch in the old continent.[70]

---

67. A.L. Steigman, U.S. legation-Lagos to Secretary of State, 10 January 1973, RG 59, Subject Numeric Files: Social, Box 3095, *NARA-CP*.

68. Howard Fuller, *No Struggle, No Progress*, 154.

69. Oral History, Otis Cunningham, 12 December 2009, *Columbia College-Chicago*.

70. Richard Gibson to Paul Hansen, 9 December 1975, Box 3, *Richard Gibson Papers*.

Baraka called him "Dear Richard" and, per usual, was "very, very glad to hear from you."[71] When Baraka shifted from a kind of Black Nationalism to Maoism,[72] Gibson congratulated him on his "correct" shift.[73]

Among those arriving with the substantial U.S. delegation for "6PAC" was the poet and activist once known as Don L. Lee, also from Black Chicago, who was displeased by Baraka's shift—but assuredly not on pro-Moscow grounds. Now under the moniker Haki Madhubuti, he was unsparing in his analysis of what he witnessed. "For the nine days of the Congress," he said, "I sat and listened, taped, took notes and interviewed people. I grew angrier and angrier and wiser. This trip was a significant point," he noted thoughtfully, "in my internal and external growth and development...." The gathering also proved important in the broader ideological evolution of Black America, still being liberated from Jim Crow in a process that carried the price of sacrificing their left-wing polestar—Robeson most notably—which left this delegation ill-equipped to engage with leaders of independent Africa, deeply influenced by doctrines of class struggle and grateful to the aid rendered by the Soviet Union. The Afro-Americans were sometimes not even aware how deeply they had been influenced by rudimentary anticommunism, which for some merged with China's ever sharper critique of Moscow.

Sekou Touré of Guinea-Conakry had rushed to the aid of Nkrumah when he was ousted and many in the U.S. delegation identified—at least abstractly—with both men. But when the Guinean leader contemptuously dismissed "skin color" as a basis for unity, it clashed fundamentally with the experience of many Afro-Americans who in a white supremacist society had united on this basis from time to time, even as "race traitors," like current U.S. Supreme Court Justice Clarence Thomas, were dismissed peremptorily. What emerged in Dar as a result was an ideological donnybrook with the "class vs. race," combatants often talking past one another, oblivious to what they shared and flummoxed by what separated them.

"The major lines of conflict and confrontation" said Madhubuti, "could be classified as Black Nationalism versus Marxist-Leninist". (I would amend this sweeping statement by saying that the division turned on the extent to which one side or another thought class

71. Amiri Baraka to Richard Gibson, 28 October 1975, Box 3.

72. *New York Times,,* 27 December 1974.

73. Richard Gibson to Amiri Baraka, 27 December 1974, Box 12, *Richard Gibson Papers.*

or "race" predominated in their own local context and the extent to which there was a recognition of the role of the socialist camp in weakening U.S. imperialism, the ultimate foe of all assembled). Madhubuti and those aligned with him may have acknowledged the latter point abstractly but seemed to think that Afro-Americans, just barely emerging from Jim Crow, and Africa, still ensnared by imperialism and neo-colonialism, did not require the force of the socialist camp in confronting their foes. This wholly unrealistic viewpoint objectively consigned all peoples of African descent to continued domination.

Wounded, Madhubuti fired back, declaring that "Black Nationalism was seen by most of the participants as *provincial, racism in reverse, short sighted and at best naive.* This took many of the Nationalists by surprise", he said seemingly astonished. [emphasis his] This viewpoint was not his alone but was threaded through the U.S. delegation, which was the "largest" of all, he contended, "in excess of two hundred" delegates. Though it was estimated that this sizeable group of free spenders expended "approximately $250,000 in transportation, lodging and…artifacts," somehow the "Marxists were in command." The delegates, who included activist Sylvia Hill (who played a crucial role), writer Lerone Bennett, cleric H.H. Brookins, the educator recently known as Howard Fuller, and the poet Amiri Baraka, represented a fair cross-section of various ideological trends in Black America. As for Madhubuti, he exposed his sympathy for the PAC when he observed that the "correct name for South Afrika [sic]" was "Azania," not a choice endorsed by the ANC-led alliance.[74]

Of course, the ascendant Black Nationalists had their own critics. Sylvia Hill of Washington, D.C. thought they had conspired to exclude her from a meeting with the Tanzanian leadership—and were surprised to find her already there when they arrived.[75] She recalled an organizing meeting at Manhattan's Hilton Hotel which left her with the distinct impression that only Nationalists e.g. James Turner and Jitu Weusi of Brooklyn (whose father, tellingly, had been a Communist), Baraka "and a few others" would be the only delegates in Dar, to which she objected strenuously and prevailed. From

---

74. Haki R. Madhubuti, *Enemies: The Clash of Race*, Chicago: Third World Press, 1978, 52, 63, 66, 67, 68, 90. On the role of women at the confab see e.g. Ashley Farmer, *Remaking Black Power: How Black Women Transformed the Era*, Chapel Hill: University of North Carolina Press, 2017. Note particularly the role of Sylvia Hill of Washington, D.C.

75. Article by Mary Jane Patterson, circa 2003, Box 109, *Trans Africa Papers, Howard University, Washington, D.C.*

her viewpoint, the "race" versus "class" debate was a diversion from what should have been the main agenda item: support for liberation movements. "African Americans" she observed "sometimes can be ugly Americans" and "a few African Americans will end up being very ugly white Americans. That's very painful to see," she said reflecting on the tumult in Dar, "but it is real." Pointedly, she blamed Turner for the attempt to exclude her from important meetings in Dar.[76]

The delegation was rife with contradiction in any case. One reason why so many from the U.S. were able to travel thousands of miles to southeast Africa was because of the largesse of Carol Bernstein Ferry, a funder of numerous "Black Power" projects. It was in March 1974 that the activist, Courtland Cox, informed this affluent Euro-American woman that the thousands of dollars she had contributed to organizing efforts were "very important in our initial organizing"—but more was needed.[77]

Bill Sutherland, the Afro-American observer, also noticed the "conflict between cultural nationalists and the people who were Marxists…." He also accurately noted that the "majority of the [U.S.] delegation was in the cultural nationalist mode," which thus pitted them against (mostly) Africans. These nationalists, he said, "happened to be the people with the money and the time to take international trips." He also argues that this dramatic confrontation in Dar was a transformative moment in Baraka's evolution—and perhaps others'—from his cultural nationalist stance to a "revolutionary socialist" posture. The ideologically cocooned Afro-American nationalists, said Sutherland, were receptive to neither Touré nor Nyerere, who "were very clear that Pan Africanism must not be defined as a narrow cultural nationalism. This came as quite a shock to a number of the African-Americans." It is possible, as shall be seen, that this controversy disposed the leadership in Tanzania to take a malignant view of a melodramatic episode soon to unfold when what Sutherland called "neo-Garveyites" who wound up residing in Butiama—were well-armed, leading to the "concocted" idea that the CIA was coming to "sabotage and overthrow" the regime through them. This led to a Pan-African debacle whereby numerous Afro-Americans were "put in jail without trial," "quite a tragic moment" that led

76. La TaSha Levy, "Remembering Sixth PAC," *Black Scholar,* circa 1974, Box 109.

77. Courtland Cox to Carol Ferry, 23 March 1974, Box 4, *Sixth PAC Papers, Howard University.*

to "tremendous disillusionment" and the government increasingly reluctant to assist the Pan African Skills Project.[78]

To be fair, the U.S. cultural nationalists may have been confused by the conflicting signals sent from the continent. Though rebuked by Toure, it was well known that he and Nkrumah were as much brothers as comrades—and in 1970 the former Ghanaian leader was rebuked by the revived Mary Louise Hooper. "Dear Kwame", she wrote, "I have known the ANC—at the leadership level—for 15 years," and consequently she rejected unequivocally the "anti-ANC propaganda" she accused him of spreading. Writing from her refuge in Klamath Falls, Oregon, she reminded him of his own "experience with deserters and disaffected" that were pouring PAC propaganda into his ear. That is, the PAC line of "one settler/one bullet" gained traction in the U.S. not least because the hero Nkrumah was seen as endorsing it.[79]

Dar's previous embrace of the PAC may have confused the U.S. visitors. Prexy Nesbitt, the Afro-American who was as close to FRELIMO as any non-Mozambican, found that at a certain point "in Tanzania…the PAC's armed wing was virtually at war with the Tanzanian Army….There were rebellions going on inside of the training camps of the PAC….I found a lot of corruption going on with use of monies," he said of the PAC. "And then there was a big three, four-way split inside of the PAC organization" that fueled corruption and mutiny alike. "Some African Americans", he said, "supported the PAC because the PAC believed in a black struggle in South Africa. They did not believe, as the ANC did, in a struggle by all of those who wanted to see a…non-racial South Africa…." Some of his fellow Chicagoans, for example, "liked hearing phrases like, 'we're going to drive the whites into the sea'…" He "got attacked" because he did not accept this line. "Defending me were the Tanzanian government and also the Organization of African Unity's African Liberation Committee and many of the European groups." Thus, at a conference in West Germany a "very, ugly, ugly episode" unfolded when the PAC and their allies termed him "the Black Craig Williamson," a reference to a notorious apartheid spy said to "have killed Ruth First" with a letter bomb during her exile. "He was a spy, a master spy." And some of those who made it to Dar from Chicago—or who remained back home in the U.S.—were of like mind about him,

78. Bill Sutherland, *Guns and Gandhi*, 218-219, 230.

79. Mary Louise Hooper to "Dear Kwame," Box 2, *Mary Louise Hooper Papers*.

putting them at odds with a government they purportedly backed in Tanzania.[80]

ANC leader Duma Nokwe said he was a "little baffled" by 6PAC considering the rise of the OAU and the Afro-Asian Peoples Solidarity Organization. It was "difficult to see precisely where this body would fit in," he said, "particularly when the call made very little or no mention at all of an anti-imperialist character but characterized the 20th Century as the Century of Black Power"—which was a "bit of a misreading," he said diplomatically. "We did attend," he said of the ANC, despite the "sharp differences." Thus, "our Afro-American brothers and sisters were looking at the world from a different perspective. The result was a sharp confrontation of ideas," which "sometimes...didn't quite make sense...," though this confusion, he suggested, also encompassed "our brothers from Britain...."[81]

Though there were those in the then rising Black Consciousness Movement who denied U.S. paternity, there were parallels between and among Black Power, cultural nationalism, and the BCM. The latter also challenged the PAC in addition to rebuking the ANC for "corruption." But what united these various forms of Black Nationalism was reflected in the spirited remarks of Basil Manning in London, when he rebuked the SACP for being dominated by those "who are exploiting our people," the same people who were "running the people's army," i.e. the "white and the Indian," like "the white Communist Joseph Slovo of Russia [sic]". Then there were "the Indian Communists Mac Maharaj, Mohammed Timol and Phyllis Naidoo" and the "white Communists Ray Simons and Marius Schoon and with some Black puppet Communists like John Matshobi (Pule), Henry Makgothi (Spuires) and Thomas Nkobi."[82] The racializing of Communists and imprecations about their purportedly oversized roles was not undertaken by Manning alone. The pervasive and putrid cesspool that was white supremacy made it difficult for some to look beyond the politics of the epidermis.

Then there was the real problem with certain ANC spokesmen in the U.S. In 1972 Hooper said the group was "disgraced" by the performance of their envoy "Gladstone Ntlabati," who was "drunk" and "used foul and abusive language" at an important confab in Washington that included 25 different groups and 300 individuals,

80. Oral History, Prexy Nesbitt, April 2009, *Columbia College-Chicago*.

81. *African Agenda*, 3(Number 6, October-November 1974), *Chicago History Museum*.

82. "New BCM Leaders Slam ANC, PAC Corruption," no date, Box 88, Folder 43, Part II, *Lusaka Mission, ANC Records*.

and like so many other ACOA events was financed by the generosity of Peter Weiss. Yet the ANC delegate, contrary to the organization's outlook, focused his remarks on "the issue of killing white people, not of investments," which probably influenced attendees to believe that this perspective was mainstream in Southern Africa.[83]

Thus, on 28 May 1974, mere weeks before 6PAC, the front page of Dar's leading newspaper blared the story of the detained Afro-Americans, deemed by a subsequent scholar to be a "major turning point" for this suddenly beleaguered community. Two unnamed Negro men arrived from New York carrying goods addressed to the "Kirongwe Ujamaa Village. The Two were taking a six-ton container of goods to the Mara region for a nation building skills project. The container consisted of eighteen boxes and drums and in one of the boxes were a pistol, a rifle and bullets. Police also reported [the presence of] a telescopic fitting device, a six-channel walkie-talkie and a holster...." The authorities reacted strongly, detaining scores of Afro-Americans. This "drastically reduced the population of the Afro community," says scholar Lessie Tate, causing some to flee, others to be expelled. It may have influenced Nyerere's critique of the dominant cultural nationalist faction of the U.S. delegation at 6PAC, though his cooperation with the Pan African Skills Project had suggested otherwise.[84]

Revealingly, the U.S. cultural nationalists were pitted against those considered to be revolutionary and most hostile to Washington, though the North American sojourners thought they too were pitted against Washington. The opposing bloc included not only Guinea-Conakry but Congo-Brazzaville, Cuba, Egypt, Algeria, FRELIMO, SWAPO, the ANC—even ZANU and Tanzania itself.[85] The latter were seen as friendly forces by the cultural nationalists, who drew few lessons from their virtual isolation. This was not the finest hour for Afro-Americans as they sought to destabilize the alliance between the revolutionaries and the socialist camp—which was also a prime goal of U.S. imperialism. Interestingly enough, Washington thought that this division was being played out within the ANC

83. Mary Louise Hooper to Thami Mhlambiso, 1 May 1972, Box 2, *Mary Louise Hooper Papers*. Eyebrows could be raised about Hooper too. The right-wing Social Democrat, the Negro actor Frederick O'Neal was a "personal friend of mine," she said, a "wonderful guy" who "cooperated closely when I worked with ACOA...he never refused me...." Mary Louise Hooper memorandum, October 1969, Box 2, *Mary Louise Hooper Papers*.

84. Ibid., Lessie Tate, 189, 210; *Daily News*, 28 May 1974.

85. Ibid., Seth Markle, dissertation, 282

itself. As of 1972, the Lusaka legation reported that "Soviet influence in the ANC seems to be growing.... There has been a struggle within the ANC between the Communists—and non-Communist black nationalists."[86]

The Pretoria legation chimed in that same year to point out that "young African, Colored and Indians are increasingly referring to themselves as 'Black,'" which went beyond this terminology in the U.S. "They consider terms such as 'non-white' and 'Colored' to be demeaning." This new nomenclature cropped up "largely from the subject peoples' own search for identity," said the U.S. legation and a repudiation of past terms, e.g. "Kaffir" and "Bantu."[87] The U.S. national ,Professor Marshall Murphee, head of the Centre for Inter-Racial Studies at the University of Rhodesia—and the son of a U.S. missionary who arrived in Salisbury in 1920—saw a "Black Power Syndrome" developing there by 1972.[88]

Even Duma Nokwe, thought to be close to the SACP, was sent a text by Houser on "Black Theology and Black Power" and another by the departed State Department official "Soapy" Williams on "Africa for the Africans."[89]

Nevertheless, as it had been for some time, the socialist camp was one of the most reliable supporters of the liberation movements, as Washington was well aware. U.S. imperialism watched from the sidelines as Tambo—preceded by Amilcar Cabral of Guinea-Bissau—was hosted in Berlin in 1973 by Erich Honecker of the ruling Socialist Unity Party of the GDR, with more aid expected to flow as a result.[90]

It seemed that the "cultural nationalists" had misjudged Tanzania. The government's housing of PAC may have been misinterpreted as an endorsement of this group's anticommunism and "one settler, one bullet" philosophy, which North Americans understandably embittered by the ravages of settler colonialism found appealing (but which even the PAC did not consistently follow, as their attachment to the settler Patrick Duncan showed). The decision to provide them refuge was more a function of the ecumenical eclecticism of

86. Report from Lusaka legation, 25 January 1972, RG 59, Subject Numeric Files: Politics & Defense, Box 2577, *NARA-CP*.

87. R.P. Smith, Pretoria legation to Secretary of State, 21 July 1972, RG 59, Subject Numeric Files: Social, Box 3095.

88. W.P. O'Neill, Cape Town legation to Secretary of State, 13 December 1972, RG 59, Subject Numeric Files: Social, Box 3095.

89. George Houser to Duma Nokwe, 12 September 1972, Box 150, *ACOARA*.

90. U.S. Legation-Berlin to Secretary of State, 20 December 1972, RG 59, Subject Numeric Files: Politics & Defense, Box 2577, *NARA-CP*.

Tanzania, which opened its doors to liberation movements of various stripes. Cultural nationalists should have paid attention to what the SACP journal noticed in 1970: Tanzania moved to circumscribe what was called "Soul Music," a product of Black America and generally hailed in all quarters among Afro-Americans. Dar rejected this music on the grounds that it spurred the idea that Afro-Americans were models of success—hardly accurate—and that the U.S. itself was a great nation willing to absorb those previously scorned. The fact that those who overthrew Nkrumah in Ghana had embraced this cultural product also did not recommend it.[91]

Though it sought to build bridges to Black America, the SACP was also capable of criticizing this community. Thus in 1973 readers of their journal could absorb "Black Americans in Africa: A Critical View", which focused on some of the more troubling aspects of this presence, including imperialism's attempt to weaponize this group as a Trojan Horse, an inevitable outgrowth of some being inducted into elite circles. "The Afro-American especially the middle-class Afro-American," it was stressed with some justification "is a liberal *par excellence*"—a descriptor not intended as complimentary. (What should have been noted is that the routing of the likes of Robeson ideologically warped the nation and had been noticeably devastating for Black America—but the critique was not limited to the U.S., as the Nigerian future Nobel winner Wole Soyinka was also scorned as "right-wing".)[92] To bolster their case, the *African Communist* turned its ire against the anticommunist writer Richard Gibson, who specialized in assailing the ANC, MPLA, and others thought to be too close to Moscow.[93]

Some of those designated as "cultural nationalists" did not help their overall case by adopting positions questionable to even their comrades. The *Black News* of Brooklyn, for example, like almost within this tendency, highlighted the PAC and their frequent attacks on leftists and spoke of a tie between the government of Forbes Burnham of Guyana and the PAC. They also hosted Jorge Sangumba of UNITA and praised this group,[94] despite its CIA ties. UNITA, however, purported to be "pro-Black" in alleged contrast to the MPLA,

---

91. J.K. Obatala, "U.S. 'Soul' Music in Africa," *African Communist*, (Number 41, Second Quarter, 1970): 80-89, 80, 88-89.

92. J.K. Obatala, "Black Americans in Africa: A Critical View," *African Communist*, (Number 52, 2nd Quarter, 1973): 88-98, 92, 97.

93. Review of Richard Gibson's work on African Liberation Movements, *African Communist*, (Number 51, 4th Quarter, 1972): 117-121.

94. *Black News*, January 1972 and 28 January 1974 and 21 March 1974.

which harbored non-Africans (the same charge wielded by the PAC against the ANC, to likewise positive effect in North America).

As the war for Southern African became more intense, it became more difficult for some to choose sides thoughtfully, particularly when anticommunism had become so endemic in the U.S., making too many skeptical of the ANC and MPLA. But it was not just Southern Africa. After the brutal dictator Idi Amin came to power in Uganda, he made a special—and not unsuccessful—appeal to Afro-Americans. Roy Innis, whose roots were in the Virgin Islands, which was apparent in his faint accent, came to head the Congress of Racial Equality, which shared right-wing Social Democratic roots with Houser and the ACOA. By 1975 he was recruiting mercenaries to fight the MPLA in Angola, but as early as 1973, he was seeking to emulate the Pan African Skills Project by sending Negro technicians to Kampala, filling the void created by the expulsion of Ugandans and others of South Asian descent.[95]

Still such weaknesses were not Afro-Americans' alone. They reflected the sweep and breadth of the Red Scare that debilitated the U.S. progressive movement generally—witness Robeson's CAA—and was then exported globally, e.g. to Southern Africa. It was also an effect of the slow demise of Robeson's unacknowledged heirs: The Black Panther Party. By 1974, this group—which had sought to popularize the socialist alternative—was on its last legs. "FBI Subversion of the Black Panthers" was an all too accurate headline.[96]

One can also follow this trend in the peregrinations of George Houser, who in 1972 made his 15th trip to Africa. The red carpet was rolled out for him in Lusaka as he met with Kaunda for 45 minutes in the State House—but he also spoke at length with Jonas Savimbi's comrade Jorge Sangumba, whose organization was soon to become a hallowed cause for U.S. reactionaries. Even SWAPO, said Houser, spoke "well" of UNITA. He found time to confer with Shelton Siwela of the Rhodesian splinter group FROLIZI, who like so many suspicious characters in the region had studied in the U.S. Naturally, Houser also traveled to Kinshasa to confer with Roberto.[97]

Alarm bells should have rung loudly when Roberto told him that he and the Congolese dictator once known as Joseph Mobutu were more than good friends, they were like brothers. The elusive Roberto also claimed that he was close to the man the dictator helped

95. *African Agenda*, April 1973, Box 4, Folder 2, *Chicago Anti-Apartheid Collection, Columbia College-Chicago.*

96. *Guardian* [U.K.], 28 May 1974.

97. Report, 5 September 1972, Box 1, *George Houser Papers.*

to slay, the sainted Patrice Lumumba, and he claimed to know the celebrated Frantz Fanon, who he said was a brilliant man who influenced him more than any other person. He and Houser chatted about Roberto's journey to Accra in 1958 for an important conference and his subsequent trip to Manhattan, where he bonded further with the ACOA before returning to Kinshasa by July 1960. Roberto said that his group had excellent relations with China and also received aid from Turkey and Tunisia.[98]

Not helpful in this regard was the activity of Charles Evers, a prominent Negro politician in Mississippi whose credibility was enhanced by the fact that the martyred leader Medgar Evers was his brother. Evers advocated trade relations with African businessmen in South Africa, to destroy the "wall of segregation," though this effort was contrary to the global movement to boycott and isolate Pretoria. Following in his footsteps was the Negro businessman Charles Young of Meridian, Mississippi, a cosmetics manufacturer, who sought to forge trade ties in South Africa.[99]

Such attempts to ease the isolation of apartheid were opposed hotly by Congressman Charles Diggs. In response segregationist Senator Eastland of Mississippi denounced him,[100] threateningly.[101] Senator Eastland remained staunch in his support for Salisbury, declaring in 1974 that "Rhodesia has done absolutely nothing that we, as colonies, didn't do ourselves 200 years ago."[102]

It was also apparent that when in 1974 Salisbury cried "immigrants wanted," Rhodesia would receive more than a pro forma hearing from Senator Eastland.[103] Agreeing was Charles St. Thomas, a businessman in Johannesburg who had migrated from the U.S. a decade earlier: "I would say that the United States is a fertile ground for immigration recruitment,"[104] he told his fellow apartheid supporters, speaking of those disgusted with the forced retreat from Jim Crow. Despite the upsurge in activism, there were too many bonds linking apartheid and the Jim Crow legacy to untangle them easily.

---

98. Report, 6 August 1973, Box 1, *George Houser Papers*.

99. Clipping, no date, Box 14, File 2, Subseries 4, *James O. Eastland Papers*.

100. Press Release, 22 May 1973, Box 85, File 3, Subseries 1, *James O. Eastland Papers*.

101. Ibid.

102. Senator Eastland to John Crowe, 25 January 1974, Box 85 File 3, Subseries 1, *James O. Eastland Papers*.

103. "Rhodesian Commentary," February 1974, Box 85, File 3, Subseries 1.

104. *Financial Gazette* [South Africa], 25 January 1974.

In 1972, for example, Washington had considered purchasing the Cactus guided missile system from Pretoria.[105]

By 1970 the U.S. based *American Southern Africa Review* opened an office in Rhodesia headed by U.S. national, John Slinkman and his spouse Carol. Born in Maryland and educated at the segregationist University of Mississippi, he was described as "deeply committed to the Rhodesian cause and has already joined the [ruling] Rhodesian Front." The elated couple were pictured alongside Prime Minister Ian Smith. Slinkman, it was said enthusiastically by an observant journalist, "who looks and sounds like an American is, I'm happy to report, a Rhodesian now...."[106] But hedging its bets, two Rhodesians, John Roger Nicholson and Alfred Trevor Gallaher, had been convicted by Salisbury in the previous months for spying for the CIA. They had been in touch with U.S. Consul General Paul O'Neill. The breadth of right-wing ideology in the U.S. stained all from there—perhaps understandably, as the ACOA knew well. Thus, when the celebrated Negro journalist and diplomat Carl Rowan was headed to the vicinity, he too was said to be "reputed in Washington to be a CIA operative...."[107]

Barely visible threads continued to tie apartheid and colonialism to Uncle Sam's apron strings. By 1973 a chief consul of Pretoria in Mozambique, Louis Vorster, had a German spouse and both, said a U.S. emissary there, were "well disposed towards Americans.... He often recalls the racial situation in [the] Southern part of the United States fifteen years ago," speaking of 1958 "when he was assigned to Washington...." Like his U.S. counterparts, he did not think Lisbon was up to the task of controlling this vast colony, seeing "Portuguese security efforts as undisciplined with much wastage of both time and personnel."[108]

It was also apparent that Congressman Diggs was becoming a bete noire in the eyes of both Mississippi and apartheid South Africa, boding ill for his future, which was to be punctuated by scandal and imprisonment, as shall be seen. By 1971 he had secured a visa from

---

105. *Anti-Apartheid News*, September 1972, Box 128, *Leroy Walker Africa News Service Archive, Duke University*.

106. *American Southern Africa Review*, December 1970, *University of Kansas-Lawrence*.

107. *American Southern Africa Review*, July 1971, *University of Kansas-Lawrence*.

108. Consul General-Lourenco Marques to Secretary of State, 16 October 1973, RG 59, Subject Numeric Files: Political and Defense, Box 2584, *NARA-CP*.

Pretoria and was to be found in South Africa. It had been a long time, said the *Rand Daily Mail*, since "a visitor from abroad excited as much antagonism from the white South Africans" as Diggs inspired during his "nine-day visit." Dismissively, the paper noted that he was "frequently late for appointments," while his visit was unfavorably compared with the recent visit of Malwai's Hastings Banda,[109] who was feted lavishly.

This harsh evaluation aside, Congressman Diggs was unmeasured in his criticism of Ford and General Motors, major forces in the political economy of his home state of Michigan, because of their brutal exploitation of cheap African labor thereby undermining U.S. workers.[110] The feisty lawmaker also took a potshot at Hollywood, threatening a boycott if the blockbuster film *The Godfather* was shown before racially segregated audiences in South Africa.[111] It was also in 1971 that Congressman Diggs chaired a Washington hearing in which Kenneth Williams of the "Polaroid Revolutionary Workers Movement" denounced his employer as "the leader of American firms supporting apartheid, that it is bringing back to the United States the techniques in slavery that it is learning in South Africa."[112]

The increased frequency of travel between North America and South Africa also buoyed the magazine *Southern Africa*, based in Manhattan, which by late 1974 had sent a member of their collective to the region for six weeks of reportage. Janet Hooper and Stephanie Urdang, members of the collective, were gleeful to find "the response to the magazine from members of the liberation movements such as FRELIMO, MPLA, SWAPO, ZANU, ANC was extremely supportive and enthusiastic." "FRELIMO's and MPLA's only complaint," it was said with happiness, "was that the magazine was whisked away by eager militants as soon as it arrives and some don't get a chance to see it....The same response from PAIGC" in Guinea-Bissau was observed.[113] Jennifer Davis, a South African exile in the U.S., was part of the magazine's delegation and she would eventually replace Houser at the helm of the ACOA. By 1973 she was also working for

109. *Rand Daily Mail*, 21 August 1971.

110. Telegram from Pretoria, 17 August 1971, RG 59, Subject Numeric Files: Social, Box 3094, *NARA-*

111. Telegram from Pretoria, 21 August 1972, RG 59, Subject Numeric Files: Social, Box 3095.

112. "Informal Report" from State Department, 3 May 1971, RG 59, Subject Numeric Files: Social, Box 3094, *NARA-CP.*

113. Janet Hooper and Stephanie Urdang to Carol Bernstein Ferry, Box 20, *Carol Bernstein Ferry and Ping Ferry Papers, Indiana University Purdue University, Indianapolis.*

the group's "Africa Fund" which, she said, monitored "more than 50 African and European journals and newspapers," the gleanings from which often made their way into the pages of *Southern Africa.* "One member of our 2 person staff," she said, "played an important role in tracing and monitoring all U.S. imports of chrome" from Rhodesia; "the flow of information," she said accurately, "helped keep alive protest which included the boycott of several ships by the [International Longshore Association], [and] demonstrations against sanctions breaking in Burnside, near New Orleans...."[114]

This was becoming a trend. In 1972 Baltimore stevedores chose not to unload 92 drums of nickel from Rhodesia.[115] In November 1973 rank-and-file stevedores in Philadelphia refused for 24 hours to cross a picket line organized by the newly formed Coalition to Stop Rhodesian Imports, leaving unloaded "blue fiber" asbestos from the ship "African Sun." Though "essentially spontaneous," this action morphed into organized struggle.[116] Weeks after regime change in Lisbon, the inspired West Coast stevedores, traditionally progressive, donated $200 to the ANC-SACP-allied South African Congress of Trade Unions.[117]

In short, relationships between North American and Southern African progressives were blossoming as a direct result of the victories of the anti-Jim Crow movement, which empowered Afro-Americans and improved their own balance sheet. By 1970 Thulani Gcabashe, his spouse Hilda, and their four children had migrated from Durban to Atlanta. She was the daughter of the late Chief Luthuli and they moved into the home of the leading Afro-American scholar Vincent Harding. Gcabashe began working alongside this historian at the institute recently formed in name of the slain Dr. King.[118] (After the family's arrival, Thandi Gcabashe was asked by skeptical Georgians, "Why Atlanta...why go from the frying pan to the fire?" That is, why flee apartheid for a former capital of Jim Crow?)[119] Still, according

114. Jennifer Davis to Carol Bernstein Ferry Papers, 5 November 1974, Box 1, *Carol Bernstein Ferry Papers.*

115. Judge William Booth to William Halle, President of the ILA, 28 July 1972, Box 149, *ACOARA.*

116. Statement, January 1975, Box 74, *ACOARA.*

117. Mary Louise Hooper to Nadia Walsh, 28 May 1974, Box 1, *Mary Louise Hooper Papers.*

118. Charles Runyon to Elliott Goldstein, 24 August 1970, RG 59, Subject Numeric Files: Political and Defense, Box 2584, *NARA-CP.*

119. Undated article from Tandi Gchabashe, Bo Greater Regional Office, Southern Africa Peace Education Program, 1970s-1992, *AFSC.*

to the U.S. envoy in Johannesburg, by 1971, the PAC's Sobukwe too was seeking "permanent residence" in the U.S.[120]

Washington was finding that African students at Fort Hare University, who might have been expected to be sympathetic to U.S. imperialism, instead had "strong criticism of U.S. foreign policy." This "major center of African intellectuals," which had once housed Robert Mugabe and Nelson Mandela, was full of criticism for "U.S. imports from Rhodesia...."[121]

This surveillance of Fort Hare was an aspect of a larger effort to track the Mandelas, particularly the spouse of the imprisoned leader. In the early fall of September 1970, the attorney Joel Carlson held a party for his clients, including Winnie Mandela. Present was Marvine Howe of the *New York Times*. A U.S. envoy was told by "Lois" that she "spent quite a while talking to Winnie Mandela only, she asked my connection to which I replied that I was a secretary at the American Consulate-General. It was an awkward type setting.... [Clients] certainly weren't overly conversant except for Winnie...." Mandela was described as "young and absolutely beautiful," with an "abundance of sex appeal," a frequent topic of conversation at the legation. "Lois" and the journalist "didn't participate in the dancing but"—like besotted voyeurs— "enjoyed watching....They sure can dance!" The dancers also "stood giving the Black Power salute," meaning a clenched fist, as did Carlson. "I left with a terrible uneasy feeling about these people. The 'Black Power' salute and the intensity of the singing shook me. They appeared far more intelligent than the average man on the street...." She then leapt to the conclusion that spoke more about her own—and perhaps her class's—anxieties: the "feeling that these were a trained group of people who wouldn't hesitate for a moment cutting my head off or cutting Mr. Carlson's head off if or when the time comes." She was heartened by the lingering idea that apartheid torturer "Colonel Swanepoel's statement that he will get them in the end will prove true...."[122]

Retrospectively it is not easy to unpack this level of anxiety, though it is fair to infer that the spectacle of unbowed Africans stirred racial and class fears from those who came from a nation undergoing a

120. Confidential Telegram from Consul General-Johannesburg to Secretary of State, 25 November 1970, RG 59, Subject Numeric Files: Political and Defense, Box 2581.

121. Cape Town Embassy to Secretary of State, 15 May 1973, RG 59, Subject and Numeric Files: Political and Defense, Box 2584, *NARA-CP*.

122. "Lois" to La Rue Lutkins, 21 September 1970, RG 59, Subject Numeric Files: Politics & Defense, Box 2580.

wrenching transition from a dark status quo that had yet to fade decisively.

These anxieties may have been stirred by the collapse of the regime in Portugal in April 1974, which had been prefigured by the advances in Mozambique, which in turn brought those like Mandela closer to power. ACOA arranged for $10,000 from the affluent Peter Weiss and Dan Bernstein to be donated to Janet Mondlane's Mozambique Institute, a major source of sustenance for refugees.[123] As of 1970 Tambo, writing as "Acting President" of the ANC, addressed Houser from Tanzania, telling him that it would be a "fruitful exercise to meet and have a discussion with you after the lapse of many years," with the aim of getting a check.[124] But since the ACOA ended the year with "several thousand dollars deficit," as Houser told Marcelino dos Santos of FRELIMO,[125] it was unclear if Tambo could be accommodated. Moreover, despite the ACOA's attempt to accommodate the U.S. elite, the group was being investigated by the Internal Revenue Service. They were not alone, as the Nixon regime fought back, making "everybody," said Houser, "exceedingly cautious."[126] Thus, by 1972 it was unclear if Houser would be able to meet the "special request" of SWAPO's Sam Nujoma to "provide monthly financial assistance" to Theo Ben Gurirab, eventually Foreign Minister of Namibia.[127]

This was part of the advance and retreat of the movement that finally advanced decisively in Lisbon. But the advance was not accepted willingly by the U.S. ruling elite as an inevitable turn in history's tides. In July 1973 George Kennan, the architect of Washington's Cold War, defended Portuguese colonialism in the pages of the *New York Times*.[128] He had previously endorsed the "separate

---

123. George Houser to Janet Mondlane, 30 June 1969, Box 142, Series III, ACOARA. Later the Ford Foundation donated a hefty $100, 000 to the Mozambique Institute. See Report, 10 August 1973, Box 1, *George Houser Papers*.

124. Oliver Tambo to George Houser, 17 July 1970, Box 142, Series III, *ACOARA*.

125. George Houser to Marcelino dos Santos, 5 January 1971, Box 142, Series III, *ACOARA*.

126. George Houser to Janet Mondlane, 13 September 1971, Box 142, Series III, *ACOARA*.

127. Sam Nujoma to George Houser, 4 July 1972,

128. *New York Times*, 25 July 1973.

but equal" underpinning of Jim Crow and found that too much was being made of the ravages of apartheid.[129]

Appropriately, in order to attain liberation, the movement would have to repel the retrogressive anticommunist thinking that Kennan helped to shape.

---

129. African Impressions, 1967, Box 196, *George Kennan Papers, Princeton University-New Jersey*.

Chapter 15

Will Cuban Troops Invade Rhodesia, Namibia and South Africa, 1975-1976?

PRESIDENT Nixon's forced resignation in 1974 was debilitating for the overall position of U.S. imperialism, bogged down in a losing war in Indochina that would end in defeat. The April 1974 overthrow of the right-wing regime in Lisbon was also a hinge moment, giving shape to the previous and coming eras alike.

Still, even with the heavy magnitude of developments, things were to an extent outweighed by what was to come: the defeat of U.S. imperialism in Indochina in April 1975, followed by the liberation of Mozambique a few months later, and then the capstone event: Angolan independence in November, which was met by a South African invasion that was ultimately repelled by Cuban troops. The latter angered Washington tremendously, leading to attacks on détente with Moscow—seen falsely as Cuba's puppet-master—and prompting the defining move of U.S. imperialism: counter-revolution. It was shortly after the Angolan victory that President Jimmy Carter, elected with a tremendous number of Black votes in 1976, fueled an insurgency in Afghanistan, on the border of the Soviet Union, in league with religious zealots, whose scorched earth policies have yet to be extirpated. This "repayment" of Moscow served to undermine the Soviet Union, leading to its collapse by 1991.

The hysteria that beset Washington in late 1975 is difficult to overestimate. And it may have been a factor in what has turned out to be a miscalculation in leaning so decisively to China. Chester Crocker, who fought fearsomely in the 1980s to oust Cuban troops from Southern Africa, wrote that the Angola crisis "had left a deep scare in American political memory." Moscow and Havana, he said ruefully, "with the active connivance of pro-Communist elements of the Portuguese government effectively installed the MPLA regime" in Luanda. He singled out for invective Admiral Rosa Coutinho, "Lisbon's man in Luanda at the time," who "actively facilitated the insertion of hundreds of Cuban advisers" beginning—purportedly—in January 1975. By June, said Crocker, he was conferring with the comrades in Havana and by September Cuban troops had begun to arrive. This entire episode, Crocker argued with some accuracy, induced "trauma" among U.S. policymakers, which may have been true even in the clinical sense.[1]

The fright was captured by a writer from Salisbury given space in the pro-business *Wall Street Journal* in March 1976. "The black-white war long forecast for this part of the world may be almost upon us," it was said tremulously. This meant "repercussions not only for Southern Africa but for the whole Western world," since "blacks with Communist allies are doing the attacking." Worse, it was said was that despite this Black-Red alliance, "Few in America have had the courage to stand up and say that black is not always beautiful…."[2]

Despite the apparent weakness of U.S. imperialism at the time of Nixon's resignation, Washington counterattacked by seeking to nominate the ultra-rightist columnist and key Nixon backer Patrick J. Buchanan as ambassador to South Africa.[3] Buchanan thought that Salisbury and Pretoria were "natural allies in the Cold War," the right-wing consensus.[4] This was ominous since the White House already knew that Pretoria, as one aide put it, "constantly seeks ways to end-run the State Department," which would only increase in the event of Buchanan's appointment.[5] Though Buchanan was blocked from the desired position, another conservative eminence, Melvin Laird—a powerful former Congressman and Pentagon chief—was conferring with his comrades in South Africa by April 1975.[6]

Magnus Malan, an important military man in Pretoria, was "proud of his own formal military training, especially his attendance at the regular Command and General Staff Officers' Course in the United

1. Chester Crocker, *High Noon in Southern Africa: Making Peace in a Tough Neighborhood*, New York: Norton, 1982, 39, 42, 145.

2. *Wall Street Journal*, 5 March 1976.

3. Tom Korologos, Assistant to Gerald Ford to Senator Barry Goldwater, 17 September 1974, Box 45, *National Security Adviser, Presidential Country Files.*

4. Patrick J. Buchanan, *Nixon's White House Wars: The Battles that Made and Broke a President and Divided America Forever*, New York: Crown Forum, 2917, 388-389.

5. Hal Horan to Brent Scowcroft, 5 November 1974, Box 45, *National Security Adviser, Presidential Country Files.*

6. Clipping, 5 April 1975, Box 247, *Leroy Walker Africa News Service Archive, Duke University.*

States in 1962-63."[7] He recalled vividly a 1975 meeting with apartheid's leading figures where all were understandably "concerned about the political climate in the U.S. The press had initially been fairly positive but had lately condemned South Africa's presence in Angola in harsh terms and in part this induced [Pretoria's] decision to commence the withdrawal from Angola," which left the dictator in Kinshasa "very upset."[8] He was not the only man upset. P.W. Botha, yet another key shaper of apartheid, insisted that as Minister of Defense, "we went into Angola with America's knowledge and approval—and they left us in the lurch."[9] By February 1976, Prime Minister Vorster was fuming. He told his U.S. visitor that "the Angolan experience had made him lose confidence in the U.S." and that "the failure of the West to act has whetted Cuban-Soviet appetites in Africa…." Exaggerating perhaps, he thought that "the Cubans and the Russians could be so bold as to make landing in Saldanha Bay or Cape Agulhas and the U.S. would not lift a finger," which may have been true. The visitor thought that the irate Vorster "reflects the mood of the country. The Angolan experience has greatly heightened South Africa's sense of vulnerability,"[10] a steppingstone to 1994.

Botha, Vorster and their clique found it hard to understand that as the U.S. was compelled to erode the more egregious aspects of Jim Crow, Afro-American voters were thereby empowered and could hardly be ignored. Meeting with Botha in May 1976, the Secretary of State was blunt in his evisceration of Pretoria. "We are not trying to reform you. We are trying to prevent the radicalization of Black Africa and a race war. We want to avoid you having to face a coalition of 46 African states—and supported by the Cubans, North Koreans, North Vietnamese…." It was true, it was reported, that the Secretary did not "have any ideas for a solution" but he knew that "history is against you, but we want to buy time at least."[11]

Accumulated contradictions in Black America reached a stormy crescendo as a result, an irony given that the roots of many

7. Chester Crocker, *High Noon in Southern Africa*, 116.

8. Magnus Malan, *My Life with the Defense Force*, Pretoria: Proton, 2006, 130.

9. Remarks in House of Assembly, 17 April 1978 in Pieter–Dirk Uys, compiler, *P.W. Botha: In His Own Words*, Middlesex, U.K.: Penguin, 1987, 59.

10. Report of Meeting, February 1976, *National Security Adviser, Presidential Country Files for Africa*.

11. Minutes of Meeting, 14 May 1976, 5 PM, *National Security Adviser's Memoranda of Conversations Collection, Gerald Ford [Digital] Presidential Library*. Accessed 22 June 2016.

Afro-Americans lay in Angola.[12] Professor Emma Jones of the University of California-Davis law school told her colleague Henry Richardson at Temple University that there needed to be reconsideration of the push for a "criminal prosecution" of the Congress of Racial Equality, once a bulwark of the anti-Jim Crow movement now "engaged in recruiting mercenaries" to fight in Angola. This was "distressing" though she insisted "we must not invoke the Justice Department against another Black organization," even if it was in bed with Pretoria.[13] "Black Vets Recruited" for Angola was the story in the Washington press of January 1976; reportedly 200 had signed up, many of whom had fought in Indochina.[14] CORE specialized in recruiting Negro mercenaries for Savimbi's UNITA.[15] For his part, Richardson—who was to join the national security staff of incoming president Jimmy Carter—thought it was inappropriate for the National Conference of Black Lawyers to take a position on diplomatic recognition of the MPLA regime in Luanda. He was also disappointed that he was not briefed before the leader of the group, Lennox Hinds (who had roots in the Caribbean island of Trinidad), departed for Angola in early 1976.[16]

The ability to recruit Negro mercenaries for combat in Angola was constrained by Pretoria. The CIA agent John Stockwell, who was on the scene, pointed out that his then employer was often distrustful of Negro agents because of racism, hampering the agency's operations in Africa. The agency was also worried about backlash against non-racialism, "because of the South African involvement." Nonetheless, the CIA recruited mercenaries to fight in Southern Africa.[17] This apartheid policy hampered the ability of the CIA to infiltrate into the sub-region with some of its wiliest agents, like James "Ted" Harris, a Negro and former leader of the U.S. Student Association, who was a graduate of Princeton and a Ford Foundation executive who also had experience with the African American Institute.[18]

12. Gerald Horne, *The Deepest South: The U.S., Brazil and the African Slave Trade*, New York: New York University Press, 2008, passim.

13. Emma Jones to Henry Richardson, 6 April 1976, Box 191, *Gerald Horne Papers*.

14. *Washington Post*, 27 January 1976.

15. *Washington Star*, 28 January 1976.

16. Henry Richardson to Lennox Hinds, 24 February 1976m Box 190, *Gerald Horne Papers*.

17. John Stockwell, *In Search of Enemies: A CIA Story*, New York: Norton, 1978, 168, 75, 182-185.

18. Aida Parker, *Secret War Against South Africa*, Johannesburg: South Africa Today, 1977, 27.

As with 6PAC in Dar in 1974, there were Black Americans who were swayed by UNITA's cry that it was authentically "Black", unlike the MPLA—said to be dominated by Communists and so-called "mixed race" elements. Florence Tate, who was close to the future Mayor of Washington, D.C.—Marion Barry, an activist in his own right—confessed unashamedly that she backed UNITA.[19] She too was close to Richard Gibson, known to have murky ties to U.S. intelligence: Gibson was "shocked" to learn "of the murder of Sister Chinosole, born Patricia Thornton" who "went to Angola to work with UNITA," known for its gangster tactics: this was his sad message to Tate, which may have restrained her wanderlust in traveling to the frontlines of battle.[20] Undeterred, Gibson assailed Senator Edward Kennedy, heir to a presidential legacy, because of his wariness of UNITA: "you should talk with my old friend Amiri Baraka",[21] he counselled in order to gain devastating intelligence on MPLA. Baraka thought that Gibson was brimming with "clear insights. Most of these views are the same as ours,"[22] he gushed, a view which did not bode well for the ideological viability of an important strand of Black Nationalism.

Despite these ideological twists and turns that conceivably could bolster Pretoria, apartheid insisted in pursuing its own self-defeating rules. Just as the armed forces were about to overturn the status quo in Lisbon, setting in motion a chain of events in the sub-region, a U.S. Negro official—Richard Saunders of the U.S. Information Service—and his spouse, Emily were told to leave a nightclub at the Blue Waters Hotel in Durban, because of their visible African ancestry. "As a rule," said Congressman Diggs grumpily, "Black Americans are not permitted to visit South Africa," making it very difficult for Negro CIA agents to seek meetings in Pretoria.[23]

Stockwell recalled that in Angola the CIA "had organized four mercenary units, right down to such details as the purchase of life insurance" for some. "There were as many as 24 U.S. advisors working with Angolan rebels at any one time;" a third of his staff were "propagandists and they worked closely with UNITA and FNLA

19. Letter from Florence Tate, 4 December 1975, Box 3, *Richard Gibson Papers.*

20. Richard Gibson to Florence Tate, 21 October 1975, Box 3.

21. Richard Gibson to Florence Tate, 4 November 1975, Box 3.

22. Amiri Baraka to Richard Gibson, 19 March 1975, Box 12, *Richard Gibson Papers.*

23. Statement by Congressman Diggs, May 1974, Box 14, *Washington Office on Africa Papers.*

publicists in New York." "The CIA funded these activities through a bank account in Bonn so that they could tell Congress that they were not giving money to anyone inside the U.S." Yes, he confessed, "U.S. personnel in the region were collaborating extremely closely with South Africans. U.S. planes regularly flew into Kinshasa in the dead of night to be met by South African planes which would then fly U.S. arms shipments the final leg into Angola," providing further plausible deniability—the gold standard—to the contention that there was direct CIA aid to the rebels.[24] "I left behind communications equipment" for UNITA, said Stockwell. "I sent in trainers.... [and] he [Savimbi] had been functioning for years with help from the North Koreans and the Chinese...." When UNITA and MPLA sought to work out their many differences, Washington ordered crudely, "knock it off."[25]

CIA meddling had incalculable consequences, not only in terms of retarding liberation but in stirring suspicions too. Mary Louise Hooper, who had worked side-by-side with the ANC for years, told her "dearest brother" Tambo that "another ANC leader has been telling people..." that "I've been a CIA agent." Moses Mabhida, the SACP leader, "wrote me this," she said.[26] (It is to be hoped that Nokwe was wrong and Mabhida was right since by late 1975 Tambo was sharing intimate details between and among Africans and non-Africans in the ANC that would have been pure catnip for the CIA if they had known.[27] If Dumisani Makhaye is to be believed, Mabhida's judgment could be relied upon. Born in KwaZulu Natal in 1955, he was a SACP member who found his leader to be a "strange person. Only a standard seven in terms of education but a real Communist who had a rare insight" and, besides, was "one of the most loyal members of the ANC....")[28]

U.S. Negroes were rejected for work in Southern Africa, though they may have not been so easily detectable at first glance.[29] Pretoria

---

24. John Stockwell, "Five Big Lies of the CIA," 5 February 1986, Box 19, *Washington Office on Africa Papers.*

25. "Ties that Bind," Newsletter of "Blacks Against Contra Aid," January 1988, Box 163, *Gerald Horne Papers, Schomburg Center, New York Public Library.*

26. Mary Louise Hooper to Oliver Tambo, 10 August 1969, Box 4, *Mary Louise Hooper Papers.*

27. Oliver Tambo to Mary Louise Hooper, 7 March 1975, Box 4, *Mary Louise Hooper Papers.*

28. Oral History, Dumisani Makhaye, 20 January 2004, *University of Connecticut-Storrs.*

29. James Sanders, *Apartheid's Friends: The Rise and Fall of South Africa's Secret Service*, London: John Murray, 2000, 52.

and Washington missed an opportunity because some U.S. Negroes were quite willing to cooperate with imperialism. The writer Louis Lomax much earlier confessed that he was "unnerved" by Zimbabwean patriot Joshua Nkomo and anti-apartheid writer Bloke Modisane. "What bothered me most," he asserted, "was the fact that Africans are totally unwilling to accept whites as coequals and partners in a free government"—a wildly inaccurate misreading— "yet they have no qualms about accepting money from" the Soviets. "The impact of Russia…on these exiles" he averred "is a cause for concern…." This was an obvious misunderstanding and reflected the retreat of certain Negroes from radical ideology and the incapability of seeing global matters beyond the limited prism of "race."[30]

While some U.S. Negroes and their government were misreading the Southern Africa scene, London had noticed what was obvious: Angola was hurtling toward confrontation. This was having knock-on effects in Rhodesia, since mercenaries were fungible. London noticed this too[31] and had also found that Salisbury was taking advantage of Teheran's long-time relations with Pretoria by seeking to "recruit British and American servicemen in Iran as mercenaries." There was "no point in trying to engage the Iranian authorities on this,"[32] it was said conveniently. Some British subjects who thought they were applying to Pretoria for "enlistment" in various posts found they were "getting Rhodesian Army literature." Working from bars, hotels, and clubs in Isfahan, Shiraz, and Ahvaz, and near Iranian military centers, Rhodesian recruiters were quite busy, offering salaries up to $3000 monthly and were receiving a favorable hearing from U.S. nationals and British subjects alike. These men were frustrated by the difficulty of living conditions in Iran and were willing to renege on their contracts. An appeal was made to their "basic conservatism", i.e. the "free world against Communism," which was also effective in drawing recruits to Angola, particularly since "sometimes the sales pitch is blatantly racist." Bell helicopter had just fired "at least…one hundred eighty instructor pilots following a strike over work and living conditions" and "at least a dozen of those guys wound up in Rhodesia…." Apparently, some went to Angola as well; a "captured American mercenary" had in his pocket

30. Louis Lomax, *The Reluctant African*, New York: Harper, 1960, 15, 23.
31. Report, FCO35/1872, *NAUK-London*.
32. "Confidential" Report, 30 June 1976, FCO36/1874, *NAUK-London*.

the "rather tawdry come-ons found in the magazines which circulate among American gun-freaks,"[33] said London.

U.S. mercenaries were arriving steadily in Southern Africa, with Fort Bragg, North Carolina—a huge military base teeming with veterans with experience in Indochina—the center for recruitment.[34] In early 1976, the Washington newspapers were bulging with stories and advertisements about mercenaries.[35]

Thus, I rebuked the poet Amiri Baraka and the African Liberation Support Committee after they—consonant with their pro-China orientation—denounced the Cuban intervention in Angola as an example of what was termed "Soviet Social Imperialism."[36] This latter phrase became a buzzword in certain left-wing U.S. circles, users oblivious to the fact that it placed them in the trenches alongside Pretoria. Like many, Bill Sales, who had participated in the tumultuous student uprising at Columbia University in 1968,[37] declared passionately "Southern Africa/Black America: Same Struggle, Same Fight." But unlike many he also denounced the "revisionist example" of "Soviet Social Imperialism," seen as a "real and present danger in Southern Africa."[38] Florence Tate, a Negro activist in Washington, denounced the "twin imperialist powers," meaning the U.S. and USSR, as she saluted the U.S.-backed UNITA.[39] The Sino-Soviet conflict provided a passageway for those uncomfortable with being on the same side as Moscow to remain "militant" while siding with Pretoria. This trend was also manifest in Canada.[40] Tate went a step further: She registered as a foreign agent on behalf of those she

---

33. "Confidential" Report and attachment, 17 June 1976, FCO36/1874, *NAUK-London.*

34. *Africa News*, 9 February 1976, Box 33, *Leroy Walker Africa News Service Archive.*

35. *Washington Post*, 8 February 1976. See particularly the *Washington Star*, 8 February 1976, 15 February 1976, 27 January 1976, 25 January 1976: see below on the attempt by Pretoria to purchase this periodical covertly.

36. Gerald Horne, "Maoism-Trojan Horse of Imperialism in Angola," *Black Liberation Journal* 1(Number 1, 1976): 31,

37. Stefan Bradley, *Harlem v. Columbia University: Black Student Power in the Late 1960s*, Urbana: University of Illinois Press, 2009.

38. Pamphlet by Bill Sales, 1977, Box 171, *Gerald Horne Papers.*

39. *Washington Star*, 29 August 1975.

40. Hardial Bains, "Against Soviet Social Imperialism and for National Liberation: What Kind of Friendship?" Toronto: Norman Bethune Institute, 1976.

supported politically.[41] She received $45,000 from UNITA by March 1980 and $20,000 by July.[42]

Fortunately, Congressman Diggs of Black Detroit remained focused, observing "we do not know Dr. Kissinger's grand design for [Southern Africa] since he has not found the time to discuss his diplomatic activities with the [Congressional Black Caucus]."[43] Diggs joined with Congressman Charles Rangel of Harlem to "condemn the intervention of the U.S. and all other external powers in Angola's Civil War," which was leading to "another Vietnam...." They were "particularly concerned about the convergence of U.S. interests with those of racist South Africa so that they are on the same side in support of the FNLA-UNITA forces," i.e. Holden Roberto and Jonas Savimbi.[44] Other members of the Afro-American delegation in Washington rejected anticommunism—even of the left—and zeroed in on racism, stressing, "because we are African Americans and because we know that the destiny of Blacks in America and Blacks in Africa is inextricably intertwined", they were forced to intervene against U.S. policy in Southern Africa most notably.[45] From the other side, Congressman John Rarick departed Washington in 1975 and became a correspondent for the periodical of the Ku Klux Klan, the *Fiery Cross*.[46]

The strength of the ultra-right complicated this conflict over Angola and helped to effectively split the anti-apartheid movement, contributing to what journalist saw as a "hot war in Angola"—and a "cold war in New York City," as an ALSC meeting at Columbia University descended into chaos.[47] The ANC envoy in Manhattan, Thami Mhlambiso, observed that when the then U.S. Communist leader Tony Monteiro, who specialized in Southern African affairs, spoke at Brooklyn College "students literally exchanged blows when it came to the question of Angola....People like Monteiro

---

41. Note for File on Florence Tate Statement, 19 September 1980, Box 61, *Washington Office on Africa Papers*.

42. Registration Statement, 22 September 1980, Box 61, *Washington Office on Africa Papers*.

43. Statement by Congressman Charles Diggs, 1 September 1976, Box 171, *Gerald Horne Papers*.

44. Statement by Congressmen Rangel and Diggs, January 1976, Box 9, *International Affairs Department Country Files, AFL-CIO*.

45. Statement by Congressman Diggs and Congresswoman Yvonne B. Burke, 17 September 1976, Box 171, *Gerald Horne Papers*.

46. Ibid., Zoe Hyman, 211.

47. *Soho Weekly News*, 12 February 1976.

are dividing the African people," he asserted.[48] This was an overstatement at best. Monteiro was the type of comrade that Mhlambiso should have embraced. For it was Monteiro who presented the 100,000 signatures gathered in the U.S. demanding the expulsion of South Africa from the U.N to Guinea-Conakry's representative, Jeanne Martin Cisse.[49] Sponsors included writers, like Maya Angelou, Toni Morrison, and Alice Childress; activists including Jesse Jackson; the actor-playwright, Ossie Davis; scholar Ewart Guinier; and union leader Bill Lucy. I was among those who presented the signatures with Monteiro, giving the statement, "Angola must not become another Vietnam."[50]

The Angola controversy in Black America became quite subjective and intensely personal. The activist Howard Fuller, who survived attack from Portuguese armed forces during his foray into pre-1975 liberated zones in Mozambique, recalled the question as to whether leaders were "married to white women" became a badge of degradation (if one were)—or elevation (if not). A similar criterion was invoked to degrade certain MPLA leaders. Fuller recollected that "the debate over African liberation groups in Angola turned particularly nasty;" at one contentious meeting at Howard University, the capstone of Negro education in Washington, D.C., "word got around that dudes were going to kill me." He had begun—like many others—to lean toward socialism as a result, though he eventually became a comrade of future U.S. president George W. Bush.[51]

But this was not the end of the skein of complications. What had supposedly led China into the arms of U.S. imperialism was fear of being attacked by the Soviet Union, but in April 1975 a "top secret" study found its way into the White House that found the purported "Soviet Military Threat" to China to be overblown, though the analyst had difficulty in understanding why it was trumpeted.[52] Admittedly, this was before the Angola crisis, which worsened relations between and among the major powers, including China and the Soviet Union. As this crisis flared in late November 1975, an editorial

48. Thambi Mhlambiso to "Comrades," 26 September 1976, Box 14, Folder 24, *Lusaka Mission, ANC Records*.

49. *Bilalian News*, 13 February 1976.

50. "Campaign for One Million Voices for Expulsion of South Africa from the United Nations," 26 December 1975, Box 163, *Gerald Horne Papers*.

51. Howard Fuller, *No Struggle, No Progress*, 154, 9.

52. "The Chinese Assessment of the Soviet Military Threat," April 1975, Box 2, *Dale Van Atta Papers, Gerald Ford Presidential Library-Ann Arbor, Michigan*.

in the *New York Times* assailed Moscow's role in Angola: the "prime Soviet purpose" was "to counter Chinese influence" via Holden Roberto and Jonas Savimbi.[53]

More typical of official U.S. commentary on this conflict was the remark by Congressman Lester Wolff who after returning from China said war between the neighboring Communist nations was "inevitable."[54] Surely, Washington was pleased when in a Spring 1976 Security Council debate, as South African was denigrated, China exchanged a bitter philippic with the Cubans and Soviets.[55]

Washington harped on this anti-Moscow theme and saw a developing alliance with China as a trump card in turning the tide in Southern Africa. By early August 1975, weeks after independence, the CIA was joyous about Mozambique's apparent differences with Moscow and their sidling closer to China, an intermittent trend in coming years.[56]

In the early days of the Gerald Ford administration—successor to the disgraced Nixon, compelled to resign-- China was not the only preoccupation. Somehow, the U.S. envoy in Kinshasa thought that U.S. Air Force "assistance" would make "points for U.S.-African relations and for president's relations with U.S. blacks," the latter a growing fixation, given their voting strength (That is, "assistance" to a boxing match.).[57]

The effort to woo Black voters figured into the calculations as to whether to aid preparations for the upcoming heavyweight boxing match in Kinshasa involving Muhammad Ali. The exiled South African trumpeter Hugh Masekela, described by the Kinshasa legation as the "former husband of Miriam Makeba," the famed singer "whose political views he does not share," requested U.S. aircraft to transport equipment.[58] Though the legation was concerned with

53. *New York Times*, 26 November 1975.

54. *Washington Star*, 27 April 1976.

55. Executive Secretariat, Telegraphic Summary, 1 April 1976, Box 15, *Dale Van Atta Papers*.

56. "Staff Notes," 4 August 1975, Box 4, *Dale Van Atta Papers*.

57. Report to Henry Kissinger from U.S. legation-Kinshasa, 7 September 1974, Box 7, *National Security Adviser, Presidential Country Files for Africa, 1974-1977, Gerald Ford Presidential Library*.

58. Report from Kinshasa legation to Secretary of State, September 1974, Box 7, *National Security Adviser, Presidential Country Files for Africa:* The trumpeter sough to "assure that.... they have nothing whatsoever to do with Henry Schwartz, V.P. of Video Techniques and kingpin of entire fight preparations. Schwartz's nefarious dealings well-known and informed sources

"risks" in "association with shady characters to say nothing of possibly crooks," the recommendation was made that "every effort be made promptly to make C-141 or C-130 [aircraft] available," which could impress Negro voters back home.[59]

The dictator in Kinshasa once known as Joseph Mobutu had mixed feelings about this U.S. role. He backed the fight and stood to benefit greatly from it, but he was becoming nervous about the sight of gigantic U.S. aircraft landing in his line of vision. These gigantic aircraft could just as well be carrying armed transporters. By June 1975 he was fretting that the U.S. was "implicated" in an attempt to dislodge him from power. As he peered across the Congo River, he detected arms "and money...pouring" in from Moscow—"even from Yugoslavia"—for the MPLA, gearing up to seize power in Luanda and possibly extend their influence into his backyard. Mobutu's comrade Holden Roberto was backed only by his regime and China, he thought. "Time is running out very rapidly," he worried, and he wanted the U.S. to supply Roberto and Jonas Savimbi of UNITA via his regime,[60] allowing for skimming and corruption on his part (which went unmentioned).

An irate Washington blamed Moscow for the rumors that the United States wanted to overthrow Mobutu. The dictator himself, perhaps influenced by Pretoria, went further and blamed the "Jewish Underground" and the banker David Rockefeller, who also "might be involved." He was reminded by a U.S. envoy that it was the U.S. that had trained his security team. He was told further that "such things as big boxing events, like the Ali-[George] Foreman fight (for which I complimented him warmly) often brought in their train unsavory characters from the international underworld," which Mobutu could have seen as another veiled threat that there were plans to e.g. import snipers and blame the "underworld." Yet "Mobutu nodded when I said that lots of money was probably won and lost in questionable ways in connection with the fight."[61] For his part, Ali assuaged concern about his previous antiwar activism by reportedly stating that he was ready to box in South Africa itself.[62]

---

tell us he was arrested last week in London for fraud and extortion in connection with last March Foreman-Norton fight in Caracas."

59. Report from Kinshasa legation, September 1974, Box 7, *National Security Adviser, Presidential Country Files for Africa.*

60. Report from Kinshasa legation, June 1975, Box 7, *National Security Adviser, Presidential Country Files for Africa.*

61. Report from Kinshasa legation, July 1975, Box 7, *National Security Adviser, Presidential Country Files.*

62. *Johannesburg Star*, 4 January 1975.

Secretary of State Kissinger was moved to inform President Ford in a "confidential" message that "in the wake of President Mobutu's charges of U.S. Government involvement in a plot against him," bilateral ties had been "severely strained," potentially jeopardizing the Angolan adventure. The dictator in Kinshasa had a "real suspicion that we had conspired to obtain his assassination." This was not good, said the former professor, since "our economic interests in Zaire [Congo] are large," given the "enormous energy and mineral wealth." The country was Washington's "largest market in black Africa after Nigeria."[63] By January 1976 the MPLA and their Cuban allies were advancing, buoyed by a mid-December vote in Congress reproaching the U.S. intervention in Angola, which—said a U.S. agent in Kinshasa— "has created the most serious doubt in Mobutu's mind."[64]

It left CIA chief William Colby unsettled too. As the congressional vote was being considered, he told Vice President Nelson Rockefeller, scion to a major fortune and at the apex of the ruling elite, that matters were "not at all cheerful" after receiving a report on "how determined the Soviets will be in support of the MPLA." Still, a silver lining could be found in "evidence of disagreement in the Kremlin on Angola" since "consensus behind the current Angola policy is not deep,"[65] leaving plenty of room for manipulation.

President Ford told Congress that Moscow had begun escalating in Angola as early as fall 1974 and went into overdrive during 1975. By the end of that year there were an estimated 10,000 Cuban troops there, necessitating "grave concern over the international consequences of the situation in Angola,"[66] a nagging threat to détente, as he saw things. East Germany did not have 2000 nationals in Angola, as was thought, but more like 200—the inflation by sheer dismay. In a "secret" missive, Vice President Rockefeller was told that "next to the Soviets and Cubans the East Germans have been the principal

63. Henry Kissinger to President Ford, circa July 1975, Box 7, *National Security Adviser, Presidential Country Files.*

64. Report by U.S. legation-Kinshasa, January 1976, Box 7, *National Security Adviser, Presidential Country Files.*

65. William Colby to Vice President Rockefeller, 23 December 1975, Box 9, FA 385, Series 15, Speeches, *Nelson A. Rockefeller Vice Presidential Foreign Affairs and National Security Records, Rockefeller Archive Center, Sleepy Hollow, New York.*

66. Gerald Ford to House Speaker, 27 January 1976, Box 9, FA 385, Series 15, Speeches.

provider of assistance to Angola,"[67] offering enhanced incentive to destabilize the GDR.

Still, Washington was panicking. On 27 June 1975 Kissinger was joined by other men who were to play a prime role in shaping the basic policies of U.S. imperialism in coming years, including Brent Scowcroft, William Colby of the CIA, James Schlesinger, and Donald Rumsfeld, later the military mind behind the disastrous 2003 invasion of Iraq. "We believe it highly unlikely," it was reported, "that the MPLA will be able to vanquish its rivals and achieve complete control of Angola in the next several months;" if that were to occur, it was said with concern, this party "would almost certainly demand control over Gulf Oil's operations," a vital interest of U.S. imperialism. They intently discussed not only Soviet aid to the MPLA but Yugoslav aid as well, which did not bode well for either regime.[68]

Also, before these plotting men was a memorandum detailing the forces shaping U.S. policy. Gulf Oil had arrived in Cabinda in 1966 and thereafter half the oil extracted was shipped directly to the U.S., no small factor considering the recent oil boycott of the U.S. by Arab producers in protest of anti-Palestinian, pro-Israeli policies. Thus, the U.S. was "by far" the "most important foreign investor in Angola," given the additional presence of Texaco, Exxon, Sun Oil, Hess, Cities Service, Occidental, Amoco, Conoco, Tenneco—and other plunderers interested in gold, diamonds, sulfur, and gypsum. Savimbi's was considered to be the "weakest of the three movements," though that was to change as Roberto faded and UNITA was backed by Pretoria and Washington. Both Lusaka and Kinshasa were dependent upon the Benguela railway, which bisected Angola, making this nation even more important than it appeared. The problem was the MPLA, said to be founded in 1956 "with the aid of the small, clandestine Angola Communist Party." By 1971, the group's leader, Agostinho Neto, had journeyed to China but "came away empty-handed." There were "increasing racial tensions" in Angola, which the MPLA sought to resolve but which its rivals sought to exploit.[69]

Still, the significant oil discoveries in Cabinda insured that Angola would not be ignored. By late 1973 as the oil boycott was beginning

---

67. Jon Howe to Vice President Rockefeller, 13 April 1976, Box 9, FA 385, Series 15.

68. "Secret" Memorandum prepared for 27 June 1975 meeting, Box 10, *U.S. National Security Council Institutional Files, 1974-1977, Gerald Ford Presidential Library.*

69. National Security Study Memorandum 224, 16 June 1975, Box 36, *U.S. National Council Institutional Files, 1974-1977, Gerald Ford Presidential Library.*

to sting in the U.S., Oliver Tambo told his spouse that it was "certainly having repercussions;" astutely he saw that "people who have investments...see their assets being eaten away by market depressions and inflation making things worse still....People who have been living affluent lives, will have to change and this is all to the good...."[70]

Thus, Mobutu and his Washington paymaster—and certainly his interlocutors—were concerned about another major fight beyond Ali-Foreman: who would prevail in Angola. Mobutu, said the legation, had "taken from his reserve stocks"—code for U.S. supplies—"and sent to Angola enough equipment for five battalions (5000 men) plus nine armored cars and a few heavy mortars and anti-tank weapons and he is now getting ready to ship the existing equipment of five of his paratroop battalions."[71] Mobutu leaped into Angola with both feet, fearing that the rise of the MPLA would threaten his already shaky rule. The U.S. legation felt he was over-extending himself unnecessarily, creating problems at home. "We had better tell Mobutu [to] slow down" was the wise counsel suggested.[72] Mobutu had good reason to fret: it was not long before Belgium and France and the U.S. intervened in already unsteady Shaba province to repress an uprising that could have threatened his misrule.[73]

Mobutu's miscalculations aside, the crisis in Angola was preoccupying Washington. As early as 12 August 1975, a CIA analysis noted sourly that the MPLA was "almost in complete control of Luanda"[74] and domination of the capital was critical to national sovereignty, a point forgotten when the decision was made in Washington to downplay Pretoria's invasion of Angola and stress the fraudulent point that the invasion had nothing to do with the Cuban response. A few days later, the agency said further that the MPLA was "increasingly dominant."[75] A few days after that the CIA found that

---

70. Oliver Tambo to Adelaide Tambo, 12 December 1973, Reel 1, *Oliver Tambo Papers.*

71. Report from Kinshasa legation, July 1975, Box 7, *National Security Adviser, Presidential Country Files.*

72. Report from Kinshasa legation, September 1975, *National Security Adviser, Presidential Country Files.*

73. Chester Crocker, *High Noon in Southern Africa: Making Peace in a Tough Neighborhood,* New York: Norton, 1992, 54.

74. National Intelligence Bulletin, 12 August 1975, Box 5, *Dale Van Atta Papers.*

75. National Intelligence Bulletin, 20 August 1975, Box 5, *Dale Van Atta Papers.*

the MPLA "having succeeded in driving the two rival nationalist groups"—that of the old ACOA friends Holden Roberto and Jonas Savimbi— "from Luanda," was now "jockeying with the Portuguese for political control."[76]

Just as Washington was willing to cooperate with the PAC in South Africa despite its "one settler/one bullet" rhetoric—which one would have thought to be off-putting to the settler regime in North America—an "analytical summary" of Roberto's group prepared in June 1975 underlined the "racist image" of his group "resulting from indiscriminate attacks on whites in the early 1960s...." There were compensating factors, however: China had been aiding him at least since 1974. Mobutu found his rival, MPLA, "intolerable." Still, it was said balefully, "the principal disadvantage the FNLA faces is Roberto's continued refusal to appear in Angola, apparently out of fear of assassination...."[77]

At the same time, U.S. intelligence had found that Roberto's FNLA—National Front for the Liberation of Angola—was "receiving the bulk" of Chinese "military aid" in Angola; this group, it was reported, "would have been in worse shape" if China "had not acceded to a new request for arms...." Why? China was "thoroughly disenchanted" with MPLA's "growing ties to Moscow" and was also "attempting to curry favor" with Kinshasa, which was close to Roberto; aid was also being rendered to Savimbi's UNITA.[78] U.S. intelligence also found China to be a major player in Tanzania, which had been the case for some time—a direct result of their construction of the railway from Zambia—which was essential to its relationship with FRELIMO, which in turn helped its ties to ZANU, steadily gaining momentum in the battle to overthrow Rhodesia.[79]

By September Mobutu was elated with the substantial inflow of U.S. military materiel that had just arrived by ship for use in Angola by Roberto's forces. The bespectacled leader was "pleased" with the arrival of "4.2 mortars, the 106 ammo" and the rest; with anger, "he categorically stated that both North Koreans and Chinese had

---

76. CIA Weekly Review, 22 August 1975, Box *Dale Van Atta Papers*.

77. "Analytical Summary," 18 June 1975, Box 10, *National Security Council Institutional Files, 1974-1977, Gerald Ford Presidential Library*.

78. National Intelligence Bulletin, 25 August 1975, Box 5, *Dale Van Atta Papers*. See also "Secret Nonforn", Jon Howe to the Vice President, 18 July 1975, Box 9, FA 385, Series 19, *Nelson A. Rockefeller Vice Presidential Foreign Affairs and National Security Records, Rockefeller Archive Center, Sleepy Hollow, New York*.

79. "Staff Notes," CIA, 3 September 1975, Box 6, *Dale Van Atta Papers*.

refused to allow their arms" to "be used inside Angola." The U.S. and Mobutu wanted Tanzania to release "80 tons" of Chinese weapons "for Savimbi" but it was doubtful that Nyerere would acquiesce. Making "arrangements with the Israelis for 8000 rounds" was suggested as a substitute. Mobutu's air transport planes were "working night and day" to ferry arms to his comrades in Angola—to the point that his pilots had reached their "limit" and he wanted the U.S. to take over.[80] But Mobutu was getting nervous since Moscow had just declared him a "grave menace," delivering a reportedly "provocative warning" about his interference in Angola, spurring a "tirade" against the Soviets.[81]

Washington had become frustrated with Nyerere too. By January 1976 he had abandoned the idea of a Government of National Unity with a ruling troika of Neto, Roberto, and Savimbi—this after Mobutu—according to a U.S. official in Dar— "thought [he] could dictate [the] whole future of Angola by its support for FNLA…."[82]

By late October 1975, U.S. intelligence determined that Moscow and its allies had delivered 8500 tons of weapons to Angola, necessary to repel invading South African forces.[83] Moreover, said the CIA, "Soviet media" was "emphasizing Angola issue," stressing that the U.S., China, and South Africa were "working 'side by side.'"[84] But by 5 November the CIA had determined that China was "lowering the visibility of its involvement in Angola," since aid to Roberto and Savimbi had "resulted in a blow up this summer" with Tanzania. This could have simply meant that they'd be shipping aid to Roberto from Kinshasa rather than Dar.[85]

Days after the proclamation of Angolan independence, the Nigerian leader Joseph Garba was cited as saying that "African support for MPLA is snowballing and the only way to stop it is to get

80. Report from Kinshasa legation, September 1975, Box 7, *National Security Adviser, Presidential Country Files.*

81. Report from Kinshasa legation, October 1975, Box 7, *National Security Adviser, Presidential Country Files.*

82. Report on Meeting, January 1976, Box 6, *National Security Adviser, Presidential Country Files.*

83. Defense Intelligence Agency, Weekly Intelligence Summary, 31 October 1975, Box 7, *Dale Van Atta Papers.*

84. CIA's National Intelligence Daily, 5 November 1975, Box 8, *Dale Van Atta Papers.*

85. National Intelligence Bulletin, 5 November 1975, Box 8, *Dale Van Atta Papers.*

South Africa out of Angola."[86] From nearby Accra, the U.S. Ambassador Shirley Temple Black—a former Hollywood child star—was reported to be "concerned by the widely held African view that the U.S. is the power behind South African intervention in Angola" and suggested that "we turn off the alleged U.S.-South African connection without delay."[87] At the same time Peter Killen, who handled the State Department's African portfolio, was meeting in Pretoria with the Foreign Minister, Hilgard Muller, and expressed concern about the "growing trade with Luanda," conducted by Pretoria and Windhoek alike, "primarily in foodstuffs and medicines," presenting not only an "incongruity" but jeopardizing the profitability of affected apartheid firms.[88]

By January 1976, U.S. intelligence declared a "turning point" had been reached in Angola, as Holden Roberto's forces were on the verge of "collapse," which could lead to a revolt in Shaba province in the nation then known as Zaire, along with "serious problems for South Africa."[89] By October of that year the U.S. legation in Pretoria was reporting that these developments had induced "shock" among apartheid rulers, along with "bitterness" and "depression." They were "amazed at the turn of events," with many among the European minority now fearing a "sell-out, particularly on the part of the [government]," contributing to "dismay" with "chaos [feared]," all meaning an "exodus" was imminent, further weakening the regime.[90]

Just before this "turning point," the Ugandan dictator, Idi Amin—a favorite of some Black Nationalists in the U.S., particularly after he expelled South Asians—had a "secret" meeting in Kampala with U.S. officialdom where he endorsed the U.S. role in Angola. Airily, he dismissed as "without foundation" stories about Pretoria's intervention, along with reports of the flood of mercenaries from the North Atlantic nations. He agreed to lobby the Organization of African Unity meeting that was also attended by an envoy from the Federal Republic of Germany. During this hour-long conversation,

86. "Executive Secretariat, Telegraphic Summary," 25 November 1975, Box 9, *Dale Van Atta Papers*.

87. "Executive Secretariat, Telegraphic Summary," 3 December 1975, Box 9, *Dale Van Atta Papers*.

88. Report of Meeting, December 1975, Box 4, *National Security Adviser, Presidential Country Files for Africa*.

89. National Intelligence Bulletin, 19 January 1976, Box 9, *Dale Van Atta Papers*.

90. Report on Meeting, October 1976, Box 6, *National Security Adviser, Presidential Country Files for Africa*.

he pledged his fidelity to the bedrock faith of anticommunism and stressed his "disenchantment" with Libya,[91] whose regime would be toppled by the U.S. and its allies by 2011. From Toronto the PAC's Trofomo Sono joined the amen chorus, praising Amin as a "true, African Black leader."[92]

On 3 March 1976 at 3:30 PM, Kissinger was to be found in his office with Ambassador Black. He was worried. "When the Cubans go into Rhodesia," which had been bruited, along with a march to Pretoria, "I may want to get involved even if no one else does," which was brave talk but unrealistic. "This has nothing to do with the white minority in Rhodesia," he said meretriciously, adding with like inaccuracy, "if the Africans want to make war over that question there is no problem for us but if Cuba is involved, there is." The cool Ambassador Black replied, "the thing that brings blood to the eye of black Africans is South African involvement." Dauntlessly, Kissinger responded, "The thing that brings blood to my eye is Cuban involvement," more accurately elaborating, "for several reasons Angola was a disaster for the United States." He added, "we are the victims of our own impotence," arguing that Havana was "contributing to a racial war that could be transported to the Western Hemisphere." "The Africans have not understood this problem. It is not an African problem, it is a geo-political problem. South African involvement in Angola was very damaging. It is very unfortunate that they came in," the translation being: it was unfortunate they were defeated by the Cubans and Angolans. "If we could have hired mercenaries," which the U.S. did unofficially, "South Africa could have stayed out," probably false too.

Ambassador Black was unconvinced. The seemingly ubiquitous Congressman Diggs came to her residence in Accra, supposedly to discuss cocoa. "But it turned out that he wanted to talk about Angola. He was very critical of the United States in my house. Everyone was very emotional and agreed with Diggs," a group that included other envoys. "The Ethiopian said he would take money from the devil to defeat South Africa." "I said," stated Black "that is exactly what you have done."

When Kissinger concluded the meeting by telling her that she was "the only ambassador in Africa I would willingly come to see," it was hard to say if he was agreeing with her analysis or—more

91. Report on "Secret" Meeting, 2 January 1976, Box 2, *National Security Adviser, Presidential Country Files for Africa, 1974-1977.*

92. *Contrast* [Toronto], 8 December 1977.

likely—simply being his usual unctuous self.[93] Whatever the case, she sensed instinctively what Nyerere told Kissinger's colleague, William Schaufele: "Africans tend to see Southern Africa as a single issue,"[94] and were not as concerned with Cuban intervention as Washington tended to be.

As the remarks of the emissary from Addis suggested, Kissinger and the class he represented were not only concerned about the immediate impact of Angola on the sub-region—which was disastrous—but the global impact which was similarly devastating, raising far-reaching questions about the potency of U.S. imperialism. These fears are what led this class to install Reagan in the White House by 1980 and push steadily for disintegration of the Soviet Union—except the price was a closer tie to the ally in Angola, meaning China, which was to place this most populous of nations in the passing lane, potentially surpassing U.S. imperialism itself. Weeks after the Kissinger-Black sit-down, his own State Department Bureau of Intelligence and Research reported on "The Latin American Arms Market and the Effect of Angola." The fear was that even U.S. neighbors, impressed by Cuba's performance, would turn to Moscow for arms—weakening a major U.S. cash cow—leading the island's Latin American neighbors to ally with Havana, meaning a loss for U.S. imperialism.[95] Similarly, it was then that Zimbabwean leader Joshua Nkomo accused Washington of having "bolstered" Salisbury with its excessive focus on Havana, which would only backfire ultimately. Even the Kenyan Foreign Minister said Nairobi would be willing to "accept Soviet and Cuban…troops," since this would be "better than minority rule" on the continent. The "French Cooperation Minister" informed "our ambassador in Togo that Angola has traumatized African states and engendered fear" since it showed the U.S.-dominated status quo was untenable,[96] though the alternative was unclear, fomenting anxiety.

In January 1976 in Paris, Joseph Sisco, Helmut Sonnefeldt, and other State Department heavyweights met with their peers and concluded parallel to that of the French Minister, finding Africa in a "semi-state of shock" as a result of Angola, either "numb or resigned." The list

93. Transcript, 3 March 1976, Box 13, *Dale Van Atta Papers.*

94. Report on Meeting, August 1976, Box 6, *National Security Adviser, Presidential Country Files for Africa.*

95. Report by State Department, 17 March 1976, Box 14, *Dale Van Atta Papers.*

96. "Executive Secretariat, Telegraphic Summary," 26 March 1976, Box 14, *Dale Van Atta Papers.*

of countries so afflicted included Ivory Coast, Senegal, Gabon, and particularly Zaire [Congo-Kinshasa]. The Gabonese leadership was "scared." Omar Bongo, Libreville's corrupt leader, was frightened about "internal problems" and "survival"; if he built up "too strong an army or a presidential guard" it could dislodge him and, perhaps, call on foreign forces to vouchsafe their triumph. He was also concerned that the Roberto-Savimbi "confrontation" was "becoming worse" and might "become a catastrophe." The two combatants "actually" had "come to blows a few weeks ago…."[97]

Back in Libreville, days later, Bongo threatened to create "trouble" for Ethiopia in its then restive province of Eritrea in "retaliation for [Addis'] recognition of MPLA." But belying his fury was the fact that the U.S. observer present found him to be "somewhat depressed at military reverses in Angola…." Thus, the "steam seems to have gone out of his efforts against MPLA…."[98] Bongo's "uneasiness," said this U.S. observer, "had been further stimulated by recent rumors that Cuban forces might next be engaged in either Namibia or Rhodesia, actions which would trigger conflagration in Southern Africa."[99] At a private meeting in newly independent Mozambique, paramount leader Samora Machel left the distinct impression that he too might welcome Cuban troops to repel raids launched by Salisbury.[100] The Cuban sword of Damocles hanging over Salisbury and Pretoria helped to soften their posture, making negotiations likely. The problem was that after independence the Cubans frequently were not there to enforce agreements brokered, a relief to the region's exploiting class.

Angola was a game changer, a transformational development. It was not only Bongo who sensed this. In a "secret sensitive" report from March 1976, reference was made to the "Angolan debacle" and the spread of Cuban troops continentally. The recommendation from the U.S. National Security Council? Consider "support" for the "PRC [Chinese] assisted ZANU faction" in Zimbabwe, which would foil the presumed Cuban-Soviet faction headed by Joshua Nkomo.[101]

---

97. Report on Meeting, January 1976, Box 2, *National Security Adviser, Presidential Country Files for Africa.*

98. Report on Meeting, January 1976, Box 2, *National Security Adviser, Presidential Country Files for Africa.*

99. Report on Meeting, February 1976, Box 2, *National Security Adviser, Presidential Country Files for Africa.*

100. Report on Meeting, August 1976, Box 4, *National Security Adviser, Presidential Country Files for Africa.*

101. "Secret Sensitive" Report, 11 March 1976, Box 44, *U.S. National Security Council, Institutional Files, 1974-1977, Gerald Ford Presidential Library.*

Subsequently, Chester Crocker, draftsman of the disastrous U.S. policy in Africa in the 1980s, asserted enthusiastically that Nkomo's ostensible competitor, Robert Mugabe, was "not fond of nor beholden to Moscow."[102]

The staggered Kissinger even ordered an opinion on "legal aspects of Cuban Armed Intervention in Rhodesia, Namibia and South Africa." Worrisomely, the counselor, Monroe Leigh, told him that Salisbury and Windhoek were "uniquely vulnerable to such interventions."[103] Vice President Rockefeller was told in a reassuring fashion that the "Cuban role in the Rhodesian insurgency has been a minor one, limited to a few training cadres in Mozambique. The presence of a sizable Cuban force in Angola, however, is a reminder to all participants in the Rhodesian problem of the potential for Cuban involvement in Rhodesia",[104] a looming threat that factored into the Rhodesians' more reasonable attitude at the Lancaster House talks that led to independence in 1980.

Nonetheless, Kaunda's aide Mark Chona already had sensed the kind of forces in Mozambique that would push for the ill-fated Nkomati Accord, leading to Maputo's expulsion of many ANC cadre. FRELIMO, he said, was playing a double game in Angola, not as pro-MPLA as it seemed because of nervousness about a vicious reaction in Pretoria.[105] A Cuban detachment could have blunted this but Angola—despite fears to the contrary—was absorbing Havana's military. But Chona may have had his own agenda since he then rebuked visiting British Foreign Secretary, James Callaghan, for not being more resolute on "Africa's Czechoslovakia," a reference to the Soviet intervention of 1968. Chona was hoping that Kissinger would react by pressing London further to the right, according to a U.S. agent.[106] But Chona too may have had more than one agenda, allegedly telling the Lusaka legation that he was critical of the Cubans' intervention—since if Pretoria evacuated southern Angola, Havana's

---

102. Chester Crocker, *High Noon in Southern Africa: Making Peace in a Tough Neighborhood*, New York: Norton, 1992, 39.

103. Monroe Leigh to Henry Kissinger, 5 March 1976, Box 44, *National Security Council Institutional Files.*

104. "Secret Noforn" Report, 14 October 1976, Box 9, FA 385, Series 19, *Nelson A. Rockefeller Vice Presidential Foreign Affairs and National Security Records*

105. Report from Lusaka legation, December 1975, Box 8, *National Security Adviser, Presidential Country Files for Africa.*

106. Report from Lusaka legation, December 1975, Box 8, *National Security Adviser, Presidential Country Files for Africa.*

forces "would race south to Namibian border," making it "Cuba's next stop." Besides, the "Soviet grand strategy probably included Zimbabwe" too.[107]

Assuming Chona made these provocative remarks, the objective impact was to reinforce the narrative of an imminent arrival of Cubans in Salisbury—or even Pretoria—which would be hard to countenance for political reasons. Chona may have been pleased to hear the early report that Lusaka was cooperating with the CIA in backing UNITA.[108] In any case, the force of events was not in accord with his presumed theses. Chester Crocker, the chief U.S. negotiator in the sub-region during the 1980s, suggested that Cuban muscle in Angola compelled Lusaka to expel UNITA and then welcome Soviet leader Nikolai Podgorny in March 1977.[109]

Nonetheless, Kaunda was said to be considering sending Chona to Washington to "offset negative influence of Nigerian[s]," perceived as pro-MPLA. "Nigerians had been exceedingly active and effective in lobbying with members of U.S. Congress, especially... Congressman Diggs...."[110] Washington had to be consoled by the report received from Lusaka indicating that as of January 1976, Kaunda was assailing the MPLA and their Moscow ally[111]—but this was to change soon too.

The ACOA was not absent as this drama unfolded in 1975. Earlier that year Houser arrived in Angola, staying there from 15-25 March. He was handicapped since "few people speak English" he found, while he spoke no Portuguese. He did manage to speak with Agostinho Neto. The "atmosphere" was "tense," he said with "soldiers everywhere." In fact, "many political leaders carried revolvers." There were "few Africans driving cars," a legacy of colonialism that deprived most of the population of this form of mobility. "Settlers still dominate the economy," he found, which may have been a revelation to Houser alone. He also visited UNITA offices in Lobito and Luanda and found "a good minority of Portuguese were on hand going through the procedure of taking out membership," which did

107. Report from Lusaka legation, January 1976, Box 8, *National Security Adviser, Presidential Country Files for Africa.*

108. Andy De Roche, *Kenneth Kaunda*, 58.

109. Chester Crocker, *High Noon in Southern Africa: Making Peace in a Tough Neighborhood*, New York: Norton, 1992, 54.

110. Report from Lusaka legation, January 1976, Box 8, *National Security Adviser, Presidential Country Files for Africa.*

111. Report from Lusaka legation, January 1976, Box 7, *National Security Adviser, Presidential Country Files for Africa.*

not alarm him. China, he said, was "training" FNLA troops,[112] a process that had reportedly begun as early as 1974 with 300 instructors.[113]

Tanzania, however, continued to have problems in bilateral relations with the U.S. Just as Gerald Ford was being sworn in, yet another U.S. national was being detained in southeast Africa. William Whitfield of Arkansas was arrested in Arusha for reasons that remained unclear and held indefinitely while his spouse and two children were kept under house arrest. He had been living in the country for the past year.[114]

In short, U.S. imperialism remained dissatisfied with Tanzania but was constrained in its ability to act on this feeling. By the end of 1975 South African Broadcasting, though pleased with Chinese attacks on the Soviet Union over Angola, was upset by this Asian giant's continued aid to Mozambique and Tanzania. Moreover, these two African nations compounded the purported sin by backing the MPLA. On the other hand it was said glowingly, "Ivory Coast [and] Zaire" were in the same boat as Pretoria in that they all tended to "understand alike the danger of Russian imperialism and together with China oppose the intervention in Angola....Peking [as] a champion of the safety of the Cape sea route" came in for special praise.[115] As tensions mounted in the weeks preceding Angolan independence, J.Z. Gryffenberg, an emissary at the South African legation in Washington, chided the United States for its own repellent racism, which—he thought—discredited any attempt to chide his nation similarly—an old tactic in Pretoria.[116]

Others supposedly opposed to apartheid still shared an ideological trench with Pretoria. This could have been said for Kwado Akpan, Publicity Director of the PAC in the U.S., who by 1974 had accepted an invitation from Savimbi to visit his secluded headquarters in Angola.[117] As the Angola crisis escalated in May 1976, Steve Biko of the Black Consciousness Movement was under oath in an apartheid hearing. He was being grilled about a movement that was to petrify Pretoria in coming years: divestment from U.S. corporations with

112. Report by George Houser, 26 May 1975, Box 9, *Carol Bernstein Ferry and Ping Ferry Papers*.

113. Andy De Roche, *Kenneth Kaunda: The United States and Southern Africa*, London: Bloomsbury Academic, 2016, 42.

114. Letter from Robert Whitfield, 8 August 1974, Box 4, *White House Central Files, Subject File, Gerald Ford Presidential Library*.

115. SABC commentary, Box 120, *Leroy Walker Africa News Service*.

116. *Philadelphia Inquirer*, 7 October 1975.

117. *Azania Combat*, 1974, Box 144, *Leroy Walker Africa News Service*.

South African holdings. In a circuitous manner, he affirmed the obvious: "Church groups from America and England [are] specifically coming to investigate the position of their firms inside this country...." He went on to criticize Polaroid since their donation of part of their profits to certain South Africa groups was "paternalistic."[118]

The defeat in Vietnam, the Cubans' confidence in intervening in faraway Angola without evident fear of blowback from U.S. imperialism, and the apparent deterioration of Washington's global position ignited a vociferous round of backbiting in the former slaveholding republic. Henry Kissinger, the vicar of U.S. foreign policy, was targeted with the perception that he was executing a policy too congenial to Moscow. In the spring of 1976 Ronald Reagan challenged Gerald Ford for the Republican Party presidential nomination and almost toppled him, running hard to the right, particularly on foreign policy. The man who became Reagan's Vice President in 1980—George Herbert Walker Bush—was signed by Southern Africa too: Senator Frank Church of Idaho—seen by the *New York Times* as the "hottest liberal dark horse" for the White House in 1976[119]—in turn sought to destabilize the competition by opposing Bush's appointment as CIA Director (which he got anyway) since he was "hoping... President [Ford] will choose him as a running mate.... All this contributed to Biko's candor, doubtlessly impelling his activism too."[120]

President Ford was running scared in any case. In the battleground state of Florida, he exhorted that his regime "would accept no further Cuban adventures" in Africa but this was misinterpreted in Pretoria, according to one of his constituents. Malcolm Butler said that Pretoria did not understand the "Florida [party] primary context" and could easily make "unrealistic and dangerous assumptions" about U.S. aid to halt a Cuban advance in the region,[121] putting Washington more obviously and blatantly on the side of apartheid. In McAllen, Texas, on the border with Mexico, attorney Charles Thompson knew why there was a "surge of voters into the Reagan ranks" in his state: Kissinger's "vicious and unrelenting attacks upon Rhodesia and South Africa...."[122]

---

118. Millard Arnold, ed., *Steve Biko: Black Consciousness in South Africa*, New York: Random House, 1978, 33-34, 37.

119. *New York Times*, 15 June 1975.

120. Senator Church to Mercer Hufford, 9 December 1975, Box 4, *Frank Church Papers, Boise State University-Idaho*.

121. Malcom Butler to Brent Scowcroft, 3 March 1976, Box 4, *National Security Adviser, Presidential Country Files*.

122. Letter from Charles Thompson, 6 May 1976, Box 4, *White House Central File, Subject File, Gerald Ford Presidential Library*.

Dixie Republicans may have noticed how the deteriorating situation in Southern Africa allowed Afro-American politicos to hold meetings with the Secretary of State, opening doors that Dixie would have preferred to remain shut. This would increase Black leverage on foreign policy, igniting the fear that it would be wielded against the heinous system of Jim Crow and its legacy. By late August 1976 even the *New York Times* had noticed that the Reverend Jesse Jackson, soon to run for president with apartheid as a major issue, and his comrade, Manhattan Borough President Percy Sutton, met with Dr. Kissinger about Southern Africa.[123]

Dixie's hold on reality could be questioned, a twisted perspective that was rarely a sound basis for formulating policy. At a Rotary Club luncheon in Greenville, Mississippi in April 1976 with no Afro-Americans present, Congressman David Bowen argued that Salisbury and Pretoria were capitals of the continent's only democracies. He said these societies were completely integrated but in the next breath admitted that there were apartheid-like conditions in housing, schools, and hospitals. Naturally, he was silent—or obstinate—as the anti-Jim Crow movement arose in the Magnolia State.[124]

But it was not just in Dixie, perpetually worried about the fate of Jim Crow, that Ford was being challenged from the right. Harold Peter Stern, Chairman of the Republican Party in posh Harrison, New York in Westchester Country, was studiously neutral in the Ford vs. Reagan showdown. But even he was angry that the incumbent had "permitted Congress to abandon Angola to the Communists," while Kissinger's apologia during his tour of Africa "really shocked me." He was adamant: "Do not leave the white settlers there defenseless."[125] In nearby New Jersey, Carl McIntire of the International Council of Christian Churches—with offices in Amsterdam, launching pad for migration to the Cape in 1652—denounced U.S. policy in Southern Africa. "Mozambique is Communist," he said in May 1976, yet still maintained relations with Washington: "it is clear that Mr. Kissinger is now helping Communism directly," he charged. "Africa is being delivered into Communist hands," he contended "and we are on Communists' side…." In Angola, "there is not a single missionary left," not because it was a war zone but because of

123. *New York Times*, 24 August 1976.

124. Statement by Owen Brooks of Delta Ministry, circa 1976, Box 14, *Washington Office on Africa Papers*.

125. Letter from Harold Peter Stern, 28 April 1976, Box 4, *White House Central File, Subject File. Gerald Ford Presidential Library*.

the MPLA—while he could not even snag a meeting in the White House.[126]

Meeting with President Ford, Kissinger acknowledged the obvious: "after Angola," he said, "the pace of events accelerated with the radicals predominating. The pro-Western states were in a panic because they thought of a fate like Angola's awaited them.... All of Africa was being pushed into radicalism...." Hence, the "only way we could stop the radicalization process," he said, was "to push majority rule" in Rhodesia while "[giving] the whites more time to work things out" in South Africa. But this rational response to a setback for U.S. imperialism was not accepted with equanimity by many of Ford's voters.[127]

By April 1976 Kissinger, on the cusp of being overwhelmed by onrushing events, had sped to Tanzania where he met with Nyerere. It was "swelteringly hot," he said, as they met "alone at his private residence." The "substantive atmosphere was nearly as warm," said the U.S. Secretary of State, as he sought to woo this influential African. He described the Tanzanian as "sharp, clever, gregarious and fascinating...." He was man of broad "intellectual range," imbued with "subtlety, sophistication and wit...." He was "quick on the uptake and understanding in response." He was the "Chou en Lai of Africa," said Kissinger, dispensing with reserve in equating the Tanzanian with the Chinese leader with whom he had cut an anti-Soviet deal, a premonition of what he hoped to gain in Dar.[128] Yet these encomia notwithstanding, Kissinger may have known that Tanzania in 1975 had seized Chinese arms to be delivered to UNITA in Angola.[129]

The unrestrained Kissinger was a bit more circumspect publicly about his private meetings with those like Nyerere, but his general tone was suggestive of the unavoidable fact that a page of history was turning and that minority regimes were in danger—and it was this assessment that so enraged the grandees of the ruling Republican Party, placing President Ford's future in dire jeopardy.

---

126. Carl McIntire to Gerald Ford, 3 May 1976, Box 45, *White House Central File, Subject File.*

127. Minutes of Meeting, circa Spring 1976, *National Security Adviser's Memoranda of Conversations Collection. Gerald Ford [Digital] Presidential Library.* Accessed 22 June 2016.

128. Henry Kissinger to Brent Scowcroft, 26 April 1976, Box 32, *National Security Adviser, Trip Briefing Books and Cables for Henry Kissinger, Kissinger Trip File, Gerald Ford Presidential Library.*

129. Linda Heywood, *Contested Power in Angola, 1840s to the Present*, Rochester: University of Rochester Press, 2000, 200.

After the glow of the meeting had faded, Kissinger revealed that he "first disabused Nyerere of any notion that this [African] initiative was an electoral advantage to us. I pointed out that the hostile mail we got and the fact that American blacks and liberals vote Democratic anyway, and white conservatives may rebel against us… for the same reason I feel strongly that at this point we should not hype the African initiative at home,"[130] but it was too late: Ford was perceived by the base of his party of selling out white supremacists abroad, suggesting he could easily do the same at home.

While conferring with President Ford in the Oval Office at the White House before his departure for Africa, Kissinger was even more candid. He worried that he would be greeted with the catcalls and riots that met Vice President "Nixon in Latin America in '59…." "I am fatalistic," he mused, since "basically I am with the whites in South Africa…."[131]

When Chancellor Helmut Kohl of Germany visited the White House, Kissinger sought to win him over by telling him that "about one third of the population of the Palatinate migrated" to Philadelphia, while "there was a strong emigration from the Old Reich into" Rhodesia and South Africa, which was another basis for Berlin's interest.[132] Racial unity—of even the trans-oceanic variety—was unavailing in the face of armed Cubans.

His whirlwind journey brought Kissinger to meet Mobutu too and he was accorded "just as warm and lavish a reception as in Dar or Lusaka." The mood was different, however, as there was an "intense siege mentality in the wake of Angola," coupled with "insecurity". That "theme has dominated all our talks." A poor predictor, he told the African strongman that Ford was "certain to win" the upcoming election and that "would allow us to conduct a more forceful foreign policy."[133] Though a specialist in foreign policy, the busy Kissinger took time to receive updates on Democratic Party primary results

---

130. Brent Scowcroft to President Ford (quoting Kissinger), 15 September 1976, Box 42, *National Security Adviser, Trip Briefing Books and Cables for Henry Kissinger, Kissinger Trip File.*

131. Minutes of Meeting, 21 April 1976, 9:20-9:55 AM, *National Security Adviser's Memoranda of Conversation Collection, Gerald Ford [Digital] Presidential Library,* accessed 22 June 2016.

132. Minutes of Meeting, 4 May 1976, *National Security Adviser's Memoranda of Conversations Collection.*

133. Henry Kissinger to Brent Scowcroft, 28 April 1976, Box 32, National *Security Adviser, Trip Briefing Books and Cables for Henry Kissinger, Kissinger Trip File.*

in Pennsylvania.[134] But his detractors were monitoring Republican Party primaries and though President Ford was to prevail, he was weakened by Governor Reagan's stiff challenge, which was propelled by a failed Africa policy. The popular television personality Barbara Walters interrogated Dr. Kissinger about this in May 1976, as she suggested that his maladroit position on Africa was hurting Ford; a question about the possibility of Cuban troops in Rhodesia was designed to stir disfavor as it mixed the volatile combination of socialism versus white supremacy.[135]

South Carolina's Hugh Beasley thought Kaunda reminded him of the slain Dr. King, which was not intended as a compliment. But it was Kissinger who really inflamed the Southerner's temper. He had just heard him on the radio speaking at a congressional hearing and being queried by "Senator [Jacob] Javits, a Jew who is a rabid supporter of Israel, a country that was formed by the Jews coming in through Palestine and by force taking over the country from the people who had been living there...."[136] Hank Mullenhard of North Augusta, South Carolina concurred. Kissinger, he said, was "against every Christian principle.... I just thank God that Kissinger wasn't around when we were fighting for our liberty as a new nation...."[137]

Edward Benjamin of New Orleans also objected to U.S. policy: "while Kissinger's family was living in the ghettos of Europe," he said, "stout Dutchmen went out to South Africa and discovered gold and diamonds...." Thus, "if the Dutch and the British do not want to mingle their bloodlines with Negroes, that is their business...." Sadly enough, he said with a sigh, "Many Jews feel much more kindly disposed toward intermingling with Negroes than other peoples...."[138]

These Southerners would have been even more outraged if they had been able to read Kissinger's message to Nyerere on the eve of the Summit of the Non-Aligned Movement in Colombo, Sri Lanka.

---

134. Report, 27 April 1976, Box 32, National *Security Adviser, Trip Briefing Books and Cables for Henry Kissinger, Kissinger Trip File.*

135. Report on Walters interview with Kissinger, 17 May 1976, Box 248, *Leroy Walker Africa News Service Archive.*

136. Hugh Beasley to Congressman Derrick, 13 May 1976, Box 2, *Butler Derrick Papers*: He continued, "don't forget that the traitor, Alger Hiss, was one of the main architects of the United Nations," now bedeviling Washington. "The Swedes and Socialistic experts," he declaimed "can argue all they want to, but there is something lacking in the Negroid Race."

137. Hank Mullenhard to "Dear Butler," 11 May 1976, Box 2, *Butler Derrick Papers.*

138. Edward Benjamin to Gerald Ford, 13 July 1976, Box 45, *White House Central Files, Subject File, Gerald Ford Presidential Library.*

Verbally prostrating himself, he pled emotionally with this African leader not to raise the sticky matter of the U.S. colony of Puerto Rico there,[139] a sign of the rapidly changing correlation of forces that Reagan's triumph in 1980 was designed to overturn. Unassuaged, Nyerere was furious: Kissinger's effort to prevent him from committing an "unfriendly act" had "triggered [a] violent emotional reaction" in the Tanzanian leader, interpreting it as a "war" threat.[140]

But it was Beasley—whose son was in the U.S. Navy—who repeatedly raised searching questions about Southern Africa. "The Russians and their Cuban mercenaries," he said accusingly, were "establishing a Naval Base" in Angola. He knew since he had "visited Rhodesia twice and expect[ed] to try again...." There he found that "Rhodesian whites are of the same racial strains as we are in our section." While thumbing through the "Rhodesian Telephone Directory" in Salisbury he noticed that there was a "Derrick Oils located there" and, in fact, there were "11 different Butlers' in the Directory," who may have been his or his interlocutor's blood relatives, further basis for a U.S. intervention. He encountered "several Americans" who had "retired and gone there to live," another reason for U.S. concern. "Frankly," he said, "if I had no family ties and were a young man, I would move there myself...." Never forget, he said, "Rhodesia was the only [nation] that offered to send a combat team to Vietnam...."[141]

The Cuban presence in Angola and the seeming unraveling in Salisbury was creating momentum for an even more muscular U.S. role in the region. Senator Thurmond of South Carolina was told that Washington should be "selling more arms and equipment to South Africa," internationally recognized boycotts be damned. "Missiles, planes, small arms" should be sent forthwith and then the legislator was instructed that he "should be speaking up for the minorities in South West Africa," meaning Europeans. The writer making these suggestions, identified as "Mrs. Charles Gervin," was fretful, demanding "they must not lose all (as the Portuguese settlers in Angola) to these terrorists...."[142]

---

139. Henry Kissinger to Julius Nyerere, July 1976, Box 6, *National Security Adviser, Presidential Country Files for Africa.*

140. Report from Dar es Salaam legation, July 1976, Box 6, *National Security Adviser, Presidential Country Files for Africa.*

141. Hugh Beasley to Congressman Derrick, 2 March 1976, Box 2, *Butler Derrick Papers.*

142. "Mrs. Charles Gervin" to Senator Thurmond, Box 6, Subject Correspondence, *J. Strom Thurmond Papers.*

Perhaps Ford's opponents would have been more favorable to him if they had known how his fellow Michigander, the fabulously wealthy John McGoff, was seeking to execute a covert policy to back Pretoria through the offices of Connie Mulder, South Africa's Minister of Information, and the Secretary of that ministry, Eschel Rhoodie.[143] "We broadcast to sixty five countries worldwide," boasted McGoff as he was en route to South Africa.[144] The stocky, cocky, silver-haired McGoff was in Africa during the previous world war and had visited South Africa as recently as 1968.[145] "I am not an agent…for the Republic of South Africa," was his unintentionally revealing riposte to the accusation that he was seeking to buy the *Washington Star* with millions funneled to him from Pretoria.[146] He did, however, own a huge game farm in the northeast of South Africa.[147]

The right-wing *Washington Times* debuted in 1982 and was tied not only to McGoff but the South Korean Christian evangelist Sun Myung Moon. The scandal called "Muldergate" was revealed ultimately to involve spending $73 million on 160 secret propaganda projects across the globe. When McGoff arrived in Pretoria he was said to have been handed a cool $12 million for the purchase of the *Washington Star* and a share in the television branch of the then collapsing United Press International, billed as "the second largest news-film producer in the world." Not all their various ideas took flight but in December 1975 McGoff was able to buy the *Sacramento Union*, based in the capital of California, then well on its way to becoming the most powerful and populous U.S. state—and by some estimates the 5th largest economy in the world.[148]

In addition to President Ford, McGoff was also close to former governor of Texas, John Connally, who was in the limousine with President Kennedy when he was assassinated in November 1963, and then went on to become a crony of his antagonist Nixon. McGoff's South African comrade Rhoodie, a primary funnel for Muldergate

143. See Box 45, *White House Central Files, Subject File, Gerald Ford Presidential Library*. This container includes many notes from McGoff seeking to establish ties between Ford and Mulder.

144. John McGoff to Brent Scowcroft, 5 March 1976, Box 45, *White House Central Files, Subject File.*

145. *Columbia Journalism Review*, 1979, Box 2, *Thompson/Day Papers on South Africa, Michigan State University-East Lansing.*

146. *Lansing State Journal*, 18 July 1979, Box 2, *Thompson/Day Papers on South Africa.*

147. *Washington Post*, 27 June 1978.

148. "Washington Notes on Africa," Summer 1982, Box 2, *Group Research Archives, Columbia University, New York City.*

funds, bought a home in sunny Miami with his ill-gotten gains. Rhoodie had been posted to the U.S. as early as 1966. The South African golfer Gary Player was implicated in Rhoodie's schemes, paid with secret Pretoria funds to host U.S. corporate bosses in South Africa for lush "golfing holidays" in a bid to stem the anti-investment tide. It seemed that Rhoodie's long-term goal was to form a pro-Pretoria publishing empire based in the U.S. Indiana conservative Beurt SerVaas, yet another wealthy publishing magnate (he controlled the *Saturday Evening Post*), who was for decades a major force in statewide politics, had investments in South Africa and was implicated in the Rhoodie scandal and was thought to be a former CIA agent. Another Republican titan, Richard Mellon Scaife, principal heir to a billion-dollar fortune in banking and oil and precious metals, was a business partner of McGoff and had been involved with the CIA through World Forum Features, a London news agency identified as a CIA front. Such connections raised the question of whether the CIA was a witting partner in this entire scheme.[149]

By 1978 the well-connected McGoff crony Governor Connally, had journeyed to South Africa himself, where according to press reports, he "boosted the hopes of whites."[150] His junket was arranged by SerVaas, who maintained an overseas bureau in Cape Town.[151]

McGoff, the press baron, had a convenient excuse for collecting often sensitive information. By January 1976 he was meeting in the White House with Les Devilliers, Pretoria's Deputy Secretary for Information, and Brent Scowcroft, a Lieutenant General of the Air Force, seconded to President Ford's staff. "We have offices in...Moscow, Salisbury and Luanda," he boasted, and in the latter city he was able to report helpfully that "there are several hundred East Europeans at the Hotel Tivoli in Luanda" and "over 8000 Cubans, one Congolese Liaison officer and one Portuguese Communist" close by. Pretoria's man admitted that "we have agonized over this" and "we have decided to pull out in eight days" as a result of the adverse correlation of forces. McGoff was beyond angry, castigating U.S. Senators "[John] Tunney and [Dick] Clark." "I think that our Congress has been penetrated," he concluded, leading to a massive and successful campaign to defeat both men—with South African funding. There was a general worry that ripples from Angola would spread

149. Mervyn Rees and Chris Day, *Muldergate*, 47, 139, 163, 186, 193, 195, 200. See also *Rand Daily Mail*, 27 June 1979.

150. *Philadelphia Bulletin*, 3 September 1978.

151. *Indianapolis Star*, 23 March 1980.

to the "Middle East" in favor of Moscow.[152] (Eschel Rhoodie confessed later that groups opposed to women's reproductive freedom were used as conduits through which he and his comrades shoveled $250,000 in Iowa to defeat Clark and $150,000 in California to subdue Tunney.)[153]

Pretoria managed to spend a considerable amount in defeating these pesky Senators, a stern lesson to others who might seek to emulate them and a boon to U.S. nationals like Sydney Baron and Andrew Hatcher, who were also reputedly conduits for this campaign cash.[154] Pretoria also unstintingly praised Daniel Patrick Moynihan. As of January 1976, South African Broadcasting hailed him for having "condemned Russia for its bid to colonize Africa." By November, propelled by such inflamed rhetoric, he had become a U.S. Senator from New York.[155] When Rhoodie claimed credit for these senatorial setbacks (and advances) he was not exaggerating.[156]

Ultimately it was revealed that the South Africa Foundation and related sugar interests provided campaign contributions, free jet trips, and airplane tickets from at least 1971 to 1976 to Congressman William Poage of Texas and fellow legislators including William Wampler of Virginia, David Bowen of Mississippi, and John Flynt of Georgia.[157] The PAC demanded that the U.S. Congress investigate charges that Pretoria was funding U.S. pols, but there was little impulse to act on Capitol Hill.[158] Quite typically, in July 1978 five Congressmen were reported to be winging their way to South Africa on a Pretoria-financed junket.[159] De facto bribes went to various U.S.

---

152. Minutes, 26 January 1976, *National Security Adviser's Memoranda of Conversation Collection, Gerald Ford Presidential [Digital] Library*, accessed 22 June 2016. Hereafter Ford Digital Library.

153. Note, Summer 1982, Box 62, *Washington Office on Africa Papers*.

154. Mervyn Rees and Chris Day, *Muldergate*, 200. For more on the defeat of the two legislators, see Clipping, 13 June 1979, Box 245, *Leroy Walker Africa News Service Archive*.

155. South African Broadcasting Corporation Commentary, 29 January 1976, Box 120, *Leroy Walker Africa News Service Archive*.

156. *Trans Africa Forum*, October 1982, Box 1, *Cheryl Johnson-Odim Papers, Columbia College of Chicago*.

157. *Washington Star*, 23 August 1978.

158. PAC Statement, 19 March 1979, Box 237, *Leroy Walker Africa News Service Archive*.

159. *Washington Post*, 12 July 1978: The list included these Congressmen: John Dent of Pennsylvania; Richard Ichord of Missouri; Harold Runnels of New Mexico; Bob Wilson of California; and Senator Carl Curtis of Nebraska.

periodicals in the form of large and expensive advertisements garlanding apartheid with hearty hosannas.[160]

Before and after 1976, Pretoria had been quite active in Washington, seeking to increase exports of sugar[161] and seal fur from the Cape.[162] The sugar issue particularly, perhaps because it intersected with the ever sensitive matter of Cuba, attracted considerable attention.[163] World prices were rising in the 1970s, which could benefit Havana—and/or Pretoria.[164] Congressman Parren Mitchell of the Congressional Black Caucus took a vanguard role in restricting Pretoria's sugar quota. By 1974 he was told of activists' distress about the "success South Africa is having in convincing moderates in the United States that things are really changing"[165]—though by 1976 this false perception had begun to fade.

Congressman Diggs argued that the Pretoria sugar quota hurt competitors in Swaziland, Malawi, Madagascar, and Mauritius, since South Africa's quota was much larger than the individual quotas of the other four. When he visited sugar plantations in Natal he found racist segregation.[166] It was also Congressman Diggs who engineered creative litigation designed to cripple South African Airways, Pretoria's advertising in U.S. periodicals, and importation of Rhodesian chrome.[167]

Pretoria was successful in convincing U.S. intelligence (the extremely covert National Security Agency) to aid the secret, underground "Silvermine" communications center at the Simonstown Naval Station in South Africa (which was later revealed to have been penetrated by Soviet intelligence).[168] Meeting in Nairobi in November 1975, the World Council of Churches, which was becoming more active on the anti-apartheid front, passed a blisteringly worded

---

160. *Washington Post*, 5 July 1978.

161. *Washington Afro-American*, 11-15 June 1974.

162. Michael Peay of Lawyers Committee for Civil Rights to "Interested Parties," 20 August 1975, Box 244, *Leroy Walker Africa News Archive*.

163. *New York Times*, 8 June 1971 and 10 June 1971.

164. *Johannesburg Star*, 25 November 1972. See also *Johannesburg Star*, 25 November 1972: "Sugar threatened by rain" in Natal.

165. Ted and Chris Root to Congressman Mitchell, 7 June 1974, Box 14, *Washington Office on Africa Papers, Yale University*.

166. Statement by Congressman Diggs, May 1974, Box 14, *Washington Office on Africa Papers*.

167. Goler Teal Butcher, "Southern African Issues in United States Courts," *Howard Law Journal*, 26(Number 2, 1983): 601-643.

168. *CounterSpy* [U.S.], Spring 1976, Box 244, *Leroy Walker Africa News Service Archive*.

resolution on nuclear collaboration with Pretoria and its "military implications," with General Electric [GE] of the U.S. singled out for castigation.[169] Following suit, the Organization of African Unity cracked down on Iran for supplying oil to apartheid (and investing i[illegible]-to-oil programs), which simultaneously sent a message to [illegible] giants similarly implicated.[170]

[illegible]ria's leverage over its primary ally in Washington was not [illegible] rhetorical. South Africa was an essential partner in a new [illegible]n cartel which was probed for antitrust violations, months [illegible]Angolan independence.[171] Washington was accused of ship-[illegible]hough weapons-grade uranium to South Africa to make [illegible]tomic bombs.[172] By 1978 an atomic detonation by Pretoria in [illegible]a caused global outrage.

[illegible]outh African press headlined "how America depends on [illegible]frica" in the rarified realm of raw materials. At a hearing [illegible] by Congressman Diggs on this topic, a journalist noticed an "official from the South Africa Embassy was as usual taking notes."[173]

As Pretoria stepped up its lobbying in Washington, a predictable backlash ensued. By 1975 Howard University, the leader in Negro higher education, headquartered in Washington, moved to fire Professor Leslie Rubin, a South African national. He had taught there for 13 years but was accused of skipping classes, being disrespectful to students, and the like.[174]

Protests against South Africa were also becoming more prevalent. Even the *New York Times*, which preferred to imagine that there were no voices in the nation to the left of liberalism, noticed that representatives of the National Conference of Black Lawyers, of which I was a leader, was active supporting the MPLA: "Angolans reported to talk in Cuba with U.S. backers" was their pithy report about NCBL.[175]

Pressed by activists and the disturbing reports about U.S. mercenaries fighting in Angola, a few states acted. By April 1976 a grand jury in Connecticut was probing arms sales by state firms in South

---

169. Resolution of WCC, 23 November-10 December 1975, Box 114, *Leroy Walker Africa News Service Archive*

170. "Africa Bureau Fact Sheet," November-December 1975, Box 120, *Leroy Walker Africa News Service Archive*.

171. *Washington Post*, 19 August 1975 and *Christian Science Monitor*, 6 October 1975.

172. *Washington Post*, 14 April 1975.

173. *Johannesburg Star*, 19 June 1976, cited in *Azania Combat*, August-September 1976, Box 139, *Leroy Walker Africa News Service Archive*.

174. *Washington Post*, 9 November 1975 and 12 November 1975.

175. *New York Times*, 28 February 1976.

Africa. These included Colt, Remington, Olin, and Winchester. Walter Plowman pled guilty of providing false information on his export license for U.S. pistols destined for South Africa via West Germany.[176]

The foregoing notwithstanding, it was the fearsome presence of Cuban troops that altered the equation in Southern Africa, creating a cul de sac for apartheid from which there was no easy exit.

176. *Hartford Courant*, 30 April 1976.

Chapter 16

Soweto's Reverberations, 1976-1978

IF the combustible era of 1974-1975 started the countdown to the electoral defeat of apartheid in 1994, 1976 served to accelerate what had become a frenetic pace. "1976 has been an amazing year," said George Houser of the ACOA. "We have been working in the field of African liberation for more than 20 years now," but this crucial year "seemed to usher in a new era." Houser averred that "American people" were "more conscious than ever before of the importance of Southern Africa"—though the "growing edge for action on Southern Africa lies in the Black community."[1] By January 1978 Houser observed that ACOA had "sold somewhere over $12,000 in literature during" the previous year. "Compared with the two years ago when sales were something less than $4000 this is quite an accomplishment."[2]

It was not just ACOA riding the decolonization wave. Tami Hultman of *Africa News* in Durham, North Carolina found that by mid-1977 "a surprising number of our readers are in Africa....The Nigerian Sunday newspaper 'Punch' with a circulation of more than 150,000 uses 'Africa News' regularly, as does the 'Tanzania Daily News.'"[3] In the months leading up to the Spring of 1978, subscriptions to *the Africa News* digest had risen from 170 to 1264 and its granular reporting on Southern Africa was a primary reason.[4]

The intervention of Cuban troops electrified Southern Africa, as it frightened authoritarian leaders to the north and dismayed Washington. The changed balance of forces in the sub-region was further indicated by the Soweto Uprising in South Africa in June

1. George Houser to Carol Bernstein Ferry and Ping Ferry, 16 December 1976, Box 9, *Carol Bernstein Ferry and Ping Ferry Papers.*

2. George Houser to Carol Bernstein Ferry and Ping Ferry, 5 January 1978, Box 9, *Bernstein Ferry Papers.*

3. Letter from Tami Hultman, 18 July 1977, Box 16, *Bernstein Ferry Papers.*

4. Memorandum, 16 May 1978, Box 16, *Bernstein Ferry Papers.*

1976, ostensibly sparked by the reluctance of young Africans to dispense with studying in English in favor of Afrikaans. In the U.S., the Republican Party primaries indicated mass alienation from the awkward misrule of President Ford and his foreign policy guru, Dr. Kissinger. This shifted the party further to the right with the rise of Ronald Reagan, many of whose supporters sat on their hands as the peanut farmer from Georgia, Governor Jimmy Carter, was elected U.S. president in 1976 with mass support from Black Americans, and notably the Reverend Andrew Young, who became his controversial Ambassador to the United Nations. "The President was elected by votes of black people," was the uncontroversial assessment of a White House aide in 1977.[5] With that electoral configuration, Carter was compelled to follow up on Dr. Kissinger's stated goal of pressing for negotiations with the rebel regime in Salisbury, leading to Zimbabwean independence in 1980. But, again, this development further angered the potent pro-Pretoria faction with influence at the highest levels of the U.S. government—who struck back with a vengeance in November 1980 by ousting Carter and electing the bridesmaid of 1976, Ronald W. Reagan.

These overlapping developments also had incalculable ideological impact, not only in improving the profile of Cuba and socialism in the Pan-African world but also, to opposing effect, by bolstering pro-China forces among U.S. Negroes who excoriated Moscow and Havana alike. Nine years after Reagan's victory, the Berlin Wall came tumbling down, igniting the Soviet collapse two years later and ushering Cuba into crisis, which may have hampered the island's role as the ultimate guarantor of the liberation of Southern Africa

As 1976 was about to dawn, Ted Lockwood of the Washington Office on Africa, a sister organization of ACOA, found himself and his colleagues "up to our ears in the Angola business," as Congress debated cutting aid to pro-apartheid factions there. "Liberals are quite squishy," he assured a funder, "but there seems to some disposition to ask for justification for covert intervention that may not have been present before,"[6] which was an emblem of Cuba's heroism and Pretoria's perfidy.

From behind bars on Robben Island, Ahmed Kathrada sensed instinctively the "gravity of developments" when "Fidel Castro

---

5. Henry Richardson to David Aaron, 17 December 1977, Box 115, *National Security Council Staff Material, North/South, Jimmy Carter Presidential Library-Atlanta.*

6. Ted Lockwood to Carol Bernstein Ferry, 10 December 1975, Box 22, *Carol Bernstein Ferry and Ping Ferry Papers.*

issued the ominous warning that continued South African aggression in Angola could very lead to full-scale war, which was likely to overflow not only Namibia but into South Africa itself;" a warning that Washington could hardly ignore in crafting policy.[7] The entire sub-region could have gone up in flames, jeopardizing the enormous super-profits gleaned by vampire-like U.S. corporations. It was in August 1977 that Nyerere of Tanzania managed to appear on U.S. television and issued his own warning, declaring that if Pretoria entered the war in Rhodesia, so would Tanzania. Tactfully, he gave routine praise to President Carter but then acquainted his audience with a history lesson most had forgotten. Responding to the plaint that Cubans and Soviets were supposedly colonizing Africa, he said, "Your own country was assisted by the French, but I don't really believe you wanted to get rid of the British so that the French should take over your country."[8]

This was the backdrop to the precipitous rise of Governor Carter to the White House. Aware of the generally conservative attitudes of many Euro-Americans, particularly regarding overt challenges to white supremacy, a Carter aide was told as early as 1975 that "as much as possible the issue of Southern Africa should not be emphasized," even though it proved to be a winning tack among Afro-Americans. "Most groups which are aware of this issue," said this advisor to Congressman John Jenrette of South Carolina, "take polar positions and a high profile on Southern Africa is likely to alienate more than the number of friends which could be won, no matter what position you take."[9]

By August 1976, however, with the Angola crisis still brewing, one of Carter's main advisors, Richard Holbrooke, warned that Africa "'would become and will become one of the major foreign policy issues of the coming decade…." "This is especially" the case for the voters who would be needed to push the Georgian over the finish line in November, i.e. "the millions of our citizens who find an important part of their heritage in Africa." But any support from

7. Ahmed Kathrada, "Indian South Africans-A Future Bound with the Cause of the African Majority," in Mac Maharaj, *Reflections in Prison*, 97-124, 122.

8. Transcript of "Issues and Answers," American Broadcasting Corporation, 7 August 1977, Box 9, *Gwendolen Carter Papers, University of Florida-Gainesville*.

9. John J. Clark to Stuart Eizenstat, 27 April 1975, Box 1, *Jimmy Carter Pre-Presidential 1976 Campaign Issues Office, Stuart Eizenstat Papers, Jimmy Carter Presidential Library-Atlanta, Georgia*.

Carter for African liberation would have to be laced with the poison pill of firm "opposition to Soviet expansionism,"[10] which not only paved the way for the rise of Reagan, who was capable of taking a harder line than his fellow governor, but also would handicap any post-independence redistribution of the wealth or prosecution of war crimes—since both efforts would be perceived as playing into the hands of Moscow and/or Havana. Unsurprisingly, just before the inauguration, Carter's main foreign policy advisor, Zbigniew Brzezinski, who had close ties to anticommunist Poles, was told unreservedly of "the Africans' suspicions of our motives."[11] (A Salisbury operative retained a political cartoon that featured Ian Smith of Salisbury exclaiming "ethnic purity! That's the phrase I've been looking for!"[12]—a sarcastic reference to a gaffe ridden catch phrase popularized by Carter that paved the way for Reagan's more sincere invocation.)

From prison, an encouraged Walter Sisulu forthrightly rejected the anticommunist predicates upon which Washington relied. Provocatively invoking the U.S. in remarks entitled "We Shall Overcome," he then pivoted to praise "V.I. Lenin, the architect of the October Revolution and one of the world's greatest revolutionary strategists and tacticians." It was "no longer open to doubt," said Mandela's comrade, "that the imperialists have long used the cloak of anticommunism to impede the struggles of the colonial and former colonial peoples," citing the experiences of Chile, Cuba, and Congo under Lumumba.[13]

Some Africans may have noticed an article in the Washington press during the early days of the Carter administration about more Rhodesians and Afrikaners moving to the U.S. The combined rate of immigration was about 3000 per month and since the number of Europeans in Rhodesia was rarely above 250,000, this meant a disastrous leakage of those needed to fight a racist war. A similar number were decamping to Britain, Australia, and New Zealand.[14] Texas, a conservative redoubt, was understandably attracting those who had

10. Richard Holbrooke to Stuart Eizenstat, 21 August 1976, Box 1, *Stuart Eizenstat Papers*.

11. Peter Tarnoff to Zbigniew Brzezinski, 1 January 1977, Box 70, *Brzezinski Material, National Security Affairs, Jimmy Carter Presidential Library*.

12. *Chicago Sun-Times*, 21 April 1976, Box 1, *Kenneth Towsey Papers*.

13. Walter Sisulu, "We Shall Overcome," in Mac Maharaj, ed., *Reflections in Prison: Voices from the South African Liberation Struggle*, Amherst: University of Massachusetts Press, 2001, 71-90, 73.

14. *Washington Post*, 6 November 1977.

been comfortable with apartheid. This process was "accelerated," it was said, by the twin bombshells of Angola and Soweto. By 1977 the U.S was reported to be accepting five times as many South Africans as it had in 1975.[15]

Pretoria did not seem to be happy with the U.S. accepting so many of its fleeing nationals. Appropriately enough it was the South African newspaper *Citizen* that tweaked the presumed hypocrisy of U.S. immigration policy, pointing out that the acceptance of many South Africans of European heritage came while the country was expelling "illegals" from south of the border, a racially tinged policy not unlike Pretoria's.[16]

For a decade beginning in 1961, about 150,000 English-speaking migrants arrived in South Africa, principally from Great Britain—but this only raised old Boer-Briton tensions. Besides, with London acceding to what was to become the European Union, there was stiffer competition from Europe for those seeking to migrate. (Interestingly, Portuguese and Greeks were said to assimilate more readily in South Africa.)[17]

Moving in a like-minded direction was a river of mercenaries apparently incapable of being dammed. J.C. Harrison of London's "Rhodesian Department" found that by late 1976 there were "350 to 400" U.S. mercenaries in Rhodesia.[18] H.M.S. Reid of London's Central and Southern Africa Department saw this as nothing new; "recruitment of mercenaries for service in the South African armed forces has probably been going on rather quietly for a long time...."[19] Major Ronald Gatewood of the U.S., stationed at the Pretoria legation, might have been able to shed light on this matter but by 1978 he barely escaped intact when his private plane caught fire, leaving a total wreck.[20]

By early 1977 one source estimated that 30% of Rhodesia's forces had roots in the U.S., U.K., or South Africa (and Australia could have been added too).[21] A report by the Quakers from roughly 1977 found "600-800 U.S. mercenaries in Rhodesia...."[22] By 1978 the Quakers

15. *Washington Post*, 3 June 1978.

16. *Citizen* [South Africa], 14 June 1977.

17. *Guardian* [U.K.], 4 November 1972.

18. Report, 30 November 1976, FCO36/1876, *NAUK-London*.

19. Report, 23 November 1976, FCO36/1876.

20. *Sunday Times* [South Africa], 13 August 1978.

21. *Africa News* [U.S.], 24 January 1977.

22. Report, circa 1977, PED PROGRAM RESOURCES SOUTHERN AFRICA ADMIN-PROJECTS-SA STUDY TOUR FWCC SEMINAR & MEETING, *AFSC*.

received a handwritten report from Mozambique that exclaimed that there were "2000!" U.S. mercenaries in Rhodesia, "mostly Vietnam Vets, unemployed and not regarded as war heroes at home." They were "highly paid to come and kill...."[23] More conservatively, the NAACP estimated in 1978 that "700 American volunteers—all of whom are white—are serving in the Rhodesian army." They demanded that Washington "apply...the law of conspiracy to those who participate in the recruitment of Americans for the Rhodesian army,"[24] though this may have been too much to ask of the Carter regime, already in retreat from its early promise.

Whatever the number, by the Summer of 1977, well into the advent of a Carter regime elected with significant Afro-American support, the progressive attorney Lennox Hinds spoke authoritatively of the "complicity of the U.S. State Department and Justice Department in the recruitment of mercenaries."[25] Contemporaneously, the British legation in the U.S. had a similar concern about U.S. lassitude, doubting if any prosecutions of mercenary recruiters would emerge.[26] As often happened in the mercantile republic, money was at play. The journalist Robin Wright found by early 1977 that Robert "Bob" Brown, a prime recruiter of fighters, was "making a small fortune" in doing so.[27] In late 1976 Brown could be found in Salisbury, making his second visit since 1974.[28] There he may have encountered a fellow U.S. national, Frank Sweeney, who declared that Rhodesia was then crawling with mercenaries who were "racialists as I am."[29] Some of these warriors for hire, brimming with global experience in terror, then moved on to Nicaragua where they proved handy in destabilizing the Sandinista government in the 1980s.[30]

Other mercenaries were not as mobile. This included a number who were captured in Angola and were visited by U.S. Senator George McGovern in 1978. George Gause was born in Florida in

---

23. "Letter from Mozambique," 15 September 1978, ID ADMINISTRATION AFRICA PROGRAMS SOUTHERN MOZAMBIQUE-MEDICAL PROG., *AFSC*.

24. NAACP Task Force on Africa: Report and Recommendations, 1978, Box 35, *Washington Office on Africa Papers*.

25. Lennox Hinds to Carol Bernstein Ferry and Ping Ferry, 2 August 1977, Box 14, *Bernstein Ferry Papers*.

26. R.J.S. Muir to J.C. Harrison, 4 January 1977, FCO36/2064, *NAUK-London*.

27. *Washington Post*, 3 January 1977. See Robert K. Brown, *I Am a Soldier of Fortune: Dancing with Devils*, Philadelphia: Casemate, 2013.

28. *Sunday Mail*, FCO36/1876, *NAUK-London*.

29. *Johannesburg Star*, 20 July 1976.

30. Sam Hall, *Counter-Terrorist*, New York: Donald Fine, 1987.

1928 and had resided in North Dakota but had lived "on and off since 1968," in Angola he told the legislator. "It was a contract for Cabinda Gulf" that brought him there. He left in 1971 and returned, cohabitating with a young woman of Vietnamese origin who was born in Angola. He bought a farm and seemed to be doing well—but then the MPLA government nationalized his property and he chafed at having to work for them. In 1975 he was jailed, he claimed, "for the reason that I had a hunting rifle. And a revolver. Without a license." Why? "We have a lot of…boa constrictors and a lot of wild animals," that had to be slaughtered and "I do some hunting too…." "I can't say that I've been treated badly" in prison, he told McGovern, though there were 36 others in his cell with him. He confessed to the Senator, "you're the first visitor I've had in 18 months…." He and a fellow mercenary were in "very good shape," absorbing "no abuse. Some of them are good friends," meaning the guards.

Senator McGovern was told otherwise that Gause's Argentina-born comrade Gustavo Grillo was hit with gunfire in battle and captured on 13 February 1976 and then was tried in June, receiving a 30-year sentence. "Technically nobody recruited me," he said. "I'm the one that made the contact with David Bufkin," who worked "indirectly…for the CIA…." "I came over on my interests," he conceded. "Then finally I made contact with Holden Roberto," ACOA's friend. "I'm very passionate for adventure," he said by way of explaining his plight—"and of course money," since he was paid a "few thousand dollars a month"—though he was only "3 days in combat" before being captured. It was a "very tense ambush. There were only 12 of us against… maybe a battalion…." He had served "4 years in the United States Marine Corps" in Vietnam. "As a combat soldier?" queried McGovern; "nonstop" was his terse reply. His immigration status was murky, claiming that his parents were "American citizens," though doubt persisted. "Why didn't you leave when the May uprising occurred in '77," asked the inquisitive McGovern, since "they opened the doors of the prison." Simple, he said, "we were put against the wall to be shot," i.e. "by the people that came in here on the 27th," meaning "the fractionists." He was "lucky the Cubans were here in time" to rescue the grateful inmate. "The Cubans came just in time to prevent you from being executed?" asked McGovern. "Yes" was the response. The unlucky Daniel Gearhart was executed; "he was with me at the ambush," said Grillo. Grillo had been in Angola for three years as of 1978, though "living 3 years in here is like 6 or 9 years…." The New Jersey resident said, "I love the United States." The fact that he had spent time in Cuba, apparently on behalf of the CIA, raised eyebrows further and complicated his release.

Another prisoner, Gary Acker, was afflicted with malaria and various "skin diseases." Recruited by Bufkin from Fresno, he jumped at the opportunity to earn a hefty $2500 monthly. He departed for Angola from Kinshasa in what he described as a Roberto-sponsored venture. "We have a lot of Vietnam veterans," he said of his fellow soldiers of fortune, who came from a "lot of army camps." Since veterans "had the highest unemployment rate" in the U.S., this was incentive to take his chances in Africa.[31]

Arriving in Angola in February 1981, Jennifer Davis of ACOA met a deserter, Jose Ricardo Belmondo, who fought with the apartheid invaders. He told her that his commander was "Colonel Carpenter the man who in 1975 led some of the South African forces into Angola and was later responsible for setting up the Buffalo Battalion....[He] was an American veteran who had fought in Zaire and Vietnam....A light machine gun, which had belonged to a South African pilot shot down over Angola was of U.S. origin, stamped American International Corporation, SCL, Utah...."[32]

The influx of U.S. mercenaries to Southern Africa was hardly a secret or even required subterfuge. In a "confidential" report, a London official said, "there is no way in which HMG [Her Majesty's Government] can control the activities of Major Lamprecht in Rhodesia or of his contacts in the United States,"[33] where he reaped a huge bounty of mercenaries. London knew that these Euro-Americans were "flying helicopters and fighter planes" and "participating in special missions along the Mozambique border;" specialized positions hard to fill. Invariably they were embittered veterans of the failed war in Vietnam, thirsting for revenge against real and imagined Communists.[34]

In the summer of 1976 the BBC in London interviewed one from this group in Rhodesia who confided that the "idea of fighting in the American [military] that's populated with...it's made up with Black [soldiers] didn't appeal to me at all" since, he countered, "I have a strong affinity with European culture...." The BBC host then said, "some eighty veterans have reportedly just joined the Rhodesian army and at the Fort McPherson Officers' Club in Atlanta, Georgia,

---

31. Interviews, 13 December 1978, Box 648, *George McGovern Papers, Princeton University-New Jersey.*

32. Jennifer Davis, "Report on a Visit to Angola (February 1-10, 1981), ID AFRICA ADMINISTRATION....SOUTH S AFR IAP S AFR REP TAMAPSA, *AFSC.*

33. "Confidential" report from P.J. Barlow, 21 July 1976, FCO65/1767.

34. Undated article by Robin Moore, FCO36/2064, *NAUK-London.*

Bob Brown tried to persuade serving American officers to follow them...." There were "hundreds of American gun publications" that carried "ads for mercenaries and direct recruitment of mercenaries." Stunningly, few of the mercenaries who responded to recruitment mentioned money, suggesting that racist ideology was the driving concern.[35]

In a perhaps unrelated development, in 1977 the highest court in New York state upheld the publishing of advertisements for jobs in South Africa.[36] U.S. courts, which had been touted by NAACP leaders as the guarantor of equality, proved to be conspicuously supportive of Pretoria's tenuous claims during the apartheid era. Consider, for example, an earlier case decided in favor of the blatantly discriminatory South African Airways, which regularly landed its planes in U.S. airports.[37] By 1982 the unavoidable happened: two men pled guilty in Houston after seeking to transport arms to South Africa via this airline, including 790 MA6 automatic rifles, 350 shorter versions of this weapon, 100 grenade launchers, and more. The accused, in what was then billed as the largest illegal arms cache confiscated in the U.S. in recent memory, were both British.[38] Congressman Mickey Leland of the Black Caucus sought to bar the airline from landing in Texas—before perishing in a plane crash in Ethiopia.[39]

In May 1976 a London journalist poking around "70 yards from the White House.... counted six sporting magazines" in local bookstores "carrying advertisements for 'able bodied fighting men' for service in Rhodesia." This, he said, represented a lack of "American sympathy for overturning white rule in Africa," a fact reflected in Ronald Reagan's surprising challenge to Gerald Ford deploying a manipulative invocation of African issues. Like others he was taken aback since there was "no move in Washington to enforce [the] law" against recruiting mercenaries.[40]

Reagan distinguished himself successfully from his opponent Ford by portraying the incumbent as unable to stand up effectively to Africans and Communists, a devastating one-two punch. By May 1976 Vice President Nelson A. Rockefeller, who knew something about demagogy, was appalled. "His concerns about Angola were

---

35. Transcript, 19 July 1976, FCO65/1767, *NAUK-London*.

36. *New York Times*, 11 February 1977.

37. Clipping, 10 November 1970, Box 244, *Leroy Walker Africa News Service Archive*.

38. *Houston Chronicle*, 18 May 1982. See also *Financial Times*, 14 May 1981.

39. *Houston Chronicle*, 8 October 1982.

40. *Daily Express*, 7 May 1976.

totally misleading to the American people," he scoffed, saying their effect was "either...due to ignorance or it is due to demagoguery." The "covert action" there was working, claimed the vice-president, before somebody "leaked" the details, leading to congressional circumscribing of the CIA. Sadly, he thought, the CIA's supposedly noble deed was posed falsely as, "did we support the blacks or were we supporting a racist or apartheid white group"—not his preferred framing: foiling Reds. At a press conference at the Biltmore Hotel in Los Angeles, a skeptical journalist captured the fragility of the Ford campaign by asking Rockefeller if his candidate should resign since Reagan was beating him so badly.[41] Robert "Bud" McFarlane, who would coordinate Reagan's foreign policy and was then driven to the brink of suicide as a result of its macabre folly, was at this juncture "truly astonished by the alarming performance of Governor Reagan," referring to "his remarks concerning the possible use of United States forces in Rhodesia" on behalf of Salisbury. His startling comments were marked as "approved by General Scowcroft," President Ford's National Security Advisor.[42]

In an opposing direction, the ANC-SACP alliance was inspired by a late 1970s journey to Vietnam, which provoked alterations in their strategy, leading ultimately to the negotiations and elections down the line.[43] The delegation, which included Slovo, Tambo, Joe Modise, Thabo Mbeki, and Cassius Make, was a watershed on the road to 1994,[44] helping to undergird the efforts to launch a mass uprising against apartheid that would make this system of cruelty ungovernable. Study of Vietnam and its lessons was a staple of the anti-apartheid movement. Even the ideologically flexible Joe Matthews admitted after the dust had cleared in 2000 that "I read a lot about the Vietnamese struggle...."[45] He was not alone.[46]

---

41. Press Conference, 5 May 1976, Box 1, FA 383, Series 15, Speeches, *Nelson A. Rockefeller Vice Presidential Records, Rockefeller Archive Center, Sleepy Hollow, New York*

42. Robert McFarlane to Jon Howe, et.al., no date, Box 9, Series 19, FA 385, Nelson *A. Rockefeller Vice Presidential Foreign Affairs and National Security Records,*

43. Alan Wieder, *Ruth First and Joe Slovo in the War Against Apartheid*, New York: Monthly Review Press, 2013.

44. Luli Callinicos, *Oliver Tambo*, 394, 522.

45. Oral History, Joe Matthews, 2 October 2000, *University of Connecticut-Storrs.*

46. Oral History, Sindiso Gregory Mfenyana, 28 January 2001, *University of Connecticut-Storrs.*

It was well that the South African comrades consulted with experts, for according to Episcopalian activists, there were apartheid "secret agents working in the United States,"[47] a fact confirmed by the South African press.[48] The Episcopalians, one among many religious denominations in the vanguard of anti-apartheid activism, reported that apartheid police officers were arriving in the U.S. to study riot control—a praxis honed in communities from Harlem to Watts during the unrest of the 1960s. These visitors could be found conferring with the delegates at the International Association of Chiefs of Police convention in Los Angeles.[49] It was also the Episcopalians' William Johnston who publicized the report that the U.S. granted almost 1000 visas annually to Pretoria officialdom over five years, which facilitated closer collaboration.[50]

One outlet went a step further and claimed that the CIA was training South African intelligence agents.[51] When in late 1977 H.H. de Villiers of the South African legation in Washington asked his fellow rightist William Rusher of the U.S. for "2000 names" of "influential Conservatives" and "Moderates" in the U.S., it would have been reasonable to infer that he was fishing for more agents to toil in the U.S.[52] Rusher would not have to look far for recruits: in 1977 the popular Alaskan Lieutenant Governor Lowell Thomas, Jr., son of a famous reporter, visited South Africa, where he found Africans were "not ready" to vote,[53] and then asserted that interracial marriage was "against nature."[54] As it turned out, this was not an unusual view for a U.S. elected official, demonstrated when New Hampshire Governor Meldrin Thomson argued strenuously against the prospect of holding elections in what is now Namibia.[55] More respectably, the

47. Press Release from Episcopal Churchmen for South Africa, 8 August 1977, Box 61, *Washington Office on Africa Papers.*

48. *Sunday Times,* 24 July 1977.

49. Press Release from Episcopal Churchmen, 17 September 1977, Box 245, *Leroy Walker Africa News Service Archive.*

50. William Johnston to Don Patterson, Director of South African Affairs-State Department, 29 January 1978, Box 245, *Leroy Walker Africa News Service Archive.*

51. *Weekend World,* 14 August 1977, Box 245, *Leroy Walker Africa News Service Archive.*

52. H.H. de Villiers to William Rusher, 21 December 1977, Box 84, *William Rusher Papers.*

53. *Wall Street Journal,* 27 November 1977.

54. *Durham Morning Herald* [North Carolina], 2 December 1977.

55. *Rand Daily Mail,* 25 January 1978.

besieged Pretoria hired the potent flack Sydney Baron of Chicago to act as their lobbyist.[56]

Perhaps unsurprisingly, it was at this point that James Gilliland, who served almost two decades in the Foreign Ministry of Pretoria, suggested that South Africa should become the 51st U.S. state. A self-described "lifelong Nationalist," he argued that by joining the North American republic, "South Africa would no longer have to fear a Communist onslaught." Sure, it might mean one person-one vote; then again, the rescued European minority would be part of a heavily conservative "white" majority.[57] A few years later, this cuckoo opinion was echoed in the *New York Times*.[58]

This student of U.S. affairs might have agreed with the maunderings of the Rhodesian Eric Campbell, who took heart from the vehement 1970s protests against school desegregation in Boston, as he wrote for the "Rhodesia White People's Party" in Bulawayo.[59] Similarly, South African Broadcasting denounced affirmative action measures to uplift Afro-Americans and women of all ancestries, deriding this delicate mechanism as a "quota system," a position mirrored on the U.S. right. The case of Allan Bakke, a Californian who claimed that he was deprived admission to medical school because of affirmative action, was adopted as a holy crusade in Pretoria.[60] "The circumstances of the Bakke case," it was announced in mid-1978—a case I worked on, incidentally, as a lawyer opposing his interests—"disqualify the American administration as a mentor to race relations and confirm the merit of South Africa's approach."[61]

Even when humans were not moving across borders, capital was. Senator Church of Idaho was thought to be a contender for the White House in 1976, propelled by his confrontations with the CIA and other intelligence agencies over their multiple misdeeds. But by 1977 he was just another backbencher in the shadow of President Carter. It was then that the retired Major General Julius Klein told him about "my good friend Colonel (Dr.) Emmanuel Rosenblat," a "top ten oil expert" who with "his group have invested more than $12 million

---

56. Letter from WOA to Friends in Chicago, 19 December 1978, Box 62, *Washington Office on Africa Papers*.

57. *Sunday Times* [South Africa], 31 July 1977,

58. *New York Times*, 13 August 1985.

59. Eric Campbell, *Rhodesia Today: Race War & Race Suicide*, Liverpool: White Power Publications, no date, *Michigan State University-East Lansing*.

60. South African Broadcasting Corporation Commentary, 4 July 1978, Box 120, *Leroy Walker Africa News Service Archive*.

61. South African Broadcasting Corporation Commentary, 11 July 1978, Box 120, *Leroy Walker Africa News Service Archive*.

in the Etosha Basin" in what is now Namibia. There were "huge oil deposits" sure to attract Idahoans and other U.S. nationals.[62] Near that same time Clifford Robedeaux of the U.S. visited South Africa, scouting for real estate for his clients and himself.[63] These investors had not sensed wholly what a London report was to detail: an oil boycott, said the *London Times* in mid-1978, "could cripple Vorster in two years."[64] Muscat too was in an oil-rich neighborhood and Smith Hempstone, a well-connected conservative and Africa hand, was seeking to help a "friend" with Rhodesian ties get a job in Washington.[65]

Moreover, investors from the U.S. in the South Africa were profiting substantially from their extensive holdings. Charles Engelhard had passed from the scene, but by 1978 like a dead hand from the grave he sought to implant his name on the library at the newly formed Kennedy School at Harvard, leading to stormy anti-apartheid protests.[66] If they had been paying attention, however, the investor class would have sought to adjust their portfolios, since by early 1978, the progressive Hospital Workers Union in New York—for whom I used to provide legal counsel—moved to bar their pension funds from investing in corporations with money in South Africa.[67] Weeks later the United Auto Workers Union followed suit.[68]

This was a kind of sanction against apartheid, a movement that gathered steam in coming years when it was imposed over the firm objection of Ronald Reagan. By 1978 a notorious "sanctions buster" on Pretoria's behalf was jailed in Chicago. Richard Beck was held in a relatively plush prison. The complex was "new," said a Johannesburg reporter, "everyone refers to it as the Holiday Inn," and "Beck has his own bedroom with private dresser." In case there was any doubt, the warden avowed that "he certainly is physically comfortable." Beck enjoyed such comfort after shipping 300,000 rand worth of guns and ammunition to South Africa via Switzerland, disguised as playground equipment. Michigan arms dealer Seymour Freilich was charged alongside him.[69] By mid-1979 this Johannesburg

62. Major General Julius Klein to Senator Church, 16 November 1977, Box 23, *Frank Church Papers*.

63. *Rand Daily Mail*, 24 August 1978.

64. *Sunday Times* [London], 11 June 1978.

65. Smith Hempstone to Anthony Ashworth, 18 May 1979, Box 3, *Kenneth Towsey Papers*.

66. *Sydney Morning Herald*, 23 October 1978.

67. Press Release, 29 January 1978, Box 244, *Leroy Walker Africa News Service Archive*.

68. *Wall Street Journal*, 7 March 1978.

69. *Sunday Times* [South Africa], 17 December 1978.

arms dealer was freed from his comfortable confinement.[70] Minority regimes attracted parasites effortlessly. That same year Louis Steinberg, yet another Chicago fraudster, accused of embezzling millions in what was described as "one of the largest bank frauds in the nation's history" fled to Rhodesia, a nation with which the U.S. had no legitimate extradition treaty.[71] "Everywhere you look in Rhodesia," said a Salisbury journal kept by the regime's man in Washington, "Americans are coming out of the woodwork, carving niches for themselves," e.g. Neville Romain, born in Connecticut but who fought alongside South Africa during World War II. Then he moved to Los Angeles to sell burglar alarms, this after toiling in U.S. counter-espionage, losing a fortune—before arriving in Rhodesia in the late 1970s to work alongside sellout Africans.[72]

More serious still was the 1977 report that despite inflamed anti-apartheid rhetoric in Washington, the U.S. was working with South Africa on a nuclear weapon and was selling uranium stockpiled in Oak Ridge, Tennessee.[73]

The affluent Michigander John McGoff—who knew more than most about the strength of organized labor—called on his "old friend" Gerald Ford to assist him in getting a visa for Admiral Hugo Biermann, Pretoria's Defense chief, to visit the U.S. Connie Mulder, whose surname was soon to be associated with a smelly scandal, had managed to buy a 420-acre retirement estate in the Transvaal on a government salary. He continued to be friendly with the anticommunist McGoff but would find that with the new regime in Washington the press baron would be lucky to escape relatively unscathed.[74] By 1979 it was estimated that Pretoria had poured $11 million into U.S. media via McGoff.[75] Fellow press baron John O'Hara of the conservative *Reader's Digest* was of like mind. By 1978 he was seeking to entice more readers by offering South African Defense bonds as a prize for subscribing.[76]

Buttressing his plan was a commentary from South African Broadcasting stating that it was ludicrous to think that anti-Jim Crow principles had taken root in the U.S. "Racial segregation—uncontrolled,

70. *Rand Daily Mail*, 5 June 1979.
71. *Chicago Tribune*, 24 February 1979.
72. *Illustrated Rhodesia*, 13 October 1977, Box 1, *Kenneth Towsey Papers*.
73. *Christian Science Monitor*, 11 August 1977.
74. *Los Angeles Times*, 19 February 1977.
75. *New York Times*, 20 June 1979.
76. John O'Hara to Tim Smith, Inter-Faith Center for Corporate Responsibility, 19 July 1978, Box 38, *Leroy Walker Africa News Service Archive*.

disordered, demoralizing and destructive—increases," as "fearful whites move to the suburbs...." There was "little wonder the Carter men [sic] suffer a guilt complex...but they should not suppose," it was said obstinately, "they can pass it off on to us."[77]

What had intervened to change minds was the Soweto Uprising, which increased mass mobilization inside South Africa, eventually making the nation incapable of governance and paving the way for the release of political prisoners and negotiations with the regime. Soweto had considerable impact in Africa as a whole. Cheryl Johnson Odim, who was to play a pivotal role in the anti-apartheid movement in Chicago, was matriculating in Nigeria then and recalled "people were talking about it.... People were just up in arms...."[78] Pretoria was quite sensitive about this revolt. When Ambassador Andrew Young was slated to visit the region in 1977, his Negro colleague Henry Richardson thought that "one of the reasons why the South Africans are so opposed to Andy's visit is the possibility that he will speak to Soweto students."[79] Writing from South Africa, General Walton Walker was beyond furious about Ambassador Young, who he considered a dupe of Communists at best. Young, it was said, was a product of what had become a familiar theme in Pretoria: the U.S. was "paralyzed" over "her guilt about the treatment of her own Negroes," a worrisome trend heightened by "Carter's reliance on the Negro vote," leading to the Young appointment.[80] And Pretoria was determined to demonstrate decisively that "guilt" over maltreatment of Africans was the height of folly.

Whether or not Young was barred, Carter was under pressure to continue hiring high-level Negro officials. His key aide Peter Tarnoff more precisely noted that, there were "two blacks (both State Department employees) among the 97 personnel presently assigned to South Africa," and there was desire in Washington for more but, he said, "South Africa is not a country to which black Americans wish to serve...." Tarnoff also pushed for more "presidential attention to detained black dissidents in South Africa (as has been done in the case of Russian dissidents)," a major concession. In any case,

77. South African Broadcasting Corporation Commentary, 7 June 1977, Box 120, *Leroy Walker Africa News Service Archive.*

78. Oral History, Cheryl Johnson Odim, 4 December 2009, *Columbia College-Chicago.*

79. Henry Richardson to Zbigniew Brzezinski, 12 May 1977, Box 69, *Brzezinski Materials.*

80. General Walton Walker, *The Bear at the Door: The Soviet Threat to the West's Lifeline in Africa,* Sandton [South Africa]: Valiant, 1978, xviii, 119.

he continued, he wanted the "Ambassador or Deputy Chief of Mission to attend all political trials,"[81] meaning more personnel to be assigned and more opportunity for conflict with Pretoria.

Early on, Carter's National Security Council surveyed governmental connections to Pretoria and found that five agencies had "ties which are 'heavy' and 5 have 'very heavy' ties...." "Nearly half of the agencies questioned have ties with South Africa," said Richardson, while "those with heavy ties included" the Civil Aeronautics Board and the Export-Import Bank. Those with "very heavy" ties included the Department of Justice, the Treasury Department, the Pentagon, and the State Department—i.e. heavyweight departments with opportunities ripe to be cultivated in Pretoria.[82] When Henry Richardson of the National Security Council warned in mid-1977 that "Botha may also be trying to go over the head of the USG [Carter],"[83] he was also indicating that Pretoria had powerful cards to play.

Pretoria, in sum, was not simply a client on its knees. "It is worth remembering," said one journalist "that U.S. ferro-alloy producers still can't do without [South African] ores."[84] In the prelude to his election Carter's staff collected material that indicated that South Africa had the "western world's largest holder of reserves and identified resources of manganese ore (93%), vanadium (90%), platinum group metals (89%), chrome ore (84%), gold (64%) and fluorspar (46%) as well as of the andalusite group refractory minerals (21%)."[85] Even if they so desired, Young's—and Carter's—ability to shift U.S. policy toward the sub-region was constrained severely.

Soweto also served to boost the ANC since the organization could accommodate the militant youth fleeing apartheid more easily than their rivals by bringing them to military bases in Angola or training centers in Eastern Europe. The ANC contacted the chapter of the Afro-Asian Peoples Solidarity Organization in East Germany, requesting aid to youth fleeing after the uprising, including tons of powdered milk, soap, toothbrushes, malaria tablets, and penicillin.[86]

81. Memorandum from Peter Tarnoff, 1 February 1978, Box 70, *Brzezinski Materials.*

82. Henry Richardson to Zbigniew Brzezinski, 22 August 1977, Box 71, *Brzezinski Material.*

83. Henry Richardson to David Aaron, 2 June 1977, Box 115, *NSC Staff Material, North/South, President Jimmy Carter Presidential Library-Atlanta.*

84. *Financial Mail*, [South Africa], 10 April 1977.

85. Material from South Africa Department of Mines, circa 1976, Box 223. *Stuart Eizenstat Papers.*

86. Memorandum, May 1978, Box 86, Folder 29, Part I, *Lusaka Mission, ANC Records.*

The PAC did not have as much latitude. When youth arrived at their Tanzanian bases, says Afro-American activist Prexy Nesbitt, they were disappointed by the squalor and corruption they found.[87] George Nene recalled that "the ANC engaged us, they took us to a safe house and we [were] given books to read, unlike in the PAC camp where we were given alcohol to drink." From a camp he was transported to the Soviet Union for more training and by 1977 was in Angola—before moving on to Mozambique, then to Swaziland, then to Tanzania. The adept training he received led to his leading the ANC mission in Nigeria by 1988. The PAC was unable to establish a similar infrastructure for training cadre.[88]

Success breeds success, and the ability of the ANC to take advantage of its more extensive global network allowed it to recruit more effectively. The poet and writer Wally Serote emerged from what he termed a "very politicized family;" his "great grandfather had fought against the Afrikaners on the side of the British." But coming to maturity he opposed Marxism "because I said no, this comes from Europe, it has nothing to do with us." This brought him to Black Consciousness, "a movement which really emerged from among students," he said. The South African writer Barney Simon helped him in his move to Columbia University in the 1970s where he encountered "Angela Davis," then a U.S. Communist. "I knew her and had lots of common platforms and discussions with her," facilitated by the fact that the nation was "sharply divided in terms of black and white, because I was more…within black America, than I was within white America." By 1977 he was in Botswana and "integrated into the underground" and "trained militarily"; then it was on to Angola for "upgrading" and "further…upgrading in the Soviet Union…."[89] Serote was yet another mark of the success of the ANC network.

But Nesbitt, a man of the radical left, did not necessarily reflect the obtaining ideology among Negro youth, most notably the many of whom were quite taken with the PAC's "one settler/one bullet" rhetoric. In 1978 David Sibeko, the PAC man in Manhattan, blasted Nesbitt, accusing him of "maliciously" engaging in "slander" against his group with "malign" purposes. Sibeko, who soon was to be slain because of internal conflicts, disputed that his group was wracked

87. Oral History, Prexy Nesbitt, 1 April 2009, *Columbia College-Chicago.*

88. Oral History, George Nene, 9 October 2004, *University of Connecticut-Storrs.*

89. Oral History, Wally Serote, 4 October 2000, *University of Connecticut-Storrs.*

by "tremendous internal political struggles," though he was soon to fall victim to same. Nesbitt, he charged, was seeking to "curry favor with political dregs whose singular achievement in the land of Malcolm X and George Jackson is to front for decadent and bogus parties.... Nesbitt should tell us which PAC officials he met" that purportedly so misled him.[90]

Nesbitt attracted this unwanted invective when he counseled the World Council of Churches to cut off funding to the PAC. "I concluded in my report, in a very detailed and lengthy report, that the PAC was an ineffectual liberation movement and that the World Council should no longer give any money to the PAC, just concentrate on supporting the ANC. That finding," he said later, "and my report, became the subject of a tremendous internal [conflict] with many of the PAC's external supporters taking on the staff of the World Council of Churches, specifically me, for having written this report." This report also brought stiff criticism in Chicago from pro-PAC backers.[91]

In 1977 Henry Isaacs of the PAC leadership revealed this split when he committed the sin of criticizing Chinese policy in Africa—a blunder in the eyes of many of his comrades. He tied himself in knots, arguing that "despite the fact that the FNLA's troops were trained by Chinese instructors," the idea that China backed Holden Roberto's detachments was "pure calumny."[92] By 1978 a PAC gathering in Tanzania, the first there in years, led to the expulsion of seven Central Committee members and a spate of internal turmoil.[93] Isaacs termed this report to be "shoddy journalism" but Sibeko's corpse was suggestive of the real deadliness of this turmoil.[94]

Yes, the PAC had friends in the U.S. It was appreciated when their jailed leader, Sobukwe, was reported to have spoken of the "beauty of America because we represented democracy." Andrew Young compared him favorably to Dr. King and his children, Miliswa and Dini, arrived at Young's home in Atlanta. Anthony Lewis, liberal anticommunist columnist for the *New York Times*, praised Sobukwe's "authentic greatness." But, alas, these men were hardly capable

90. David Sibeko to George Houser, 29 September 1978, Box 81, *ACOARA*.

91. Oral History, Prexy Nesbitt, 1 April 2009, *Columbia College-Chicago*.

92. Henry Issacs, "Southern Africa: Soviet Dominator or Self Determination," 1977, Box 144, *Leroy Walker Africa News Service Archive*.

93. *Guardian* [U.S.], 19 July 1978.

94. Henry Isaacs, Acting Chief Representative and Member of the Central Committee of PAC to "Africa News," 19 July 1978, Box 144, *Leroy Walker Africa News Service Archive*.

of providing the kind of aid that the ANC could obtain in Eastern Europe.[95] Sobukwe's obituary in this august newspaper praised him since he was "staunchly opposed to any attempts by Communists to join" his PAC: "there are no Communists in South Africa," he cracked, "only Communist quacks."[96] It was not only Sobukwe who found a friend in Young. It was the ambassador who "strongly recommended" that Carter meet with Harry Oppenheimer, the foremost South African businessman, described as a "friend of the United States," who "can be a powerful ally…."[97] Soon Mondale was angling for a meeting with this financial behemoth. But he was counseled by staff not to over-estimate Oppenheimer's influence; he may have been the "nearest thing to an effective white opposition to the Nationalist Party" but it was unclear if that counted for much in 1977.[98]

Despite the PAC's popularity in the U.S., the ANC continued to maintain adherents there too. In 1975 Mary Louise Hooper, the long-time ACOA worker, told Ezekiel Mphahlele that she was "still convinced that our ANC is the only instrument we have for fighting oppression in [South Africa], so we must stick to it and be loyal…."[99]

Like one hand washing another, Soweto also boosted anti-apartheid organizing in the U.S., which led to more corporations divesting from apartheid, contributing to the crisis in Pretoria. With atypical reserve, the ANC emissary in Manhattan, Thami Mhlambiso, said at the time that the "Soweto Uprising helped to boost the moral[e] of many of our activists in America…."[100] In June 1976, as the embers in Soweto were still burning, the left-wing *Guardian* in New York City reported on a Soweto-inspired demonstration of hundreds occurring in Times Square, in the throbbing heart of Manhattan. A member of the National Conference of Black Lawyers, headquartered in Harlem, identified as "Jerry Horne" was quoted as stating that "Kissinger was shaking hands with Spinola of Portugal, then Pinochet of Chile and now Vorster…. IBM, Coca-Cola and

---

95. Benjamin Pogrund *How Can a Man Die Better*, 325, 337.

96. *New York Times*, 28 February 1978.

97. Memorandum from Peter Tarnoff, 30 September 1977, Box 48, *Brzezinski Material*.

98. Christine Dodson to Denis Clift, 11 October 1977, Box 115, *NSA Staff Material, North/South, Jimmy Carter Presidential Library*.

99. Mary Louise Hooper to Ezekiel Mphahlele, 26 February 1975, Box 2, *Mary Louise Hooper Papers*.

100. Thami Mhlambiso to "Comrades," 26 September 1976, Box 14, Folder 24, *Lusaka Mission, ANC Records-Fort Hare University*.

General Electric have their tentacles in South Africa. It's one struggle and one fight—down with apartheid, stop the genocide."[101]

The speaker was making a thinly veiled reference to U.S. imperialism's comeback in Lisbon, a point validated indirectly by the Socialist leader Mario Soares when he appeared in Washington in January 1978. "I grant you that there may be some activities of the CIA in Portugal," he said, as he admitted what could not be denied. To his credit, he lavished praise on Alvaro Cunhal, Portuguese Communist leader, "a man of the greatest personal courage" who "suffered the persecution of the previous regime" when "underground for ten years," not to mention his "ten years in prison, of which six [were] in solitary confinement." Even Soares knew that "events in Angola have very strong repercussions on the domestic situation in Portugal"—and vice versa, insuring the dedicated attention of those busily taking in his words. "In the last two months," for example, "there was the hurried inflow into Portugal of about 400,000 people" from Angola, creating a budgetary burden and fertile soil for the CIA.[102]

By that point, I had arranged the publication of *The Facts on Angola*, a compendium of clippings from the international press on the crisis there that highlighted the perfidy of U.S. imperialism and China. It was advertised in Chicago's *African Agenda*,[103] a reliable source for news that was endorsed by Agostinho Neto, founding father of the new Angola.[104] The journal boasted it was "read by people in the African countries including the African liberation movements and in Europe, Asia, the Middle East, Latin America and the Caribbean...."[105] Harold Rogers, the main force behind *African Agenda*, was well respected within the ANC and SACP, calling Nzo, the Secretary General of the former, "Alf" and speaking of the "many times...spent" with Duma Nokwe.[106]

---

101. *Guardian*, 30 June 1976.

102. Transcript of Mario Soares, 17 January 1978, Box 4, *International Affairs Country Files-AFL-CIO, University of Maryland-College Park.*

103. See ad in *African Agenda*, 5(Number 1, 1976), 16, Box 3, *Chicago Anti-Apartheid Movement Collection, Columbia College-Chicago*: The address given for this booklet—530 West 112th Street, #62 in Manhattan—was my then address.

104. *African Agenda*, 4(Number 2, 1975): 2.

105. *African Agenda*, 3(Number 2, February-March 1974), *Chicago History Museum*.

106. Harold Rogers to "Dear Alf," 2 May 1978, Box 6, Folder 39, *Lusaka Mission, ANC Records*.

More to the point, in sketching the "way forward from Soweto," the SACP warned of the attempt to "weaken the influence" of the ANC by "catchphrases such as 'Black Power,'" still seen as a U.S. import designed for an African minority. "Recently the U.S. State Department announced," said the SACP statement, "that it was preparing scholarship places in the U.S. educational institutions for the hundreds of young militants" pouring out of the country, many of whom made their way to military bases in Angola. U.S. campuses were seen as a diversion from this path, creating a "meeting point between enemy strategy and [Black Power] activities...."[107] In a virtuous circle, the ANC, which was receiving assistance from the socialist bloc, requested aid for Rogers' ventures. "He is a close friend of ANC," said Administrative Secretary, Joe Nhlanhla, "member of the party in the USA. He accompanied Angela Davis to Africa some years back."[108]

Thus, by 1978 Francis Meli, an ANC leader in Lusaka, was telling a "dear comrade" that "delivery of 'Sechaba' [ANC periodical] from Berlin," where it was printed, had been delayed. "The diplomatic bag is not always the quickest way" to ship it "and we suggest that Berlin send us a ticket so that we can take it there ourselves each month," rather than rely upon GDR diplomats. There was then a "paper shortage" in Berlin, meaning that "we produce 20,000" issues "which is not sufficient for our propaganda needs...."[109] Still, the ANC could rely upon Berlin in a way that the PAC could not, to the detriment of the latter.

That same year, Moscow's legation in Lusaka was informed that Tambo's "and his wife's holiday in the USSR," set to coincide with the Communist Party congress, should be extended.[110] Black Sea resorts were a frequent haunt of ANC and SACP leaders and dwarfed the kinds of locale available to PAC cadre.

Another telling sign came that same year when SACP leader Moses Kotane died in Moscow. He served as "Treasurer General" of the ANC and "General Secretary" of the SACP, with his ties in Eastern Europe proving to be valuable in his ANC post. He was elected

---

107. "The Way Forward from Soweto," Report by Plenary of Central Committee of SACP, April 1977, in *South African Communists Speak*, 417-432, 426.

108. Joe Nhalalanhla to Reddy Mazimba, 13 June 1978, Box 6, Folder 59, *Lusaka Mission, ANC Records*.

109. Francis Meli to "Dear Comrade," 28 April 1978, Reel 7, *Oliver Tambo Papers*.

110. Alfred Nzo to Anatoli Melnikov, 21 July 1978, Box 88, Folder 51, Part II, *Lusaka Mission, ANC Records*.

as General Secretary in 1939 and a member of the National Executive Committee of the ANC by 1946. He travelled to Moscow for training in 1931 and again in 1935. With Mandela, he was a founding member of the ANC's armed wing and was therefore exiled in 1963.[111] The wider point is that the ANC's growing strength was shaped by its external ties, many of which the PAC simply did not enjoy.

But the ANC continued to have difficulty in recruiting able personnel to staff what should been a plum post in Manhattan, near the United Nations and a buzzing Harlem alike. As early as 1972, the ANC delegate in New York sought to take advantage of the presence of substantial numbers of residents there with roots in the Caribbean by seeking to entice these small nations to aid the ANC, something that Jamaica had been doing in any case.[112] Considering that Antigua had become a base for the shipment of shotguns and other arms to South Africa, this thrust in the Caribbean was even more advisable.[113] There was an offer to assist from Trinidad too but Thami Mhlambiso found that "different excuses are now being given" for reneging, meaning a "very tough campaign here and we should not hope for any financial support to come for quite some time. We seem also to be targets of people who come here and collect funds" on false pretenses.[114] Then the typewriter was stolen from their office, "so things have been very hard," he claimed.[115]

The ANC headquarters in Lusaka was not so sure about his protestations, however. Just before Carter was elected president, Mhlambiso, the delegate at this important Manhattan address, was summoned to Zambia by the ANC leadership to discuss various sensitive matters, including "my association with Roy Innis," the notorious recruiter of Negro mercenaries to fight in Angola. "Lack of funds" was the root problem the envoy countered, though the "National Council of Churches" had "helped to pay our rent…." Houser of the ACOA offered to help but only after "long and painful lectures"—but then the goateed activist would scurry to those same churches that were funding the ANC and boast of the funding his

111. Obituary, 25 May 1978, Reel 7, *Oliver Tambo Papers*.

112. Monique Bedasse, *Jah Kingdom: Rastafairans, Tanzania and the Pan-Africanism in the Age of Decolonization*, Chapel Hill: University of North Carolina Press, 2017.

113. Clipping, 27 December 1978, Box 245, *Leroy Walker Africa News Service Archive*.

114. Thami Mhlambiso to Alfred Nzo, 9 November 1972, Box 13, Folder 35, *Lusaka Mission*.

115. Thami Mhlambiso to Mendi Msimang, 22 February 1973, Box 13, Folder 35, *Lusaka Mission*.

organization was providing the ANC, seeking money to make up the alleged shortfall. The "SWAPO representative has similar experiences," he asserted—but at least they had the advantage of funding from the U.N. Council on Namibia. He also "discussed this" with Tony Monteiro, the point man on Africa for U.S. Communists, and got "numerous promises from him," most unmet.

His wrath rising, he declared that "none of the so-called support groups have any business to complain about our ineffectiveness," a call that had reached Lusaka. It was "an eye-opener" to find that these groups "do not really mean well…." This meant, he said angrily, that he and his office were "dependent upon the availability of funds from my wife who is working as a Nurse!" Furiously, he said, "I have lacked funds for bus fare." Yes, he had gotten $3000 from the "Defense and Aid Fund" in London after he had "received a court order" mandating his "eviction," but that barely kept his head above water.

He praised the ANC folks in Philadelphia—though "only two in number"—and Boston too ("about 25 members"). California was better endowed but going there was like travelling to London in its onerousness and resultant jet lag. "Some of the traditional support groups," as the ACOA example indicated, "saw us as a threat to their own survival" and were unhelpful. There were "rumblings of discontent," from all sides, he found. Gladstone Ntlabati, who Mary Louise Hooper had renounced, "posed" many "difficulties" still. Thus, despite obvious advantages globally, the PAC found a "decided preference" in the U.S. "American officials and some individuals would like to have the ANC smashed," not to mention certain U.S. Negroes too. "If the ANC is destroyed it will be an easy step to crush the PAC or even if they do not crush the PAC, they [are] assured that by smashing the ANC, the Soviet Union of Communist influence will be kept at bay as far as South Africa is concerned…."

Turning to the basis for his being summoned to Zambia, Mhlambiso detailed how after the Soweto Uprising, there was a march from "our office" to the U.N. Monteiro and Stokely Carmichael, Black Power eminence, both spoke. 500 were amassed, causing Mhlambiso to assert haughtily, "how then do people come to allege that I work with Savimbi?"—though Carmichael's presence would have raised flags about the turn of so many Black Power figures away from the MPLA. What happened was that Innis' sister-in-law offered her home as a venue for the ANC to raise funds with allies from Moscow, Tunis, Accra, and Mbabane. Monteiro was present, which should have reassured the doubters, though it turned out that the venue happened to be Innis' home. This was in October 1975, just as Innis had begun to recruit mercenaries. Perhaps sensing the frailty of his position, Mhlambiso turned on Monteiro and his group, NAIMSAL (a group that I worked for too), charging that the campaign to expel South Africa from the U.N. was conducted in a unilateral fashion. Then in early 1976 Monteiro headed to Luanda, where the then Communist was accused of repeating this tawdry story of Innis, he thought. "How strange at times mankind can behave," he philosophized.

Mhlambiso was surely worthy of criticism, but he noted—with a degree of accuracy that was difficult for some comrades to comprehend—that the ANC's problem in the U.S. was that "we have a reputation of being 'integrationists'...a terrible label in the U.S.," at least among a sector of militant Afro-Americans. Duma Nokwe had arrived in Manhattan with a "South African white woman," a faux pas. The ANC could not "afford the luxury of being seen with South African white women—militant or not, especially at this time that we are accused of being led by whites...." When "Comrade Nokwe collapsed and was in hospital" with the presence of his companion, matters were complicated unduly.

But he undercut his case by assailing the respected economist Sean Gervasi as "ultra-leftist...not so reputable.... Who at one time was [purporting] to be an advisor to ANC & ZAPU, a man who was alleging that he was advisor to President Kaunda. All lies of course." Then he turned on fellow ANC member Johnstone Mfanafuthi Makhathini, who had served the group competently in Algeria, and Ben Magubane, a preeminent South African scholar with deep roots in Los Angeles. Magubane, Mhlambiso said, was "spreading stories that I work with the CIA. They have gone on to implicate Monteiro in the schemes."

Mhlambiso may have assured the Lusaka comrades by pointing to his "serious discussion" with "Comrade Henry Winston," the Afro-American chair of the U.S. Communist Party who was the moving force behind Monteiro's NAIMSAL. SACP leaders may have been pleased to read his assertion that "for our purposes there is [no] support group whose loyalty and dedication to the ANC can... surpass that of the Communist Party, USA," though in a nation reeking with anticommunism this may have been a dubious distinction. "I challenge anyone to deny this," he said. He undercut his case and perhaps assured that he would be redeployed elsewhere by attacking ANC leader Nzo as possessing low energy.

Mhlambiso did not directly respond to the explosive charge that he was all too close to 8 recent expellees from the ANC. Instead he threw himself on the mercy of those who were judging him, wailing that "I have given the best part of my youth to this organization and I intend to go on doing so." But the fact that he almost "exchanged blows" with a comrade on a recent visit to Dar sealed his fate, and soon he was evicted from Manhattan altogether.[116]

One point Mhlambiso made in his extraordinarily lengthy missive was undeniable It was confirmed by K.W. Kgositsile in a message to Nzo that there was "a lot of tension between Comrades Mhlambiso and Makhathini....They cannot work together"—and the arrival of the latter in Manhattan mandated the departure of the former.[117] "This problem needs our immediate attention," said an ANC member in New York, since it was "important that Comrade Thami is made to feel and accept that his removal from this position is an ordinary transfer and not a demotion or being discredited," in order to "ease the tensions that existed." He "reportedly fails to attend important meetings.... This is the general complaint....This of course is taken advantage of by the PAC...."[118]

As tensions climbed in Pretoria and Washington alike, driven in part by the crisis in Angola, conflicts accelerated accordingly in the U.S. more broadly. In 1977 at the University of North Carolina-Chapel Hill (where I was to teach two decades later) the ANC's Makhathini and the PAC's soon-to-be-slain David Sibeko clashed sharply in what almost exceeded a verbal scrap.[119] This fracas occurred in the context of intensely bitter relations between the two groups, evidenced by the denunciatory statement on the PAC submitted by the ANC at an OAU meeting in Dar in 1978.[120] By that point, a fratricidal conflict beset the PAC, contributing to an attempted palace coup in Dar in November 1977.[121]

By early 1978 it was left to the Swedish Social Democrat Bernt Carlsson to lecture Sibeko (in a message he shared with Tambo). The ANC, he said, was founded in 1912 "five years before the Bolshevik Revolution," and was "not set up by the Soviet Union for the benefit

---

116. Thami Mhlambiso to "Comrades," 26 September 1976, Box 14, Folder 24, *Lusaka Mission, ANC Records*.

117. K.W. Kgositsile to "Comrade Alf," 21 July 1977, Box 6, Folder 39, *Lusaka Mission, ANC Records*.

118. Letter to "Dear Comrades", 26 November [year unclear], Box 6, Folder 39, Part II, *Lusaka Mission*.

119. "The Diplomatic Report," 12(Number 135, 20 November 1977), Box 14, Folder 24, *Lusaka Mission*.

120. ANC Statement on PAC, June 1978, Box 16, Folder 69, *Lusaka Mission*.

121. Statement by T.M.l Ntantala, Deputy Chair of Central Committee of PAC, circa 1978, Box 16, Folder 69, *Lusaka Mission*.

of the Russians as the PAC apparently now claims...." "With regret," this diplomat reminded Sibeko that "you have not felt it necessary to contact the Socialist International before now."[122] Sibeko, then serving as Director of Foreign Affairs of the PAC, told the U.N. that the writings of Du Bois "played a significant role in shaping the political thinking" of his organization, but he was apparently unaware of the late leader's solidarity with the ANC and friendliness toward Moscow.[123]

Having lived in Chapel Hill, I can attest that the PAC would have had more supporters there. The group's line was much more in tune with the Black Power sentiment that gripped so many Afro-Americans. The PAC also had an ally just across the border in what was to become Zimbabwe. In 1978 a writer for ZANU, corresponding from Chimoio, Mozambique, attacked détente between Moscow and Washington—which would have pleased Ronald Reagan—terming it an "un-Marxist attempt" that was "typical of revisionist tendencies who are afraid of war and turn liberal." It was comparable, the writer said, to the discredited "détente" that Pretoria had sought to effectuate with Lusaka, which—of course—was not the same as relaxation of tensions between two social systems armed to the teeth with nuclear weapons and clashing dangerously then in neighboring Angola.[124]

By May 1978 the ANC had consulted with Prexy Nesbitt of Chicago who was also close to FRELIMO. There was a "lengthy discussion" about the "ineffectiveness of the organization in the USA." The Chicagoan was candid in stating that the PAC and some Black Consciousness Movement elements "were stealing the show in the United States at the expense of the ANC," an opinion given credence by the judgment that "Mr. Nesbitt appeared to be a genuine man," with his analysis of Mhlambiso as evidence. Nesbitt told the comrades what they should have known: "in America today," he said, "the Black community is divided on ideological lines and that in some American [colleges]...more white students [were] involved in campaigns aimed at the total isolation of South Africa than Afro-Americans.... Most Americans have never heard of the Freedom Charter, and let alone of our official organ, 'Sechaba'...." Nesbitt was "disturbed to

122. Bernt Carlsson to David Sibeko, 20 January 1978, Reel 19, *Oliver Tambo Papers.*

123. Remarks by David Sibeko, 23 February 1978, *E.S. Reddy Collection, Schomburg Center, New York Public Library.*

124. "Chitepo Bulletin," 30 September 1978, Box 89, Folder 58, Part II, *Lusaka Mission, ANC Records.*

hear that we had invited" boxer Muhammad Ali to various events since "Ali is unpopular in certain American circles because...he had agreed to fight in [the notorious Bantustan] Bophuthatswana...and only retracted after pressure had been brought to bear...."[125]

* * *

In previous years Pretoria had objected to a newly enlightened Washington seeking to send Negro diplomats to South Africa. The appointment of former aide to Dr. King, Andrew Young, to be a major emissary abroad was bound to create waves. Early on the United Church of Christ hailed the "recent appointment of a fellow UCC minister, the Reverend Andrew Young," prompting the denomination to announce "plans to mobilize Black Americans and others of goodwill to support vigorously the liberation struggle in Southern Africa...."[126] The hostile response by Pretoria to Young's appointment may have led Young's fellow Negro Henry Richardson, then on the White House staff, to argue for "non-discrimination against Andy Young." "If the press concludes that the United States backed off and condoned South Africa's rejection" of him, the unavoidable deduction would be that Washington "is permitting South African racial discrimination" to guide the U.S. This would anger "Afro-Americans, the Frontline States," meaning Tanzania, Zambia, etc., "and the Patriotic Front" of soon to be independent Zimbabwe.[127]

Pretoria's worst fears about Ambassador Young may have been confirmed when shortly after entering office he proclaimed that an "Africa war would start one [in the] U.S.," an opinion garnished by his protocol-breaking description of fellow public servants Nixon, Ford, and Kissinger as "racists."[128]

Ambassador Young was tallying a lengthening list of antagonists, which guaranteed his tenure would be limited. It was not just his provocative statements, it was the very presence of a man of African descent intervening on global matters, a sensitive issue historically whose strategic importance was not well understood in Washington. Ambassador Young did little to dissuade his detractors when he appeared at the United Nations in early 1978, praising Du Bois,

---

125. Minutes of Meeting, 23 May 1978, Box 44, Folder 8, Part II, *Lusaka Mission*.

126. Press Release, 7 February 1977, Box 55, Series II, *ACOARA*.

127. Henry Richardson to Zbigniew Brzezinski, 12 May 1977, Box 69, *Brzezinski Material*.

128. *New York Times*, 6 July 1977.

then dead for 15 years but whose legacy lived on. "As a young man growing up in our native South," he said, "I heard almost nothing of W.E.B. Du Bois and when I heard of him and wanted to buy his books, I found it extremely difficult to find any writings of [his] in an American bookstand." After unmasking U.S. "freedom of expression" with this challenge to basic U.S. propagandistic cant, he compared Dixie to "neo-colonialism" in Africa.[129]

This was the atmosphere when the apartheid leadership met with Vice President Walter Mondale and his delegation in Europe in the early Spring of 1977. Exhibiting the familial ties that had linked Pretoria and Washington for generations, White House aide Stuart Eizenstat spread the word that "a cousin of mine who lives in South Africa had been approached by Dr. Connie Mulder," soon to be ensnared in a major influence peddling scandal, "with a request that an early *nonpublic*_meeting be arranged in Washington with you," speaking of Brzezinski, because of the impending downturn in bilateral relations.[130] [emphasis original]

Seemingly unaware of the rudimentary political dynamic, Prime Minister Vorster whiningly responded to President Carter, "why must we confront one another…why must we quarrel with each other?" Apparently not well-briefed, the apartheid leader did not understand that Carter had been elected in part because of a significant turnout by Afro-American voters and could not altogether ignore their revulsion at the continued existence of state-sanctioned racism. Perhaps he was simply stalling, trying to wait out Carter, knowing that the friendlier Reagan loomed in the background. Thus, Vorster threw a curveball at the U.S. president, telling him that "the demands of time and the grave magnitude of the issues involved in the search for peace make the use of normal diplomatic channels inappropriate."[131] Maybe he thought he could employ his nonexistent charm to wrong-foot Carter.

Vorster should not have been surprised by the chilliness of this meeting, given the sizeable sums Pretoria had spent in Washington.[132] Brand Fourie, for example, had been a diplomat for 38 of his

---

129. Remarks by Andrew Young, 23 February 1978, *E.S. Reddy Collection, Schomburg Center, New York Public Library*: In the same collection, see also

130. Stuart Eizenstat to Zbigniew Brzezinski, 12 April 1977, Box 14, *Brzezinski Material.*

131. Prime Minister Vorster to President Carter, 23 March 1977, Box 14, *Brzezinski Material.*

132. See early 1977 letters between Carter and Vorster, Box 18, *Brzezinski Material.*

61 years by the time he started meeting with Carter regime officialdom in 1977. Possessing a degree from New York University, he was described as "friendly toward American officials…."[133] Marthinius Steyn of the Orange Free State, Administrator General of what was to become Namibia, had served during World War II under the aegis of U.S. General Mark Clark.[134]

Pretoria may not have been so optimistic if they'd had access to what Mondale was telling Carter. He flatly rejected Nixon's "sole objective of keeping the Soviets out" of the region. "This led the South Africans—the key actors in the area—to believe that we cared little about *apartheid* and that any solution that kept the Russians at bay would be acceptable…." [emphasis original] "The purpose of my meeting with Vorster would be to convey a different message." Echoing Kissinger's Angola-induced hysteria, the Vice President declaimed, "we are concerned of the growing possibility of a transcontinental race war in Southern Africa that would radicalize black Africans, open the door to Soviet and Cuban penetration"—and, he could have added, potentially jeopardize U.S. investments in the sub-region. Understatedly, he said, if his scenario were to materialize "there could be adverse political consequences in many other countries, including our own…." He boldly declared that "this will be the first time such a message will have been delivered to South Africa" and "it is a message that will profoundly change the nature of our relationship."[135]

The May 1977 meeting between the two in Vienna did not go well. Vorster took umbrage when he thought that the Vice President was seeking to equate Afro-Americans with the Africans in his nation. The latter were "separate nations" he contended hotly.[136] South African Broadcasting was enraged. Didn't Mondale say in 1971 that "America was coming to resemble South Africa. America's 'reserves' and Bantustans he said were the ghettoes of the inner cities, 'and our apartheid,' he went on, 'is all the more disgusting for being insidious and unproclaimed [sic]…?" Getting personal, the sword was twisted in Carter, who was said to have "suffered a guilt complex because of his slowness in rallying to the cause of racial justice in the American

133. "Your Meeting with Brand Fourie, Friday, November 11," 1977, Box 70. *Brzezinski Material.*

134. Memorandum from State Department, July 1977, Box 48, *Brzezinski Material.*

135. Vice President Mondale to President Carter, 8 April 1977, Box 14, *Brzezinski Material.*

136. *Sydney Morning Herald*, 21 May 1977.

South and...now he was endeavoring to compensate by crusading for black rights in South Africa...." How dare Mondale and Carter seek to "compensate for the failure of America's race policies" by attacking Pretoria.[137] Again and again, SABC beat the drum about the "guilt factor in Washington." In the midst of praising their new best friend, Senator Daniel Patrick Moynihan of New York, who had demonized the Negro family generally and Negro women particularly, the Pretoria authorities declared without evidence that those who pushed for one person/one vote were driven by guilt.[138]

By late 1977 Pretoria was again considering what it had done in 1975: expelling CIA spies.[139] By 1978 Pretoria may have had a premonition of what Mondale meant. That year William Rourke Jordan, a U.S. national resident in South Africa since 1975, was arrested on charges of possessing illegal firearms. He was said to be a former Brigadier General in the U.S. Marines but was nonetheless found guilty and deported. The pro-apartheid U.S. analyst Aida Parker claimed that he was a CIA cover operative who was close to Henrik van den Bergh, one of Pretoria's most trusted intelligence and police operatives. It was becoming difficult to figure out where Washington's remit began, and Pretoria's ended. The International Freedom Foundation in Washington was effectively run from Johannesburg and had been initiated in the first instance by Russell Crystal, a militant South African anticommunist of the sort that became fashionable in the U.S. by November 1980. Jonathan Pollard, a U.S. spy who turned over his nation's most closely held secrets to Israel, was quite close to a college friend who was a senior South African intelligence officer, leading the CIA to believe that much of what he revealed to Israel was instantaneously handed over to Pretoria. These included details of U.S. covert operations in South Africa, which the CIA had somehow neglected to coordinate with Pretoria.[140] In sum, the advent of Carter led to a vicious counterattack by Pretoria that was to prepare the path for the rise of Reagan.

These vignettes were also suggestive of the presumed reach of the CIA, whose specter—if not reality—was feared by all sides. In about 1978 Anna Tekere, thought to be a Zimbabwean patriot, was accused

137. South African Broadcasting Commentary, 5 July 1977, Box 120, *Leroy Walker Africa News Service Archive*.

138. South African Broadcasting Commentary, 4 June 1977, Box 120, *Leroy Walker Africa News Service Archive*.

139. *Rand Daily Mail*, 18 October 1977.

140. James Sanders, *Apartheid's Friends: The Rise and Fall of South Africa's Secret Service*, London: John Murray, 2000, 126, 189, 316.

of being "sent out by the CIA...." She was "on the payroll of the CIA contracted between the CIA and herself in 1975 while she was in America," when she was "known by her maiden name as Miss Anne Mejeni...." (Edgar Tekere was a rival of ZANU leader Robert Mugabe, to whom the undated letter was addressed). Citing the French intellectual Regis Debray, it was said that "in ZANU...our leadership purports to be a Democratic Socialist Party guided by Mao's Thought"[141]—which, given the entente between China and the U.S., often placed these two powers—and their intelligence agencies—on the same side.

Despite Mondale's audacious words, by mid-1977 U.S. activists were fighting an attempt to deny aid to Mozambique and Angola. "*Aid* to Mozambique and Angola has been denied without documented evidence of human rights violations," said the Washington Office on Africa, "yet aid to *South Africa* has not been prohibited despite well-documented evidence of torture, deaths in detention, police shootings in the street," and other clear signs of a regime in severe distress.[142] [emphasis original]

Unfortunately, WOA's allies were sending mixed signals. Implicitly reversing the disastrous import of their leader Roy Wilkins' endorsement of the role of U.S. business in South Africa, by 1978 the NAACP demanded a total cessation by the nation's corporate sector from investment in apartheid.[143] The group was contradicted quickly by the erstwhile civil rights leader, U.S. Negro Vernon Jordan, who served on the board of Xerox, who had emulated Wilkins by visiting South Africa and concluded that a pullout would be ill-advised.[144]

Snapping back to right-wing reality, the NAACP then sought to cut a deal with U.S. oil interests, leading the staid columnist William Raspberry to wonder if the group had executed a "sellout." It was suspected that their leader Benjamin Hooks had not read the agreement linking the group ever closer to "Big Oil," with an apartheid-friendly agenda that included "deregulation and wider use of nuclear power," ignoring the "effects" on "low income people." In a remarkable display of the class-biased inefficiency that often characterized the organization, it was speculated that a

141. Undated Letter to Kenneth Kaunda, Robert Mugabe, et.al., Box 89, Folder 58, Part II, *Lusaka Records, ANC Records*.

142. Statement, July 1977, Box 14, *Washington Office on Africa Papers*.

143. *New York Times*, 20 January 1978.

144. *New York Times*, 4 July 1978.

"handful of [Negroes] who work for Big Oil" hijacked the statement unbeknownst to Hooks.[145]

The columnist may have been too generous to the NAACP. A few years after Wilkins' whitewash of the role of U.S. business under apartheid, in 1956 Dr. W. Montague Cobb—another NAACP leader—visited South Africa, where he bonded with Dr. Phillip Tobias of Witwatersrand University and asked him to give a lecture at Howard University in Washington, D.C. which was "very well received." Then near the time of the November 1976 election, Dr. Cobb got a visa and again flew to South Africa to meet with both Botha and Vorster, who was "most courteous." So was Dr. Cobb when he suggested the unsustainable—even bizarre—course of "liberalizing apartheid," not destroying it. It did not help that he repeated this depiction to Vice President Mondale, who might have thought it represented mainstream Negro politics.[146]

As ever, it would be an error to focus unduly on the mishaps of the NAACP in gauging Afro-American activism in Southern Africa. For at the same time, the National Conference of Black Lawyers—which I once led—sought to "study the needs of South African refugees in Angola, Mozambique and Zambia," according to Lennox Hinds, who added accurately that "South Africa has been one of our priority concerns for quite some time."[147]

Part of the general problem with both the anti-apartheid and anti-Jim Crow movements was that they were heavily dependent upon affluent donors rather than a broad membership base. This allowed those like Carol Bernstein Ferry of New York to become kinds of unseen puppet masters.[148] "We don't think you are going in a very good direction," she bluntly told *Southern Africa* magazine in November 1976 when they were struggling to cover the ins-and-outs of the Angola crisis.[149] By 1977 Jennifer Davis, a Southern African exile soon to replace Houser at the ACOA, was editing the magazine "half time at a salary of $5000 a year,"[150] a mere pittance even then,

---

145. *Washington Post*, 27 January 1978.

146. Dr. W. Montague Cobb to Walter Mondale, circa 1976, Box CO-53, *White House Central Files, Subject File, President Jimmy Carter Presidential Library*.

147. Lennox Hinds to Carol Bernstein Ferry and Ping Ferry, 10 July 1978, Box 14, *Bernstein Ferry Papers*.

148. See her informative obituary, *New York Times*, 14 June 2001.

149. Carol Bernstein Ferry to Janet Hooper, November 1976, Box 19, *Carol Bernstein Ferry and Ping Ferry Papers*.

150. Jennifer Davis to Carol Bernstein Ferry, 12 May 1977, Box 19, *Bernstein Ferry Papers*.

underscoring the need for Ferry—and her power in the movement. The magazine was in dire straits, inducing "pessimism" among the staff. They were "subsidizing issues with borrowed money," digging a deeper hole that might start to fill if they were able to "bring our circulation up to 10,000,"[151] entailing more unseen dependence upon Bernstein Ferry. Bernstein Ferry, as she was eager to point out, had been among "major supporters" of ACOA; however, her commanding, even peremptory tone underlined that this was done "for a good reason—that it was hard to get other Americans to focus on Africa and its problems when it was hardly ever in the news,"[152] a comment that highlighted her foundation's important role.

This problem was, like so many others, an outgrowth of the Cold War. Anticommunism necessitated the sapping of left-wing unions, who would have ordinarily been the source of funding for left-wing organizations, but their decline left affluent individuals to fill the vacuum—which was certainly better than no funding but was problematic nevertheless. Thus, in December 1976 Lennox Hinds of the National Conference of Black Lawyers spoke correctly of a "state of confusion within the Black community" in the U.S. "in light of the most recent developments in Angola." He sought to "send a fact-finding delegation to Luanda" and, possibly, to so-called "terrorism" trials in South Africa in a search for clarity.[153] Bernstein Ferry's ample funds were requested, per usual.

Houser and the ACOA, which had come into existence in the wake of the defenestration of Robeson's CAA, was having second thoughts about what he—and they—had wrought. By 1978, he was upset with Holden Roberto of Angola, who he had known for years, since "the line they are taking appeals to the worst in the American fear psychosis of Cuban and Soviet intervention in Africa." With vivid nostalgia he recalled "their old headquarters in Kinshasa, which I had visited many times over the years," but which had just "closed." "The headquarters is Holden Roberto's home, which I also visited," Houser said, speaking warmly of this "large villa surrounded by a big fence" on "two or three acres of land. Undoubtedly it belonged

151. Stephanie Urdang and Craig Howard to Carol Bernstein Ferry and Ping Ferry, undated, Box 20, *Bernstein Ferry Papers*.

152. Carol Bernstein Ferry to "Dear George," 21 December 1976, Box 9, *Bernstein Ferry Papers*.

153. Lennox Hinds to Carol Bernstein Ferry, 23 December 1976, Box 14, *Bernstein Ferry Papers*.

to a rich Belgian in the period before 1960" and independence.[154] But this dewy-eyed recollection of class and colonialism did not lead him to see that there was perhaps something inherently amiss about an ecumenical approach to African liberation that involved consorting with CIA assets like Roberto.

The anticommunism embedded in the fling with Roberto handcuffed ACOA, limiting the effectiveness of its other efforts. Unfortunately, the Democratic Party, to which Negro voters flocked, was a shaky vehicle for decolonization, and by early 1978, South African Broadcasting was claiming a victory within its ranks, which would only prepare the ground for Reagan by 1980. "The power struggle in President Carter's inner council," the network reported, "is turning in favor" of Brzezinski, the anticommunist tribune obsessed with Moscow. "He is insisting that the East-West balance must be maintained in Africa as well as elsewhere" in order to block "Moscow's imperialist aims in Africa,"[155] a posture which dovetailed with that of China and its U.S. acolytes. This meant a laser-like focus on Cuban troops in Angola, seen rightfully as a mortal threat to apartheid—but also the extension of this concern to Havana's role throughout the region, particularly in Lesotho, surrounded by South Africa, and a natural transmission belt for activism and ideology into the land of apartheid itself.[156]

Ironically, Brzezinski was telling Carter then what SABC was broadcasting. In December 1978 the flinty Polish-American announced that "the basic reason why our difficulties are mounting" in the sub-region "is that our middle-of-the-road solutions are collapsing as the situation becomes polarized" and, thus, "neither the whites nor the blacks take us very seriously...." His regime, he said sadly, was "visibly reluctant to press the Soviet-Cuban issue" or "to apply sanctions to the whites...." In other words, Afro-American voters were pressing for sanctions while adherents to the anticommunist consensus were still in panic mode about the "Soviet-Cuban issue" stemming from 1975, leading to policy paralysis.[157]

The ideological trends then brewing in Black America combined with the demonstrated weaknesses of the ACOA and their partner in

---

154. George Houser to Jennifer Davis, Paul Irish, et.al., 26 May 1978, Box 94, *ACOARA*.

155. South African Broadcasting Corporation Commentary, 16 March 1978, Box 120, *Leroy Walker Africa News Service Archive*.

156. *Rand Daily Mail*, 6 June 1978.

157. Zbigniew Brzezinski to President Carter, 2 December 1978, Box 42, *Brzezinski Materials*.

liberal anticommunism, the NAACP, to create an opening for a new group. By 1977 Trans-Africa, based in Washington and headed by the charismatic lawyer Randall Robinson, who had earned his spurs by organizing the boycott of Gulf Oil, presented itself as "newly organized" and was seeking to raise $100,000. Present at the creation were Robinson's old friend from their native Virginia, the tennis star Arthur Ashe; the ever present Congressman Diggs; the writer Lerone Bennett, who had been a delegate at the "6PAC" in Dar; the union leader Bill Lucy; and the anticommunist academic Ronald Walters.[158] This group faced an uphill climb, however, and despite luminous victories during the 1980s, it was unable to survive the fall of apartheid, ironically. Part of the problem may have been Robinson's attempt to reject the reigning philosophy of the era, anticommunism, which in the Washington of that era placed him beyond the pale—to a degree.[159]

Only to a degree because despite his often brave words, in 1981 Trans-Africa announced that it "views the Soviet Union as an imperialistic power just like the United States....Socialism as a strategy for development has proven to be no panacea...."[160] Such verbiage would be viewed suspiciously by the ANC-SACP alliance, the MPLA and other forces that counted on ample support from Moscow (though these words were unremarkable in Washington).

Perhaps to bolster his own position, Henry Richardson of Carter's staff instructed Brzezinski that Diggs and his fellow members of the Congressional Black Caucus were "increasingly influential... both in Washington and in Afro-America....Diggs is entirely correct that concern with South Africa is not limited in the black community to those expressly concerned with foreign affairs. Other kinds of black groups and groupings are coherently expressing their anger and concern....This trend has been building for several years but only now seems visible in Washington,"[161] instantly enhancing the role of Richardson as one of the few who saw what others seemed to miss.

Still, Richardson was on to something in stressing the role of Trans-Africa, informing Brzezinski in December 1977 that "we had a

158. Press Release, 24 September 1977, Box 3, *Robert Van Lierop Papers.*

159. Randall Robinson, *Defending the Spirit: A Black Life in America,* New York: Dutton, 1998, 210.

160. "Policy Statement of Trans-Africa," December 1981, Box 1, Folder 17, *Cheryl Johnson Odim Papers, Columbia College-Chicago*

161. Henry Richardson to Zbigniew Brzezinski, 8 December 1977, Box 115, *NSA Staff Material, North/South.*

holiday so far from *serious* Afro-America pressure towards economic sanctions against South Africa" but now there was "a harbinger of the end of the grace period" since, he emphasized once more "*all* major black organizations are paying increasing attention to the subject."[162] [emphasis original] When the labor leader Douglas Fraser of the United Auto Workers Union was told by President Carter that South Africa—along with nuclear disarmament, the Middle East, and the Panama Canal—was "one of the four principal elements of our foreign policy," he indicated that "serious Afro-America pressure" was not a chimera.[163] (Fraser's union made his priorities known when $3000 from their coffers was donated to ACOA.)[164]

But like a law of nature this pressure met a countervailing force. The "arms embargo is becoming porous," said Richardson in 1978, speaking of the halt in flow of the weapons to Pretoria. "The Republicans appear to be staking out the accomodationist [sic] position on Southern African issues, including John Connally's reception in South Africa"—speaking of the Nixon ally-- which was rapturous. "His views may be expressing public attitudes unfettered by accurate information,"[165] an accommodation to apartheid that was to become the norm in the White House after 1980.

However, there were other trends that Richardson did not share with Brzezinski, detailed by the left-leaning *African Agenda* in 1976. The magazine reprimanded the "fuzzy ideologists with their romantic notions and political action based on skin color alone," PAC oriented views which "tapped the deeply rooted sentiments of our people about Africa." Reference was made to the mass marches that had been organized by the African Liberation Support Committee beginning in 1972. Then 6PAC in Dar occurred, itself partly an attack on these "fuzzy ideologists" and "the reaction of most U.S. delegates was one of shock and dismay" but "even more disturbing," it was stressed, was "a profound IGNORANCE of the political debates, taking place in the world today." With the demise of Robeson, et al., and despite the romantic invocation of Africa, many of the U.S. "ideologists" were woefully unaware of basic political realities. The editorial saluted the hundreds who came to Chicago in the fall of 1973 for the founding of NAIMSAL, with which I worked.

---

162. Henry Richardson to Zbigniew Brzezinski, 8 December 1977, Box 115.

163. President Carter to Doug Fraser, 8 June 1978, Box 115.

164. Douglas Fraser to ACOA, 7 March 1980, Box 84, *ACOARA*.

165. Henry Richardson to Zbigniew Brzezinski, 25 September 1978, Box 115.

This group backed MPLA, unlike "[Amiri] Baraka and what is left of the African Liberation Support Committee," which "continue to support UNITA and FNLA." Also assailed were mercenary recruiter Roy Innis and the activist and soon to be investment banker Vernon Jordan, who opposed sanctioning apartheid. But despite their brio, the forces behind NAIMSAL and *African Agenda* were also not long for this world. As early as May 1977 the latter was moaning that "in the last few months we have suffered from financial constraints and have been unable to publish on our scheduled dates.... If we do not receive your help, we will be forced to stop our publication"—which happened shortly thereafter.[166]

The same fate, as noted, had befallen the once mighty African Liberation Support Committee. There was much rockiness internally. As Carter entered office various chapters were barely hanging on as they were making unrealistic assessments: "the USSR [was] posing as a friend of the liberation forces [while maintaining] its own imperialist plans for Africa"[167]—a position which, whatever its merits, would have brought the group into strategic and tactical conflict with the MPLA and ANC particularly, then surviving because of Moscow's beneficence.

Similar forces at a program applauding Robert Mugabe's ZANU chanted, "Carter-Brezhnev you can't hide, the people of Zimbabwe will decide." This ALSC program denounced the "Soviet Social Imperialism" that was thought to be embodied by Moscow's paramount leader, Leonid Brezhnev, substantiating this claim with the words of Mugabe himself from a recent August 1977 trip to China.[168] Weeks later, Richard Gibson was working with Baraka and the PAC in plotting an "international conference on the Social-Imperialist threat to Europe", i.e. an anti-Moscow extravaganza.[169] This pro-China posturing had consequences. Shortly after Soweto 1976 it was reported that China was involved in the "death or disappearance of nearly 50 guerilla recruits" in Tanzania, thought to be opposed

---

166. *African Agenda*, 6(Number 2, April-May 1977), *Chicago History Museum*.

167. "The Struggle in ALSC: What Direction? Sectarianism or Fighting Imperialism? By the Following [ALSC] Chapters": Chicago, Indianapolis, Lafayette, Indiana; Atlanta; Birmingham, Baltimore, Circa 1977, Box 258, *Leroy Walker Africa News Service Archive*.

168. Undated Pamphlet, "Zimbabwe Liberation Day," Box 258, *Leroy Walker Africa News Service Archive*.

169. Richard Gibson to Amiri Baraka, 28 September 1977, Box 12, *Richard Gibson Papers*.

to their political line[170]—a story retained by Rhodesia's man in Washington.

Nevertheless, "fuzzy" ideology could not overwhelm the volcanic impact of Soweto 1976, which led directly to the deposing of the apartheid regime 18 years later.

---

170. *Washington Post*, 23 August 1976, Box 1, *Kenneth Towsey Papers*.

Chapter 17

The U.S. Unable to Stem Apartheid's Crisis, 1978-1980

THE recalcitrant right embodied by Ronald Reagan made an electoral comeback in November 1980. The former governor of California had rocketed into the favor of these malodorous forces in the Spring of 1976 when he challenged the incumbent, Gerald Ford, from the right in party primaries with the issue of Southern Africa in the forefront. Then he began his successful presidential campaign in the backwater of Philadelphia, Mississippi in August 1980—infamous as the site of the state-aided slaying of anti-Jim Crow crusaders in 1964—illustrating once again how counter-revolution has been a major theme of the history of the U.S.[1]

The champagne corks were popping in Pretoria and bureaucrats were dancing in the hallways as a result, though the arrival of African majority rule in neighboring Zimbabwe was chastening.[2] Speaking at the palatial Waldorf-Astoria Hotel in Manhattan, recently elected Robert Mugabe conceded that independence had arrived earlier than expected but gave a hint of turmoil to come when he said that undeveloped farms would be seized by the state.[3] (For years, Salisbury had thought that Mugabe was less influenced by Moscow than Nkomo, making him appear to be less dangerous; thus as early as 1966 Salisbury stressed the number of Nkomo's forces

---

1. Gerald Horne, *The Counter-Revolution of 1776: Slave Resistance and the Origins of the United States of America*, New York: New York University Press, 2014.

2. Gerald Horne, *From the Barrel of a Gun: The U.S. and the War Against Zimbabwe, 1965-1980.*

3. Remarks by Robert Mugabe, 26 August 1980, Box 10, *Gwendolen Carter Papers.*

who were studying in Eastern Europe: 45 in the Soviet Union; 10 in Czechoslovakia; 12 in Yugoslavia; 11 in East Germany.)[4]

Still, the glee among those who admired apartheid was uncontainable at the prospect that this system of wickedness would be extended. But ironically, it was precisely during the Reagan regime that sanctions would be slapped on Pretoria—which, along with the mass movement in the sub-region, led directly to February 1990: the release of Mandela and other political prisoners and the beginning of negotiations leading to majority rule in 1994. But alas, the forces of evil proved more formidable than thought, as they managed to escape without being subjected to trials for war crimes, not to mention mass expropriation of their dearly held property. One inference that should be drawn, assuredly relevant to strugglers in North America, is that settler colonialism grounded in white supremacy may be the most formidable opponent of the politically aware and sophisticated.

Joy was also soaring among the right-wing Christian base that propelled Reagan into the White House. This rise in happiness included one who had sought a leadership role in the Republican Party. The Reverend Pat Robertson, who was host of a popular television show, presided over a vast array of economic interests that included diamond mines in the former Belgian Congo.[5] He had flown on the private jet of the dictator Mobutu and supped at the yacht of his consistent ally in Kinshasa. The sly cleric also maintained close ties to Frederick Chiluba, the diminutive Zambian who was to oust Kaunda in Lusaka.[6]

Robertson was hardly singular. In fact, one of the many reasons why the right wing remained so potent in Washington was the gigantic sums to be made from cooperating with Pretoria and its numerous corporate backers. William Keyes arrived in Washington in 1985, then a 32-year-old Negro without a nickel. Soon he was representing the apartheid regime as a lobbyist to the tune of $390,000–$500,000 annually. His ostensible target was the Afro-American community, but more accurately he was a well-paid symbol of an artificial nonracialism as Pretoria sought to soften its hard-edged racist image by

4. Memo from Special Branch Headquarters, 7 April 1966, Box 1, *Kenneth Towsey Papers*.

5. Alec Foege, *The Empire God Built: Inside Pat Robertson's Media Machine*, New York: Wiley, 1996, 217-218.

6. Robert Boston, *The Most Dangerous Man in America? Pat Robertson and the Rise of the Christian Coalition*, Amherst, New York: Prometheus, 1996, 197, 201, 203.

hiring those with brown-skinned faces.[7] Keyes' Negro comrade J.A. Parker received a mere $35,000.[8]

It was not only Negroes who hopped aboard the gravy train eagerly. By 1980 Pretoria had hired Congressman James Symington and former Senator George Smathers to lobby, at a reported $300,000 annually apiece.[9] It was unclear how much U.S. neo-fascist leader Lyndon La Rouche was paid when he prepared profiles on anti-apartheid leaders for the use of Pretoria, as he sought to "win friends and allies" there.[10]

A firm foundation had been laid for Reagan's rise by preceding events, notably the growth of rightists in the U.S. disturbed by gains of the liberation movements. Dana Brown of St. Louis was in this camp. He financed the production of "Safari" coffee but by 1977 was complaining to Senator Eastland of Mississippi that "because of the loss of Angola coffee crops," he was now "paying and will continue to pay billions of extra dollars for coffee."[11] Dr. Robert McCully was similarly upset. Born and educated in Mississippi, by 1977 he was teaching in the Department of Pathology at the University of Stellenbosch in South Africa, a position arranged for him by Chapman Binford of apartheid's Armed Forces Institute of Pathology. The outraged academic equated newly empowerd Africans with their U.S. counterparts in that both have "power completely out of proportion to their numbers [or] their contribution to society" and were now collaborating with despised Communists besides.[12]

Senator Eastland of Mississippi, a fervent backer of apartheid and Jim Crow alike, was similarly perturbed, terming in 1978 the "murder of settlers in Zaire [Congo] by guerrilla Africans trained by the Cubans" an "international disgrace."[13] But even his bluster was

---

7. *Washington Post*, 21 November 1985; "Group Research Report," no date, Box 2, *Group Research Archives, Columbia University, New York.*

8. *Africa News* [U.S.], 16 December 1985.

9. Clipping, circa 1980, Box 237, *Leroy Walker Africa News Service Archive.*

10. *Our Town* [U.S,], 4 November 1979, Box 60, *Washington Office on Africa Papers.*

11. Dana Brown to Senator Eastland, 11 March 1977, FS 3 SS1 Box 91, *James Eastland Papers.* Brown's hometown newspaper carried a cartoon featuring an African resembling a gorilla in a business suit, fishing with a hammer and sickle hook while sitting on a briefcase carrying the inscription, "Rhodesia." *St. Louis Globe-Democrat*, 2 September 1977.

12. Chapman Binford to Senator Eastland and Dr. Robert McCully to Chapman Binford, 3 February 977, FS 3 SS1, Box 91, *James Eastland Papers.*

13. Senator Eastland to Mike Quayle, FS 3 SS1, Box 95, *James Eastland Papers.* The legislator's defense of minority rule was echoed by economist,

surpassed by that of Soviet dissident, Alexander Solzhenitsyn, who claimed that the presence of Cuban troops in Angola meant "the first blow has been struck in the Fourth World War. This will decide the future of the world," he exhorted. (The compelled U.S. withdrawal from Vietnam in 1975 meant that "the Third World War is now over. The West lost.")[14]

An indicator of the direction of the prevailing winds in Washington was visible in 1982 when newly appointed CIA chief William Casey, a canny investor who once had regulated Wall Street, took a lengthy trip to the sub-region, visiting Zimbabwe, South Africa, and Zambia. He had visited 33 years earlier, during a different era, as a director of the Intercontinental Hotels Corporation. Upon his return he was contemptuously defaming, alleging that "the native has little education, will or inclination for our world.... Those living in the primitive tribal state seem happier than those in the city...." Like such visitors before and since he also claimed that "the [white] South Africa is much like the American," auguring an ever-closer tie. He was delighted to find that Pretoria was more than willing to aid his counter-revolutionary crusade in Nicaragua, just as they forged a new level of cooperation in seeking to oust the MPLA from Angola, which became an obsession.[15] Soon it was reported South African pilots were delivering aid to Nicaraguan "contras."[16]

Casey's counterpart Niel Barnard, like his cohorts, looked to cooperation on nuclear strategy, in addition to cooperation in aiding the twin terrorist groupings—UNITA in Angola and RENAMO in Mozambique—to overthrow MPLA and FRELIMO. Barnard seemed to suggest that real men in Pretoria wanted to go further and see that "Tanzania should come under South Africa's control—indeed the entire continent south of the equator." Perhaps restraining the heritage of anti-Semitism in Pretoria was apartheid's interconnection with Israel, including advanced training from the disreputable Mossad. Intelligence cooperation between Pretoria and Washington became more intense during the 1980s too. This "intelligence relationship" said Barnard "goes back a long way." He met face-to-face with the inscrutable Casey, known for his inarticulate mumbling,

---

Milton Friedman: *Newsweek*, 3 May 1976.

14. Newsletter of Canadian Intelligence Service, May 1977, FS 3 SS1, Box 91, *James Eastland Papers*.

15. Joseph Perisco, *Casey: From the OSS to the CIA*, New York: Viking, 1990, 1982, 299, 332.

16. Stephen Ellis and Tsepo Sechaba, *Comrades Against Apartheid*, 110.

during what was described as a "highly secret visit" to the region in 1983. He saw no problem with this since "numbers of aspirant spies from the ANC were trained" by the East Germans. Since he claimed to have "numerous sources" within the ANC, this knowledge was hardly a secret in Pretoria. Lennox Sebe of the Bantustan that was Ciskei also provided intelligence to the CIA.[17]

His brother Charles Sebe, an intelligence agent, was said, "like many black South Africans," to have "hero worshipped a stereotype of the cool, self-sufficient American black who intimidates whites. He studied videocassettes of American tv programs and movies that conformed to that image," said journalist Joseph Lelyveld. Yet ironically, when speaking before Europeans he tended to make fun of U.S. Negroes since "black American hemming and hawing" often "inspired laughter and cheers" among a certain group of South Africans, who no doubt were able to calm their frazzled nerves about the specter of militant African Americans.[18] Sebe's simultaneous emulation and denigration of African Americans was a reflection not just of his own psychosis but also the contradictory tugs felt by African defenders of apartheid, compelled to lance those seen as opposed to this system of cruelty even as they imitated them.

Barnard was probably among those celebrating when Reagan was elected, for it was in 1979 that three U.S. officials were ousted from South Africa on charges of espionage.[19] Then there were the merely suspicious episodes, e.g. when that same year Ruth and Sheldon Stafford from Kansas City landed their private plane unannounced in Windhoek, concluding their 22nd crossing of the Atlantic.[20]

As so often happened in a nation where the Euro-American majority leaned decisively in a conservative direction, the Carter regime—heavily dependent upon Afro-American voters—wound up preparing the path for the rise of Reagan, trapped as it was between its "human rights" rhetoric and the sympathy for Salisbury and Pretoria that had accumulated over the decades. This surrender did not spare his administration from brutal attacks from the right, who see concession as a sign of weakness and imminent surrender.[21]

---

17. Niel Barnard, as told to Tobie Wiese, *Secret Revolution: Memoirs of a Spy Boss*, Cape Town: Tafelberg, 2015, 16, 44-46, 65, 67, 76, 79, 82, 83, 85.

18. Joseph Lelyveld, *Move Your Shadow: South Africa, Black and White*, New York: Times Books, 1985, 174.

19. *Washington Post*, 13 April 1979.

20. *Windhoek Observer*, 12 May 1979.

21. "ACSA Foundation Newsletter," 3(Number 12, January 1978), Box 301, *Group Research Archives-Columbia University, New York City.*

Thus, instead of seeing the 12-day visit to South Africa by Dr. King's former aide, the Reverend Jesse Jackson, as an opportunity to pressure Pretoria, it was viewed as an unwelcome intervention. Brzezinski told President Carter that the journey "generated more excitement and controversy than any other visiting American since the trip of Bobby Kennedy in 1966," but it "created a white backlash against the South African government" for allowing it. He was obsessed with how the minority viewed Jackson: "*whites also reacted strongly* to Jackson's visit," he stressed. They "reacted sharply to the epithets—such as 'terroristic dictatorship'—used by Jackson," though the pastor was, I believe, accurate in having "compared apartheid to the 'ungodly acts of Hitler.'" Veritably seeing majority sentiment as irrelevant, the Carter aide found that "on balance, South African whites have been dismayed that a voice as powerful as Jesse Jackson's has spoken out against their system of government in such harsh terms." The Chicagoan also "stated publicly his intention to speak with you," meaning Carter, which exacerbated Pretoria's irritation.[22]

Secretary of Commerce Juanita Kreps also weighed in, advising the White House that the progressive pastor "has stated that the South African subsidiaries of General Motors and Ford are supplying trucks, cars and military and para-military equipment to the South African armed forces and police." She dissented, claiming that "sales of commercial vehicles by GM and Ford South African subsidiaries to [Pretoria] would not necessarily constitute a violation of U.S. law." She took time to note "diversions" of U.S. military materiel from Greece, Canary Islands, Mozambique, Swaziland, Lesotho, and Botswana, in any case. This included shotguns and ammunition. Computers for the police continued to arrive too, including a potent digital computer from Britain destined for apartheid's air force.[23]

Secretary Kreps tactfully neglected to mention how Lockheed—in Carter's own Georgia—had an Italian subsidiary implicated in Pretoria's military build-up that went far beyond the provision of shotguns to include fighter jets.[24] Space Research Corporation of

---

22. Zbigniew Brzezinski to President Carter, 2 August 1979, Box 48, *Brzezinski Material.*

23. Juanita Kreps to President Carter, 4 October 1979, Box 134, Office of Staff Secretary, Presidential Files, *Jimmy Carter Presidential Library.*

24. Ann Seidman and Neva Makgleta, "Transnational Corporate Involvement in South Africa's Military Build-up," United Nations, New York: Centre Against Apartheid, October 1978, Box 128, *Leroy Walker Africa News Service Archive.*

the U.S. was fortunately convinced to plead guilty to sending long-range artillery to Pretoria that proved quite useful in killing Africans and Cubans on the battlefields of Angola.[25] Subsequently, the U.S. exported shock batons to Pretoria, quite useful in suppressing mass protests.[26]

Reverend Jackson's headline-grabbing trip was emblematic of a rising tide against apartheid in the U.S. and elsewhere that Carter was unable to tame, and Reagan was unable to resist. In 1979 a record number of shareholder resolutions were submitted to banks and corporations seeking to restrain U.S. investment in South Africa.[27] As this movement was gaining momentum, a Negro pastor from Philadelphia issued the "Sullivan Principles," a code for so-called responsible investing in apartheid, designed to sanitize this odious practice. But for an inflexible Pretoria even his mild restraint on investment was a bridge too far. Just before the November 1980 election, the author of this monstrosity—Reverend Leon Sullivan—arrived in South Africa and was greeted with a hailstorm of catcalls. South African Broadcasting was scalding: "Acting probably on the principle that it is easier to solve the problems of others than your own, we have in South Africa right now," the Reverend Sullivan; "from the country that gave us the Reverend Jesse Jackson to solve South Africa's problems we now have the Reverend Leon Sullivan."[28] Sarcasm aside, SABC was reacting to what a staffer for the Quakers, Michael Simmons, noticed in 1979: "the movement around divestment appears to be intensifying on college campuses across the country,"[29] compelling U.S. corporations to withdraw from South Africa.

The Reverend Sullivan happened to be present at an important 1979 "exclusive meeting" of 300 university trustees and officials at the Ford Foundation, along with Richard Moose, Assistant Secretary of State for Africa. Also present was Dumisani Khumalo of ACOA—later to be the post-1994 South African ambassador at the U.N. Anticipating the waves of student anti-apartheid activism that were about

25. Press Release from Department of Justice, 25 March 1980, Box 244, *Leroy Walker Africa News Service Archive*.

26. Report by Washington Office on Africa, October 1982, Box 244, *Leroy Walker Africa News Service Archive*.

27. "Kenneth Propp, "The Domestic Debate Over Apartheid," 1979, Box 36, *Records of the Study Commission on U.S. Policy Toward Southern Africa, Schomburg Center, New York Public Library*.

28. South African Broadcasting Corporation Commentary, 3 September 1980, Box 120, *Leroy Walker Africa News Service Archive*.

29. Michael Simmons to Peace Education staff, 13 March 1979, PED 1979 SOUTHERN AFRICA PROGRAM, *AFSC*.

to rock the nation, Hugh Calkins of Harvard University provided the advice, "whenever students take over a building don't call the police. The resulting publicity will only benefit the students."[30] The Ford Foundation was itself skittish about this matter. They were concerned then that the "withdrawal or substantial reduction of Foundation activity in Sub-Sahara activity not only would entail adverse repercussions in Africa but would also be viewed by groups in the U.S. in which the Foundation has a strong interest"—meaning Negroes— "as a decision based on race or color,"[31] unavoidably igniting a backlash.

While Jackson and Sullivan were flying to South Africa, arriving from Pretoria was P.G.J. Koornhof, Minister of Cooperation and Development, who by June 1979 was installed at the plush Hilton Riviera Hotel in Palm Springs, California, where he addressed an audience.[32] But it was evident even then that in light of prevailing trends in the sub-region, Washington had begun to hedge—which sheds light on why the day after Koornhof spoke, David Thebehali, Mayor of Soweto, could be found in this resort town.[33] This contradictory pattern was refracted when Professor Gwendolen Carter, the U.S.-based scholar, spoke at Potchefstroom University, an outpost of Afrikanerdom, at the same moment. She was asked, on the one hand, why the U.S. Senate chose not to ban the export of torture implements to South Africa, while another thought the remedy for Pretoria's problems included deporting Africans en masse to North America.[34]

Professor Carter was not considered a friend of apartheid; soon thereafter security police detained her for a couple of hours at Johannesburg's airport and strip-searched her. This occurred even though, as her friend Thomas Karis recalled, "she was often met at airports by Ford Foundation or American embassy officials."[35] Her rough treatment sent a clear signal.

---

30. Report by Dumisani Khumalo, 6 June 1979, PED 1979 SOUTHERN AFRICA PROGRAM.

31. Report, December 1970, Box 267, 005996, Reports 3255-6161 (FA 739b), *Ford Foundation Records, Rockefeller Archive Center, Sleepy Hollow, New York.*

32. Speech by P.G.J. Koornhof, 19 June 1979, Box 10, *Gwendolen Carter Papers.*

33. Speech by David Thebehali, 20 June 1979, Box 10, *Gwendolen Carter Papers.*

34. Session with Final Year Law Class-Potchefstroom University, circa 1979, Box 10, *Gwendolen Carter Papers.*

35. Remarks by Thomas Karis, 25 November 1991, Box 3, *Gwendolen Carter Papers.*

Congressional delegations to South Africa were also becoming common as the election approached. Early 1980 found Senator Paul Tsongas of Massachusetts in Soweto. There he encountered "raw anger" combined with contempt for the "hypocrisy" of the U.S.: "talking to another white liberal" did not seem to delight them either.[36] On their trip to Africa, Congressman William Gray of the Black Caucus and fellow House potentate Jim Wright of Texas had barely landed in Lagos before being accorded what was described as "shock treatment." Nigeria, it was reported, was willing to back the U.S.'s counter-revolutionary aims in Iran and Afghanistan—in return for backing of African aims in Rhodesia and South Africa: a trade which may have seemed reasonable at the time but in retrospect was misguided given the real potential for alienating Tehran and the resultant chaos in Kabul which prevails to this very day, serving to ignite religious zealotry in the form of today's Boko Haram, now terrorizing the Nigerian countryside.[37] Nigeria could not be ignored easily, for as I wrote in 1981, the "volume of U.S. trade with Nigeria is twice as big as U.S. trade with South Africa."[38]

The Wright-Gray delegation was necessary since Salisbury was busily maneuvering as the tenure of this corrupt regime was expiring. Ian Smith himself was slated to visit the U.S. just before the 1978 election and—according to Senator Frank Church—had the aim of mobilizing right-wing sentiment further.[39]

Congressman Gray found time to confer with Lord Soames, London's negotiator on Zimbabwe, and was unimpressed by this "arrogant, aristocratic British racist bastard" with a "regal attitude about himself." The British peer was "caustic in his attack on Mugabe" and wrongly predicted that the elections then unfolding there would lead to a "coalition of at least three parties. It will be Nkomo, [Abel] Muzorewa [Rhodesian toady] and the whites. Everything possible is being done to cut out Mugabe,"[40] who prevailed, suggesting once again that London may have been more out of touch with reality than Washington—no small feat.

Leading Negro intellectual Tilden Le Melle was present at the subsequent Zimbabwean election as part of an ACOA delegation that included George Houser and Cynthia Cannady. They were detained

---

36. Briefing by Senator Tsongas, 25 January 1980, Box 15, *Washington Office on Africa Papers*.

37. Briefing, 22 January 1980, Box 15, *Washington Office on Africa Papers*.

38. *Carolina Times*, 19 September 1981.

39. *Houston Chronicle*, 6 October 1978.

40. Briefing, 22 January 1980, Box 15, *Washington Office on Africa Papers*.

temporarily because of their insistence on observance of democratic norms.[41] On the other hand, Bayard Rustin—who once advised Dr. King—signaled the continuing rightward drift of mainstream Negro leadership when he endorsed the fraudulent 1979 pro-Rhodesian elections, intended to scupper the 1980 election. Also typical was the response of ACOA's Judge William Booth, who in denouncing Rustin compared the 1979 election to those held in the Soviet Union, the chief ally of liberation forces.[42]

Rustin's response was not unusual but signified how far to the right the U.S. political spectrum had moved under the combined weight of blindly maniacal anticommunism and anti-Sovietism. Thus, Allard Lowenstein, viewed correctly as a tribune of "liberalism" who had incurred the wrath of Pretoria when he had entered South West Africa in the late 1950s, was by 1979 also sanctioning bogus elections in Rhodesia and—according to his sympathetic biographer—"found himself in the anomalous position of being on the same side as Jesse Helms,"[43] the most retrograde of U.S. Senators.

Kabul and Tehran were very much on the minds of anti-apartheid leader Randall Robinson and U.S. diplomat, the Negro Johnny Carson, who had a conversation described as "confidential." In a throwback to the era when the NAACP sought to broker ties between the CIA and ANC leader Z.K. Matthews, Robinson had been meeting with the agency's Cord Meyer who told him that the CIA was focused on Afghanistan, Angola, and Jamaica. Then Robinson and his colleagues C. Payne Lucas and Walter Carrington were invited to Carter's White House to attend a special briefing on Iran and Afghanistan for the foreign policy elite. That Trans-Africa was invited could be seen to signal the acceptance of Negroes at the highest level—or, more likely, crude co-optation. Alarmingly, besides Robinson and his coterie present were banker David Rockefeller, labor misleader Lane Kirkland, reactionary academic Samuel Huntington, and discredited former advisor to discredited President Johnson, McGeorge Bundy.[44] Ironically, the defeat of Carter saved Trans-Africa from descending further into such perilous relationships.

Seeking to move the Carter regime from the precipice of the right-wing ledge to which it had crawled—though ever cognizant of the danger provided by the rise of the hardline right in the U.S.—our

41. Release, 19 February 1980, Box 149, *ACOARA*.

42. Judge William Booth to "Dear Sirs," 20 April 1979, Box 149, *ACOARA*.

43. William Chafe, *Never Stop Running: Allard Lowenstein and the Struggle to Save American Liberalism*, New York: Basic, 1993, 137, 531.

44. Briefing, 11 January 1980, Box 15, *Washington Office on Africa Papers*.

movement saw little alternative to organizing what we termed a "big demonstration at the Democratic National Convention" to be held in Manhattan in 1980.[45]

Perhaps the outreach to Robinson was a sign of desperation in the White House, as Communist-backed liberation marches seemed to be on the march. For also by 1979 the dislodging of the corrupt Eric Gairy regime in Grenada had occurred and the resultant New Jewel Movement aligned itself with the organization I was to head: the National Conference of Black Lawyers.[46]

Perhaps that is why the CIA reportedly hired a magician as a consultant on their "project in the manipulation of human behavior"; magicians renowned at "getting people to look in the wrong direction at the right time" were seen as matched well with U.S. intelligence.[47] Worse than magic was the CIA campaigns on "mind control," especially the effort to ascertain "whether a human being could be induced secretly to commit an assassination against his will."[48]

Rather than keeping faith with many of the voters that elected him—not to mention adding substance to his otherwise vacuous "human rights" verbiage—Carter capitulated to anticommunism. A 1979 CIA analysis argued that the ANC "lacks the leadership, organization and trained manpower to play a significant role in destabilizing South Africa in the immediate or near future, although its capabilities have increased in the past two years" with "military aid from USSR, Cuba and East Germany…." Suspiciously, "leaders" of the group, "many of whom are members of the [SACP]," held reins of influence. The SACP maintained "considerable influence in the ANC" which "led to a strong pro-Soviet alignment." The ANC, it was said with apparent frustration, had "long been dependent on Soviet funding…." Tambo had just spent nine days in Havana, while the Soviet press agency Novosti published ANC material from Luanda. Mandela "remains the symbolic leader" and "still has more backing than any other militant black South African leader."[49]

---

45. Minutes of meeting of the Coalition for the Liberation of Southern Africa, 25 June 1980, Box 179, *Gerald Horne Papers*.

46. Invitation, 14 June 1982, Box 191, *Gerald Horne Papers* (Unison Whiteman, Foreign Minister, to be greeted at reception at 777 U.N. Plaza in Manhattan.) In same box see also "International Law Seminar and Excursion" to Grenada, 9-16 March 1981.

47. Clipping, 4 August 1977, Box 3, Folder 35, *Prexy Nesbitt Papers, Columbia College-Chicago*.

48. *New York Times*, 10 February 1978.

49. CIA analysis, 9 February 1979, Box 115, *NSA Staff Material, North/South, Jimmy Carter Presidential Library*.

Thus, the Carter regime was highly vulnerable to the anticommunist implication when in a 1977 meeting Vorster offered to handover to Mondale a document purportedly written by Mandela: he "wrote a thesis," it was said, on "How to be a Good Communist."[50]

Vorster had a point. Shortly after he volunteered to prove that Mandela was a "Good Communist," the ANC office in Lusaka was contacting "Comrade Shubin, Soviet Afro-African Committee" in Moscow, telling him that "in addition to the other invaluable Soviet literature which we receive and for which we are so thankful we want to make a special request for more of the following for our Provisional HQ offices" including "*International Affairs...New Times* and *Soviet Military Review*."[51]

The same could be said about events surrounding the impending independence of Zimbabwe. It was in March 1980, as the Carter regime was on the verge of expiring, that the ANC's Alfred Nzo made an urgent request of the Central Committee of the Soviet Communist Party: "for a long time," he said, "our Department of Communications has enjoyed the assistance of a Soviet specialist," who was "seconded to work with ZAPU in the same field" across the border; this aid "significantly helped our cadres in establishing our communications"[52] and the sovereignty of Zimbabwe should not circumscribe its importance, he beseeched.

Naturally, the SACP continued to receive assistance of various types from Moscow, and by mid-1979 Sonia Bunting was enthusiastically reporting to the ANC about the "success of my tour of Africa on behalf of Inkululeko Publications", the party's publishing arm, which distributed the *African Communist* from London "Without the help of the ANC," she proclaimed, "the work itself would have been impossible" but because of this aid, "on every area of my visit—Angola, Zambia, Botswana, Mozambique and Tanzania I came across the same willingness to help" in spreading the gospel of socialism,[53] a spread Washington was sworn to overcome.

After regime change in Lisbon in April 1974, the successful Cuban intervention in Angola in 1975, and the Soweto Uprising of 1976,

50. "Secret" Minutes of Meeting, 20 May 1977, NLC 133 13 276 4.6, *Jimmy Carter Presidential Library*.

51. Draft Letter to "Comrade Shubin," 27 July 1979, Box 88, Folder 43, Part II, *Lusaka Mission, ANC Records*.

52. Alfred Nzo to Central Committee, 21 March 1980, Box 88, Folder 43, Part II, *Lusaka Mission, ANC Records*.

53. Sonai Bunting to Secretary General, ANC, 24 June 1979, Box 89, Folder 55, Part II, *Lusaka Mission, ANC Records*.

Moscow's aid to the ANC accelerated accordingly. By 1979 South African radicals Eil and Violet Weinberg were beaming, since the ANC had "granted us the rare privilege of a medical check-up and rest period in the Soviet Union," for which they exuded "deep humble gratitude."[54] Carter was trapped, unable or unwilling to butt heads with the anticommunist consensus. When in October 1978, Helen Suzman, touted widely as a "liberal" alternative to apartheid, came to Columbia University in Manhattan and promptly denounced the "Soviet bloc" as more repressive than her native land, it more tightly boxed-in the peanut farmer.[55]

But he was constrained from the other side too, as suggested by reports that Washington was gravely concerned about the political reliability of Negro troops if the U.S. was forced to intervene militarily in Africa.[56]

The ongoing restlessness of Afro-Americans did not help Carter's case with the Euro-American majority that leaned decisively to the right. Months before his crushing electoral defeat in 1980, South African Broadcasting was commenting with smug satisfaction that Miami was "in flames" after the slaying of a Negro businessman during a typically bruising confrontation with the police. Black Miami erupted and SABC scolded: "America's framework of reference...must be questioned: the assumption that large bodies of men of different colour and cultural inheritance can be accommodated" was foolish.[57] Curiously, further imperiling Carter's already meager electoral chances, a putatively phony memorandum began to circulate widely—purportedly from Brzezinski—that mandated driving an even deeper cleavage between Afro-Americans and Africans.[58]

---

54. Eli and Violet Weinberg to Alfred Nzo, 16 August 1979, Box 88, Folder 43, Part II, *Lusaka Mission, ANC Records*.

55. Speech by Helen Suzman, 31 October 1978, Box 35, *Records of the Study Commission on U.S. Policy Toward Southern Africa, Schomburg Center, New York Public Library*.

56. Clipping, 26 October 1979, Box 245, *Leroy Walker Africa News Service Archive*.

57. South African Broadcasting Corporation Commentary, 20 May 1980, Box 237, *Leroy Walker Africa News Service Archive*.

58. *Rand Daily Mail*, 31 October 1980. For a text of this document, see "National Security Council Memorandum 46," 17 March 1978, Box 66, *Leon Sullivan Papers, Emory University-Atlanta*: This "secret" memo considered "durable contacts between radical African leaders and leftist leaders of the U.S. black community....Nationalist liberation movement in black Africa can act as a catalyst with far-reaching effects on the American black community....Such a result would be likely if Zaire went the way of Angola

Carter's inability to reverse the overthrow of his—and apartheid's—ally, the Shah of Iran, in 1979 ruined his reputation nationally among the all-important hawks; at the same time the decision by the new regime in Tehran to curtail oil supply to South Africa further isolated Pretoria, increasing anger there and among U.S. allies.[59] So moved, the Organization of Petroleum Exporting Countries—at the behest of the OAU—then tightened its oil embargo on Pretoria, which been imposed initially in 1974.[60] Stung to the quick, Pretoria frantically sought to impose fines on those who published information on oil supplies,[61] and diverted more tax revenue (that could have been directed towards armament) toward expensive programs seeking to convert coal to petroleum. Oil quickly became what the *Rand Daily Mail* called "our worst threat."[62] Pretoria began paying what was estimated to be an "80 percent premium" for oil.[63] Apparently keeping up with the news, by mid-1980, the ANC was accused of bombing a coal-to-oil facility.[64] This trend was punctuated when Tehran furiously broke diplomatic relations with Pretoria.[65] The oil crisis hamstrung nations besides South Africa. It led to a more dedicated search for uranium—which the colony to be named Namibia supplied—and other nuclear alternatives, which then empowered Pretoria.[66] But this move toward nuclear was complicated by the

and Mozambique....possibility of joint action by U.S. blacks and African nationalist movement....re-emergence of Pan-African ideals....extremist actions in the style of the defunct Black Panther Party" in motion; "internationally damage could be done to the United States by coordinated activity of African states designed to condemn U.S. policy toward South Africa and to initiate discussion on the U.S. racial issue at the United Nations, where the African representation constitutes a powerful bloc with about one-third of all the votes...the idea of economic assistance to black Americans shared by some African regimes could be realized by their placing orders in the United States mainly with companies owned by blacks, they could a limited influence on the U.S. black community....may refocus their attention on the Arab-Israeli conflict....their sympathies would like with the Arabs...inhibit coordinated activity of black movement in the United States....."

59. *Washington Post*, 2 February 1979.

60. *Business Week*, 5 March 1979.

61. Clipping, 24 January 1979, Box 237, *Leroy Walker Africa News Service Archive.*

62. *Rand Daily Mail*, 24 February 1979.

63. *Financial Times*, 20 February 1979.

64. Clipping, 29 June 1980, Box 115, *Leroy Walker Africa News Service Archive.*

65. *New York Times*, 5 March 1979.

66. *African Business*, April 1980, Box 295, *Leroy Walker Africa News Service Archive.*

Three Mile Island near nuclear meltdown in Pennsylvania in 1979[67] and the Israel-South Africa collaboration that led to a nuclear blast in what is now Namibia that same year.[68] Carter's reaction to both events was criticized roundly by the powerful U.S. right wing, further harming his re-election bid.

Still, stories kept appearing about this dangerous turn of events. The U.S. corporation Allis Chalmers was accused credibly of supplying Pretoria with its research reactor— "Safari I"—while the U.S. itself provided uranium for the sinister nuclear blast in Namibia. It turned out that between 1955 and 1977 about 100 technicians from South Africa were seconded to the U.S.'s Atomic Energy Commission.[69] By late 1980 it was reported that ESCOM, the Electricity Supply Commission of South Africa, employed four of the U.S.'s leading nuclear plant operators— all from the Tennessee Valley Authority— at "top salaries."[70] The U.S. movement maintained good sources on this kind of deviltry, not only from close monitoring of the press but also through its even closer ties with the liberation movements.

Thus, the future Foreign Minister of Namibia—Theo-Ben Gurirab—was a dear friend and in January 1981 was reported missing from a meeting with activists: he was "not able to make it," said the minutes, "because of pressing problems re: current negotiations."[71] SWAPO often briefed us about nuclear and related matters, pointing us to relevant sources.

As Israel's collaboration with apartheid became more obvious, the National Conference of Black Lawyers began to raise searching questions about this settler colonial state, which led to rebukes by Negro leaders, e.g. Vernon Jordan (an eventual investment banker) and Benjamin Hooks, a Republican Party insider who headed the NAACP. They termed solidarity with Palestinians as a "sideshow" while NCBL critiqued "Mr. Hooks' comment that Blacks should leave foreign affairs to the State Department," which was the essence

67. J. Samuel Walker, *Three Mile Island: A Nuclear Crisis in Historical Perspective*, Berkeley: University of California Press, 2004.

68. *TIME*, 3 March 1980; CBS News Transcript, 21 February 1980: "Israel got most of its help" for its own nuclear capability from Pretoria; CBS News Transcript, 22 February 1980: Here commentator Walter Cronkite, sought to amend the 21 February report: all the foregoing can be found in Box 114, *Leroy Walker Africa News Service Archive*.

69. Louis Schneider to "Washington Post," 1 November 1979, PED 1979 SOUTHERN AFRICA PROGRAM, *AFSC*.

70. *Johannesburg Star*, 27 November 1980.

71. Minutes in hand of Horne, 21 January 1981, Box 180, *Gerald Horne Papers*.

of the bargain that led to the simultaneous crushing of Robeson and the agonizing retreat of Jim Crow.[72] Interestingly, as Afro-Americans spoke out more vigorously about Palestine and Israel's collaboration with apartheid, there began to emerge more stories about purported "Black Anti-Semitism" (though rarely was the real anti-Jewish fervor of Pretoria a topic in the mainstream press).[73]

The blow inflicted by Iran served to heighten the importance of U.S. oil giants in keeping apartheid afloat. The bilateral tie to Washington also was complicated by the continuing importance of South African gold. "The price of gold is very linked to that of the dollar," said South African Broadcasting in 1979; hence, problems in the U.S. reverberated in South Africa. When the dollar "weakened," often the price of gold was "strengthened." Pretoria, it was said with pleasure, "welcomes the bonanza she is receiving [since] every ten dollar increase in the gold price adds 200 million rand to our credit over a year."[74] Gold rising and dollar weakening became a kind of mantra chanted in Pretoria for more than good luck.

As the 1980 presidential election approached, South Africa seemed to be doing well economically, which encouraged Reagan supporters to push even harder for victory, so as to keep the profits from there flowing. "Among those harvesting the rewards of this booming economy are subsidiaries of more than 300 American companies who are making historic highs in profits up to 49 percent here, 80 percent there," according to an observer cited in the *Washington Post* in August 1980. The "value of American exports to South Africa rose 30 percent in 1979 and South African imports went up 16 percent."[75]

Anti-apartheid forces were also pleased during this moment, despite the disappointments of Carter. The PAC, however, was still wracked with dissension. David Sibeko, the rotund and articulate leader, was slain as a result of internecine conflict in 1979, just after addressing a program honoring the deceased leader Malcolm X. He was mourned tearfully in Brooklyn, New York, in some ways the citadel of cultural nationalist stances.[76] His widow had visited the house of drummer Max Roach in the U.S. in 1978, accompanied by a PAC comrade. "The assassins gained entrance into the apartment,"

72. NCBL Statement, 16 October 1979, Box 191, *Gerald Horne Papers*.

73. Report by Bill Sutherland on U.S. tour, January 1979, PED SOUTHERN AFRICA PROGRAM, *AFSC*.

74. South African Broadcasting Corporation Commentary, 24 July 1979, Box 109, *Leroy Walker Africa News Service Archive*.

75. *Washington Post*, 23 August 1980.

76. *Black News* [U.S.], 15 February 1979 and June-July 1979,

said Elizabeth Sibeko, that was "owned" by "Vus" Make, another PAC leader, "and shot down David in cold blood and missing Vus by an inch."[77] In their obituary, *Azania News* included a picture of him hugging Black Panther founder Huey P. Newton. "In May 1965 he was sent on a journalism course" in China, where he was "converted to the revolutionary doctrines of Mao…." The former Communist Harry Haywood spoke at his memorial.[78] An ANC leader in Washington, Dumi Matabane, said then that "PAC is dying a natural death yet there are still forces that would like to see it survive,"[79] which was not far from the mark.

Unfortunately, the PAC was implicated during the murderous reign of the Khmer Rouge in Cambodia, as an outgrowth of the group's relationship to China. According to *Azania Today*, there were "20 PAC members who spent approximately two years in Democratic Kampuchea," the name adopted during the era of tyrannical misrule in southeast Asia. Profitably, an ANC delegation had visited Vietnam, which overturned the despotism of its neighbor, while the PAC was seeking to learn from the Khmer Rouge. Thus, the PAC denounced "Vietnam's barbarous and brutal invasion and pro-social imperialist role," code for Moscow, made more explicit when also reproached was the "brutal and barbarous invasion of Kampuchea by the Soviet-backed Hanoi regime…."[80] Just after Reagan's electoral triumph, there was a conference in Montreal targeting "Soviet Imperialism" sponsored by the "League of Revolutionary Struggle-Marxist Leninist" that included religious zealots from the "Free Afghanistan Alliance," the "Patriotic and Democratic Front of the Great National Union of Kampuchea," and, of course, the PAC. "A common theme running throughout the entire weekend," it was

77. Elizabeth Sibeko to Max Roach, 16 January 1980, Box 78, *Max Roach Papers, Library of Congress-Washington, D.C.*

78. *Azania News*, 14(Numbers 9-12, 1979), Box 144, *Leroy Walker Africa News Service Archive*. The influential Haywood was also close to the ubiquitous Richard Gibson. See Doug Rae to Gibson, 20 April 1978, Box 12, *Richard Gibson Papers*: "…Appreciate if you could act as our authorized agent in the negotiation of foreign publishing rights to [Haywood's] *Black Bolshevik*….. sales of the book are going very well in the U.S……Harry said to send his regards and tell you that he too is going to China." Doug Rae to Gibson, 21 March 1978, Box 12: "Robert Williams suggested that we send you a copy" of this book.

79. Dumi Matabane to Alfred Nzo, 8 May 1980, Box 14, Folder 24, *Lusaka Mission, ANC Records*.

80. *Azania Today*, 1(Number 2, March-April 1980), Box 144, *Leroy Walker Africa News Service Archive*.

said, "was the importance of recognizing the Soviet Union as the more dangerous of the two superpowers...."[81]

The 1979-1980 conflict between Vietnam and Cambodia ensnared the SACP too. Shortly after the Soviet intervention in Afghanistan in 1979, which had been induced in part by Washington's attempt to destabilize the left-wing regime in Kabul, the SACP endorsed Moscow's move, and in that context spoke of the "hatred of the Soviet Union" which "has united China with the imperialists" as an "ally of imperialists against the world revolutionary movement...." "China's brazen invasion of Vietnam," supposedly launched to teach Hanoi a lesson and bloody its nose for dislodging the Khmer Rouge, "was accompanied not by the threat of sanctions but by a frenzied rush of Western businessmen to negotiate trade deals with Peking." Meanwhile, "French invasions in Africa and continued occupation of African territories" were "ignored" by China and its African allies.[82]

Binding itself even closer to China, a PAC ally across the ocean in New Zealand charged that the World Council of Churches' Programme to Combat Racism was "infiltrated by ANC/Moscow supporters." The victory of ZANU in the Spring 1980 election that led to the establishment of Zimbabwe was portrayed as a setback for these infiltrators since Prime Minister Mugabe was "known for his strong anti-Soviet stance" and "has shown an unwillingness even to allow a Russian diplomatic presence in the new Zimbabwe." The South African poet Breyten Breytenback was praised because of his anti-SACP stance.[83] The PAC continued to attack the ANC relentlessly, in broadsides that included the Afro-Asian Peoples Solidarity Organization and its 1967 decision to designate "authentic" liberation movements—which did not include the PAC.[84]

On the other hand, the PAC's devolution tended to boost the ANC to the point that by November 1980 the group was boasting that it had access to the "OAU printing press," supplementing its usual source in East Berlin.[85]

But it was not necessarily smooth sailing for the ANC. By early 1979, Paula Whatley, who taught at Howard University and was

81. *Unity*, 5 December 1980, Box 179, *Gerald Horne Papers*.

82. Statement by SACP on "The Situation in Afghanistan," January 1980 in *South African Communists Speak*, 467-469, 468.

83. "Abosa," New Zealand section, 30 October 1980, Box 144, *Leroy Walker Africa News Service Archive*.

84. *Azania Today*, 1(Number 1, 1980), Box 139, *Leroy Walker Africa News Service Archive*.

85. Memorandum from OAU, 13 November 1980, Reel 7, *Oliver Tambo Papers*.

married to ANC representative in Washington Dumi Matabane, was reporting to ANC headquarters in Lusaka, that "in the main the white groups" in the U.S. "don't even attempt in the paltriest fashion to politicize white workers' though Vietnam has shaken things up." The African Liberation Support Committee "foundered on Maoism" in Angola and "its present main political activity" was "spreading anti-Sovietism" and demonizing those who would not go along, the ANC and MPLA and their many supporters most notably. Unnamed "mistakes" had led to the foundering of NAIMSAL, she said. She praised the United Auto Workers Union and the Coalition of Black Trade Unionists but "the A. Philip Randolph Institute and Bayard Rustin" were to be avoided as corrupt right-wing Social Democrats linked tightly to the CIA and labor misleader George Meany. Still, it would not be "wise for ANC to have too overtly a reliance on the CPUSA as this would only bring ANC into internal feuds in the USA."[86] She was not alone in questioning the integrity of U.S. labor. In the pages of the *African Communist*, Meany and Irving Brown were subjected to brutal critique.[87] Bluntly, *Sechaba*—the ANC periodical—termed Brown to be a "CIA agent."[88]

Whatley's spouse was not necessarily upbeat either. In the waning days of the Carter regime he visited West Virginia and found "coal miners are losing jobs because of the American companies importing coal from South Africa." These bedraggled workers "were shocked to learn that a black mine worker in South Africa is paid 5 [rand] a day," whereas they "got $60 or $70." As Pretoria's coal-to-oil scheme ramped up after the downturn in relations with Iran, miners in South Africa came under even more pressure, contributing to unrest. Wisely, Dumi Matabane told the ANC leadership in words that had held relevance since at least the 19th century, "we have to strengthen our propaganda in this country since it is the centre of operation for our enemies...." The ANC returned the favor, as expressed when he "met Rev. Ben Chavis" who gave "many thanks to ANC for the part it played in the fight for the release of the Wilmington 10," political prisoners in North Carolina of which Chavis was the leader." This cleric, who was to lead the NAACP briefly, was "ready to work" with the ANC. The wider problem here, however, was the difficulty in working out a process with the group's representative at the

86. Report by Paula Whatley, January 1979, Box 14, Folder 24, *Lusaka Mission, ANC Records*.

87. R.S. Nyamenko, "U.S. Bid to Derail South African Trade Union Movement," *African Communist*, (First Quarter 1983, Number 92): 33-37.

88. Editorial, *Sechaba*, (November 1982): 1-2.

U.N., the respected Makhathini, about lines of authority[89]—perhaps inevitable given the importance of both New York and Washington nationally and internationally.

Whatley had put her finger on a real problem: as the anti-apartheid movement grew, the machinations of white supremacy in the U.S. meant that those who were defined as "white" would receive informal preference for positions in the movement, although this seemed to be counter-intuitive. This dynamic arose among the Quakers, one of the more politically engaged religious denominations, which—as was typical—debated if "preference will be given to Black Americans" in Southern African posts, with the expected negative response. Reactions ranged from the usual dodge, "'color is totally irrelevant,' to the feeling that a Black American would have more difficulty and be less effective than a white American… One person asked whether a Black American could effectively address the white power structure in America."[90] The consensus among the deciders, mostly "white," was that "all other things being equal, the responses were negative."[91]

Bill Sutherland, one of the few Afro-Americans on the staff of the Quakers, who had one of the longest records of service in Africa, stretching from Nkrumah's Ghana to Tanzania, was subjected to repetitive critique. A graduate of Bates College, he was jailed because of his pacifism during the previous World War, was a co-founder of CORE—whose anticommunism under Roy Innis was merely an exaggeration more than a deviation—and moved to Ghana in 1954.[92] He was treated dismissively despite his credentials when he was being considered for a post as the Angola crisis was percolating in 1975. Sukie Rice of the New England staff asked, "we are still unclear up here as to just what his connection is at this time, or previous to this, to AFSC or Quakers….He sounds like what some might call an agitator…."[93] David Birmingham, described rhapsodically by a staffer as a "warm, straightforward professorial Quaker gentleman," was noticeably hostile to Sutherland, who "couldn't have been worse for building bridges between whites and blacks in Southern Africa,"

89. Dumi Matabane to Alfred Nzo, 8 May 1980, Box 14, Folder 24, Part II, *Lusaka Mission, ANC Records*.

90. "Jack H." to "Dear Lorraine", 13 April 1974, IAD U.S. PROG. CON'T RYP/PUERTO RICO (PARTICIPANTS-TRIPS) ISD ADMINISTRATION AFRICA, *AFSC*.

91. Harry Abrahamson in Lusaka to Lorraine Cleveland, 11 April 1974, *IAD* U.S. PROG. CON'T…. *AFSC*.

92. Information sheet on Sutherland, no date, ID 1975, *AFSC*.

93. Memorandum on Bill Sutherland, 8 July 1975, ID 1975, *AFSC*.

though his job was precisely to "build bridges between social change people in Southern Africa and America." There was a "great deal of misunderstanding still befogging perceptions" of such matters internally—which was truer than realized.[94]

Sutherland was sufficiently close to the leadership in Dar es Salaam that he worked for the Foreign Ministry and applied for citizenship.[95] Rather breezily in December 1975, Sutherland provided a list of the regional leaders he knew "personally," which dwarfed any comparable list from all of his colleagues.[96] In 1975 he had an "extended personal discussion" with the Rhodesian sellout leader Bishop Muzorewa; had "several short meetings" with Victoria Chitepo, en route to becoming Zimbabwe's First Lady before the assassination of her spouse; and a "long discussion" with Nobel Laureate Sean McBride.[97] In 1978 ZANU's Mugabe himself wrote Sutherland "personally to request...urgent help for our Party...following the attack on two of our transit camps in Mozambique...."[98] Shortly thereafter, aid was en route.[99] When the Quakers sought to send personnel to Mozambique, they were told by Janet Mondlane that Maputo was "quite leery of Americans" – "don't hold your breath for change"—but this was not necessarily true of Sutherland.[100] It was Sutherland who intervened with the Tanzanian government, requesting "reconsideration of the refusal to allow" AFSC to initiate "registration" of

94. David Sogge to Pat Hunt, 19 March 1976, IAD U.S. PROG. CON'T...... *AFSC.*

95. David Sogge to U.N. Special Committee, circa 1976, IAD U.S. PROG. CON'T......*AFSC.*

96. Bill Sutherland to Dave Edler, 28 December 1975, ID 975, *AFSC*: "These are the people [in Mozambique alone] who I know personally..... Holder Martins, Minister of Health.....Janet Mondlane, Ministry of Health, President Samora Machel....Vice President Marcelino dos Santos.....Jorge Ribello, Minister of Information.....Joaquim Chissano, Minister for Foreign Affairs.....Safferdeen Khan, Ministry of Foreign Affairs...."

97. Bill Sutherland to "Steve and Dave," 16 August 1975, ID 1975, *AFSC.* As late as 1977 a misguided journalist for a prestigious newspaper said that Muzorewa "commands the overwhelming support of Rhodesia's Black majority." *New York Times*, 18 December 1977. The cleric had spent time in the U.S., was ordained by the United Methodists and studied at Central Methodist College in Missouri: *Washington Post*, 25 April 1979.

98. Robert Mugabe to Bill Sutherland, 5 January 1978, ID 1978 AFRICA PROGRAM-CON'T SOUTHERN AFR REGION.... *AFSC.*

99. Jeanne Newman to Robert Mugabe, 29 March 1978, ID 1978 AFRICA PROGRAM-CON'T SOUTHERN AFR REGION.... *AFSCI.*

100. "David" from Mozambique to AFSC, 29 September 1978, ID 1978 AFRICA PROGRAM-CON'T SOUTHERN......*AFSC.*

the group's shipping of five tons of supplies to refugees in Botswana and ten tons to Zambia via Dar, though the government there was still gun-shy from the Pan-African debacle that led to the 1974 detention of U.S. Negroes for alleged smuggling.[101]

When an informed and eloquent spokesman was needed to address a shareholders meeting at Fluor, the Southern California corporation that had invested in a coal liquefaction plant in South Africa deemed essential for apartheid's energy future, it was Sutherland who was deployed.[102] Interestingly, as the battle for Angola raged, Sutherland was accused of being "concerned that too little news of Black group[s] supporting the MPLA...had reached the African news media" while "extensive publicity" was accorded Roy Innis and his recruitment of Negro mercenaries.[103] When future Nobel Laureate Desmond Tutu asserted in 1979 that the Quakers were "very knowledgeable" about his South Africa, he probably had the likes of Sutherland in mind.[104]

Yet, writing from tony Montecito, California, one of the more opulent towns in the U.S., Libby Jackman—after noting that "the number of [Quakers] in South Africa is about 80"—found that many "stated their distrust of Bill Sutherland's activities" and, to be fair, "of Lyle Tatum and the AFSC in general...."[105] It was Tatum, one of the Quakers' longest serving staffers, who in 1979 went to a pro-Zimbabwe meeting in London and was disappointed to find an "audience which was heavily Communist....I never saw a better argument for the AFSC Peace Education Program on Southern Africa," seen as an effective antidote and congruent with the liberal anticommunist consensus back home.[106] To be sure, Sutherland emerged from this same consensus but the ironic contradiction was that because he was a Negro in the U.S., he was expected to defer to

101. Bill Sutherland to Tanzanian government, 10 August 1978, ID 1978 AFRICA PROGRAM-CON'T SOUTHERN

102. *Los Angeles Times*, 11 March 1979.

103. David Sogge to Southern Africa Committee, IAD U.S. PROG. CON'T, *AFSC*.

104. *Kairos* [South African Council of Churches newspaper], July 1979, PED SOUTHERN AFRICA PROGRAM, *AFSC*.

105. Libby Jackman to David Sogge, 26 October 1977, PED PROGRAM RESOURCES SOUTHERN AFRICA ADMIN-PROJECTS-SA STUDY TOUR FWCC SEMINAR & MEETING, *AFSC*.

106. Lyle Tatum to David Sogge, 22 September 1979, INTERNATIONAL DIVISION 1979 ADMINISTRATION AFRIA PROGRAMS ADMINISTRATION SOUTHERN...MOZAMBIQUE, *AFSC*.

his Euro-American cohorts. Thus, Sutherland worked closely with the PAC's Templeton Ntantala.[107]

As for Sutherland, he ruffled feathers in the group when he said reproachfully that "nonviolent black militant movements" in the region, soulmates of AFSC theoretically, "often do want contact with *white* people," he emphasized "but are quite open to contact with those they feel have suffered their same oppression, e.g. Blacks from USA. Now white South Africans find this very hard to take"[108]—and, it seems, so did some of his colleagues. Nevertheless, Sutherland was accused of the ultimate sin by a fellow staffer: endorsing armed struggle in Southern Africa.[109] "South African Friends never mentioned giving up of white privilege" was another insight offered, which should not have come as a surprise either.[110]

Other AFSC staff then in the sub-region included Jim Seawell, a Negro who was graying and bearded,[111] and whose spouse was Euro-American and, apparently, felt "their marriage could be a positive factor in their work for social reconciliation in Zimbabwe." He had worked in Nkrumah's Ghana on curriculum reform and physics instruction.[112] He was friendly with Mike Williams, a UCLA graduate who reported for the sub-regional press, centered in Zambia and Zimbabwe.[113] Seawell too was reprimanded for providing funds to individual PAC members.[114]

Despite her acute insight, Whatley may have been unaware of some of the hardly visible currents in the solidarity movement.

---

107. Report by James and Patricia Seawell, 3 December 1980, ID AFRICA PROGS TAMPSA ZAMBIA, *AFSC*.

108. Bill Sutherland to Dear David, 4 November 1977, PED PROGRAM RESOURCES SOUTHERN AFRICA ADMIN-PROJECTS……*AFSC*.

109. Louis Schneider to "Members of the Board of Directors," 27 July 1979, South Africa File, *AFSC*.

110. Report, Circa 1977, PED PROGRAM RESOURCES SOUTHERN AFRICA……*AFSC*.

111. Clipping, 15 June 1981, PED SOUTHERN AFRICA…. TAO, *AFSC*.

112. Memo from Tom Draisma, 2 February 1981, ID, AFRICA ADMINISTRATION…. SOUTH S AFR IAP S AFR REP TAMAPSA, *AFSC*.

113. The Seawells to Magham Keita, 2 December 1980, ID AFRICA PROGS TAMPSA ZAMBIA, *AFSC*. UCLA, which contained a formidable African Studies program, also had ties to Rhodesia. See S.D. O'Donnell to Kenneth Towsey, 2 October 1975, Box 2, *Kenneth Towsey Papers*: The "friend" of Rhodesian operatives, Professor John Hutchinson of UCLA "was at my home for dinner last night" after meeting with Nkomo—and then briefed Salisbury.

114. D. Sogge to the Seawells, 29 January 1981, ID AFRICA PROGS TAMPSA ZAMBIA, *AFSC*.

For example, as the Rhodesian revolt was hurtling toward resolution, 40 U.S. nationals in the colony sought bravely to intervene in opposition to the so-called "Internal Settlement,"[115] a capitulation to settler colonialism. There were about 20 U.S. nationals in Mozambique as of 1979, according to AFSC staff, including the Afro-American architect Roberta Washington, then designing a health clinic,[116] and later a resident of Harlem, where I worked alongside her in the movement. One Quaker correspondent said that she was "greatly respected in the country. She was invited to attend the Fourth Congress" of the ruling party,[117] further indicating her prestige.

Matabane's sobriety notwithstanding, there were indications of imminent change, even in the U.S. Arriving steadily were those fleeing conscription by Pretoria, reluctant to fight in Angola and Namibia and elsewhere. "A number of war resisters are starting to arrive in the U.S.A.," said organizer Don Morton in late 1978, who desperately was seeking to "find them jobs, lawyers, places to stay."[118] Even in Brooklyn, Morton was worried by the long arm of Pretoria. By late 1979 he expressed "caution in discussing" his campaign since he well knew that South Africa's "Defense Force despises Omkeer," the draft resisters' network he coordinated. When their newsletter appeared, the SADF journal went to some length to denounce them. "We make it a policy not to openly discuss such matters as who pays for or who prints this 'subversive literature'" because of this nervous apprehension. Remarkably, he had "procured lists from the Defense Force itself," that contained "well over 5000 draftees inducted into the army since 1977, with their home addresses and broken down by religious denomination…." This was an "unbelievable breakthrough." The group's "mission is so vital that it can't be overstated." Pretoria, he said, "will be furious when they realize the scope of our operation…." He was also studying how "the successful GI movement was built in the U.S. during the war against Indo-China…." Like U.S. soldiers who had reached out to their supposed

115. "Japowell" from Dar to Peter Molotsi of AFSC, 3 March 1978, ID 1978 AFRICA PROGRAM-CON'T SOUTHERN…. *AFSC.*

116. "Daily" of University of Washington-Seattle, 10 October 1979, INTERNATIONAL DIVISION 1979 ADMINISTRATION AFRICA PROGRAMS ADMINISTRATION SOUTHERN…. *AFSC.*

117. Patricia Hunt, Memo to File on Conversation with Susan McCord, 17 August 1983, ID 1983 Africa-E to Africa-SA, Mozambique, S. Africa, IAP Zambia, *AFSC.*

118. Don Morton to Carol Bernstein Ferry and Ping Ferry, 11 December 1978, Box 18, *Bernstein Ferry Papers.*

adversaries in Indochina, Morton was organizing a "conference... with SWAPO" in Chicago in November 1979.[119]

Morton was seeking funding for these efforts from Carol Bernstein Ferry, the affluent New Yorker, who had problems of her own. "I've never joined the Communists or the Socialists" she said later; nonetheless, her "house was burglarized in a very peculiar way;" it was "very, very queer" and "nothing was stolen." The "file cabinet in our bedroom...was opened and stuff was strewn all over our room...."[120] Shortly thereafter Randall Robinson of Trans-Africa, the Black American lobby arm that targeted apartheid, said his group had suffered "weekly break-ins for months." Daniel Opperman of South Africa was asked to leave the U.S. during this time based on reports of his involvement of harassment of anti-apartheid organizations.[121] It was in early 1978 that the anti-apartheid activist and academic Richard Lapchick was beaten severely in his office by two masked men.[122] In May 1979 Caryl Murphy of the *Washington Post* called Millard Arnold in Windhoek, inquiring about troop movements and political trends, when suddenly the telephone line went dead. Earlier this journalist had been followed ominously in London.[123]

"Everybody lived with constant surveillance, constant" reiterated the seasoned activist Prexy Nesbitt. His mail was "always messed with" and he constantly discovered "tapped telephones." He recalled the now infamous slaying of Black Panther leader Fred Hampton in the wee hours of the Chicago morning of 4 December 1969 by agents of the state. "There is no doubt in my mind," he insisted, that this was "related to Fred Hampton's tremendous and growing international outreach....I remember introducing Fred Hampton and Bobby Rush, now Congressman Rush, to representatives of the Mozambique Liberation Front" in Chicago.[124]

---

119. Don Morton to Carol Bernstein Ferry and Ping Ferry, 23 October 1979, Box 18, *Bernstein Ferry Papers*.

120. Oral History, Carol Bernstein Ferry, 12 October 1994, Box 23, *Bernstein Ferry Papers*.

121. *Guardian* [London], no date, circa 1982, Box 237, *Leroy Walker Africa News Service Archive*.

122. *Washington Post*, 24 February 1978. See also *New York Times*, 1 August 1981: New York attorney, Catherine Julia Tobin, 29, slain in Durban, "stabbed in the chest, arms and hands". Robbery ruled out as a motive. She was a graduate of the law school of New Jersey's Rutgers University, a hotbed of political activism, including the anti-apartheid variety.

123. Richard Pollak, *Up Against Apartheid: The Role and Plight of the Press of South Africa*, Carbondale: Southern Illinois University Press, 1981, 85-86.

124. Oral History, Prexy Nesbitt, 1 April 2009, *Columbia College-Chicago*.

It remains unclear who rifled Bernstein's files and why Lapchick was brutalized. What was obvious was that the rise of Reagan combined with a troubled global climate—the overthrow of the Shah in Iran, the Soviet intervention in Afghanistan, the dislodging of the Khmer Rouge in Cambodia, Pretoria's heightened aid to "contra" forces in Mozambique and Angola, the election of Robert Mugabe in the new nation of Zimbabwe, continuing unrest in South Africa itself, to name only a few key events—was frazzling tempers all around.

* * *

And in the U.S., which Dumi Matabane accurately identified as Pretoria's main source of support, an anti-apartheid movement was reaching new heights of fervor. This was manifested heavily on the cultural front: in music, movies, and sports, most notably. South Africa's relatively small population of European descent had produced an outsized number of personalities in these fields, including luminaries, e.g. golfer Gary Player, tennis whiz Cliff Drysdale, actor and dancer Juliet Prowse, African musicians like Hugh Masekela and Abdullah Ibrahim, and many more. Pressure on this front was destined to receive press coverage, given the personalities and profit involved.

Just like the nations themselves, there had been a lengthy cross-fertilization between the music of South Africa and the U.S. In the 1920s the recorded music of country star Jimmy Rodgers—who was deeply influenced by Negro culture and music—was widely available in Durban and exerted an influence on Zulu music. So-called "Black Face Minstrelsy" had arrived from the U.S. to South Africa by 1862 and vaudeville in Cape Town had largely developed parallel to and in sync with its North American counterpart. The spread of the phonograph and radio led to the further assertion of a cultural and racial identity between Africans in South Africa and U.S. Negroes. The music called jazz was seen by many in South Africa as a modified form of what was there termed "Bantu" music and dance.[125]

Subsequently, Muhammad Ali, the Afro-American champion, had been prevailed on to decline taking his immense talents to a Bantustan: by 1978 his attempt to fight there was foiled because of protest, said the promoter Robert Arum.[126] Arum was determined to

125. Erich Nunn, *Sounding the Color Line: Music and Race in the Southern Imagination*, Athens: University of Georgia Press, 2015, 70, 72, 64.

126. Clipping, 11 March 1978, Box 247, *Leroy Walker Africa News Service Archive*.

promote boxing matches in South Africa nonetheless. Speaking from South Africa, he criticized the Afro-American boxer Larry Holmes after he refused adamantly to consider fighting there.[127] The Negro champion Bob Foster was also pressured not to fight Pierre Fourie in South Africa.[128] But a setback for the movement arrived in 1979 when the Negro boxer John Tate defeated Kallie Knoetze in a Bantustan. When they fought in Miami earlier, demonstrations occurred against the South African, who had been working as a policeman and had once shot an African child in the leg, who was said to be fleeing from a robbery.[129] These protests led to the U.S. revoking Knoetze's visa on grounds of moral turpitude,[130] which earned censure from a conservative columnist in Orlando, Florida.[131]

The attempt to travel to South Africa by the Negro tennis player Arthur Ashe, who also was personally close to Trans-Africa's Randall Robinson, occupied considerable attention in Nixon's White House[132]—and beyond. It was at the urging of Congressman Diggs that the legation in Mbabane delivered to Ashe a message discouraging a trip to South Africa: "you would be subjected to degrading experience, urge reconsideration."[133] Unlike other sporting sojourners there, however, Ashe styled himself as an anti-apartheid crusader. In 1970, amid klieg lights, cameras, and hordes of reporters—with U.N. official Ralph Bunche nearby, a Negro purportedly complicit in the devastation of the Congo—the man with the devastating backhand addressed the matter of apartheid before the United Nations committee with oversight. Described as "calm, polite and moderate" by an Euro-American observer, the acceptable mode for Negroes in this envoy's preference—"[he] did not seek at any time to be militant": this envoy was also exuberant that "his reference to our embassy in Pretoria was the only repeat only reference he made to [U.S. policy]…."[134]

127. *Rand Daily Mail*, 5 February 1979.

128. *Guardian* [U.K.], 1 June 1973.

129. *New York Times*, 3 June 1979.

130. *New York Times*, 10 January 1979.

131. *Orlando Sentinel Star*, 14 January 1979.

132. William Rountree to President Nixon, 28 January 1970, Box 65, *Nixon Presidential Materials Project, White House Central Files, Subject Files, Richard M. Nixon Presidential Library*.

133. Telegram, 19 August 1969, RG 59, Box 3095, Subject Numeric Files: Social, *NARA-CP*.

134. Airgram, 14 April 1970, Box 3095, RG 59, Subject Numeric Files, *NARA-CP*.

Ever since I.W. Schlesinger arrived at the southern tip of Africa from the U.S. at the turn of the 20th century, the products of the industry that had come to be metonymized as "Hollywood" had been quite popular in South Africa. In 1970 it was estimated that 20% of all films entering South Africa were "banned" from being viewed by Africans and others not defined as "white." This list included *Sweet Charity, Boston Strangler, Rosemary's Baby, West Side Story, The Mercenaries, Che,* and *Valley of the Dolls*. Banned for Africans but not Indians nor Coloureds were *Tom Jones, The Dirty Dozen, Darling, The Magnificent Seven, From Russia with Love, Spartacus, A Farewell to Arms, Zulu,* and *One Hundred Rifles*. Illustrative of the contradictions of apartheid which restrained capitalism was the estimate that at that point only 7% of Africans had ever seen a movie. The warmth between Pretoria and Washington was demonstrated when the South African Information Service film—*Kutlwanong: A Place of Hearing*—won a Gold Camera Award from the U.S. Industrial Film Festival in May 1970. Likewise, it was then that Hollywood studio MGM appointed Andre Pieterse of South Africa as Vice President for Foreign Distribution. Accommodating U.S. airlines censored the films they showed and advertised en route to South Africa, so as not to offend the tender sensibilities of apartheid. Reportedly, Pan American Airways dropped *For Love of Ivy*, with Afro-American actors Sidney Poitier and Abbey Lincoln (soon to be renamed Aminata Moseka). In 1965 sixty odd U.S. artists signed a declaration stating they would do all in their power to prevent their work from being issued or used in South Africa, but actors for hire could hardly control what studios did with their handiwork—unless they were considered to be mega-stars.[135]

By 1979 it was estimated that Hollywood was losing an estimated $100 million annually from piracy, with South Africa designated by one analyst as the "biggest problem."[136] Ironically, as apartheid gained the global spotlight, the incentive arose to make more Hollywood fare with Southern African backdrops, which created more opportunities for piracy and related problems. By 1978 the Negro actor Richard Roundtree, then encased in celebrity because of his role as the private detective Shaft, was to be found in South Africa starring in a movie about the war in Rhodesia. Apparently not viewed as an "honorary white" an unnamed "Black U.S. actress"

135. Report on Cultural Boycott, 18 June 1970, Reel 5, #583, Part II, *ACOA Papers-Library of Congress*.

136. *Business Week*, 9 April 1979.

was treated roughly at a local bistro, incurring her wrath[137] and illustrating once more that Pretoria and Washington were operating on separate tracks. Cinema converted cutthroat mercenaries into heroes in movies like *The Wild Geese*, starring Richard Burton,[138] seen as one of the brightest stars in the cinematic firmament.

There were dissenting voices, including the iconoclastic Afro-American actor/comedian Richard Pryor, who told a U.S. television audience that "angry black people in this country, who are carrying guns around should go to South Africa and kill some white people," which NBC—then broadcasting his incendiary words—bleeped or deleted, including what was described as an "unspecified obscenity."[139] Less controversially, an ANC member was nominated for a prestigious "Oscar" nomination from Hollywood for producing the music for the well-attended movie about Steve Biko, *Cry Freedom*.[140]

In New York, we made a point of throwing up picket-lines at theaters exhibiting movies whitewashing apartheid. This included the 1980 blockbuster *The Dogs of War*, a paean to mercenaries, a screening of which at an 86th Street theater in Manhattan we leafleted.[141] Our most extensive campaign was against the South African-backed movie *The Gods Must be Crazy*.[142]

As the nomination for the Biko movie indicated, musicians were playing an ever-larger role in the anti-apartheid movement. In February 1980 at the spectacular Church of St. John the Divine at 112th Street and Amsterdam Avenue in Manhattan, I chaired a committee that raised thousands of dollars for the use of ZANU and ZAPU in the upcoming election—weeks away—that led to the independence of Zimbabwe. This was the first of many fundraisers featuring jazz artists raising money for the cause, with this one starring South African luminaries Hugh Masekela and Abdullah Ibrahim, along with Jimmy Owens and Cuban percussionist Machito.[143] (We were hardly

137. Clipping, 22 October 1978, Box 259, *Leroy Walker Africa News Service Archive*.

138. Clipping, 7 December 1978, Box 259, *Leroy Walker Africa News Service Archive*.

139. *Los Angeles Times*, 20 May 1979.

140. Stephen Ellis and Tsepo Sechaba, *Comrades Against Apartheid*, 133.

141. Leaflet, circa 1984, Box 180, *Gerald Horne Papers*. In the same box, see "Outreach," October 1984: the movie was exhibited at the 68ith Street Playhouse in Manhattan.

142. Leaflet, circa 1984, Box 180, *Gerald Horne Papers*.

143. "Zimbabwe Emergency Concert," 9 February 1980, Box 179, *Gerald Horne Papers*. In the same box, see material on "Emergency Conference" on Zimbabwe, 11 January 1980.

alone in raising funds for the liberation of Zimbabwe; in 1977, ACOA sent $1500 to Robert Mugabe in Mozambique[144] and $2500 to his rival, Joshua Nkomo, "which comes from a friend of ours."[145] In 1979 Houser sent a "scanner machine" to the ZANU office in Maputo.)[146]

In 1979 we organized an analogous concert featuring the brilliant violinist Noel Pointer and the prominent saxophonist Sonny Fortune.[147] The politicized Fortune organized an anti-apartheid discussion on the New Jersey based radio station WBGO-FM. There it was mentioned that not only did the pianist Chick Corea perform in South Africa but recorded there too and thanked Pretoria in his liner notes for their aid. At his anti-apartheid performance, Fortune's combo consisted of the stellar musicians Billy Hart, Stanley Cowell and Reggie Workman—the latter bassist was a workhorse on behalf of good causes.[148] These concerts involved intensive labor; minutes of the organizing meeting of the latter event revealed that "press releases have to be written, flyers have to be dropped off...posters have to be posted...phone calls have to be made...."[149]

We did not neglect the mighty financial powers behind the music industry—and other industries—which is why we could be found in June 1980 at what we called a "mass demonstration" in the heart of finance capital, at Wall and Broad Streets, home of the New York Stock Exchange. Our slogan? "Remember Soweto."[150]

The cultural boycott also included a spirited protest targeting the Museum of Natural History in Manhattan since they collaborated with their apartheid peers in a paleo-anthropological exhibit displaying the bones of long deceased African ancestors.[151]

Thus, it came as no surprise when in 1969 a Cape Town pianist then known as Adolf "Dollar" Brand described himself to a potential U.S. donor as a "thirty year South African pianist, composer and arranger." "I left [South Africa] about four years ago," he continued,

---

144. George Houser to Robert Mugabe, 19 September 1977, Box 93, *ACOARA*.

145. George Houser to Joshua Nkomo, 11 May 1977, Box 93, *ACOARA*.

146. E.Z. Tekere to George Houser, 20 October 1979, Box 149, *ACOARA*.

147. Minutes of South African Freedom Day Coalition meeting, 17 June 1979, Box 179, *Gerald Horne Papers*. See also *Guardian* [N.Y.] 8 February 1984.

148. *Daily World* [N.Y.], 18 February 1984.

149. Minutes of 7 November 1983 meeting at District 65, Box 180, *Gerald Horne Papers*.

150. Leaflet, 16 June 1980, Box 179, *Gerald Horne Papers*.

151. Petition to Thomas Nicolson of Museum of Natural History, circa 1984, Box 180, *Gerald Horne Papers*. In the same collection, Box 171, see Leaflet on protest.

where he met the Negro musician Duke Ellington, who brought him to the U.S.[152] In 1963 Ellington and the famed saxophonist John Coltrane had checked out Brand in Switzerland, and it was in 1966 that Ellington heaped praise on his fellow pianist, in a recommendation that helped him enter the nation.[153] Dollar Brand had first became intimately familiar with jazz at the age of 14 in Cape Town, a port city where U.S. Negroes had been visiting for decades. But he first heard the sweet sounds when an ice cream truck he passed blared the music of Louis Jordan over the loudspeakers. Soon he was playing at clubs in Johannesburg but to audiences composed of Europeans only by law and regulation. His pointillistic music was influenced by the playing of Theolonius Monk, the North Carolina-born Afro-American pianist, while his sideman Kippie Moeketi was influenced by the saxophone renderings of the Kansas City-born Negro Charlie "Bird" Parker.[154]

But like so many exiles from Africa, this musician did not adapt very well to the peculiar folkways of the U.S. He "appeared to be suffering from various forms of alienation," said one observer: "both artistic and social. He seemed to be just plain homesick for Africa at times. Also, his music was so specifically African in source and so linked to contemporary dissonant sounds that he felt himself to be outside of the American jazz world," a feeling that had a "corrosive effect on his ability to concentrate solely on his studies."[155]

As this disgruntled exile was applying for funds, the Euro-American horn player Stan Getz was playing in South Africa—for "whites only in Johannesburg, Cape Town and Durban," according to the jazz bible, *Downbeat*, which seemed to think this was acceptable as long as he found time to play for Africans only too. Getz was billed as the first prominent jazz musician to play in the nation since Bud Shank visited in 1958.[156]

The "cultural nationalists" centered in Brooklyn saw jazz, of which Ibrahim was an embodiment, as essential to their, well, "culture." Their headquarters—called "The East"—featured performances by signature musicians such as Pharoah Sanders, McCoy

---

152. Adolf "Dollar" Brand to Gerald Freund, 1 November 1969, Box 299, RG 1.2 (FA 387), Series 200: US, Subseries 200 r: US, *RFR Projects, Rockefeller Archive Center*.

153. Duke Ellington Immigration and Naturalization Service, 4 February 1966, Box 299, RG 1.2 (FA 387).

154. Jack Lind, "Dollar Brand," *Downbeat* [U.S.] 30(Number 30, 21 November 1963): 13, 34, 13

155. Hall Overton to Norman Lloyd, 19 May 1968, Box 299, RG 1.2 (FA 387).

156. *Downbeat*, 37(Number 15, 6 August 1970): 8.

Tyner, Rashaan Roland Kirk, Dewey Redman, Sun Ra, Lee Morgan, and—notably—Max Roach. Lectures by Black Power luminaries like Stokely Carmichael and H. Rap Brown guaranteed that the PAC would receive a favorable reception.[157]

Roach was one of the more politicized musicians. Just after the Soweto Revolt, he joined with fellow politicized musician, Archie Shepp, in a concert in Rome where they performed "Sweet Mao"—in honor of the Chinese leader—and "Suid Afrika '76."[158] This was a continuation of a pattern; earlier Roach's stimulating "Freedom Now Suite," devoted to the anti-Jim Crow cause, was banned in South Africa. This boomeranged, he said, and "created the kind of curiosity that sold it. It was distributed much more widely than a record like that perhaps would have been….People heard it….When Dollar Brand [Abdullah Ibrahim] and Hugh Masekela and folks like that came to the States," said the drummer, "they would say to me, 'it really gave us a lot of inspiration to know that other people were thinking about what was going on over here.'"[159] Roach, the activist, had joined with others in picketing a concert at Manhattan's Carnegie Hall held by the dynamic duo of Miles Davis, trumpeter extraordinaire, and Gil Evans. "We had a picket line…. Miles stopped the concert, took me off the stage…. It was really a political issue." At stake were matters concerning the principals in this stellar event implicated in ties to apartheid.[160]

Roach may have been the U.S. artist most deeply involved in the anti-apartheid cause. He was not singular, however. The future famed poet Maya Angelou reminded him in 1961 that when the talented singer Billie Holiday died, "they had a day of quiet in South Africa…. I would never have known," she said, "that Billie was liked or known or anything" there.[161]

Angelou's close companion was the PAC's Vusumzi Make and it was he who in 1961 praised Roach's tune, "Tears for Johannesburg", which led him to ask the composer to write an article on Sharpeville:

---

157. Kwasi Konadu, *A View from the East: Black Cultural Nationalism and Education in New York City*, Syracuse: Syracuse University Press, 2009, 28.

158. Interview, 2 September 1979, Box 57, *Max Roach Papers, Library of Congress-Washington, D.C.*

159. Interview, 3 June 1989, Box 57, *Max Roach Papers*.

160. Interview, 26 April 1992, Box 57, *Max Roach Papers*.

161. Maya Angelou to "Dearest Max and Abbey," 6 January 1961, Box 70, *Max Roach Papers*.

it "will be very widely circulated in South Africa, Africa and many parts of the world," he assured.[162]

The South African R.B. Shogoe, who had served time in prison with the PAC's Sobukwe, told Roach in 1961 that "people like you, Charles Mingus, Abbey Lincoln, Coleman Hawkins"—skilled Negro musicians all—were a "real inspiration to us Freedom Fighters here in Africa....Your disc—'We Insist'—is a personal pride to every young jazz collector here in Johannesburg. I was very lucky to get a direct copy from the States before it was censored by the government...." So inspired, Shogoe "composed" a "song...only played on the black notes of the piano and is typically Xhosa...." He told Roach that he had a "clash" with "Marcus Garvey when he said a piano cannot only be played on white notes...."[163] He was not the only South African artist who contacted Roach for sustenance. The novelist Zakes Mda told the percussionist, "it is through desperation that I write to you" since "I have known you to be sympathetic to the struggle of the people of South Africa."[164]

In 1970 there was a segregated production of the musical *Cabaret* that arrived from Manhattan to South Africa, led by producer Harold Prince.[165] The Negro singer Percy Sledge—who had climbed the music charts with his affecting "When a Man Loves a Woman"—showed no love for Africans when he arrived to perform in South Africa that same year. He was placed in a hotel that barred Africans, then was induced to take all his meals in his room.[166] "I don't know nothin'" he was quoted as saying, "I jes comes to sing and to see me some wild animals" (though the quotation in dialect cast questions of authenticity on the essence of these words).[167] The German actor Marlene Dietrich, who was a frequent resident in the U.S., was expected to follow.[168] Dame Margot Fonteyn, a British subject who was also popular in the U.S., was denounced in 1972 by the Southern Africa Liberation Group of Evanston, Illinois when she performed in

---

162. Vusumzi Make to Max Roach, 27 February 1961, Box 75, *Max Roach Papers*.

163. R.B. Shogoe to Max Roach, 10 July 1962, Box 66, *Max Roach Papers*.

164. Zakes Mda to Max Roach, 26 July 1972, Box 78, *Max Roach Papers*.

165. *Southern Africa: A Monthly Survey of News and Opinion*, 33(Number 6, July-August 1970), Box 55, Series II, *ACOA*. This periodical was published by the Southern Africa Committee, 637 West 125th Street in Harlem.

166. *Cape Times*, 30 May 1970.

167. Press Release, 28 June 1971, Reel 5, Part II, *ACOA Papers-Library of Congress*.

168. Clipping, 22 April 1970, Reel 5, Part II.

Cape Town before audiences comprised exclusively of the European minority.[169]

But how could one complain about Sledge and the other scofflaws when, as of 1970, the playwright Athol Fugard, attaining notoriety because of his plays about apartheid, opposed the boycott of apartheid?[170] Even the Detroit chanteuse Aretha Franklin was planning a three-week tour of South Africa in 1971 (though given her antipathy to aviation, her arrival would be necessarily cumbersome).[171] Thus, she cancelled her tour but arriving in her stead were the performers Brook Benton and Judy Clay. Also scheduled to arrive were Lloyd Price, the Isley Brothers, Muhammad Ali, Ray Charles, and Count Basie.[172] Already there was the unfunny comic Shelley Berman.[173] He may have felt at home alongside Eartha Kitt,[174] also in South Africa, while the Negro golfer Lee Elder was expected any day.[175] Also slated to arrive was the Broadway hit musical *Hello, Dolly!*, expected to play before segregated audiences (though it was unclear what these audiences would make of the star singer/actor Carol Channing, who appeared to be "white" but was thought to have African ancestry.)[176]

The tug of anti-racism created friction as it jerked furiously against the braided cord of apartheid. Frank Marcus, who wrote *The Killing of Sister George*, an early lesbian play turned movie, said ignore the boycott of apartheid and he was denounced swiftly by Edward Albee, the prize-winning U.S. playwright.[177]

However, as the flames of unrest leapt ever higher, the music adjusted accordingly. A revealing episode unfolded in Portugal in late 1971 where the politicized Euro-American bassist Charlie Haden chose to play protest music before an engaged crowd of 10,000. "Song for Che," was his selection, an homage to the Argentine revolutionary. There were repercussions: the concert the following day was cancelled by the police and he and his band—which included trailblazing saxophonist Ornette Coleman—were asked to leave the country. At the airport, Haden said, "I was taken to the security room and told I would have to come with the policemen.... I began to get

169. Press Release, July 1972, Reel 5, Part II.
170. *New York Times*, 6 July 1970.
171. Press Release, 28 June 1971, Reel 5, Part II, *ACOA*.
172. **Tan**, September 1971, Reel 5, Part II.
173. Undated Clipping, Reel 5, Part II.
174. *Newsweek*, 22 November 1971.
175. *New York Times*, 21 December 1971.
176. *Johannesburg Star*, 10 April 1965.
177. Clipping, 27 July 1970, Reel 5, Part II.

scared." Then it was on to police headquarters where he was interrogated for five hours—before all could board a departing plane. The good news was that this action placed the right-wing country, then enmeshed in losing wars in Africa, into an unflattering spotlight.[178]

U.S. cultural exports—in music and film in particular—had begun to set a global standard, and depriving polecat nations like pre-1974 Portugal and South Africa of these products was psychologically asphyxiating. The "cultural boycott" as it came to be called played an instrumental role in bringing apartheid to its knees after Reagan's 1980 election, precisely when it was thought that the Pretoria regime had received an extended reprieve.

* * *

The anti-apartheid movement began to flourish on campuses, as students linked the local—college endowment investments—with the global: apartheid's horrors. Into this maelstrom stepped the Reverend Leon Sullivan, who despite his role as a kind of antipode to Jesse Jackson—who would run for U.S. president in 1984 and thereafter on an explicit anti-apartheid platform—was still reviled by the obtuse Afrikaner elite whenever he arrived in South Africa, as during his July 1979 jaunt.[179] Typically, Lynette Volker was irate in responding to Sullivan's entreaties, asking angrily in 1979 "should these principles not also be applied to the USA?" After all, she said sardonically, "people who live in White Houses should not throw Little Rocks," a poisonous reference to the bitter desegregation crisis of 1957.[180] The writer did not realize that the pastor was seeking to save Pretoria by moving it to a U.S. model, sidelining the radical left by dint of minor concessions to desegregation. But the Philadelphia clergyman did not realize that the U.S. bargain would be far more difficult to execute as long as there was an African majority to satisfy. The writer may have thought that the cleric was much too reminiscent of an earlier visitor, Robert Kennedy who was accused during his controversial visit to South Africa of calling for a "New Deal" for African workers, the ultimate transgression.[181]

---

178. *Downbeat*, 39(Number 1, 20 January 1972): 9.

179. 17-19 July 1979 visit, Box 64, *Leon Sullivan Papers.*

180. Lynette Volker to Leon Sullivan, 9 November 1979, Box 55, *Leon Sullivan Papers.*

181. Clipping, *Sunday Times*, 1 January 1967, box 12, *International Affairs Department, Country Files, AFL-CIO.*

Thus, after Sullivan's 1980 visit to South Africa just before the election, U.S. businesses there were reported to be "sore and dismayed" with him and his code. Sullivan was "very much dissatisfied" that only 140 of 300 businesses there had signed on to his vaunted principles. Colgate Palmolive flatly refused to recognize a union with African members, despite his protest. Others, hiding under their desks, conceded that he provided a "pretext" for remaining in the land of lush profits.[182] But when S.G. Marzullo of Mobil forwarded a $7000 check, an "assessment as a member of the Sullivan Committee,"[183] a signal was sent as to how profitable monitoring apartheid could be, opening the door to various types of corruption. Mobil Oil was playing various angles, placing an advertisement in 1979 declaring baldly, "the NAACP needs help."[184]

More than "sore and dismayed" was Keith McKennon, Vice President of Dow Chemical, who sternly admonished the progressive Reverend William Howard of the National Council of Churches, based in Manhattan—with whom I traveled to Cuba in the 1970s. "If the key raw materials the U.S. imports from [South Africa] were cut off from us, the U.S. automobile, steel and chemical industries would be brought to their knees within a few months and that chaos and heavy unemployment would undoubtedly follow," as a result of Howard's presumed "myopic and misguided" call for divestment from apartheid.[185] The U.S. Congress backed this analysis when it floated the idea of a "resource war in Southern Africa" because of "western dependence on key strategic minerals" from the subregion.[186] By early 1983, NAIMSAL denounced a television broadcast on CBS that had criticized the NCC for supporting "freedom fighters of South Africa and Namibia."[187]

Sullivan's liberal anticommunist allies were not united behind this code. George Houser of the ACOA told him that "our organization has been critical of the codes of conduct approach to change in South Africa" and surmised, "I have the sneaking suspicion that you may

182. *The Economist*, 20 September 1980, Box 55.

183. S.G. Marzullo to Jim Rawlings of Union Carbide, 16 March 1981, Box 55.

184. Advertisement, 4 January 1979, Box 35, *Washington Office on Papers.*

185. Keith McKennon to Reverend William Howard, 22 September 1980, Box 55.

186. "The Possibility of a Resource War in Southern Africa, Hearing Before the Subcommittee on Africa of the Committee on Foreign Affairs," First Session, 8 July 1981, 119, Box 2, *Cheryl Johnson-Odim Papers, Columbia College-Chicago.*

187. NAIMSAL Press Release, 31 January 1983, Box 179, *Gerald Horne Papers.*

have more questions about this approach than you did when you began...."[188] Sullivan told his fellow pastor and ally Ben Hooks of the NAACP that "the waves are getting a little rough but I intend to hang in there a little longer...,"[189] but he was almost capsized nonetheless.

Thus, the veteran academic Gwendolen Carter said, explicitly in reference to the code, that cosmetic "changes" by U.S. corporations "do no tackle the fundamental issue of political change in that country."[190] Similarly, while visiting South Africa before the election, Senator Paul Tsongas told those assembled that the Sullivan Principles were a "joke."[191] "I directed a project that exposed Sullivan and what he was all about," boasted grizzled activist Prexy Nesbitt.[192] The Episcopalians, one of the more active Christian denominations against apartheid, denounced the Sullivan Principles.[193] A self-described "member of the industry steering committee that advises Reverend Sullivan," Paul Gibson of Menlo Park (future headquarters of what came to be known as Silicon Valley), "tend[ed] to disagree" with Professor Carter, seeming to suggest that he rejected "majority rule" and "one man, one vote."[194]

Born in West Virginia in 1922, the tall, fair-skinned cleric with a booming voice was shaped early in life by the example of the Reverend Adam Clayton Powell of Harlem, yet another pastor who entered politics—elected to Congress in the early 1940s. In 1961 Sullivan led a boycott in his new home, Philadelphia, on behalf of jobs for Negroes, from the pulpit of the largest Protestant church in this metropolis: his 6000 parishioners formed a solid base of support. In 1964, financed by the Ford Foundation, he opened a job training center which came to have branches in 150 cities, providing him with even wider reach.[195] Yet the activist Brooklyn pastor Milton Galamison objected that "most people never separate Dr. Sullivan from" his Opportunities Industrialization Center "and those who attack his position," who were legion, "often confront OIC staff and

188. George Houser to Leon Sullivan, 17 October 1980, Box 55.

189. Leon Sullivan to Benjamin Hooks, 31 October 1980, Box 55.

190. Gwendolen Carter to Paul Gibson, 24 November 1979, Box 55.

191. Briefing by Senator Tsongas, 25 January 1980, Box 15, *Washington Office on Africa Papers*.

192. Oral History, Prexy Nesbitt, 1 April 2009, *Columbia College-Chicago*.

193. Report by Episcopal Churchmen, May 1982, Box 244, *Leroy Walker Africa News Service Archive*.

194. Paul Gibson to Gwendolen Carter, 29 October 1979, Box 55.

195. Biographical sketch, 25 September 1978, Box 63, *Leon Sullivan Papers-Emory University*.

Board Members,"[196] making them uncomfortable and staining their reputations for being complicit with apartheid. This included Galamison himself, who had led stormy protests against school segregation in Brooklyn but was now being undermined because he was on OIC's board.

The "Sullivan Principles," a corporate code of conduct, were developed during the midst of the 1976 electoral season. A member of the Board of Directors of General Motors, Sullivan's attempt to entice profit-making enterprises to impose at their facilities general principles of non-discrimination were contrary to apartheid and, thus, could be seen either as naïve, subversive, or a cover for continuing exploitation. David Rockefeller of the Chase Manhattan Bank, whose brother had served as U.S. Vice President, had been in and out of Southern Africa for years, busily counting his many ducats along the way. In 1976 he hemmed and hawed and parsed his words furiously when Sullivan reached him. The pastor's code, he insisted, "doesn't apply to the bank. We have only a two-man representative office in Johannesburg, not a full-scale bank."[197] He ducked the stickier matter of capital investment and loans. He may have forgotten that as early as 1972 Dillon Read, the uber Wall Street firm with which he maintained close ties, was said by Salisbury to "very ready to assist the Rhodesian government to raise moneys in the Euro bond dollar market or through bank credits from the U.S.A" since "the freeze is obviously over."[198]

Speaking of the corporate response, Donald Ming, Bishop of the AME denomination in Cape Town, found that "most of the rhetoric is nothing but 'lip service,'" while telling Sullivan not contradictorily that "your program...seems to be catching on."[199] By 1979 Sullivan was gratified to find that 160 corporations had signed on to his code, though "companies from other parts of the world" mostly had not.[200] This opened loopholes, either allowing non-U.S. corporations to feast on apartheid, while restraining Sullivan's signees—or

196. Milton Galamison to Reverend Euton Williams, 10 September 1980, Box 55, *Leon Sullivan Papers.*

197. David Rockefeller to Leon Sullivan, 9 April 1976, Box 54, *Leon Sullivan Papers-Emory University.*

198. D.W. Young, Ministry of Finance to Kenneth Towsey, 7 February 1972, Box 2, *Kenneth Towsey Papers.*

199. Donald Ming to Leon Sullivan, 4 January 1978, Box 54, *Leon Sullivan Papers.*

200. Leon Sullivan to Reverend William Pauly, 17 October 1979, Box 55, *Leon Sullivan Papers.*

allowing the latter to differentiate foreign subsidiaries of U.S. giants and to invest unmolested.

As had been the case for some time, wily corporate executives knew that in hindering the deployment of [African] human capital, apartheid was strangling the economy. In 1979 S.G. Marzullo of Mobil Oil sent Sullivan a news item about the shortage of skilled workers in South Africa, which could be resolved by "bring[ing] non-whites into the system," words underlined by the sender.[201]

* * *

Skillful evasion became the preferred mode for dealing with the code, though political activists were hardly fooled by this choreography. Sullivan also fused his concerns with that of the likeminded, e.g. W.H. Shuenyane of the Careers Development Project of Johannesburg, who told the cleric in 1979 of his "deepest gratitude for the warm welcome" during his U.S. junket, though he reduced his effectiveness as an ally when he spoke derisively of the "impotence of Black South Africans in uplifting themselves," veritably ignoring the flaccidity of apartheid,[202] a crisis Washington proved incapable of stemming.

201. S.G. Marzullo to Leon Sullivan, 29 October 1979, Box 55, *Leon Sullivan Papers*: the news item was from the *Wall Street Journal*, 29 October 1979.

202. W.H. Shuenyane to Leon Sullivan, 3 January 1979, Box 54, *Leon Sullivan Papers*.

Chapter 18

The Tide Turns 1980-1984

REAGAN'S inauguration in January 1981 was thought to mark the initiation of a prelapsarian Eden, a return to halcyon days before the retreat of Jim Crow and the assault on apartheid. A commentary on South African Broadcasting said as much.[1] But, alas, mass movements have a repetitive habit of interrupting the dreams of the most determined and imposing weavers of nightmares. Such was the case in the 1980s when sanctions were slapped on Pretoria, heightening a crisis already in motion, induced by the attempt spearheaded by the ANC's on-the-ground ally, the United Democratic Front, to make the nation "ungovernable."

Reagan, a mediocre actor for much of his adult life, was eminently suited to be putty in the hands of the ultra-right forces that had lusted for power since Carter's election in 1976. Just as several liberation movement leaders had Afro-American spouses, a number of U.S. shapers of policy toward the sub-region had spouses from the European minority, serving to generate even more sympathy for beset "kith and kin." This included the academic Edwin Munger, praised in the apartheid press, whose wife was South African[2]—and Chester Crocker, who had a Rhodesian spouse.[3] Reagan's regime, says Crocker, his chief negotiator in Southern Africa, was not only the "most conservative in modern U.S. history" but complementarily, the president—said his Secretary of State Alexander Haig—was "not too steeped on the issues" of the sub-region. Early on Pretoria continued its historic pattern, revealed by "Muldergate" and John

1. South African Broadcasting Corporation Commentary, 21 January 1981, Box 237, *Leroy Walker Africa News Service Archive*.

2. *Cape Argus*, 14 January 1970: Munger was "one of the few American specialists on Africa who truly deserves the title of 'expert'" and had "lived for several years" in South Africa.

3. Gerald Horne, *From the Barrel of a Gun*, passim.

McGoff, of blanketing Washington with lobbyists and propagandists, willing to supply three-martini lunches and rewards of various sorts to guileful legislators. Reagan was berated after he cowardly and strangely explained that it would be wrong to abandon an ally in Pretoria that had stood with the U.S. during the Second World War—though it was well-known that many of the country's leaders had been interned because of pro-Berlin sympathies. Even Crocker felt that his bizarre words "epitomized the insensitivity that would be the sad hallmark of his sporadic personal involvement in the years to come," which concluded in January 1989. "Did he realize," said a wondrous Crocker, "that hundreds of thousands of black Africans in Zambia, Kenya, Zimbabwe, Nigeria, Madagascar, Mali, Senegal, Chad, Togo, Ghana, Niger and—yes—South Africa had fought with the Allies in both world wars. Or that the National Party of South Africa…agitated on the Nazi side and against South African entry into the war."

Tragically, Reagan was not alone in his pro-Pretoria bias. Senator Jesse Helms of North Carolina sought to force Crocker to fire his "senior deputy" in these complicated sub-regional negotiations and replace him with a "staffer who had very close ties to the intelligence apparatus in Pretoria," which was thought to have penetrated Washington thoroughly in any case. Nevertheless, at Crocker's confirmation hearing, occurring shortly after the inauguration, "some of the questions," he recalled, "appeared to have been inspired by people on the right fringe of [the] National Party who distrusted P.W. Botha's own reformist [sic] agenda!" Even the leak of his policy papers to the left was actually an operation by the right wing to embarrass him further. His nominal supervisor, William Clark—who famously confused Mauretania and Mauritius and almost undermined the "wrong" government—was naïve: his "diplomatic experience was nil" and his "political instincts toward the Botha government were warm and often uncritical, just like Reagan's."

Niel Barnard, Pretoria's intelligence maven, was "cold toward my team," Crocker carped, "due in part to my role in discouraging his research in the United States in matters relating to nuclear technology acquisition while I was still at Georgetown University!" But Barnard should have realized that Crocker was on his side, for the bespectacled, mustachioed negotiator with a rapidly receding hairline was furious about the Clark Amendment, named after former Senator Dick Clark, and defeated in part by a tidal wave of campaign donations from Pretoria. This proviso would bar various kinds of aid to Angolan rebels. Angola, Crocker yelped, was the "only country in the world subject to such a legislative ban on U.S. covert involvement."[4] A central priority of the new regime in Washington was overturning the Clark Amendment in 1981, but they failed "overwhelmingly", it was said, "due in part to strong Black Caucus opposition...."[5]

Indicative of the importance of this amendment, both Savimbi and Mobutu made the long trip from Africa to Washington as the vote to repeal it was pushed.[6] In some ways this debate was a typical Washington charade, in that despite the presumed malevolence of the Clark Amendment, Savimbi claimed that he was getting U.S. aid nonetheless; and, in any case, Mobutu was ultra-concerned about the talks of his puppet-master in Washington with the MPLA, which he thought should simply be overthrown.[7] Even the PAC, whose specialty was blistering attacks on the ANC, found time to remind the ill-informed Reagan that the "present ruling Nationalist Party in South Africa actively supported the Nazis. The former [Prime Minister] Vorster.... The former head of the Bureau of State Security...General Hendrik van den Berghe" were all "interned" due to an association with the "Ox Wagon Sentinel," which "sabotaged the British war effort!"[8] And that of the U.S. too.

Crocker was not exaggerating about Pretoria's widespread influence in Washington during the Reagan years. Just as Dick Clark and John Tunney had been singled out by Pretoria and then ousted, their next target was Congressman Howard Wolpe of Michigan, a former scholar of the region, who had the misfortune of coming from the same vicinity as the morally and financially compromised John McGoff, one of Pretoria's closest allies in the U.S. "When the survival of South Africa is at stake," as it was announced at the time, "rules don't apply." Connie Mulder himself joined McGoff in what became a successful attempt to dislodge Wolpe from Congress.[9] The scholar David Wiley felt compelled to rise to the defense of one of Randall Robinson's closest congressional allies. Howard Pollock, a staunch Reagan follower, argued passionately that Congressman Wolpe was "helping Communist causes in Africa...."[10] Also, on Pretoria's

---

4. Chester Crocker, *High Noon in Southern Africa*, 66, 91, 97, 116, 137.

5. Paul Thompson to William Clark, 30 September 1983, Box 38, WHORM Subject File, CO Countries, CO006, Angola.

6. Press Release, 1 December 1981, Box 15, *Washington Office on Africa Papers*.

7. Chester Crocker to Secretary of State, 29 January 1982, Box 4, Executive Secretariat, NSC, Country File, Africa, S. Africa.

8. *Azania Today*, 2(Numbers 1 &2, 1981), 5-7.

9. "Washington Notes on Africa," Autumn 1982, Box 23, *Jean Sindab Papers*.

10. David Wiley to Editor, "Kalamazoo Gazette," 22 September 1984, Box 36, *Washington Office on Africa Papers*.

payroll then, as well paid lobbyists, were Republican Party honchos Stuart Spencer and John Sears, both of whom were close to Reagan personally.[11]

Wolpe was seen as too squishy on the bedrock matter of support for Savimbi's UNITA, a sacred cause for the ruling Republicans. Revealingly, Washington was somehow skeptical of Pretoria's backing of this Angolan, perhaps underscoring the age-old aphorism that there is no honor among thieves. "We have good reason for keeping our contacts with Savimbi—including our messages to him," said the legation in Cape Town, "outside of South African channels."[12] The cutthroats in Pretoria and Washington had good reason to suspect that their erstwhile comrades would engage in backstabbing in a nano-second.

At times, Washington's allies would not stay bought and veered from the path chosen for them. This is what the White House was told in early 1982 when Mobutu's emissary at the United Nations "double crossed us" on an important vote on Israel's annexation of the Golan Heights, forcing a U.S. veto and bitter recriminations, along with "more heat." It was "not yet clear" if this maneuver was executed at the emissary's behest or on "secret last-minute instructions" from Mobutu, reinforcing concerns that he could be an untrustworthy ally.[13]

Gatsha Buthelezi, the Zulu chauvinist, was also seen by Washington as an ally, but there was doubt about him too. The Consul General in Durban met with him in 1981 and was stunned when the man sitting across from him said "neither he nor the ordinary African is afraid of Communism;" blasphemy personified. Anticommunism was "so much political piffle," said the Zulu leader, little more than "political blustering by a government which has nowhere to [go]." It would be like London portraying the "Irish problem as a sinister Communist plot" and added for good measure, "I might even have more reason to fear American intentions in South Africa than I have to fear Russian intentions…." These words augured "disaster" said the Consul General, since "he continues to harbor a latent anti-Americanism which still hampers relations with him."[14]

11. "Washington Notes on Africa," Summer/Autumn 1983, Box 22, *Jean Sindab Papers, Schomburg Center, New York Public Library*.

12. Cape Town legation to Chester Crocker, 10 November 1981, Box 4, Executive Secretariat, NSC, Country File, S. Africa, *Reagan Presidential Library*.

13. Fred Wettering to Judge Clark, 27 January 1982, Box 4, Executive Secretariat, NSC, Country File, Africa, S. Africa.

14. Consul General-Durban to Secretary of State, November 1981, Box 9 [] Box 2], African Affairs Directorate, NSC, *Reagan Presidential Library*.

What the diplomat should have asked is to what extent did the historic strain of "anti-Americanism" embedded within the Afrikaner elite trickle down and outward, and what was the implication for policy?

This was not the only issue on the mind of Washington. Their cabal also included the South Korean evangelist Sun Myung Moon, who launched the right-wing *Washington Times*, a reliable ally of Pretoria. James Whelan, who formerly served McGoff as an editor and executive at his Panax Corporation, then leapfrogged to take the helm at this newly born newspaper. This gang also counted as a member Smith Hempstone, quite close to the European minority in Kenya, where he was to serve as U.S. ambassador. He traveled to Angola in 1981 to confer with the ultra-right's favorite, Savimbi. He then penned a laudatory article about the bearded counter-revolutionary for *Reader's Digest*, yet another mouthpiece for the right wing.[15]

Crocker was not engaging in puffery when he spoke of Pretoria's anger at his apparent refusal to acquiesce immediately to nuclear cooperation. This was a major priority of Pretoria,[16] leading to U.S. firms aiding this treacherous quest.[17] "All the major western powers are seeking assured supplies of uranium," said one journalist, "as the oil crisis concentrates their efforts on the nuclear alternatives."[18] The vast enterprises that survived the death of the once ubiquitous Charles Engelhard and Westinghouse, yet another vast conglomerate, were implicated in this shady business.[19] Yet by late 1981 the *Wall Street Journal* headlined, "Uranium Industry boom goes bust as growth of nuclear power falters",[20] further diverting apartheid's already troubled trajectory. This may have been premature, since by mid-1982 there were reports of enhanced nuclear collaboration between Pretoria and Washington.[21] By 1982, Edward Teller, often

15. "Washington Notes on Africa," Summer 1982, Box 23, *Jean Sindab Papers*.

16. James V. Zimmerman, Assistant Director of Export/Import and International Safeguards, U.S. Nuclear Regulatory Commission to Carlton Stoiber, Director of Office of Nuclear Export and Import Control of State Department, 20 April 1982, Box 244, *Leroy Walker Africa News Service Archive*: application from Transnuclear Incorporated for license to export nuclear material to South Africa.

17. *Washington Post*, 6 April 1982.

18. *African Business*, April 1980, Box 295, *Leroy Walker Africa News Service Archive*.

19. *Wall Street Journal*, 13 January 1981.

20. *Wall Street Journal*, 3 November 1981.

21. *Johannesburg Star*, 19 May 1982.

described as the "father" of U.S. atomic weapons, was headed to South Africa.[22] In 1983 demonstrations erupted in Baltimore when South African uranium docked; part of what drove picketers was the possibility of a toxic leak.[23] When the U.S. reportedly planned to place cruise missiles in South Africa, a Cuban journalist accused Washington of "atomic blackmail,"[24] indicating that nuclear collaboration had failed to cease.

Israeli-South African nuclear collaboration continued apace, and as a byproduct, Israeli migrants continued to arrive at the Cape, at a figure estimated to be 30,000 by 1982.[25] This sinister relationship disoriented many in the U.S. who were concerned with the concomitant fraying of Black-Jewish relations in sites like New York City, especially Brooklyn. Interestingly, the star Negro athlete Arthur Ashe kept a file on Israel-South African relations that included much underlining of relevant passages.[26]

Despite this setback, economic relations between apartheid and the U.S. intensified during the 1980s. Harry Oppenheimer, at the summit of the apartheid economy, increased his investments in the U.S. and Canada, via the company known as Minorco, which controlled hundreds of millions of dollars in North American coal, uranium, gold, and copper. He was said to control assets worth $2 billion in this Bermuda subsidiary. On Minorco's board were Walter Wriston of Citicorp, a major New York bank, and Felix Rohatyn, an investment banker who presided over the 1970s attempt to financially strangle New York City. Minorco, in typically complex financing, was invested in Phibro to the tune of 27%, which in turn was invested in Salomon Brothers, yet another huge Wall Street firm. Phibro had been spun off from Engelhard Minerals and Chemical—controlled by the late campaign donor to President Johnson. Minorco was the largest stakeholder in Engelhard.[27] Oppenheimer's importance as a business figure was signaled when he met at a South African airport the visiting dignitary Henry Kissinger—who called Foreign Minister Pik Botha, an "old friend."[28]

---

22. *The Citizen* [Johannesburg], 27 March 1982.
23. Clipping, March 1983, Box 295, *Leroy Walker Africa News Service Archive.*
24. *Granma*, 26 December 1982.
25. *Sunday Times* [South Africa], 16 May 1982.
26. File, no date, Box 34, *Arthur Ashe Papers, Schomburg Center, New York Public Library.*
27. *ANC Weekly News Briefing*, 6(Number 21, 9 May 1982), *Leroy Walker Africa News Service.*
28. *Sowetan*, 30 August 1982.

Oppenheimer's growing profile in South Africa—as a major booster of a liberal anticommunist successor to apartheid, not unlike what was engineered in the U.S. after the crushing of Robeson—was an aspect of the larger story of closer relations between U.S. and South African corporations, often conducted secretly for fear of a public relations backlash. Military relations were part of this story.[29]

It seemed that U.S. visitors were imposing wear and tear on the red carpets laid out for them upon arrival in South Africa, given the horde that was crossing the Atlantic in a southeastward direction. The list was to include Governor John Brown of Kentucky, but he cancelled his visit after meeting with ANC and NAACP members. He skipped his visit, though Kentucky coal was part of the coal-to-oil scheme designed to rescue Pretoria from the still biting boycott on petroleum exports imposed by Iran.[30] The Negro federal judge Leon Higginbotham did not turn down an invitation to visit South Africa, then returned complaining that it was like Germany in the 1930s. "I felt it was back in the state of Mississippi in 1850," said his accompanying clerk Sarah Mitchell.[31]

Arriving in South Africa at this dangerous moment was Irving Brown, the U.S. labor operative who was close to the CIA and had ties to the ACOA.[32] The AFL-CIO, which Brown represented, was becoming increasingly unpopular. The union involved in motor assembly in South Africa snubbed the U.S. labor federation's delegation after they gave an award to Gatsha Buthelezi,[33] the Zulu nationalist who was to play a major role in succeeding years. There was a "regular flow of black trade union leaders from home" into Washington, said the ANC's delegate there. "The AFL-CIO is busy recruiting our people" but contrastingly, "the people, especially the Afro-American people are as ever our ally in the struggle against racism."[34]

Congressman Wolpe was despised by these forces, which was understandable since along with Congressman Ronald V. Dellums of the Black Caucus, he was a moving force for sanctions legislation that helped to weaken Pretoria. In Grand Rapids, Michigan, where Gerald Ford and McGoff had both been prominent, pro-Pretoria groups were formed to weaken Wolpe, including the "Christian

29. *Die Burger*, 11 September 1982.

30. *Rand Daily Mail*, 27 August 1982.

31. *Cape Times*, 27 August 1982.

32. Editorial, *Sechaba*, November 1982,

33. *Sowetan*, 14 September 1982.

34. Dumi Matabane to "Dear Comrade Joe," 3 March 1982, Box 35, Folder 27, *Lusaka Mission, ANC Records*.

Psychology Association" and "Americans Concerned for South Africa." This city best known for manufacturing furniture also contained a sizeable population of Dutch origin, which correspondingly linked it with Pretoria. Intriguingly, South African David Mabunda, who worked with the Reverend Sullivan's Opportunities Industrialization Center, was seen as the key man in this setup. This former student at Michigan State University had also been associated with Holden Roberto of Angola and reputedly had ties to professors with similar intelligence connections.[35]

London, which under Prime Minister Margaret Thatcher was to form a toxic companion to the ill-informed Reagan, monitored the ally in its "special relationship" relentlessly. Days after the physically faltering president's inauguration, the Washington legation identified, in a "confidential" report, a "Breeze of Bourbonism" in the air. "There is a strong body of opinion in the Republican Party," it was discerned, "that would positively welcome an early confrontation" with Moscow and its allies. This "would force the U.S. to side with South Africa (something which they maintain is an American strategic and political interest)." That the "Africans not the Americans would suffer most from bad relations between them" was not a negligible factor. There was a sharp focus on "Cubanism" and "concern about Soviet activity in the Third World...."[36] It was well for London to monitor Washington and its ties to Pretoria, since by 1982 South Africa was sending missiles to Argentina during the conflict with Britain over the Falklands/Malvinas,[37] as if it saw Buenos Aires as a proxy redeeming the "Boer" defeat decades earlier at the hands of London. This was part and parcel of Pretoria's increasingly aggressive posture in the Americas, driven perhaps by the pummeling Pretoria was absorbing at the hands of Havana. Months after Reagan's swearing in, unwinding in the small Caribbean island of Dominica was a joint enterprise led by what was called the "American underworld" and the terrorist Ku Klux Klan: it was an attempted coup intended to establish a "free port" that, said a reporter, was "to be used for the trans-shipment of oil and arms to South Africa"[38]—and, perhaps, harass Cuba in its backyard, in the bargain. In anticipation of the 1983 invasion of the tiny Caribbean island of Grenada, the White House began complaining early on about the airport Cuban

35. "Doug" to "Ken", no date, Box 38, *Washington Office on Africa Papers*.

36. Report, February 1981, FCO106/207, *NAUK-London*.

37. *Washington Post*, 25 May 1982.

38. *Tennessean*, 7 May 1981, Box 130, *Leroy Walker Africa News Service Archive*.

workers were building there, portrayed misleadingly as a "refueling stop in their African adventures...."[39]

The Quakers also sent a delegate to the Caribbean. Bill Sutherland was so designated, and after a hair-raising ride to the airport in St. Lucia and being caught up in a regional strike, he made it to Antigua, the center of the Space Research Corporation scandal, concerning the U.S. corporation that armed apartheid with heavy artillery and sought to transship via Antigua. There he was briefed by the late journalist and activist Tim Hector,[40] whose sterling presence continues to be missed.

Weeks after the inauguration, Reagan's National Security Advisor—Richard Allen—was briefed by former U.S. envoy Marion Smoak, just back from his second trip to Windhoek, in words that would have not been deemed surprising in London. He enjoyed a "long personal visit with Foreign Minister [Pik] Botha, an old friend from his service here as an ambassador." Smoak, then a lobbyist for the illegal occupation of what became Namibia by 1990, was optimistic—like others—that Reagan would prolong the agony of this colony.[41] An "era of good feelings" was once more emerging between Pretoria and Washington. Days after the Republican victory in November 1980, a headline trumpeted "Expensive Europe is spurned," as South African tourists headed to the U.S.[42] Those lining up to enter the U.S. may have included Aaron Michael Rosholt of South Africa, chairman of Barlow Rand, the conglomerate with multiple interests in Zimbabwe and illegally occupied Namibia. He happened to have a dedicated interest in reading about the U.S. Civil War, though it was unclear if he was seeking tips on the impending conflict in his own nation.[43]

By June 1982 South African Broadcasting was happily reporting the arrival—at the airport named after Jan Smuts in Johannesburg (now carrying the name of Tambo)—of a U.S. airline, Pan American, for "the first time since 1978." "Some 60,000 North Americans visited the Republic last year," in pursuit of an "extensive network of interests—in trade, finance, manufacture, mining and

39. *Miami Herald*, 20 December 1981.

40. Report by Bill Sutherland, January 1982, PED PROGRAM RESOURCES SOUTHERN AFRICA.... TAO, *AFSC*.

41. Marion Smoak to "Dear Dick," 26 February 1981, Box 163, WHORM, Subject File, *Ronald Reagan Presidential Library-Simi Valley, California*.

42. Clipping, 29 November 1980, Box 244, *Leroy Walker Africa News Service Archive*.

43. *New York Times*, 11 April 1982.

tourism—which has developed in recent years to make the United States South Africa's leading supplier and business partner."[44] As early as March 1980, the number of U.S. tourists in South Africa was increasing at a rapid clip of 10%.[45] This back-and-forth was aided immeasurably by the fact that South African Airways was one of the earliest carriers to purchase from Boeing their 747 jumbo jet.[46]

Richard Allen was a known commodity in Pretoria. After leaving the White House in 1973 as the Nixon regime was decomposing, he was hired by powerful business interests in Portugal as a lobbyist and in that capacity arranged junkets to colonized Angola and Mozambique by the likeminded Congressman Philip Crane and the pro-colonialist scholar Lewis Gann.[47]

What likely emerged from these confidential conversations was further planning to destabilize South Africa's newly independent neighbors. Days afterwards George Houser was to be found in Maputo and was "taken aback when I asked one of my American friends where Joe Massinga was. He said to me, 'Haven't you heard? He was arrested for working with the CIA.'" Houser, who had known the detainee when "he was a student here in the U.S.," found that he was "recruited by the CIA when he was a student at Fordham [University]" in New York City. "One of the CIA agents," Houser found "asked all kinds of questions relating to ANC military bases," a prelude to a brutal bombarding of Mozambique by Pretoria, which was to force FRELIMO a few years later to demand their comrades' exit via the ill-considered Nkomati Accord.[48] Intriguingly enough, it was Houser who supplied the book-stuffed library at the Ministry of Foreign Affairs administered by the accused, an erstwhile FRELIMO dissident, once tied to their antagonist, COREMO but who had—supposedly—returned to the fold by 1975. Massinga received a new Volvo sedan and $300 monthly from his CIA handler—according to the detainee's confession.[49]

According to Cuban sources, there was an extensive CIA spy network in Mozambique,[50] understandable given its proximity to the

44. South African Broadcasting Corporation Commentary, 3 June 1982, Box 237, *Leroy Walker Africa News Service Archive*.

45. Clipping, 5 March 1980, Box 115, *Leroy Walker Africa News Service Archive*.

46. *Financial Gazette*, 31 July 1970.

47. "Washington Notes on Africa," Summer 1980, Box 23, *Jean Sindab Papers, Schomburg Center, New York Public Library*.

48. Houser remarks, circa 1981, Box 1, *George Houser Papers*.

49. Note, Circa 1981, Box 1, *George Houser Papers*.

50. *Granma* [Cuba], 6 April 1981: Those identified as working alongside the CIA were: Frederick B. Lundahl; his spouse Karen; James Douglas Smith;

U.S. ally in South Africa. Recruiting pilots—and aviation specialists generally—was a priority. At least two CIA station chiefs in Maputo were trained as pilots and paratroopers.[51] (This tendency has taken on added resonance considering the still mysterious death of President Samora Machel in a plane crash on South African soil, discussed below).

Soon congressional hearings were held that sought to portray the ANC and SWAPO as dupes of Moscow. The spectacle was presided over by Senator Jeremiah Denton of Alabama; a diehard bigot embittered by his role in the failed war in Indochina, he possessed the requisite racism and anticommunism to succeed in Washington. From late 1981 through early 1982 he dispatched two staffers to South Africa on what was described as a "mystery mission" to uncover "Soviet links" with the ANC.[52]

Dumi Matabane, the ANC representative in Washington, was fuming about the "fabrications that our movements [are] engaged in the training of terrorists (American) in this country," one of the central contentions of the U.S. right. This was evidence of the unavoidable: "the government's relation with S. Africa is growing stronger by [the] day…."[53]

Senator Denton, however, might have countered by pointing to the December 1980 appearance of the ANC Secretary General at a fundraiser in Oakland, California for the newspaper of the U.S. Communist Party,[54] to argue the relation between the ANC and U.S. radicals was growing stronger by the day, in order to justify his flyspecking investigation.

Among the witnesses who wound up testifying in Washington was Nokonono Delphine Kava, a former member of the ANC then tied to Steve Biko. He was hailed by Denton as a "nationalist" rather than a Communist, an important distinction then—even though the witness asserted, "I am not a nationalist…. I am a Black Consciousness Activist." Acute attention was paid to the July 1981 remarks of Tambo and Moses Mabhida at the 60th anniversary gathering of

---

Sandra Adeline Taber; Lavone Lorraine Tate; Walter Caetano de Andrade; Frederocl Wetering; Jimmy Joseph Kolker; Barbara Smith; Shirley M. Smith; Shirley Trego; Ginger Lee Ollivier; Arthur Russel; Louis Leon Ollivier; Patricia Russel.

51. *Granma*, 6 April 1981.

52. *Newsweek*, 25 January 1982.

53. Dumi Matabane to "Dear Comrade Joe," 3 March 1982, Box 35, Folder 27, *Lusaka Mission, ANC Records*.

54. Text of Speech by Alfred Nzo, 13 December 1980, Box 35, Folder 27, *Lusaka Mission, ANC Records*.

the SACP in London, where the latter chose to "condemn in absolute terms the conspiracy between the Reagan administration and racist, fascist South Africa." Unpersuaded, Senator Denton emphasized that "presidents of both SWAPO and the ANC have repeatedly acknowledged the importance of Soviet support.... [and] high officials of SWAPO and the ANC were among the speakers at the XXVIth Congress" of the Soviet Communist Party in March 1981. SWAPO, he said, "received 90 percent of its military support and 60 percent of its overall support from Communist sources." And 10 of the 22 members of the National Executive Committee of the ANC were simultaneously SACP members, it was said.[55] By September 1981, two Soviet lieutenant colonels had been killed by South African military forces in Southern Africa alongside SWAPO combatants, heightening the hysteria about Moscow.[56] The ANC charged that in order to directly assist Senator Denton, Carl Noffke, a senior official in Pretoria, "arranged for a consignment of captured Communist weapons to be sent to Washington" for Denton to flash dramatically at his hearing.[57]

Though Senator Denton was excoriated by some for his red-baiting, his critics did not include South African Broadcasting, which congratulated the Alabamian for holding a tight focus on the SACP and Moscow.[58] A number of those who did object signed an "Open Letter to President Reagan" in response to the hearings. Publicized by the ANC, these U.S. nationals lambasted the "smear campaign" that reeked of the worst excesses of the Red Scare. Denton's investigation was an "immoral equivalent of a U.S. agency investigating 'Jewish Subversion' with the aid of the Gestapo in Germany in 1938," the letter charged. The signatories included Randall Robinson, scholar Ronald Walters, attorneys Gay McDougall (who I knew well and who was photographed besides Mandela when he first voted in 1994) and Franklin Williams (accused of involvement in the coup

55. U.S. Congress. Senate. Committee on the Judiciary. Subcommittee on Security and Terrorism. 97th Congress, Second Session. *The Role of the Soviet Union, Cuba and East Germany in Fomenting Terrorism in South Africa*, 22, 24-25, 29, 31 March 1982, Volume I, Washington, D.C.: Government Printing Office, 1982m, 4m, 12, 34, 191. See also Volume II: documents purporting to prove allegations.

56. South African Broadcasting Corporation Commentary, 10 September 1981, Box 120, *Leroy Walker Africa News Service Archive*.

57. *ANC Weekly News Briefing*, 6(Number 16, 17 April 1982), *Leroy Walker Africa News Service*.

58. South African Broadcasting Corporation Commentary, 29 March 1982, Box 120, *Leroy Walker Africa News Service Archive*.

against Nkrumah in 1966), then Communist leader Angela Davis, and feminist writer June Jordan.[59]

Apartheid had long been a pet cause of the Washington right and this accelerated in the 1980s. Even Senator Samuel Haykawa, one of the few Japanese-Americans in this body, was part of this tendency, informing Pretoria that the White House wanted to make South Africa an ever-closer ally.[60]

This obsessive anticommunism, which reached a deafening crescendo in the 1980s, is what drew U.S. attention to the sub-region, the scholar Ufo Ike Okeke has argued: U.S. interest accelerated in response to Moscow's interest. In this regard, Okeke also stresses the importance of the maniacally anticommunist National Security Study Memorandum 39, drafted by Henry Kissinger in 1969.[61] At this juncture, according to Maqsud Ulhasan Nuri, Moscow provided "$80 million worth of weapons each year" to the ANC and "supplied some 90 percent of…ANC weapons".[62] In addition to the role played by Cuban troops in draining Pretoria's military in southern Angola, the liberation forces were heavily dependent upon the socialist bloc—which meant its impending setback would haunt these movements even after Mandela's election in 1994.

In 1982-1983 veteran U.S. intelligence agent Duane Claridge—code name: "Dewey Maroni"—was providing briefings on the destabilization campaign in Central America to "General Van der Westhuizen, Chief of South African Military Intelligence during his visit to Langley," Virginia. The South African graciously "invited me to come to South Africa to see how his organization provided logistics support to Jonas Savimbi" in Angola. Pretoria "had solved the logistics problem of supplying Savimbi's guerrillas, the enigma that still haunted us in Nicaragua. The South Africans had made some interesting innovations in airdrop techniques from which the CIA sought to profit. "We had information to share with them as well," he continued, since "Savimbi's UNITA troops were facing some of the Cuban paramilitary personnel whom we had captured in Grenada," the tiny Caribbean island invaded by the U.S. in 1983. "The names of these Cubans might be useful to the South Africans and Savimbi

59. *ANC Weekly News Briefing*, 6(Number 10, 2 March 1982), *Leroy Walker Africa News Service.*

60. *Johannesburg Star,* 5 July 1982.

61. Ufo Ike Okeke, "American Reaction to Soviet Influence in Southern Africa," Ph.d. dissertation, University of South Carolina, 1981, 54.

62. Maqsud Ulhasan Nuri, "Cuban Policy in Africa: The Limits of the Proxy Model," Ph.d. dissertation, University of South Carolina, 1990, 392.

in inducing defections." Clardige also sought to "explore potential South African support for anticommunist Afghan rebels",[63] whose war was to stretch well into the 21st century, including a bombing of Manhattan on 11 September 2001.

But Assemblyman Herman Farrell of New York State Legislature took a diametrically different tack, telling the wrinkling president that he was aghast at hearing the report that Prime Minister Botha was coming to the US., remarking mockingly that he had "hope that this announcement was only a ploy of the media to discredit your administration…."[64] This visit did not ultimately occur but in the first weeks of the new regime 5 high-level South African intelligence officials did arrive, indicating the importance of the CIA to U.S. policy in Southern Africa. Congressmen Walter Fauntroy and William Gray of the Black Caucus called for the "immediate replacement" of U.N. Ambassador Jeanne Kirkpatrick,[65] seen to be responsible for this overt attempt to heighten collaboration with apartheid. W.N. du Plessis, described as "Chief of Staff for Intelligence" within the South African military, was among those arriving in Washington, the "first high ranking military officer" from Pretoria to make such a visit since 1974.[66] Kirkpatrick herself managed to have a secret huddle with a leader of this ill-famed delegation, P.W. Van Der Westhuizen, yet another military intelligence official.[67] Disingenuously, she denied knowing who he was (presumably she met any stranger with an Afrikaner accent who turned up in Manhattan or Washington.)[68] Perhaps unrelatedly, a few months after this controversial meeting, U.S. Ensign Stephen Baba, 21 years old, faced court martial for sending electronic warfare secrets to Pretoria.[69]

This arrival of a high-level delegation from Pretoria so soon after the advent of the new regime in Washington may have resulted from a split at the top, as suggested by the previously quoted memoir of Chester Crocker, lead negotiator for the sub-region. Secretary of State Haig "instructed" the legation in Cape Town to "call on" Pretoria's

---

63. Duane R. Claridge, *A Spy for All Seasons: My Life in the CIA*, New York: Scribner, 1997, 280-281.

64. Assemblyman Herman Farrell to President Reagan, 25 March 1981, Box 163, WHORM, Subject File.

65. Congressmen Fauntroy and Gray to President Reagan, 30 March 1981, Box 163, WHORM, Subject File.

66. *Africa News*, 23 March 1981, Box 237, *Leroy Walker Africa News Service Archive*.

67. *New York Post*, 21 March 1981.

68. *New York Times*, 25 March 1981.

69. *New York Times*, 18 December 1981.

man, Brand Fourie, to "lodge oral complaints…on misleading methods used…to obtain visas for four high ranking…military officers." This, said Haig, was an "abuse of diplomatic protocol."[70] It may have actually been an expression of confidence in Pretoria that—as the saying went at the time—the right hand often did not know what the far-right hand was doing.

Whatever the case, National Security Advisor Richard Allen was briefed after the meeting with the South African visitors and the briefer was decidedly unimpressed with their acumen. "Diplomacy is not the South Africans' long suit," said Fred Wettering, though he did acknowledge that this may have been the product of an apartheid society where rule of the "*baas*"—or boss—was law, leaving little need for the powerful to develop negotiating skills. One among their number struck him as "manipulative," while another had a "simple Manichean view of everything," devoid of nuance. Worse, the visitors "will likely misrepresent much of what I said" on returning to Pretoria, since the regime there was so desperate for good news that they would at times manufacture it.[71]

Commenting at the time of these meetings, South African Broadcasting espied a convergence of interests between the North Atlantic bloc and Pretoria, with both seeing Moscow as Enemy Number 1. "There is an obvious analogy," it was said, "between the relationship of the United States to the Third World and South Africa to Southern Africa,"[72] with the Soviet Union being a stumbling block in both cases. SABC thought the impending journey to Washington by Foreign Minister Pik Botha was the "most important visit abroad by a Foreign Minister since this country left the Commonwealth," which was not hyperbolic; it probably was fair to call it a "historic turning point…."[73]

The problem for U.S. imperialism was that although Robeson and his comrades had been routed on the basis of anticommunism—and the 6PAC had become a debacle partially because of the corrosive impact of anticommunism on some Negro delegates—Washington was unable to make an effective anticommunist argument concerning

70. Secretary of State Haig to Consul General-Cape Town, 7 April 1981, Box 4, Executive Secretariat, NSC, Country File, Africa, S. Africa.

71. Fred Wettering to Richard Allen, 13 March 1981, Box 4, Executive Secretariat, NSC, Country Filem, Africa, S. Africa.

72. South African Broadcasting Corporation Commentary, 20 March 1981, Box 120, *Leroy Walker Africa News Service Archive.*

73. South African Broadcasting Corporation Commentary, 8 May 1981, Box 120, *Leroy Walker Africa News Service Archive.*

Southern Africa—certainly not to the extent that was executed with the disastrous covert action in Afghanistan. The so-called Reagan Doctrine, maniacal anticommunism in so many words, was applied consistently in Kabul but Pretoria continued to carry so much racist baggage as to compromise apartheid in a Washington officially sworn to an opposing course, making it difficult to maintain the same kind of approach consistently in Southern Africa.[74]

Activists did not light a fire under Reagan accidentally. David Lampel was Vice President of Inner City Broadcasting Corporation, sited in the same Manhattan office building that housed both the ANC and SWAPO—801 Second Avenue. ICBC controlled a talk radio station that targeted the millions from the African diaspora that lived within reach of their broadcast signal and, as a result, apartheid was a frequent topic of discussion. I was residing in Manhattan during the Reagan years myself and appeared more than once on these airwaves. It was Lampel who forwarded many letters our movement helped to generate about apartheid to Congressman Mario Biaggi of the Bronx, who sent them in turn to the White House.[75] South African Broadcasting noticed worriedly Pretoria's "obvious interest in the growing Afro-American confrontation over its role in international politics."[76]

Despite these avid protests, Secretary of State Alexander Haig—a beribboned military man—informed the president in May 1981 that "we have effectively ended the unproductive ostracism" of Pretoria while "restoring our military attaché link and Coast Guard training for South African sea and air rescue personnel." "On the nuclear matter," quite critical, "we will seek relief" for Pretoria and "make a best effort on fuel supply for their reactors…."[77] A scant year later South African Broadcasting congratulated Washington's relaxation of the arms embargo on ARMSCOR, Pretoria's military procurer, altering a policy that had been in place for 20 years. "Nonmilitary goods," an amorphous phrasing, could now be sent to the police and military.[78] By June 1982, Senator Orrin Hatch of Utah, a reliable Republican,

74. James M. Scott, *Deciding to Intervene: The Reagan Doctrine and American Foreign Policy*, Durham: Duke University Press, 1996, 5.

75. David Lampel to Congressman Biaggi, 3 April 1981, Box 163, WHORM, Subject File.

76. South African Broadcasting Corporation Commentary, 3 April 1981, Box 237, *Leroy Walker Africa News Service Archive*.

77. Secretary Haig to President Reagan, 20 May 1981, Box 4, Executive Secretariat, NSC, Country File, Africa, S. Africa.

78. Johannesburg legation to Secretary of State, March 1982, Box 9 [Box 4], African Affairs Directorate, NSC, *Reagan Presidential Library*.

seemed open to providing Pretoria with "incentives" to negotiate reasonably on evacuating illegally occupied Namibia. What "they seem to be very concerned about," he told the White House, "is the isolation from our military and intelligence activities." They wanted the U.S. to "sell them aircraft and associated surveillance equipment,"[79] and he seemed willing to comply.

Secretary Haig's optimism was understandable but premature. As he was promising the rebirth of friendship between Washington and Pretoria, activists in New York City were plotting a contrary course. In 1981 a South African rugby team was scheduled to play in this metropolis. Raucous demonstrations erupted, in which I participated. The city's mayor, Edward Koch, was known as a fervent Zionist; thus, the headline in the leading Harlem weekly blared, "Koch welcomes S. African team? Would he welcome PLO?"[80] A few days later, there was the predictable headline: "Koch cancels rugby match,"[81] no minor matter in the isolation of sports-mad Pretoria. Days after that there was another combustible headline: "Powerful bomb…exploded outside the downtown Schenectady offices of the Eastern Rugby Union," apartheid's local partner; "no one was injured."[82] The "Stop Apartheid Rugby Tour"—SART—was quite successful in demonstrating against these unwelcome visitors, not only in New York City and upstate New York but Los Angeles and Chicago too.[83]

While activists were harassing South Africans in the U.S., Prexy Nesbitt of Chicago had managed by 1983 to infiltrate the land of apartheid. "I was inside South Africa illegally, when I worked for the World Council of Churches", he recalled later. "I worked with some of these nuns and priests" of Irish origin, "when I was illegally in South Africa and had to be smuggled out." It was a time of "intense struggle, whether you were directly a soldier of the struggle, or whether you were doing support work. And intelligence [was] gathered, at … those levels, for the underground of the African National Congress, [which] necessitated and drew in people who

79. Senator Hatch to Judge Clark, 23 June 1982, Box 9, 10, 12[Box 4], Robert Lilac Files Race, *Reagan Presidential Library*.

80. *New York Amsterdam News*, 25 July 1981.

81. *New York Times*, 8 August 1981.

82. *Albany Times Union*, [New York], 23 September 1981. See also File on "Capital District Coalition Against Apartheid" embedded in "Anti-Apartheid Movements: File of Clippings and Miscellanea," *Michigan State University*.

83. See *Guardian* [New York], articles from Fall 1981, Box 247, *Leroy Walker Africa News Service Archive*.

were from some of these church bodies." Nesbitt was engaged in labor "benefiting not just the African National Congress and various people fighting against apartheid in South Africa, it was also work [involving] the struggle going on in Angola, the struggle going on in Zimbabwe." "The World Council of Churches," for which he toiled, "had given special help to the educational effort and the medical effort supporting Zimbabwean refugees...."[84]

SART and Nesbitt's cloak and dagger derring-do were simply part of a larger mosaic of protest that included a general expansion of the cultural boycott during the 1980s. Actor and singer Ben Vereen was cajoled into canceling his tour of South Africa but the O'Jays, whose music ironically had more substantive content than his, were not persuaded likewise.[85] Having famously sung about the love of money being the source of evil, the O'Jays had those sentiments tossed back in their faces.[86]

Appearing at the apartheid resort known as Sun City were the little singer with the big voice, Stephanie Mills,[87] and schmaltz purveyor Neil Sedaka[88] When the Staple Singers appeared in South Africa and claimed they had never heard of the boycott, an observer noticed that the "atmosphere became tense."[89] The *Sowetan*, growingly militant on this front, named and shamed an elongated list of boycott violators, which by late 1982 included numerous Afro-American performers, including The Supremes, The Temptations, Shirley Scott, Shirley Bassey, Stanley Turrentine, Dakota Station, The Mighty Clouds of Joy, Brook Benton, Jimmy Smith, Millie Jackson, Two Tons of Fun, Lou Donaldson, and Ray Charles—who was picketed in New York as a result.[90] The Black Consciousness Movement was also busily upbraiding these Negro artists, focusing on boycott scofflaws Ray Charles, the Temptations, and Betty Wright. Millie Jackson, yet another target, was emphatic in denouncing those hounding her, telling them "I'm here for dollars. I'm not interested in the black struggle." Besides, she countered, "Afro-Americans are lazy and have criminal tendencies."[91]

---

84. Oral History, Prexy Nesbitt, 1 April 2009, *Columbia College-Chicago*.

85. *Sunday Times* [South Africa], 29 April 1981.

86. Flyer on O'Jays, no date, Box 1, *Southern Africa Collective Collection, Schomburg Center, New York Public Library*.

87. *Rand Daily Mail*, 17 May 1982.

88. *Johannesburg Star*, 20 May 1982.

89. *Sowetan*, 18 May 1982.

90. *Sowetan*, 17 December 1982.

91. Press Release, 17 March 1981, Box 4, *Dennis Brutus Papers, Schomburg Center, New York Public Library*.

Jackson was attacked mercilessly but she was joined in this circle of infamy by Chick Corea, Tina Turner, Eartha Kitt, George Benson, Sha Na Na, and many more.[92] (In 1984, the NAACP withdrew awards for Tina Turner and Dannie Bell because they had performed in South Africa.)[93] Naturally, bias was embedded in this process. The crooner Frank Sinatra received $1.79 million for his mere nine concerts in 1981. Even factoring in his inflated reputation, this was larger than what Negro performers received by several orders of magnitude—and indicated how desperate apartheid backers were to break the curtain of isolation that had descended.[94] (Personally, I recall being struck by how Don King was flayed repeatedly in the mainstream press, while his fiercest competitor, Bob Arum, who actively promoted violating the cultural boycott, was not; of course, King is of African ancestry and Arum is not). The hall of shame into which these U.S. artists should be inducted is quite extensive.[95]

In direct response, "Artists and Athletes Against Apartheid" was formed in 1983, marking yet another sturdy signpost in the road to 1994. Arthur Ashe, once reviled for traveling to South Africa himself, was a moving force in this group, along with his long-time friend from Richmond, Virginia, Randall Robinson. Joining them were basketball superstar Kareem Abdul-Jabbar and fellow celebrated hoopster, Wilt 'The Stilt' Chamberlain; singer Tony Bennett; actor and comedian Bill Cosby; actor and playwright Ossie Davis and his spouse, Ruby Dee; comedian Dick Gregory; boxer Larry Holmes; composer Quincy Jones; boxing promoter Don King; actor Paul Newman; actor Sidney Poitier; and actor Jane Fonda.[96]

---

92. Press Release, 25 September 1982, Box 1, *Southern Africa Collective Collection, Schomburg Center, New York Public Library.*

93. *Los Angeles Times*, 5 December 1984.

94. Undated brochure, Box 1, *Southern Africa Collective Collection, Schomburg Center, New York Public Library.*

95. Undated list compiled by Patrice Lumumba Coalition of Harlem and Los Angeles and Michael Beaubien of violators of cultural boycott, Box 179, *Gerald Horne Papers*: Osmonds; Village People; Billy Cobham; Goldie Hawn; Curtis Mayfield; Liza Minelli; Helen Reddy; Tim Reid; Shirley Scott; George Shearing; Edwin Starr; Stanley Turrentine. See also an undated list of violators of the cultural boycott, circa 1983, PED NARMIC, Program Resources, S. Africa, 1983: Cher, Glen Campbell, Wilson Pickett, Paul Anka, the Beach Boys, Chick Corea, Lou Donaldson, Aretha Franklin, Nikki Giovanni, Goldie Hawn, Isaac Hayes, Eartha Kitt, Curtis Mayfield, Johnny Mathis, Helen Reddy, George Shearing, The Temptations, Tina Turner.

96. Stationery of Artists and Athletes Against Apartheid, circa 1983, Box 27, *Arthur Ashe Papers, Schomburg Center, New York Public Library.*

Pretoria betrayed its own uneasiness about this movement when South African Broadcasting attacked Fonda, along with the students at Witwatersrand University and Rhodes University who invited her to speak.[97]

New York City, the main population center in the republic, was a beacon of cosmopolitan activism that did not ignore other nations. Thus, in 1981 activists there organized a global conference in solidarity with the sub-region, held at the Riverside Church in upper Manhattan (a conference that I helped to organize and publicize).[98] It was a success in bringing diverse forces together on a common militant platform; attendees included Bill Sutherland.[99] The success was indicated ironically by the vicious attack on this gathering made by the U.S. ultra-right, including Senator Jesse Helms of North Carolina.[100]

The ACOA remained an active force and by 1980 was publishing a "Student Anti-Apartheid Movement Newsletter" detailing protests on scores of U.S. campuses.[101] This was grounded in earlier efforts, e.g. the 1960s sit-ins at Chase Manhattan Bank as a result of their tie to apartheid, a protest spearheaded by Students for a Democratic Society.[102] But there was no better barometer of how the tide against apartheid had turned than the student movement. By 1982 more than 30 colleges and universities had divested more than $190 million dollars from banks and corporations operating in South Africa and actions demanding further divestment had roiled the waters on hundreds of campuses.[103] It was not only campuses that had become a hotbed of pro-divestment sentiment. The journalist Linn Washington recalled that roughly "fifty years ago, 15,000 Philadelphians volunteered to help defend Ethiopia against Mussolini's invasion"

97. South African Broadcasting Corporation Commentary, 18 June 1981, Box 237, *Leroy Walker Africa News Service Archive.*

98. *Carolina Times*, 3 October 1981. Horne: "epoch making conference on Southern Africa" At the time I wrote a weekly column for the Afro-American press that often targeted Pretoria. See e.g. *Norfolk Journal & Guide*, 16 September 1981.

99. *New York Daily News*, 9 October 19811

100. *Red Locusts: Soviet Support for Terrorism in South Africa*, no publishing details, *University of Texas-Austin.*

101. "Student Anti-Apartheid Movement Newsletter," December 1980, Box 237, *Leroy Walker Africa News Service Archive.*

102. *Southern Africa Magazine*, March-April 1981, Box 237, *Leroy Walker Africa News Service Archive.*

103. Brochure from "Africa Fund" of ACOA, circa 1983, Box 5, *Dennis Brutus Papers, Schomburg Center, New York Public Library.*

and "in 1982 Philadelphia became the first big city…to pass divestment legislation," demonstrating that "anti-apartheid is not simply an elite concern here…."[104]

It was becoming increasingly untenable to make the fundamentally silly argument that investment in South Africa was detachable from support for apartheid itself. This claim should have been exposed by even faint familiarity with the case of U.S. journalist Nat Gibson, charged in August 1981 with unauthorized publication of potentially "embarrassing or alarming statements" about the South African military. The controversy stemmed from a report on a strike In the Eastern Cape in June 1980 where it was revealed that the military was protecting "factories against strikers." That the case was dropped did not change its clear implications in favor of divestment.[105]

Early on the White House faced the contradiction that Gulf Oil generally opposed its anti-MPLA, anti-Cuban policy, not least since these forces were protecting oil facilities in Cabinda from being ransacked by Jonas Savimbi, quickly becoming the hero of the hard right.[106] The mouthpiece of business, the *Wall Street Journal*, reported faithfully this concern.[107]

Appearing before a congressional committee a few months after the inauguration, Melvin Hill, President of Gulf Oil Exploration and Production—who also was active in Nigeria, Cameroon, Gabon, and Zaire—praised the MPLA, as if he were a party cadre, and warned menacingly against alignment with Pretoria. For that would mean "sanctions" imposed by Nigeria, the continent's emerging heavyweight, and would include "the use of oil as a political weapon." Recall, Hill said, how BP was nationalized in Nigeria because of disgust with London's Rhodesia policy.[108]

Increasingly, Nigeria became a pressing concern in Washington. L. Paul Bremer III—who was to be the U.S. viceroy in Baghdad after the catastrophic overthrow of Saddam Hussein in 2003—told Richard Allen in 1981 that a Washington priority should be accentuating the

104. Pacific News Service article, 1984, PED Program Resources, Southern Africa, 1984, *AFSC*.

105. Secretary of State to Consul General-Johannesburg, February 1982, Box 9 [Box 2], African Affairs Directorate, NSC, *Reagan Presidential Library*.

106. Fred Wettering to Richard Allen, 6 July 1981, Box 38, WHORM, Subject File, CO Countries, CO006 Angola.

107. *Wall Street Journal*, 27 March 1981.

108. Testimony of Melvin Hill, 1 April 1981, Box 15, *Washington Office on Africa Papers*.

"moderating role the Nigerians play among the Front Line States,"[109] led by Tanzania and Zimbabwe. The details of this priority were left to the imagination but given past praxis this could easily mean discrediting or otherwise deposing of Nigerians unwilling to play a "moderating role."

But Gulf faced a rising chorus of protest in response. James Willis of Pensacola found it hard to believe that "the Export-Import Bank loaned $ 5 million dollars to Angola...." He was incredulous. "Did Gulf help?" he asked disbelievingly. "Why is our government loaning money to Russia's sidekick and why should we subsidize Gulf explorations. I support President Reagan," lest there be any doubt, he insisted, who was the "best president we have since George Washington," a major slaveholder.[110]

Other than Gulf's acquiescence to the Cuban presence in Angola, another surprising aspect of ruling elite foreign policy was their approach to Harare. In late June 1981 the doddering Reagan met with Australian Prime Minister Malcolm Fraser. It was at this meeting that Secretary Haig made the surprising point that Pretoria was no longer suspicious of Mugabe and wanted him to survive. The man from Canberra "recalled that British intelligence had been dead wrong about [Mugabe], forgetting that he hated the Soviets," the primary target, and "had had ties to the Chinese and was a Christian...."[111]

Diplomacy toward Harare was crucial given its proximity to Pretoria. The "popularity" of the ZANU regime was "beginning to wane," Reagan said in 1981. He blamed the "very deliberate and pragmatic approach to land resettlement and the rising cost of living" as "primarily responsible for much of the criticism...."[112]

Washington in short was ambivalent about the newly installed regime in the city formerly known as Salisbury. U.S. officials clearly wanted to destabilize but it was unclear what would come next. Part of Washington's problem was summarized by the Cape Town legation in 1981: apparently, Pretoria's Foreign Minister, Pik Botha, was concerned about South Africa's "sizable and vulnerable financial

---

109. L. Paul Bremer III to Richard Allen, 2 October 1981, Box 4, Executive Secretariat, NSC, Country File, Africa, S. Africa, *Reagan Presidential Library*.

110. James Willis to Edwin Meese, 5 November 1981, Box 38, WHORM Subject Files, CO Countries CO006 Angola, *Reagan Presidential Library*.

111. Minutes of Meeting, 30 June 1981, Box 14, Executive Secretariat, NSC, Subject File, Memcons, *Reagan Presidential Library*.

112. President Reagan to Clement Zablocki, 17 December 1981, Box 159, WHORM Subject File, Zimbabwe, *Reagan Presidential Library*.

exposure in Zimbabwe," decrying the "blunder of leaving sizable South Africa funds vulnerable to black Marxist governments...."[113] Just as Harare started to feel more comfortable about surviving land reform—the expropriation of the European minority after 1994—Washington and its allies were feeling more comfortable about punishing Harare, propelled by pent-up complaints.

Smith's dead regime remained a pet cause of the ruling Republican Party, which had not relinquished the harebrained idea of overturning African majority rule. Writing from Harare, Tom Schaaf, a shady figure, wanted to broker a meeting between Smith and the hardliner Senator Helms of North Carolina. Smith was also elusive since "what he says in public will of course be quite different from [what] he will say in confidence," probably a veiled reference to coup plotting.[114]

William Askin was among those badgering the White House about a "continuing series of abuses which American citizens have suffered at the hands of Zimbabwe officials...." He was Executive Director of Game Conservative International, whose board chair, Harry Lee Tennison, was a "prominent Republican industrialist of Fort Worth," Texas. This sturdy conservative was "detained, harassed, embarrassed and reviled" by the Zimbabwean authorities at a "border crossing post of [Kazungula]," and this was "totally uncalled for...."[115]

Congressman Gerald Solomon demanded that aid to Harare be reduced. The "profound sense of outrage that many members of Congress felt at Zimbabwe's abstention from the United Nations vote that condemned the shooting down of Korean Airlines flight 707" in 1983 and "recent sponsorship with Nicaragua of a United Nations resolution condemning the American liberation [sic] of Grenada is a gratuitous slap at our country."[116] It was likely that Washington was displeased with the ZANU Congress that occurred months later. Kaunda and Machel were featured but also among the honored guests was the Vice President of the Democratic People's Republic of Korea, then—as now—at sword's point with the U.S.

---

113. Consul General-Cape Town to Secretary of State, 10 November 1981, Box 4, Executive Secretariat, NSC, Country File, Africa, S. Africa, *Reagan Presidential Library*.

114. Tom Schaaf to Edwin Meese, 13 September 1982, Box 159, WHORM, Subject File, Zimbabwe, *Reagan Presidential Library*.

115. William Askin to President Reagan, 15 September 1983, Box 159, WHORM, Subject File, Zimbabwe

116. Congressman Gerald Solomon to President Reagan, 17 November 1983, Box 159, WHORM, Subject File, Zimbabwe.

"Mugabe gave Oliver Tambo star billing," said a Quaker observer, which diminished the opportunity to use the PAC as a wedge in the region.[117]

As had been the case since at least the Angola crisis of 1975, China continued to play a dastardly role in the sub-region, aligning with the North Atlantic bloc in pursuit of anti-Soviet nirvana. In a "secret" report from 1981, London uncovered what was already well known: China chose to "applaud the firm public stance adopted by the President towards the Soviet Union."[118] At that juncture, China was still discussing aiding UNITA in Angola in league with the U.S.[119] This consideration continued even though London reported, in a "confidential" memo, that there was reason to believe that Savimbi was overrated and did not control the territory he claimed.[120]

It was not only China defecting from the socialist consensus. As the 1980s unwound, Thabo Mbeki reported that "Polish workers who have resettled in South Africa (reported by people inside the country) have become more vicious than white South African workers"[121]—and one of their number became the assassin of SACP leader Chris Hani.

In the 1980s reproach of Savimbi was heretical in the corridors of power in Washington. Robert Cleaves, a Los Angeles businessman, told the White House in 1983 that he had "just returned from an extensive visit to Southern Africa," where he had spent "considerable time with Dr. Jonas Savimbi...," who he learned was enamored with Reagan. "I have been able to generate contacts and develop intelligence which I will hope will continue to be of benefit to you," he told the president.[122] Cleaves was "an old friend," the White House was told, and "on the 'short list' for consideration as ambassador to South Africa. He also accompanied Ian Smith when Smith visited President Reagan in our Los Angeles offices (in 1979, as I recall) ...."[123]

---

117. Letter to "Dear Friends," 17 August 1984, ID Africa-S S S Afri-IAP Zimbabwe-TAMAPSA, 1984, *AFSC*.

118. Report, 1981, FCO105/548, *NAUK-London*.

119. Letter to "Dear Brian," 13 July 1981, FCO106/298, *NAUK-London*.

120. Report, 21 July 1981, FCO106/298, *NAUK-London*.

121. Jerry Herman to Bill Taylor, et.al., 9 May 1985, PED Program Resources, Southern Africa, 1984, *AFSC*.

122. Robert Cleaves to President Reagan, 4 October 1983, Box 38, WHORM Subject File, CO Countries, CO006, Angola, *Reagan Presidential Library*.

123. Peter Hannaford to Kathleen Osborne, 4 November 1983, Box 38, WHORM Subject File, CO Countries, CO006, Angola.

Other than China, the problem in Angola—and to a degree in Mozambique—was that it had become harder to galvanize solidarity for radical regimes holding power, as opposed to national liberation movements promising radicalism. Once the reins of power were seized, there seemed to be a drop in support for these newly installed regimes.[124] It was as if there were many more of those who could sympathize with armed struggle—or the sight of struggling Africans—than who sympathized with Africans seeking to wrestle knotty matters of state administration.

Thus, not all the news from the anti-apartheid movement was promising. The Washington Office on Africa had been formed with the assistance of ACOA but now on the scene, within walking distance from the White House, was Trans-Africa, headed by Randall Robinson. There was an uneasy division of labor between the two. Chris Root of WOA thought that Robinson "tends to the division along racial lines and then transposes his own bias in favor of working with the national elite to the 'white side' of things as well as to his primary focus on the 'National Black Leadership,'" whereas Root's group "tend to lean more towards the importance of being a resource to local groups...." It was "Randall's perception that we are a little politically 'purist'" as a result.[125]

Another WOA functionary expressed dismay with the work of six Afro-American women, quite active in a capital that was—after all—predominantly Afro-American. In a "confidential" missive, Connie Street spoke of her clash with one of these women, Sylvia Hill, who also had been present at 6PAC in Dar. The "overall problem," said Street, was "complete centralization of power with 6 women: Sylvia Hill, Sandra Hill, Kathy Flewellen, Cecilie Counts, Shery Gardner and Adwoa Dunn." Street was "fed up." Their Southern Africa Support Project, formed around 1978, was not playing a positive role, she thought: "there is a Marxist study group that these women are in which also includes Damu [Smith]." "Ken Jones might be in it" too. "That group," like the SACP peer, "tries through its members to control SASP, the D.C. chapter of the Alliance Against Racist and Political Repression," known to be close to the U.S. Communist Party, and the "Venceremos Brigade," known to be close to Havana. Asking a question that U.S. intelligence would like answered too, this functionary wondered speculatively, "the other thing we talked about

124. William Minter, *Apartheid's Contras: An Inquiry into the Roots of War in Angola and Mozambique*, Johannesburg: Witwatersrand University Press, 1994, 153.

125. Chris Root to Jean Sindab, 2 June 1980, Box 23, *Jean Sindab Papers*.

that neither of us knew the answer to was the connection between the Marxist Study Group [and] the Communist Party."[126]

WOA was misguided in its perception, perhaps having spent too much time in a Reagan-dominated Washington. But the fault lines revealed were not those of Washington alone. During the same time in Atlanta, site of a bourgeoning Negro population, the legislator and NAACP leader Julian Bond was told that anti-apartheid activism should include "any white liberal legislators, whoever they are and if they can be trusted," since their presence served as camouflage in a state where movements comprised wholly of Afro-Americans were viewed with suspicion by the majority. Despite the dedicated activism of religious denominations over the years, in Georgia "churches" were "a bummer," difficult to organize. "Moralistic suasion," a specialty of churches "will be counter-productive," it was said with sadness.[127]

Amiri Baraka, the writer once known as LeRoi Jones, had attained a kind of renown after he backed UNITA during the Angola crisis of 1975. He did not shrink from his stance and clashed sharply with fellow Afro-American poet Antar Mberi, known to be close to the U.S. Communist Party, at a writers' congress: this time the issue was the perennial ANC vs. PAC debate, with Baraka defending the latter strenuously.[128]

These conflicts reflected colonialism's death spiral in the subregion, causing its defenders to redouble their efforts, combined with the difficulty in the U.S. in dealing with raw anticommunism, which not only engendered ideological feebleness but uncertain tactics too. That is, all sides had weaknesses. Shortly after the mentally faltering Reagan moved into the White House, E.S. Reddy of the U.N. Special Committee Against Apartheid told the ANC about reservations about his own work. "Dear Oliver," he wrote in salutation to the ANC's Tambo, "last Wednesday Mr. Makhathini," the group's U.N. envoy, "told me categorically that that the Special Committee Against Apartheid was ineffective and not helpful to the liberation movement and compared badly with the Council for Namibia," the U.N.'s companion grouping. "He made it very clear that I was *personally* responsible," he stressed dejectedly. Reddy, who had assumed

126. "Confidential" Report, 25 June 1981, Box 23, *Jean Sindab Papers*.

127. Ike Miller, Canterbury Center for Spiritual Life to Julian Bond, 15 June 1981, Atlanta Regional Office, Southern Africa Peace Education Program, *AFSC*.

128. "U.S. Writers Fight for ANC's Cause," *Sechaba*, March 1982, *Columbia College-Chicago*.

his post in 1963 and claimed to work "70 hours a week," confessed unashamedly that this contention "hurt me deeply."[129]

Despite the hosannas of praise for the Council on Namibia, the negotiations leading to independence slowed down in the early stages of the new regime in Washington. Pretoria was maneuvering furiously, seeking to place so-called Francophone states alongside the Frontline States led by Tanzania and Zimbabwe, in order to weaken the latter. This would include Gabon, Ivory Coast, Senegal, Togo, and Zaire. Even the U.S. Consul General in Cape Town saw this effort as unlikely to succeed; just an awkward way to foil Libya, which supposedly wanted to become involved in the negotiations.[130]

The PAC was—per usual—writhing in internecine conflict. One of its leaders, Henry Isaacs, chose this moment to quit, perhaps seeking to avoid the deadly fate of his late comrade David Sibeko. According to an observant journalist, the group he departed "increasingly identified with China's political line." The ANC continued in its policy of "refusing to share a platform with the PAC—a position that has posed a problem by some U.S. support organizations, which have been reluctant to take sides"—an accurate reflection of what I experienced at the time. The article mentioned that one of my Harlem comrades, the late Elombe Brath and his group, the Patrice Lumumba Coalition, "had traditionally been close to the PAC," which was true given his own history as an avatar of Black Nationalism. But unlike some who carried this descriptor, Elombe was always willing to bend to intelligence and by April 1982 he and the PLC "decided" to "support ANC exclusively…."[131] This head-spinning change may have been a reaction to the real threat perceived by the rise of the hard right in the U.S. in the 1980 and what it portended.

Bill Sutherland observed some of the tensions that had driven Elombe to abandon the PAC when he toured the U.S. in 1982. He began on 3 October in Massachusetts, where he found "the Boston chapter of Trans-Africa headed by Professor Willard Johnson may be one of the most effective in the country…." In Portland he saw that "Black Nationalism may be growing stronger and organizers would do well to consider encouraging *parallel* action rather than integrated action", e.g. organizing separately in Black and

---

129. E.S. Reddy to "Dear Oliver," 29 April 1981, Reel 19, *Oliver Tambo Papers*.

130. Report by Consul General-Cape Town, 17 March 1982, Box 4, Executive Secretariat, NSC, Country File, Africa, S. Africa, *Reagan Presidential Library*.

131. *Africa News* [U.S.], 7 June 1982.

non-Black communities. "Very few of Stanford's Afro-American students attended and here is a case where *parallel action* may be the method.... Denver was yet another example of how the presence of Africans in a community provides an informed nucleus for Southern Africa work...." [emphasis original] In other words, unlike Afro-Americans, Africans were often not as skeptical of the alleged beneficence of the bulk of Euro-Americans and could be more effective organizing beside this community. In Tampa, Sutherland's "audience was primarily white, raising once again the issue in my mind of when is Parallel Action rather than Integrated Coalition action more effective in community outreach."[132]

Sutherland's was an understandable reaction to the unwillingness of U.S. Jim Crow to retreat altogether. Thus, religious denominations were quite active against apartheid but often on "parallel" tracks. In 1982 Paul A. Wee, General Secretary of Lutheran World Ministries, reminded the typically uninformed Reagan that his denomination in what was to become Namibia had a "combined baptized membership" that comprised a goodly percentage of the colony. He detailed the "cries of agony and suffering of the Namibian people" and the "tyranny" of Pretoria.[133]

These tensions were endemic in the sub-region. In 1984, a Quaker who had lived in Malawi for six years remained "concerned about the tension that is still present between AFSC [American Friends Service Committee] and Quakers in South Africa...."[134] Another kind of problem confronted the Quakers' delegate in Harare. As the Free South Africa Movement was being concocted, which helped to dig a deeper grave for apartheid, Edgar Lockwood announced morosely, "I think the fact that I am [a] white American and an expatriate is a particular hindrance in a country like Zimbabwe where the revolution was fought as a basically nationalist revolution rather than a revolution for class reasons. Only a very few whites are deeply trusted," while Washington was "seen as a dubious ally of liberation, if not an outright co-conspirator" against decolonization. Then there was the "use of secret agents" by the U.S., casting suspicion upon Euro-Americans generally in the sub-region.[135]

---

132. Memo from Bill Sutherland on 1982 Tour, PED PROGRAM RESOURCES SOUTHERN AFRICA.... TAO, *AFSC*.

133. Paul A. Wee to President Reagan, 12 November 1982, Box 164, WHORM, Subject File, *Reagan Presidential Library*.

134. "Jane" to AFSC, 22 October 1984, ID Africa-E Africa- 1984, *AFSC*.

135. Report by Edgar Lockwood, 25 January 1984, South Africa File, *AFSC*. (Also found in ID 1983 Africa-E to Africa-SA Mozambique S. Africa IAP Zambia)

* * *

I was friendly with Barbara Masekela—sister of the musician—and had visited her comfortable apartment in upper Manhattan when she was teaching at Rutgers University. I was surprised as any when she gave it all up. "I have decided to make myself available to the ANC on a full-time basis," she announced in February 1982. "I have no pre-conditions to make," she told ANC leader Alfred Nzo, saying she was "available to come to Lusaka at the end of June at the earliest...."[136] She did move and became a close aide to the freed Mandela, then her nation's chief envoy in Paris. Her abandonment of the comforts of Manhattan for Lusaka was yet another sign that the tide had turned against apartheid.

136. Barbara Masekela to Alfred Nzo, 16 February 1982, Box 35, Folder 27, *Lusaka Mission, ANC Records.*

Chapter 19

The CIA Cabal Strikes Back, 1984-1985

BY early November 1984, champagne corks were popping again in Pretoria's hallways of influence. "Reagan victory delights [Pretoria]," was the headline to a story in which top leader P.W. Botha was said to be "grateful" for the result.[1] Apartheid's critical ally, the former GE pitchman Reagan, was re-elected with overwhelming support from the all important Euro-American constituency. Anti-apartheid activists, myself included, were frustrated. But that same month, Randall Robinson and several his cohorts launched the "Free South Africa Movement," unleashing civil disobedience that led to mass arrests first at the South African legation in Washington, and then spreading to consulates from New York to Los Angeles. This deft maneuver captured headlines. It engaged a mass audience as it became fashionable to be arrested protesting, with celebrities flocking to Washington, New York, and Los Angeles to demonstrate. (I coordinated the arrests at the South African consulate on the East Side of Manhattan --and represented arrestees in court-- and was besieged with requests from those who wished to be arrested.[2] I had a sense that a Rubicon of sorts had been crossed in terms of reaching a new stage in our movement when the Attorney General of the state of New York, Robert Abrams—a cautious man like most bourgeois politicians—chose to be arrested there.)[3]

The momentum for this upsurge was driven by the presidential campaign of Jesse Jackson, who made anti-apartheid and

1. *South Africa Digest*, 16 November 1984, Box 120, *Leroy Walker Africa News Service Archive*.

2. Sky Kershner, Fairfield United Methodist Church, Fairfield, New Jersey to Gerald Horne, Box 190, *Gerald Horne Papers*: "Thanks for representing us on Feb. 15 [at] the South African Consulate.... may see you on March 4th..."

3. *Daily Challenge* [New York], 10 January 1985.

decolonization a major plank in his platform while seeking the Democratic Party nomination. This in turn gave momentum to a lagging campaign to slap punitive sanctions on Pretoria and helped to exacerbate the crisis the nation already was enduring as the attempt to make South African ungovernable gained enormous traction. This movement also forced Pretoria to sanction itself. Even before the November 1984 demonstrations, Pretoria decided not to place a consulate in Denver, due to stern local opposition.[4] When Pretoria denied a visa to the Reverend Jackson in 1984, it was not a sign of strength but of self-isolation.[5] When the U.S. filmmaker Woody Allen moved in 1985 to disallow his movies from being shown in South Africa, it was a further signal of apartheid's increasing isolation.[6] Another portent came when Tyne Daly of the popular U.S. TV show *Cagney and Lacey* donated her earnings from South Africa to anti-apartheid causes, dismissing the filthy lucre as "bloody money."[7]

Decisions by liberal filmmakers and actors aside, the turning point for the unraveling of apartheid debatably arrived months after the re-election of the shambling Reagan. By August 1985 the White House was aflutter about a proposed debt moratorium in South Africa, frightening Wall Street. Pretoria's premier banker was deep in conversation with the Federal Reserve's Paul Volcker, monetary chieftain. "The main problem," according to Reagan aide Phillip Ringdahl, "is that American [banks] hold $600 million in short-term notes due next week which the banks are 'not inclined' to roll over, nor are any European or other banks willing to pick them up." South Africa also held "$7 billion [in] debt which comes due in the next six months" and Pretoria was deathly concerned with a "panic," a "run on the banks" that would see depositors rush to withdraw their funds, causing a liquidity crisis.[8] Something had to give.

A shaken aide, Robert McFarlane, took this concern directly to the bumbling Reagan. The situation was causing a "significant loss of private banking confidence," he said gravely. Speaking on 27 August, he was, like Ringdahl, worried that "about $600 million will come due...this week." Also, like Ringdahl, he emphasized that U.S. banks "will refuse to roll these debts over" and that it was "unlikely

4. *Rocky Mountain News*, 9 September 1983.
5. *Sydney Morning Herald*, 1 September 1984.
6. *Sydney Morning Herald*, 28 July 1985.
7. *Johannesburg Star*, 17 October 1983.
8. Phillip Ringdahl to Robert McFarlane, 27 August 1985, African Affairs Directorate, NSC, RAC Box 9 [Box 2], *Reagan Presidential Library*.

that Japan will roll them over too," exacerbating the incipient crisis.[9] The only way out seemed to be the most consequential: an elongated process of regime change in Pretoria, eventuating in democratic elections less than a decade later.

There were also telltale signs that the Robinson-led effort was a political earthquake already in motion, which along with the debt crisis exerted enormous strain on apartheid. On 30 November 1984 Republican Senators Richard Lugar of Indiana and Nancy Kassenbaum of Kansas were warning the increasingly incoherent Reagan, who may have already had Alzheimer's, that "over the past four years there has been a gradual erosion of support in the Congress for the Southern Africa policy...."[10] The legislators may have had in mind what had happened just weeks before when—as Congressman George Crockett of Detroit and the Black Caucus told the White House—Congress "overwhelmingly approved bipartisan Resolutions calling upon" Pretoria to "immediately release the Mandelas"—not only Nelson from Robben Island but also his oft jailed spouse, Winnie.[11] Of the latter, Mary O. Ross of the Women's Convention of the National Baptist Convention told the White House of her "concern for the welfare of Winnie Mandela....We appeal to you in support of [her]," she implored, "because, like her, we are Black and have borne the burdens of racial oppression...."[12]

The Caucus was also in alignment with Trans-Africa, which assailed the Reagan regime's removal of export controls, bolstering apartheid, particularly in the contested realms of the military and police. They also castigated the White House's demagogy in demanding removal of Cuban troops from Angola[13]—while the U.S. itself would not have been formed but for the presence of French troops. Beyond the work of committed activists, most indicative of how and why sanctions would soon be slapped on Pretoria was the December 1984 hand delivery by Congresswoman Lynn Martin, a staunch Republican Party activist, of a protest to South African envoy B.G. Fourie demanding an end to apartheid. It was signed by other leading

---

9. Robert McFarlane to President Reagan, African Affairs Directorate, NSC Records, RAC Box 16 [Box 9], *Reagan Presidential Library*.

10. Senators Lugar and Kassenbaum to President Reagan, 30 November 1984, Box 165, WHORM, Subject File, *Reagan Presidential Library*.

11. Congressman George Crockett to President Reagan, 11 October 1984, Box 165, WORHM, Subject File,

12. Mary O. Ross to President Reagan, no date, Box 168, WHORM, Subject File.

13. Report by Trans-Africa, circa 1984, Box 24, *William Gray Papers, Schomburg Center, New York Public Library*.

congressional Republicans, who added "we are for the most part, politically conservative," a signal of the breadth of anti-apartheid sentiment sweeping the nation.[14] Symptomatic of the strains now induced by alliance with apartheid, in 1985 U.S. Communist leader Angela Davis clashed with the president's daughter, Maureen Reagan, at a U.N. confab in Nairobi, with Davis cheered by thousands.[15]

The cross-border raids launched by Pretoria against its neighbors, in blatant violation of international law, were serving to galvanize support for Cuban troops in the sub-region, the removal of whom was a top priority for Washington. In sum, U.S. policy—like the president--was quite typically incoherent: building support for the opposite of what it desired.

The problem was that the hardliners who tended to predominate at the upper reaches of the Republican Party were unrepentant in their support for Pretoria, considering their mutual interest in racist despotism. As the U.S. was celebrating its annual 4 July holiday in 1984, the White House was briefed by Howard Pollock, who was not only president of the National Rifle Association—the gun lobby that was possibly the most important force within the Republican Party—but also a former Congressman from Alaska. "I have just returned from my sixth visit to Southern Africa in the past five years," he said, "having journeyed into both Namibia and Angola...." In the latter nation, which he likely entered illegally without a visa, he conferred with the leadership "at the bushveldt [sic] headquarters at Jamba, Angola." "I met with Dr. Jonas Savimbi" and "his Cabinet of Ministers," he said proudly. "Dr. Savimbi asked me to personally convey to you," he told the president, "his need for U.S. assistance in the form of effective and anti-aircraft missiles," meaning the "Stingers" already deployed with potent result to the religious zealots in Afghanistan. The missiles were needed, he said, "to bring down the Cuban and Portuguese [sic] piloted aircraft."[16] Pollock's journey to the region, the White House was told, was "totally funded by that government,"[17] meaning Pretoria, a point reflected in his overheated conclusions. Bluntly, Pollock told the generally ignorant Reagan to

---

14. Release, 5 December 1984, Box 17, *William Gray Papers*.

15. *Sydney Morning Herald*, 18 July `1985.

16. Howard Pollock to President Reagan, 4 July 1984, Box 175, OF WHORM, CO 141, South Africa, 592000 and CO 143 Namibia, *Reagan Presidential Library*.

17. Robert Kimmitt to Frederick Ryan, 20 May 1985, Box 166, WHORM, Subject File, *Reagan Presidential Library*.

either adopt his course or be accused of mimicking his now discredited predecessors, Jimmy Carter and Andrew Young.[18]

Pollock insisted that aid to Savimbi be increased, the reaction of the Frontline States be damned. "To my knowledge," he asserted "this is the only area in the world where we refuse to support anti-Communists who seek freedom and independence from a Communist regime," referring to the MPLA in Luanda.[19]

Pollock's comrade Jack Abramoff—who was to become a scandal-plagued producer of an anticommunist movie about the sub-region—said in the prelude to the election that he and his fellow "College Republicans" harbored "intense opposition to any diplomatic recognition of the Cuban backed regime currently ruling Angola....This decision could signal the beginning of the end of the anticommunist regime with which your administration is identified around the world."[20]

Another source of "intelligence" on South Africa promoted by U.S. allies of Pretoria was Stanton D. Anderson, a senior partner in a prominent Washington law firm. After his visit to the Cape, he did accurately relay that the "right wing of the ruling Nationalist Party is now fractured into several groups, the most extreme of which would make George Lincoln Rockwell feel right at home," a reference to the U.S. Nazi leader. "As I drove around Soweto," he said, "I never feared for my own safety. I stopped at a number of homes and I never felt threatened as one might feel on Fourteenth Street" in the heart of Black Washington.[21]

Pat Buchanan, who was to become an ultra-right presidential candidate himself, instructed the frantic Reagan in 1985 that Angola should become the linchpin of his foreign policy. It was the "single place," he insisted, "where America can best send back a message that the one-sided rules of détente" with Moscow "do not apply in the Reagan Era." This was the "same place where in 1975," he said, still smarting from the pain of it all, "it was made evident that détente was a Western delusion...." If the "Eagle," meaning the U.S.,

18. Howard Pollock to President Reagan, 12 April 1985, Box 166, WHORM, Subject File, *Reagan Presidential Library*.

19. Attached Report by Howard Pollock, 4-16 June 1984, Box 175, OF WHORM, CO 141, South Africa, 59200 and CO 143 Namibia.

20. Jack Abramoff to President Reagan, 28 September 1984, Box 38, WHORM, Subject File CO Countries, CO006 Angola, *Reagan Presidential Library*.

21. Memo from Stanton Anderson, no date, Box 2, OA 14170-14170, *David Chew Papers, Reagan Presidential Library*.

was "holding out the olive branch of 'people-to-people exchanges,'" it should make clear that it "still has something else in the other claw," e.g. a trusty weapon.[22] Angola, a wound still throbbing in Washington a decade after independence, was a major Cold War battleground and yet another reason to push for dissolution of the Soviet Union and overthrow of Fidel Castro.

Angola was a dedicated object of attention not only because of the presence of Cuban troops but also as a training ground for ANC militants, a factor that took on added importance after the Nkomati Accord reduced the number of ANC cadre across the continent in Mozambique. Winding up there was Fannie Phakola, who was born in 1957 and began as a pro-PAC and Black Consciousness Movement militant before departing for Swaziland. "There was no PAC in Swaziland," said Phakola, until 1979. When the monarch, King Sobhuza, died in 1982, things changed since he was "supportive of our struggle"—so it was off to Mozambique, where there was "no PAC also," he found. It seemed that the ANC's regional and global ties had monumental local consequence, impelling those fleeing the nation into their ranks. In any case, the issue was "which PAC do you want to join, because" the group was "divided into five in Dar," which, he said, "discouraged me." By 1983, it was off to Angola for an ANC military training camp. "There were courses in topography, artillery, firearms, tactics, and politics"—the "bulk of the training" in the latter category. Conditions were difficult, leading to a mutiny and the "killing of each other." Top commander Chris Hani arrived to settle things down. By 1985 Phakola was off to the Soviet Union for ideological training, "doing Marx and Lenin" with students from a "hundred countries," including Palestine, Nigeria, Ghana, over a "ten-month course." Then the peripatetic revolutionary moved on to Cuba— "Thabo Mbeki then was still a member of the party," he recalled. But retrospectively, it seemed that his stint in Angola was the transformative part of his journey.[23]

One problem for overturning MPLA rule in Luanda was the presence of a Gulf Oil facility in Cabinda, defended by Cuban troops. In June 1985 the U.S. Secretary of State sent out a worldwide alert denouncing a "raid" there by Pretoria. "We have told [Pretoria] privately and publicly that we do not consider its explanation…satisfactory. Given the presence of American citizens at the Malongo

22. Pat Buchanan to President Reagan, 7 November 1985, Box 38, WHORM, Subject File, CO Countries CO006, Angola, *Reagan Presidential Library.*

23. Oral History, Fannie Phakola, 14 October 2004, *University of Connecticut-Storrs.*

facility," it was said, the "danger to American lives arising from the [Pretoria] action" was unacceptable. Legations around the globe were requested to "signal our displeasure," while Ambassador Herman Nickel in South Africa was asked to voice "our intense displeasure."[24]

As ever, the ultra-right placed the survival of their ideology, imperialism and capitalism itself, over human life—even that of those defined as "white." A commentator in the *Washington Post* argued correctly that Savimbi was "overtly appealing to black nationalist attitudes and antiwhite bias," which kept him popular among certain U.S. Negroes. But he "proudly claimed to have attacked the installations of American and other western companies," infuriating Gulf Oil to his detriment.[25]

Pressure to align more closely with Pretoria was emerging from diverse quarters. Before the election, Walter Annenberg—a leading donor to the coffers of the Republican Party—became an intermediary, transmitting messages to the White House from the Bantustan that was the Transkei, written by their leader G.M. Matanzima, who had a relationship with the late Shah of Iran, who had also been a favorite of Republican bigwigs.[26] The continuing conflict between Tehran and Washington dictated that the pleas of counter-revolutionary Iranians backed by Bantustan Africans could hardly be ignored. Knowing this, Matanzima pressed Washington to grant his mini-state full diplomatic recognition.[27]

It was not just rock-ribbed Republicans like Annenberg, Pollock and Abramoff who were cheerleading for a harder line in the subregion. Mburumba Kerina, also known as William Eric Getzen, was born in what is now Namibia and graduated from Lincoln University in Pennsylvania in 1957. By early November 1984 he was writing

---

24. Secretary of State George Shultz to legations in Maputo, Lusaka, Harare, Moscow, Beijing, Brasilia, Tokyo, etc., June 1985, African Affairs Directorate, NSC, RAC, Box 9 [Box 2], *Reagan Presidential Library*.

25. *Washington Post*, 26 January 1986.

26. Walter Annenberg to President Reagan, 22 February 1984, Box 16 [Box 7], RAC, *Reagan Presidential Library*: "During the last years in the life of the late Shah of Iran these gentlemen came to see me with an offer from the Transkei government to provide the Shah with an enormous tract of land where he could establish a permanent and secure residence.....I did arrange for these South Africans to meet with the Shah's sister and brother-in-law and only deteriorating illness precluded the Shah from following through on the Republic of Transkei's gesture."

27. G.M. Matanzima to President Reagan, 17 February 1984, Box 223, WHORM Subject File, CO 178, Zambia, *Reagan Presidential Library*.

from Brooklyn to express to the virulently anticommunist Reagan his "congratulations on mentioning the Namibia problem in your recent debate with" opponent Walter Mondale. He pleaded with the Republican leader to "protect the people of Namibia from being dragged behind the Soviet 'Iron Curtain.'"[28]

Unfortunately, it was not just Angola and Namibia that were in the crosshairs. Mozambique too was in a perilous position in 1984. It was then that P.W. Botha—the Prime Minister who was to become the first President of South Africa that year—told his counterpart in Washington that "we and other African countries are very concerned about the influence exercised" in Maputo by "Indian, white and Mestizo advisers…most of whom are hardline Communists," an approach that eerily mirrored that of the PAC in conflating ancestry and ideology. "The KGB has considerable influence on the Mozambique intelligence service," he charged, a reference to Moscow's routinely demonized intelligence service. "Where you have dispatched your diligent diplomats," he said misleadingly, "the Soviets have deployed Cuban forces…." He was thankful to Washington that "with the very able support of your diplomatic representatives we now have a draft security treaty prepared for negotiation with Mozambique"—the disastrous Nkomati Accord, which led to the ouster of ANC cadre and, ultimately, the death of President Samora Machel himself. Botha was pleased that the reactionary Reagan was running for re-election: this was "welcome news."[29]

It was also "welcome news" to Botha when the U.S. thumbed its nose at the arms embargo against Pretoria. In early 1984 it was reported that Washington "quietly licensed the commercial export of more than $28.3 million worth of military technology to South Africa during the last three years…."[30] Surveying the landscape, South African Broadcasting said with satisfaction in November 1983 that "in Southern Africa during the past three years the United States has altogether overshadowed Europe."[31]

The growing Soviet role in the sub-region that irked Botha may have been a reaction to the arrest of Dieter Gerhardt, a commander at

---

28. Mburumba Kerina to President Reagan, 2 November 1984, Box 175, OF WHORM CO 141 South Africa 59200 and CO 143 Namibia, *Reagan Presidential Library.*

29. P.W. Botha to President Reagan, 14 February 1984, Box 16[Box 8], AAD RAC Reagan *Presidential Library.* s

30. Clipping, 28 January 1984, Box 244, *Leroy Walker Africa News Service Archive.*

31. South African Broadcasting Corporation Commentary, 29 November 1983, Box 120, *Leroy Walker Africa News Service Archive.*

the strategic Simon's Town naval dockyard in South Africa who was taken into custody in New York City in 1983, charged with spying for Moscow.[32] A few months later South African Broadcasting raised an alarm about a spate of Soviet and other Eastern European spies detained in South Africa, indicating—it was said— Moscow's escalating interest in undermining apartheid.[33]

Due east in the Seychelles, a handful of mercenaries with South African ties had been arrested and Pretoria was compelled to reject a proposal to swap them for Mandela's freedom.[34] This defection and the arrests should have been interpreted in Pretoria as symptoms of regime rot, a signal that a severe course correction was direly needed. After all, a mere decade after the "victory" of 1984, the Nationalists would be escorted out of power. Other examples of festering rot were bubbling to the surface. That same year, for example, a man known as Peter Harris—actually Andre Charles Stander—a former top detective and police captain in South Africa who was the son of a major general—and accused of bank robbery in Johannesburg—fled to Fort Lauderdale, Florida, where he was slain in a confrontation with a police officer.[35]

Another telltale sign was that despite the increasing coziness between Pretoria and Washington, the apartheid regime was seeking to bar press coverage of the deteriorating domestic situation there. As early as March 1983, the American Broadcasting Corporation was complaining that it took nearly a year to gain visas to send a crew to make a documentary film on unions. Upon arrival, *TV Guide* said, "South Africa welcomed them—with sabotage and surveillance."[36]

The television network should have recognized that Pretoria had become increasingly sensitive to the power of unions, particularly since they were being boosted by their U.S. peers. Just before the 1984 election Richard Trumka, leader of the United Mine Workers in the U.S., offered assistance to South African miners,[37] whose starvation

32. *TIME*, 7 February 1983.

33. South African Broadcasting Corporation Commentary, 2 January 1984, Box 120, *Leroy Walker Africa News Service Archive*: The accused spies included Yuri Loginov, exchanged for 10 West German agents; Major Aleksei Moslov, exchanged for Sapper Johan van der Mescht; Yugoslav Miro Malek and Czechs Josef Kohout and Jaro Hladek.

34. *Observer* [U.K.], 13 February 1983.

35. *TIME*, 27 February 1984.

36. *TV Guide*, 18 May 1983, Box 275, *Leroy Walker Africa News Service Archive*.

37. Press Release, 17 September 1984, Box 273, *Leroy Walker Africa News Service Archive*.

wages had been undermining their West Virginia counterparts for years. Trumka had employed Nomonde Ngubo, a South African who had matriculated at Fort Hare—the alma mater of Mandela, Tambo, and Mugabe—and had been involved with South African unions. It was this activist who proposed to ACOA a "Shell Boycott," focusing on the oil giant.[38] The increasing involvement of U.S. unions on behalf of their Southern African counterparts was one of the most important aspects of the solidarity movement that was to force sanctions over the unyielding objections of Republican hardliners.[39] This imposing trend was brought into sharp relief when Lynn Williams of the Steelworkers and Milan Stone, President of the United Rubber, Cork, Linoleum, Plastic Workers berated John Cahill, president of BTR, Inc. of Providence, Rhode Island after his South African subsidiary chose to "dismiss…strikers and [illegible] them with scabs," upbraiding "management's willingness [illegible] the South African military and police" against workers, an[illegible] precedent with North American implications.[40]

Regrettably, the news was not as positiv[illegible] represented by the miners, or the "Free South Africa Mov[illegible] for that matter. Perhaps not accidentally, as FSAM was be[illegible]hed, newspaper headlines brayed "PLO told of support [illegible]ck Lawyers." My comrade in the National Conference of [illegible]wyers Adrien K. Wing, who was to travel with me to Khart[illegible] London in a failed attempt to mediate the war in Sudan t[illegible] lead to the emergence of South Sudan, had been photographed at an international conference embracing Chairman Yasser Arafat, the Palestinian leader often demonized on these shores.[41] Our Harlem headquarters, which had been an anchor of the anti-apartheid movement, was besieged as a result.[42] As our statement at the time indicated, our office was "threatened with bombings and death threats….Donors cancelled grants…." It was "no secret," it was said perceptively, "that certain forces oppose African Americans speaking out on foreign

38. Nomonde Ngubo to Jennifer Davis, 24 November 1985, Box 84, *ACOARA*.

39. Harold Rogers, "U.S. Trade Union Action Against Apartheid," circa 1981, Box 179, *Gerald Horne Papers*.

40. Lynn Williams and Milan Stone to John Cahill, 2 January 1986, Box 84, *ACOARA*.

41. *New York Daily News*, 26 November 1984; *Detroit Free Press*, 26 November 1984.

42. See Sound Device Permit, 15 June 1984, Box 190, *Gerald Horne Papers*: For rally at Harlem State Office Building on 125th Street in Manhattan, six blocks from our office on 119th Street.

policy generally and the Middle East specifically…." Reference was made to the "sacking" of Andrew Young after apparently authorized contact with the Palestinians, the "harassment" of the Reverend Jackson of late on similar grounds, and the "attack" on Gil Noble, a local television journalist of rare integrity and repute who was also unafraid to tackle the controversial.[43] "Even as I write," said former Boston judge Margaret Burnham, "phone callers are threatening us with physical and financial harm," and we were "required to post a police guard."[44] Sensing the compelled liquidation of the organization, our leadership proclaimed that Wing "spoke for herself," not NCBL.[45] Though Palestine was the ostensible spark for this controversy, lurking was the relationship of Israel to apartheid and our broadcasting of this fraught matter. The pro-Israel lobby was also exasperated with the ANC, which NCBL supported adamantly. Their organ was upset when the ANC's Makhathini reputedly referred to the policies of Israel as "'Zionist Nazism.'" Nor were they pleased when an ANC speaker addressed a fundraiser for U.S. Communists.[46]

Though it had been clear for some time that Afrikaner nationalism—which in its latest iteration was exemplified by Eugene Terre Blanche, the Afrikaner Resistance Movement, and their symbol, which not coincidentally resembled a swastika—often entailed a virulent anti-Semitism, there seemed to be more concern among the Zionists about the left.[47]

Donald Woods, the anti-apartheid editor, denounced "Mr. Apartheid," P.W. Botha, in the pages of the *New York Times*, reminding those who may have forgotten "how openly your party admired Hitler" and that apartheid was "the first cousin to Hitler's Nuremberg laws against the Jews." "In 1943," Woods continued, "you were chief organizer in Cape Province of the party that tried to stop General Smuts' allowing Jewish refugees into South Africa"—but by the 1980s the pro-Zionist movement in the U.S. was seemingly more concerned about the work of African American activists.[48]

Certainly, there was more concern among the ossified right wing about NCBL, which one of their propagandists termed an

---

43. Press Release, 5 December 1984, Box 196, *Gerald Horne Papers*.

44. Margaret Burnham to "Dear Friend," 12 December 1984, Box 196, *Gerald Horne Papers*.

45. *New York Post*, 2 December 1984; NCBL Statement, 27 November 1984, Box 196, *Gerald Horne Papers*.

46. *Bulletin of Anti-Defamation League*, May 1986, *Gwendolen Carter Papers*.

47. *New York Times*, 23 August 1981.

48. *New York Times*, 10 June 1984.

"organization of Marxist and revolutionary lawyers."[49] When NCBL—and myself—rose to defend ANC member Fred Dube, then teaching at the State University of New York at Stony Brook, who was sacked because of allegations of anti-Semitism, such attacks increased in intensity. Dube, who had been jailed on Robben Island, was forced to depart New York.[50]

An angry correspondent neatly captured the furor that engulfed New York City in particular, where what was called "Black –Jewish Relations" had rested uneasily on tenterhooks for some time. Ben Morrow compared Wing to Jackson and Nation of Islam leader Louis Farrakhan before adding contemptuously, "...why should I care about discrimination in South Africa?" "You are the enemy," he cried, and "[we] don't love the enemy. We eliminate the enemy!" Typical of the time, he concluded by saying, "I went to Boston University with Martin Luther King," as if that excused or made legitimate his threats.[51]

Not unaffected, David Dinkins—the City Clerk who would become the mayor who greeted Mandela effusively in 1990—expressed his "great dismay," not about the threats but about solidarity with Palestinians.[52] The august *New York Times* turned over the valuable real estate of its front page to an account of this story.[53]

This death defying episode split the organization. It had been preceded by a debate in which I was on one side pushing for more global engagement, and the eminent law professor Derrick Bell was on the other. Bell, who was to serve as a mentor to Barack Obama at Harvard Law School, told us "we should exercise great caution in committing NCBL budget to national projects and should not make our major effort the identification with foreign governments and the freedom efforts of Third World peoples around the world. I do not underestimate the importance of those efforts to the eventual liberation of American blacks," he said. "I realize this suggestion will not be warmly received," he said accurately. But he worried about the "alienation of black lawyers"—not the most politically sophisticated

49. John Rees, "Reds are Turning the Heat on South Africa," 9 January 1985, Box 38, *Mack Mattingly Papers, University of Georgia-Athens.*

50. Brochure of Committee to Support Professor Dube, circa 1983, Box 163, *Gerald Horne Papers.*

51. Ben Morrow to A.K. King, 24 November 1984, Box 196, *Gerald Horne Papers.*

52. David Dinkins to Haywood Burns, 27 November 1984, Box 196, *Gerald Horne Papers.*

53. *New York Times,* 12 December 1984.

Negroes—due to global campaigns and that this would "increase the difficulty of obtaining foundation grants," which also was accurate.[54]

Despite such reversals, the anti-apartheid movement continued to grow, given a boost by the Free South Africa Movement, which quickly became a *cause célèbre* in South Africa itself, indicative of its reach.[55] Almost from its inception, FSAM received press coverage in Johannesburg.[56] NCBL was, among other organizations, crucial in this development, its efforts extending beyond legal counsel to mobilizing neighborhoods. Among its leaders in Chicago was Stan Willis, born in 1941, who had—informally—studied "Marxism Leninism" at the University of Chicago and developed "socialist thoughts…." "We studied the thoughts of African socialists," he said, and "we were following developments in Cuba" too. "More than once" he met with Dullah Omar, Mandela's lawyer. Then, he said, "It was easy to get an audience with you know Chris Hani," the SACP leader, "I remember spending many days doing that…." In the 1980s he was among those picketing Pretoria's Chicago consulate on Michigan Avenue.[57] Omar, born in 1934, was an early member of the Non-European Unity Movement, and then worked for the Black Consciousness Movement and the PAC. "I think I am the lawyer," he said in 2000, "who visited Robben Island more than any other lawyer in this country. First acting for the PAC," then serving the Mandelas faithfully.[58]

Simultaneously in Chicago, there was a campaign to elect the progressive African American lawyer Harold Washington as Mayor. Curtis Black was among those who detected a synergy between the two movements.[59] Helen Shiller was among those picketing the South African consulate; her previous experience included typesetting and designing *ZANU News*, which was shipped to Mozambique during the anti-Rhodesian struggle.[60] She was joined by Anne Evens, who had lived in Mozambique for 7 years and returned to Chicago with a daughter who was half Mozambican. She recalled during her U.S. activism "a lot of conflict between those that supported the ANC versus those that supported the PAC…." Undeterred, she "got

54. Derrick Bell to NCBL, 2 August 1984, Box 190, *Gerald Horne Papers.*

55. *Rand Daily Mail*, 5 December 1984; *Cape Argus*, 4 December 1984; *Johannesburg Star*, 7 December 1984.

56. *Johannesburg Star*, 22 November 1984.

57. Oral History, Stan Willis, 25 April 2010, *Columbia College-Chicago.*

58. Oral History, Dullah Omar, 6 October 2000, *University of Connecticut-Storrs.*

59. Oral History, Curtis Black, 22 April 2010, *Columbia College-Chicago.*

60. Oral History, Helen Shiller, 22 April 2010, *Columbia College-Chicago.*

arrested related to anti-apartheid work about 23 times" and "spent some nights in jail...."[61] Jean Kracher, born in Chicago in 1957, distinguished the "more internationalist approach" of her hometown's Prexy Nesbitt with the "nationalist faction" with which he clashed, as manifested at 6PAC in Dar in 1974. Her father owned a tavern and was "pretty strict" but "one song we all loved" was Hugh Masekela's "Grazing in the Grass."[62] Josephine Wyatt was another African American active on the picket line. Born in 1921, her spouse was a porter on a railroad where he was subjected to vicious racism, something she knew from her native Georgia. As for South Africa, she said, "I understood what they must have been experiencing and I could identify with them...." "To this day I don't buy Shell gasoline," she said in 2010, "and it all started back then." She knew the Black Communist leader Claude Lightfoot. "I used to listen to a lot of his speeches and I read his book" and found his indictment to be a "witch hunt...about intimidation and punishment for people who were trying to bring about a change...."[63] Another Chicago picketer was Carol Thompson. Of Czechoslovak and German parentage—she spoke German—she also found Nesbitt to be an "inspiration," along with his comrades Lisa Brock and Cheryl Johnson-Odim.[64]

A well-traveled scholar, Johnson-Odim—born in 1948—met Chester Crocker, the top Reagan diplomat on the sub-region and left unimpressed with this "beady eyed...apologist for apartheid." The church of the Reverend Jeremiah Wright, later known as the pastor who ministered to Barack Obama, was "very active" on the anti-apartheid front too. He "really worked with me and the Trans-Africa Support Committee," she recalled later. For example, there was spirited demonstration at the Michigan Avenue consulate, with a "thousand people" on "one of the coldest days of that year" in a city well-known for frigidity. It was "below zero with the wind chill factor," but they soldiered on.[65]

Funeka Sihlali, born in 1948 in the same Eastern Cape neighborhood as Steve Biko, wound up in Chicago. A speaker of Xhosa, he too fondly recalled the pastorate of the Reverend Wright, which "always had a sign outside his church that said, 'Free South Africa' from 1979

61. Oral History, Anne Evens, 4 May 2009, *Columbia College-Chicago*.

62. Oral History, Jean Kracher, 31 March 2010, *Columbia College-Chicago*.

63. Oral History, Josephine Wyatt, 1 April 2010, *Columbia College-Chicago*.

64. Oral History, Carol Thompson, 16 April 2009, *Columbia College-Chicago*.

65. Oral History, Cheryl Johnson-Odim, 4 December 2009, *Columbia College-Chicago*.

on," while "visitors from South Africa were always welcome there" to be hosted by this "well read" cleric.[66]

As for the Reverend Wright, he was on the Board of Directors of Trans-Africa. Born in 1941, by the early 1970s he was teaching seminary students, several whom were South African. As NCBL could attest, he came to realize the admonition "don't mention Israel" and Pretoria together, for "they say you're anti-Semitic." He was "against Leon Sullivan" and his supposed "Principles" for corporate engagement with apartheid, which did not lead to Wright's embrace by Big Business. He too admired Nesbitt and Lisa Brock.[67]

Even as the anti-apartheid movement was progressing, setbacks did occur. Even the immense importance of the Free South Africa Movement, initiated by Randall Robinson, created its own complications. A wounded Jennifer Davis of ACOA, who had replaced Houser, was irked by the perception that Robinson had seized the spotlight by downplaying her group's contributions. "I would hope that we will find better ways of working co-operatively," she told him stiffly. FSAM, she complained, "makes not even passing mention of the divestment campaign we have spearheaded over the last five years on campuses, in many communities, cities and states…."[68] She had a point: the tightening noose around the mottled neck of apartheid was significantly aided by the ACOA-inspired campaign for divestment. It was Davis who congratulated Governor Thomas Kean of New Jersey—a Republican—on "your principled and courageous decision to withstand White House pressure and sign the divestment bill," seeking to undermine the "unique evil of apartheid…."[69]

Weeks after this monumental initiative that was FSAM had been launched, the Washington Office on Africa—ACOA's companion—argued that it also had "caused pain" for WOA, consigning this struggling group to "a kind of second class citizenship." With rare candor it was acknowledged that there was an "unrecognized problem" of having a mostly "white staff," as the movement had yet to overcome the still lingering impact of the decline of Robeson's CAA, a phenomenon pointed to by Nesbitt.[70] WOA had problems beyond

66. Oral History, Funeka Sihlali, 1 December 2009, *Columbia College-Chicago.*

67. Oral History, Jeremiah Wright, 24 April 2009, *Columbia College-Chicago.*

68. Jennifer Davis to Randall Robinson, 11 February 1986, Box 84, *ACOARA.*

69. Jennifer Davis to Governor Kean, 22 August 1985, Box 108, *ACOARA.*

70. Karl Mathiasen II and Martin Timin to WOA, 14 December 1984, Box 1, *Washington Office on Africa Papers-Yale University.*

the competitive challenge provided by Trans-Africa, however. Just as Robinson was preparing to commit civil disobedience at the South African legation, operatives of the politically suspect Lyndon LaRouche, who purported to be on the left but was deemed by his detractors to be a unique neo-fascist, attacked a WOA press conference with vigor.[71] Targeting anti-apartheid activism, LaRouche's colleagues also disrupted a press conference of Catholic bishops that had targeted apartheid.[72]

WOA was suffering in more ways than one. The budget had grown from $60,000 in 1980 to $103,000 by 1983, though the Executive Director was earning a meager $17,000 yearly.[73] By 1985 their top leader, the brilliant Jean Sindab, had an annual salary of a mere $22,500 while the comrade who was to replace her, Damu Smith, had a yearly wage of a mere $18,000.[74] That same year, Smith succeeded Sindab and was congratulated by the Reverend Earl Neil of the Episcopal Church—one of the more active denominations—"irregardless [sic] of his being Black." "Over the last few years," he complained, "several Black Administrators have felt a need to maintain an 'integrated' staff in order to be 'fair' and project a certain 'image,'" all of which was "detrimental." There was much too much consideration, he carped, of asking "'what will our white friends think?", rather than "what is best for the organization's role in the liberation struggle.'"[75]

In short, the emergence of the Free South Africa Movement presented a kind of existential crisis for WOA and its Manhattan partner, ACOA (Houser served on their board and helped to form the group in 1972 as a branch of ACOA, which then incorporated separately in 1977).[76] As Sindab was stepping down from leading WOA, a debate erupted about why the group "was excluded" from FSAM. There was a "historical perception" that WOA was a "'white'

---

71. Press Release, 20 November 1984, Box 60, *Washington Office on Africa Papers*. See Dennis King, *Lyndon LaRouche and the New American Fascism*, New York: Doubleday, 1989.

72. *National Catholic Reporter*, 23 November 1984, Box 60, *Washington Office on Africa Papers*.

73. "Confidential" letter from Jean Sindab, 21 March 1984, Box 154, *ACOARA*.

74. Jean Sindab to Executive Committee, Box 22, *Jean Sindab Papers, Schomburg Center, New York Public Library*.

75. Reverend Earl Neil to Jean Sindab, 20 June 1985, Box 22, *Jean Sindab Papers*.

76. Karl Mathissen, Management Assistance Group to WOA, 14 December 1984, Box 154, *ACOARA*.

organization," and amid the heightened racism fostered by Reagan's rise, this was a difficult hurdle to mount. FSM "wanted this to be solely a Black Movement. They wanted black control," while WOA was "ultimately controlled by churches' white leaders." Back and forth went the debate of the WOA staff, arguing at a time when one would have thought celebration was in order. When the African American Sindab arrived at WOA, "black folks did not want her to take the job," it was said. "They wanted WOA to close & TA [Trans-Afrca] to survive," and thus she was termed a "traitor" or "stupid" or both. Her predecessor Ted Lockwood "left the white legacy" while "George Houser was as rotten as hell" in that regard. "He controlled Africa stuff and didn't let black people" in. Robinson was also viewed sourly, and there were those who worked with him "despite…their dislike" of him. The Reverend Jesse Jackson, whose presidential race helped to catapult apartheid into mass consciousness, was dismissed as a "wild card."[77]

But brickbats casually tossed at rivals—real or imagined—could not mask the underlying problems of WOA. By 1983 Trans-Africa was said to have a mailing list of about 10,000, and their annual dinner—a major fundraiser—attracted about 1500 of the well-dressed and well-coiffed. WOA was sponsored by 9 Protestant denominations, ACOA, and the United Auto Workers—but had a mailing list of about 3500 and was not as well-funded as Trans-Africa by a long shot.[78]

Moreover, all WOA's ostensible backers—even in the ordinarily reliable religious community—were not consistently supportive. It was in the pivotal year of 1984 that Canon Edward B. Geyer, Jr., the Executive for National Mission in Church and Society of the Episcopalians in New York City, told Sindab that though he was opposed to apartheid, "it grieves us to learn of your group's politicized posture regarding the Reagan Administration…." Thus, he departed from the ranks regretfully.[79]

Though it was easy to be deluded in assuming that the mainstream press was on the side of the anti-apartheid angels, this was not consistently the case. Jerry Herman of the Quakers met with Gerhard Pieterse of the *Sunday Express* of London, who interviewed him and "followed with a story that was not only inaccurate" but defaming;

77. Minutes of Staff Meeting, 6 December 1984, Box 22, *Jean Sindab Papers.*

78. Edgar Lockwood to Simon Stocker, 19 June 1983, ID Africa-S S Afri-IAP Zimbabwe-TAMAPSA, 1984, *AFSC.*

79. Canon Edward Geyer to Jean Sindab, 21 March 1984, Box 154, *ACOARA.*

he suggested that the ACOA boycott Pieterse but this was easier said than done.[80] L. Clayton Willis of Willis Media of Oklahoma billed himself as a "Reagan-Bush supporter" who had "written for the Afrikaans and English speaking media in South Africa" and further, "was honored to escort [George H.W. Bush's] step-mother-in-law Mrs. Marvin Pierce to your inauguration," he told the stumbling Reagan. Given this background, his one-sided coverage of apartheid was what could be expected.[81] Arnaud de Borchgrave, chief editor of the *Washington Times*—financed by the South Korean evangelist, the fanatically anticommunist Sun Myung Moon—was in close touch with Reagan aide Patrick J. Buchanan, who he sent the many articles published in his periodical whitewashing apartheid.[82]

As apartheid became a matter of global concern, commentators leaped to cover it, no matter how ill-informed, adding to confusion. Writing for the *Sydney Morning Herald*, the popular writer Christopher Hitchens confused the African National Council of Zimbabwe with the ANC and placed Joe Slovo in the ranks of the former. Then he nattered on about the funeral of Douglas Lilford of the Rhodesian Front, whose daughter was the leader of the Elvis Presley Fan Club[83]—a typical performance by North Atlantic journalists forced to confront struggles of which they knew little and were often unprepared to study.

Predictably, Robinson's heightened profile brought incoming fire—and not just from movement competitors. Amid the red-baiting of the ANC and claims that the Communists had "won control of the ANC leadership" in 1947, which led to the ANC's publications being produced at the Weimert Publishing House in East Germany, Trans-Africa was hit by a similar fusillade. This "lobby for the left" was launched in May 1978, it was said by detractors, growing out of a September 1976 meeting and 1977 formation.[84] The White House chose to retain a commentary by South African Broadcasting that accused Trans-Africa of being a "Communist Front."[85] When Trans-Africa, it was reported, "successfully infiltrated the reception held"

---

80. Jerry Herman to Jennifer Davis, 16 March 1983, Box 154, *ACOARA*.

81. L. Clayton Willis to President Reagan, 27 August 1985, Box 167, WHORM, Subject Files, *Reagan Presidential Library*.

82. Arnaud de Borchgrave to Pat Buchanan, 30 October 1985, Box 168, WHORM, Subject File, *Reagan Presidential Library*.

83. *Sydney Morning Herald*, 16 December 1985.

84. "Trans-Africa: A Lobby for the Left," Lincoln Institute for Research and Education, Box 35, *Washington Office on Africa Papers*.

85. Pretoria legation to Secretary of State, February 1985, African Affairs Directorate, NSC, RAC Box 9 [Box 2], *Reagan Presidential Library*.

at the South African embassy, hosted by the Negro lobbyist William Keyes and designed to "promote minority business ventures in South Africa," howls of outrage were emitted at their attempt to discourage Negro investment in apartheid.[86] Washington may have known that Robinson approached Dr. Rudolph Yossiphov, First Secretary of the U.N. Mission of Bulgaria, in his capacity with the Council on Nambia, seeking "funding" for FSAM.[87] Of course, this did not signal a pro-Communist commitment on Robinson's part, he was simply responding to the U.N. appointment of a Bulgarian, but anticommunists were known for muddying the waters unnecessarily. Thus, the Washington Office on Africa also contacted Dr. Yossiphov for funding for a "SWAPO Cultural Tour," featuring Namibian artists.[88] (It was a matter of routine when I invited U.N. officials to one of our many fundraising concerts for anti-apartheid activism.)[89] The obdurately right wing Senator Mack Mattingly of Georgia retained a publication that pointed to Robinson's participation in the historic solidarity conference at Manhattan's Riverside Church in 1981 to make his tenuous point that "Reds are turning the heat on South Africa;" the "founding members of the Trans-Africa Board of Directors," he claimed awkwardly, were "Left. Lefter. Leftest."[90]

While legitimate anti-apartheid movements were under siege, the Reverend Leon Sullivan of Philadelphia continued to build his own faux movement purportedly against corporate involvement in South Africa.[91] His movement was important camouflage for the corporate sector. As the columnist Jack Anderson, revealed, the U.S. stake in apartheid had been understated. The "true investment," he wrote in 1983, was "almost six times larger" than thought—about

86. "Lisa" to "Staff," 10 December 1985, Box 60, *Washington Office on Africa Papers*.

87. Randall Robinson to Dr. Yossiphov, 19 March 1985, Box 5, *Washington Office on Africa Papers*.

88. Damu Smith to Dr. Yossphov, 7 August 1985, Box 5, *Washington Office on Africa Papers*.

89. Gerald Horne to Executive Secretary, Organization of African Unity and Chair, U.N. Special Committee Against Apartheid, 7 February 1984, Box 190, *Gerald Horne Papers*.

90. John Rees, "Reds are Turning the Heat on South Africa," 9 January 1985, Box 38, *Mack Mattingly Papers, University of Georgia-Athens*.

91. See "Progress Report on the Application of Sullivan Principles by U.S. Companies in South Africa," 1984, Box 24, *William Gray Papers, Schomburg Center, New York Public Library*: Efforts mostly involved desegregation of the workplace, promotion of Africans and Coloureds to middle management in U.S. corporations such as Dow, Monsanto, Du Pont, Xerox, etc.

$14.6 billion, along with $4 billion in bank loans that encompassed about half of the Fortune 500 listing of the major U.S. corporate behemoths.[92]

The Permanent Secretary of the Cabinet in Maseru, Lesotho was not fooled. J.R.L. Kotsokoane rebuked Sullivan for his apparent naiveté about the role of foreign investment in apartheid. "For heaven sake," he said with exasperation, "let us not confuse reality and myth."[93] He may have been thinking of what prompted Tim Smith of the Inter-Faith Center for Corporate Responsibility to tell the pastor: "Stanford Oil of California," he said, "has just sent an official letter telling us that [Pretoria] has served an order on them requiring them to sell to the [South African] police and military. This is an amazing development," he said wondrously, "because it indicates the whole oil industry falls under this order, and thus are commercial 'partners' with the police and military."[94] By way of contrast, the Secretary of Foreign Affairs for Bophuthatswana—a Bantustan created by Pretoria—spoke warmly to Sullivan of his "great pleasure in [making] your acquaintance at the Moral Re-Armament Conference" in Switzerland, a gathering place for various oddball reactionaries; he was "inviting" him "at government expense to visit."[95].

Just back from South Africa, Robert Vitale told the pastor that his vaunted "Principles" were considered there to be "less than helpful" by anti-apartheid forces: "I trust you will not take offense,"[96] he said of his gentle reprimand. More to the point, the *New York Times* was told by Arthur Reynolds and Bonnie Cohen of the Retirement Board of Washington, D.C. that their investment portfolio, divested of apartheid-related stocks and bonds, had outperformed the market; a "positive investment strategy" hard to ignore.[97]

As Pretoria came under unremitting pressure, a musty idea was revived. John Williams of Florida told Sullivan that he wanted South Africa to become involved in "seeking admission to membership in the United States of English Speaking People....Becoming the 51st through 55th state...down the road," since next in line would be

92. *Washington Post*, 30 July 1983.

93. J.R.L. Kotsokoane to Reverend Sullivan, 24 November 1982, Box 56, *Leon Sullivan Papers-Emory University*.

94. Tim Smith to Reverend Sullivan, 11 March 1983, Box 56, *Leon Sullivan Papers*.

95. Secretary for Foreign Affairs to Reverend Sullivan, 25 October 1983, Box 56, *Leon Sullivan Papers*.

96. Robert Vitale to Leon Sullivan, 8 August 1985, Box 57, *Leon Sullivan Papers*.

97. *New York Times*, 31 October 1985.

Australia and New Zealand in a polity that "should be open to any nation willing to become English speaking"—though it was doubtful if he had Ghana or Tanzania in mind.[98]

Perhaps buoyed by such piffle, Sullivan sought to make his "Principles" global, hoping to induce Canada, France, Finland, and other nations to adopt some version of what U.S. signees had applied to apartheid.[99]

The besieged Washington Office on Africa was nonetheless a formidable foe to Sullivan. As the Free South Africa Movement was about to be launched, they reminded one and all of the devastating impact of investment in apartheid on U.S. job prospects. "Since 1975 imports of South African steel have increased 5000 percent," it was said, while "international competitiveness of South Africa steel is built on the systematic denial of democratic rights to the black majority," a point studiously circumvented by the Principles. "Most South Africa steel is produced by the government owned... ISCOR [Iron and Steel Corporation]," paeans to "private enterprise" notwithstanding. "Companies such as U.S. Steel, ARMCO, Phelps Dodge, Allegheny Ludlum and Standard Pressed Steel Co. have pumped billions of dollars' worth of capital" into South Africa. They were joined by banks including Chase, Citi, First Boston, Merrill Lynch, and Manufacturers Hanover. Meanwhile, Chicago steelworkers were being laid off, as Chicago buildings were being constructed with South African steel.[100]

WOA's rebuke was echoed by the pro-Reagan Heritage Foundation, a sign that the liberal anticommunism of Sullivan was now being undermined by rightists determined to impose a hardline consensus. The Principles were derided as a "bureaucratic quagmire," though the corporations paid a "stiff fee for the privilege" of being signees. "$100,000 on the in house paperwork alone" meant multiple opportunities for corruption in Philadelphia. This was "coercive." By the late 1970s, Sullivan's companion, Opportunities Industrialization Center, had 160 offices in 40 states with 5000 full-time workers and a budget of $150 million with 90% coming from governments. By 1969 OIC had gone global, sited in 8 African nations and interests in 5 others, including "Marxist" Zimbabwe. Reagan was now cutting back on OIC, finding even Sullivan's palliatives too harsh.

98. John Williams to Leon Sullivan, 31 October 1985, Box 57, *Leon Sullivan Papers*.

99. Leon Sullivan to Shirley Carr, 14 February 1984, Box 60, *Leon Sullivan Papers*.

100. Brochure, September 1984, Box 67, *Leon Sullivan Papers*.

Since 1970, said HF, Sullivan's organizations received $500 million from federal, state, and local governments as a result of Sullivan's "blackmail."[101]

Tim Smith's group was sponsored by Christian religious denominations, many of which played a pioneering role in the anti-apartheid movement, filling the vacuum left by the routing of Robeson's comrades. Reverend William Howard of the National Council of Churches took the lead in upbraiding Sullivan, instructing him in 1985 that during the "recent debate over Assemblyman Willie Brown's bill for divestment" in California, "opponents...repeatedly used the Sullivan Principles as an argument against" sanctions and divestment. These "Principles" had "become a euphemism for moderation and economic 'constructive engagement,'" a derisive reference to the term affixed to the Reagan policy of conciliation with apartheid.[102]

* * *

The Principles arrived at an inopportune moment for by the advent of the Reagan regime, the campus divestment movement was steadily growing. As early as 1982, Jennifer Davis—who had replaced Houser as leader of ACOA—told Abdul Minty, the veteran campaigner, that her group had a "very solid 'anti-apartheid' base on campuses. This spring more than 70 campuses responded to our call for 'two weeks of Action in Solidarity with the Liberation Movements'."[103] By May 1985 there had been anti-apartheid demonstrations of various dimensions on at least 100 U.S. campuses.[104] One of the campuses rocked was that of Northwestern University, just outside of Chicago, where May 1985 saw the most dramatic protests there since the war in Vietnam, as a massive sit-in was staged.[105] That month also saw 7 protesters acquitted after supposedly trespassing at the Chicago consulate of South Africa, with the defense of "necessity" to prevent a larger harm—apartheid—was accepted, setting a possible precedent for 91 Northwestern protesters.[106] Even at the

101. "The Institution Analysis," 12 September 1984, Box 69, *Leon Sullivan Papers*.

102. Reverend William Howard to Reverend Sullivan, 24 May 1985, Box 57, *Leon Sullivan Papers*.

103. Jennifer Davis to Abdul Minty, 28 July 1982, Box 93, *ACOARA*.

104. *Guardian* [U.S.], 8 May 1985.

105. *Daily Northwestern*, 10 May 1985.

106. *Daily Northwestern*, 20 May 1985.

University of Utah, not renowned as a hotbed of activism, there were three shantytowns built on campus by May 1986 in solidarity with anti-apartheid.[107]

By August 1985, this movement had mushroomed and came up in a five-hour meeting Reagan aide Robert McFarlane held with visiting Foreign Minister "Pik" Botha. McFarlane thought that his interlocutor had a "primitive understanding of the strategic stakes in our Congress and public at large," suggesting that Botha thought Washington—like Pretoria—could be guided dictatorially. But he did "understand fully the President's vulnerability on the issue and the likelihood that pressure will increase when school starts in the fall," making him "extremely grateful" for Washington's ample aid.[108]

By 1983 stevedores in Baltimore were protesting uranium shipments that came via South Africa.[109] By 1984 an injunction had to be obtained to compel stevedores in San Francisco to offload South African cargo.[110] This extraordinary measure was taken after hundreds of stevedores refused to unload a ship containing auto parts, steel, and wines destined for U.S. markets.[111]

South Africa was a critical node in the worldwide chain of energy because of the uranium it controlled in Namibia. But at the same time, Pretoria needed Washington's aid in propelling its own energy and power source. Congressman Edward Markey charged that U.S. nationals were employed by the Electricity Supply Commission of South Africa [ESCOM], a putative violation of the Atomic Energy Act of 1954.[112] By 1985, according to U.S. Secretary of Energy John Herrington, "40 U.S. citizens were employed as reactor operators at ESCOM'S Koeberg nuclear power plant" in South Africa—with more en route.[113] Press reports retained by the White House staff

107. *Daily Utah Chronicle*, 2 April 1986, Box 13, *Washington Office on Africa Papers*.

108. Robert McFarlane to NSDRF, 8 August 1985, African Affairs Directorate, NSC RAC Box 9[Box 2], *Reagan Presidential Library*.

109. Memo from Daki Napata, 28 March 1983, PED, NARMIC, Program Resources, S. Africa, 1983, *AFSC*.

110. Miloanne H. Yecathorn to Jerry Herman, 8 December 1984, PED Program Resources, Southern Africa, 1984, *AFSC*.

111. Release from Public Media Center, 27 November 1984, PED Program Resources Southern Africa 1984, *AFSC*.

112. Congressman Edward Markey to John Herrington, 1 March 1985, Box 168, WHORM, Subject File.

113. John Herrington to Congressman Markey, 15 February 1985, Box 168, WHORM, Subject File.

indicated that some of these U.S. employees at Koeberg had salaries soaring beyond $100,000 annually.[114]

The United Mine Workers of the U.S. also got involved, demanding "action be taken to ban the direct and indirect importation of coal and coal products mined" in South Africa, a mortal threat to their members' livelihood. These imports, it was said accurately, "[have] caused and continues to cause serious injury to the UMWA...."[115] A leader of the miners, Richard Trumka, who was to lead all of U.S. labor as head of the AFL-CIO, reiterated his standing offer of assistance to South African miners.[116] Concurring was Congressman Walter Fauntroy of the Black Caucus, who informed a North Carolina audience that cheap apartheid labor meant the loss of employment in the U.S.[117]

The ever active Quakers were expanding their project, meeting with European activists in Brussels, London, Paris, Munich, and Geneva on a common anti-apartheid platform.[118] There was little cause for surprise when the Quakers' Jerry Herman spoke to an aroused crowd of 25,000 in Trafalgar Square in London to condemn apartheid.[119] These global winds helped to propel the movement in the U.S., aiding it in overcoming the stout ultra-rightists harbored there. David Acquah of the Ghana National Committee Against Apartheid, told Herman that it was "reassuring to learn that your analysis of the Southern Africa situation is in complete accord with that of our Committee...."[120]

Lockwood chose to address an audience in Zimbabwe when he spoke in detail about the upsurge of the U.S. movement, creating unyielding pressure on the White House.[121] Still, it was the energy of South African protesters that was driving the agenda; shootings,

---

114. *Reuters*, 22 January 1985, Box 9[Box 2], African Affairs Directorate, NSC, *Reagan Presidential Library*. See also *Guardian*, [U.K.], 22 January 1985: "as many as 40 skilled American nuclear workers may be in [South Africa]."

115. United Mine Workers to William Von Raab, U.S. Commissioner of Customs, 12 July 1985, Box 169, WHORM, Subject File.

116. Press Release, 17 September 1984, Box 273, *Leroy Walker Africa News Service Archive*.

117. *Raleigh News & Observer*, 17 May 1985.

118. Memo from Jerry Herman, 23 September 1983, PED, NARMIC, Program Resources, S. Africa, 1983, *AFSC*.

119. Report from Bob Hughes, Chair of Anti-Apartheid Movement-U.K., 15 July 1985, PED Southern Africa TAO Youth & Militarism, 1985, *AFSC*.

120. David Acquah to Jerry Herman, 11 March 1983, PED, NARMIC, Program Resources, S. Africa, 1983, *AFSC*.

121. *Herald* [Harare], 1 August 1985.

executions, mass demonstrations, and the like attracted global attention. "South Africa has become the #1 issue," Jerry Herman was told in 1985 by a San Franciscan. "I got up this morning early to hear what was happening in South Africa and the BBC, TV and radio news were leading with South African news."[122] The press attention in turn attracted the curious and committed to the ranks of anti-apartheid movements, already energized by the Free South Africa Movement.

Thus, the U.S. legation in London reported almost mundanely in 1985 that "the autumn parade of South African visitors to London continues," including Desmond Tutu, "Transvaal political boss" F.W. de Klerk, and South African Broadcasting's General Riaan Eksteen. Tambo addressed the Labour Party while de Klerk was being told he should send Mandela abroad "for medical treatment" by way of release. F.W. de Klerk "demurred" on this proposal to defuse the pressing matter. An unnamed Pretoria dignitary claimed that de Klerk was in Britain to reassure friends— "all two of them," it was said waggishly. P.W. Botha, the ultimate boss in Pretoria, had entered politics in 1948, as apartheid dawned and was seen as incapable of dismantling its legacy. Astutely, de Klerk, who had entered politics in 1972, was seen as capable of executing this difficult task.[123]

A sign of the difficulty Washington faced was the posture of its erstwhile partner in the much ballyhooed "special relationship." Britain, said the U.S. legation, was "more politically divided" than the U.S. on apartheid. Tambo, still viewed suspiciously as a SACP placeman in Washington, got a warm "bear hug" from Labour's leader Neil Kinnock, a possible Prime Minister-in-waiting. His spouse, Glynnis, had refused a wedding ring since it might contain gold from South Africa.[124] His embrace of Kinnock did not deter Tambo from contacting the Central Committee of the Soviet Communist Party in 1985, requesting that "Soviet instructors [be] attached to our camps in Angola," along with "interpreters" and a "counter intelligence specialist…."[125] The South African legation in Washington did not include Tambo on their list of "Key Communists" in the ANC leadership but did include Yusuf Dadoo, Nzo, Dan Tloome, Reg September,

122. Letter to "Dear Jerry," 28 August 1985, PED Southern Africa TAO Youth & Militarism, 1985, *AFSC*.

123. Report from London legation, October 1985, African Affairs Directorate, NSC, Box 9[Box 2], *Reagan Presidential Library*.

124. Report from London legation, October 1985, African Affairs Directorate, NSC, Box 9[Box 2].

125. Oliver Tambo to Central Committee of Soviet Communist Party, 27 September 1985, Reel 15, *Oliver Tambo Papers*.

and Joe Slovo—but not Thabo Mbeki, Thomas Nkobi, Joe Modise, or Jacob Zuma (though others disagreed).[126] Yet this did not halt the red-baiting of Tambo. Nor did it prevent the stauncher ANC critics from doing the same. The hardline president of Boston University, John Silber, took to the pages of the *New York Times* to charge that the ANC was "dominated by leaders voicing strident Communism," singling out Moses Mabhida for his backing of the Soviet intervention in Afghanistan. Winnie Mandela, it was said, fervently desired to "impose on fellow South Africans a dictatorship as brutal as that imposed by Moscow on the Ethiopians and Afghans." Distinguished positively was Gatsha Buthelezi.[127]

While Tambo was requesting Soviet aid, the anticommunist opposition in Mozambique was complaining about same. Afonso Dhklama of the so-called "National Resistance," MNR, observed that "about 70 percent of the attacks on our men are by air—MIG 17s, 19s and helicopters"—all of Soviet provenance—and "from mid-1985 until now [mid-1986] we have shot down MIGs and 11 helicopters."[128]

* * *

Tracking the Quakers and Reverend Howard was the Southern Christian Leadership Conference [SCLC], founded by Dr. Martin Luther King, Jr. and headquartered in Atlanta. They launched a boycott of the grocery chain Winn Dixie, which imported South African fruit.[129] The chain had sought to gain immunity by donating to Historically Black Colleges and Universities, including Florida's Bethune Cookman, which balked at joining the boycott since Winn Dixie "has been a heavy contributor."[130] SCLC did not rely solely on moral suasion to convince the corporation of the error of their ways. By late 1985, there were mass arrests at their store in East Point, Georgia.[131] The Reverend Joseph Lowery, a faithful heir to Dr. King's formidable legacy, demanded "equitable re-investment in the Black community"

126. "Southern Africa: Soviet Front Organizations," Washington, D.C.: Ministry of Information and South African Embassy, August 1983, Box 38, *Mack Mattingly Papers, University of Georgia-Athens.*

127. *New York Times*, 9 October 1986.

128. "What Mozambique Watchers are Saying...Interview with President Dhklama," 12 July 1986, Box 34, *Washington Office on Africa Papers.*

129. *Atlanta Journal & Constitution*, 24 September 1985.

130. Oswald Bronson to Reverend Joseph Lowery, 27 September 1979, Box 132, *Southern Christian Leadership Conference Papers-Emory University*. Hereafter denoted as SCLC Papers.

131. *Atlanta Journal & Constitution*, 7 December 1985.

at home, not in apartheid; Winn Dixie did "no business with black attorneys, real estate agencies, accountants, ad agencies," etc.—and this had to change.[132] Labor joined this campaign in the form of the United Steelworkers, the American Federation of Teachers, the United Food and Commercial Workers Union, etc.[133] They were all joined by Vernon Bellecourt of the American Indian Movement and the National Organization for Women.[134]

As so often happened, corporations willing to invest in apartheid also had repugnant racial records domestically too. Winn Dixie, true to its name, had a lengthy history of racist discrimination at its 1300 stores in the U.S. South. African Americans, disproportionately sited in this region, bought a third of the hefty $7 billion in sales registered in 1984 but made up less than 9% of the managerial force.[135]

Atlanta had long been a crucible of the anti-Jim Crow movement and soon became a bastion of the anti-apartheid movement. City Councilman John Lewis and State Representative Tyrone Brooks were among the protesters arrested at demonstration outside a stockholders' meeting of IBM, targeted for its complicity with apartheid.[136]

Neither the Reverend Sullivan nor his right-wing critics could stem the overflowing anti-apartheid tide then symbolized by the Free South Africa Movement. The accumulated pressure forced Pretoria to allow Lord Nicholas Bethell of Britain to visit Robben Island. By early 1985 Gay McDougall, an African American attorney who was an anti-apartheid leader, had been briefed on this epic turn of events. He described Mandela's cell as a "large room with six beds, plenty of books and adequate facilities for washing and toilet. The cell door is open almost all day" and there was a ping pong table and a small tennis court close by. The prisoner, described as an over "6 ft. tall lean figure with silvering hair," was in the process of imprisoning his jailers metaphorically. He averred that "in my first ten years on Robben Island conditions were really very bad. We were physically assaulted. We were subjected to psychological persecution. We had to work every day in the lime quarry from 7 A.M. to 4 P.M. with a one-hour break, wearing shorts and sandals, with no socks or underwear and just a calico jacket. It was hard, boring, unproductive

132. Reverend Lowery to Dr. Gibson, 28 December 1982, Box 243, *SCLC Papers*.

133. Peggy Perry to Reverend Albert Love, 24 October 1985, Box 243, *SCLC Papers*.

134. Various Materials, circa 1985, Box 243, *SCLC Papers*.

135. SCLC Release, 27 September 1985, Box 132, *SCLC Papers*.

136. *Atlanta Journal & Constitution*, 30 April 1985.

work and on rainy days in the winter it was very cold.... Diet was maize porridge for breakfast with half a teaspoon of sugar, boiled grain for lunch with puzamadla, a drink made from maize...porridge with vegetables in the evening," and "a lot of tension between guards and prisoners" besides. Helen Suzman recalled of this time that there were "guards with Alsatian dogs...sometimes with swastikas on their wrists...." But things began to change in 1974, coincidental with the Portuguese Revolution. Mandela said "I am in good health...not true that I have cancer...not true that I had a toe amputated. I get up [quite early] every morning, do two hours physical exercise.... Then I read and study...the South African newspapers as well as the 'Guardian Weekly' and 'TIME'...." There was a "radio in the cell" too, though only local stations were available—not the BBC. "I cultivate my garden...tomatoes, broccoli, beans, cucumber and strawberries." Amnesty International would not back the Free Mandela campaign because of his endorsement of armed struggle but he seemed to shrug it off, adding boldly, "Personally I am a socialist and I believe in a classless society.... I appreciate the Soviet Union because it was the one country that long ago condemned racialism...." He also asserted, "I was grateful, too, by the way to Emperor Haile Selassie of Ethiopia who received me in 1962."[137]

This visit and the resultant publicity were signs that Pretoria was responding to the pressure unleashed by Wall Street and FSAM alike. During his first 18 years in prison Mandela had not been allowed to even hold hands with his spouse on her few sanctioned visits, highly corrosive to their marriage. Nor was he allowed to attend the funeral of his eldest son, similarly disruptive of familial relations.[138] But as the regime in Pretoria felt the heat, it reacted accordingly, allowing Mandela and his fellow prisoner Toivo ya Toivo to play tennis, for example. "He used to beat me," the Namibian confessed. "And scrabble too but it was mainly chess.... If you could play chess with Mandela in a day," the South African "would only move two or three pieces, the man could take his time and I had no patience for that," as Mandela practiced for the bruising negotiations that soon were to unfold with the authorities. Somehow, Toivo ya Toivo found a copy

137. Letter, 8 February 1985, Box 222, *Gay McDougall Papers, Columbia University-New York City*.

138. Alec Russell, *Bring me My Machine Gun: The Battle for the Soul of South Africa from Mandela to Zuma*, New York: Public Affairs, 2009, 31.

of the work of Karl Marx on Robben Island too, which may have steeled the resolve of both.[139]

Mandela's organization was also encountering problems. "A sum of $400 a month in this country is too little to expect one to be able to do what I'm supposed to be doing here," complained the ANC's envoy in Washington, Dumi Matabane, in 1982. His spouse, a professor, was "not well paid at Howard" University and things were becoming more problematic amid "allegations that our movement are engaged in training of terrorist[s] in the USA"; thus, he was "requesting a total yearly living allowance of $8000 monthly...."[140] In a sense, this was a problem of growth: the fact that an envoy could request a substantial raise in salary was indicative of growing ambition and rising horizons. The same could be said when African Americans began inquiring about joining the ANC.[141]

Mandela's sudden surfacing was hardly accidental. As the crisis deepened in Pretoria, there was maneuvering designed to detach him from his organization and arrange a "Muzorewa" style deal, of the kind that had just failed ignominiously in Zimbabwe. In the Oval Office at the White House, Zambia's Kenneth Kaunda advised that talks should be held with the jailed Mandela and Walter Sisulu and "forget about Tambo." Avoiding such a split became a strategic task of the ANC in coming years. The Zambian leader "dodged a question"

---

139. Transcript of Interview with Toivo ya Toivo by Gerald Horne, March 1997, Box 169, *Gerald Horne Papers*.

140. Dumi Matabane to Thomas Nkobi, 3 March 1982, Part II, Box 6, Folder 40, *Lusaka Mission, ANC Records*.

141. Cheryl Yvonne Worthy to Alfred Nzo, 26 December 1985, Part II, Box 6, Folder 37, *Lusaka Mission*: She "first encountered racism in the United States" at the "age of three;" later, her "entrance into Cuba was...illegal, sequestering an airplane.... I did not know I was violating Cuban national law" by doing so. She was pregnant at the time: "my child and I were released from prison after having served only 14 months of a 13-year sentence" and then she met ANC emissary Mpho Mmutle and fell "seriously in love." Now she desired to join the ANC. Valerie O'Connor Makhathini to O.R. Tambo, 3 July 1985, Box 9, Folder 72, *O.R. Tambo Papers, Fort Hare University*: She was married to the ANC envoy at the United Nations and was now pregnant and complained that "abuse and dehumanization began on the weekly day, which was more like a funeral...or should I say worse than a funeral." Writing from Mount Vernon, New York, she noted "the constant reminder" from her mother: "I told you never to marry a Black man," a reference to Johnstone Makhathini, who was "insensitive and heartless."

on the Cubans and Savimbi but this too was a victory of sorts for Pretoria in that he could have been expected to act otherwise.[142]

* * *

All this reflected the struggle in the sub-region where Reagan's consigliere Chester Crocker was working with Pretoria in seeking to compel the withdrawal of Cuban troops from Angola. Crocker was contemptuous of President Dos Santos in Luanda, along with his "Soviet wife" and "Soviet engineering degree." He was less hostile to his Angolan counterpart, Kito Rodrigues, who was educated in part by U.S. Protestant missionaries and, perhaps as a result had developed a "special taste for American college and professional basketball." Yet his pen dripping with acid, Crocker reamed his Pretoria peers and the "rampant strife in their ranks," often fueled by excess; "like paint remover the non-stop alcohol intake stripped away any veneer of Afrikaner solidarity. They disagreed about everything." In one marathon negotiating session in Cape Verde, "one wondered about the 'policy process' among grown men who took such evident delight in making spectacles of themselves in the presence of foreigners, strangers and their own young countrymen (and women) from South African Airways...." Crocker "warned the South Africans that the growing township unrest," then a fixture on U.S. television, "and their response to it were becoming a more serious political issue in the United States."

With his constant references to Angolan "mestizos," Crocker himself was part of the problem, as his hold on the situation in the sub-region was unsteady. He sensed that Pretoria and the CIA were conspiring against him and was loath to admit that Pretoria's

142. Memorandum of Conversation, 30 March 1983, 11:30 AM, Box 14, Executive Secretariat, NSC, Subject File, MEMCONS, *Reagan Presidential Library*. See also Interview with Alistair Sparks, 21 January 1985, Box 10, *Gwendolen Carter Papers*: "The government wants Nelson [Mandela] to do a Sobukwe" but "he will never accept the conditions they want to put on.... I have a feeling that I can't substantiate about AZAPO [Azanian People's Organization]. Many of its members are Indian, admirers of Louis Farrakhan...the old Black Muslim Islamic link up.... Biko defined Black as not white and thereby included all the Blacks and some of the Coloureds and Indians. The militant Indians were delighted. So now Indians are running AZAPO.... [Allan] Boesak runs scared but has the ability and organizational skills.... Tutu is too keen on publicity and couldn't organize teddy bear's picnic....Albertina [Sisulu] is a rock of strength but not a leader"—and by default matters fell to Mandela.

repeated defeats at the hands of Cuban troops were the critical factor driving negotiations and the entire process. Part of U.S. strategy seemed to be distinguishing Maputo and favoring it over Luanda but that only set up President Samora Machel for the disaster that was the Nkomati Accord, forcing the evacuation of ANC cadre and, ultimately, his death. Still, by 1985 Maputo was becoming the largest recipient of U.S. aid in Sub-Saharan Africa; yet during his tenure with Reagan— "eight and a half years," said Crocker— "no battle was more bitter" than those involving Mozambique, in part because right-wing Christian evangelicals, like Pat Robertson, were major backers of the terrorist RENAMO, or Mozambican National Resistance opposition.

As the Cubans had battered Pretoria, another blow arrived in July 1985 when spooked U.S. banks refused to rollover South African debt, leaving the nation "sitting on a financial volcano," according to Crocker. "Two thirds of the country's foreign obligations were concentrated in short-term loans, due within one year, nearly 40 percent were due in six months." Pretoria closed the exchange markets and declared a unilateral moratorium on debt repayment, a red flag to creditors. Pretoria was also pressed by an "alliance" between Robinson and the cleric Desmond Tutu—and this was "paralleled by the links between [Pretoria's] narrowing circle of security advisers and a network of conservatives [in Washington]," along with the "evangelical movement and within the intelligence community and the White House staffs."[143] When Archbishop Tutu received the Nobel Peace Prize in 1984, it amplified his voice. His denunciation of Reagan as a "racist" the following year was bound to shake the rafters in the White House.[144] That same year, Zenani Mandela-Dlamini echoed this unassailable assertion when she charged that White House policies on apartheid were untenable, as she received an award from an African American museum in Detroit on behalf of her persecuted parents, Nelson and Winnie Mandela.[145]

Though reliably right-wing, Crocker was viewed suspiciously by the ultra-right. By 1985 the apartheid mass media was reporting that both he and Ambassador Herman Nickel were about to be ousted. Phil Christiansen, an aide to Senator Richard Lugar, said the White

143. Chester A. Crocker, *High Noon in Southern Africa,* 137, 145, 161, 216, 217, 168, 209, 231, 292, 322, 247, 249, 250, 267,

144. *Washington Post,* 10 November 1985.

145. *New York Times,* 29 August 1985.

House was "unhappy" with both.[146] In mid-1985, Crocker stopped by the office of National Security Council chief Robert McFarlane. He "asked to have a personal meeting with you," McFarlane was told; "my sense," said Phillip Ringdahl "is that he feels particularly embattled at this time over his stewardship of our African policy and wishes to reassure himself"[147]—doubtlessly because of the imprecations often directed at him by the hard right.

As suggested by Crocker's focus on Maputo, the U.S. was playing a double game in Mozambique, seeming to extend the olive branch while ultra-rightists brazenly backed an armed opposition renowned for slicing off noses and limbs and lips of their victims. "Security in our area is bad," said a Quaker emissary in late 1985 in Mozambique. "Bandits" had just been "caught in an area where I was going to establish rice fields. He was part of a band of 17 which had the previous week murdered 17 innocent women and children.... Bandits also have warned foreign governments that cooperantes [expatriate workers like himself] are targets for kidnapping." Besides, he concluded gloomily, "I have malaria and feel rotten."[148]

U.S. policy toward Maputo was a textbook case of coercive diplomacy, engaging while destabilizing. By early 1985 the White House was debating the possibility of a visit by President Machel. A visit "would bolster Machel's confidence and prestige," said aide Robert Kimmitt, "at a time when he is coming under sharp attack from anti-West hardliners and other opponents...."[149] But Kimmitt had to contend with his own "hardliners," led by fellow aide Patrick J. Buchanan, who exploded at the very idea of a Machel visit. He was a "Marxist," he fumed with "an atrocious human rights record, a long history of association with the Soviets, who is facing a tremendous opposition from 'RENAMO'...." Seemingly he backed the Nkomati Accord: "the South Africans have done a deal with Machel—he kicks out the ANC; they cut off the anti-Machel guerrillas," a bargain Pretoria was bound not to uphold. A Machel visit, said Buchanan, was "going to cause serious negative reactions across the conservative movement, among the neo-conservatives and even among some

146. Phil Ringdahl to Robert McFarlane, 20 May 1985, Box 166, WHORM, Subject File, *Reagan Presidential Library*.

147. Phillip Ringdahl to Robert McFarlane, 11 June 1985, Box 16, WHORM, Subject File, CO 001 CONT.-GEO AREAS, *Reagan Presidential Library*.

148. Letter from Maputo, 18 November 1985, ID Africa-E Africa-S 1985, *AFSC*.

149. Robert Kimmitt to F.J. Ryan, 5 February 1985, Box 133, WHORM, Co Countries CO 108 Mozambique, *Reagan Presidential Library*.

human rights activists...."[150] The question was: should Machel be toppled or wooed? The answer: both.

Chester Crocker intimated that irrespective of stated U.S. policy, the ultra-right free-lanced. The CIA director, for example, "has the resources to make a serious run at becoming a rival Foreign Minister. He has the networks, the budget and personnel resources, the private and dedicated communications capabilities and the access to senior levels in Washington and abroad. He is in a position to play the role of prosecutor, judge and jury in the highly judgmental business of analyzing the world." When the CIA was tied to the growing hysteria in Pretoria, pressed as it was by what it called a "total onslaught" of the SACP-Soviet-Cuban alliance, blood was bound to flow copiously—along with attacks on supposed allies. Pretoria "hawks," cried Crocker, "tried every device they could think of to undercut; feeding information to hostile Senators," for example, who then grilled him at highly publicized congressional hearings. "The hawks had their own diplomatic service, with their own message, code language, channels, delivery system and network of friends scattered amongst conservative circles" in his hometown, Washington. "This lobbying campaign was directed by Americans working for the military intelligence directorate" in Pretoria. Lobbyists included, he said, Stuart Spencer, a former campaign manager for Reagan himself, guaranteeing high-level access and leverage. He suggested that even CIA director William Casey was complicit in this cabal. Pat Buchanan, also ideologically aligned with the hardliners, deemed the State Department to be "enemy country." Crocker thought the MNR—RENAMO—Mozambican "resistance" to be an "African Khmer Rouge," wholly beyond the pale. "Sadly," said the naïve Crocker, "Reagan failed to convey a sense of outrage on racial issues," given this morally compromised leader's backing of apartheid.[151]

A key figure in the Mozambican terrorist opposition was Leo Milas, a founder of the so-called Mozambique National Resistance. Prexy Nesbitt considered him to be a "notorious...Afro-American agent provocateur...."[152] He was thought, in short, to have U.S. roots and posed as a Mozambican. Once he had worked for Planned

---

150. Patrick J. Buchanan to Michael Deaver, 14 February 1985, WHORM, Box 133, CO Countries CO 108 Mozambique, *Reagan Presidential Library*.

151. Chester Crocker, *High Noon in Southern Africa*, 279, 281, 283, 284, 293, 287, 319.

152. Prexy Nesbitt, Review Essay, "Toward Understanding National Liberation Movements," *Africa Today*, 19(Number 4, Autumn 1972): 83-88, 85.

Parenthood, according to Lockwood. "At one time he used a Muslim name," Lockwood said, "and may have been involved in some way in the Southern Sudan Civil War" too. FRELIMO's late founder Mondlane "apparently brought in some American detective agencies to trace his background," since he "claimed he was born in Inhambane" in the southern part of the country but moved to the U.S.A. for his education—though he spoke Portuguese with a Brazilian accent. He may have worked as a stevedore in San Pedro, California. Reputedly, his mother and father still resided there. "MNR has some CIA connections" and purportedly, "the Americans persuaded the British to supply MNR from Oman."[153]

Milas had powerful supporters in the U.S. Mozambique, said Prexy Nesbitt, "was at war against an enemy that was backed by South Africa and backed up by major conservative organizations in the United States like Coors Foundation, or like the American Free Enterprise Institute…or individuals like Pat Robertson. The 'Pat Robertson Club' had the rebel movement of RENAMO [MNR] on its show several times." These forces were joined by Senator Jesse Helms of North Carolina, the Republican panjandrum who was a "frequent and regular visitor to the South African apartheid regime. He got briefings from the South African government. He got money from the South African government. He was a regular apologist for the South African government."[154] Alongside him were fellow Republicans in the bulk of the North Carolina congressional delegation, which worked closely with the billionaire-funded American Legislative Exchange Council, which coordinated pro-apartheid measures in state legislatures. He visited South West Africa on their behalf.[155]

* * *

As Toivo ya Toivo of Namibia put it, "I was delighted when in 1985 NCBL under the leadership of [Dr.] Gerald Horne organized a trip for me [to the U.S.] …to publicize SWAPO." He met with Chester Crocker ("a nut, we had arguments") and Mayor Harold Washington of Chicago, who gave him the key to the city. (Though he found France to be the most sympathetic of the capitalist bloc, he insisted that "East Germans were our comrades, they supported us

153. Edgar Lockwood to "Dear Friends," 22 March 1985, ID Africa A-E Africa-S, 1985, *AFSC*.

154. Oral History, Prexy Nesbitt, 1 April 2009, *Columbia College-Chicago*.

155. Memo from WOA, 25 April 1984, Box 274, *ACOARA*.

considerably….Nor could I see people sleeping in the streets," unlike in the U.S.)[156] He was not impressed with U.S. imperialism—"at the time," he said, "I was not a person who was generally fond of Americans" because of "their government's decisions to side with South Africa"—and found the hawkish Reagan to be "openly hostile to our cause….You never [hear] him talking about the release of Nelson Mandela" while he was perpetually beating the drum on behalf of Soviet dissidents. He spoke at Harvard Law School, met with U.S. Communist Angela Davis (he "had read a lot about her"), and was introduced to his future spouse, "Vicki…[a] member of the Communist Party of the United States…."[157]

Yes, the CIA cabal was energetic but one of the lessons of the liberation of Southern Africa is that if one is properly organized—and able to evade ideological snares—as the Vietnamese and others have shown, the most determined imperialists can be brought to heel, particularly if one has on one's side one as charismatic as Namibia's founding father, Toivo ya Toivo.

---

156. Transcript of Interview with Toivo ya Toivo by Horne, March 1997, Box 169, *Gerald Horne Papers*.

157. Andimba Toivo ya Tovo, *On Trial for My Country*, 226, 228.

Chapter 20

Sanctions Imposed on Apartheid, 1985-1986

THE Comprehensive Anti-Apartheid Act of 1986 was enacted in the face of adamant opposition from the White House. The presidential elections of 1980 and 1984 were thought to have inaugurated a new spirit of amity between Washington and Pretoria, and surely this was the goal of both regimes. But global public opinion intervened (especially from steadfast Frontline States); the Free South Africa Movement, the campus divestment movement, (and the South African financial crisis) turned the tide, pushing Washington to the left of some of its European allies, and forcing imperialism to adjust accordingly, which then placed even more pressure on Pretoria. These factors, along with the strength of the mass movement within South Africa itself, ably assisted by the Frontline States, would lead in February 1990 to the unbanning of the ANC and SACP and the freedom of political prisoners, led by Nelson Mandela.

Reagan vetoed the bill, which was then overridden by the House 313 to 83—49 more than the two-thirds required—and the Senate followed with a 78 to 21 margin, the first override of a foreign policy issue since the War Powers Act was enacted over Nixon's veto in 1973 during the height of the conflict in Indochina.[1]

The bill's passage was a rebuke to the so-called "Reagan Doctrine" of rolling back of liberation movements and socialism, though, admittedly, on the larger chessboard, the increased expenditures made by Moscow and its allies in Southern Africa harmed the struggle in Nicaragua, Grenada, Southern Yemen, and—most of all—Afghanistan, where punishment was inflicted relentlessly in league with religious

---

1. Chapter from book on Senator Edward M. Kennedy, Box 2, *Adam Clymer Papers, John F. Kennedy Presidential Library.*

zealots ("freedom fighters" soon to be designated as "terrorists.")[2] Tambo retained an article that suggested that U.S. imperialism was frightened that sanctions would stanch the seemingly ceaseless flow of Southern African raw materials to the then deteriorating industrial machine in the U.S., putting the "economy and military preparedness" of U.S. imperialism at risk.[3] But, again, there is no honor among thieves; Canberra—not unsympathetic to apartheid—hastened to push quietly for sanctioning Pretoria in order to profit and seize South African export markets in coal, manganese, iron ore, chrome, uranium, asbestos, and vanadium.[4] China rejected the proliferating rumors that it was collaborating with Pretoria to ship enriched uranium and share nuclear technology.[5]

Kader Asmal, who was to become a member of Mandela's 1994 Cabinet, cautioned that "the list of sanctions may appear wide. But they are associated with approaches which are meant to isolate the ANC and to disarm it in the vital stage of the armed struggle....[The association] of terrorism with the activities of the ANC and the support the Frontline States is legally incorrect and politically impermissible."[6] Like other South African leaders, Asmal well knew that the "Black congressional lobby worked very hard" to overturn Reagan's ill-advised veto of the bill.[7] It was the wise Tambo who early on said—as recounted by his comrade, Mazizi Kunene—"definitely, absolutely, we must mobilize America, especially the African people,"[8] a decision which was to pay huge dividends.

Tambo was also advised by my colleague in the National Conference of Black Lawyers, Jeanne Woods, that this bill was a "victory" though "anything but comprehensive." It did "little to curb U.S. corporate collaboration with the regime and contain[ed] numerous loopholes," including allowing the reinvestment of profits and "intelligence sharing." It called for "an investigation of 'the extent to which Communists have infiltrated'" the anti-apartheid movement, an open invitation for the perpetration of dirty tricks. This was little

2. James M. Scott, *Deciding to Intervene: The Reagan Doctrine and American Foreign Policy*, Durham: Duke University Press, 1996, 5.

3. *Business Day*, 23 August 1985, Reel 13, *Oliver Tambo Papers*.

4. *Sydney Morning Herald*, 1 September 1986.

5. *Sydney Morning Herald*, 27 September 1986. See also *Worldwide Report*, 21 February 1986. For more on allegations concerning Chinese technology transfers to South Africa, see *New Statesman*, 12 September 1986.

6. Memo from Kader Asmal, 29 October 1986, Reel 11, *Oliver Tambo Papers*.

7. Oral History, Kader Asmal, 5 July 2001, *University of Connecticut-Storrs*.

8. Oral History, Mazizi Kunene, 27 April 2001, *University of Connecticut-Storrs*.

more than "pretexts for the acceleration of harassment," said Woods, and it was combined with "thinly veiled threats against the Frontline States" in its opposition to supposed "cross border terrorism,"[9] portending the continued destabilizing of Harare, Luanda, and Maputo particularly. Attorney Woods augmented Tambo's legal arsenal when she sent him a detailed report on "legal obligations of States with respect to apartheid."[10] Thus, the U.S. movement had become an essential component of the resistance to Pretoria, manifested not only in astute legal analysis but also in the $1196 sent in 1986 to Cyril Ramaphosa of the National Union of Mineworkers in South Africa by Jennifer Davis of ACOA, raised by San Francisco forces allied with the Reverend Jesse Jackson's "Rainbow Coalition."[11] When Anthony Mongalo, Tambo's secretary, conveyed to Woods "deep appreciation and sincere thanks" on behalf of his principal, it was more than a pro forma gesture.[12]

Fortunately for the ANC, their ties in the U.S. stretched beyond the usual precincts of African Americans and the rather small left wing. After sanctions were slapped on Pretoria, Tambo prepared to visit the U.S., and would this time be accorded red carpet treatment. He was slated to meet with the Chief Executive Officers of IBM, Johnson and Johnson, and other corporate giants, including General Motors, Burroughs, and Citibank. "They had dinner with Harry Oppenheimer the other night," the South African business titan, "and it is my sense," said his informant, "that he raised their apprehension level a bit.... They will want to talk about nationalization, violence and Communism (the standard fare...[usual] trilogy)." Tambo's well-placed interlocutor, Peggy Dulany, the fourth child of uber-banker David Rockefeller, added casually, "you will also be meeting with my father again," then even more informally adding, "if you would like me to, I could easily call John Whitehead, the Deputy Secretary of State," though "he is likely to view you as a terrorist and the ANC as a dangerous organization...."[13]

---

9. Jeanne Woods, "Analysis of the Anti-apartheid Act of 1986," circa 1986, Reel 3, *Oliver Tambo Papers*.

10. Jeanne Woods to "Dear Comrade Oliver Tambo," 26 October 1984, Reel 11, *Oliver Tambo Papers*.

11. Jennifer Davis to Cyril Ramaphosa, 25 September 1986, Box 84, *ACOARA*.

12. Anthony Mongalo to Jeanne Woods, 6 February 1987, Reel 3, *Oliver Tambo Papers*.

13. "Peggy" to Oliver Tambo, 17 October 1986, Box 9, Folder 73, *O.R. Tambo File, ANC Archives, Fort Hare University*.

Assuredly, the U.S. elite continued to be obsessed with the alleged influence of the SACP. A *New York Times* journalist found in 1986 that in Alexandria Township in Johannesburg there was a neighborhood known suspiciously as "Cuba," while Pretoria reported anxiously that 23 of the 30 members of the ANC leadership were simultaneously SACP leaders. Per Woods' warning, pursuant to the recently passed legislation—and consistent with Section 509 of the bill—the White House transmitted to Congress a report on the SACP recounting the history of the party, along with the painful memory of Angola 1975, the Cuban intervention, and the 1977 visit to the region of Soviet leader Nikolai Podgorny.[14]

The passage of the bill sanctioning Pretoria stunned the Republican Party, which thought it had provided an impermeable firewall protecting apartheid. A baffled Phil Nicolaides of the White House staff stated in July 1986 that "most Americans know little and care less about South Africa. Ronald Reagan is the most popular president of modern times"—and more than willing to back Pretoria with his final dying breath. Yet his "policy" was "greeted by such a negative response—even from key legislators in his own party."[15] Nicalaides refused to analyze the impact of the divestment movement, nor FSAM, nor Wall Street's worries about South African debt, so he looked within and blamed the State Department for these developments, principally Chester Crocker, the increasingly convenient whipping boy. He did not weigh the October 1985 report that 2700 had been arrested in FSAM protests over the past year. A conservative organ was reduced to terming Randall Robinson—falsely—as an "apostle of Marxist revolutionaries."[16]

Robinson admitted that he was "overwhelmed by the success" of FSAM, though it meant "our work doubled while our already small staff remained the same," leading to a "very long delay of our newsletter," hampering organizing.[17] More bad news arrived when NAACP chief Benjamin Hooks announced that "due to our financial crisis, we will not be able to purchase a table" for Robinson's annual fundraiser.[18]

---

14. Report, no date, Box 222, *Gay McDougall Papers, Columbia University*.

15. Phil Nicolaides to Patrick Buchanan, 23 July 1986, Box 2, Series 1, Subject File, *Pat Buchanan Files, Reagan Presidential Library*.

16. *Wall Street Journal*, 7 October 1985.

17. Randall Robinson to "Dear Member," 19 September 1985, Box VIII: 480, *NAACP Papers*.

18. Benjamin Hooks to Dick Hatcher, 2 April 1984, Box VIII: 480, *NAACP Papers*.

Yet their opponents seemed to be bogged down with their own problems. When the virtual house organ of the Republican Right—the *Washington Times*—reported that the president's "advisers" were "split" on the sticky matter of apartheid, it was not an incorrect conclusion.[19]

For his part, Crocker maintained that "every major element of our Southern African policies...was the object of one form of sabotage or another" perpetrated by the "domestic White House" (meaning Patrick Buchanan), "the CIA or Defense," even the National Security Council, tasked with bringing coherence to the unwieldy and often conflicting bureaucratic organs and preventing precisely what occurred: open warfare among conflicting factions. He denounced the "treacherous conduct of our 'colleagues' in other agencies."[20] Crocker did not seem to realize that part of the problem was that there were those who were willing to bend to new realities and those who thought they could recreate the reality of, say, 1973. Thus, by August 1986, the White House was told dejectedly that there was a faulty "assumption that veto of the sanctions legislation could be sustained by the Senate," especially since Republicans themselves were split. Remarkably the Republican vote count, which was "overly optimistic" about sustaining the veto, was "prepared," according to Will Ball, by "Jody Baldwin, a paid consultant to the South African government."[21]

It was not just Crocker who was seen as an enemy within the gates by the ultra-right. Constantine Menges, a leader of those unwilling to compromise on apartheid, thought Crocker's superior—Secretary of State Shultz—was the real problem. Menges— quite appropriately nicknamed "Constant Menace"—was a hawk on Angola, like most of his ilk.[22]

Operatives on behalf of apartheid were insinuated at the highest levels of the ruling party in Washington and tilted analyses—wrongly and misleadingly—in their favor. Other pro-apartheid forces—State Senator John Marchi of Staten Island, for example—descended into the bog of absurdity in order to uphold their flagging cause. Marchi told Congressman Guy Molinari, a Republican, to reconsider his pro-sanctions stance since, after all, "our first president was a slave

19. *Washington Times*, 18 July 1986.

20. Chester Crocker, *High Noon in Southern Africa*, 330.

21. Will Ball to "DTR", 28 August 1986, Box 168, WHORM, Subject File.

22. Constantine Menges, *Inside the National Security Council: The True Story of the Making and Unmaking of Reagan's Foreign Policy*, New York: Simon & Schuster, 1988, 231.

owner who in his wisdom manumitted his property in his last Will and Testament,"[23] suggesting, perhaps, that apartheid could evolve to vitiate apartheid.

Flummoxed by the prospect of attacking Wall Street—a source of lush campaign donations—and possibly underestimating the impact on public opinion of FSAM and the divestment movement, the White House staff turned with a vengeance on the State Department. Buchanan, the engine of much of this propaganda, was told by September 1986 that "State Department mail…has been running 'very heavily against sanctions," a reaction to the claim that the "preponderance of public opinion" was "against sanctions…." In fact, "mail to the President on this issue tabulated since August 20, 1985 to the present" revealed "pro-sanctions: 3467" and "anti-sanctions 5737…."[24]

Among the latter may have been John J. Murphy, Chairman and President of Dresser Industries. He informed Senator J. Strom Thurmond of South Carolina that "as an employer in your state" he "strongly oppose[d]" the "anti-apartheid act" since "we are a longtime employer in South Africa and currently employ 750 South Africans…."[25]

Dresser was swimming against a rising wave. U.S. corporations were fleeing South Africa. Just before the launching of FSAM there were 350 of them there, but then suddenly 70 of the biggest either pulled out or announced their intention to do so, a direct response to the mushrooming divestment movement.[26] By 1986 it was reported that Coca-Cola, under fire in its home base of Atlanta—where the Reverend Joseph Lowery and fellow pastors and congregants were threatening a boycott—had decided to divest from South Africa. "Until earlier this year," said the *Wall Street Journal*, "it was the second largest U.S. employer in that country," but the "company won't lose any money" as a result of finagling.[27] Carl Ware, the company's leading Negro, told South Africa exile Tandi Gcabashe, the daughter of the late Chief Luthuli then toiling in exile, about the "decision

---

23. John Marchi to Congressman Molinari, 18 September 1986, Box 169, WHORM, Subject File.

24. Phil Nacolaides to Patrick Buchanan, 23 September 1986 and 22 September 1986, Box 171, WHORM, Subject File.

25. John J. Murphy to Senator Thurmond, 8 July 1985, CMS 1986, Box 023, *J. Strom Thurmond Papers, Clemson University.*

26. "Legislative Research Commission. State Investments with South African Investors. Report to the 1987 General Assembly of North Carolina," *University of North Carolina-Chapel Hill.*

27. *Wall Street Journal*, 18 September 1986.

to complete…divestment from South Africa…."[28] Predictably, the White House was upset.

Suggestive of how anti-apartheid pressure was redounding to the benefit of certain Negroes, the company had sought to fortify its position by adding Donald McHenry—who had replaced Andrew Young as ambassador to the U.N. after he was sacked—as a well-paid board member.[29] The "widely heralded $10 million for various black development projects" from Coke was "negotiated by…board member Don McHenry who completely caved" to Tutu and "UDF [United Democratic Front] radicals, who demanded that Buthelezi be excluded from the largesse. "This type of corporate activity," complained Reagan aide Phillip Ringdahl, "is adding to problems between already divided blacks…."[30]

Buoyed by the movement against Coca-Cola, Atlanta was becoming a center of anti-apartheid resistance. Both Lowery and State Senator Julian Bond compelled the football coach at the University of Georgia, Vince Dooley, to delay a booster trip to South Africa, which would have compromised their many African American stars.[31] Perhaps in response, the respected widow of the deceased Dr. King—Coretta Scott King—was recruited by the company to provide a clean bill of health, which she did, adding that Coke's "record of support for the African American community in the United States reinforces my confidence in its contributions to South Africa. Black South African leaders," she insisted, "including Archbishop Desmond Tutu and Dr. Nthato Motlana have praised the Coca Cola [company]…."[32]

Lowery's activism was foiling his fellow pastor, the Reverend Leon Sullivan, who was still providing U.S. corporations authorization to invest in apartheid. As of 1986 even African entrepreneurs at Witwatersrand University "seemed to be most critical", said an observer, of the Philadelphian's campaign.[33]

Still, staunch opposition from diehards continued. Dick Winchell of the Palmetto State informed Senator Thurmond that "if I were a white in S. Africa, I would support apartheid because if each person had one vote, the illiterate majority would VOTE themselves my

28. Carl Ware to "Dear Tandi", 26 March 1987, Box Atlanta Regional Office, Southern Africa Peace Program, *AFSC*.

29. *Atlanta Journal &Constitution*, 18 September 1986.

30. Phillip Ringdahl to John Poindexter, 26 March 1986, Box 9, 10 [Box 3], African Affairs Directorate, NSC Records, RAC, *Reagan Presidential Library*.

31. *Atlanta Journal & Constitution*, 30 March 1984.

32. *Atlanta Journal & Constitution*, 19 June 1990.

33. Cable from State Department, March 1986, Box 58, *Leon Sullivan Papers*.

wealth…." Like those similarly situated over the decades, he insisted that "in the early days of our country, should the colonists of the original 13 colonies have extended the franchise to all of the Indians throughout the land…."[34]

Even the usually revered Reagan was coming under attack by reactionaries for supposedly pulling the rug out from under apartheid. "I don't think that apartheid is repugnant," said Gordon Mellish of Toledo, Ohio; "the problem is that the blacks want what the whites have. The answer to [their] greed is apartheid"— "Reagan can go to hell," since" there is something wrong with the Negro's ability. Look at Haiti and Africa…they have accomplished nothing…."[35] "As for your statement that South Africa's domestic policies are 'very controversial,'" said Marjorie Wing of Houston, disputing Senator Lloyd Bentsen of Texas, "certainly they are no more controversial than United States racial policies in the South as late as in the 1950s…." For good measure, she red-baited ACOA and Trans-Africa.[36]

It is unclear if the White House had tabulated the 750 postcards from San Francisco denouncing the Reagan policy of "constructive engagement" with apartheid, transmitted in April 1986 by Senator Barbara Boxer.[37] Definitely escaping this tabulation was the letter from Dr. Levi Watkins, Jr. of Johns Hopkins Hospital—perhaps the leading facility of its type globally—to Nancy Reagan, the president's adoring spouse. "I am a heart surgeon" he told her in November 1986 and knew the late Dr. Martin Luther King, Jr.— "he was my pastor as a child," and then a "close friend." He had brought him and his wife, Coretta Scott King, and Desmond Tutu, former Ambassador Andrew Young, and many others to this world class hospital to speak. Now he wanted to bring Winnie Mandela there. "In view of Mr. Reagan's concern for human rights," he said without sarcasm, "particularly in the Soviet Union, I plead with him to extend that concern to Mrs. Mandela…."[38]

Bamboozled, the White House found it difficult to maintain and pursue a consistent line. So, from attacking the State Department, suddenly Buchanan switched: "the problem lies with the U.S.

34. Dick Winchell to Senator Thurmond, 7 August 1985, CMS 1985, Box 38, *J. Strom Thurmond Papers.*

35. Gordon and Juanita Mellish, 22 August 1985, CMS 1985, Box 38.

36. Marjorie Wing to Senator Bentsen, 24 August 1985, CMS 1985, Box 38.

37. Senator Boxer to President Reagan, 3 April 1986, Box 168, WHORM, Subject File.

38. Dr. Levi Watkins, Jr. to Nancy Reagan, 6 November 1986, Box 172, WHORM, Subject File.

Senate," he told one of its members, Senator Carl Curtis of Nebraska. Frustratingly, "they cannot see that the battle for the future is not between segregation and de-segregation but the Soviet Empire and the West...."[39]

Buchanan, a future White House aspirant himself, was among the hardest of the hardliners. South Africa, he said, was "arguably the only successful country on the continent" and the U.S. "should be at South Africa's side." Instead, "Congress has cast our lot with those attempting to kick South Africa to death for sins of segregation of which America herself was guilty for decades...." UNITA and MNR were "assets": a victory by the latter in "overthrowing the Marxist regime in Maputo, would end Soviet influence in Mozambique and leave Prime Minister Robert ('Comrade Bob') Mugabe in Zimbabwe with no friendly outlet to the sea," imperiling his regime too. "Expulsion of the East Bloc personnel from Zimbabwe," he concluded "could be made a nonnegotiable demand and the same squeeze could be applied to landlocked Zambia,"[40] collapsing the Frontline States, like falling dominoes.

Mugabe was becoming a bête noire for the likes of Buchanan. By 1986 he was Chairman of the Non-Aligned Movement, a fierce opponent of the "constructive engagement" policy toward apartheid.[41] Mugabe was also presiding over a nation that had become a beehive of anti-apartheid activism by U.S. nationals, often conducted to the consternation of Washington. Among such figures was Carol Thompson, who raised concern about nuclear ties between the U.S. and South Africa.[42]

A new low in Harare-Washington bilateral relations was reached in July 1986 when Jimmy Carter was joined by British and West German diplomats in storming out of a Zimbabwean reception marking the U.S. national holiday after an African official asked why the U.S. bombed Libya and not South Africa. Aid cuts were threatened in a spectacle made all the more explosive by the former president's exit from his nation's own embassy.[43]

---

39. Patrick Buchanan to Senator Curtis, 3 November 1986, Box 172, WHORM, Subject File.

40. Patrick J. Buchanan, *Right from the Beginning*, Washington, D.C.: Regnery, 1990, 374-375.

41. Speech by Robert Mugabe, 2 October 1986, Box 10, *Gwendolen Carter Papers*.

42. *Herald* [Zimbabwe], 11 December 1985.

43. *Australia Financial Review*, 10 July 1986.

Pretoria's closeness to the White House may have amounted to a catastrophic victory, allowing for the circulation of misleading analyses of the correlation of forces. Nicholas Platt of the State Department complained that P.W. Botha "continues his recent practice of bypassing the State Department apparently in an effort to establish a separate channel to the White House," and did so, said Platt, in a "tone" that is "inappropriate for a communication to the President,"[44] reeking of swaggering influence.

Platt may have had in mind Carl Shipley of the pretentiously titled "Americans for President Reagan's Foreign Policy." He had been registered as a foreign agent for Pretoria's "interests in Namibia," said Platt. "He is no longer registered" but was still lobbying; thus, said Platt, "it would be inappropriate to answer Mr. Shipley's letter as a private U.S. citizen."[45]

Shipley could be ignored, but the White House found it harder to dismiss the action taken by their acolytes at Dartmouth College, who destroyed a shantytown on campus, meant to symbolize the school's intertwined ties to apartheid.[46] No such counter-offensive occurred at Columbia University on the edge of Harlem, where I was an advisor to student activists in my capacity as leader of the National Conference of Black Lawyers. As I was featured on the front page of the school's newspaper at one of many campus demonstrations,[47] the Reverend Jackson was meeting with Ivy League campus presidents pressuring them to divest their endowments from apartheid.[48] College presidents were busily meeting on this matter, including at an important gathering in Boulder, Colorado.[49]

The rationalizations for the blood money from apartheid were becoming more threadbare. In Boulder some alleged that sanctions

44. Nicholas Platt to John Poindexter, 18 June 1986, Box 169, WHORM, Subject File.

45. Nicholas Platt to John Poindexter, 14 March 1986, Box 175, WHORM, CO 141, South Africa 59200 and CO 143 Namibia, *Reagan Presidential Library*.

46. *Washington Post*, 6 February 1986.

47. *Columbia Spectator*, 7 April 1985.

48. *New York Times*, 21 June 1985.

49. "Conference on South Africa for College Presidents.... Issues and Options Concerning University of Colorado Treasury Investments in Entities Doing Business in South Africa and Other Initiatives" by C. William Fisher, Vice President for Budget and Finance, 28 September 1985, Box 74, Brooking Institution Program Files, *Warren Cikins Papers, John F. Kennedy Presidential Library*.

harmed funding for African college students.[50] On the West Coast, students at the University of California-Berkeley barred the unloading of goods from South Africa at the docks of San Francisco, refuting the policy of their school.[51] Due south in Austin, students at the University of Texas faced death threats, assaults, and break-ins as a result of their vibrant activism.[52]

Reciprocally, workers in Elandsfontein, South Africa staged a half day walkout in solidarity with 3M workers in Freehold, New Jersey whose audio and video tape plant was being closed. The latter were also backed by the well-known troubadours Willie Nelson and Bruce Springsteen, whose hometown was nearby. In South Africa the workers—250 strong—were all wearing Freehold t-shirts in solidarity with the 160 in New Jersey.[53]

The cultural boycott too was gaining traction. A boycott of Channel 13 in Los Angeles was launched after it broadcast *Shaka Zulu,* which Howard Rosenberg of the *Los Angeles Times* said "may be the most violent TV production ever shown nationally in America...also the nudest production ever shown on American non-cable TV. That includes male rear-ends and female bare breasts...." The program was burnished with "intrusive...commercial breaks," guaranteeing profits. It was "unwatchable," he said with disgust, as the "script" was "awful at worst." Unsaid was that the apartheid portrayals of Africans had the subsidiary "benefit" of sliming African-Americans and augmenting domestic racism.[54] Protests erupted in San Francisco as a result of this broadcast.[55] The U.N. showed that, boycotts aside, U.S. nationals continued to engage in sporting contacts with apartheid too.[56]

But Botha, sensing that pro-apartheid sentiments were deeply entrenched among a goodly portion of Euro-Americans, pressed his advantage. He was "obviously extremely exercised," said Buchanan,

---

50. James Moulder to Warren Cikins, 6 November 1985, Box 74, *Warren Cikins Papers.*

51. "Student Anti-Apartheid Newsletter," 4 March 1986, Box: Greater Regional Office, Southern Africa Peace Education Program, *AFSC.*

52. "Student Anti-Apartheid Newsletter," March-April 1986, Box Atlanta Regional Office, Southern Africa Peace Program, *AFSC.*

53. "Labor Against Apartheid Newsletter," Spring 1986, *Anti-Apartheid Movements: File of Clippings and Miscellenea, Michigan State University-East Lansing.*

54. *Los Angeles Times,* 21 November 1986.

55. *San Francisco Examiner,* 2 December 1986.

56. "Register of Sports Contacts with South Africa," 1 December 1985, Box 1, *E.S. Reddy Collection, Schomburg Center, New York Public Library.*

"over the fact that President Reagan's communications with him have ceased to be written," a decision which "indicated a desire *not* to have a written record of some of what was transmitted." Reagan's unwillingness to memorialize his discussions with Botha was a signal that the tides of history were turning against apartheid. "Obviously the State President is extremely agitated at a time of historic crisis for his country," Buchanan said. "He feels besieged and isolated, unsure as to whether he is even in communication any longer with the President,"[57] who had begun to hedge his bets and communicate mostly through the U.S. ambassador in Pretoria, Herman Nickel. Sarcasm dripping, John Sears—a key man at the White House—remarked that Botha did "not understand the State Department's strategy of trashing his country...."[58] [emphasis original] There was "tremendous suspicion of our State Department on the part of the South Africans," said Buchanan. "Sears contends that President Reagan remains tremendously popular inside South Africa,"[59] casually disregarding the reality that this analysis ignored the majority of the population there.

Phillip Ringdahl of the White House staff was among those who found Botha "demeaning" of the U.S., as if he did not realize that he was the client and Washington was the superpower. Ringdahl summoned a diplomat from the Washington legation, who "handed over" yet another demeaning "response saying it was self-explanatory, then walked out of the room"—this after the U.S. voted against Pretoria at the U.N., castigating the latest raid on Cabinda, Angola where Gulf Oil pumped oil protected by Cuban troops. Savimbi was upset too. But it was Ringdahl who was left to fret over "U.S. domestic fallout" as a result of being on the wrong side of Botha.[60]

The White House was being squeezed by this recalcitrant "ally" on one side, and being confronted by FSAM, campus divestment, ungovernable South Africa backed by the Frontline States (and the socialist camp too) and resultant fallout on Wall Street on the other. The State Department too had the effrontery to report bad news, e.g.

57. Patrick Buchanan to John Poindexter, 13 June 1986, Box 169, WHORM, Subject File.

58. John Sears to Patrick Buchanan, 5 June 1986, Box 169, WHORM, Subject File.

59. Patrick Buchanan to Donald Reagan and John Poindexter, 22 August 1986, Box 169, WHORM, Subject File.

60. Phillip Ringdahl to Robert McFarlane, 3 July 1985, Box 9, 10 [Box 3], African Affairs Directorate, NSC Records, RAC, *Reagan Presidential Library.*

the intelligence that France had recalled its ambassador in Pretoria and was seeking to "halt all new investment there." Paris may have been stealing a march on a post-apartheid regime since it was "taking the lead" against Pretoria "both within" the Security Council and what became the European Union, "no doubt due in part to pressure from Francophone Africa,"[61] e.g. Guinea-Conakry. This divergence by France was castigated by Chester Crocker, who said bitingly, "we owed nothing to the French, who had spent much of the past three years making hay in the Third World at the expense of our policies."[62]

After conferring with Ambassador Herman Nickel in Pretoria, the White House was told that South Africa was "clearly in the 'thump' phase of their dual track 'thump and talk' policy" since there was now an "upsurge in anti-American attitudes by [Pretoria's] leaders including"—most prominently—"President Botha" himself. The "business community" was "especially worried about sanctions," though there was "no sign of [South African] gratitude or even acknowledgment" of the aid rendered Pretoria by Washington. "They assume that our policies are driven by pursuit of our interests, not theirs," an accurate assessment on Pretoria's part. Botha was "really rankled" by the fact that Tutu and Buthelezi were "received in the Oval Office but not him," as if he were a mistress who had to be hidden from sight. Even his spouse raised this slight.[63] Botha was falling apart and would have to be replaced, for it seemed he was enduring a nervous breakdown. From the "Situation Room" at the White House came the report that he was "buckling under pressure," "frustrated and 'rattled,'" and enmeshed in an "angry siege mentality" with "barely controlled anger." He had few friends beyond the closest of family—and even they had their doubts. He would have to step down soon.[64]

At least Botha was able to escape the indignity accorded Buthelezi after his Oval Office visit, who was scorned by Randall Robinson in the pages of the *New York Times*.[65] Buthelezi received a cold shoulder from Black America during his visit. He found the questions posed

61. Report from Executive Secretariat, Bureau of Intelligence and Research, 25 July 1985, Box 9 [Box 2], African Affairs Directorate, NSC, RAC, *Reagan Presidential Library*.

62. Chester Crocker, *High Noon in Southern Africa*, 342.

63. Phillip Ringdahl to Robert McFarlane, 20 June 1985, Box 9 [Box 2], African Affairs Directorate, NSC, RAC, *Reagan Presidential Library*.

64. "Situation Room Checklist," 29 March 1985, African Affairs Directorate, NSC RAC Box 9 [Box 2], *Reagan Presidential Library*.

65. *New York Times*, 5 June 1985.

by the Washington Association of Black Journalists at a tumultuous press conference to be "hostile and insulting." Dennis Schatzman of the *Los Angeles Sentinel* cited the polemicist H.L. Mencken when he told the beset visitor, "it's hard to believe that a man is telling the truth when you know that you would lie if you were in his place."[66] It turned out that Robinson's group had circulated a list of hostile queries to be posed to this besieged visitor,[67] as he campaigned for weeks in front of television cameras and journalists' tape recorders.[68]

Freedom House of Manhattan, an anticommunist clearinghouse of some note, found the Zulu visitor to have a "very delicate hide for a politician," making him susceptible to jabs from his many opponents in Black America. His handlers "tried, softly, to tell him that one must develop rhino skin" but he was loath to listen. Back home he did not "have the control over the younger Inkatha people that he'd like to have," referring to his chauvinist troops; a "fair amount of 'persuasion' (I hate to use the word 'coercion')" was "used to get people signed up" with his group, increasing their volatility. Since "Inkatha members have social and economic advantages, as well as a leg up when it comes to employment in KwaZulu [Natal]," this enhanced their recruiting prospects.[69]

Buthelezi remained a favorite of the hard right, a status solidified when he received an honorary doctorate from Boston University, headed by one of his fans, John Silber.[70] Of course, consistent with past patterns, there were those in Black America who seemed more concerned with alleged Communist advance than the stark reality of apartheid. These included Bayard Rustin, a former aide to Dr. King, who had become a frequent visitor to South Africa. His comrades in Freedom House deemed it "inconceivable that [Pretoria] would even consider one-man-one vote," the non-negotiable demand of their many opponents; after all, it was said, it "took American blacks 101 years"—post-1865—to reach this goal in a nation and region where they were generally outnumbered.[71]

Snubbing Botha was becoming a popular sport, indulged in by Coretta Scott King, the widow of Dr. King, when she visited South

---

66. *Washington Times*, 28 November 1986.

67. *Washington Times*, 13 November 1986.

68. *Washington Times*, 17 November 1986.

69. Letter, 24 January 1985, Box 85, *Freedom House Archives, Princeton University*.

70. Luli Callinicos, *Oliver Tambo*, 507.

71. Memo, 22 March 1985, Box 85, *Freedom House Archives*.

Africa in 1986.[72] Actually, with a liberal naïveté, she had sought to meet with him in a kind of mediating role until the United Democratic Front, backed by the ANC, objected. Even Tutu distanced himself from her because of this outreach to Pretoria. Backpedaling furiously, she then cancelled a meeting with Buthelezi.[73] Instead she conferred with Winnie Mandela and told her that her late husband had called for sanctions against apartheid in 1962 in a statement co-signed by Chief Luthuli.[74] (Mrs. King was coming under assault from various quarters: the leading activist in Los Angeles, Ron Wilkins, assailed her for speaking at the Crystal Cathedral in Garden Grove after they barred the ANC's Nzo on anticommunist grounds.)[75]

Ms. Mandela had won few friends at the White House when earlier she said Washington was a main prop of the "racist white regime" in Pretoria.[76] Audrey Burroughs, a U.S. Negro who also visited South Africa in 1986, was not given the opportunity to snub Botha, but she did say that her U.S. accent most likely spared her the routine disrespect accorded Africans, yet another black eye for Pretoria in the U.S.[77] Beth Burris, yet another African American sojourner in South Africa, would have disagreed. This church worker charged that officers of the law beat her, leaving serious cuts on her body. "If I had been white," she said accusingly, "they wouldn't have touched me" during her journey to northern Transvaal. "There was blood all over my clothes," said this Lutheran missionary.[78]

Botha, on the other hand, had to consider a weightier matter: how to respond when the ANC bombed an oil pipeline and chemical plant in Durban.[79]

* * *

John Sears had been close to President Nixon before becoming one of the most trusted aides to the graceless President Reagan. In early 1986 he was told by Patrick Buchanan that "an old friend who

72. *Washington Post*, 10 September 1986.
73. *Los Angeles Times*, 10 September 1986.
74. *Guardian* [U.K.], 12 September 1986.
75. *Los Angeles Sentinel*, 23 October 1986.
76. *New York Times*, 25 January 1986.
77. *New York Times*, 16 April 1986.
78. *Washington Post*, 15 March 1986; Clipping, 11 March 1986, Box 144, *Leroy Walker Africa News Service Archive*.
79. *Los Angeles Times*, 23 June 1986.

represents the South Africans" wanted to get a message to the White House but "they fear that the State Department will trash it at the same they leak its contents,"[80] a thinly veiled reference to Crocker's purported perfidy. Most definitely, as Robert McFarlane—yet another top White House aide—was told, "economic sanctions... was not our initiative" and "gives the world the impression that we were shamed into it."[81] The operative verb was actually "pressured" since the Republican Right was devoid of shame.

The road to this pivotal moment was less than smooth. By mid-July 1986, a host of Republican Congressmen, led by Paul Crane, Duncan Hunter, Dan Lungren, Robert Dornan, Henry Hyde, and Jack Kemp—18 altogether—reminded the White House that weeks earlier the House of Representatives voted 369 to 49 that no U.S. assistance should go to the ANC "until such times as the ANC's controlling body no longer includes members" of the SACP. The ANC was derided as a "typical Soviet backed 'liberation' movement;" thus, "to oppose and expose the ANC is to take the high moral ground" in contravention of this "Communist Front practicing terrorism." Moreover, in a tactic stretching back at least to the attempt to woo Z.K. Matthews during his sojourn in the U.S. in the early 1950s, Washington would take an "'open arms' attitude towards any well meaning non-Communists in the ANC who wish to disassociate themselves from the ANC...." It was concluded that "any policy that implicitly accepts the ANC/SACP alliance as legitimate...would be a moral outrage...."[82] Instead of engaging with the ANC, 11 members of Congress, including Newt Gingrich of Georgia and Dick Armey of Texas, wanted a South African Constitution of "five chambers", elected, variously, by Africans, "whites," Coloured, Indians—and another for the Bantustans, with laws having to be passed by 3 of 5 to pass.[83] This suggestion came as these same Congressmen were braying about non-racialism at home which in practice meant wielding the Euro-American majority to strengthen racial privilege, while advocating another way to protect this same privilege in South Africa.

---

80. Patrick Buchanan to John Sears, 28 January 1986, Box 168, WHORM, Subject File, *Reagan Presidential Library*.

81. John Lenxzowski to Robert McFarlane, 26 September 1985, Box 168, WHORM, Subject File.

82. Congressmen Burton, et.al. to John Poindexter, 17 July 1986, Box 170, WHORM, Subject File, *Reagan Presidential Library*.

83. Newt Gingrich, et.al., to President Reagan, 15 August 1986, Box 169, WHORM, Subject File.

This was an obvious reflection of a mossback stance that ill prepared Washington to adapt to imminent changes on the horizon. Yet, the fact that hardliners felt compelled to intervene so stridently was indicative that events were outpacing their control of the situation. In particular, the Republican Party base was furious with the decision to adapt to changing currents by engaging with the ANC and seeking to split it; the hardliners preferred that the ANC, better still, be liquidated.

Typical of their constituency was the reaction of Charles Stockell of Beaufort, South Carolina who in 1986 informed Patrick Buchanan that "last night I could not sleep and as I sat through the long hours turning this matter over in my mind," his cogitation skidded into the "depths of…profound disillusionment." The source of his depression was the idea that the U.S. was acquiescing to the purported Red tide rather than seeking to stem it. "Are we to side with Communist organizations and further Soviet goals?"[84] As Stockell saw things, the ANC was "Communist dominated" and "Communist controlled." "I am a Regular Army Officer," he cried. "I have been wounded four times in the service of my nation" and "for 35 years I have been a Soviet specialist" who had lived in the Soviet Union too. He also chose to "travel in and study the South African region," his claim to insight into regional affairs and the ANC most notably.[85] This experience contributed to his exceedingly negative reaction to the congressional testimony of Chester Crocker, Washington's point man on the sub-region whose own conservatism was weak tea as far as the ultra-right was concerned.

Stockell was not singular. Richard Sanders of Seattle was a delegate to the Republican convention in 1976 and voted for Reagan over the incumbent Gerald Ford for the Republican presidential nomination. But Reagan's policy as articulated by Crocker "makes me sick." "Your administration," he told Buchanan, "is trying to pull the rug out from under the Afrikaners,"[86] a serious charge indeed. Buchanan was sympathetic, praising these "insightful thoughts on South

84. Charles Stockell to Patrick Buchanan, 17 March 1986, Box 168, WHORM, Subject File, *Reagan Presidential Library*.

85. Charles Stockell to President Reagan, 17 March 1986, Box 168, WHORM, Subject File.

86. Richard Sanders to Patrick Buchanan, 11 March 1986, Box 168, WHORM. Subject File.

Africa. You are not alone. I've received numerous letters expressing similar sentiments."[87]

As the nature of his correspondence showed, Buchanan—a pugnacious man of Irish Catholic descent—was the hardest of the hardliners in the White House. As the bill promoting sanctions against apartheid was winding its way through Congress, he was told, "quite simply no one in the United States or anywhere else, knows this issue better than you."[88] This was an exaggeration that nonetheless made a point: no one in the U.S. was more pro-apartheid and, in a position, to do something about it.

So encouraged, Phil Nicolaides told Buchanan that the ANC was "every bit as much a Soviet controlled and supplied operation" as the Sandinistas, then reeling from a U.S.-inspired insurgency, or the reviled Palestine Liberation Organization. Thus, he defended the prospect of murderous raids by Pretoria on Zimbabwe, Botswana, and Zambia against "terrorist bases."[89] In fact, he asserted that ANC and SACP leader Joe Slovo was a "KGB Colonel."[90] This unsupported charge had become boilerplate in Washington, propelling increased U.S. spying on the ANC. One U.S. spy was irate, terming the ANC "bad guys.... Soviet pawns, stalking horses for the Soviets."[91]

Of like mind was former White House Senior Policy Advisor John McLaughry, writing from Concord, Vermont—or as he put it, "out here in the Real America—outside the Beltway." "People do not see any good reason why we should use our sanctions to bring down a Christian government which fought beside us in three wars"—a canard often repeated by the White House—"in order to install in power a bunch of Communist-led savages."[92] Wirt A. Yeager of Jackson, Mississippi, told "Dear Ron" that his lieutenant—Crocker—was "despicable": "fire him or reassign him," he advised, "without moment's delay." As for Secretary of State George Shultz, he was furious with his "insubordination and lack of respect" for the president. The "State Department has not been thoroughly cleaned out

87. Pat Buchanan to Richard Sanders, 21 May 1986, Box 168, WHORM, Subject Files.

88. Anthony Dolan to Patrick Buchanan, 11 July 1986, Box 2, Series 1, Subject File, *Pat Buchanan Files, Reagan Presidential Library.*

89. Phil Nicolaides to Patrick Buchanan, 20 May 1986, Box 169, WHORM, Subject Files.

90. Phil Nicolaides to Patrick Buchanan, 11 July 1986, Box 2, Series 1, Subject File, *Pat Buchanan Files, Reagan Presidential Library.*

91. *Sydney Morning Herald*, 24 July 1986.

92. John McLaughry to President Reagan, no date, Box 169, WHORM, Subject Files.

in 50 years and you yourself have said how critically important this [is],"[93] he reminded pointedly.

Eva Lopatkin Easton of Sloatsburg, New York took the time to monitor the "comings and goings of the leaders of the ANC in the Communist world over Radio Moscow and Radio Havana." The latter was "offering Americans who want to communicate directly to Nelson Mandela the opportunity to do so." They played the singer Stevie Wonder singing birthday greetings to the jailed leader, followed by the Reverend Jesse Jackson stating the same.[94] She too may have noticed that in the U.S. Congress, Black Caucus leader George Crockett continued to gather support for his "Mandela Freedom Resolution," which received unanimous approval in the House Foreign Affairs Committee, accompanied by 137 co-sponsors.[95]

Crockett, who had been jailed decades earlier because of his zealous defense of African American Communist Party-USA leader Ben Davis,[96] was also pressing the State Department to hire more Negroes, which could only compromise relations with apartheid. There was rampant "racial discrimination against Black Foreign Service Officers," he was told. "The State Department still insists on projecting an…'all white male' image to the world…." One of the victims of this bias, Odie Fields, was "fed up," though activism was hampered since professionals like himself did not have "many ties with Black political leaders because most of our service is abroad…."[97]

Crockett's activism was not his alone. Anti-apartheid had become a top priority for the Caucus and its constituents. Addressing his colleagues in June 1986, Congressman William Gray of the CBC was forceful: "why do we resist using our economic and political might on behalf of black South Africans," he asked imploringly, "when we have done it so freely on behalf of others?" Since the U.S. had been dragged away from Jim Crow screaming, Washington had become quite sensitive to the credible charge that it executed a racist foreign policy, something Gray well knew. In his appearance before the House Banking Committee, the solon dismissed peremptorily

93. Wirt A. Yeager to "Dear Ron," 23 June 1986, Box 170, WHORM, Subject Files.

94. Eva Lopatkin Easton to Patrick Buchanan, 26 July 1986, Box 171. WHORM, Subject Files.

95. Randall Robinson to Benjamin Hooks, 28 August 1984, Box VIII: 480, *NAACP Papers.*

96. Gerald Horne, *Black Liberation/Red Scare: Ben Davis and the Communist Party*, Newark: University of Delaware Press, 1994.

97. Odie Fields, et.al. to Congressman Crockett, 4 June 1986, Box 58, *Leon Sullivan Papers.*

"predictions of a Communist takeover." Instead, he asked dramatically, "what is the difference between swastika in 1936 and swastika in 1986? ...[apartheid] has no less dangerous implications than Nazism for world peace and stability."[98]

A problem for Washington was that when it came to the ANC, the Negro elite was not as susceptible as others to red-baiting. Instead, they took advantage of Pretoria's unseemly ties to Nazism to discredit apartheid. This was a staple for the Reverend Jackson too, who at a press conference unloaded on "Nazi apartheid in South Africa" as he described "Botha [as] the successor to Hitler...."[99] The Reverend Jackson had attained a new level of prominence in 1984, when he ran for the Democratic Party nod for president. Preceding him in the attempt to forge a left within a major political party was Senator Edward M. Kennedy, brother of the slain president and the assassinated Attorney General. He walked in the footsteps of the latter when he visited South Africa in 1985, incurring the wrath of Pretoria, which begrudgingly admitted him. Dismissively, South African Broadcasting accused him of spouting the "chic slogans of East Coast liberalism" during his tumultuous visit.[100]

Again, Tutu was at the nub of this visit, seizing the opportunity to denounce Ambassador Nickel at an "apologist for apartheid" before global cameras, which may have influenced the testy quality of Kennedy's subsequent meeting with Botha. Senator Kennedy renewed his request to visit the imprisoned Mandela, while Nickel attacked him and divestment in introducing him to an audience. Botha reportedly was satisfied, "impressed and grateful" as a result. Kennedy in turn attacked Reagan, as denunciations flew back and forth,[101] including a harsh critique of the legislator by AZAPO [Azanian People's Organization].[102] Nickel was congratulated by White House aide John Poindexter for "the way you handled" the U.S. visitor.[103] The White House seemed overjoyed by the difficulties encountered by Senator Kennedy in South Africa. "Radical blacks and moderate

98. Testimony of Congressman Gray, 10 June 1986, Box 22, *William Gray Papers, Schomburg Center, New York Public Library.*

99. Remarks by Jesse Jackson, 19 June 1986, Box 17, *William Gray Papers.*

100. South African Broadcasting Corporation Commentary, 7 January 1985, Box 120, *Leroy Walker Africa News Service Archive.*

101. Chapter from book on Senator Kennedy, Box 2, *Adam Clymer Papers, John F. Kennedy Presidential Library.*

102. Report by AZAPO, 24 September 1986.

103. John Poindexter to Admiral Poindexter, 11 January 1985, Executive Secretariat, NSC, Country File, Africa, S. Africa, Box 4, *Reagan Presidential Library.*

whites," chortled aide Robert Kimmitt, were "both upset" with him. Pretoria was "beside itself," a familiar posture, seeing the visitor as "provocative and insulting...." At one point "P.W. Botha" was "on the verge of expelling Kennedy from the country"[104]—though if this had occurred, it would have given another positive jolt to the anti-apartheid movement.

The atmosphere had become polarized, with fewer and fewer accepting the White House rationale for "constructive engagement" with the "ally" in Pretoria. When William Robertson, the highest ranking Negro in the State Department, spoke at the famed Ebenezer Church in Atlanta, he hailed Reagan, asserting that the president was "crying 'end apartheid.'" The response was heckling and what was described as a "hostile reaction," with one voice yelling, "funny, funny."[105]

Fortunately for the White House, there was an important segment of their base of support that was not splintering. Buchanan praised his friend Bill Cheshire, who directed the predictably right-wing editorial page of the *Washington Times*, saying "nobody has given us more supporting fire on our stand against sanctions that you folks on the *Times'* editorial pages; and it is recognized in the Oval Office [by Reagan] and mightily appreciated here."[106]

Unsurprisingly, when J.W.H. Meiring, a Nationalist Party leader and parliamentarian visited the U.S., he was pleased, telling the errant Reagan how "impressed" he was "by the positive and sympathetic interest that I found everywhere in your country," not to mention his enthusiastic "admiration" of the president personally.[107] Alfred H. Honikman felt similarly. Born in Cape Town in 1910, this architect served as mayor of his hometown from 1961 to 1963, before moving to Southern California, where his son and family lived.[108]

Historically, Washington had relied heavily upon a distinct minority of Negroes to deodorize their policy toward apartheid and this moment was not different. Buchanan told key White House aides Donald Regan and John Poindexter that "the Administration is giving greater visibility to black Americans in the framing of South

---

104. Robert Kimmitt to Phillip Ringdahl, 14 January 1985, African Affairs Directorate, NSC, RAC, Box 9 [Box 2], *Reagan Presidential Library*.

105. *Washington Times*, 20 January 1986.

106. Patrick Buchanan to "Dear Bill" Cheshire, 1 August 1986, Box 170, WHORM, Subject Files.

107. J.W.H. Meiring to President Reagan, 3 September 1986, Box 170, WHORM, Subject Files.

108. Alfred Honikman to Congressman R.J. Lagomarsino, 1 September 1986, Box 170, WHORM, Subject Files.

African and Southern African policy," referencing Alan Keyes—a future senatorial candidate defeated by Barack Obama in Illinois—and writer Walter Williams, who was "interested in the Ambassadorship to South Africa...."[109] This was a direct reaction to the development described by *Wall Street Journal* columnist Suzanne Garment, referring to the impact of campus protests, FSAM and the like: "South Africa becomes a part of U.S. politics."[110]

Another columnist, Mona Charen, sensed something similar. "The left adores this issue," she stressed, speaking of anti-apartheid. "It carries them back to the old civil rights struggle," a relief since "things have gone badly for the left since those glory days...which is one reason they've been salivating to get South Africa onto the front pages." To her credit, she found it "inconsistent for one thing to say you're against sanctions in [South] Africa because it'll hurt the people; and yet we punish the Nicaraguan and Cuban regimes without reference to this...standard...."[111]

As such, Buchanan was bent on undermining Trans-Africa, which was "engaged in a remarkably single-minded and successful campaign." "Urgently needed," he declared, "is a new broad-based, multi-racial non-partisan organization of Americans interested in this hugely important continent"—"let's give it a working title of American Coalition for African Freedom"[112]—but aligning with a White House-inspired lobby on Africa was an idea designed to crash and burn. Almost magically, the press soon reported that a "U.S. Black Group seeks support for South Africa," i.e. the "Black Silent Majority Committee," led by Clay Claiborne which was fervent in opposition to Cuban troops in Angola.[113]

A logical candidate for such a group would have been the entertainer Sammy Davis, Jr., who had wounded his popularity a few years earlier by embracing Richard M. Nixon. But it was this singer and actor who rebutted the fatuous Reagan after he sought to convince him of the correctness of his policy on apartheid.[114] Davis

---

109. Patrick Buchanan to Donald Regan and John Poindexter, 25 July 1986, Box 168, WHORM, Subject Files.

110. *Wall Street Journal*, 25 July 1986.

111. Mona Charen to Patrick Buchanan, 29 July 1986, Box 171, WHORM, Subject Files.

112. Memorandum from Patrick Buchanan, May 1986, Box 169, WHORM, Subject Files.

113. *Rocky Mountain News*, 25 April 1986.

114. Ronald Reagan to Sammy Davis, Jr., 24 June 1986, Box 169, WHORM, Subject Files.

was unconvinced, instructing him "as my friend and as my President, please do something about South Africa."[115]

One reason it was difficult for Buchanan's idea to take flight was that it could hardly receive majority support on this hugely important continent, in South Africa not least. At the southern tip of Africa resided Nobel Laureate Desmond Tutu, who had become increasingly acerbic in his denunciations of the vacuous Reagan, a tendency that had become so flagrant that Carl McIntire of the International Council of Christian Churches, part of the Republicans' hardline religious base, fortified the White House by taking the time to forward an annotated list of Tutu's hardest hitting assessments.[116]

Included was a quote reportedly from Tutu, designed to inflame the Euro-American majority: "I have said before and I say it again now that I hate capitalism."[117] Tutu was becoming an object of derision among hardliners, with the Reverend Jerry Falwell of Virginia calling him a "phony."[118] D. Kent-Brown, Pretoria's Vice-Consul in New York, asked the hard-right U.S. journalist William Rusher to "investigate" him on the grounds that his "Tutu Refugee Fund" was requesting U.S. nationals "to support ANC terrorists," making him worthy of indictment.[119] The pummeling of Tutu may have made him more susceptible to persuasion. It was in 1986 that the cleric and his daughter, Naomi Tutu-Seavers, expressed their "grave concern about the growing trend in the anti-apartheid solidarity movement

---

115. Sammy Davis, Jr. to President Reagan, 13 June 1986, Box 169, WHORM, Subject Files.

116. Carl McIntire to President Reagan, 26 August 1986, Box 170, WHORM, Subject Files: Included were pages from a Tutu book with relevant passages underlined, e.g.: "white compatriots went into transports of ecstatic delight when Ronald Reagan won……anything that pleases most White South Africans cannot fail to depress most Blacks…. those feelings are not without reason……" Particularly upsetting to this correspondent was Tutu's unmasking of the myth of Pretoria's solidarity during the previous world war: "somebody needs lessons in elementary history for surely nearly everybody ought to know that certainly in World War II many Afrikaners were opposed: to U.K., U.S." and "hoped for a Nazi victory……..I no longer attend U.S. embassy functions nor do I see Reagan administration people…….the U.S. government does not really care Blacks. Poles are different. They are White……will your CIA now be out to get me?" he asked challengingly.

117. *New York Times*, 23 August 1986.

118. *New York Times*, 24 August 1985.

119. D. Kent-Brown to William Rusher, 28 February 1986, Box 84, *William Rusher Papers*.

to deny public forums to Black South Africans sympathetic to the philosophy of Black Consciousness or the [PAC]...." "These Black South Africans," they implored, "represent a legitimate and popular trend in our just struggle...."[120] Leah Tutu, on the other hand, was denounced as she allegedly "had no business traveling to this free [sic] society criticizing our ally South Africa's policy of apartheid." This was as "absurd," said the Georgia Coalition for Divestment, as the "insinuation that Leah Tutu likes communism."[121]

It was not only the Tutus who may have been influenced by the increasingly shrill anticommunism, sensing yet another defeat was in store, worsening the pain of Angola 1975. Dumi Matabane, the ANC's man in Washington, told Tambo that for FSAM "at present the demonstrations have taken a form of pure anti-apartheid expression and no commitance [sic] to a particular liberation movement. The name of our movement can hardly be heard nor one placard calling for support of our organization." He reiterated his firm refusal to share a platform with the PAC, referring to an invitation Tambo received to the National Black Leadership Roundtable from Congressman Walter Fauntroy of the Black Caucus that was to occur at Howard University Law School in March 1985.[122]

While obstinate Republicans were flaying Archbishop Tutu, they were embracing Jonas Savimbi of Angola. In February 1986 he arrived in the U.S. for a 10-day visit. It was a "major success," crowed John Fisher of the American Security Council, one of his non-governmental allies. He "held substantive talks with President Reagan, Vice President Bush, Secretary Shultz, Secretary [Casper] Weinberger [of the Pentagon] and CIA Director Casey...." He also conferred privately "with the Senate Intelligence Committee and House Foreign Affairs Committee, the Arms Control and Foreign Policy Caucus," of the Congress, the "Senate Republican leadership, the House Republican Study Committee, the Senate Steering Committee and key Democratic [Party] lawmakers" besides.[123] Rarely has a leader—let alone an African leader—been accorded such entrée

---

120. "Against Racism: Newsletter of the Ant-Racism Literature Project," May-June 1986, Box 163, *Gerald Horne Papers*. This widely circulated Tutu letter can also be found in the attached letter from L. Makhanda to "Dear Friends," 10 February 1986, Box 81, *ACOARA*.

121. *Atlanta Daily World*, 13 January 1986.

122. Dumi Matabane to "Dear Comrade Chief," 13 January 1985, Reel 10, *Oliver Tambo Papers*.

123. John Fisher to John Poindexter, 28 February 1986, Box 38, WHORM Subject File, CO Countries, CO006 Angola, *Reagan Presidential Library*.

into the U.S. political elite, an indicator of how badly Angola 1975 had stung and how determined Washington was to reverse this defeat. Moreover, given that ANC militants were being trained in Angola, overthrowing the MPLA in Luanda could also strike a blow for apartheid too. "I spent a great deal of time with Jonas Savimbi when he was here," was the blunt confession of Vice President—and former CIA Director—Bush, though this could have been said of others in the chain of command.[124] Thus, in the ultimate gesture of respect, the Angolan rode to a reception at the office of the conservative Heritage Foundation in the Secretary of State's limousine. This gesture, said Crocker, was designed to "assure Savimbi that we support him" and "will not abandon him,"[125] a refrain commonly endured by erstwhile U.S. allies, as certain Vietnamese could have attested.

But this broad base of support was insufficient. Since the U.S. had been compelled in recent decades to espouse a non-racial creed, it was embarrassing to be on the same side as Pretoria on the matter of Savimbi. More Negroes had to be recruited to provide a patina of respectability. But the Angolan's many supporters were to be sorely disappointed when his glitzy dinner at the Capital Hilton in Washington on 4 February 1986 was boycotted by a good deal of the African American leadership. Savimbi's handler, Fisher, found it "deplorable" that "members of the Congressional Black Caucus"— "these so-called black leaders", he wailed—shunned him in this alleged "free society" and refused to "debate the issues." He bumped into Randall Robinson, who "ran away" rather than engage. This was outrageous, he declaimed, since "Angola is a key to Southern Africa. Southern Africa is a key to Africa" and "Africa is a key to Europe," still the site of massive U.S. direct foreign investment. Thus, in 1978 "during the MPLA sponsored Shaba War, the price of cobalt," a necessary component of emerging technologies, "went up three, four and five times." It was this almost hysterical concern with Angola that led to the collapse of détente and a renewed push to overthrow the Soviet Union, which was to be achieved a scant five years later.[126]

124. George H.W. Bush to Congressman Jim Courter, 15 March 1986, Box 16, WHORM Subject Files, CO 001 Cont.-GEO. Areas, *Reagan Presidential Library*.

125. Chester Crocker to Secretary of State Shultz, 6 February 1986, in Kenneth Mokoena, ed., *South Africa and the United States: The Declassified History*, New York: New Press, 1993, 293-294.

126. Memorandum by John Fisher, 4 February 1986, Box 38, WHORM, Subject File, CO Countries, CO 006 Angola, *Reagan Presidential Library*.

The ultra-right was fixated on the point that socialist encroachment in Africa was jeopardizing Europe. John Davenport of New Jersey—a former editor at both *Barron's* and *Fortune,* both essential reading on Wall Street—fabricated when he said that "according to Lenin the road to the communization of Europe lay through the heart of Africa."[127]

The rationale for treating this supposed problem with Savimbi was threadbare. If Angola—and Mozambique and Zimbabwe— "ceased being Marxist [sic]," said right-wing ideologue John Lenczowski, and ditched their "strong sympathies for the Communist ANC," then Pretoria "would no longer feel as threatened." "How could this come about?" he asked rhetorically. "Supporting the anticommunist resistance in Angola" was the critical first step.[128]

Counter-revolutionary Washington had an embarrassment of riches in its ultimately failed attempt to overthrow the MPLA in Luanda. Addressing Congress in 1986, shortly after Savimbi's departure from Washington, Stan Atkinson said, "I have covered insurgents and counter-insurgents in [Indochina]" but "other than the Cambodian resistance—specifically the KPNLF, the Khmer People's National Liberation Front," the recently ousted genocidal Khmer Rouge, backed by China and the U.S.—"I have never seen resistance forces as well-disciplined militarily" as the FNLA of Holden Roberto,[129] not Savimbi's UNITA. Roberto, whose roots in the U.S. were deeper than Savimbi's, reaped the benefit of these ties, including a warm relationship with Israel. According to Moshe Leshem, the former chief Israeli diplomat in Kinshasa, "a number of Angolans came to Israel to be trained" and were "furnished some equipment.... Holden Roberto visited with me in Copenhagen," while he was Israeli ambassador in Denmark.[130]

Savimbi's father was an evangelical pastor, which allowed him to win the confidence and support of the proliferating conservative Christian constituencies in Texas, Louisiana, Oklahoma, and Dixie generally. "He was riding high in those friendly environments," said

---

127. John Davenport, "The Freeman," August 1985, Box 85, *Freedom House Archives, Princeton University.*

128. John Lenczowski to Robert McFarlane, 26 September 1985, Box 16 [Box 8], AAD, RAC, *Reagan Presidential Library.*

129. Testimony of Stan Atkinson, "The Struggle for Freedom in Angola," Hearing Before the Task Force on Foreign Affairs, Republican Study Committee, U.S. House of Representatives, 10 April 1986, Box 11, OA 16258 16591, *Carl Anderson Files, Reagan Presidential Library.*

130. Testimony of Moshe Leshem, in Ibid., "The Struggle for Freedom in Angola," 10 April 1986.

Herman Cohen, an African specialist in the State Department. "All" of his movements in the U.S., said Cohen, "were professionally coordinated by American lobbying firms financed by South Africa...."[131]

As Israel went, increasingly so did the growingly influential organized Jewish-American community. Max Fisher of the National Jewish Coalition weighed in as the sanctions bill proceeded. "As Jews," he told Senator Bob Dole of Kansas, a future Republican presidential nominee, "our concern" was that the "resolution of South Africa's problems be peaceful," since this benighted land was "home to 118,000 Jews whose future under a government controlled or dominated by the ANC would be bleak,"[132] neatly eliding the presence of Slovo and a raft of others of Jewish heritage in the ranks of the left. Ignoring these figures, Nathan Perlmutter and David Evanier of the Anti-Defamation League took a "closer look" at the ANC and concluded that "the fall of South Africa to such a Soviet-oriented and Communist influenced force would be a severe setback,"[133] presumably to anticommunism and U.S. imperialism. "The pro-Israel community is very opposed to the amendment to the South African sanctions bill," said Max Green, "that would cut off aid to those countries which the president certifies are in violation of the international arms embargo of South Africa", a proviso that would ensnare Israel. But symptomatic of the strength of the anti-apartheid movement was Green's admonition that "opposition would probably take the form of quite quiet lobbying."[134] Again and again, the National Jewish Coalition returned to the issue of "118,000 Jews whose future under a government controlled or dominated by the ANC would be bleak" since "many radical blacks in South Africa have already exhibited hostility towards South Africa's Jews...."[135] (Green need not have worried about the arms embargo

---

131. Herman Cohen, *The Mind of the African Strongman: Conversations with Dictators, Statesmen and Father Figures*, Washington, D.C.: New Academia, 2015, 143

132. Max Fisher to Senator Dole, 30 September 1986, Box 6, Series 1, Subject Files, *Katherine Chumachenko Files, Reagan Presidential Library.*

133. Nathan Perlmutter and David Evanier, "The African National Congress: A Closer Look," *ADL Bulletin*, 43 (Number 5, May 1986): 1, Box 23, Series II, Subject Files, *Max Green Files, Reagan Presidential Library.*

134. Max Green to Patrick Buchanan, 12 September 1986, Box 168, WHORM, Subject Files.

135. R.J. Fox, M.M. Fisher and Gordon Zacks to Senator Bob Dole, 10 September 1986, Box 171, WHORM, Subject Files.

since it was hedged with qualifications and primarily symbolic.)[136] The Anti-Defamation League was staunchly anticommunist and was displeased when ANC speakers appeared at events sponsored by the U.S. Communist Party,[137] a not infrequent occurrence. Thus, sabotaging the sanctions bill was a must.

Left unmentioned was what a Florida newspaper later revealed. Sited in the northern part of the state was "Tadiran," an Israeli company that had a lucrative contract supplying military radios to Pretoria and would have been impacted significantly by a sanctions bill.[138] Already this relationship had attracted the dedicated attention of activists.[139] Speaking of Tallahassee, a local paper termed the presence of this company to be the "city's shame."[140] Soon Koor—the entity that included Tadiran—was seeking a bailout from Israel, as pressure mounted against their tie to Pretoria.[141]

Buchanan, who had been accused of anti-Semitism, was a critical force mobilizing pro-Zionist sentiment against sanctioning apartheid. After the Republican leader Senator Richard Lugar "clopped us across the face" in backing the sanctions bill, the White House aide thought he had a weapon with which to clop him back. "As the sanctions bill requires us to cut off aid to any country making military sales to South Africa," he announced with confidence, "this will bring us the all-out support of the Jewish Coalition—and perhaps even the quiet support of AIPAC,"[142] the major pro-Israel lobby.

Undeterred, Fisher's line was pushed by the pro-Israel lobby in order to derail sanctions against apartheid. Also, part of this phalanx was the American Israel Public Affairs Committee, which sent its well-connected top leaders to "lobby in person," according to Max Green. The Anti-Defamation League of B'nai B'rith sent Dave Brody to "visit key Senators." Zulu chauvinist Gatsha Buthelezi and novelist Alan Paton "might visit" too "to make certain [they are] not typecast as creatures from the far right...." Also enlisted in this ground

136. William Minter, "Destructive Engagement: The United States and South Africa in the Reagan Era," in Phyllis Johnson and David Martin, eds., *Destructive Engagement: Southern Africa at War*, Harare: Zimbabwe Publishing House, 1986, 281-320, 284.

137. *ADL Bulletin*, May 1986, Box 10, *Gwendolen Carter Papers*.

138. *Tallahassee Democrat*, 11 May 1988.

139. *Tallahassee Democrat*, 20 September 1988.

140. *Florida Flambeau*, 21 September 1988.

141. *New York Times*, 22 October 1988.

142. Patrick Buchanan to Donald Regan, 13 September 1986, Box 170, WHORM, Subject Files.

force were elements from the AFL-CIO (U.S. labor movement) and the wickedly pro-Israel Washington journal *The New Republic*.[143]

Buthelezi was joining Savimbi as a favored African in Washington. The increasingly forgetful Reagan remembered to tell the Zulu leader that he "appreciated your support" for his pro-apartheid policy, "which I believe is similar in some ways to our own."[144] Responding, Buthelezi saluted the alleged "great compassion and statesmanship" of his correspondent while emphasizing the "urgency of releasing Dr. Nelson Mandela…."[145] One White House aide called Buthelezi "a friend" who "enjoyed my columns on Bishop Tutu," reproaching the cleric severely.[146]

Reciprocating, John Hutchinson of the University of California-Los Angeles contacted William Casey of the CIA and demanded funding for the "Inkatha Labor Federation," tied to Buthelezi, along with the United Workers Union of South Africa. He assailed the ANC-SACP allied Congress of South Africa Trade Unions. "I have had many international telephone conversations with South Africans since I was last there in 1985" and thought this money would be more than helpful. Dropping names, he referenced "Bill Buckley," patron saint of modern conservatism, to substantiate his good faith. This funding was needed since he found a "note of desperation" in Pretoria "that was not there even just a year ago"—it "reminds me of…Rhodesia," a troubling sign. Perhaps "partition" of South Africa was the way out, with a band of territory stretching from Cape Town to the Mozambican border with "whites on the west side (embracing Johannesburg and the gold fields)" with all others left with the remains. The alternative, he warned Casey, was "carnage and a Soviet subsidiary…."[147]

It was then that William Rusher, one of Buckley's closest comrades, made his seventh trip to South Africa in recent years, finding this one "easily the most informative" of all. He "did not see a cloud

---

143. Max Green to Mari Maseng, 24 September 1986, Box 6, Series 1, Subject Files, *Katherine Chumachenko Files*.

144. President Reagan to Gatsha Buthelezi, 15 August 1986, Box 169, WHORM, Subject Files.

145. Gatsha Buthelezi to President Reagan, 11 July 1986, Box 169, WHORM, Subject Files.

146. Phillip Ringdahl to John Poindexter, 21 November 1986, Box 170, WHORM, Subject Files.

147. John Hutchinson to William Casey, 28 September 1986, Box 171, WHORM, Subject Files. See also Ray S. Cline and Yonah Alexnder, *Terrorism: The Soviet Connection*, New York: Crane Russak, 1984: Highlighted here are ANC and SWAPO ties to Moscow.

in the sky during my entire stay," he enthused, and was so energized he made a personal donation to an apartheid propaganda arm.[148] But it would take more than handouts from reactionaries to stem apartheid's steady erosion.

Republicans were scrambling to find Africans who would join the anti-sanctions parade. One Republican, battling amnesia, sought to recall a "Bishop who led millions of Black South Africans" and "was strongly opposed to sanctions" and could not "recall his name"—was it "Moreno or Moranerema?" After consulting the South African legation, the message was transmitted that he may have been thinking of "Bishop Barnabas Lekganyane, head of the Zion Christian Church," or maybe it was "Isaac Mokoena."[149]

Not on board with the anti-sanctions movement was Richard Trumka of the Mine Workers Union, who reminded the White House that "in the past you have spoken out forcefully on behalf of...Solidarity in Poland," the anticommunist union that was essential to the destabilization of socialism in Eastern Europe. "I strongly urge you to do the same for these black mineworkers,"[150] but Trumka must have known that there was a distinct difference between support for the destabilizing of socialism and the destabilizing of apartheid.

While the MPLA leadership was being eviscerated, President Samora Machel of Mozambique visited the White House, but this only fomented rifts in the Republican Party elite, some of whom thought he should be toppled, not wooed. Dana Rohrbacher, who had served as a speechwriter for the faux articulate Reagan, was seething about the "departure statement" made by the president as the Mozambican leader was leaving Washington.[151] As sanctions were in the process of being imposed against Pretoria, more blows were raining down on Maputo. Pretoria was expelling Mozambican expatriate workers, endangering the Mozambican economy, and MNR "appears to have put the regime in jeopardy." "There is talk," the White House was told, "of Machel calling for East Bloc

---

148. William Rusher to Helga De Beer, Director, Southern Africa Forum, 11 March 1985, Box 150, *William Rusher Papers, Library of Congress.*

149. *Reuters*, 13 August 1986, Box 3, OA 13157, *Thomas Gibson Files, Reagan Presidential Library.*

150. Richard Trumka to President Reagan, 14 January 1986, Box 23, Series II, Subject Files, *Max Green Files, Ronald Reagan Presidential Library.*

151. Dana Rohrbacher to Patrick Buchanan, 19 September 1985, Box 133, WHORM, CO Countries, CO 108, Mozambique, *Reagan Presidential Library.*

intervention."[152] It seemed Maputo's choice was to either weather regime change or endure more terrorist attacks.

It would not be easy for Buchanan to find African American adherents for this artificially derived cause. In fact, White House aide John Poindexter was told there was "potential for U.S. Blacks to become radicalized by events" in Southern Africa.[153] Buchanan, the conduit to the hardliners seeking to overthrow FRELIMO, acknowledged that the chosen vessel for this onerous task, the so-called Mozambican National Resistance [MNR or RENAMO], was "not the Army of Northern Virginia in terms of gallantry toward its enemies," an arcane reference to the alleged "gallantry" of a group who fought to preserve the enslavement of Africans; what mattered was that "they are assuredly anti-Communist and anti-Soviet...."[154] But the hardliners were difficult to satisfy: Congressmen Dan Burton, Vin Weber, Duncan Hunter, and "four or five others" were upset with U.S. policy toward these Lusophone nations: this was the word passed to Chief of Staff Donald Regan.[155] Senator Malcolm Wallop was among those who demanded overt—not covert—aid to MNR.[156]

Senator Wallop was noticeably hyperactive, joining with segregationist Senator Strom Thurmond of South Carolina in trying to get $50 million in military aid for UNITA simultaneously.[157] Chester Crocker said accurately that these terrorists and bandits had access to the highest levels of the White House and the Pentagon.[158] And the opprobrious term "bandit" was not rhetorical excess, as even the U.S. ambassador in Mozambique denounced MNR in this fashion.[159]

Anne Evens of Chicago thought similarly. This activist worked in Mozambique in the 1980s, building schools and clinics and working

152. Patrick Buchanan to President Reagan, 17 October 1986, Box 170, WHORM, Subject Files.

153. Helen E. Soos to John Poindexter, 7 February 1986, Box 173, WHORM, Subject Files.

154. Patrick Buchanan to Chief of Staff, 30 September 1985, Box 133, WHORM, CO Countries, CO 108, Mozambique, *Reagan Presidential Library*.

155. Max Friedersdorf and M.B. Oglesby to Donald Regan, 8 October 1985, Box 133, WHORM, CO Countries, CO 108, Mozambique.

156. Senator Malcolm Wallop to James Dyer, 19 March 1986, Box 133, WHORM, CO Countries, CO 108, Mozambique.

157. Strom Thurmond to Neal Blair, 15 January 1986, CMS 1986, Box 023, *Strom Thurmond Papers, Clemson University*. See also "Angola's Struggle for Victory Over Communism.... Special Report from the Conservative Caucus Foundation...." Vienna, Virginia, circa 1985, *University of Kansas-Lawrence*.

158. Chester Crocker, *High Noon in Southern Africa*, 338.

159. Iain Christie, *Samora Machel*, 115.

on road and water projects; "latrines" were a specialty. She studied the local language and conferred "many times" with Graca Machel, a leader in her own right in addition to being the spouse of FRELIMO's leader. Yes, it was "challenging" and "stressful," she conceded later, as well as "sad" and "scary." In Manica province, where travel often involved military personnel with guns— "kind of like Chicago," she said half-joking—one could easily "hear shooting pretty often" because of banditry.[160]

By May 1986, there was dancing in the suites of the White House when an MRN office was opened in Washington. An unnamed "American who was recently with [Afonso] Dhklama [of MNR] in his jungle sanctuary is the chief organizer…." Though he had been swept out of office in 1980, Ian Smith was en route to Washington, and "in anticipation of his visit has had meetings"[161] with Botha and, presumably, Dhklama too.

The purveyor of this message, Thomas Schaaf, was also known as Tom Curran and worked for Salisbury at the highest level as late as 1978 before leaving Zimbabwe hurriedly in 1986. He worked closely with Luis Serapiao, the MNR's man in Washington, who was also based at Howard University. They were joined by James Blanchard, an affluent Louisiana businessman who donated tens of thousands of dollars to the cause, and Robert MacKenzie—also surnamed McKenna—who served with Salisbury's armed forces in the 1970s and by the mid-1980s was in and out of Mozambique surreptitiously and was tied in turn to Senator Jesse Helms of North Carolina.[162] Adopting a mask, Schaaf was portrayed to the inquiring *Washington Post* not as a representative for Mozambican bandits but a delegate of the apparently more high-minded "Mozambique Research Center," "of which I am chairman," said Neal Blair, who also served as Chairman of the Agency for International Freedom.[163]

Finally, in the Fall of 1986 Samora Machel died—perhaps killed—in a suspicious plane crash on South African territory after his experienced pilot sailed into a mountain range, apparently misdirected by a deceitful beacon— "downed 200 yards within South African territory," according to the Reverend Jesse Jackson, who was among

160. Oral History, Anne Evens, 4 May 2009, *Columbia College-Chicago*.

161. Thomas Schaaf to Patrick Buchanan, 5 June 1986, Box 169, WHORM, Subject Files.

162. Alex Vines, *RENAMO: From Terrorism to Democracy in Mozambique?* London: James Currey, 1991, 43, 44.

163. Neal Blair to "Washington Post," 11 November 1987, Box 133, WHORM, Co Countries, CO 108, Mozambique, *Reagan Presidential Library*.

the mourners at his funeral. Upon his return, Jackson warned the enfeebled Reagan that "another major trauma like the death of President Machel could turn Southern Africa into another Lebanon." He found "circumstantial evidence" to be "mounting" of "South Africa's involvement in the plane crash." He was disturbed by the "absence of any American foreign policy official at the funeral," the latest insult to Maputo. This was "perceived by many in Southern Africa," said the respected pastor, "to be a 'non-interference' move with respect to South Africa's policy of military aggression,"[164] a reasonable inference. Jackson, who had come to know Machel as they bonded over their mutual interest in pugilism, was shaken by his death.[165]

A scholar who examined this tragic death wrote that "I realized that it was no accident." To discredit the idea that it was an assassination, Pretoria screened a documentary "narrated by an American accented voice," said Daniel Douek, presumably to lend missing gravitas. A "portable beacon" diverted the plane maliciously, a tactic "widely used by the Americans in the Vietnam War and elsewhere." This was the final insult heaped on Machel and Mozambique, following his 1985 Washington visit, where officialdom ignored his immense documentation of Pretoria's support for the terrorist MNR. Instead, he was pressured to compromise with these outlaws and to increase cooperation with the U.S.-dominated World Bank and its thieving companion, the International Monetary Fund, entailing the enhanced privatizing of public goods like health care and education.[166] His death, said Chester Crocker, led to a "mounting surge of right wing sabotage against our Mozambique policy," which was already in tatters.[167]

The ability of imperialism and its agents to rampage in the subregion was invigorating them further. Congressman Butler Derricks of South Carolina was told by a constituent that he "learned…that South Africa had more than 50 advanced type of nuclear weapons," and he had "talked to at least three men in public office who had contact with South African troops in Korea in World War II [sic] and

164. Reverend Jesse Jackson to President Reagan, 6 November 1986, Box 133, WHORM CO Countries, CO 108, Mozambique.

165. Iain Christie, *Samora Machel*, 167.

166. Daniel L. Douek, "New Light on the Samora Machel Assassination: 'I Realized that it was no Accident,'" *Third World Quarterly*, (2017): 1.21, 11, 17. See also *New Times* [Moscow], Number 25, 1987, Box 181, *Gerald Horne Papers*: a "false radio beacon" from South Africa brought down Machel's plane.

167. Chester Crocker, *High Noon in Southern Africa*, 330.

they made a statement that these South Africans will wipe out those Blacks entirely if we are not careful...."[168]

Machel's death was a victory for apartheid and its U.S. supporters, which included a good deal of the ruling Republican Party. It was an unfortunate punctuation to the Nkomati Accord whereby Maputo thought it had a deal with Pretoria in which the expulsion of ANC militants would lead to a cessation of the war against FRELIMO. This momentous pact, it was said by Charles Hill of the U.S. National Security Council, was taken "after a great deal of American prodding" and was, therefore, a "severe setback for Soviet policies."[169] Ostensibly, what was driving U.S. imperialism in the sub-region was the fear of socialist—and Soviet—advance. This Botha knew well, and it doubtlessly informed his 1986 proposal to free Mandela if Moscow freed so-called dissidents, e.g. Natan Sharansky and Andrei Sakharov.[170]

But this desperate ploy by Pretoria was doomed—like apartheid itself; just another reminder that sanctions were beginning to bite into the meaty flesh of this system of cruelty.

---

168. Hugh Beasley to Congressman Derricks, 17 September 1985, Box 26, *Butler Derricks Papers, University of South Carolina-Columbia.*

169. Charles Hill to Robert McFarlane, 13 March 1984, Box 4, Executive Secretariat, NSC, Country File, Africa, S. Africa, *Reagan Presidential Library.*

170. *Los Angeles Times,* 1 February 1986.

Chapter 21

Endgame, 1987-1990

WASHINGTON hardliners were apoplectic. Oliver Tambo, who was thought only recently to be the head of a Communist-dominated "terrorist" organization—a "tool" of Moscow, no less—was being entertained at the highest levels in Washington. Those who were upset found it hard to swallow that combined pressure from anti-apartheid activists—especially in South Africa, which had made the nation ungovernable—and soaring anxiety on Wall Street about Pretoria's debt, along with ample backing from the Frontline States and the socialist camp, had compelled U.S. imperialism to finally acknowledge reality. But never-say-die Washington did not surrender altogether; it continued to contribute to the slow walk to Namibian freedom by stressing the unrelated matter of Cuban troops in Angola, while turning up the heat on the socialist camp, which paid off in 1989 when these Eastern European regimes began to crumble.

Adroitly, it was that moment when Pretoria chose to negotiate with an ANC, which was not as strong as it appeared in light of the incipient crumbling of one of its chief bases of support. By 2001, Kader Asmal, one of the shrewdest of ANC leaders, observed that "anybody who says that the apartheid house was a pack of cards which...will fall down at the slightest touch is suffering from amnesia, political amnesia." Yes, the Nationalists did "know they were going to lose power" in negotiations, "but they were still going to fight." The ANC, on the other hand, "didn't have an intelligence force" to "prepare analyses of the weaknesses of the government's negotiating position," nor did many of their allies.[1]

But in 1987 none of this was apparently on the horizon. Robert L. Monaghan, president of the Cal-Mon Oil Company in Midland, Texas—where Vice President George H.W. Bush had augmented his inherited fortune—was among the legions who were terribly upset.

---

1. Oral History, Kader Asmal, 5 July 2001, *University of Connecticut-Storrs.*

"Having served as your Regional Chairman in 1976, 1980 and 1984 for most of the West Texas area," he told the often forgetful Reagan, "I am not a bomb throwing right wing radical," he unconvincingly contended. He remained irate about the meeting between Tambo and Secretary of State Shultz.[2]

He was not alone. B. Franklin Reinauer II had a "mutual friend" with the White House's Admiral John Poindexter in "Ron Marryott who is currently President of the Naval War College," a major military think tank. Reinauer had the "honor of being President of the Naval War College Foundation." His imperialist credentials confirmed, he moved swiftly to the main point. He had just spent six weeks in South Africa and was angry about the meeting with Tambo. Why, he sputtered, dealing with this gentle, bespectacled leader "would [be] like dealing with [Ayatollah] Khomeni when he was in Paris…." Going further, he wondered querulously "why Mandela was not executed instead of imprisoned is a puzzlement," adding futilely "he should not be released from prison." Though, he said on second thought, doing so could mean a "struggle for leadership" and internecine conflict. He seemed even more upset with the "young radicals" spearheading the divestment movement on campus,[3] a movement so profound that the mainstream *New York Times* found it difficult to ignore.[4]

Since the CIA had reportedly hired South African pilots to fly aid to the so-called "contras" in Central America,[5] it was hard for those like Reinauer to turn a cold shoulder to Pretoria. In response, in 1987 the Farabundi Marti Liberation Front of El Salvador met in Luanda—after having convened in Harare—and issued a joint statement with liberation forces.[6]

The growing relationship between the conflicts in Central America and Southern Africa was exposed further when Bob Brister of St. Petersburg, Florida was at a warehouse in Tampa loading a container destined for Nicaraguan victims of the contra war. There, he said, "I discovered huge rolls of newsprint from South Africa bound for the *St. Petersburg Times*," a major player in the regional discourse

2. Robert L. Monaghan to President Reagan, 22 January 1987, Box 172, WHORM, Subject Files, *Reagan Presidential Library*.

3. B. Franklin Reinauer to Admiral Poindexter, 30 June 1986, Box 9. 10 [Box 3] African Affairs Directorate, *Reagan Presidential Library*.

4. *New York Times*, 2 February 1986.

5. *Sydney Morning Herald*, 29 January 1987.

6. Joint Statement, November 1987, Reel 7, *Oliver Tambo Papers*.

on apartheid and, thereby, compromised[7]—despite adamant denials from the paper and even the original accuser.[8]

Herman Cohen, who was to play a vanguard role in shaping U.S. policy toward Africa, also found "considerable opposition to the planned meeting because the ANC is heavily infiltrated by Communists…." He asked plaintively, "do we work with the black nationalists in the organization to help them get rid of Communists," a familiar stratagem in Washington, abroad and at home. He thought there was a "lot of tension between the Communists (many of whom are whites) and the black nationalist factions" that could be manipulated. "Black nationalists like Tambo"—a confusing designation at best— "need our help in eventually defeating the Communists," he concluded uneasily.[9]

The intelligence community did not seem to be pleased by the meeting with Tambo either. "The Soviets identify the ANC as the leading opposition organization," it was announced sternly in February 1987, and "provide virtually all of its military supplies and much of its training. The ANC is Moscow's primary long-term ally in South Africa"[10] and now was being courted by Washington in the face of even sterner opposition from the Pretoria ally.

Conceding to reality, Buchanan sought to blunt the effects of this Tambo-Shultz confab by arranging a meeting with what he called the "anti-ANC prelate," Bishop Isaac Mokoena. This "would send an excellent message," he told Frank Carlucci, whose shenanigans in Africa stretched back to the murder of Lumumba and now extended to his current tour of duty in the Pentagon.[11]

If the intelligence community had been able to scrutinize Tambo's correspondence, their most dire and febrile fears would have been realized. In early 1987 he made an "urgent request" to the Central Committee of the Soviet Communist Party "for a group of 4 or 5 of our comrades to be given an intensive 2-3 months course of training in Military Combat Work…with specialization in intelligence." He

---

7. Bob Brister to the Editor, 17 November 1988, Box Atlanta Regional Office Southern Africa Peace Education Program, *AFSC*.

8. Bob Brister to Mr. Barnes, 5 December 1988, Box: Atlanta Regional Office Southern Africa Peace Education Program, *AFSC*.

9. Herman Cohen to "VADM Donald S. Jones, USN," 20 January 1987, Box 9, 10 [Box 3], African Affairs Directorate, NSC Records, RAC.

10. Special National Intelligence Estimate, "Prospects for South Africa: Stability, Reform and Violence," Circa 6 February 1987, Box 9, 10[Box 3], African Affairs Directorate, NSC Records, RAC.

11. Patrick Buchanan to Frank Carlucci, 22 January 1987, Box 173, WHORM, Subject Files.

did not stint in giving "thanks to the training being currently given to a group [of]...cadres in response to the request we submitted in November 1986."[12] Writing from Lusaka, Chris Hani (the leader of the ANC's armed wing) informed Alfred Nzo, the group's overall Secretary General, that he was "keen to have services of...7...Soviet specialists on" various subjects including "Propaganda." He was en route to Angola "to discuss with the Party and Government... the continued rendering of services by Soviet specialists to the Movement...."[13] Hani's enhanced profile had been marked when unnamed intelligence agents sought to besmirch his reputation by accusing him of trying to build "his own Xhosa army."[14]

In Angola Hani would have been pleased to see the wreckage of Pretoria's ambitious plans. In the preceding months of 1988 the Cuban forces and their Southern African allies unleashed a withering defeat for Pretoria at Cuito Cuanavale, which turned the tide in favor of liberation. Cuban pilots flying MIG-23 fighter jets of Soviet make proved to be decisive, further angering hawks in Washington. Israel denied that it was fighting alongside the apartheid military; others were not so sure.[15] Whatever the case, it was downhill from here for apartheid with Namibian independence becoming more likely and the ouster of the humbled Nationalist Party veritably assured.

As Cuban troops were administering hammer blows against apartheid forces, the United Democratic Front and other forces in South Africa were busily undermining Pretoria. Thus, as Cuito Cuanavale was determining the destiny of the sub-region, in the Transvaal, Popo Molefe, "Terror" Lekota, and other comrades were on trial. Part of the bill of indictment was that the ANC reportedly termed the "Reagan Administration" as "firmly and unequivocally among the bandit forces that are conducting a reign of terror throughout Africa." Cited were the "criminal invasion of Grenada, the undeclared war against Nicaragua," and other misdeeds. "We heard evidence from various witnesses," it was said at trial, "that ANC recruits are taught the principles of Marxism"[16]—and yet, official Washington was now conferring with the ANC at the highest level.

12. Oliver Tambo to Central Committee of Soviet Communist Party, 19 March 1987, Reel 7, *Oliver Tambo Papers*.

13. Chris Hani to Alfred Nzo, 3 October 1989, Reel 7, *Oliver Tambo Papers*.

14. "Insider," no date, Box 181, *Gerald Horne Papers*.

15. Namibia Information Service, 6 June 1988, Box 163, *Gerald Horne Papers*.

16. Trial Transcript, 1988, Box 1, *South Africa Conspiracy Trial Case Papers, New York Public Library-Schomburg Center*.

Indicative of the alignment of forces, in early 1987 SACP Chairman Dan Tloome wrote "Dear Comrade Tambo," making a "formal request" that Joe Slovo, now General Secretary of the SACP, be accorded a "release...from his functions as Chief of Staff of Umkhonto we Sizwe," the ANC's armed wing ("his association with our People's Army," it was added with relish, "began on the very day of its foundation....")[17]

Cubans, often armed by Moscow, were better known for their combat role in the sub-region but—congruent with Hani's prioritizing of "Propaganda"—Barbara Masekela, now stationed in Lusaka, wanted authorization in 1987 for Cuban filmmakers to make a film on South Africa.[18] Soon, with the advent of perestroika and glasnost in Moscow, such requests would receive short shrift, allowing Pretoria to seize the time and embark on negotiations with a weakened foe.

But it was not just the ANC. Andimba Toivo ya Toivo noted that SWAPO cadre, like Abel S. Haluteni, received military training in the Soviet Union. Maxton J. Mutongolume, on the other hand, received military training in China. Johannes Otto Nankudhu received his military training in the Soviet Union and returned with a group of guerillas in 1965 to fight the occupiers. Leonard Philemon, called "Castro," also received his military training thanks to Moscow, as did Messag Victory and Lazarus Shakala; while Ngarikutuke Tjiriange studied law in the Soviet Union and became Namibia's first Minister of Justice.[19]

Niel Barnard, Pretoria's spy chief—while noting ruefully that "numbers of aspirant spies from the ANC were trained by the Stasi," East German intelligence—pointed out that a "high level secret communications channel" was opened with Moscow by early 1988 and actual talks began by May. The ANC, he said, did not have the "military capability to overthrow" his regime, and once Moscow began pressing Angola for a settlement—where the ANC had important bases—Tambo's forces were weakened further. In any case, says Barnard, he had "numerous sources within the ANC," which made his task simpler.[20]

---

17. Dan Tloome to Tambo, 10 February 1987, Reel 19, *Oliver Tambo Papers*.

18. Barbara Masekela to Administrative Secretary of Politico-Military Council, 6 January 1987, Reel 7, *Oliver Tambo Papers*.

19. Andimba Toivo ya Toivo, *On Trial for My Country*, 263, 278, 284-287, 292, 284.

20. NIel Barnard, *Secret Revolution: Memoirs of a Spy Boss*, Cape Town: Tafelberg, 2015, 85, 92, 106.

It was not just the ANC that was penetrated: Thomas Joseph Dolce of Maryland admitted to espionage on behalf of Pretoria for ideological and not monetary reasons.[21] When a Highway Patrol Superintendent in Ohio, Jack Walsh, was fired after a junket in South Africa, it was not clear if he was in a category like Dolce's.[22]

Whatever the case, illicit ties between Pretoria and Washington did not seem to be diminishing as the turning point of February 1990 approached, when Mandela was freed and the ANC and SACP unbanned. In late 1988 three U.S. nationals were arrested for importing AK-47 machine guns from South Africa, while three South Africans were also charged, two of whom lived in Namibia and were part of the South African military fighting in Angola. They were also selling the products of endangered species, including rhino horns and leopard mounts.[23]

But as Barnard sensed when talks were opened with Moscow, serious changes were afoot that would eventuate with the collapse of the Soviet Union. It was in July 1989 when SACP leader Jack Simons reached Tambo from Lusaka with a disturbing report on "new Soviet thinking about South Africa." In pointed remarks, Dr. Viteley Vasilkov raised worrisome questions about Moscow's sole support for the ANC, terming this "unilateral and narrow." It supposedly "scares away whites and blacks," he said. In fact, U.S. imperialism's gambit of aligning with religious zealots to drain Moscow in Afghanistan was working to the extent that a rattled Soviet Union was being forced to reassess what had been thought to be fundamental precepts.[24]

Republican Congressmen were furious nevertheless, seemingly not understanding the forces at play: the spreading unrest in South Africa; the specter of Cuban troops just across the border, which had been haunting Washington since 1975; the uncontrollable campus divestment movement boosted by organized labor; and the nervous bankers. Instead, Congressmen Jack Kemp, Dan Burton, Jim Courter, and Robert Livingston, whined that Washington's "policy has gone astray in Southern Africa." They cited the words of Winnie Mandela in Moscow's *Pravda*, where she was quoted as saying that the "Soviet

21. *Washington Post*, 12 October 1988.

22. *Washington Times*, 17 May 1989; *New York Times*, 17 May 1989.

23. Department of Justice Press Release, 3 November 1988, Box 175, WHORM, CO 141, South Africa, 59200 and CO 143 Namibia, *Reagan Presidential Library*.

24. Jack Simons to Oliver Tambo, 1 July 1989, Reel 5, *Oliver Tambo Papers*. See the column by Henry Richardson: *Philadelphia Inquirer*, 25 June 1988.

Union is the torchbearer for all our hopes and aspirations." The outraged legislators demanded overt backing for MNR in response. "Nowhere has U.S. foreign policy strayed so far from your expressed beliefs as in Africa,"[25] they irritably informed the addled Reagan.

The White House could have objected to this line with good reason since, after all, they did not seek to halt massive ultra-right support to MNR, a tack consistent with their line of privatizing of governmental functions. In 1988 the Quaker investigator Carole Collins uncovered "involvement of right-wing religious groups" from the U.S., "many with conservative political agendas openly hostile to the Marxist FRELIMO." Indeed, "some groups, based in the U.S... have been suspected of using their religious status as a cover for pro-MNR activities. One former missionary who worked in Zimbabwe for many years, Tom Schaaf," a confederate of Patrick Buchanan in the White House, "now heads the Mozambique Information Office in Washington" and "claims to represent the MNR."[26] Neighboring Malawi, she said, was crawling with right-wing religious activity, symbolized by the Blantyre Christian Center, which was "set up four years ago" and was "known to have helped arrange visits by right-wing Americans, journalists and others to RENAMO [MNR] held areas...." In addition to Schaaf, others assisted by the BCC included Jack Wheeler and Robert MacKenzie "of the mercenary magazine 'Soldier of Fortune.'" MacKenzie, a veteran of the war in Vietnam and former officer in the Rhodesian and South African special forces, then headed "Freedom Inc." while Wheeler ran the "Freedom Research Foundation...."[27]

The supposed gap that separated ultra-right versus mainline right-wing Republicans was disappearing rapidly under the heat of pressure from the anti-apartheid movement and African banditry alike, a point validated when Senator Bob Dole of Kansas was won over by MNR, which helped to bring along Bruce Fein, a conservative attorney who became a lobbyist for MNR.[28] Though it may have merely been a switch from extreme hardliners to simple hardliners, it was then that MNR apparently endured a leadership change, "with the

---

25. Jack Kemp, et.al. to President Reagan, 9 April 1987, Box 9, 10 [Box 3], African Affairs Directorate, NSC Records, RAC, *Reagan Presidential Library*.

26. Carole Collins, "Mozambique: Rebuilding Amidst War", 20-30 June 1988, Box: ID Africa-S/ Afr-IAP, *AFSC*.

27. Carole Collins to Ed Reed, 12 November 1989, Box: ID Africa Administration Africa-E Africa-S, *AFSC*.

28. Alex Vines, *RENAMO: From Terrorism to Democracy in Mozambique?* London: James Currey, 1991, 48, 72.

blessing of the CIA," according to FRELIMO, wresting "control of the MNR from the South African military to help clean up its image"[29]—not necessarily its reality. Another alleged beacon of liberty was the International Freedom Foundation, deemed by one left-wing analyst as the "most reactionary and aggressive right wing think tank" of all, though their competitors would have dissented. IFF too was closely associated with Pretoria, and Jack Abramoff—soon to epitomize the essence of Washington scandal and money-grubbing—was part of the Board of Directors.[30] During the 1980s there were repeated attempts to supply official U.S. aid to MNR.[31]

The U.S. televangelist Jimmy Swaggart was quite popular in South Africa, controlling a large office and what was called a "spiritual supermarket" in Johannesburg. South African Broadcasting transmitted his program. Pat Robertson, yet another member of this growing fraternity of huckster pastors, was also a force in South Africa.[32] The religious right was closely connected in turn to a growing corps of Negro conservatives that included Clarence Thomas—soon to be appointed to the U.S. Supreme Court, he was then on the board of the "Lincoln Review," edited and founded by Jay Parker, a paid agent of Pretoria who was Thomas's mentor and a member of the board of the World Anti-Communist League, which was obsessed with Moscow and its presumed surrogates, e.g. the SACP.[33] MNR's Dhklama was pictured holding a copy of the *Aida Parker Newsletter*, a journal of these bitterly anticommunist forces—indicating the deepening of a Reactionary Black International, augured years ago by Max Yergan's break with Robeson and endorsement of Pretoria.[34]

WACL was suspected of sponsoring a glossy magazine published in South Africa that warned the European minority not to follow Washington because this government was much too influenced by

29. Central Committee Report from FRELIMO's Fifth Congress, October 1989, Box: ID Africa Administration Africa-E Africa-S 1989, *AFSC*.

30. David Ivon, "Touting for South Africa: International Freedom Foundations," *Covert Action*, (Number 31, Winter 1989): 62-64, Box 33, *Washington Office on Africa Papers*.

31. See S 1665, 1983, Box 3, Intelligence, *American Civil Liberties Union Papers, Princeton University*: aid to MNR was to extend to 1987 to the amount of $5 million.

32. Clipping, March 1988, Box 274, *ACOARA*.

33. Jeffrey Marishane, "Prayer, Profit and Power: American Religious Right Wing and Foreign Policy," March 1990, University of Amsterdam: Govan Mbeki Fund, March 1990, Box 274, *ACOARA*.

34. *Aida Parker Newsletter*, Spring 1988, Box 274, *ACOARA*.

African Americans to be trusted.[35] Douglas Kagan, Chairman of Nebraska Conservatives for Freedom in Omaha, exposed the none too covert ties between the ruling party and less respectable elements when he took to the pages of this periodical to declaim "we are supporters of the people" of South Africa, a category that surely did not include the majority.[36] Attacks on the ANC issued frequently from their arsenal: "is it mere coincidence," it was asked wondrously, "that one of Mandela's grandchildren is named Gaddafi," after the Libyan leader,[37] who helped to fund the ANC.

Those who were to the right of the Republican Party still sought to coordinate with the White House, notably through Buchanan. This included Howard Phillips of the Conservative Caucus, founded in 1974 coincidentally enough, the moment when the roof covering apartheid began to collapse with the Portuguese Revolution. He focused on Southern Africa, which proved to be lucrative since he was getting funding from Pretoria. He was among those pressuring Chevron and others to depart Angola. Devilishly, in the mid-1980s, he hired 65 Negro clergymen from Kentucky to dress in Cuban combat fatigues to conduct a mock activity, which included a rented helicopter used to harass a Chevron stockholders' meeting taking place in Atlanta. He was also tied to Don McAlvany, who ran a precious metals business in Denver that was purportedly dependent upon South Africa for supplies. From 1976 to 1989 he had made 30 trips to South Africa, where he had access to cabinet members—even President Botha—and spoke at military bases sprinkled throughout the sub-region. He was also a comrade of Major General John Singlaub—present at the creation of the CIA—who had spent two weeks with MNR, providing the kind of military advice that he was uniquely qualified to dispense.[38]

McAlvany was also part of the fanatically anticommunist John Birch Society and joined with Robert Hoy of the Virginia-based "American-Afrikaner Union," whose obdurate stance did not preclude "partition" of South Africa on racist grounds. Both were sending their forces to South Africa to advocate their demented views

35. "VAT Update", June-August 1989, Box 149, *Leroy Walker Africa News Service Archive.*

36. "VAT Update," November-December 1989, Box 149, *Leroy Walker Africa News Service Archive.*

37. "Vat Update," March-February 1990, Box 149, *Leroy Walker Africa News Service Archive.*

38. Lynora Williams, Center for Democratic Renewal to Jennifer Davis, 24 April 1989, Box 234, *A*

and fortify like-minded groups.[39] The closer apartheid crept toward defeat, the more energized its U.S. supporters appeared. In 1988 right-wing radicals vandalized the headquarters of the Washington Office on Africa,[40] already weakened because of lackluster fund-raising. Eugene Valberg, apparently inspired by the "American-Afrikaner Union," was a U.S. national teaching at Lesotho University forced to flee after students denounced him as a racist for praising apartheid.[41]

U.S. opponents of these forces were not unaware of their malevolence, which led to an early 1989 conference on Pretoria's aggression against Mozambique and Angola. There it was revealed that a South African national spying on behalf of Moscow had been arrested in New York and then spirited directly to South Africa, where he faced an uncertain fate, further evidence—if any were needed—of the endurance of the Pretoria-Washington tie-up. The veteran activist Prexy Nesbitt spoke at length about how Jonas Savimbi employed the firm led by Paul Manafort—later known as a comrade of Donald J. Trump in his journey to the White House. The CIA was still active in Mozambique, he said—as the role of Singlaub may have indicated—and a growing number of U.S. Negroes had been recruited to support UNITA, including the iconoclastic comedian Dick Gregory, who had visited their headquarters in Jamba, Angola.[42] The late humorist was certainly not among those protesting the 1989 appearance of UNITA's Jardo Muekalia at the posh headquarters of the Council on Foreign Relations on the East Side of Manhattan, where this envoy seemed baffled by the "rancor" expressed by those demonstrating.[43] Savimbi, billed as having trained in China, was also present.[44]

"Blacks Against Contra Aid" were among the groups protesting and, in a turnabout, the CIA's former point man in Angola during the 1975 debacle, John Stockwell, was providing them with intelligence, By the 1980s U.S. operatives Oliver North and Richard Secord were diverting aid and twisting arms to get other nations to fund UNITA. North himself admitted to having flown long distances

39. Center for Democratic Renewal Update, 2 April 1990, Box 274, *ACOARA*.

40. *Guardian*, [New York], 8 June 1988.

41. Press Release, 1988, Box 274, *ACOARA*.

42. Jerry Herman to AFSC, 2 February 1989, Box: ID Africa Administration East South West, *AFSC*.

43. Jardo Muekalia to CFR, 16 October 1989, Box 532, *Council on Foreign Relations Papers*.

44. Announcement of Savimbi Luncheon, 10 October 1989, Box 532, *Council on Foreign Relations Papers-Princeton University*.

to meet Savimbi and that some of the funds raised for his embattled forces were raised in Iran, Saudi Arabia, and Brunei.[45] Still, as Euro-American men in bespoke suits ambled along the thickly carpeted floors of the CFR, there was a dawning recognition that all-out support for UNITA was inconsistent with the stated aim of improving ties with the Frontline States.[46] When a CIA plane loaded with arms to UNITA crashed in Angola, killing 4 U.S. nationals aboard, symbolically crashing along with it was U.S. courting of Savimbi, who would be swept aside in the next few years.[47]

Savimbi also was backed by anticommunist African leaders, including Senegal's Leopold Senghor. "When I asked him why he did this," said Herman Cohen of the State Department, "his reply was based on Negritude. He said that the leaders of the MPLA government" in Luanda "were all people of mixed African and Portuguese [heritage] who did [not] speak African languages. Savimbi and his UNITA," he said, "were pure Africans…." Similarly inclined was Felix Houphouet-Boigny, founding father of Ivory Coast, Senegal's neighbor. He was Savimbi's mentor. "The place I met [Savimbi] most often was in the home of President Houphouet-Boigny in Abidjian"; in this capital Savimbi was also provided with money laundering services meant to disguise his various sources of funds, which proved to be truly munificent. Savimbi had an agent there who received diamonds from couriers and converted them into various currencies. This was just one aspect of Abidjan's crucial role. Across the continent, Kenyan leader Daniel Arap Moi had similar motivation in backing MNR. He knew Dhklama quite well, as they were both evangelical Christians and similarly susceptible to the influence of the fountainhead of this trend in the U.S. itself. Kaunda's successor in Lusaka also pledged support to these counter-revolutionaries, given Frederick Chiluba's awareness of the ethnic ties that existed between Savimbi and a sector of Zambians. As for Cohen, he first met Savimbi in Lusaka in 1965 when he was a lower-level U.S. envoy.[48]

* * *

45. "Ties that Bind," Newsletter of "Blacks Against Contra Aid," January 1988, Box 163, *Gerald Horne Papers*.

46. See e.g. Minutes of State Department Advisory Committee on South Africa, 6 May 1986, Box 58, *Leon Sullivan Papers*.

47. *Washington Post*, 30 November 1989.

48. Herman J. Cohen, *The Mind of the African Strongman*, Washington, D.C.: New Academia, 2015, 7, 21, 47, 56, 59, 69. The MNR's leader surname has been rendered as 'Dhlakama'.

It was not only policy toward Pretoria that the ultra-right found upsetting. The often inattentive Reagan found time to write a draft of a letter by hand to one of his first donors, way back in the mid-1960s when ran for governor of California. "Your concern about Mozambique," he told the Los Angeles industrialist Henry Salvatori, was legitimate. "Our conservative friends are upset" about not going for the kill in Maputo and overthrowing FRELIMO "and unfortunately we can't reassure them without giving away some secrets, better left undisturbed"—a shrouded reference to covert aid to MNR, the terrorist bandits then being funded by White House cohorts. Mozambique, where massive offshore energy supplies were soon to be found, "nurse[s] a desire to sever existing ties with the East," meaning Moscow and its allies. He conceded that "RENAMO," or MNR, "does not fall under the title of 'freedom fighters,'" certainly not for lack of trying by hardliners. "We won't do anything foolish. Nancy sends her love to Gracie [Salvatori], as do I," he concluded familiarly.[49] Conveniently, Reagan was often cited for the proposition that "sometimes my right hand doesn't know [what] my far right hand is doing," which presumably immunized him against charges of backing bandits and terrorists in Mozambique.[50]

Like many industrialists, Salvatori was hardly enthusiastic about anti-apartheid sanctions. His class viewed dourly such restrictions on capital movement. Terry Eckel, President of Eckel International of Odessa, Texas continued to rail against sanctions even after they were imposed, telling the sympathetic Senator Strom Thurmond of South Carolina that he was "vigorously oppose[d]" to this legislation. "We are a manufacturing company" that had been "exporting our equipment to South Africa since 1983." This entity was essential to the gold mining industry.[51]

Like others, Eckel was quite concerned that sanctions would be stiffened further. Even the Democratic Party leader, Congressman John Dingell of Michigan, was worried that a new bill could result in a cutoff of minerals vital to the production of auto emission control

49. President Reagan to Henry Salvatori, 18 June 1987, Box 133, WHORM, CO Countries, CO 108, Mozambique, *Reagan Presidential Library.*

50. William Minter, "Destructive Engagement: The United States and South Africa in the Reagan Era, "in Phyllis Johnson and David Martin, eds., *Destructive Engagement: Southern Africa at War*, Harare: Zimbabwe Publishing House, 1988, 281-320, 288.

51. Terry Eckel to Senator Thurmond, 20 September 1988, CMS 1988, Box 001, *Strom Thurmond Papers.*

equipment, which would be a blow to General Motors, Ford, and Chrysler.[52]

Correspondingly, there was an attempt by the South African giant Minorco to buy Consolidated Gold Fields, which had "important potential implications for U.S. national security," said Senator Tim Wirth of Colorado. Consolidated had 50% of its assets in the U.S., including a 49% share in Newmont Mining, which then held a major share of Peabody Coal.[53] Washington state Senator Brock Adams was concerned about the proposed acquisition of Consolidated Gold Fields by Anglo-American Gold Mining and De Beers of South Africa. "The largest minerals syndicate in South Africa," he warned, "would secure operational control of the largest gold mining company" in the U.S., along with the "largest coal production company" in the U.S. and "the only source of titanium feedstocks."[54] In other words, as the divestment movement spread, South African corporations continued to control—or tried to control—major U.S. corporations. By the 1980s, as divestment movements surged on U.S. campuses, Anglo-American of South Africa began funneling capital into the U.S. and quickly became the largest foreign investor there, displacing Shell Oil, a development of gargantuan political consequence.[55] A problem for these moneymakers was the campus movement, which had a secret weapon. By 1988, the ANC had reason to believe there were "more than 3000 South African students in the USA. Some of our people in the USA," said one Lusaka official of the liberation movement, "believe that the figure is much more than that…."[56] They were not only a source of detailed information about the apartheid economy but were also motivated to act on this intelligence.

The attempt to manacle apartheid was proceeding apace. In early 1988, Jennifer Davis of the ACOA contacted the scholar Dan O'Meara in Montreal with a proposal to extend U.S.-style sanctions north of

52. Herman Cohen to Paul Schott Stevens, 20 June 1988, Box 16 [Box 8], African Affairs Directorate, RAC, *Reagan Presidential Library*.

53. Senator Tim Wirth to President Reagan, 21 October 1988, Box 174, WHORM, Subject Files, *Reagan Presidential Library*.

54. Senator Brock Adams to President Reagan, 21 October 1988, Box 175, WHORM, CO 141, South Africa, 592000 and CO 143 Namibia, *Reagan Presidential Library*.

55. Ruth Kaplan, "Anglo American Corporation of South Africa, Ltd., Investments in North America," circa 1980s, Box 3, *Robert Massie Papers, Princeton University*.

56. Memo from M. Piliso, Director of Department of Manpower Development of ANC, 27 April 1988, Reel 12, *Oliver Tambo Papers*.

the border. "At the end of 1987", she said, "Congress abolished the ability of U.S. companies to write off taxes paid in South Africa and Namibia against U.S. taxes," hampering investment in apartheid and colonialism. This "could raise the effective tax rate of the South African operations of U.S. companies" from 57% to 72%. "Mobil corporation," an oil behemoth, was then the "largest U.S. investor in South Africa" and, thus, "reacted strongly", since it, along with Caltex were destined to be "hard hit." To head off a successful lobbying campaign to overturn this development, she wanted to increase the pressure by extending similar sanctions to Canada.[57] On 16 June 1988 in a spirited "Remember Soweto" demonstration in the heart of Manhattan, protesters amassed at Mobil Oil's headquarters at 150 East 42nd Street, heeding a "call for Mobil Oil and Royal Dutch Shell to cut their lifeline to apartheid South Africa."[58] The demonstration—coordinated by myself—was amplified by the presence of a sophisticated sound system, disrupting the solemnity of usually unruffled midtown shoppers.[59] Midtown regulars were becoming accustomed to our presence since Mobil Oil was one of our chief targets. Earlier, on the birthday of the slain Dr. King, we assembled there and were pleased by the excellent press coverage we received—which was not a norm, since we were often ignored—as hundreds participated in civil disobedience.[60]

Mobil got the message. By May 1989 Richard Trumka of the United Mine Workers and Joseph Misbrener, leader of the International Union of Oil, Chemical and Atomic Workers, were congratulating Allen E. Murray, Chairman and CEO of Mobil, for selling South African assets, even though there had not been a complete withdrawal. Murray was urged to meet with unions in the land of apartheid.[61]

As the crisis of apartheid deepened, U.S. opponents smelled blood in the water and acted accordingly. In a show of solidarity toward South Africa's National Union of Mineworkers, Trumka's union and others marched in front of Shell Oil's Washington office.[62]

As U.S. corporations were forced by duress to depart South Africa, Japan stepped in and by 1988 had surpassed the U.S. as South Africa's

57. Jennifer Davis to Dan O'Meara, 14 March 1988, Box 73, *ACOARA*.

58. Leaflet, 16 June 1988, Box 163, *Gerald Horne Papers*.

59. Sound Device Permit, 4 April 1988, Box 163, *Gerald Horne Papers*.

60. Report by Gerald Horne and Donna Katzin, 28 January 1988, Box 181, *Gerald Horne Papers*.

61. Richard Trumka and Joseph Misbrener, 19 May 1989, Box 73, *ACOARA*.

62. J.J. Barry, International President of International Brotherhood of Electrical Workers to Matthew Pinsker, 14 March 1989, Box 1, *Robert Massie Papers, Princeton University*.

top trading partner—but that only increased unease in Tokyo, suggesting that apartheid was in a death spiral from which there was no easy escape.[63] Thus, in 1987 picket lines greeted those entering the "American Club" in Tokyo for a tasting of South African wines. Protesters included the Japan Afro-American Friendship Association and the Japan Anti-Apartheid Committee, who were attacked by disgruntled—perhaps intoxicated—wine tasters.[64]

But it was not only Tokyo and Mobil that were feeling the white heat of protest. At Fairview High School in Colorado, students voted 309-229 to remove 2 vending machines selling Coca Cola from their facility in order to protest apartheid, a troubling signal for this consumer giant.[65] This vote did not materialize magically; instead, it was the product of years of organizing by Quakers in particular, who in a single year had produced 24,000 buttons, t-shirts, stickers—and a budget for a coordinator, postage, travel, and the like for a "Coke Divestment Campaign."[66]

"Did you know that the military in South Africa eat Kellogg's cereals" was the question posed by New York's Educators Against Apartheid, referring to the corporation based in Battle Creek, Michigan.[67] Scores of U.S. corporations had crept across the border to set up shop in Zimbabwe, including Colgate, Caltex, Coca Cola, Cummins Engine, Goodyear Rubber, Pfizer, 3M, and Union Carbide.[68]

Sanctions were not simply biting Big Business. P.B. Williams of Laurens, South Carolina would have concurred. "My wife inherited a few South African gold mine stocks from her father in 1978," he told Senator Strom Thurmond, but "nothing like the amount in terms of the 40% raise in salary you received recently," he added acerbically. In any case, Pretoria "withheld…15% in taxes from the dividends these companies paid. Up to 1988 in filing income taxes she was allowed a credit on South Africa taxes withheld. Now she has been informed" that "Congress has passed a law disallowing

63. *Christian Science Monitor*, 5 April 1988.

64. *Japan Times*, 29 May 1987.

65. *Denver Post*, 5 May 1989; *Rocky Mountain News*, 5 May 1989.

66. "Budget for One Year Coke Divestment Campaign, June 1986-June 1987," Box: Atlanta Regional Office, Southern Africa Peace Education Program, *AFSC*.

67. Educators Against Apartheid Newsletter, May 1988, Box 163, *Gerald Horne Papers*.

68. Memorandum from Allison Hernick, 18 June 1990, Box 175, *Junior Achievement Records, Indiana University Purdue University-Indianapolis.*

this credit," leaving him fulminating angrily.[69] He would also be displeased by the campaign against Kruger-rands, the apartheid gold coin that delivered bounteous profits in Pretoria.

Carlucci, taking a growing role in the sub-region, acknowledged that "there is a lot we don't know about RENAMO [MNR] compared to UNITA" in Angola, which was as close to U.S. imperialism as a moustache and a top lip. Both Zimbabwe and Tanzania had been drawn into the fight in Mozambique too, which argued—from Washington's viewpoint—for escalating, so as to weaken two of the Frontline States. Carlucci knew that "support" from Pretoria "has continued despite the Nkomati Accord," which Washington sought to broker and then watched with feigned helplessness as it was violated.[70]

Savimbi continued to be an honored visitor in the U.S., though his mid-1988 tour of the U.S. South saw protesters—mostly African American—outnumbering supporters at a rate of 3-1. The majority thought apartheid was the issue, while the minority fixated on "communism" and flocked to the bearded terrorist's side. Charles Evers, brother of the martyred Medgar, was among the latter, presenting Savimbi an award.[71]

According to Herman Cohen, a prominent U.S. official, "the prime Reagan Doctrine cause in Africa" was that of Savimbi. The only amendment one might make to this sweeping assertion would be to elevate the importance of his UNITA on the totem pole of counter-insurgencies backed by Washington as part of a Cold War strategy to weaken Havana and Moscow, which were supporting Luanda. A problem there, however, was the fact that the mainstream Negro leaders were reluctant to follow the White House. Cohen was also "encountering difficulties in scheduling any presidential meetings with African leaders," though such photo opportunities "helped to strengthen [Reagan's] anti-apartheid image." Since these cosmetic sit-downs were also designed to either woo Negro voters or convince wavering Euro-Americans that Reagan's policies were not as racist as they appeared to be, Cohen emphasized to White House aide Colin Powell that this was "something the domestic side of the White House should care about." Thus, the slated meeting with Zambia's Kaunda "helped the White House escape the intense

69. P.B. Williams to Senator Thurmond, 19 March 1990, Box 20, Constituent Correspondence, Box 20, *J. Strom Thurmond Papers*.

70. Frank Carlucci to Robert S. Tuttle, 19 June 1987, Box 134, CO Countries, CO 108, Mozambique, *Reagan Presidential Library*.

71. *Washington Post*, 26 June 1988.

African criticism" of his pro-apartheid policies. The president was also advised to meet with Nigeria's leader, Ibrahim Babangida, "since he is trying—at considerable price—to broker national reconciliation in Angola on behalf of Jonas Savimbi,"[72] an African with otherwise polecat status.

Washington continued to curry favor with Kaunda, not least because he was seen as more pliable than Mugabe. This was not easy since the Zambian clashed with Canada's Prime Minister Brian Mulroney and Britain's Margaret Thatcher "over Southern African policy" in a manner that "became quite acrimonious," according to Frank Carlucci.[73] Ties with Lusaka became so warm that Kaunda ludicrously sought to nominate the bellicose U.S. president for the Nobel Peace Prize.[74]

Both Carlucci and his ostensible supervisor Reagan were treading carefully since MNR was not reluctant to attack U.S. nationals and those close to them in Mozambique. The White House was told as much by Roy Sano of the World Division, Board of Global Ministries of the United Methodist Church, joined by Peggy Billings, General Secretary of the World Division. In Cambine, Mozambique on 2 September 1987, at about 4 A.M., they said, "armed bandits' began an attack" on a school. "Fifteen church members were killed and five others, including at least one pastor and one church leader, were taken away by force" to an uncertain fate. "School buildings were burned and looted. Homes were robbed and destroyed…the Hospital was broken into and all medicines taken."[75]

The Methodists were not singular in their solidarity with Southern Africa. There were the Quakers, of course, and the Lutheran World Federation too, quite active on the Namibian front. Carl Mau, born in Seattle, who headed the LWF from 1974-1985, was described by Toivo ya Toivo as taking an "uncompromising position against apartheid…." Abisai Shejavali, whose doctorate was obtained in Dubuque, Iowa, was General Secretary of the Council of Churches in Namibia until his 1992 retirement.[76]

---

72. Herman Cohen to Colin Powell, 29 January 1988, Box 16, WHORM, Subject Files, CO 001 Cont-Geo. Areas, *Reagan Presidential Library*.

73. Frank Carlucci to President Reagan, circa 1987, Box 223, WHORM, Subject File, CO 178, Zambia, *Reagan Presidential Library*.

74. Kenneth Kaunda to President Reagan, 11 October 1987, Box 223, WHORM Subject File, CO 178, Zambia.

75. Roy Sano and Peggy Billings to President Reagan, 16 September 1987, Box 134, WHORM, Co Countries, CO 108, Mozambique.

76. Andimba Toivo ya Toivo, *On Trial for My Country*, 276, 287.

But Carlucci was haunted by a fact that had apparently escaped the purblind Buchanan. He had focused intently on the "state and local government actions against American firms" in South Africa which had caused them to flee or consider doing so.[77] This local issue had reached the highest level: Secretary of State Shultz instructed the Attorney General to intervene in Baltimore in "challenging that city's divestment measure." This, he intoned solemnly, "deserve[s] the immediate coordinated attention of the Executive Branch."[78]

Shultz's attempted intervention in Baltimore may not have assuaged the growing chorus of voices on the hard right opposing his policies. When his deputy, Chester Crocker, met with Foreign Minister Pik Botha, in Geneva in 1988, the bespectacled and rapidly balding Assistant Secretary of State had not "spoken to him" in two years, he recounted,[79] a decision bound to inflame the ire of his—and Shultz's—detractors.

The Congressional Black Caucus remained a crowbar chipping away at apartheid. On their behalf Congressman Charles Rangel reminded Reagan that the Comprehensive Anti-Apartheid Act of 1986 required more sanctions unless Mandela was freed—and he remained incarcerated.[80] Tambo told Congressman Fauntroy of the Caucus that "our visit to the [U.S.] represents a milestone in our global mobilization," which—if anything—was an understatement. "[I] remember with particular fondness and satisfaction," he said reminiscing, "the Sunday morning service at the New Bethel Baptist Church," not to mention the "financial contribution collected on that morning...."[81] The ANC spent considerable time counting the money collected for Tambo, who also chose to "remember most fondly" his "visit to....Operation PUSH," led by Jesse Jackson in Chicago and the "absolutely overwhelming welcome that you and the PUSH family gave us." Making the trip even more memorable was

77. Frank Carlucci to James Miller III, 25 March 1987, Box 173, WHORM, Subject Files.

78. George Shultz to Edwin Meese, 9 April 1987, Box 9, 10[Box 3], African Affairs Directorate, NSC Records, RAC, *Reagan Presidential Library*.

79. Chester Crocker, *High Noon in Southern Africa*, 330.

80. Congressman Rangel to President Reagan, 5 October 1987, Box 174, WHORM, Subject Files. The letter was signed by inter alia, Congressmen Crockett of Detroit; Major Owens of Brooklyn; Mervyn Dymally of Los Angeles; Alan Wheat of Kansas City; Gus Savage of Chicago, Edolphus Towns of Brooklyn; and Kweisi Mfume of Baltimore.

81. Oliver Tambo to Congressman Fauntroy, 2 June 1987, Reel 16, *Oliver Tambo Papers*.

the "generous gift of $20,000."[82] This was not the only cash donation made by U.S. nationals to those fighting imperialism. In August 1987, a 17-member delegation from the United Methodist Church and the Quakers of the U.S. were pictured handing a $2,000 check to Major General Jevan Maseko of the Zimbabwe Defense Force on behalf of their herculean effort in guarding the Beira Corridor, protecting trade and transport between his nation and Mozambique against the ravages of apartheid-sponsored banditry[83]

Then there was the incalculable ideological support rendered to the Frontline States, e.g. the 1987 Angola report authored by the Quakers' Carole Collins noting that "the Slave Trade so depopulated the country that in 1960 it was estimated to have about the same population that it had in 1600 prior to the slave trade."[84]

The African American community had become a material force in the sub-region—to the point where the president's daughter, Maureen Reagan, "had originally thought of doing a trip" to Mozambique, said diplomat Herman Cohen, in order to "pre-empt a possible visit" there by "presidential candidate Jesse Jackson."[85] Predictably, the White House sought to split the Caucus. In what Alison Fortier called their "sanctions strategy," the administration sought "more responsible members of the Black Caucus," which seemed to mean anyone but Congressman Ronald V. Dellums of Berkeley[86] — one of the unsung heroes of the attempt to end apartheid.[87]

Though holding an opposing viewpoint, Neely B. Coble of Nashville understood what was going on. "Because of our large black population in the United States," he told the newly appointed White House Chief of Staff, Howard Baker, "apartheid has gotten to be a political issue. Practically all our American politicians are trying to

---

82. Oliver Tambo to the Reverend Jackson, 2 June 1987, Reel 16, *Oliver Tambo Papers*.

83. *Herald* [Zimbabwe], 25 August 1987.

84. Carole Collins, "Report on a Trip to Angola, 30 August-19 September 1987," Box: ID Africa.... South S AFR-IAP...TAMAPSA.... Mozambique...." *AFSC*.

85. Herman Cohen to Colin Powell, 30 July 1988, Box 16, WHORM, Subject Files, CO 001, Cont.-Geo. Areas, *Reagan Presidential Library*.

86. Letter to Alison Fortier, 5 August 1988, Box 18-20 [Box 5]. RAC, *Alison Fortier Papers, Reagan Presidential Library*.

87. "Congressional Black Caucus: Selected Efforts to Influence U.S. Toward South Africa, 1971-1989," Box 4, *Robert Massie Papers, Princeton University*: "Prepared Under Dellums' Auspices," 26 September 1990.

'woo' votes from our American black Community" and, he added portentously, "this will increase."[88]

Leading moviemakers including Woody Allen, Jonathan Demme, Spike Lee, Martin Scorsese, and Susan Seidelman echoed Rangel when they told the White House that "our goal is to have motion pictures become part of the United Nations endorsed cultural and business boycott" of apartheid.[89] Simultaneously, they were promoting "A World Apart," an affecting dramatization of the lives of Joe Slovo and Ruth First.[90] Even Big Business got into the act. From her perch at an elite law firm, Washington insider Carla Hills told Carlucci with a hint of exasperation "why it is poor public policy to force Chevron out of Angola,"[91] where it was pumping petroleum profitably, under the benevolent protection of well-armed Cuban troops.

The prickly matter of Cuban troops in Angola was a bone still caught in the throat of U.S. imperialism, convincing some on the ultra-right that they were not as strong as they seemed, a situation which—they thought—called for a firmer response. Their problem was that their ally in Pretoria was not actually as strong as it appeared, at least when it came to facing down the Cubans. In 1988 Carole Collins of the Quakers spoke to a Cuban diplomat in the sub-region who told her that his military "directly face[d] SADF [South African Defense Forces] lines close to the Namibian border, raising the possibility of a direct confrontation." Should that occur, "Cuban troops would not necessarily be able to refrain from entering Namibia, which opens a wholly new military situation for South Africa," a hint that they might not stop advancing until they reached Pretoria itself. The recalcitrant ally, perhaps drunk on the intoxication of white supremacy—according to this diplomat—balked at the participation of the U.S. in negotiations with the Cubans over their Angolan presence, while their opponents—principally the ANC—did not.[92]

Again, there was an obvious cleavage at the highest level of the U.S. ruling elite, with Carla Hills and those like her willing to

---

88. Neely B. Coble to Howard Baker, Box 174, WHORM, Subject Files, *Reagan Presidential Library*.

89. Filmmakers United Against Apartheid to the White House, 2 November 1987, Box 174, WHORM, Subject Files.

90. Announcement, 15 June 1988, Box 181, *Gerald Horne Papers*.

91. Carla Hills of Weil, Gosthal and Manges to "Dear Frank" Carlucci, 19 June 1987, Box 38, WHORM, Subject File, CO Countries, CO006, Angola, *Reagan Presidential Library*.

92. Carole Collins to Mohulatsi Mokeyane, 14 May 1988, Box: PED NARMIC Program Resources Southern Africa, *AFSC*.

compromise—or at least recognize reality—and others who were not. Straddling the fence were members of Secretary of State Shultz's Advisory Committee on South Africa, which included Franklin Thomas of the Ford Foundation, former civil rights leader turned investment banker Vernon Jordan, and the much criticized Reverend Leon Sullivan. The essence of the matter was revealed in the dissent filed by committee member Owen Bieber of the United Auto Workers, who demanded stiffer sanctions on apartheid. Committee co-chair, the affluent Negro attorney William Coleman found "the utter lack of indignation and the acceptance of the status quo among a small number of people" in the U.S. to be "upsetting." Against the Bieber dissent, the State Department's Lawrence Eagleburger and General Motors' Roger Smith issued their own "alternative recommendations."[93]

The stance of the wily Jordan, often found on the winning side when elite debates erupted, was telling. During his journey to South Africa he found "negative feelings" toward Washington and "especially negative feelings toward President Reagan" among the nation's majority. "The U.S. and everything American is hated," he reported. Buthelezi, seen as a savior by the White House, was similarly viewed as a "collaborator, as an enemy of the people...." According to Thomas, he believed that "black relations with the U.S. are at an all-time low." Mandela, it was said soberly, had the "status of God," seen in "almost messianic" terms. Jordan, who happened to be quite dark-skinned, "did not like or believe the [Pretoria] officials whom he met." Referring to a local rube, he said they "make Roy Harris from Augusta...look like a flaming liberal...." Jordan did not think much of Foreign Minister Botha either. The Congress of South African Trade Unions, tied to the ANC-SACP alliance, was "suspicious of the AFL-CIO." There was "still some good feelings toward American blacks," but it was unclear how long this would last. Jordan's views were not unique to him but shared by the graying leader of IBM, Frank Cary.[94]

Thomas too was criticized by different forces when he hosted a breakfast meeting sponsored by the Council on Foreign Relations for Washington's favorite African, Jonas Savimbi.[95] He had won few

---

93. "Report of the Secretary of State's Advisory Committee on South Africa," 29 January 1987, Box 222, *Gay McDougall Papers.*

94. State Department Advisory Committee on South Africa: Minutes, 6 May 1986, Box 58, *Leon Sullivan Papers.*

95. Report, 23 June 1988, Box 532, *Council on Foreign Relations Papers, Princeton University.*

friends on the left when his Ford Foundation subsidized a study on South Africa that carried no recommendations on Namibia, or on UNITA for that matter.[96]

Elite visitors to South Africa returning with tales of woe had become a familiar sight in Washington. The latest was Alison Rosenberg, who told Colin Powell—the top Negro in the White House—that her just concluded visit in early 1988 was "by far the most discouraging visit I have made to South Africa in the past seven years." Helen Suzman, viewed as a "liberal" in Pretoria, was frustrated and "ready to retire." "Only the Conservatives are on a roll," she said, as they were attacking the ruling Nationalists from the right. They tended to "attract the economically disenfranchised—poor farmers, low skilled laborers and the like…." As for Botha, "his domestic and foreign policy decisions do not reflect a sensitivity to U.S. interests"—and thus would soon be replaced by F.W. de Klerk. Under Botha, Pretoria remained "willing to score points at the expense of the U.S…."[97]

The beleaguered Sullivan was getting hit from all sides. Fred Dube of the ANC said accusingly that the pastor "didn't contribute a bloody thing to our struggle,"[98] while New York City Comptroller Harrison Goldin was "deeply troubled"—not by Sullivan's Principles, which tended to sanctify investment in apartheid, but by the fact that "you have given Louis Farrakhan a forum in your church," referring to the controversial cleric and leader of the Nation of Islam who was, it was charged, a tribune of "anti-Semitism and bigotry." Goldin self-righteously claimed to oppose "racism" and "bigotry" whether such occurred in "South Africa or here at home and whether…espoused by Botha, a [Meir] Kahane [the Israeli terrorist] or a Farrakhan."[99]

By 1988, the much criticized Sullivan Principles were being battered once more. The U.S. Consul General in Durban lamented the failure of this code to accomplish the anti-apartheid goal it was presumably designed to effectuate. Thus, said F. Allen Harris, there needed be a "search for a prominent black American leader to serve"

96. Ibid., William Minter, "Destructive Engagement," 286.

97. Alison P. Rosenberg to Colin Powell, 31 March 1988, Box 14, 17, 18 [Box 4]. RAC, *Alison Fortier Papers, Reagan Presidential Library.*

98. Oral History, Fred Dube, 24 July 2001, *University of Connecticut-Storrs.* On the Dube case, see the editorial in the *New York Times*, 24 February 1987.

99. Harrison Goldin to Reverend Sullivan, 6 December 1988, Box 58, *Leon Sullivan Papers.*

alongside Sullivan to restore the code's flagging credibility.[100] Despite this flaying from all sides, the ideologically compromised NAACP chose this moment to endorse the Sullivan Principles.[101]

But if Sullivan had not existed, he would have had to be invented, a point illustrated when "Sullivan lite" initiatives began to flourish. The U.S. Corporate Council on South Africa played a similar role with this code, just as General Motors was a major donor to the Institute for Democratic Alternatives in South Africa, headed by Frederic van Zyl Slabbert and Alex Boraine, who were seeking a post-apartheid dispensation that left capital in the driver's seat. The well-known advertising firm the Ogilvy Group constructed free advertising for the Progressive Federal Party—a grouping akin to IDASA.[102]

As Israel came under fire from African Americans for collusion with apartheid, charges of anti-Semitism rose accordingly. The Reverend Jesse Jackson became a repeated target for what the hardline Young Americans for Freedom called his "anti-Jewish racist sentiments" and his "active support of Soviet backed terrorist groups," i.e. the ANC and SWAPO. Actor and comedian Bill Cosby was also protested on similar grounds and Eastman Kodak, which had hired him to promote their products, was urged to purge him because of his support for the ANC. YAF demanded a halt to the "McCarthy Style U.N. Cultural Boycott" and its replacement by the reverse: targeting ANC and SWAPO supporters.[103]

The charge that critics of Israel were bigoted did not seem to halt the searching inquiry about the relationship between Zionism and apartheid. Highly publicized was the report that the air force in Pretoria got two Boeing 707s from Israel, which were then converted to in flight fueling tankers, while another converted aircraft was used as an airborne electronic warfare control center to direct air attacks against Angola.[104]

Part of Sullivan's problem was that he was seen as seeking to put a liberal face on a backwards, reactionary regime. The ANC chose to retain a study by Willie Esterhuys of the University of Stellenbosch, the citadel of Afrikanerdom, which found that by 1988 the European

---

100. Memorandum of Conversation between F. Allen Harris and Reid Weedon of Arthur D. Little, 27 February 1988, Box 16[Box 10], RAC, *Reagan Presidential Library.*

101. Press Release, 20 February 1985, Box 70, *Leon Sullivan Papers.*

102. Memorandum, circa 1988, Box 14, 17, 18 [Box 4], RAC, *Alison Fortier Papers, Reagan Presidential Library.*

103. "Young Americans for Freedom and Restore a More Benevolent Order Coalition," no date, Box 275, *Leroy Walker Africa News Service Archive.*

104. Report by Abdul Minty, 15 April 1988, Box 154, *ACOARA.*

minority made up 20% of the nation's population though "control of the modern sector of the economy, excluding agriculture, is mainly in the hands of English speakers"—yet "between 70-80 percent" of the "political system, including the civil service and agriculture are controlled by Afrikaners," who were often the backbone of reaction, complicating the possibility of a deal to ease the Nationalists out of power. "In the election of 1977," he said, "the NP gained 82 percent of the seats in the white parliament and 66.1 percent of the votes" overall—"its peak since 1948"—while "anti-American rhetoric especially against the Carter Administration played an important role in the campaign."[105] And though Reagan was now in power and had sought to do their bidding, sanctions were in place, auguring further setbacks.

Alternatively, SACP leader Jack Simons was optimistic. By September 1989 he was crowing that the "NP suffered its first decline since 1948." If the "alliance"—meaning ANC/SACP/COSATU [Congress of South African Trade Unions]— "sticks to its election promises," and the "liberation movement steps up its revolution & struggle, we see a glimmering of hope of a non-violent transition to majority rule." Yes, he acknowledged, "the tide flows strongly against socialism everywhere—even in the fatherland of the proletarians!" This was weeks before the fall of the Berlin Wall and the Copernican changes in Eastern Europe. "Swedes claim that the Mensheviks have triumphed over the Bolsheviks," he said, "& perestroika seems to confirm their claims...." He was not enthused about the new leader in Moscow: "[Mikhail] Gorbachev," had "difficulty in fitting his revisionism into the structure of 'scientific socialism.'"[106]

But just as the tide had shifted in South Africa towards liberation, it became more difficult to dam the massive waves generated by anti-apartheid forces. In early 1987 a committee I chaired in New York City sponsored yet another "Music Against Apartheid" concert with all funds going to the ANC and featuring Abdullah Ibrahim [Dollar Brand] and an accompanying chanteuse, his spouse Sathima 'Bea' Benjamin, along with the West African drum/dance troupe of Olatunji.[107] The next year, the pianist and vocalist joined forces again

---

105. Willie Esterhuys, "Through White Eyes: South Africa Today," 1988, Box 17, Folder 33, *Washington Mission, ANC Records-Fort Hare University*.

106. Jack Simons to Anna, 10 September 1989, C1.1, *Papers of Jack Simons & Ray Alexander, University of Cape Town*.

107. Leaflet, 27 February 1987, Box 163, *Gerald Horne Papers*.

in a Manhattan concert I helped to organize on behalf of the ANC.[108] In September 1987, we feted the exiled South African writer Keorapetse Kgositsile[109] at Riverside Church in Manhattan.[110] Months later, yet another South African in exile—former political prisoner Dennis Goldberg—was celebrated at the Harlem home of writer Jean Carey Bond and her architect spouse, Max Bond.[111] Liberation movement leaders were arriving steadily in Manhattan. By May 1988 Jennifer Davis of ACOA was hosting a "small informal dinner" for Sam Nujoma of SWAPO at her cozy West Side apartment.[112]

By September it was back to the streets—or more precisely, the tennis court—where I served, as the *New York Amsterdam News* wrote, as "coordinator of the Ad Hoc Committee to Combat Apartheid in U.S. Tennis," to protest the appearance of "at least 21 South Africans" at the prestigious U.S. Open. "For the most part," said the observant journalist, "tennis fans at the first day of the Open sneaked peeks at the demonstrators...."[113] Our press conference at City Hall also attracted media attention.[114] A local periodical carried my picture holding a sign saying "Close the U.S. Open to Apartheid" and quoted me: "when you don't care you lose track of your humanity.... We were about 100 strong and 40 yards away from the [courts]. With our sound system they heard us inside. Television crews showed up.... We need to be concerned as people should have during the 1936 Olympics when the Holocaust was starting."[115]

The exceptional press coverage we received did not materialize accidentally. The scholar and activist Richard Lapchick, whose father had been a well-known basketball coach in New York, provided solid pointers on the protest.[116] Based on his suggestions, I

---

108. "A Birthday Tribute to Nelson Mandela," 6 August 1988, Box 163, *Gerald Horne Papers*.

109. Minutes written by author, 8 August 1987, Box 181, *Gerald Horne Papers*.

110. Announcement of fete, 27 September 1987, Box 181, *Gerald Horne Papers*.

111. Announcement of reception, 20 May 1988, Box 181, *Gerald Horne Papers*.

112. Invitation, 8 May 1988, Box 181, *Gerald Horne Papers*.

113. *New York Amsterdam News*, 5 September 1987.

114. *People's Daily World*, 3 September 1987. See also *New York Newsday*, 2 September 1987; *Guardian* [New York], 12 August 1987.

115. *City Sun* [Brooklyn], 9-15 September 1987.

116. Richard Lapchick to "Dear Gerald" Horne, 25 March 1987, Box 181, *Gerald Horne Papers*: "Good to hear from you after so many years....I would suggest we obtain a list from the USTA [United States Tennis Association]

contacted the tennis authorities, stating that "more South Africans have made more appearances in Tennis Grand Prix tournaments in the United States than in all other countries combined during the current year."[117]

The South African golfer Gary Player continued to attract irked attention, especially after it was revealed that he had developed a golf course in Ypsilanti, Michigan in conjunction with Eastern Michigan University, which hosted a complement of already dissatisfied African American students.[118] Also on the sports front, the city of Albany, New York was forced to pay $47,000 to harassed demonstrators who had protested the presence of rugby players from South Africa.[119]

More controversial was our reprimanding the U.S. musician Paul Simon for breaking the cultural boycott by traveling to South Africa. The ANC agreed but some musicians disagreed.[120] Nonplussed, we termed Simon's *Graceland* "Dis-Graceland: Selling out the Cultural Boycott" in a forum at Harlem's Harriet Tubman School featuring radio personalities Elombe Brath and Bob Law alongside South African exile Sikhulu Shange.[121] The popularity of Simon's attempt to fuse South African music with U.S. forms helped to bring more attention to talented African musicians, including Jonas Gwangwa. This horn player, songwriter, and producer arrived in the U.S., like others, during the dying days of apartheid, by his own admission, he "was very excited"—though it "wasn't what I thought it was, of course." As "the taxi went through Harlem," he was appalled; "phew!" he said with disgust, at this "deflating" experience. "This is America! Ja, it's a slum." His experience of Simon in the U.S. also mirrored apartheid in that "you had a white artist standing there and miming and the black guy singing behind the curtain, that happened many times...."

His fellow musician Hugh Masekela was of like mind. "I had idols who became role models," he said late in his fruitful career as a trumpeter and vocalist, including the premier African American artists "Louis Armstrong and Miles Davis and Dizzy Gillespie and Clifford

---

and try to meet—with Arthur Ashe's help—each South African player to get them to make an anti-apartheid stand. If they commit, they're OK. If not, they become the focus of activities." In the same box, see City of New York Sound Device Permit for U.S. Open Tennis, 1 September 1987.

117. Gerald Horne to USTA, 23 August 1987, Box 181, *Gerald Horne Papers*.

118. *Lansing State Journal*, 5 January 1988.

119. Clipping, no date, circa 1988, Box 163, *Gerald Horne Papers*.

120. *People's Daily World*, 11 April 1987.

121. Leaflet, 14 May 1987, Box 191, *Gerald Horne Papers*.

Brown and Duke Ellington," which drew him like filings to a magnet to the U.S. But he said with asperity, "they were in a country" that "was worse than South Africa, where they were being lynched...." He was unhappy because while in this alleged land of liberty, "we lived under the surveillance by the security agencies, especially the FBI. We were aware of it. There was a car always parked outside my flat." He was perceived as an antagonist of the Pretoria ally and a comrade of the ANC-SACP alliance besides. Although he was to return repeatedly, he departed the U.S. in 1972. "I had like peaked there," he said later. "When you're successful in the States, besides Civil Rights there's nothing much that you can do. Except conspicuous consumption," and of that he had enough.[122]

Success begets success. Simon notwithstanding, the anti-apartheid movement was striding from gain to gain. By mid-1987 Tambo was busily signing letters to Sidney Poitier, Harry Belafonte, and the music mogul Dick Griffey, thanking them profusely for their assistance to the ANC.[123] Griffey had knocked together the "Coalition for a Free Africa," which specialized in generating aid for refugees in camps in Angola, Tanzania, etc., and included leading politico Maxine Waters, entrepreneur Danny Bakewell, Congressman Fauntroy, philanthropist and Democratic Party donor Stanley Sheinbaum, and music producer and executive Clarence Avant.[124]

The presence of Poitier, Belafonte, and other stars in the anti-apartheid ranks illustrated the defensive crouch into which Pretoria had been placed on the all-important cultural front. But apartheid was hardly finished in this crucial realm, as was indicated when the scandal-ridden Washington insider Jack Abramoff helped to produce *Red Scorpion*, a pro-UNITA film financed by the First Bank of Minneapolis and slated to be distributed by Warner Bros.—which then dropped it after forceful protests.[125] Though defended by UNITA forces while filming in Southern Africa, the film set came under fierce attack by Luanda.[126] It was not just Abramoff who was

122. Hilda Bernstein, *The Rift: The Experience of South Africans*, London: Jonathan Cape, 1994, 339, 343.

123. Letters from Tambo to Poitier, Belafonte, Griffey, et.al., 5 June 1987, Reel 3, *Oliver Tambo Papers*.

124. Coalition for a Free Africa to "Dear Friend," 24 May 1989, Box 73, *ACOARA*.

125. Namibia Information Service, 6 June 1988, Box 163, *Gerald Horne Papers*.

126. Peter H. Stone, *Heist: Superlobbyist Jack Abramoff, his Republican Allies and the Buying of Washington*, New York: Farrar, Straus and Giroux, 2006, 45-46, 47.

attracted to the region. Filmmaker Steven Spielberg was there "anonymously," according to a journalist, scouting for sites for a future cinematic treatment of a book by Afrikaner author Laurens van der Post. Apparently, he did not venture to Swaziland, though Abramoff did—and was booted out.[127]

Abramoff had become a major player not only in the domestic hard right but the global one too. He worked closely with Adolfo Calero, leader of the counter-revolutionary forces in Nicaragua and a former manager of the Coca Cola bottling plant in Managua. This global counter-revolutionary upsurge was symbolized when Abramoff arrived at Savimbi's headquarters in Jamba, Angola alongside the tycoon Lewis Lehrman, who gifted to the UNITA leadership a copy of the U.S. Declaration of Independence and a letter from Reagan. Also speaking there were Ghulam Warduk, a leader of the counter-revolutionary forces in Afghanistan, and Pa Kao Her, who headed up the counter-revolutionary forces in Laos.[128]

Inevitably our activism attracted unwanted attention. A publication from the Christian right —the *Family Protection Scorecard*— termed the divestment movement a "proven Soviet active measure." The conference we held a few years earlier at Riverside Church was denounced. Citing the testimony of the FBI's Edward O'Malley before Congress, this important meeting was grouped "among examples of specific Soviet active measures…." As for Randall Robinson, it was said that he "may or may not be a Communist…." The author Tomas D. Schulman was a defector from the Soviet Union who had departed "with CIA assistance"—by his own admission—from his role at Radio Moscow.[129] Perhaps in response, Robinson took to the pages of the *Washington Post* to call for sanctions against the regime in Ethiopia, then one of Moscow's closest allies on the continent.[130]

Robinson was under fire, perceived accurately as the linchpin of the proliferating anti-apartheid movement. *The New Republic*, a pro-Israel journal close to the Democratic Party—which was to bill itself as the in-flight journal of Air Force One under President Bill Clinton—denounced Robinson for being too soft on Cuban troops

127. *The Namibian*, 4 December 1987.

128. Jack Abramoff, *Capital Punishment: The Hard Truth about Washington Corruption from America's Most Notorious Lobbyist*, Washington, D.C.: WND, 2011, 38, 40, 41.

129. "Family Protection Scorecard," 1987, Box 181, *Gerald Horne Papers*.

130. *Washington Post*, 4 October 1987.

in Angola and too hard on F.W. de Klerk in Pretoria while exhibiting "blindness to ANC's faults."[131]

The attack on Robinson was taking a toll, though the success of FSAM may have indicated otherwise. By late 1988 he was telling one of his main donors, Carol Bernstein Ferry, that "unfortunately, some of our long term core funders have retreated from funding U.S. organizations working on international issues," leading to "cash flow problems" for his Trans-Africa, meaning that "needed now are bridge funds" if the doors to his headquarters were not to be shuttered.[132] Ferry had informed him earlier that given the respectability of his group, she expected Trans-Africa to be able to raise sufficient funds among African Americans, but the news here was mixed. Robinson was planning a "Freedom Fest in support of our anti-apartheid work" with "Don King Productions," but this eponymously named firm was headed by a man whose reputation for probity was mixed.[133] The Washington Office on Africa had seen Robinson's group as a rival but by 1988 they were in the same dilemma: their leader Damu Smith was considering "drastic measures…taken to cut our staff and staff pay…."[134]

Ferry and her spouse had problems of their own. "We both have a CIA file," she said later, "and [an FBI file too]." They "sued the CIA…. We were the first people to win," though the "suit had taken years:" "really, five or six years" and "was very time consuming and expensive," detracting from their ability to donate to groups like Robinson's. There were "quite a number of years when you really had to be practically Ronald Reagan to write us a good letter and explain what you needed and not get three thousand dollars" but expensive litigation eroded this philanthropy. "We used to be the ace in the hole for all sorts of people," she said, "who just couldn't get it anywhere else and people knew that" but the times—and their bank account—had changed.[135]

Nonetheless, we continued to press Pretoria, often coordinating with the figures who would become leading legal scholars in

---

131. *The New Republic*, 9-16 July 1990, Box 84, *ACOARA*.

132. Randall Robinson to Carol Bernstein Ferry, 9 December 1988, Box 21, *Ferry Papers, Indiana University Purdue University- Indianapolis*.

133. Randall Robinson to Carol Bernstein and Ping Ferry, 28 September 1987, Box 21, *Ferry Papers*.

134. Damu Smith to WOA executive, 22 November 1988, Box 1, *Washington Office on Africa Papers, Yale University*.

135. Oral History, Carol Bernstein Ferry, 12 October 1994, Box 23, *Ferry Papers*.

post-1994 South Africa, including Kader Asmal and Albie Sachs.[136] One of our proposals was to initiate a project in Lusaka, sponsored by the National Conference of Black Lawyers and National Lawyers Guild, that would prepare litigation against U.S. corporations in the sub-region on various grounds.[137] When one of the preeminent legal scholars and litigators of his era, Michael Tigar of the University of Texas, supported this idea, Pretoria should have been worried.[138] Intriguingly, progressive U.S. lawyers were monitoring elections in Dixie and then taking that experience and applying it to the elections in 1989 that led to Namibian independence.[139] Earlier, Attorney Jeanne Woods made a proposal to the U.N. Special Committee Against Apartheid to fund an "Anti-Apartheid Litigation Project" that would focus, for example, on covert aid to UNITA in Angola, covert backing of U.S. mercenaries in the sub-region, enforcing Decree Number 1 barring the looting of Namibia's resources, and blocking the landings of South African Airways globally—and more.[140]

Tambo's trip to Washington was also the sounding of the starter's pistol for a race to the post-apartheid dispensation. It was then that even regime lawyers began maneuvering—said the ANC's PM Maduna—in a "controversy over funds from the U.S.," leading to a search for "alternative sources" of financing. But this led to an impasse too since these sources included signatories to the Sullivan Principles and others who "specifically declare their hostility toward the ANC."[141] Undeterred, left wing U.S. lawyers had already begun a Commission of Inquiry into the Crimes of Apartheid that included Congressman Crockett, Lennox Hinds of NCBL, Vicki Erenstein (who was to become the spouse of Toivo ya Toivo), and others.[142] Responding in kind, the Foreign Relations Committee of the U.S. Senate launched an investigation of their own: the focus was on

136. Kader Asmal to Michael Ratner, 19 January 1987, Box 203, *Gerald Horne Papers*.

137. Marguerite Hiken to National Lawyers Guild, circa 1987, Box 203, *Gerald Horne Papers*.

138. Michael Tigar to Marguerite Hiken, 5 March 1987, Box 203, *Gerald Horne Papers*.

139. International Association of Democratic Lawyers Observer Mission to Namibia, 19-25 October 1989, Reel 10, *Oliver Tambo Papers*.

140. Jeanne Woods to Abdennous Abrous, 8 September 1983, Box 191, *Gerald Horne Papers*.

141. P.M. Maduna to Oliver Tambo, 16 February 1987, Reel 11, *Oliver Tambo Papers*.

142. Memo on Commission of Inquiry, circa 1988, Reel 11, *Oliver Tambo Papers*.

"human rights abuses" by "liberation movements," notably in their sites of exile, e.g. Tanzania.[143]

The activism of left-wing U.S. lawyers was indicative of how close they had gotten to liberation movements and ruling parties in the sub-region. For example, W. Haywood Burns—a founder of NCBL and active in the NLG too—was part of a Manhattan law firm that represented Cuba, Angola, Algeria, Kenya, Tanzania, and others. It counseled Luanda in purchasing U.S. manufactured civilian aircraft, among other crucial tasks.[144]

As for U.S. courts, it was in 1988 that the ANC's Fred Dube filed suit against the State University of New York after he was denied tenure, a decision thought to be motivated by his stinging critique of Israel. Joining him in this litigation were fellow professors Leslie Owens and Amiri Baraka and he was represented by Lennox Hinds of the National Conference of Black Lawyers and Frank Deale of the Center for Constitutional Rights.[145] By 1989 he was fleeing New York for the Pacific Northwest, after his Long Island home was ransacked by assailants described as "Zionist thugs."[146]

The man born as Ernest Frederick Dube in 1929 matriculated, like so many, at Adams College in South Africa, which had a strong U.S. influence. There a principal from the U.S. objected to the dancing of Zulu women, feeling "they shouldn't kick their legs up," an encounter that apparently shaped Dube's view of Euro-Americans when he left to study in the U.S. He received a doctorate at Cornell University in 1975, a center of the rising "Black Power" ideology, whose influence eased his admission to this august institution. But the influence was bilateral since, he said, "I changed them because they were narrow nationalists.... They were supporters of PAC, not ANC"—but "they began to support the ANC after I had been there...." Many, he thought, were naïve about politics until their experience at the Sixth Pan African Congress in Tanzania in the 1970s. He was forced to depart Stony Brook unwillingly but remained in the U.S. until 1997 before repatriating.[147]

---

143. Max Sisulu, ANC Department of Economics and Planning to "Dear Comrade", 12 January 1989, Reel 15, *Oliver Tambo Papers*.

144. "Description of the Law Firm", circa 1980s, Reel 11, *Oliver Tambo Papers*.

145. E.F. Dube, et.al. vs. SUNY, 14 October 1988, Reel 16, *Oliver Tambo Papers*.

146. *The Militant*, 22 September 1989.

147. Oral History, Fred Dube, 24 July 2001, *University of Connecticut-Storrs*.

The fact that we were not able to save Dube's job was indicative of a wider point: despite the admitted strength of the anti-apartheid movement, it was imbedded in a nation with a formidable ultra-right that could claim with some justification that it founded the republic in the first instance. As Tambo was preparing to come to Washington for his trailblazing meeting with the Secretary of State, activists in Denver were "alarmed by the problem" of "our failure to make progress in engaging the Black community." The "Black religious community has never offered more than rhetorical support" and "one unidentified 'prominent' Minister advised caution because of her perception that AFSC [Quakers] is a Communist organization."[148] I shall never forget the experience of living in Harlem during this same time and going to collect signatures on various anti-apartheid petitions and encountering members of the "First World Alliance" who dismissed our efforts, for reasons that remain unclear, but may have had something to do with seeing the racist oppression of Africans as an embarrassment inconsistent with their vision of a heroic African past.

That was not the only problem we faced then. One of our cardinal attainments was the production of a weekly television program, *South Africa Now*, expertly produced by Danny Schecter. But just as the turning point of February 1990 loomed, the show was removed from the airwaves in the major market of Los Angeles. Schecter termed this a "bonehead" maneuver, but the reason echoed the earlier critique of Tutu—it was biased in favor of the ANC, a charge made repeatedly by the leftist turned right-winger David Horowitz, who led the crusade against Schecter's work.[149] Understandably, Schecter saw this as not his setback alone. Since 1985, he charged, there had been "less coverage" of apartheid in the mainstream U.S. news media as "press bans" by Pretoria were working. This was combined, he said, with a "tendency to take UNITA's claims at face value," inflating its importance dangerously.[150]

Another contradiction was revealed when Congressman Mervyn Dymally of the Black Caucus retreated from the push for sanctions against apartheid diamonds when an importer—Maurice Tempelsman, whose tentacles had extended in the region for decades and who was better known as a consort for Jacqueline Kennedy—decided

148. Linda Mizell Taylor to Jerry Herman, 17 November 1986, Box: PED NARMIC Program Resources Southern Africa, *AFSC*.

149. *Los Angeles Times*, 26 October 1990.

150. *Extra!* Newsletter of Fairness and Accuracy in Reporting, 4 March 1988, Box 163, *Gerald Horne Papers*.

to back his scholarship program.[151] The role of Dymally became even more controversial when he reportedly began to press Luanda to grant concessions to Dick Griffey, the music mogul. Angola needed help to combat the trade embargo and Dymally was willing to help—for a price. The congressman also was supportive of the kleptocrat once known as Joseph Mobutu, who—coincidentally—donated $250,000 to a Griffey charity.[152] For reasons that remained unclear Congressman Gus Savage of the Caucus also began to praise Mobutu, though mercenary motives were suspected.[153] Apparently these charges were not wholly false insofar as Jennifer Davis of ACOA chose to circulate the underlying news reports to Thabo Mbeki, TheoBen-wwGurirab of SWAPO, and many others.[154] In some ways, this maneuvering anticipated what befell the region after apartheid was finally removed when grasping profiteering skyrocketed, replacing what was thought to have been moral rectitude.

It was not just the premature counting of riches that was beginning to bedevil the movement. Again, in Los Angeles, politico Maxine Waters was accused by the activist Bud Day of acting similarly. She was tied to Robinson's Free South Africa Movement and, he said, had a "history of excluding other anti-apartheid groups"— "similar tactics are underway again," he said mournfully.[155] By the time Mandela visited in 1990, this cry had become an oratorio shouted from coast to coast about similar forms of exclusion.

The Quakers, who had global reach, faced a different problem in Southern Africa. "Because of its many hostile and warmongering activities in Southern Africa over the past 30 years," said their representatives Mackie McLeod and Zubaida Price, "the U.S. and those affiliated with it are considered enemies or at least treated with great suspicion by many influential people and institutions." Thus "any organizations with 'American' as part of its name immediately sets off warning alarms"—and this included the "American Friends," or the Quakers— "and makes the simplest transactions more complicated...." There was a saving grace, said the two informed

151. *Washington Post*, 25 January 1990.

152. *Washington Post*, 2 January 1990.

153. Undated column by Jack Anderson and Dale Van Atta, Box 1, *Carol Thompson/Bud Day Papers on South Africa, Michigan State University-East Lansing*.

154. Jennifer Davis to Thabo Mbeki, et.al., 4 January 1990, Box 73, *ACOARA*. See also Jennifer Davis to the Reverend William Howard, et.al., 8 June 1988, Box 73, *ACOARA*.

155. Bud Day to Lindiwe Mabuza, 10 June 1990, Box 4, *Thompson/Day Papers on South Africa, Michigan State University-East Lansing*.

correspondents: "the fact that we are African Americans with a track record of support for Southern Africa development has worked in our favor."[156] But even their obvious ancestry could not override the "commonly held belief that American NGOs are fair weather friends" at best, leading to a "deep mistrust of U.S. based institutions and their motives by Southern Africans."[157] This external suspicion of the Quakers then fed internal conflict, as when their staffer Carole Collins was accused of "institutionalized racism" and "manipulation," among other transgressions.[158]

U.S. nationals weren't the only ones facing problems. In South Africa, the ANC was grappling with the fact that Winnie Mandela had become close to Robert Brown, a Negro Republican from North Carolina and a wealthy public relations man who had been close to President Nixon. Apparently, she gave him authority to exploit the family name, but her husband balked. Brown also raised $100,000 so that she could obtain a new home (doubtlessly in anticipation of further enrichment as a result of this act of "charity.") The duplicitous Reagan had wanted to appoint him as the ambassador in Pretoria but accusations of union busting against his firm helped to scuttle this effort. He also opposed sanctions, making him an odd match for Mandela.[159] Lindiwe Mabuza, an ANC envoy in the U.S., found the "connection with Robert Brown bothersome" and, thus suggested there was the "need" for "guidance" from headquarters in order to respond.[160]

Still, the sudden appearance of Brown, a skilled manipulator, was suggestive of a wider and ultimately more profound point: the vultures were circling, waiting to pounce on the decaying apartheid system.

---

156. Mackie McLeod and Zubaida Price, Monthly Letter #1, July-August 1990, Box: ID Africa Administration East South West, *AFSC*.

157. Mackie McLeod and Zubaida Price to AFSC, 17 April 1990, Box: ID Africa Administration East South West, *AFSC*.

158. Memo on Collins, 27 April 1990, Box: ID Africa Administration East South West, *AFSC*.

159. *Washington Post*, 8 March 1989.

160. Lindiwe Mabuza to "Dear Zwelakhe," 9 March 1990, Box 15, Folder 1, *Washington Mission, ANC Records*.

Chapter 22

Liberation, 1990-1994

BY February 1990 I was teaching at the lovely Santa Barbara campus of the University of California. On an early Sunday morning I was returning from a festive weekend in neighboring Los Angeles when the dulcet tones of National Public Radio commentator Daniel Schorr announced that Nelson Mandela had been freed and the ANC and SACP unbanned.

I had heard this was coming and I also knew that Pretoria was facing an unrivalled crisis, but I confess I was taken aback by this announcement. What unfolded over the next four years was a round-robin of negotiations, leading to elections in the Spring of 1994, combined with bloody violence unleashed to weaken the ANC-SACP alliance at the behest of apartheid's recalcitrant defenders and their stooges. Tragically, as Mandela was being freed, Tambo's health was deteriorating; the man who had led the movement was collapsing just as the finish line was being reached. Tellingly, he received medical aid from a Black Sea facility in the similarly collapsing Soviet Union, in East Germany and Bulgaria—as well as Sweden.[1]

Apparently, de Klerk sped up this inevitable announcement. The so-called Afrikaner Resistance Movement threatened the Reverend Jesse Jackson as he prepared to travel to South Africa, inducing Pretoria—according to one journalist—to free Mandela before the pastor's arrival so that he could not take any credit for the heralded release.[2] As early as August 1988 then Vice President Bush had been told that "the South Africans are considering releasing Mandela soon."[3]

---

1. Luli Callinicos, *Oliver Tambo*, 613.

2. *Reuters*, 1 February 1990, Box 139, *Leroy Walker Africa News Service Archive.*

3. Donald Gregg to Vice President Bush, 23 August 1988, OA/ID 19872, *Donald Gregg Files, George Bush Presidential Library, College Station, Texas.*

Pretoria had chosen a propitious moment to exit center stage. The collapse of the Berlin Wall in November 1989 foretold the impending collapse of the socialist camp itself, debilitating a bulwark for anti-apartheid forces. Speaking before parliament in February 1990, de Klerk admitted as much, speaking of the "unstoppable tide" then sweeping through Eastern Europe. He also denounced the "brutal violence" that, he said, characterized Beijing's rule. "The year of 1989," he announced confidently, "will go down in history as the year in which Stalinist Communism expired," and this, he insisted, was "of decisive importance in Africa...."[4] Apartheid's spy chief, Niel Barnard—of German descent and who grew to maturity in Namibia and, typically, referred to English as the "language of the conqueror"—gloated that the collapse of the socialist camp "offered" a "unique chance" to press the ANC. In the same context he noted the "paramilitary assistance" offered to the Zulu chauvinist forces of Gatsha Buthelezi, which contributed to an ocean of bloodletting and the further weakening of the ANC as negotiations commenced.[5]

Buthelezi was still shunned by most African Americans. The Reverend Joseph Lowery termed him an "Uncle Tom,"[6] the ultimate put-down. By way of contrast, former ANC leader Joe Matthews was by the early 1990s a major figure of the Inkatha Freedom Party and called its leader Buthelezi "my best friend."[7] Standing with Lowery was veteran Chicago activist Prexy Nesbitt, who persuaded the Reverend Jesse Jackson to disinvite Buthelezi from speaking alongside him.[8]

The gushing of blood in South Africa captured the attention of the U.S. Congress through the impassioned testimony of Gay McDougall, a leading African American attorney who was frequently in South Africa during this time. In July 1992 she testified that "during recent months political violence in South Africa has reached the highest levels ever in its history." "Parallels between the Los Angeles riots and South Africa's violence have often been drawn in the past few months," she said in reference to a recent racially tinged conflagration in California. In L.A. pressure caused the disbanding

---

4. Speech by F.W. de Klerk, 2 February 1990, Second Session of 9th Parliament of South Africa, Box 20, *William Gray, New York Public Library, Schomburg Center.*

5. Niel Barnard as told to Tobie Wiese, *Secret Revolution*, 131, 139, 151.

6. *Atlanta Journal Constitution*, 17 June 1991.

7. *Johannesburg Star*, 8 July 1993.

8. Prexy Nesbitt to Operation PUSH, 9 February 1991, Box 4, Folder 40, *Prexy Nesbitt Papers.*

of a unit "accused…of operating an elite spy network"—why could not Pretoria act similarly, she asked plaintively.[9] McDougall's intervention was another sign that attorneys remained in the vanguard of anti-apartheid resistance. Thus, Jeanne Woods had continued to send detailed analyses to Tambo of "the current U.S. sanctions against South Africa."[10]

President de Klerk had been primed for this moment, having gained requisite international experience necessary for such a maneuver during the tumultuous year of 1975 by serving as chief envoy to the United Nations and the United States too.[11] A U.S. publication captured the tumult of the times when a cover story in February 1990 featured a picture of Mandela and above him the apparently unrelated headline: "Life After Lenin: Gorbachev's Biggest Gamble."[12]

Days before President de Klerk's epochal announcement about Mandela, Foreign Minister Roelof "Pik" Botha was to be found in Budapest, seeking—as was the historical tendency—labor that could be defined as "white" in order to bolster his faltering regime. The ANC condemned the welcome he was granted but it was simply one more sign of the radical change in the global climate.[13] The search for skilled labor in Eastern Europe was monitored by the ANC.[14] The group was kept busy as legions were lining up at South African legations in search of a new home in Africa. By early March 1990 an estimated 21,000 Hungarians had applied for visas for South Africa.[15]

Mendi Msimang of the ANC sought urgent consultations with the Hungarian envoy in London, Dr. Josef Gyorke. The South African leader found Botha's visit to be "disturbing" and a "grave concern," but this was only the beginning of a chain of turnabouts. The Hungarian explained that there were already "50,000 ethnic Hungarians in South Africa" and, in any case, "there was a new situation in Hungary; there was a new political picture" and the ANC would simply have to adjust to it.[16]

---

9. Testimony of Gay McDougall, 23 July 1992, Box 3, File 18, *Prexy Nesbitt Papers, Columbia College-Chicago.*

10. Jeanne Woods to Oliver Tambo, 9 June 1988, Reel 3, *Oliver Tambo Papers.*

11. Biographical Details on de Klerk, no date, Box 20, *William Gray Papers.*

12. *Newsweek*, 19 February 1990.

13. *Los Angeles Times*, 6 January 1990.

14. Clipping, 19 January 1990, Box 63, Folder 116, *Lusaka Mission, ANC Records.*

15. *The Age*, 19 April 1990, Box 63, Folder 116. *Lusaka Mission.*

16. Minutes of Meeting, 16 January 1990, Reel 10, *Oliver Tambo Papers.*

There was a new situation globally. Pik Botha secretly visited China[17] and by December 1991 President de Klerk himself was in Moscow, one of the last heads of state to visit the imploding Soviet Union.[18]

The ANC found that this was simply the beginning. Pretoria also launched an advertising campaign in West Germany in order to attract, as one journalist wrote, "skilled East Germans" to South Africa. At this juncture, it was said, South Africa counted 13,000 Poles, 6,000 Hungarians, and 3,000 Slovaks and Czechs among those defined as "white"—with more in the pipeline.[19] It was not just attracting migrants. "Childless white South African couples," said one observer, "are poised to descend on Romania for an orphan shopping spree."[20] By one account, as early as April 1990, "30,000" from Eastern Europe had migrated to South Africa in search of what was called a "promised land."[21] This population shift had an added advantage for Pretoria in serving to heighten already conflicted race relations: "South African Blacks uneasy about immigrant influx," was a headline from 1992.[22]

Weeks after de Klerk's bold move, Namibian independence was proclaimed, a direct result of the heroic role of Cuban troops who bested the apartheid military on the battlefield, narrowing Pretoria's options. This vast territory, which had suffered from the worst examples of colonialism—that of pre-Nazi Germany, and then apartheid South Africa—was finally able to escape from tyranny. Prexy Nesbitt was compelled to celebrate. "I was invited to Namibia's independence [as a] guest," he recalled later, but could not find a place to stay. But he had to witness this important moment in history when the new Namibian flag was unfurled at an elaborate independence ceremony, "so I slept for three nights on a chair in the Kalahari Sands Hotel, Namibia's biggest hotel....I had no money...most of us who did this work, we had nothing, we had no money...." However, like his preceding work, he found it fulfilling, nonetheless. "I was privileged to be at one of the most extraordinary moments probably of my whole career," he exulted, "which was the night the flag raised for the Independence of Namibia and I just, just was teary-eyed, goose bumps all over me." But even then Namibia was just an

17. *Sydney Morning Herald*, 14 October 1991.
18. *Australian Financial Review*, 9 December 1991.
19. *The Economist*, 20 January 1989.
20. *The Independent* [U.K.], 18 January 1990.
21. *The Independent*, 17 April 1990.
22. *Reuters*, 29 February 1992.

appetizer before the main course. For when the new president, Sam Nujoma, was introduced there was "this incredible bellow of sound" from the masses there assembled. "But when Mandela was brought up into the stadium a few minutes later, they went bananas they just went berserk," a preview of the sustained applause the newly freed political prisoner would receive when he toured the U.S. a few months later.[23]

This turn of events left U.S. imperialism in an uneasy position. On the one hand, the long held dream of the dissolution of the Soviet Union seemed well within sight, yet somehow Washington was unable to block the rise of the ANC-SACP alliance, the thwarting of which was an essential aspect of anticommunism. This setback was an outgrowth of another troubling sign: the refusal of African Americans to be seduced—to the same extent as others—by the siren song of anticommunism, which hampered Washington's ability to achieve a full victory. This was the backdrop for a telephone conversation between de Klerk and President George H.W. Bush on 10 February 1990. At 12:30 in the afternoon, Bush was to be found at Camp David, the presidential retreat in Maryland, where the South African stressed that "there is a risk of mass mobilization that can be dangerous," speaking of the unleashing of pent-up anti-apartheid sentiments. "You are the leader of the free world, Mr. President" were his unctuous and archaic words, exposing the debility of a formulation— "free world"? —that somehow included a suffocating apartheid. "I hope we can avoid having checklists," de Klerk insisted, "that make it look like we in South Africa are being forced by the outside world" to change, but this was inevitable since external pressure was a sine qua non for the retreat of apartheid. Bush sought to shore up the embattled leader, inviting him to the U.S. while recognizing correctly that "there will be some criticism here on the left...." Then he provided unsolicited analytical advice, telling de Klerk, "you have problems, like we all do in elective governments. Yours are on your right." In response de Klerk seemed to suggest that his prime concern was not internal party politics but the fact that "there is great cohesion in the ANC," including "strong party discipline...."[24]

President de Klerk proved to be oily and unctuous in his dealings with the White House. "We recognize your courage in the Gulf," he told Bush in the Cabinet Room on 24 September 1990, referring to the

23. Oral History, Prexy Nesbitt, 1 April 2009, *Columbia College-Chicago*.

24. Telephone Conversation, 10 February 1990, Box 2, OA/ID CF 01297-013, *John M. Ordway Files, Bush Presidential Library*.

crisis in Kuwait and Iraq. "We support you," he insisted as if there might have been doubt. "I just saw Savimbi," he confided, and "he is positively inclined" too. Yet, again, his prime concern was that "the ANC, the PAC and the trade unions," all "must be moved away from socialism." In Madagascar, he told Bush, "they told us not to create a black majority government," seeding false hope. President Joaquim Chissano in Maputo "says to us he is against sanctions"—which, if an accurate representation, was also misreading the forces capable of imposing sanctions. "Only Mugabe," he said acerbically, "still displays hostility on our Marshall Plan for the region for the eleven states." Bush had his own grievances: "I took some flak on calling for a peaceful solution with Mandela. Jesse Jackson jumped on me," he added ruefully. But de Klerk repetitively returned to his major theme: "ANC policies militate against your own economic values," he said. "They must moderate their policies." He also reinforced the message from Bush's own base: Mandela, he asserted, "is tied up with things you don't believe in.... Qadhafi [sic] is their comrade." "Castro is another one," added Bush agreeably.[25]

In yet another telephone conversation, de Klerk continued pounding Mandela. After thanking Bush and "European leaders" for their aid to his tottering regime, he launched into another diatribe against Mandela who—he claimed— "has problems with his middle management." Bush, on the same wavelength, chose to "raise the question" of the SACP. "When Mandela was here," he said, I touched on it and reported to you that I raised it with him. I noticed a big gathering with the Communist leaders. What is the state of play with the Communist Party and an end of violence," he asked of two disconnected issues? "The alliance is coming under stress," was de Klerk's reply about the ANC, SACP, and their union comrades. "The wisdom of continuing the alliance as in the past is very much a subject which is alive. I think the Communists will become an albatross around their neck. My biggest problem with the moderates is not the ANC," he said slyly, "but the Communist factors in the ANC...."[26]

Mandela disconcerted de Klerk when, in one of his first public remarks on 11 February 1990 in Cape Town, he said unequivocally, "I salute the South African Communist Party for its sterling

---

25. Minutes of Meeting between Bush and de Klerk, 24 September 1990, Box 1, *John Ordway Files, Bush Presidential Library*.

26. Telephone Conversation between President Bush and President de Klerk, 13 August 1990, 9:31-9:41 A.M., Box 1, *John Ordway Files, Bush Presidential Library*.

contribution to the struggle for democracy.... I salute General Secretary Joe Slovo, one of our finest patriots."[27]

Bush was being tugged by his base and the overall anticommunist atmosphere at a moment that simultaneously saw maximum crisis in the socialist camp and mass anti-apartheid sentiment domestically and globally. Perforce this had to produce a compromise. Pretoria was wise to stress their support for the White House on Iraq, seeking to compel the ANC to do the same. "We were disturbed that you took exception" to the ANC statement on this matter, Mandela said to Bush in a March 1991 message. The ANC leader was opposed to any concession to weakening sanctions for South African Airways. "Apartheid is still being practiced," he said. "I didn't expect the ANC to support us," said Bush in reply, adding with a twist, "when the South African government supported us, we welcomed it." "I don't want to mislead you," he said, an oblique reference to his dilemma in seeking to prop up de Klerk and unravel the ANC while appearing not to do so. Nonplussed, Mandela ended the telephone conversation by saying cheerily, "I feel good, especially having heard your voice today. I'm planning to leave for a month's vacation,"[28] he added in a carefree flourish that belied the complications he was facing.

By May 1991, Mandela remained exuberant. Speaking by telephone to Bush, then ensconced in the Oval Office, he began familiarly, telling the beleaguered president, "I have a one year old grandson. He runs to the telephone every time it rings and yells, 'Bush! Bush,'' a reaction to the frequent incoming calls from the White House, an abrupt change from not so distant days when the ANC was derided by Washington as little more than a "Communist Front." Pleasantries aside, Mandela returned to the grimness of the moment, detailing the "wave of violence in Soweto" that was breathtaking. "The government is doing nothing. In the Transvaal since last year ten thousand people have lost their lives. The government has failed to respond.... There can be no question of talking to the government" as a result. The Yale-educated president could only muster wanly, "Oh dear," before adding, "you know our last phone call they tried

27. Remarks by Mandela, 11 February 1990, in Nelson Mandela, *Let Freedom Reign: The Words of Nelson Mandela*, Northampton, Massachusetts: Interlink, 2010, 76-83, 78.

28. Telephone Conversation between President Bush and Deputy President Mandela, 6 March 1991, Box 1, *John Ordway Files*.

to make it as if there was some big division between us." Mandela: "Yes, I know, thank you." End of conversation.[29]

Perhaps tact and diplomacy prevented Mandela from noting what the press was reporting. As of early 1991 U.S. corporations continued to ship shotguns to South Africa for unavoidably malign purposes.[30] And General Dynamics of the U.S. continued to sell small aircraft to Pretoria ideal for aerial surveillance of assembled masses.[31]

Mandela's pique was becoming harder to shroud in light of the bloodshed in South Africa to which Pretoria turned a blind eye, at best or aided actively, at worst. When in 1993 the White House wanted the ANC leader to come together with de Klerk in Philadelphia on the 4th of July, "tempers were extremely high," said the ANC's Lindiwe Mabuza, at a "meeting of the anti-apartheid coalition" there. The joint appearance was viewed as "a mockery and outrage," a "counter-coup." "There are some who want to picket because ANC is deemed insensitive to the historical consequences of an independence celebration that kept the African enslaved and the Native American dispossessed of land...." Old tensions were rising; it was thought that Jerry Herman of the Quakers was "nursing an old grudge against ANC" and encouraging protests as a result. Then there was the related question of "singling Coke out of all the U.S. companies," which "had become problematic since Coke had become responsive in terms of black empowerment, social responsibility, etc."[32] As it turned out, there was a protest.[33] (But it was not only Coke that caused consternation in the ranks. Annette Hutchins of Soft Sheen in Chicago, which specialized in converting the kinky locks of African women's hair to a texture more like those of their European counterparts, wanted to invade the South Africa market, though this may not have been a blow against white supremacy.[34])

F.W. de Klerk was not thrilled about this Philadelphia meeting either. "In front of us in a wide and leafy mall stretching into the distance there was a crowd of several thousand people, most of them black Americans." Sufficiently inspired, the Reverend Leon Sullivan

---

29. Telephone conversation between President Bush and Deputy President Mandela, 3 May 1991, Box 1, *John Ordway Files*.

30. *Washington Post*, 17 January 1991.

31. *Business Week*, 25 June 1990.

32. Lindiwe Mabuza to Thabo Mbeki, 1 June 1993, Box 15, Folder 1, *Washington Mission, ANC Records*.

33. *Philadelphia Daily News*, 17 June 1992.

34. Annette Hutchins to Lindiwe Mabuza, 2 December 1992, Box 15, Folder 2, *Washington Mission*.

uttered remarks that de Klerk found distasteful. But in retrospect this assembly should have been a symbol of what was to come: the ANC, weakened by the erosion of the socialist camp, had been convinced by Washington to provide not only an unsightly photo opportunity of a faux reconciliation between victims and victimizers, but also an indication that the latter would not be subjected to war crimes' trials or even meaningful expropriation but saluted as "realistic" negotiators.[35]

In that context the pummeling of Mozambique should be considered, which immeasurably weakened the Frontline States as it sent a foreboding signal to them all. By 1991, the expulsion of ANC militants from Maputo was still being felt, as Tambo informed "Dear Comrade President Chissano" that "I have not had contact with you for a very long time and this is indeed regrettable"[36]—and damaging. How could anti-apartheid forces advance without simple coordination at the top? When Tambo bumped into the widow of Samora Machel in Manhattan, he had to apologize: "how could I have made the mistake of not knowing that I was talking to you in New York,"[37] he said apologetically, a further indication of lack of coordination at the highest level. The infamous Nkomati Accord had taken its toll.

F.W. de Klerk should have considered himself lucky to have escaped the fate usually meted out to the final figurehead of a tyrannical system. He complained that sensitive matters were "being hidden from me," referring to "secret projects" to fan discord and bloodshed among anti-apartheid forces. His lack of sympathy for anti-apartheid measures in the U.S. suggested how effective these bills were. His 1990 visit to Washington should have illustrated the true balance of forces, as he was embraced warmly, which even he found surprising. He was "caught...off guard" when he was "received with full military honors," including the playing of the Afrikaner anthem, "Die Stem." "I found it difficult to hold back my tears," he said unashamedly. He and his spouse "struck up a warm personal relationship" with the Bushes, "which has continued ever since then."[38]

The response of the Congressional Black Caucus to the new dispensation in South Africa was mixed. By late February 1990 Congressmen William Gray and Ronald V. Dellums, who had performed yeoman service on the anti-apartheid front, were headed to Lusaka

---

35. F.W. de Klerk, *The Last Trek*, 281.
36. Oliver Tambo to President Chissano, 21 May 1991, Reel 3, *Tambo Papers*.
37. Oliver Tambo to Graca Machel, 21 May 1991, Reel 3, *Tambo Papers*.
38. F.W. de Klerk, *The Last Trek*, 152, 188, 190.

to confer with the freed leader and his comrades. It was reported they had "far-reaching conversations" with the ANC leadership while Mandela himself deftly stressed the "importance of the American legislature's independence of the Executive."[39]

Also on the list of questionable proposals was the one made by Walter Fauntroy, an erstwhile force in the Congressional Black Caucus, who wanted to establish a telephone line to raise funds for the ANC—with his firm taking a considerable slice of the proceeds.[40] Mandela than agreed to a two-hour interview hosted by BET [Black Entertainment Television] of Washington, where he promised to mention Fauntroy's proposal.[41] By February 1992, Fauntroy had landed a hefty $700,000 contract in return for raising funds and lobbying for the ANC.[42] As the ANC got closer to power, they spent considerable time fielding profit-making ideas from allies, the very process of which was baneful.

Perhaps more compatible with the movement's aims was the offer by mega-musician Quincy Jones to release his latest album—*Back on the Block*—in South Africa and "donate my portion of the royalties to the ANC."[43] This was becoming a popular idea: Stevie Wonder offered to donate royalties from his *Keep our Love Alive* album to the ANC too.[44] Mandela replied to Jones, flattering him as he proposed that Jones bring together other stars—including Whitney Houston, Stevie Wonder, and LL Cool J for ANC fundraising concerts.[45] Jones was enthusiastic. "When the fires of rage over the Rodney King verdict exploded here in our own Los Angeles, it was quite tempting to wonder if USA didn't actually mean 'Union of South Africa,'" a reference to a celebrated case of racist injustice involving the acquittal of "white" police officers caught on tape administering a vicious beating to an African-American motorist. So motivated, Jones agreed

39. Minutes of Meeting, 28 February-5 March 1990, Box 18, *William Gray Papers, Schomburg Center*. See also *Philadelphia Tribune*, 2 March 1990.

40. Walter Fauntroy to Lindiwe Mabuza, 27 November 1991, Box 23, Folder 16, *Washington Mission,*

41. Nelson Mandela to "Dear Walter" Fauntroy, 17 December 1991, Box 23, Folder 16, *Washington Mission.*

42. *Sunday Times*, February 1992, Box 23, Folder 16, *Washington Mission.*

43. Quincy Jones to Thomas Nkobi, 1 August 1990, Box 16, Folder 6. *Washington Mission.*

44. Lennox Hinds and Maurice Garber to Lindiwe Mabuza, 20 March 1991, Box 27, Folder 54, *Washington Mission.*

45. Nelson Mandela to Quincy Jones, 27 March 1992, Box 16, Folder 7, *Washington Mission.*

to organize "three concerts for the ANC in South Africa," punctuating the accord with a "proud yes!"[46]

Mandela's breakthrough into the rarified realm of celebrity was evidenced further when the then popular late night chat show hosted by Arsenio Hall wanted to feature him and his spouse "as our special guests" for a television audience estimated in the millions.[47] Soon Mandela was thanking Wonder for "your most enormous gift" as he noted that the "richness and strength of the music generated by African Americans and by you in particular have [been] a constant source of enormous inspiration to me...."[48] A similar note was sent to "Bill and Camille" Cosby, the comic actor and his spouse, "for the very generous donation...."[49]

The youthful filmmaker Spike Lee had a similar interest. "We're [seeking] to have him in Malcolm X," he said speaking of slotting Mandela in his latest movie. "This is one of the most important films in the history of CINEMA," he emphasized.[50] Lindiwe Mabuza of the ANC mulled the idea of having her leader "as a teacher at the end of the film in a Soweto classroom," though she was not as skeptical as others.[51] "Madiba [Mandela] would give a lesson or present Malcolm X's 'By Any Means Necessary' speech...Our own recommendation is that this gets the movement's endorsement."[52] In September 1991 she told the moviemaker, "we finally have approval."[53]

But suddenly there was an abrupt reversal, causing Lee to complain directly to "Dear Nelson" that "your letter was a shock.... I think someone is giving you misinformation about the film. We do not want you to play Malcolm X," he insisted.[54] Mandela had told him that "after careful consideration and discussion with my

---

46. Quincy Jones to Nelson Mandela, Spring 1992, Box 24, Folder 19, *Washington Mission.*

47. Velda Fennell, Talent Coordinator to Lindiwe Mabuza, 19 December 1991, Box 16, Folder 8, *Washington Mission, ANC Records.*

48. Nelson Mandela to Stevie Wonder, 10 June 1990, Box 17, Folder 19, *Washington Mission.*

49. Nelson Mandela to "Bill and Camille" Cosby, circa 1990, Box 17, Folder 19.

50. Spike Lee to "Dear Lindiwe", 15 March 1991, Box 17, Folder 15, *Washington Mission, ANC Records.*

51. Lindiwe Mabuza to Pallo Jordan, 1 May 1991, Box 17, Folder 15.

52. Lindiwe Mabuza to Saki Macozoma, 20 July 1991, Box 17, Folder 15.

53. Lindiwe Mabuza to "Dear Spike," 19 September 1991, Box 17, Folder 15.

54. Spike Lee to "Dear Nelson," no date, Box 17, Folder 15. See also in the same box and folder, Preston Holmes to Nelson Mandela, 31 December 1991.

colleagues" he had decided not to "participate in the film you propose...."[55] Another looming setback was the 1992 decision by boxer Muhammad Ali to visit South Africa. As Mabuza put it, he "will come first and foremost as a Moslem. This might be fine in a Moslem country" but not South Africa.[56]

But as the ANC was being accepted by the notoriously unprogressive U.S. mainstream, compromise was ineluctable. By 1992, Mandela told tennis star Arthur Ashe that he was "deeply grieved to learn of your illness" (he soon would die of AIDS). Forgotten was the controversy surrounding the athlete's violation of the cultural and sports boycott. (I recall confronting Ashe personally about this violation in Manhattan in the 1970s at a book signing.) Mandela, who had written critically about "Black Consciousness," now said it "was an important part of our political growth and development. You must take some credit for that," which went beyond flattery to cant. "I can never forget my own joy at meeting you," he concluded, which was likely accurate.[57]

Subtly but directly, the U.S. elite media and their often unwitting Negro sidekicks sought to force Mandela and the ANC into a framework that elided armed struggle and alignment with the socialist camp with something more familiar: Mandela as Martin Luther King in a grand moral struggle. Mabuza was asked to arrange for the ANC leader to pose "alone looking at the statue of Abraham Lincoln at the Lincoln Memorial,"[58] as Dr. King might have done.

This incipient trend was buoyed by the presidential defeat of the Republican Party in 1992, as the new Democratic Party regime led by Bill Clinton was thought to be less sympathetic to apartheid. Combined with the erosion of the socialist camp, the need to conciliate the victorious Democrats—who, after all, did not obtain the majority of the votes in 1992—helped to push the ANC further down the road of compromise, which could easily veer into opportunism. These trends did not deter Randall Robinson from lambasting Clinton after it was revealed that he had profited from investment in De [Beers, the South African giant. It was an "outrage," Robinson charged, "it goes beyond uninformed [in]sensitivity," the norm for

55. Nelson Mandela to Spike Lee, 30 December 1991, Box 17, Folder 15.

56. Lindiwe Mabuza to Andrew Dipela, 22 March 1992, Box 22, Folder 1, *Washington Mission, ANC Records.*

57. Nelson Mandela to Arthur Ashe, 24 April 1992, Box 22, Folder 2, *Washington Mission, ANC Records.*

58. Letter to Lindiwe Mabuza, 22 June 1990, Box 28, Folder 6, *Washington Mission.*

Democrats.[59] But even this justifiable criticism may have been weakening to anti-apartheid forces who no longer enjoyed the unalloyed backstop of the socialist camp.

Then there were those who sought to become involved in the post-apartheid dispensation but were rejected by the ANC. This list included Professor Albert Blaustein of Rutgers University, who had been asked by Buthelezi to participate in drafting the constitution, but the ANC and SACP objected because of his firmly declared anticommunism.[60] The shunning of Blaustein was one piece of a larger mosaic: as the ANC had evolved to become accepted by the U.S. mainstream—which often leaned to the right—how should it react? Sidmel Estes-Sumpter was a former president of the National Association of Black Journalists, a group whose members were more likely to be favorable to the ANC than the mainstream press. Yet, as she told the ANC's Pallo Jordan, the firm hired to handle the flood of press coverage garnered by Mandela was inadequate: "I have never been treated as discourteously and rudely and capriciously," she complained.[61]

It was evident that Washington was masquerading as an honest broker, an umpire, but was actually a player, adroitly seeking to weaken the ANC—which was not difficult considering the continuing crisis in the Soviet Union—though it should have been known that the Nationalist Party was a frail reed still.

By July 1991 Mandela was not as cheery in light of the U.S. move to lift sanctions. "Sanctions applied by the U.S. in the CAAA," said Mandela of the Comprehensive Anti-Apartheid Act, "have helped immeasurably. And we are grateful." With his own deftness, Mandela told Bush that "on lifting the sanctions we differ on timing," not the actual fact, which could have meant: lift sanctions after the ANC wins elections. "Your action is premature," said Mandela, since "one can do damage if there are two parties talking to each other and a third party with a reputation for impartiality"—a presumed reference to Bush— "appears to be acting in favor of one or another of the parties," problems ensue. What this colloquy reflected was the ANC's weakened position in light of Moscow's retreat. "The abolition of apartheid is not complete," he declaimed correctly. What

59. *Washington Times*, 9 July 1992.

60. *Reuters*, 22 January 1992, Box 15, Folder 1, *Washington Mission, ANC Records*.

61. Sidmel Estes-Sumpter to Pallo Jordan, circa 1990, Folder 16, Folder 7, *Washington Mission*.

about political prisoners and their release, he asked properly. "Violence is raging in the country," he added.[62]

By mid-1992 Bush's popularity after the apparent victory over Iraq was fading rapidly, contributing to his defeat in November. It had been known for some time that African Americans were not as supportive of the Gulf War as others, with one analyst arguing that the White House's policy of "constructive engagement" with Pretoria had soured them on the president.[63] "I know you have been calling," Bush told Mandela. "I'm sorry I didn't have the time to take the call. I've been running around as busy as a chicken with its neck cut off," he said in an oblique reference to his impending electoral beheading. Sticking to his talking points, Mandela replied, "our demands are very reasonable.... We have already ma[d]e a compromise twice," since "all the constitutions in the past ...have been adopted by a simple majority." "This is the first time they have suggested a larger majority," he said of the de Klerk bloc. "This is a problem, since we have a constituency which wants a 51 percent majority." Bush feinted by adding "I remember your triumphant visit here.... You should take it easy. I'm no spring chicken and you're older than I am."

In this state of flux, when the old was heading for the exit but the new was yet to be born (or even reveal itself fully), Washington was hedging its bets. Even before conversing with de Klerk, the White House arranged a meeting with Major General H.B. Holomisa, Chairman of the Military Council of Transkei—an illegitimate "Bantustan." Bush's aide David Passage had breakfast with him on 31 January though he was forced to acknowledge, "we fully realize that the U.S. has no relations with Transkei...."[64] Before that, Bush's National Security Advisor Brent Scowcroft was orchestrating a U.S. visit by Albertina Sisulu, described not as the spouse of the presumed Communist Walter Sisulu, but, more respectably, as "matriarch of... South Africa's 'Black Consciousness' Movement...."[65]

Bush, a center-rightist from Texas, was not trusted fully by the hard right base of the Republican Party. He had never been elected to statewide office in Texas as a result, the usual launching pad for national office. By November 1984, as the Free South Africa Movement was

62. Telephone conversation between President Bush and Deputy President Mandela, 10 July 1991, Box 1, *John Ordway Files.*

63. *New York Times*, 2 March 1991.

64. Memorandum, 1 February 1990, Box 1, OA/ID CFOO212, *David Passage Files, Bush Presidential Library.*

65. Brent Scowcroft to President Bush, 10 May 1989, Box 2, OA/ID CF01297-013, *John Ordway Files, George Bush Presidential Library.*

taking off, an aide of his fretted that "nobody's defending the South Africans but the issue is becoming who can attack them the loudest."[66] By 1986, with Bush gearing up to run for the White House in 1988, his aides debated if he should be so bold as to speak on South Africa at the NAACP convention. "U.S. policy on South Africa is in flux," it was counseled, "and now under review," making such a speech inadvisable.[67]

Part of the problem for political figures like Bush was that his more affluent campaign donors were often comfortable with the status quo in South Africa. The Dallas real estate developer Trammel Crow was among these. "I have been to South Africa," he told the Vice President in mid-1987, "and there is no distortion as wild and weird today as that is being promoted about Africa." He managed to admit that apartheid was "wrong," but countered quickly that also wrong was "the provision in the Liberian constitution that prevents white people from owning property." He forwarded an article that for good measure railed vituperatively against the "Communist controlled" ANC.[68]

Still, what was most telling in Bush's pre-presidential deliberations about apartheid was the counsel of his aide Thaddeus Garrett—who happened to be a Negro. "Do not use the term 'constructive engagement,'" he advised his boss, as it had been discredited by the anti-apartheid movement. "Do not refer to the 'Sullivan Principles'" either, Bush was told, since massive ideological bombardment had forced the Philadelphia pastor to become a backer of divestment, denuding his previous campaign of respectability. "Do not say that sanctions don't work" because it was clear to anyone sentient that they did.[69] Instead, maintain credibility by demanding freedom for Mandela. In other words, as Bush was on the verge of seizing the highest office in the land, he was reduced to making his prime demand freedom for a man thought to be a trusted cadre of the SACP, just as their presumed patron in Moscow was on the cusp of imploding. "For both domestic and foreign policy reasons," General Scowcroft was told in October 1989, "the U.S. needs to be among [those] pushing for change away from apartheid." In other words,

66. Memorandum, 30 November 1984, OA/ID 19780, *Donald Gregg Files, Bush Presidential Library.*

67. Memorandum, 1 July 1986, OA/ID 19816, *Donald Gregg Files.*

68. Trammel Crow to Vice President Bush, 10 June 1987, OA/ID 19835, *Donald Gregg Files.*

69. Thaddeus Garrett to David Bates, 12 January 1988, OA/ID 19872, *Donald Gregg Files.*

at that moment the former slaveholders' republic could not afford to show its true face, since this was alienating at home and compromising abroad.[70]

Unsurprisingly, the hard right base of the Republican Party did not accept the idea of demanding Mandela's freedom with equanimity. Mara and Ray Croissant were among those upset by the embrace of Mandela, who—they argued— "admires the arch foes of our western, liberal, democratic philosophy—Gadhafi [sic], Castro, Puerto Rican terrorists and Arafat." Worse, they said, "if we support Mandela, we support this sort of philosophy in the United States as well as in South Africa. There are serious implications for both countries," they reminded.[71] Carl McIntire, a religious zealot and prime cheerleader for the ruling party, was "strongly" in "protest."[72] Earle M. Craig of Newport Beach, California, one of the wealthier suburbs in the nation, expressed his "disapproval" of Mandela, "an avowed Communist and terrorist." Instead, he implored, "please keep supporting Jonas Savimbi…." Craig was no stranger to the president, giving his words added meaning. "[I] always enjoy hearing from my father and mother," he added with a fillip, "about their visits with you and Mrs. Bush in the White House."[73] "Explain to me," groused Jeff Ohly of Greenville, South Carolina "why we have welcomed with open arms a Marxist revolutionary," meaning Mandela. "He should not have even been granted a visa," let alone have the red carpet rolled out for him, which is what occurred. "His beliefs and values," he told Senator J. Strom Thurmond, a veteran race-baiter, "are contrary to our capitalist free enterprise society and he has been rightly branded anti-American."[74] Also displeased were the bulk of the estimated 100,000 Europeans who had left Zimbabwe for South Africa since independence in 1980 and now were faced with the prospect of a replay in their new home. Some of these migrants were early joiners of the curiously named "World Apartheid Movement,"

---

70. David Miller, Jr. to General Scowcroft, 27 October 1989, NSC, Box 1, *David Passage Files, Bush Presidential Library.*

71. Mara and Ray Croissant to President Bush, 21 June 1990, WHORM, Subject Files, CO, Subseries 141, Case No. 1321118-159630, *Bush Presidential Library.*

72. Carl McIntire to President Bush, 5 February 1990, Box 1, WHORM, Subject Files, CO, Subseries CO 141, Case No. 070533-119247, *Bush Presidential Library.*

73. Earle M. Craig to President Bush, circa 1990, Box 1, WHORM, Subject Files, CO, Subseries CO 141, Case No. 132118-159630,

74. Jeff Ohly to Senator Thurmond, 21 June 1990, Box 20, Constituent Correspondence, *J. Strom Thurmond Papers.*

also known as the "World Preservationist Movement," which maintained ties to the Ku Klux Klan in the U.S.[75]

Similarly dissenting was the American-Afrikaner Union, closely tied to South Africa's Conservative Party. Taking the notion of "Bantustan" to its illogical conclusion, it vowed to deliver a so-called "homeland" for the population defined as "white," which in practical terms meant Afrikaners.[76] From the viewpoint of the U.S. ultra-right, the Conservative Party was unreliable since some within their ranks backed Saddam Hussein as Washington was poised to wage war against him in 1991. Robert van Tonder of the so-called Boerestaat Party was in accord with their pro-apartheid comrades, while the ruling Nationalists were not—but the latter had proven themselves incapable of keeping a lid on unrest and could therefore not avoid being sacrificed.[77]

* * *

Those perceived to be close to Mandela were often reproached. At the top of the list was Randall Robinson, who was assailed as leading the "politically correct wing of the American parasite class."[78] Arthur Ashe, Robinson's friend since their youth, conversely argued that "Mr. Mandela gives Randall much credit for freeing him...."[79] Though Ashe's health was deteriorating rapidly, he still managed to lobby against attempts by some within the World Boxing Council to authorize boxing matches in South Africa.[80]

Jack Abramoff described routinely as a "Super-Lobbyist" in Washington and also described as a "devoted and fierce backer of Israel" at this tense moment of transition, was Executive Director of the so-called International Freedom Foundation, which focused heavily on undermining the credentials of several major opponents of apartheid, including Mandela and Tambo. The IFF was handsomely funded by Pretoria to the tune of $1.5 million annually and was

---

75. Johann van Rooyen, *Hard Right: The New White Power in South Africa*, London: Tauris, 1994, 96. See also *Vrye Weekblad*, 30 November 1990.

76. Zoe L. Hyman, "American Segregationist Ideology and White Southern Africa, 1948-1975," 236.

77. *Washington Post*, 19 January 1991.

78. *Business Day*, 17 November 1992, Box 15, Folder 1, *Washington Mission, ANC Records.*

79. Letter from Arthur Ashe, 4 December 1991, Box 1, *Arthur Ashe Papers, Schomburg Center.*

80. World Boxing Council to Arthur Ashe, 9 December 1991, Box 1, *Arthur Ashe Papers.*

generally successful in attracting to its fraying banner conservative Republicans e.g. Congressmen Dan Burton and Bob "B-1" Dornan.[81]

These reactionaries had their most hysterical fears confirmed when Mandela in a nationally televised June 1990 broadcast from Harlem's City College of New York refused to back away from his support for Fidel Castro, Yasser Arafat, and Muammar Gaddafi, though support for the latter two in the former slaveholding republic was equated virtually with anti-Semitism and support for Havana seen as wobbliness on the bedrock matter of anticommunism.[82]

Mandela's embrace of Arafat was a sore point for the pro-Israel community in the U.S. Cecil Eprile, who was Jewish, sent an open letter to the ANC leader from his home in Del Mar, California. They were friends 35 years ago in Johannesburg, he said. "Shortly before your arrest," he wrote, "you got one of your aides to bring me to your hiding place…because you trusted me." But now he felt betrayed by the embrace of Arafat.[83] Strikingly, Mandela's historic tour of the U.S. was hounded by pro-Israel zealots, not least in New York City.[84] As had been typical, these zealots ignored the real anti-Semitism flowing out of South Africa, e.g. when J.A. Marais, a leader of a rigidly racist pro-apartheid party, blamed the erosion of minority influence as Mandela was poised to take office on Slovo—"a Jew as most probably also Trevor Manuel," a "Coloured" leader.[85]

It could have been worse. Minister Louis Farrakhan of the Nation of Islam "declined the invitation to participate" in the questioning of Mandela since, as the group's spokesman said, "wise Caucasian people sit behind closed doors and iron out their differences, develop strategies" and the like and Africans should act similarly.[86]

Mandela did not win many friends among the Republican Party base when he said, addressing a joint session of Congress in Washington on 26 June 1990, that "too many among our white compatriots

---

81. Peter H. Stone, *Heist: Superlobbyist Jack Abramoff, His Republican Allies and the Buying of Washington*, New York: Farrar, Straus and Giroux, 2006, 45-46.

82. Transcript of Nelson Mandela Interview with Ted Koppel, 21 June 1990, Box 275, *Leroy Walker Africa News Service*,

83. Cecil Eprile to Nelson Mandela, 15 March 1990, Box 61, Folder 145, *Washington Mission, ANC Records*.

84. Marjorie N. Feld, *American Jews and the Struggle Over Apartheid*, New York City: Palgrave, 2014, 127-134.

85. J.A. Marais, "The Founders of the New South Africa," Arabi, Louisiana: Christian Defense League, 1994, *Michigan State University-East Lansing*.

86. Leonard Farrakhan Muhammad to Lindiwe Mabuza, 15 June 1990, Box 16, Folder 8, *Washington Mission, ANC Records*.

are [too] steeped in the ideology of racism to admit easily that change must come…." On the other hand, Mandela thrilled his own supporters when he invoked the iconic names of John Brown and Sojourner Truth, who crusaded against slavery, as well as not only Dr. Martin Luther King, Jr. but also W.E.B. Du Bois and Marcus Garvey.[87]

The criticism Mandela received for this appearance was symptomatic of a wider trend. Though celebrated generally in the U.S., he was reviled by the base of the Republican Party. By June 1990 a full-page advertisement in Atlanta's most widely read newspaper greeted his arrival in this Dixie redoubt. He was pictured standing next to Slovo with the accompanying inscription that the ANC was a "Communist dominated, terrorist organization." Included were Mandela's handwritten notes from his 1964 trial: "We Communist Party members are the most advanced revolutionaries in modern history." It was paid for by the fanatically anticommunist John Birch Society.[88] "Birchers" pursued Mandela relentlessly, terming him as "little more than a terrorist. "His warm embrace of Yasir Arafat," it was said, "should have opened the eyes of most Americans…." Senator Jeremiah Denton reported with dismay that, as early as 1982 18 of the top 33 ANC leaders were also SACP members—including Mandela.[89]

Linking Mandela with Arafat was bound to stoke outrage in the influential pro-Israel community. By early 1991 it was reported that "South African Jews ask end to sanctions," an initiative endorsed by co-religionists in the Houston Jewish community which, it was reported, "has a large number of former South African Jews," some of whom "went ballistic over [Mandela's] condemnation of Israeli policies."[90] Promptly, Israel moved to remove its tepid anti-apartheid sanctions, imposed in the first instance to dampen U.S. criticism of their untrammeled dealings with Pretoria. In any case, only official aspects of the relationship—state visits, sports, and cultural links—were ever curtailed, as Israel's enormous military commerce with apartheid increased after "sanctions" were established.[91] Israel's cooperation included training of Buthelezi's formidable intelligence

---

87. Remarks by Nelson Mandela at Joint Session of Congress, 26 June 1990, Box 19, *William Gray Papers, Schomburg Center.*

88. *Atlanta Journal-Constitution*, 25 June 1990.

89. Letter to Jim Daley, 6 June 1990, 157-25073-987, *Nelson Mandela FBI File, FBI-Washington, D.C.*

90. "Israeli Foreign Affairs," 24 April 1991, Box 61, Folder 144, *Washington Mission, ANC Records.*

91. "Israel Foreign Affairs," 9 July 1991, Box 61, Folder 144.

corps,[92] while a former leader of the Israel lobby in Washington, Morris Amtay, also served as a lobbyist for UNITA.[93]

Birchers were, in a sense, emulating the FBI, which had similar concerns. When Mandela visited Oakland in 1990 the agency ascertained that the CPUSA, "using the name Northern California Reception Committee," was the force behind Mandela's gala visit. This was further confirmation, it was said, of the reality illustrated by the "open presence" of the Chicago comrades in the Free South Africa Movement. More cautiously, it was observed that "our description of the ANC as a Soviet Front is an over-simplification which fails to recognize the complex and paradoxical nature of that particular organization (which was, of course, founded before the Russian Revolution.)"[94] Confirming the FBI's fears, the ANC's Jeff Radebe—who had studied international law in Leipzig, East Germany—arrived in Chicago to accept yet another ambulance, which would be helpful in transporting the wounded to hospitals in South Africa; beginning in 1989 and up to about 1994, this Midwestern metropolis had donated 18 such vehicles.[95]

Tens of thousands greeted Mandela in the local baseball stadium in Oakland. "Our news coverage" of the visit, said Barbara Rodgers of a local television station, was "well received," more reason for the FBI to fret.[96] The Bureau's report noted that the "ANC has also supported various Soviet interests such as the invasions of Czechoslovakia and Afghanistan and professed solidarity with the PLO [Palestine Liberation Organization] and Cuba." Moreover, it highlighted that Moscow's aid to the group was "substantial," while also repeating the familiar theme of the SACP's purported domination of the ANC.[97]

Atlanta was among the cities whose governments received threatening telephone calls when Mandela visited. The "Aryan Knights" claimed there were two bombs waiting to be detonated as he traversed the metropolis.[98] One "threat against the life" of Mandela, said the FBI, was particularly ominous: the "voice sounded like that

---

92. "Israel Foreign Affairs," 21 August 1991, Box 61, Folder 144.

93. "Israel Foreign Affairs," November 1990, Box 61, Folder 145.

94. Memorandum, 1 August 1990, 185-2255-2, *Mandela FBI File*.

95. *Chicago Defender*, 28 September 1994, Box 3, Folder 34, *Prexy Nesbitt Papers*.

96. Barbara Rodgers to Lindiwe Mabuza, circa 1990, Box 16, Folder 6, *Washington Mission*.

97. Memorandum, August 1990, 185-2255-2, *Mandela FBI File*.

98. Memorandum, 14 June 1990, 157-25073-987, *Nelson Mandela FBI File, FBI-Washington, D.C.*

of a middle aged white male" with "no accent." The "call was possibly made from an airport" and the "caller stated that he and his two companions had spent their lives trying to stop Mandela" and "had received military training" besides.[99] Dixie exploded in rancor when Mandela visited, as if it were recognized that his visit assuredly represented yet another chapter in the ongoing declension of white supremacy. "Remember John F. Kennedy in Dallas?" was the chillingly ominous query from Houston. Well, it said, "bring this black murderer to Houston and we will give him a welcome that the world will not forget!" Assassination was promised.[100] In Miami, the self-styled "Cuba Liberation Front" pledged mayhem too when Mandela arrived.[101]

Then there was a hitherto unknown neo-Nazi group that the FBI thought would "attempt and act against" Mandela, impelling the Nation of Islam's "Fruit of Islam"—the paramilitary arm of the African American religious group—to intervene.[102] The Black Lawyers Association in South Florida wanted the city boycotted because of the snubbing of Mandela by local authorities.[103] James Joseph, an African American who was to serve as a post-apartheid ambassador in Pretoria, "shared the indignation of those in Miami and elsewhere who condemned the snub" of Mandela.[104] Miami was becoming a regional reactionary citadel, a dubious distinction solidified when Buthelezi headed there after being hosted by the pro-Israel lobby in Los Angeles. The latter's comrades, the Cuban American National Foundation, were slated to host him but a demonstration by Dr. King's Southern Christian Leadership Conference convinced the Zulu leader to cancel the event and head home.[105]

New Orleans was also worthy of boycott thought Carl Galmon since, he said, it was "the only major city" in the nation "with a Black

99. FBI Atlanta office to FBI Director, June 1990, 185A B5 53252 14, *Nelson Mandela FBI File.*

100. Handwritten note from Houston, 6 June 1990, 185 A HQ 28286 4, *Mandela FBI File.*

101. FBI-Atlanta to FBI Director, 29 June 1990, 185-2255-2, *Mandela FBI File.*

102. FBI Miami to FBI Director, 27 June 1990, 185-1110, *Mandela FBI File.*

103. *Miami Times*, 26 July 1990.

104. James A. Joseph, *Saved for a Purpose: A Journal from Private Virtues to Public Values*, Durham: Duke University Press, 2015, 163.

105. "Israel Foreign Affairs," 10 July 1992, Box 61, Folder 144, *Washington Mission, ANC Records.*

Mayor and a majority Black City Council without"—he stressed—a *Selective Purchasing Divestment Ordinance*" that targeted Pretoria.[106]

But it was not just Dixie that was up in arms. When Mandela visited Chicago in 1993 the FBI spotted a man with binoculars "peering through the window…directly opposite the hall" where the ANC leader was speaking. A brief investigation revealed the presence of a rifle, along with a "blow-gun and one cross-bow…nunchuks, hunting knife and two swords…." The rifle was of Chinese origin "with a four inch blue barrel," along with "60 live rounds of 7.62 full metal jacket ammunition…."[107] Fortunately, the suspect was subdued before mayhem could ensue.

Los Angeles too was the scene of disturbances during Mandela's visit, albeit not as alarming. I was in the 90,000 seat Coliseum when he spoke and I estimate that it was at least 2/3 full. But I was not involved in the organizing and was taken aback when my old comrade Ron Wilkins charged that "Mandela's tour" was "controlled by political opportunists." Singled out for invective was the leading politico Maxine Waters, soon to join the Congressional Black Caucus, who—he said—possessed a "proven history of not respecting or acknowledging a range of anti-apartheid formations locally…." "She has not worked with us," he said of his own Patrice Lumumba Coalition. In New York City, Elombe Brath of the PLC was making a similar accusation. "Unchecked control of money collected for the ANC in the past has been misappropriated and never received," he charged, espying the vultures circling.[108] At that point there were an estimated 100 South African writers, students, and the like in Southern California who could have been deployed more effectively than they were.[109] But with all the problems, the value of Mandela's long journey was ratified when music executive Dick Griffey told Tambo that the visit was a "terrific success," an understatement in light of the $50 million he offered to raise for a scholarship fund for South African youth.[110]

Still, Brath said he felt "totally isolated" from the organizing for Mandela's trip, while Mayor David Dinkins was forced to admonish pro-Israel leaders, instructing them that it would be "'very, very unwise'" to picket Mandela, the need for this intervention a symptom

---

106. Carl Galmon to Reverend Avery Alexander, 12 December 1991, Box 16, Folder 6, *Washington Mission, ANC Records.*

107. Memorandum, 9 July 1993, 185-0-5023, *Mandela FBI File.*

108. *Los Angeles Sentinel*, 21-27 June 1990.

109. *Los Angeles Times*, 23 May 1990.

110. Dick Griffey to Oliver Tambo, 3 July 1990, Reel 3, *Tambo Papers.*

of the fractured coalition that hardly positioned anti-apartheid forces to pressure Washington further.[111]

Some of the objections came in response to Mandela's venturesome itinerary. Native Americans wanted him to speak on 12 October 1992, a date that "signifies 500 years of their resistance to colonization," according to the ANC's Lindiwe Mabuza[112] and, it was no secret that if he had accepted this invitation, controversy would have reigned despite the clear parallels between settler colonialism in Southern Africa and North America. During Mandela's 1990 visit the Lakota people of the Dakotas deemed it a "singular honor and great pleasure" to meet with the ANC.[113]

The ANC sought to operate strategically in deploying Mandela. For honorary degrees, "Georgetown would top the list," said Mabuza, possibly because its location in Washington afforded maximal publicity. Then there were "universities with historical links to [the] ANC," e.g. Oberlin College, which a previous ANC president had attended; and "universities or colleges with good anti-apartheid record[s]" were to be favored.[114]

By this juncture, Israel—a key ally of Pretoria over the years—had become a major antagonist of the ANC, as the grilling of Mandela in Manhattan suggested. Shortly thereafter it was revealed that agents of Israel's closest domestic allies in the U.S.—including the Anti-Defamation League—were monitoring anti-apartheid activism in league with Pretoria between 1987 and 1991—at minimum. The chief agent, Roy Bullock, seemed to be a freelance spy and provocateur.[115] It turns out that in 1986 Bullock learned that the South African Consul General in Los Angeles was speaking in Las Vegas at a meeting organized by the Liberty Lobby's Willis Carto, an infamous anti-Semite. His arrival there led to a relationship with Pretoria, ties that also revealed his links to both the CIA and Israeli intelligence.[116]

---

111. *Village Voice*, 26 June 1990.

112. Lindiwe Mabuza to Thabo Mbeki, 31 January 1991, Box 15, Folder 1, *Washington Mission, ANC Records*.

113. Two Crows of Lakota Elders Survival Fund to ANC, 14 August 1990, Box 16, Folder 7, *Washington Mission*.

114. Lindiwe Mabuza to Jesse Duarte, circa 1990, Box 15, Folder 1, *Washington Mission, ANC Records*.

115. Jeremy Kalmaofsky, "Defaming the Anti-Defamation League," *Moment*, Box 163, *Gerald Horne Papers*. See also *Washington Post*, 19 October 1993.

116. *Village Voice*, 11 May 1993. On "ADL's extensive intelligence unit", see *San Francisco Chronicle*, 23 April 1993.

It turns out that I was one of those being monitored, surveillance which increased after I hosted a program featuring Chris Hani of the SACP and ANC in Los Angeles, where it may have been noticed that his security cordon was permeable, information that may have contributed to his subsequent assassination in South Africa. One of my co-plaintiffs in a lawsuit against the ADL was Congressman Dymally of the Congressional Black Caucus.[117] "I would very much to discuss this matter with you," was the message I received from Albert Mokhiber of the Arab-American Anti-Discrimination Committee.[118] According to papers filed in the U.S. District Court for the Central District of California, my name appeared in the "[Tom] Gerard files," belonging to an officer in the San Francisco Police Department who cooperated with the spies.[119] One purported spy read the U.S. Communist press for anti-apartheid news and then sent resultant items to Bullock. The alleged spy, David Gurvitz, contributed to the file on Hani kept by the Los Angeles office of the ADL. "There is also a Los Angeles ADL file on University of California at Santa Barbara Professor Gerald Horne," according to a court exhibit. It was unclear if this intelligence was reported to Pretoria—though Bullock acknowledged sending reports regularly to South African agents.[120] By one account, 10,000 names of activists appeared in Bullock's files.[121]

In retrospect it is evident that this spying operation was hardly trivial. The surveillance of Hani in Los Angeles is notably unnerving, given his subsequent assassination and the esteem in which he was held among the working class and poor in South Africa. Born in 1942 he was a graduate of Fort Hare University who by 1967 was fighting in Rhodesia. He spent 7 years in Lesotho, providing him with regional contacts. As leader of the ANC's armed wing, he helped to grow this force from a few hundred militants to thousands.[122] Sonia Bunting, a member since 1942 of the Communist Party that also housed Hani, spoke movingly in 2000 about the impact of Hani's loss. "He had a photographic memory" that proved indispensable in military maneuvers. He "could recite Shakespeare and he always

117. Press Advisory, 21 October 1993, Box 163, *Gerald Horne Papers*.

118. Albert Mokhiber to Gerald Horne, 19 August 1993, Box 163, *Gerald Horne Papers*.

119. Gerald Horne, et.al. vs. ADL, et.al., 1993, Box 163, *Gerald Horne Papers*.

120. Exhibits H and B, 1993, Box: Greater Regional Office, Southern Africa Peace Education Program, 1970s-1992, *AFSC*.

121. Report, 24 April 1993, Box 3, Folder 16, *Prexy Nesbitt Papers*.

122. "The Monitor," October 1990, Box 23, Folder 15, *Washington Mission, ANC Records*.

had a pocket book of Shakespeare with him," suggestive of the expanse of his intellect. "There were thousands" of armed militants in the ANC "and he knew them all, he knew their background... he knew about their mothers and their fathers and they adored him...."[123] Swaminathan Gouden agrees that "masses worshipped Chris Hani...."[124] Interestingly, the *Washington Post* headlined "Communists in U.S. Host ANC Leader," in reference to Hani, revealing the longstanding dual anxiety about ties between the SACP and CPUSA.[125] Many of their readers would have been even more concerned had they known that Hani met his spouse, Dimpho Hani of Lesotho, in Moscow.[126]

* * *

Arnon Milchan, a Hollywood producer and a major donor to Democratic Party grandees, was accused of laundering illicit funds for Pretoria's propaganda operations and was said to have sought nuclear secrets for Israel. He was the "front man," according to a close observer, for this vast right-wing conspiracy. He too was close to the ADL and was apparently a witting accomplice when Israel supplied tritium for South Africa's nuclear weapons.[127]

These retrograde elements, among them spies, were not assuaged by the curiously timed revelation—accompanying Mandela's release and arrival in the U.S.—that Washington may have had a role in the leader's arrest and 28-year imprisonment. Gerard Ludi of South African intelligence claimed that he had infiltrated the SACP and that there was also a "deep cover" agent within the ANC too. As one journalist wrote, "Ludi said the secret informant's case officer was Ludi's longtime friend, Millard Shirley, a high-ranking CIA official in South Africa."[128]

---

123. Oral History, Sonai Bunting, 4 October 2000, *University of Connecticut-Storrs*.

124. Oral History, Swaminathan Gounden, 16 April 2001, *University of Connecticut-Storrs*.

125. *Washington Post*, no date, Box 23, Folder 15, *Washington Mission, ANC Records*.

126. Oral History, Mac Maharaj, 10 October 2000, *University of Connecticut-Storrs*.

127. "Israel Foreign Affairs," 13 April 1993, Box 61, Folder 144, *Washington Mission, ANC Records*.

128. *Washington Post*, 11 June 1990. Cf. Nicholas Grant, *Winning our Freedoms Together*, 11: Here the culprit is said to be Donald Rickford.

Given such skullduggery, the murders and executions of that tumultuous time are more explicable. This interregnum between Mandela's release in 1990 and his swearing-in as president involved one of the bloodiest rounds of killings since the end of the so-called Anglo-Boer War at the end of the 19th century. Supposedly, one Afrikaner leader was able to assemble a force of 100,000 armed men and set up clandestine cells. Here Mandela's two-year correspondence course in Afrikaans may have come in handy. Kobie Coetsee, an Afrikaner leader, had met with Mandela dozens of times prior to his release and Pretoria's spy chief, more than sixty times.[129]

This initiative was not necessarily embraced warmly by Mandela's comrades. There was even antipathy to the publication of his autobiography, smuggled out of confinement. According to Mac Maharaj, one of the men closest to him, Mandela "would have to watch himself, there would be some among his own comrades whose support he could not take for granted." Part of the problem was not only the ideological destabilization sponsored by Pretoria and Washington, but a division on Robben Island that continued afterward—and, arguably, to this very day—often depicted as a cleavage between SACP cadre grouped around Govan Mbeki (or even Harry Gwala) and those around Mandela. Certainly the split was not based on hostility toward the SACP. "I had seldom seen anyone defend the alliance with the Communist Party," said Maharaj, "as Madiba [Mandela] had defended it from the perspective of the prisoner." Yet this useful point needs to be placed in the context of other remarks by Maharaj, e.g. the "suspicions and rumors about Mandela's involvement [in] circles abroad" and the highlighting of his status as a political prisoner above others "because there were uncomfortable rumors that Madiba [Mandela] was [selling] out.... Rumors from the time of the Lusaka Manifesto that Madiba had been brought clandestinely to the State House of Kenneth Kaunda and had engaged in secret meetings with John Vorster...." Mandela also "maintained a warm correspondence" with Buthelezi, fanning the flames further.[130]

---

129. John Carlin, *Knowing Mandela: A Personal Portrait*, New York: Harper Perennial, 2013, 52, 75, 81, 85.

130. Padraig O'Malley, *Shades of Difference: Mac Maharaj and the Struggle for South Africa*, New York: Viking, 2007, 309, 214, 296, 300. On the sparring in prison between Mandela, on the one hand, and Mbeki and Gwala on the other, see Alec Russell, *Bring Me My Machine Gun: The Battle for the Soul of South Africa from Mandela to Zuma*, New York: Public Affairs, 2009, 70.

Conversely, as the U.S. ruling party inspected Mandela's words upon his release its hard right base felt that its fears had been confirmed. Speaking to ANC members in Lusaka days after his release, the graying leader asserted, "we have received enormous support from the Soviet Union and socialist countries" and "the fact of that alliance" with the SACP "has made it easy for us to get the maximum support from the socialist countries," which happened to be an accurate assessment.[131] Brian Bunting, a veteran Communist, recalled with satisfaction Vladimir Shubin's arrival at an ANC congress in 1990 in Durban, as a representative of Soviet Communists. "When he got up to speak," said Bunting, "the whole hall erupted because practically everybody there knew him....He's a remarkable personality...."[132] Some there assembled might have known of the massive Soviet aid to the anti-apartheid struggle, including—says Mac Maharaj—"a radio communication system with encryption in it" that was then "developed" by his spouse, a "computer specialist and mathematician,"[133] which proved to be quite useful.

By 1993, one report indicated, that of the 50 persons on the National Executive Committee of the ANC, the highest decision making body, about 33 were SACP members. The latter, it was said, headed all the ANC's most sensitive administrative structures, including the all-important Political and Military Council. This meant, said this analyst, that the SACP "closely controls the entire ideological training and 'mental colonization' of the ANC civilian cadres and...military personnel...."[134] As had been the case for decades, the North Atlantic community was obsessed with the extent to which ANC leaders were simultaneously SACP cadre. "Of the five men who are to represent the ANC at the next round of talks with [Pretoria]," it was reported in August 1990, "Mr. [Joe] Slovo is a Communist...Nzo may be...Mbeki is said to be by his enemies. Of the 22 party members whom the party has now identified as its 'internal leadership,' nine sit on the ANC's National Executive Committee...."[135] When Pretoria sought unsuccessfully to bar Slovo from negotiations with

---

131. Remarks by Mandela, 2 March 1990, Reel 16, *Oliver Tambo Papers*.

132. Oral History, Brian Bunting, 3 October 2000, *University of Connecticut-Storrs*.

133. Oral History, Mac Maharaj, 10 October 2000, *University of Connecticut-Storrs*.

134. "Spotlight on Africa," May-June 1993, published by "America African Association", Box 259, *Leroy Walker Africa News Service*.

135. *The Economist*, 4 August 1990.

the ANC that eventuated in 1994 elections,[136] it reflected this kind of analysis.

Part of the problem was—sadly enough—that a number of anti-apartheid champions—in the U.S. most notably—were unaware of how dependent their campaign was on the existence of a socialist camp now engaged in headlong retreat. With befuddlement Robinson of Trans-Africa, Jennifer Davis of ACOA, and Aubrey McCutcheon of the Washington Office on Africa wrote the new Soviet leader, Mikhail Gorbachev, to express their "extreme dismay" at Moscow's "intention to tour the internationally acclaimed Moscow Circus in South Africa"—and with "equal dismay," they said, "we read of your agreement to trade rough diamonds through De Beers…."[137] It was a clear sign of changing times when the ANC threatened to picket the Moscow Circus if it performed in South Africa.[138] In any case, since these U.S. leaders would not have dared to praise Moscow before 1989, their critique then was hard to take seriously.

Since the eclipsing of Robeson and the purging of Du Bois from the NAACP, the left had been on the defensive in Black America—the pulsating heartbeat of the movement—and, yet, this grievous development was hardly acknowledged. And with the drain on Moscow induced by the U.S. intervention in Kabul, Gorbachev decided to run up the white flag and, as the heroic fables of settler colonialism projected, decided to "come out with his hands up."

Thus, by November 1990 Jennifer Davis of ACOA was distressed since she and a co-worker "for the third time in a couple of months" were "holding off on our early pay checks—and you may have heard," she told Abdul Minty in Norway, that the Washington Office on Africa was "facing a similar plight."[139] In early 1991 the

136. *Reuters*, 29 April 1990. Stephen Ellis and Tsepo Sechaba, *Comrades Against Apartheid*, 150: As of June 1985, there were only 8 non-Communists among the ANC's highest body, the National Executive Committee. See also Padraig O'Malley, *Shades of Difference*, 63: "Among Party members never publicized for political reasons were Walter Sisulu, Thomas Nkobi…Alfred Nzo…and most likely for a brief period, Nelson Mandela, according to old colleagues." One of today's moguls in South Africa—Tokyo Sexwale—a former ANC militant, studied guerrilla tactics in Moscow: see Alec Russell, *Bring me My Machine Gun*, 162. For background on his first name, see Gerald Horne, *Facing the Rising Sun: African Americans, Japan and the Rise of Afro-Asian Solidarity*, New York: New York University Press, 2018.

137. Randall Robinson, et.al. to Mikhail Gorbachev, 13 August 1990, Box 90, *ACOARA*.

138. *Canberra Times*, 25 July 1990.

139. Jennifer Davis to Abdul Minty, 7 November 1990, Box 93, *ACOARA*.

old hand Prexy Nesbitt, then operating from the Mozambique Solidarity office in Chicago, told Randall Robinson and Jennifer Davis bluntly of the "increasing concern that the anti-apartheid and solidarity work in this country is steadily drifting into purposelessness and confusion...."[140] Nesbitt had a particular concern: in yet another blow to solidarity, by January 1991 he was no longer on the Maputo payroll; "remove me from the list of registered 'foreign agents,'" he instructed the U.S. Department of Justice.[141] On the verge of Mandela's election in 1994, during what was thought to be a period of unrivalled joy, Imani Countess of the Washington Office on Africa seemed slightly depressed. She stressed that "*basic operating expenses for the remainder of 1994*" were hardly present since there had been a "decline in foundation support for Africa work." Though WOA was "not on the brink of closure,"[142] it was close.

To a degree it was inevitable that with the ANC and SACP unbanned and on a glide path to seizing power, and with Namibia free, the solidarity movements would be forced to adapt. But what was only dimly recognized at the time was that the ongoing collapse of the socialist camp which had buoyed left-wing movements of all types would inexorably serve to deflate the Southern Africa solidarity movement too.

The solidarity movement's financial difficulties were coupled with longstanding political difficulties: e.g., the extent to which the movement should be a local adjunct of the ANC versus carving out another role. Back then I was firmly in the former camp—today, I am not so sure. In any case, by the Spring of 1992, ACOA's Mike Fleshman was "increasingly concerned about the political thrust" of Lennox Hinds, known to be close to the ANC, who he also provided legal counsel.[143] This was the prelude to a pro-ANC conference slated to take place in Manhattan.

Hinds and Cleveland Robinson, a union leader who had roots in the Caribbean, had assembled at Manhattan's Riverside Church in late 1992, despite Fleshman's concern, bringing together an impressive array of personalities in support of the ANC and their allies, including Mayor David Dinkins of New York City, former

140. Prexy Nesbitt to Jennifer Davis and Randall Robinson, 27 March 1991, Box 57, *ACOARA*.

141. Prexy Nesbitt to Joseph Clarkson, Chief Registration Unit, Internal Security Section, Criminal Division, Department of Justice, Box 57, *ACOARA*.

142. Imani Countess to the Ferrys, 25 March 1994, Box 22, *Ferry Papers, IUPUI-Indianapolis*.

143. Mike Fleshman to Jennifer Davis, 27 April 1992, Box 96, *ACOARA*.

presidential hopeful Jesse Jackson, Coretta Scott King, Congressman Maxine Waters, investor Maurice Tempelsman, erstwhile Congressman Howard Wolpe, and many more. Thabo Mbeki provided the keynote, in indicator of the importance of the gathering.[144]

The movement's post-1994 adjustment was far from smooth. By 1995 a group of Nigerians were upbraiding Randall Robinson and Trans-Africa, a mighty fall from the halcyon days. Robinson was beginning to focus on human rights violations in this West African nation. With sarcasm and no small amount of accuracy, it was said, "we realize that an organization such as yours needs a popular emotional cause to remain functional and relevant.... We do not begrudge your fund raising scheme.... We will forever remember how you and your organization ducked for cover during our political crisis in 1993."[145]

Still, it was striking that as the solidarity movements retrenched in the U.S., those who had either been willing to compromise with apartheid or remained silent began to march forward. By 1990, for example, Junior Achievement International, a so-called "free market" beacon based in the U.S., had begun to cooperate with the U.S. authorities and Kellogg, the Michigan based corporation, in South Africa initiated a project the top diplomat in Pretoria praised for "accomplishing many goals" that he and his corporate backers supported.[146] JA also cooperated in the development of an "economics and business training program" sited in strategically located Botswana, "which gives young people practical enterprise in the free enterprise program."[147] A similar initiative was launched in Swaziland,[148] along with proposals to expand in Zimbabwe and Namibia.[149] Because of such efforts by June 1990 there were scores of U.S. corporations based in Zimbabwe and extending their tentacles outward, including Colgate, Coca-Cola, Cummins Engine, Goodyear, Mobile,

---

144. National Conference in Support of the ANC and other Democratic Forces, 13-15 November 1992, Box 19, *ACOARA*.

145. *New York Times*, 20 April 1995. A copy of this can be found in Box 22 of the *Jean Sindab Papers, Schomburg Center*.

146. David Loose to Joseph Stewart, 10 December 1990, Box 169, *Junior Achievement Records-Indiana University Purdue University Indiana-Indianapolis*.

147. Memorandum of Understanding Between JA International and US AID mission, 1 July 1993, Box 175, *Junior Achievement Records-Indiana University Purdue University Indiana-Indianapolis*.

148. David Loose to Valerie Dickson-Horton, 17 November 1992, Box 175, *Junior Achievement Records*.

149. Proposals, 1990s, Box 239, *Junior Achievement Records*.

Pfizer, 3M, Union Carbide, and many more—as if liberation from colonialism and neo-colonialism meant hardly anything.[150]

Mac Maharaj was among the comrades who knew how difficult it was for U.S. corporations to break altogether with the region. Still, as a result of pressure from unions and students and African Americans within both groups, 40 U.S. companies left South Africa by 1984, and 50 more by the next year—though admittedly in some cases they simply decamped across the border to Zimbabwe.[151] Even corporations like Coca-Cola, which had sworn that they had exited South Africa, was reported as of 1991 to still be there, leading to an enhanced call for a boycott of their malnourishing product.[152]

But the U.S. foreign policy fixation on Moscow carried with it a stiff price. It involved an entente with China that led to massive U.S. direct foreign investment in this most populous of nations, though it was not predicted at the time that this could create a gargantuan power that would come to the verge of surpassing U.S. imperialism and limiting its options further. Then there was the de facto alliance with religious zealots in Afghanistan—and globally—that would serve to drain Washington's treasury in seemingly never-ending wars.[153]

* * *

President George H.W. Bush's new regime seemed not to know how to take "yes" for an answer. His aide Brent Scowcroft was told in April 1989, before the Berlin Wall was reduced to rubble, that Moscow was "still exporting revolution in Southern Africa," which "hardly seem[s] to square with Gorbachev's announced opposition to exporting revolution…." Scowcroft was told further that umbrage had been taken with the Soviet leader's words on a recent visit to Havana, leading to a journalist for the *Washington Post* "who should know better" writing, "no export of revolution: This seeming renunciation of conducting class war by armed struggle is what the West has been hoping to hear for 70 years." Yet, with seeming incomprehension it was reported that "in a March 31 press conference in Harare, Soviet First Deputy Foreign Minister Adamishin said that the Soviet Union was the only major source of weapons for the [ANC] and

150. Memorandum, 18 June 1990, Box 169, *Junior Achievement Records*.

151. Padraig O'Malley, *Shades of Difference*, 551, 555.

152. *Springfield Union News*, 22 March 1991.

153. Gerald Horne, *Blows Against the Empire: U.S. Imperialism in Crisis*, New York: International, 2008.

would continue supplying it. He added, 'Those who think we are going to stop supplying the ANC with arms to force it into negotiations are engaged in wishful thinking.'" Incredulously, it was noted that Moscow did not pledge to halt what had been "over twenty years of bankrolling, arming and training SWAPO...." Indeed, the analyst morosely concluded that the "Soviets are bound to have a great deal of influence and considerable presence in SWAPO-controlled Namibia...."[154]

The vast array of raw materials and the seemingly inexhaustible supply of cheap labor were not the only factors engaging the attention of the White House and their minions. By 1988 there were about 27,000 ships circling the Cape carrying around 75% of the strategic raw materials of the North Atlantic bloc, while 8000 tankers moved 70% of Western Europe's oil supplies and 30% of the U.S.'s imported oil.[155]

As the pivotal year of 1989 was unfolding the ANC and emissaries from Moscow were to be found frequently in extended huddles. One such meeting took place in Lusaka in March, with the ANC team led by Reg September and Moscow's team seeking briefing on matters concerning the increasingly controversial Winnie Mandela: the minutes noted that the meeting "lasted two hours."[156] But as part of the "new thinking" in Moscow, the PAC—which had been an unremitting critic of the Soviet Communist Party and its allies—travelled to Russia to confer.[157] When the PAC sent a delegation in 1992 to confer with the Chinese Communist Party, the ANC may have had reason to believe that it was being outflanked diplomatically.[158]

This warming of relations occurred even though serious questions continued to be raised about the PAC, e.g. the tendency of their leaders to drive expensive cars and reside in expensive homes in Tanzania and their involvement in what was described to Oliver Tambo as "car-cum-mandrax racketeering."[159] In 1991, Thabo Mbeki upset the PAC when he requested that the United Nations oust their envoy

---

154. Memorandum to Brent Scowcroft, 26 April 1989, OA/ID CF00207, *Peter Rodman Files, George H.W. Bush Presidential Library, Texas A&M University, College Station, Texas.*

155. *Sydney Morning Herald*, 21 March 1988.

156. Minutes of Meeting, 25 March 1989, Reel 5, *Oliver Tambo Papers.*

157. Report on PAC Delegation, circa 1988, Box 10, Folder 38, *Lusaka Mission, ANC Records.*

158. Press Release, 30 June 1992, Box 81, *ACOARA.*

159. Memorandum, circa 1989, Reel 15, *Oliver Tambo Papers.*

from a briefing he was holding.[160] Nor did this entente with Moscow indicate that the PAC was enjoying a similar warming in the U.S. By 1993 the group's Gora Ebrahim was expressing irritation with the Quakers because of various real and imagined slights.[161] But the upsetting developments took a new twist when Soviet Foreign Minister Eduard Shevardnadze met with Savimbi in Washington in December 1990, a clear signal to the MPLA, Cuba, and the ANC that the faucet of subsidies would soon be turned off.[162]

The new line was announced by Vladimir Tikhomirov, who said that "at present academics and politicians in the USSR do not see the ANC-SACP alliance as the only 'true representative' of the people of South Africa...."[163]

When the ANC delegation arrived in Moscow no red carpet was rolled out. Unlike in 1986 when the group conferred with Mikhail Gorbachev himself, in 1989 they were snubbed, given only a meeting with a non-voting member of the Political Bureau of the Communist Party.[164] Still, the statement issued after a April 1989 visit to Moscow that involved consultations with the Soviet Afro-Asian Solidarity Committee, stressed—unlike previous communiqués—that there had been "no pressure at all" to compel the ANC to "abandon the armed struggle...or that the USSR is considering abandoning support for the ANC...." This unusual admission was also confirmed by the ANC envoy in Moscow, Simon Makana.[165] Times were changing. It had not been so long ago that Alfred Nzo, "in response to the generous offer" from Moscow, had decided to "submit the following list of the fourteen comrades for rest and treatment" at a Soviet spa, including cadre from Lusaka, Maputo, Dar, and London.[166]

By then Ms. Mandela was bathed in controversy, particularly after the mysterious death of Dr. Abu-Baker Asvat led to fingers

---

160. "Media Release," 27 November 1991, Box 64, Folder 172, *Washington Mission, ANC Records.*

161. Ken Martin to Jerry Herman, 8 April 1993, Box: PED.... Southern Africa....1992, *AFSC.*

162. *Kwacha News*, January 1991, *University of Kansas-Lawrence.*

163. Vladimir Tikhomirov, "Contemporary Politics in South Africa and the Soviet Policy Towards Southern Africa" in Anatoly Gromyko and John Kane-Berman, eds., *The Moscow Papers: The USSR and South Africa: Similarities, Problems and Opportunities*, Johannesburg: SAIRR, 1991, 7-15, 12.

164. *Australian*, 14 March 1989.

165. Statement of South African Delegation to USSR, 1-10 April 1989, Reel 17, *Oliver Tambo Papers.*

166. Alfred Nzo to Soviet Embassy, no date, circa 1980s, Box 88, Folder 43, *Lusaka Mission, Part II, ANC Records.*

of accusation being pointed at her. The so-called Mandela Football Club was seen by some as a questionable grouping tied to her. This led to the United Democratic Front and the Congress of South African Trade Unions, allies of the ANC, distancing themselves from her, enhancing disunity.[167]

This trend had arrived at an unwelcome moment. Months earlier WOA was drowning in sorrows, lamenting that "1989 has been one of the most difficult years" they had endured in their history despite the recent SWAPO victory at the polls that led to independence in March 1990. There was "conflict and confusion" resulting and absent funding from "August-November"; they were "closed for nearly three weeks" and "office hours were decreased...."[168]

Yet amid the bad news, there was one glimmer of sunshine. The *Wall Street Journal* was stunned to ascertain that as Communists in Eastern Europe and elsewhere reeled, the SACP had surged.[169] The profundity of the socialist camp's impending dissolution also impacted the PAC. This group was displeased when Harare endorsed negotiations with Pretoria, inducing a rift that became difficult to heal.[170]

In the same vein, UNITA and Savimbi began to shrivel as Namibian independence loomed and the Cubans took control of the skies over the sub-region. By April 1989 it was reported that the group's Tito Chingunji was attacked by Savimbi, who suspected him of plotting with the U.S. behind his back. Savimbi was also excoriated by the usually friendly journalist Fred Bridgland, which did not aid his case in Washington, his base of support. In response, the number of junkets from the U.S. to his headquarters in Jamba increased, as the bearded leader sought to substantiate his contention that Chingunji was involved in "witchcraft."[171] But Savimbi's days were numbered.

---

167. Document on death of Dr. Abu-Baker Asvat and related press coverage, 1988, Box 1, *South Africa Black Consciousness Movement Collection, New York Public Library-Schomburg Center.*

168. Minutes of WOA Board Meeting, 30 November 1989, Box 90, *ACOARA.*

169. *Wall Street Journal*, 30 July 1990; *New York Times*, 29 July 1990.

170. *Guardian* [U.K.], 7 March 1990.

171. "Africa Confidential," 14 April 1989, Box 10, Folder 38, *Lusaka Mission, ANC Records*. See also William Minter, ed., *Accounts from Angola: UNITA as Described by Ex-Participants and Foreign Visitors*, Amsterdam, Netherlands: AWEEPA, 1990. See also R. Bruce McColm to Max Kampelman, 1 April 1992, Box 60, *Freedom House Archives*: "Angola mayhem...N'Zau Puna comes from the royal family line of the northern enclave of oil-rich Cabinda. During the mid-1960s Puna abandoned his title of 'Baron' and joined UNITA. He was

The Cuban onslaught leading to Namibian independence, the continued strength of the divestment movement, and the refusal of the movement to isolate the ANC-SACP alliance meant UNITA was losing its utility too. The conservative bible, *National Review*, assailed him and, in the ultimate indignity, compared him to Soviet and Chinese Communist leaders. Radek Sikorski launched this philippic after spending 10 weeks in Jamba.

* * *

Mandela's arrival in the U.S. in 1990 was a landmark event. Rarely has an African leader been treated with such reverence and rapture by such a broad-based U.S. audience, let alone one thought to be a member of a Communist Party. Though there had been widespread support in Black America for the PAC and skepticism about the ANC's ties to Moscow, even those who held such beliefs were seemingly swept up in the laudation.

More to the point, Mandela raised about $4 million while traipsing from the Atlantic to the Pacific. Revealingly, Detroit—a complement to Port Elizabeth, it was the capital of automobile manufacturing and housed an African American majority besides—raised more money than any other U.S. city. Nearly 50,000 attendees paid from $10 to $10,000 to attend a packed rally at the local baseball stadium on 28 June 1990. Advertisers paid up to $1,250 a page for a souvenir journal that sold for $5 each.[172]

Cities jostled and competed to establish their anti-apartheid bona fides. "I pioneered municipal anti-apartheid legislation," boasted Mayor David Dinkins of New York City.[173]

Still, it is important to recall that the Mandela visit was not writing on a blank slate. As the preceding pages have suggested, there had been solidarity and interest in South Africa stretching back decades, at least since the so-called Anglo-Boer War of the late 19th century. Thus, in Los Angeles—the nation's second most populous city—Michael Zinzun was playing a leading role in The Friends of

---

trained in China…number two person in UNITA…defected to Portugal" on 1 March and "provided the MPLA information with inside information on the organization's strategy…his cousin, who is Luanda's Minister of Defense…."

172. Clipping, unclear provenance, 26 February 1991, Box 158, *ACOARA*: By then the ANC had yet to receive all the funds raised in the Motor City, making it "the only city that has failed to release money", according to Lennox Hinds.

173. Mayor Dinkins to the Ferrys, 2 October 1991, Box 18, *Ferry Papers*.

the African National Congress & Frontline States, which had reached its second year of operation as Mandela arrived—though members had been active for decades, working closely with local ANC members. They had organized a visit by Tambo in 1987 and subsequently placed ANC members on local television shows. They sent 7 people to Namibia to produce a video on the election and independence celebrations. Their mailing list of 2,000 included many who actively participated in the group.[174] Their activism was similar to what was unfolding in the much smaller city of Pittsburgh, where the NAACP chapter was involved in sending textbooks to South Africa.[175]

Sadly, solidarity shriveled after 1994, as the liberation movement became a ruling party and—presumably—decided that a grassroots base in the U.S. ran contrary to their interests. This was simply one mistake among many.

---

174. Michael Zinzun to Rachel Kagan, 12 June 1990, Box 115, *ACOARA*.

175. Memorandum from NAACP-Pittsburgh, 22 June 1990, Box 115, *ACOARA*. See attached article from *Pittsburgh Courier*, 20 December 1988.

Epilogue

WHEN Nelson Mandela was inaugurated in 1994, some of the stormiest applause from the masses assembled was appropriately directed at the Cuban delegation led by President Fidel Castro. It was, after all, the Cuban defeat of apartheid forces on the battlefield that turned the tide against the regime, forcing more reasonable postures upon them, leading to democratic elections. But by the time Mandela was sworn into office, the once mighty socialist camp had eroded significantly, as U.S. imperialism preened as the "sole remaining superpower," capable of tipping the scales in favor of its sub-regional allies and U.S. corporate interests that were staunchly unwilling to relinquish their misbegotten gains. As a result, by 2019—if not before—there was grumbling and grousing among many, both in Southern Africa and abroad, about what had been wrought, though often this conversation was curiously lacking the salient factors noted in the sentences above. Perhaps it was because the depth of anticommunism hampered comprehension of the crucial role played by the socialist camp. To be sure, there were self-inflicted wounds, some of which were real head-scratchers: the dislodging of Thabo Mbeki in favor of Jacob Zuma and the ouster of the latter in 2018, for instance. Frank Chikane, a key Mbeki advisor, blamed "foreign intelligence agencies" and "foreign entities" for this regime change and it did not require a seer to divine that this was an allusion to Washington and its post-1994 policy of keeping the ANC-SACP-COSATU [Congress of South African Trade Unions] alliance off-balance, unable to move effectively against U.S. imperialism and its many local allies.[1]

Even before he joined the ancestors—and more so after his passing—an image of Mandela as a squishy liberal uninterested in wealth redistribution, still the pivotal issue, was wielded adeptly by the myrmidons of apartheid. Taking to the pages of the *Wall Street Journal* in 2015, the bible of the Republican Party, F.W. de Klerk, praised the "exemplary leadership of Nelson Mandela," eliding the imprecations he once tossed at the deceased leader. He even reproached the "coup" that dislodged Mbeki, another leader who he had denounced routinely. Now, he lamented, "unqualified ANC cadres" were slotted in "key positions," and the SACP "now controls

1. Frank Chikane, *Eight Days in September: The Removal of Thabo Mbeki*, Johannesburg: Picador Africa, 2012, 4.

the Secretary-Generalship of the ANC and 12 key cabinet posts with dominant influence within the presidency and ministries dealing with economic policy…." There was "greater state intervention in the economy," which may have been true but, neglected was the "state intervention" on behalf of Afrikaners that long undergirded the discredited policy of apartheid. There had been a "fundamental change in the ownership and control of land," a point that evaded the wider concern that a European minority still overwhelmingly controlled this resource. "ANC's policies," de Klerk said with anger, "have benefited only the top 15% of the black population,"[2] though when socialism and massive wealth redistribution were blocked by de Klerk and his acolytes during the negotiations leading to 1994, such a result became unavoidable. South Africa, he bragged, "has the largest mineral resources in the world," which was why readers in the wealthiest precincts of North America should pay attention to Pretoria, a familiar argument.

Despite escaping war crimes prosecutions and retaining a good deal of their obscenely obtained holdings, the forces represented by de Klerk were still dissatisfied. The SACP, he said irritably, was "granted fully 12.5 per cent of the seats in Parliament" via its representation within the ANC. His predecessor, Botha, called him on the carpet, peppering him with increasingly poisoned questions about the "evil conspiracy" that led to this result, including the "New World Order" that purportedly bound him to the White House. Upset, de Klerk stormed away.[3]

Sindiso Gregory Mfenyana, born in 1940 and posted by the ANC in Moscow, recalled in 2001 that "we had been used to getting all this assured support" from Eastern Europe before Tambo "realized that we could not rely on the Soviet Union for our support." Thus, "he built up relations with the Frontline States and made them the main bastion of our support"—though Nkomati seriously complicated this strategy. Mfenyana, who joined the ANC in 1952, recalled that Nkomati was a setback: "if you had seen the faces of our cadres on that day," he said, still seemingly stunned, "they behaved as if the struggle was being pushed back for years"—which may have been an accurate assessment. "An indication of things to come," he said with remaining asperity, "was the banning of the Soviet daily 'Pravda'" in the GDR. "It was clear that President Honecker" in Berlin "was not happy with some developments in the Soviet Union under Mikhail Gorbachev," reservations that were widespread from

2. *Wall Street Journal*, 20 August 2015.
3. F.W. de Klerk, *The Last Trek*, 336, 374.

Havana to Hanoi. Inexorably, this impacted negotiations with Pretoria; even before, when talks between Mandela and Botha were revealed, "the first reaction among the cadres was disbelief and alarm…. It was a difficult time…."[4]

Like Mfenyana, thankfully, those present at the creation of the new dispensation were relatively clear about the dimensions and import of the apartheid regime's ouster.[5] Peter Peyise was born in 1932 and trained in Odessa, where he learned "skills, underground skills," including "how to make false bottoms in a suitcase." He was present in the GDR in 1973 for an important youth festival—"we saw many comrades of ours" there, he said in 2001. He was then posted in Algeria for "20 years" and "it was tough." But he too sees the negotiations to have been driven by apartheid's weaknesses in the Angola-Namibia theater, "because they knew that if they're annihilated there, that force will pass through South Africa and liberate South Africa"—forcibly. "Because South Africa was not guarded, South Africa was empty, all the soldiers were not there in South Africa,"[6] they were overextended in the region stretching from Luanda southward to Windhoek and beyond. Yet despite this weakness, apartheid had the advantage of being backed by the self-proclaimed sole remaining superpower.

Fannie Phakola, an SACP member who spent time in Cuba, is of like mind. "Thabo Mbeki was still a member of the party" then, he recalled in 2005, and was present at negotiations, along with his father, Govan. In 1990 "people thought that Mandela was selling us out," and Phakola was among them. Yet he also knew that "with the collapse of the Eastern Bloc…capitalism took over. Where were we going to get support?" The besieged Frontline States, as heroic as they were, could hardly fill the vacuum. Since his spouse was Angolan, he had even more reason to be aware of this phenomenon.[7]

On the other side of the fence, Father Michael Lapsley, born in New Zealand and influenced by Maori militancy as a youth, has been much more critical. Ultimately this Anglican priest who had been based in Durban fell victim to an apartheid letter bomb. "Cuba offered me medical treatment," he said later. "The PLO [Palestine

---

4. Oral History, Sindiso Gregory Mfenyana, 28 January 2001, *University of Connecticut-Storrs.*

5. Oral History, Kader Asmal, 5 July 2001, *University of Connecticut-Storrs.*

6. Oral History, Peter Peyise, 23 February 2001, *University of Connecticut-Storrs.*

7. Oral History, Fannie Phakola, 14 October 2005, *University of Connecticut-Storrs.*

Liberation Organization] offered to pay for my medical treatment." Perhaps the nature of his experience led him to the searing conclusion that the failure of the ANC regime to act more decisively on "reparations" represents a "moral failure."[8] Lisa Brock, who not only marched in Chicago against apartheid but communed in Maputo with Hani and Slovo, said in 2009 that if she could speak with Mandela she would ask him, "why he didn't nationalize De Beers." "I still don't completely understand that," she confessed, asking why not "make it a parastatal?"[9] These kinds of perceptions were understandably displeasing to the proud Mandela. One observer recalled how during a talk he gave in November 2009, the leader noted, "my people said I was afraid....They said I was a coward because I reached out to the Afrikaner."[10] By 2015, one U.S. publication blared the headline "Rebranding Mandela as a Sellout," adding that "today's youth [in South Africa] are frustrated over continued white dominance of the economy and persistent poverty" and now "resent the compromises Mandela made." Highlighted was Julius Malema, a former comrade of President Zuma, who broke with him to found the "Economic Freedom Fighters." Malema "openly" criticized Mandela, which was another way to reprimand the ANC and its allies, charging that the now deceased icon had "sold out."[11] Of course, mainstream U.S. publications—like the one that published this article—were not averse to shifting the spotlight from imperialism's outsized role in delivering the results to which Malema objected, via decades of anticommunist policy that culminated in the retreat of the socialist camp and made problematic the effort to engage in widescale wealth redistribution.

This negative perception of Mandela and what he had wrought was fed by President Robert Mugabe. Strikingly, weeks before he himself was deposed in 2017, he rebuked his fellow leader: "Everything is in the whites' hands," said Mugabe with rising ire, speaking of South Africa. "The most important thing for [Mandela] was his release from prison and nothing else," he charged. An observant journalist wrote, "Mugabe claimed that this view of Mandela was even shared by members of President Jacob Zuma's cabinet." The slow pace of land reform was seen as particularly galling. "Last

8. Oral History, Father Michael Lapsley, 6 October 2000, *University of Connecticut-Storrs*.

9. Oral History, Lisa Ann Brock, 8 December 2009, *Columbia College-Chicago*.

10. John Carlin, *Knowing Mandela: A Personal Portrait*, New York: Harper Perennial, 2013, 139.

11. *The Week*, 18 December 2015.

March [2017] faced with claims that 40,000 of the whites owned 80 percent of the land Zuma moved to expropriate white owned land without compensation," as tardiness in redistribution only enhanced his growing unpopularity.[12]

To be sure, Trevor Manuel, who was once in charge of the post-1994 economy in South Africa, had a point when he announced balefully in December 2016, "I only regret that the government that took over in '94 wasn't more honest about the pillaging of the economy by the apartheid government. I wish more people would talk about how the country was ransacked before it was handed over to the black people. I wish more people would talk about the fact that billions were taken out the country, never to be seen again."[13] But to do so would invite rebuke from Washington in defense of its ousted racial comrades.

Part of the disappointment—again—stemmed from unrealistic expectations driven by an inadequate assessment of the impact of Moscow's retreat. Curtis Black, a Chicago activist, was "disappointed" with Mandela's U.S. visit since "he was here as a diplomat, really to court the Bush Administration and I wanted someone to come here and teach the American people about making a revolution,"[14] which was beyond Mandela's brief—even had he possessed the magic potion. For his part, Mandela continued to honor the anti-Jim Crow cause, referencing Dr. King in his own speech on becoming a Nobel Laureate. But what he said afterwards was probably even more profound: the final victory over apartheid "will finally bring to a close a history of 500 years of African colonization."[15] The spring of 1994 did mark the beginning of a new era, the full dimensions of which that have yet to be measured.

* * *

Russel Maphanga was born in 1941. A cosmopolitan, he was sufficiently familiar with his homeland to discern that "Zulu, Xhosa and Ndbele are interrelated languages." By 1989 he was in the Soviet Union. "I was sent to a sanatorium," he said, "where you enjoy a rest and cure...." But this unwinding did not distract him from his critique of the negotiations leading to 1994. "Cyril Ramaphosa...was

12. *New York Amsterdam News*, 21-27 September 2017.
13. *Financial Times*, 17-18 December 2016.
14. Oral History, Curtis Black, 22 April 2010, *Columbia College-Chicago*.
15. Mandela Remarks, 10 December 1993, in Nelson Mandela, *Let Freedom Reign*, 90-93, 91.

a trained legal person and trade unionist and a politician" he said of the ANC's primary negotiator, "but lacked the skill of negotiating on military issues. The whole team had that shortcoming," he said in 2003 of a delegation that included Slovo, a commander of the ANC's armed wing, "and that is why we are suffering today."[16]

It is also difficult to overestimate the impact of the Nkomati Accord, which weakened not only the ANC but the Frontline States too. This pact had a knock-on effect. John Daniel of South Africa, who studied at both Western Michigan University and the State University of New York-Buffalo, recalled later that after Nkomati there was a not unrelated crackdown in Swaziland, leading to "gun battles," further debilitating the ANC. As for the apartheid regime, he says, "I don't think that they saw it as giving up in 1990" with the unbanning of the opposition. "I think they saw it as a change in tactics.... They were of the view that with the collapse of the Communist system that the ANC had lost its lifeline...." They "seemed to believe that they could defeat the ANC electorally," as they were "pleasantly surprised by the success of what they had done in Namibia where they had created this anti-SWAPO coalition," the so-called Democratic Turnhalle Alliance, which seemed to be gaining support—for a while.[17]

Sipho Magagula, who was born in South Africa but grew to maturity in Swaziland, has a similarly dyspeptic view. "You would see people walking in the streets" in Mbabane "hand in hand, black and white;" it was possible to "feel so free" there. But this outward pleasantness masked an uglier reality since the government worked "hand in hand" with Pretoria.[18] Tim Jenkin, born in 1948, was tasked by the ANC with blowing up the so-called "Coloured Parliament." "They wanted me to be Guy Fawkes," he said in 2000. His importance to the group was underscored when in the 1980s he arranged communication between Mandela's attorney and the Lusaka-based leadership, an important conduit. But he wound up in Angola, he says, since the ANC "felt that Maputo was too dangerous for South Africans", a reasonable conclusion but also an admission of weakness given Mozambique's proximity to the battlefield.[19]

16. Oral History, Russel Maphanga, 30 July 2003, *University of Connecticut-Storrs.*

17. Oral History, John Daniel, 13 December 2003, *University of Connecticut-Storrs.*

18. Oral History, Sipho Magagula, 30 August 2004, *University of Connecticut-Storrs.*

19. Oral History, Tim Jenkin, 6 October 2000, *University of Connecticut-Storrs.*

Kay Moonsamy too was well aware of the importance of the Frontline States. This SACP member was born in 1944 and like Mandela was conversant with the pamphlet "How to be a Good Communist." During those "dark days," he recalled in 2000, "it was not the Western countries that gave us asylum but it was Africa!" Early on he was involved in "underground activities," a "great strain and harsh times for my dear wife and our dear children," he said. But he knew of the upward climb of the SACP from "2000 members" in 1950 at the time of banning and reinvention to "60,000 to 70,000" by 1990, despite harsh anticommunist repression encouraged by Washington. He was in exile by 1965 and returned in 1990 knowing that the "socialist countries were also a powerful group that supported our struggle, that is starting with the Soviet Union." He spent two months studying at the Lenin Party School in Moscow, and then spent 2 weeks in underground training and "military training."[20]

Albert Dlomo was born in Durban in 1935 and during the struggle was on the frontlines, supplying chemicals to the ANC's armed wing via SACP militant Ronnie Kasrils. He recalled a "Reverend Tremble" or "Trimble" in Natal who was a U.S. national who was also helpful in this process. He also feels that when the ANC negotiated "we were in a weak position where the ANC…itself had been infiltrated." When "Tambo fell ill," "we had a crisis." There was also a split between those who wanted a "Castro way," i.e. the seizure of power, and others not so inclined: "we were caught with our pants down" he concluded sourly.[21]

Nkosinathi Benson Fihla, born in Port Elizabeth in 1932, agrees that differences within the leadership created problems, often represented as a Mbeki-Mandela split. "But the real difference was between [Comrade Harry] Gwala and the leadership."[22] Gwala, a "committed Stalinist" according to the biographer of Jacob Zuma, "sparred relentlessly with Mandela."[23] Though the SACP understandably presented a face of monolithic unity in public, this masked a deeper reality. Speaking of her spouse Lionel Forman, Sadie Forman of the SACP recalled that when Belgrade was

---

20. Oral History, Kay Moonsamy, 7 December 2000, *University of Connecticut-Storrs.*

21. Oral History, Albert Dlomo, 24 April 2000, *University of Connecticut-Storrs.*

22. Oral History, Nkosinathi Benson Fihla, 24 July 2005, *University of Connecticut-Storrs.*

23. Alec Russell, *Bring me My Machine Gun*, 56.

under fire from Moscow, he fought in Prague to prevent Yugoslav delegates from being expelled from the International Union of Students.[24] Also in Prague was Gertrude Shope, born in 1925, an ANC leader whose spouse served with the World Federation of Trade Unions,[25] derided in Washington as little more than a "Communist Front."

Indres Naidoo, a Communist, who boasted "I'm the first MK soldier," or armed ANC fighter, was well aware of these differences, recalling that many thought armed struggle was "adventurism." Indeed the "Indian Congress was in fact split down the middle" on this and other matters, as "more senior members...rejected" this turn. But not Naidoo. "I was the first MK soldier to be shot by the enemy," he said. By 1985 this former ANC envoy in Berlin found that his militancy meant the U.S. refused him a visa but, with his usual zest, "I put up a hell of a fight" and won, though he was still barred from veering beyond a 25-mile radius of the United Nations. He also knew that it was not only the apartheid regime that had penetrated the ranks of its opponents. "We too infiltrated the state machinery," he said in 2000, and had "our spies in the military," among them was present cabinet member Derek Hanekom. By 1989 he was traveling with an Indian passport, like other comrades. But he too recalled with concern the disagreements about the deal cut with the apartheid regime, disagreements that included not only Gwala but current SACP leader Blade Nzimande, Brian Bunting, and others. He compared the process to the Lancaster House talks that led to Zimbabwean independence in 1980, a process that likewise represented a bitter compromise for many.[26]

Winnie Ngwenya, born in 1953 and also imprisoned, agrees that the movement had infiltrated the regime. "The prison warders were black and they treated us like humans. But when they saw Afrikaners they pretended not to like us.... They used to help us to communicate...some of them were members of unions."[27]

Like others within the SACP, Phyllis Naidoo was cosmopolitan, speaking Zulu, Afrikaans, Tamil, and English. The ability of the

24. Oral History, Sadie Forman, 19 December 2001, *University of Connecticut-Storrs.*

25. Oral History, Gertrude Shope, 11 October 2000, *University of Connecticut-Storrs.*

26. Oral History, Indres Naidoo, 3 October 2000, *University of Connecticut-Storrs.*

27. Oral History, Winnie Ngwenya, 29 September 2005, *University of Connecticut-Storrs.*

SACP to attract those of her mettle was indicative of why it was a force that could not be ignored easily. Though like others with roots on the Indian Ocean coast, she found that her parents "hate the British so much.... My grandfather said 'never, never use that language in my home,'" meaning English. She was born in 1928 and her parents arrived in South Africa from Tamil Nadu in 1902. She lived in the same neighborhood as the vaunted Gwala and Mabhida and later joined the armed wing of the ANC, then wound up on Robben Island where she—like some other comrades—aided the PAC. She later went to Zimbabwe, suggesting that her generosity while imprisoned did not hurt her in Harare, where ZANU was in control and "they were PAC people...."[28]

Billy Nair, a Central Committee member of the SACP, born in Durban in 1929—albeit with roots in India and Mauritius—also spoke of "English speaking whites of Natal [as] just as racist" as the more demonized Afrikaners. More to the point, he was sufficiently alert to assess the impact on his homeland of the altered correlation of forces.[29] Fatima Seedat, a Communist born in 1922, also had a father who was hostile to London. He visited both the Soviet Union and China in 1951[30] and too was able to acknowledge what the collapse of socialism meant.

Dr. Somalingum Ponnusamy, was also born in Durban, in 1958. Two decades later he was in India, a key ally of the anti-apartheid forces— "there was this period whereby South Africans of Indian descent could further their education in India"—and there contacted the ANC. By 1987 it was on to Lusaka, then Angola. "I was also a member of MK [ANC's] Military Intelligence....I trained in the Soviet Union," receiving a "three month course in military intelligence," dealing with "explosives, reconnaissance, gathering information, being able to evade people that are following you, being able to follow somebody without being spotted, topography and deployment of troops," along with "military engineering...." He too sees Nkomati as a negative turning point, a decision made without consulting the ANC. From 1978 to 1992 he was in exile but as of 2001 still retained appreciation for Delhi's influence on the struggle. It was "tremendous," particularly when apartheid sought to construct a

---

28. Oral History, Phyllis Naidoo, 23 November 2000, *University of Connecticut-Storrs.*

29. Oral History, Billy Nair, 10 February 2000, *University of Connecticut-Storrs.*

30. Oral History, Fatima Seedat, 8 August 2000, *University of Connecticut-Storrs.*

so-called "tri-cameral parliament," co-opting Indians, but only 15% of this community voted.[31]

Also of South Asian descent was Sunny Singh, born in 1939 and a member of the ANC's armed wing. By 1976 he left for Swaziland, then to Mozambique, then Tanzania, then Angola, then to the GDR for "military training"—more pointedly, "urban warfare." Then it was back to Angola and Mozambique, then service under Jacob Zuma's supervision. After Nkomati he was sent to Holland as chief ANC delegate, where he found "amazing" support from the masses—not so much from the government.[32]

Dumisani Makhaye, a Communist born in 1955, also points to the SACP—albeit in a difference manner—in seeking to understand the fate of post-apartheid South Africa. "We have not, the party has not yet survived," he said, in reference to the 1986 passing of SACP titan Moses Mabhida. Speaking in 2004, he lamented the "fatal blow... suffered when that great man passed away." He was not simply one of [the] first best commissars of [MK] who did not only theorize" but "led from the front." He also "operated from Swaziland," influencing this small, strategically sited kingdom in the process. Makhaye knew of what he spoke, since he trained cadre in Angolan camps studied in Cuba and East Germany. Revealingly, "there was no PAC in Angola nor AZAPO in Angola" and "few members of the PAC in Tanzania and Uganda during the days of [Idi] Amin," the erratic leader of the 1970s—yet "the ANC was everywhere. "There were times when we would actually feed members of the PAC," he said. But this ideological hegemony was difficult to disconnect from the pervasive influence of Mabhida.[33]

Angela Sangweni was also exiled in Swaziland—Lesotho too, along with Zambia and Holland. In Mbabane, she found a dearth of conflict between the PAC and ANC, the kind of peaceful coexistence not seen in, for example, New York City. Thus, when Chief Luthuli died, "a memorial was conducted, and it was done by both [parties]." Suggestive of the cross-border ties, she served as Secretary at the Angolan legation in Lusaka for five years and also spent a decade in Kenya with the United Nations, until 1992.[34] Stanislaus

31. Oral History, Dr. Somalingum Ponnusamy, 23 July 2001, *University of Connecticut-Storrs.*

32. Oral History, Sunny Singh, 23 July 2001, *University of Connecticut-Storrs.*

33. Oral History, Dumisani Makhaye, 20 January 2004, *University of Connecticut-Storrs.*

34. Oral History, Angela Sangweni, 5 July 2001, *University of Connecticut-Storrs.*

Sangweni became a courier between Lusaka and Lesotho, and as a U.N. employee also managed to coordinate with Chris Hani and forces in Addis Ababa too.[35]

Like so many ANC militants, Ernest Frederick Dube matriculated at Adams College of South Africa, begun by U.S. missionaries in the 19th century. He eventually made his way to New York, where he became hostile to the Reverend Leon Sullivan— "he didn't contribute a bloody thing to our struggle," he concluded with lingering bitterness. He remained in the U.S. until 1997, but by 2001 he had grasped one of the central problems of the anti-imperialist movement globally: the movement was far too weak in the U.S. itself, which gave Washington too much latitude, especially after the dissolution of the Soviet Union. "There are also some Communists in the United States," he said accurately and "those were in full support of our struggle" but they were numerically small and politically weak. "The people who seemed to understand very little were those in the trade unions," which had been purged of radicals during the Cold War. Thus, even if the ANC "had won with the barrel of the gun," the wider question would remain: could a nation of 55 million, with a 5-million strong European minority largely tied at the apron strings to world imperialism, prevail completely?[36] In that context, Swaminathan Gounden, born in 1927, agreed with the ending of the armed struggle: "we didn't want things to happen like what happened in India…millions lost their lives…."[37]

Joe Matthews, the son of the famed ANC leader Z.K. Matthews, hailed from a family that was tied to both Adams College and the American Mission Board, and in which knowledge of Afrikaans, Zulu, Sesotho, Tswana, and English was common. He acknowledged the obvious in terming his father a "very strong supporter" of the U.S. and a "great admirer" of President Roosevelt, who "worked closely with blacks in the United States," which meant he "argued" with Robeson precisely about the Communist Party that Dube saluted. But he said in 2000, "once the Soviet Union collapsed and you got new attitudes developing," liberation became possible. Though he had become close to Buthelezi, he dismissed the PAC and the Black Consciousness Movement; "we had people coming

35. Oral History, Stanislaus Sangweni, 6 July 2001, *University of Connecticut-Storrs.*

36. Oral History, Ernest Frederick Dube, 24 July 2001, *University of Connecticut-Storrs.*

37. Oral History, Swaminathan Gounden, 16 April 2001, *University of Connecticut-Storrs.*

even from the [U.S.] to study" both but, he sniffed, "we never really thought from their activities they were a significant political force." There were those who called the ANC "Mbombela," a train that has "no classes" and takes miners into the mines. At a moment when he was no longer close to either organization, he distilled an essential truth—often neglected—when he opined that the ANC had as much—or more—influence on the SACP, than vice versa.[38]

Cosmopolitan is also an apt descriptor for Alven Bennie Pemba, born in Port Elizabeth in 1930, who spoke Afrikaans and Xhosa and worked closely with Govan Mbeki. He liaised with unions in this industrial center and was influential in persuading other nations not to offload apartheid exports. "We got a success with the Arabs" he recalled proudly in 2002.[39]

Also part of Adams College was Epainette Mbeki, born in 1916. She became a teacher at a night school sponsored by the Communists, where she collaborated with Kotane, Dadoo, and other "high ups.... We were working together...." But her family was touched by misfortune beyond the lengthy imprisonment of her spouse, Govan. Her grandson—the child of her son Thabo— "just disappeared.... We don't know what happened to him," a tragedy making this First Family like so many other families.[40]

Moreover, the endurance of Ms. Mbeki was not unique to her. Baleka Mbete, born in 1949, also symbolizes the problems faced by women in the struggle. As the principal parent of her teenage children, she had difficulty with them when she was enduring divorce. The "situation that faces a woman," she said sagely in 2001, "is very unique and very particular to being a woman...." Her spouse imbibed alcohol unduly, she said, and U.S. friends sent her funds to help him overcome his addiction; he too was unemployed and found it difficult to handle her being in the spotlight. Her father had been involved in the Communist Party, but she had not been. "I wanted to be and tried to be a member,"[41] however, suggesting the popularity of an entity that faced scorn and rebuke in the U.S.

Ms. Mbete's travails indicate how apartheid had damaged not only the marrow of society but the sensitive chords of familial ties.

---

38. Oral History, Joe Matthews, 2 October 2000, *University of Connecticut-Storrs*.

39. Oral History, Alven Bennie Pemba, 10 June 2002, *University of Connecticut-Storrs*.

40. Oral History, Epainette Mbeki, 14 June 2001, *University of Connecticut-Storrs*.

41. Oral History, Baleka Mbete, 9 May 2001, *University of Connecticut-Storrs*.

By 1992 Mandela himself split from his spouse, wrecking fantasies about a supposed revolutionary union. This came after Winnie was sentenced to six years in prison for her part in the 1988 kidnapping of a number of youths, one of whom was murdered (she managed to escape incarceration). In 1998 he married the widow of Mozambique's Founding Father, Graca Machel.[42] Decades of imprisonment took an obvious toll on the Mandelas, as their personal lives became fodder for lurid journalism. He accused her of "brazen infidelity," alleging that she "never entered his bedroom while he was awake. He called himself 'the loneliest man,'"[43] a sad coda for a man whose face was his passport and a savage indictment of the ravages inflicted by apartheid.

U.S. imperialism had a dual advantage; at once a defender of apartheid and home to a population of African descent—often with mercurial politics—capable of influencing the anti-apartheid majority. Mandla Langa, born in 1950, and later trained in Angola, early on displayed his own capability by winning a contest sponsored by an Anglo-American conglomerate on "what it means to be South African." At the time, he recalled later, "I...had read Ralph Ellison's... 'Invisible Man,'" an iconic anticommunist Negro novel, and the Oklahoman's *Shadow and Act* too. These were "inspirational texts for me," he confessed. He concedes he wrote a "liberal" essay based on these questionable sources found on a visit to a Pretoria library. Yet he also read the work of James Baldwin, another African-American writer. His Harlem-inflected play *Blues for Mr. Charlie* was then banned, yet Langa found it to be "very powerful." He acknowledged that the "Black Consciousness Movement" in his homeland was "majorly influenced by what was happening in the United States" but he added cogently that like socialism, this trend would have to embody South African characteristics if it were to take root.[44] Even de Klerk was struck when in a highly regarded address, Thabo Mbeki quoted the Harlem Bard Langston Hughes in commenting on African exasperation in May 1998, when he asked, "What happens to a dream deferred"—does it explode?[45]

Prema Naidoo, born in 1945, was also alert to the influence of the BCM. His father was quite familiar with M.K. Gandhi, which could be said of other anti-apartheid leaders too. Yet he too thought BCM was driven by "Stokely Carmichael, Huey Newton," not to mention

---

42. Note in Nelson Mandela, *Let Freedom Reign*, 89, 114.
43. *Washington Post*, 1 March 1997.
44. Oral History, Mandla Langa, no date, *University of Connecticut-Storrs*.
45. F.W. de Klerk, *The Last Trek*, 394.

Frantz Fanon. "It was a global thing," or more precisely, a U.S. "thing" with global dimensions.[46]

The impact of U.S. white supremacy on Africans was not uniform. Wally Serote, born in Sophiatown in 1944, was part of the underground in Botswana before honing his skills in Angola and the Soviet Union. "The impact of U.S. white supremacy on Africans was pervasive. Wally Serote, ANC militant, was among those struck by the de facto apartheid in the U.S."[47]

Zenzile Ngalo, born in 1930, was among the many who were displeased with the influence of U.S. imperialism, recalling in 2001 that the "CIA," which played a major role in shaping events in the sub-region, plotted to kill ANC leaders, including Tambo. This former ANC envoy to Cairo also contends "we were living better then," speaking of pre-1994 exile, "we were better off than we are today...."[48]

Simon Makana was the chief ANC envoy in Moscow from 1987 through December 1990 and thus, was in a position to take the measure of Cold War tensions. He later recalled a "young chap" from the U.S. who told him, "I'm sent here by the U.S. Administration to establish working relations with the ANC." A skeptical Thabo Mbeki replied, "what do you mean?" The North American said, "I know you people don't trust us," which was beyond true. "We don't trust you either, but we go[t] to work together to save that situation in South Africa," meaning preserving capitalism and the vast holdings of the European minority. "Their main worry," says Makana, "was the Communist flag or ideology in the ANC." It became easier for Washington to worry less once the socialist camp began eroding.[49]

Mlamli Faku of South Africa, born in 1947, suggests that pessimism about post-apartheid South Africa must be counterbalanced by the real gains of the ANC regime, including the increased provision of water and electricity.[50] This occurred, suggests Ebrahim Ebrahim, in the face of overwhelming odds, including the drugging of political prisoners.[51] Given the close cooperation between

46. Oral History, Prema Naidoo, 12 July 2001, *University of Connecticut-Storrs*.

47. Oral History, Wally Serote, 4 October 2000, *University of Connecticut-Storrs*.

48. Oral History, Zenzile Ngalo, 5 July 2001, *University of Connecticut-Storrs*.

49. Oral History, Simon Makana, 17 August 2001, *University of Connecticut-Storrs*.

50. Oral History, Mlamli Faku, no date, *University of Connecticut-Storrs*.

51. Oral History, Ebrahim Ebrahim, 20 October 2000, *University of Connecticut-Storrs*.

Washington and Pretoria over the years, it is chilling to reflect on the 1979 words of Senator Frank Church of Idaho, who headed a congressional investigation on the subject, that "on mind control and behavioral experiments they only scratched the surface" in their purportedly comprehensive inquiry.[52]

This raises another issue, not often considered: the ongoing psychic impact of apartheid and how it continues to haunt the imagination. According to Ben Turok, Issie Hayman was crumbling, "he'd already tried to cut his wrists twice."[53] Wolfie Kodesh, a leading Communist, did not move in this direction, yet this cadre, who "never married" in part because of his devotion to the cause, recalled in 2000 that "people who [were] political [in South Africa were] in danger always of arrest," creating severe emotional strain. When Mandela was arrested, he broke down and "cried for hours."[54] By May 1994 one would have thought that the Quaker representative in the region, John Stewart, would be euphoric. Instead, he confessed, "I'm emerging from deep depression," a state of mind "partly related to the cost paid in achieving the major step forward for the world, that the South African change has been; costs of lives and values," the "friends dead, lost; and with what's happening in Rwanda (and Burundi,)" a reference to massacres then unfolding. He was "frustrated too by the blockages and trying to find a way" that seemed beyond his immediate grasp.[55] Apartheid imposed a heavy cost, the price of which remains difficult to calculate precisely. Anxiety did not disappear post-apartheid either: years after he had stepped down from power, a close Mandela advisor conceded that even after taking power, the president feared that the security forces might try to sabotage his regime.[56]

I too suffered a personal loss when the ANC envoy at the United Nations, "Johnny" Makhathini, passed away in 1988. We worked closely together for years and, like so many others, I was taken with his charm and bonhomie. Born in Durban in 1932, he too attended Adams College and was part of the ANC in the prelude to the Rivonia trial. In Dar es Salaam at an assemblage singing the praises of Mandela, he suddenly walked in wearing a holster with

52. Interview, 29 April 1979, Box 4, *Ashby-Gramer Research Files, Boise State University-Idaho*.

53. Oral History, Ben Turok, 5 October 2000, *University of Connecticut-Storrs*.

54. Oral History, Wolfie Kodesh, 4 October 2000, *University of Connecticut-Storrs*.

55. John Stewart to Mary Massaro, 18 May 1994, Box: ID Africa-S, *AFSC*.

56. Alec Russell, *Bring me My Machine Gun*, 32.

a pistol and looking like an accomplished soldier. Such incidents became part and parcel of his ANC representation, particularly during his long tenure in North Africa, where he honed his French language skills. As his obituary noted, he "paid special attention to the solidarity movement" in the U.S.,[57] a fact to which I can well attest.

Sindiso Gregory Mfenyana concurs. The diminutive envoy with the bright smile and mischievous humor was "my personal mentor," he said. "He had the OAU and later the UN eating out of his hand. That's the man," he exulted of the diplomat, "buried in Zambia." When Nicaragua wanted to send an envoy to the U.N., Washington was "very hostile," he recalled, and so the Central Americans went to the Cubans for counsel who advised, "'Go to Makhathini.'" Even Ivory Coast's Houphouet-Boigny, a neo-colonialist of the rankest sort, was charmed by him and doled out "assistance" to the ANC as a result; the same was true for Banda of Malawi.[58] The loss of Makhathini as negotiations were beginning with apartheid was incalculable.

But even charm has its limits, and our grief at the profound loss of Makhathini should not obscure the wider reality that Ivory Coast and Senegal were also among the prized supporters of the UNITA bandits. Apparently, the military in Rwanda had been cooperating with Savimbi also. This Pan-African influence combined with backing from the hard right in Washington to make Savimbi an inflexible bargaining partner. When 18 heads of state gathered in Gbadolite in what is now the Democratic Republic of the Congo to broker an accord with Luanda in 1989, the U.S. diplomat Herman Cohen recollected that the UNITA chief found his arm twisted. He signed, but the "fact that he could instruct his lobbyist to contact Secretary [of State James] Baker on a Sunday afternoon and dictate U.S. policy reflected his remarkable influence on a large segment of the American body politic." Baker reversed field, disapproved of the pact, and said so publicly. By 1992 another UNITA leader, Tito Chingunji, was recalled to headquarters in Angola and, said Cohen, "assassinated in a voodoo type ritual." "This news caused tremendous consternation in Washington," leaving a "decided sour taste." This led to a U.S. split with UNITA over the 1992 election in Angola, creating a predictable rift between the Republicans and the harder right, with the

57. Obituary of Makhathini, December 1988, Reel 15, *Oliver Tambo Papers.*

58. Oral History, Sindiso Gregory Mfenyana, 28 January 2001, *University of Connecticut-Storrs.*

Heritage Foundation leading the charge on behalf of the latter. What followed, says Cohen, were "ten years of fighting after the 1992 election," which "caused more hardship to the Angolan people than the war between 1966 and 1991"—before events took a turn for the better and Savimbi was killed. Cohen celebrated, since "I knew in my heart that the Angolan people had been spared the rule of a tyrannical disciple of Mao Zedong."[59] Of course, after the collapse of the Soviet Union, it was easier to pull the plug on despots like Savimbi.

Besides, Cohen and his diabolical colleagues could rest assured that there was a dividend to be taken from the apparent demise of UNITA. Many of their fighters found their way into the mercenary firms that mushroomed simultaneously in South Africa, including "Executive Outcomes," which controlled planes, armored vehicles, and helicopters, and had the capability to field hundreds of fighters, who found work in Sierra Leone most notably. In any case, despite the decline of UNITA, its companion in mayhem, RENAMO in Mozambique, continued as an opposition force as late as 2019, illustrating the utter vacuity of Nkomati.[60]

Back in South Africa, those who had profited from the crimes of apartheid were managing to hold on to what was important to them: their wealth. Among the celebrants were those of Cosmo City, South Africa. With its fancy Tuscan homes with fake campaniles and pastel-shaded villas with giant, engraved bronze gates, it also featured a curiously named "United States of America Boulevard," interpreted by one observer as a "solid symbol of the vanquishing of the old order," a dubious proposition given the opulence there. There was a profusion of U.S. street names in the wealthier areas of Cosmo City, including Tennessee Street and Las Vegas Crescent, as if this naming would serve as a talisman frightening potential expropriators. African Americans continued to be an unwelcome presence in South Africa, as they had been for decades. Post-1994, one from this group—a reporter—was in a Johannesburg queue at "Thrupps, the Whole Foods" of this metropolis, when "an elderly white woman" complimented her insultingly on the "good taste

59. Herman J. Cohen, *The Mind of the African Strongman*, 7, 144, 145, 149, 152-153.

60. *The Guardian* [U.K.], 8 March 1997, Box 1, Folder 57, *Prexy Nesbitt Papers*.

your madam has;" an insult greeted with the icy response, "I am the madam."[61]

From the other side of the street, the U.S. Negro diplomat James Joseph, who served in South Africa, grappled with the Mandela legacy in the context of his current sainthood. It was "correct," he said, to emphasize Mandela's "African-ness," though in the U.S. this would be seen as a disruptive "identity politics." In 1994 in Tunis, he watched as Mandela spoke eloquently of the giants of Africa, including Nasser, Nkrumah, Lumumba, Du Bois, and Garvey. When Thabo Mbeki delivered his now famous "I am an African" oration, Mandela—said Joseph— "was one of the first to leap to his feet in applause." Still, like many of his comrades, Mandela was multi-lingual. Joseph was "surprised at how well Mandela spoke Afrikaans and how much he knew about their culture and history." Yet, says Joseph, "our relationship was seriously threatened" when a "deliberate leak of a confidential cable...was distorted," though not falsified, in averring, "American Ambassador calls Mandela a Marxist." Ambassador Joseph, in office from 1996-1999, oversaw an expansion of staff in the republic from 182 to 300, representing a hefty 23 agencies and offices, while Foreign Service nationals or local employees mushroomed to more than 400, providing ample opportunity for interference in the internal affairs of the infant regime.[62]

By the time, then First Lady Hillary Rodham Clinton arrived in Southern Africa in early 1997, the U.S. legation in Pretoria housed 203 U.S. nationals and 252 South Africans, a small army capable of much mischief. Tellingly, her staff prepared her to respond to the following queries: "What is your reaction to those who accuse the U.S. of trying to dictate foreign policy in South Africa?" and "Why is Peace Corps opening a new program in South Africa while closing programs elsewhere in Southern Africa?"[63]

Her briefers informed her that in Zimbabwe the "ruling party" was "riven with ethnic, generational and regional divisions...exacerbated by uncertainty over who will succeed" Mugabe, an issue that was resolved by palace intrigue in November 2017 leading to the forced retirement of the elderly leader. "Repeat of the inter-tribal violence of

61. Alec Russell, *bring me My Machine Gun*, 42. Interestingly, one of the neighborhoods in Pretoria was known as "Brooklyn", apparent homage to the New York City borough. See F.W. de Klerk, *The Last Trek*, 143.

62. James A. Joseph, *Saved for a Purpose: A Journal from Private Virtues to Public Values*, Durham: Duke University Press, 2015, 221-222, 227, 229, 220.

63. Briefing Book, 15-29 March 1997, 2006-0457-F, Box 1, National Security Council African Affairs, *Bill Clinton Presidential Library-Little Rock, Arkansas.*

the 1980s is highly unlikely," it was said, a crude description of the political unrest that rocked Matabeleland. There remained in Zimbabwe, "roughly 100,000 whites and 60,000 Indians," both of which played a major role in the economy. Her ventriloquist suggested that she repeat endlessly that Harare and Washington "have an excellent bilateral relationship," a cosmetic rendering that could not obscure the deterioration of ties, including the imposition of stiff sanctions, after Zimbabwe moved toward land reform and, simultaneously, sent a signal to the ANC to tread carefully on this sensitive matter.[64]

On the other hand, when President Mugabe visited Washington just before the First Lady's journey—his fourth official visit to the U.S.—President Clinton "applauded President Mugabe's leadership in launching a comprehensive economic structural adjustment," a euphemism obscuring how Washington's ideological hegemony meant the erosion of the state's role in guaranteeing a reasonable standard of living and subsidies for health and education and food most notably—which in turn hastened land reform, inaugurating punishing sanctions.[65] Moreover, Washington congratulated Harare on agreeing to hold joint military exercises, though it was budget draining for this small nation and, in addition, empowered the military while bringing it closer to U.S. imperialism, all of which were conditions precedent for regime change in November 2017.[66] At the same time, Washington reproached Harare for "problems" in the "tender process" which "hamper[s] U.S. investment…." "Mineral rich Zimbabwe is the hub of the Southern African region with good transportation and communication links to neighboring markets," Washington noted, underscoring why this South African neighbor was viewed as critical.[67] By December 1996 Washington was fielding "serious complaints by U.S. firms and others about the lack of transparency and fairness in the…tender process" in Harare, specifically "on two major energy and telecommunications tenders" and the "lack of intellectual property rights protection." Harare wanted to "liquidate some para-statals, commercialize others and wholly or partially privatize the rest" in their attempt to "increase Black

64. Ibid., Briefing Book, 15-29 March 1997.

65. Press Release from White House, 18 May 1995, from "Official Working Visit of President Mugabe…." In Box 1, National Security Council African Affairs.

66. Memorandum, July 1995, Box 3, National Security Council African Affairs.

67. U.S. Embassy to State Department, December 1995, Box 3, National Security Council African Affairs.

ownership of economic assets."[68] This conflict between U.S. imperialism and the national bourgeoisie—indeed, the nation as a whole—had become a primary contradiction after independence. Thus, in February 1997 there was a flap between Coca-Cola and Harare after the latter was accused of adopting a "lackadaisical approach" to the former's concerns, causing their executives to depart hastily from Zimbabwe. This amounted to "mixed signals" on the primary matter of foreign investment.[69]

In August 1996 Washington was worried, since "pressure for indigenization is increasing" in Zimbabwe. The government was "pressing multinational corporations," many of which were of U.S. origin, "to appoint Black Zimbabweans CEOs at the end of foreign white managers' tours...." A distinguishing characteristic of U.S. imperialism is that not only did it wish to profit—often obscenely—but wanted to be in total control as well, particularly in Africa where its slaveholding fortune was grounded.[70] Thus, by December 1997 Washington was informed that "U.S. investment in Zimbabwe continues to grow, despite troubling recent developments," i.e. "aggressive land acquisition,"[71] the pretext for the punitive sanctions soon to be imposed.

Still, the kerfuffle accompanying land reform in Zimbabwe highlighted that attacks on the European minority tended to drown out what may have been even more episodes of this type in South Africa itself. Though she was not a settler in South Africa, Amy Biehl was a Euro-American spending time in Cape Town in 1993 when she was murdered by youth purportedly shouting, "you deserve to die because you are a settler," a reflection of unresolved tensions concerning the trinity of race, class, and gender.[72]

Despite the brave words of Mandela on receiving his Nobel Laureate, 500 years of colonialism may have come to a close in 1994 but reverberations will continue to sound for years to come. Part of the problem has been the reluctance to seriously engage the question

---

68. Memorandum, December 1996, Box 4, National Security Council African Affairs.

69. Memorandum, February 1997, Box 4, National Security Council African Affairs.

70. Memorandum, August 1996, Box 4, National Security Council African Affairs.

71. U.S. Embassy to State Department, December 1997, Box 5, National Security Council African Affairs.

72. Memorandum from U.S. Embassy-Pretoria, August 1993, FOIA 2009, -0960, WHORM Subject Files General ME 001-03 035406 OA/ID 17740, Box 1, *Clinton Presidential Library*.

of wealth redistribution, which has helped to engender racialized class anger against "settlers" more generally, even those on the side of the angels—as Ms. Biehl apparently was. And the essence of this problem has been the longstanding U.S. creed of anticommunism, which received a new birth with the collapse of the Soviet Union and has therefore not been inspected sufficiently, notably in terms of how it handicaps the crucial issue of wealth redistribution. When Mandela was being invited to Washington in 1998 to receive a medal, the matter arose once more. "Is Chris Hani too controversial—Communist—for POTUS [President of the United States] to praise?" though he was a "hero" in South Africa itself. In other words, praising Communists was still beyond the pale in the U.S., even if it would help woo a purported ally.[73]

Also roiling relations with Harare—and the ANC to a degree—was the refusal of these newly minted governments to toe the U.S. line on Cuba. By 1996 a Foreign Ministry official acknowledged that Harare "might disappoint the United States on Cuba," which was gross understatement given the sub-region's continuing gratitude to Havana for its rescue operation and stern refusal to join the U.S. embargo of the island.[74] There were also concerns about Harare's ties to both Iran and Libya—with the latter regime overthrown forcibly by U.S. imperialism and its North Atlantic allies in 2011, followed by the graphic murder of the preeminent leader in Tripoli.[75]

A few years after Joseph's tenure had concluded, the more than ample staff got a workout in 2001 when the U.N. sponsored a global conference on racism and xenophobia in Durban. Quickly overshadowed by the attack on New York and Washington on 11 September, the dominant conflict appeared to be that between Thabo Mbeki and Colin Powell, the Jamaican-American U.S. Secretary of State. "This became a major grievance," said a Powell ally, particularly after the "nightmare" of being heckled severely while speaking at the University of Witwatersrand. This observer claimed he was "held a virtual hostage for an hour by left wing students," then received "identical treatment" when he returned in 2002.[76]

---

73. David Halperin to Anthony Blinken, 21 September 1998, Box 2, OA/ID 17740, *Clinton Presidential Library*.

74. U.S. Embassy to State Department, June 1996, Box 3, National Security Council African Affairs.

75. Memorandum, August 1996, Box 4, National Security Council African Affairs.

76. R.W. Johnson, *South Africa's Brave New World: The Beloved Country Since the End of Apartheid*, London: Allen Lane, 2009, 343, 344.

There were those in the U.S. who might have cheered the protesters. Assuredly, Chicago activists were among those who had been subjected to internecine conflict, particularly in combat with the PAC. Lisa Brock recalled an encounter with Conrad Worrill, a PAC supporter, during a protest against an apartheid rugby tour. "He looks down at me," said the small activist, "and says you're the leader of the white group," an insult as far as he was concerned.[77] Her spouse, Otis Cunningham, an African American born in 1949, spent considerable time in his youth reading "Malcolm…Ho…Che," though "we didn't read Maoist stuff," nor did he truck with "PAC" and "Black Consciousness Movement"—"we didn't work with them…in a very deliberate way…." A "huge influence on me," he says in retrospect "was Prexy" Nesbitt, the long-time Chicago based politico.[78]

Rachel Rubin was also influenced by Nesbitt. Her mother was born in Palestine, and Rubin herself travelled to Mozambique and to South Africa by 1992. She was concerned about the ties between Israel and South Africa—it was "always a very sticky issue," she said in 2009. Like others in Chicago she was among those who praised Anne Evens, who "locked herself in the South African consulate and the police had to break in to get her out and they actually broke her finger or broke her hand."[79]

Rosetta Daylie worked full time for the American Federation of State, County and Municipal Employees, which had one of the larger African-American memberships of any union. She was president of her local affiliate and part of the Coalition of Black Trade Unionists too, whose leader—Bill Lucy, also an AFSCME officer—paid for her to "go to South Africa and work for Nelson Mandela's election,"[80] a task she shared with others. Willie Williamson, born in Grenada, Mississippi in 1948, was part Native American and he was among those who saw the parallel between Jim Crow and apartheid, which drove his activism.[81] Tim Wright was born in Los Angeles in 1955, where he witnessed the Watts Revolt of 1965, a turning point in the struggle against Jim Crow. Early on, he travelled to Angola and met President Neto and worked closely with Angela Davis besides. He

---

77. Oral History, Lisa Brock, 8 December 2009, *Columbia College-Chicago.*

78. Oral History, Otis Cunningham, 12 December 2009, *Columbia College-Chicago.*

79. Oral History, Rachel Rubin, 20 April 2009, *Columbia College-Chicago.*

80. Oral History, Rosetta Daylie, 27 November 2009, *Columbia College-Chicago.*

81. Oral History, Willie Williamson, 21 November 2009, *Columbia College-Chicago.*

was part of a legal defense team in Chicago that used the "necessity defense" to evade the conviction of 17 defendants accused of invading the South African consulate. Not guilty was the verdict. Wright compared Jim Crow to apartheid, while he likened Compton, California to Soweto. Interestingly, he worked closely with President Bill Clinton and then toiled in South Africa itself between 2003 and 2006, where he left with a harsh opinion of President Mugabe who, he said, was seeking to "destroy" Zimbabwe. He worked with the National Lawyers Guild and not the National Conference of Black Lawyers.[82]

Then there was the Reverend Jeremiah Wright of Chicago, who had served as a pastor and confidante at one time to Senator Barack Obama. Born in 1941, he was on the board of Trans-Africa ("Randall Robinson's mother and my mother were at each other's weddings," he said) and like so many others he was critical of his fellow pastor Leon Sullivan and his "Principles." Sullivan was "dead wrong," he said. Wright also served as a leader of the Commission for Racial Justice of the United Church of Christ, which backed many controversial political cases. In 2009 he said, "Law enforcement screwed me, and all of us who sat on the commission from that point on had files in terms of being watched by the government," since they were seen as "dangerous subversive types...." At his pastorate in Chicago, he boasted, "we had grown to be largest church in the denomination."[83] Funeka Sihlali, was born in Johannesburg in 1948 in the same neighborhood as Steve Biko, was exiled in Chicago. "he's well read," Sihlali said in December 2009, speaking admiringly of the pastor.[84]

Father Time remains undefeated, and so it was when Hugh Masekela, the celebrated South African musician, passed away in January 2018. President Clinton had praised his "incomparable music," which galvanized so many during the height of the anti-apartheid movement.[85] Like the trumpeter, South African writer Keorapetse Kgositsile, who died just before Masekela, was a major influence on African American artists and, in fact, married and fathered a daughter with an African American woman.[86] The bonds of singular intimacy that spanned the Atlantic helped to insure that the ongoing

82. Oral History, Tim Wright, 25 November 2009, *Columbia College-Chicago.*

83. Oral History, Jeremiah Wright, 24 April 2009, *Columbia College-Chicago.*

84. Oral History, Funeka Sihlali, 1 December 2009, *Columbia College-Chicago.*

85. President Clinton to Molly Biehl, 28 April 1994, Box 2, OA/ID 17740, *Clinton Presidential Library.*

86. *New York Times*, 17 January 2018.

movements against Jim Crow and apartheid would be mutually reinforcing.

When Mandela died in 2013 it was an occasion to take stock not only of his legacy but the braided history of racism on both sides of the Atlantic that helped to define him. Typically, the Federal Bureau of Investigation inventoried reactions, including that of Eric West—"who claims to be a 'conservative' living in South Africa"—who asserted "Mandela was a terrorist—not a freedom fighter!" This man was seemingly unaware that there were those who felt that the now lionized leader was being upbraided, even as he was interred, for not taking a more hostile approach to settlers, particularly in placing them on trial for ramified transgressions and expropriating their ill-gotten wealth. Dozens of heads of state were confirmed for his funeral and almost a dozen more former heads of state, a list that included presidents Obama, Carter, Clinton, George W. Bush, and their spouses. In his eulogy, President Obama sought to draw comparisons between the struggles in the nation he led and South Africa, though skirting the essential difference between fighting for national liberation in a country where Africans were the majority and fighting for rights in a nation where a European majority often stood in the way of simple principles of racial equality.[87]

Yet what still united these two citadels of inequality was that wealth redistribution remained the order of the day. Until that lofty goal is attained, there will ever be unrest and the potential for revolution.

87. See remarks by Eric West, 5 December 2013; Report on funeral, 9 December 2013; Remarks by President Obama, 11 December 2013, all from *Mandela FBI File—Federal Bureau of Investigation, Washington, D.C.*

Index